October 23-26, 2011
Cascais, Portugal

**Association for
Computing Machinery**

Advancing Computing as a Science & Profession

SOSP'11

Proceedings of the Twenty-Third ACM

Symposium on Operating Systems Principles

Sponsored by:

ACM SIGOPS and INESC-ID

Supported by:

**Microsoft Research, National Science Foundation, Infosys,
VMware, Google, HP, NetApp, Intel, HiPEAC,
IBM Research, Facebook, Citrix, Akamai, SAP**

**Association for
Computing Machinery**

Advancing Computing as a Science & Profession

The Association for Computing Machinery
2 Penn Plaza, Suite 701
New York, New York 10121-0701

Notice to Past Authors of ACM-Published Articles
ACM intends to create a complete electronic archive of all articles and/or other material previously published by ACM. If you have written a work that has been previously published by ACM in any journal or conference proceedings prior to 1978, or any SIG Newsletter at any time, and you do NOT want this work to appear in the ACM Digital Library, please inform permissions@acm.org, stating the title of the work, the author(s), and where and when published.

ISBN: 978-1-4503-0977-6

Additional copies may be ordered prepaid from:

ACM Order Department
PO Box 30777
New York, NY 10087-0777, USA

Phone: 1-800-342-6626 (US and Canada)
+1-212-626-0500 (Global)
Fax: +1-212-944-1318
E-mail: acmhelp@acm.org
Hours of Operation: 8:30 am – 4:30 pm ET

Printed in the USA

Foreword

Dear Reader,

Welcome to the Proceedings of the 23rd ACM Symposium on Operating Systems Principles (SOSP 2011), held in Cascais, Portugal. This year's program includes 28 papers, and touches on a wide range of computer systems topics, from data center computing, storage systems and geo-replication to operating system architecture, virtualization, concurrency, security, and mobile platforms. The program committee made every effort to identify and include some of the most creative and thought-provoking ideas in computer systems today. Each accepted paper was shepherded by a program committee member to make sure the papers are as readable and complete as possible. We hope you will enjoy the program as much as we did in selecting it.

This year's proceedings are, for the first time, published digitally on a USB key with no paper copy distributed at the conference. The cost to the environment of so many reams of printed paper, plus the difficulty of shipping printed material to the conference site, made this an easy decision. The workshop proceedings appear on the conference USB key as well. You will find two copies of each of this year's SOSP papers: a traditional 2-column version designed for printing, and a one-column version intended for reading on a computer. In addition, the USB key contains a copy of every SOSP paper from each of the previous 22 instances of the conference, starting in 1967. The very nature of publishing is changing as we speak. We look forward to your feedback about the appropriate form and format for future SOSP proceedings.

We are most grateful to the authors of the 157 papers who chose to submit their work to SOSP (five papers were subsequently withdrawn by the authors). Their ideas and efforts are the basis of the conference's success. Selecting the program out of so many quality submissions was a difficult task. A program committee consisting of 28 leading scholars in the broad area of computer systems conducted a three-stage reviewing process and online discussion; final selections were made during a physical meeting in Boston, MA, which was attended by a core of 13 PC members. Each submission received at least three PC reviews, with a maximum of eight. All in all, 719 reviews were produced. The PC made every effort to provide detailed and constructive feedback, which should help authors to further improve their work. Author anonymity was maintained throughout the reviewing and selection process; PC members were removed from the deliberations of any paper with which they had a conflict of interest (co-author, same institution, recent collaborator, former student/adviser).

The organizing committee is pleased to be able to follow the informal tradition of locating every third SOSP in Europe. Doing so would not have been possible this year without the tireless efforts of Luís Rodrigues and João Leitão as well as the support of the Instituto de Engenharia de Sistemas e Computadores Investigação e Desenvolvimento em

Lisboa (INESC-ID) which is conference co-sponsor along with ACM SIGOPS. For the first time, SOSP is co-located with the ACM Symposium on Cloud Computing (SOCC), to take place on October 27th and 28th. SOCC, a conference now in its second year, is co-sponsored by SIGOPS, SIGMOD and INESC-ID, and it should provide an excellent counterpoint to SOSP in a very topical area of research.

Following the lead of SOSP 2009, this year's conference also offers a full slate of workshops on the Sunday before the main event. These workshops cover a range of topics related to operating systems: programming languages (PLOS), mobile handheld systems (MobiHeld), power-aware computing (HotPower), and the management of large scale systems through log analysis and machine learning (SLAML). We would like to thank the organizers and sponsors of all four workshops as well as Rama Kotla and Rodrigo Rodrigues, who served as workshop chairs. We welcome community feedback on ideas for future co-located workshops.

We are especially thankful this year for our generous corporate and governmental donors. These donors make it possible to host SOSP in an environment that is conducive to collegial interaction and, this year, they have provided funds for full travel grants to over 70 students from a wide range of countries and institutions. Special thanks go to Brett Fleisch who assembled our NSF grant application, and to the folks at UC Riverside for administering the resulting grant.

SOSP is a great conference mostly because it attracts so many high-quality submissions, and we would like to again thank all the authors who submitted. We also thank the PC members for the tremendous amount of work they did: reviewing the submissions, providing feedback, and shepherding the accepted submissions. We are grateful to the external reviewers who provided an additional perspective on a few papers. SOSP has always been organized by volunteer efforts from a host of people; we would like to thank all the following people who have dedicated so much of their time to the conference: Luís Rodrigues (local arrangements), João Leitão (registration), John MacCormick (treasurer), Chandu Thekkath, J.P. Martin, and Sape Mullender (sponsorships), David Lie, Nickolai Zeldovich, and Dilma Da Silva (scholarships), Nuno Carvalho (website), Paarijaat Aditya (submissions website), Rama Kotla and Rodrigo Rodrigues (workshops), Bryan Ford and George Candea (WIPs/Posters), and Junfeng Yang and Rodrigo Rodrigues (publicity).

Finally, we would like to especially thank Andrew Birrell who assembled the conference USB key and guided the production of "camera-ready" copy.

We hope that you will find the program interesting and inspiring, and trust that the symposium will provide you with a valuable opportunity to network and share ideas with researchers and practitioners from institutions around the world.

Ted Wobber	Peter Druschel
General Chair	Program Chair

Contents

Key-Value

Chair: Marvin Theimer

Storage

Chair: Eddie Kohler

Security

Chair: Adrian Perrig

Reality

Chair: George Candea

Virtualization

Chair: Gernot Heiser

OS Architecture

Chair: Nickolai Zeldovich

Detection and Tracing

Chair: Rebecca Isaacs

Threads and Races

Chair: Bryan Ford

Geo-Replication

Chair: Ant Rowstron

Sponsors

Supporters

vmware   Google   hp   NetApp   intel   HiPEAC
COMPILATION ARCHITECTURE

IBM Research   facebook   EuroSys   CiTRIX   Akamai   SAP

Organizers

General Chair:	Ted Wobber, MSR Silicon Valley
Program Chair:	Peter Druschel, MPI-SWS
Treasurer:	John MacCormick, Dickinson College
Sponsorship Chairs:	Sape Mullender, Alcatel-Lucent
	Jean-Philippe Martin, MSR Silicon Valley
	Chandu Thekkath, MSR Silicon Valley
Workshop Chairs:	Ramakrishna Kotla, MSR Silicon Valley
	Rodrigo Rodrigues, MPI-SWS
Publicity Chairs:	Junfeng Yang, Columbia University
	Rodrigo Rodrigues, MPI-SWS
Registration:	João Leitão, INESC-ID/IST
Local Arrangements:	Luís Rodrigues, INESC-ID/IST
Scholarship Committee:	David Lie, U. of Toronto
	Dilma da Silva, IBM
	Nickolai Zeldovich, MIT
Webmaster:	Nuno Carvalho, INESC-ID/IST
Poster and WIP Chairs:	George Candea, EPFL
	Bryan Ford, Yale
Publications:	Andrew Birrell, MSR Silicon Valley
Program Committee:	Andrew Birrell, MSR Silicon Valley
	George Candea, EPFL
	Mike Dahlin, UT Austin
	Jeff Dean, Google
	Peter Druschel, MPI-SWS
	Bryan Ford, Yale
	Greg Ganger, CMU
	Steve Gribble, UW
	Steve Hand, Cambridge
	Tim Harris, MSR Cambridge
	Gernot Heiser, UNSW/NICTA
	Rebecca Isaacs, MSR Silicon Valley
	Sam King, UIUC
	Eddie Kohler, UCLA/Harvard
	Philip Levis, Stanford
	Petros Maniatis, Intel Research Berkeley
	Robert Morris, MIT
	Andrew Myers, Cornell
	Adrian Perrig, CMU
	Robbert van Renesse, Cornell
	Ant Rowstron, MSR Cambridge
	Margo Seltzer, Harvard
	Marvin Theimer, Amazon
	Geoff Voelker, UCSD
	Emmett Witchel, UT Austin
	Nikolai Zeldovich, MIT
	Lidong Zhou, MSR Asia
	YY Zhou, UCSD

SILT: A Memory-Efficient, High-Performance Key-Value Store

Hyeontaek Lim[1], Bin Fan[1], David G. Andersen[1], Michael Kaminsky[2]

[1]Carnegie Mellon University, [2]Intel Labs

ABSTRACT

SILT (Small Index Large Table) is a memory-efficient, high-performance key-value store system based on flash storage that scales to serve billions of key-value items on a single node. It requires only 0.7 bytes of DRAM per entry and retrieves key/value pairs using on average 1.01 flash reads each. SILT combines new algorithmic and systems techniques to balance the use of memory, storage, and computation. Our contributions include: (1) the design of three basic key-value stores each with a different emphasis on memory-efficiency and write-friendliness; (2) synthesis of the basic key-value stores to build a SILT key-value store system; and (3) an analytical model for tuning system parameters carefully to meet the needs of different workloads. SILT requires one to two orders of magnitude less memory to provide comparable throughput to current high-performance key-value systems on a commodity desktop system with flash storage.

Categories and Subject Descriptors

D.4.2 [**Operating Systems**]: Storage Management; D.4.7 [**Operating Systems**]: Organization and Design; D.4.8 [**Operating Systems**]: Performance; E.1 [**Data**]: Data Structures; E.2 [**Data**]: Data Storage Representations; E.4 [**Data**]: Coding and Information Theory

General Terms

Algorithms, Design, Measurement, Performance

Keywords

Algorithms, design, flash, measurement, memory efficiency, performance

1. INTRODUCTION

Key-value storage systems have become a critical building block for today's large-scale, high-performance data-intensive applications. High-performance key-value stores have therefore received substantial attention in a variety of domains, both commercial and academic:

Metric	2008 → 2011	Increase
CPU transistors	731 → 1,170 M	60 %
DRAM capacity	0.062 → 0.153 GB/$	147 %
Flash capacity	0.134 → 0.428 GB/$	219 %
Disk capacity	4.92 → 15.1 GB/$	207 %

Table 1: From 2008 to 2011, flash and hard disk capacity increased much faster than either CPU transistor count or DRAM capacity.

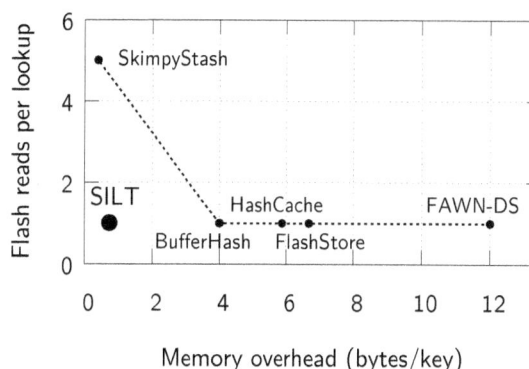

Figure 1: The memory overhead and lookup performance of SILT and the recent key-value stores. For both axes, smaller is better.

e-commerce platforms [21], data deduplication [1, 19, 20], picture stores [7], web object caching [4, 30], and more.

To achieve low latency and high performance, and make best use of limited I/O resources, key-value storage systems require efficient indexes to locate data. As one example, Facebook engineers recently created a new key-value storage system that makes aggressive use of DRAM-based indexes to avoid the bottleneck caused by multiple disk operations when reading data [7]. Unfortunately, DRAM is up to 8X more expensive and uses 25X more power per bit than flash, and, as Table 1 shows, is growing more slowly than the capacity of the disk or flash that it indexes. As key-value stores scale in both size and importance, index memory efficiency is increasingly becoming one of the most important factors for the system's scalability [7] and overall cost effectiveness.

Recent proposals have started examining how to reduce per-key in-memory index overhead [1, 2, 4, 19, 20, 32, 40], but these solutions either require more than a few bytes per key-value entry in memory [1, 2, 4, 19], or compromise performance by keeping all or part of the index on flash or disk and thus require many flash reads or disk seeks to handle each key-value lookup [20, 32, 40] (see Figure 1 for the design space). We term this latter problem *read amplification* and explicitly strive to avoid it in our design.

This paper presents a new flash-based key-value storage system, called SILT (Small Index Large Table), that significantly reduces per-key memory consumption with predictable system performance and lifetime. SILT requires approximately 0.7 bytes of DRAM per key-value entry and uses on average only 1.01 flash reads to handle lookups. Consequently, SILT can saturate the random read I/O on our experimental system, performing 46,000 lookups per second for 1024-byte key-value entries, and it can potentially scale to billions of key-value items on a single host. SILT offers several knobs to trade memory efficiency and performance to match available hardware.

This paper makes three main contributions:

- The design and implementation of three basic key-value stores (LogStore, HashStore, and SortedStore) that use new fast and compact indexing data structures (partial-key cuckoo hashing and entropy-coded tries), each of which places different emphasis on memory-efficiency and write-friendliness.
- Synthesis of these basic stores to build SILT.
- An analytic model that enables an explicit and careful balance between memory, storage, and computation to provide an accurate prediction of system performance, flash lifetime, and memory efficiency.

2. SILT KEY-VALUE STORAGE SYSTEM

Like other key-value systems, SILT implements a simple exact-match hash table interface including PUT (map a new or existing key to a value), GET (retrieve the value by a given key), and DELETE (delete the mapping of a given key).

For simplicity, we assume that keys are *uniformly distributed* 160-bit hash values (e.g., pre-hashed keys with SHA-1) and that data is fixed-length. This type of key-value system is widespread in several application domains such as data deduplication [1, 19, 20], and is applicable to block storage [18, 36], microblogging [25, 38], WAN acceleration [1], among others. In systems with lossy-compressible data, e.g., picture stores [7, 26], data can be adaptively compressed to fit in a fixed-sized slot. A key-value system may also let applications choose one of multiple key-value stores, each of which is optimized for a certain range of value sizes [21]. We discuss the relaxation of these assumptions in Section 4.

Design Goals and Rationale The design of SILT follows from five main goals:

1. **Low read amplification**: Issue at most $1 + \varepsilon$ flash reads for a single GET, where ε is configurable and small (e.g., 0.01).
   Rationale: Random reads remain the read throughput bottleneck when using flash memory. Read amplification therefore directly reduces throughput.
2. **Controllable write amplification and favoring sequential writes**: It should be possible to adjust how many times a key-value entry is rewritten to flash over its lifetime. The system should issue flash-friendly, large writes.
   Rationale: Flash memory can undergo only a limited number of erase cycles before it fails. Random writes smaller than the SSD log-structured page size (typically 4 KiB[1]) cause extra flash traffic.

---
[1]For clarity, binary prefixes (powers of 2) will include "i", while SI prefixes (powers of 10) will appear without any "i".

Optimizations for memory efficiency and garbage collection often require data layout changes on flash. The system designer should be able to select an appropriate balance of flash lifetime, performance, and memory overhead.

3. **Memory-efficient indexing**: SILT should use as little memory as possible (e.g., less than one byte per key stored).
   Rationale: DRAM is both more costly and power-hungry per gigabyte than Flash, and its capacity is growing more slowly.
4. **Computation-efficient indexing**: SILT's indexes should be fast enough to let the system saturate the flash I/O.
   Rationale: System balance and overall performance.
5. **Effective use of flash space**: Some data layout options use the flash space more sparsely to improve lookup or insertion speed, but the total space overhead of any such choice should remain small – less than 20% or so.
   Rationale: SSDs remain relatively expensive.

In the rest of this section, we first explore SILT's high-level architecture, which we term a "multi-store approach", contrasting it with a simpler but less efficient single-store approach. We then briefly outline the capabilities of the individual store types that we compose to form SILT, and show how SILT handles key-value operations using these stores.

Conventional Single-Store Approach A common approach to building high-performance key-value stores on flash uses three components:

1. *an in-memory filter* to efficiently test whether a given key is stored in this store before accessing flash;
2. *an in-memory index* to locate the data on flash for a given key; and
3. *an on-flash data layout* to store all key-value pairs persistently.

Unfortunately, to our knowledge, no existing index data structure and on-flash layout achieve all of our goals simultaneously. For example, HashCache-Set [4] organizes on-flash keys as a hash table, eliminating the in-memory index, but incurring random writes that impair insertion speed. To avoid expensive random writes, systems such as FAWN-DS [2], FlashStore [19], and SkimpyStash [20] append new values sequentially to a log. These systems then require either an in-memory hash table to map a key to its offset in the log (often requiring 4 bytes of DRAM or more per entry) [2, 20]; or keep part of the index on flash using multiple random reads for each lookup [20].

Multi-Store Approach BigTable [14], Anvil [29], and Buffer-Hash [1] chain multiple stores, each with different properties such as high write performance or inexpensive indexing.

Multi-store systems impose two challenges. First, they require effective designs and implementations of the individual stores: they must be efficient, compose well, and it must be efficient to transform data between the store types. Second, it must be efficient to query multiple stores when performing lookups. The design must keep read amplification low by not issuing flash reads to each store. A common solution uses a compact in-memory filter to test whether a given key can be found in a particular store, but this filter can be memory-intensive—e.g., BufferHash uses 4–6 bytes for each entry.

SILT's multi-store design uses a series of *basic key-value stores*, each optimized for a different purpose.

1. Keys are inserted into a write-optimized store, and over their lifetime flow into increasingly more memory-efficient stores.

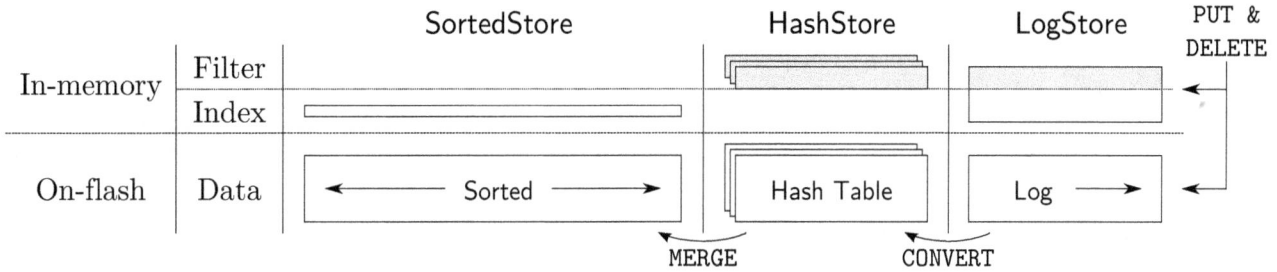

Figure 2: Architecture of SILT.

		SortedStore (§3.3)	HashStore (§3.2)	LogStore (§3.1)
Mutability		Read-only	Read-only	Writable
Data ordering		Key order	Hash order	Insertion order
Multiplicity		1	≥ 0	1
Typical size		> 80% of total entries	< 20%	< 1%
DRAM usage		0.4 bytes/entry	2.2 bytes/entry	6.5 bytes/entry

Table 2: Summary of basic key-value stores in SILT.

2. Most key-value pairs are stored in the most memory-efficient basic store. Although data outside this store uses less memory-efficient indexes (e.g., to optimize writing performance), the average index cost per key remains low.

3. SILT is tuned for high worst-case performance—a lookup found in the last and largest store. As a result, SILT can avoid using an in-memory filter on this last store, allowing all lookups (successful or not) to take $1 + \varepsilon$ flash reads.

SILT's architecture and basic stores (the LogStore, HashStore, and SortedStore) are depicted in Figure 2. Table 2 summarizes these stores' characteristics.

LogStore is a write-friendly key-value store that handles individual PUTs and DELETEs. To achieve high performance, writes are appended to the end of a log file on flash. Because these items are ordered by their insertion time, the LogStore uses an in-memory hash table to map each key to its offset in the log file. The table doubles as an in-memory filter. SILT uses a memory-efficient, high-performance hash table based upon cuckoo hashing [34]. As described in Section 3.1, our *partial-key cuckoo hashing* achieves 93% occupancy with very low computation and memory overhead, a substantial improvement over earlier systems such as FAWN-DS and BufferHash that achieved only 50% hash table occupancy. Compared to the next two read-only store types, however, this index is still relatively memory-intensive, because it must store one 4-byte pointer for every key. SILT therefore uses only one instance of the LogStore (except during conversion to HashStore as described below), with fixed capacity to bound its memory consumption.

Once full, the LogStore is converted to an immutable *HashStore* in the background. The HashStore's data is stored as an on-flash hash table that does not require an in-memory index to locate entries. SILT uses multiple HashStores at a time before merging them into the next store type. Each HashStore therefore uses an efficient in-memory filter to reject queries for nonexistent keys.

SortedStore maintains key-value data in sorted key order on flash, which enables an extremely compact index representation (e.g., 0.4 bytes per key) using a novel design and implementation of *entropy-coded tries*. Because of the expense of inserting a single item into sorted data, SILT periodically merges in bulk several HashStores

along with an older version of a SortedStore and forms a new SortedStore, garbage collecting deleted or overwritten keys in the process.

Key-Value Operations Each PUT operation inserts a (key, value) pair into the LogStore, even if the key already exists. DELETE operations likewise append a "delete" entry into the LogStore. The space occupied by deleted or stale data is reclaimed when SILT merges HashStores into the SortedStore. These lazy deletes trade flash space for sequential write performance.

To handle GET, SILT searches for the key in the LogStore, Hash-Stores, and SortedStore in sequence, returning the value found in the youngest store. If the "deleted" entry is found, SILT will stop searching and return "not found."

Partitioning Finally, we note that each physical node runs multiple SILT instances, responsible for disjoint key ranges, each with its own LogStore, SortedStore, and HashStore(s). This partitioning improves load-balance (e.g., virtual nodes [37]), reduces flash overhead during merge (Section 3.3), and facilitates system-wide parameter tuning (Section 5).

3. BASIC STORE DESIGN

3.1 LogStore

The LogStore writes PUTs and DELETEs sequentially to flash to achieve high write throughput. Its in-memory partial-key cuckoo hash index efficiently maps keys to their location in the flash log, as shown in Figure 3.

Partial-Key Cuckoo Hashing The LogStore uses a new hash table based on *cuckoo hashing* [34]. As with standard cuckoo hashing, it uses two hash functions h_1 and h_2 to map each key to two candidate buckets. On insertion of a new key, if one of the candidate buckets is empty, the key is inserted in this empty slot; if neither bucket is available, the new key "kicks out" the key that already resides in one of the two buckets, and the displaced key is then inserted to its own alternative bucket (and may kick out other keys). The insertion algorithm repeats this process until a vacant position is found, or it reaches a maximum number of displacements (e.g., 128 times in our

3

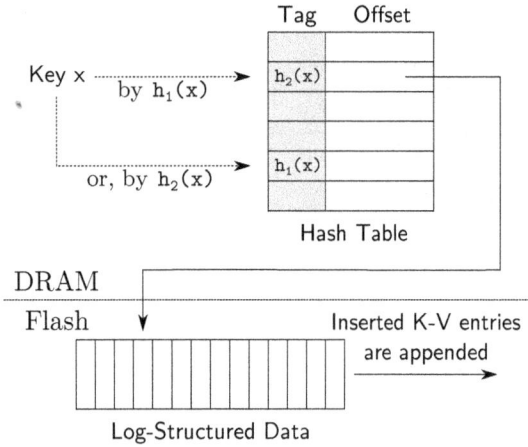

Figure 3: Design of LogStore: an in-memory cuckoo hash table (index and filter) and an on-flash data log.

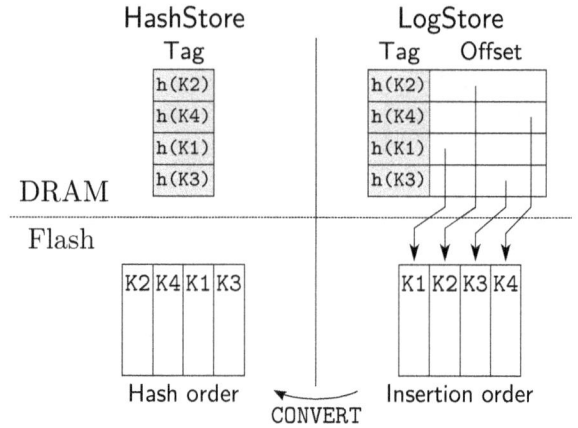

Figure 4: Convert a LogStore to a HashStore. Four keys K1, K2, K3, and K4 are inserted to the LogStore, so the layout of the log file is the insert order; the in-memory index keeps the offset of each key on flash. In HashStore, the on-flash data forms a hash table where keys are in the same order as the in-memory filter.

implementation). If no vacant slot found, it indicates the hash table is almost full, so SILT freezes the LogStore and initializes a new one without expensive rehashing.

To make it compact, the hash table does not store the entire key (e.g., 160 bits in SILT), but only a "tag" of the actual key. A lookup proceeds to flash only when the given key matches the tag, which can prevent most unnecessary flash reads for non-existing keys. If the tag matches, the full key and its value are retrieved from the log on flash to verify if the key it read was indeed the correct key.

Although storing only the tags in the hash table saves memory, it presents a challenge for cuckoo hashing: moving a key to its alternative bucket requires knowing its other hash value. Here, however, the full key is stored only on flash, but reading it from flash is too expensive. Even worse, moving this key to its alternative bucket may in turn displace another key; ultimately, each displacement required by cuckoo hashing would result in additional flash reads, just to insert a single key.

To solve this costly displacement problem, our *partial-key cuckoo hashing* algorithm stores the index of the alternative bucket as the tag; in other words, partial-key cuckoo hashing uses the tag to reduce flash reads for non-existent key lookups *as well as* to indicate an alternative bucket index to perform cuckoo displacement without any flash reads. For example, if a key x is assigned to bucket $h_1(x)$, the other hash value $h_2(x)$ will become its tag stored in bucket $h_1(x)$, and vice versa (see Figure 3). Therefore, when a key is displaced from the bucket a, SILT reads the tag (value: b) at this bucket, and moves the key to the bucket b without needing to read from flash. Then it sets the tag at the bucket b to value a.

To find key x in the table, SILT checks if $h_1(x)$ matches the tag stored in bucket $h_2(x)$, or if $h_2(x)$ matches the tag in bucket $h_1(x)$. If the tag matches, the (key, value) pair is retrieved from the flash location indicated in the hash entry.

Associativity Standard cuckoo hashing allows 50% of the table entries to be occupied before unresolvable collisions occur. SILT improves the occupancy by increasing the associativity of the cuckoo hashing table. Each bucket of the table is of capacity four (i.e., it contains up to 4 entries). Our experiments show that using a 4-way set associative hash table improves space utilization of the table to about 93%,[2] which matches the known experimental result for

various variants of cuckoo hashing [24]; moreover, 4 entries/bucket still allows each bucket to fit in a single cache line.[3]

Hash Functions Keys in SILT are 160-bit hash values, so the LogStore finds $h_1(x)$ and $h_2(x)$ by taking two non-overlapping slices of the low-order bits of the key x.

By default, SILT uses a 15-bit key fragment as the tag. Each hash table entry is 6 bytes, consisting of a 15-bit tag, a single valid bit, and a 4-byte offset pointer. The probability of a false positive retrieval is 0.024% (see Section 5 for derivation), i.e., on average 1 in 4,096 flash retrievals is unnecessary. The maximum number of hash buckets (not entries) is limited by the key fragment length. Given 15-bit key fragments, the hash table has at most 2^{15} buckets, or $4 \times 2^{15} = 128$ Ki entries. To store more keys in LogStore, one can increase the size of the key fragment to have more buckets, increase the associativity to pack more entries into one bucket, and/or partition the key-space to smaller regions and assign each region to one SILT instance with a LogStore. The tradeoffs associated with these decisions are presented in Section 5.

3.2 HashStore

Once a LogStore fills up (e.g., the insertion algorithm terminates without finding any vacant slot after a maximum number of displacements in the hash table), SILT freezes the LogStore and converts it into a more memory-efficient data structure. Directly sorting the relatively small LogStore and merging it into the much larger Sorted-Store requires rewriting large amounts of data, resulting in high write amplification. On the other hand, keeping a large number of Log-Stores around before merging could amortize the cost of rewriting, but unnecessarily incurs high memory overhead from the LogStore's index. To bridge this gap, SILT first converts the LogStore to an immutable HashStore with higher memory efficiency; once SILT accumulates a configurable number of HashStores, it performs a

---

[2]Space utilization here is defined as the fraction of used entries (not used buckets) in the table, which more precisely reflects actual memory utilization.

[3]Note that, another way to increase the utilization of a cuckoo hash table is to use more hash functions (i.e., each key has more possible locations in the table). For example, FlashStore [19] applies 16 hash functions to achieve 90% occupancy. However, having more hash functions increases the number of cache lines read upon lookup and, in our case, requires more than one tag stored in each entry, increasing overhead.

bulk merge to incorporate them into the SortedStore. During the LogStore to HashStore conversion, the old LogStore continues to serve lookups, and a new LogStore receives inserts.

HashStore saves memory over LogStore by eliminating the index and reordering the on-flash (key, value) pairs from insertion order to hash order (see Figure 4). HashStore is thus an on-flash cuckoo hash table, and has the same occupancy (93%) as the in-memory version found in LogStore. HashStores also have one in-memory component, a filter to probabilistically test whether a key is present in the store without performing a flash lookup.

Memory-Efficient Hash Filter Although prior approaches [1] used Bloom filters [12] for the probabilistic membership test, SILT uses a hash filter based on partial-key cuckoo hashing. Hash filters are more memory-efficient than Bloom filters at low false positive rates. Given a 15-bit tag in a 4-way set associative cuckoo hash table, the false positive rate is $f = 2^{-12} = 0.024\%$ as calculated in Section 3.1. With 93% table occupancy, the effective number of bits per key using a hash filter is $15/0.93 = 16.12$. In contrast, a standard Bloom filter that sets its number of hash functions to optimize space consumption requires at least $1.44 \log_2(1/f) = 17.28$ bits of memory to achieve the same false positive rate.

HashStore's hash filter is also efficient to create: SILT simply copies the tags from the LogStore's hash table, in order, discarding the offset pointers; on the contrary, Bloom filters would have been built from scratch, hashing every item in the LogStore again.

3.3 SortedStore

SortedStore is a static key-value store with very low memory footprint. It stores (key, value) entries sorted by key on flash, indexed by a new *entropy-coded trie* data structure that is fast to construct, uses 0.4 bytes of index memory per key on average, and keeps read amplification low (exactly 1) by directly pointing to the correct location on flash.

Using Sorted Data on Flash Because of these desirable properties, SILT keeps most of the key-value entries in a single SortedStore. The entropy-coded trie, however, does not allow for insertions or deletions; thus, to merge HashStore entries into the SortedStore, SILT must generate a new SortedStore. The construction speed of the SortedStore is therefore a large factor in SILT's overall performance.

Sorting provides a natural way to achieve fast construction:

1. Sorting allows efficient bulk-insertion of new data. The new data can be sorted and sequentially merged into the existing sorted data.
2. Sorting is well-studied. SILT can use highly optimized and tested sorting systems such as Nsort [33].

Indexing Sorted Data with a Trie A trie, or a prefix tree, is a tree data structure that stores an array of keys where each leaf node represents one key in the array, and each internal node represents the longest common prefix of the keys represented by its descendants.

When fixed-length key-value entries are sorted by key on flash, a trie for the *shortest unique prefixes* of the keys serves as an index for these sorted data. The shortest unique prefix of a key is the shortest prefix of a key that enables distinguishing the key from the other keys. In such a trie, some prefix of a lookup key leads us to a leaf node with a direct index for the looked up key in sorted data on flash.

Figure 5 shows an example of using a trie to index sorted data. Key prefixes with no shading are the shortest unique prefixes which are used for indexing. The shaded parts are ignored for indexing

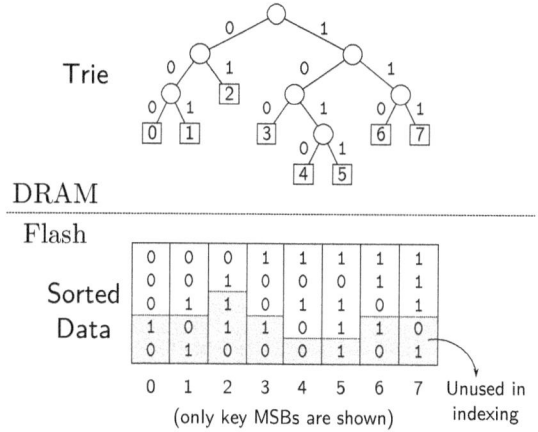

Figure 5: Example of a trie built for indexing sorted keys. The index of each leaf node matches the index of the corresponding key in the sorted keys.

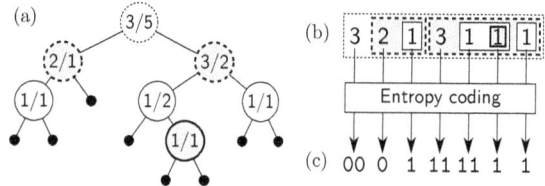

Figure 6: (a) Alternative view of Figure 5, where a pair of numbers in each internal node denotes the number of leaf nodes in its left and right subtries. (b) A recursive form that represents the trie. (c) Its entropy-coded representation used by Sorted-Store.

because any value for the suffix part would not change the key location. A lookup of a key, for example, 10010, follows down to the leaf node that represents 100. As there are 3 preceding leaf nodes, the index of the key is 3. With fixed-length key-value pairs on flash, the exact offset of the data is the obtained index times the key-value pair size (see Section 4 for extensions for variable-length key-value pairs). Note that a lookup of similar keys with the same prefix of 100 (e.g., 10000, 10011) would return the same index even though they are not in the array; the trie guarantees a correct index lookup for stored keys, but says nothing about the presence of a lookup key.

Representing a Trie A typical tree data structure is unsuitable for SILT because each node would require expensive memory pointers, each 2 to 8 bytes long. Common trie representations such as level-compressed tries [3] are also inadequate if they use pointers.

SortedStore uses a compact recursive representation to eliminate pointers. The representation for a trie T having L and R as its left and right subtries is defined as follows:

$$\text{Repr}(T) \; := \; |L| \; \text{Repr}(L) \; \text{Repr}(R)$$

where $|L|$ is the number of leaf nodes in the left subtrie. When T is empty or a leaf node, the representation for T is an empty string. (We use a special mark (-1) instead of the empty string for brevity in the simplified algorithm description, but the full algorithm does not require the use of the special mark.)

```
# @param  T    array of sorted keys
# @return      trie representation
def construct(T):
  if len(T) == 0 or len(T) == 1:
    return [-1]
  else:
    # Partition keys according to their MSB
    L = [key[1:] for key in T if key[0] == 0]
    R = [key[1:] for key in T if key[0] == 1]
    # Recursively construct the representation
    return [len(L)] + construct(L) + construct(R)
```

Algorithm 1: Trie representation generation in Python-like syntax. key[0] and key[1:] denote the most significant bit and the remaining bits of key, respectively.

Figure 6 (a,b) illustrates the uncompressed recursive representation for the trie in Figure 5. As there are 3 keys starting with 0, $|L| = 3$. In its left subtrie, $|L| = 2$ because it has 2 keys that have 0 in their second bit position, so the next number in the representation is 2. It again recurses into its left subtrie, yielding 1. Here there are no more non-leaf nodes, so it returns to the root node and then generates the representation for the right subtrie of the root, 3 1 1 1.

Algorithm 1 shows a simplified algorithm that builds a (non-entropy-coded) trie representation from sorted keys. It resembles quicksort in that it finds the partition of keys and recurses into both subsets. Index generation is fast (≥ 7 M keys/sec on a modern Intel desktop CPU, Section 6).

Looking up Keys Key-lookup works by incrementally reading the trie representation (Algorithm 2). The function is supplied the lookup key and a trie representation string. By decoding the encoded next number, *thead*, SortedStore knows if the current node is an internal node where it can recurse into its subtrie. If the lookup key goes to the left subtrie, SortedStore recurses into the left subtrie, whose representation immediately follows in the given trie representation; otherwise, SortedStore recursively decodes and discards the entire left subtrie and then recurses into the right. SortedStore sums *thead* at every node where it recurses into a right subtrie; the sum of the *thead* values is the offset at which the lookup key is stored, if it exists.

For example, to look up 10010, SortedStore first obtains 3 from the representation. Then, as the first bit of the key is 1, it skips the next numbers (2 1) which are for the representation of the left subtrie, and it proceeds to the right subtrie. In the right subtrie, SortedStore reads the next number (3; not a leaf node), checks the second bit of the key, and keeps recursing into its left subtrie. After reading the next number for the current subtrie (1), SortedStore arrives at a leaf node by taking the left subtrie. Until it reaches the leaf node, it takes a right subtrie only at the root node; from $n = 3$ at the root node, SortedStore knows that the offset of the data for 10010 is ($3 \times$ key-value-size) on flash.

Compression Although the above uncompressed representation uses up to 3 integers per key on average, for *hashed* keys, SortedStore can easily reduce the average representation size to 0.4 bytes/key by compressing each $|L|$ value using *entropy coding* (Figure 6 (c)). The value of $|L|$ tends to be close to half of $|T|$ (the number of leaf nodes in T) because fixed-length hashed keys are uniformly distributed over the key space, so both subtries have the same probability of storing a key. More formally, $|L| \sim Binomial(|T|, \frac{1}{2})$. When $|L|$ is small enough (e.g., ≤ 16), SortedStore uses static, glob-

```
# @param  key    lookup key
# @param  trepr  trie representation
# @return        index of the key
#                in the original array
def lookup(key, trepr):
  (thead, ttail) = (trepr[0], trepr[1:])
  if thead == -1:
    return 0
  else:
    if key[0] == 0:
      # Recurse into the left subtrie
      return lookup(key[1:], ttail)
    else:
      # Skip the left subtrie
      ttail = discard_subtrie(ttail)
      # Recurse into the right subtrie
      return thead + lookup(key[1:], ttail)

# @param  trepr  trie representation
# @return        remaining trie representation
#                with the next subtrie consumed
def discard_subtrie(trepr):
  (thead, ttail) = (trepr[0], trepr[1:])
  if thead == -1:
    return ttail
  else:
    # Skip both subtries
    ttail = discard_subtrie(ttail)
    ttail = discard_subtrie(ttail)
    return ttail
```

Algorithm 2: Key lookup on a trie representation.

ally shared Huffman tables based on the binomial distributions. If $|L|$ is large, SortedStore encodes the difference between $|L|$ and its expected value (i.e., $\frac{|T|}{2}$) using Elias gamma coding [23] to avoid filling the CPU cache with large Huffman tables. With this entropy coding optimized for hashed keys, our entropy-coded trie representation is about twice as compact as the previous best recursive tree encoding [16].

When handling compressed tries, Algorithm 1 and 2 are extended to keep track of the number of leaf nodes at each recursion step. This does not require any additional information in the representation because the number of leaf nodes can be calculated recursively using $|T| = |L| + |R|$. Based on $|T|$, these algorithms choose an entropy coder for encoding len(L) and decoding thead. It is noteworthy that the special mark (-1) takes no space with entropy coding, as its entropy is zero.

Ensuring Constant Time Index Lookups As described, a lookup may have to decompress the entire trie, so that the cost of lookups would grow (large) as the number of entries in the key-value store grows.

To bound the lookup time, items are partitioned into 2^k buckets based on the first k bits of their key. Each bucket has its own trie index. Using, e.g., $k = 10$ for a key-value store holding 2^{16} items, each bucket would hold in expectation $2^{16-10} = 2^6$ items. With high probability, no bucket holds more than 2^8 items, so the time to decompress the trie for bucket is both bounded by a constant value, and small.

This bucketing requires additional information to be stored in memory: (1) the pointers to the trie representations of each bucket and (2) the number of entries in each bucket. SILT keeps the amount of this bucketing information small (less than 1 bit/key) by using a simpler version of a compact select data structure, semi-direct-

Comparison	"Deleted"?	Action on K_{SS}	Action on K_{HS}
$K_{SS} < K_{HS}$	any	copy	–
$K_{SS} > K_{HS}$	no	–	copy
$K_{SS} > K_{HS}$	yes	–	drop
$K_{SS} = K_{HS}$	no	drop	copy
$K_{SS} = K_{HS}$	yes	drop	drop

Table 3: Merge rule for SortedStore. K_{SS} **is the current key from SortedStore, and** K_{HS} **is the current key from the sorted data of HashStores. "Deleted" means the current entry in** K_{HS} **is a special entry indicating a key of SortedStore has been deleted.**

16 [11]. With bucketing, our trie-based indexing belongs to the class of data structures called monotone minimal perfect hashing [10, 13] (Section 7).

Further Space Optimizations for Small Key-Value Sizes For small key-value entries, SortedStore can reduce the trie size by applying *sparse indexing* [22]. Sparse indexing locates the *block* that contains an entry, rather than the exact offset of the entry. This technique requires scanning or binary search within the block, but it reduces the amount of indexing information. It is particularly useful when the storage media has a minimum useful block size to read; many flash devices, for instance, provide increasing I/Os per second as the block size drops, but not past a certain limit (e.g., 512 or 4096 bytes) [31, 35]. SILT uses sparse indexing when configured for key-value sizes of 64 bytes or smaller.

SortedStore obtains a sparse-indexing version of the trie by pruning some subtries in it. When a trie has subtries that have entries all in the same block, the trie can omit the representation of these subtries because the omitted data only gives in-block offset information between entries. Pruning can reduce the trie size to 1 bit per key or less if each block contains 16 key-value entries or more.

Merging HashStores into SortedStore SortedStore is an immutable store and cannot be changed. Accordingly, the merge process generates a new SortedStore based on the given HashStores and the existing SortedStore. Similar to the conversion from LogStore to HashStore, HashStores and the old SortedStore can serve lookups during merging.

The merge process consists of two steps: (1) sorting HashStores and (2) sequentially merging sorted HashStores data and SortedStore. First, SILT sorts all data in HashStores to be merged. This task is done by enumerating every entry in the HashStores and sorting these entries. Then, this sorted data from HashStores is sequentially merged with already sorted data in the SortedStore. The sequential merge chooses newest valid entries, as summarized in Table 3; either copy or drop action on a key consumes the key (i.e., by advancing the "merge pointer" in the corresponding store), while the current key remains available for the next comparison again if no action is applied to the key. After both steps have been completed, the old SortedStore is atomically replaced by the new SortedStore. During the merge process, both the old SortedStore and the new SortedStore exist on flash; however, the flash space overhead from temporarily having two SortedStores is kept small by performing the merge process on a single SILT instance at the same time.

In Section 5, we discuss how frequently HashStores should be merged into SortedStore.

Application of False Positive Filters Since SILT maintains only one SortedStore per SILT instance, SortedStore does not have to

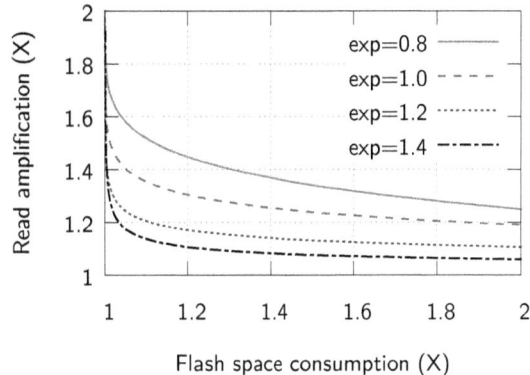

Figure 7: Read amplification as a function of flash space consumption when inlining is applied to key-values whose sizes follow a Zipf distribution. "exp" is the exponent part of the distribution.

use a false positive filter to reduce unnecessary I/O. However, an extension to the SILT architecture might have multiple SortedStores. In this case, the trie index can easily accommodate the false positive filter; the filter is generated by extracting the key fragments from the sorted keys. Key fragments can be stored in an in-memory array so that they have the same order as the sorted data on flash. The extended SortedStore can consult the key fragments before reading data from flash.

4. EXTENDING SILT FUNCTIONALITY

SILT can support an even wider range of applications and workloads than the basic design we have described. In this section, we present potential techniques to extend SILT's capabilities.

Crash Tolerance SILT ensures that all its in-memory data structures are backed-up to flash and/or easily re-created after failures. All updates to LogStore are appended to the on-flash log chronologically; to recover from a fail-stop crash, SILT simply replays the log file to construct the in-memory index and filter. For HashStore and SortedStore, which are static, SILT keeps a copy of their in-memory data structures on flash, which can be re-read during recovery.

SILT's current design, however, does not provide crash tolerance for *new* updates to the data store. These writes are handled asynchronously, so a key insertion/update request to SILT may complete before its data is written durably to flash. For applications that need this additional level of crash tolerance, SILT would need to support an additional synchronous write mode. For example, SILT could delay returning from write calls until it confirms that the requested write is fully flushed to the on-flash log.

Variable-Length Key-Values For simplicity, the design we presented so far focuses on fixed-length key-value data. In fact, SILT can easily support variable-length key-value data by using *indirection with inlining*. This scheme follows the existing SILT design with fixed-sized slots, but stores (`offset`, `first part of (key, value)`) pairs instead of the actual (`key, value`) in HashStores and SortedStores (LogStores can handle variable-length data natively). These offsets point to the remaining part of the key-value data stored elsewhere (e.g., a second flash device). If a whole item is small enough to fit in a fixed-length slot, indirection can be avoided; consequently, large data requires an extra flash read (or write), but small data incurs no additional I/O cost. Figure 7 plots an analytic result on the tradeoff of this scheme with different slot sizes. It uses key-value pairs whose sizes range between 4 B and 1 MiB and follow a Zipf distribution, assuming a 4-byte header (for key-value lengths), a 4-byte offset pointer, and an uniform access pattern.

For specific applications, SILT can alternatively use segregated stores for further efficiency. Similar to the idea of simple segregated storage [39], the system could instantiate several SILT instances for different fixed key-value size combinations. The application may choose an instance with the most appropriate key-value size as done in Dynamo [21], or SILT can choose the best instance for a new key and return an opaque key containing the instance ID to the application. Since each instance can optimize flash space overheads and additional flash reads for its own dataset, using segregated stores can reduce the cost of supporting variable-length key-values close to the level of fixed-length key-values.

In the subsequent sections, we will discuss SILT with fixed-length key-value pairs only.

Fail-Graceful Indexing Under high memory pressure, SILT may temporarily operate in a degraded indexing mode by allowing higher read amplification (e.g., more than 2 flash reads per lookup) to avoid halting or crashing because of insufficient memory.

(1) Dropping in-memory indexes and filters. HashStore's filters and SortedStore's indexes are stored on flash for crash tolerance, allowing SILT to drop them from memory. This option saves memory at the cost of one additional flash read for the SortedStore, or two for the HashStore.

(2) Binary search on SortedStore. The SortedStore can be searched without an index, so the in-memory trie can be dropped even without storing a copy on flash, at the cost of $\log(n)$ additional reads from flash.

These techniques also help speed SILT's startup. By memory-mapping on-flash index files or performing binary search, SILT can begin serving requests before it has loaded its indexes into memory in the background.

5. ANALYSIS

Compared to single key-value store approaches, the multi-store design of SILT has more system parameters, such as the size of a single LogStore and HashStore, the total number of HashStores, the frequency to merge data into SortedStore, and so on. Having a much larger design space, it is preferable to have a systematic way to do parameter selection.

This section provides a simple model of the tradeoffs between write amplification (WA), read amplification (RA), and memory overhead (MO) in SILT, with an eye towards being able to set the system parameters properly to achieve the design goals from Section 2.

$$\text{WA} = \frac{\text{data written to flash}}{\text{data written by application}}, \quad (1)$$

$$\text{RA} = \frac{\text{data read from flash}}{\text{data read by application}}, \quad (2)$$

$$\text{MO} = \frac{\text{total memory consumed}}{\text{number of items}}. \quad (3)$$

Model A SILT system has a flash drive of size F bytes with a lifetime of E erase cycles. The system runs P SILT instances locally, each of which handles one disjoint range of keys using one Log-Store, one SortedStore, and multiple HashStores. Once an instance

Symbol	Meaning	Example
SILT design parameters		
d	maximum number of entries to merge	7.5 M
k	tag size in bit	15 bits
P	number of SILT instances	4
H	number of HashStores per instance	31
f	false positive rate per store	2^{-12}
Workload characteristics		
c	key-value entry size	1024 B
N	total number of distinct keys	100 M
U	update rate	5 K/sec
Storage constraints		
F	total flash size	256 GB
E	maximum flash erase cycle	10,000

Table 4: Notation.

has d keys in total in its HashStores, it merges these keys into its SortedStore.

We focus here on a workload where the total amount of data stored in the system remains constant (e.g., only applying updates to existing keys). We omit for space the similar results when the data volume is growing (e.g., new keys are inserted to the system) and additional nodes are being added to provide capacity over time. Table 4 presents the notation used in the analysis.

Write Amplification An update first writes one record to the Log-Store. Subsequently converting that LogStore to a HashStore incurs $1/0.93 = 1.075$ writes per key, because the space occupancy of the hash table is 93%. Finally, d total entries (across multiple Hash-Stores of one SILT instance) are merged into the existing Sorted-Store, creating a new SortedStore with N/P entries. The total write amplification is therefore

$$\text{WA} = 2.075 + \frac{N}{d \cdot P}. \quad (4)$$

Read Amplification The false positive rate of flash reads from a 4-way set associative hash table using k-bit tags is $f = 8/2^k$ because there are eight possible locations for a given key—two possible buckets and four items per bucket.

This 4-way set associative cuckoo hash table with k-bit tags can store 2^{k+2} entries, so at 93% occupancy, each LogStore and Hash-Store holds $0.93 \cdot 2^{k+2}$ keys. In one SILT instance, the number of items stored in HashStores ranges from 0 (after merging) to d, with an average size of $d/2$, so the average number of HashStores is

$$H = \frac{d/2}{0.93 \cdot 2^{k+2}} = 0.134 \frac{d}{2^k}. \quad (5)$$

In the *worst-case* of a lookup, the system reads once from flash at the SortedStore, after $1+H$ failed retrievals at the LogStore and H HashStores. Note that each LogStore or HashStore rejects all but an f fraction of false positive retrievals; therefore, the expected total number of reads per lookup (read amplification) is:

$$\text{RA} = (1+H)f + 1 = \frac{8}{2^k} + 1.07\frac{d}{4^k} + 1. \quad (6)$$

By picking d and k to ensure $1.07d/4^k + 8/2^k < \varepsilon$, SILT can achieve the design goal of read amplification $1 + \varepsilon$.

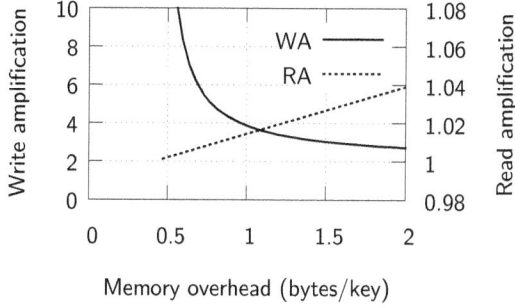

Figure 8: WA and RA as a function of MO when N=100 M, P=4, and k=15, while d is varied.

Memory Overhead Each entry in LogStore uses $(k+1)/8+4$ bytes (k bits for the tag, one valid bit, and 4 bytes for the pointer). Each HashStore filter entry uses $k/8$ bytes for the tag. Each SortedStore entry consumes only 0.4 bytes. Using one LogStore, one SortedStore, and H HashStores, SILT's memory overhead is:

$$\text{MO} = \frac{\left(\left(\frac{k+1}{8}+4\right)\cdot 2^{k+2}+\frac{k}{8}\cdot 2^{k+2}\cdot H+0.4\cdot\frac{N}{P}\right)\cdot P}{N}$$

$$= \left((16.5+0.5k)2^k+0.067\,kd\right)\frac{P}{N}+0.4. \quad (7)$$

Tradeoffs Improving either write amplification, read amplification, or memory amplification comes at the cost of one of the other two metrics. For example, using larger tags (i.e., increasing k) reduces read amplification by reducing both f the false positive rate per store and H the number of HashStores. However, the HashStores then consume more DRAM due to the larger tags, increasing memory overhead. Similarly, by increasing d, SILT can merge HashStores into the SortedStore less frequently to reduce the write amplification, but doing so increases the amount of DRAM consumed by the HashStore filters. Figure 8 illustrates how write and read amplification change as a function of memory overhead when the maximum number of HashStore entries, d, is varied.

Update Rate vs. Flash Life Time The designer of a SILT instance handling U updates per second wishes to ensure that the flash lasts for at least T seconds. Assuming the flash device has perfect wear-leveling when being sent a series of large sequential writes [15], the total number of writes, multiplied by the write amplification WA, must not exceed the flash device size times its erase cycle budget. This creates a relationship between the lifetime, device size, update rate, and memory overhead:

$$U\cdot c\cdot \text{WA}\cdot T \;\leq\; F\cdot E. \quad (8)$$

Example Assume a SILT system is built with a 256 GB MLC flash drive supporting 10,000 erase cycles [5] ($E=10000$, $F=256\times 2^{30}$). It is serving $N=100$ million items with $P=4$ SILT instances, and $d=7.5$ million. Its workload is 1 KiB entries, 5,000 updates per second ($U=5000$).

By Eq. (4) the write amplification, WA, is 5.4. That is, each key-value update incurs 5.4 writes/entry. On average the number of HashStores is 31 according to Eq. (5). The read amplification, however, is very close to 1. Eq. (6) shows that when choosing 15 bits for the key fragment size, a GET incurs on average 1.008 of flash reads even when all stores must be consulted. Finally, we can see how the SILT design achieves its design goal of memory efficiency: indexing a total of 102.4 GB of data, where each key-value pair

takes 1 KiB, requires only 73 MB in total or 0.73 bytes per entry (Eq. (7)). With the write amplification of 5.4 from above, this device will last 3 years.

6. EVALUATION

Using macro- and micro-benchmarks, we evaluate SILT's overall performance and explore how its system design and algorithms contribute to meeting its goals. We specifically examine (1) an end-to-end evaluation of SILT's throughput, memory overhead, and latency; (2) the performance of SILT's in-memory indexing data structures in isolation; and (3) the individual performance of each data store type, including flash I/O.

Implementation SILT is implemented in 15 K lines of C++ using a modular architecture similar to Anvil [29]. Each component of the system exports the same, basic key-value interface. For example, the classes which implement each of the three stores (LogStore, HashStore, and SortedStore) export this interface but themselves call into classes which implement the in-memory and on-disk data structures using that same interface. The SILT system, in turn, unifies the three stores and provides this key-value API to applications. (SILT also has components for background conversion and merging.)

Evaluation System We evaluate SILT on Linux using a desktop equipped with:

CPU	Intel Core i7 860 @ 2.80 Ghz (4 cores)
DRAM	DDR SDRAM / 8 GiB
SSD-L	Crucial RealSSD C300 / 256 GB
SSD-S	Intel X25-E / 32 GB

The 256 GB SSD-L stores the key-value data, and the SSD-S is used as scratch space for sorting HashStores using Nsort [33]. The drives connect using SATA and are formatted with the ext4 filesystem using the `discard` mount option (TRIM support) to enable the flash device to free blocks from deleted files. The baseline performance of the data SSD is:

Random Reads (1024 B)	48 K reads/sec
Sequential Reads	256 MB/sec
Sequential Writes	233 MB/sec

6.1 Full System Benchmark

Workload Generation We use YCSB [17] to generate a key-value workload. By default, we use a 10% PUT / 90% GET workload for 20-byte keys and 1000-byte values, and we also use a 50% PUT / 50% GET workload for 64-byte key-value pairs in throughput and memory overhead benchmarks. To avoid the high cost of the Java-based workload generator, we use a lightweight SILT client to replay a captured trace file of queries made by YCSB. The experiments use four SILT instances ($P=4$), with 16 client threads concurrently issuing requests. When applicable, we limit the rate at which SILT converts entries from LogStores to HashStores to 10 K entries/second, and from HashStores to the SortedStore to 20 K entries/second in order to prevent these background operations from exhausting I/O resources.

Throughput: SILT can sustain an average insert rate of 3,000 1 KiB key-value pairs per second, while simultaneously supporting 33,000 queries/second, or 69% of the SSD's random read capacity. With no inserts, SILT supports 46 K queries per second (**96%** of the drive's raw capacity), and with no queries, can sustain an insert rate of approximately 23 K inserts per second. On a deduplication-like

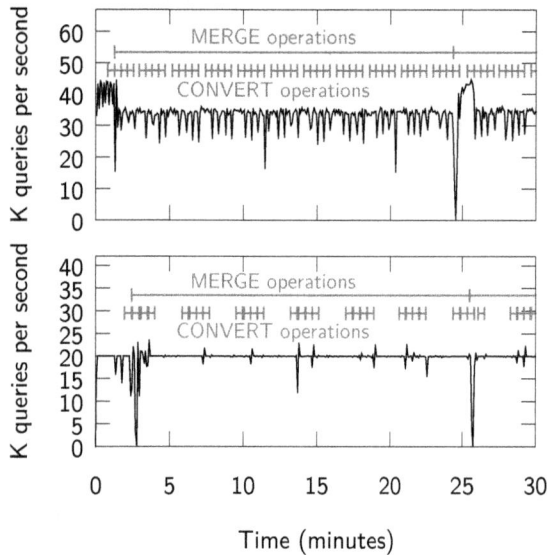

Figure 9: GET throughput under high (upper) and low (lower) loads.

<table>
<thead>
<tr><th>Type</th><th>Cuckoo hashing
(K keys/s)</th><th>Trie
(K keys/s)</th></tr>
</thead>
<tbody>
<tr><td>Individual insertion</td><td>10182</td><td>–</td></tr>
<tr><td>Bulk insertion</td><td>–</td><td>7603</td></tr>
<tr><td>Lookup</td><td>1840</td><td>208</td></tr>
</tbody>
</table>

Table 5: In-memory performance of index data structures in SILT on a single CPU core.

the full SILT configuration. The upper right configuration instead omits the SortedStore, and consumes four times as much memory. Finally, the upper left configuration uses only the basic LogStore, which requires nearly 10x as much memory as SILT. To make this comparison fair, the test generates unique new items so that garbage collection of old entries cannot help the SortedStore run faster.

The figures also help understand the modest cost of SILT's memory efficiency. The LogStore-only system processes the 50 million inserts (500 million total operations) in under 170 minutes, whereas the full SILT system takes only 40% longer–about 238 minutes–to incorporate the records, but achieves an order of magnitude better memory efficiency.

Latency: SILT is fast, processing queries in 367 μs on average, as shown in Figure 11 for 100% GET queries for 1 KiB key-value entries. GET responses are fastest when served by the LogStore (309 μs), and slightly slower when they must be served by the SortedStore. The relatively small latency increase when querying the later stores shows the effectiveness (reducing the number of extra flash reads to $\varepsilon < 0.01$) and speed of SILT's in-memory filters used in the Log and HashStores.

In the remaining sections, we evaluate the performance of SILT's individual in-memory indexing techniques, and the performance of the individual stores (in-memory indexes plus on-flash data structures).

6.2 Index Microbenchmark

The high random read speed of flash drives means that the CPU budget available for each index operation is relatively limited. This microbenchmark demonstrates that SILT's indexes meet their design goal of computation-efficient indexing.

Experiment Design This experiment measures insertion and lookup speed of SILT's in-memory partial-key cuckoo hash and entropy-coded trie indexes. The benchmark inserts 126 million total entries and looks up a subset of 10 million random 20-byte keys.

This microbenchmark involves memory only, no flash I/O. Although the SILT system uses multiple CPU cores to access multiple indexes concurrently, access to individual indexes in this benchmark is single-threaded. Note that inserting into the cuckoo hash table (LogStore) proceeds key-by-key, whereas the trie (SortedStore) is constructed en mass using bulk insertion. Table 5 summarizes the measurement results.

Individual Insertion Speed (Cuckoo Hashing) SILT's cuckoo hash index implementation can handle 10.18 M 20-byte key insertions (PUTs or DELETEs) per second. Even at a relatively small, higher overhead key-value entry size of 32-byte (i.e., 12-byte data), the index would support 326 MB/s of incoming key-value data on one CPU core. This rate exceeds the typical sequential write speed of a single flash drive: inserting keys into our cuckoo hashing is unlikely to become a bottleneck in SILT given current trends.

workload with 50% writes and 50% reads of 64 byte records, SILT handles 72,000 requests/second.

SILT's performance under insert workloads is limited by the time needed to convert and merge data into HashStores and SortedStores. These *background operations* compete for flash I/O resources, resulting in a tradeoff between query latency and throughput. Figure 9 shows the sustainable query rate under both high query load (approx. 33 K queries/second) and low query load (22.2 K queries/second) for 1 KiB key-value pairs. SILT is capable of providing predictable, low latency, or can be tuned for higher overall throughput. The middle line shows when SILT converts LogStores into HashStores (periodically, in small bursts). The top line shows that at nearly all times, SILT is busy merging HashStores into the SortedStore in order to optimize its index size.[4] In Section 6.3, we evaluate in more detail the speed of the individual stores and conversion processes.

Memory overhead: SILT meets its goal of providing high throughput with low memory overhead. We measured the time and memory required to insert 50 million new 1 KiB entries into a table with 50 million existing entries, while simultaneously handling a high query rate. SILT used at most 69 MB of DRAM, or 0.69 bytes per entry. (This workload is worst-case because it is never allowed time for SILT to compact all of its HashStores into the SortedStore.) For the 50% PUT / 50% GET workload with 64-byte key-value pairs, SILT required at most 60 MB of DRAM for 100 million entries, or 0.60 bytes per entry.

The drastic improvement in memory overhead from SILT's three-store architecture is shown in Figure 10. The figure shows the memory consumption during the insertion run over time, using four different configurations of basic store types and 1 KiB key-value entries. The bottom right graph shows the memory consumed using the full SILT system. The bottom left configuration omits the intermediate HashStore, thus requiring twice as much memory as

---

[4]In both workloads, when merge operations complete (e.g., at 25 minutes), there is a momentary drop in query speed. This is due to bursty TRIMming by the ext4 filesystem implementation (discard) used in the experiment when the previous multi-gigabyte SortedStore file is deleted from flash.

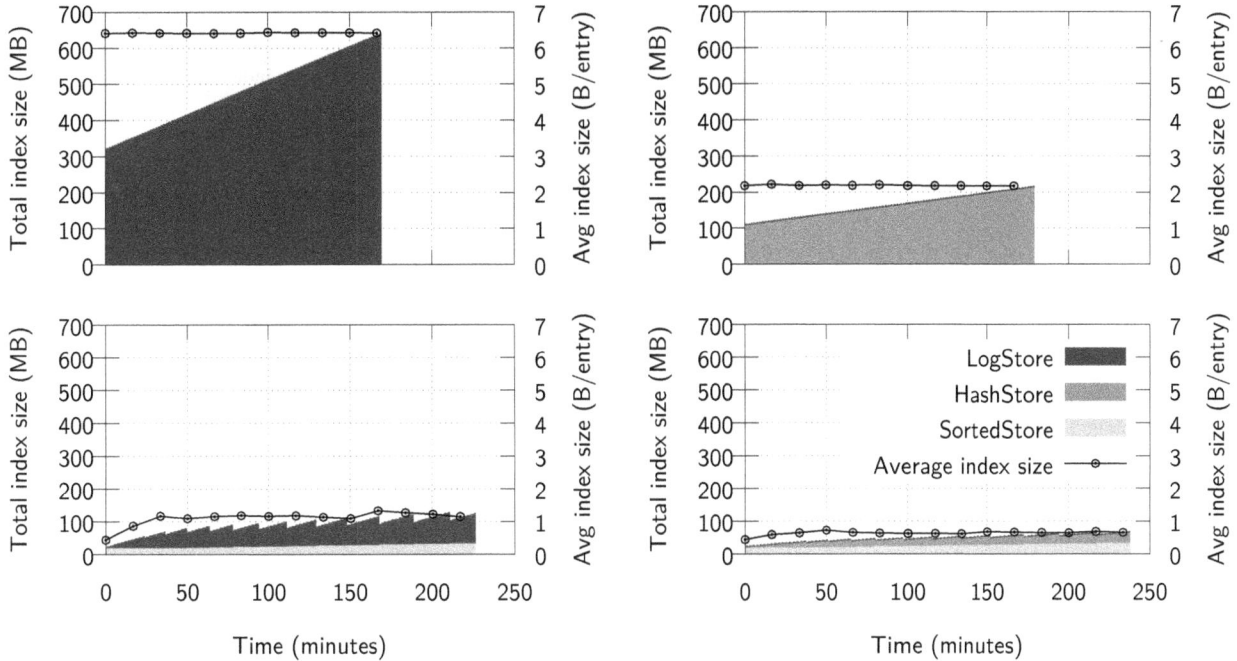

Figure 10: Index size changes for four different store combinations while inserting new 50 M entries.

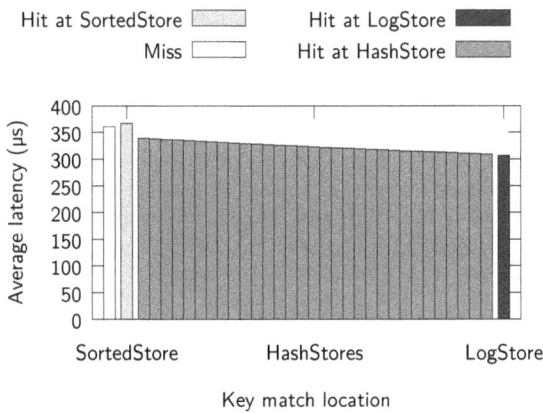

Figure 11: GET query latency when served from different store locations.

Bulk Insertion Speed (Trie) Building the trie index over 126 million pre-sorted keys required approximately 17 seconds, or 7.6 M keys/second.

Key Lookup Speed Each SILT GET operation requires a lookup in the LogStore and potentially in one or more HashStores and the SortedStore. A single CPU core can perform 1.84 million cuckoo hash lookups per second. If a SILT instance has 1 LogStore and 31 HashStores, each of which needs to be consulted, then one core can handle about 57.5 K GETs/sec. Trie lookups are approximately 8.8 times slower than cuckoo hashing lookups, but a GET triggers a lookup in the trie only after SILT cannot find the key in the LogStore and HashStores. When combined, the SILT indexes can handle about $1/(1/57.5 \text{ K} + 1/208 \text{ K}) \approx 45$ K GETs/sec with one CPU core.

Type	Speed (K keys/s)
LogStore (by PUT)	204.6
HashStore (by CONVERT)	67.96
SortedStore (by MERGE)	26.76

Table 6: Construction performance for basic stores. The construction method is shown in the parentheses.

Insertions are faster than lookups in cuckoo hashing because insertions happen to only a few tables at the same time and thus benefit from the CPU's L2 cache; lookups, however, can occur to any table in memory, making CPU cache less effective.

Operation on Multiple Cores Using four cores, SILT indexes handle 180 K GETs/sec in memory. At this speed, the indexes are unlikely to become a bottleneck: their overhead is on-par or lower than the operating system overhead for actually performing that many 1024-byte reads per second from flash. As we see in the next section, SILT's overall performance is limited by sorting, but its index CPU use is high enough that adding many more flash drives would require more CPU cores. Fortunately, SILT offers many opportunities for parallel execution: Each SILT node runs multiple, completely independent instances of SILT to handle partitioning, and each of these instances can query many stores.

6.3 Individual Store Microbenchmark

Here we measure the performance of each SILT store type in its entirety (in-memory indexing plus on-flash I/O). The first experiment builds multiple instances of each basic store type with 100 M key-value pairs (20-byte key, 1000-byte value). The second experiment queries each store for 10 M random keys.

Type	SortedStore (K ops/s)	HashStore (K ops/s)	LogStore (K ops/s)
GET (hit)	46.57	44.93	46.79
GET (miss)	46.61	7264	7086

Table 7: Query performance for basic stores that include in-memory and on-flash data structures.

Table 6 shows the construction performance for all three stores; the construction method is shown in parentheses. LogStore construction, built through entry-by-entry insertion using PUT, can use 90% of sequential write bandwidth of the flash drive. Thus, SILT is well-suited to handle bursty inserts. The conversion from LogStores to HashStores is about three times slower than LogStore construction because it involves bulk data reads and writes from/to the same flash drive. SortedStore construction is slowest, as it involves an external sort for the entire group of 31 HashStores to make one SortedStore (assuming no previous SortedStore). If constructing the SortedStore involved merging the new data with an existing SortedStore, the performance would be worse. The large time required to create a SortedStore was one of the motivations for introducing HashStores rather than keeping un-merged data in LogStores.

Table 7 shows that the minimum GET performance across all three stores is 44.93 K ops/s. Note that LogStores and HashStores are particularly fast at GET for non-existent keys (more than 7 M ops/s). This extremely low miss penalty explains why there was only a small variance in the average GET latency in Figure 11 where bad cases looked up 32 Log and HashStores and failed to find a matching item in any of them.

7. RELATED WORK

Hashing *Cuckoo hashing* [34] is an open-addressing scheme to resolve hash collisions efficiently with high space occupancy. Our partial-key cuckoo hashing—storing only a small part of the key in memory without fetching the entire keys from slow storage on collisions—makes cuckoo hashing more memory-efficient while ensuring high performance.

Minimal perfect hashing is a family of collision-free hash functions that map n distinct keys to n consecutive integers $0 \ldots n-1$, and is widely used for memory-efficient indexing. In theory, any minimal perfect hash scheme requires at least 1.44 bits/key [27]; in practice, the state-of-the-art schemes can index any static data set with 2.07 bits/key [10]. Our entropy-coded trie achieves 3.1 bits/key, but it also preserves the lexicographical order of the keys to facilitate data merging. Thus, it belongs to the family of monotone minimal perfect hashing (MMPH). Compared to other proposals for MMPH [8, 9], our trie-based index is simple, lightweight to generate, and has very small CPU/memory overhead.

External-Memory Index on Flash Recent work such as Micro-Hash [40] and FlashDB [32] minimizes memory consumption by having indexes on flash. MicroHash uses a hash table chained by pointers on flash. FlashDB proposes a self-tuning B^+-tree index that dynamically adapts the node representation according to the workload. Both systems are optimized for memory and energy consumption of sensor devices, but not for latency as lookups in both systems require reading multiple flash pages. In contrast, SILT achieves very low memory footprint while still supporting high throughput.

Key-Value Stores HashCache [4] proposes several policies to combine hash table-based in-memory indexes and on-disk data layout for caching web objects. FAWN-DS [2] consists of an on-flash data log and in-memory hash table index built using relatively slow CPUs with a limited amount of memory. SILT dramatically reduces DRAM consumption compared to these systems by combining more memory-efficient data stores with minimal performance impact. FlashStore [19] also uses a single hash table to index all keys on flash similar to FAWN-DS. The flash storage, however, is used as a cache of a hard disk-backed database. Thus, the cache hierarchy and eviction algorithm is orthogonal to SILT. To achieve low memory footprint (about 1 byte/key), SkimpyStash [20] moves its indexing hash table to flash with linear chaining. However, it requires on average 5 flash reads per lookup, while SILT only needs $1 + \varepsilon$ per lookup.

More closely related to our design is BufferHash [1], which keeps keys in multiple equal-sized hash tables—one in memory and the others on flash. The on-flash tables are guarded by in-memory Bloom filters to reduce unnecessary flash reads. In contrast, SILT data stores have different sizes and types. The largest store (SortedStore), for example, does not have a filter and is accessed at most once per lookup, which saves memory while keeping the read amplification low. In addition, writes in SILT are appended to a log stored on flash for crash recovery, whereas inserted keys in BufferHash do not persist until flushed to flash in batch.

Several key-value storage libraries rely on caching to compensate for their high read amplifications [6, 28], making query performance depend greatly on whether the working set fits in the in-memory cache. In contrast, SILT provides uniform and predictably high performance regardless of the working set size and query patterns.

Distributed Key-Value Systems Distributed key-value storage clusters such as BigTable [14], Dynamo [21], and FAWN-KV [2] all try to achieve high scalability and availability using a cluster of key-value store nodes. SILT focuses on how to use flash memory-efficiently with novel data structures, and is complementary to the techniques used in these other systems aimed at managing failover and consistency.

Modular Storage Systems BigTable [14] and Anvil [29] both provide a modular architecture for chaining specialized stores to benefit from combining different optimizations. SILT borrows its design philosophy from these systems; we believe and hope that the techniques we developed for SILT could also be used within these frameworks.

8. CONCLUSION

SILT combines new algorithmic and systems techniques to balance the use of memory, storage, and computation to craft a memory-efficient, high-performance flash-based key value store. It uses two new in-memory index structures—partial-key cuckoo hashing and entropy-coded tries—to reduce drastically the amount of memory needed compared to prior systems. SILT chains the right combination of basic key-value stores together to create a system that provides high write speed, high read throughput, and uses little memory, attributes that no single store can achieve alone. SILT uses in total only 0.7 bytes of memory per entry it stores, and makes only 1.01 flash reads to service a lookup, doing so in under 400 microseconds. Our hope is that SILT, and the techniques described herein, can form an efficient building block for a new generation of fast data-intensive services.

ACKNOWLEDGMENTS

This work was supported by funding from National Science Foundation award CCF-0964474, Google, the Intel Science and Technology Center for Cloud Computing, by CyLab at Carnegie Mellon under grant DAAD19-02-1-0389 from the Army Research Office. Hyeontaek Lim is supported in part by the Korea Foundation for Advanced Studies. We thank the SOSP reviewers, Phillip B. Gibbons, Vijay Vasudevan, and Amar Phanishayee for their feedback, Guy Blelloch and Rasmus Pagh for pointing out several algorithmic possibilities, and Robert Morris for shepherding this paper.

REFERENCES

[1] A. Anand, C. Muthukrishnan, S. Kappes, A. Akella, and S. Nath. Cheap and large CAMs for high performance data-intensive networked systems. In *NSDI'10: Proceedings of the 7th USENIX conference on Networked systems design and implementation*, pages 29–29. USENIX Association, 2010.

[2] D. G. Andersen, J. Franklin, M. Kaminsky, A. Phanishayee, L. Tan, and V. Vasudevan. FAWN: A fast array of wimpy nodes. In *Proc. SOSP*, Oct. 2009.

[3] A. Andersson and S. Nilsson. Improved behaviour of tries by adaptive branching. *Information Processing Letters*, 46(6):295–300, 1993.

[4] A. Badam, K. Park, V. S. Pai, and L. L. Peterson. HashCache: Cache storage for the next billion. In *Proc. 6th USENIX NSDI*, Apr. 2009.

[5] M. Balakrishnan, A. Kadav, V. Prabhakaran, and D. Malkhi. Differential RAID: Rethinking RAID for SSD reliability. In *Proc. European Conference on Computer Systems (Eurosys)*, 2010.

[6] Berkeley DB. http://www.oracle.com/technetwork/database/berkeleydb/, 2011.

[7] D. Beaver, S. Kumar, H. C. Li, J. Sobel, and P. Vajgel. Finding a needle in Haystack: Facebook's photo storage. In *Proc. 9th USENIX OSDI*, Oct. 2010.

[8] D. Belazzougui, P. Boldi, R. Pagh, and S. Vigna. Theory and practise of monotone minimal perfect hashing. In *Proc. 11th Workshop on Algorithm Engineering and Experiments*, ALENEX '09, 2009.

[9] D. Belazzougui, P. Boldi, R. Pagh, and S. Vigna. Monotone minimal perfect hashing: searching a sorted table with O(1) accesses. In *Proceedings of the twentieth Annual ACM-SIAM Symposium on Discrete Algorithms*, SODA '09, pages 785–794, 2009.

[10] D. Belazzougui, F. Botelho, and M. Dietzfelbinger. Hash, displace, and compress. In *Proceedings of the 17th European Symposium on Algorithms*, ESA '09, pages 682–693, 2009.

[11] D. K. Blandford, G. E. Blelloch, and I. A. Kash. An experimental analysis of a compact graph representation. In *Proc. 6th Workshop on Algorithm Engineering and Experiments*, ALENEX '04, 2004.

[12] B. H. Bloom. Space/time trade-offs in hash coding with allowable errors. *Communications of the ACM*, 13(7):422–426, 1970.

[13] F. C. Botelho, A. Lacerda, G. V. Menezes, and N. Ziviani. Minimal perfect hashing: A competitive method for indexing internal memory. *Information Sciences*, 181:2608–2625, 2011.

[14] F. Chang, J. Dean, S. Ghemawat, W. C. Hsieh, D. A. Wallach, M. Burrows, T. Chandra, A. Fikes, and R. E. Gruber. Bigtable: A distributed storage system for structured data. In *Proc. 7th USENIX OSDI*, Nov. 2006.

[15] L.-P. Chang. On efficient wear leveling for large-scale flash-memory storage systems. In *Proceedings of the 2007 ACM symposium on Applied computing (SAC '07)*, Mar. 2007.

[16] D. R. Clark. *Compact PAT trees*. PhD thesis, University of Waterloo, Waterloo, Ontario, Canada, 1998.

[17] B. Cooper, A. Silberstein, E. Tam, R. Ramakrishnan, and R. Sears. Benchmarking cloud serving systems with YCSB. In *Proc. 1st ACM Symposium on Cloud Computing (SOCC)*, June 2010.

[18] F. Dabek, M. F. Kaashoek, D. Karger, R. Morris, and I. Stoica. Wide-area cooperative storage with CFS. In *Proc. 18th ACM Symposium on Operating Systems Principles (SOSP)*, Oct. 2001.

[19] B. Debnath, S. Sengupta, and J. Li. FlashStore: High throughput persistent key-value store. *Proc. VLDB Endowment*, 3:1414–1425, September 2010.

[20] B. Debnath, S. Sengupta, and J. Li. SkimpyStash: RAM space skimpy key-value store on flash-based storage. In *Proc. International Conference on Management of Data*, ACM SIGMOD '11, pages 25–36, 2011.

[21] G. DeCandia, D. Hastorun, M. Jampani, G. Kakulapati, A. Lakshman, A. Pilchin, S. Sivasubramanian, P. Vosshall, and W. Vogels. Dynamo: Amazon's highly available key-value store. In *Proc. 21st ACM Symposium on Operating Systems Principles (SOSP)*, Oct. 2007.

[22] J. Dong and R. Hull. Applying approximate order dependency to reduce indexing space. In *Proc. ACM SIGMOD International Conference on Management of data*, SIGMOD '82, pages 119–127, 1982.

[23] P. Elias. Universal codeword sets and representations of the integers. *IEEE Transactions on Information Theory*, 21(2):194–203, Mar. 1975.

[24] Ú. Erlingsson, M. Manasse, and F. Mcsherry. A cool and practical alternative to traditional hash tables. In *Proc. 7th Workshop on Distributed Data and Structures (WDAS'06)*, 2006.

[25] Facebook. http://www.facebook.com/, 2011.

[26] Flickr. http://www.flickr.com/, 2011.

[27] E. A. Fox, L. S. Heath, Q. F. Chen, and A. M. Daoud. Practical minimal perfect hash functions for large databases. *Communications of the ACM*, 35:105–121, Jan. 1992.

[28] S. Ghemawat and J. Dean. LevelDB. https://code.google.com/p/leveldb/, 2011.

[29] M. Mammarella, S. Hovsepian, and E. Kohler. Modular data storage with Anvil. In *Proc. SOSP*, Oct. 2009.

[30] Memcached: A distributed memory object caching system. http://www.danga.com/memcached/, 2011.

[31] S. Nath and P. B. Gibbons. Online maintenance of very large random samples on flash storage. In *Proc. VLDB*, Aug. 2008.

[32] S. Nath and A. Kansal. FlashDB: Dynamic self-tuning database for NAND flash. In *Proc. ACM/IEEE International Conference on Information Processing in Sensor Networks*, Apr. 2007.

[33] C. Nyberg and C. Koester. Ordinal Technology - NSort. http://www.ordinal.com/, 2011.

[34] R. Pagh and F. Rodler. Cuckoo hashing. *Journal of Algorithms*, (2):122–144, May 2004.

[35] M. Polte, J. Simsa, and G. Gibson. Enabling enterprise solid state disks performance. In *Proc. Workshop on Integrating Solid-state Memory into the Storage Hierarchy*, Mar. 2009.

[36] S. Quinlan and S. Dorward. Venti: A new approach to archival storage. In *Proc. USENIX Conference on File and Storage Technologies (FAST)*, pages 89–101, Jan. 2002.

[37] I. Stoica, R. Morris, D. Karger, M. F. Kaashoek, and H. Balakrishnan. Chord: A scalable peer-to-peer lookup service for Internet applications. In *Proc. ACM SIGCOMM*, Aug. 2001.

[38] Twitter. http://www.twitter.com/, 2011.

[39] P. Wilson, M. Johnstone, M. Neely, and D. Boles. Dynamic storage allocation: A survey and critical review. *Lecture Notes in Computer Science*, 1995.

[40] D. Zeinalipour-Yazti, S. Lin, V. Kalogeraki, D. Gunopulos, and W. A. Najjar. MicroHash: An efficient index structure for flash-based sensor devices. In *Proc. 4th USENIX Conference on File and Storage Technologies*, Dec. 2005.

Scalable Consistency in Scatter

Lisa Glendenning   Ivan Beschastnikh   Arvind Krishnamurthy   Thomas Anderson

Department of Computer Science & Engineering
University of Washington

ABSTRACT

Distributed storage systems often trade off strong semantics for improved scalability. This paper describes the design, implementation, and evaluation of Scatter, a scalable and consistent distributed key-value storage system. Scatter adopts the highly decentralized and self-organizing structure of scalable peer-to-peer systems, while preserving linearizable consistency even under adverse circumstances. Our prototype implementation demonstrates that even with very short node lifetimes, it is possible to build a scalable and consistent system with practical performance.

Categories and Subject Descriptors

H.3.4 [**Information Storage and Retrieval**]: Systems and Software—*Distributed systems*

General Terms

Design, Reliability

Keywords

Distributed systems, consistency, scalability, fault tolerance, storage, distributed transactions, Paxos

1. INTRODUCTION

A long-standing and recurrent theme in distributed systems research is the design and implementation of efficient and fault tolerant storage systems with predictable and well-understood consistency properties. Recent efforts in peer-to-peer (P2P) storage services include Chord [36], CAN [26], Pastry [30], OpenDHT [29], OceanStore [16], and Kademlia [22]. Recent industrial efforts to provide a distributed storage abstraction across data centers include Amazon's Dynamo [10], Yahoo!'s PNUTS [8], and Google's Megastore [1] and Spanner [9] projects. Particularly with geo-

graphic distribution, whether due to using multiple data centers or a P2P resource model, the tradeoffs between efficiency and consistency are non-trivial, leading to systems that are complex to implement, complex to use, and sometimes both.

Our interest is in building a storage layer for a very large scale P2P system we are designing for hosting planetary scale social networking applications. Purchasing, installing, powering up, and maintaining a very large scale set of nodes across many geographically distributed data centers is an expensive proposition; it is only feasible on an ongoing basis for those applications that can generate revenue. In much the same way that Linux offers a free alternative to commercial operating systems for researchers and developers interested in tinkering, we ask: what is the Linux analogue with respect to cloud computing?

P2P systems provide an attractive alternative, but first generation storage layers were based on unrealistic assumptions about P2P client behavior in the wild. In practice, participating nodes have widely varying capacity and network bandwidth, connections are flaky and asymmetric rather than well-provisioned, workload hotspots are common, and churn rates are very high [27, 12]. This led to a choice for application developers: weakly consistent but scalable P2P systems like Kademlia and OpenDHT, or strongly consistent data center storage.

Our P2P storage layer, called Scatter, attempts to bridge this gap – to provide an open-source, free, yet robust alternative to data center computing, using only P2P resources. Scatter provides scalable and consistent distributed hash table key-value storage. Scatter is robust to P2P churn, heterogeneous node capacities, and flaky and irregular network behavior. (We have left robustness to malicious behavior, such as against DDoS attacks and Byzantine faults, to future work.) In keeping with our goal of building an open system, an essential requirement for Scatter is that there be no central point of control for commercial interests to exploit.

The base component of Scatter is a small, self-organizing group of nodes, each managing a range of keys, akin to a BigTable [6] tablet. A set of groups together partition the table space to provide the distributed hash table abstraction. Each group is responsible for providing consistent read/write access to its key range, and for reconfiguring as necessary to meet performance and availability goals. As nodes are added, as nodes fail, or as the workload changes for a region of keys, individual groups must merge with neighboring groups, split into multiple groups, or shift responsibility over parts of the key space to neighboring groups, all while maintaining consistency. A lookup overlay topology connects the Scatter groups in a ring, and groups execute distributed transactions in a decentralized fashion to modify the topology consistently and atomically.

A key insight in the design of Scatter is that the consistent group abstraction provides a stable base on which to layer the optimizations needed to maintain overall system performance and availability goals. While existing popular DHTs have difficulty maintaining consistent routing state and consistent name space partitioning in the presence of high churn, these properties are a direct consequence of Scatter's design. Further, Scatter can locally adjust the amount of replication, or mask a low capacity node, or merge/split groups if a particular Scatter group has an unusual number of weak/strong nodes, all without compromising the structural integrity of the distributed table.

Of course, some applications may tolerate weaker consistency models for application data storage [10], while other applications have stronger consistency requirements [1]. Scatter is designed to support a variety of consistency models for application key storage. Our current implementation provides linearizable storage within a given key; we support cross-group transactions for consistent updates to meta-data during group reconfiguration, but we do not attempt to linearize multi-key application transactions. These steps are left for future work; however, we believe that the Scatter group abstraction will make them straightforward to implement.

We evaluate our system in a variety of configurations, for both micro-benchmarks and for a Twitter-style application. Compared to OpenDHT, a publicly accessible open-source DHT providing distributed storage, Scatter provides equivalent performance with much better availability, consistency, and adaptability. We show that we can provide practical distributed storage even in very challenging environments. For example, if average node lifetimes are as short as three minutes, therefore triggering very frequent reconfigurations to maintain data durability, Scatter is able to maintain overall consistency and data availability, serving its reads in an average of 1.3 seconds in a typical wide area setting.

2. BACKGROUND

Scatter's design synthesizes techniques from both highly scalable systems with weak guarantees and strictly consistent systems with limited scalability, to provide the best of both worlds. This section overviews the two families of distributed systems whose techniques we leverage in building Scatter.

Distributed Hash Tables (DHTs): DHTs are a class of highly distributed storage systems providing scalable, key based lookup of objects in dynamic network environments. As a distributed systems building primitive, DHTs have proven remarkably versatile, with application developers having leveraged scalable lookup to support a variety of distributed applications. They are actively used in the wild as the infrastructure for peer-to-peer systems on the order of millions of users.

In a traditional DHT, both application data and node IDs are hashed to a key, and data is stored at the node whose hash value immediately precedes (or follows) the key. In many DHTs, the node storing the key's value replicates

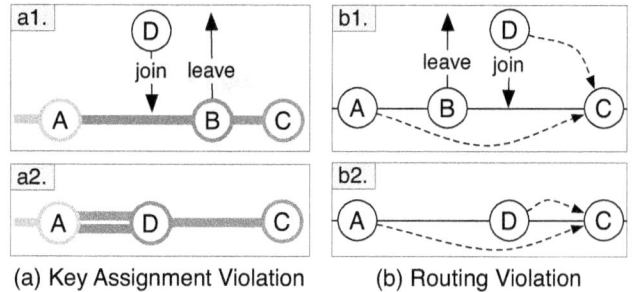

(a) Key Assignment Violation   (b) Routing Violation

Figure 1: Two examples demonstrating how (a) key assignment consistency and (b) routing integrity may be violated in a traditional DHT. Bold lines indicate key assignment and are associated with nodes. Dotted lines indicate successor pointers. Both scenarios arise when nodes join and leave concurrently, as pictured in (a1) and (b1). The violation in (a2) may result in clients observing inconsistent key values, while (b2) jeopardizes overlay connectivity.

the data to its neighbors for better reliability and availability [30]. Even so, many DHTs suffer inconsistencies in certain failure cases, both in how keys are assigned to nodes, and in how requests are routed to keys, yielding inconsistent results or reduced levels of availability. These issues are not new [12, 4]; we recite them to provide context for our work.

Assignment Violation: A fundamental DHT correctness property is for each key to be managed by at most one node. We refer to this property as *assignment consistency*. This property is violated when multiple nodes claim ownership over the same key. In the figure, a section of a DHT ring is managed by three nodes, identified by their key values A, B, and C. A new node D joins at a key between A and B and takes over the key-range $(A, D]$. However, before B can let C know of this change in the key-range assignment, B fails. Node C detects the failure and takes over the key-range $(A, B]$ maintained by B. This key-range, however, includes keys maintained by D. As a result, clients accessing keys in $(A, D]$ may observe inconsistent key values depending on whether they are routed to node C or D.

Routing Violation: Another basic correctness property stipulates that the system maintains consistent routing entries at nodes so that the system can route lookup requests to the appropriate node. In fact, the correctness of certain links is essential for the overlay to remain connected. For example, the Chord DHT relies on the consistency of node successor pointers (routing table entries that reference the next node in the key-space) to maintain DHT connectivity [35]. Figure 1b illustrates how a routing violation may occur when node joins and leaves are not handled atomically. In the figure, node D joins at a key between B and C, and B fails immediately after. Node D has a successor pointer correctly set to C, however, A is not aware of D and incorrectly believes that C is its successor (When a successor fails, a node uses its locally available information to set its successor pointer to the failed node's successor). In this scenario, messages routed through A to keys maintained by D will skip over node D and will be incorrectly forwarded to node C. A more complex routing algorithm that allows for backtracking may avoid this scenario, but such tweaks come at the risk of routing loops [35]. More generally, such routing inconsistencies jeopardize connectivity and may lead to system partitions.

Both violations occur for keys in DHTs, e.g., one study of OpenDHT found that on average 5% of the keys are owned by multiple nodes simultaneously even in settings with low churn [31]. The two examples given above illustrate how such a scenario may occur in the context of a Chord-like system, but these issues are known to affect all types of self-organizing systems in deployment [12].

Needless to say, inconsistent naming and routing can make it challenging for developers to understand and use a DHT. Inconsistent naming and routing also complicates system performance. For example, if a particular key becomes a hotspot, we may wish to shift the load from nearby keys to other nodes, and potentially to shift responsibility for managing the key to a well-provisioned node. In a traditional DHT, however, doing so would increase the likelihood of naming and routing inconsistencies. Similarly, if a popular key happens to land on a node that is likely to exit the system shortly (e.g., because it only recently joined), we can improve overall system availability by changing the key's assignment to a better provisioned, more stable node, but only if we can make assignment changes reliably and consistently.

One approach to addressing these anomalies is to broadcast all node join and leave events to all nodes in the system, as in Dynamo. This way, every node has an eventually consistent view of its key-range, at some scalability cost. Since key storage in Dynamo is only eventually consistent, applications must already be written to tolerate temporary inconsistency. Further, since all nodes in the DHT know the complete set of nodes participating in the DHT, routing is simplified.

Coordination Services: In enterprise settings, applications desiring strong consistency and high availability use coordination services such as Chubby [2] or ZooKeeper [14]. These services use rigorous distributed algorithms with provable properties to implement strong consistency semantics even in the face of failures. For instance, ZooKeeper relies on an atomic broadcast protocol, while Chubby uses the Paxos distributed consensus algorithm [18] for fault-tolerant replication and agreement on the order of operations.

Coordination services are, however, scale-limited as every update to a replicated data object requires communication with some *quorum* of all nodes participating in the service; therefore the performance of replication protocols rapidly degrades as the number of participating nodes increases (see Figure 9(a) and [14]). Scatter is designed with the following insight: what if we had many instances of a coordination service, cooperatively managing a large scale storage system?

3. SCATTER OVERVIEW

We now describe the design of Scatter, a scalable consistent storage layer designed to support very large scale peer-to-peer systems. We discuss our goals and assumptions, provide an overview of the structure of Scatter, and then discuss the technical challenges in building Scatter.

3.1 Goals and Assumptions

Scatter has three primary goals:

1. **Consistency:** Scatter provides linearizable consistency semantics for operations on a single key/value pair, despite (1) lossy and variable-latency network connections, (2) dynamic system membership including uncontrolled departures, and (3) transient, asymmetric communication faults.

2. **Scalability:** Scatter is designed to scale to the largest deployed DHT systems with more than a million heterogeneous nodes with diverse churn rates, computational capacities, and network bandwidths.

3. **Adaptability:** Scatter is designed to be self-optimizing to a variety of dynamic operating conditions. For example, Scatter reconfigures itself as nodes come and go to preserve the desired balance between high availability and high performance. It can also be tuned to optimize for both WAN and LAN environments.

Our design is limited in the kinds of failures it can handle. Specifically, we are not robust to malicious behavior, such as Byzantine faults and denial of service attacks, nor do we provide a mechanism for continued operation during pervasive network outages or correlated and widespread node outages. We leave adding these features to future work.

3.2 Design Overview

While existing systems partially satisfy some of our requirements outlined in the preceding paragraphs, none exhibit all three. Therefore, we set out to design a new system, Scatter, that synthesizes techniques from a spectrum of distributed storage systems.

The first technique we employ to achieve our goals is to use self-managing sets of nodes, which we term *groups*, rather than individual nodes as building blocks for the system. Groups internally use a suite of replicated state machine (RSM) mechanisms [33] based on the Paxos consensus algorithm [18] as a basis for consistency and fault-tolerance. Scatter also implements many standard extensions and optimizations [5] to the basic Paxos algorithm, including: (a) an elected leader to initiate actions on behalf of the group as a whole, and (b) reconfiguration algorithms [19] to both exclude failed members and include new members over time.

As groups maintain internal integrity using consensus protocols with provable properties, a simple and aggressive failure detector suffices. Nodes that are excluded from a group after being detected as failed can not influence any future actions of the group. On the other hand, the failure to quickly detect a failed node will not impede the liveness of the group because only a quorum of the current members are needed to make progress.

Scatter implements a simple DHT model in which a circular key-space is partitioned among groups (see Figure 2). Each group maintains up-to-date knowledge of the two neighboring groups that immediately precede and follow it in the key-space. These consistent lookup links form a global ring topology, on top of which Scatter layers a best-effort routing policy based on cached hints. If this soft routing state is stale or incomplete, then Scatter relies on the underlying consistent ring topology as ground truth.

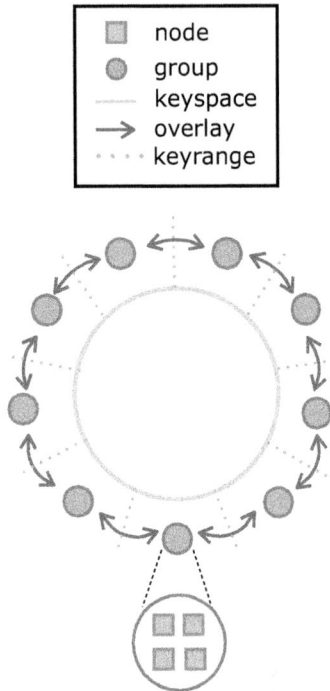

Figure 2: Overview of Scatter architecture

Carefully engineered groups go a long way to meeting our stated design goals for Scatter. However, a system composed of some static set of groups will be inherently limited in many ways. For example, if there is a burst of failures or sufficient disparity between the rate of leaves and joins for a particular group, then that group is at risk of losing a functional quorum. Not only is a static set of groups limited in robustness, but it is also restricted in both scalability and the ability to adapt gracefully to dynamic conditions. For instance, the performance of consensus algorithms degrades significantly as the number of participants increases. Therefore, a static set of groups will not be able to incrementally scale with the online addition of resources. As another example, if one group is responsible for a hotspot in the keyspace, it needs some way of coordinating with other groups, which may be underutilized, to alleviate the hotspot.

Therefore, we provide mechanisms to support the following *multi-group operations*:

- *split*: partition the state of an existing group into two groups.
- *merge*: create a new group from the union of the state of two neighboring groups.
- *migrate*: move members from one group to a different group.
- *repartition*: change the key-space partitioning between two adjacent groups.

Although our approach is straightforward and combines well-known techniques from the literature, we encountered a number of technical challenges that may not be apparent from a cursory inspection of the high-level design.

Atomicity: Multi-group operations modify the routing state across multiple groups, but as we discussed in Sec-

tion 2, strong consistency is difficult or impossible to guarantee when modifications to the routing topology are not atomic. Therefore, we chose to structure each multi-group operation in Scatter as a distributed transaction. We illustrate this design pattern, which we call nested consensus, in Figure 3. We believe that this general idea of structuring protocols as communication between replicated participants, rather than between individual nodes, can be applied more generally to the construction of scalable, consistent distributed systems.

Nested consensus uses a two-tiered approach. At the top tier, groups execute a two-phase commit protocol (2PC), while within each group the actions that the group takes are agreed on using consensus protocols. Multi-group operations are coordinated by whichever group decides to initiate the transaction as a result of some local policy. As Scatter is decentralized, multiple groups can concurrently initiate conflicting transactions. Section 4 details the mechanisms used to coordinate distributed transactions across groups.

Performance: Strong consistency in distributed systems is commonly thought to come with an unacceptably high performance or availability costs. The challenge of maximizing system performance influenced every level of Scatter's design and implementation — whether defined in terms of latency, throughput, or availability — without compromising core integrity. Although many before us have shown that strongly consistent replication techniques can be implemented efficiently at small scale, the bigger challenge for us was the additional layer of "heavy-weight" mechanisms — distributed transactions — on top of multiple instantiations of independent replicated state machines.

Self Organization: Our choice of complete decentralization makes the design of policies non-trivial. In contrast to designs in which a system deployment is tuned through human intervention or an omnipotent component, Scatter is tuned by the actions of individual groups using local information for optimization. Section 6 outlines various techniques for optimizing the resilience, performance, and load-balance of Scatter groups using local or partially sampled non-local information.

4. GROUP COORDINATION

In this section, we describe how we use nested consensus to implement multi-group operations. Section 4.1 characterizes our requirements for a consistent and available overlay topology. Section 4.2 details the nested consensus technique, and Section 4.3 walks through a concrete example of the group split operation.

4.1 Overlay Consistency Requirements

Scatter's overlay was designed to solve the consistency and availability problems discussed in Section 2. As Scatter is defined in terms of groups rather than nodes, we will slightly rephrase the assignment consistency correctness condition as the following system invariant: groups that are adjacent in the overlay agree on a partitioning of the key-space between them. For individual links in the overlay to remain highly available, Scatter maintains an additional invariant: a group can always reach its adjacent groups. Although these invariants are locally defined they are sufficient to provide global consistency and availability properties for Scatter's overlay.

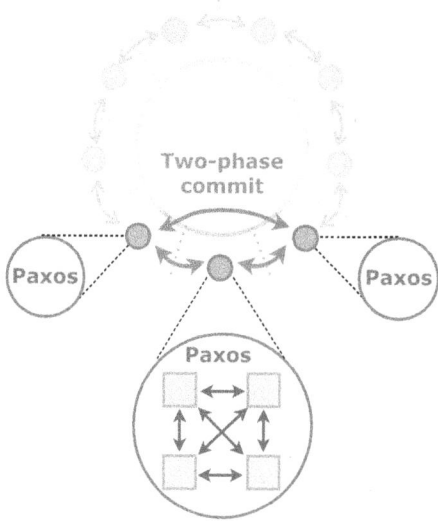

Figure 3: Overview of nested consensus. Groups coordinate distributed transactions using a two-phase commit protocol. Within each group, nodes coordinate using the Paxos distributed consensus algorithm.

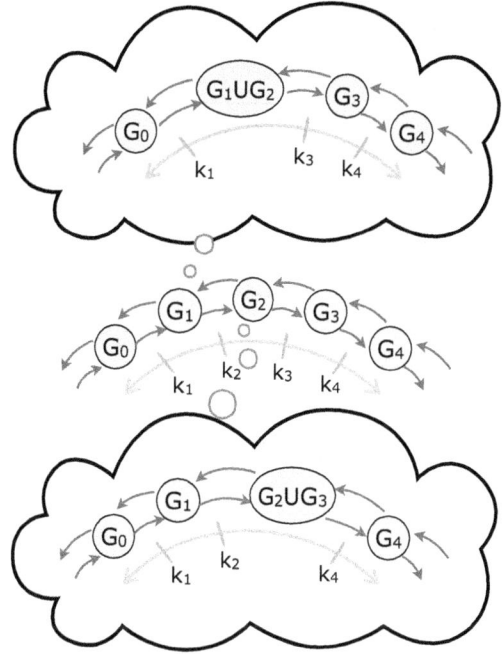

Figure 4: Scenario where two adjacent groups, G_1 and G_2, propose a merge operation simultaneously. G_1 proposes a merge of G_1 and G_2, while G_2 proposes a merge of G_2 and G_3. These two proposals conflict.

We can derive further requirements from these conditions for operations that modify either the set of groups, the membership of groups, or the partitioning of the key-space among groups. For instance, in order for a group G_a to be able to communicate directly with an adjacent group G_b, G_a must have knowledge of some subset of G_b's members. The following property is sufficient, but perhaps stronger than necessary, to maintain this connectivity: every adjacent group of G_b has up-to-date knowledge of the membership of G_b. This requirement motivated our implementation of operations that modify the membership of a group G_b to be *eagerly replicated* across all groups adjacent to G_b in the overlay.

In keeping with our goal to build on classic fault-tolerant distributed algorithms rather than inventing ad-hoc protocols, we chose to structure group membership updates as distributed transactions across groups. This approach not only satisfied our requirement of eager replication but provided a powerful framework for implementing the more challenging multi-group operations such as group splits and merges. Consider, for example, the scenario in Figure 4 where two adjacent groups, G_1 and G_2, propose a merge operation simultaneously. To maintain Scatter's two overlay consistency invariants, the adjacent groups G_0 and G_4 must be involved as well. Note that the changes required by G_1's proposal and G_2's proposal conflict — i.e., if both operations were executed concurrently they would violate the structural integrity of the overlay. These anomalies are prevented by the atomicity and concurrency control provided by our transactional framework.

4.2 Nested Consensus

Scatter implements distributed transactions across groups using a technique we call *nested consensus* (Figure 3). At a high level, groups execute a two-phase commit protocol

(2PC); before a group executes a step in the 2PC protocol it uses the Paxos distributed consensus algorithm to internally replicate the decision to execute the step. Thus distributed replication plays the role of write-ahead logging to stable storage in the classic 2PC protocol.

We will refer to the group initiating a transaction as the *coordinator* group and to the other groups involved as the *participant* groups. The following sequence of steps loosely captures the overall structure of nested consensus:

1. The coordinator group replicates the decision to initiate the transaction.
2. The coordinator group broadcasts a transaction *prepare* message to the nodes of the participant groups.
3. Upon receiving the *prepare* message, a participant group decides whether or not to commit the proposed transaction and replicates its vote.
4. A participant group broadcasts a *commit* or *abort* message to the nodes of the coordinator group.
5. When the votes of all participant groups is known, the coordinator group replicates whether or not the transaction was committed.
6. The coordinator group broadcasts the outcome of the transaction to all participant groups.
7. Participant groups replicate the transaction outcome.
8. When a group learns that a transaction has been committed then it executes the steps of the proposed transaction, the particulars of which depend on the multi-group operation.

Note that nested consensus is a non-blocking protocol. Provided a majority of nodes in each group remain alive and connected, the two phase commit protocol will terminate. Even if the previous leader of the coordinating group

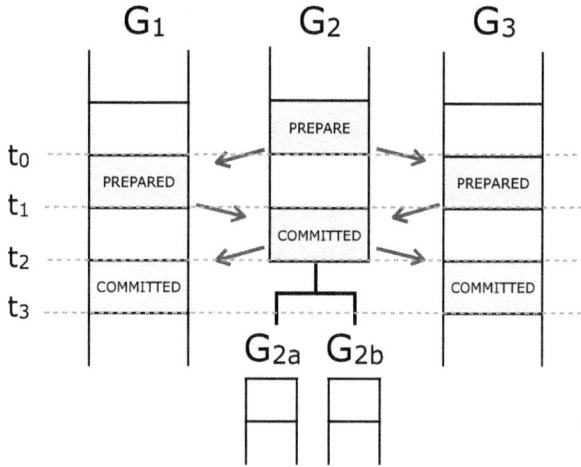

Figure 5: Group G_2 splits into two groups, G_{2a} and G_{2b}. Groups G_1, G_2, and G_3 participate in the distributed transaction. Causal time advances vertically, and messages between groups are represented by arrows. The cells beneath each group name represent the totally-ordered replicated log of transaction steps for that group.

fails, another node can take its place and resume the transaction. This is not the case for applying two phase commit to managing routing state in a traditional DHT.

In our implementation the leader of a group initiates every action of the group, but we note that a judicious use of broadcasts and message batching lowers the apparently high number of message rounds implied by the above steps. We also think that the large body of work on optimizing distributed transactions could be applied to further optimize performance of nested consensus, but our experimental evaluations in Section 7 show that performance is reasonable even with a relatively conservative implementation.

Our implementation encourages concurrency while respecting safety. For example, the storage service (Section 5) continues to process client requests during the execution of group transactions except for a brief period of unavailability during any reconfiguration required by a committed transaction. Also, groups continue to serve lookup requests during transactions that modify the partitioning of the key-space provided that the lookups are serialized with respect to the transaction commit.

To illustrate the mechanics of nested consensus, the remainder of the section walks through an example group split operation and then considers the behavior of this mechanism in the presence of faults and concurrent transactions.

4.3 Example: Group Split

Figure 5 illustrates three groups executing a split transaction. For clarity, this example demonstrates the necessary steps in nested consensus in the simplest case — a non-faulty leader and no concurrent transactions. At t_0, G_2 has replicated its intent to split into the two groups G_{2a} and G_{2b} and then sends a 2PC PREPARE message to G_1 and G_3. In parallel, G_1 and G_3 internally replicate their vote to commit the proposed split before replying to G_0. After each group

has learned and replicated the outcome (COMMITTED) of the split operation at time t_3, then the following updates are executed by the respective group: (1) G_1 updates its successor pointer to G_{2a}, (2) G_3 updates its predecessor pointer to G_{2b}, and (3) G_2 executes a *replicated state machine reconfiguration* to instantiate the two new groups which partition between them G_2's original key-range and set of member nodes.

To introduce some of the engineering considerations needed for nested consensus, we consider the behavior of this example in more challenging conditions. First, suppose that the leader of G_1 fails after replicating intent to begin the transaction but before sending the PREPARE messages to the participant groups. The other nodes of G_1 will eventually detect the leader failure and elect a new leader. When the new leader is elected, it behaves just like a restarted classical transaction manager: it queries the replicated write-ahead log and continues executing the transaction. We also implemented standard mechanisms for message timeouts and re-deliveries, with the caveat that individual steps should be implemented so that they are idempotent or have no effect when re-executed.

We return to the question of concurrency control. Say that G_1 proposed a merge operation with G_2 simultaneously with G_2's split proposal. The simplest response is to enforce mutual exclusion between transactions by participant groups voting to abort liberally. We implemented a slightly less restrictive definition of conflicting multi-group operations by defining a lock for each link in the overlay. Finer-grained locks reduce the incidence of deadlock; for example, two groups, G_1 and G_3, that are separated by two hops in the overlay would be able to update their membership concurrently; whereas with complete mutual exclusion these two operations would conflict at the group in the middle (G_2).

5. STORAGE SERVICE

A consistent and scalable lookup service provides a useful abstraction onto which richer functionality can be layered. This section describes the storage service that each Scatter group provides for its range of the global key-space. To evaluate Scatter, we implemented a peer-to-peer Twitter-like application layered on a standard DHT-interface. This allowed us to do a relatively direct comparison with OpenDHT in Section 7.

As explained in Section 4, each group uses Paxos to replicate the intermediate state needed for multi-group operations. Since multi-group operations are triggered by environmental changes such as churn or shifts in load, our design assumes these occur with low frequency in comparison to normal client operations. Therefore Scatter optimizes each group to provide low latency and high throughput client storage.

To improve throughput, we partition each group's storage state among its member nodes (see Figure 6). Storage operations in Scatter take the form of a simple read or write on an individual key. Each operation is forwarded to the node of the group assigned to a particular key – referred to as the *primary* for that key.

The group leader replicates information regarding the assignment of keys to primaries using Paxos, as it does with the state for multi-group operations. The key assignment is cached as soft state by the routing service in the other Scat-

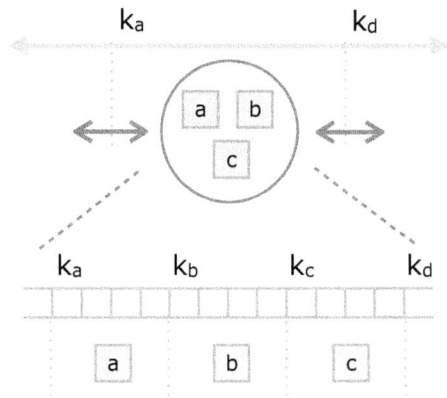

Figure 6: Example Scatter group composed of three nodes (a, b, c) and assigned to the key-range $[k_a, k_d]$. The group's key-range is partitioned such that each node of the group is the *primary* for some subset of the group's key-space. The primary of a key-range owns those keys and both orders and replicates all operations on the keys to the other nodes in the group; e.g., a is assigned $[k_a, k_b]$ and replicates all updates to these keys to b and c using Paxos.

ter groups. All messages are implemented on top of UDP, and Scatter makes no guarantees about reliable delivery or ordering of client messages. Once an operation is routed to the correct group for a given key, then any node in the group will forward the operation to the appropriate primary. Each primary uses Paxos to replicate operations on its key-range to all the other nodes in the group – this provides linearizability. Our use of the Paxos algorithm in this case behaves very much like other primary-backup replication protocols – a single message round usually suffices for replication, and operations on different keys and different primaries are not synchronized with respect to each other.

In parliamentary terms [18], the structure within a group can be explained as follows. The group nodes form the group *parliament* which elects a parliamentary leader and then divides the law into disjoint areas, forming a separate *committee* to manage each resulting area of the law independently. All members of parliament are also a member of every committee, but each committee appoints a different committee chair (i.e., the primary) such that no individual member of parliament is unfairly burdened in comparison to his peers. Because the chair is a distinguished proposer in his area, in the common case only a single round of messages is required to pass a committee decree. Further, since committees are assigned to disjoint areas of the law, decrees in different committees can be processed concurrently without requiring a total ordering of decrees among committees.

In addition to the basic mechanics described in this section and the previous section, Scatter implements additional optimizations including:

- **Leases**: Our mechanisms for delegating keys to primaries does not require time-based leases; however, they can be turned on for a given deployment. Leases allow primaries to satisfy reads without communicating to the rest of the group; however, the use of leases can also delay the execution of certain group opera-

	Load Balance	Latency	Resilience
Low churn Uniform latency	✓		
Low churn Non-uniform latency	✓	✓	
High churn Non-uniform latency	✓	✓	✓

Table 1: Deployment settings and system properties that a Scatter policy may target. A ✓ indicates that we have developed a policy for the combination of setting and property.

tions when a primary fails.

- **Diskless Paxos**: Our implementation of Paxos does not require writing to disk. Nodes that restart just rejoin the system as new nodes.
- **Relaxed Reads**: All replicas for a given key can answer read requests from local – possibly stale – state. Relaxed reads violate linearizability, but are provided as an option for clients.

6. SAMPLE POLICIES

An important property of Scatter's design is the separation of policy from mechanism. For example, the mechanism by which a node joins a group does not prescribe how the target group is selected. Policies enable Scatter to adapt to a wide range of operating conditions and are a powerful means of altering system behavior with no change to any of the underlying mechanisms.

In this section we describe the policies that we have found to be effective in the three experimental settings where we have deployed and evaluated Scatter (see Section 7). These are: (1) low churn and uniform network latency, (2) low churn and non-uniform network latency, and (3) high churn and non-uniform network latency. Table 1 lists each of these settings, and three system properties that a potential policy might optimize. A ✓ in the table indicates that we have developed a policy for the corresponding combination of deployment setting and system property. We now describe the policies for each of the three system properties.

6.1 Resilience

Scatter must be resilient to node churn as nodes join and depart the system unexpectedly. A Scatter group with $2k+1$ nodes guarantees data availability with up to k node failures. With more than k failures, a group cannot process client operations safely. To improve resilience, Scatter employs a policy that prompts a group to merge with an adjacent group if its node count is below a predefined threshold. This maintains high data availability and helps prevent data loss. This policy trades-off availability for performance since smaller groups are more efficient.

To determine the appropriate group size threshold we carried out a simulation, parameterized with the base reconfiguration latency plotted in Figure 12(b). Figure 7 plots the probability of group failure for different group sizes for two node churn rates with node lifetimes drawn from heavy-tailed Pareto distributions observed in typical peer-to-peer systems [3, 32]. The plot indicates that a modest group size of 8-12 prevents group failure with high probability.

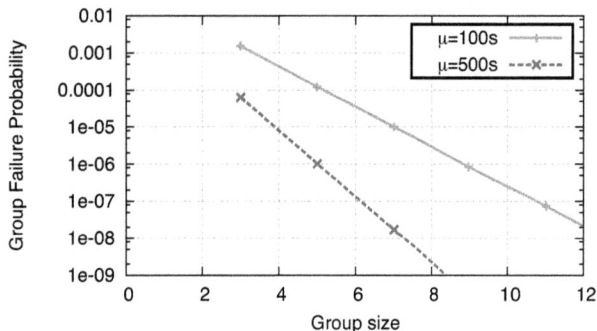

Figure 7: Impact of group size on group failure probability for two Pareto distributed node churn rates, with average lifetimes $\mu = 100s$ and $\mu = 500s$.

The resilience policy also directs how nodes join the system. A new node samples k random groups and joins the group that is most likely to fail. The group failure probability is computed using node lifetime distribution information, if available. In the absence of this data, the policy defaults to having a new node join the sampled group with the fewest nodes. The default policy also takes into account the physical diversity of nodes in a group, e.g., the number of distinct BGP prefixes spanned by the group. It then assigns a joining node to a group that has the smallest number of nodes and spans a limited number of BGP prefixes in order to optimize for both uncorrelated and correlated failures. We performed a large-scale simulation to determine the impact of the number of groups sampled and found that checking four groups is sufficient to significantly reduce the number of reconfiguration operations performed later. If multiple groups have the expected failure probability below the desired threshold, then the new node picks the target group based on the policy for optimizing latency as described below.

6.2 Latency

Client latency depends on its time to reach the primary, and the time for the primary to reach consensus with the other replicas. A join policy can optimize client latency by placing new nodes into groups where their latencies to the other nodes in the group will be low. The *latency-optimized join* policy accomplishes this by having the joining node randomly select k groups and pass a `no-op` operation in each of them as a pseudo primary. This allows the node to estimate the performance of operating within each group. While performing these operations, nodes do not explicitly join and leave each group. The node then joins the group with the smallest command execution latency. Note that latency-optimized join is used only as a secondary metric when there are multiple candidate groups with the desired resiliency properties. As a consequence, these performance optimizations are not at the cost of reduced levels of physical diversity or group robustness. Experiments in Section 7.1.1 compare the latency-optimized join policy with $k = 3$ against the random join policy.

The *latency-optimized leader selection* policy optimizes the RSM command latency in a different way – the group elects the node that has the lowest Paxos agreement latency as the leader. We evaluate the impact of this policy on reconfiguration, merge, and split costs in Section 7.1.3.

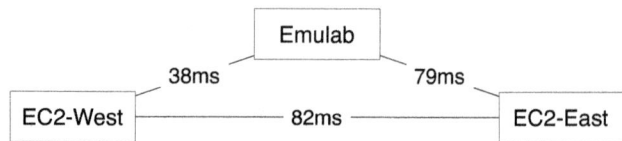

Figure 8: Inter-site latencies in the multi-cluster setting used in experiments.

6.3 Load Balance

Scatter also balances load across groups in order to achieve scalable and predictable performance. A simple and direct method for balancing load is to direct a new node to join the group that is heavily loaded. The *load-balanced join* policy does exactly this – a joining node samples k groups, selects groups that have low failure probability, and then joins the group that has processed the most client operations in the recent past. The load-balance policy also repartitions the keyspace among adjacent groups when the request load to their respective keyspaces is skewed. In our implementation, groups repartition their keyspaces proportionally to their respective loads whenever a group's load is a factor of 1.6 or above that of its neighboring group. As this check is performed locally between adjacent groups, it does not require global load monitoring, but it might require multiple iterations of the load-balancing operation to disperse hotspots. We note that the overall, cumulative effect of many concurrent locally optimal modifications is non-trivial to understand. A thorough analysis of the effect of local decisions on global state is an intriguing direction for future work.

7. EVALUATION

We evaluated Scatter across three deployment environments, corresponding to the churn/latency settings listed in Table 1: (1) **single cluster**: a homogeneous and dedicated Emulab cluster to evaluate the low churn/uniform latency setting; (2) **multi-cluster**: multiple dedicated clusters (Emulab and Amazon's EC2) at LAN sites connected over the wide-area to evaluate the low churn/non-uniform latency setting; (3) **peer-to-peer**: machines from PlanetLab in the wide-area to evaluate the high churn/non-uniform latency setting.

In all experiments Scatter ran on a single core on a given node. On Emulab we used 150 nodes with 2.4GHz 64-bit Xeon processor cores. On PlanetLab we used 840 nodes, essentially all nodes on which we could install both Scatter and OpenDHT.

For multi-cluster experiments we used 50 nodes each from Emulab (Utah), EC2-West (California) and EC2-East (Virginia). The processors on the EC2 nodes were also 64-bit processor cores clocked at 2.4GHz. Figure 8 details the inter-site latencies for the multi-cluster experiments. We performed our multi-cluster experiments using nodes at physically distinct locations in order to study the performance of our system under realistic wide-area network conditions.

We used Berkeley-DB for persistent disk-based storage, and a memory cache to pipeline operations to BDB in the background.

Section 7.1 quantifies specific Scatter overheads with deployments on dedicated testbeds (single-cluster, multi-cluster). We then evaluate Scatter at large scales on PlanetLab with

(a) Single Cluster

(b) Multi-Cluster

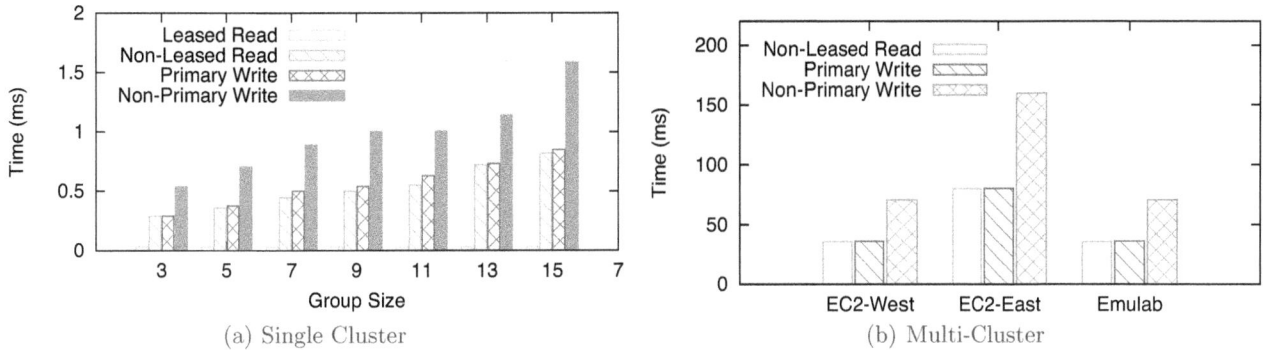

Figure 9: Latency of different client operations in (a) a single-cluster deployment for groups of different sizes, and (b) a multi-cluster deployment in which no site had a majority of nodes in the group.

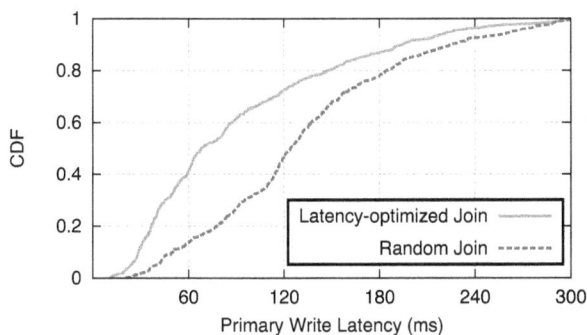

Figure 10: The impact of join policy on write latency in two PlanetLab deployments. The latency-optimized join policy is described in Section 6.2. The random join policy directs nodes to join a group at random.

varying churn rates in the context of a Twitter-like publish-subscribe application called Chirp in Section 7.2, and also compare it to a Chirp implementation on top of OpenDHT.

7.1 Microbenchmarks

In this section we show that a Scatter group imposes a minor latency overhead and that primaries dramatically increase group operation processing throughput. Then, we evaluate the latency of group reconfiguration, split and merge. The results indicate that group operations are more expensive than client operations, but the overheads are tolerable since these operations are infrequent.

7.1.1 Latency

Figure 9 plots a group's client operation processing latency for single cluster and multi-cluster settings. The plotted latencies do not include the network delay between the client and the group. The client perceived latency will have an additional delay component that is simply the latency from the client to the target group. We present the end-to-end application-level latencies in Section 7.2.

Figure 9(a) plots client operation latency for different operations in groups of different sizes. The latency of leased reads did not vary with group size – it is processed locally by the primary. Non-leased reads were slightly faster than pri-

mary writes as they differ only in the storage layer overhead. Non-primary writes were significantly slower than primary-based operations because the primary uses the faster leader-Paxos for consensus.

In the multi-cluster setting no site had a node majority. Figure 9(b) plots the latency for operations that require a primary to coordinate with nodes from at least one other site. As a result, inter-cluster WAN latency dominates client operation latency. As expected, operations initiated by primaries at EC2-East had significantly higher latency, while operations by primaries at EC2-West and Emulab had comparable latency.

To illustrate how policy may impact client operation latency, Figure 10 compares the impact of latency-optimized join policy with $k = 3$ (described in Section 6.2) to the random join policy on the primary's write latency in a PlanetLab setting. In both PlanetLab deployments, nodes joined Scatter using the respective policy, and after all nodes joined, millions of writes were performed to random locations. The effect of the latency-optimized policy is a clustering of nodes that are close in latency into the same group. Figure 10 shows that this policy greatly improves write performance over the random join policy – median latency decreased by 45%, from 124ms to 68ms.

Latencies in the PlanetLab deployment also demonstrate the benefit of majority consensus in mitigating the impact of slow-performing outlier nodes on group operation latency. Though PlanetLab nodes are globally distributed, the 124ms median latency of a primary write (with random join policy) is not much higher than that of the multi-cluster setting. Slow nodes impose a latency cost but they also benefit the system overall as they improve fault tolerance by consistently replicating state, albeit slowly.

7.1.2 Throughput

Figure 11 plots write throughput of a single group in single cluster and multi-cluster settings. Writes were performed on randomly selected segments. Throughput was determined by varying both the number of clients (up to 20) and the number of outstanding operations per client (up to 100).

The figure demonstrates the performance benefit of using primaries. In both settings, a single leader becomes a scalability bottleneck and throughput quickly degrades for groups with more nodes. This happens because the message overhead associated with executing a group command is linear in group size. Each additional primary, however, adds

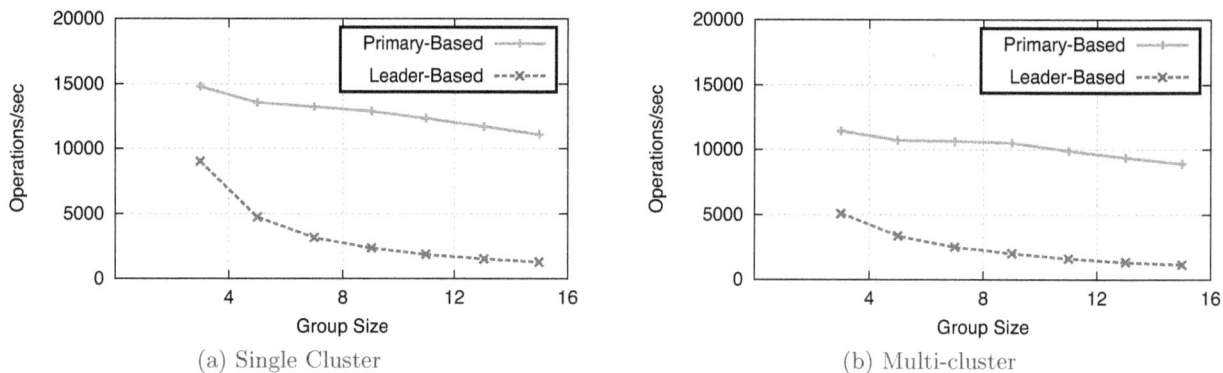

(a) Single Cluster

(b) Multi-cluster

Figure 11: Scatter group throughput in single cluster and multi-cluster settings.

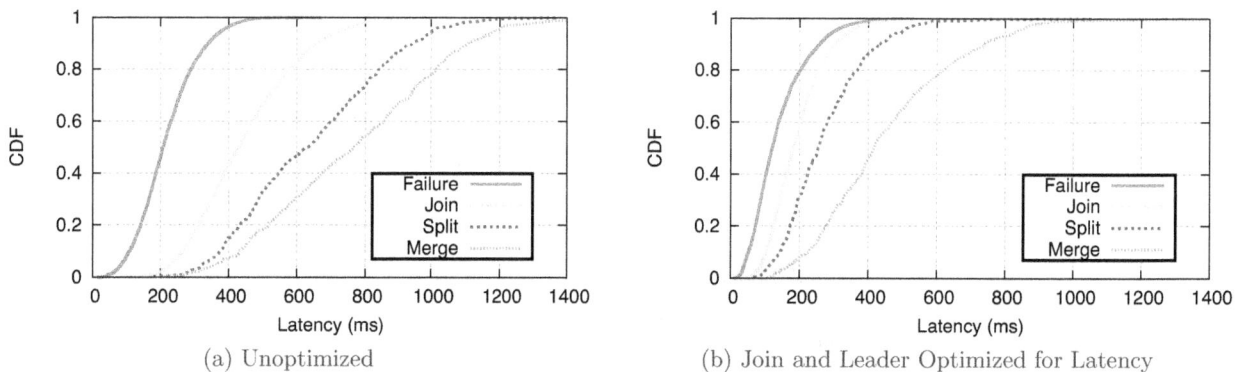

(a) Unoptimized

(b) Join and Leader Optimized for Latency

Figure 12: CDFs of group reconfiguration latencies for a P2P setting with two sets of policies: (a) random join and random leader, and (b) latency-optimized join and latency-optimized leader.

extra capacity to the group since primaries process client operations in parallel and also pipeline client operations. The result is that in return for higher reliability (afforded by having more nodes) a group's throughput decreases only slightly when using primaries.

Though the latency of a typical operation in the multi-cluster deployment is significantly higher than the corresponding operation in the single cluster setting, group throughput in the multi-cluster setting (Figure 11(a)) is within 30% of the group throughput in a single cluster setting (Figure 11(b)). And for large groups this disparity is marginal. The reason for this is the pipelining of client requests by group primaries, which allows the system to mask the cost of wide-area network communication.

7.1.3 Reconfiguration, Split, and Merge

We evaluated the latency cost of group reconfiguration, split, and merge operations. In the case of failure, this latency is the duration between a failure detector sensing a failure and the completion of the resulting reconfiguration. Table 2 lists the average latencies and standard deviations for single and multi- cluster settings across thousands of runs and across group sizes 2-13. These measurements do not account for data transfer latency.

Basic single cluster latency. In the single cluster setting all operations take less than 10ms. Splitting and merging are the most expensive operations as they require co-

	Single cluster	Multi-cluster (Unopt.)	Multi-cluster (Opt. leader)
Failure	2.04 ± 0.44	90.9 ± 31.8	55.6 ± 7.6
Join	3.32 ± 0.54	208.8 ± 48.8	135.8 ± 15.2
Split	4.01 ± 0.73	246.5 ± 45.4	178.5 ± 15.1
Merge	4.79 ± 1.01	307.6 ± 69.8	200.7 ± 24.4

Table 2: Group reconfiguration, split, and merge latencies in milliseconds and standard deviations for different deployment settings.

ordination between groups, and merging is more expensive because it involves more groups than splitting.

Impact of policy on multi-cluster latency. The single-cluster setting provides little opportunity for optimization due to latency homogeneity. However, in the multi-cluster settings, we can decrease the latency cost with a leader election policy. Table 2 lists latencies for two multi-cluster deployments, one with a random leader election policy, and one that used a latency-optimized leader policy described in Section 6.2. From the table, the latency optimizing policy significantly reduced the latency cost of all operations.

Impact of policy on PlanetLab latency. Figure 12 plots CDFs of latencies for the PlanetLab deployment. It compares the random join with random leader policies (Figure 12(a)) against latency-optimized join and latency-optimized leader policies described in Section 6.2 (Figure 12(b)). In combination, the two latency optimizing policies shift the CDF curves to the left, decreasing the latency of all operations – reconfiguration, split and merge.

7.2 Application-level Benchmarks

To study the macro-level behavior of Scatter, we built and deployed Chirp, a Twitter-like application. In this section we compare PlanetLab deployments of Chirp on top of Scatter and OpenDHT. We compare our implementation with OpenDHT, which is an open-source DHT implementation that is currently deployed on PlanetLab. OpenDHT uses lightweight techniques for DHT maintenance, and its access latencies are comparable to that of other DHTs [28]. It therefore allows us to evaluate the impact of the more heavy-weight techniques used in Scatter.

For a fair comparison, both Scatter and OpenDHT send node heartbeat messages every 0.5s. After four consecutive heartbeat failures OpenDHT re-replicates failed node's keys, and Scatter reconfigures to exclude the failed node and re-partitions the group's keyspace among primaries. Additionally, Scatter used the same base-16 recursive routing algorithm as is used by OpenDHT. Only forward and reverse group pointers were maintained consistently in Scatter, but it relied on these only when the soft routing state turned out to be inconsistent. In both systems the replication factor was set to provide at least seven 9s of reliability, i.e., with an average lifetime of 100 seconds, we use 9 replicas (see Figure 7).

To induce churn we use two different lifetime distributions, Poisson and Pareto. Pareto is a typical way of modeling churn in P2P systems [3, 32], and Poisson is a common reference distribution. For both churn distributions a node's join policy joined the group with the lowest expected residual lifetime — for Poisson this is equivalent to joining the group with the fewest nodes.

7.2.1 Chirp overview

Chirp works much like Twitter; to participate in the system a user u creates a user-name, which is associated with two user-specific keys, $K^u_{updates}$ and $K^u_{follows}$, that are computed by hashing u's user-name. A user may write and post an *update*, which is at most 140 characters in length; *follow* another user; or fetch updates posted by the users being followed. An update by a user u is appended to the value of $K^u_{updates}$. When u follows u', the key $K^{u'}_{updates}$ is appended to $K^u_{follows}$, which maintains the list of all users u is following.

Appending to a key value is implemented as a non-atomic read-modify-write, requiring two storage operations. This was done to more fairly compare Scatter and OpenDHT. A key's maximum value was 8K in both systems. When a key's value capacity is exceeded (e.g., a user posts over 57 maximum-sized updates), a new key is written and the new key is appended to the end of the value of the old key, as a pointer to the continuation of the list. The Chirp client application caches previously known tails of each list accessed by the user in order to avoid repeatedly scanning through the list to fetch the most recent updates. In addition, the pointer to the tail of the list is stored at its header so that a user's followers can efficiently access the most recent updates of the user.

We evaluated the performance of Chirp on Scatter and

OpenDHT by varying churn, the distribution of node lifetimes, and the popularity distribution of keys. For the experiments below, we used workloads obtained from Twitter measurement studies [17, 15]. The measurements include both the updates posted by the users and the structure of the social network over which the updates are propagated.

7.2.2 Impact of Churn

We first evaluate the performance by using node lifetime distributions that are Poisson distributed and by varying the mean lifetime value from 100 seconds to 1000 seconds. We based our lifetime distributions on measurements of real-world P2P systems such as Gnutella, Kazaa, FastTrack, and Overnet [32, 13, 7, 34]. For this experiment, the update/fetch Chirp workload was synthesized as follows: we played a trace of status updates derived from the Twitter measurement studies, and for each user u posting an update, we randomly selected one of u's followers and issued a request from this user to the newly posted update. Figure 13 plots performance, availability, and consistency of the fetches in this workload as we vary churn. Each data point represents the mean value for a million fetch operations.

Figure 13(a) indicates that the performance of both systems degrades with increasing churn as routing state becomes increasingly stale, and the probability of the value residing on a failed node increases. OpenDHT slightly outperforms Scatter in fetch latency because a fetch in Scatter incurs a round of group communication.

Figure 13(b) shows that Scatter has better availability than OpenDHT. The availability loss in OpenDHT was often due to the lack of structural integrity, with inconsistent successor pointer information or because a key being fetched has not been assigned to any of the nodes (see Figure 1). To compute the fetch failure for Scatter in Figure 13(b) an operation was considered to have failed if a response has not been received within three seconds. The loss of availability for Scatter was because an operation may be delayed for over three seconds when the destination key belonged to a group undergoing reconfiguration in response to churn.

Figure 13(c) compares the consistency of the values stored in the two systems. OpenDHT's inconsistency results confirmed prior studies, e.g., [31] — even at low churn rates over 5% of the fetches were inconsistent. These inconsistencies stem from a failure to keep replicas consistent, either because an update to a replica failed or because different nodes have different views regarding how the keyspace is partitioned. In contrast, Scatter had no inconsistencies across all experiments.

7.2.3 Heavy tailed node lifetimes

Next, we considered a node lifetime distribution in which nodes are drawn from a heavy-tailed Pareto distribution that is typical of many P2P workloads. Heavy-tailed distributions exhibit "memory", i.e., nodes who have been part of the system for some period of time are more likely to persist than newly arriving nodes. Scatter provides for a greater ability to optimize for skewed node lifetime distribution due to its group abstraction. Note that all of the keys associated with a group are replicated on the same set of nodes, whereas in OpenDHT each node participates in multiple different replica sets. In this setting, Scatter takes into account the measured residual lifetime distribution in the various reconfiguration operations, e.g., which group an arriving node

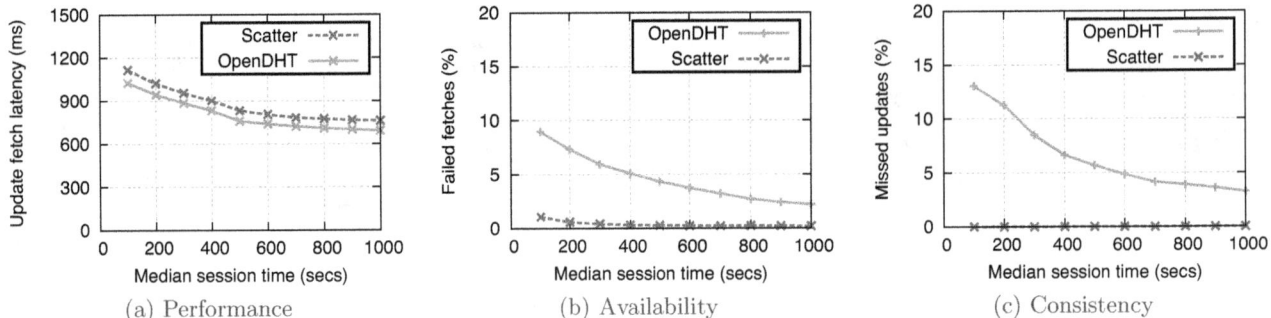

(a) Performance   (b) Availability   (c) Consistency

Figure 13: Impact of varying churn rates for Poisson distributed lifetimes. The graphs plot measurements for P2P deployments of Chirp for both Scatter (dashed line), and OpenDHT (solid line).

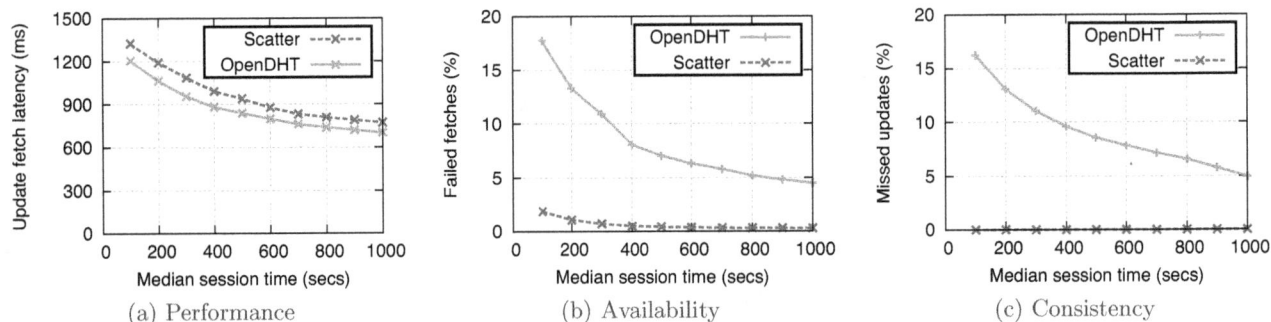

(a) Performance   (b) Availability   (c) Consistency

Figure 14: Impact of varying churn rates for Pareto distributed lifetimes ($\alpha = 1.1$).

should join, when should groups merge or split, and in determining the optimal size of the group to meet the desired (seven 9s) availability guarantee. For these experiments the workload was generated in the same way as the workload used in Section 7.2.2.

OpenDHT slightly outperformed Scatter with respect to access latency (see Figure 14(a)). However, Scatter's availability fared better under the heavy-tailed churn rate than that of OpenDHT (Figure 14(b)). As before, Scatter had no inconsistencies, while OpenDHT was more inconsistent with the heavy tailed churn rate (Figure 14(c)).

7.2.4 Non-uniform load

In the next experiment, we studied the impact of high load on Scatter. For this experiment, we batched and issued one million updates from the Twitter trace, and after all of the updates have been posted, the followers of the selected users fetched the updates. The fetches were issued in a random order and throttled to a rate of 10,000 fetches per second for the entire system. Note that in this experiment the keys corresponding to popular users received more requests, as the load is based on social network properties. The load is further skewed by the fact that users with a large number of followers are more likely to post updates [17].

Figure 15(a) shows that Scatter had a slightly better fetch latency than OpenDHT due to its better load balance properties. However, latency in Scatter tracked OpenDHT's latency as in prior experiments (Figures 13(a) and 14(a)).

Figure 15(b) plots the normalized node load for Scatter and OpenDHT. This was computed in both systems by tracking the total number of fetch requests processed by a

node, and then dividing this number by the mean. The figure shows that Scatter's load-balance policy (Section 6.3) is effective at distributing load across nodes in the system. OpenDHT's load distribution was more skewed.

7.2.5 Scalability

For our final set of experiments, we evaluated the scalability of Scatter and its ability to adapt to variations in system load. We also compared Scatter with ZooKeeper, a system that provides strongly consistent storage. As ZooKeeper is a centralized and scale-limited system, we built a decentralized system comprising of multiple ZooKeeper instances, where the global keyspace is statically partitioned across the different instances. We also optimized the performance of this ZooKeeper-based alternative by basing the keyspace partitioning on the historical load estimates of the various key values; we split our workload into two halves, used the first half to derive the keyspace partitioning, and then performed the evaluations using the second half of the trace. Each ZooKeeper instance comprised of five nodes. We performed these experiments without node churn, as the system based on ZooKeeper did not have a management layer for dealing with churn.

Figure 16 plots the average throughput results with standard deviations as we vary the number of nodes in the system. The throughput of Scatter is comparable to that of the ZooKeeper-based system for small number of nodes, indicating that Scatter stacks up well against a highly optimized implementation of distributed consensus. As we increase the number of nodes, the performance of ZooKeeper-based alternative scales sub-linearly. This indicates that, even though

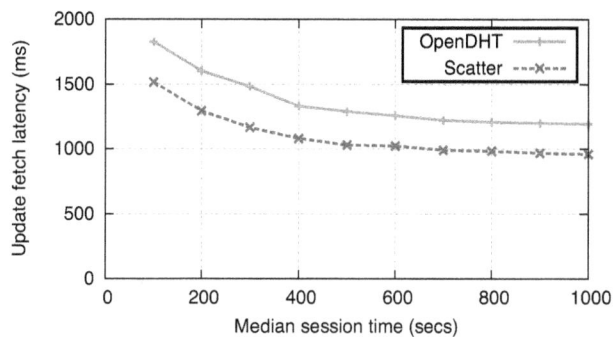

(a) Latency

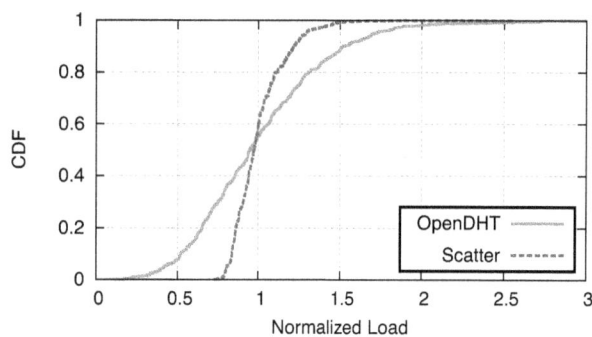

(b) Node Load

Figure 15: High load results for Chirp with node churn distributed as Pareto($\alpha = 1.1$). (a) Scatter has better latency than OpenDHT at high loads; (b) Scatter maintains a more balanced distribution of load among its nodes than OpenDHT.

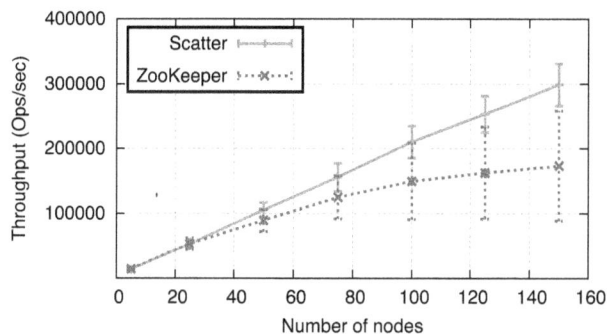

Figure 16: Comparison of Scatter with a system that composes multiple ZooKeeper instances. The figure provides the throughput of the two systems as we vary the number of nodes.

the keyspace partitioning was derived based on historical workload characteristics, the inability to adapt to dynamic hotspots in the access pattern limits the scalability of the ZooKeeper-based system. Further, the variability in the throughput also increases with the number of ZooKeeper instances used in the experiment. In contrast, Scatter's throughput scales linearly with the number of nodes, with only a small amount of variability due to uneven group sizes and temporary load skews.

8. RELATED WORK

Our work is made possible by foundational techniques for fault tolerant distributed computing such as Paxos [18], replicated state machines [33], and transactions [20]. In particular, our design draws inspiration from the implementation of distributed transactions across multiple replication groups in Viewstamped Replication [25].

A number of recent distributed systems in industry also rely on distributed consensus algorithms to provide strongly consistent semantics — such systems provide a low-level control service for an ecosystem of higher-level infrastructure applications. Well-known examples of such systems include Google's Chubby lock service [2] and Yahoo's ZooKeeper

coordination service [14]. Scatter extends the techniques in such systems to a larger scale.

At another extreme, peer-to-peer systems such as distributed hash tables (DHTs) [26, 30, 22, 29] provide only best-effort probabilistic guarantees, and although targeted at planetary scale have been found to be brittle and slow in the wild [27, 28]. Still, the large body of work on peer-to-peer system has numerous valuable contributions. Scatter benefits from many decentralized self-organizing techniques such as sophisticated overlay routing, and the extensive measurements on workload and other environmental characteristics in this body of work (e.g. [11]) are invaluable to the design and evaluation of effective policies [23].

One recent system showing that DHTs are a valuable abstraction even in an industrial setting is Amazon's Dynamo [10], a highly available distributed key-value store supporting one of the largest e-commerce operations in the world. Unlike Scatter, Dynamo chooses availability over consistency, and this trade-off motivates a different set of design choices.

Lynch et al. [21] propose the idea of using state machine replication for atomic data access in DHTs. An important insight of this theoretical work is that a node in a DHT can be made more robust if it is implemented as a group of nodes that execute operations atomically using a consensus protocol. An unsolved question in the paper is how to atomically modify the ring topology under churn, a question which we answer in Scatter with our principled design of multi-group operations.

Motivated by the same problems with large scale DHTs (as discussed in Section 2), Castro et al. developed MSPastry [4]. MSPastry makes the Pastry [30] design more dependable, without sacrificing performance. It does this with robust routing, active probes, and per-hop acknowledgments. A fundamental difference between MSPastry and Scatter is that Scatter provides provable consistency guarantees. Moreover, Scatter's group abstraction can be reused to support more advanced features in the future, such as consistency of multi-key operations.

Although we approached the problem of scalable consistency by starting with a clean slate, other approaches in the literature propose mechanisms for consistent operations layered on top of a weakly-consistent DHT. Etna [24] is a representative system of this approach. Unfortunately such systems inherit the structural problems of the underlying data system, resulting in lower object availability and system efficiency. For example, inconsistencies in the underlying routing protocol will manifest as unavailability at the higher layers (see Figures 13(b) and 14(b)).

9. CONCLUSION

This paper presented the design, implementation and evaluation of Scatter — a scalable distributed key-value storage system that provides clients with linearalizable semantics. Scatter organizes computing resources into fault-tolerant groups, each of which independently serve client requests to segments of the keyspace. Groups employ self-organizing techniques to manage membership and to coordinate with other groups for improved performance and reliability. Principled and robust group coordination is the primary contribution of our work.

We presented detailed evaluation results for various deployments. Our results demonstrate that Scatter is efficient in practice, scales linearly with the number of nodes, and provides high availability even at significant node churn rates. Additionally, we illustrate how Scatter provides tunable knobs to effectively adapt to the different deployment settings for significant improvements in load balance, latency, and resilience.

Acknowledgments.

This work was supported in part by grant CNS-0963754 from the National Science Foundation. We would like to thank Vjekoslav Brajkovic and Justin Cappos for their contributions to earlier versions of Scatter. We would also like to thank our shepherd Ant Rowstron and the anonymous reviewers for their feedback.

10. REFERENCES

[1] J. Baker, C. Bond, J. Corbett, J. Furman, A. Khorlin, J. Larson, J.-M. Leon, Y. Li, A. Lloyd, and V. Yushprakh. Megastore: Providing Scalable, Highly Available Storage for Interactive Services. In *Proc. of CIDR*, 2011.

[2] M. Burrows. The Chubby lock service for loosely-coupled distributed systems. In *Proc. of OSDI*, 2006.

[3] F. Bustamante and Y. Qiao. Friendships that last: Peer lifespan and its role in P2P protocols. In *Proc. of IEEE WCW*, 2003.

[4] M. Castro, M. Costa, and A. Rowstron. Performance and dependability of structured peer-to-peer overlays. In *Proc. of DSN*, 2004.

[5] T. D. Chandra, R. Griesemer, and J. Redstone. Paxos Made Live: An Engineering Perspective. In *Proc. of PODC*, 2007.

[6] F. Chang, J. Dean, S. Ghemawat, W. C. Hsieh, D. A. Wallach, M. Burrows, T. Chandra, A. Fikes, and R. E. Gruber. Bigtable: A Distributed Storage System for Structured Data. *ACM Transactions on Computer Systems*, 26(2), 2008.

[7] J. Chu, K. Labonte, and B. N. Levine. Availability and Locality Measurements of Peer-To-Peer File Systems. In *Proc. of ITCom*, 2002.

[8] B. F. Cooper, R. Ramakrishnan, U. Srivastava, A. Silberstein, P. Bohannon, H.-A. Jacobsen, N. Puz, D. Weaver, and R. Yerneni. PNUTS: Yahoo!'s Hosted Data Serving Platform. *Proc. VLDB Endow.*, 1:1277–1288, August 2008.

[9] J. Dean. Large-Scale Distributed Systems at Google: Current Systems and Future Directions, 2009.

[10] G. DeCandia, D. Hastorun, M. Jampani, G. Kakulapati, A. Lakshman, A. Pilchin, S. Sivasubramanian, P. Vosshall, and W. Vogels. Dynamo: Amazon's Highly Available Key-value Store. In *Proc. of SOSP*, 2007.

[11] J. Falkner, M. Piatek, J. P. John, A. Krishnamurthy, and T. Anderson. Profiling a Million User DHT. In *Proc. of IMC*, 2007.

[12] M. J. Freedman, K. Lakshminarayanan, S. Rhea, and I. Stoica. Non-transitive connectivity and DHTs. In *Proc. of WORLDS*, 2005.

[13] P. K. Gummadi, R. J. Dunn, S. Saroiu, S. D. Gribble, H. M. Levy, and J. Zahorjan. Measurement, Modeling, and Analysis of a Peer-to-Peer File-Sharing Workload. In *Proc. of SOSP*, 2003.

[14] P. Hunt, M. Konar, F. P. Junqueira, and B. Reed. ZooKeeper: Wait-Free Coordination for Internet-scale systems. In *Proc. of USENIX ATC*, 2010.

[15] J. Yang and J. Leskovec. Temporal Variation in Online Media. In *Proc. of WSDM*, 2011.

[16] J. Kubiatowicz, D. Bindel, D. Bindel, Y. Chen, S. Czerwinski, P. Eaton, D. Geels, R. Gummadi, S. Rhea, H. Weatherspoon, W. Weimer, C. Wells, and B. Zhao. OceanStore: An Architecture for Global-Scale Persistent Storage. In *Proc. of ASPLOS*, 2000.

[17] H. Kwak, C. Lee, H. Park, and S. Moon. What is Twitter, a social network or a news media? In *Proc. of WWW*, 2010.

[18] L. Lamport. The Part-Time Parliament. *ACM Transactions on Computer Systems*, 16(2), 1998.

[19] L. Lamport, D. Malkhi, and L. Zhou. Reconfiguring a State Machine. *ACM SIGACT News*, 41(1), 2010.

[20] B. W. Lampson and H. E. Sturgis. Crash recovery in a distributed data storage system. Technical report, Xerox Parc, 1976.

[21] N. A. Lynch, D. Malkhi, and D. Ratajczak. Atomic Data Access in Distributed Hash Tables. In *Proc. of IPTPS*, 2002.

[22] P. Maymounkov and D. Mazières. Kademlia: A Peer-to-Peer Information System Based on the XOR Metric. In *Proc. of IPTPS*, 2002.

[23] M. Mitzenmacher. The Power of Two Choices in Randomized Load Balancing. *IEEE Transactions on Parallel and Distributed Systems*, 12(10), 2001.

[24] A. Muthitacharoen, S. Gilbert, and R. Morris. Etna: A fault-tolerant algorithm for atomic mutable DHT data. Technical Report MIT-LCS-TR-993, MIT, June 2005.

[25] B. M. Oki and B. H. Liskov. Viewstamped Replication: A New Primary Copy Method to Support Highly-Available Distributed Systems. In *Proc. of PODC*, 1988.

[26] S. Ratnasamy, P. Francis, M. Handley, R. Karp, and S. Schenker. A Scalable Content-Addressable Network. In *Proc. of SIGCOMM*, 2001.

[27] S. Rhea, B. Chun, J. Kubiatowicz, and S. Shenker. Fixing the Embarrassing Slowness of OpenDHT on PlanetLab. In *Proc. of WORLDS*, 2005.

[28] S. Rhea, D. Geels, T. Roscoe, and J. Kubiatowicz. Handling Churn in a DHT. In *Proc. of USENIX ATC*, 2004.

[29] S. Rhea, B. Godfrey, B. Karp, J. Kubiatowicz, S. Ratnasamy, S. Shenker, I. Stoica, and H. Yu. OpenDHT: A Public DHT Service and Its Uses. In *Proc. of SIGCOMM*, 2005.

[30] A. Rowstron and P. Druschel. Pastry: Scalable, distributed object location and routing for large-scale peer-to-peer systems. In *Proc. of Middleware*, 2001.

[31] S. Sankararaman, B.-G. Chun, C. Yatin, and S. Shenker. Key Consistency in DHTs. Technical Report UCB/EECS-2005-21, UC Berkeley, 2005.

[32] S. Saroiu, P. Gummadi, and S. Gribble. A Measurement Study of Peer-to-Peer File Sharing Systems. In *Proc. of MMCN*, 2002.

[33] F. B. Schneider. Implementing Fault-Tolerant Services Using the State Machine Approach: A Tutorial. *ACM Computing Surveys*, 22(4), 1990.

[34] S. Sen and J. Wang. Analyzing Peer-to-Peer Traffic Across Large Networks. *IEEE/ACM Transactions on Networking*, 2004.

[35] I. Stoica, R. Morris, D. Liben-Nowell, D. Karger, M. F. Kaashoek, F. Dabek, and H. Balakrishnan. Chord: A Scalable Peer-to-Peer Lookup Protocol for Internet Applications. Technical Report MIT-LCS-TR-819, MIT, Mar 2001.

[36] I. Stoica, R. Morris, D. Liben-Nowell, D. R. Karger, M. F. Kaashoek, F. Dabek, and H. Balakrishnan. Chord: A Scalable Peer-to-Peer Lookup Protocol for Internet Applications. *IEEE/ACM Transactions on Networking*, 11(1), 2003.

Fast Crash Recovery in RAMCloud

Diego Ongaro, Stephen M. Rumble, Ryan Stutsman,
John Ousterhout, and Mendel Rosenblum

Stanford University

ABSTRACT

RAMCloud is a DRAM-based storage system that provides inexpensive durability and availability by recovering quickly after crashes, rather than storing replicas in DRAM. RAMCloud scatters backup data across hundreds or thousands of disks, and it harnesses hundreds of servers in parallel to reconstruct lost data. The system uses a log-structured approach for all its data, in DRAM as well as on disk; this provides high performance both during normal operation and during recovery. RAMCloud employs randomized techniques to manage the system in a scalable and decentralized fashion. In a 60-node cluster, RAMCloud recovers 35 GB of data from a failed server in 1.6 seconds. Our measurements suggest that the approach will scale to recover larger memory sizes (64 GB or more) in less time with larger clusters.

Categories and Subject Descriptors

D.4.7 [**Operating Systems**]: Organization and Design—*Distributed systems*; D.4.2 [**Operating Systems**]: Storage Management—*Main memory*; D.4.5 [**Operating Systems**]: Reliability—*Fault-tolerance*; D.4.8 [**Operating Systems**]: Performance—*Measurements*

General Terms

Design, Measurement, Performance, Reliability, Experimentation

Keywords

Storage systems, Main memory databases, Crash recovery, Scalability

1. INTRODUCTION

The role of DRAM in storage systems has been increasing rapidly in recent years, driven by the needs of large-scale Web applications. These applications manipulate very large datasets with an intensity that cannot be satisfied by disks alone. As a result, applications are keeping more and more of their data in DRAM. For example, large-scale caching systems such as memcached [3] are being widely used (in 2009 Facebook used a total of 150 TB of DRAM in memcached and other caches for a database containing

200 TB of disk storage [15]), and the major Web search engines now keep their search indexes entirely in DRAM.

Although DRAM's role is increasing, it still tends to be used in limited or specialized ways. In most cases DRAM is just a cache for some other storage system such as a database; in other cases (such as search indexes) DRAM is managed in an application-specific fashion. It is difficult for developers to use DRAM effectively in their applications; for example, the application must manage consistency between caches and the backing storage. In addition, cache misses and backing store overheads make it difficult to capture DRAM's full performance potential.

RAMCloud is a general-purpose storage system that makes it easy for developers to harness the full performance potential of large-scale DRAM storage. It keeps all data in DRAM all the time, so there are no cache misses. RAMCloud storage is durable and available, so developers need not manage a separate backing store. RAMCloud is designed to scale to thousands of servers and hundreds of terabytes of data while providing uniform low-latency access (5-10 μs round-trip times for small read operations).

The most important factor in the design of RAMCloud was the need to provide a high level of durability and availability without impacting system performance. Replicating all data in DRAM would have solved some availability issues, but with 3x replication this would have tripled the cost and energy usage of the system. Instead, RAMCloud keeps only a single copy of data in DRAM; redundant copies are kept on disk or flash, which is both cheaper and more durable than DRAM. However, this means that a server crash will leave some of the system's data unavailable until it can be reconstructed from secondary storage.

RAMCloud's solution to the availability problem is fast crash recovery: the system reconstructs the entire contents of a lost server's memory (64 GB or more) from disk and resumes full service in 1-2 seconds. We believe this is fast enough to be considered "continuous availability" for most applications.

This paper describes and evaluates RAMCloud's approach to fast recovery. There are several interesting aspects to the RAMCloud architecture:

- **Harnessing scale**: RAMCloud takes advantage of the system's large scale to recover quickly after crashes. Each server scatters its backup data across all of the other servers, allowing thousands of disks to participate in recovery. Hundreds of *recovery masters* work together to avoid network and CPU bottlenecks while recovering data. RAMCloud uses both data parallelism and pipelining to speed up recovery.

- **Log-structured storage**: RAMCloud uses techniques similar to those from log-structured file systems [21], not just for information on disk but also for information in DRAM.

The log-structured approach provides high performance and simplifies many issues related to crash recovery.

- **Randomization**: RAMCloud uses randomized approaches to make decisions in a distributed and scalable fashion. In some cases randomization is combined with refinement: a server selects several candidates at random and then chooses among them using more detailed information; this provides near-optimal results at low cost.

- **Tablet profiling**: RAMCloud uses a novel dynamic tree structure to track the distribution of data within tables; this helps divide a server's data into partitions for fast recovery.

We have implemented the RAMCloud architecture in a working system and evaluated its crash recovery properties. Our 60-node cluster recovers in 1.6 seconds from the failure of a server with 35 GB of data, and the approach scales so that larger clusters can recover larger memory sizes in less time. Measurements of our randomized replica placement algorithm show that it produces uniform allocations that minimize recovery time and that it largely eliminates straggler effects caused by varying disk speeds.

Overall, fast crash recovery allows RAMCloud to provide durable and available DRAM-based storage for the same price and energy usage as today's volatile DRAM caches.

2. RAMCLOUD

Crash recovery and normal request processing are tightly intertwined in RAMCloud, so this section provides background on the RAMCloud concept and the basic data structures used to process requests. We have omitted some details because of space limitations.

2.1 Basics

RAMCloud is a storage system where every byte of data is present in DRAM at all times. The hardware for RAMCloud consists of hundreds or thousands of off-the-shelf servers in a single datacenter, each with as much DRAM as is cost-effective (24 to 64 GB today). RAMCloud aggregates the DRAM of all these servers into a single coherent storage system. It uses backup copies on disk or flash to make its storage durable and available, but the performance of the system is determined by DRAM, not disk.

The RAMCloud architecture combines two interesting properties: low latency and large scale. First, RAMCloud is designed to provide the lowest possible latency for remote access by applications in the same datacenter. Our goal is end-to-end times of 5-10 μs for reading small objects in datacenters with tens of thousands of machines. This represents an improvement of 50-5,000x over existing datacenter-scale storage systems.

Unfortunately, today's datacenters cannot meet RAMCloud's latency goals (Ethernet switches and NICs typically add at least 200-500 μs to round-trip latency in a large datacenter). Thus we use low-latency Infiniband NICs and switches in our development environment as an approximation to the networking hardware we hope will be commonplace in a few years; this makes it easier to explore latency issues in the RAMCloud software. The current RAMCloud system supports 5 μs reads in a small cluster, and each storage server can handle about 1 million small read requests per second.

The second important property of RAMCloud is scale: a single RAMCloud cluster must support thousands of servers in order to provide a coherent source of data for large applications. Scale creates several challenges, such as the likelihood of frequent component failures and the need for distributed decision-making to avoid bottlenecks. However, scale also creates opportunities, such as the

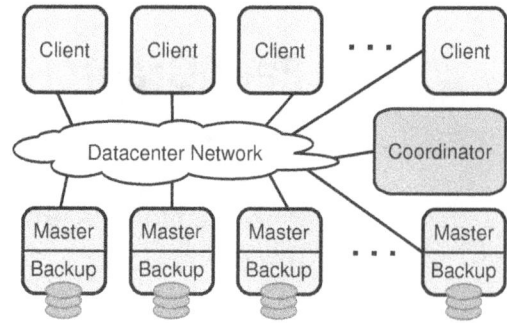

Figure 1: RAMCloud cluster architecture. Each storage server contains a master and a backup. A central coordinator manages the server pool and tablet configuration. Client applications run on separate machines and access RAMCloud using a client library that makes remote procedure calls.

ability to enlist large numbers of resources on problems like fast crash recovery.

RAMCloud's overall goal is to enable a new class of applications that manipulate large datasets more intensively than has ever been possible. For more details on the motivation for RAMCloud and some of its architectural choices, see [18].

2.2 Data Model

The current data model in RAMCloud is a simple key-value store. RAMCloud supports any number of tables, each of which contains any number of objects. An object consists of a 64-bit identifier, a variable-length byte array (up to 1 MB), and a 64-bit version number. RAMCloud provides a simple set of operations for creating and deleting tables and for reading, writing, and deleting objects within a table. Objects are addressed with their identifiers and are read and written in their entirety. There is no built-in support for atomic updates to multiple objects, but RAMCloud does provide a conditional update ("replace the contents of object O in table T only if its current version number is V"), which can be used to implement more complex transactions in application software. In the future we plan to experiment with more powerful features such as indexes, mini-transactions [4], and support for large graphs.

2.3 System Structure

As shown in Figure 1, a RAMCloud cluster consists of a large number of storage servers, each of which has two components: a *master*, which manages RAMCloud objects in its DRAM and services client requests, and a *backup*, which stores redundant copies of objects from other masters using its disk or flash memory. Each RAMCloud cluster also contains one distinguished server called the *coordinator*. The coordinator manages configuration information such as the network addresses of the storage servers and the locations of objects; it is not involved in most client requests.

The coordinator assigns objects to storage servers in units of *tablets*: consecutive key ranges within a single table. Small tables are stored in their entirety on a single storage server; larger tables are split across multiple servers. Client applications do not have control over the tablet configuration; however, they can achieve some locality by taking advantage of the fact that small tables (and adjacent keys in large tables) are stored together on a single server.

The coordinator stores the mapping between tablets and storage servers. The RAMCloud client library maintains a cache of this information, fetching the mappings for each table the first time it is accessed. Clients can usually issue storage requests directly to the relevant storage server without involving the coordinator. If a client's cached configuration information becomes stale because a tablet has moved, the client library discovers this when it makes a request to a server that no longer contains the tablet, at which point it flushes the stale data from its cache and fetches up-to-date information from the coordinator. Clients use the same mechanism during crash recovery to find the new location for data.

2.4 Managing Replicas

The internal structure of a RAMCloud storage server is determined primarily by the need to provide durability and availability. In the absence of these requirements, a master would consist of little more than a hash table that maps from ⟨table identifier, object identifier⟩ pairs to objects in DRAM. The main challenge is providing durability and availability without sacrificing performance or greatly increasing system cost.

One possible approach to availability is to replicate each object in the memories of several servers. However, with a typical replication factor of three, this approach would triple both the cost and energy usage of the system (each server is already fully loaded, so adding more memory would also require adding more servers and networking). The cost of main-memory replication can be reduced by using coding techniques such as parity striping [20], but this makes crash recovery considerably more expensive. Furthermore, DRAM-based replicas are still vulnerable in the event of power failures.

Instead, RAMCloud keeps only a single copy of each object in DRAM, with redundant copies on secondary storage such as disk or flash. This makes replication nearly free in terms of cost and energy usage (the DRAM for primary copies will dominate both of these factors), but it raises two issues. First, the use of slower storage for backup might impact the normal-case performance of the system (e.g., by waiting for synchronous disk writes). Second, this approach could result in long periods of unavailability or poor performance after server crashes, since the data will have to be reconstructed from secondary storage. Section 2.5 describes how RAMCloud solves the performance problem, and Section 3 deals with crash recovery.

2.5 Log-Structured Storage

RAMCloud manages object data using a logging approach. This was originally motivated by the desire to transfer backup data to disk or flash as efficiently as possible, but it also provides an efficient memory management mechanism, enables fast recovery, and has a simple implementation. The data for each master is organized as a log as shown in Figure 2. When a master receives a write request, it appends the new object to its in-memory log and forwards that log entry to several backup servers. The backups buffer this information in memory and return immediately to the master without writing to disk or flash. The master completes its request and returns to the client once all of the backups have acknowledged receipt of the log data. When a backup's buffer fills, it writes the accumulated log data to disk or flash in a single large transfer, then deletes the buffered data from its memory.

Backups must ensure that buffered log data is as durable as data on disk or flash (i.e., information must not be lost in a power failure). One solution is to use new DIMM memory modules that incorporate flash memory and a super-capacitor that provides enough power for the DIMM to write its contents to flash after a power outage [2]; each backup could use one of these modules to hold all of its buffered log data. Other alternatives are per-server battery backups that extend power long enough for RAMCloud to flush buffers, or enterprise disk controllers with persistent cache memory. RAMCloud manages its logs using techniques similar to those in log-structured file systems [21]. Each master's log is divided into

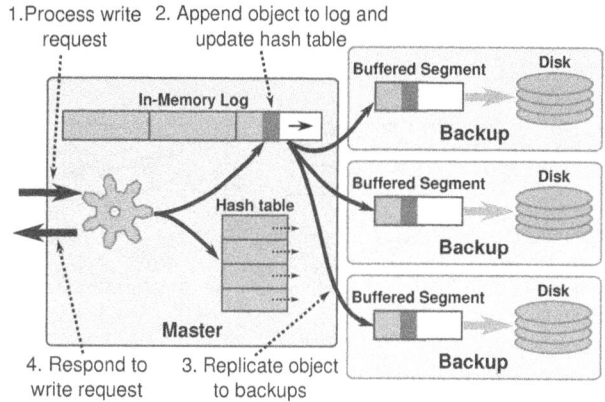

Figure 2: When a master receives a write request, it updates its in-memory log and forwards the new data to several backups, which buffer the data in their memory. The data is eventually written to disk or flash in large batches. Backups must use an auxiliary power source to ensure that buffers can be written to stable storage after a power failure.

8 MB *segments*. The master keeps a count of unused space within each segment, which accumulates as objects are deleted or overwritten. It reclaims wasted space by occasionally invoking a *log cleaner*; the cleaner selects one or more segments to clean, reads the live records from the segments and rewrites them at the head of the log, then deletes the cleaned segments along with their backup copies. Segments are also the unit of buffering and I/O on backups; the large segment size enables efficient I/O for both disk and flash.

RAMCloud uses a log-structured approach not only for backup storage, but also for information in DRAM: the memory of a master is structured as a collection of log segments identical to those stored on backups. This allows masters to manage both their in-memory data and their backup data using a single mechanism. The log provides an efficient memory management mechanism, with the cleaner implementing a form of generational garbage collection. In order to support random access to objects in memory, each master keeps a hash table that maps from ⟨table identifier, object identifier⟩ pairs to the current version of an object in a segment. The hash table is used both to look up objects during storage operations and to determine whether a particular object version is the current one during cleaning (for example, if there is no hash table entry for a particular object in a segment being cleaned, it means the object has been deleted).

The buffered logging approach allows writes to complete without waiting for disk operations, but it limits overall system throughput to the bandwidth of the backup storage. For example, each RAMCloud server can handle about 300,000 100-byte writes/second (versus 1 million reads/second) assuming 2 disks per server, 100 MB/s write bandwidth for each disk, 3 disk replicas of each object, and a 100% bandwidth overhead for log cleaning. Additional disks can be used to boost write throughput.

3. RECOVERY

When a RAMCloud storage server crashes, the objects that had been present in its DRAM must be reconstructed by replaying its log. This requires reading log segments from backup storage, processing the records in those segments to identify the current version of each live object, and reconstructing the hash table used for storage operations. The crashed master's data will be unavailable until the hash table has been reconstructed.

Fortunately, if the period of unavailability can be made very short, so that it is no longer than other delays that are common in

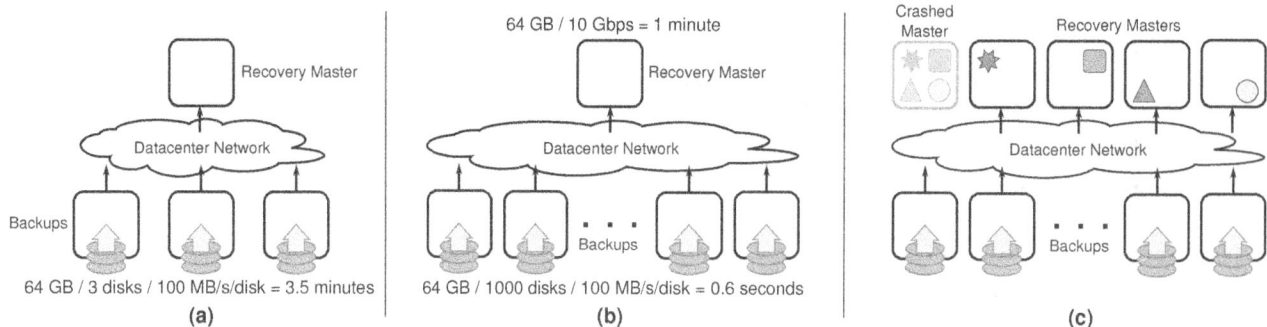

Figure 3: (a) Disk bandwidth is a recovery bottleneck if each master's data is mirrored on a small number of backup machines. (b) Scattering log segments across many backups removes the disk bottleneck, but recovering all data on one recovery master is limited by the network interface and CPU of that machine. (c) Fast recovery is achieved by partitioning the data of the crashed master and recovering each partition on a separate recovery master.

normal operation, and if crashes happen infrequently, then crash recovery will be unnoticeable to the application's users. We believe that 1-2 second recovery is fast enough to constitute "continuous availability" for most applications; our goal is to achieve this speed for servers with at least 64 GB of memory.

3.1 Using Scale

The key to fast recovery in RAMCloud is to take advantage of the massive resources of the cluster. This subsection introduces RAMCloud's overall approach for harnessing scale; the following subsections describe individual elements of the mechanism in detail.

As a baseline, Figure 3a shows a simple mirrored approach where each master chooses 3 backups and stores copies of all its log segments on each backup. Unfortunately, this creates a bottleneck for recovery because the master's data must be read from only a few disks. In the configuration of Figure 3a with 3 disks, it would take about 3.5 minutes to read 64 GB of data.

RAMCloud works around the disk bottleneck by using more disks during recovery. Each master scatters its log data across all of the backups in the cluster (each segment on a different set of backups) as shown in Figure 3b. During recovery, these scattered log segments can be read simultaneously; with 1,000 disks, 64 GB of data can be read into memory in less than one second.

Once the segments have been read from disk into backups' memories, they must be combined to find the most recent version for each object (no backup can tell in isolation whether a particular object in a particular segment is the most recent version). One approach is to send all the log segments to a single *recovery master* and replay the log on that master, as in Figure 3b. Unfortunately, the recovery master is a bottleneck in this approach: with a 10 Gbps network interface, it will take about 1 minute to read 64 GB of data, and the master's CPU will also be a bottleneck.

To eliminate the recovery master as the bottleneck, RAMCloud uses multiple recovery masters as shown in Figure 3c. During recovery RAMCloud divides the objects of the crashed master into *partitions* of roughly equal size. Each partition is assigned to a different recovery master, which fetches the log data for the partition's objects from backups and incorporates those objects into its own log and hash table. With 100 recovery masters operating in parallel, 64 GB of data can be transferred over a 10 Gbps network in less than 1 second. As will be shown in Section 4, this is also enough time for each recovery master's CPU to process the incoming data.

Thus, the overall approach to recovery in RAMCloud is to combine the disk bandwidth, network bandwidth, and CPU cycles of

thousands of backups and hundreds of recovery masters. The subsections below describe how RAMCloud divides its work among all of these resources and how it coordinates the resources to recover in 1-2 seconds.

3.2 Scattering Log Segments

For fastest recovery the log segments for each RAMCloud master should be distributed uniformly across all of the backups in the cluster. However, there are several factors that complicate this approach:

- Segment placement must reflect failure modes. For example, a segment's master and each of its backups must reside in different racks, in order to protect against top-of-rack switch failures and other problems that disable an entire rack.

- Different backups may have different bandwidth for I/O (different numbers of disks, different disk speeds, or different storage classes such as flash memory); segments should be distributed so that each backup uses the same amount of time to read its share of the data during recovery.

- All of the masters are writing segments simultaneously; they should coordinate to avoid overloading any individual backup. Backups have limited buffer space.

- Storage servers are continuously entering and leaving the cluster, which changes the pool of available backups and may unbalance the distribution of segments.

Making decisions such as segment replica placement in a centralized fashion on the coordinator would limit RAMCloud's scalability. For example, a cluster with 10,000 servers could back up 100,000 or more segments per second; this could easily cause the coordinator to become a performance bottleneck.

Instead, each RAMCloud master decides independently where to place each replica, using a combination of randomization and refinement. When a master needs to select a backup for a segment, it chooses several candidates at random from a list of all backups in the cluster. Then it selects the best candidate, using its knowledge of where it has already allocated segment replicas and information about the speed of each backup's disk (backups measure the speed of their disks when they start up and provide this information to the coordinator, which relays it on to masters). The best backup is the one that can read its share of the master's segment replicas most quickly from disk during recovery. A backup is rejected if it is in the same rack as the master or any other replica for the current segment. Once a backup has been selected, the master contacts that backup to reserve space for the segment. At this point the backup can reject the request if it is overloaded, in which case the master selects another candidate.

The use of randomization eliminates pathological behaviors such as all masters choosing the same backups in a lock-step fashion. Adding the refinement step provides a solution nearly as optimal as a centralized manager (see [17] and [5] for a theoretical analysis). For example, if a master scatters 8,000 segments across 1,000 backups using a purely random approach, backups will have 8 segments on average. However, some backups are likely to end up with 15-20 segments, which will result in uneven disk utilization during recovery. Adding just a small amount of choice makes the segment distribution nearly uniform and also allows for compensation based on other factors such as disk speed (see Section 4.4). This mechanism also handles the entry of new backups gracefully: a new backup is likely to be selected more frequently than existing backups until every master has taken full advantage of it.

RAMCloud masters mark one of the replicas for each segment as the *primary replica*. Only the primary replicas are read during recovery (unless they are unavailable), and the performance optimizations described above consider only primary replicas.

We considered the possibility of storing one of the backup replicas on the same machine as the master. This would reduce network bandwidth requirements, but it has two disadvantages. First, it would reduce system fault tolerance: the master already has one copy in its memory, so placing a second copy on the master's disk provides little benefit. If the master crashes, the disk copy will be lost along with the memory copy; it would only provide value in a cold start after a power failure. Second, storing one replica on the master would limit the burst write bandwidth of a master to the bandwidth of its local disks. In contrast, with all replicas scattered, a single master can potentially use the disk bandwidth of the entire cluster (up to the limit of its network interface).

3.3 Failure Detection

RAMCloud detects server failures in two ways. First, RAMCloud clients will notice if a server fails to respond to a remote procedure call. Second, RAMCloud checks its own servers to detect failures even in the absence of client activity; this allows RAMCloud to replace lost replicas before multiple crashes cause permanent data loss. Each RAMCloud server periodically issues a ping RPC to another server chosen at random and reports failures to the coordinator. This is another example of using a randomized distributed approach in place of a centralized approach. The probability of detecting a crashed machine in a single round of pings is about 63% for clusters with 100 or more nodes; the odds are greater than 99% that a failed server will be detected within five rounds.

In either case, server failures are reported to the coordinator. The coordinator verifies the problem by attempting to communicate with the server itself, then initiates recovery if the server does not respond. Timeouts must be relatively short (tens of milliseconds) so that they don't significantly delay recovery. See Section 5 for a discussion of the risks introduced by short timeouts.

3.4 Recovery Flow

The coordinator supervises the recovery process, which proceeds in three phases:

1. **Setup.** The coordinator finds all replicas of all log segments belonging to the crashed master, selects recovery masters, and assigns each recovery master a partition to recover.

2. **Replay.** Recovery masters fetch log segments in parallel and incorporate the crashed master's partitions into their own logs.

3. **Cleanup.** Recovery masters begin serving requests, and the crashed master's log segments are freed from backup storage.

These phases are described in more detail below.

3.5 Setup

3.5.1 Finding Log Segment Replicas

At the start of recovery, replicas of the crashed master's segments must be located among the cluster's backups. RAMCloud does not keep a centralized map of replicas since it would be difficult to scale and would hinder common-case performance. Only masters know where their segments are replicated, but this information is lost when they crash.

The coordinator reconstructs the locations of the crashed master's replicas by querying all of the backups in the cluster. Each backup responds with a list of the replicas it has stored for the crashed master (backups maintain this index in memory). The coordinator then aggregates the responses into a single location map. By using RAMCloud's fast RPC system and querying multiple backups in parallel, the segment location information is collected quickly.

3.5.2 Detecting Incomplete Logs

After backups return their lists of replicas, the coordinator must determine whether the reported segment replicas form the entire log of the crashed master. The redundancy in RAMCloud makes it highly likely that the entire log will be available, but the system must be able to detect situations where some data is missing (such as network partitions).

RAMCloud avoids centrally tracking the list of the segments that comprise a master's log by making each log self-describing; the completeness of the log can be verified using data in the log itself. Each segment includes a *log digest*, which is a list of identifiers for all segments in the log at the time this segment was written. Log digests are small (less than 1% storage overhead even when uncompressed, assuming 8 MB segments and 8,000 segments per master).

This leaves a chance that all the replicas for the newest segment in the log are unavailable, in which case the coordinator would not be able to detect that the log is incomplete (the most recent digest it could find would not list the newest segment). To prevent this, when a master creates a new segment replica it makes its transition to the new digest carefully. First, a new digest is inserted in the new replica, and it is marked as *active*. Then, after the new active digest is durable, a final update to the prior active digest marks it as inactive. This ordering ensures the log always has an active digest, even if the master crashes between segments. Two active log digests may be discovered during recovery, but the coordinator simply ignores the newer one since its segment must be empty.

If the active log digest and a replica for each segment cannot be found, then RAMCloud cannot recover the crashed master. In this unlikely case, RAMCloud notifies the operator and waits for backups to return to the cluster with replicas for each of the missing segments. Alternatively, at the operator's discretion, RAMCloud can continue recovery with loss of data.

3.5.3 Starting Partition Recoveries

Next, the coordinator must divide up the work of recovering the crashed master. The choice of partitions for a crashed master is made by the master itself: during normal operation each master analyzes its own data and computes a set of partitions that would evenly divide the work of recovery. This information is called a *will* (it describes how a master's assets should be divided in the

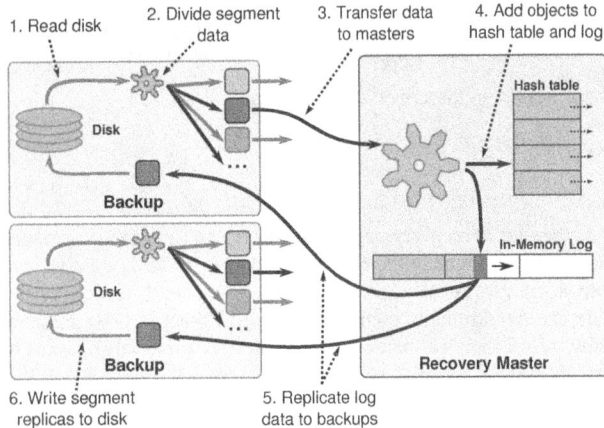

Figure 4: During recovery, segment data flows from disk or flash on a backup over the network to a recovery master, then back to new backups as part of the recovery master's log.

event of its demise). Masters periodically upload their wills to the coordinator. Section 3.9 describes how masters compute their wills efficiently.

During recovery setup, the coordinator assigns each of the partitions in the crashed master's will to an existing master within the cluster. Each of these recovery masters receives two things from the coordinator: a list of the locations of all the crashed master's log segments and a list of tablets that the recovery master must recover and incorporate into the data it manages.

3.6 Replay

The vast majority of recovery time is spent replaying segments to reconstruct partitions on the recovery masters. During replay the contents of each segment are processed in six stages (see Figure 4):

1. The segment is read from disk into the memory of a backup.

2. The backup divides the records in the segment into separate groups for each partition based on table and object identifiers in the log records.

3. The records for each partition are transferred over the network to the recovery master for that partition.

4. The recovery master incorporates the data into its in-memory log and hash table.

5. As the recovery master fills segments in memory, it replicates those segments over the network to backups with the same scattering mechanism used in normal operation.

6. The backups write the new segment replicas to disk or flash.

RAMCloud harnesses concurrency in two dimensions during recovery. The first dimension is data parallelism: different backups read different segments from disk in parallel, different recovery masters reconstruct different partitions in parallel, and so on. The second dimension is pipelining: all of the six stages listed above proceed in parallel, with a segment as the basic unit of work. While one segment is being read from disk on a backup, another segment is being partitioned by that backup's CPU, and records from another segment are being transferred to a recovery master; similar pipelining occurs on recovery masters. For fastest recovery all of the resources of the cluster should be kept fully utilized, including disks, CPUs, and the network.

3.7 Segment Replay Order

In order to maximize concurrency, recovery masters and backups operate independently. As soon as the coordinator contacts each backup to obtain its list of segments, the backup begins prefetching segments from disk and dividing them by partition. At the same time, masters fetch segment data from backups and replay it. Ideally backups will constantly run ahead of masters, so that segment data is ready and waiting whenever a recovery master requests it. However, this only works if the recovery masters and backups process segments in the same order. If a recovery master accidentally requests the last segment in the backup's order then the master will stall: it will not receive any data to process until the backup has read all of its segments.

In order to avoid pipeline stalls, each backup decides in advance the order in which it will read its segments. It returns this information to the coordinator during the setup phase, and the coordinator includes the order information when it communicates with recovery masters to initiate recovery. Each recovery master uses its knowledge of backup disk speeds to estimate when each segment's data is likely to be loaded. It then requests segment data in order of expected availability. (This approach causes all masters to request segments in the same order; we could introduce randomization to avoid contention caused by lock-step behavior.)

Unfortunately, there will still be variations in the speed at which backups read and process segments. In order to avoid stalls because of slow backups, each master keeps several concurrent requests for segment data outstanding at any given time during recovery; it replays segment data in the order that the requests return.

Because of the optimizations described above, recovery masters will end up replaying segments in a different order than the one in which the segments were originally written. Fortunately, the version numbers in log records allow the log to be replayed in any order without affecting the result. During replay each master simply retains the version of each object with the highest version number, discarding any older versions that it encounters.

Although each segment has multiple replicas stored on different backups, only the primary replicas are read during recovery; reading more than one would waste valuable disk bandwidth. Masters identify primary replicas when scattering their segments as described in Section 3.2. During recovery each backup reports all of its segments, but it identifies the primary replicas and only prefetches the primary replicas from disk. Recovery masters request non-primary replicas only if there is a failure reading the primary replica.

3.8 Cleanup

After a recovery master completes the recovery of its assigned partition, it notifies the coordinator that it is ready to service requests. The coordinator updates its configuration information to indicate that the master now owns the tablets in the recovered partition, at which point the partition is available for client requests. Clients with failed RPCs to the crashed master have been waiting for new configuration information to appear; they discover it and retry their RPCs with the new master. Recovery masters can begin service independently without waiting for other recovery masters to finish.

Once all recovery masters have completed recovery, the coordinator contacts each of the backups again. At this point the backups free the storage for the crashed master's segments, since it is no longer needed. Recovery is complete once all of the backups have been notified.

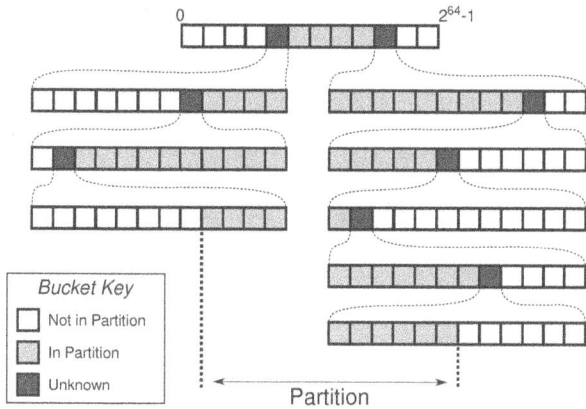

Figure 5: A tablet profile consists of a hierarchical collection of bucket arrays; buckets are subdivided dynamically when their counts become large. The tree structure creates (bounded) uncertainty when assigning partition boundaries, since counts in ancestor buckets may represent objects either before or after the boundary.

3.9 Tablet Profiling

Each master is responsible for creating a *will*, which describes how its objects should be partitioned during recovery. A partition consists of one or more tablets. The master should balance its partitions so that they require roughly equal time to recover, and the partitions should be sized based on the desired recovery time. The master's storage is not actually partitioned during normal operation as this would create unnecessary overheads; partitioning only occurs during recovery. The master uploads its will to the coordinator and updates the will as its data evolves.

RAMCloud computes wills using *tablet profiles*. Each tablet profile tracks the distribution of resource usage within a single table or tablet in a master. It consists of a collection of buckets, each of which counts the number of log records corresponding to a range of object identifiers, along with the total log space consumed by those records. Tablet profiles are updated as new log records are created and old segments are cleaned, and the master periodically scans its tablet profiles to compute a new will.

Unfortunately, it isn't possible to choose the buckets for a tablet profile statically because the space of object identifiers is large (2^{64}) and clients can allocate object identifiers however they wish. With any static choice of buckets, it is possible that all of the objects in a table could end up in a single bucket, which would provide no information for partitioning. Buckets must be chosen dynamically so that the contents of each bucket are small compared to the contents of a partition.

RAMCloud represents a tablet profile as a dynamic tree of bucket arrays, as shown in Figure 5. Initially the tree consists of a single bucket array that divides the entire 64-bit identifier space into buckets of equal width (in the current implementation there are 256 buckets in each array). Whenever a master creates a new log record it updates the appropriate bucket. If a bucket becomes too large (the number of records or space usage exceeds a threshold) then a child bucket array is created to subdivide the bucket's range into smaller buckets. Future log records are profiled in the child bucket array instead of the parent. However, the counts in the parent bucket remain (RAMCloud does not attempt to redistribute them in the child bucket array since this could require rescanning a large portion of the log). The master decrements bucket counts when it cleans log segments. Each bucket array records the position of the log head when that array was created, and the master uses this information during cleaning to decrement the same bucket that was incremented

when the record was created (thus, over time the counts in non-leaf buckets are likely to become small). Bucket arrays are collapsed back into their parents when usage drops.

To calculate partitions, a master scans its tablet profiles in a depth-first search, accumulating counts of records and space usage and establishing partition boundaries whenever the counts reach threshold values. For example, one policy might be to assign partitions based on log space usage so that no partition has more than 600 MB of log data or more than three million objects.

The tablet profile structure creates uncertainty in the actual usage of a partition, as illustrated in Figure 5. If a partition boundary is placed at the beginning of a leaf bucket, it isn't possible to tell whether counts in ancestor buckets belong to the new partition or the previous one. Fortunately, the uncertainty is bounded. For example, in the current RAMCloud implementation, there could be up to 7 ancestor buckets, each of which could account for 8 MB of data (the threshold for subdividing a bucket), for a worst-case uncertainty of 56 MB for each partition boundary. In order to bound recovery times, RAMCloud pessimistically assumes that unknown counts fall within the current partition.

In the configuration used for RAMCloud, the memory overhead for tablet profiles is 0.6% in the worst case (8 levels of bucket array for 8 MB of data). The parameters of the tablet profile can be changed to make trade-offs between the storage overhead for profiles and the accuracy of partition boundaries.

3.10 Consistency

We designed RAMCloud to provide a strong form of consistency (linearizability [13], which requires exactly-once semantics), even across host failures and network partitions. A full discussion of RAMCloud's consistency architecture is beyond the scope of this paper, and the implementation is not yet complete; however, it affects crash recovery in two ways. First, a master that is suspected of failure (a *sick master*) must stop servicing requests before it can be recovered, to ensure that applications always read and write the latest version of each object. Second, when recovering from suspected coordinator failures, RAMCloud must ensure that only one coordinator can manipulate and serve the cluster's configuration at a time.

RAMCloud will disable a sick master's backup operations when it starts recovery, so the sick master will be forced to contact the coordinator to continue servicing writes. The coordinator contacts backups at the start of recovery to locate a replica of every segment in the sick master's log, including the active segment to which the master may still be writing. Once a backup with a replica of the active segment has been contacted, it will reject backup operations from the sick master with an indication that the master must stop servicing requests until it has contacted the coordinator. Masters will periodically check in with their backups, so disabling a master's backup operations will also stop it from servicing read requests by the time recovery completes.

Coordinator failures will be handled safely using the ZooKeeper service [14]. The coordinator will use ZooKeeper to store its configuration information, which consists of a list of active storage servers along with the tablets they manage. ZooKeeper uses its own replication mechanisms to provide a high level of durability and availability for this information. To handle coordinator failures, the active coordinator and additional standby coordinators will compete for a single coordinator lease in ZooKeeper, which ensures that at most one coordinator runs at a time. If the active coordinator fails or becomes disconnected, its lease will expire and it will stop servicing requests. An arbitrary standby coordinator will acquire the lease, read the configuration information from ZooKeeper, and resume service. The configuration information is small, so we expect to recover from coordinator failures just as quickly as other server failures.

3.11 Additional Failure Modes

Our work on RAMCloud so far has focused on recovering the data stored in the DRAM of a single failed master. The sections below describe several other ways in which failures can occur in a RAMCloud cluster and some preliminary ideas for dealing with them; we defer a full treatment of these topics to future work.

3.11.1 Backup Failures

RAMCloud handles the failure of a backup server by creating new replicas to replace the ones on the failed backup. Every master is likely to have at least one segment replica on the failed backup, so the coordinator notifies all of the masters in the cluster when it detects a backup failure. Each master checks its segment table to identify segments stored on the failed backup, then it creates new replicas using the approach described in Section 3.2. All of the masters perform their rereplication concurrently and the new replicas are scattered across all of the disks in the cluster, so recovery from backup failures is fast. If each master has 64 GB of memory then each backup will have about 192 GB of data that must be rewritten (assuming 3 replicas for each segment). For comparison, 256 GB of data must be transferred to recover a dead master: 64 GB must be read, then 192 GB must be written during rereplication.

3.11.2 Multiple Failures

Given the large number of servers in a RAMCloud cluster, there will be times when multiple servers fail simultaneously. When this happens, RAMCloud recovers from each failure independently. The only difference in recovery is that some of the primary replicas for each failed server may have been stored on the other failed servers. In this case the recovery masters will use secondary replicas; recovery will complete as long as there is at least one replica available for each segment. It should be possible to recover multiple failures concurrently; for example, if a RAMCloud cluster contains 5,000 servers with flash drives for backup, the measurements in Section 4 indicate that a rack failure that disables 40 masters, each with 64 GB storage, could be recovered in about 2 seconds.

If many servers fail simultaneously, such as in a power failure that disables many racks, RAMCloud may not be able to recover immediately. This problem arises if no replicas are available for a lost segment or if the remaining masters do not have enough spare capacity to take over for all the lost masters. In this case RAMCloud must wait until enough machines have rebooted to provide the necessary data and capacity (alternatively, an operator can request that the system continue with some loss of data). RAMCloud clusters should be configured with enough redundancy and spare capacity to make situations like this rare.

3.11.3 Cold Start

RAMCloud must guarantee the durability of its data even if the entire cluster loses power at once. In this case the cluster will need to perform a "cold start" when power returns. Normally, when a backup restarts, it discards all of the segments stored on its disk or flash, since they have already been rereplicated elsewhere. However, in a cold start this information must be preserved. Backups will contact the coordinator as they reboot, and the coordinator will instruct them to retain existing data; it will also retrieve a list of their segments. Once a quorum of backups has become available, the coordinator will begin reconstructing masters. RAMCloud can use the same partitioned approach described above, but it may make

CPU	Xeon X3470 (4x2.93 GHz cores, 3.6 GHz Turbo)
RAM	16 GB DDR3 at 1333 MHz
Disk 1	WD 2503ABYX (7200 RPM, 250 GB)
	Effective read/write: 105/110 MB/s
Disk 2	Seagate ST3500418AS (7200 RPM, 500 GB)
	Effective read/write: 108/87 MB/s
Flash Disks	Crucial M4 CT128M4SSD2 (128GB)
	Effective read/write: 269/182 MB/s
NIC	Mellanox ConnectX-2 Infiniband HCA
Switches	5x 36-port Mellanox InfiniScale IV (4X QDR)

Table 1: Experimental cluster configuration. All 60 nodes have identical hardware. Effective disk bandwidth is the average throughput from 1,000 8 MB sequential accesses to random locations in the first 72 GB of the disk. Flash drives were used in place of disks for Figure 9 only. The cluster has 5 network switches arranged in two layers. Each port's maximum network bandwidth is 32 Gbps, but nodes are limited to about 25 Gbps by PCI Express. The switching fabric is oversubscribed, providing at best about 22 Gbps of bisection bandwidth per node when congested.

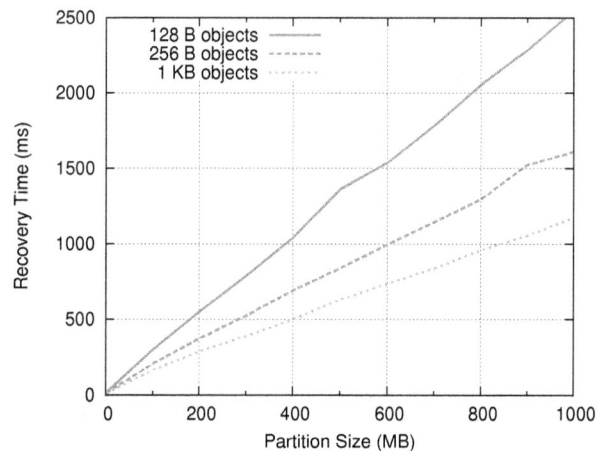

Figure 6: Recovery time as a function of partition size with a single recovery master and 60 backups. Each curve uses objects of a single uniform size.

more sense to use a different approach where masters are reconstructed exactly as they existed before the cold start. This will be faster than the partitioned approach because masters will not need to write any backup data: the existing backups can continue to serve after the masters are reconstructed.

The current RAMCloud implementation does not perform cold starts.

4. EVALUATION

We implemented the RAMCloud architecture described in Sections 2 and 3, and we evaluated the performance and scalability of crash recovery using a 60-node cluster. The cluster hardware consists of standard off-the-shelf components (see Table 1) with the exception of its networking equipment, which is based on Infiniband; with it our end hosts achieve both high bandwidth (25 Gbps) and low latency (user-level applications can communicate directly with the NICs to send and receive packets, bypassing the kernel).

The default experimental configuration used one backup server on each machine, with a single disk. A subset of these machines also ran recovery masters. One additional machine ran the coordinator, the crashed master, and the client application. In order to increase the effective scale of the system, some experiments ran two independent backup servers on each machine (each with one disk).

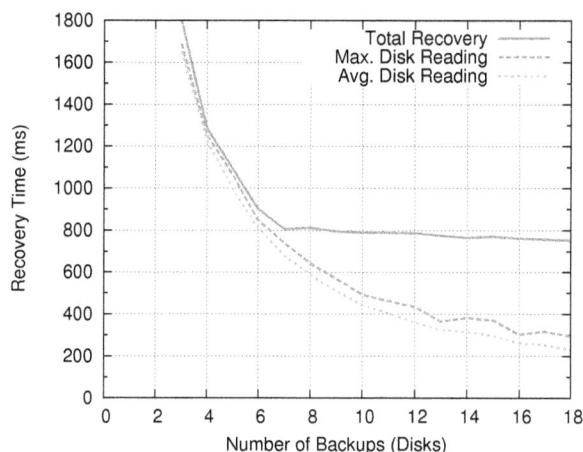

Figure 7: Recovery time as a function of the number of disks, with a single recovery master, one 600 MB partition with 1,024 byte objects, and each disk on a separate machine. "Avg. Disk Reading" measures the average elapsed time (across all disks) to read backup data during recovery; "Max. Disk Reading" graphs the longest time for any disk in the cluster. Once 6-8 disks are available recovery time is limited by the network of the recovery master.

In each experiment a client application observed and measured a crash of a single master and the subsequent recovery. The client initially filled the master with objects of a single size (1,024 bytes by default). It then sent a magic RPC to the coordinator which caused it to recover the master. The client waited until all partitions had been successfully recovered, then read a value from one of those partitions and reported the end-to-end recovery time. All experiments used a disk replication factor of 3 (i.e., 3 replicas on disk in addition to one copy in DRAM). The CPUs, disks, and networks were idle and entirely dedicated to recovery (in practice, recovery would have to compete for resources with application workloads, though we would argue for giving priority to recovery).

Each of the subsections below addresses one question related to the performance of recovery. The overall results are:

- A 60-node cluster can recover lost data at about 22 GB/sec (a crashed server with 35 GB storage can be recovered in 1.6 seconds), and recovery performance scales with cluster size. However, our scalability measurements are limited by the small size of our test cluster.

- The speed of an individual recovery master is limited primarily by network speed for writing new segment replicas.

- The segment scattering algorithm distributes segments effectively and compensates for varying disk speeds.

- Fast recovery significantly reduces the risk of data loss.

4.1 How Large Should Partitions Be?

Our first measurements provide data for configuring RAMCloud (partition size and number of disks needed per recovery master). Figure 6 measures how quickly a single recovery master can process backup data, assuming enough backups to keep the recovery master fully occupied. Depending on the object size, a recovery master can replay log data at a rate of 400-800 MB/s, including the overhead for reading the data from backups and writing new backup copies. With small objects the speed of recovery is limited by the cost of updating the hash table and tablet profiles. With large objects recovery is limited by the network speed during writes to new backups (for example, with 600 MB partitions and a disk

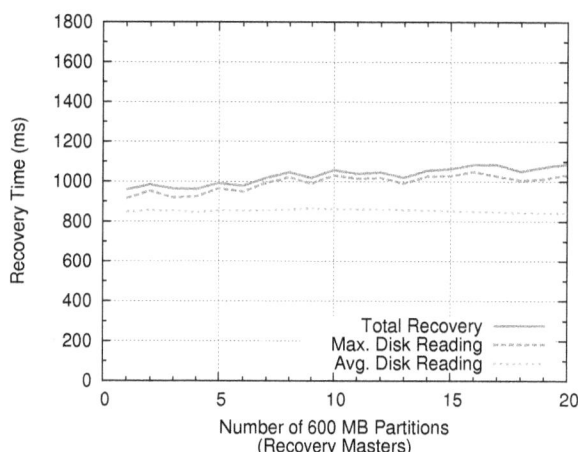

Figure 8: Recovery performance under proportional scaling (one recovery master and 6 backups for each 600 MB partition of data to recover). Each recovery master shared a host with 2 backups, and each point is an average of 5 runs (Figure 11 shows the variance between runs). A horizontal line would indicate perfect scalability. Recovery time is limited by disk bandwidth.

replication factor of 3, the recovery master must write 1.8 GB of data to backups).

For 1-second recovery Figure 6 suggests that partitions should be limited to no more than 800 MB and no more than 3 million log records (with 128-byte objects a recovery master can process 400 MB of data per second, which is roughly 3 million log records). With 10 Gbps Ethernet, partitions must be limited to 300 MB due to the bandwidth requirements for rereplication.

In our measurements we filled the log with live objects, but the presence of deleted versions will, if anything, make recovery faster. The master's memory has the same log structure as the backup replicas, so the amount of log data to read will always be equal to the size of the master's memory, regardless of deleted versions. However, deleted versions may not need to be rereplicated (depending on the order of replay).

4.2 How Many Disks Are Needed for Each Recovery Master?

Each of our disks provided an effective bandwidth of 100-110 MB/s when reading 8 MB segments; combined with Figure 6, this suggests that RAMCloud will need about 6-8 disks for each recovery master in order to keep the pipeline full. Figure 7 graphs recovery performance with one recovery master and a varying number of disks and reaches the same conclusion. With large numbers of disks, the speed of recovery is limited by outbound network bandwidth on the recovery master.

4.3 How Well Does Recovery Scale?

The most important issue in recovery for RAMCloud is scalability: if one recovery master can recover 600 MB of data in one second, can 10 recovery masters recover 6 GB in the same time, and can 100 recovery masters recover 60 GB? Unfortunately, the disk bandwidth available in our cluster limited us to 20 recovery masters (120 backups), which is only about 20% the number we would expect in a full-size RAMCloud recovery. Nonetheless, within this limited range RAMCloud demonstrates excellent scalability. Figure 8 graphs recovery time as the amount of lost data is increased and the cluster size is increased to match. For each 600 MB partition of lost data, the cluster includes one recovery master and 6 backups with one disk each. With 20 recovery masters and 120

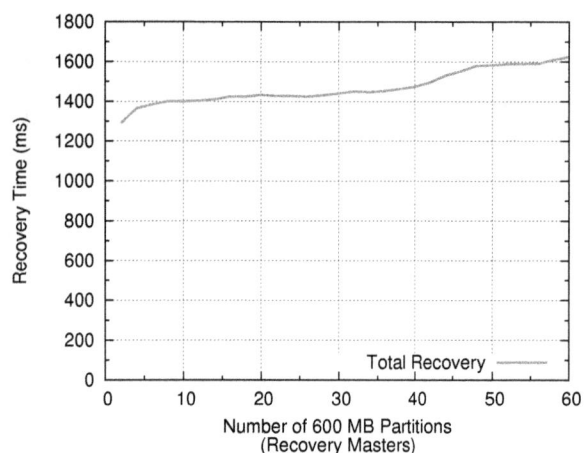

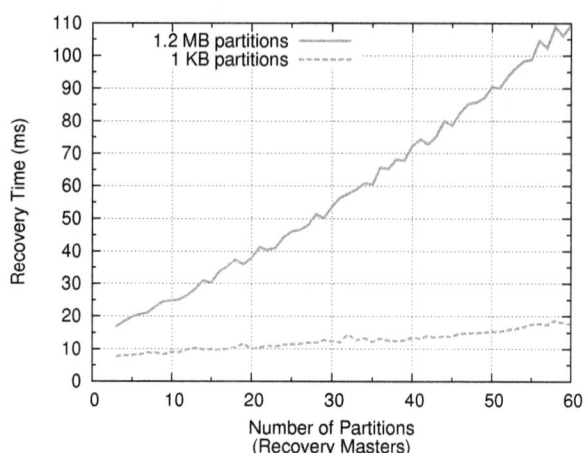

Figure 9: Recovery time under proportional scaling, using flash drives instead of disks. Each partition contained 600 MB of data, and there were 2 backups for each recovery master. As with Figure 8, scaling is proportional: the number of recovery masters and backups increases with the number of partitions being recovered. Each point is an average of 5 runs. A horizontal line would indicate perfect scalability. Recovery is slower than in Figure 8 for a number of reasons: less disk bandwidth available per master (540 MB/s vs. 600-660 MB/s), network saturation, and processor and memory contention between the master and backups on each node.

Figure 10: Management overhead as a function of system scale. Partition size is reduced to 16 KB and segment replicas are stored in DRAM in order to eliminate overheads related to data size or disk. For "1 KB partitions" each partition only contains a single object; this measures the coordinator's overheads for contacting masters and backups. "1.2 MB partitions" maintains the same number of segments (and roughly the same number of RPCs) as in Figure 8; it measures the overhead for masters to contact more and more backups as cluster size increases. Each data point is the average over 5 runs, and there were 2 backups for each recovery master.

disks, RAMCloud can recover 11.7 GB of data in under 1.1 seconds, which is only 13% longer than it takes to recover 600 MB with a single master and 6 disks.

In order to allow more recovery masters to participate in recovery, we replaced all the disks in our cluster with flash drives, each of which provided 270 MB/s read bandwidth (as opposed to 110 MB/s for the disks). With this configuration we were able to run recoveries that used 60 recovery masters, as shown in Figure 9. The system still scales well: with 60 recovery masters RAMCloud can recover 35 GB of data from a lost server in about 1.6 seconds, which is 26% longer than it takes 2 recovery masters to recover 1.2 GB of data.

It is important to keep the overhead for additional masters and backups small, so that recovery can span hundreds of hosts in large clusters. In order to isolate these overheads, we ran additional experiments with artificially small segments (16 KB) and kept all segment replicas in DRAM to eliminate disk overheads. Figure 10 (bottom curve) shows the recovery time using trivial partitions containing just a single 1 KB object; this measures the cost for the coordinator to contact all the backups and masters during the setup phase. Our cluster scales to 60 recovery masters with only about a 10 ms increase in recovery time (thanks in large part to fast RPCs).

Figure 10 also shows recovery time using 1.2 MB partitions and 16 KB segments (upper curve). In this configuration the cluster performs roughly the same number of RPCs as it does in Figure 8, but it has very little data to process. This exposes the fixed overheads for recovery masters to communicate with backups: as the system scale increases, each master must contact more backups, retrieving less data from each individual backup. Each additional recovery master adds only about 1.5 ms of overhead, so work can be split across 100 recovery masters without substantially increasing recovery time.

4.4 How Well Does Segment Scattering Work?

Figure 11 shows that the segment placement algorithm described in Section 3.2 works well. We measured three different variations of the placement algorithm: the full algorithm, which considers both disk speed and number of segments already present on each backup; a version that uses purely random placement; and an in-between version that attempts to even out the number of segments on each backup but does not consider disk speed. The top graph in Figure 11 shows that the full algorithm improves recovery time by about 33% over a purely random placement mechanism. Much of the improvement came from evening out the number of segments on each backup; considering disk speed improves recovery time by only 12% over the even-segment approach because the disks did not vary much in speed.

To further test how the algorithm handles variations in disk speed, we also took measurements using the configuration of our cluster when it first arrived. The fans were shipped in a "max speed" debugging setting, and the resulting vibration caused large variations in speed among the disks (as much as a factor of 4x). In this environment the full algorithm provided an even larger benefit over purely random placement, but there was relatively little benefit from considering segment counts without also considering disk speed (Figure 11, bottom graph). RAMCloud's placement algorithm compensates effectively for variations in the speed of disks, allowing recovery times almost as fast with highly variable disks as with uniform disks. Disk speed variations may not be significant in our current cluster, but we think they will be important in large datacenters where there are likely to be different generations of hardware.

4.5 Will Scattering Result in Data Loss?

RAMCloud's approach of scattering segment replicas allows faster recovery, but it increases the system's vulnerability in the event of simultaneous node failures. For example, consider a cluster with 1,000 nodes and 2x disk replication. With RAMCloud's scattering approach to segment placement, there is a 5% chance that data will be lost if any 3 nodes fail simultaneously (the three nodes will account for the master and both backups for at least one segment). In contrast, if each master concentrates all its segment replicas on two backups, as in Figure 3a, the probability of data loss drops to less than 10^{-5} with 3 simultaneous failures.

Fortunately, the fast recovery enabled by scattering makes it

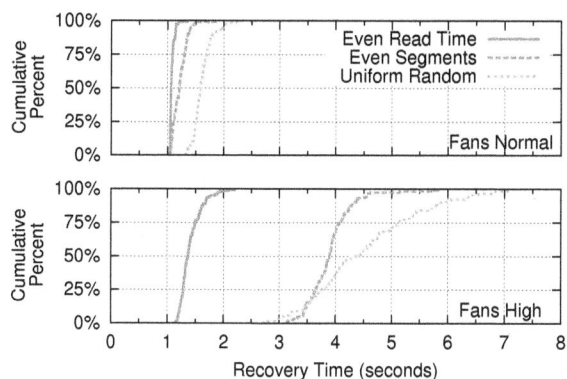

Figure 11: Impact of segment placement on recovery time. Each line is a cumulative distribution of 120 recoveries of twenty 600 MB partitions, showing the percent of recoveries that completed within a given time. "Even Read Time" uses the placement algorithm described in Section 3.2; "Uniform Random" uses a purely random approach; and "Even Segments" attempts to spread segments evenly across backups without considering disk speed. The top graph measured the cluster in its normal configuration, with relatively uniform disk performance; the bottom graph measured the system as it was shipped (unnecessarily high fan speed caused vibrations that degraded performance significantly for some disks). With fans at normal speed, "Even Read Time" and "Even Segments" perform nearly the same since there is little variation in disk speed.

unlikely that a second or third failure will occur before a first failure has been recovered, and this more than makes up for the additional vulnerability, as shown in Figure 12. With one-second recovery the probability of data loss is very low (about 10^{-5} in one year even with a 100,000-node cluster). The risk of data loss rises rapidly with reduced recovery time: if recovery takes 1,000 seconds, then RAMCloud is likely to lose data in any one-year period. The line labeled "100s" corresponds roughly to the recovery mechanisms in other systems such as GFS and HDFS (these systems keep 3 replicas on disk, vs. 1 replica in DRAM and 2 replicas on disk for the corresponding RAMCloud); with large cluster sizes these other systems may be vulnerable to data loss. Using a concentrated approach rather than scattering improves reliability, but the benefit from faster recovery is much larger: a 10x improvement in recovery time improves reliability more than a 1,000x reduction in scattering.

One risk with Figure 12 is that it assumes server failures are independent. There is considerable evidence that this is not the case in datacenters [23, 8]; for example, it is not unusual for entire racks to become inaccessible at once. Thus it is important for the segment scattering algorithm to consider sources of correlated failure, such as rack boundaries. If there are unpredictable sources of correlated failure, they will result in longer periods of unavailability while RAMCloud waits for one or more of the backups to reboot (RAMCloud is no better or worse than other systems in this respect).

Although we made all of the performance measurements in this section with 3x disk replication to be conservative, Figure 12 suggests that the combination of two copies on disk and one copy in DRAM should be quite safe. The main argument for 3x disk replication is to ensure 3-way redundancy even in the event of a datacenter power outage, which would eliminate the DRAM copies. With 3x disk replication in addition to the DRAM copy, the likelihood of data loss is extremely small: less than 1% in a year even with 100,000 servers and 1,000-second recovery times.

4.6 What Is the Fastest Possible Recovery?

Assuming that recovery is scalable, it should be possible to recover even faster than 1-2 seconds by using more backups and more

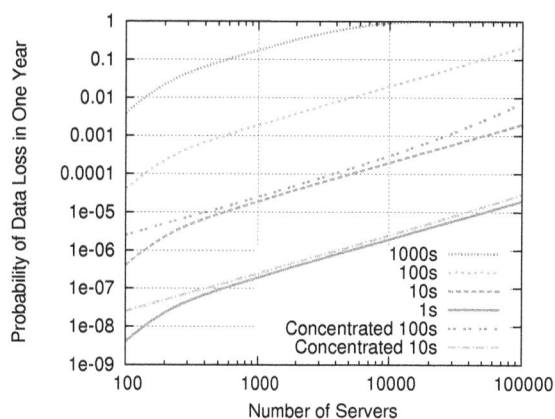

Figure 12: Probability of data loss in one year as a function of cluster size, assuming 8,000 segments per master, two disk replicas for each DRAM copy, and two crashes per year per server with a Poisson arrival distribution. Different lines represent different recovery times. Lines labeled "Concentrated" assume that segments are concentrated instead of scattered: each master picks 2 backups at random and replicates all of its segments on each of those backups.

recovery masters, with smaller partitions. However, we think that it will be difficult to recover faster than a few hundred milliseconds without significant changes to the recovery mechanism. For example, RAMCloud currently requires 150 milliseconds just to detect failure, and the time for the coordinator to contact every backup may approach 100 ms in a large cluster. In addition, it takes nearly 100 ms to read a single segment from disk (but this could be reduced if flash memory replaces disk for backup storage).

5. RISKS

There are three risks associated with RAMCloud's recovery mechanism that we have not been able to fully evaluate yet. We hope to learn more about these risks (and devise solutions, if necessary) as we gain more experience with the system.

Scalability. The measurements of scalability in Section 4.3 are encouraging, but they are based on a cluster size about one-fifth of what we would expect in production. It seems likely that larger clusters will expose problems that we have not yet seen.

Over-hasty recovery. In order to recover quickly, RAMCloud must also detect failures quickly. Whereas traditional systems may take 30 seconds or more to decide that a server has failed, RAMCloud makes that decision in 150 ms. This introduces a risk that RAMCloud will treat performance glitches as failures, resulting in unnecessary recoveries that could threaten both the performance and the integrity of the system. Furthermore, fast failure detection precludes some network protocols. For example, most TCP implementations wait 200 ms before retransmitting lost packets; if TCP is to be used in RAMCloud, either its retransmit interval must be shortened or RAMCloud's failure detection interval must be lengthened. The current implementation of RAMCloud supports several transport protocols for its RPC system (including TCP), most of which support fast failure detection.

Fragmented partitions. Our approach to recovery assumes that a master's objects can be divided into partitions during recovery. However, this changes the locality of access to those objects, which could degrade application performance after recovery. Our current data model does not benefit much from locality, but as we experiment with richer data models, this issue could become important.

6. RELATED WORK

There are numerous examples where DRAM has been used to improve the performance of storage systems. Early experiments in the 1980s and 1990s included file caching [19] and main-memory database systems [10, 11]. In recent years, large-scale Web applications have found DRAM indispensable to meet their performance goals. For example, both Google and Yahoo! keep their entire Web search indexes in DRAM; Facebook offloads its database servers by caching tens of terabytes of data in DRAM with memcached [3]; and Bigtable allows entire column families to be loaded into memory [6]. RAMCloud differs from these systems because it keeps all data permanently in DRAM (unlike Bigtable and Facebook, which use memory as a cache on a much larger disk-based storage system) and it is general-purpose (unlike the Web search indexes).

There has recently been a resurgence of interest in main-memory databases. One example is H-Store [16], which keeps all data in DRAM, supports multiple servers, and is general-purpose. However, H-Store is focused more on achieving full RDBMS semantics and less on achieving large scale or low latency to the same degree as RAMCloud. H-Store keeps redundant data in DRAM and does not attempt to survive coordinated power failures.

A variety of "NoSQL" storage systems have appeared recently, driven by the demands of large-scale Web applications and the inability of relational databases to meet their needs. Examples include Dynamo [9] and PNUTS [7]. Many of these systems use DRAM in some form, but all are fundamentally disk-based and none are attempting to provide latencies in the same range as RAMCloud. These systems provide availability using symmetric replication instead of fast crash recovery.

RAMCloud is similar in many ways to Google's Bigtable [6] and GFS [12]. Bigtable, like RAMCloud, implements fast crash recovery (during which data is unavailable) rather than online replication. Bigtable also uses a log-structured approach for its (meta)data, and it buffers newly-written data in memory, so that write operations complete before data has been written to disk. GFS serves a role for Bigtable somewhat like the backups in RAMCloud. Both Bigtable and GFS use aggressive data partitioning to speed up recovery. However, Bigtable and GFS were designed primarily for disk-based datasets; this allows them to store 10-100x more data than RAMCloud, but their access latencies are 10-100x slower (even for data cached in DRAM).

Caching mechanisms such as memcached [3] appear to offer a particularly simple mechanism for crash recovery: if a caching server crashes, its cache can simply be re-created as needed, either on the crashed server (after it restarts) or elsewhere. However, in large-scale systems, caching approaches can cause large gaps in availability after crashes. Typically these systems depend on high cache hit rates to meet their performance requirements; if caches are flushed, the system may perform so poorly that it is essentially unusable until the cache has refilled. This happened in an outage at Facebook in September 2010 [1]: a software error caused 28 TB of memcached data to be flushed, rendering the site unusable for 2.5 hours while the caches refilled from slower database servers.

Randomization has been used by several previous systems to allow system management decisions to be made in a distributed and scalable fashion. For example, consistent hashing uses randomization to distribute objects among a group of servers [24, 9]. Mitzenmacher and others have studied the theoretical properties of randomization with refinement and have shown that it produces near-optimal results [17, 5].

RAMCloud's log-structured approach to storage management is similar in many ways to log-structured file systems (LFS) [21]. However, log management in RAMCloud is simpler and more efficient than in LFS. RAMCloud is simpler because the log need not contain metadata to enable random-access reads as in LFS: the hash table enables fast access to data in DRAM, and the disk log is never read except during recovery, at which time the entire log is read. Thus the log consists primarily of object records and *tombstones* that mark their deletion. RAMCloud does not require checkpoints as in LFS, because it replays the entire log during recovery. RAMCloud is more efficient than LFS because it need not read data from disk during cleaning: all live data is always in memory. The only I/O during cleaning is to rewrite live data at the head of the log; as a result, RAMCloud consumes 3-10x less bandwidth for cleaning than LFS (cleaning cost has been a controversial topic for LFS; see [22], for example).

7. CONCLUSION

In this paper we have demonstrated that the resources of a large-scale storage system can be used to recover quickly from server crashes. RAMCloud distributes backup data across a large number of secondary storage devices and employs both data parallelism and pipelining to achieve end-to-end recovery times of 1-2 seconds. Although we have only been able to evaluate RAMCloud on a small cluster, our measurements indicate that the techniques will scale to larger clusters. Our implementation uses a simple log-structured representation for data, both in memory and on secondary storage, which provides high write throughput in addition to enabling fast recovery.

Fast crash recovery is a key enabler for RAMCloud: it allows a high-performance DRAM-based storage system to provide durability and availability at one-third the cost of a traditional approach using online replicas.

8. ACKNOWLEDGMENTS

Asaf Cidon reeducated us on the fundamentals of probability and assisted us with several calculations, including Figure 12. Nanda Kumar Jayakumar helped us with performance measurements and some of the figures in the paper. Several people provided helpful feedback on the paper, including Asaf Cidon, Ankita Kejriwal, Kay Ousterhout, George Varghese, the anonymous SOSP reviewers, and our shepherd Geoff Voelker. This work was supported by the Gigascale Systems Research Center and the Multiscale Systems Center, two of six research centers funded under the Focus Center Research Program, a Semiconductor Research Corporation program, and by Facebook, Mellanox, NEC, NetApp, SAP, and Samsung. This work was also partially supported by NSF Cybertrust awards CNS-0716806 and CNS-1052985 (CT-T: A Clean-Slate Infrastructure for Information Flow Control). Diego Ongaro is supported by The Junglee Corporation Stanford Graduate Fellowship. Steve Rumble is supported by a Natural Sciences and Engineering Research Council of Canada Postgraduate Scholarship.

9. REFERENCES

[1] More Details on Today's Outage | Facebook, Sept. 2010. http://www.facebook.com/note.php?note_id=431441338919.

[2] Agiga tech agigaram, Mar. 2011. http://www.agigatech.com/agigaram.php.

[3] memcached: a distributed memory object caching system, Jan. 2011. http://www.memcached.org/.

[4] M. K. Aguilera, A. Merchant, M. Shah, A. Veitch, and C. Karamanolis. Sinfonia: A new paradigm for building scalable distributed systems. *ACM Trans. Comput. Syst.*, 27:5:1–5:48, November 2009.

[5] Y. Azar, A. Z. Broder, A. R. Karlin, and E. Upfal. Balanced allocations (extended abstract). In *Proceedings of the twenty-sixth annual ACM symposium on theory of computing*, STOC '94, pages 593–602, New York, NY, USA, 1994. ACM.

[6] F. Chang, J. Dean, S. Ghemawat, W. C. Hsieh, D. A. Wallach, M. Burrows, T. Chandra, A. Fikes, and R. E. Gruber. Bigtable: A distributed storage system for structured data. *ACM Trans. Comput. Syst.*, 26:4:1–4:26, June 2008.

[7] B. F. Cooper, R. Ramakrishnan, U. Srivastava, A. Silberstein, P. Bohannon, H.-A. Jacobsen, N. Puz, D. Weaver, and R. Yerneni. Pnuts: Yahoo!'s hosted data serving platform. *Proc. VLDB Endow.*, 1:1277–1288, August 2008.

[8] J. Dean. Keynote talk: Evolution and future directions of large-scale storage and computation systems at google. In *Proceedings of the 1st ACM symposium on Cloud computing*, Jun 2010.

[9] G. DeCandia, D. Hastorun, M. Jampani, G. Kakulapati, A. Lakshman, A. Pilchin, S. Sivasubramanian, P. Vosshall, and W. Vogels. Dynamo: amazon's highly available key-value store. In *Proceedings of twenty-first ACM SIGOPS symposium on operating systems principles*, SOSP '07, pages 205–220, New York, NY, USA, 2007. ACM.

[10] D. J. DeWitt, R. H. Katz, F. Olken, L. D. Shapiro, M. R. Stonebraker, and D. A. Wood. Implementation techniques for main memory database systems. In *Proceedings of the 1984 ACM SIGMOD international conference on management of data*, SIGMOD '84, pages 1–8, New York, NY, USA, 1984. ACM.

[11] H. Garcia-Molina and K. Salem. Main memory database systems: An overview. *IEEE Trans. on Knowl. and Data Eng.*, 4:509–516, December 1992.

[12] S. Ghemawat, H. Gobioff, and S.-T. Leung. The google file system. In *Proceedings of the nineteenth ACM symposium on Operating systems principles*, SOSP '03, pages 29–43, New York, NY, USA, 2003. ACM.

[13] M. P. Herlihy and J. M. Wing. Linearizability: a correctness condition for concurrent objects. *ACM Trans. Program. Lang. Syst.*, 12:463–492, July 1990.

[14] P. Hunt, M. Konar, F. P. Junqueira, and B. Reed. Zookeeper: wait-free coordination for internet-scale systems. In *Proceedings of the 2010 USENIX annual technical conference*, USENIX ATC '10, pages 11–11, Berkeley, CA,

USA, 2010. USENIX Association.

[15] R. Johnson and J. Rothschild. Personal Communications, March 24 and August 20, 2009.

[16] R. Kallman, H. Kimura, J. Natkins, A. Pavlo, A. Rasin, S. Zdonik, E. P. C. Jones, S. Madden, M. Stonebraker, Y. Zhang, J. Hugg, and D. J. Abadi. H-store: a high-performance, distributed main memory transaction processing system. *Proc. VLDB Endow.*, 1:1496–1499, August 2008.

[17] M. D. Mitzenmacher. *The power of two choices in randomized load balancing.* PhD thesis, University of California, Berkeley. 1996. AAI9723118.

[18] J. Ousterhout, P. Agrawal, D. Erickson, C. Kozyrakis, J. Leverich, D. Mazières, S. Mitra, A. Narayanan, D. Ongaro, G. Parulkar, M. Rosenblum, S. M. Rumble, E. Stratmann, and R. Stutsman. The case for ramcloud. *Commun. ACM*, 54:121–130, July 2011.

[19] J. K. Ousterhout, A. R. Cherenson, F. Douglis, M. N. Nelson, and B. B. Welch. The sprite network operating system. *Computer*, 21:23–36, February 1988.

[20] D. A. Patterson, G. Gibson, and R. H. Katz. A case for redundant arrays of inexpensive disks (raid). In *Proceedings of the 1988 ACM SIGMOD international conference on management of data*, SIGMOD '88, pages 109–116, New York, NY, USA, 1988. ACM.

[21] M. Rosenblum and J. K. Ousterhout. The design and implementation of a log-structured file system. *ACM Trans. Comput. Syst.*, 10:26–52, February 1992.

[22] M. Seltzer, K. A. Smith, H. Balakrishnan, J. Chang, S. McMains, and V. Padmanabhan. File system logging versus clustering: a performance comparison. In *Proceedings of the USENIX 1995 Technical Conference*, TCON'95, pages 21–21, Berkeley, CA, USA, 1995. USENIX Association.

[23] K. Shvachko, H. Kuang, S. Radia, and R. Chansler. The hadoop distributed file system. In *Proceedings of the 2010 IEEE 26th Symposium on Mass Storage Systems and Technologies (MSST)*, MSST '10, pages 1–10, Washington, DC, USA, 2010. IEEE Computer Society.

[24] I. Stoica, R. Morris, D. Liben-Nowell, D. R. Karger, M. F. Kaashoek, F. Dabek, and H. Balakrishnan. Chord: a scalable peer-to-peer lookup protocol for internet applications. *IEEE/ACM Trans. Netw.*, 11:17–32, February 2003.

Design Implications for Enterprise Storage Systems via Multi-Dimensional Trace Analysis

Yanpei Chen, Kiran Srinivasan*, Garth Goodson*, Randy Katz
University of California, Berkeley, *NetApp Inc.
{ychen2, randy}@eecs.berkeley.edu, *{skiran, goodson}@netapp.com

ABSTRACT

Enterprise storage systems are facing enormous challenges due to increasing growth and heterogeneity of the data stored. Designing future storage systems requires comprehensive insights that existing trace analysis methods are ill-equipped to supply. In this paper, we seek to provide such insights by using a new methodology that leverages an objective, multi-dimensional statistical technique to extract data access patterns from network storage system traces. We apply our method on two large-scale real-world production network storage system traces to obtain comprehensive access patterns and design insights at user, application, file, and directory levels. We derive simple, easily implementable, threshold-based design optimizations that enable efficient data placement and capacity optimization strategies for servers, consolidation policies for clients, and improved caching performance for both.

Categories and Subject Descriptors

C.4 [**Performance of Systems**]: Measurement techniques; D.4.3 [**Operating Systems**]: File Systems Management—*Distributed file systems*

1. INTRODUCTION

Enterprise storage systems are designed around a set of data access patterns. The storage system can be specialized by designing to a specific data access pattern; e.g., a storage system for streaming video supports different access patterns than a document repository. The better the access pattern is understood, the better the storage system design. Insights into access patterns have been derived from the analysis of existing file system workloads, typically through trace analysis studies [1, 3, 17, 19, 24]. While this is the correct general strategy for improving storage system design, past approaches have critical shortcomings, especially given recent changes in technology trends. In this paper, we present a new design methodology to overcome these shortcomings.

The data stored on enterprise network-attached storage systems is undergoing changes due to a fundamental shift in the underlying technology trends. We have observed three such trends, including:

- *Scale*: Data size grows at an alarming rate [12], due to new types of social, business and scientific applications [20], and the desire to "never delete" data.
- *Heterogeneity*: The mix of data types stored on these storage systems is becoming increasingly complex, each having its own requirements and access patterns [22].
- *Consolidation*: Virtualization has enabled the consolidation of multiple applications and their data onto fewer storage servers [6, 23]. These virtual machines (VMs) also present aggregate data access patterns more complex than those from individual clients.

Better design of future storage systems requires insights into the changing access patterns due to these trends. While trace studies have been used to derive data access patterns, we believe that they have the following shortcomings:

- *Unidimensional:* Although existing methods analyze many access characteristics, they do so one at a time, without revealing cross-characteristic dependencies.
- *Expertise bias:* Past analyses were performed by storage system designers looking for specific patterns based on prior workload expectations. This introduces a bias that needs to be revisited based on the new technology trends.
- *Storage server centric:* Past file system studies focused primarily on storage servers. This creates a critical knowledge gap regarding client behavior.

To overcome these shortcomings, we propose a new design methodology backed by the analysis of storage system traces. We present a *method that simultaneously analyzes multiple characteristics and their cross dependencies*. We use a multi-dimensional, statistical correlation technique, called k-means [2], that is completely agnostic to the characteristics of each access pattern and their dependencies. The K-means algorithm can analyze hundreds of dimensions simultaneously, providing added objectivity to our analysis. To further reduce expertise bias, we involve as many relevant characteristics as possible for each access pattern. In addition, we analyze patterns at different granularities (e.g., at the user session, application, file level) on the storage server as well as the client, thus addressing the need for understanding client patterns. The resulting design insights enable policies for building new storage systems.

Client side observations and design implications	Server side observations and design implications
1. Client sessions with IO sizes >128KB are read only or write only. ⇒ Clients can consolidate sessions based on only the read-write ratio.	7. Files with >70% sequential read or write have no repeated reads or overwrites. ⇒ Servers should delegate sequentially accessed files to clients to improve IO performance.
2. Client sessions with duration >8 hours do ≈10MB of IO. ⇒ Client caches can already fit an entire day's IO.	8. Engineering files with repeated reads have random accesses. ⇒ Servers should delegate repeatedly read files to clients; clients need to store them in flash or memory.
3. Number of client sessions drops off linearly by 20% from Monday to Friday. ⇒ Servers can get an extra "day" for background tasks by running at appropriate times during week days.	9. All files are active (have opens, IO, and metadata access) for only 1-2 hours in a few months. ⇒ Servers can use file idle time to compress or deduplicate to increase storage capacity.
4. Applications with <4KB of IO per file open and many opens of a few files do only random IO. ⇒ Clients should always cache the first few KB of IO per file per application.	10. All files have either all random access or >70% sequential access. (Seen in past studies too) ⇒ Servers can select the best storage medium for each file based on only access sequentiality.
5. Applications with >50% sequential read or write access entire files at a time. ⇒ Clients can request file prefetch (read) or delegation (write) based on only the IO sequentiality.	11. Directories with sequentially accessed files almost always contain randomly accessed files as well. ⇒ Servers can change from per-directory placement policy (default) to per-file policy upon seeing any sequential IO to any files in a directory.
6. Engineering applications with >50% sequential read and sequential write are doing code compile tasks, based on file extensions. ⇒ Servers can identify compile tasks; server has to cache the output of these tasks.	12. Some directories aggregate only files with repeated reads and overwrites. ⇒ Servers can delegate these directories entirely to clients, tradeoffs permitting.

Table 1: Summary of design insights, separated into insights derived from client access patterns and server access patterns.

We analyze two recent, network-attached storage file system traces from a production enterprise datacenter. Table 1 summarizes our key observations and design implications, they will be detailed later in the paper. Our methodology leads to observations that would be difficult to extract using past methods. We illustrate two such access patterns, one showing the value of multi-granular analysis (Observation 1 in Table 1) and another showing the value of multi-feature analysis (Observation 8).

First, we observe (Observation 1) that *sessions with more than 128KB of data reads or writes are either read-only or write-only.* This observation affects shared caching and consolidation policies across sessions. Specifically, client OSs can detect and co-locate cache sensitive sessions (read-only) with cache insensitive sessions (write-only) using just one parameter (read-write ratio). This improves cache utilization and consolidation (increased density of sessions per server).

Similarly, we observe (Observation 8) that *files with >70% sequential read or sequential write have no repeated reads or overwrites.* This access pattern involves four characteristics: read sequentiality, write sequentiality, repeated read behavior, and overwrite behavior. The observation leads to a useful policy: sequentially accessed files do not need to be cached at the server (no repeated reads), which leads to an efficient buffer cache.

These observations illustrate that our methodology can derive unique design implications that leverage the correlation between different characteristics. To summarize, our contributions are:

- Identify storage system access patterns using a multi-dimensional, statistical analysis technique.
- Build a framework for analyzing traces at different granularity levels at both server and client.
- Analyze our specific traces and present the access patterns identified.
- Derive design implications for various storage system components from the access patterns.

In the rest of the paper, we motivate and describe our analysis methodology (Sections 2 and 3), present the access patterns we found and the design insights (Section 4), provide the implications on storage system architecture (Section 5), and suggest future work (Section 6).

2. MOTIVATION AND BACKGROUND

Past trace-based studies have examined a range of storage system protocols and use cases, delivering valuable insights for designing storage servers. Table 2 summarizes the contributions of past studies. Many studies predate current technology trends. Analysis of real-world, corporate workloads or traces have been sparse, with only three studies among the ones listed [13, 15, 18]. A number of studies have focused on NFS trace analysis only [8, 10]. This focus somewhat neglects systems using the Common Internet File System (CIFS) protocol [5], with only a single CIFS study [15]. CIFS systems are important since CIFS is the network storage protocol for Windows, the dominant OS on commodity platforms. Our work uses the same traces as [15], but we perform analysis using a methodology that extracts multi-dimensional insights at different layers. This methodology is sufficiently different from prior work as to make the analysis findings not comparable. The following discusses the need for this methodology.

2.1 Need for Insights at Different Layers

We divide our view of the storage system into behavior at clients and servers. Storage *clients* interface directly with users, who create and view content via applications. Separately, *servers* store the content in a durable and efficient fashion over the network. Past network storage system trace studies focus mostly on storage servers (Table 2). Storage client behavior is underrepresented primarily due to the reliance on stateless NFS traces. This leaves a knowledge gap about access patterns at storage clients. Specifically, these questions are unanswered:

- Do applications exhibit clear access patterns?
- What are the user-level access patterns?
- Any correlation between users and applications?
- Do all applications interact with files the same way?

Study	Date of Traces	File System	N/w FS	Multi-Dim.	Multi-Layer	Data Set	Trace Info	Insights/Contributions
Ousterhout, *et al.* [17]	1985	BSD				Eng	Live	Seminal patterns analysis: Large, sequential read access; limited read-write; bursty I/O; short file lifetimes, etc.
Ramakrishnan, *et al.* [18]	1988-89	VAX/VMS	✓			Eng, HPC, Corp	Live	Relationship between files and processes - on usage patterns, sharing, etc.
Baker, *et al.* [3]	1991	Sprite	✓			Eng	Live	Analysis of distributed file system; comparison to [17], caching effects.
Gribble, *et al.* [10]	1991-97	Sprite, NFS, VxFS	✓			Eng, Backup	Live, Snap	Workload self-similarity
Douceur, *et al.* [7]	1998	FAT, FAT32, NTFS				Eng	Snap	Analysis of file and directory attributes: size, age, lifetime, directory depth
Vogels [24]	1998	FAT, NTFS				Eng, HPC	Live, Snap	Supported past observations and trends in NTFS
Zhou *et al.* [25]	1999	VFAT				PC	Live	Analysis of personal computer workloads
Roselli, *et al.* [19]	1997-00	VxFS, NTFS				Eng, Server	Live	Increased block lifetimes, caching strategies
Ellard, *et al.* [8]	2001	NFS	✓			Eng, Email	Live	NFS peculiarities, pathnames can aid file layout
Agrawal, *et al.* [1]	2000-04	FAT, FAT32, NTFS				Eng	Snap	Distribution of file size and type in namespace, change in file contents over time
Leung, *et al.* [15]	2007	CIFS	✓			Corp, Eng	Live	File re-open, sharing, activity characteristics; changes compared to previous studies
Kavalanekar, *et al.* [13]	2007	NTFS				Web, Corp	Live	Study of web (live maps, web content, etc.) workloads in servers via events tracing.
This paper	2007	CIFS	✓	✓	✓	Corp, Eng	Live	Section 4

Table 2: **Past studies of storage system traces.** "Corp" stands for corporate use cases. "Eng" stands for engineering use cases. "Live" implies live requests or events in traces were studied, "Snap" implies snapshots of file systems were studied.

Insights on these access patterns lead to better design of *both* clients and servers. They enable server capabilities such as per session quality of service (QoS), or per application service level objectives (SLOs). They also inform various consolidation, caching, and prefetching decisions at clients.

Each of these access patterns is visible only at a particular semantic layer within the client: users or applications. We define each such layer as an *access unit*, with the observed behaviors at each access unit being an *access pattern*. The analysis of client side access units represents an improvement on prior work.

On the server side, we extend the previous focus on files. We need to also understand how files are grouped within a directory, as well as cross-file dependencies and directory organization. Thus, we perform multi-layer and cross-layer dependency analysis on the server also. This is another improvement on past work.

2.2 Need for Multi-Dimensional Insights

Each access unit has certain inherent characteristics. Characteristics that can be quantified are *features* of that access unit. For example, for an application, the read size in bytes is a feature; the number of unique files accessed is another. Each feature represents an independent mathematical dimension that describes an access unit. We use the terms dimension, feature, and characteristic interchangeably. The global set of features for an access unit is limitless. Picking a good feature set requires domain knowledge.

Many recent studies analyze access patterns *only one feature at a time*. This represents a key limitation. The resulting insights, although valuable, lead to *uniform policies* around a single design point. For example, study [15] revealed that most bytes are transferred from larger files. Although this is an useful observation, it does not reveal other characteristics of such large files: Do they have repeated reads? Do they have overwrites? Do they have many metadata requests? And so on. Adding these dimensions breaks up the predominant access pattern into smaller, *minority* access patterns, each may require a specific storage policy.

Understanding minority access patterns is increasingly important, because the trend toward data heterogeneity implies that no "common case" will dominate storage system behavior. Minority access patterns become visible only upon analyzing multiple features simultaneously, hence the need for multi-dimensional insights. We also need to select a reasonable number of features. Doing so allows us to fully describe the access patterns and reduce the bias in picking any one feature.

Manually identifying multi-feature dependencies is difficult, and can lead to an untenable analysis. Therefore, we need techniques that analyze a large number of features, scale to a high number of analysis data points, and do not require a priori knowledge of any cross-feature dependencies. Multi-dimensional statistics techniques have solved similar problems in other domains [4, 9, 21]. We can apply similar techniques and combine them with domain specific knowledge of the storage systems being analyzed.

In short, the need for multi-layered and multi-dimensional insights motivates our methodology.

3. METHODOLOGY

In this section, we describe our analysis method in detail. We start with a description of the traces we analyzed, followed by a description of the access units selected for our study. Next, we describe key steps in our analysis process, including selecting the right features for each access unit, using the k-means data clustering algorithm to identify access patterns, and additional information needed to interpret and generalize the results.

3.1 Traces Analyzed

We collected CIFS traces from two large-scale, enterprise-class file servers deployed at our corporate datacenters. One server covers roughly 1000 employees in marketing, sales, finance, and other corporate roles. We call this the *corporate trace*. The other server covers roughly 500 employees in various engineering roles. We call this the *engineering trace*. We described the trace collecting infrastructure in [15].

The corporate trace reflects activities on 3TB of active storage from 09/20/2007 to 11/21/2007. It contains activity from many Windows applications. The engineering trace reflects activities on 19TB of active storage from 08/10/2007 to 11/14/2007. It interleaves activity from both Windows and Linux applications. In both traces, many clients use virtualization technologies. Thus, we believe we have representative traces with regards to the technology trends in scale, heterogeneity, and consolidation. Also, since protocol-independent users, applications, and stored data remain the primary factors affecting storage system behavior, we believe our analysis is relevant beyond CIFS.

3.2 Access Units

As mentioned in Section 2.1, we analyze access patterns at multiple access units at the server and the client. Selecting access units is subjective. We chose access units that form clear semantic design boundaries. On the client side, we analyze two access units:

- *Sessions*: Sessions reflect aggregate behavior of an user. A CIFS session is bounded by matching session connect and logoff requests. CIFS identifies it by a tuple - {client IP address, session ID}.
- *Application instance*: Analysis at this level leads to application specific optimizations in client VMs. CIFS identifies each application instance by the tuple - {client IP address, session ID, and process ID}.

We also analyzed file open-closes, but obtained no useful insights. Hence we omit that access unit from the paper.

We also examined two server side access units:

- *File*: Analyzing file level access patterns facilitates per-file policies and optimization techniques. Each file is uniquely identified by its full path name.
- *Deepest subtree*: This access unit is identified by the directory path immediately containing the file. Analysis at this level enables per-directory policies.

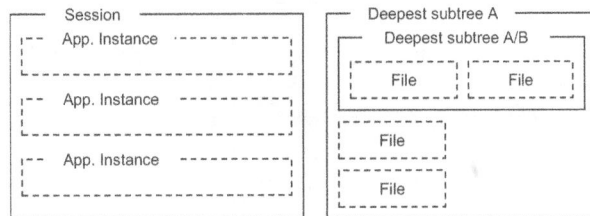

Figure 1: Access units analyzed. At clients, each session contains many application instances. At servers, each subtree contains many files.

Figure 1 shows the semantic hierarchy among different access units. At clients, each session contains many application instances. At servers, each subtree contains many files.

3.3 Analysis Process

Our method (Figure 2) involves the following steps:

1. Collect network storage system traces (Section 3.1).
2. Define the descriptive features for each access unit. This step requires domain knowledge about storage systems (Section 3.3.1).
3. Extract multiple instances of each access unit, and compute from the trace the corresponding numerical feature values of each instance.
4. Input those values into k-means, a multi-dimensional statistical data clustering technique (Section 3.3.2).
5. Interpret the k-means output and derive access patterns by looking at only the relevant subset of features. This step requires knowledge of both storage systems and statistics. We also need to extract considerable additional information to support our interpretations (Section 3.3.3).
6. Translate access patterns to design insights.

We give more details about Steps 2, 4, and 5 below.

3.3.1 Selecting features for each access unit

Selecting the set of descriptive features for each access unit requires domain knowledge about storage systems (Step 2 in Figure 2). It also introduces some subjectivity, since the choice of features limits on how one access pattern can differ from another. The human designer needs to select some basic features initially, e.g., total IO size and read-write ratio for a file. We will not know whether we have a good set of features until we have completed the entire analysis process. If the analysis results leave some design choice ambiguities, we need to add new features to clarify those ambiguities, again using domain knowledge. For example, for the deepest subtrees, we compute various percentiles (25th, 50th, and 75th) of certain features like read-write ratio because the average value for those features did not clearly separate the access patterns. We then repeat the analysis process using the new feature set. This iterative process leads to a long feature set for all access units, somewhat reducing the subjective bias of a small feature set. We list in Section 4 the chosen features for each access unit.

Most of the features used in our analysis (Section 4) are self-explanatory; some ambiguous or complex features require precise definitions, such as:

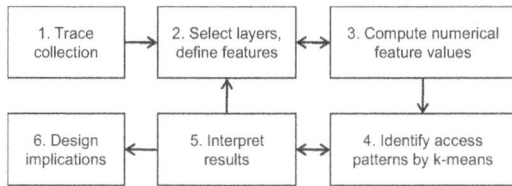

Figure 2: Methodology overview. The two-way arrows and the loop from Step 2 through Step 5 indicate our many iterations between the steps.

IO: We use "IO" as a substitute for "read and write".

Sequential reads or writes: We consider two read or writes requests to be sequential if they are consecutive in time, and the file offset + request size of the first request equals the file offset of the second request. A single read or write request is by definition not sequential.

Repeated reads or overwrites: We track accesses at 4KB block boundaries within a file, with the offset of the first block being zero. A read is considered repeated if it accesses a block that has been read in the past half hour. We use an equivalent definition for overwrites.

3.3.2 Identifying access patterns via k-means

A key part of our methodology is the k-means multi-dimensional correlation algorithm. We use it to identify access patterns simultaneously across many features (Step 4 in Figure 2). K-means is a well-known, statistical correlation algorithm. It identifies sets of data points that congregate around a region in n-dimensional space. These congregations are called *clusters*. Given data points in an n-dimensional space, k-means picks k points at random as initial cluster centers, assigns data points to their nearest cluster centers, and recomputes new cluster centers via arithmetic means across points in the cluster. K-means iterates the assignment-recompute process until the cluster centers become stationary. K-means can run with multiple sets of initial cluster centers and return the best result [2].

For each access unit, we extract different instances of it from the trace, i.e., all session instances, application instances, etc. For each instance, we compute the numerical values of all its features. This gives us a data array in which each row correspond to an instance, i.e., a data point, and each column correspond to a feature, i.e., a dimension. We input the array into k-means, and the algorithm finds the natural clusters across all data points. *We consider all data points in a cluster as belonging to a single equivalence class, i.e., a single access pattern.* The numerical values of the cluster centers indicate the characteristics of each access pattern.

We choose k-means for two reasons. First, k-means is algorithmically simple. This allows rapid processing on large data sets. We used a modified version of the k-means C library [14], in which we made some improvements to limits the memory footprint when processing large data sizes. Second, k-means leads to intuitive labels of the cluster centers. This helps us translate the statistical behavior extracted from the traces into tangible insights. Thus, we prefer k-

means to other clustering algorithms such as hierarchical clustering and k-means derivatives [2].

K-means requires us to specify k, the number of clusters. This is a difficult task since we do not know a priori the number of "natural" clusters in the data. We compute the intra-cluster "residual" variance from the k-means results - the sum of squared distances from each data point to its assigned cluster center. This is a standard metric for cluster quality, and gives us a lower bound on k. We cannot set k so small that the residual variance forms a large fraction of the total variance, i.e., residual variance ≈ the sum of squared distances from each data point to the global average of all data points. We optionally increase k beyond the lower bound until some key access patterns can be separated. Concurrently, we take care not to increase k too high, to prevent having an unwieldy number of access patterns and design targets. We applied this reasoning to set k at each client and server access unit.

3.3.3 Interpreting and generalizing the results

The k-means algorithm gives us a set of access patterns with various characteristics. We need additional information to understand the significance of the results. This information comes from computing various secondary data outside of k-means analysis (Step 5 in Figure 2:

- We gathered the start and end times of each session instance, aggregated by times of the day and days of the week. This gave us insight into how users launch and end sessions.
- We examine filename extensions of files associated with every access pattern belonging to these access units: application instances, files, and deepest subtrees. This information connects the access patterns to more easily recognizable file extensions.
- We perform correlation analysis between the file and deepest subtrees access units. Specifically, we compute the number of files of each file access pattern that is located within directories in each deepest subtree access pattern. This information captures the organizations of files in directories.

Such information gives us a detailed picture about the semantics of the access patterns, resulting in human understandable labels to the access patterns. Such labels help us translate observations to design implications.

Furthermore, after identifying the design implications, we explore if the design insights can be extrapolated to other trace periods and other storage system use cases. We accomplish this by repeating our exact analysis over multiple subsets of the traces, for example, a week's worth of traces at a time. This allow us to examine how our analysis would be different had we obtained only a week's trace. Access patterns that are consistent, stable across different weeks would indicate that they are likely to be more general than just our tracing period or our use cases.

4. ANALYSIS RESULTS & IMPLICATIONS

This section presents the access patterns we identified and the accompanying design insights. We discuss client and

(a). Descriptive features for each session			
Duration	Total metadata requests	Overwrite ratio	Directories accessed
Total IO size	Avg. time between IO requests	Tree connects	Application instances seen
Read:write ratio by bytes	Read sequentiality	Unique trees accessed	
Total IO requests	Write sequentiality	File opens	
Read:write ratio by requests	Repeated read ratio	Unique files opened	

(b). Corporate session access patterns	Full day work	Half day content viewing	Short content viewing	Short content generation	Supporting metadata	Supporting read-write
% of all sessions	0.5%	0.7%	1.2%	0.2%	96%	1.4%
Duration	8 hrs	4 hrs	10 min	70 min	7 sec	10 sec
Total IO size	11 MB	3 MB	128 KB	3 MB	0	420 B
Read:write ratio by bytes	3:2	1:0	1:0	0:1	0:0	1:1
Metadata requests	3000	700	230	550	1	20
Read sequentiality	70%	80%	0%	-	-	0%
Write sequentiality	80%	-	-	90%	-	0%
File opens:files	200:40	80:15	30:7	50:15	0:0	6:3
Tree connect:Trees	5:2	3:2	2:2	2:2	1:1	2:2
Directories accessed	10	7	4	6	0	2
Application instances	4	3	2	2	0	1

(c). Engineering session access patterns	Full day work	Human edit small files	Application generated backup/copy	Short content generation	Supporting metadata	Machine generated update
% of all sessions	0.4%	1.0%	4.4%	0.4%	90%	3.6%
Duration	1 day	2 hrs	1 min	1 hr	10 sec	10 sec
Total IO size	5 MB	5 KB	2 MB	2 MB	0	36 B
Read:write ratio	7:4	1:1	1:0	0:1	0:0	1:0
Metadata requests	1700	130	40	200	1	0
Read sequentiality	60%	0%	90%	-	-	0%
Write sequentiality	70%	0%	-	90%	-	-
File opens:files	130:20	9:2	6:5	15:6	0:0	1:1
Tree connect:Trees	1:1	1:1	1:1	1:1	1:1	1:1
Directories accessed	7	2	1	3	0	1
Application instances	4	2	1	1	0	1

Table 3: Session access patterns. (a): Full list of descriptive features. (b) and (c): Short names and descriptions of sessions in each access pattern; listing only the features that help separate the access patterns.

serve side access patterns (Section 4.1, 4.2). We also check if these patterns persist across time (Section 4.3).

For each access unit, we list the descriptive features (only some of which help separate access patterns), outline how we derived the high-level name (label) for each access pattern, and discuss relevant design insights.

4.1 Client Side Access Patterns

As mentioned in Section 3.2, we analyze sessions and application instances at clients.

4.1.1 Sessions

Sessions reflect aggregate behavior of human users. We used 17 features to describe sessions (Table 3). The corporate trace has 509,076 sessions, and the engineering trace has 232,033.

In Table 3, we provide quantitative descriptions and short names for all the session access patterns. We derive the names from examining the significant features: duration, read-write ratio, and IO size.

We also looked at the aggregate session start and end times to get additional semantic knowledge about each access pattern. Figure 3 shows the start and end times for selected session access patterns. The start times of corporate full-day work sessions correspond exactly to the U.S. work day – 9am start, 12pm lunch, 5pm end. Corporate content generation sessions show slight increase in the evening and towards Friday, indicating rushes to meet daily or weekly deadlines. In the engineering trace, the application generated backup and

machine generated update sessions depart significantly from human workday and work week patterns, leading us to label them as application and machine (client OS) generated.

One surprise was that the 'supporting metadata' sessions account for >90% of all sessions in both traces. We believe these sessions are not humanly generated. They last roughly 10 seconds, leaving little time for human mediated interactions. Also, the session start rate averages to roughly one per employee per minute. We are certain that our colleagues are not connecting and logging off every minute of the entire day. However, the shape of the start time graphs have a strong correlation with the human work day and work week. We call these supporting metadata sessions – machine generated in support of human user activities. These metadata sessions form a sort of "background noise" to the storage system. We observe the same background noise at other layers both at clients and servers.

Observation 1: The sessions with IO sizes greater than 128KB are either read-only or write-only, except for the full-day work sessions. Among these sessions, only read-only sessions utilize buffer cache for repeated reads and prefetches. Write-only sessions only use the cache to buffer writes. Thus, if we have a cache eviction policy that recognizes their write-only nature and releases the buffers immediately on flushing dirty data, we can satisfy many write-only sessions with relatively little buffer cache space. We can attain better consolidation and buffer cache utilization by managing the ratio of co-located read-only and write-only sessions. This insight can be used by virtualization managers and client operating systems to manage a shared buffer cache between sessions. Recognizing such read-only and write-only sessions

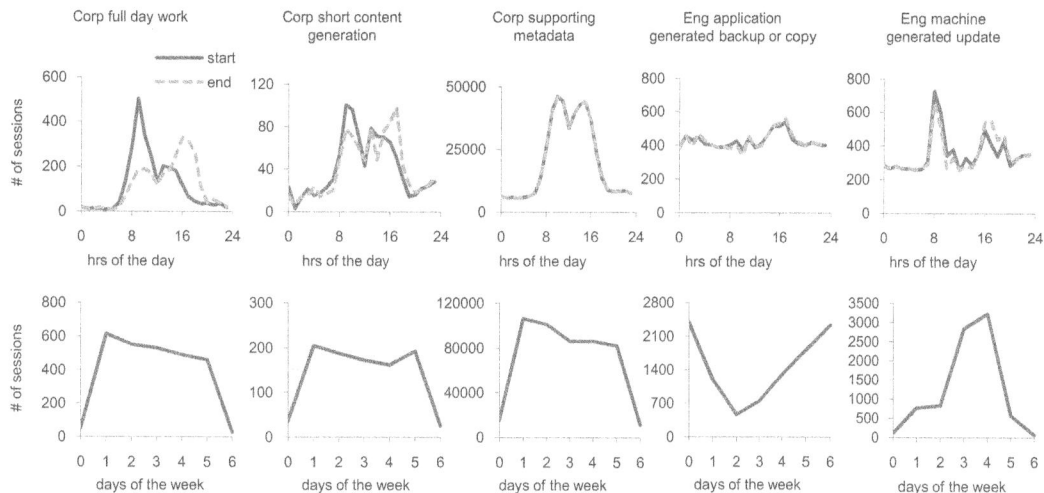

Figure 3: Number of sessions that start or ends at a particular time. Number of session starts and ends in times of the day (top) and session starts in days of the week (bottom). Showing only selected access patterns.

is easy. Examining a session's total read size and write size reveals their read-only or write-only nature. *Implication 1: Clients can consolidate sessions efficiently based only on the read-write ratio.*

Observation 2: The full-day work, content-viewing, and content-generating sessions all do ≈10MB of IO. This means that a client cache of 10s of MB can fit the working set of a day for most sessions. Given the growth of flash devices on clients for caching, despite large-scale consolidation, clients should easily cache a day's worth of data for all users. In such a scenario, most IO requests would be absorbed by the cache, reducing network latency and bandwidth utilization, and load on the server. Moreover, complex cache eviction algorithms are unnecessary. *Implication 2: Clients caches can already fit an entire day's IO.*

Observation 3: The number of human-generated sessions and supporting sessions peaks on Monday and decreases steadily to 80% of the peak on Friday (Figure 3). This is true for all human generated sessions, including the ones not shown in Figure 3. There is considerable "slack" in the server load during evenings, lunch times, and even during working hours. This implies that the server can perform background tasks such as consistency checks, maintenance, or compression/deduplication, at appropriate times during the week. A simple count of active sessions can serve as an effective start and stop signal. By computing the area under the curve for session start times by days of the week, we estimate that background tasks can squeeze out roughly one extra day's worth of processing without altering the peak demand on the system. This is a 50% improvement over a setup which performs background tasks only during weekends. In the engineering trace, the application generated backup or copy sessions seem to have been already designed this way. *Implication 3: Servers get an extra "day" for background tasks by running them at appropriate times during week-days.*

4.1.2 Application instances

Application instance access patterns reflects application behavior, facilitating application specific optimizations. We

used 16 features to describe application instances (Table 4). The corporate trace has 138,723 application instances, and the engineering trace has 741,319.

Table 4 provides quantitative descriptions and short names for all the application instance access patterns. We derive the names from examining the read-write ratio, IO size, and file extensions accessed (Figures 4 and 5).

We see again the metadata background noise. The supporting metadata application instances account for the largest fraction, and often do not even open a file.

There are many files without a file extension, a phenomenon also observed in recent storage system snapshot studies [16]. We notice that file extensions turn out to be poor indicators of application instance access patterns. This is not surprising because we separate access patterns based on read/write properties. A user could either view a `.doc` or create a `.doc`. The same application software has different read/write patterns. This speaks to the strength of our multi-layer framework. Aggregating IO by application instances gives clean separation of patterns; while aggregating just by application software or file extensions will not.

We also find it interesting that most file extensions are immediately recognizable. This means that *what* people use network storage systems for, i.e., the file extensions, remains easily recognizable, even though *how* people use network storage systems, i.e., the access patterns, is ever changing and becoming more complex.

Observation 4: The small content viewing application and content update application instances have <4KB total reads per file open and access a few unique files many times. The small read size and multiple reads from the same files means that clients should prefetch and place the files in a cache optimized for random access (flash/SSD/memory). The trend towards flash caches on clients should enable this transfer.

Application instances have bi-modal total IO size - either

very small or large. Thus, a simple cache management algorithm suffices; we always keep the first 2 blocks of 4KB in cache. If the application instance does more IO, it is likely to have IO size in the 100KB-1MB range, so we evict it from the cache. We should note that such a policy makes sense even though we proposed earlier to cache all 11MB of a typical day's working set - 11MB of cache becomes a concern when we have many consolidated clients. *Implication 4: Clients should always cache the first few KB of IO per file per application.*

Observation 5: We see >50% sequential read and write ratio for the content update applications instances (corporate) and the content viewing applications instances for human-generated content (both corporate and engineering). Dividing the total IO size by the number of file opens suggest that these application instances are sequentially reading and writing entire files for office productivity (`.xls`, `.doc`, `.ppt`, `.pdf`, etc.) and multimedia applications.

This implies that the files associated with these applications should be prefetched and delegated to the client. Prefetching means delivering the whole file to the client before the whole file is requested. Delegation means giving a client temporary, exclusive access to a file, with the client periodically synchronizing to server to ensure data durability. CIFS does delegation using opportunistic locks, while NFSv4 has a dedicated operation for delegation. Prefetching and delegation of such files will improve read and write performance, lower network traffic, and lighten server load.

The access patterns again offer a simple, threshold-based decision algorithm. If an application instance does more than 10s of KB of sequential IO, and has no overwrite, then it is likely to be a content viewing or update application instance; such files are prefetched and delegated to the clients. *Implication 5: Clients can request file prefetch (read) and delegation (write) based on only IO sequentiality.*

Observation 6: Engineering applications with >50% sequential reads and >50% sequential writes are doing code compile tasks. We know this from looking at the file extensions in Figure 5. These compile processes show read sequentiality, write sequentiality, a significant overwrite ratio and large number of metadata requests. They rely on the server heavily for data accesses. We need more detailed client side information to understand why client caches are ineffective in this case. However, it is clear that the server cache needs to prefetch the read files for these applications. The high percentage of sequential reads and writes gives us another threshold-based algorithm to identify these applications. *Implication 6: Servers can identify compile tasks by the presence of both sequential reads and writes; server has to cache the output of these tasks.*

4.2 Server Side Access Patterns

As mentioned in Section 3.2, we analyzed two kinds of server side access units: files and deepest subtrees.

4.2.1 Files

File access patterns help storage server designers develop per-file placement and optimization techniques. We used 25 features to describe files (Table 5). Note that some of

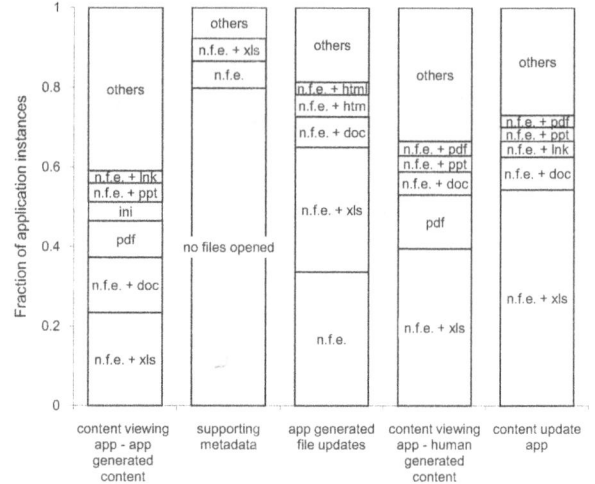

Figure 4: File extensions for corporate application instance access patterns. For each access pattern (column), showing the fraction of the two most frequent file extensions that are accessed together within a single application instance. "n.f.e." denotes files with "no file extension".

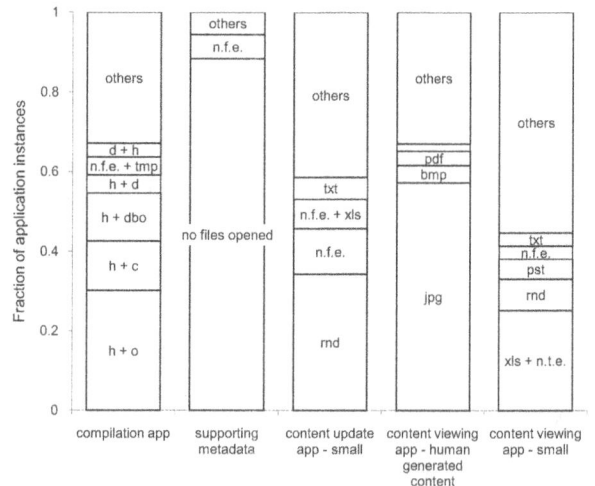

Figure 5: File extensions for engineering application instance access patterns. For each access pattern (column), showing the fraction of the two most frequent file extensions that are accessed together within a single application instance. "n.f.e." denotes files with "no file extension".

the features include different percentiles of a characteristic, e.g., read request size as percentiles of all read requests. We believe including different percentiles rather than just the average would allow better separation of access patterns. The corporate trace has 1,155,099 files, and the engineering trace has 1,809,571.

In Table 5, we quantitative descriptions and short names for all the file access patterns. Figures 6 and 7 give the most common file extensions in each. We derived the names by examining the read-write ratio and IO size. For the engineering trace, examining the file extensions also proved useful, leading to labels such as "edit code and compile output", and "read only log/backup".

(a). Descriptive features for each application instance			
Total IO size	Total metadata requests	Repeated read ratio	File opens
Read:write ratio by bytes	Avg. time between IO requests	Overwrite ratio	Unique files opened
Total IO requests by bytes	Read sequentiality	Tree connects	Directories accessed
Read:write ratio by requests	Write sequentiality	Unique trees accessed	File extensions accessed

(b). Corporate application instance access patterns	Content viewing app - app generated content	Supporting metadata	App generated file updates	Content viewing app - human generated content	Content update app
% of all app instances	16%	56%	14%	8.8%	5.1%
Total IO	100 KB	0	1 KB	800 KB	3.5 MB
Read:write ratio	1:0	0:0	1:1	1:0	2:3
Metadata requests	130	5	50	130	500
Read sequentiality	5%	-	0%	80%	50%
Write sequentiality	-	-	0%	-	80%
Overwrite ratio	-	-	0%	-	5%
File opens:files	19:4	0:0	10:4	20:4	60:11
Tree connect:Trees	2:2	0:0	2:2	2:2	2:2
Directories accessed	3	0	3	3	4
File extensions accessed	2	0	2	2	3

(c). Engineering application instance access patterns	Compilation app	Supporting metadata	Content update app - small	Content viewing app - human generated content	Content viewing app - small
% of all app instances	1.6%	93%	0.9%	2.0%	2.5%
Total IO	2 MB	0	2 KB	1 MB	3 KB
Read:write ratio	9:1	0:0	0:1	1:0	1:0
Metadata requests	400	1	14	40	15
Read sequentiality	50%	-	-	90%	0%
Write sequentiality	80%	-	0%	-	-
Overwrite ratio	20%	-	0%	-	-
File opens:files	145:75	0:0	3:1	5:4	2:1
Tree connect:Trees	1:1	0:0	1:1	1:1	1:1
Directories accessed	15	0	1	1	1
File extensions accessed	5	0	1	1	1

Table 4: Application instance access patterns. (a): Full list of descriptive features. (b) and (c): Short names and descriptions of application instances in each access pattern; listing only the features that help separate the access patterns.

We see that there are groupings of files with similar extensions. For example, in the corporate trace, the small random read access patterns include many file extensions associated with web browser caches. Also, multi-media files like .mp3 and .jpg congregate in the sequential read and write access patterns. In the engineering trace, code libraries group under the sequential write files, and read only log/backup files contain file extensions .0 to .99. However, the most common file extensions in each trace still spread across many access patterns, e.g., office productivity files in the corporate trace and code files in the engineering trace.

Observation 7: For files with >70% sequential reads or sequential writes, the repeated read and overwrite ratios are close to zero. This implies that there is little benefit in caching these files at the server. They should be prefetched as a whole and delegated to the client. Again, the bimodal IO sequentiality offers a simple algorithm for the server to detect which files should be prefetched and delegated – if a file has any sequential access, it is likely to have a high percentage of sequential access, therefore it should be prefetched and delegated to the client. Future storage servers can suggest such information to clients, leading to delegation requests. *Implication 7: Servers should delegate sequentially accessed files to clients to improve IO performance.*

Observation 8: In the engineering trace, only the edit code and compile output files have a high % of repeated reads. Those files should be delegated to the clients as well. The repeated reads do not show up in the engineering application instances, possibly because a compilation process launches many child processes repeatedly reading the same files. Each child process reads "fresh data," even though the server sees repeated reads. With larger memory or flash caches at clients, we expect this behavior to drop. The working set issues that lead to this scenario need to be examined. If the repeated reads come from a single client, then the server can suggest that the client cache the appropriate files.

We can again employ a threshold-based algorithm. Detecting any repeated reads at the server signals that the file should be delegated to the client. At worst, only the first few reads will hit the server. Subsequent repeated reads are stopped at the client. *Implication 8: Servers should delegate repeatedly read files to clients.*

Observation 9: Almost all files are active (have opens, IO, and metadata access) for only 1-2 hours over the entire trace period, as indicated by the typical opens/read/write activity of all access patterns. There are some regularly accessed files, but they are so few that they do not affect the k-means analysis. The lack of regular access for most files means that there is room for the server to employ techniques to increase capacity by doing compaction on idle files.

Common techniques include deduplication and compression. The activity on these files indicate that the IO performance impact should be small. Even if run constantly, compaction has a low probability of affecting an active file. Since common libraries like gzip optimize for decompression [11], decompressing files at read time should have only slight performance impact. *Implication 9: Servers can use file idle time to compress or deduplicate data to increase storage capacity.*

(a). Descriptive features for each file

Number of hours with 1, 2-3, or 4 file opens	Read sequentiality
Number of hours with 1-100KB, 100KB-1MB, or >1MB reads	Write sequentiality
Number of hours with 1-100KB, 100KB-1MB, or >1MB writes	Read:write ratio by bytes
Number of hours with 1, 2-3, or 4 metadata requests	Repeated read ratio
Read request size - 25th, 50th, and 75th percentile of all requests	Overwrite ratio
Write request size - 25th, 50th, and 75th percentile of all requests	
Avg. time between IO requests - 25th, 50th, and 75th percentile of all request pairs	

(b). Corporate file access patterns	Metadata only	Sequential write	Sequential read	Small random write	Smallest random read	Small random read
% of all files	59%	4.0%	4.1%	4.7%	19%	9.2%
Opens activity	2hrs, 1 open	1hr, 2-3 opens	1hr, 2-3 opens	1hr, 2-3 opens	1hr, 1 open	1hr, 1 open
Read activity	0	0	1hr, 100KB-1MB	0	1hr, 1-100KB	1hr, 1-100KB
Write activity	0	1hr, 100KB-1MB	0	1hr, 1-100KB	0	0
Read request size	-	-	4-32KB	-	2KB	32KB
Write request size	-	60KB	-	4-22KB	-	-
Read sequentiality	-	-	70%	-	0%	0%
Write sequentiality	-	80%	-	0%	-	-
Read:write ratio	0:0	0:1	1:0	0:1	1:0	1:0

(c). Engineering file access patterns	Metadata only	Sequential write	Small random read	Edit code & compile output	Sequential read	Read-only log/backup
% of all files	42%	1.9%	32%	7.3%	8.3%	8.1%
Opens activity	1hr, 1 open	1hr, 2-3 opens	1hr, 2-3 opens	1hr, 2-3 opens	1hr, 2-3 opens	2hrs, 2-3 opens
Read activity	0	0	1hr, 1-100KB	1hr, 1-100KB	1hr, 1-100KB	2hrs, 1-100KB
Write activity	0	1hr, >1MB	0	0	0	0
Read request size	-	-	3-4KB	4KB	8-16KB	1KB
Write request size	-	64KB	-	-	-	-
Read sequentiality	-	-	0%	0%	70%	0%
Write sequentiality	-	90%	-	-	-	-
Repeated read ratio	-	-	0%	50%	0%	0%
Read:write ratio	0:0	0:1	1:0	1:0	1:0	1:0

Table 5: File access patterns. (a): Full list of descriptive features. (b) and (c): Short names and descriptions of files in each access pattern; listing only the features that help separate the access patterns.

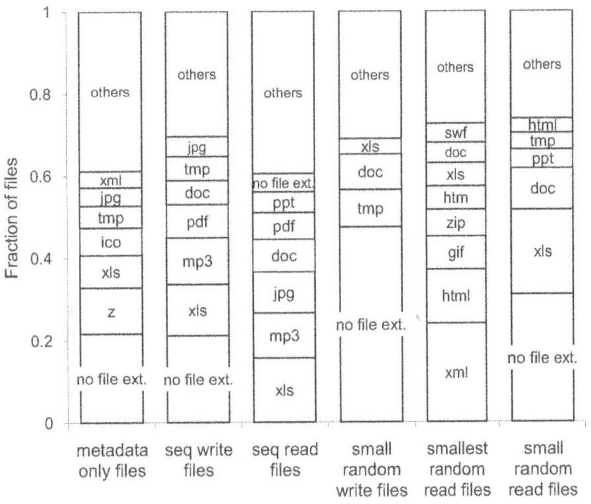

Figure 6: File extensions for corporate files. Fraction of file extensions in each file access pattern.

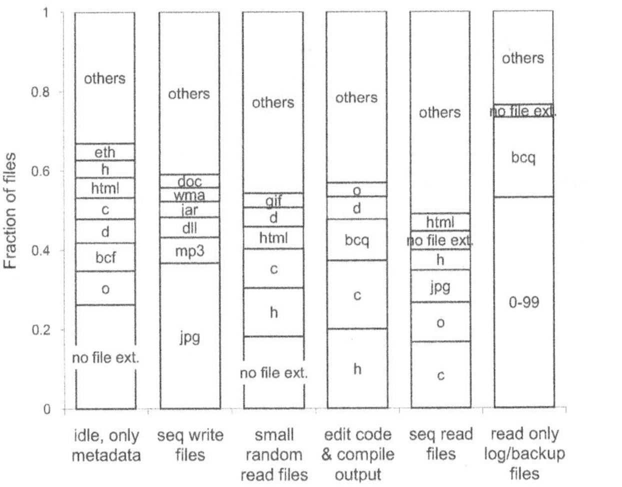

Figure 7: File extensions for engineering files. Fraction of file extensions in each file access pattern.

Observation 10: All files have either all random access or >70% sequential access. The small random read and write files in both traces can benefit from being placed on media with high random access performance, such as solid state drives (SSDs). Files with a high percentage of sequential access can reside on traditional hard disk drives (HDDs), which already optimize for sequential access. The bimodal IO sequentiality offers yet another threshold-based placement algorithm – if a file has any sequential access, it is likely to have a high percentage of sequential access; therefore place it on HDDs. Otherwise, place it on SSDs. We

note that there are more randomly accessed files than sequentially accessed files. Even though sequential files tend to be larger, we still need to do a working set analysis to determine the right size of server SSDs for each use case. *Implication 10: Servers can select the best storage medium for each file based only on access sequentiality.*

4.2.2 Deepest subtrees

Deepest subtree access patterns help storage server designers develop per-directory policies. We used 40 features to describe deepest subtrees (Table 6). Some of the features

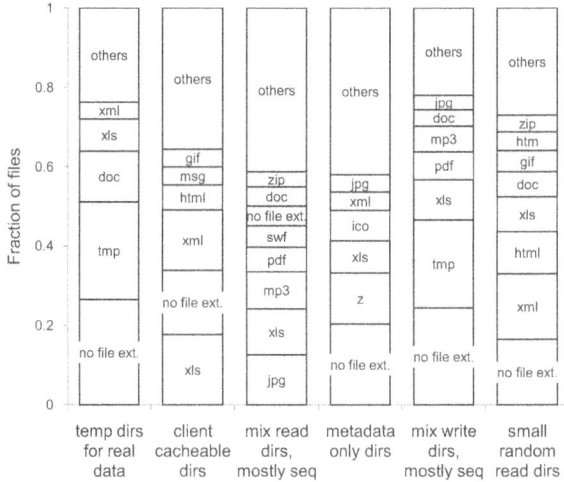

Figure 8: File extensions for corporate deepest subtrees. Fraction of file extensions in deepest subtree access patterns.

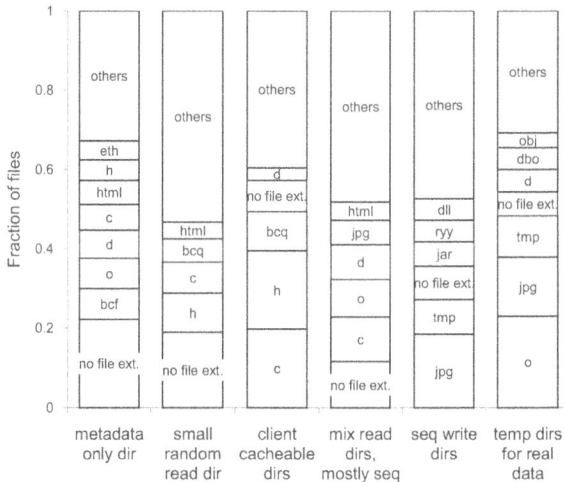

Figure 9: File extensions for engineering deepest subtrees. Fraction of file extensions in deepest subtree access patterns.

include different percentiles of a characteristic, e.g. per file read sequentiality as percentiles of all files in a directory. Including different percentiles rather than just the average allows better separation of access patterns. The corporate trace has 117,640 deepest subtrees, and the engineering trace has 161,858. We use "directories" and "deepest subtrees" interchangeably.

In Table 6, we provide quantitative descriptions and short names for all the deepest subtree access patterns. We derive the names using two types of information. First, we analyze the file extensions in each subtree access pattern (Figures 8 and 9). Second, we examine how many files of each file access patterns are within each subtree pattern (Figures 10). For brevity, we show only the graph for corporate deepest subtrees. The graph for the engineering deepest subtrees conveys the same information with regard to our design insights.

For example, the "random read" and "client cacheable" labels come from looking at the IO patterns. "Temporary directories" accounted for the .tmp files in those directories. "Mix read" and "mix write" directories considered the presence of both sequential and randomly accessed files in those directories.

The metadata background noise remains visible at the subtree layer. The spread of file extensions is similar to that for file access patterns – some file extensions congregate and others spread evenly. Interestingly, some subtrees have a large fraction of metadata-only files that do not affect the descriptions of those subtrees.

Some subtrees contain only files of a single access pattern (e.g., small random read subtrees in Figures 10). There, we can apply the design insights from the file access patterns to the entire subtree. For example, the small random read subtrees can reside on SSDs. Since there are more files than subtrees, per-subtree policies can lower the amount of policy information kept at the server.

In contrast, the mix read and mix write directories contain both sequential and randomly accessed files. Those subtrees need per-file policies: Place the sequentially accessed files on HDDs and the randomly accessed files on SSDs. Soft links to files can preserve the user-facing directory organization, while allowing the server optimize per-file placement. The server should automatically decide when to apply per-file or per-subtree policies.

Observation 11: Directories with sequentially accessed files almost always contain randomly accessed files also. Conversely, some directories with randomly access files will not contain sequentially accessed files. Thus, we can default all subtrees to per-subtree policies. Concurrently, we track the IO sequentiality per subtree. If the sequentiality is above some threshold, then the subtree switches to per-file policies. *Implication 11: Servers can change from per-directory placement policy (default) to per-file policy upon seeing any sequential IO to any files in a directory.*

Observation 12: The client cacheable subtrees and temporary subtrees aggregate files with repeated reads or overwrites. Additional computation showed that the repeated reads and overwrites almost always come from a single client. Thus, it is possible for the entire directory to be prefetched and delegated to the client. Delegating entire directories can preempt all accesses that are local to a directory, but consumes client cache space. We need to understand the tradeoffs through a more in-depth working set and temporal locality analysis at both the file and deepest subtree levels. *Implication 12: Servers can delegate repeated read and overwrite directories entirely to clients, tradeoffs permitting.*

4.3 Access Pattern Evolutions Over Time

We want to know if the access patterns are restricted to our particular tracing period or if they persist across time. Only if the design insights remain relevant across time can we rationalize their existence in similar use cases.

We do not have enough traces to generalize beyond our monitoring period. We investigate the reverse problem - if we

(a). Descriptive features for each subtree	
Number of hours with 1, 2-3, or 4 file opens	Read:write ratio - 25th, 50th, and 75th percentile of files
Number of hours with 1-100KB, 100KB-1MB, or >1MB reads	Repeated read ratio - 25th, 50th, and 75th percentile of files
Number of hours with 1-100KB, 100KB-1MB, or >1MB writes	Overwrite ratio - 25th, 50th, and 75th percentile of files
Number of hours with 1, 2-3, or 4 metadata requests	Read sequentiality - aggregated across all files
Read request size - 25th, 50th, and 75th percentile of all requests	Write sequentiality - aggregated across all files
Write request size - 25th, 50th, and 75th percentile of all requests	Read:write ratio - aggregated across all files
Avg. time between IO requests - 25th, 50th, and 75th percentile of all request pairs	Repeated read ratio - aggregated across all files
Read sequentiality - 25th, 50th, and 75th percentile of files in the subtree	Overwrite ratio - aggregated across all files
Write sequentiality - 25th, 50th, and 75th percentile of files in the subtree	

(b). Corp. subtree access patterns	Temp dirs for real data	Client cache-able dirs	Mix read dirs, mostly sequential	Metadata only dirs	Mix write dirs, mostly sequential	Small random read dirs
% of all subtrees	2.3%	4.1%	5.6%	64%	3.5%	21%
Opens activity	3hrs, >4 opens	3hr, 1 open	2hr, 1 open	2hr, 1 open	1hr, >4 opens	1hr, >4 opens
Read activity	3hrs, 1-100KB	2hrs, 1-100KB	1hr, 1-100KB	0	0	1hr, 1-100KB
Write activity	2hrs, 0.1-1MB	0	0	0	1hr, >1MB	0
Read request size	4KB	4-10KB	4-32KB	-	-	1-8KB
Write request size	4KB	-	-	-	64KB	-
Read sequentiality	10-30%	0%	50-70%	-	-	0%
Write sequentiality	50-70%	-	-	-	70-80%	-
Repeat read ratio	20-50%	50%	0%	-	-	0%
Overwrite ratio	30-70%	-	-	-	0%	-
Read:write ratio	1:0 to 0:1	1:0	1:0	0:0	0:1	1:0

(c). Eng. subtree access patterns	Metadata only dirs	Small random read dirs	Client cache-able dirs	Mixed read dirs, mostly sequential	Sequential write dirs	Temp dirs for real data
% of all subtrees	59%	25%	6.1%	7.1%	1.9%	1.3%
Opens activity	1hr, 2-3 opens	1hr, >4 opens	1hr, >4 opens	1hr, >4 opens	1hr, >4 opens	3hrs, >4 opens
Read activity	0	1hr, 1-100KB	1hr, 1-100KB	1hr, 0.1-1MB	0	3hrs, 1-100KB
Write activity	0	0	0	0	1hr, 0.1-1MB	1hr, 1-100KB
Read request size	-	1-4KB	2-4KB	8-10KB	-	4-32KB
Write request size	-	-	-	-	32-60KB	4-60KB
Read sequentiality	-	0%	0%	40-70%	-	10-65%
Write sequentiality	-	-	-	-	70-90%	60-80%
Repeat read ratio	-	0%	50-60%	0%	-	0-40%
Overwrite ratio	-	-	-	-	0%	0-30%
Read:write ratio	0:0	1:0	1:0	1:0	0:1	1:0 to 0:1

Table 6: Deepest subtree access patterns. (a): Full list of descriptive features. (b) and (c): Short names and descriptions of subtrees in each access pattern; listing only the features that help separate access patterns.

had to analyze traces from only a subset of our tracing period, how would our results differ? We divided our traces into weeks and repeated the analysis for each week. For brevity, we present only the results for weekly analysis of corporate application instances and files. These two layers have yielded the most interesting design insights and they highlight separate considerations at the client and server.

Figure 11 shows the result for files. All the large access patterns remain steady across the weeks. However, the access pattern corresponding to the smallest number of files, the small random write files, comes and goes week to week. There are exactly two, temporary, previously unseen access patterns that are very similar to the small random files. The peaks in the metadata only files correspond to weeks that contain U.S. federal holidays or weeks immediately preceding a holiday long weekend. Furthermore, the numerical values of the descriptive features for each access pattern vary in a moderate range. For example, the write sequentiality of the sequentiality write files ranges from 50% to 90%.

Figure 12 shows the result for application instances. We see no new access patterns, and the fractional weight of each access pattern remains nearly constant, despite holidays. Furthermore, the numerical values of descriptive features also remain nearly constant. For example, the write sequentiality of the content update applications varies in a narrow range from 80% to 85%.

Thus, if we had done our analysis on just a week's traces, we would have gotten nearly identical results for application instances, and qualitatively similar result for files. We believe that the difference comes from the limited duration of client sessions and application instances, versus the long-term persistence of files and subtrees.

Based on our results, we are confident that the access patterns are not restricted just to our particular trace period. Future storage systems should continuously monitor the access patterns at all levels, automatically adjusting policies as needed, and notify designers of previously unseen access patterns.

We should always be cautious when generalizing access patterns from one use case to another. For use cases with the same applications running on the same OS file API, we expect to see the same application instance access patterns. Session access patterns such as daily work sessions are also likely to be general. For the server side access patterns, we expect the files and subtrees with large fractional weights to appear in other use cases.

5. ARCHITECTURAL IMPLICATIONS

Section 4 offered many specific optimizations for placement, caching, delegation, and consolidation decisions. We combine the insights here to speculate on the architecture of future enterprise storage systems.

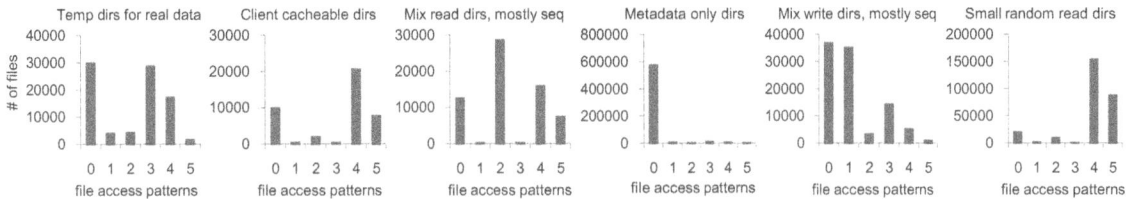

Figure 10: Corporate file access patterns within each deepest subtree. For each deepest subtree access pattern (i.e., each graph), showing the number of files belonging to each file access pattern that belongs to subtrees in the subtree access pattern. Corporate file access pattern indices: 0. metadata only files; 1. sequential write files; 2. sequential read files; 3. small random write files; 4. small random read files; 5. less small random read files.

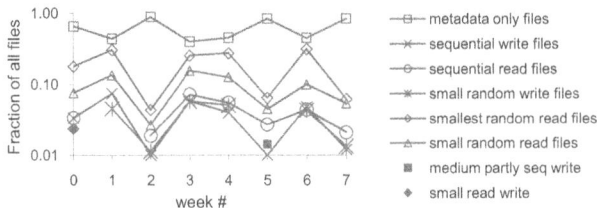

Figure 11: Corporate file access patterns over 8 weeks. All patterns remain (hollow markers), but the fractional weight of each changes greatly between weeks. Some small patterns temporarily appear and disappear (solid markers).

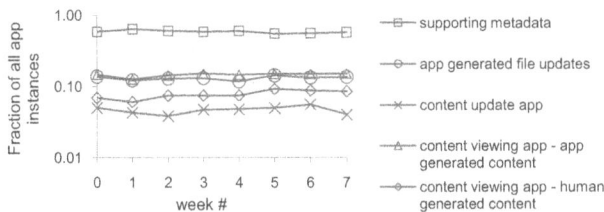

Figure 12: Corporate application instance access patterns over 8 weeks. All patterns remain with near constant fractional weight. No new patterns appear.

We see a clear separation of roles for clients and servers. The client design can target high IO performance by a combination of efficient delegation, prefetching and caching of the appropriate data. The servers should focus on increasing their aggregated efficiency across clients: collaboration with clients (on caching, delegation, etc.) and exploiting user patterns to schedule background tasks. Automating background tasks such as offline data deduplication delivers capacity savings in a timely and hassle-free fashion, i.e., without system downtime or explicit scheduling. Regarding caching at the server, we observe that very few access patterns actually leverage the server's buffer cache for data accesses. Design insights 4-6, 8 and 12 indicate a heavy role for the client cache and Design insight 7 suggests how *not* to use the server buffer cache - caching metadata only and acting as a warm/backup cache for clients would result in lower latencies for many access patterns.

We also see simple ways to take advantage of new storage media such as SSDs. The clear identification of sequential and random access file patterns enables efficient device-

specific data placement algorithms (Design insights 10 and 11). Also, the background metadata noise seen at all levels suggests that storage servers should both optimize for metadata accesses and redesign client-server interactions to decrease the metadata chatter. Depending on the growth of metadata and the performance requirements, we also need to consider placing metadata on low latency, non-volatile media like flash or SSDs.

Furthermore, we believe that storage systems should introduce many monitoring points to dynamically adjust the decision thresholds of placement, caching, or consolidation policies. We need to monitor both clients and servers. For example, when repeated read and overwrite files have been properly delegated to clients, the server would no longer see files with such access patterns. Without monitoring points at the clients, we would not be able to quantify the file delegation benefits. Storage systems should make extensible tracing APIs to expedite the collection of long-term future traces. This will facilitate future work similar to ours.

6. CONCLUSIONS AND FUTURE WORK

We must address the storage technology trends toward ever-increasing scale, heterogeneity, and consolidation. Current storage design paradigms that rely on existing trace analysis methods are ill equipped to meet the emerging challenges because they are unidimensional, focus only on the storage server, and are subject to designer bias. We showed that a multi-dimensional, multi-layered trace-driven design methodology leads to more objective design points with highly targeted optimizations at both storage clients and servers. Using our corporate and engineering use cases, we present a number of insights that informs future designs. We described in some detail the access patterns we observed, and we encourage fellow storage system designers to extract further insights from our observations.

Future work includes exploring the dynamics of changing working sets and access sequences, with the goal of anticipating data accesses before they happen. Another worthwhile analysis is to look for optimization opportunities *across clients*; this requires collecting traces at different clients, instead of only at the server. Also, we would like to explore opportunities for deduplication, compression, or data placement. Doing so requires extending our analysis from *data movement* patterns to also include *data content* patterns. Furthermore, we would like to perform on-line analysis in live storage systems to enable dynamic feedback on placement and optimization decisions. In addition, it would be useful to build tools to synthesize the access patterns, to enable designers to evaluate the optimizations we proposed here.

We believe that storage system designers face an increasing challenge to anticipate access patterns. Our paper builds the case that system designers can longer accurately anticipate access patterns using intuition only. We believe that the corporate and engineering traces from our corporate headquarters would have similar use cases at other traditional and high-tech businesses. Other use cases would require us to perform the same trace collection and analysis process to extract the same kind of "ground truth". We also need similar studies at regular intervals to track the evolving use of storage system. We hope that this paper contributes to an objective and principled design approach targeting rapidly changing data access patterns.

NetApp, the NetApp logo, and Go further, faster are trademarks or registered trademarks of NetApp, Inc. in the United States and/or other countries.

7. REFERENCES

[1] N. Agrawal, W. J. Bolosky, J. R. Douceur, and J. R. Lorch. A Five-Year Study of File-System Metadata. In *FAST 2007*.

[2] E. Alpaydin. *Introduction to Machine Learning*. MIT Press, Cambridge, Massachusetts, 2004.

[3] M. G. Baker, J. H. Hartman, M. D. Kupfer, K. W. Shirriff, and J. K. Ousterhout. Measurements of a distributed file system. In *SOSP 1991*.

[4] P. Bodik, M. Goldszmidt, A. Fox, D. B. Woodard, and H. Andersen. Fingerprinting the datacenter: automated classification of performance crises. In *EuroSys 2010*.

[5] Common Internet File System Technical Reference. Storage Network Industry Association, 2002.

[6] IDC Whitepaper: The economics of Virtualization. `www.vmware.com/files/pdf/Virtualization-application-based-cost-model-WP-EN.pdf`.

[7] J. R. Douceur and W. J. Bolosky. A Large-Scale Study of File-System Contents. In *SIGMETRICS 1999*.

[8] D. Ellard, J. Ledlie, P. Malkani, and M. Seltzer. Passive NFS Tracing of Email and Research Workloads. In *FAST 2003*.

[9] A. Ganapathi, H. Kuno, U. Dayal, J. L. Wiener, A. Fox, M. Jordan, and D. Patterson. Predicting Multiple Metrics for Queries: Better Decisions Enabled by Machine Learning. In *ICDE 2009*.

[10] S. Gribble, G. S. Manku, E. Brewer, T. J. Gibson, and E. L. Miller. Self-Similarity in File Systems: Measurement and Applications. In *SIGMETRICS 1998*.

[11] The gzip algorithm. `http://www.gzip.org/algorithm.txt`.

[12] IDC Report: Worldwide File-Based Storage 2010-2014 Forecast Update. `http://www.idc.com/getdoc.jsp?containerId=226267`.

[13] S. Kavalanekar, B. L. Worthington, Q. Zhang, and V. Sharda. Characterization of storage workload traces from production Windows Servers. In *IISWC 2008*.

[14] Open Source Clustering Software - C Clustering Library. `http://bonsai.hgc.jp/~mdehoon/software/cluster/software.htm`, 2010.

[15] A. Leung, S. Pasupathy, G. Goodson, and E. Miller. Measurement and analysis of large-scale network file system workloads. In *USENIX ATC 2008*.

[16] D. T. Meyer and W. J. Bolosky. A Study of Practical Deduplication. In *FAST 2010*.

[17] J. K. Ousterhout, H. D. Costa, D. Harrison, J. A. Kunze, M. Kupfer, and J. G. Thompson. A trace-driven analysis of the Unix 4.2 BSD file system. In *SOSP 1985*.

[18] K. K. Ramakrishnan, P. Biswas, and R. Karedla. Analysis of file I/O traces in commercial computing environments. In *SIGMETRICS 1992*.

[19] D. Roselli, J. Lorch, and T. Anderson. A comparison of file system workloads. In *USENIX 2000*.

[20] I. Stoica. A Berkeley View of Big Data: Algorithms, Machines and People. UC Berkeley EECS Annual Research Symposium, 2011.

[21] K. Thomas, C. Grier, J. Ma, V. Paxson, and D. Song. Design and evaluation of a real-time URL spam filtering service. In *IEEE Symposium on Security and Privacy 2011*.

[22] R. Villars. The Migration to Converged IT: What it Means for Infrastructure, Applications, and the IT Organization. IDC Directions Conference 2011.

[23] VMware Whitepaper: Server Consolidation and Containment. `www.vmware.com/pdf/server_consolidation.pdf`.

[24] W. Vogels. File system usage in Windows NT 4.0. In *SOSP 1999*.

[25] M. Zhou and A. J. Smith. Analysis of Personal Computer Workloads. In *MASCOTS 1999*.

Differentiated Storage Services

Michael Mesnier, Feng Chen, Tian Luo[*]

Intel Labs
Intel Corporation
Hillsboro, OR

Jason B. Akers

Storage Technologies Group
Intel Corporation
Hillsboro, OR

ABSTRACT

We propose an I/O classification architecture to close the widening semantic gap between computer systems and storage systems. By *classifying* I/O, a computer system can request that different classes of data be handled with different storage system *policies*. Specifically, when a storage system is first initialized, we assign performance policies to predefined classes, such as the filesystem journal. Then, online, we include a classifier with each I/O command (e.g., SCSI), thereby allowing the storage system to enforce the associated policy for each I/O that it receives.

Our immediate application is caching. We present filesystem prototypes and a database proof-of-concept that classify all disk I/O — with very little modification to the filesystem, database, and operating system. We associate caching policies with various classes (e.g., large files shall be evicted before metadata and small files), and we show that end-to-end file system performance can be improved by over a factor of two, relative to conventional caches like LRU. And caching is simply one of many possible applications. As part of our ongoing work, we are exploring other classes, policies and storage system mechanisms that can be used to improve end-to-end performance, reliability and security.

Categories and Subject Descriptors

D.4 [**Operating Systems**]; D.4.2 [**Storage Management**]: [Storage hierarchies]; D.4.3 [**File Systems Management**]: [File organization]; H.2 [**Database Management**]

General Terms

Classification, quality of service, caching, solid-state storage

1. INTRODUCTION

The block-based storage interface is arguably the most stable interface in computer systems today. Indeed, the primary read/write functionality is quite similar to that used

[*]The Ohio State University

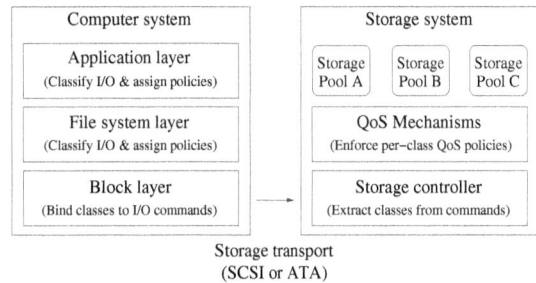

Figure 1: High-level architecture

by the first commercial disk drive (IBM RAMAC, 1956). Such stability has allowed computer and storage systems to evolve in an independent yet interoperable manner, but at at a cost – it is difficult for computer systems to optimize for increasingly complex storage system internals, and storage systems do not have the semantic information (e.g., on-disk FS and DB data structures) to optimize independently.

By way of analogy, shipping companies have long recognized that *classification* is the key to providing differentiated service. Boxes are often classified (kitchen, living room, garage), assigned different policies (deliver-first, overnight, priority, handle-with-care), and thusly treated differently by a shipper (hand-carry, locked van, truck). Separating classification from policy allows customers to pack and classify (label) their boxes once; the handling policies can be assigned on demand, depending on the shipper. And separating policy from mechanism frees customers from managing the internal affairs of the shipper, like which pallets to place their shipments on.

In contrast, modern computer systems expend considerable effort attempting to manage storage system internals, because different classes of data often need different levels of service. As examples, the "middle" of a disk can be used to reduce seek latency, and the "outer tracks" can be used to improve transfer speeds. But, with the increasing complexity of storage systems, these techniques are losing their effectiveness — and storage systems can do very little to help because they lack the semantic information to do so.

We argue that computer and storage systems should operate in the same manner as the shipping industry — by utilizing I/O classification. In turn, this will enable storage systems to enforce per-class QoS policies. See Figure 1.

Differentiated Storage Services is such a classification framework: I/O is classified in the computer system (e.g., filesystem journal, directory, small file, database log, index, ...), policies are associated with classes (e.g., an FS journal requires low-latency writes, and a database index requires low-latency reads), and mechanisms in the storage system enforce policies (e.g., a cache provides low latency).

Our approach only slightly modifies the existing block interface, so eventual standardization and widespread adoption are practical. Specifically, we modify the OS block layer so that every I/O request carries a classifier. We copy this classifier into the I/O command (e.g., SCSI CDB), and we specify policies on classes through the management interface of the storage system. In this way, a storage system can provide block-level differentiated services (performance, reliability, or security) — and do so on a class-by-class basis. The storage system does not need any knowledge of computer system internals, nor does the computer system need knowledge of storage system internals.

Classifiers describe what the data is, and policies describe how the data is to be managed. Classifiers are handles that the computer system can use to assign policies and, in our SCSI-based prototypes, a classifier is just a number used to distinguish various filesystem classes, like metadata versus data. We also have user-definable classes that, for example, a database can use to classify I/O to specific database structures like an index. Defining the classes (the classification scheme) should be an infrequent operation that happens once for each filesystem or database of interest.

In contrast, we expect that policies will vary across storage systems, and that vendors will differentiate themselves through the policies they offer. As examples, storage system vendors may offer service levels (platinum, gold, silver, bronze), performance levels (bandwidth and latency targets), or relative priority levels (the approach we take in this paper). A computer system must map its classes to the appropriate set of policies, and I/O classification provides a convenient way to do this dynamically when a filesystem or database is created on a new storage system. Table 1 shows a hypothetical mapping of filesystem classes to available performance policies, for three different storage systems.

Beyond performance, there could be numerous other policies that one might associate with a given class, such as replication levels, encryption and integrity policies, perhaps even data retention policies (e.g., secure erase). Rather than attempt to send all of this policy information along with each I/O, we simply send a classifier. This will make efficient use of the limited space in an I/O command (e.g., SCSI has 5 bits that we use as a classifier). In the storage system the classifier can be associated with any number of policies.

We begin with a priority-based performance policy for cache management, specifically for non-volatile caches composed of solid-state drives (SSDs). That is, to each FS and DB class we assign a caching policy (a relative priority level). In practice, we assume that the filesystem or database vendor, perhaps in partnership with the storage system vendor, will provide a default priority assignment that a system administrator may choose to tune.

FS Class	Vendor A: Service levels	Vendor B: Perf. targets	Vendor C: Priorities
Metadata	Platinum	Low lat.	0
Journal	Gold	Low lat.	0
Small file	Silver	Low lat.	1
Large file	Bronze	High BW	2

Table 1: An example showing FS classes mapped to various performance policies. This paper focuses on priorities; lower numbers are higher priority.

We present prototypes for Linux Ext3 and Windows NTFS, where I/O is classified as metadata, journal, directory, or file, and file I/O is further classified by the file size (e.g., $\leq$4KB $\leq$16KB, ..., >1GB). We assign a caching priority to each class: metadata, journal, and directory blocks are highest priority, followed by regular file data. For the regular files, we give small files higher priority than large ones.

These priority assignments reflect our goal of reserving cache space for metadata and small files. To this end, we introduce two new block-level caching algorithms: *selective allocation* and *selective eviction*. Selective allocation uses the priority information when allocating I/O in a cache, and selective eviction uses this same information during eviction. The end-to-end performance improvements of selective caching are considerable. Relative to conventional LRU caching, we improve the performance of a file server by 1.8x, an e-mail server by 2x, and metadata-intensive FS utilities (e.g., `find` and `fsck`) by up to 6x. Furthermore, a TCO analysis by Intel IT Research shows that priority-based caching can reduce caching costs by up to 50%, as measured by the acquisition cost of hard drives and SSDs.

It is important to note that in both of our FS prototypes, we do not change which logical blocks are being accessed; we simply classify I/O requests. Our design philosophy is that the computer system continues to see a single logical volume and that the I/O into that volume be classified. In this sense, classes can be considered "hints" to the storage system. Storage systems that know how to interpret the hints can optimize accordingly, otherwise they can be ignored. This makes the solution backward compatible, and therefore suitable for legacy applications.

To further show the flexibility of our approach, we present a proof-of-concept classification scheme for PostgreSQL [33]. Database developers have long recognized the need for intelligent buffer management in the database [10] and in the operating system [45]; buffers are often classified by type (e.g., index vs. table) and access pattern (e.g., random vs. sequential). To share this knowledge with the storage system, we propose a POSIX file flag (`O_CLASSIFIED`). When a file is opened with this flag, the OS extracts classification information from a user-provided data buffer that is sent with each I/O request and, in turn, binds the classifier to the outgoing I/O command. Using this interface, we can easily classify all DB I/O, with only minor modification to the DB and the OS. This same interface can be used by any application. Application-level classes will share the classification space with the filesystem — some of the classifier bits can be reserved for applications, and the rest for the filesystem.

This paper is organized as follows. Section 2 motivates the need for Differentiated Storage Services, highlighting the shortcomings of the block interface and building a case for block-level differentiation. Alternative designs, not based on I/O classification, are discussed. We present our design in Section 3, our FS prototypes and DB proof-of-concept in Section 4, and our evaluation in Section 5. Related work is presented in Section 6, and we conclude in Section 7.

2. BACKGROUND & MOTIVATION

The contemporary challenge motivating Differentiated Storage Services is the integration of SSDs, as caches, into conventional disk-based storage systems. The fundamental limitation imposed by the block layer (lack of semantic information) is what makes effective integration so challenging. Specifically, the block layer abstracts computer systems from the details of the underlying storage system, and *vice versa*.

2.1 Computer system challenges

Computer system performance is often determined by the underlying storage system, so filesystems and databases must be smart in how they allocate on-disk data structures. As examples, the journal (or log) is often allocated in the middle of a disk drive to minimize the average seek distance [37], files are often created close to their parent directories, and file and directory data are allocated contiguously whenever possible. These are all attempts by a computer system to obtain some form differentiated service through intelligent block allocation.

Unfortunately, the increasing complexity of storage systems is making intelligent allocation difficult. Where is the "middle" of the disk, for example, when a filesystem is mounted atop a logical volume with multiple devices, or perhaps a hybrid disk drive composed of NAND and shingled magnetic recording? Or, how do storage system caches influence the latency of individual read/write operations, and how can computer systems reliably manage performance in the context of these caches? One could use models [27, 49, 52] to predict performance, but if the predicted performance is undesirable there is very little a computer system can do to change it.

In general, computer systems have come to expect only best-effort performance from their storage systems. In cases where performance must be guaranteed, dedicated and over-provisioned solutions are deployed.

2.2 Storage system challenges

Storage systems already offer differentiated service, but only at a coarse granularity (logical volumes). Through the management interface of the storage system, administrators can create logical volumes with the desired capacity, reliability, and performance characteristics — by appropriately configuring RAID and caching.

However, before an I/O enters the storage system, valuable semantic information is stripped away at the OS block layer, such as user, group, application, and process information. And, any information regarding on-disk structures is obfuscated. This means that all I/O receives the same treatment within the logical volume.

For a storage system to provide any meaningful optimization within a volume, it must have semantic computer system information. Without help from the computer system, this can be very difficult to get. Consider, for example, that a filename could influence how a file is cached [26], and what would be required for a storage system to simply determine the the name of a file associated with a particular I/O. Not only would the storage system need to understand the on-disk metadata structures of the filesystem, particularly the format of directories and their filenames, but it would have to track all I/O requests that modify these structures. This would be an extremely difficult and potentially fragile process. Expecting storage systems to retain sufficient and up-to-date knowledge of the on-disk structures for each of its attached computer systems may not be practical, or even possible, to realize in practice.

2.3 Attempted solutions & shortcomings

Three schools of thought have emerged to better optimize the I/O between a computer and storage system. Some show that computer systems can obtain more knowledge of storage system internals and use this information to guide block allocation [11, 38]. In some cases, this means managing different storage volumes [36], often foregoing storage system services like RAID and caching. Others show that storage systems can discover more about on-disk data structures and optimize I/O accesses to these structures [9, 41, 42, 43]. Still others show that the I/O interface can evolve and become more expressive; object-based storage and type-safe disks fall into this category [28, 40, 58].

Unfortunately, none of these approaches has gained significant traction in the industry. First, increasing storage system complexity is making it difficult for computer systems to reliably gather information about internal storage structure. Second, increasing computer system complexity (e.g., virtualization, new filesystems) is creating a moving target for semantically-aware storage systems that learn about on-disk data structures. And third, although a more expressive interface could address many of these issues, our industry has developed around a block-based interface, for better or for worse. In particular, filesystem and database vendors have a considerable amount of intellectual property in how blocks are managed and would prefer to keep this functionality in software, rather than offload to the storage system through a new interface.

When a new technology like solid-state storage emerges, computer system vendors prefer to innovate above the block level, and storage system vendors below. But, this tug-of-war has no winner as far as applications are concerned, because considerable optimization is left on the table.

We believe that a new approach is needed. Rather than teach computer systems about storage system internals, or *vice versa*, we can have them agree on shared, block-level goals — and do so through the existing storage interfaces (SCSI and ATA). This will not introduce a disruptive change in the computer and storage systems ecosystem, thereby allowing computer system vendors to innovate above the block level, and storage system vendors below. To accomplish this, we require a means by which block-level goals can be communicated with each I/O request.

3. DESIGN

Differentiated Storage Services closes the semantic gap between computer and storage systems, but does so in a way that is practical in an industry built around blocks. The problem is not the block interface, *per se*, but a lack of information as to how disk blocks are being used.

We must careful, though, to not give a storage system too much information, as this could break interoperability. So, we simply *classify* I/O requests and communicate block-level goals (policies) for each class. This allows storage systems to provide meaningful levels of differentiation, without requiring that detailed semantic information be shared.

3.1 Operating system requirements

We associate a classifier with every block I/O request in the OS. In UNIX and Windows, we add a classification field to the OS data structure for block I/O (the Linux "BIO," and the Windows "IRP") and we copy this field into the actual I/O command (SCSI or ATA) before it is sent to the storage system. The expressiveness of this field is only limited by its size, and in Section 4 we present a SCSI prototype where a 5-bit SCSI field can classify I/O in up to 32 ways.

In addition to adding the classifier, we modify the OS I/O scheduler, which is responsible for coalescing contiguous I/O requests, so that requests with different classifiers are never coalesced. Otherwise, classification information would be lost when two contiguous requests with different classifiers are combined. This does reduce a scheduler's ability to coalesce I/O, but the benefits gained from providing differentiated service to the uncoalesced requests justify the cost, and we quantify these benefits in Section 5.

The OS changes needed to enable filesystem I/O classification are minor. In Linux, we have a small kernel patch. In Windows, we use closed-source filter drivers to provide the same functionality. Section 4 details these changes.

3.2 Filesystem requirements

First, a filesystem must have a *classification scheme* for its I/O, and this is to be designed by a developer that has a good understanding of the on-disk FS data structures and their performance requirements. Classes should represent blocks with similar goals (e.g., journal blocks, directory blocks, or file blocks); each class has a unique ID. In Section 4, we present our prototype classification schemes for Linux Ext3 and Windows NTFS.

Then, the filesystem developer assigns a policy to each class; refer back to the hypothetical examples given in Table 1. How this policy information is communicated to the storage system can be vendor specific, such as through an administrative GUI, or even standardized. The Storage Management Initiative Specification (SMI-S) is one possible avenue for this type of standardization [3]. As a reference policy, also presented in Section 4, we use a priority-based performance policy for storage system cache management.

Once mounted, the filesystem classifies I/O as per the classification scheme. And blocks may be reclassified over time. Indeed, block reuse in the filesystem (e.g., file deletion or defragmentation) may result in frequent reclassification.

3.3 Storage system requirements

Upon receipt of a classified I/O, the storage system must extract the classifier, lookup the policy associated with the class, and enforce the policy using any of its internal mechanisms; legacy systems without differentiated service can ignore the classifier. The mechanisms used to enforce a policy are completely vendor specific, and in Section 4 we present our prototype mechanism (priority-based caching) that enforces the FS-specified performance priorities.

Because each I/O carries a classifier, the storage system does not need to record the class of each block. Once allocated from a particular storage pool, the storage system is free to discard the classification information. So, in this respect, Differentiated Storage Services is a stateless protocol. However, if the storage system wishes to later move blocks across storage pools, or otherwise change their QoS, it must do so in an informed manner. This must be considered, for example, during de-duplication. Blocks from the same allocation pool (hence, same QoS) can be de-duplicated. Blocks from different pools cannot.

If the classification of a block changes due to block re-use in the filesystem, the storage system must reflect that change internally. In some cases, this may mean moving one or more blocks across storage pools. In the case of our cache prototype, a classification change can result in cache allocation, or the eviction of previously cached blocks.

3.4 Application requirements

Applications can also benefit from I/O classification; two good examples are databases and virtual machines. To allow for this, we propose a new file flag O_CLASSIFIED. When a file is opened with this flag, we overload the POSIX scatter/gather operations (readv and writev) to include one extra list element. This extra element points to a 1-byte user buffer that contains the classification ID of the I/O request. Applications not using scatter/gather I/O can easily convert each I/O to a 2-element scatter/gather list. Applications already issuing scatter/gather need only create the additional element.

Next, we modify the OS virtual file system (VFS) in order to extract this classifier from each readv() and writev() request. Within the VFS, we know to inspect the file flags when processing each scatter/gather operation. If a file handle has the O_CLASSIFIED flag set, we extract the I/O classifier and reduce the scatter/gather list by one element. The classifier is then bound to the kernel-level I/O request, as described in Section 3.1. Currently, our user-level classifiers override the FS classifiers. If a user-level class is specified on a file I/O, the filesystem classifiers will be ignored.

Without further modification to POSIX, we can now explore various ways of differentiating user-level I/O. In general, any application with complex, yet structured, block relationships [29] may benefit from user-level classification. In this paper, we begin with the database and, in Section 4, present a proof-of-concept classification scheme for PostgreSQL [33]. By simply classifying database I/O requests (e.g., user tables versus indexes), we provide a simple way for storage systems to optimize access to on-disk database structures.

4. IMPLEMENTATION

We present our implementations of Differentiated Storage Services, including two filesystem prototypes (Linux Ext3 and Windows NTFS), one database proof-of-concept (Linux PostgreSQL), and two storage system prototypes (SW RAID and iSCSI). Our storage systems implement a priority-based performance policy, so we map each class to a priority level (refer back to Table 1 for other possibilities). For the FS, the priorities reflect our goal to reduce small random access in the storage system, by giving small files and metadata higher priority than large files. For the DB, we simply demonstrate the flexibility of our approach by assigning caching policies to common data structures (indexes, tables, and logs).

4.1 OS changes needed for FS classification

The OS must provide in-kernel filesystems with an interface for classifying each of their I/O requests. In Linux, we do this by adding a new classification field to the FS-visible kernel data structure for disk I/O (`struct buffer_head`). This code fragment illustrates how Ext3 can use this interface to classify the OS disk buffers into which an inode (class 5 in this example) will be read:

```
bh->b_class = 5;      /* classify inode buffer */
submit_bh(READ, bh); /* submit read request  */
```

Once the disk buffers associated with an I/O are classified, the OS block layer has the information needed to classify the block I/O request used to read/write the buffers. Specifically, it is in the implementation of `submit_bh` that the generic block I/O request (the BIO) is generated, so it is here that we copy in the FS classifier:

```
int submit_bh(int rw, struct buffer_head * bh) {
    ...
    bio->bi_class = bh->b_class /* copy in class */
    submit_bio(rw, bio);       /* issue read   */
    ...
    return ret;
}
```

Finally, we copy the classifier once again from the BIO into the 5-bit, vendor-specific *Group Number* field in byte 6 of the SCSI CDB. This one-line change is all that is need to enable classification at the SCSI layer:

```
SCpnt->cmnd[6] = SCpnt->request->bio->bi_class;
```

These 5 bits are included with each WRITE and READ command, and we can fill this field in up to 32 different ways (2^5). An additional 3 reserved bits could also be used to classify data, allowing for up to 256 classifiers (2^8), and there are ways to grow even beyond this if necessary (e.g., other reserved bits, or extended SCSI commands).

In general, adding I/O classification to an existing OS is a matter of tracking an I/O as it proceeds from the filesystem, through the block layer, and down to the device drivers. Whenever I/O requests are copied from one representation to another (e.g., from a buffer head to a BIO, or from a BIO to a SCSI command), we must remember to copy the classifier. Beyond this, the only other minor change is to the I/O scheduler which, as previously mentioned, must be modified so that it only coalesces requests that carry the same classifier.

Block layer	LOC	Change made
bio.h	1	Add classifier
blkdev.h	1	Add classifier
buffer_head.h	13	Add classifier
bio.c	2	Copy classifier
buffer.c	26	Copy classifier
mpage.c	23	Copy classifier
bounce.c	1	Copy classifier
blk-merge.c	28	Merge I/O of same class
direct-io.c	60	Classify file sizes
sd.c	1	Insert classifier into CDB

Table 2: Linux 2.6.34 files modified for I/O classification. Modified lines of code (LOC) shown.

Overall, adding classification to the Linux block layer requires that we modify 10 files (156 lines of code), which results in a small kernel patch. Table 2 summarize the changes. In Windows, the changes are confined to closed-source filter drivers. No kernel code needs to be modified because, unlike Linux, Windows provides a stackable filter driver architecture for intercepting and modifying I/O requests.

4.2 Filesystem prototypes

A filesystem developer must devise a classification scheme and assign storage policies to each class. The goals of the filesystem (performance, reliability, or security) will influence how I/O is classified and policies are assigned.

4.2.1 Reference classification scheme

The classification schemes for the Linux Ext3 and Windows NTFS are similar, so we only present Ext3. Any number of schemes could have been chosen, and we begin with one well-suited to minimizing random disk access in the storage system. The classes include metadata blocks, directory blocks, journal blocks, and regular file blocks. File blocks are further classified by the file size ($\leq$4KB, $\leq$16KB, $\leq$64KB, $\leq$256KB, ..., $\leq$1GB, $>$1GB) — 11 file size classes in total.

The goal of our classification scheme is to provide the storage system with a way of prioritizing which blocks get cached and the eviction order of cached blocks. Considering the fact that metadata and small files can be responsible for the majority of the disk seeks, we classify I/O in such a way that we can separate these random requests from large-file requests that are commonly accessed sequentially. Database I/O is an obvious exception and, in Section 4.3 we introduce a classification scheme better suited for the database.

Table 3 (first two columns) summarizes our classification scheme for Linux Ext3. Every disk block that is written or read falls into exactly one class. Class 0 (unclassified) occurs when I/O bypasses the Ext3 filesystem. In particular, all I/O created during filesystem creation (`mkfs`) is unclassified, as there is no mounted filesystem to classify the I/O. The next 5 classes (superblocks through indirect data blocks) represent filesystem metadata, as classified by Ext3 after it has been mounted. Note, the unclassified metadata blocks will be re-classified as one of these metadata types when they are first accessed by Ext3. Although we differentiate metadata classes 1 through 5, we could have combined them into one class. For example, it is not critical that we

Ext3 Class	Class ID	Priority
Superblock	1	0
Group Descriptor	2	0
Bitmap	3	0
Inode	4	0
Indirect block	5	0
Directory entry	6	0
Journal entry	7	0
File <= 4KB	8	1
File <= 16KB	9	2
...	...	...
File > 1GB	18	11
Unclassified	0	12

Table 3: Reference classes and caching priorities for Ext3. Each class is assigned a unique SCSI Group Number and assigned a priority (0 is highest).

Ext3	LOC	Change made
balloc.c	2	Classify block bitmaps
dir.c	2	Classify inodes tables
ialloc.c	2	Classify inode bitmaps
inode.c	94	Classify indirect blocks, inodes, dirs, and file sizes
super.c	15	Classify superblocks, journal blocks, and group descriptors
commit.c	3	Classify journal I/O
journal.c	6	Classify journal I/O
revoke.c	2	Classify journal I/O

Table 4: Ext3 changes for Linux 2.6.34.

differentiate superblocks and block bitmaps, as these structures consume very little disk (and cache) space. Still, we do this for illustrative purposes and system debugging.

Continuing, class 6 represents directory blocks, class 7 journal blocks, and 8-18 are the file size classes. File size classes are only approximate. As a file is being created, the file size is changing while writes are being issued to the storage system; files can also be truncated. Subsequent I/O to a file will reclassify the blocks with the latest file size.

Approximate file sizes allow the storage system to differentiate small files from large files. For example, a storage system can cache all files 1MB or smaller, by caching all the file blocks with a classification up to 1MB. The first 1MB of files larger than 1MB may also fall into this category until they are later reclassified. This means that small files will fit entirely in cache, and large files may be partially cached with the remainder stored on disk.

We classify Ext3 using 18 of the 32 available classes from a 5-bit classifier. To implement this classification scheme, we modify 8 Ext3 files (126 lines of code). Table 4 summarizes our changes.

The remaining classes (19 through 31) could be used in other ways by the FS (e.g., text vs. binary, media file, bootable, read-mostly, or hot file), and we are exploring these as part of our future work. The remaining classes could also be used by user-level applications, like the database.

4.2.2 Reference policy assignment

Our prototype storage systems implement 16 priorities; to each class we assign a priority (0 is the highest). Metadata, journal, and directory blocks are highest priority, followed by the regular file blocks. 4KB files are higher priority than 16KB files, and so on. Unclassified I/O, or the unused metadata created during file system creation, is assigned the lowest priority. For this mapping, we only require 13 priorities, so 3 of the priority levels (13-15) are unused. See Table 3.

This priority assignment is specifically tuned for a file server workload (e.g., SPECsfs), as we will show in Section 5, and reflects our bias to optimize the filesystem for small files and metadata. Should this goal change, the priorities could be set differently. Should the storage system offer policies other than priority levels (like those in Table 1), the FS classes would need to be mapped accordingly.

4.3 Database proof-of-concept

In addition to the kernel-level I/O classification interface described in Section 4.1, we provide a POSIX interface for classifying user-level I/O. The interface builds on the scatter/gather functionality already present in POSIX.

Using this new interface, we classify all I/O from the PostgreSQL open source database [33]. As with FS classification, user-level classifiers are just numbers used to distinguish the various I/O classes, and it is the responsibility of the application (a DB in this case) to design a classification scheme and associate storage system policies with each class.

4.3.1 A POSIX interface for classifying DB I/O

We add an additional scatter/gather element to the POSIX readv and writev system calls. This element points to a user buffer that contains a classifier for the given I/O. To use our interface, a file is opened with the flag O_CLASSIFIED. When this flag is set, the OS will assume that all scatter/gather operations contain $1 + n$ elements, where the first element points to a classifier buffer and the remaining n elements point to data buffers. The OS can then extract the classifier buffer, bind the classifier to the kernel-level I/O (as described in Section 4.1), reduce the number of scatter gather elements by one, and send the I/O request down to the filesystem. Table 5 summarizes the changes made to the VFS to implement user-level classification. As with kernel-level classification, this is a small kernel patch.

The following code fragment illustrates the concept for a simple program with a 2-element gathered-write operation:

```
unsigned char class = 23;  /* a class ID */
int fd = open("foo", O_RDWR|O_CLASSIFIED);
struct iovec iov[2];        /* an sg list */

iov[0].iov_base = &class; iov[0].iov_len = 1;
iov[1].iov_base = "Hello, world!";
iov[1].iov_len = strlen("Hello, world!");
rc = writev(fd, iov, 2);   /* 2 elements */
close(fd);
```

The filesystem will classify the file size as described in Section 4.2, but we immediately override this classification with the user-level classification, if it exists. Combining user-level and FS-level classifiers is an interesting area of future work.

OS file	LOC	Change made
filemap.c	50	Extract class from sg list
mm.h	4	Add classifier to readahead
readahead.c	22	Add classifier to readahead
mpage.h	1	Add classifier to page read
mpage.c	5	Add classifier to page read
fs.h	1	Add classifier to FS page read
ext3/inode.c	2	Add classifier to FS page read

Table 5: Linux changes for user-level classification.

DB class	Class ID
Unclassified	0
Transaction Log	19
System table	20
Free space map	21
Temporary table	22
Random user table	23
Sequential user table	24
Index file	25
Reserved	26-31

Table 6: A classification scheme PostgreSQL. Each class is assigned a unique number. This number is copied into the 5-bit SCSI Group Number field in the SCSI WRITE and READ commands.

4.3.2 A DB classification scheme

Our proof-of-concept PostgreSQL classification scheme includes the transaction log, system tables, free space maps, temporary tables, user tables, and indexes. And we further classify the user tables by their access pattern, which the PostgreSQL database already identifies, internally, as random or sequential. Passing this access pattern information to the storage system avoids the need for (laborious) sequential stream detection.

Table 6 summarizes our proof-of-concept DB classification scheme, and Table 7 shows the minor changes required of PostgreSQL. We include this database example to demonstrate the flexibility of our approach and the ability to easily classify user-level I/O. How to properly assign block-level caching priorities for the database is part of our current research, but we do share some early results in Section 5 to demonstrate the performance potential.

4.4 Storage system prototypes

With the introduction of solid-state storage, storage system caches have increased in popularity. Examples include LSI's CacheCade and Adaptec's MaxIQ. Each of these systems use solid-state storage as a persistent disk cache in front of a traditional disk-based RAID array.

We create similar storage system caches and apply the necessary modification to take advantage of I/O classification. In particular, we introduce two new caching algorithms: *selective allocation* and *selective eviction*. These algorithms inspect the relative priority of each I/O and, as such, provide a mechanism by which computer system performance policies can be enforced in a storage system. These caching algorithms build upon a baseline cache, such as LRU.

DB file	LOC	Change made
rel.h	6	Pass classifier to storage manager
xlog.c	7	Classify transaction log
bufmgr.c	17	Classify indexes, system tables, and regular tables
freelist.c	7	Classify sequential vs. random
smgr.c/md.c	21	Assign SCSI groups numbers
fd.c	20	Add classifier to scatter/gather and classify temp. tables

Table 7: PostgreSQL changes.

4.4.1 Our baseline storage system cache

Our baseline cache uses a conventional write-back cache with LRU eviction. Recent research shows that solid-state LRU caching solutions are not cost-effective for enterprise workloads [31]. We confirm this result in our evaluation, but also build upon it by demonstrating that a conventional LRU algorithm *can* be cost-effective with Differentiated Storage Services. Algorithms beyond LRU [13, 25] may produce even better results.

A solid-state drive is used as the cache, and we divide the SSD into a configurable number of allocation units. We use 8 sectors (4KB, a common memory page size) as the allocation unit, and we initialize the cache by contiguously adding all of these allocation units to a *free list*. Initially, this free list contains every sector of the SSD.

For new write requests, we allocate cache entries from this free list. Once allocated, the entries are removed from the free list and added to a *dirty list*. We record the entries allocated to each I/O, by saving the mapping in a hash table keyed by the logical block number.

A *syncer daemon* monitors the size of the free list. When the free list drops below a low watermark, the syncer begins cleaning the dirty list. The dirty list is sorted in LRU order. As dirty entries are read or written, they are moved to the end of the dirty list. In this way, the syncer cleans the least recently used entries first. Dirty entries are read from the SSD and written back to the disk. As entries are cleaned, they are added back to the free list. The free list is also sorted in LRU order, so if clean entries are accessed while in the free list, they are moved to the end of the free list.

It is atop this baseline cache that we implement selective allocation and selective eviction.

4.4.2 Conventional allocation

Two heuristics are commonly used by current storage systems when deciding whether to allocate an I/O request in the cache. These relate to the size of the request and its access pattern (random or sequential). For example, a 256KB request in NTFS tells you that the file the I/O is directed to is at least 256KB in size, and multiple contiguous 256KB requests indicate that the file may be larger. It is the small random requests that benefit most from caching, so large requests or requests that appear to be part of a sequential stream will often bypass the cache, as such requests are just as efficiently served from disk. There are at least two fundamental problems with this approach.

First, the block-level request size is only partially correlated with file size. Small files can be accessed with large requests, and large files can be accessed with small requests. It all depends on the application request size and caching model (e.g., buffered or direct). A classic example of this is the NTFS Master File Table (MFT). This key metadata structure is a large, often sequentially written file. Though when read, the requests are often small and random. If a storage system were to bypass the cache when the MFT is being written, subsequent reads would be forced to go to disk. Fixing this problem would require that the MFT be distinguished from other large files and, without an I/O classification mechanism, this would not be easy.

The second problem is that operating systems have a maximum request size (e.g., 512KB). If one were to make a caching decision based on request size, one could not differentiate file sizes that were larger than this maximum request. This has not been a problem with small DRAM caches, but solid-state caches are considerably larger and can hold many files. So, knowing that a file is, say, 1MB as opposed to 1GB is useful when making a caching decision. For example, it can be better to cache more small files than fewer large ones, which is particularly the case for file servers that are seek-limited from small files and their metadata.

4.4.3 Selective allocation
Because of the above problems, we do not make a cache allocation decision based on request size. Instead, for the FS prototypes, we differentiate metadata from regular files, and we further differentiate the regular files by size.

Metadata and small files are always cached. Large files are conditionally cached. Our current implementation checks to see if the syncer daemon is active (cleaning dirty entries), which indicates cache pressure, and we opt to not cache large files in this case (our configurable cut-off is 1MB or larger — such blocks will bypass the cache). However, an idle syncer daemon indicates that there is space in the cache, so we choose to cache even the largest of files.

4.4.4 Selective eviction
Selective eviction is similar to selective allocation in its use of priority information. Rather than evict entries in strict LRU order, we evict the lowest priority entries first. This is accomplished by maintaining a dirty list for each I/O class. When the number of free cache entries reaches a low watermark, the syncer cleans the lowest priority dirty list first. When that list is exhausted, it selects the next lowest priority list, and so on, until a high watermark of free entries is reached and the syncer is put to sleep.

With selective eviction, we can completely fill the cache without the risk of priority inversion. For an FS, this allows the caching of larger files, but not at the expense of evicting smaller files. Large files will evict themselves under cache pressure, leaving the small files and metadata effectively pinned in the cache. High priority I/O will only be evicted after all lower priority data has been evicted. As we illustrate in our evaluation, small files and metadata rarely get evicted in our enterprise workloads, which contain realistic mixes of small and large file size [29].

4.4.5 Linux implementation
We implement a SW cache as RAID level 9 in the Linux RAID stack (MD).[1] The mapping to RAID is a natural one. RAID levels (e.g., 0, 1, 5) and the nested versions (e.g., 10, 50) simply define a static mapping from logical blocks within a volume to physical blocks on storage devices. RAID-0, for example, specifies that logical blocks will be allocated round-robin. A Differentiated Storage Services architecture, in comparison, provides a dynamic mapping. In our implementation, the classification scheme and associated policies provide a mapping to either the cache device or the storage device, though one might also consider a mapping to multiple cache levels or different storage pools.

Managing the cache as a RAID device allows us to build upon existing RAID management utilities. We use the Linux *mdadm* utility to create a cached volume. One simply specifies the storage device and the caching device (devices in /dev), both of which may be another RAID volume. For example, the cache device may be a mirrored pair of SSDs, and the storage device a RAID-50 array. Implementing Differentiated Storage Services in this manner makes for easy integration into existing storage management utilities.

Our SW cache is implemented in a kernel RAID module that is loaded when the cached volume is created; information regarding the classification scheme and priority assignment are passed to the module as runtime parameters. Because the module is part of the kernel, I/O requests are terminated in the block layer and never reach the SCSI layer. The I/O classifiers are, therefore, extracted directly from the block I/O requests (BIOs), not the 5-bit classification field in the SCSI request.

4.4.6 iSCSI implementation
Our second storage system prototype is based on iSCSI [12]. Unlike the RAID-9 prototype, iSCSI is OS-independent and can be accessed by both Linux and Windows. In both cases, the I/O classifier is copied into the SCSI request on the host. On the iSCSI target the I/O classifier is extracted from the request, the priority of the I/O class is determined, and a caching decision is made. The caching implementation is identical to the RAID-9 prototype.

5. EVALUATION
We evaluate our filesystem prototypes using a file server workload (based on SPECsfs [44]), an e-mail server workload (modeled after the Swiss Internet Analysis [30]), a set of filesystem utilities (`find`, `tar`, and `fsck`), and a database workload (TPC-H [47]).

We present data from the Linux RAID-9 implementation for the filesystem workloads; NTFS results using our iSCSI prototype are similar. For Linux TPC-H, we use iSCSI.

5.1 Experimental setup
All experiments are run on a single Linux machine. Our Linux system is a 2-way quad-core Xeon server system (8 cores) with 8GB of RAM. We run Fedora 13 with a 2.6.34 kernel modified as described in Section 4. As such, the Ext3

---

[1]RAID-9 is not a standard RAID level, but simply a way for us to create cached volumes in Linux MD.

File size	File server	E-mail server
1K	17%	0
2K	16%	24%
4K	16%	26%
8K	7%	18%
16K	7%	12%
32K	9%	6%
64K	7%	5%
128K	5%	3%
256K	5%	2%
512K	4%	2%
1M	3%	1%
2M	2%	0%
8M	1%	0%
10M	0%	1%
32M	1%	0%

Table 8: File size distributions.

filesystem is modified to classify all I/O, the block layer copies the classification into the Linux BIO, and the BIO is consumed by our cache prototype (a kernel module running in the Linux RAID (MD) stack).

Our storage device is a 5-disk LSI RAID-1E array. Atop this base device we configure a cache as described in Section 4.4.5, or 4.4.6 (for TPC-H); an Intel®32GB X25-E SSD is used as the cache. For each of our tests, we configure a cache that is a fraction of the used disk capacity (10-30%).

5.2 Workloads

Our file server workload is based on SPECsfs2008 [44]; the file size distributions are shown in Table 8 (File server). The setup phase creates 262,144 files in 8,738 directories (SFS specifies 30 files per directory). The benchmark performs 262,144 transactions against this file pool, where a transaction is reading an existing file or creating a new file. The read/write ratio is 2:1. The total capacity used by this test is 184GB, and we configure an 18GB cache (10% of the file pool size). We preserve the file pool at the end of the file transactions and run a set of filesystem utilities. Specifically, we search for a non-existent file (`find`), archive the filesystem (`tar`), and then check the filesystem for errors (`fsck`).

Our e-mail server workload is based on a study of e-mail server file sizes [30]. We use a request size of 4KB and a read/write ratio of 2:1. The setup phase creates 1 million files in 1,000 directories. We then perform 1 million transactions (reading or creating an e-mail) against this file pool. The file size distribution for this workload is shown in Table 8 (E-mail server). The total disk capacity used by this test is 204GB, and we configure a 20GB cache.

Finally, we run the TPC-H decision support workload [47] atop our modified PostgreSQL [33] database (Section 4.3). Each PostgreSQL file is opened with the flag `O_CLASSIFIED`, thereby enabling user-level classification and disabling file size classification from Ext3. We build a database with a scale factor of 8, resulting in an on-disk footprint of 29GB, and we run the I/O intensive queries (2, 17, 18, and 19) back-to-back. We compare 8GB LRU and LRU-S caches.

5.3 Test methodology

We use an in-house, file-based workload generator for the file and e-mail server workloads. As input, the generator takes a file size distribution, a request size distribution, a read/write ratio, and the number of subdirectories.

For each workload, our generator creates the specified number of subdirectories and, within these subdirectories, creates files using the specified file and write request size distribution. After the pool is created, transactions are performed against the pool, using these same file and request size distributions. We record the number of files written/read per second and, for each file size, the 95th percentile (worst case) latency, or the time to write or read the entire file.

We compare the performance of three storage configurations: no SSD cache, an LRU cache, and an enhanced LRU cache (LRU-S) that uses selective allocation and selective eviction. For the cached tests, we also record the contents of the cache on a class-by-class basis, the read hit rate, and the eviction overhead (percentage of transferred blocks related to cleaning the cache). These three metrics are performance indicators used to explain the performance differences between LRU and LRU-S. Elapsed time is used as the performance metric in all tests.

5.4 File server

Figure 2a shows the contents of the LRU cache at completion of the benchmark (left bar), the percentage of blocks written (middle bar), and the percentage of blocks read (right bar). The cache bar does not exactly add to 100% due to round-off.[2] Although the cache activity (and contents) will naturally differ across applications, these results are representative for a given benchmark across a range of different cache sizes.

As shown in the figure, the LRU breakdown is similar to the blocks written and read. Most of the blocks belong to large files — a tautology given the file sizes in SPECsfs2008 (most files are small, but most of the data is in large files). Looking again at the leftmost bar, one sees that nearly the entire cache is filled with blocks from large files. The smallest sliver of the graph (bottommost layer of cache bar) represents files up to 64KB in size. Smaller files and metadata consume less than 1% and cannot be seen.

Figure 2b shows the breakdown of the LRU-S cache. The write and read breakdown are identical to Figure 2a, as we are running the same benchmark, but we see a different outcome in terms of cache utilization. Over 40% of the cache is consumed by files 64KB and smaller, and metadata (bottommost layer) is now visible. Unlike LRU eviction alone, selective allocation and selective eviction limit the cache utilization of large files. As utilization increases, large-file blocks are the first to be evicted, thereby preserving small files and metadata.

Figure 3a compares read hit rates. With a 10% cache, the read hit rate is approximately 10%. Given the uniformly random distribution of the SPECsfs2008 workload, this result is expected. However, although the read hit rates are

---

[2]Some of the classes consume less than 1% and round to 0.

(a) LRU cache and I/O breakdown

(b) LRU-S cache and I/O breakdown

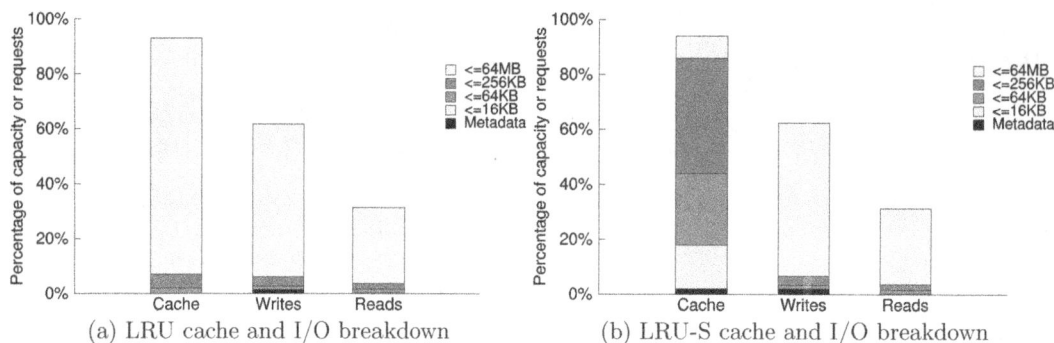

Figure 2: SFS results. Cache contents and breakdown of blocks written/read.

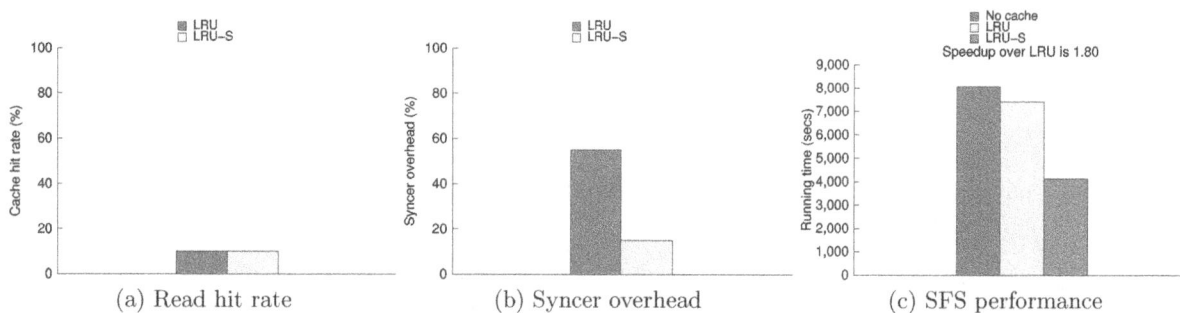

(a) Read hit rate

(b) Syncer overhead

(c) SFS performance

Figure 3: SFS performance indicators

identical, the miss penalties are not. In the case of LRU, most of the hits are to large files. In the case of LRU-S, the hits are to small files and metadata. Given the random seeks associated with small file and metadata, it is better to miss on large sequential files.

Figure 3b compares the overhead of the syncer daemon, where overhead is the percentage of transferred blocks due to cache evictions. When a cache entry is evicted, the syncer must read blocks from the cache device and write them back to the disk device — and this I/O can interfere with application I/O. Selective allocation can reduce the job of the syncer daemon by fencing off large files when there is cache pressure. As a result, we see the percentage of I/O related to evictions drop by more than a factor or 3. This can translate into more available performance for the application workload.

Finally, Figure 3c shows the actual performance of the benchmark. We compare the performance of no cache, an LRU cache, and LRU-S. Performance is measured in running time, so smaller is better. As can be seen in the graph, an LRU cache is only slightly better than no cache at all, and an LRU-S cache is 80% faster than LRU. In terms of running time, the no-cache run completes in 135 minutes, LRU in minutes 124, and LRU-S in 69 minutes.

The large performance difference can also be measured by the improvement in file latencies. Figures 4a and 4b compare the 95th percentile latency of write and read operations, where latency is the time to write or read an entire file. The x-axis represents the file sizes (as per SPECsfs2008) and the y-axis represents the reduction in latency relative to no

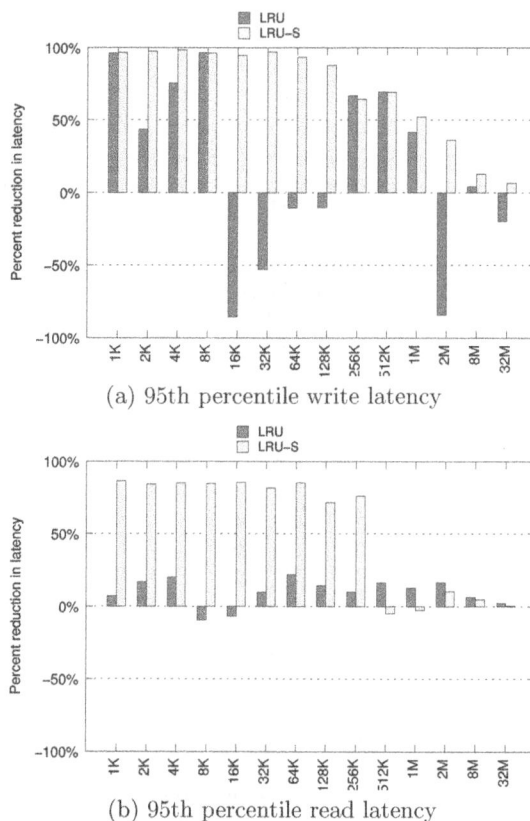

(a) 95th percentile write latency

(b) 95th percentile read latency

Figure 4: SFS file latencies

cache at all. Although LRU and LRU-S reduce write latency equally for many of the file sizes (e.g., 1KB, 8KB, 256KB, and 512KB), LRU suffers from outliers that account for the increase in 95th percentile latency. The bars that extend below the x-axis indicate that LRU *increased* write latency relative to no cache, due to cache thrash. And the read latencies show even more improvement with LRU-S. Files 256KB and smaller have latency reductions greater than 50%, compared to the improvements in LRU which are much more modest. Recall, with a 10% cache, only 10% of the working set can be cached. Whereas LRU-S uses this 10% to cache small files and metadata, standard LRU wastes the cache on large, sequentially-accessed files. Stated differently, the cache space we save by evicting large files allows for many more small files to be cached.

5.5 E-mail server

The results from the e-mail server workload are similar to the file server. The read cache hit rate for both LRU and LRU-S is 11%. Again, because the files are accessed with a uniformly random distribution, the hit rate is correlated with the size of the working set that is cached. The miss penalties are again quite different. LRU-S reduces the read latency considerably. In this case, files 32KB and smaller see a large read latency reduction. For example, the read latency for 2KB e-mails is 85ms, LRU reduces this to 21ms, and LRU-S reduces this to 4ms (a reduction of 81% relative to LRU).

As a result of the reduced miss penalty and lower eviction overhead (reduced from 54% to 25%), the e-mail server workload is twice as fast when running with LRU-S. Without any cache, the test completes the 1 million transactions in 341 minutes, LRU completes in 262 minutes, and LRU-S completes in 131 minutes.

Like the file server, an e-mail server is often throughput limited. By giving preference to metadata and small e-mails, significant performance improvements can be realized. This benchmark also demonstrates the flexibility of our FS classification approach. That is, our file size classification is sufficient to handle both file and e-mail server workloads, which have very different file size distributions.

5.6 FS utilities

The FS utilities further demonstrate the advantages of selective caching. Following the file server workload, we search the filesystem for a non-existent file (`find`, a 100% read-only metadata workload), create a tape archive of an SFS subdirectory (`tar`), and check the filesystem (`fsck`).

For the `find` operation, the LRU configuration sees an 80% read hit rate, compared to 100% for LRU-S. As a result, LRU completes the find in 48 seconds, and LRU-S in 13 (a 3.7x speedup). For `tar`, LRU has a 5% read hit rate, compared to 10% for LRU-S. Moreover, nearly 50% of the total I/O for LRU is related to syncer daemon activity, as LRU write-caches the tar file, causing evictions of the existing cache entries and leading to cache thrash. In contrast, the LRU-S fencing algorithm directs the tar file to disk. As as result, LRU-S completes the archive creation in 598 seconds, compared to LRU's 850 seconds (a 42% speedup).

Finally, LRU completes `fsck` in 562 seconds, compared to 94 seconds for LRU-S (a 6x speedup). Unlike LRU, LRU-S retains filesystem metadata in the cache, throughout all of the tests, resulting in a much faster consistency check of the filesystem.

5.7 TPC-H

As one example of how our proof-of-concept DB can prioritize I/O, we give highest priority to filesystem metadata, user tables, log files, and temporary tables; all of these classes are managed as a single class (they share an LRU list). Index files are given lowest priority. Unused indexes can consume a considerable amount of cache space and, in these tests, are served from disk sufficiently fast. We discovered this when we first began analyzing the DB I/O requests in our storage system. That is, the classified I/O both identifies the opportunity for cache optimization, and it provides a means by which the optimization can be realized.

Figure 5 compares the cache contents of LRU and LRU-S. For the LRU test, most of the cache is consumed by index files; user tables and temporary tables consume the remainder. Because index files are created after the DB is created, it is understandable why they consume such a large portion of the cache. In contrast, LRU-S fences off the index files, leaving more cache space for user tables, which are often accessed randomly.

The end result is an improved cache hit rate (Figure 6a), slightly less cache cleaning overhead (Figure 6b), and a 20% improvement in query time (Figure 6c). The non-cached run completes all 4 queries in 680 seconds, LRU in 463 seconds, and LRU-S in 386 seconds. Also, unlike the file and e-mail server runs, we see more variance in TPC-H running time when not using LRU-S. This applies to both the non-cached run and the LRU run. Because of this, we average over three runs and include error bars. As seen in Figure 6c, LRU-S not only runs faster, but it also reduces performance outliers.

6. RELATED WORK

File and storage system QoS is a heavily researched area. Previous work focuses on QoS guarantees for disk I/O [54], QoS guarantees for filesystems [4], configuring storage systems to meet performance goals [55], allocating storage bandwidth to application classes [46], and mapping administrator-specified goals to appropriate storage system designs [48]. In contrast, we approach the QoS problem with I/O classification, which benefits from a coordinated effort between the computer system *and* the storage system.

More recently, providing performance differentiation (or isolation) has been an active area of research due to the increasing level in which storage systems are being shared within a data center. Such techniques manage I/O scheduling to achieve fairness within a shared storage system [17, 50, 53]. The work presented in this paper provides a finer granularity of control (classes) for such systems.

Regarding caching, numerous works focus on flash and its integration into storage systems as a conventional cache [20, 23, 24]. However, because enterprise workloads often exhibit such poor locality of reference, it can be difficult to make conventional caches cost-effective [31]. In contrast, we show

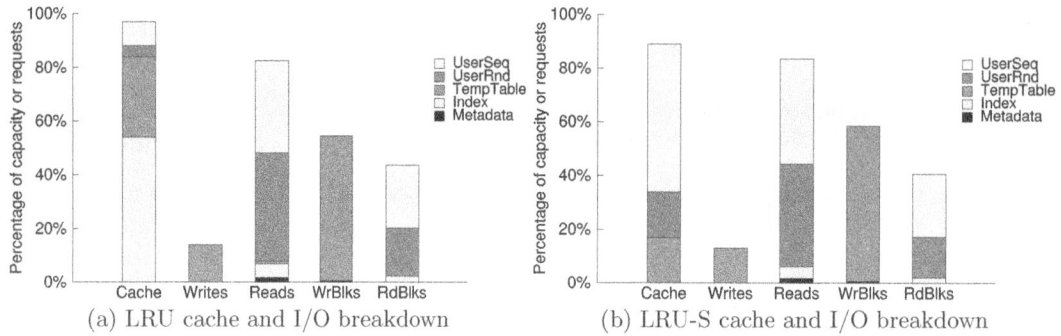

Figure 5: TPC-H results. Cache contents and breakdown of blocks written/read.

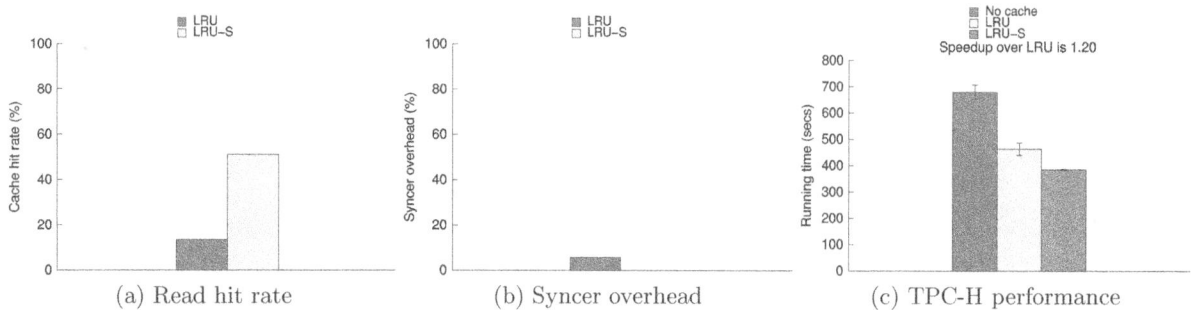

Figure 6: TPC-H performance indicators

that *selective* caching, even when applied to the simplest of caching algorithms (LRU) can be cost effective. Though we introduce selective caching in the context of LRU [39], any of the more advanced caching algorithms could be used, such as LRU-K [32], CLOCK-Pro [13], 2Q [15], ARC [25], LIRS [14], FBR [35], MQ [59], and LRFU [19].

Our block-level selective caching approach is similar to FS-level approaches, such as Conquest [51] and zFS [36], where faster storage pools are reserved for metadata and small files. And there are other block-level caching approaches with similar goals, but different approaches. In particular, Hystor [6] uses data migration to move metadata and other latency sensitive blocks into faster storage, and Karma [57] relies on *a priori* hints on database block access patterns to improve multi-level caching.

The characteristics of flash [7] make it attractive as a medium for persistent transactions [34], or to host flash-based filesystems [16]. Other forms of byte-addressable non-volatile memory introduce additional filesystem opportunities [8].

Data migration [1, 2, 5, 6, 18, 21, 56], in general, is a complement to the work presented in this article. However, migration can be expensive [22], so it is best to allocate storage from the appropriate storage during file creation, whenever possible. Many files have well-known patterns of access, making such allocation possible [26].

And we are not the first to exploit semantic knowledge in the storage system. Most notably, semantically-smart disks [43] and type-safe disks [40, 58] explore how knowledge of on-disk data structures can be used to improve performance,

reliability, and security. But we differ, quite fundamentally, in that we send higher-level semantic information with each I/O request, rather than detailed block information (e.g., inode structure) through explicit management commands. Further, unlike this previous work, we do not offload block management to the storage system.

7. CONCLUSION

The inexpressive block interface limits I/O optimization, and it does so in two ways. First, computer systems are having difficulty optimizing around complex storage system internals. RAID, caching, and non-volatile memory are good examples. Second, storage systems, due to a lack of semantic information, experience equal difficulty when trying to optimize I/O requests.

Yet, an entire computer industry has been built around blocks, so major changes to this interface are, today, not practical. Differentiated Storage Services addresses this problem with I/O classification. By adding a small classifier to the block interface, we can associate QoS policies with I/O classes, thereby allowing computer systems and storage system to agree on shared, block-level policies. This will enable continued innovation on both sides of the block interface.

Our filesystem prototypes show significant performance improvements when applied to storage system caching, and our database proof-of-concept suggests similar improvements.

We are extending our work to other realms such as reliability and security. Over time, as applications come to expect differentiated service from their storage systems, additional usage models are likely to evolve.

Acknowledgments

We thank our Intel colleagues who helped contribute to the work presented in this paper, including Terry Yoshii, Mathew Eszenyi, Pat Stolt, Scott Burridge, Thomas Barnes, and Scott Hahn. We also thank Margo Seltzer for her very useful feedback.

8. REFERENCES

[1] M. Abd-El-Malek, W. V. C. II, C. Cranor, G. R. Ganger, J. Hendricks, A. J. Klosterman, M. Mesnier, M. Prasad, B. Salmon, R. R. Sambasivan, S. Sinnamohideen, J. D. Strunk, E. Thereska, M. Wachs, and J. J. Wylie. Ursa Minor: versatile cluster-based storage. In *Proceedings of the 4th USENIX Conference on File and Storage Technologies*, San Francisco, CA, December 2005. The USENIX Association.

[2] A. C. Arpaci-Dusseau and R. H. Arpaci-Dusseau. Information and Control in Gray-Box Systems. In *Proceedings of the 18nd ACM Symposium on Operating Systems Principles (SOSP 01)*, Chateau Lake Louise, Banff, Canada, October 2001.

[3] S. N. I. Association. A Dictionary of Storage Networking Terminology. http://www.snia.org/education/dictionary.

[4] P. R. Barham. A Fresh Approach to File System Quality of Service. In *Proceedings of the IEEE 7th International Workshop on Network and Operating System Support for Digital Audio and Video (NOSSDAV 97)*, St. Louis, MO, May 1997.

[5] M. Bhadkamkar, J. Guerra, L. Useche, S. Burnett, J. Liptak, R. Rangaswami, and V. Hristidis. BORG: Block-reORGanization for Self-optimizing Storage Systems. In *Proceedings of the 7th USENIX Conference on File and Storage Technologies (FAST 09)*, San Francisco, CA, February 2009. The USENIX Association.

[6] F. Chen, D. Koufaty, and X. Zhang. Hystor: Making the best use of solid state drives in high performance storage systems. In *Proceedings of the 25th ACM International Conference on Supercomputing (ICS 2011)*, Tucson, AZ, May 31 - June 4 2011.

[7] F. Chen, D. A. Koufaty, and X. Zhang. Understanding Intrinsic Characteristics and System Implications of Flash Memory based Solid State Drives. In *Proceedings of the International Conference on Measurement and Modeling of Computer Systems (SIGMETRICS 2009)*, Seattle, WA, June 2009. ACM Press.

[8] J. Condit, E. B. Nightingale, C. Frost, E. Ipek, D. Burger, B. C. Lee, and D. Coetzee. Better I/O Through Byte-Addressable, Persistent Memory. In *Proceedings of the 22nd ACM Symposium on Operating Systems Principles (SOSP 09)*, Big Sky, MT, October 2009.

[9] X. Ding, S. Jiang, F. Chen, K. Davis, and X. Zhang. DiskSeen: Exploiting Disk Layout and Access History to Enhance I/O Prefetch. In *Proceedings of the 2007 USENIX Annual Technical Conference*, Santa Clara, CA, June 2007. The USENIX Association.

[10] W. Effelsberg and T. Haerder. Principles of database buffer management. *ACM Transactions on Database Systems (TODS)*, 9(4):560–595, December 1984.

[11] H. Huang, A. Hung, and K. G. Shin. FS2: Dynamic Data Replication in Free Disk Space for Improving Disk Performance and Energy Consumption. In *Proceedings of 20th ACM Symposium on Operating System Principles*, pages 263–276, Brighton, UK, October 2005. ACM Press.

[12] Intel Corporation. Open Storage Toolkit. http://www.sourceforge.net/projects/intel-iscsi.

[13] S. Jiang, F. Chen, and X. Zhang. CLOCK-Pro: An Effective Improvement of the CLOCK Replacement. In *Proceedings of the 2005 USENIX Annual Technical Conference (USENIX ATC 2005)*, Anaheim, CA, April 10-15 2005. The USENIX Association.

[14] S. Jiang and X. Zhang. LIRS: An Efficient Low Inter-reference Recency Set Replacement Policy to Improve Buffer Cache Performance. In *Proceedings of the International Conference on Measurement and Modeling of Computer Systems (SIGMETRICS 2002)*, Marina Del Rey, CA, June 15-19 2002. ACM Press.

[15] T. Johnson and D. Shasha. 2Q: A Low Overhead High Performance Buffer Management Replacement Algorithm. In *Proceedings of the 20th International Conference on Very Large Data Bases (VLDB'94)*, Santiago Chile, Chile, September 12-15 1994. Morgan Kaufmann.

[16] W. K. Josephson, L. A. Bongo, D. Flynn, and K. Li. DFS: A File System for Virtualized Flash Storage. In *Proceedings of the 8th USENIX Conference on File and Storage Technologies (FAST 10)*, San Jose, CA, February 2010. The USENIX Association.

[17] M. Karlsson, C. Karamanolis, and X. Zhu. Triage: performance differentiation for storage systems using adaptive control. *ACM Transactions on Storage*, 1(4):457–480, November 2006.

[18] S. Khuller, Y.-A. Kim, and Y.-C. J. Wan. Algorithms for data migration with cloning. In *Proceedings of the 22nd ACM SIGMOD-SIGACT-SIGART Symposium on Principles of Database Systems*, San Diego, CA, June 2003. ACM Press.

[19] D. Lee, J. Choi, J. Kim, S. H. Noh, S. L. Min, Y. Cho, and C. S. Kim. LRFU: A Spectrum of Policies that Subsumes the Least Recently Used and Least Frequently Used Policies. *IEEE Transactions on Computers*, 50(12):1352–1361, December 2001.

[20] A. Leventhal. Flash storage memory. In *Communications of the ACM*, volume 51(7), pages 47–51, July 2008.

[21] C. Lu, G. A. Alvarez, and J. Wilkes. Aqueduct: online data migration with performance guarantees. In *Proceedings of the 1st USENIX Conference on File and Storage Technologies (FAST 02)*, Monterey, CA, January 2002. The USENIX Association.

[22] P. Macko, M. Seltzer, and K. A. Smith. Tracking Back References in a Write-Anywhere File System. In *Proceedings of the 8th USENIX Conference on File and Storage Technologies (FAST 10)*, San Jose, CA, February 2010. The USENIX Association.

[23] B. Marsh, F. Douglis, and P. Krishnan. Flash memory file caching for mobile computers. In *Proceedings of the 27th Hawaii Conference on Systems Science*, Wailea, HI, Jan 1994.

[24] J. Matthews, S. Trika, D. Hensgen, R. Coulson, and K. Grimsrud. Intel Turbo Memory: Nonvolatile disk caches in the storage hierarchy of mainstream computer systems. In *ACM Transactions on Storage (TOS)*, volume 4, May 2008.

[25] N. Megiddo and D. S. Modha. Outperforming LRU with an Adaptive Replacement Cache Algorithm. *IEEE Computer Magazine*, 37(4):58–65, April 2004.

[26] M. Mesnier, E. Thereska, G. Ganger, D. Ellard, and M. Seltzer. File classification in self-* storage systems. In *Proceedings of the 1st International Conference on Autonomic Computing (ICAC-04)*, New York, NY, May 2004. IEEE Computer Society.

[27] M. Mesnier, M. Wachs, R. R. Sambasivan, A. Zheng, and G. R. Ganger. Modeling the relative fitness of storage. In *Proceedings of the International Conference on Measurement and Modeling of Computer Systems (SIGMETRICS 2007)*, San Diego, CA, June 2007. ACM Press.

[28] M. P. Mesnier, G. R. Ganger, and E. Riedel. Object-based Storage. *IEEE Communications*, 44(8):84–90, August 2003.

[29] D. T. Meyer and W. J. Bolosky. A Study of Practical Deduplication. In *Proceedings of the 9th USENIX Conference on File and Storage Technologies (FAST 11)*, San Jose, CA, Feb 15-17 2011. The USENIX Association.

[30] O. Muller and D. Graf. Swiss Internet Analysis 2002. http://swiss-internet-analysis.org.

[31] D. Narayanan, E. Thereska, A. Donnelly, S. Elnikety, and A. Rowstron. Migrating Server Storage to SSDs: Analysis of Tradeoffs. In *Proceedings of the 4th ACM European Conference on Computer systems (EuroSys '09)*, Nuremberg, Germany, March 31 - April 3 2009. ACM Press.

[32] E. J. O'Neil, P. E. O'Neil, and G. Weikum. The LRU-K page replacement algorithm for database disk buffering. In *Proceedings of the 1993 ACM International Conference on Management of Data (SIGMOD '93)*, Washington, D.C., May 26-28 1993. ACM Press.

[33] PostgreSQL Global Development Group. Open source database. http://www.postgresql.org.

[34] V. Prabhakaran, T. L. Rodeheffer, and L. Zhou. Transactional Flash. In *Proceedings of the 8th USENIX Symposium on Operating Systems Design and Implementation (OSDI 08)*, San Diego, CA, December 2008. The USENIX Association.

[35] J. T. Robinson and M. V. Devarakonda. Data Cache Management Using Frequency-Based Replacement. In *Proceedings of the International Conference on Measurement and Modeling of Computer Systems (SIGMETRICS 1990)*, Boulder, CO, May 22-25 1990. ACM Press.

[36] O. Rodeh and A. Teperman. zFS - A Scalable Distributed File System Using Object Disks. In *Proceedings of the 20th Goddard Conference on Mass Storage Systems (MSS'03)*, San Diego, CA, April 2003. IEEE.

[37] C. Ruemmler and J. Wilkes. Disk shuffling. Technical Report HPL-91-156, Hewlett-Packard Laboratories, October 2001.

[38] J. Schindler, J. L. Griffin, C. R. Lumb, and G. R. Ganger. Track-aligned Extents: Matching Access Patterns to Disk Drive Characteristics. In *Proceedings of the 1st USENIX Conference on File and Storage Technologies (FAST 02)*, Monterey, CA, January 2002. The USENIX Association.

[39] A. Silberschatz, P. B. Galvin, and G. Gagne. *Operating Systems Concepts*. Wiley, 8th edition, 2009.

[40] G. Sivathanu, S. Sundararaman, and E. Zadok. Type-safe Disks. In *Proceedings of the 7th USENIX Symposium on Operating Systems Design and Implementation (OSDI 06)*, Seattle, WA, November 2006. The USENIX Association.

[41] M. Sivathanu, L. N. Bairavasundaram, A. C. Arpaci-Dusseau, and R. H. Arpaci-Dusseau. Life or Death at Block Level. In *Proceedings of the 6th Symposium on Operating Systems Design and Implementation (OSDI 04)*, pages 379–394, San Francisco, CA, December 2004. The USENIX Association.

[42] M. Sivathanu, V. Prabhakaran, A. C. Arpaci-Dusseau, and R. H. Arpaci-Dusseau. Improving Storage System Availability with D-GRAID. In *Proceedings of the 3rd USENIX Conference on File and Storage Technologies (FAST 04)*, pages 15–30, San Francisco, CA, March 2004. The USENIX Association.

[43] M. Sivathanu, V. Prabhakaran, F. I. Popovici, T. E. Denehy, A. C. Arpaci-Dusseau, and R. H. Arpaci-Dusseau. Semantically-Smart Disk Systems. In *Proceedings of the 2th USENIX Conference on File and Storage Technologies (FAST 03)*, San Francisco, CA, March-April 2003. The USENIX Association.

[44] Standard Performance Evaluation Corporation. Spec sfs. http://www.storageperformance.org.

[45] M. Stonebraker. Operating system support for database management. *Communications of the ACM*, 2(7):412–418, July 1981.

[46] V. Sundaram and P. Shenoy. A Practical Learning-based Approach for Dynamic Storage Bandwidth Allocation. In *Proceedings of the Eleventh International Workshop on Quality of Service (IWQoS 2003)*, Berkeley, CA, June 2003. Springer.

[47] Transaction Processing Performance Council. TPC Benchmark H. http://www.tpc.org/tpch.

[48] S. Uttamchandani, K. Voruganti, S. Srinivasan, J. Palmer, and D. Pease. Polus: Growing Storage QoS Management Beyond a "4-Year Old Kid". In *Proceedings of the 3rd USENIX Conference on File and Storage Technologies (FAST 04)*, San Francisco, CA, March 2004. The USENIX Association.

[49] M. Uysal, G. A. Alvarez, and A. Merchant. A modular, analytical throughput model for modern disk arrays. In *Proceedings of the 9th International Symposium on Modeling Analysis and Simulation of Computer and Telecommunications Systems (MASCOTS-2001)*, Cincinnati, OH, August 2001. IEEE/ACM.

[50] M. Wachs, M. Abd-El-Malek, E. Thereska, and G. R. Ganger. Argon: Performance Insulation for Shared Storage Servers. In *Proceedings of the 5th USENIX Conference on File and Storage Technologies (FAST 07)*, San Jose, CA, February 2007. The USENIX Association.

[51] A.-I. A. Wang, P. Reiher, G. J. Popek, and G. H. Kuenning. Conquest: Better performance through a Disk/Persistent-RAM hybrid file system. In *Proceedings of the 2002 USENIX Annual Technical Conference (USENIX ATC 2002)*, Monterey, CA, June 2002. The USENIX Association.

[52] M. Wang, K. Au, A. Ailamaki, A. Brockwell, C. Faloutsos, and G. R. Ganger. Storage device performance prediction with CART models. In *Proceedings of the 12th International Symposium on Modeling Analysis and Simulation of Computer and Telecommunications Systems (MASCOTS-2004)*, Volendam, The Netherlands, October 2004. IEEE.

[53] Y. Wang and A. Merchant. Proportional share scheduling for distributed storage systems. In *Proceedings of the 5th USENIX Conference on File and Storage Technologies (FAST 07)*, San Jose, CA, February 2007. The USENIX Association.

[54] R. Wijayaratne and A. L. N. Reddy. Providing QoS guarantees for disk I/O. *Multimedia Systems*, 8(1):57–68, February 2000.

[55] J. Wilkes. Traveling to Rome: QoS specifications for automated storage system management. In *Proceedings of the 9th International Workshop on Quality of Service (IWQoS 2001)*, Karlsruhe, Germany, June 2001.

[56] J. Wilkes, R. Golding, C. Staelin, and T. Sullivan. The HP AutoRAID Hierarchical Storage System. *ACM Transactions on Computer Systems (TOCS)*, 14(1):108–136, February 1996.

[57] G. Yadgar, M. Factor, and A. Schuster. Karma: Know-it-All Replacement for a Multilevel cAche. In *Proceedings of the 5th USENIX Conference on File and Storage Technologies (FAST 07)*, San Jose, CA, February 2007. The USENIX Association.

[58] C. Yalamanchili, K. Vijayasankar, E. Zadok, and G. Sivathanu. DHIS: discriminating hierarchical storage. In *Proceedings of The Israeli Experimental Systems Conference (SYSTOR 09)*, Haifa, Israel, May 2009. ACM Press.

[59] Y. Zhou, J. F. Philbin, and K. Li. The Multi-Queue Replacement Algorithm for Second Level Buffer Caches. In *Proceedings of the 2001 USENIX Annual Technical Conference*, Boston, MA, June 25-30 2001. The USENIX Association.

A File is Not a File: Understanding the I/O Behavior of Apple Desktop Applications

Tyler Harter, Chris Dragga, Michael Vaughn,
Andrea C. Arpaci-Dusseau, Remzi H. Arpaci-Dusseau
Department of Computer Sciences
University of Wisconsin, Madison
{harter, dragga, vaughn, dusseau, remzi}@cs.wisc.edu

ABSTRACT

We analyze the I/O behavior of *iBench*, a new collection of productivity and multimedia application workloads. Our analysis reveals a number of differences between iBench and typical file-system workload studies, including the complex organization of modern files, the lack of pure sequential access, the influence of underlying frameworks on I/O patterns, the widespread use of file synchronization and atomic operations, and the prevalence of threads. Our results have strong ramifications for the design of next generation local and cloud-based storage systems.

1. INTRODUCTION

The design and implementation of file and storage systems has long been at the forefront of computer systems research. Innovations such as namespace-based locality [21], crash consistency via journaling [15, 29] and copy-on-write [7, 34], checksums and redundancy for reliability [5, 7, 26, 30], scalable on-disk structures [37], distributed file systems [16, 35], and scalable cluster-based storage systems [9, 14, 18] have greatly influenced how data is managed and stored within modern computer systems.

Much of this work in file systems over the past three decades has been shaped by *measurement*: the deep and detailed analysis of workloads [4, 10, 11, 16, 19, 25, 33, 36, 39]. One excellent example is found in work on the Andrew File System [16]; detailed analysis of an early AFS prototype led to the next-generation protocol, including the key innovation of callbacks. Measurement helps us understand the systems of today so we can build improved systems for tomorrow.

Whereas most studies of file systems focus on the corporate or academic intranet, most file-system users work in the more mundane environment of the *home*, accessing data via desktop PCs, laptops, and compact devices such as tablet computers and mobile phones. Despite the large number of previous studies, little is known about home-user applications and their I/O patterns.

Home-user applications are important today, and their importance will increase as more users store data not only on local devices but also in the cloud. Users expect to run similar applications across desktops, laptops, and phones; therefore, the behavior of these applications will affect virtually every system with which a user interacts. I/O behavior is especially important to understand since it greatly impacts how users perceive overall system latency and application performance [12].

While a study of how users typically exercise these applications would be interesting, the first step is to perform a detailed study of I/O behavior under typical but controlled workload tasks. This style of *application study*, common in the field of computer architecture [40], is different from the *workload study* found in systems research, and can yield deeper insight into how the applications are constructed and how file and storage systems need to be designed in response.

Home-user applications are fundamentally large and complex, containing millions of lines of code [20]. In contrast, traditional UNIX-based applications are designed to be simple, to perform one task well, and to be strung together to perform more complex tasks [32]. This modular approach of UNIX applications has not prevailed [17]: modern applications are standalone monoliths, providing a rich and continuously evolving set of features to demanding users. Thus, it is beneficial to study each application individually to ascertain its behavior.

In this paper, we present the first in-depth analysis of the I/O behavior of modern home-user applications; we focus on productivity applications (for word processing, spreadsheet manipulation, and presentation creation) and multimedia software (for digital music, movie editing, and photo management). Our analysis centers on two Apple software suites: iWork, consisting of Pages, Numbers, and Keynote; and iLife, which contains iPhoto, iTunes, and iMovie. As Apple's market share grows [38], these applications form the core of an increasingly popular set of workloads; as device convergence continues, similar forms of these applications are likely to access user files from both stationary machines and moving cellular devices. We call our collection the *iBench task suite*.

To investigate the I/O behavior of the iBench suite, we build an instrumentation framework on top of the powerful DTrace tracing system found inside Mac OS X [8]. DTrace allows us not only to monitor system calls made by each traced application, but also to examine stack traces, in-kernel functions such as page-ins and page-outs, and other details required to ensure accuracy and completeness. We also develop an application harness based on AppleScript [3] to drive each application in the repeatable and automated fashion that is key to any study of GUI-based applications [12].

Our careful study of the tasks in the iBench suite has enabled us to make a number of interesting observations about how applications access and manipulate stored data. In addition to confirming standard past findings (*e.g.*, most files are small; most bytes accessed are from large files [4]), we find the following new results.

A file is not a file. Modern applications manage large databases of information organized into complex directory trees. Even simple word-processing documents, which appear to users as a "file", are

SOSP '11, October 23-26, 2011, Cascais, Portugal.

in actuality small file systems containing many sub-files (*e.g.*, a Microsoft .doc file is actually a FAT file system containing pieces of the document). File systems should be cognizant of such hidden structure in order to lay out and access data in these complex files more effectively.

Sequential access is not sequential. Building on the trend noticed by Vogels for Windows NT [39], we observe that even for streaming media workloads, "pure" sequential access is increasingly rare. Since file formats often include metadata in headers, applications often read and re-read the first portion of a file before streaming through its contents. Prefetching and other optimizations might benefit from a deeper knowledge of these file formats.

Auxiliary files dominate. Applications help users create, modify, and organize content, but user files represent a small fraction of the files touched by modern applications. Most files are helper files that applications use to provide a rich graphical experience, support multiple languages, and record history and other metadata. File-system placement strategies might reduce seeks by grouping the hundreds of helper files used by an individual application.

Writes are often forced. As the importance of home data increases (*e.g.*, family photos), applications are less willing to simply write data and hope it is eventually flushed to disk. We find that most written data is explicitly forced to disk by the application; for example, iPhoto calls fsync thousands of times in even the simplest of tasks. For file systems and storage, the days of delayed writes [22] may be over; new ideas are needed to support applications that desire durability.

Renaming is popular. Home-user applications commonly use atomic operations, in particular rename, to present a consistent view of files to users. For file systems, this may mean that transactional capabilities [23] are needed. It may also necessitate a rethinking of traditional means of file locality; for example, placing a file on disk based on its parent directory [21] does not work as expected when the file is first created in a temporary location and then renamed.

Multiple threads perform I/O. Virtually all of the applications we study issue I/O requests from a number of threads; a few applications launch I/Os from hundreds of threads. Part of this usage stems from the GUI-based nature of these applications; it is well known that threads are required to perform long-latency operations in the background to keep the GUI responsive [24]. Thus, file and storage systems should be thread-aware so they can better allocate bandwidth.

Frameworks influence I/O. Modern applications are often developed in sophisticated IDEs and leverage powerful libraries, such as Cocoa and Carbon. Whereas UNIX-style applications often directly invoke system calls to read and write files, modern libraries put more code between applications and the underlying file system; for example, including "cocoa.h" in a Mac application imports 112,047 lines of code from 689 different files [28]. Thus, the behavior of the framework, and not just the application, determines I/O patterns. We find that the default behavior of some Cocoa APIs induces extra I/O and possibly unnecessary (and costly) synchronizations to disk. In addition, use of different libraries for similar tasks within an application can lead to inconsistent behavior between those tasks. Future storage design should take these libraries and frameworks into account.

This paper contains four major contributions. First, we describe a general tracing framework for creating benchmarks based on interactive tasks that home users may perform (*e.g.*, importing songs, exporting video clips, saving documents). Second, we deconstruct the I/O behavior of the tasks in iBench; we quantify the I/O behavior of each task in numerous ways, including the types of files ac-

cessed (*e.g.*, counts and sizes), the access patterns (*e.g.*, read/write, sequentiality, and preallocation), transactional properties (*e.g.*, durability and atomicity), and threading. Third, we describe how these qualitative changes in I/O behavior may impact the design of future systems. Finally, we present the 34 traces from the iBench task suite; by making these traces publicly available and easy to use, we hope to improve the design, implementation, and evaluation of the next generation of local and cloud storage systems:

```
http://www.cs.wisc.edu/adsl/Traces/ibench
```

The remainder of this paper is organized as follows. We begin by presenting a detailed timeline of the I/O operations performed by one task in the iBench suite; this motivates the need for a systematic study of home-user applications. We next describe our methodology for creating the iBench task suite. We then spend the majority of the paper quantitatively analyzing the I/O characteristics of the full iBench suite. Finally, we summarize the implications of our findings on file-system design.

2. CASE STUDY

The I/O characteristics of modern home-user applications are distinct from those of UNIX applications studied in the past. To motivate the need for a new study, we investigate the complex I/O behavior of a single representative task. Specifically, we report in detail the I/O performed over time by the Pages (4.0.3) application, a word processor, running on Mac OS X Snow Leopard (10.6.2) as it creates a blank document, inserts 15 JPEG images each of size 2.5MB, and saves the document as a Microsoft .doc file.

Figure 1 shows the I/O this task performs (see the caption for a description of the symbols used). The top portion of the figure illustrates the accesses performed over the full lifetime of the task: at a high level, it shows that more than 385 files spanning six different categories are accessed by eleven different threads, with many intervening calls to fsync and rename. The bottom portion of the figure magnifies a short time interval, showing the reads and writes performed by a single thread accessing the primary .doc productivity file. From this one experiment, we illustrate each finding described in the introduction. We first focus on the single access that saves the user's document (bottom), and then consider the broader context surrounding this file save, where we observe a flurry of accesses to hundreds of helper files (top).

A file is not a file. Focusing on the magnified timeline of reads and writes to the productivity .doc file, we see that the file format comprises more than just a simple file. Microsoft .doc files are based on the FAT file system and allow bundling of multiple files in the single .doc file. This .doc file contains a directory (Root), three streams for large data (WordDocument, Data, and 1Table), and a stream for small data (Ministream). Space is allocated in the file with three sections: a file allocation table (FAT), a double-indirect FAT (DIF) region, and a ministream allocation region (Mini).

Sequential access is not sequential. The complex FAT-based file format causes random access patterns in several ways: first, the header is updated at the beginning and end of the magnified access; second, data from individual streams is fragmented throughout the file; and third, the 1Table stream is updated before and after each image is appended to the WordDocument stream.

Auxiliary files dominate. Although saving the single .doc we have been considering is the sole purpose of this task, we now turn our attention to the top timeline and see that 385 different files are accessed. There are several reasons for this multitude of files. First, Pages provides a rich graphical experience involving many images and other forms of multimedia; together with the 15 inserted JPEGs, this requires 118 multimedia files. Second, users

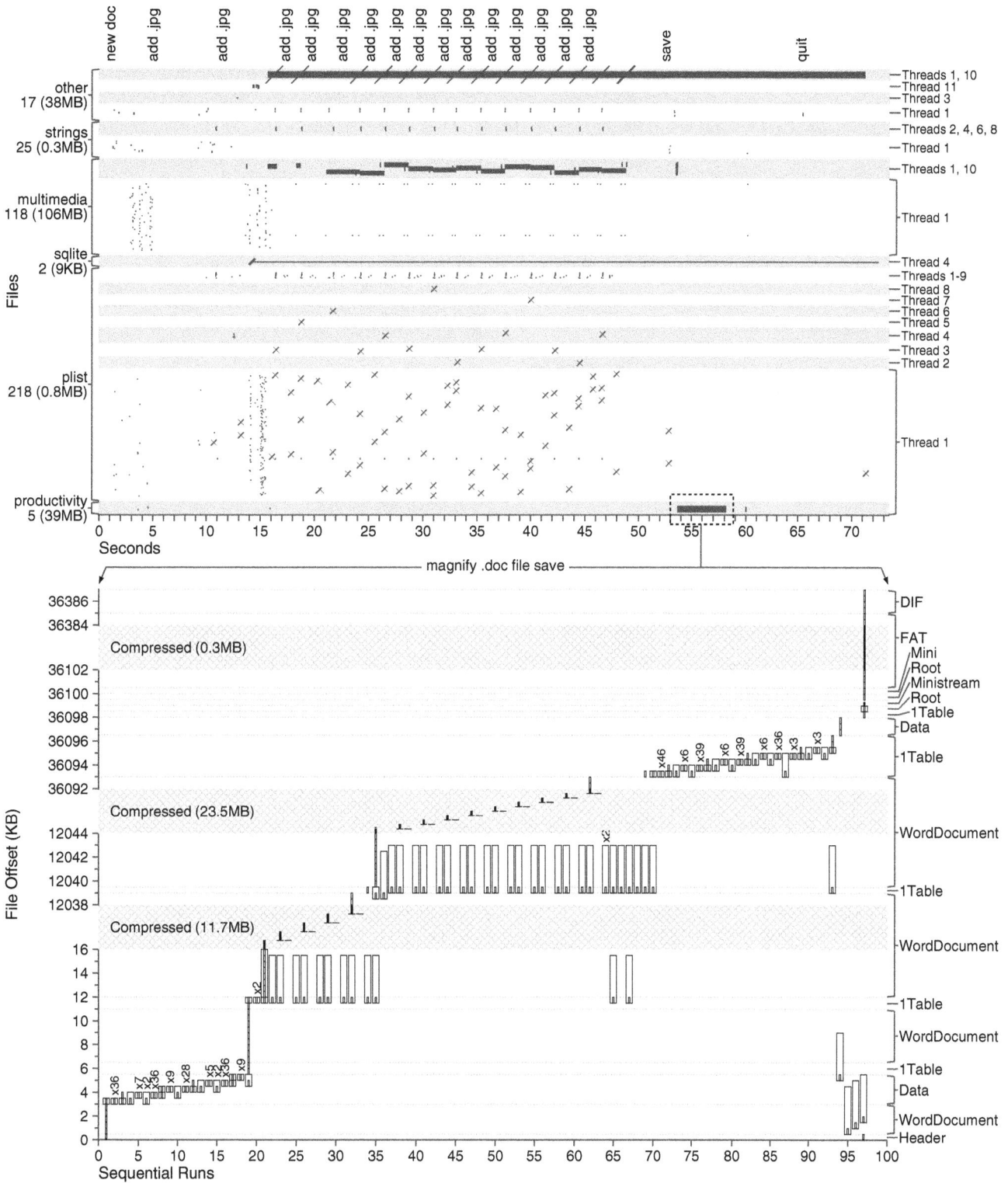

Figure 1: **Pages Saving A Word Document.** The top graph shows the 75-second timeline of the entire run, while the bottom graph is a magnified view of seconds 54 to 58. In the top graph, annotations on the left categorize files by type and indicate file count and amount of I/O; annotations on the right show threads. Black bars are file accesses (reads and writes), with thickness logarithmically proportional to bytes of I/O. / is an fsync; \ is a rename; X is both. In the bottom graph, individual reads and writes to the .doc file are shown. Vertical bar position and bar length represent the offset within the file and number of bytes touched. Thick white bars are reads; thin gray bars are writes. Repeated runs are marked with the number of repetitions. Annotations on the right indicate the name of each file section.

want to use Pages in their native language, so application text is not hard-coded into the executable but is instead stored in 25 different .strings files. Third, to save user preferences and other metadata, Pages uses a SQLite database (2 files) and a number of key-value stores (218 .plist files).

Writes are often forced; renaming is popular. Pages uses both of these actions to enforce basic transactional guarantees. It uses fsync to flush write data to disk, making it durable; it uses rename to atomically replace old files with new files so that a file never contains inconsistent data. The timeline shows these invocations numerous times. First, Pages regularly uses fsync and rename when updating the key-value store of a .plist file. Second, fsync is used on the SQLite database. Third, for each of the 15 image insertions, Pages calls fsync on a file named "tempData" (classified as "other") to update its automatic backup.

Multiple threads perform I/O. Pages is a multi-threaded application and issues I/O requests from many different threads during the experiment. Using multiple threads for I/O allows Pages to avoid blocking while I/O requests are outstanding. Examining the I/O behavior across threads, we see that Thread 1 performs the most significant portion of I/O, but ten other threads are also involved. In most cases, a single thread exclusively accesses a file, but it is not uncommon for multiple threads to share a file.

Frameworks influence I/O. Pages was developed in a rich programming environment where frameworks such as Cocoa or Carbon are used for I/O; these libraries impact I/O patterns in ways the developer might not expect. For example, although the application developers did not bother to use fsync or rename when saving the user's work in the .doc file, the Cocoa library regularly uses these calls to atomically and durably update relatively unimportant metadata, such as "recently opened" lists stored in .plist files. As another example, when Pages tries to read data in 512-byte chunks from the .doc, each read goes through the STDIO library, which only reads in 4 KB chunks. Thus, when Pages attempts to read one chunk from the 1Table stream, seven unrequested chunks from the WordDocument stream are also incidentally read (offset 12039 KB). In other cases, regions of the .doc file are repeatedly accessed unnecessarily. For example, around the 3KB offset, read/write pairs occur dozens of times. Pages uses a library to write 2-byte words; each time a word is written, the library reads, updates, and writes back an entire 512-byte chunk. Finally, we see evidence of redundancy between libraries: even though Pages has a backing SQLite database for some of its properties, it also uses .plist files, which function across Apple applications as generic property stores.

This one detailed experiment has shed light on a number of interesting I/O behaviors that indicate that home-user applications are indeed different than traditional workloads. A new workload suite is needed that more accurately reflects these applications.

3. IBENCH TASK SUITE

Our goal in constructing the iBench task suite is two-fold. First, we would like iBench to be *representative* of the tasks performed by home users. For this reason, iBench contains popular applications from the iLife and iWork suites for entertainment and productivity. Second, we would like iBench to be relatively *simple* for others to use for file and storage system analysis. For this reason, we automate the interactions of a home user and collect the resulting traces of I/O system calls. The traces are available online at this site: http://www.cs.wisc.edu/adsl/Traces/ibench. We now describe in more detail how we met these two goals.

3.1 Representative

To capture the I/O behavior of home users, iBench models the actions of a "reasonable" user interacting with iPhoto, iTunes, iMovie, Pages, Numbers, and Keynote. Since the research community does not yet have data on the exact distribution of tasks that home users perform, iBench contains tasks that we believe are common and uses files with sizes that can be justified for a reasonable user. iBench contains 34 different tasks, each representing a home user performing one distinct operation. If desired, these tasks could be combined to create more complex workflows and I/O workloads. The six applications and corresponding tasks are as follows.

iLife iPhoto 8.1.1 (419): digital photo album and photo manipulation software. iPhoto stores photos in a library that contains the data for the photos (which can be in a variety of formats, including JPG, TIFF, and PNG), a directory of modified files, a directory of scaled down images, and two files of thumbnail images. The library stores metadata in a SQLite database. iBench contains six tasks exercising user actions typical for iPhoto: starting the application and importing, duplicating, editing, viewing, and deleting photos in the library. These tasks modify both the image files and the underlying database. Each of the iPhoto tasks operates on 400 2.5 MB photos, representing a user who has imported 12 megapixel photos (2.5 MB each) from a full 1 GB flash card on his or her camera.

iLife iTunes 9.0.3 (15): a media player capable of both audio and video playback. iTunes organizes its files in a private library and supports most common music formats (*e.g.*, MP3, AIFF, WAVE, AAC, and MPEG-4). iTunes does not employ a database, keeping media metadata and playlists in both a binary and an XML file. iBench contains five tasks for iTunes: starting iTunes, importing and playing an album of MP3 songs, and importing and playing an MPEG-4 movie. Importing requires copying files into the library directory and, for music, analyzing each song file for gapless playback. The music tasks operate over an album (or playlist) of ten songs while the movie tasks use a single 3-minute movie.

iLife iMovie 8.0.5 (820): video editing software. iMovie stores its data in a library that contains directories for raw footage and projects, and files containing video footage thumbnails. iMovie supports both MPEG-4 and Quicktime files. iBench contains four tasks for iMovie: starting iMovie, importing an MPEG-4 movie, adding a clip from this movie into a project, and exporting a project to MPEG-4. The tasks all use a 3-minute movie because this is a typical length found from home users on video-sharing websites.

iWork Pages 4.0.3 (766): a word processor. Pages uses a ZIP-based file format and can export to DOC, PDF, RTF, and basic text. iBench includes eight tasks for Pages: starting up, creating and saving, opening, and exporting documents with and without images and with different formats. The tasks use 15 page documents.

iWork Numbers 2.0.3 (332): a spreadsheet application. Numbers organizes its files with a ZIP-based format and exports to XLS and PDF. The four iBench tasks for Numbers include starting Numbers, generating a spreadsheet and saving it, opening the spreadsheet, and exporting that spreadsheet to XLS. To model a possible home user working on a budget, the tasks utilize a five page spreadsheet with one column graph per sheet.

iWork Keynote 5.0.3 (791): a presentation and slideshow application. Keynote saves to a .key ZIP-based format and exports to Microsoft's PPT format. The seven iBench tasks for Keynote include starting Keynote, creating slides with and without images, opening and playing presentations, and exporting to PPT. Each Keynote task uses a 20-slide presentation.

	Name	Description	Files	(MB)	Accesses	(MB)	RD%	WR%	Accesses / CPU Sec	I/O MB / CPU Sec
iLife — iPhoto	Start	Open iPhoto with library of 400 photos	779	(336.7)	828	(25.4)	78.8	21.2	**151.1**	4.6
	Imp	Import 400 photos into empty library	5900	(1966.9)	8709	(3940.3)	74.4	25.6	26.7	**12.1**
	Dup	Duplicate 400 photos from library	2928	(1963.9)	5736	(2076.2)	52.4	47.6	**237.9**	**86.1**
	Edit	Sequentially edit 400 photos from library	12119	(4646.7)	18927	(12182.9)	69.8	30.2	19.6	**12.6**
	Del	Sequentially delete 400 photos; empty trash	15246	(23.0)	15247	(25.0)	21.8	78.2	**280.9**	0.5
	View	Sequentially view 400 photos	2929	(1006.4)	3347	(1005.0)	98.1	1.9	24.1	7.2
iLife — iTunes	Start	Open iTunes with 10 song album	143	(184.4)	195	(9.3)	54.7	45.3	**72.4**	3.4
	ImpS	Import 10 song album to library	68	(204.9)	139	(264.5)	66.3	33.7	**75.2**	**143.1**
	ImpM	Import 3 minute movie to library	41	(67.4)	57	(42.9)	48.0	52.0	**152.4**	**114.6**
	PlayS	Play album of 10 songs	61	(103.6)	80	(90.9)	96.9	3.1	0.4	0.5
	PlayM	Play 3 minute movie	56	(77.9)	69	(32.0)	92.3	7.7	2.2	1.0
iLife — iMovie	Start	Open iMovie with 3 minute clip in project	433	(223.3)	786	(29.4)	99.9	0.1	**134.8**	5.0
	Imp	Import 3 minute .m4v (20MB) to "Events"	184	(440.1)	383	(122.3)	55.6	44.4	29.3	**9.3**
	Add	Paste 3 minute clip from "Events" to project	210	(58.3)	547	(2.2)	47.8	52.2	**357.8**	1.4
	Exp	Export 3 minute video clip	70	(157.9)	546	(229.9)	55.1	44.9	2.3	1.0
iWork — Pages	Start	Open Pages	218	(183.7)	228	(2.3)	99.9	0.1	**97.7**	1.0
	New	Create 15 text page document; save as .pages	135	(1.6)	157	(1.0)	73.3	26.7	**50.8**	0.3
	NewP	Create 15 JPG document; save as .pages	408	(112.0)	997	(180.9)	60.7	39.3	**54.6**	9.9
	Open	Open 15 text page document	103	(0.8)	109	(0.6)	99.5	0.5	**57.6**	0.3
	PDF	Export 15 page document as .pdf	107	(1.5)	115	(0.9)	91.0	9.0	**41.3**	0.3
	PDFP	Export 15 JPG document as .pdf	404	(77.4)	965	(110.9)	67.4	32.6	**49.7**	5.7
	DOC	Export 15 page document as .doc	112	(1.0)	121	(1.0)	87.9	12.1	**44.4**	0.4
	DOCP	Export 15 JPG document as .doc	385	(111.3)	952	(183.8)	61.1	38.9	**46.3**	8.9
iWork — Numbers	Start	Open Numbers	283	(179.9)	360	(2.6)	99.6	0.4	**115.5**	0.8
	New	Save 5 sheets/column graphs as .numbers	269	(4.9)	313	(2.8)	90.7	9.3	9.6	0.1
	Open	Open 5 sheet spreadsheet	119	(1.3)	137	(1.3)	99.8	0.2	**48.7**	0.5
	XLS	Export 5 sheets/column graphs as .xls	236	(4.6)	272	(2.7)	94.9	5.1	8.5	0.1
iWork — Keynote	Start	Open Keynote	517	(183.0)	681	(1.1)	99.8	0.2	**229.8**	0.4
	New	Create 20 text slides; save as .key	637	(12.1)	863	(5.4)	92.4	7.6	**129.1**	0.8
	NewP	Create 20 JPG slides; save as .key	654	(92.9)	901	(103.3)	66.8	33.2	**70.8**	8.1
	Play	Open and play presentation of 20 text slides	318	(11.5)	385	(4.9)	99.8	0.2	**95.0**	1.2
	PlayP	Open and play presentation of 20 JPG slides	321	(45.4)	388	(55.7)	69.6	30.4	72.4	10.4
	PPT	Export 20 text slides as .ppt	685	(12.8)	918	(10.1)	78.8	21.2	**115.2**	1.3
	PPTP	Export 20 JPG slides as .ppt	723	(110.6)	996	(124.6)	57.6	42.4	**61.0**	7.6

Table 1: **34 Tasks of the iBench Suite.** The table summarizes the 34 tasks of iBench, specifying the application, a short name for the task, and a longer description of the actions modeled. The I/O is characterized according to the number of files read or written, the sum of the maximum sizes of all accessed files, the number of file accesses that read or write data, the number of bytes read or written, the percentage of I/O bytes that are part of a read (or write), and the rate of I/O per CPU-second in terms of both file accesses and bytes. Each core is counted individually, so at most 2 CPU-seconds can be counted per second on our dual-core test machine. CPU utilization is measured with the UNIX `top` utility, which in rare cases produces anomalous CPU utilization snapshots; those values are ignored.

Table 1 contains a brief description of each of the 34 iBench tasks as well as the basic I/O characteristics of each task when running on Mac OS X Snow Leopard 10.6.2. The table illustrates that the iBench tasks perform a significant amount of I/O. Most tasks access hundreds of files, which in aggregate contain tens or hundreds of megabytes of data. The tasks typically access files hundreds of times. The tasks perform widely differing amounts of I/O, from less than a megabyte to more than a gigabyte. Most of the tasks perform many more reads than writes. Finally, the tasks exhibit high I/O throughput, often transferring tens of megabytes of data for every second of computation.

3.2 Easy to Use

To enable other system evaluators to easily use these tasks, the iBench suite is packaged as a set of 34 system call traces. To ensure reproducible results, the 34 user tasks were first automated with AppleScript, a general-purpose GUI scripting language. Apple-Script provides generic commands to emulate mouse clicks through menus and application-specific commands to capture higher-level operations. Application-specific commands bypass a small amount of I/O by skipping dialog boxes; however, we use them whenever possible for expediency.

The system call traces were gathered using DTrace [8], a kernel and user level dynamic instrumentation tool. DTrace is used to instrument the entry and exit points of all system calls dealing with the file system; it also records the current state of the system and the parameters passed to and returned from each call.

While tracing with DTrace was generally straightforward, we addressed four challenges in collecting the iBench traces. First, file sizes are not always available to DTrace; thus, we record every file's initial size and compute subsequent file size changes caused by system calls such as `write` or `ftruncate`. Second, iTunes uses the `ptrace` system call to disable tracing; we circumvent this block by using `gdb` to insert a breakpoint that automatically returns without calling `ptrace`. Third, the `volfs` pseudo-file system in HFS+ (Hierarchical File System) allows files to be opened via their inode number instead of a file name; to include pathnames in the trace, we instrument the `build_path` function to obtain the full path when the task is run. Fourth, tracing system calls misses I/O resulting from memory-mapped files; therefore, we purged memory and instrumented kernel page-in functions to measure the amount of memory-mapped file activity. We found that the amount of memory-mapped I/O is negligible in most tasks; we thus do not include this I/O in the iBench traces or analysis.

To provide reproducible results, the traces must be run on a single file-system image. Therefore, the iBench suite also contains snapshots of the initial directories to be restored before each run; initial state is critical in file-system benchmarking [1].

4. ANALYSIS OF IBENCH TASKS

The iBench task suite enables us to study the I/O behavior of a large set of home-user actions. As shown from the timeline of I/O behavior for one particular task in Section 2, these tasks are likely to access files in complex ways. To characterize this complex behavior in a quantitative manner across the entire suite of 34 tasks, we focus on answering four categories of questions.

- What different types of files are accessed and what are the sizes of these files?
- How are files accessed for reads and writes? Are files accessed sequentially? Is space preallocated?
- What are the transactional properties? Are writes flushed with fsync or performed atomically?
- How do multi-threaded applications distribute I/O across different threads?

Answering these questions has two benefits. First, the answers can guide file and storage system developers to target their systems better to home-user applications. Second, the characterization will help users of iBench to select the most appropriate traces for evaluation and to understand their resulting behavior.

All measurements were performed on a Mac Mini running Mac OS X Snow Leopard version 10.6.2 and the HFS+ file system. The machine has 2 GB of memory and a 2.26 GHz Intel Core Duo processor.

4.1 Nature of Files

Our analysis begins by characterizing the high-level behavior of the iBench tasks. In particular, we study the different types of files opened by each iBench task as well as the sizes of those files.

4.1.1 File Types

The iLife and iWork applications store data across a variety of files in a number of different formats; for example, iLife applications tend to store their data in libraries (or data directories) unique to each user, while iWork applications organize their documents in proprietary ZIP-based files. The extent to which tasks access different types of files greatly influences their I/O behavior.

To understand accesses to different file types, we place each file into one of six categories, based on file name extensions and usage. *Multimedia* files contain images (*e.g.*, JPEG), songs (*e.g.*, MP3, AIFF), and movies (*e.g.*, MPEG-4). *Productivity* files are documents (*e.g.*, .pages, DOC, PDF), spreadsheets (*e.g.*, .numbers, XLS), and presentations (*e.g.*, .key, PPT). *SQLite* files are database files. *Plist* files are property-list files in XML containing key-value pairs for user preferences and application properties. *Strings* files contain strings for localization of application text. Finally, *Other* contains miscellaneous files such as plain text, logs, files without extensions, and binary files.

Figure 2 shows the frequencies with which tasks open and access files of each type; most tasks perform hundreds of these accesses. Multimedia file opens are common in all workloads, though they seldom predominate, even in the multimedia-heavy iLife applications. Conversely, opens of productivity files are rare, even in iWork applications that use them; this is likely because most iWork tasks create or view a single productivity file. Because .plist files act as generic helper files, they are relatively common. SQLite files only have a noticeable presence in iPhoto, where they account for a substantial portion of the observed opens. Strings files occupy a significant minority of most workloads (except iPhoto and iTunes). Finally, between 5% and 20% of files are of type "Other" (except for iTunes, where they are more prevalent).

Figure 3 displays the percentage of I/O bytes accessed for each file type. In bytes, multimedia I/O dominates most of the iLife tasks, while productivity I/O has a significant presence in the iWork tasks; file descriptors on multimedia and productivity files tend to receive large amounts of I/O. SQLite, Plist, and Strings files have a smaller share of the total I/O in bytes relative to the number of opened files; this implies that tasks access only a small quantity of data for each of these files opened (*e.g.*, several key-value pairs in a .plist). In most tasks, files classified as "Other" receive a more significant portion of the I/O (the exception is iTunes).

Summary: Home applications access a wide variety of file types, generally opening multimedia files the most frequently. iLife tasks tend to access bytes primarily from multimedia or files classified as "Other"; iWork tasks access bytes from a broader range of file types, with some emphasis on productivity files.

4.1.2 File Sizes

Large and small files present distinct challenges to the file system. For large files, finding contiguous space can be difficult, while for small files, minimizing initial seek time is more important. We investigate two different questions regarding file size. First, what is the distribution of file sizes accessed by each task? Second, what portion of accessed bytes resides in files of various sizes?

To answer these questions, we record file sizes when each unique file descriptor is closed. We categorize sizes as very small (< 4KB), small (< 64KB), medium (< 1MB), large (< 10MB), or very large (≥ 10MB). We track how many accesses are to files in each category and how many of the bytes belong to files in each category.

Figure 4 shows the number of accesses to files of each size. Accesses to very small files are extremely common, especially for iWork, accounting for over half of all the accesses in every iWork task. Small file accesses have a significant presence in the iLife tasks. The large quantity of very small and small files is due to frequent use of .plist files that store preferences, settings, and other application data; these files often fill just one or two 4 KB pages.

Figure 5 shows the proportion of the files in which the bytes of accessed files reside. Large and very large files dominate every startup workload and nearly every task that processes multimedia files. Small files account for few bytes and very small files are essentially negligible.

Summary: Agreeing with many previous studies (e.g., [4]), we find that while applications tend to open many very small files (< 4 KB), most of the bytes accessed are in large files (> 1 MB).

4.2 Access Patterns

We next examine how the nature of file accesses has changed, studying the read and write patterns of home applications. These patterns include whether files are used for reading, writing, or both; whether files are accessed sequentially or randomly; and finally, whether or not blocks are preallocated via hints to the file system.

4.2.1 File Accesses

One basic characteristic of our workloads is the division between reading and writing on open file descriptors. If an application uses an open file only for reading (or only for writing) or performs more activity on file descriptors of a certain type, then the file system may be able to make more intelligent memory and disk allocations.

To determine these characteristics, we classify each opened file descriptor based on the types of accesses–read, write, or both read and write–performed during its lifetime. We also ignore the actual flags used when opening the file since we found they do not accurately reflect behavior; in all workloads, almost all write-only file descriptors were opened with O_RDWR. We measure both the

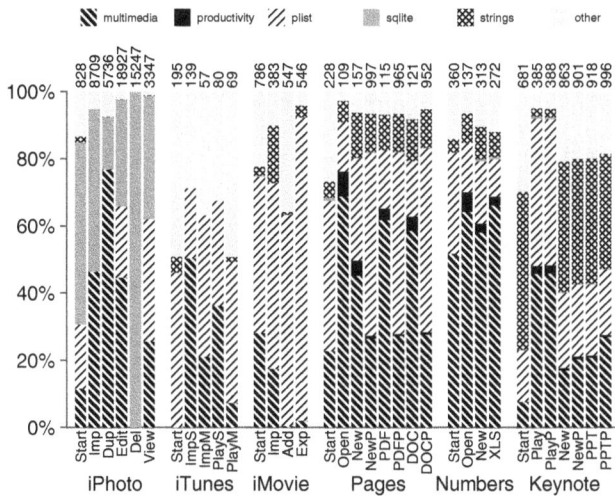

Figure 2: **Types of Files Accessed By Number of Opens.** This plot shows the relative frequency with which file descriptors are opened upon different file types. The number at the end of each bar indicates the total number of unique file descriptors opened on files.

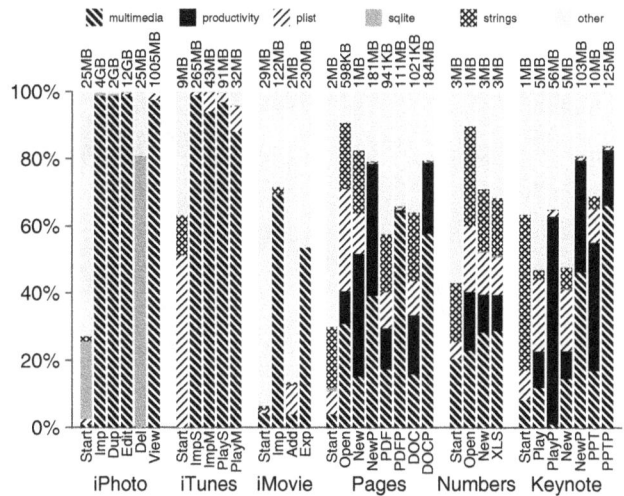

Figure 3: **Types of Files Opened By I/O Size.** This plot shows the relative frequency with which each task performs I/O upon different file types. The number at the end of each bar indicates the total bytes of I/O accessed.

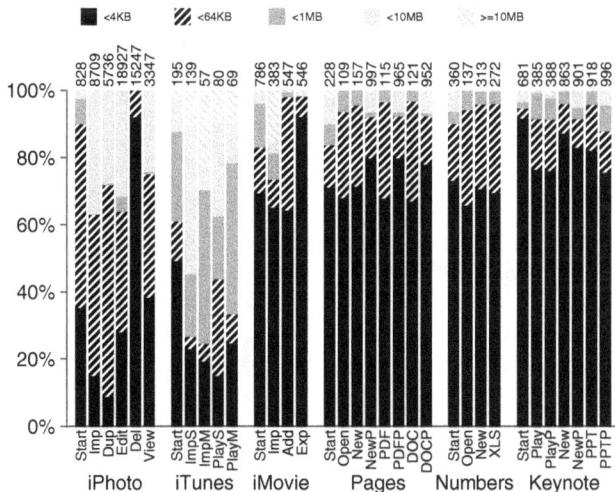

Figure 4: **File Sizes, Weighted by Number of Accesses.** This graph shows the number of accessed files in each file size range upon access ends. The total number of file accesses appears at the end of the bars. Note that repeatedly-accessed files are counted multiple times, and entire file sizes are counted even upon partial file accesses.

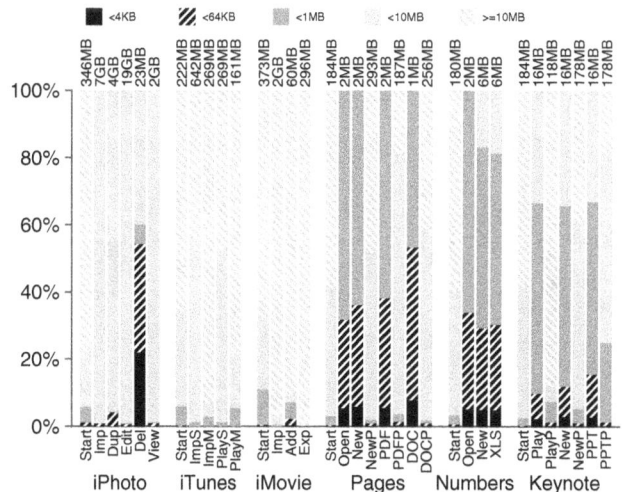

Figure 5: **File Sizes, Weighted by the Bytes in Accessed Files.** This graph shows the portion of bytes in accessed files of each size range upon access ends. The sum of the file sizes appears at the end of the bars. This number differs from total file footprint since files change size over time and repeatedly accessed file are counted multiple times.

proportional usage of each type of file descriptor and the relative amount of I/O performed on each.

Figure 6 shows how many file descriptors are used for each type of access. The overwhelming majority of file descriptors are used exclusively for reading or writing; read-write file descriptors are quite uncommon. Overall, read-only file descriptors are the most common across a majority of workloads; write-only file descriptors are popular in some iLife tasks, but are rarely used in iWork.

We observe different patterns when analyzing the amount of I/O performed on each type of file descriptor, as shown in Figure 7. First, even though iWork tasks have very few write-only file descriptors, they often write significant amounts of I/O to those descriptors. Second, even though read-write file descriptors are rare, when present, they account for relatively large portions of total I/O (particularly when exporting to .doc, .xls, and .ppt).

Summary: While many files are opened with the O_RDWR flag, most of them are subsequently accessed write-only; thus, file open flags cannot be used to predict how a file will be accessed. However, when an open file is both read and written by a task, the amount of traffic to that file occupies a significant portion of the total I/O. Finally, the rarity of read-write file descriptors may derive in part from the tendency of applications to write to a temporary file which they then rename as the target file, instead of overwriting the target file; we explore this tendency more in §4.3.2.

4.2.2 Sequentiality

Historically, files have usually been read or written entirely sequentially [4]. We next determine whether sequential accesses are dominant in iBench. We measure this by examining all reads and writes performed on each file descriptor and noting the percentage

77

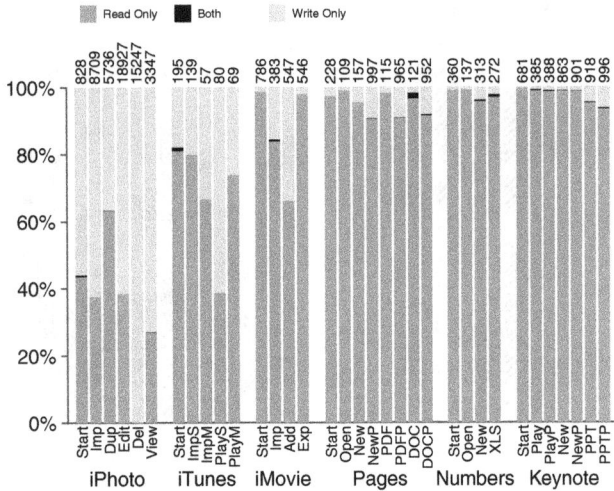

Figure 6: **Read/Write Distribution By File Descriptor.** File descriptors can be used only for reads, only for writes, or for both operations. This plot shows the percentage of file descriptors in each category. This is based on usage, not open flags. Any duplicate file descriptors (*e.g.*, created by dup) are treated as one and file descriptors on which the program does not perform any subsequent action are ignored.

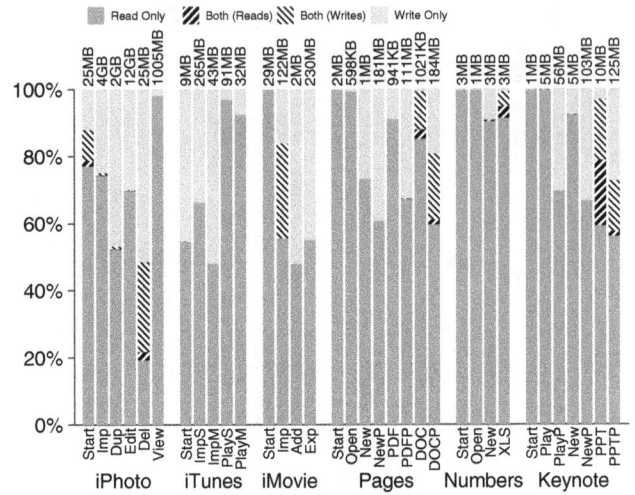

Figure 7: **Read/Write Distribution By Bytes.** The graph shows how I/O bytes are distributed among the three access categories. The unshaded dark gray indicates bytes read as a part of read-only accesses. Similarly, unshaded light gray indicates bytes written in write-only accesses. The shaded regions represent bytes touched in read-write accesses, and are divided between bytes read and bytes written.

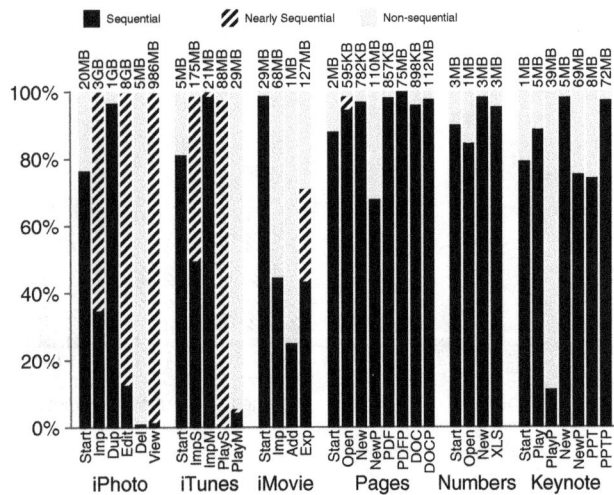

Figure 8: **Read Sequentiality.** This plot shows the portion of file read accesses (weighted by bytes) that are sequentially accessed.

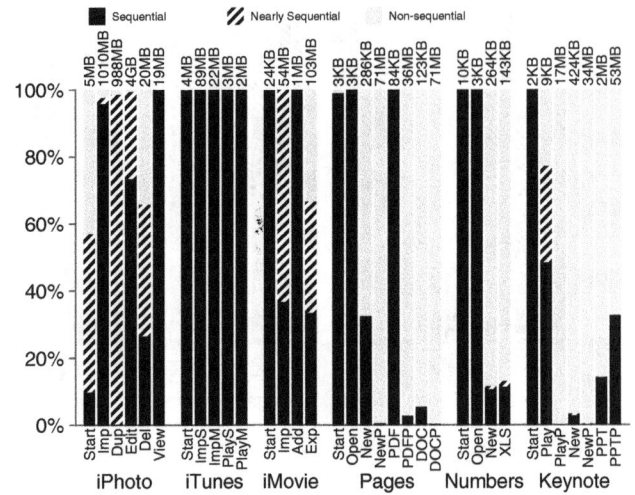

Figure 9: **Write Sequentiality.** This plot shows the portion of file write accesses (weighted by bytes) that are sequentially accessed.

of files accessed in strict sequential order (weighted by bytes).

We display our measurements for read and write sequentiality in Figures 8 and 9, respectively. The portions of the bars in black indicate the percent of file accesses that exhibit pure sequentiality. We observe high read sequentiality in iWork, but little in iLife (with the exception of the Start tasks and iTunes Import). The inverse is true for writes: most iLife tasks exhibit high sequentiality; iWork accesses are largely non-sequential.

Investigating the access patterns to multimedia files more closely, we note that many iLife applications first touch a small header before accessing the entire file sequentially. To better reflect this behavior, we define an access to a file as "nearly sequential" when at least 95% of the bytes read or written to a file form a sequential run. We found that a large number of accesses fall into the "nearly sequential" category given a 95% threshold; the results do not change much with lower thresholds.

The slashed portions of the bars in Figures 8 and 9 show observed sequentiality with a 95% threshold. Tasks with heavy use of multimedia files exhibit greater sequentiality with the 95% threshold for both reading and writing. In several workloads (mainly iPhoto and iTunes), the I/O classified almost entirely as non-sequential with a 100% threshold is classified as nearly sequential. The difference for iWork applications is much less striking, indicating that accesses are more random.

Summary: A substantial number of tasks contain purely sequential accesses. When the definition of a sequential access is loosened such that only 95% of bytes must be consecutive, then even more tasks contain primarily sequential accesses. These "nearly sequential" accesses result from metadata stored at the beginning of complex multimedia files: tasks frequently touch bytes near the beginning of multimedia files before sequentially reading or writing the bulk of the file.

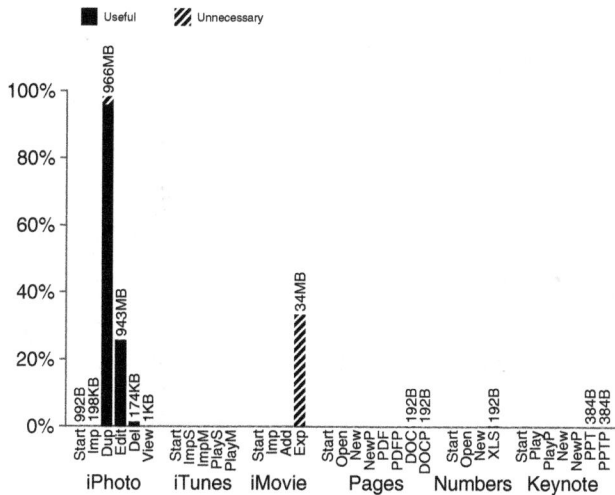

Figure 10: **Preallocation Hints.** The sizes of the bars indicate which portion of file extensions are preallocations; unnecessary preallocations are diagonally striped. The number atop each bar indicates the absolute amount preallocated.

4.2.3 Preallocation

One of the difficulties file systems face when allocating contiguous space for files is not knowing how much data will be written to those files. Applications can communicate this information by providing hints [27] to the file system to preallocate an appropriate amount of space. In this section, we quantify how often applications use preallocation hints and how often these hints are useful.

We instrument two calls usable for preallocation: pwrite and ftruncate. pwrite writes a single byte at an offset beyond the end of the file to indicate the future end of the file; ftruncate directly sets the file size. Sometimes a preallocation does not communicate anything useful to the file system because it is immediately followed by a single write call with all the data; we flag these preallocations as unnecessary.

Figure 10 shows the portion of file growth that is the result of preallocation. In all cases, preallocation was due to calls to pwrite; we never observed ftruncate preallocation. Overall, applications rarely preallocate space and preallocations are often useless.

The three tasks with significant preallocation are iPhoto Dup, iPhoto Edit, and iMovie Exp. iPhoto Dup and Edit both call a copyPath function in the Cocoa library that preallocates a large amount of space and then copies data by reading and writing it in 1 MB chunks. iPhoto Dup sometimes uses copyPath to copy scaled-down images of size 50-100 KB; since these smaller files are copied with a single write, the preallocation does not communicate anything useful. iMovie Exp calls a Quicktime append function that preallocates space before writing the actual data; however, the data is appended in small 128 KB increments. Thus, the append is not split into multiple write calls; the preallocation is useless.

Summary: Although preallocation has the potential to be useful, few tasks use it to provide hints, and a significant number of the hints that are provided are useless. The hints are provided inconsistently: although iPhoto and iMovie both use preallocation for some tasks, neither application uses preallocation during import.

4.3 Transactional Properties

In this section, we explore the degree to which the iBench tasks require transactional properties from the underlying file and storage system. In particular, we investigate the extent to which ap-

plications require writes to be durable; that is, how frequently they invoke calls to fsync and which APIs perform these calls. We also investigate the atomicity requirements of the applications, whether from renaming files or exchanging inodes.

4.3.1 Durability

Writes typically involve a trade-off between performance and durability. Applications that require write operations to complete quickly can write data to the file system's main memory buffers, which are lazily copied to the underlying storage system at a subsequent convenient time. Buffering writes in main memory has a wide range of performance advantages: writes to the same block may be coalesced, writes to files that are later deleted need not be performed, and random writes can be more efficiently scheduled.

On the other hand, applications that rely on durable writes can flush written data to the underlying storage layer with the fsync system call. The frequency of fsync calls and the number of bytes they synchronize directly affect performance: if fsync appears often and flushes only several bytes, then performance will suffer. Therefore, we investigate how modern applications use fsync.

Figure 11 shows the percentage of written data each task synchronizes with fsync. The graph further subdivides the source of the fsync activity into six categories. *SQLite* indicates that the SQLite database engine is responsible for calling fsync; *Archiving* indicates an archiving library frequently used when accessing ZIP formats; *Pref Sync* is the PreferencesSynchronize function call from the Cocoa library; *writeToFile* is the Cocoa call writeToFile with the atomically flag set; and finally, *FlushFork* is the Carbon FSFlushFork routine.

At the highest level, the figure indicates that half the tasks synchronize close to 100% of their written data while approximately two-thirds synchronize more than 60%. iLife tasks tend to synchronize many megabytes of data, while iWork tasks usually only synchronize tens of kilobytes (excluding tasks that handle images).

To delve into the APIs responsible for the fsync calls, we examine how each bar is subdivided. In iLife, the sources of fsync calls are quite varied: every category of API except for Archiving is represented in one of the tasks, and many of the tasks call multiple APIs which invoke fsync. In iWork, the sources are more consistent; the only sources are Pref Sync, SQLite, and Archiving (for manipulating compressed data).

Given that these tasks require durability for a significant percentage of their write traffic, we next investigate the frequency of fsync calls and how much data each individual call pushes to disk. Figure 12 groups fsync calls based on the amount of I/O performed on each file descriptor when fsync is called, and displays the relative percentage each category comprises of the total I/O.

These results show that iLife tasks call fsync frequently (from tens to thousands of times), while iWork tasks call fsync infrequently except when dealing with images. From these observations, we infer that calls to fsync are mostly associated with media. The majority of calls to fsync synchronize small amounts of data; only a few iLife tasks synchronize more than a megabyte of data in a single fsync call.

Summary: Developers want to ensure that data enters stable storage durably, and thus, these tasks synchronize a significant fraction of their data. Based on our analysis of the source of fsync calls, some calls may be incidental and an unintentional side-effect of the API (*e.g.*, those from SQLite or Pref Sync), but most are performed intentionally by the programmer. Furthermore, some of the tasks synchronize small amounts of data frequently, presenting a challenge for file systems.

Figure 11 legend: SQLite · Pref Sync · Archiving · writeToFile · FlushFork · Other · No fsync

iPhoto · iTunes · iMovie · Pages · Numbers · Keynote

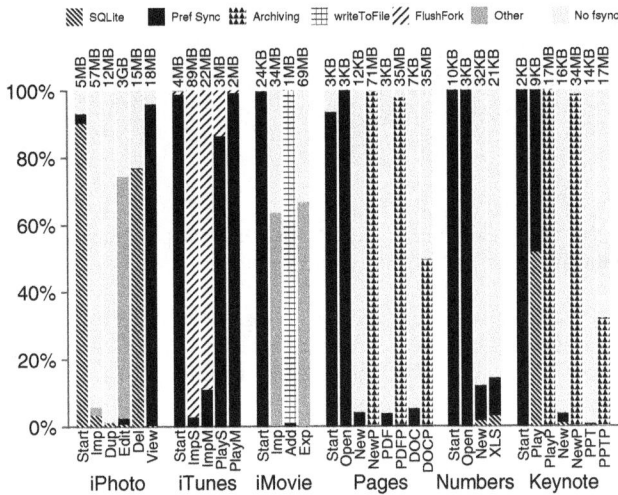

Figure 11: **Percentage of Fsync Bytes.** The percentage of fsync'd bytes written to file descriptors is shown, broken down by cause. The value atop each bar shows total bytes synchronized.

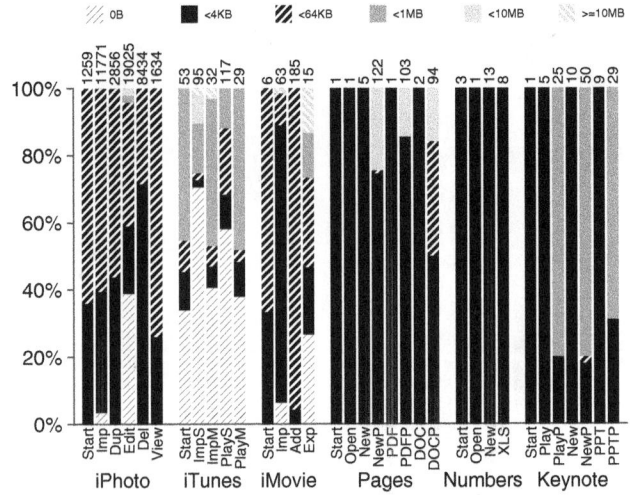

Figure 12 legend: 0B · <4KB · <64KB · <1MB · <10MB · >=10MB

iPhoto · iTunes · iMovie · Pages · Numbers · Keynote

Figure 12: **Fsync Sizes.** This plot shows a distribution of fsync sizes. The total number of fsync calls appears at the end of the bars.

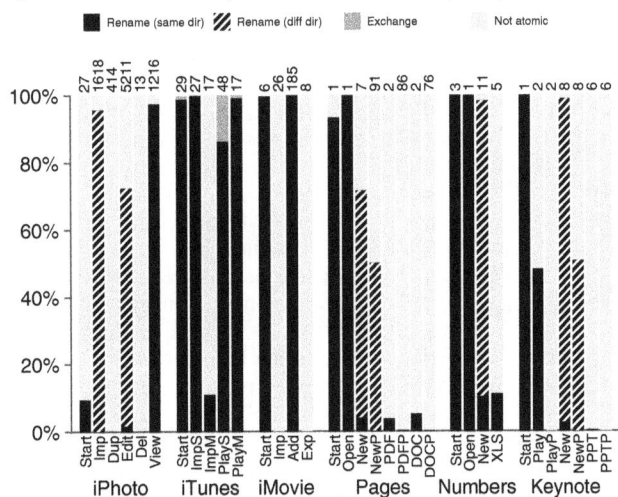

Figure 13 legend: Rename (same dir) · Rename (diff dir) · Exchange · Not atomic

iPhoto · iTunes · iMovie · Pages · Numbers · Keynote

Figure 13: **Atomic Writes.** The portion of written bytes written atomically is shown, divided into groups: (1) rename leaving a file in the same directory; (2) rename causing a file to change directories; (3) exchangedata which never causes a directory change. The atomic file-write count appears atop each bar.

Figure 14 legend: Pref Sync · writeToFile · movePath · FSRenameUnicode · Other

iPhoto · iTunes · iMovie · Pages · Numbers · Keynote

Figure 14: **Rename Causes.** This plot shows the portion of rename calls caused by each of the top four higher level functions used for atomic writes. The number of rename calls appears at the end of the bars.

4.3.2 Atomic Writes

Applications often require file changes to be atomic. In this section, we quantify how frequently applications use different techniques to achieve atomicity. We also identify cases where performing writes atomically can interfere with directory locality optimizations by moving files from their original directories. Finally, we identify the causes of atomic writes.

Applications can atomically update a file by first writing the desired contents to a temporary file and then using either the rename or exchangedata call to atomically replace the old file with the new file. With rename, the new file is given the same name as the old, deleting the original and replacing it. With exchangedata, the inode numbers assigned to the old file and the temporary file are swapped, causing the old path to point to the new data; this allows the file path to remain associated with the original inode number, which is necessary for some applications.

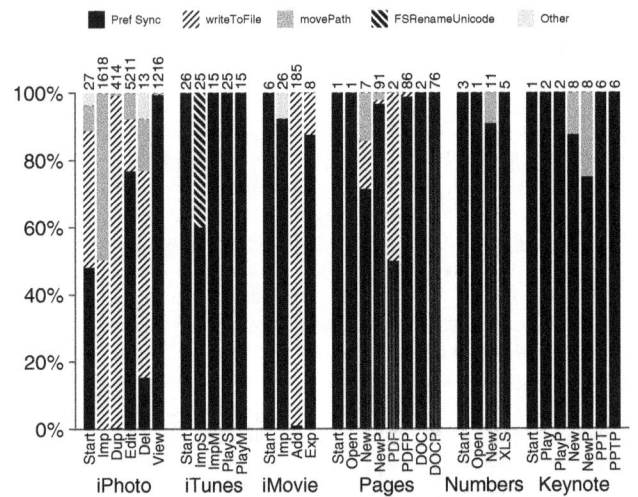

Figure 13 shows how much write I/O is performed atomically with rename or exchangedata; rename calls are further subdivided into those which keep the file in the same directory and those which do not. The results show that atomic writes are quite popular and that, in many workloads, all the writes are atomic. The breakdown of each bar shows that rename is frequent; a significant minority of the rename calls move files between directories. exchangedata is rare and used only by iTunes for a small fraction of file updates.

We find that most of the rename calls causing directory changes occur when a file (*e.g.*, a document or spreadsheet) is saved at the user's request. We suspect different directories are used so that users are not confused by seeing temporary files in their personal directories. Interestingly, atomic writes are performed when files are saved to Apple formats, but not when exporting to Microsoft formats. We suspect that the interface between applications and the Microsoft libraries does not specify atomic operations well.

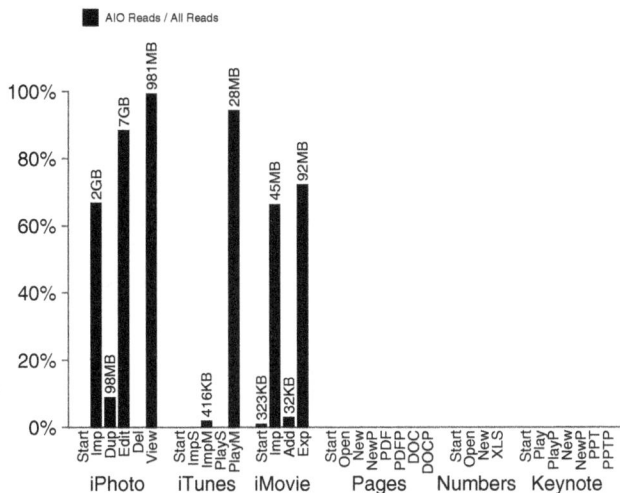

Figure 15: **Asynchronous Reads.** This plot shows the percentage of read bytes read asynchronously via `aio_read`. The total amount of asynchronous I/O is provided at the end of the bars.

Figure 14 identifies the APIs responsible for atomic writes via `rename`. *Pref Sync*, from the Cocoa library, allows applications to save user and system wide settings in .plist files. *WriteToFile* and *movePath* are Cocoa routines and *FSRenameUnicode* is a Carbon routine. A solid majority of the atomic writes are caused by Pref Sync; this is an example of I/O behavior caused by the API rather than explicit programmer intention. The second most common atomic writer is writeToFile; in this case, the programmer is requesting atomicity but leaving the technique up to the library. Finally, in a small minority of cases, programmers perform atomic writes themselves by calling movePath or FSRenameUnicode, both of which are essentially `rename` wrappers.

Summary: Many of our tasks write data atomically, generally doing so by calling `rename`. The bulk of atomic writes result from API calls; while some of these hide the underlying nature of the write, others make it clear that they act atomically. Thus, developers desire atomicity for many operations, and file systems will need to either address the ensuing renames that accompany it or provide an alternative mechanism for it. In addition, the absence of atomic writes when writing to Microsoft formats highlights the inconsistencies that can result from the use of high level libraries.

4.4 Threads and Asynchronicity

Home-user applications are interactive and need to avoid blocking when I/O is performed. Asynchronous I/O and threads are often used to hide the latency of slow operations from users. For our final experiments, we investigate how often applications use asynchronous I/O libraries or multiple threads to avoid blocking.

Figure 15 shows the portion of read operations performed asynchronously with `aio_read`; none of the tasks use `aio_write`. We find that asynchronous I/O is used rarely and only by iLife applications. However, in those cases where asynchronous I/O is performed, it is used quite heavily.

Figure 16 investigates how threads are used by these tasks: specifically, the portion of I/O performed by each of the threads. The numbers at the tops of the bars report the number of threads performing I/O. iPhoto and iTunes leverage a significant number of threads for I/O, since many of their tasks are readily subdivided (*e.g.*, importing 400 different photos). Only a handful of tasks perform all their I/O from a single thread. For most tasks, a small

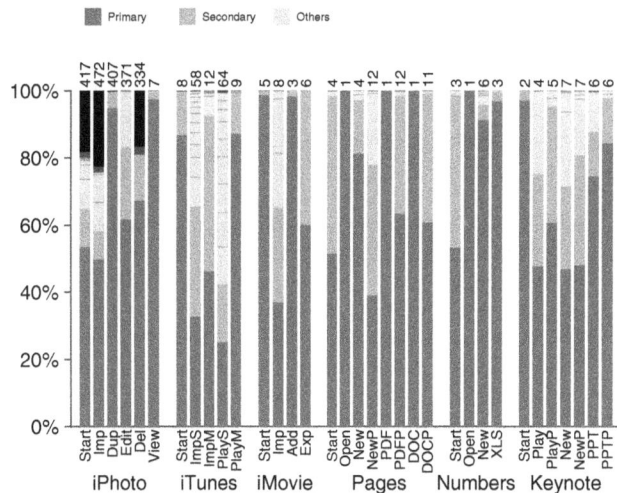

Figure 16: **I/O Distribution Among Threads.** The stacked bars indicate the percentage of total I/O performed by each thread. The I/O from the threads that do the most and second most I/O are dark and medium gray respectively, and the other threads are light gray. Black lines divide the I/O across the latter group; black areas appear when numerous threads do small amounts of I/O. The total number of threads that perform I/O is indicated next to the bars.

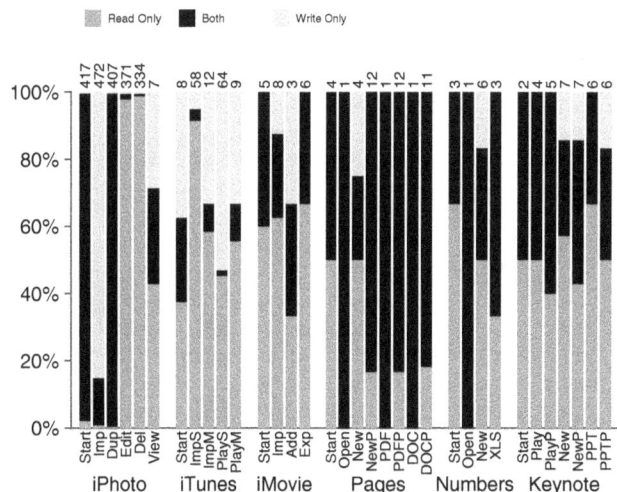

Figure 17: **Thread Type Distribution.** The plot categorizes threads that do I/O into three groups: threads that read, threads that write, or threads that both read and write. The total number of threads that perform I/O is indicated next to the bars.

number of threads are responsible for the majority of I/O.

Figure 17 shows the responsibilities of each thread that performs I/O, where a thread can be responsible for reading, writing, or both. The measurements show that significantly more threads are devoted to reading than to writing, with a fair number of threads responsible for both. These results indicate that threads are the preferred technique to avoiding blocking and that applications may be particularly concerned with avoiding blocking due to reads.

Summary: Our results indicate that iBench tasks are concerned with hiding long-latency operations from interactive users and that threads are the preferred method for doing so. Virtually all of the applications we study issue I/O requests from multiple threads, and some launch I/Os from hundreds of different threads.

5. RELATED WORK

Although our study is unique in its focus on the I/O behavior of individual applications, a body of similar work exists both in the field of file systems and in application studies. As mentioned earlier, our work builds upon that of Baker [4], Ousterhout [25], Vogels [39], and others who have conducted similar studies, providing an updated perspective on many of their findings. However, the majority of these focus on academic and engineering environments, which are likely to have noticeably different application profiles from the home environment. Some studies, like those by Ramakrishnan [31] and by Vogels, have included office workloads on personal computers; these are likely to feature applications similar to those in iWork, but are still unlikely to contain analogues to iLife products. None of these studies, however, look at the characteristics of individual application behaviors; instead, they analyze trends seen in prolonged usage. Thus, our study complements the breadth of this research with a more focused examination, providing specific information on the causes of the behaviors we observe, and is one of the first to address the interaction of multimedia applications with the file system.

In addition to these studies of dynamic workloads, a variety of papers have examined the static characteristics of file systems, starting with Satyanarayanan's analysis of files at Carnegie-Mellon University [36]. One of the most recent of these examined metadata characteristics on desktops at Microsoft over a five year time span, providing insight into file-system usage characteristics in a setting similar to the home [2]. This type of analysis provides insight into long term characteristics of files that ours cannot; a similar study for home systems would, in conjunction with our paper, provide a more complete image of how home applications interact with the file system.

While most file-system studies deal with aggregate workloads, our examination of application-specific behaviors has precedent in a number of hardware studies. In particular, Flautner et al.'s [13] and Blake et al.'s [6] studies of parallelism in desktop applications bear strong similarities to ours in the variety of applications they examine. In general, they use a broader set of applications, a difference that derives from the subjects studied. In particular, we select applications likely to produce interesting I/O behavior; many of the programs they use, like the video game Quake, are more likely to exercise threading than the file system. Finally it is worth noting that Blake et al. analyze Windows software using event tracing, which may prove a useful tool to conduct a similar application file-system study to ours in Windows.

6. DISCUSSION AND CONCLUSIONS

We have presented a detailed study of the I/O behavior of complex, modern applications. Through our measurements, we have discovered distinct differences between the tasks in the iBench suite and traditional workload studies. To conclude, we consider the possible effects of our findings on future file and storage systems.

We observed that many of the tasks in the iBench suite frequently force data to disk by invoking fsync, which has strong implications for file systems. Delayed writing has long been the basis of increasing file-system performance [34], but it is of greatly decreased utility given small synchronous writes. Thus, more study is required to understand why the developers of these applications and frameworks are calling these routines so frequently. For example, is data being flushed to disk to ensure ordering between writes, safety in the face of power loss, or safety in the face of application crashes? Finding appropriate solutions depends upon the answers to these questions. One possibility is for file systems to expose new interfaces to enable applications to better express their exact needs and desires for durability, consistency, and atomicity. Another possibility is that new technologies, such as flash and other solid-state devices, will be a key solution, allowing writes to be buffered quickly, perhaps before being staged to disk or even the cloud.

The iBench tasks also illustrate that file systems are now being treated as repositories of highly-structured "databases" managed by the applications themselves. In some cases, data is stored in a literal database (e.g., iPhoto uses SQLite), but in most cases, data is organized in complex directory hierarchies or within a single file (e.g., a .doc file is basically a mini-FAT file system). One option is that the file system could become more application-aware, tuned to understand important structures and to better allocate and access these structures on disk. For example, a smarter file system could improve its allocation and prefetching of "files" within a .doc file: seemingly non-sequential patterns in a complex file are easily deconstructed into accesses to metadata followed by streaming sequential access to data.

Our analysis also revealed the strong impact that frameworks and libraries have on I/O behavior. Traditionally, file systems have been designed at the level of the VFS interface, not breaking into the libraries themselves. However, it appears that file systems now need to take a more "vertical" approach and incorporate some of the functionality of modern libraries. This vertical approach hearkens back to the earliest days of file-system development when the developers of FFS modified standard libraries to buffer writes in block-sized chunks to avoid costly sub-block overheads [21]. Future storage systems should further integrate with higher-level interfaces to gain deeper understanding of application desires.

Finally, modern applications are highly complex, containing millions of lines of code, divided over hundreds of source files and libraries, and written by many different programmers. As a result, their own behavior is increasingly inconsistent: along similar, but distinct code paths, different libraries are invoked with different transactional semantics. To simplify these applications, file systems could add higher-level interfaces, easing construction and unifying data representations. While the systems community has developed influential file-system concepts, little has been done to transition this class of improvements into the applications themselves. Database technology does support a certain class of applications quite well but is generally too heavyweight. Future storage systems should consider how to bridge the gap between the needs of current applications and the features low-level systems provide.

Our evaluation may raise more questions than it answers. To build better systems for the future, we believe that the research community must study applications that are important to real users. We believe the iBench task suite takes a first step in this direction and hope others in the community will continue along this path.

Acknowledgments

We thank the anonymous reviewers and Rebecca Isaacs (our shepherd) for their tremendous feedback, as well as members of our research group for their thoughts and comments on this work at various stages.

This material is based upon work supported by the National Science Foundation under CSR-1017518 as well as by generous donations from Network Appliance and Google. Tyler Harter and Chris Dragga are supported by the Guri Sohi Fellowship and the David DeWitt Fellowship, respectively.

Any opinions, findings, and conclusions or recommendations expressed in this material are those of the authors and do not necessarily reflect the views of NSF or other institutions.

7. REFERENCES

[1] N. Agrawal, A. C. Arpaci-Dusseau, and R. H. Arpaci-Dusseau. Generating Realistic Impressions for File-System Benchmarking. In *FAST '09*, San Jose, CA, February 2009.

[2] N. Agrawal, W. J. Bolosky, J. R. Douceur, and J. R. Lorch. A Five-Year Study of File-System Metadata. In *FAST '07*, San Jose, CA, February 2007.

[3] Apple Computer, Inc. AppleScript Language Guide, March 2011.

[4] M. Baker, J. Hartman, M. Kupfer, K. Shirriff, and J. Ousterhout. Measurements of a Distributed File System. In *SOSP '91*, pages 198–212, Pacific Grove, CA, October 1991.

[5] W. Bartlett and L. Spainhower. Commercial Fault Tolerance: A Tale of Two Systems. *IEEE Transactions on Dependable and Secure Computing*, 1(1):87–96, January 2004.

[6] G. Blake, R. G. Dreslinski, T. Mudge, and K. Flautner. Evolution of Thread-level Parallelism in Desktop Applications. *SIGARCH Comput. Archit. News*, 38:302–313, June 2010.

[7] J. Bonwick and B. Moore. ZFS: The Last Word in File Systems. http://opensolaris.org/os/community/zfs/docs/zfs_last.pdf, 2007.

[8] B. Cantrill, M. W. Shapiro, and A. H. Leventhal. Dynamic Instrumentation of Production Systems. In *USENIX '04*, pages 15–28, Boston, MA, June 2004.

[9] G. DeCandia, D. Hastorun, M. Jampani, G. Kakulapati, A. Lakshman, A. Pilchin, S. Sivasubramanian, P. Vosshall, and W. Vogels. Dynamo: Amazon's Highly Available Key-Value Store. In *SOSP '07*, Stevenson, WA, October 2007.

[10] J. R. Douceur and W. J. Bolosky. A Large-Scale Study of File-System Contents. In *SIGMETRICS '99*, pages 59–69, Atlanta, GA, May 1999.

[11] D. Ellard and M. I. Seltzer. New NFS Tracing Tools and Techniques for System Analysis. In *LISA '03*, pages 73–85, San Diego, CA, October 2003.

[12] Y. Endo, Z. Wang, J. B. Chen, and M. Seltzer. Using Latency to Evaluate Interactive System Performance. In *OSDI '96*, Seattle, WA, October 1994.

[13] K. Flautner, R. Uhlig, S. Reinhardt, and T. Mudge. Thread-level Parallelism and Interactive Performance of Desktop Applications. *SIGPLAN Not.*, 35:129–138, November 2000.

[14] S. Ghemawat, H. Gobioff, and S.-T. Leung. The Google File System. In *SOSP '03*, pages 29–43, Bolton Landing, NY, October 2003.

[15] R. Hagmann. Reimplementing the Cedar File System Using Logging and Group Commit. In *SOSP '87*, Austin, TX, November 1987.

[16] J. Howard, M. Kazar, S. Menees, D. Nichols, M. Satyanarayanan, R. Sidebotham, and M. West. Scale and Performance in a Distributed File System. *ACM Transactions on Computer Systems*, 6(1), February 1988.

[17] B. Lampson. Computer Systems Research – Past and Present. SOSP 17 Keynote Lecture, December 1999.

[18] E. K. Lee and C. A. Thekkath. Petal: Distributed Virtual Disks. In *ASPLOS VII*, Cambridge, MA, October 1996.

[19] A. W. Leung, S. Pasupathy, G. R. Goodson, and E. L. Miller. Measurement and Analysis of Large-Scale Network File System Workloads. In *USENIX '08*, pages 213–226, Boston, MA, June 2008.

[20] Macintosh Business Unit (Microsoft). It's all in the numbers... blogs.msdn.com/b/macmojo/archive/2006/11/03/it-s-all-in-the-numbers.aspx, November 2006.

[21] M. K. McKusick, W. N. Joy, S. J. Leffler, and R. S. Fabry. A Fast File System for UNIX. *ACM Transactions on Computer Systems*, 2(3):181–197, August 1984.

[22] J. C. Mogul. A Better Update Policy. In *USENIX Summer '94*, Boston, MA, June 1994.

[23] J. Olson. Enhance Your Apps With File System Transactions. http://msdn.microsoft.com/en-us/magazine/cc163388.aspx, July 2007.

[24] J. Ousterhout. Why Threads Are A Bad Idea (for most purposes), September 1995.

[25] J. K. Ousterhout, H. D. Costa, D. Harrison, J. A. Kunze, M. Kupfer, and J. G. Thompson. A Trace-Driven Analysis of the UNIX 4.2 BSD File System. In *SOSP '85*, pages 15–24, Orcas Island, WA, December 1985.

[26] D. Patterson, G. Gibson, and R. Katz. A Case for Redundant Arrays of Inexpensive Disks (RAID). In *SIGMOD '88*, pages 109–116, Chicago, IL, June 1988.

[27] R. H. Patterson, G. A. Gibson, E. Ginting, D. Stodolsky, and J. Zelenka. Informed Prefetching and Caching. In *SOSP '95*, pages 79–95, Copper Mountain, CO, December 1995.

[28] R. Pike. Another Go at Language Design. http://www.stanford.edu/class/ee380/Abstracts/100428.html, April 2010.

[29] V. Prabhakaran, A. C. Arpaci-Dusseau, and R. H. Arpaci-Dusseau. Analysis and Evolution of Journaling File Systems. In *USENIX '05*, pages 105–120, Anaheim, CA, April 2005.

[30] V. Prabhakaran, L. N. Bairavasundaram, N. Agrawal, H. S. Gunawi, A. C. Arpaci-Dusseau, and R. H. Arpaci-Dusseau. IRON File Systems. In *SOSP '05*, pages 206–220, Brighton, UK, October 2005.

[31] K. K. Ramakrishnan, P. Biswas, and R. Karedla. Analysis of File I/O Traces in Commercial Computing Environments. *SIGMETRICS Perform. Eval. Rev.*, 20:78–90, June 1992.

[32] D. M. Ritchie and K. Thompson. The UNIX Time-Sharing System. In *SOSP '73*, Yorktown Heights, NY, October 1973.

[33] D. Roselli, J. R. Lorch, and T. E. Anderson. A Comparison of File System Workloads. In *USENIX '00*, pages 41–54, San Diego, CA, June 2000.

[34] M. Rosenblum and J. Ousterhout. The Design and Implementation of a Log-Structured File System. *ACM Transactions on Computer Systems*, 10(1):26–52, February 1992.

[35] R. Sandberg. The Design and Implementation of the Sun Network File System. In *Proceedings of the 1985 USENIX Summer Technical Conference*, pages 119–130, Berkeley, CA, June 1985.

[36] M. Satyanarayanan. A Study of File Sizes and Functional Lifetimes. In *SOSP '81*, pages 96–108, Pacific Grove, CA, December 1981.

[37] A. Sweeney, D. Doucette, W. Hu, C. Anderson, M. Nishimoto, and G. Peck. Scalability in the XFS File System. In *USENIX 1996*, San Diego, CA, January 1996.

[38] M. Tilmann. Apple's Market Share In The PC World Continues To Surge. maclife.com, April 2010.

[39] W. Vogels. File system usage in Windows NT 4.0. In *SOSP '99*, pages 93–109, Kiawah Island Resort, SC, December 1999.

[40] S. C. Woo, M. Ohara, E. Torrie, J. P. Shingh, and A. Gupta. The SPLASH-2 Programs: Characterization and Methodological Considerations. In *ISCA '95*, pages 24–36, Santa Margherita Ligure, Italy, June 1995.

CryptDB: Protecting Confidentiality with Encrypted Query Processing

Raluca Ada Popa, Catherine M. S. Redfield, Nickolai Zeldovich, and Hari Balakrishnan
MIT CSAIL

ABSTRACT

Online applications are vulnerable to theft of sensitive information because adversaries can exploit software bugs to gain access to private data, and because curious or malicious administrators may capture and leak data. CryptDB is a system that provides practical and provable confidentiality in the face of these attacks for applications backed by SQL databases. It works by *executing SQL queries over encrypted data* using a collection of efficient SQL-aware encryption schemes. CryptDB can also *chain encryption keys to user passwords*, so that a data item can be decrypted only by using the password of one of the users with access to that data. As a result, a database administrator never gets access to decrypted data, and even if all servers are compromised, an adversary cannot decrypt the data of any user who is not logged in. An analysis of a trace of 126 million SQL queries from a production MySQL server shows that CryptDB can support operations over encrypted data for 99.5% of the 128,840 columns seen in the trace. Our evaluation shows that CryptDB has low overhead, reducing throughput by 14.5% for phpBB, a web forum application, and by 26% for queries from TPC-C, compared to unmodified MySQL. Chaining encryption keys to user passwords requires 11–13 unique schema annotations to secure more than 20 sensitive fields and 2–7 lines of source code changes for three multi-user web applications.

Categories and Subject Descriptors: H.2.7 [**Database Management**]: Database Administration—*Security, integrity, and protection.*

General Terms: Security, design.

1 INTRODUCTION

Theft of private information is a significant problem, particularly for online applications [40]. An adversary can exploit software vulnerabilities to gain unauthorized access to servers [32]; curious or malicious administrators at a hosting or application provider can snoop on private data [6]; and attackers with physical access to servers can access all data on disk and in memory [23].

One approach to reduce the damage caused by server compromises is to encrypt sensitive data, as in SUNDR [28], SPORC [16], and Depot [30], and run all computations (application logic) on clients. Unfortunately, several important applications do not lend themselves to this approach, including database-backed web sites that process queries to generate data for the user, and applications

that compute over large amounts of data. Even when this approach is tenable, converting an existing server-side application to this form can be difficult. Another approach would be to consider theoretical solutions such as fully homomorphic encryption [19], which allows servers to compute arbitrary functions over encrypted data, while only clients see decrypted data. However, fully homomorphic encryption schemes are still prohibitively expensive by orders of magnitude [10, 21].

This paper presents CryptDB, a system that explores an intermediate design point to provide confidentiality for applications that use database management systems (DBMSes). CryptDB leverages the typical structure of database-backed applications, consisting of a DBMS server and a separate application server, as shown in Figure 1; the latter runs the application code and issues DBMS queries on behalf of one or more users. CryptDB's approach is to *execute queries over encrypted data*, and the key insight that makes it practical is that SQL uses a well-defined set of operators, each of which we are able to support efficiently over encrypted data.

CryptDB addresses two threats. The first threat is a curious database administrator (DBA) who tries to learn private data (e.g., health records, financial statements, personal information) by snooping on the DBMS server; here, CryptDB prevents the DBA from learning private data. The second threat is an adversary that gains complete control of application and DBMS servers. In this case, CryptDB cannot provide any guarantees for users that are logged into the application during an attack, but can still ensure the confidentiality of logged-out users' data.

There are two challenges in combating these threats. The first lies in the tension between minimizing the amount of confidential information revealed to the DBMS server and the ability to efficiently execute a variety of queries. Current approaches for computing over encrypted data are either too slow or do not provide adequate confidentiality, as we discuss in §9. On the other hand, encrypting data with a strong and efficient cryptosystem, such as AES, would prevent the DBMS server from executing many SQL queries, such as queries that ask for the number of employees in the "sales" department or for the names of employees whose salary is greater than $60,000. In this case, the only practical solution would be to give the DBMS server access to the decryption key, but that would allow an adversary to also gain access to all data.

The second challenge is to minimize the amount of data leaked when an adversary compromises the application server in addition to the DBMS server. Since arbitrary computation on encrypted data is not practical, the application must be able to access decrypted data. The difficulty is thus to ensure that a compromised application can obtain only a limited amount of decrypted data. A naïve solution of assigning each user a different database encryption key for their data does not work for applications with shared data, such as bulletin boards and conference review sites.

CryptDB addresses these challenges using three key ideas:

- The first is to execute SQL queries over encrypted data. CryptDB implements this idea using a *SQL-aware encryption strategy*, which leverages the fact that all SQL queries are made up of a

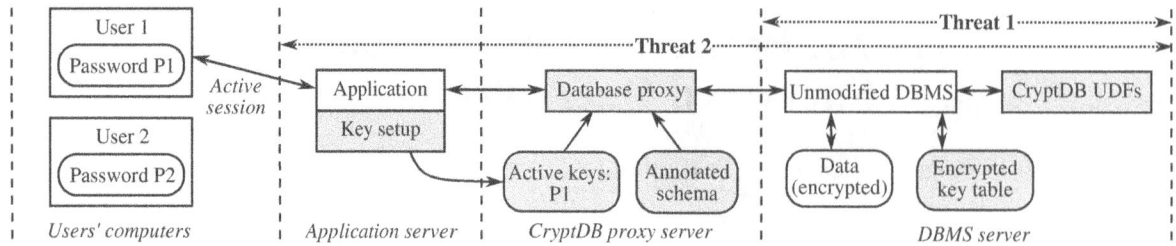

Figure 1: CryptDB's architecture consisting of two parts: a *database proxy* and an unmodified *DBMS*. CryptDB uses user-defined functions (UDFs) to perform cryptographic operations in the DBMS. Rectangular and rounded boxes represent processes and data, respectively. Shading indicates components added by CryptDB. Dashed lines indicate separation between users' computers, the application server, a server running CryptDB's database proxy (which is usually the same as the application server), and the DBMS server. CryptDB addresses two kinds of threats, shown as dotted lines. In threat 1, a curious database administrator with complete access to the DBMS server snoops on private data, in which case CryptDB prevents the DBA from accessing any private information. In threat 2, an adversary gains complete control over both the software and hardware of the application, proxy, and DBMS servers, in which case CryptDB ensures the adversary cannot obtain data belonging to users that are not logged in (e.g., user 2).

well-defined set of primitive operators, such as equality checks, order comparisons, aggregates (sums), and joins. By adapting known encryption schemes (for equality, additions, and order checks) and using a new privacy-preserving cryptographic method for joins, CryptDB encrypts each data item in a way that allows the DBMS to execute on the transformed data. CryptDB is efficient because it mostly uses symmetric-key encryption, avoids fully homomorphic encryption, and runs on unmodified DBMS software (by using user-defined functions).

- The second technique is *adjustable query-based encryption*. Some encryption schemes leak more information than others about the data to the DBMS server, but are required to process certain queries. To avoid revealing all possible encryptions of data to the DBMS *a priori*, CryptDB carefully *adjusts* the SQL-aware encryption scheme for any given data item, depending on the queries observed at run-time. To implement these adjustments efficiently, CryptDB uses *onions of encryption*. Onions are a novel way to compactly store multiple ciphertexts within each other in the database and avoid expensive re-encryptions.

- The third idea is to *chain encryption keys to user passwords*, so that each data item in the database can be decrypted only through a chain of keys rooted in the password of one of the users with access to that data. As a result, if the user is not logged into the application, and if the adversary does not know the user's password, the adversary cannot decrypt the user's data, even if the DBMS and the application server are fully compromised. To construct a chain of keys that captures the application's data privacy and sharing policy, CryptDB allows the developer to provide policy annotations over the application's SQL schema, specifying which users (or other principals, such as groups) have access to each data item.

We have implemented CryptDB on both MySQL and Postgres; our design and most of our implementation should be applicable to most standard SQL DBMSes. An analysis of a 10-day trace of 126 million SQL queries from many applications at MIT suggests that CryptDB can support operations over encrypted data for 99.5% of the 128,840 columns seen in the trace. Our evaluation shows that CryptDB has low overhead, reducing throughput by 14.5% for the phpBB web forum application, and by 26% for queries from TPC-C, compared to unmodified MySQL. We evaluated the security of CryptDB on six real applications (including phpBB, the HotCRP conference management software [27], and the OpenEMR medical records application); the results show that CryptDB protects most sensitive fields with highly secure encryption schemes. Chaining encryption keys to user passwords requires 11–13 unique schema annotations to enforce privacy policies on more than 20 sensitive

fields (including a new policy in HotCRP for handling papers in conflict with a PC chair) and 2–7 lines of source code changes for three multi-user web applications.

The rest of this paper is structured as follows. In §2, we discuss the threats that CryptDB defends against in more detail. Then, we describe CryptDB's design for encrypted query processing in §3 and for key chaining to user passwords in §4. In §5, we present several case studies of how applications can use CryptDB, and in §6, we discuss limitations of our design, and ways in which it can be extended. Next, we describe our prototype implementation in §7, and evaluate the performance and security of CryptDB, as well as the effort required for application developers to use CryptDB, in §8. We compare CryptDB to related work in §9 and conclude in §10.

2 SECURITY OVERVIEW

Figure 1 shows CryptDB's architecture and threat models. CryptDB works by intercepting all SQL queries in a *database proxy*, which rewrites queries to execute on encrypted data (CryptDB assumes that all queries go through the proxy). The proxy encrypts and decrypts all data, and changes some query operators, while preserving the semantics of the query. The DBMS server never receives decryption keys to the plaintext so it never sees sensitive data, ensuring that a curious DBA cannot gain access to private information (threat 1).

To guard against application, proxy, and DBMS server compromises (threat 2), developers annotate their SQL schema to define different *principals*, whose keys will allow decrypting different parts of the database. They also make a small change to their applications to provide encryption keys to the proxy, as described in §4. The proxy determines what parts of the database should be encrypted under what key. The result is that CryptDB guarantees the confidentiality of data belonging to users that are not logged in during a compromise (e.g., user 2 in Figure 1), and who do not log in until the compromise is detected and fixed by the administrator.

Although CryptDB protects data confidentiality, it does not ensure the integrity, freshness, or completeness of results returned to the application. An adversary that compromises the application, proxy, or DBMS server, or a malicious DBA, can delete any or all of the data stored in the database. Similarly, attacks on user machines, such as cross-site scripting, are outside of the scope of CryptDB.

We now describe the two threat models addressed by CryptDB, and the security guarantees provided under those threat models.

2.1 Threat 1: DBMS Server Compromise

In this threat, CryptDB guards against a curious DBA or other external attacker with full access to the data stored in the DBMS server. Our goal is confidentiality (data secrecy), not integrity or availability. The attacker is assumed to be *passive*: she wants to learn confidential data, but does not change queries issued by the application, query results, or the data in the DBMS. This threat includes DBMS software compromises, root access to DBMS machines, and even access to the RAM of physical machines. With the rise in database consolidation inside enterprise data centers, outsourcing of databases to public cloud computing infrastructures, and the use of third-party DBAs, this threat is increasingly important.

Approach. CryptDB aims to protect data confidentiality against this threat by executing SQL queries over encrypted data on the DBMS server. The proxy uses secret keys to encrypt all data inserted or included in queries issued to the DBMS. Our approach is to allow the DBMS server to perform query processing on encrypted data as it would on an unencrypted database, by enabling it to compute certain functions over the data items based on encrypted data. For example, if the DBMS needs to perform a GROUP BY on column c, the DBMS server should be able to determine which items in that column are equal to each other, but not the actual content of each item. Therefore, the proxy needs to enable the DBMS server to determine relationships among data necessary to process a query. By using SQL-aware encryption that adjusts dynamically to the queries presented, CryptDB is careful about what relations it reveals between tuples to the server. For instance, if the DBMS needs to perform only a GROUP BY on a column c, the DBMS server should not know the order of the items in column c, nor should it know any other information about other columns. If the DBMS is required to perform an ORDER BY, or to find the MAX or MIN, CryptDB reveals the order of items in that column, but not otherwise.

Guarantees. CryptDB provides confidentiality for data content and for names of columns and tables; CryptDB does not hide the overall table structure, the number of rows, the types of columns, or the approximate size of data in bytes. The security of CryptDB is *not perfect:* CryptDB reveals to the DBMS server relationships among data items that correspond to the *classes of computation* that queries perform on the database, such as comparing items for equality, sorting, or performing word search. The granularity at which CryptDB allows the DBMS to perform a class of computations is an entire column (or a group of joined columns, for joins), which means that even if a query requires equality checks for a few rows, executing that query on the server would require revealing that class of computation for an entire column. §3.1 describes how these classes of computation map to CryptDB's encryption schemes, and the information they reveal.

More intuitively, CryptDB provides the following properties:

- Sensitive data is never available in plaintext at the DBMS server.

- The information revealed to the DBMS server depends on the classes of computation required by the application's queries, subject to constraints specified by the application developer in the schema (§3.5.1):

  1. If the application requests no relational predicate filtering on a column, nothing about the data content leaks (other than its size in bytes).

  2. If the application requests equality checks on a column, CryptDB's proxy reveals which items repeat in that column (the histogram), but not the actual values.

  3. If the application requests order checks on a column, the proxy reveals the order of the elements in the column.

- The DBMS server cannot compute the (encrypted) results for queries that involve computation classes not requested by the application.

How close is CryptDB to "optimal" security? Fundamentally, optimal security is achieved by recent work in theoretical cryptography enabling any computation over encrypted data [18]; however, such proposals are prohibitively impractical. In contrast, CryptDB is practical, and in §8.3, we demonstrate that it also provides significant security in practice. Specifically, we show that all or almost all of the most sensitive fields in the tested applications remain encrypted with highly secure encryption schemes. For such fields, CryptDB provides optimal security, assuming their value is independent of the pattern in which they are accessed (which is the case for medical information, social security numbers, etc). CryptDB is not optimal for fields requiring more revealing encryption schemes, but we find that most such fields are semi-sensitive (such as timestamps).

Finally, we believe that a passive attack model is realistic because malicious DBAs are more likely to read the data, which may be hard to detect, than to change the data or query results, which is more likely to be discovered. In §9, we cite related work on data integrity that could be used in complement with our work. An active adversary that can insert or update data may be able to indirectly compromise confidentiality. For example, an adversary that modifies an email field in the database may be able to trick the application into sending a user's data to the wrong email address, when the user asks the application to email her a copy of her own data. Such active attacks on the DBMS fall under the second threat model, which we now discuss.

2.2 Threat 2: Arbitrary Threats

We now describe the second threat where the application server, proxy, and DBMS server infrastructures may be compromised arbitrarily. The approach in threat 1 is insufficient because an adversary can now get access to the keys used to encrypt the entire database.

The solution is to encrypt different data items (e.g., data belonging to different users) with different keys. To determine the key that should be used for each data item, developers annotate the application's database schema to express finer-grained confidentiality policies. A curious DBA still cannot obtain private data by snooping on the DBMS server (threat 1), and in addition, an adversary who compromises the application server or the proxy can now decrypt only data of currently logged-in users (which are stored in the proxy). Data of currently inactive users would be encrypted with keys not available to the adversary, and would remain confidential.

In this configuration, CryptDB provides strong guarantees in the face of *arbitrary* server-side compromises, including those that gain root access to the application or the proxy. CryptDB leaks at most the data of currently active users for the duration of the compromise, even if the proxy behaves in a Byzantine fashion. By "duration of a compromise", we mean the interval from the start of the compromise until any trace of the compromise has been erased from the system. For a read SQL injection attack, the duration of the compromise spans the attacker's SQL queries. In the above example of an adversary changing the email address of a user in the database, we consider the system compromised for as long as the attacker's email address persists in the database.

3 QUERIES OVER ENCRYPTED DATA

This section describes how CryptDB executes SQL queries over encrypted data. The threat model in this section is threat 1 from §2.1. The DBMS machines and administrators are not trusted, but the application and the proxy are trusted.

CryptDB enables the DBMS server to execute SQL queries on encrypted data almost as if it were executing the same queries on plaintext data. Existing applications do not need to be changed. The DBMS's query plan for an encrypted query is typically the same as for the original query, except that the operators comprising the query, such as selections, projections, joins, aggregates, and orderings, are performed on ciphertexts, and use modified operators in some cases.

CryptDB's proxy stores a secret master key MK, the database schema, and the current encryption layers of all columns. The DBMS server sees an anonymized schema (in which table and column names are replaced by opaque identifiers), encrypted user data, and some auxiliary tables used by CryptDB. CryptDB also equips the server with CryptDB-specific user-defined functions (UDFs) that enable the server to compute on ciphertexts for certain operations.

Processing a query in CryptDB involves four steps:

1. The application issues a query, which the proxy intercepts and rewrites: it anonymizes each table and column name, and, using the master key MK, encrypts each constant in the query with an encryption scheme best suited for the desired operation (§3.1).

2. The proxy checks if the DBMS server should be given keys to adjust encryption layers before executing the query, and if so, issues an UPDATE query at the DBMS server that invokes a UDF to adjust the encryption layer of the appropriate columns (§3.2).

3. The proxy forwards the encrypted query to the DBMS server, which executes it using standard SQL (occasionally invoking UDFs for aggregation or keyword search).

4. The DBMS server returns the (encrypted) query result, which the proxy decrypts and returns to the application.

3.1 SQL-aware Encryption

We now describe the encryption types that CryptDB uses, including a number of existing cryptosystems, an optimization of a recent scheme, and a new cryptographic primitive for joins. For each encryption type, we explain the security property that CryptDB requires from it, its functionality, and how it is implemented.

Random (RND). RND provides the maximum security in CryptDB: indistinguishability under an adaptive chosen-plaintext attack (IND-CPA); the scheme is probabilistic, meaning that two equal values are mapped to different ciphertexts with overwhelming probability. On the other hand, RND does not allow any computation to be performed efficiently on the ciphertext. An efficient construction of RND is to use a block cipher like AES or Blowfish in CBC mode together with a random initialization vector (IV). (We mostly use AES, except for integer values, where we use Blowfish for its 64-bit block size because the 128-bit block size of AES would cause the ciphertext to be significantly longer).

Since, in this threat model, CryptDB assumes the server does not change results, CryptDB does not require a stronger IND-CCA2 construction (which would be secure under a chosen-ciphertext attack). However, it would be straightforward to use an IND-CCA2-secure implementation of RND instead, such as a block cipher in UFE mode [13], if needed.

Deterministic (DET). DET has a slightly weaker guarantee, yet it still provides strong security: it leaks only which encrypted values correspond to the same data value, by deterministically generating the same ciphertext for the same plaintext. This encryption layer allows the server to perform equality checks, which means it can perform selects with equality predicates, equality joins, GROUP BY, COUNT, DISTINCT, etc.

In cryptographic terms, DET should be a pseudo-random permutation (PRP) [20]. For 64-bit and 128-bit values, we use a block cipher with a matching block size (Blowfish and AES respectively); we make the usual assumption that the AES and Blowfish block ciphers are PRPs. We pad smaller values out to 64 bits, but for data that is longer than a single 128-bit AES block, the standard

CBC mode of operation leaks prefix equality (e.g., if two data items have an identical prefix that is at least 128 bits long). To avoid this problem, we use AES with a variant of the CMC mode [24], which can be approximately thought of as one round of CBC, followed by another round of CBC with the blocks in the reverse order. Since the goal of DET is to reveal equality, we use a zero IV (or "tweak" [24]) for our AES-CMC implementation of DET.

Order-preserving encryption (OPE). OPE allows order relations between data items to be established based on their encrypted values, without revealing the data itself. If $x < y$, then $OPE_K(x) < OPE_K(y)$, for any secret key K. Therefore, if a column is encrypted with OPE, the server can perform range queries when given encrypted constants $OPE_K(c_1)$ and $OPE_K(c_2)$ corresponding to the range $[c_1, c_2]$. The server can also perform ORDER BY, MIN, MAX, SORT, etc.

OPE is a weaker encryption scheme than DET because it reveals order. Thus, the CryptDB proxy will only reveal OPE-encrypted columns to the server if users request order queries on those columns. OPE has provable security guarantees [4]: the encryption is equivalent to a random mapping that preserves order.

The scheme we use [4] is the first provably secure such scheme. Until CryptDB, there was no implementation nor any measure of the practicality of the scheme. The direct implementation of the scheme took 25 ms per encryption of a 32-bit integer on an Intel 2.8 GHz Q9550 processor. We improved the algorithm by using AVL binary search trees for batch encryption (e.g., database loads), reducing the cost of OPE encryption to 7 ms per encryption without affecting its security. We also implemented a hypergeometric sampler that lies at the core of OPE, porting a Fortran implementation from 1988 [25].

Homomorphic encryption (HOM). HOM is a secure probabilistic encryption scheme (IND-CPA secure), allowing the server to perform computations on encrypted data with the final result decrypted at the proxy. While fully homomorphic encryption is prohibitively slow [10], homomorphic encryption for specific operations is efficient. To support summation, we implemented the Paillier cryptosystem [35]. With Paillier, multiplying the encryptions of two values results in an encryption of the sum of the values, i.e., $HOM_K(x) \cdot HOM_K(y) = HOM_K(x+y)$, where the multiplication is performed modulo some public-key value. To compute SUM aggregates, the proxy replaces SUM with calls to a UDF that performs Paillier multiplication on a column encrypted with HOM. HOM can also be used for computing averages by having the DBMS server return the sum and the count separately, and for incrementing values (e.g., SET $id=id+1$), on which we elaborate shortly.

With HOM, the ciphertext is 2048 bits. In theory, it should be possible to pack multiple values from a single row into one HOM ciphertext for that row, using the scheme of Ge and Zdonik [17], which would result in an amortized space overhead of $2\times$ (e.g., a 32-bit value occupies 64 bits) for a table with many HOM-encrypted columns. However, we have not implemented this optimization in our prototype. This optimization would also complicate partial-row UPDATE operations that reset some—but not all—of the values packed into a HOM ciphertext.

Join (JOIN and OPE-JOIN). A separate encryption scheme is necessary to allow equality joins between two columns, because we use different keys for DET to prevent cross-column correlations. JOIN also supports all operations allowed by DET, and also enables the server to determine repeating values between two columns. OPE-JOIN enables joins by order relations. We provide a new cryptographic scheme for JOIN and we discuss it in §3.4.

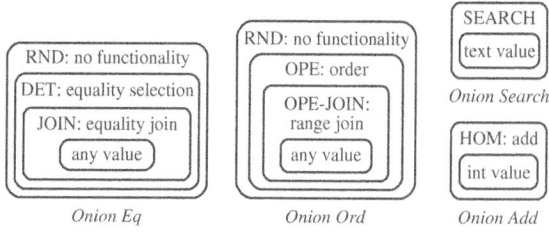

Figure 2: Onion encryption layers and the classes of computation they allow. Onion names stand for the operations they allow at some of their layers (Equality, Order, Search, and Addition). In practice, some onions or onion layers may be omitted, depending on column types or schema annotations provided by application developers (§3.5.2). DET and JOIN are often merged into a single onion layer, since JOIN is a concatenation of DET and JOIN-ADJ (§3.4). A random IV for RND (§3.1), shared by the RND layers in *Eq* and *Ord*, is also stored for each data item.

Word search (SEARCH).   SEARCH is used to perform searches on encrypted text to support operations such as MySQL's LIKE operator. We implemented the cryptographic protocol of Song et al. [46], which was not previously implemented by the authors; we also use their protocol in a different way, which results in better security guarantees. For each column needing SEARCH, we split the text into keywords using standard delimiters (or using a special keyword extraction function specified by the schema developer). We then remove repetitions in these words, randomly permute the positions of the words, and then encrypt each of the words using Song et al.'s scheme, padding each word to the same size. SEARCH is nearly as secure as RND: the encryption does not reveal to the DBMS server whether a certain word repeats in multiple rows, but it leaks the number of keywords encrypted with SEARCH; an adversary may be able to estimate the number of distinct or duplicate words (e.g., by comparing the size of the SEARCH and RND ciphertexts for the same data).

When the user performs a query such as SELECT * FROM *messages* WHERE *msg* LIKE "% alice %", the proxy gives the DBMS server a token, which is an encryption of alice. The server cannot decrypt the token to figure out the underlying word. Using a user-defined function, the DBMS server checks if any of the word encryptions in any message match the token. In our approach, all the server learns from searching is whether a token matched a message or not, and this happens only for the tokens requested by the user. The server would learn the same information when returning the result set to the users, so the overall search scheme reveals the minimum amount of additional information needed to return the result.

Note that SEARCH allows CryptDB to only perform full-word keyword searches; it cannot support arbitrary regular expressions. For applications that require searching for multiple adjacent words, CryptDB allows the application developer to disable duplicate removal and re-ordering by annotating the schema, even though this is not the default. Based on our trace evaluation, we find that most uses of LIKE can be supported by SEARCH with such schema annotations. Of course, one can still combine multiple LIKE operators with AND and OR to check whether multiple independent words are in the text.

3.2   Adjustable Query-based Encryption

A key part of CryptDB's design is *adjustable query-based encryption*, which dynamically adjusts the layer of encryption on the DBMS server. Our goal is to use the most secure encryption schemes that enable running the requested queries. For example, if the application issues no queries that compare data items in a column, or that sort a

column, the column should be encrypted with RND. For columns that require equality checks but not inequality checks, DET suffices. However, the query set is not always known in advance. Thus, we need an adaptive scheme that dynamically adjusts encryption strategies.

Our idea is to encrypt each data item in one or more *onions*: that is, each value is dressed in layers of increasingly stronger encryption, as illustrated in Figures 2 and 3. Each layer of each onion enables certain kinds of functionality as explained in the previous subsection. For example, outermost layers such as RND and HOM provide maximum security, whereas inner layers such as OPE provide more functionality.

Multiple onions are needed in practice, both because the computations supported by different encryption schemes are not always strictly ordered, and because of performance considerations (size of ciphertext and encryption time for nested onion layers). Depending on the type of the data (and any annotations provided by the application developer on the database schema, as discussed in §3.5.2), CryptDB may not maintain all onions for each column. For instance, the *Search* onion does not make sense for integers, and the *Add* onion does not make sense for strings.

For each layer of each onion, the proxy uses the same key for encrypting values in the same column, and different keys across tables, columns, onions, and onion layers. Using the same key for all values in a column allows the proxy to perform operations on a column without having to compute separate keys for each row that will be manipulated. (We use finer-grained encryption keys in §4 to reduce the potential amount of data disclosure in case of an application or proxy server compromise.) Using different keys across columns prevents the server from learning any additional relations. All of these keys are derived from the master key *MK*. For example, for table *t*, column *c*, onion *o*, and encryption layer *l*, the proxy uses the key

$$K_{t,c,o,l} = \text{PRP}_{MK}(\text{table } t, \text{column } c, \text{onion } o, \text{layer } l), \quad (1)$$

where PRP is a pseudorandom permutation (e.g., AES).

Each onion starts out encrypted with the most secure encryption scheme (RND for onions *Eq* and *Ord*, HOM for onion *Add*, and SEARCH for onion *Search*). As the proxy receives SQL queries from the application, it determines whether layers of encryption need to be removed. Given a predicate *P* on column *c* needed to execute a query on the server, the proxy first establishes what onion layer is needed to compute *P* on *c*. If the encryption of *c* is not already at an onion layer that allows *P*, the proxy strips off the onion layers to allow *P* on *c*, by sending the corresponding onion key to the server. The proxy never decrypts the data past the least-secure encryption onion layer (or past some other threshold layer, if specified by the application developer in the schema, §3.5.1).

CryptDB implements onion layer decryption using UDFs that run on the DBMS server. For example, in Figure 3, to decrypt onion *Ord* of column 2 in table 1 to layer OPE, the proxy issues the following query to the server using the DECRYPT_RND UDF:

```
UPDATE Table1 SET
          C2-Ord = DECRYPT_RND(K, C2-Ord, C2-IV)
```

where *K* is the appropriate key computed from Equation (1). At the same time, the proxy updates its own internal state to remember that column *C2-Ord* in *Table1* is now at layer OPE in the DBMS. Each column decryption should be included in a transaction to avoid consistency problems with clients accessing columns being adjusted.

Note that onion decryption is performed entirely by the DBMS server. In the steady state, no server-side decryptions are needed, because onion decryption happens only when a new class of computation is requested on a column. For example, after an equality

Employees		Table1							
ID	Name	C1-IV	C1-Eq	C1-Ord	C1-Add	C2-IV	C2-Eq	C2-Ord	C2-Search
23	Alice	x27c3	x2b82	xcb94	xc2e4	x8a13	xd1e3	x7eb1	x29b0

Figure 3: Data layout at the server. When the application creates the table shown on the left, the table created at the DBMS server is the one shown on the right. Ciphertexts shown are not full-length.

check is requested on a column and the server brings the column to layer DET, the column remains in that state, and future queries with equality checks require no decryption. This property is the insight into why CryptDB's overhead is modest in the steady state (see §8): the server mostly performs typical SQL processing.

3.3 Executing over Encrypted Data

Once the onion layers in the DBMS are at the layer necessary to execute a query, the proxy transforms the query to operate on these onions. In particular, the proxy replaces column names in a query with corresponding onion names, based on the class of computation performed on that column. For example, for the schema shown in Figure 3, a reference to the *Name* column for an equality comparison will be replaced with a reference to the *C2-Eq* column.

The proxy also replaces each constant in the query with a corresponding onion encryption of that constant, based on the computation in which it is used. For instance, if a query contains WHERE Name = 'Alice', the proxy encrypts 'Alice' by successively applying all encryption layers corresponding to onion *Eq* that have not yet been removed from *C2-Eq*.

Finally, the server replaces certain operators with UDF-based counterparts. For instance, the SUM aggregate operator and the + column-addition operator must be replaced with an invocation of a UDF that performs HOM addition of ciphertexts. Equality and order operators (such as = and <) do not need such replacement and can be applied directly to the DET and OPE ciphertexts.

Once the proxy has transformed the query, it sends the query to the DBMS server, receives query results (consisting of encrypted data), decrypts the results using the corresponding onion keys, and sends the decrypted result to the application.

Read query execution. To understand query execution over ciphertexts, consider the example schema shown in Figure 3. Initially, each column in the table is dressed in all onions of encryption, with RND, HOM, and SEARCH as outermost layers, as shown in Figure 2. At this point, the server can learn nothing about the data other than the number of columns, rows, and data size.

To illustrate when onion layers are removed, consider the query:

SELECT ID FROM Employees WHERE Name = 'Alice',

which requires lowering the encryption of *Name* to layer DET. To execute this query, the proxy first issues the query

UPDATE Table1 SET
    C2-Eq = DECRYPT_RND($K_{T1,C2,Eq,RND}$, C2-Eq, C2-IV),

where column *C2* corresponds to *Name*. The proxy then issues

SELECT C1-Eq, C1-IV FROM Table1 WHERE C2-Eq = x7..d,

where column *C1* corresponds to *ID*, and where x7..d is the *Eq* onion encryption of "Alice" with keys $K_{T1,C2,Eq}$.JOIN and $K_{T1,C2,Eq}$.DET (see Figure 2). Note that the proxy must request the random IV from column C1-IV in order to decrypt the RND ciphertext from C1-Eq. Finally, the proxy decrypts the results from the server using keys $K_{T1,C1,Eq,RND}$, $K_{T1,C1,Eq,DET}$, and $K_{T1,C1,Eq,JOIN}$, obtains the result 23, and returns it to the application.

If the next query is SELECT COUNT(*) FROM Employees WHERE Name = 'Bob', no server-side decryptions are necessary, and the proxy directly issues the query SELECT COUNT(*) FROM

Table1 WHERE C2-Eq = xbb..4a, where xbb..4a is the *Eq* onion encryption of "Bob" using $K_{T1,C2,Eq}$.JOIN and $K_{T1,C2,Eq,DET}$.

Write query execution. To support INSERT, DELETE, and UPDATE queries, the proxy applies the same processing to the predicates (i.e., the WHERE clause) as for read queries. DELETE queries require no additional processing. For all INSERT and UPDATE queries that set the value of a column to a constant, the proxy encrypts each inserted column's value with each onion layer that has not yet been stripped off in that column.

The remaining case is an UPDATE that sets a column value based on an existing column value, such as *salary=salary*+1. Such an update would have to be performed using HOM, to handle additions. However, in doing so, the values in the OPE and DET onions would become stale. In fact, any hypothetical encryption scheme that simultaneously allows addition and direct comparison on the ciphertext is insecure: if a malicious server can compute the order of the items, and can increment the value by one, the server can repeatedly add one to each field homomorphically until it becomes equal to some other value in the same column. This would allow the server to compute the difference between any two values in the database, which is almost equivalent to knowing their values.

There are two approaches to allow updates based on existing column values. If a column is incremented and then only projected (no comparisons are performed on it), the solution is simple: when a query requests the value of this field, the proxy should request the HOM ciphertext from the *Add* onion, instead of ciphertexts from other onions, because the HOM value is up-to-date. For instance, this approach applies to increment queries in TPC-C. If a column is used in comparisons after it is incremented, the solution is to replace the update query with two queries: a SELECT of the old values to be updated, which the proxy increments and encrypts accordingly, followed by an UPDATE setting the new values. This strategy would work well for updates that affect a small number of rows.

Other DBMS features. Most other DBMS mechanisms, such as transactions and indexing, work the same way with CryptDB over encrypted data as they do over plaintext, with no modifications. For transactions, the proxy passes along any BEGIN, COMMIT, and ABORT queries to the DBMS. Since many SQL operators behave differently on NULLs than on non-NULL values, CryptDB exposes NULL values to the DBMS without encryption. CryptDB does not currently support stored procedures, although certain stored procedures could be supported by rewriting their code in the same way that CryptDB's proxy rewrites SQL statements.

The DBMS builds indexes for encrypted data in the same way as for plaintext. Currently, if the application requests an index on a column, the proxy asks the DBMS server to build indexes on that column's DET, JOIN, OPE, or OPE-JOIN onion layers (if they are exposed), but not for RND, HOM, or SEARCH. More efficient index selection algorithms could be investigated.

3.4 Computing Joins

There are two kinds of joins supported by CryptDB: *equi-joins*, in which the join predicate is based on equality, and *range joins*, which involve order checks. To perform an equi-join of two encrypted columns, the columns should be encrypted with the same key so that the server can see matching values between the two columns. At the same time, to provide better privacy, the DBMS server should not be able to join columns for which the application did not request a join, so columns that are never joined should not be encrypted with the same keys.

If the queries that can be issued, or the pairs of columns that can be joined, are known *a priori*, equi-join is easy to support: CryptDB can use the DET encryption scheme with the same key for each group of columns that are joined together. §3.5 describes how the proxy learns the columns to be joined in this case. However, the challenging case is when the proxy does not know the set of columns to be joined *a priori*, and hence does not know which columns should be encrypted with matching keys.

To solve this problem, we introduce a new cryptographic primitive, JOIN-ADJ (*adjustable join*), which allows the DBMS server to adjust the key of each column at runtime. Intuitively, JOIN-ADJ can be thought of as a keyed cryptographic hash with the additional property that hashes can be adjusted to change their key *without access to the plaintext*. JOIN-ADJ is a deterministic function of its input, which means that if two plaintexts are equal, the corresponding JOIN-ADJ values are also equal. JOIN-ADJ is collision-resistant, and has a sufficiently long output length (192 bits) to allow us to assume that collisions never happen in practice.

JOIN-ADJ is non-invertible, so we define the JOIN encryption scheme as $\text{JOIN}(v) = \text{JOIN-ADJ}(v) \parallel \text{DET}(v)$, where $\parallel$ denotes concatenation. This construction allows the proxy to decrypt a $\text{JOIN}(v)$ column to obtain v by decrypting the DET component, and allows the DBMS server to check two JOIN values for equality by comparing the JOIN-ADJ components.

Each column is initially encrypted at the JOIN layer using a different key, thus preventing any joins between columns. When a query requests a join, the proxy gives the DBMS server an onion key to adjust the JOIN-ADJ values in one of the two columns, so that it matches the JOIN-ADJ key of the other column (denoted the *join-base* column). After the adjustment, the columns share the same JOIN-ADJ key, allowing the DBMS server to join them for equality. The DET components of JOIN remain encrypted with different keys.

Note that our adjustable join is transitive: if the user joins columns A and B and then joins columns B and C, the server can join A and C. However, the server cannot join columns in different "transitivity groups". For instance, if columns D and E were joined together, the DBMS server would not be able to join columns A and D on its own.

After an initial join query, the JOIN-ADJ values remain transformed with the same key, so no re-adjustments are needed for subsequent join queries between the same two columns. One exception is if the application issues another query, joining one of the adjusted columns with a third column, which causes the proxy to re-adjust the column to another join-base. To avoid oscillations and to converge to a state where all columns in a transitivity group share the same join-base, CryptDB chooses the first column in lexicographic order on table and column name as the join-base. For n columns, the overall maximum number of join transitions is $n(n-1)/2$.

For range joins, a similar dynamic re-adjustment scheme is difficult to construct due to lack of structure in OPE schemes. Instead, CryptDB requires that pairs of columns that will be involved in such joins be declared by the application ahead of time, so that matching keys are used for layer OPE-JOIN of those columns; otherwise, the same key will be used for all columns at layer OPE-JOIN. Fortunately, range joins are rare; they are not used in any of our example applications, and are used in only 50 out of 128,840 columns in a large SQL query trace we describe in §8, corresponding to just three distinct applications.

JOIN-ADJ construction. Our algorithm uses elliptic-curve cryptography (ECC). JOIN-ADJ$_K(v)$ is computed as

$$\text{JOIN-ADJ}_K(v) := P^{K \cdot \text{PRF}_{K_0}(v)}, \tag{2}$$

where K is the initial key for that table, column, onion, and layer, P is a point on an elliptic curve (being a public parameter), and PRF_{K_0} is a pseudo-random function [20] mapping values to a pseudorandom number, such as $\text{AES}_{K_0}(\text{SHA}(v))$, with K_0 being a key that is the

same for all columns and derived from MK. The "exponentiation" is in fact repeated geometric addition of elliptic curve points; it is considerably faster than RSA exponentiation.

When a query joins columns c and c', each having keys K and K' at the join layer, the proxy computes $\Delta K = K/K'$ (in an appropriate group) and sends it to the server. Then, given JOIN-ADJ$_{K'}(v)$ (the JOIN-ADJ values from column c') and ΔK, the DBMS server uses a UDF to adjust the key in c' by computing:

$$(\text{JOIN-ADJ}_{K'}(v))^{\Delta K} = P^{K' \cdot \text{PRF}_{K_0}(v) \cdot (K/K')}$$

$$= P^{K \cdot \text{PRF}_{K_0}(v)} = \text{JOIN-ADJ}_K(v).$$

Now columns c and c' share the same JOIN-ADJ key, and the DBMS server can perform an equi-join on c and c' by taking the JOIN-ADJ component of the JOIN onion ciphertext.

At a high level, the security of this scheme is that the server cannot infer join relations among groups of columns that were not requested by legitimate join queries, and that the scheme does not reveal the plaintext. We proved the security of this scheme based on the standard Elliptic-Curve Decisional Diffie-Hellman hardness assumption, and implemented it using a NIST-approved elliptic curve. We plan to publish a more detailed description of this algorithm and the proof on our web site [37].

3.5 Improving Security and Performance

Although CryptDB can operate with an unmodified and unannotated schema, as described above, its security and performance can be improved through several optional optimizations, as described below.

3.5.1 Security Improvements

Minimum onion layers. Application developers can specify the lowest onion encryption layer that may be revealed to the server for a specific column. In this way, the developer can ensure that the proxy will not execute queries exposing sensitive relations to the server. For example, the developer could specify that credit card numbers should always remain at RND or DET.

In-proxy processing. Although CryptDB can evaluate a number of predicates on the server, evaluating them in the proxy can improve security by not revealing additional information to the server. One common use case is a SELECT query that sorts on one of the selected columns, without a LIMIT on the number of returned columns. Since the proxy receives the entire result set from the server, sorting these results in the proxy does not require a significant amount of computation, and does not increase the bandwidth requirements. Doing so avoids revealing the OPE encryption of that column to the server.

Training mode. CryptDB provides a training mode, which allows a developer to provide a trace of queries and get the resulting onion encryption layers for each field, along with a warning in case some query is not supported. The developer can then examine the resulting encryption levels to understand what each encryption scheme leaks, as described in §2.1. If some onion level is too low for a sensitive field, she should arrange to have the query processed in the proxy (as described above), or to process the data in some other fashion, such as by using a local instance of SQLite.

Onion re-encryption. In cases when an application performs infrequent queries requiring a low onion layer (e.g., OPE), CryptDB could be extended to re-encrypt onions back to a higher layer after the infrequent query finishes executing. This approach reduces leakage to attacks happening in the time window when the data is at the higher onion layer.

3.5.2 Performance Optimizations

Developer annotations. By default, CryptDB encrypts all fields and creates all applicable onions for each data item based on its type. If many columns are not sensitive, the developer can instead provide explicit annotations indicating the sensitive fields (as described in §4), and leave the remaining fields in plaintext.

Known query set. If the developer knows some of the queries ahead of time, as is the case for many web applications, the developer can use the training mode described above to adjust onions to the correct layer *a priori*, avoiding the overhead of runtime onion adjustments. If the developer provides the exact query set, or annotations that certain functionality is not needed on some columns, CryptDB can also discard onions that are not needed (e.g., discard the *Ord* onion for columns that are not used in range queries, or discard the *Search* onion for columns where keyword search is not performed), discard onion layers that are not needed (e.g., the adjustable JOIN layer, if joins are known *a priori*), or discard the random IV needed for RND for some columns.

Ciphertext pre-computing and caching. The proxy spends a significant amount of time encrypting values used in queries with OPE and HOM. To reduce this cost, the proxy pre-computes (for HOM) and caches (for OPE) encryptions of frequently used constants under different keys. Since HOM is probabilistic, ciphertexts cannot be reused. Therefore, in addition, the proxy pre-computes HOM's Paillier r^n randomness values for future encryptions of any data. This optimization reduces the amount of CPU time spent by the proxy on OPE encryption, and assuming the proxy is occasionally idle to perform HOM pre-computation, it removes HOM encryption from the critical path.

4 MULTIPLE PRINCIPALS

We now extend the threat model to the case when the application infrastructure and proxy are also untrusted (threat 2). This model is especially relevant for a multi-user web site running a web and application server. To understand both the problems faced by a multi-user web application and CryptDB's solution to these problems, consider phpBB, a popular online web forum. In phpBB, each user has an account and a password, belongs to certain groups, and can send private messages to other users. Depending on their groups' permissions, users can read entire forums, only forum names, or not be able to read a forum at all.

There are several confidentiality guarantees that would be useful in phpBB. For example, we would like to ensure that a private message sent from one user to another is not visible to anyone else; that posts in a forum are accessible only to users in a group with access to that forum; and that the name of a forum is shown only to users belonging to a group that's allowed to view it. CryptDB provides these guarantees in the face of arbitrary compromises, thereby limiting the damage caused by a compromise.

Achieving these guarantees requires addressing two challenges. First, CryptDB must capture the application's access control policy for shared data at the level of SQL queries. To do this, CryptDB requires developers to annotate their database schema to specify principals and the data that each principal has access to, as described in §4.1.

The second challenge is to reduce the amount of information that an adversary can gain by compromising the system. Our solution limits the leakage resulting from a compromised application or proxy server to just the data accessible to users who were logged in during the compromise. In particular, the attacker cannot access the data of users that were not logged in during the compromise. Leaking the data of active users in case of a compromise is unavoidable: given the impracticality of arbitrary computation on encrypted data, some data for active users must be decrypted by the application.

In CryptDB, each user has a key (e.g., her application-level password) that gives her access to her data. CryptDB encrypts different data items with different keys, and enforces the access control policy using chains of keys starting from user passwords and ending in the encryption keys of SQL data items, as described in §4.2. When a user logs in, she provides her password to the proxy (via the application). The proxy uses this password to derive onion keys to process queries on encrypted data, as presented in the previous section, and to decrypt the results. The proxy can decrypt only the data that the user has access to, based on the access control policy. The proxy gives the decrypted data to the application, which can now compute on it. When the user logs out, the proxy deletes the user's key.

4.1 Policy Annotations

To express the data privacy policy of a database-backed application at the level of SQL queries, the application developer can annotate the schema of a database in CryptDB by specifying, for any subset of data items, which *principal* has access to it. A principal is an entity, such as a user or a group, over which it is natural to specify an access policy. Each SQL query involving an annotated data item requires the privilege of the corresponding principal. CryptDB defines its own notion of principals instead of using existing DBMS principals for two reasons: first, many applications do not map application-level users to DBMS principals in a sufficiently fine-grained manner, and second, CryptDB requires explicit delegation of privileges between principals that is difficult to extract in an automated way from an access control list specification.

An application developer annotates the schema using the three steps described below and illustrated in Figure 4. In all examples we show, italics indicate table and column names, and bold text indicates annotations added for CryptDB.

Step 1. The developer must define the *principal types* (using PRINCTYPE) used in her application, such as users, groups, or messages. A *principal* is an instance of a principal type, e.g., principal 5 of type user. There are two classes of principals: external and internal. External principals correspond to end users who explicitly authenticate themselves to the application using a password. When a user logs into the application, the application must provide the user password to the proxy so that the user can get the privileges of her external principal. Privileges of other (internal) principals can be acquired only through delegation, as described in Step 3. When the user logs out, the application must inform the proxy, so that the proxy forgets the user's password as well as any keys derived from the user's password.

Step 2. The developer must specify which columns in her SQL schema contain sensitive data, along with the principals that should have access to that data, using the ENC_FOR annotation. CryptDB requires that for each private data item in a row, the name of the principal that should have access to that data be stored in another column in the same row. For example, in Figure 4, the decryption of *msgtext* x37a21f is available only to principal 5 of type msg.

Step 3. Programmers can specify rules for how to delegate the privileges of one principal to other principals, using the speaks-for relation [49]. For example, in phpBB, a user should also have the privileges of the groups she belongs to. Since many applications store such information in tables, programmers can specify to CryptDB how to infer delegation rules from rows in an existing table. In particular, programmers can annotate a table T with (a x) SPEAKS_FOR (b y). This annotation indicates that each row present in that table specifies that principal a of type x speaks for

```
PRINCTYPE physical_user EXTERNAL;
PRINCTYPE user, msg;

CREATE TABLE privmsgs (
  msgid   int,
  subject  varchar(255) ENC_FOR (msgid msg),
  msgtext text        ENC_FOR (msgid msg) );

CREATE TABLE privmsgs_to (
  msgid int,  rcpt_id int,  sender_id int,
  (sender_id user) SPEAKS_FOR (msgid msg),
  (rcpt_id user)   SPEAKS_FOR (msgid msg) );

CREATE TABLE users (
  userid int,  username varchar(255),
  (username physical_user) SPEAKS_FOR (userid user) );
```

Example table contents, without anonymized column names:

Table *privmsgs*

msgid	subject	msgtext
5	xcc82fa	x37a21f

Table *users*

userid	username
1	'Alice'
2	'Bob'

Table *privmsgs_to*

msgid	rcpt_id	sender_id
5	1	2

Figure 4: Part of phpBB's schema with annotations to secure private messages. Only the sender and receiver may see the private message. An attacker that gains complete access to phpBB and the DBMS can access private messages of only currently active users.

principal b of type y, meaning that a has access to all keys that b has access to. Here, x and y must always be fixed principal types. Principal b is always specified by the name of a column in table T. On the other hand, a can be either the name of another column in the same table, a constant, or $T2.col$, meaning *all* principals from column col of table $T2$. For example, in Figure 4, principal "Bob" of type physical_user speaks for principal 2 of type user, and in Figure 6, all principals in the *contactId* column from table *PCMember* (of type contact) speak for the *paperId* principal of type review. Optionally, the programmer can specify a predicate, whose inputs are values in the same row, to specify a condition under which delegation should occur, such as excluding conflicts in Figure 6. §5 provides more examples of using annotations to secure applications.

4.2 Key Chaining

Each principal (i.e., each instance of each principal type) is associated with a secret, randomly chosen key. If principal B speaks for principal A (as a result of some SPEAKS_FOR annotation), then principal A's key is encrypted using principal B's key, and stored as a row in the special *access_keys* table in the database. This allows principal B to gain access to principal A's key. For example, in Figure 4, to give users 1 and 2 access to message 5, the key of msg 5 is encrypted with the key of user 1, and also separately encrypted with the key of user 2.

Each sensitive field is encrypted with the key of the principal in the ENC_FOR annotation. CryptDB encrypts the sensitive field with onions in the same way as for single-principal CryptDB, except that onion keys are derived from a principal's key as opposed to a global master key.

The key of each principal is a combination of a symmetric key and a public–private key pair. In the common case, CryptDB uses the symmetric key of a principal to encrypt any data and other principals' keys accessible to this principal, with little CPU cost. However, this

is not always possible, if some principal is not currently online. For example, in Figure 4, suppose Bob sends message 5 to Alice, but Alice (user 1) is not online. This means that CryptDB does not have access to user 1's key, so it will not be able to encrypt message 5's key with user 1's symmetric key. In this case, CryptDB looks up the public key of the principal (i.e., user 1) in a second table, *public_keys*, and encrypts message 5's key using user 1's public key. When user 1 logs in, she will be able to use the secret key part of her key to decrypt the key for message 5 (and re-encrypt it under her symmetric key for future use).

For external principals (i.e., physical users), CryptDB assigns a random key just as for any other principal. To give an external user access to the corresponding key on login, CryptDB stores the key of each external principal in a third table, *external_keys*, encrypted with the principal's password. This allows CryptDB to obtain a user's key given the user's password, and also allows a user to change her password without changing the key of the principal.

When a table with a SPEAKS_FOR relation is updated, CryptDB must update the *access_keys* table accordingly. To insert a new row into *access_keys* for a new SPEAKS_FOR relation, the proxy must have access to the key of the principal whose privileges are being delegated. This means that an adversary that breaks into an application or proxy server cannot create new SPEAKS_FOR relations for principals that are not logged in, because neither the proxy nor the adversary have access to their keys. If a SPEAKS_FOR relation is removed, CryptDB revokes access by removing the corresponding row from *access_keys*.

When encrypting data in a query or decrypting data from a result, CryptDB follows key chains starting from passwords of users logged in until it obtains the desired keys. As an optimization, when a user logs in, CryptDB's proxy loads the keys of some principals to which the user has access (in particular, those principal types that do not have too many principal instances—e.g., for groups the user is in, but not for messages the user received).

Applications inform CryptDB of users logging in or out by issuing INSERT and DELETE SQL queries to a special table *cryptdb_active* that has two columns, *username* and *password*. The proxy intercepts all queries for *cryptdb_active*, stores the passwords of logged-in users in memory, and never reveals them to the DBMS server.

CryptDB guards the data of inactive users at the time of an attack. If a compromise occurs, CryptDB provides a bound on the data leaked, allowing the administrators to not issue a blanket warning to *all* the users of the system. In this respect, CryptDB is different from other approaches to database security (see §9). However, some special users such as administrators with access to a large pool of data enable a larger compromise upon an attack. To avoid attacks happening when the administrator is logged in, the administrator should create a separate user account with restricted permissions when accessing the application as a regular user. Also, as good practice, an application should automatically log out users who have been inactive for some period of time.

5 APPLICATION CASE STUDIES

In this section, we explain how CryptDB can be used to secure three existing multi-user web applications. For brevity, we show simplified schemas, omitting irrelevant fields and type specifiers. Overall, we find that once a programmer specifies the principals in the application's schema, and the delegation rules for them using SPEAKS_FOR, protecting additional sensitive fields just requires additional ENC_FOR annotations.

phpBB is a widely used open source forum with a rich set of access control settings. Users are organized in groups; both users and groups have a variety of access permissions that the application

```
PRINCTYPE physical_user EXTERNAL;
PRINCTYPE user, group, forum_post, forum_name;

CREATE TABLE users      ( userid int, username varchar(255),
  (username physical_user) SPEAKS_FOR (userid user) );

CREATE TABLE usergroup ( userid int, groupid int,
  (userid user) SPEAKS_FOR (groupid group) );

CREATE TABLE aclgroups ( groupid int, forumid int, optionid int,
  (groupid group) SPEAKS_FOR (forumid forum_post)
        IF optionid=20,
  (groupid group) SPEAKS_FOR (forumid forum_name)
        IF optionid=14);

CREATE TABLE posts      ( postid int, forumid int,
  post text ENC_FOR (forumid forum_post) );

CREATE TABLE forum      ( forumid int,
  name varchar(255) ENC_FOR (forumid forum_name) );
```

Figure 5: Annotated schema for securing access to posts in phpBB. A user has access to see the content of posts in a forum if any of the groups that the user is part of has such permissions, indicated by *optionid* 20 in the *aclgroups* table for the corresponding *forumid* and *groupid*. Similarly, *optionid* 14 enables users to see the forum's name.

administrator can choose. We already showed how to secure private messages between two users in phpBB in Figure 4. A more detailed case is securing access to posts, as shown in Figure 5. This example shows how to use predicates (e.g., IF *optionid*=...) to implement a conditional speaks-for relation on principals, and also how one column (*forumid*) can be used to represent multiple principals (of different type) with different privileges. There are more ways to gain access to a post, but we omit them here for brevity.

HotCRP is a popular conference review application [27]. A key policy for HotCRP is that PC members cannot see who reviewed their own (or conflicted) papers. Figure 6 shows CryptDB annotations for HotCRP's schema to enforce this policy. Today, HotCRP cannot prevent a curious or careless PC chair from logging into the database server and seeing who wrote each review for a paper that she is in conflict with. As a result, conferences often set up a second server to review the chair's papers or use inconvenient out-of-band emails. With CryptDB, a PC chair cannot learn who wrote each review for her paper, even if she breaks into the application or database, since she does not have the decryption key.[1] The reason is that the SQL predicate "NoConflict" checks if a PC member is conflicted with a paper and prevents the proxy from providing access to the PC chair in the key chain. (We assume the PC chair does not modify the application to log the passwords of other PC members to subvert the system.)

grad-apply is a graduate admissions system used by MIT EECS. We annotated its schema to allow an applicant's folder to be accessed only by the respective applicant and any faculty using (*reviewers.reviewer_id* reviewer), meaning all reviewers, SPEAKS_FOR (*candidate_id* candidate) in table *candidates*, and ... SPEAKS_FOR (*letter_id* letter) in table *letters*. The applicant can see all of her folder data except for letters of recommendation. Overall, grad-apply has simple access control and therefore simple annotations.

---

[1]Fully implementing this policy would require setting up two PC chairs: a main chair, and a backup chair responsible for reviews of the main chair's papers. HotCRP allows the PC chair to impersonate other PC members, so CryptDB annotations would be used to prevent the main chair from gaining access to keys of reviewers assigned to her paper.

```
PRINCTYPE physical_user EXTERNAL;
PRINCTYPE contact, review;

CREATE TABLE ContactInfo   ( contactId int, email varchar(120),
  (email physical_user) SPEAKS_FOR (contactId contact) );

CREATE TABLE PCMember     ( contactId int );
CREATE TABLE PaperConflict ( paperId int, contactId int );
CREATE TABLE PaperReview  (
  paperId      int,
  reviewerId   int    ENC_FOR (paperId review),
  commentsToPC text ENC_FOR (paperId review),
  (PCMember.contactId contact) SPEAKS_FOR
      (paperId review) IF NoConflict(paperId, contactId) );

NoConflict (paperId, contactId):      /* Define a SQL function */
  (SELECT COUNT(*) FROM PaperConflict c WHERE
      c.paperId = paperId AND c.contactId = contactId) = 0;
```

Figure 6: Annotated schema for securing reviews in HotCRP. Reviews and the identity of reviewers providing the review will be available only to PC members (table *PCMember* includes PC chairs) who are not conflicted, and PC chairs cannot override this restriction.

6 DISCUSSION

CryptDB's design supports most relational queries and aggregates on standard data types, such as integers and text/varchar types. Additional operations can be added to CryptDB by extending its existing onions, or adding new onions for specific data types (e.g., spatial and multi-dimensional range queries [43]). Alternatively, in some cases, it may be possible to map complex unsupported operation to simpler ones (e.g., extracting the month out of an encrypted date is easier if the date's day, month, and year fields are encrypted separately).

There are certain computations CryptDB cannot support on encrypted data. For example, it does not support both computation and comparison on the same column, such as WHERE $salary >$ $age*2+10$. CryptDB can process a part of this query, but it would also require some processing on the proxy. In CryptDB, such a query should be (1) rewritten into a sub-query that selects a whole column, SELECT $age*2+10$ FROM ..., which CryptDB computes using HOM, and (2) re-encrypted in the proxy, creating a new column (call it *aux*) on the DBMS server consisting of the newly encrypted values. Finally, the original query with the predicate WHERE $salary > aux$ should be run. We have not been affected by this limitation in our test applications (TPC-C, phpBB, HotCRP, and grad-apply).

In multi-principal mode, CryptDB cannot perform server-side computations on values encrypted for different principals, even if the application has the authority of all principals in question, because the ciphertexts are encrypted with different keys. For some computations, it may be practical for the proxy to perform the computation after decrypting the data, but for others (e.g., large-scale aggregates) this approach may be too expensive. A possible extension to CryptDB to support such queries may be to maintain multiple ciphertexts for such values, encrypted under different keys.

7 IMPLEMENTATION

The CryptDB proxy consists of a C++ library and a Lua module. The C++ library consists of a query parser; a query encryptor/rewriter, which encrypts fields or includes UDFs in the query; and a result decryption module. To allow applications to transparently use CryptDB, we used MySQL proxy [47] and implemented a Lua module that passes queries and results to and from our C++ module. We implemented our new cryptographic protocols using NTL [44]. Our

	Databases	Tables	Columns
Complete schema	8,548	177,154	1,244,216
Used in query	1,193	18,162	128,840

Figure 7: Number of databases, tables, and columns on the sql.mit.edu MySQL server, used for trace analysis, indicating the total size of the schema, and the part of the schema seen in queries during the trace period.

CryptDB implementation consists of ∼18,000 lines of C++ code and ∼150 lines of Lua code, with another ∼10,000 lines of test code.

CryptDB is portable and we have implemented versions for both Postgres 9.0 and MySQL 5.1. Our initial Postgres-based implementation is described in an earlier technical report [39]. Porting CryptDB to MySQL required changing only 86 lines of code, mostly in the code for connecting to the MySQL server and declaring UDFs. As mentioned earlier, CryptDB does not change the DBMS; we implement all server-side functionality with UDFs and server-side tables. CryptDB's design, and to a large extent our implementation, should work on top of any SQL DBMS that supports UDFs.

8 EXPERIMENTAL EVALUATION

In this section, we evaluate four aspects of CryptDB: the difficulty of modifying an application to run on top of CryptDB, the types of queries and applications CryptDB is able to support, the level of security CryptDB provides, and the performance impact of using CryptDB. For this analysis, we use seven applications as well as a large trace of SQL queries.

We evaluate the effectiveness of our annotations and the needed application changes on the three applications we described in §5 (phpBB, HotCRP, and grad-apply), as well as on a TPC-C query mix (a standard workload in the database industry). We then analyze the functionality and security of CryptDB on three more applications, on TPC-C, and on a large trace of SQL queries. The additional three applications are OpenEMR, an electronic medical records application storing private medical data of patients; the web application of an MIT class (6.02), storing students' grades; and PHP-calendar, storing people's schedules. The large trace of SQL queries comes from a popular MySQL server at MIT, sql.mit.edu. This server is used primarily by web applications running on scripts.mit.edu, a shared web application hosting service operated by MIT's Student Information Processing Board (SIPB). In addition, this SQL server is used by a number of applications that run on other machines and use sql.mit.edu only to store their data. Our query trace spans about ten days, and includes approximately 126 million queries. Figure 7 summarizes the schema statistics for sql.mit.edu; each database is likely to be a separate instance of some application.

Finally, we evaluate the overall performance of CryptDB on the phpBB application and on a query mix from TPC-C, and perform a detailed analysis through microbenchmarks.

In the six applications (not counting TPC-C), we only encrypt sensitive columns, according to a manual inspection. Some fields were clearly sensitive (e.g., grades, private message, medical information), but others were only marginally so (e.g., the time when a message was posted). There was no clear threshold between sensitive or not, but it was clear to us which fields were definitely sensitive. In the case of TPC-C, we encrypt all the columns in the database in single-principal mode so that we can study the performance and functionality of a fully encrypted DBMS. All fields are considered for encryption in the large query trace as well.

8.1 Application Changes

Figure 8 summarizes the amount of programmer effort required to use CryptDB in three multi-user web applications and in the single-principal TPC-C queries. The results show that, for multi-principal mode, CryptDB required between 11 and 13 unique schema annotations (29 to 111 in total), and 2 to 7 lines of code changes to provide user passwords to the proxy, in order to secure sensitive information stored in the database. Part of the simplicity is because securing an additional column requires just one annotation in most cases. For the single-principal TPC-C queries, using CryptDB required no application annotations at all.

8.2 Functional Evaluation

To evaluate what columns, operations, and queries CryptDB can support, we analyzed the queries issued by six web applications (including the three applications we analyzed in §8.1), the TPC-C queries, and the SQL queries from sql.mit.edu. The results are shown in the left half of Figure 9.

CryptDB supports most queries; the number of columns in the "needs plaintext" column, which counts columns that cannot be processed in encrypted form by CryptDB, is small relative to the total number of columns. For PHP-calendar and OpenEMR, CryptDB does not support queries on certain sensitive fields that perform string manipulation (e.g., substring and lowercase conversions) or date manipulation (e.g., obtaining the day, month, or year of an encrypted date). However, if these functions were precomputed with the result added as standalone columns (e.g., each of the three parts of a date were encrypted separately), CryptDB would support these queries.

The next two columns, "needs HOM" and "needs SEARCH", reflect the number of columns for which that encryption scheme is needed to process some queries. The numbers suggest that these encryption schemes are important; without them, CryptDB would be unable to support those queries.

Based on an analysis of the larger sql.mit.edu trace, we found that CryptDB should be able to support operations over all but 1,094 of the 128,840 columns observed in the trace. The "in-proxy processing" shows analysis results where we assumed the proxy can perform some lightweight operations on the results returned from the DBMS server. Specifically, this included any operations that are not needed to compute the set of resulting rows or to aggregate rows (that is, expressions that do not appear in a WHERE, HAVING, or GROUP BY clause, or in an ORDER BY clause with a LIMIT, and are not aggregate operators). With in-proxy processing, CryptDB should be able to process queries over encrypted data over all but 571 of the 128,840 columns, thus supporting 99.5% of the columns.

Of those 571 columns, 222 use a bitwise operator in a WHERE clause or perform bitwise aggregation, such as the Gallery2 application, which uses a bitmask of permission fields and consults them in WHERE clauses. Rewriting the application to store the permissions in a different way would allow CryptDB to support such operations. Another 205 columns perform string processing in the WHERE clause, such as comparing whether lowercase versions of two strings match. Storing a keyed hash of the lowercase version of each string for such columns, similar to the JOIN-ADJ scheme, could support case-insensitive equality checks for ciphertexts. 76 columns are involved in mathematical transformations in the WHERE clause, such as manipulating dates, times, scores, and geometric coordinates. 41 columns invoke the LIKE operator with a column reference for the pattern; this is typically used to check a particular value against a table storing a list of banned IP addresses, usernames, URLs, etc. Such a query can also be rewritten if the data items are sensitive.

8.3 Security Evaluation

To understand the amount of information that would be revealed to the adversary in practice, we examine the steady-state onion levels of different columns for a range of applications and queries. To

Application	Annotations	Login/logout code	Sensitive fields secured, and examples of such fields
phpBB	31 (11 unique)	7 lines	23: private messages (content, subject), posts, forums
HotCRP	29 (12 unique)	2 lines	22: paper content and paper information, reviews
grad-apply	111 (13 unique)	2 lines	103: student grades (61), scores (17), recommendations, reviews
TPC-C (single princ.)	0	0	92: all the fields in all the tables encrypted

Figure 8: Number of annotations the programmer needs to add to secure sensitive fields, lines of code to be added to provide CryptDB with the passwords of users, and the number of sensitive fields that CryptDB secures with these annotations, for three different applications. We count as one annotation each invocation of our three types of annotations and any SQL predicate used in a SPEAKS_FOR annotation. Since multiple fields in the same table are usually encrypted for the same principal (e.g., message subject and content), we also report unique annotations.

Application	Total cols.	Consider for enc.	Needs plaintext	Needs HOM	Needs SEARCH	Non-plaintext cols. with MinEnc: RND	SEARCH	DET	OPE	Most sensitive cols. at HIGH
phpBB	563	23	0	1	0	21	0	1	1	6 / 6
HotCRP	204	22	0	2	1	18	1	1	2	18 / 18
grad-apply	706	103	0	0	2	95	0	6	2	94 / 94
OpenEMR	1,297	566	7	0	3	526	2	12	19	525 / 540
MIT 6.02	15	13	0	0	0	7	0	4	2	1 / 1
PHP-calendar	25	12	2	0	2	3	2	4	1	3 / 4
TPC-C	92	92	0	8	0	65	0	19	8	—
Trace from `sql.mit.edu`	128,840	128,840	1,094	1,019	1,125	80,053	350	34,212	13,131	—
... with in-proxy processing	128,840	128,840	571	1,016	1,135	84,008	398	35,350	8,513	—
... col. name contains *pass*	2,029	2,029	2	0	0	1,936	0	91	0	—
... col. name contains *content*	2,521	2,521	0	0	52	2,215	52	251	3	—
... col. name contains *priv*	173	173	0	4	0	159	0	12	2	—

Figure 9: Steady-state onion levels for database columns required by a range of applications and traces. "Needs plaintext" indicates that CryptDB cannot execute the application's queries over encrypted data for that column. For the applications in the top group of rows, sensitive columns were determined manually, and only these columns were considered for encryption. For the bottom group of rows, all database columns were automatically considered for encryption. The rightmost column considers the application's most sensitive database columns, and reports the number of them that have MinEnc in HIGH (both terms are defined in §8.3).

quantify the level of security, we define the MinEnc of a column to be the weakest onion encryption scheme exposed on any of the onions of a column when onions reach a steady state (i.e., after the application generates all query types, or after running the whole trace). We consider RND and HOM to be the strongest schemes, followed by SEARCH, followed by DET and JOIN, and finishing with the weakest scheme which is OPE. For example, if a column has onion *Eq* at RND, onion *Ord* at OPE and onion *Add* at HOM, the MinEnc of this column is OPE.

The right side of Figure 9 shows the MinEnc onion level for a range of applications and query traces. We see that most fields remain at RND, which is the most secure scheme. For example, OpenEMR has hundreds of sensitive fields describing the medical conditions and history of patients, but these fields are mostly just inserted and fetched, and are not used in any computation. A number of fields also remain at DET, typically to perform key lookups and joins. OPE, which leaks order, is used the least frequently, and mostly for fields that are marginally sensitive (e.g., timestamps and counts of messages). Thus, CryptDB's adjustable security provides a significant improvement in confidentiality over revealing all encryption schemes to the server.

To analyze CryptDB's security for specific columns that are particularly sensitive, we define a new security level, HIGH, which includes the RND and HOM encryption schemes, as well as DET for columns having no repetitions (in which case DET is logically equivalent to RND). These are highly secure encryption schemes leaking virtually nothing about the data. DET for columns with repeats and OPE are not part of HIGH as they reveal relations to the DBMS server. The rightmost column in Figure 9 shows that most of the particularly sensitive columns (again, according to manual inspection) are at HIGH.

For the `sql.mit.edu` trace queries, approximately 6.6% of columns were at OPE even with in-proxy processing; other encrypted columns (93%) remain at DET or above. Out of the columns that were at OPE, 3.9% are used in an ORDER BY clause with a LIMIT, 3.7% are used in an inequality comparison in a WHERE clause, and 0.25% are used in a MIN or MAX aggregate operator (some of the columns are counted in more than one of these groups). It would be difficult to perform these computations in the proxy without substantially increasing the amount of data sent to it.

Although we could not examine the schemas of applications using `sql.mit.edu` to determine what fields are sensitive—mostly due to its large scale—we measured the same statistics as above for columns whose names are indicative of sensitive data. In particular, the last three rows of Figure 9 show columns whose name contains the word "pass" (which are almost all some type of password), "content" (which are typically bulk data managed by an application), and "priv" (which are typically some type of private message). CryptDB reveals much less information about these columns than an average column, almost all of them are supported, and almost all are at RND or DET.

Finally, we empirically validated CryptDB's confidentiality guarantees by trying real attacks on phpBB that have been listed in the CVE database [32], including two SQL injection attacks (CVE-2009-3052 & CVE-2008-6314), bugs in permission checks (CVE-2010-1627 & CVE-2008-7143), and a bug in remote PHP file inclusion (CVE-2008-6377). We found that, for users not currently logged in, the answers returned from the DBMS were encrypted; even with root access to the application server, proxy, and DBMS, the answers were not decryptable.

8.4 Performance Evaluation

To evaluate the performance of CryptDB, we used a machine with two 2.4 GHz Intel Xeon E5620 4-core processors and 12 GB of RAM to run the MySQL 5.1.54 server, and a machine with eight 2.4 GHz AMD Opteron 8431 6-core processors and 64 GB of RAM to run the CryptDB proxy and the clients. The two machines were connected over a shared Gigabit Ethernet network. The higher-provisioned client machine ensures that the clients are not the bottleneck in any experiment. All workloads fit in the server's RAM.

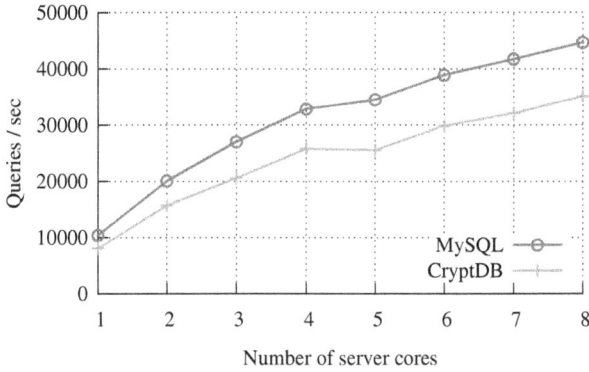

Figure 10: Throughput for TPC-C queries, for a varying number of cores on the underlying MySQL DBMS server.

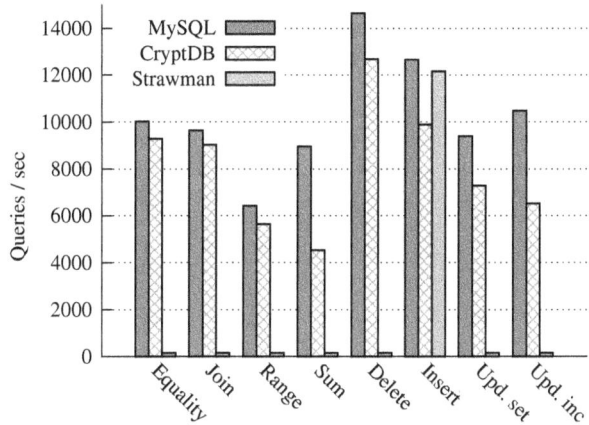

Figure 11: Throughput of different types of SQL queries from the TPC-C query mix running under MySQL, CryptDB, and the strawman design. "Upd. inc" stands for UPDATE that increments a column, and "Upd. set" stands for UPDATE which sets columns to a constant.

8.4.1 TPC-C

We compare the performance of a TPC-C query mix when running on an unmodified MySQL server versus on a CryptDB proxy in front of the MySQL server. We trained CryptDB on the query set (§3.5.2) so there are no onion adjustments during the TPC-C experiments. Figure 10 shows the throughput of TPC-C queries as the number of cores on the server varies from one to eight. In all cases, the server spends 100% of its CPU time processing queries. Both MySQL and CryptDB scale well initially, but start to level off due to internal lock contention in the MySQL server, as reported by SHOW STATUS LIKE 'Table%'. The overall throughput with CryptDB is 21–26% lower than MySQL, depending on the exact number of cores.

To understand the sources of CryptDB's overhead, we measure the server throughput for different types of SQL queries seen in TPC-C, on the same server, but running with only one core enabled. Figure 11 shows the results for MySQL, CryptDB, and a *strawman* design; the strawman performs each query over data encrypted with RND by decrypting the relevant data using a UDF, performing the query over the plaintext, and re-encrypting the result (if updating rows). The results show that CryptDB's throughput penalty is greatest for queries that involve a SUM (2.0× less throughput) and for incrementing UPDATE statements (1.6× less throughput); these are the queries that involve HOM additions at the server. For the other types of queries, which form a larger part of the TPC-C mix, the throughput overhead is modest. The strawman design performs poorly for almost all queries because the DBMS's indexes on the

Query (& scheme)		MySQL Server	CryptDB		
			Server	Proxy	Proxy⋆
Select by =	(DET)	0.10 ms	0.11 ms	0.86 ms	0.86 ms
Select join	(JOIN)	0.10 ms	0.11 ms	0.75 ms	0.75 ms
Select range	(OPE)	0.16 ms	0.22 ms	**0.78** ms	28.7 ms
Select sum	(HOM)	0.11 ms	0.46 ms	0.99 ms	0.99 ms
Delete		0.07 ms	0.08 ms	0.28 ms	0.28 ms
Insert	(all)	0.08 ms	0.10 ms	**0.37** ms	16.3 ms
Update set	(all)	0.11 ms	0.14 ms	**0.36** ms	3.80 ms
Update inc	(HOM)	0.10 ms	0.17 ms	**0.30** ms	25.1 ms
Overall		0.10 ms	0.12 ms	**0.60** ms	10.7 ms

Figure 12: Server and proxy latency for different types of SQL queries from TPC-C. For each query type, we show the predominant encryption scheme used at the server. Due to details of the TPC-C workload, each query type affects a different number of rows, and involves a different number of cryptographic operations. The left two columns correspond to server throughput, which is also shown in Figure 11. "Proxy" shows the latency added by CryptDB's proxy; "Proxy⋆" shows the proxy latency without the ciphertext pre-computing and caching optimization (§3.5). Bold numbers show where pre-computing and caching ciphertexts helps. The "Overall" row is the average latency over the mix of TPC-C queries. "Update set" is an UPDATE where the fields are set to a constant, and "Update inc" is an UPDATE where some fields are incremented.

Scheme	Encrypt	Decrypt	Special operation
Blowfish (1 int.)	0.0001 ms	0.0001 ms	—
AES-CBC (1 KB)	0.008 ms	0.007 ms	—
AES-CMC (1 KB)	0.016 ms	0.015 ms	—
OPE (1 int.)	9.0 ms	9.0 ms	Compare: 0 ms
SEARCH (1 word)	0.01 ms	0.004 ms	Match: 0.001 ms
HOM (1 int.)	9.7 ms	0.7 ms	Add: 0.005 ms
JOIN-ADJ (1 int.)	0.52 ms	—	Adjust: 0.56 ms

Figure 13: Microbenchmarks of cryptographic schemes, per unit of data encrypted (one 32-bit integer, 1 KB, or one 15-byte word of text), measured by taking the average time over many iterations.

RND-encrypted data are useless for operations on the underlying plaintext data. It is pleasantly surprising that the higher security of CryptDB over the strawman also brings better performance.

To understand the latency introduced by CryptDB's proxy, we measure the server and proxy processing times for the same types of SQL queries as above. Figure 12 shows the results. We can see that there is an overall server latency increase of 20% with CryptDB, which we consider modest. The proxy adds an average of 0.60 ms to a query; of that time, 24% is spent in MySQL proxy, 23% is spent in encryption and decryption, and the remaining 53% is spent parsing and processing queries. The cryptographic overhead is relatively small because most of our encryption schemes are efficient; Figure 13 shows their performance. OPE and HOM are the slowest, but the ciphertext pre-computing and caching optimization (§3.5) masks the high latency of queries requiring OPE and HOM. Proxy⋆ in Figure 12 shows the latency without these optimizations, which is significantly higher for the corresponding query types. SELECT queries that involve a SUM use HOM but do not benefit from this optimization, because the proxy performs decryption, rather than encryption.

In all TPC-C experiments, the proxy used less than 20 MB of memory. Caching ciphertexts for the 30,000 most common values for OPE accounts for about 3 MB, and pre-computing ciphertexts and randomness for 30,000 values at HOM required 10 MB.

8.4.2 Multi-User Web Applications

To evaluate the impact of CryptDB on application performance, we measure the throughput of phpBB for a workload with 10 parallel clients, which ensured 100% CPU load at the server. Each client continuously issued HTTP requests to browse the forum, write and

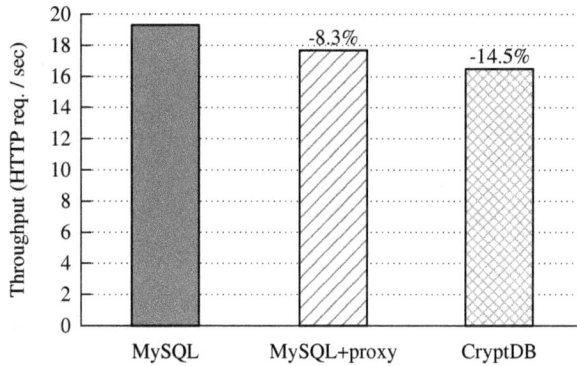

Figure 14: Throughput comparison for phpBB. "MySQL" denotes phpBB running directly on MySQL. "MySQL+proxy" denotes phpBB running on an unencrypted MySQL database but going through MySQL proxy. "CryptDB" denotes phpBB running on CryptDB with notably sensitive fields annotated and the database appropriately encrypted. Most HTTP requests involved tens of SQL queries each. Percentages indicate throughput reduction relative to MySQL.

DB	Login	R post	W post	R msg	W msg
MySQL	60 ms	50 ms	133 ms	61 ms	237 ms
CryptDB	67 ms	60 ms	151 ms	73 ms	251 ms

Figure 15: Latency for HTTP requests that heavily use encrypted fields in phpBB for MySQL and CryptDB. R and W stand for read and write.

read posts, as well as write and read private messages. We pre-loaded forums and user mailboxes with messages. In this experiment, we co-located the MySQL DBMS, the CryptDB proxy, and the web application server on a single-core machine, to ensure we do not add additional resources for a separate proxy server machine to the system in the CryptDB configuration. In practice, an administrator would likely run the CryptDB proxy on another machine for security.

Figure 14 shows the throughput of phpBB in three different configurations: (1) connecting to a stock MySQL server, (2) connecting to a stock MySQL server through MySQL proxy, and (3) connecting to CryptDB, with notably sensitive fields encrypted as summarized in Figure 9, which in turn uses a stock MySQL server to store encrypted data. The results show that phpBB incurs an overall throughput loss of just 14.5%, and that about half of this loss comes from inefficiencies in MySQL proxy unrelated to CryptDB. Figure 15 further shows the end-to-end latency for five types of phpBB requests. The results show that CryptDB adds 7–18 ms (6–20%) of processing time per request.

8.4.3 Storage

CryptDB increases the amount of the data stored in the DBMS, because it stores multiple onions for the same field, and because ciphertexts are larger than plaintexts for some encryption schemes. For TPC-C, CryptDB increased the database size by 3.76×, mostly due to cryptographic expansion of integer fields encrypted with HOM (which expand from 32 bits to 2048 bits); strings and binary data remains roughly the same size. For phpBB, the database size using an unencrypted system was 2.6 MB for a workload of about 1,000 private messages and 1,000 forum posts generated by 10 users. The same workload on CryptDB had a database of 3.3 MB, about 1.2× larger. Of the 0.7 MB increase, 230 KB is for storage of *access_keys*, 276 KB is for *public_keys* and *external_keys*, and 166 KB is due to expansion of encrypted fields.

8.4.4 Adjustable Encryption

Adjustable query-based encryption involves decrypting columns to lower-security onion levels. Fortunately, decryption for the more-

secure onion layers, such as RND, is fast, and needs to be performed only once per column for the lifetime of the system.[2] Removing a layer of RND requires AES decryption, which our experimental machine can perform at ∼200 MB/s per core. Thus, removing an onion layer is bottlenecked by the speed at which the DBMS server can copy a column from disk for disk-bound databases.

9 RELATED WORK

Search and queries over encrypted data. Song et al. [46] describe cryptographic tools for performing keyword search over encrypted data, which we use to implement SEARCH. Amanatidis et al. [2] propose methods for exact searches that do not require scanning the entire database and could be used to process certain restricted SQL queries. Bao et al. [3] extend these encrypted search methods to the multi-user case. Yang et al. [51] run selections with equality predicates over encrypted data. Evdokimov and Guenther present methods for the same selections, as well as Cartesian products and projections [15]. Agrawal et al. develop a statistical encoding that preserves the order of numerical data in a column [1], but it does not have sound cryptographic properties, unlike the scheme we use [4]. Boneh and Waters show public-key schemes for comparisons, subset checks, and conjunctions of such queries over encrypted data [5], but these schemes have ciphertext lengths that are exponential in the length of the plaintext, limiting their practical applicability.

When applied to processing SQL on encrypted data, these techniques suffer from some of the following limitations: certain basic queries are not supported or are too inefficient (especially joins and order checks), they require significant client-side query processing, users either have to build and maintain indexes on the data at the server or to perform sequential scans for every selection/search, and implementing these techniques requires unattractive changes to the innards of the DBMS.

Some researchers have developed prototype systems for subsets of SQL, but they provide no confidentiality guarantees, require a significant DBMS rewrite, and rely on client-side processing [9, 12, 22]. For example, Hacigumus et al. [22] heuristically split the domain of possible values for each column into partitions, storing the partition number unencrypted for each data item, and rely on extensive client-side filtering of query results. Chow et al. [8] require trusted entities and two non-colluding untrusted DBMSes.

Untrusted servers. SUNDR [28] uses cryptography to provide privacy and integrity in a file system on top of an untrusted file server. Using a SUNDR-like model, SPORC [16] and Depot [30] show how to build low-latency applications, running mostly on the clients, without having to trust a server. However, existing server-side applications that involve separate database and application servers cannot be used with these systems unless they are rewritten as distributed client-side applications to work with SPORC or Depot. Many applications are not amenable to such a structure.

Companies like Navajo Systems and Ciphercloud provide a trusted application-level proxy that intercepts network traffic between clients and cloud-hosted servers (e.g., IMAP), and encrypts sensitive data stored on the server. These products appear to break up sensitive data (specified by application-specific rules) into tokens (such as words in a string), and encrypt each of these tokens using an order-preserving encryption scheme, which allows token-level searching and sorting. In contrast, CryptDB supports a richer set of operations (most of SQL), reveals only relations for the necessary classes of computation to the server based on the queries issued by the application, and allows chaining of encryption keys to user passwords, to restrict data leaks from a compromised proxy.

---

[2]Unless the administrator periodically re-encrypts data/columns.

Disk encryption. Various commercial database products, such as Oracle's Transparent Data Encryption [34], encrypt data on disk, but decrypt it to perform query processing. As a result, the server must have access to decryption keys, and an adversary compromising the DBMS software can gain access to the entire data.

Software security. Many tools help programmers either find or mitigate mistakes in their code that may lead to vulnerabilities, including static analysis tools like PQL [29, 31] and UrFlow [7], and runtime tools like Resin [52] and CLAMP [36]. In contrast, CryptDB provides confidentiality guarantees for user data even if the adversary gains complete control over the application and database servers. These tools provide no guarantees in the face of this threat, but in contrast, CryptDB cannot provide confidentiality in the face of vulnerabilities that trick the user's client machine into issuing unwanted requests (such as cross-site scripting or cross-site request forgery vulnerabilities in web applications). As a result, using CryptDB together with these tools should improve overall application security.

Rizvi et al. [41] and Chlipala [7] specify and enforce an application's security policy over SQL views. CryptDB's SQL annotations can capture most of these policies, except for result processing being done in the policy's view, such as allowing a user to view only aggregates of certain data. Unlike prior systems, CryptDB enforces SQL-level policies cryptographically, without relying on compile-time or run-time permission checks.

Privacy-preserving aggregates. Privacy-preserving data integration, mining, and aggregation schemes are useful [26, 50], but are not usable by many applications because they support only specialized query types and require a rewrite of the DBMS. Differential privacy [14] is complementary to CryptDB; it allows a trusted server to decide what answers to release and how to obfuscate answers to aggregation queries to avoid leaking information about any specific record in the database.

Query integrity. Techniques for SQL query integrity can be integrated into CryptDB because CryptDB allows relational queries on encrypted data to be processed just like on plaintext. These methods can provide integrity by adding a MAC to each tuple [28, 42], freshness using hash chains [38, 42], and both freshness and completeness of query results [33]. In addition, the client can verify the results of aggregation queries [48], and provide query assurance for most read queries [45].

Outsourced databases. Curino et al. advocate the idea of a relational cloud [11], a context in which CryptDB fits well.

10 CONCLUSION

We presented CryptDB, a system that provides a practical and strong level of confidentiality in the face of two significant threats confronting database-backed applications: curious DBAs and arbitrary compromises of the application server and the DBMS. CryptDB meets its goals using three ideas: running queries efficiently over encrypted data using a novel SQL-aware encryption strategy, dynamically adjusting the encryption level using onions of encryption to minimize the information revealed to the untrusted DBMS server, and chaining encryption keys to user passwords in a way that allows only authorized users to gain access to encrypted data.

Our evaluation on a large trace of 126 million SQL queries from a production MySQL server shows that CryptDB can support operations over encrypted data for 99.5% of the 128,840 columns seen in the trace. The throughput penalty of CryptDB is modest, resulting in a reduction of 14.5–26% on two applications as compared to unmodified MySQL. Our security analysis shows that CryptDB protects most sensitive fields with highly secure encryption schemes for six applications. The developer effort consists of 11–13 unique schema annotations and 2–7 lines of source code changes to express relevant privacy policies for 22–103 sensitive fields in three multi-user web applications.

The source code for our implementation is available for download at `http://css.csail.mit.edu/cryptdb/`.

ACKNOWLEDGMENTS

We thank Martin Abadi, Brad Chen, Carlo Curino, Craig Harris, Evan Jones, Frans Kaashoek, Sam Madden, Mike Stonebraker, Mike Walfish, the anonymous reviewers, and our shepherd, Adrian Perrig, for their feedback. Eugene Wu and Alvin Cheung also provided useful advice. We also thank Geoffrey Thomas, Quentin Smith, Mitch Berger, and the rest of the `scripts.mit.edu` maintainers for providing us with SQL query traces. This work was supported by the NSF (CNS-0716273 and IIS-1065219)'and by Google.

REFERENCES

[1] R. Agrawal, J. Kiernan, R. Srikant, and Y. Xu. Order preserving encryption for numeric data. In *Proceedings of the 2004 ACM SIGMOD International Conference on Management of Data*, Paris, France, June 2004.

[2] G. Amanatidis, A. Boldyreva, and A. O'Neill. Provably-secure schemes for basic query support in outsourced databases. In *Proceedings of the 21st Annual IFIP WG 11.3 Working Conference on Database and Applications Security*, Redondo Beach, CA, July 2007.

[3] F. Bao, R. H. Deng, X. Ding, and Y. Yang. Private query on encrypted data in multi-user settings. In *Proceedings of the 4th International Conference on Information Security Practice and Experience*, Sydney, Australia, April 2008.

[4] A. Boldyreva, N. Chenette, Y. Lee, and A. O'Neill. Order-preserving symmetric encryption. In *Proceedings of the 28th Annual International Conference on the Theory and Applications of Cryptographic Techniques (EUROCRYPT)*, Cologne, Germany, April 2009.

[5] D. Boneh and B. Waters. Conjunctive, subset, and range queries on encrypted data. In *Proceedings of the 4th Conference on Theory of Cryptography*, 2007.

[6] A. Chen. GCreep: Google engineer stalked teens, spied on chats. *Gawker*, September 2010. `http://gawker.com/5637234/`.

[7] A. Chlipala. Static checking of dynamically-varying security policies in database-backed applications. In *Proceedings of the 9th Symposium on Operating Systems Design and Implementation*, Vancouver, Canada, October 2010.

[8] S. S. M. Chow, J.-H. Lee, and L. Subramanian. Two-party computation model for privacy-preserving queries over distributed databases. In *Proceedings of the 16th Network and Distributed System Security Symposium*, February 2009.

[9] V. Ciriani, S. D. C. di Vimercati, S. Foresti, S. Jajodia, S. Paraboschi, and P. Samarati. Keep a few: Outsourcing data while maintaining confidentiality. In *Proceedings of the 14th European Symposium on Research in Computer Security*, September 2009.

[10] M. Cooney. IBM touts encryption innovation; new technology performs calculations on encrypted data without decrypting it. *Computer World*, June 2009.

[11] C. Curino, E. P. C. Jones, R. A. Popa, N. Malviya, E. Wu, S. Madden, H. Balakrishnan, and N. Zeldovich. Relational cloud: A database-as-a-service for the cloud. In *Proceedings of the 5th Biennial Conference on Innovative Data Systems Research*, pages 235–241, Pacific Grove, CA, January 2011.

[12] E. Damiani, S. D. C. di Vimercati, S. Jajodia, S. Paraboschi, and P. Samarati. Balancing confidentiality and efficiency in untrusted relational DBMSs. In *Proceedings of the 10th ACM Conference on Computer and Communications Security*, Washington, DC, October 2003.

[13] A. Desai. New paradigms for constructing symmetric encryption schemes secure against chosen-ciphertext attack. In *Proceedings of the 20th Annual International Conference on Advances in Cryptology*, pages 394–412, August 2000.

[14] C. Dwork. Differential privacy: a survey of results. In *Proceedings of the 5th International Conference on Theory and Applications of Models of Computation*, Xi'an, China, April 2008.

[15] S. Evdokimov and O. Guenther. Encryption techniques for secure database outsourcing. Cryptology ePrint Archive, Report 2007/335.

[16] A. J. Feldman, W. P. Zeller, M. J. Freedman, and E. W. Felten. SPORC: Group collaboration using untrusted cloud resources. In *Proceedings of the 9th Symposium on Operating Systems Design and Implementation*, Vancouver, Canada, October 2010.

[17] T. Ge and S. Zdonik. Answering aggregation queries in a secure system model. In *Proceedings of the 33rd International Conference on Very Large Data Bases*, Vienna, Austria, September 2007.

[18] R. Gennaro, C. Gentry, and B. Parno. Non-interactive verifiable computing: Outsourcing computation to untrusted workers. In *Advances in Cryptology (CRYPTO)*, Santa Barbara, CA, August 2010.

[19] C. Gentry. Fully homomorphic encryption using ideal lattices. In *Proceedings of the 41st Annual ACM Symposium on Theory of Computing*, Bethesda, MD, May–June 2009.

[20] O. Goldreich. *Foundations of Cryptography: Volume 1 Basic Tools*. Cambridge University Press, 2001.

[21] A. Greenberg. DARPA will spend 20 million to search for crypto's holy grail. *Forbes*, April 2011.

[22] H. Hacigumus, B. Iyer, C. Li, and S. Mehrotra. Executing SQL over encrypted data in the database-service-provider model. In *Proceedings of the 2002 ACM SIGMOD International Conference on Management of Data*, Madison, WI, June 2002.

[23] J. A. Halderman, S. D. Schoen, N. Heninger, W. Clarkson, W. Paul, J. A. Calandrino, A. J. Feldman, J. Appelbaum, and E. W. Felten. Lest we remember: Cold boot attacks on encryption keys. In *Proceedings of the 17th Usenix Security Symposium*, San Jose, CA, July–August 2008.

[24] S. Halevi and P. Rogaway. A tweakable enciphering mode. In *Advances in Cryptology (CRYPTO)*, 2003.

[25] V. Kachitvichyanukul and B. W. Schmeiser. Algorithm 668: H2PEC: Sampling from the hypergeometric distribution. *ACM Transactions on Mathematical Software*, 14(4):397–398, 1988.

[26] M. Kantarcioglu and C. Clifton. Security issues in querying encrypted data. In *Proceedings of the 19th Annual IFIP WG 11.3 Working Conference on Database and Applications Security*, Storrs, CT, August 2005.

[27] E. Kohler. Hot crap! In *Proceedings of the Workshop on Organizing Workshops, Conferences, and Symposia for Computer Systems*, San Francisco, CA, April 2008.

[28] J. Li, M. Krohn, D. Mazières, and D. Shasha. Secure untrusted data repository (SUNDR). In *Proceedings of the 6th Symposium on Operating Systems Design and Implementation*, pages 91–106, San Francisco, CA, December 2004.

[29] V. B. Livshits and M. S. Lam. Finding security vulnerabilities in Java applications with static analysis. In *Proceedings of the 14th Usenix Security Symposium*, pages 271–286, Baltimore, MD, August 2005.

[30] P. Mahajan, S. Setty, S. Lee, A. Clement, L. Alvisi, M. Dahlin, and M. Walfish. Depot: Cloud storage with minimal trust. In *Proceedings of the 9th Symposium on Operating Systems Design and Implementation*, Vancouver, Canada, October 2010.

[31] M. Martin, B. Livshits, and M. Lam. Finding application errors and security flaws using PQL: a program query language. In *Proceedings of the 2005 Conference on Object-Oriented Programming, Systems, Languages and Applications*, pages 365–383, San Diego, CA, October 2005.

[32] National Vulnerability Database. CVE statistics. http://web.nvd.nist.gov/view/vuln/statistics, February 2011.

[33] V. H. Nguyen, T. K. Dang, N. T. Son, and J. Kung. Query assurance verification for dynamic outsourced XML databases. In *Proceedings of the 2nd Conference on Availability, Reliability and Security*, Vienna, Austria, April 2007.

[34] Oracle Corporation. Oracle advanced security. http://www.oracle.com/technetwork/database/options/advanced-security/.

[35] P. Paillier. Public-key cryptosystems based on composite degree residuosity classes. In *Proceedings of the 18th Annual International Conference on the Theory and Applications of Cryptographic Techniques (EUROCRYPT)*, Prague, Czech Republic, May 1999.

[36] B. Parno, J. M. McCune, D. Wendlandt, D. G. Andersen, and A. Perrig. CLAMP: Practical prevention of large-scale data leaks. In *Proceedings of the 30th IEEE Symposium on Security and Privacy*, Oakland, CA, May 2009.

[37] R. A. Popa, C. M. S. Redfield, N. Zeldovich, and H. Balakrishnan. CryptDB web site. http://css.csail.mit.edu/cryptdb/.

[38] R. A. Popa, J. R. Lorch, D. Molnar, H. J. Wang, and L. Zhuang. Enabling security in cloud storage SLAs with CloudProof. In *Proceedings of 2011 USENIX Annual Technical Conference*, Portland, OR, 2011.

[39] R. A. Popa, N. Zeldovich, and H. Balakrishnan. CryptDB: A practical encrypted relational DBMS. Technical Report MIT-CSAIL-TR-2011-005, MIT Computer Science and Artificial Intelligence Laboratory, Cambridge, MA, January 2011.

[40] Privacy Rights Clearinghouse. Chronology of data breaches. http://www.privacyrights.org/data-breach.

[41] S. Rizvi, A. Mendelzon, S. Sudarshan, and P. Roy. Extending query rewriting techniques for fine-grained access control. In *Proceedings of the 2004 ACM SIGMOD International Conference on Management of Data*, Paris, France, June 2004.

[42] H. Shacham, N. Modadugu, and D. Boneh. Sirius: Securing remote untrusted storage. In *Proceedings of the 10th Network and Distributed System Security Symposium*, 2003.

[43] E. Shi, J. Bethencourt, H. Chan, D. Song, and A. Perrig. Multidimensional range query over encrypted data. In *Proceedings of the 28th IEEE Symposium on Security and Privacy*, Oakland, CA, May 2007.

[44] V. Shoup. NTL: A library for doing number theory. http://www.shoup.net/ntl/, August 2009.

[45] R. Sion. Query execution assurance for outsourced databases. In *Proceedings of the 31st International Conference on Very Large Data Bases*, pages 601–612, Trondheim, Norway, August–September 2005.

[46] D. X. Song, D. Wagner, and A. Perrig. Practical techniques for searches on encrypted data. In *Proceedings of the 21st IEEE Symposium on Security and Privacy*, Oakland, CA, May 2000.

[47] M. Taylor. MySQL proxy. https://launchpad.net/mysql-proxy.

[48] B. Thompson, S. Haber, W. G. Horne, T. S, and D. Yao. Privacy-preserving computation and verification of aggregate queries on outsourced databases. Technical Report HPL-2009-119, HP Labs, 2009.

[49] E. P. Wobber, M. Abadi, M. Burrows, and B. Lampson. Authentication in the Taos operating system. *ACM Transactions on Computer Systems*, 12(1):3–32, 1994.

[50] L. Xiong, S. Chitti, and L. Liu. Preserving data privacy for outsourcing data aggregation services. Technical Report TR-2007-013, Emory University, Department of Mathematics and Computer Science, 2007.

[51] Z. Yang, S. Zhong, and R. N. Wright. Privacy-preserving queries on encrypted data. In *European Symposium on Research in Computer Security*, 2006.

[52] A. Yip, X. Wang, N. Zeldovich, and M. F. Kaashoek. Improving application security with data flow assertions. In *Proceedings of the 22nd ACM Symposium on Operating Systems Principles*, pages 291–304, Big Sky, MT, October 2009.

Intrusion Recovery for Database-backed Web Applications

Ramesh Chandra, Taesoo Kim, Meelap Shah, Neha Narula, and Nickolai Zeldovich
MIT CSAIL

ABSTRACT

WARP is a system that helps users and administrators of web applications recover from intrusions such as SQL injection, cross-site scripting, and clickjacking attacks, while preserving legitimate user changes. WARP repairs from an intrusion by rolling back parts of the database to a version before the attack, and replaying subsequent legitimate actions. WARP allows administrators to *retroactively patch* security vulnerabilities—i.e., apply new security patches to past executions—to recover from intrusions without requiring the administrator to track down or even detect attacks. WARP's *time-travel database* allows fine-grained rollback of database rows, and enables repair to proceed concurrently with normal operation of a web application. Finally, WARP *captures and replays user input at the level of a browser's DOM*, to recover from attacks that involve a user's browser. For a web server running MediaWiki, WARP requires no application source code changes to recover from a range of common web application vulnerabilities with minimal user input at a cost of 24–27% in throughput and 2–3.2 GB/day in storage.

Categories and Subject Descriptors: H.3.5 [**Information Storage and Retrieval**]: Online Information Services—*Web-based services.*

General Terms: Security.

1 INTRODUCTION

Many web applications have security vulnerabilities that have yet to be discovered. For example, over the past 4 years, an average of 3–4 previously unknown cross-site scripting and SQL injection vulnerabilities were discovered *every single day* [27]. Even if a web application's code contains no vulnerabilities, administrators may misconfigure security policies, making the application vulnerable to attack, or users may inadvertently grant their privileges to malicious code [8]. As a result, even well-maintained applications can and do get compromised [4, 31, 33]. Furthermore, after gaining unauthorized access, an attacker could use web application functionality such as Google Apps Script [7, 9] to install persistent malicious code, and trigger it at a later time, even after the underlying vulnerability has been fixed.

Despite this prevalence of vulnerabilities that allows adversaries to compromise web applications, recovering from a newly discovered vulnerability is a difficult and manual process. Users or administrators must manually inspect the application for signs of an attack that exploited the vulnerability, and if an attack is found, they must track down the attacker's actions and repair the damage by hand.

Worse yet, this time-consuming process provides no guarantees that every intrusion was found, or that all changes by the attacker were reverted. As web applications take on more functionality of traditional desktop applications, intrusion recovery for web applications will become increasingly important.

This paper presents WARP[1], a system that automates repair from intrusions in web applications. When an administrator learns of a security vulnerability in a web application, he or she can use WARP to check whether that vulnerability was recently exploited, and to recover from any resulting intrusions. Users and administrators can also use WARP to repair from configuration mistakes, such as accidentally giving permissions to the wrong user. WARP works by continuously recording database updates, and logging information about all actions, such as HTTP requests and database queries, along with their input and output dependencies. WARP constructs a global dependency graph from this logged information, and uses it to *retroactively patch* vulnerabilities by rolling back parts of the system to an earlier checkpoint, fixing the vulnerability (e.g., patching a PHP file, or reverting unintended permission changes), and re-executing any past actions that may have been affected by the fix. This both detects any intrusions that exploited the vulnerability and reverts their effects.

To illustrate the extent of challenges facing WARP in recovering from intrusions in a web application, consider the following worst-case attack on a company's Wiki site that is used by both employees and customers, where each user has privileges to edit only certain pages or documents. An attacker logs into the Wiki site and exploits a cross-site scripting (XSS) vulnerability in the Wiki software to inject malicious JavaScript code into one of the publicly accessible Wiki pages. When Alice, a legitimate user, views that page, her browser starts running the attacker's code, which in turn issues HTTP requests to add the attacker to the access control list for every page that Alice can access, and to propagate the attack code to some of those pages. The adversary now uses his new privileges to further modify pages. In the meantime, legitimate users (including Alice) continue to access and edit Wiki pages, including pages modified or infected by the attack.

Although the Retro system previously explored intrusion recovery for command-line workloads on a single machine [14], WARP is the first system to repair from such attacks in web applications. Recovering from intrusions such as the example above requires WARP to address three challenges not answered by Retro, as follows.

First, recovering from an intrusion (e.g., in Retro) typically requires an expert administrator to detect the compromise and to track down the source of the attack, by analyzing database entries and web server logs. Worse yet, this process must be repeated every time a new security problem is discovered, to determine if any attackers might have exploited the vulnerability.

Second, web applications typically handle data on behalf of many users, only a few of which may have been affected by an attack. For a popular web application with many users, reverting all users' changes since the attack or taking the application offline for repair is not an option.

---

[1] WARP stands for Web Application RePair.

Third, attacks can affect users' browsers, making it difficult to track down the extent of the intrusion purely on the server. In our example attack, when Alice (or any other user) visits an infected Wiki page, the web server cannot tell if a subsequent page edit request from Alice's browser was caused by Alice or by the malicious JavaScript code. Yet an ideal system should revert all effects of the malicious code while preserving any edits that Alice made from the same page in her browser.

To address these challenges, WARP builds on the rollback-and-reexecute approach to repair taken by Retro, but solves a new problem—repair for distributed, web-based applications—using three novel ideas. First, WARP allows administrators to *retroactively apply security patches* without having to manually track down the source of each attack, or even having to decide whether someone already exploited the newfound vulnerability. Retroactive patching works by re-executing past actions using patched application code. If an action re-executes the same way as it did originally, it did not trigger the vulnerability, and requires no further re-execution. Actions that re-execute differently on patched application code could have been intrusions that exploited the original bug, and WARP repairs from this potential attack by recursively re-executing any other actions that were causally affected.

Second, WARP uses a *time-travel database* to determine dependencies between queries, such as finding the set of legitimate database queries whose results were influenced by the queries that an adversary issued. WARP uses these dependencies to roll back just the affected parts of the database during repair. Precise dependencies are crucial to minimize the amount of rollback and re-execution during repair; otherwise, recovering from a week-old attack that affected just one user would still require re-executing a week's worth of work. Precise dependency analysis and rollback is difficult because database queries operate on entire tables that contain information about all users, instead of individual data objects related to a single user. WARP addresses this problem by partitioning tables on popular lookup keys and using partitions to determine dependencies at a finer granularity than entire database tables. By tracking multiple versions of a row, WARP can also perform repair concurrently with the normal operation of the web application.

Third, to help users recover from attacks that involve client machines, such as cross-site scripting, WARP performs *DOM-level replay of user input*. In our example, WARP's repair process will first roll back any database changes caused by Alice's browser, then open a repaired (and presumably no longer malicious) version of the Wiki page Alice visited, and replay the inputs Alice originally provided to the infected page. Operating at the DOM level allows WARP to replay user input even if the underlying page changed (e.g., the attack's HTML and JavaScript is gone), and can often preserve legitimate changes without any user input. WARP uses a client-side browser extension to record and upload events to the server, and uses a browser clone on the server to re-execute them.

To evaluate our ideas in practice, we built a prototype of WARP, and ported MediaWiki, a popular Wiki application, to run on WARP. We show that an administrator using WARP can fully recover from six different attacks on MediaWiki, either by retroactively applying a security patch (for software vulnerabilities), or by undoing a past action (for administrator's mistakes). WARP requires no application changes, incurs a 24–27% CPU and 2–3.2 GB/day storage cost on a single server, and requires little user input.

In the rest of this paper, we start with an overview of WARP's design and assumptions in §2. We describe the key aspects of WARP's design—retroactive patching, the time-travel database, and browser re-execution—in §3, §4, and §5 respectively. §6 presents our prototype implementation, and §7 explains how all parts of WARP fit together in the context of an example. We evaluate WARP in §8, and compare it to related work in §9. §10 discusses WARP's limitations and future work, and §11 concludes.

2 OVERVIEW

The goal of WARP is to recover the integrity of a web application after it has been compromised by an adversary. More specifically, WARP's goal is to undo all changes made by the attacker to the system, including all indirect effects of the attacker's changes on legitimate actions of other users (e.g., through cross-site scripting vulnerabilities), and to produce a system state as if all the legitimate changes still occurred, but the adversary never compromised the application.

WARP's workflow begins with the administrator deciding that he or she wants to make a retroactive fix to the system, such as applying a security patch or changing a permission in the past. At a high level, WARP then rolls back the system to a checkpoint before the intended time of the fix, applies the fix, and re-executes actions that happened since that checkpoint, to construct a new system state. This produces a repaired system state that would have been generated if all of the recorded actions happened on the fixed system in the first place. If some of the recorded actions exploited a vulnerability that the fix prevents, those actions will no longer have the same effect in the repaired system state, effectively undoing the attack.

If the application is non-deterministic, there may be many possible repaired states, and WARP only guarantees to provide one of them, which may not necessarily be the one closest to the pre-repair state. In other words, non-deterministic changes unrelated to the attack may appear as a result of repair, and non-determinism may increase the number of actions re-executed during repair, but the repaired state is guaranteed to be free of effects of attack actions. Also, due to changes in system state during repair, some of the original actions may no longer make sense during replay, such as when a user edits a Wiki page created by the attacker and that page no longer exists due to repair. These actions are marked as *conflicts* and WARP asks the user for help in resolving them.

WARP cannot undo disclosures of private data, such as if an adversary steals sensitive information from Wiki pages, or steals a user's password. However, when private data is leaked, WARP can still help track down affected users. Additionally, in the case of stolen credentials, administrators can use WARP to retroactively change the passwords of affected users (at the risk of undoing legitimate changes), or revert just the attacker's actions, if they can identify the attacker's IP address.

The rest of this section first provides a short review of Retro, and then discusses how WARP builds on the ideas from Retro to repair from intrusions in web applications, followed by a summary of the assumptions made by WARP.

2.1 Review of Retro

Repairing from an intrusion in Retro, which operates at the operating system level, involves five steps. First, during normal execution, Retro records a log of all system calls and periodically checkpoints the file system. Second, the administrator must detect the intrusion, and track down the initial attack action (such as a user accidentally running a malware binary). Third, Retro rolls back the files affected by the attack to a checkpoint before the intrusion. Fourth, Retro re-executes legitimate processes that were affected by the rolled-back file (e.g., any process that read the file in the past), but avoids re-executing the attack action. Finally, to undo indirect effects of the attack, Retro finds any other processes whose inputs may have changed as a result of re-execution, rolls back any files they modified, and recursively re-executes them too.

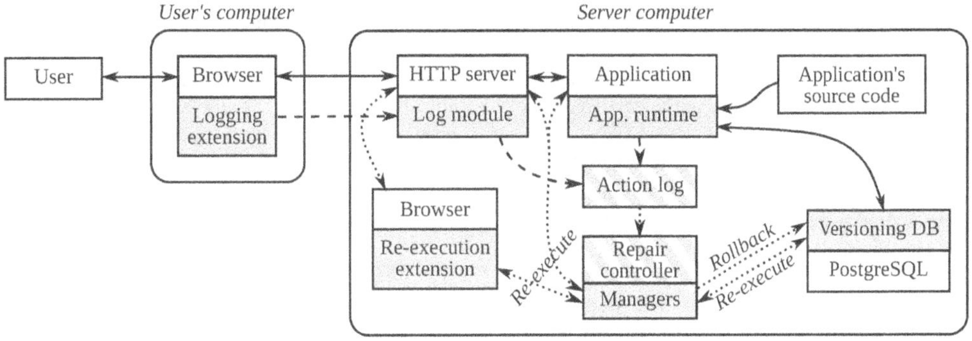

Figure 1: Overview of WARP's design. Components introduced or modified by WARP are shaded; components borrowed from Retro are striped. Solid arrows are the original web application interactions that exist without WARP. Dashed lines indicate interactions added by WARP for logging during normal execution, and dotted lines indicate interactions added by WARP during repair.

A naïve system that re-executed every action since the attack would face two challenges. First, re-execution is expensive: if the attack occurred a week ago, re-executing everything may take another week. Second, re-execution may produce different results, for reasons that have nothing to do with the attack (e.g., because some process is non-deterministic). A different output produced by one process can lead to a conflict when Retro tries to re-execute subsequent processes, and would require user input to resolve. For example, re-executing sshd can generate a different key for an ssh connection, which makes it impossible to replay that connection's network packets. Thus, while Retro needs some processes to produce different outputs (e.g., to undo the effects of an attack), Retro also needs to minimize re-execution in order to minimize conflicts that require user input, and to improve performance.

To reduce re-execution, Retro checks for *equivalence* of inputs to a process before and after repair, to decide whether to re-execute a process. If the inputs to a process during repair are identical to the inputs originally seen by that process, Retro skips re-execution of that process. Thus, even if some of the files read by a process may have been changed during repair, Retro need not re-execute a process that did not read the changed parts of the file.

Retro's design separates the overall logic of rollback, repair, and recursive propagation (the *repair controller*) from the low-level details of file system rollback and process re-execution (handled by individual *repair managers*). During normal execution, managers record information about checkpoints, actions, and dependencies into a global data structure called an *action history graph*, and periodically garbage-collect old checkpoints and action history graph entries. A node in the action history graph logically represents the history of some part of the system over time, such as all versions of a certain file or directory. The action history graph also contains actions, such as a process executing for some period of time or issuing a system call. An action has dependencies to and from nodes at a specific time, indicating the versions of a node that either influenced or were influenced by that action. During repair, the repair controller consults the action history graph, and invokes the managers as needed for rollback and re-execution. We refer the reader to Kim et al. [14] for further details.

2.2 Repairing web applications

WARP builds on Retro's repair controller to repair from intrusions in web applications. Figure 1 illustrates WARP's design, and its relation to components borrowed from Retro (in particular, the repair controller, and the structure of the action history graph). WARP's design involves the web browser, HTTP server, application code, and database. Each of these four components corresponds to a *repair*

manager in WARP, which records enough information during normal operation to perform rollback and re-execution during repair.

To understand how WARP repairs from an attack, consider the example scenario we presented in §1, where an attacker uses a cross-site scripting attack to inject malicious JavaScript code into a Wiki page. When Alice visits that page, her browser runs the malicious code, and issues HTTP requests to propagate the attack to another page and to give the attacker access to Alice's pages. The attacker then uses his newfound access to corrupt some of Alice's pages. In the meantime, other users continue using the Wiki site: some users visit the page containing the attack code, other users visit and edit pages corrupted by the attack, and yet other users visit unaffected pages.

Some time after the attack takes place, the administrator learns that a cross-site scripting vulnerability was discovered by the application's developers, and a security patch for one of the source files— say, `calendar.php`—is now available. In order to retroactively apply this security patch, WARP first determines which runs of the application code may have been affected by a bug in `calendar.php`. WARP then applies the security patch to `calendar.php`, and considers re-executing all potentially affected runs of the application. In order to re-execute the application, WARP records sufficient information during the original execution[2] about all of the inputs to the application, such as the HTTP request. To minimize the chance that the application re-executes differently for reasons *other* than the security patch, WARP records and replays the original return values from non-deterministic function calls. §3 discusses how WARP implements retroactive patching in more detail.

Now consider what happens when WARP re-executes the application code for the attacker's initial request. Instead of adding the attacker's JavaScript code to the Wiki page as it did during the original execution, the newly patched application code will behave differently (e.g., pass the attacker's JavaScript code through a sanitization function), and then issue an SQL query to store the resulting page in the database. This SQL query must logically replace the application's original query that stored an infected page, so WARP first rolls back the database to its state before the attack took place.

After the database has been rolled back, and the new query has executed, WARP must determine what other parts of the system were affected by this changed query. To do this, during original execution WARP records all SQL queries, along with their results. During repair, WARP re-executes any queries it determines may have been affected by the changed query. If a re-executed query produces results different from the original execution, WARP re-executes the

---

[2]We use the terms "original execution" and "normal execution" interchangeably.

corresponding application run as well, such as Alice's subsequent page visit to the infected page. §4 describes the design of WARP's time-travel database in more detail, including how it determines query dependencies, how it re-executes queries in the past, and how it minimizes rollback.

When the application run for Alice's visit to the infected page is re-executed, it generates a different HTTP response for Alice's browser (with the attack now gone). WARP must now determine how Alice's browser would behave given this new page. Simply undoing all subsequent HTTP requests from Alice's browser would needlessly undo all of her legitimate work, and asking Alice to manually check each HTTP request that her browser made is not practical either. To help Alice recover from such attacks, WARP provides a browser extension that records all events for each open page in her browser (such as HTTP requests and user input) and uploads this information to the server. If WARP determines that her browser may have been affected by an attack, it starts a clone of her browser on the server, and re-executes her original input on the repaired page, without having to involve her. Since Alice's re-executed browser will no longer issue the HTTP requests from the XSS attack, WARP will recursively undo the effects of those requests as well. §5 explains how WARP's browser extension works in more detail.

If a user's actions depend on changes by the attacker, WARP may be unable to replay the user's original inputs in the browser clone. For example, if the attacker created a new Wiki page, and a curious user subsequently edited that page, WARP will not be able to re-execute the user's actions once the attack is undone. In this case, WARP signals a conflict and asks the user (or administrator) to resolve it. WARP cannot rely on users being always online, so WARP queues the conflict, and proceeds with repair.

When the user next logs in, WARP redirects the user to a conflict resolution page. To resolve a conflict, the user is presented with the original page they visited, the newly repaired version of that page, and the original action that the server is unable to replay on the new page, and is asked to specify what actions they would like to perform instead. For example, the user can ask WARP to cancel that page visit altogether. Users or administrators can also use the same mechanism to undo their own actions from the past, such as if an administrator accidentally gave administrative privileges to a user. §5 further discusses WARP's handling of conflicts and user-initiated undo.

2.3 Assumptions

To recover from intrusions, WARP makes two key assumptions. First, WARP assumes that the adversary does not exploit any vulnerabilities in the HTTP server, database, or the application's language runtime, does not cause the application code to execute arbitrary code (e.g., spawning a Unix shell), and does not corrupt WARP's log. Most web application vulnerabilities fall into this category [10], and §8 shows how WARP can repair from common attacks such as cross-site scripting, SQL injection, cross-site request forgery, and clickjacking.

Second, to recover from intrusions that involve a user's browser, our prototype requires the user to install a browser extension that uploads dependency information to WARP-enabled web servers. In principle, the same functionality could be performed purely in JavaScript (see §10), but for simplicity, our prototype uses a separate extension. WARP's server trusts each browser's log information only as much as it trusts the browser's HTTP requests. This ensures that a malicious user cannot gain additional privileges by uploading a log containing user input that tries to issue different HTTP requests.

If one user does not have our prototype's extension installed, but gets compromised by a cross-site scripting attack, WARP will not be able to precisely undo the effects of malicious JavaScript code in that user's browser. As a result, server-side state accessible to that user (e.g., that user's Wiki pages or documents) may remain corrupted. However, WARP will still inform the user that his or her browser might have received a compromised reply from the server in the past. At that point, the user can manually inspect the set of changes made to his data from that point onward, and cancel his or her previous HTTP requests, if unwanted changes are detected.

3 RETROACTIVE PATCHING

To implement retroactive patching, WARP's application repair manager must be able to determine which runs of an application may have been affected by a given security patch, and to re-execute them during repair. To enable this, WARP's application repair manager interposes on the application's language runtime (PHP in our current prototype) to record any dependencies to and from the application, including application code loaded at runtime, queries issued to the database, and HTTP requests and responses sent to or from the HTTP server.

3.1 Normal execution

During normal execution, the application repair manager records three types of dependencies for the executing application code (along with the dependency's data, used later for re-execution). First, the repair manager records an input dependency to the HTTP request and an output dependency to the HTTP response for this run of the application code (along with all headers and data). Second, for each read or write SQL query issued by the application, the repair manager records, respectively, input or output dependencies to the database. Third, the repair manager records input dependencies on the source code files used by the application to handle its specific HTTP request. This includes the initial PHP file invoked by the HTTP request, as well as any additional PHP source files loaded at runtime through `require` or `include` statements.

In addition to recording external dependencies, WARP's application manager also records certain internal functions invoked by the application code, to reduce non-determinism during re-execution. This includes calls to functions that return the current date or time, functions that return randomness (such as `mt_rand` in PHP), and functions that generate unique identifiers for HTTP sessions (such as `session_start` in PHP). For each of these functions, the application manager records the arguments and return value. This information is used to avoid re-executing these non-deterministic functions during repair, as we will describe shortly.

3.2 Initiating repair

To initiate repair through retroactive patching, the administrator needs to provide the filename of the buggy source code file, a patch to that file which removes the vulnerability, and a time at which this patch should be applied (by default, the oldest time available in WARP's log). In response, the application repair manager adds a new action to WARP's action history graph, whose re-execution would apply the patch to the relevant file at the specified (past) time. The application repair manager then requests that WARP's repair controller re-execute the newly synthesized action. WARP will first re-execute this action (i.e., apply the patch to the file in question), and then use dependencies recorded by the application repair manager to find and re-execute all runs of the application that loaded the patched source code file.

3.3 Re-execution

During re-execution, the application repair manager invokes the application code in much the same way as during normal execution, with two differences. First, all inputs and outputs to and from the application are handled by the repair controller. This allows the repair controller to determine when re-execution is necessary, such as when a different SQL query is issued during repair, and to avoid re-executing actions that are not affected or changed.

Second, the application repair manager tries to match up calls to non-deterministic functions during re-execution with their counterparts during the original run. In particular, when a non-deterministic function is invoked during re-execution, the application repair manager searches for a call to the same function, from the same caller location. If a match is found, the application repair manager uses the original return value in lieu of invoking the function. The repair manager matches non-deterministic function calls from the same call site in-order (i.e., two non-deterministic function calls that happened in some order during re-execution will always be matched up to function calls in that same order during the original run).

One important aspect of this heuristic is that it is strictly an optimization. Even if the heuristic fails to match up any of the non-deterministic function calls, the repair process will still be *correct*, at the cost of increased re-execution (e.g., if the application code generates a different HTTP cookie during re-execution, WARP will be forced to re-execute all page visits that used that cookie).

4 TIME-TRAVEL DATABASE

The job of WARP's time-travel database is to checkpoint and roll back the application's persistent data, and to re-execute past SQL queries during repair. Its design is motivated by two requirements: first, the need to minimize the number of SQL queries that have to be re-executed during repair, and second, the need to repair a web application concurrently with normal operation. This section discusses how WARP addresses these requirements.

4.1 Reducing re-execution

Minimizing the re-execution of SQL queries during repair is complicated by the fact that clients issue queries over entire tables, and tables often contain data for many independent users or objects of the same type.

There are two reasons why WARP may need to re-execute an SQL query. First, an SQL query that modifies the database (e.g., an INSERT, UPDATE, or DELETE statement) needs to be re-executed in order to re-apply legitimate changes to a database after rollback. Second, an SQL query that reads the database (e.g., a SELECT statement, or any statement with a WHERE clause) needs to be re-executed if the data read by that statement may have changed as a result of repair.

To minimize re-execution of write SQL queries, the database manager performs fine-grained rollback, at the level of individual rows in a table. This ensures that, if one row is rolled back, it may not be necessary to re-execute updates to other rows in the same table. One complication lies in the fact that SQL has no inherent way of naming unique rows in a database. To address this limitation, WARP introduces the notion of a *row ID*, which is a unique name for a row in a table. Many web applications already use synthetic primary keys which can serve as row IDs; in this case, WARP uses that primary key as a row ID in that table. If a table does not already have a suitable row ID column, WARP's database manager transparently adds an extra row_id column for this purpose.

To minimize re-execution of SQL queries that read the database, the database manager logically splits the table into *partitions*, based on the values of one or more of the table's columns. During repair, the database manager keeps track of the set of partitions that have been modified (as a result of either rollback or re-execution), and avoids re-executing SQL queries that read from only unmodified

partitions. To determine the partitions read by an SQL query, the database manager inspects the query's WHERE clause. If the database manager cannot determine what partitions a query might read based on the WHERE clause, it conservatively assumes that the query reads all partitions.

In our current prototype, the programmer or administrator must manually specify the row ID column for each table (if they want to avoid the overhead of an extra row_id column created by WARP), and the partitioning columns for each table (if they want to benefit from the partitioning optimization). A partitioning column need not be the same column as the row ID. For example, a Wiki application may store Wiki pages in a table with four columns: a unique page ID, the page title, the user ID of the last user who edited the page, and the contents of that Wiki page. Because the title, the last editor's user ID, and the content of a page can change, the programmer would specify the immutable page ID as the row ID column. However, the application's SQL queries may access pages either by their title or by the last editor's user ID, so the programmer would specify them as the partitioning columns.

4.2 Re-executing multi-row queries

SQL queries can access multiple rows in a table at once, if the query's WHERE clause does not guarantee a unique row. Re-executing such queries—where WARP cannot guarantee by looking at the WHERE clause that only a single row is involved—poses two challenges. First, in the case of a query that may read multiple rows, WARP must ensure that all of those rows are in the correct state prior to re-executing that query. For instance, if some of those rows have been rolled back to an earlier version due to repair, but other rows have not been rolled back since they were not affected, naïvely re-executing the multi-row query can produce incorrect results, mixing data from old and new rows. Second, in the case of a query that may modify multiple rows, WARP must roll back all of those rows prior to re-executing that query, and subsequently re-execute any queries that read those rows.

To re-execute multi-row read queries, WARP performs *continuous versioning* of the database, by keeping track of every value that ever existed for each row. When re-executing a query that accesses some rows that have been rolled back, and other rows that have not been touched by repair, WARP allows the re-executed query to access the old value of the untouched rows from precisely the time that query originally ran. Thus, continuous versioning allows WARP's database manager to avoid rolling back and reconstructing rows for the sole purpose of re-executing a read query on their old value.

To re-execute multi-row write queries, WARP performs *two-phase re-execution* by splitting the query into two parts: the WHERE clause, and the actual write query. During normal execution, WARP records the set of row IDs of all rows affected by a write query. During re-execution, WARP first executes a SELECT statement to obtain the set of row IDs matching the new WHERE clause. These row IDs correspond to the rows that would be modified by this new write query on re-execution. WARP uses continuous versioning to precisely roll back both the original and new row IDs to a time just before the write query originally executed. It then re-executes the write query on this rolled-back database.

To implement continuous versioning, WARP augments every table with two additional columns, start_time and end_time, which indicate the time interval during which that row value was valid. Each row R in the original table becomes a series of rows in the continuously versioned table, where the end_time value of one version of R is the start_time value of the next version of R. The column end_time can have the special value ∞, indicating that row version is the current value of R. During normal execution, if an SQL query modifies a set of rows, WARP sets end_time for the modified rows to the current time, with the rest of the columns retaining their old values, and inserts a new set of rows with start_time set to the current time, end_time set to ∞, and the rest of the columns containing the new versions of those rows. When a row is deleted, WARP simply sets end_time to the current time. Read queries during normal execution always access rows with end_time $= \infty$. Rolling back a row to time T involves deleting versions of the row with start_time $\geq T$ and setting end_time $\leftarrow \infty$ for the version with the largest remaining end_time.

Since WARP's continuous versioning database grows in size as the application makes modifications, the database manager periodically deletes old versions of rows. Since repair requires that both the old versions of database rows and the action history graph be available for rollback and re-execution, the database manager deletes old rows in sync with WARP's garbage-collection of the action history graph.

4.3 Concurrent repair and normal operation

Since web applications are often serving many users, it's undesirable to take the application offline while recovering from an intrusion. To address this problem, WARP's database manager introduces the notion of *repair generations*, identified by an integer counter, which are used to denote the state of the database after a given number of repairs. Normal execution happens in the *current* repair generation. When repair is initiated, the database manager creates the *next* repair generation (by incrementing the current repair generation counter by one), which creates a fork of the current database contents. All database operations during repair are applied to the next generation. If, during repair, users make changes to parts of the current generation that are being repaired, WARP will re-apply the users' changes to the next generation through re-execution. Changes to parts of the database not under repair are copied verbatim into the next generation. Once repair is near completion, the web server is briefly suspended, any final requests are re-applied to the next generation, the current generation is set to the next generation, and the web server is resumed.

To implement repair generations, WARP augments all tables with two additional columns, start_gen and end_gen, which indicate the generations in which a row is valid. Much as with continuous versioning, end_gen $= \infty$ indicates that the row has not been superseded in any later generation. During normal execution, queries execute over rows that match start_gen $\leq$ *current* and end_gen $\geq$ *current*. During repair, if a row with start_gen $<$ *next* and end_gen $\geq$ *next* is about to be updated or deleted (due to either re-execution or rollback), the existing row's end_gen is set to *current*, and, in case of updates, the update is executed on a copy of the row with start_gen $=$ *next*.

4.4 Rewriting SQL queries

WARP intercepts all SQL queries made by the application, and transparently rewrites them to implement database versioning and generations. For each query, WARP determines the time and generation in which the query should execute. For queries issued as part of normal execution, WARP uses the current time and generation. For queries issued as part of repair, WARP's repair controller explicitly specifies the time for the re-executed query, and the query always executes in the *next* generation.

To execute a SELECT query at time T in generation G, WARP restricts the query to run over currently valid rows by augmenting its WHERE clause with AND start_time $\leq T \leq$ end_time AND start_gen $\leq G \leq$ end_gen.

During normal execution, on an UPDATE or DELETE query at time T (the current time), WARP implements versioning by making a copy of the rows being modified. To do this, WARP sets

the end_time of rows being modified in the *current* generation to T, and inserts copies of the rows with start_time $\leftarrow T$, end_time $\leftarrow \infty$, start_gen $\leftarrow G$, and end_gen $\leftarrow \infty$, where $G =$ *current*. WARP also restricts the WHERE clause of such queries to run over currently valid rows, as with SELECT queries above. On an INSERT query, WARP sets start_time, end_time, start_gen, and end_gen columns of the inserted row as for UPDATE and DELETE queries above.

To execute an UPDATE or DELETE query during repair at time T, WARP must first preserve any rows being modified that are also accessible from the *current* generation, so that they continue to be accessible to concurrently executing queries in the *current* generation. To do so, WARP creates a copy of all matching rows, with end_gen set to *current*, sets the start_gen of the rows to be modified to *next*, and then executes the UPDATE or DELETE query as above, except in generation $G =$ *next*. Executing an INSERT query during repair does not require preserving any existing rows; in this case, WARP simply performs the same query rewriting as for normal execution, with $G =$ *next*.

5 BROWSER RE-EXECUTION

To help users recover from attacks that took place in their browsers, WARP uses two ideas. First, when WARP determines that a past HTTP response was incorrect, it *re-executes the changed web page in a cloned browser* on the server, in order to determine how that page would behave as a result of the change. For example, if a new HTTP response no longer contains an adversary's JavaScript code (e.g., because the cross-site scripting vulnerability was retroactively patched), re-executing the page in a cloned browser will not generate the HTTP requests that the attacker's JavaScript code may have originally initiated, and will thus allow WARP to undo those requests.

Second, WARP performs *DOM-level replay of user input* when re-executing pages in a browser. By recording and re-executing user input at the level of the browser's DOM, WARP can better capture the user's intent as to what page elements the user was trying to interact with. A naïve approach that recorded pixel-level mouse events and key strokes may fail to replay correctly when applied to a page whose HTML code has changed slightly. On the other hand, DOM elements are more likely to be unaffected by small changes to an HTML page, allowing WARP to automatically re-apply the user's original inputs to a modified page during repair.

5.1 Tracking page dependencies

In order to determine what should be re-executed in the browser given some changes on the server, WARP needs to be able to correlate activity on the server with activity in users' browsers.

First, to correlate requests coming from the same web browser, WARP's browser extension assigns each client a unique client ID value. The client ID also helps WARP keep track of log information uploaded to the server by different clients. The client ID is a long random value to ensure that an adversary cannot guess the client ID of a legitimate user and upload logs on behalf of that user.

Second, WARP also needs to correlate different HTTP requests coming from the same page in a browser. To do this, WARP introduces the notion of a *page visit*, corresponding to the period of time that a single web page is open in a browser frame (e.g., a tab, or a sub-frame in a window). If the browser loads a new page in the same frame, WARP considers this to be a new visit (regardless of whether the frame navigated to a different URL or to the same URL), since the frame's page starts executing in the browser anew. In particular, WARP's browser extension assigns each page visit a visit ID, unique within a client. Each page visit can also have a dependency on a previous page visit. For example, if the user clicks on a link as part of page visit #1, the browser extension creates page visit #2, which depends on page visit #1. This allows WARP to check whether page visit #2 needs to re-execute if page visit #1 changes. If the user clicks on more links, and later hits the back button to return to the page from visit #2, this creates a fresh page visit #N (for the same page URL as visit #2), which also depends on visit #1.

Finally, WARP needs to correlate HTTP requests issued by the web browser with HTTP requests received by the HTTP server, for tracking dependencies. To do this, the WARP browser extension assigns each HTTP request a request ID, unique within a page visit, and sends the client ID, visit ID, and request ID along with every HTTP request to the server via HTTP headers.

On the server side, the HTTP server's manager records dependencies between HTTP requests and responses (identified by a $\langle client\_id, visit\_id, request\_id \rangle$ tuple) and runs of application code (identified by a $\langle pid, count \rangle$ tuple, where pid is the PID of the long-lived PHP runtime process, and $count$ is a unique counter identifying a specific run of the application).

5.2 Recording events

During normal execution, the browser extension performs two tasks. First, it annotates all HTTP requests, as described above, with HTTP headers to help the server correlate client-side actions with server-side actions. Second, it records all JavaScript events that occur during each page visit (including timer events, user input events, and postMessage events). For each event, the extension records event parameters, including time and event type, and the XPath of the event's target DOM element, which helps perform DOM-level replay during repair.

The extension uploads its log of JavaScript events for each page visit to the server, using a separate protocol (tagged with the client ID and visit ID). On the server side, WARP's HTTP server records the submitted information from the client into a separate per-client log, which is subject to its own storage quota and garbage-collection policy. This ensures that a single client cannot monopolize log space on the server, and more importantly, cannot cause a server to garbage-collect recent log entries from other users needed for repair.

Although the current WARP prototype implements client-side logging using an extension, the extension does not circumvent any of the browser's privacy policies. All of the information recorded by WARP's browser extension can be captured at the JavaScript level by event handlers, and in future work, we hope to implement an extension-less version of WARP's browser logging by interposing on all events using JavaScript rewriting.

5.3 Server-side re-execution

When WARP determines that an HTTP response changed during repair, the browser repair manager spawns a browser on the server to re-execute the client's uploaded browser log for the affected page visit. This re-execution browser loads the client's HTTP cookies, loads the same URL as during original execution, and replays the client's original DOM-level events. The user's cookies are loaded either from the HTTP server's log, if re-executing the first page for a client, or from the last browser page re-executed for that client. The re-executed browser runs in a sandbox, and only has access to the client's HTTP cookie, ensuring that it gets no additional privileges despite running on the server. To handle HTTP requests from the re-executing browser, the HTTP server manager starts a separate copy of the HTTP server, which passes any HTTP requests to the repair controller, as opposed to executing them directly. This allows the repair controller to prune re-execution for identical requests or responses.

During repair, WARP uses a *re-execution extension* in the server-side browser to replay the events originally recorded by the user's browser. For each event, the re-execution extension tries to locate the appropriate DOM element using its XPath. For keyboard input events into text fields, the re-execution extension performs a three-way text merge between the original value of the text field, the new value of the text field during repair, and the user's original keyboard input. For example, this allows the re-execution extension to replay the user's changes to a text area when editing a Wiki page, even if the Wiki page in the text area is somewhat different during repair.

If, after repair, a user's HTTP cookie in the cloned browser differs from the user's cookie in his or her real browser (based on the original timeline), WARP queues that client's cookie for invalidation, and the next time the same client connects to the web server (based on the client ID), the client's cookie will be deleted. WARP assumes that the browser has no persistent client-side state aside from the cookie. Repair of other client-side state could be similarly handled at the expense of additional logging and synchronization.

5.4 Conflicts

During repair, the server-side browser extension may fail to re-execute the user's original inputs, if the user's actions somehow depended on the reverted actions of the attacker. For example, in the case of a Wiki page, the user may have inadvertently edited a part of the Wiki page that the attacker modified. In this situation, WARP's browser repair manager signals a conflict, stops re-execution of that user's browser, and requires the user (or an administrator, in lieu of the user) to resolve the conflict.

Since users are not always online, WARP queues the conflict for later resolution, and proceeds with repair, assuming, for now, that subsequent requests from that user's browser do not change. When the user next logs into the web application (based on the client ID), the application redirects the user to a conflict resolution page, which tells the user about the page on which the conflict arose, and the user's input which could not be replayed. The user must then indicate how the conflict should be resolved. For example, the user can indicate that they would like to cancel the conflicted page visit altogether (i.e., undo all of its HTTP requests), and apply the legitimate changes (if any) to the current state of the system by hand.

While WARP's re-execution extension flags conflicts that arise during replay of input *from* the user, some applications may have important information that must be correctly displayed *to* the user. For example, if an online banking application displayed $1,000 as the user's account balance during the original execution, but during repair it is discovered that the user's balance should have been $2,000, WARP will not raise a re-execution conflict. An application programmer, however, can provide a *UI conflict function*, which, given the old and new versions of a web page, can signal a conflict even if all of the user input events replay correctly. For the example applications we evaluated with WARP, we did not find the need to implement such conflict functions.

5.5 User-initiated repair

In some situations, users or administrators may want to undo their own past actions. For example, an administrator may have accidentally granted administrative privileges to a user, and later may want to revert any actions that were allowed due to this mis-configuration. To recover from this mistake, the administrator can use WARP's browser extension to specify a URL of the page on which the mistake occurred, find the specific page visit to that URL which led to the mistake, and request that the page visit be canceled. Our prototype does not allow replacing one past action with another, although this is mostly a UI limitation.

Allowing users to undo their own actions runs the risk of creating more conflicts, if other users' actions depended on the action in question. To prevent cascading conflicts, WARP prohibits a regular user

Component	Lines of code
Firefox extension	2,000 lines of JavaScript / HTML
Apache logging module	900 lines of C
PHP runtime / SQL rewriter	1,400 lines of C and PHP
PHP re-execution support	200 lines of Python
Repair managers:	4,300 lines of Python, total
Retro's repair controller	400 lines of Python
PHP manager	800 lines of Python
Apache manager	300 lines of Python
Database manager	1,400 lines of Python and PHP
Firefox manager	400 lines of Python
Retroactive patching manager	200 lines of Python
Others	800 lines of Python

Table 1: Lines of code for different components of the WARP prototype, excluding blank lines and comments.

(as opposed to an administrator) from initiating repair that causes conflicts for other users. WARP's repair generation mechanism allows WARP to try repairing the server-side state upon user-initiated repair, and to abort the repair if any conflicts arise. The only exception to this rule is if the user's repair is a result of a conflict being reported to that user on that page, in which case the user is allowed to cancel all actions, even if it propagates a conflict to another user.

6 IMPLEMENTATION

We have implemented a prototype of WARP which builds on Retro. Our prototype works with the Firefox browser on the client, and Apache, PostgreSQL, and PHP on the server. Table 1 shows the lines of code for the different components of our prototype.

Our Firefox extension intercepts all HTTP requests during normal execution and adds WARP's client ID, visit ID, and request ID headers to them. It also intercepts all browser frame creations, and adds an event listener to the frame's window object. This event listener gets called on every event in the frame, and allows us to record the event. During repair, the re-execution extension tries to match up HTTP requests with requests recorded during normal execution, and adds the matching request ID header when a match is found. Our current conflict resolution UI only allows the user to cancel the conflicting page visit; other conflict resolutions must be performed by hand. We plan to build a more comprehensive UI, but canceling has been sufficient for now.

In our prototype, the user's client-side browser and the server's re-execution browser use the same version of Firefox. While this has simplified the development of our extension, we expect that DOM-level events are sufficiently standardized in modern browsers that it would be possible to replay events across different browsers, such as recent versions of Firefox and Chrome. We have not verified this to date, however.

Our time-travel database and repair generations are implemented on top of PostgreSQL using SQL query rewriting. After the application's database tables are installed, WARP extends the schema of all the tables to add its own columns, including row_id if no existing column was specified as the row ID by the programmer. All database queries are rewritten to update these columns appropriately when the rows are modified. The approach of using query rewriting was chosen to avoid modifying the internals of the Postgres server, although an implementation inside of Postgres would likely have been more efficient.

To allow multiple versions of a row from different times or generations to exist in the same table, WARP modifies database uniqueness constraints and primary keys specified by the application to include the end_ts and end_gen columns. While this allows multiple versions of the same row over time to co-exist in the same table, WARP must now detect dependencies between queries through uniqueness violations. In particular, WARP checks whether the success (or

failure) of each INSERT query would change as a result of other rows inserted or deleted during repair, and rolls back that row if so. WARP needs to consider INSERT statements only for partitions under repair. Our time-travel database implementation does not support foreign keys, so it disables them. We plan to implement foreign key constraints in the future in a database trigger. Our design is compatible with multi-statement transactions; however, our current implementation does not support them, and we did not need them for our current applications.

WARP extends Apache's PHP module to log HTTP requests that invoke PHP scripts. WARP intercepts a PHP script's calls to database functions, mt_rand, date and time functions, and session_start, by rewriting all scripts to call a wrapper function that invokes the wrapped function and logs the arguments and results.

7 PUTTING IT ALL TOGETHER

We now illustrate how different components of WARP work together in the context of a simple Wiki application. In this case, no attack takes place, but most of the steps taken by WARP remain the same as in a case with an attack.

Consider a user who, during normal execution, clicks on a link to edit a Wiki page. The user's browser issues an HTTP request to edit.php. WARP's browser extension intercepts this request, adds client ID, visit ID, and request ID HTTP headers to it, and records the request in its log (§5.1). The web server receives this request and dispatches it to WARP's PHP module. The PHP module assigns this request a unique server-side request ID, records the HTTP request information along with the server-side request ID, and forwards the request to the PHP runtime.

As WARP's PHP runtime executes edit.php, it intercepts three types of operations. First, for each non-deterministic function call, it records the arguments and the return value (§3.1). Second, for each operation that loads an additional PHP source file, it records the file name (§3.1). Third, for each database query, it records the query, rewrites the query to implement WARP's time-travel database, and records the result set and the row IDs of all rows modified by the query (§4).

Once edit.php completes execution, the response is recorded by the PHP module and returned to the browser. When the browser loads the page, WARP's browser extension attaches handlers to intercept user input, and records all intercepted actions in its log (§5.2). The WARP browser extension periodically uploads its log to the server.

When a patch fixing a vulnerability in edit.php becomes available, the administrator instructs WARP to perform retroactive patching. The WARP repair controller uses the action history graph to locate all PHP executions that loaded edit.php and queues them for re-execution; the user edit action described above would be among this set.

To re-execute this page in repair mode, the repair controller launches a browser on the server, identical to the user's browser, and instructs it to replay the user session. The browser re-issues the same requests, and the WARP browser extension assigns the same IDs to the request as during normal execution (§5.3). The WARP PHP module forwards this request to the repair controller, which launches WARP's PHP runtime to re-execute it.

During repair, the PHP runtime intercepts two types of operations. For non-deterministic function calls, it checks whether the same function was called during the original execution, and if so, re-uses the original return value (§3.3). For database queries, it forwards the query to the repair controller for re-execution.

To re-execute a database query, the repair controller determines the rows and partitions that the query depends on, rolls them back

Attack type	CVE	Description	Fix
Reflected XSS	2009-0737	The user options (wgDB*) in the live web-based installer (config/index.php) are not HTML-escaped.	Sanitize all user options with htmlspecialchars() (r46889).
Stored XSS	2009-4589	The name of contribution link (Special:Block?ip) is not HTML-escaped.	Sanitize the ip parameter with htmlspecialchars() (r52521).
CSRF	2010-1150	HTML/API login interfaces do not properly handle an unintended login attempt (login CSRF).	Include a random challenge token in a hidden form field for every login attempt (r64677).
Clickjacking	2011-0003	A malicious website can embed MediaWiki within an iframe.	Add X-Frame-Options:DENY to HTTP headers (r79566).
SQL injection	2004-2186	The language identifier, thelang, is not properly sanitized in SpecialMaintenance.php.	Sanitize the thelang parameter with wfStrencode().
ACL error	—	Administrator accidentally grants admin privileges to a user.	Revoke the user's admin privileges.

Table 2: Security vulnerabilities and corresponding fixes for MediaWiki. Where available, we indicate the revision number of each fix in MediaWiki's subversion repository, in parentheses.

to the right version (for a write operation), rewrites the query to support time-travel and generations, executes the resulting query, and returns the result to the PHP runtime (§4).

After a query re-executes, the repair controller uses the action history graph to find other database queries that depended on the partitions affected by the re-executed query (assuming it was a write). For each such query, the repair controller checks whether their return values would now be different. If so, it queues the page visits that issued those queries for re-execution.

After edit.php completes re-execution, the HTTP response is returned to the repair controller, which forwards it to the re-executing browser via the PHP module. Once the response is loaded in the browser, the WARP browser extension replays the original user inputs on that page (§5.3). If conflicts arise, WARP flags them for manual repair (§5.4).

WARP's repair controller continues repairing pages in this manner until all affected pages are re-executed. Even though no attack took place in this example, this re-execution algorithm would repair from any attack that exploited the vulnerability in edit.php.

8 EVALUATION

In evaluating WARP, we answer several questions. §8.1 shows what it takes to port an existing web application to WARP. §8.2 shows what kinds of attacks WARP can repair from, what attacks can be detected and fixed with retroactive patching, how much re-execution may be required, and how often users need to resolve conflicts. §8.3 shows the effectiveness of WARP's browser re-execution in reducing user conflicts. §8.4 compares WARP with the state-of-the-art work in data recovery for web applications [1]. Finally, §8.5 measures WARP's runtime cost.

We ported a popular Wiki application, MediaWiki [21], to use WARP, and used several previously discovered vulnerabilities to evaluate how well WARP can recover from intrusions that exploit those bugs. The results show that WARP can recover from six common attack types, that retroactive patching detects and repairs all tested software bugs, and that WARP's techniques reduce re-execution and user conflicts. WARP's overheads are 24–27% in throughput and 2–3.2 GB/day of storage.

8.1 Application changes

We did not make any changes to MediaWiki source code to port it to WARP. To choose row IDs for each MediaWiki table, we picked a primary or unique key column whose value MediaWiki assigns once during creation of a row and never overwrites. If there is no such column in a table, WARP adds a new row_id column to the table, transparent to the application. We chose partition columns for each table by analyzing the typical queries made by MediaWiki and picking the columns that are used in the WHERE clauses of a large

number of queries on that table. In all, this required a total of 89 lines of annotation for MediaWiki's 42 tables.

8.2 Recovery from attacks

To evaluate how well WARP can recover from intrusions, we constructed six worst-case attack scenarios based on five recent vulnerabilities in MediaWiki and one configuration mistake by the administrator, shown in Table 2. After each attack, users browse the Wiki site, both reading and editing Wiki pages. Our scenarios purposely create significant interaction between the attacker's changes and legitimate users, to stress WARP's recovery aspects. If WARP can disentangle these challenging attacks, it can also handle any simpler attack.

In the *stored XSS attack*, the attacker injects malicious JavaScript code into a MediaWiki page. When a victim visits that Wiki page, the attacker's JavaScript code appends text to a second Wiki page that the victim has access to, but the attacker does not. The *SQL injection* and *reflected XSS attacks* are similar in design. Successful recovery from these three attacks requires deleting the attacker's JavaScript code; detecting what users were affected by that code; undoing the effects of the JavaScript code in their browsers (i.e., undoing the edits to the second page); verifying that the appended text did not cause browsers of users that visited the second page to misbehave; and preserving all users' legitimate actions.

The *CSRF attack* is a login CSRF attack, where the goal of the attacker is to trick the victim into making her edits on the Wiki under the attacker's account. When the victim visits the attacker's site, the attack exploits the CSRF vulnerability to log the victim out of the Wiki site and log her back in under the attacker's account. The victim then interacts with the Wiki site, believing she is logged in as herself, and edits various pages. A successful repair in this scenario would undo all of the victim's edits under the attacker's account, and re-apply them under the victim's own account.

In the *clickjacking attack*, the attacker's site loads the Wiki site in an invisible frame and tricks the victim into thinking she is interacting with the attacker's site, while in fact she is unintentionally interacting with the Wiki site, logged in as herself. Successful repair in this case would undo all modifications unwittingly made by the user through the clickjacked frame.

We used retroactive patching to recover from all the above attacks, with patches implementing the fixes shown in Table 2.

Finally, we considered a scenario where the administrator of the Wiki site mistakenly grants a user access to Wiki pages she should not have been given access to. At a later point of time, the administrator detects the misconfiguration, and initiates undo of his action using WARP. Meanwhile, the user has used her elevated privileges to edit pages that she should not have been able to edit in the first place. Successful recovery, in this case, would undo all the modifications by the unprivileged user.

Attack scenario	Initial repair	Repaired?	# users with conflicts
Reflected XSS	Retroactive patching	✓	0
Stored XSS	Retroactive patching	✓	0
CSRF	Retroactive patching	✓	0
Clickjacking	Retroactive patching	✓	3
SQL injection	Retroactive patching	✓	0
ACL error	Admin-initiated	✓	1

Table 3: WARP repairs the attack scenarios listed in Table 2. The initial repair column indicates the method used to initiate repair.

For each of these scenarios we ran a workload with 100 users. For all scenarios except the ACL error scenario, we have one attacker, three victims that were subject to attack, and 96 unaffected users. For the ACL error scenario, we have one administrator, one unprivileged user that takes advantage of the administrator's mistake, and 98 other users. During the workloads, all users login, read, and edit Wiki pages. In addition, in all scenarios except the ACL error, the victims visit the attacker's web site, which launches the attack from their browser.

Table 3 shows the results of repair for each of these scenarios. First, WARP can successfully repair all of these attacks. Second, retroactive patching detects and repairs from intrusions due to all five software vulnerabilities; the administrator does not need to detect or track down the initial attacks. Finally, WARP has few user-visible conflicts. Conflicts arise either because a user was tricked by the attacker into performing some browser action, or because the user should not have been able to perform the action in the first place. The conflicts in the clickjacking scenario are of the first type; we expect users would cancel their page visit on conflict, since they did not mean to interact with the MediaWiki page on the attack site. The conflict in the ACL error scenario is of the second type, since the user no longer has access to edit the page; in this case, the user's edit has already been reverted, and the user can resolve the conflict by, perhaps, editing a different page.

8.3 Browser re-execution effectiveness

We evaluated the effectiveness of browser re-execution in WARP by considering three types of attack code, for an XSS attack. The first is a benign, *read-only* attack where the attacker's JavaScript code runs in the user's browser but does not modify any Wiki pages. The second is an *append-only* attack, where the malicious code appends text to the victim's Wiki page. Finally, the *overwrite* attack completely corrupts the victim's Wiki page.

We ran these attacks under three configurations of the client browser: First, without WARP's browser extension; second, with WARP's browser extension but without WARP's text merging for user input; and third, with WARP's complete browser extension. Our experiment had one attacker and eight victims. Each user logged in, visited the attack page to trigger one of the three above attacks, edited Wiki pages, and logged out.

Table 4 shows the results when WARP is invoked to retroactively patch the XSS vulnerability. Without WARP's browser extension, WARP cannot verify whether the attacker's JavaScript code was benign or not, and raises a conflict for every victim of the XSS attack. With the browser extension but without text-merging, WARP can verify that the *read-only* attack was benign, and raises no conflict, but cannot re-execute the user's page edits if the attacker did modify the page slightly, raising a conflict in that scenario. Finally, WARP's full browser extension is able to re-apply the user's page edits despite the attacker's appended text, and raises no conflict in that situation. When the attacker completely corrupts the page, applying user's original changes in the absence of the attack is meaningless, and a conflict is always raised.

Attack action	Number of users with conflict		
	No extension	No text merge	WARP
read-only	8	0	0
append-only	8	8	0
overwrite	8	8	8

Table 4: Effectiveness of WARP UI repair. Each entry indicates whether a user-visible conflict was observed during repair. This experiment involved eight victim users and one attacker.

Bug causing corruption	Akkuş and Goel [1]		WARP	
	FP	User input	FP	User input
Drupal – lost voting info	89 / 0	Yes	0	No
Drupal – lost comments	95 / 0	Yes	0	No
Gallery2 – removing perms	82 / 10	Yes	0	No
Gallery2 – resizing images	119 / 0	Yes	0	No

Table 5: Comparison of WARP with Akkuş and Goel's system [1]. FP reports false positives. Akkuş and Goel can also incur false negatives, unlike WARP. False positives are reported for the *best* dependency policy in [1] that has no false negatives for these bugs, although there is no single best policy for that system. The numbers shown before and after the slash are without and with table-level white-listing, respectively.

8.4 Recovery comparison with prior work

Here we compare WARP with state-of-the-art work in data recovery for web applications by Akkuş and Goel [1]. Their system uses taint tracking in web applications to recover from data corruption bugs. In their system, the administrator identifies the request that triggered the bug, and their system uses several dependency analysis policies to do offline taint analysis and compute dependencies between the request and database elements. The administrator uses these dependencies to manually undo the corruption. Each specific policy can output too many dependencies (false positives), leading to lost data, or too few (false negatives), leading to incomplete recovery.

Akkuş and Goel used five corruption bugs from popular web applications to evaluate their system. To compare WARP with their system, we evaluated WARP with four of these bugs—two each in Drupal and Gallery2. The remaining bug is in Wordpress, which does not support our Postgres database. Porting the buggy versions of Drupal and Gallery2 to use WARP did not require any changes to source code. We replicated each of the four bugs under WARP. Once we verified that the bugs were triggered, we retroactively patched the bug. Repair did not require any user input, and after repair, the applications functioned correctly without any corrupted data.

Table 5 summarizes this evaluation. WARP has three key advantages over Akkuş and Goel's system. First, unlike their system, WARP never incurs false negatives and always leaves the application in an uncorrupted state. Second, WARP only requires the administrator to provide the patch that fixes the bug, whereas Akkuş and Goel require the administrator to manually guide the dependency analysis by identifying requests causing corruption, and by whitelisting database tables. Third, unlike WARP, their system cannot recover from *attacks* on web applications, and cannot recover from problems that occur in the browser.

Workload	Page visits / second			Data stored per page visit		
	No WARP	WARP	During repair	Browser	App.	DB
Reading	8.46	6.43	4.50	0.22 KB	1.49 KB	2.00 KB
Editing	7.19	5.26	4.00	0.21 KB	1.67 KB	5.46 KB

Table 6: Overheads for users browsing and editing Wiki pages in Media-Wiki. The first numbers are page visits per second without WARP, with WARP installed, and with WARP while repair is concurrently underway. A single page visit in MediaWiki can involve multiple HTTP and SQL queries. Data stored per page visit includes all dependency information (compressed) and database checkpoints.

Attack scenario	Number of re-executed actions			Original exec. time	Repair time breakdown							
	Page visits	App. runs	SQL queries		*Total*	Init	Graph	Firefox	DB	App.	Ctrl	Idle
Reflected XSS	14 / 1,011	13 / 1,223	258 / 24,746	180.04	17.87	2.44	0.13	1.21	1.24	2.45	8.99	1.41
Stored XSS	14 / 1,007	15 / 1,219	293 / 24,740	179.22	16.74	2.64	0.12	1.12	0.98	2.45	8.23	1.20
SQL injection	22 / 1,005	23 / 1,214	524 / 24,541	177.82	29.70	2.41	0.16	1.65	0.05	4.16	17.25	4.01
ACL error	13 / 1,000	13 / 1,216	185 / 24,326	176.52	10.75	0.54	0.49	1.04	0.03	2.25	6.04	0.35
Reflected XSS (victims at start)	14 / 1,011	14 / 1,223	1,800 / 24,741	178.21	66.67	2.50	14.46	1.27	26.13	2.23	14.12	5.97
CSRF	1,005 /1,005	1,007 / 1,217	19,799 / 24,578	174.97	1,644.53	159.99	0.46	52.01	0.70	174.04	1,222.05	35.27
Clickjacking	1,011 /1,011	995 / 1,216	23,227 / 24,641	174.31	1,751.74	162.49	0.45	52.19	0.75	171.18	1,320.89	43.78

Table 7: Performance of WARP in repairing attack scenarios described in Table 2 for a workload with 100 users. The "re-executed actions" columns show the number of re-executed actions out of the total number of actions in the workload. The execution times are in seconds. The "original execution time" column shows the CPU time taken by the web application server, including time taken by database queries. The "repair time breakdown" columns show, respectively, the total wall clock repair time, the time to initialize repair (including time to search for attack actions), the time spent loading nodes into the action history graph, the CPU time taken by the re-execution Firefox browser, the time taken by re-executed database queries that are not part of a page re-execution, time taken to re-execute page visits including time to execute database queries issued during page re-execution, time taken by WARP's repair controller, and time for which the CPU is idle during repair.

Attack scenario	Number of re-executed actions			Original exec. time	Repair time breakdown							
	Page visits	App. runs	SQL queries		*Total*	Init	Graph	Firefox	DB	App.	Ctrl	Idle
Reflected XSS	14 / 50,011	14 / 60,023	281 / 1,222,656	8,861.55	48.28	11.34	10.89	1.33	0.52	2.23	21.30	0.67
Stored XSS	32 / 50,007	33 / 60,019	733 / 1,222,652	8,841.67	56.50	11.49	11.10	2.10	0.04	5.58	23.98	2.22
SQL injection	26 / 50,005	27 / 60,014	578 / 1,222,495	8,875.06	273.40	14.57	15.98	7.37	0.09	4.85	118.18	112.36
ACL error	11 / 50,000	11 / 60,016	133 / 1,222,308	8,879.55	41.81	9.20	10.25	1.07	0.08	1.74	19.10	0.37

Table 8: Performance of WARP in attack scenarios for workloads of 5,000 users. See Table 7 for a description of the columns.

8.5   Performance evaluation

In this subsection, we evaluate WARP's performance under different scenarios. In these experiments, we ran the server on a 3.07 GHz Intel Core i7 950 machine with 12 GB of RAM. WARP's repair algorithm is currently sequential. Running it on a machine with multiple cores makes it difficult to reason about the CPU usage of various components of WARP; so we ran the server with only one core turned on and with hyperthreading turned off. However, during normal execution, WARP can take full advantage of multiple processor cores when available.

Logging overhead.   We first evaluate the overhead of using WARP by measuring the performance of MediaWiki with and without WARP for two workloads: reading Wiki pages, and editing Wiki pages. The clients were 8 Firefox browsers running on a machine different from the server, sending requests as fast as possible; the server experienced 100% CPU load. The client and server machines were connected with a 1 Gbps network.

Table 6 shows the throughput of MediaWiki with and without WARP, and the size of WARP's logs. For the reading and editing workloads, respectively, WARP incurs throughput overheads of 24% and 27%, and storage costs of 3.71 KB and 7.34 KB per page visit (or 2 GB/day and 3.2 GB/day under continuous 100% load). Many web applications already store similar log information; a 1 TB drive could store about a year's worth of logs at this rate, allowing repair from attacks within that time period. We believe that this overhead would be acceptable to many applications, such as a company's Wiki or a conference reviewing web site.

To evaluate the overhead of WARP's browser extension, we measured the load times of a Wiki page in the browser with and without the WARP extension. This experiment was performed with an unloaded MediaWiki server. The load times were 0.21 secs and 0.20 secs with and without the WARP extension respectively, showing that the WARP browser extension imposes negligible overhead.

Finally, WARP indexes its logs to support incremental loading of its dependency graph during repair. In our current prototype, for convenience, indexing is implemented as a separate step after normal execution. This indexing step takes 24–28 ms per page visit

for the workloads we tested. If done during normal execution, this would add less than an additional 12% overhead.

Repair performance.   We evaluate WARP's repair performance by considering four scenarios. First, we consider a scenario where a retroactive patch affects a small, isolated part of the action history graph. This scenario evaluates WARP's ability to efficiently load and redo only the affected actions. To evaluate this scenario, we used the XSS, SQL injection, and ACL error workloads from §8.2 with 100 users, and victim page visits at the end of the workload. The results are shown in the first four rows of Table 7. The re-executed actions columns show that WARP re-executes only a small fraction of the total number of actions in the workload, and a comparison of the original execution time and total repair time columns shows that repair in these scenarios takes an order of magnitude less time than the original execution time.

Second, we evaluate a scenario where the patch affects a small part of the action history graph as before, but the affected actions in turn may affect several other actions. To test this scenario, we used the reflected XSS workload with 100 users, but with victims at the beginning of the workload, rather than at the end. Re-execution of the victims' page visits in this case causes the database state to change, which affects non-victims' page visits. This scenario tests WARP's ability to track database dependencies and selectively re-execute database queries without having to re-execute non-victim page visits. The results for this scenario are shown in the fifth row of Table 7.

A comparison of the results for both the reflected XSS attack scenarios shows that WARP re-executes the same number of page visits in both cases, but the number of database queries is significantly greater when victims are at the beginning. These extra database queries are queries from non-victim page visits which depend on the database partitions that changed as a result of re-executing victim pages. These queries are of two types: SELECT queries that need to be re-executed to check whether their result has changed, and UPDATE queries that need to be re-executed to update the rolled-back database rows belonging to the affected database partitions. From the repair time breakdown columns, we see that the graph loading for these database query actions and their re-execution are the main contributors to the longer repair time for this scenario, as compared to when victims were at the end of the workload. Furthermore, we see that the total repair time is about one-third of the time for original execution, and so WARP's repair is significantly better than re-executing the entire workload.

Third, we consider a scenario where a patch requires all actions in the history to be re-executed. We use the CSRF and clickjacking attacks as examples of this scenario. The results are shown in the last two rows of Table 7. WARP takes an order of magnitude more time to re-execute all the actions in the graph than the original execution time. Our unoptimized repair controller prototype is currently implemented in Python, and the step-by-step re-execution of the repaired actions is a significant contributor to this overhead. We believe implementing WARP in a more efficient language, such as C++, would significantly reduce this overhead.

Finally, we evaluate how WARP scales to larger workloads. We measure WARP's repair performance for XSS, SQL injection, and ACL error workloads, as in the first scenario, but with 5,000 users instead of 100. The results for this experiment are shown in Table 8. The number of actions affected by the attack remain the same, and only those actions are re-executed as part of the repair. This indicates WARP successfully avoids re-execution of requests that were not affected by the attack. Differences in the number of re-executed actions (e.g., in the stored XSS attack) are due to non-determinism introduced by MediaWiki object caching. We used a stock Media-Wiki installation for our experiments, in which MediaWiki caches results from past requests in an `objectcache` database table. During repair, MediaWiki may invalidate some of the cache entries, resulting in more re-execution.

The repair time for the 5,000-user workload is only $3\times$ the repair time for 100 users, for all scenarios except SQL injection, despite the $50\times$ increase in the overall workload. This suggests that WARP's repair time does not increase linearly with the size of the workload, and is mostly determined by the number of actions that must be re-executed during repair. The SQL injection attack had a $10\times$ increase in repair time because the number of database rows affected by the attack increases linearly with the number of users. The attack injects the SQL query `UPDATE pagecontent SET old_text = old_text || 'attack'`, which modifies every page. Recovering from this attack requires rolling back all the users' pages, and the time to do that increases linearly with the total number of users.

Concurrent repair overhead. When repair is ongoing, WARP allows the web application to continue normal operation using repair generations. To evaluate repair generations, we measured the performance of MediaWiki for the read and edit workloads from §8.5 while repair is underway for the CSRF attack.

The results are shown in the "During repair" column of Table 6. They demonstrate that WARP allows MediaWiki to be online and functioning normally while repair is ongoing, albeit at a lower performance—with 24% to 30% lower number of page visits per second than if there were no repair in progress. The drop in performance is due to both repair and normal execution sharing the same machine resources. This can be alleviated if dedicated resources (e.g., a dedicated processor core) were available for repair.

9 RELATED WORK

The two closest pieces of work related to WARP are the Retro intrusion recovery system [14] and the web application data recovery system by Akkuş and Goel [1].

While WARP builds on ideas from Retro, Retro focuses on shell-oriented Unix applications on a single machine. WARP extends Retro with three key ideas to handle web applications. First, Retro

requires an intrusion detection system to detect attacks, and an expert administrator to track down the root cause of every intrusion; WARP's retroactive patching allows an administrator to simply supply a security patch for the application's code. Second, Retro's file- and process-level rollback and dependency tracking cannot perform fine-grained rollback and dependency analysis for individual SQL queries that operate on the same table, and cannot perform on-line repair, and WARP's time-travel database can.[3] Third, repairing any network I/O in Retro requires user input; in a web application, this would require every user to resolve conflicts at the TCP level. WARP's browser re-execution eliminates the need to resolve most conflicts, and presents a meaningful UI for true conflicts that require user input.

Akkuş and Goel's data recovery system uses taint tracking to analyze dependencies between HTTP requests and database elements, and thereby recover from data corruption errors in web applications. However, it can only recover from accidental mistakes, as opposed to malicious attacks (in part due to relying on white-listing to reduce false positives), and requires administrator guidance to reduce false positives and false negatives. WARP can fully recover from data corruptions due to bugs as well as attacks, with no manual intervention (except when there are conflicts during repair). §8.4 compared WARP to Akkuş and Goel's system in more detail.

Provenance-aware storage systems [24, 26] record dependency information similar to WARP, and can be used by an administrator to track down the effects of an intrusion or misconfiguration. Margo and Seltzer's browser provenance system [20] shows how provenance information can be extended to web browsers. WARP similarly tracks provenance information across web servers and browsers, and aggregates this information at the server, but WARP also records sufficient information to re-execute browser events and user input in a new context during repair. However, our WARP prototype does not help users understand the provenance of their own data.

Ibis [28] and PASSv2 [25] show how to incorporate provenance information across multiple layers in a system. While WARP only tracks dependencies at a fixed level (SQL queries, HTTP requests, and browser DOM events), we hope to adopt ideas from these systems in the future, to recover from intrusions that span many layers (e.g., the database server or the language runtime).

WARP's idea of retroactive patching provides a novel approach to intrusion detection, which can be used on its own to detect whether recently patched vulnerabilities have been exploited before the patch was applied. Work on vulnerability-specific predicates [13] is similar in its use of re-execution (at the virtual machine level), but requires writing specialized predicates for each vulnerability, whereas WARP only requires the patch itself.

Much of the work on intrusion detection and analysis [5, 11, 15, 16, 18, 32] is complementary to WARP, and can be applied in parallel. When an intrusion is detected and found using an existing intrusion detection tool, the administrator can use WARP to recover from the effects of that intrusion in a web application.

Polygraph [19] recovers from compromises in a weakly consistent replication system. Unlike WARP, Polygraph does not attempt to preserve legitimate changes to affected files, and does not attempt to automate detection of compromises. Polygraph works well for applications that do not operate on multiple files at once. In contrast, WARP deals with web applications, which frequently access shared data in a single SQL database.

Tracking down and reverting malicious actions has been explored in the context of databases [2, 17]. WARP cannot rely purely on

---

[3]One of Retro's scenarios involved database repair, but it worked by rolling back the entire database file, and re-executing every SQL query.

database transaction dependencies, because web applications tend to perform significant amounts of data processing in the application code and in web browsers, and WARP tracks dependencies across all those components. WARP's time-travel database is in some ways reminiscent of a temporal database [29, 30]. However, unlike a temporal database, WARP has no need for more complex temporal queries; supports two time-like dimensions (wall-clock time and repair generations); and allows partitioning rows for dependency analysis.

Many database systems exploit partitioning for performance; WARP uses partitioning for dependency analysis. The problem of choosing a suitable partitioning has been addressed in the context of minimizing distributed transactions on multiple machines [3], and in the context of index selection [6, 12]. These techniques might be helpful in choosing a partitioning for tables in WARP.

Mugshot [22] performs deterministic recording and replay of JavaScript events, but cannot replay events on a changed web page. WARP must replay user input on a changed page in order to re-apply legitimate user changes after effects of the attack have been removed from a page. WARP's DOM-level replay matches event targets between record and replay even if other parts of the page differ.

10 DISCUSSION AND LIMITATIONS

While our prototype depends on a browser extension to record client-side events and user input, we believe it would be possible to do so in pure JavaScript as well. In future work, we plan to explore this possibility, perhaps leveraging Caja [23] to wrap existing JavaScript code and record all browser events and user input; the browser's same-origin policy already allows JavaScript code to perform all of the necessary logging. We also plan to verify that DOM-level events recorded in one browser can be re-executed in a different standards-compliant browser. In the meantime, we note that operators of complex web applications often already have an infrastructure of virtual machines and mobile phone emulators for testing across browser platforms, and a similar infrastructure could be used for WARP's repair.

The client-side logs, uploaded by WARP's extension to the server, can contain sensitive information. For example, if a user enters a password on one of the pages of a web application, the user's key strokes will be recorded in this log, in case that page visit needs to be re-executed at a later time. Although this information is accessible to web applications even without WARP, applications might not record or store this information on their own, and WARP must safeguard this additional stored information from unintended disclosure.

In future work, we plan to explore ways in which WARP-aware applications can avoid logging known-sensitive data, such as passwords, by modifying replay to assume that a valid (or invalid) password was supplied, without having to re-enter the actual password. The logs can also be encrypted so that the administrator must provide the corresponding decryption key to initiate repair. An alternative design—storing the logs locally on each client machine and relying on client machines to participate in the repair process—would prevent a single point of compromise for all logs, but would make complete repair a lengthy process, since each client machine will have to come online to replay its log.

WARP's current design cannot re-execute mashup web applications (i.e., those involving multiple web servers), since the event logs for each web application's frame would be uploaded to a different web server. We plan to explore re-execution of such multi-origin web applications, as long as all of the web servers involved in the mashup support WARP. The approach we imagine taking is to have the client sign each event that spans multiple origins (such as a postMessage between frames) with a private key corresponding to the source origin. This would allow WARP re-executing at the source origin's server to convince WARP on the other frame's origin server that it should be allowed to initiate re-execution for that user.

Retroactive patching by itself cannot be used to recover from attacks that resulted from leaked credentials. For example, an attacker can use an existing XSS vulnerability in an application to steal a user's credentials and use them to impersonate the user and perform unauthorized actions. Retroactive patching of the XSS vulnerability cannot distinguish the actions of the attacker's browser from legitimate actions of the user's browser, as both used the same credentials. However, if the user is willing to identify the legitimate browsers, WARP can undo the actions performed by the attacker's browser.

We plan to explore tracking dependencies at multiple levels of abstraction, borrowing ideas from prior work [14, 25, 28]. This may allow WARP to recover from compromises in lower layers of abstraction, such as a database server or the application's language runtime. We also hope to extend WARP's undo mechanism higher into the application, to integrate with application-level undo features, such as MediaWiki's revert mechanism.

In our current prototype, we instrument the web application server to log HTTP requests and database queries. This requires that the application server be fully trusted to not tamper with WARP logging, and requires modification of the application server software, which may not always be possible. It also does not support replicated web application servers, as the logs for a replica contain the local times at that replica, which are not directly comparable to local times at other replicas. In future work, we plan to explore an alternative design with WARP proxies in front of the application's HTTP load balancer and the database, and perform logging in those proxies. This design addresses the above limitations, but can lead to more re-execution during repair, as it does not capture the exact database queries made for each HTTP request.

We also plan to explore techniques to further reduce the number of application runs re-executed due to retroactive patching, by determining which runs actually invoked the patched function, instead of the runs that just loaded the patched file.

Our current prototype assumes that the application code does not change, other than through retroactive patching. While this assumption is unrealistic, fixing it is straightforward. WARP's application repair manager would need to record each time the application's source code changed. Then, during repair, the application manager would roll back these source code changes (when rolling back to a time before these changes were applied), and would re-apply these patches as the repaired timeline progressed (in the process merging these original changes with any newly supplied retroactive patches).

11 SUMMARY

This paper presented WARP, an intrusion recovery system for web applications. WARP introduced three key ideas to make intrusion recovery practical. *Retroactive patching* allows administrators to recover from past intrusions by simply supplying a new security patch, without having to even know if an attack occurred. The *time-travel database* allows WARP to perform precise repair of just the affected parts of the system. Finally, *DOM-level replay of user input* allows WARP to preserve legitimate changes with no user input in many cases. A prototype of WARP can recover from attacks, misconfigurations, and data loss bugs in three applications, without requiring any code changes, and with modest runtime overhead.

ACKNOWLEDGMENTS

We thank Victor Costan, Frans Kaashoek, Robert Morris, Jad Naous, Hubert Pham, Eugene Wu, the anonymous reviewers, and our shepherd, Yuanyuan Zhou, for their feedback. This research was partially supported by the DARPA Clean-slate design of Resilient, Adaptive, Secure Hosts (CRASH) program under contract #N66001-10-2-4089, by NSF award CNS-1053143, by Quanta, and by Google. Taesoo Kim is partially supported by the Samsung Scholarship Foundation. The opinions in this paper do not necessarily represent DARPA or official US policy.

REFERENCES

[1] İ. E. Akkuş and A. Goel. Data recovery for web applications. In *Proceedings of the 40th Annual IEEE/IFIP International Conference on Dependable Systems and Networks*, Chicago, IL, Jun–Jul 2010.

[2] P. Ammann, S. Jajodia, and P. Liu. Recovery from malicious transactions. *Transactions on Knowledge and Data Engineering*, 14:1167–1185, 2002.

[3] C. Curino, E. Jones, Y. Zhang, and S. Madden. Schism: a workload-driven approach to database replication and partitioning. *Proceedings of the VLDB Endowment*, 3(1), 2010.

[4] Damon Cortesi. Twitter StalkDaily worm post-mortem. http://dcortesi.com/2009/04/11/twitter-stalkdaily-worm-postmortem/.

[5] G. W. Dunlap, S. T. King, S. Cinar, M. Basrai, and P. M. Chen. ReVirt: Enabling intrusion analysis through virtual-machine logging and replay. In *Proceedings of the 5th Symposium on Operating Systems Design and Implementation*, pages 211–224, Boston, MA, Dec 2002.

[6] S. Finkelstein, M. Schkolnick, and P. Tiberio. Physical database design for relational databases. *ACM Transactions on Database Systems*, 13(1):91–128, 1988.

[7] C. Goldfeder. Gmail snooze with apps script. http://googleappsdeveloper.blogspot.com/2011/07/gmail-snooze-with-apps-script.html.

[8] D. Goodin. Surfing Google may be harmful to your security. *The Register*, Aug 2008. http://www.theregister.co.uk/2008/08/09/google_gadget_threats/.

[9] Google, Inc. Google apps script. http://code.google.com/googleapps/appsscript/.

[10] S. Gordeychik. Web application security statistics. http://www.webappsec.org/projects/statistics/.

[11] S. A. Hofmeyr, S. Forrest, and A. Somayaji. Intrusion detection using sequences of system calls. *Journal of Computer Security*, 6:151–180, 1998.

[12] M. Y. L. Ip, L. V. Saxton, and V. V. Raghavan. On the selection of an optimal set of indexes. *IEEE Trans. Softw. Eng.*, 9(2):135–143, 1983.

[13] A. Joshi, S. King, G. Dunlap, and P. Chen. Detecting past and present intrusions through vulnerability-specific predicates. In *Proceedings of the 20th ACM Symposium on Operating Systems Principles*, pages 91–104, Brighton, UK, Oct 2005.

[14] T. Kim, X. Wang, N. Zeldovich, and M. F. Kaashoek. Intrusion recovery using selective re-execution. In *Proceedings of the 9th Symposium on Operating Systems Design and Implementation*, pages 89–104, Vancouver, Canada, Oct 2010.

[15] S. T. King and P. M. Chen. Backtracking intrusions. *ACM Transactions on Computer Systems*, 23(1):51–76, Feb 2005.

[16] W. Lee, S. J. Stolfo, and P. K. Chan. Learning patterns from Unix process execution traces for intrusion detection. In *Proceedings of the AAAI Workshop on AI Approaches in Fraud Detection and Risk Management*, pages 50–56, Jul 1997.

[17] P. Liu, P. Ammann, and S. Jajodia. Rewriting histories: Recovering from malicious transactions. *Journal of Distributed and Parallel Databases*, 8:7–40, 2000.

[18] B. Livshits and W. Cui. Spectator: Detection and containment of JavaScript worms. In *Proceedings of the 2008 USENIX Annual Technical Conference*, Boston, MA, Jun 2008.

[19] P. Mahajan, R. Kotla, C. C. Marshall, V. Ramasubramanian, T. L. Rodeheffer, D. B. Terry, and T. Wobber. Effective and efficient compromise recovery for weakly consistent replication. In *Proceedings of the ACM EuroSys Conference*, Nuremberg, Germany, Mar 2009.

[20] D. W. Margo and M. Seltzer. The case for browser provenance. In *Proceedings of the 1st Workshop on the Theory and Practice of Provenance*, San Francisco, CA, Feb 2009.

[21] MediaWiki. MediaWiki. http://www.mediawiki.org.

[22] J. Mickens, J. Elson, and J. Howell. Mugshot: Deterministic capture and replay for JavaScript applications. In *Proceedings of the 7th Symposium on Networked Systems Design and Implementation*, San Jose, CA, Apr 2010.

[23] M. S. Miller, M. Samuel, B. Laurie, I. Awad, and M. Stay. Caja: Safe active content in sanitized JavaScript, 2008. http://code.google.com/p/google-caja/downloads/list.

[24] K.-K. Muniswamy-Reddy, D. Holland, U. Braun, and M. Seltzer. Provenance-aware storage systems. In *Proceedings of the 2006 USENIX Annual Technical Conference*, Boston, MA, May–Jun 2006.

[25] K.-K. Muniswamy-Reddy, U. Braun, D. Holland, P. Macko, D. Maclean, D. W. Margo, M. Seltzer, and R. Smogor. Layering in provenance systems. In *Proceedings of the 2009 USENIX Annual Technical Conference*, San Diego, CA, Jun 2009.

[26] K.-K. Muniswamy-Reddy, P. Macko, and M. Seltzer. Provenance for the cloud. In *Proceedings of the 8th Conference on File and Storage Technologies*, San Jose, CA, Feb 2010.

[27] National Vulnerability Database. CVE statistics. http://web.nvd.nist.gov/view/vuln/statistics, Feb 2011.

[28] C. Olston and A. D. Sarma. Ibis: A provenance manager for multi-layer systems. In *Proceedings of the 5th Biennial Conference on Innovative Data Systems Research*, Pacific Grove, CA, Jan 2011.

[29] Oracle Corporation. Oracle flashback technology. http://www.oracle.com/technetwork/database/features/availability/flashback-overview-082751.html.

[30] R. T. Snodgrass and I. Ahn. Temporal databases. *IEEE Computer*, 19(9):35–42, Sep 1986.

[31] J. Tyson. Recent Facebook XSS attacks show increasing sophistication. http://theharmonyguy.com/2011/04/21/recent-facebook-xss-attacks/, Apr 2011.

[32] C. Warrender, S. Forrest, and B. Pearlmutter. Detecting intrusions using system calls: Alternative data models. In *Proceedings of the 20th IEEE Symposium on Security and Privacy*, Oakland, CA, May 1999.

[33] K. Wickre. About that fake post. http://googleblog.blogspot.com/2006/10/about-that-fake-post.html.

Software fault isolation with
API integrity and multi-principal modules

Yandong Mao, Haogang Chen, Dong Zhou[†], Xi Wang, Nickolai Zeldovich, and M. Frans Kaashoek

MIT CSAIL, [†]Tsinghua University IIIS

ABSTRACT

The security of many applications relies on the kernel being secure, but history suggests that kernel vulnerabilities are routinely discovered and exploited. In particular, exploitable vulnerabilities in kernel modules are common. This paper proposes LXFI, a system which isolates kernel modules from the core kernel so that vulnerabilities in kernel modules cannot lead to a privilege escalation attack. To safely give kernel modules access to complex kernel APIs, LXFI introduces the notion of *API integrity*, which captures the set of contracts assumed by an interface. To partition the privileges within a shared module, LXFI introduces *module principals*. Programmers specify principals and API integrity rules through capabilities and annotations. Using a compiler plugin, LXFI instruments the generated code to grant, check, and transfer capabilities between modules, according to the programmer's annotations. An evaluation with Linux shows that the annotations required on kernel functions to support a new module are moderate, and that LXFI is able to prevent three known privilege-escalation vulnerabilities. Stress tests of a network driver module also show that isolating this module using LXFI does not hurt TCP throughput but reduces UDP throughput by 35%, and increases CPU utilization by 2.2–3.7×.

Categories and Subject Descriptors: D.4.6 [**Operating Systems**]: Security and Protection.

General Terms: Security.

1 INTRODUCTION

Kernel exploits are not as common as Web exploits, but they do happen [2]. For example, for the Linux kernel, a kernel exploit is reported about once per month, and often these exploits attack kernel modules instead of the core kernel [5]. These kernel exploits are devastating because they typically allow the adversary to obtain "root" privilege. For instance, CVE-2010-3904 reports on a vulnerability in Linux's Reliable Datagram Socket (RDS) module that allowed an adversary to write an arbitrary value to an arbitrary kernel address because the RDS page copy function missed a check on a user-supplied pointer. This vulnerability can be exploited to overwrite function pointers and invoke arbitrary kernel or user code. The contribution of this paper is LXFI, a new software fault isolation system to isolate kernel modules. LXFI allows a module developer to partition the privileges held by a single shared module into multiple *principals*, and provides annotations to enforce *API integrity* for

complex, irregular kernel interfaces such as the ones found in the Linux kernel and exploited by attackers.

Previous systems such as XFI [9] have used software isolation [26] to isolate kernel modules from the core kernel, thereby protecting against a class of attacks on kernel modules. The challenge is that modules need to use support functions in the core kernel to operate correctly; for example, they need to be able acquire locks, copy data, etc., which require invoking functions in the kernel core for these abstractions. Since the kernel does not provide type safety for pointers, a compromised module can exploit some seemingly "harmless" kernel API to gain privilege. For instance, the spin_lock_init function in the kernel writes the value zero to a spinlock that is identified by a pointer argument. A module that can invoke spin_lock_init could pass the address of the user ID value in the current process structure as the spinlock pointer, thereby tricking spin_lock_init into setting the user ID of the current process to zero (i.e., root in Linux), and gaining root privileges.

Two recent software fault isolation systems, XFI and BGI [4], have two significant shortcomings. First, neither can deal with complex, irregular interfaces; as noted by the authors of XFI, attacks by modules that abuse an over-permissive kernel routine that a module is allowed to invoke remain an open problem [9, §6.1]. BGI tackles this problem in the context of Windows kernel drivers, which have a well-defined regular structure amenable to manual interposition on all kernel/module interactions. The Linux kernel, on the other hand, has a more complex interface that makes manual interposition difficult. For example, Linux kernel interfaces often store function pointers to both kernel and module functions in data structures that are updated by modules, and invoked by the kernel in many locations.

The second shortcoming of XFI and BGI is that they cannot isolate different instances of the same module. For example, a single kernel module might be used to implement many instances of the same abstraction (e.g., many block devices or many sockets). If one of these instances is compromised by an adversary, the adversary also gains access to the privileges of all other instances as well.

This paper's goal is to solve both of these problems for Linux kernel modules. To partition the privileges held by a shared module, LXFI extends software fault isolation to allow modules to have multiple *principals*. Principals correspond to distinct instances of abstractions provided by a kernel module, such as a single socket or a block device provided by a module that can instantiate many of them. Programmers annotate kernel interfaces to specify what principal should be used when the module is invoked, and each principal's privileges are kept separate by LXFI. Thus, if an adversary compromises one instance of the module, the adversary can only misuse that principal's privileges (e.g., being able to modify data on a single socket, or being able to write to a single block device).

To handle complex kernel interfaces, LXFI introduces *API integrity*, which captures the contract assumed by kernel developers for a particular interface. To capture API integrity, LXFI uses capabilities to track the privileges held by each principal, and introduces *light-weight annotations* that programmers use to express the API integrity of an interface in terms of capabilities and principals. LXFI enforces API integrity at runtime through software fault isolation techniques.

To test out these ideas, we implemented LXFI for Linux kernel modules. The implementation provides the same basic security properties as XFI and BGI, using similar techniques, but also enforces API integrity for multiple principals. To use LXFI, a programmer must first specify the security policy for an API, using source-level annotations. LXFI enforces the specified security policy with the help of two components. The first is a compile-time rewriter, which inserts checks into kernel code that, when invoked at runtime, verify that security policies are upheld. The second is a runtime component, which maintains the privileges of each module and checks whether a module has the necessary privileges for any given operation at runtime. To enforce API integrity efficiently, LXFI uses a number of optimizations, such as *writer-set tracking*. To isolate a module at runtime, LXFI sets up the initial capabilities, manages the capabilities as they are added and revoked, and checks them on all calls between the module and the core kernel according to the programmer's annotations.

An evaluation for 10 kernel modules shows that supporting a new module requires 8–133 annotations, of which many are shared between modules. Furthermore, the evaluation shows that LXFI can prevent exploits for three CVE-documented vulnerabilities in kernel modules (including the RDS module). Stress tests with a network driver module show that isolating this module using LXFI does not hurt TCP throughput, but reduces UDP throughput by 35%, and increases CPU utilization by 2.2–3.7×.

The contributions of the paper are as follows. First, this paper extends the typical module isolation model to support multiple principals per code module. Second, this paper introduces the notion of API integrity, and provides a light-weight annotation language that helps describe the security properties of kernel and module interfaces in terms of capabilities. Finally, this paper demonstrates that LXFI is practical in terms of performance, security, and annotation effort by evaluating it on the Linux kernel.

The rest of the paper is organized as follows. The next section defines the goal of this paper, and the threat model assumed by LXFI. §3 gives the design of LXFI and its annotations. We describe LXFI's compile-time and runtime components in §4 and §5, and discuss how we expect kernel developers to use LXFI in practice in §6. §7 describes the implementation details. We evaluate LXFI in §8, discuss related work in §9, and conclude in §10.

2 GOAL AND PROBLEM

LXFI's goal is to prevent an adversary from exploiting vulnerabilities in kernel modules in a way that leads to a privilege escalation attack. Many exploitable kernel vulnerabilities are found in kernel modules. For example, Chen et al. find that two thirds of kernel vulnerabilities reported by CVE between Jan 2010 and March 2011 are in kernel modules [1, 5].

When adversaries exploit bugs in the kernel, they trick the kernel code into performing operations that the code would not normally do. For example, an adversary can trick the kernel into writing to arbitrary memory locations, or invoking arbitrary kernel code. Adversaries can leverage this to gain additional privileges (e.g., by running their own code in the kernel, or overwriting the user ID of the current process), or to disclose data from the system. The focus of LXFI is on preventing integrity attacks (e.g., privilege escalation), and not on data disclosure.

In LXFI, we assume that we will not be able to fix all possible underlying software bugs, but instead we focus on reducing the possible operations the adversary can trick the kernel into performing to the set of operations that code (e.g., a kernel module) would ordinarily be able to do. For example, if a module does not ordinarily modify the user ID field in the process structure, LXFI should prevent the module from doing so even if it is compromised by an adversary. Similarly, if a module does not ordinarily invoke kernel functions to write blocks to a disk, LXFI should prevent a module from doing so, even if it is compromised.

LXFI's approach to prevent privilege escalation is to isolate the modules from each other and from the core of the kernel, as described above. Of course, a module may legitimately need to raise the privileges of the current process, such as through setuid bits in a file system, so this approach will not prevent all possible privilege escalation exploits. However, most of the exploits found in practice take advantage of the fact that every buggy module is fully privileged, and making modules less privileged will reduce the number of possible exploits.

Another challenge in making module isolation work lies in knowing what policy rules to enforce at module boundaries. Since the Linux kernel was written without module isolation in mind, all such rules are implicit, and can only be determined by manual code inspection. One possible solution would be to re-design the Linux kernel to be more amenable to privilege separation, and to have simpler interfaces where all privileges are explicit; however, doing this would involve a significant amount of work. LXFI takes a different approach that tries to make as few modifications to the Linux kernel as possible. To this end, LXFI, like previous module isolation systems [4, 9, 26], relies on developers to specify this policy.

In the rest of this section, we will discuss two specific challenges that have not been addressed in prior work that LXFI solves, followed by the assumptions made by LXFI. Briefly, the challenges have to do with a shared module that has many privileges on behalf of its many clients, and with concisely specifying module policies for complex kernel interfaces like the ones in the Linux kernel.

2.1 Privileges in shared modules

The first challenge is that a single kernel module may have many privileges if that kernel module is being used in many contexts. For example, a system may use the dm-crypt module to manage encrypted block devices, including both the system's main disk and any USB flash drives that may be connected by the user. The entire dm-crypt module must have privileges to write to all of these devices. However, if the user accidentally plugs in a malicious USB flash drive that exploits a bug in dm-crypt, the compromised dm-crypt module will be able to corrupt all of the block devices it manages. Similarly, a network protocol module, such as econet, must have privileges to write to all of the sockets managed by that module. As a result, if an adversary exploits a vulnerability in the context of his or her econet connection, the adversary will be able to modify the data sent over any other econet socket as well.

2.2 Lack of API integrity

The second challenge is that kernel modules use complex kernel interfaces. These kernel interfaces could be mis-used by a compromised module to gain additional privileges (e.g., by corrupting memory). One approach is to re-design kernel interfaces to make it easy to enforce safety properties, such as in Windows, as illustrated by BGI [4]. However, LXFI's goal is to isolate existing Linux kernel modules, where many of the existing interfaces are complex.

To prevent these kinds of attacks in Linux, we define *API integrity* as the contract that developers intend for any module to follow when using some interface, such as the memory allocator, the PCI subsystem, or the network stack. The set of rules that make up the contract between a kernel module and the core kernel are different

```
1  struct pci_driver {
2    int (*probe) (struct pci_dev *pcidev);
3  };
4
5  struct net_device {
6    struct net_device_ops *dev_ops;
7  };
8
9  struct net_device_ops {
10   netdev_tx_t (*ndo_start_xmit)
11     (struct sk_buff *skb,
12       struct net_device *dev);
13 };
14
15 /* Exported kernel functions */
16 void pci_enable_device(struct pci_dev *pcidev);
17 void netif_rx(struct sk_buff *skb);
18
19 /* In core kernel code */
20 module_driver->probe(pcidev);
21
22 void
23 netif_napi_add(struct net_device *dev,
24       struct napi_struct *napi,
25       int (*poll) (struct napi_struct *, int))
26 {
27   dev->dev_ops->ndo_start_xmit(skb, ndev);
28   (*poll) (napi, 5);
29 }
30
31 /* In network device driver's module */
32 int
33 module_pci_probe(struct pci_dev *pcidev) {
34   ndev = alloc_etherdev(...);
35   pci_enable_device(pcidev);
36   ndev->dev_ops->ndo_start_xmit = myxmit;
37   netif_napi_add(ndev, napi, my_poll_cb);
38   return 0;
39 }
40
41 /* In network device driver's code */
42 netif_rx(skb);
```

Figure 1: Parts of a PCI network device driver in Linux.

for each kernel API, and the resulting operations that the kernel module can perform are also API-specific. However, by enforcing API integrity—i.e., ensuring that each kernel module follows the intended contract for core kernel interfaces that it uses—LXFI will ensure that a compromised kernel module cannot take advantage of the core kernel's interfaces to perform more operations than the API was intended to allow.

To understand the kinds of contracts that an interface may require, consider a PCI network device driver for the Linux kernel, shown in Figure 1. In the rest of this section, we will present several examples of contracts that make up API integrity for this interface, and how a kernel module may violate those contracts.

Memory safety and control flow integrity. Two basic safety properties that all software fault isolation systems enforce is *memory safety*, which guarantees that a module can only access memory that it owns or has legitimate access to, and *control flow integrity*, which guarantees that a module can only execute its own isolated code and external functions that it has legitimate access to. However, memory safety and control flow integrity are insufficient to provide API integrity, and the rest of this section describes other safety properties enforced by LXFI.

Function call integrity. The first aspect of API integrity deals with *how* a kernel module may invoke the core kernel's functions. These contracts are typically concerned with the arguments that the module can provide, and the specific functions that can be invoked, as we will now illustrate.

Many function call contracts involve the notion of object ownership. For example, when the network device driver module in Figure 1 calls pci_enable_device to enable the PCI device on line 35, it is expected that the module will provide a pointer to its own pci_dev structure as the argument (i.e., the one it received as an argument to module_pci_probe). If the module passes in some other pci_dev structure to pci_enable_device, it may be able to interfere with other devices, and potentially cause problems for other modules. Furthermore, if the module is able to construct its own pci_dev structure, and pass it as an argument, it may be able to trick the kernel into performing arbitrary device I/O or memory writes.

A common type of object ownership is write access to memory. Many core kernel functions write to a memory address supplied by the caller, such as spin_lock_init from the example in §1. In these cases, a kernel module should only be able to pass addresses of kernel memory it has write access to (for a sufficient number of bytes) to such functions; otherwise, a kernel module may trick the kernel into writing to arbitrary kernel memory. On the other hand, a kernel module can also have ownership of an object without being able to write to its memory: in the case of the network device, modules should not directly modify the memory contents of their pci_dev struct, since it would allow the module to trick the kernel into controlling a different device, or dereferencing arbitrary pointers.

Another type of function call contract relates to callback functions. Several kernel interfaces involve passing around callback functions, such as the netif_napi_add interface on line 23. In this case, the kernel invokes the poll function pointer at a later time, and expects that this points to a legitimate function. If the module is able to provide arbitrary function pointers, such as my_poll_cb on line 37, the module may be able to trick the kernel into running arbitrary code when it invokes the callback on line 28. Moreover, the module should be able to provide only pointers to functions that the module itself can invoke; otherwise, it can trick the kernel into running a function that it is not allowed to call directly.

Function callbacks are also used in the other direction: for modules to call back into the core kernel. Once the core kernel has provided a callback function a kernel module, the module is expected to invoke the callback, probably with a prescribed callback argument. The module should not invoke the callback function before the callback is provided, or with a different callback argument.

Data structure integrity. In addition to memory safety, many kernel interfaces assume that the actual *data* stored in a particular memory location obeys certain invariants. For example, an sk_buff structure, representing a network packet in the Linux kernel, contains a pointer to packet data. When the module passes an sk_buff structure to the core kernel on line 42, it is expected to provide a legitimate data pointer inside of the sk_buff, and that pointer should point to memory that the kernel module has write access to (in cases when the sk_buff's payload is going to be modified). If this invariant is violated, the kernel code can be tricked into writing to arbitrary memory.

Another kind of data structure integrity deals with function pointers that are stored in shared memory. The Linux kernel often stores callback function pointers in data structures. For example, the core kernel invokes a function pointer from dev->dev_ops on line 27. The implicit assumption the kernel is making is that the function pointer points to legitimate code that should be executed. However, if the kernel module was able to write arbitrary values to the function pointer field, it could trick the core kernel into executing arbitrary code. Thus, in LXFI, even though the module can write a legitimate pointer on line 36, it should not be able to corrupt it later. To address this problem, LXFI checks whether the function pointer value that is about to be invoked was a legitimate function address that the pointer's writer was allowed to invoke too.

API integrity in Linux. In the general case, it is difficult to find or enumerate all of the contracts necessary for API integrity. However, in our experience, kernel module interfaces in Linux tend to be reasonably well-structured, and it is possible to capture the contracts of many interfaces in a succinct manner. Even though these interfaces are not used as security boundaries in the Linux kernel, they are carefully designed by kernel developers to support a range of kernel modules, and contain many sanity checks to catch buggy behavior by modules (e.g., calls to BUG()).

LXFI relies on developers to provide annotations capturing the API integrity of each interface. LXFI provides a safe default, in that a kernel function with no annotations (e.g., one that the developer forgot to annotate) cannot be accessed by a kernel module. However, LXFI trusts any annotations that the developer provides; if there is any mistake or omission in an annotation, LXFI will enforce the policy specified in the annotation, and not the intended policy. Finally, in cases when it is difficult to enforce API integrity using LXFI, re-designing the interface to fit LXFI's annotations may be necessary (however, we have not encountered any such cases for the modules we have annotated).

2.3 Threat model

LXFI makes two assumptions to isolate kernel modules. First, LXFI assumes that the core kernel, the annotations on the kernel's interfaces, and the LXFI verifier itself are correct.

Second, LXFI infers the initial privileges that a module should be granted based on the functions that module's code imports. Thus, we trust that the programmer of each kernel module only invokes functions needed by that module. We believe this is an appropriate assumption because kernel developers are largely well-meaning, and do not try to access unnecessary interfaces on purpose. Thus, by capturing the intended privileges of a module, and by looking at the interfaces required in the source code, we can prevent an adversary from accessing any additional interfaces at runtime.

3 ANNOTATIONS

At a high level, LXFI's workflow consists of four steps. First, kernel developers annotate core kernel interfaces to enforce API integrity between the core kernel and modules. Second, module developers annotate certain parts of their module where they need to switch privileges between different module principals. Third, LXFI's compile-time rewriter instruments the generated code to perform API integrity checks at runtime. Finally, LXFI's runtime is invoked at these instrumented points, and performs the necessary checks to uphold API integrity. If the checks fail, the kernel panics. The rest of this section describes LXFI's principals, privileges, and annotations.

3.1 Principals

Many modules provide an abstraction that can be instantiated many times. For example, the econet protocol module provides an econet socket abstraction that can be instantiated to create a specific socket. Similarly, device mapper modules such as dm-crypt and dmraid provide a layered block device abstraction that can be instantiated for a particular block device.

To minimize the privileges that an adversary can take advantage of when they exploit a vulnerability in a module, LXFI logically breaks up a module into multiple *principals* corresponding to each instance of the module's abstraction. For example, each econet socket corresponds to a separate module principal, and each block device provided by dm-crypt also corresponds to a separate module principal. Each module principal will have access to only the privileges needed by that instance of the module's abstraction, and not to the global privileges of the entire module.

To support this plan, LXFI provides three mechanisms. First, LXFI allows programmers to define principals in a module. To avoid requiring existing code to keep track of LXFI-specific principals, LXFI names module principals based on existing data structures used to represent an instance of the module's abstraction. For example, in econet, LXFI uses the address of the socket structure as the principal name. Similarly, in device mapper modules, LXFI uses the address of the block device.

Second, LXFI allows programmers to define what principal should be used when invoking a module, by providing annotations on function types (which we discuss more concretely in §3.3). For example, when the kernel invokes the econet module to send a message over a socket, LXFI should execute the module's code in the context of that socket's principal. To achieve this behavior, the programmer annotates the message send function to specify that the socket pointer argument specifies the principal name. At runtime, LXFI uses this annotation to switch the current principal to the one specified by the function's arguments when the function is invoked. These principal identifiers are stored on a shadow stack, so that if an interrupt comes in while a module is executing, the module's privileges are saved before handling the interrupt, and restored on interrupt exit.

Third, a module may share some state between multiple instances. For example, the econet module maintains a linked list of all sockets managed by that module. Since each linked list pointer is stored in a different socket object, no single instance principal is able to add or remove elements from this list. Performing these cross-instance operations requires global privileges of the entire module. In these cases, LXFI allows programmers to switch the current principal to the module's *global* principal, which implicitly has access to the capabilities of all other principals in that module. For example, in econet, the programmer would modify the function used to add or remove sockets from this linked list to switch to running as the global principal. Conversely, a *shared* principal is used to represent privileges accessible to all principals in a module, such as the privileges to invoke the initial kernel functions required by that module. All principals in a module implicitly have access to all of the privileges of the shared principal.

To ensure that a function that switches to the global principal cannot be tricked into misusing its global privileges, programmers must insert appropriate checks before every such privilege change. LXFI's control flow integrity then ensures that these checks cannot be bypassed by an adversary at runtime. A similar requirement arises for other privileged LXFI functions, such as manipulating principals. We give an example of such checks in §3.4.

3.2 Capabilities

Modules do not explicitly define the privileges they require at runtime—such as what memory they may write, or what functions they may call—and even for functions that a module may legitimately need, the function itself may be expecting the module to invoke it in certain ways, as described in §2.2 and Figure 1.

To keep track of module privileges, LXFI maintains a set of capabilities, similar to BGI, that track the privileges of each module principal at runtime. LXFI supports three types of capabilities, as follows:

$$annotation ::= \textbf{pre}(action) \mid \textbf{post}(action) \mid \textbf{principal}(c\text{-}expr)$$
$$action ::= \textbf{copy}(caplist)$$
$$\mid \textbf{transfer}(caplist)$$
$$\mid \textbf{check}(caplist)$$
$$\mid \textbf{if} \ (c\text{-}expr) \ action$$
$$caplist ::= (c, ptr, [size])$$
$$\mid iterator\text{-}func(c\text{-}expr)$$

Figure 2: Grammar for LXFI annotations. A *c-expr* corresponds to a C expression that can reference the annotated function's arguments and its return value. An *iterator-func* is a name of a programmer-supplied C function that takes a *c-expr* argument, and iterates over a set of capabilities. *c* specifies the type of the capability (either WRITE, CALL, or REF, as described in §3.2), and *ptr* is the address or argument for the capability. The *size* parameter is optional, and defaults to sizeof(*ptr*).

WRITE (*ptr, size*). This capability means that a module can write any values to memory region [*ptr, ptr + size*) in the kernel address space. It can also pass addresses inside the region to kernel routines that require writable memory. For example, the network device module in Figure 1 would have a WRITE capability for its sk_buff packets and their payloads, which allows it to modify the packet.

REF (*t, a*). This capability allows the module to pass *a* as an argument to kernel functions that require a capability of REF type *t*, capturing the object ownership idea from §2. Type *t* is often the C type of the argument, although it need not be the case, and we describe situations in which this happens in §6. Unlike the WRITE capability, REF (*t, a*) does not grant write access to memory at address *a*. For instance, in our network module, the module should receive a REF (pci_dev, pcidev) capability when the core kernel invokes module_driver->probe on line 20, if that code was annotated to support LXFI capabilities. This capability would then allow the module to call pci_enable_device on line 35.

CALL (*a*). The module can call or jump to a target memory address *a*. In our network module example, the module has a CALL capability for netif_rx, pci_enable_device, and others; this particular example has no instances of dynamic call capabilities provided to the module by the core kernel at runtime.

The basic operations on capabilities are granting a capability, revoking all copies of a capability, and checking whether a caller has a capability. To set up the basic execution environment for a module, LXFI grants a module initial capabilities when the module is loaded, which include: (1) a WRITE capability to its writable data section; (2) a WRITE capability to the current kernel stack (does not include the shadow stack, which we describe later); and (3) CALL capabilities to all kernel routines that are imported in the module's symbol table.

A module can gain or lose additional capabilities when it calls support functions in the core kernel. For example, after a module calls kmalloc, it gains a WRITE capability to the newly allocated memory. Similarly, after calling kfree, LXFI's runtime revokes the corresponding WRITE capability from that module.

3.3 Interface annotations

Although the principal and capability mechanisms allow LXFI to reason about the privileges held by each module principal, it is cumbersome for the programmer to manually insert calls to switch principals, transfer capabilities, and verify whether a module has a certain capability, for each kernel/module API function (as in

BGI [4]). To simplify the programmer's job, LXFI allows programmers to annotate interfaces (i.e., prototype definitions in C) with principals and capability actions. LXFI leverages the clang support for attributes to specify the annotations.

LXFI annotations are consulted when invoking a function, and can be associated (in the source code) with function declarations, function definitions, or function pointer types. A single kernel function (or function pointer type) can have multiple LXFI annotations; each one describes what action the LXFI runtime should take, and specifies whether that action should be taken before the function is called, or after the call finishes, as indicated by **pre** and **post** keywords. Figure 2 summarizes the grammar for LXFI's annotations.

There are three types of annotations supported by LXFI: **pre**, **post**, and **principal**. The first two perform a specified action either before invoking the function or after it returns. The **principal** annotation specifies the name of the module principal that should be used to execute the called function, which we discuss shortly.

There are four actions that can be performed by either **pre** or **post** annotations. A **copy** action grants a capability from the caller to the callee for **pre** annotations (and vice-versa for **post**). A **transfer** action moves ownership of a capability from the caller to the callee for **pre** annotations (and vice-versa for **post**). Both **copy** and **transfer** ensure that the capability is owned in the first place before granting it. A **check** action verifies that the caller owns a particular capability; all **check** annotations are **pre**. To support conditional annotations, LXFI supports **if** actions, which conditionally perform some action (such as a **copy** or a **transfer**) based on an expression that can involve either the function's arguments, or, for **post** annotations, the function's return value. For example, this allows transferring capabilities for a memory buffer only if the return value does not indicate an error.

Transfer actions revoke the transferred capability from *all* principals in the system, rather than just from the immediate source of the transfer. (As described above, transfers happen in different directions depending on whether the action happens in a **pre** or **post** context.) Revoking a capability from all principals ensures that no copies of the capability remain, and allows the object referred to by the capability to be re-used safely. For example, the memory allocator's kfree function uses **transfer** to ensure no outstanding capabilities exist for free memory. Similarly, when a network driver hands a packet to the core kernel, a **transfer** action ensures the driver—and any other module the driver could have given capabilities to—cannot modify the packet any more.

The **copy**, **transfer**, and **check** actions take as argument the list of capabilities to which the action should be applied. In the simple case, the capability can be specified inline, but the programmer can also implement their own function that returns a list of capabilities, and use that function in an action to iterate over all of the returned capabilities. Figure 3 provides several example LXFI annotations and their semantics.

To specify the principal with whose privilege the function should be invoked, LXFI provides a **principal** annotation. LXFI's principals are named by arbitrary pointers. This is convenient because Linux kernel interfaces often have an object corresponding to every instance of an abstraction that a principal tries to capture. For example, a network device driver would use the address of its net_device structure as the principal name to separate different network interfaces from each other. Adding explicit names for principals would require extending existing Linux data structures to store this additional name, which would require making changes to the Linux kernel, and potentially break data structure invariants, such as alignment or layout.

119

Annotation	Semantics
pre(**copy**(*c*, *ptr*, [*size*]))	Check that *caller* owns capability *c* for [*ptr*, *ptr* + *size*) before calling function.
	Copy capability *c* from *caller* to *callee* for [*ptr*, *ptr* + *size*) before the call.
post(**copy**(*c*, *ptr*, [*size*]))	Check that *callee* owns capability *c* for [*ptr*, *ptr* + *size*) after the call.
	Copy capability *c* from *callee* to *caller* for [*ptr*, *ptr* + *size*) after the call.
pre(**transfer**(*c*, *ptr*, [*size*]))	Check that *caller* owns capability *c* for [*ptr*, *ptr* + *size*) before calling function.
	Transfer capability *c* from *caller* to *callee* for [*ptr*, *ptr* + *size*) before the call.
post(**transfer**(*c*, *ptr*, [*size*]))	Check that *callee* owns capability *c* for [*ptr*, *ptr* + *size*) after the call.
	Transfer capability *c* from *callee* to *caller* for [*ptr*, *ptr* + *size*) after the call.
pre(**check**(*c*, *ptr*, [*size*]))	Check that the caller has the (*c*, *ptr*, [*size*]) capability.
pre(**check**(skb_iter(*ptr*)))	Check that the caller has all capabilities returned by the programmer-supplied skb_iter function.
pre(**if** (*c-expr*) *action*)	Run the specified action if the expression *c-expr* is true; used for conditional annotations based on return value.
post(**if** (*c-expr*) *action*)	LXFI allows *c-expr* to refer to function arguments, and (for **post** annotations) to the return value.
principal(*p*)	Use *p* as the *callee* principal; in the absence of this annotation, LXFI uses the module's shared principal.

Figure 3: Examples of LXFI annotations, using the grammar shown in Figure 2, and their semantics.

One complication with LXFI's pointer-based principal naming scheme is that a single instance of an module's abstraction may have a separate data structure that is used for different interfaces. For instance, a PCI network device driver may be invoked both by the network sub-system and by the PCI sub-system. The network sub-system would use the pointer of the net_device structure as the principal name, and the PCI sub-system would use the pointer of the pci_dev structure for the principal. Even though these two names may refer to the same logical principal (i.e., a single physical network card), the names differ.

To address this problem, LXFI separates principals from their names. This allows a single logical principal to have multiple names, and LXFI provides a function called lxfi_princ_alias that a module can use to map names to principals. The special values *global* and *shared* can be used as an argument to a **principal** annotation to indicate the module's global and shared principals, respectively. For example, this can be used for functions that require access to the entire module's privileges, such as adding or removing sockets from a global linked list in econet.

3.4 Annotation example

To give a concrete example of how LXFI's annotations are used, consider the interfaces shown in Figure 1, and their annotated version in Figure 4. LXFI's annotations are underlined in Figure 4. Although this example involves a significant number of annotations, we specifically chose it to illustrate most of LXFI's mechanisms.

To prevent modules from arbitrarily enabling PCI devices, the pci_enable_device function on line 67 in Figure 4 has a **check** annotation that ensures the caller has a REF capability for the corresponding pci_dev object. When the module is first initialized for a particular PCI device, the probe function grants it such a REF capability (based on the annotation for the probe function pointer on line 45). Note that if the probe function returns an error code, the **post** annotation on the probe function transfers ownership of the pci_dev object back to the caller.

Once the network interface is registered with the kernel, the kernel can send packets by invoking the ndo_start_xmit function. The annotations on this function, on line 60, grant the module access to the packet, represented by the sk_buff structure. Note that the sk_buff structure is a complicated object, including a pointer to a separate region of memory holding the actual packet payload. To compute the set of capabilities needed by an sk_buff, the programmer writes a capability iterator called skb_caps that invokes LXFI's lxfi_cap_iterate function on all of the capabilities that make up the sk_buff. This function in turn performs the requested operation (**transfer**, in this case) based on the context in which the capability iterator was invoked. As with the PCI example above, the annota-

tions transfer the granted capabilities back to the caller in case of an error.

Note that, when the kernel invokes the device driver through ndo_start_xmit, it uses the pointer to the net_dev structure as the principal name (line 60), even though the initial PCI probe function used the pci_dev structure's address as the principal (line 45). To ensure that the module has access to the same set of capabilities in both cases, the module developer must create two names for the corresponding logical principal, one using the pci_dev object, and one using the net_device object.

To do this, the programmer modifies the module's code as shown in lines 72–73. This code creates a new name, ndev, for an existing principal with the name pcidev on line 73. The check on line 72 ensures that this code will only execute if the current principal already has privileges for the pcidev object. This ensures that an adversary cannot call the module_pci_probe function with some other pcidev object and trick the code into setting up arbitrary aliases to principals. LXFI's control flow integrity ensures that an adversary is not able to transfer control flow directly to line 73. Moreover, only direct control flow transfers to lxfi_princ_alias are allowed. This ensures that an adversary cannot invoke this function by constructing and calling a function pointer at runtime; only statically defined calls, which are statically coupled with a preceding check, are allowed.

4 COMPILE-TIME REWRITING

When compiling the core kernel and modules, LXFI uses compiler plugins to inserts calls and checks into the generated code so that the LXFI runtime can enforce the annotations for API integrity and principals. LXFI performs different rewriting for the core kernel and for modules. Since LXFI assumes that the core kernel is fully trusted, it can omit most checks for performance. Modules are not fully trusted, and LXFI must perform more extensive rewriting there.

4.1 Rewriting the core kernel

The only rewriting that LXFI must perform on core kernel code deals with invocation of function pointers that may have been supplied by a module. If a module is able to supply a function pointer that the core kernel will invoke, the module can potentially increase its privileges, if it tricks the kernel into performing a call that the module itself could not have performed directly. To ensure this is not the case, LXFI performs two checks. First, prior to invoking a function pointer from the core kernel, LXFI verifies that the module principal that supplied the pointer (if any) had the appropriate CALL capability for that function. Second, LXFI ensures that the annotations for the function supplied by the module and the function pointer type match. This ensures that a module cannot change the effective

```
43  struct pci_driver {
44    int (*probe) (struct pci_dev *pcidev, ...)
45      principal(pcidev)
46      pre(copy(ref(struct pci_dev), pcidev))
47      post(if (return < 0)
48              transfer(ref(struct pci_dev), pcidev));
49  };
50
51  void skb_caps(struct sk_buff *skb) {
52    lxfi_cap_iterate(write, skb, sizeof(*skb));
53    lxfi_cap_iterate(write, skb->data, skb->len);
54  }
55
56  struct net_device_ops {
57    netdev_tx_t (*ndo_start_xmit)
58      (struct sk_buff *skb,
59       struct net_device *dev)
60      principal(dev)
61      pre(transfer(skb_caps(skb)))
62      post(if (return == -NETDEV_BUSY)
63              transfer(skb_caps(skb)))
64  };
65
66  void pci_enable_device(struct pci_dev *pcidev)
67    pre(check(ref(struct pci_dev), pcidev));
68
69  int
70  module_pci_probe(struct pci_dev *pcidev) {
71    ndev = alloc_etherdev(...);
72    lxfi_check(ref(struct pci_dev), pcidev);
73    lxfi_princ_alias(pcidev, ndev);
74    pci_enable_device(pcidev);
75    ndev->dev_ops->ndo_start_xmit = myxmit;
76    netif_napi_add(ndev, napi, my_poll_cb);
77    return 0;
78  }
```

Figure 4: Annotations for parts of the API shown in Figure 1. The annotations follow the grammar shown in Figure 2. Annotations and added code are underlined.

```
79  handler_func_t handler;
80  handler = device->ops->handler;
81  lxfi_check_indcall(&device->ops->handler);
82                     /* not &handler */
83  handler(device);
```

Figure 5: Rewriting an indirect call in the core kernel. LXFI inserts checking code with the address of a module-supplied function pointer.

annotations on a function by storing it in a function pointer with different annotations.

To implement this check, LXFI's kernel rewriter inserts a call to the checking function lxfi_check_indcall(void **pptr, unsigned ahash) before every indirect call in the core kernel, where pptr is the address of the module-supplied function pointer to be called, and ahash is the hash of the annotation for the function pointer type. The LXFI runtime will validate that the module that writes function f to pptr has a CALL capability for f. To ensure that annotations match, LXFI compares the hash of the annotations for both the function and the function pointer type.

To optimize the cost of these checks, LXFI implements writer-set tracking. The runtime tracks the set of principals that have been granted a WRITE capability for each memory location after the last time that memory location was zeroed. Then, for each indirect-call check in the core kernel, the LXFI runtime first checks whether any principal could have written to the function pointer about to be invoked. If not, the runtime can bypass the relatively expensive capability check for the function pointer.

To detect the original memory location from which the function pointer was obtained, LXFI performs a simple intra-procedural analysis to trace back the original function pointer. For example, as shown in Figure 5, the core kernel may copy a module-supplied function pointer device->ops->handler to a local variable handler, and then make a call using the local variable. In this case LXFI uses the address of the original function pointer rather than the local variable for looking up the set of writer principals. We have encountered 51 cases that our simple analysis cannot deal with, out of 7500 indirect call sites in the core kernel, in which the value of the called pointer originates from another function. We manually verify that these 51 cases are safe.

4.2 Rewriting modules

LXFI inserts calls to the runtime when compiling modules based on annotations from the kernel and module developers. The rest of this subsection describes the types of instrumentation that LXFI performs for module C code.

Annotation propagation. To determine the annotations that should apply to a function, LXFI first propagates annotations on a function pointer type to the actual function that might instantiate that type. Consider the structure member probe in Figure 4, which is a function pointer initialized to the module_pci_probe function. The function should get the annotations on the probe member. LXFI propagates these annotations along initializations, assignments, and argument passing in the module's code, and computes the annotation set for each function. A function can obtain different annotations from multiple sources. LXFI verifies that these annotations are exactly the same.

Function wrappers. At compile time, LXFI generates wrappers for each module-defined function, kernel-exported function, and indirect call site in the module. At runtime, when the kernel calls into one of the module's functions, or when the module calls a kernel-exported function, the corresponding function wrapper is invoked first. Based on the annotations, the wrapper sets the appropriate principal, calls the actions specified in pre annotations, invokes the original function, and finally calls the actions specified in post annotations.

The function wrapper also invokes the LXFI runtime at its entry and exit, so that the runtime can capture all control flow transitions between the core kernel and the modules. The relevant runtime routines switch principals and enforce control flow integrity using a shadow stack, as we detail in the next section (§5).

Module initialization. For each module, LXFI generates an initialization function that is invoked (without LXFI's isolation) when the module is first loaded, to grant an initial set of capabilities to the module. For each external function (except those functions defined in LXFI runtime) imported in the module's symbol table, the initialization function grants a CALL capability for the corresponding function wrapper. Note that the CALL capabilities granted to the module are only for invoking wrappers. A module is not allowed to call any external functions directly, since that would bypass the annotations on those functions. For each external data symbol in the module's symbol table, the initialization function likewise grants a WRITE capability. The initial capabilities are granted to the module's shared principal, so that they are accessible to every other principal in the module.

Memory writes. LXFI inserts checking code before each memory write instruction to make sure that the current principal has the WRITE capability for the memory region being written to.

121

5 RUNTIME ENFORCEMENT

To enforce the specified API integrity, the LXFI runtime must track capabilities and ensure that the necessary capability actions are performed on kernel/module boundaries. For example, before a module invokes any kernel functions, the LXFI runtime validates whether the module has the privilege (i.e., CALL capability) to invoke the function at that address, and if the arguments passed by the module are safe to make the call (i.e., the **pre** annotations allow it). Similarly, before the kernel invokes any function pointer that was supplied by a module, the LXFI runtime verifies that the module had the privileges to invoke that function in the first place, and that the annotations of the function pointer and the invoked function match. These checks are necessary since the kernel is, in effect, making the call on behalf of the module.

Figure 6 shows the design of the LXFI runtime. As the reference monitor of the system, it is invoked on all control flow transitions between the core kernel and the modules (at instrumentation points described in the previous section). The rest of this section describes the operations performed by the runtime.

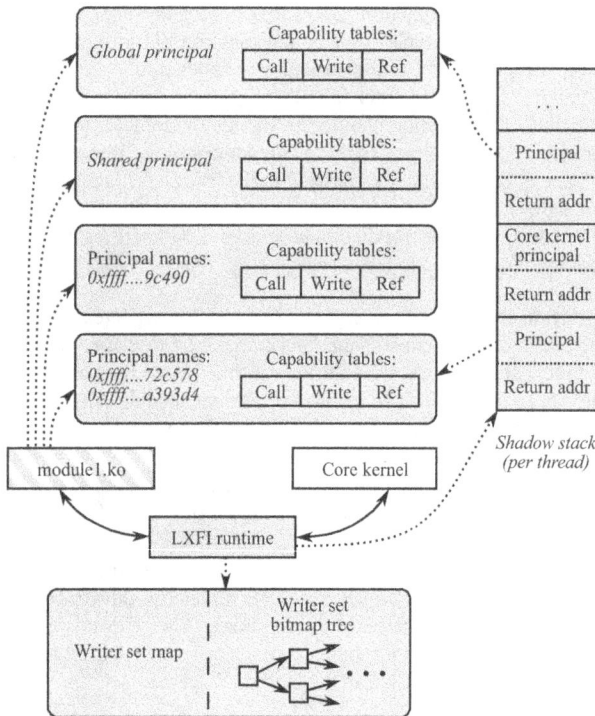

Figure 6: An overview of the LXFI runtime. Shaded components are parts of LXFI. Striped components indicate isolated kernel modules. Solid arrows indicate control flow; the LXFI runtime interposes on all control flow transfers between the modules and the core kernel. Dotted arrows indicate metadata tracked by LXFI.

Principals. The LXFI runtime keeps track of the principals for each kernel module, as well as two special principals. The first is the module's shared principal, which is initialized with appropriate initial capabilities (based on the imports from the module's symbol table); every other principal in the module implicitly has access to the capabilities stored in this principal. The second is the module's global principal; it implicitly has access to all capabilities in all of the module's principals.

Capability table. For each principal, LXFI maintains three capability tables (one per capability type), as shown in Figure 6. Efficiently managing capability tables is important to LXFI's perfor-

mance. LXFI uses a hash table for each table to achieve constant lookup time. For CALL capabilities and REF capabilities, LXFI uses function addresses and referred addresses, respectively, as the hash keys.

WRITE capabilities do not naturally fit within a hash table, because they are identified by an address range, and capability checks can happen for any address within the range. To support fast range tests, LXFI inserts a WRITE capability into all possible hash table slots covered by its address range. LXFI reduces the number of insertions by masking the least significant bits of the address (the last 12 bits in practice) when calculating hash keys. Since kernel modules do not usually manipulate memory objects larger than a page (2^{12} bytes), in our experience this data structure performs much better than a balancing tree, in which a lookup—commonly performed on WRITE capabilities—takes logarithmic time.

Shadow stack. LXFI maintains a shadow stack for each kernel thread to record LXFI-specific context. The shadow stack lies adjacent to the thread's kernel stack in the virtual address space, but is only accessible to the LXFI runtime. It is updated at the entry and the exit of each function wrapper.

To enforce control flow integrity on function returns, the LXFI runtime pushes the return address onto the shadow stack at the wrapper's entry, and validate its value at the exit to make sure that the return address is not corrupted. The runtime also saves and restores the principal on the shadow stack at the wrapper's entry and exit.

Writer-set tracking. To optimize the cost of indirect call checks, LXFI implements light-weight writer-set tracking (as described in §4.1). LXFI keeps writer set information in a data structure similar to a page table. The last level entries are bitmaps representing whether the writer set for a segment of memory is empty or not. Checking whether the writer set for a particular address is empty takes constant time. The actual contents of non-empty writer sets (i.e., what principal has WRITE access to a range of memory) is computed by traversing a global list of principals. Our experiments to date have involved a small number of distinct principals, leading to acceptable performance.

When a module is loaded, that module's shared principal is added to the writer set for all of its writable sections (including .data and .bss), because the section may contain writable function pointers that the core kernel may try to invoke. The runtime adds additional entries to the writer set map as the module executes and gains additional capabilities.

LXFI's writer-set tracking introduces both false positives and false negatives. A false positive arises when a WRITE capability of a function pointer was granted to some module's principal, but the principal did not write to the function pointer. This is benign, since it only introduces an unnecessary capability check. A false negative arises when the kernel copies pointers from a location that was modified by a module into its internal data structures, which were not directly modified by a module. At compile time, LXFI detects these cases and we manually inspect such false negatives (see §4.1).

6 USING LXFI

The most important step in enforcing API integrity is specifying the annotations on kernel/module boundaries. If a programmer annotates APIs incorrectly, then an adversary may be able to exploit the mistake to obtain increased privilege. We summarize guidelines for enforcing API integrity based on our experience annotating 10 modules.

Guideline 1. Following the principle of least privilege, grant a REF capability instead of a WRITE capability whenever possible. This ensures that a module will be unable to modify the memory contents of an object, unless absolutely necessary.

Guideline 2. For memory regions allocated by a module, grant WRITE capabilities to the module, and revoke it from the module on free. WRITE is needed because the module usually directly writes the memory it allocates (e.g., for initialization).

Guideline 3. If the module is required to pass a certain fixed value into a kernel API (e.g., an argument to a callback function, or an integer I/O port number to inb and outb I/O functions), grant a REF capability for that fixed value with a special type, and annotate the function in question (e.g., the callback function, or inb and outb) to require a REF capability of that special type for its argument.

Guideline 4. When dealing with large data structures, where the module only needs write access to a small number of the structure's members, modify the kernel API to provide stronger API integrity. For example, the e1000 network driver module writes to only five (out of 51) fields of sk_buff structure. This design requires LXFI to grant the module a WRITE capability for the sk_buff structure. It would be safer to have the kernel provide functions to change the necessary fields in an sk_buff. Then LXFI could grant the module a REF capability, perhaps with a special type of sk_buff__fields, and have the annotation on the corresponding kernel functions require a REF capability of type sk_buff__fields.

Guideline 5. To isolate instances of a module from each other, annotate the corresponding interface with principal annotations. The pointer used as the principal name is typically the main data structure associated with the abstraction, such as a socket, block device, network interface, etc.

Guideline 6. To manipulate privileges inside of a module, make two types of changes to the module's code. First, in order to manipulate data shared between instances, insert a call to LXFI to switch to the module's global principal. Second, in order to create principal aliases, insert a similar call to LXFI's runtime. In both cases, the module developer needs to preface these privileged operations with adequate checks to ensure that the functions containing these privileged operations are not abused by an adversary at runtime.

Guideline 7. When APIs implicitly transfer privileges between the core kernel and modules, explicitly add calls from the core kernel to the module to grant the necessary capabilities. For example, the Linux network stack supports packet schedulers, represented by a struct Qdisc object. When the kernel wants to assign a packet scheduler to a network interface, it simply changes a pointer in the network interface's struct net_device to point to the Qdisc object, and expect the module to access it.

7 IMPLEMENTATION

We implemented LXFI for Linux 2.6.36 running on a single-core x86_64 system. Figure 7 shows the components and the lines of code for each component. The kernel is compiled using gcc, invoking the kernel rewriting plugin (the kernel rewriter). Modules are compiled using Clang with the module rewriting plugin (the module rewriter), since Clang provides a more powerful infrastructure to implement rewriting. The current implementation of LXFI has several limitations, as follows.

The LXFI rewriter implements an earlier version of the language defined in §3. Both of the annotation languages can enforce the common idioms seen in the 10 annotated modules, however we believe the new language is more succinct. We expect that the

Component	Lines of code
Kernel rewriting plugin	150
Module rewriting plugin	1,452
Runtime checker	4,704

Figure 7: Components of LXFI.

language will evolve further as we annotate more interfaces, and discover other idioms.

The LXFI rewriter does not process assembly code, either in the core kernel or in modules. We manually inspect the assembly functions in the core kernel; none of them contains indirect calls. For modules, instrumentation is required if the assembly performs indirect calls or direct calls to an external function. In this case, developer must manually instrument the assembly by inserting calls to LXFI runtime checker. In our experience, modules use no assembly code that requires annotation.

LXFI requires all indirect calls in a module to be annotated to ensure API integrity. However, in some cases, the module rewriter fails to trace back to the function pointer declaration (e.g., due to an earlier phase of the compiler that optimized it away). In this case, developer has to modify the module's source code (e.g., to avoid the compiler optimization). For the 10 modules we annotated, such cases are rare: we changed 18 lines of code.

API integrity requires a complete set of core kernel functions to be annotated. However, in some cases, the Linux kernel inlines some kernel functions into modules. One approach is to annotate the inlined function, and let the module rewriter disable inlining of such functions. This approach, however, obscures the security boundary because these function are defined in the module, but must be treated the same as a kernel function. LXFI requires the boundary between kernel and module to be in one location by making either all or none of the functions inlined. In our experience, we have found that Linux is already well-written in this regard, and we had to change less than 10 functions (by not inlining them into a module) to enforce API integrity on 10 modules.

As pointed out in § 4.1, for indirect calls performed by the core kernel, LXFI checks that the annotation on function pointer matches the annotation on the invoked function f. Current implementation of LXFI performs checks when f has annotations, such as module functions that exported to kernel through assignment. A more strict and safe check is to enforce that f has annotations. Such check is not implemented because when f is defined in the core kernel, f may be static and has no annotation. We plan to implement annotation propagation in the kernel rewriter to solve this problem.

8 EVALUATION

This section evaluates the following 4 questions experimentally:

- Can LXFI stop exploits of kernel modules that have led to privilege escalation?

- How much work is required to annotate kernel/module interfaces?

- How much does LXFI slow down the SFI microbenchmarks?

- How much does LXFI slow down a Linux kernel module?

8.1 Security

To answer the first question we inspected 3 privilege escalation exploits using 5 vulnerabilities in Linux kernel modules revealed in 2010 that can lead to privilege escalation. Figure 8 shows three exploits and the corresponding vulnerabilities. LXFI successfully prevents all of the listed exploits as follows.

Exploit	CVE ID	Vulnerability type	Source location
CAN_BCM [17]	CVE-2010-2959	Integer overflow	`net/can/bcm.c`
Econet [18]	CVE-2010-3849	NULL pointer dereference	`net/econet/af_econet.c`
	CVE-2010-3850	Missed privilege check	`net/econet/af_econet.c`
	CVE-2010-4258	Missed context resetting	`kernel/exit.c`
RDS [19]	CVE-2010-3904	Missed check of user-supplied pointer	`net/rds/page.c`

Figure 8: Linux kernel module vulnerabilities that result in 3 privilege escalation exploits, all of which are prevented by LXFI.

CAN_BCM. Jon Oberheide posted an exploit to gain root privilege by exploiting an integer overflow vulnerability in the Linux CAN_BCM module [17]. The overflow is in the `bcm_rx_setup` function, which is triggered when the user tries to send a carefully crafted message through CAN_BCM. In particular, `bcm_rx_setup` allocates `nframes*16` bytes of memory from a slab, where `nframes` is supplied by user. By passing a large value, the allocation size overflows, and the module receives less memory than it asked for. This allows an attacker to write an arbitrary value into the slab object that directly follows the objects allocated to CAN_BCM. In the posted exploit, the author first arranges the kernel to allocate a `shmid_kernel` slab object at a memory location directly following CAN_BCM's undersized buffer. Then the exploit overwrites this `shmid_kernel` object through CAN_BCM, and finally, tricks the kernel into calling a function pointer that is indirectly referenced by the `shmid_kernel` object, leading to a root privilege escalation.

To test the exploit against LXFI, we ported Oberheide's exploit from *x86* to *x86_64*, since it depends on the size of pointer. LXFI prevents this exploit as follows. When the allocation size overflows, LXFI will grant the module a WRITE capability for only the number of bytes corresponding to the actual allocation size, rather than what the module asked for. When the module tries to write to an adjacent object in the same slab, LXFI detects that the module has no WRITE capability and raises an error.

Econet. Dan Rosenburg posted a privilege escalation exploit [18] by taking advantage of three vulnerabilities found by Nelson Elhage [8]. Two of them lie in the Econet module, and one in the core kernel. The two Econet vulnerabilities allow an unprivileged user to trigger a NULL pointer dereference in Econet. It is triggered when the kernel is temporarily in a context in which the kernel's check of a user-provided pointer is omitted, which allows a user to write anywhere in kernel space.

To prevent such vulnerabilities, the core kernel should always reset the context so that the check of a user-provided pointer is enforced. Unfortunately, kernel's `do_exit` failed to obey this rule. `do_exit` is called to kill a process when a NULL pointer dereference is captured in the kernel. Moreover, the kernel writes a zero into a user provided pointer (`task->clear_child_tid`) in `do_exit`. Along with the NULL pointer dereference triggered by the Econet vulnerabilities, the attacker is able to write a zero into an arbitrary kernel space address. By carefully arranging the kernel memory address for `task->clear_child_tid`, the attacker redirects `econet_ops.ioctl` to user space, and then gains root privilege in the same way as the RDS exploit. LXFI prevents the exploit by stopping the kernel from calling the indirect call of `econet_ops.ioctl` after it is overwritten with an illegal address.

RDS. Dan Rosenburg reported a vulnerability in the Linux RDS module in CVE-2010-3904 [19]. It is caused by a missing check of a user-provided pointer in the RDS page copying routine, allowing a local attacker to write arbitrary values to arbitrary memory locations. The vulnerability can be triggered by sending and receiving messages over a RDS socket. In the reported exploit, the attacker overwrites the `rds_proto_ops.ioctl` function pointer defined in the RDS module with the address of a user-space function. Then

it tricks the kernel to indirectly call the `rds_proto_ops.ioctl` by invoking the `ioctl` system call. As a result, the local attacker can execute his own code in kernel space.

LXFI prevents the exploit in two ways. First, LXFI does not grant WRITE capabilities for a module's read-only section to the module (the Linux kernel does). Thus, the exploit cannot overwrite `rds_proto_ops.ioctl` in the first place, since it is declared in a read-only structure. To see if LXFI can defend against vulnerabilities that allow corrupting a writable function pointer, we made this memory location writable. LXFI is able to prevent the exploit, because it checks the core kernel's indirect call to `rds_proto_ops.ioctl`. The LXFI runtime detects that the function pointer is writable by the RDS module, and then it checks if RDS has a CALL capability for the target function. The LXFI runtime rejects the indirect call because RDS module has no CALL capability for invoking a user-space function. It is worth mentioning that the LXFI runtime would also reject the indirect call if the user overwrites the function pointer with a core kernel function that the module does not have a CALL capability for.

Other exploits. Vulnerabilities leading to privilege escalation are harmful. The attacker can typically mount other types of attacks exploiting the same vulnerabilities. For example, it can be used to hide a rootkit. The Linux kernel uses a hash table (`pid_hash`) for process lookup. If a rootkit deletes a process from the hash table, the process will not be listed by `ps`' shell command, but will still be scheduled to run. Without LXFI, a rootkit can exploit the above vulnerability in RDS to unlink itself from the `pid_list` hash table. Using the same technique as in the RDS exploit, we developed an exploit that successfully hides the exploiting process. The exploit runs as an unprivileged user. It overwrites `rds_proto_ops.ioctl` to point to a user space function. When the vulnerability is triggered, the core kernel calls the user space function, which calls `detach_pid` with `current_task` (both are exported kernel symbols). As before, LXFI prevents the vulnerability by disallowing the core kernel from invoking the function pointer into user-space code, because the RDS module has no CALL capability for that code. Even if the module overwrites the `rds_proto_ops.ioctl` function pointer to point directly to `detach_pid`, LXFI still prevents this exploit, because the RDS module does not have a CALL capability for `detach_pid`.

8.2 Annotation effort

To evaluate the work required to specify contracts for kernel/module APIs, we annotated 10 modules. These modules include several device categories (network, sound, and block), different devices within a category (e.g., two sound devices), and abstract devices (e.g., network protocols). The difficult part in annotating is understanding the interfaces between the kernel and the module, since there is little documentation. We typically follow an iterative process: we annotate the obvious parts of the interfaces, and try to run the module under LXFI. When running the module, the LXFI runtime raises alerts because the module attempts operations that LXFI forbids. We then iteratively go through these alerts, understand what the module is trying to do, and annotate interfaces appropriately.

Category	Module	# Functions		# Function Pointers	
		all	unique	all	unique
net device driver	`e1000`	81	49	52	47
sound device driver	`snd-intel8x0`	59	27	12	2
	`snd-ens1370`	48	13	12	2
net protocol driver	`rds`	77	30	42	26
	`can`	53	7	7	3
	`can-bcm`	51	15	17	1
	`econet`	54	15	20	3
block device driver	`dm-crypt`	50	24	24	14
	`dm-zero`	6	3	2	0
	`dm-snapshot`	55	16	28	18
Total		334		155	

Figure 9: The numbers of annotated function prototypes and function pointers for 10 modules. An annotation is considered unique if it is used by only one module. The *Total* row reports the total number of distinct annotations.

To quantify the work involved, we count the number of annotations required to support a kernel module. The number of annotations needed for a given module is determined by the number of functions (either defined in the core kernel or other modules) that the module invokes directly, and the number of function pointers that the core kernel and the module call. As Figure 9 shows, each module calls 6–81 functions directly, and is called by (or calls) 7–52 function pointers. For each module, the number of functions and function pointers that need annotating is much smaller. For example, supporting the `can` module only requires annotating 7 extra functions after all other modules listed in Figure 9 are annotated. The reason is that similar modules often invoke the same set of core kernel functions, and that the core kernel often invokes module functions in the same way across multiple modules. For example, the interface of the PCI bus is shared by all PCI devices. This suggests that the effort to support a new module can be small as more modules are supported by LXFI.

Some functions require checking, copying, or transferring a large number of capabilities. LXFI's annotation language supports programmer-defined capability iterators for this purpose, such as `skb_caps` for handling all of the capabilities associated with an `sk_buff` shown in Figure 4. In our experience, most annotations are simple, and do not require capability iterators. For the 10 modules, we wrote 36 capability iterators to handle idioms such as for loops or nested data structures. Each module required 3-11 capability iterators.

A second factor that affects the annotation effort is the rate of change of Linux kernel interfaces. We have inspected Linux kernel APIs for 20 major versions of the kernel, from 2.6.20 to 2.6.39, by counting the numbers of both functions that are directly exported from the core kernel and function pointers that appear in shared data structures using `ctags`. Figure 10 shows our findings. The results indicate that, although the number of kernel interfaces grows steadily, the number of interfaces changed with each kernel version is relatively modest, on the order of several hundred functions. This is in contrast to the total number of lines of code changed between major kernel versions, which is on the order of several hundred thousand lines of code.

8.3 Microbenchmarks

To measure the enforcement overhead, we measure how much LXFI slows down the SFI microbenchmarks [23]. To run the tests, we turn each benchmark into a Linux kernel module. We run the tests on a desktop equipped with an Intel(R) Core(TM) i3-550 3.2 GHz CPU, 6GB memory, and an Intel 82540EM Gigabit Ethernet card. For these benchmarks, we might expect a slightly higher overhead than XFI because the stack optimizations used in SFI are not applicable

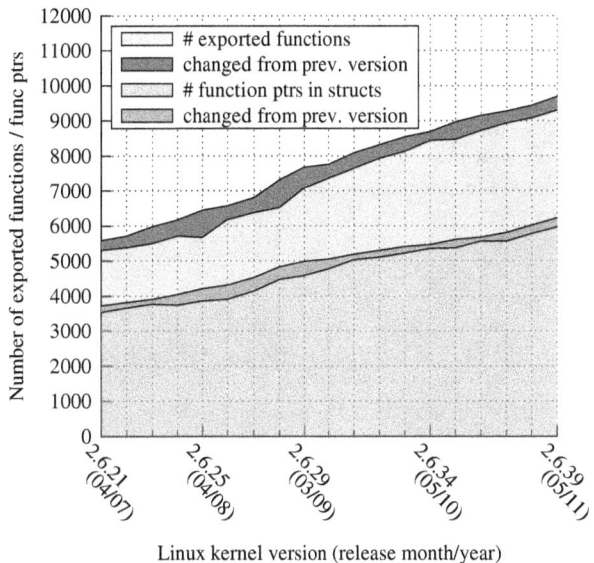

Figure 10: Rate of change for Linux kernel APIs, for kernel versions 2.6.21 through 2.6.39. The top curve shows the number of total and changed exported kernel functions; for example, 2.6.21 had a total of 5,583 exported functions, of which 272 were new or changed since 2.6.20. The bottom curve shows the number of total and changed function pointers in structs; for example, 2.6.21 had a total of 3,725 function pointers in structs, of which 183 were new or changed since 2.6.20.

to Linux kernel modules, but on the other hand LXFI, like BGI, uses a compile-time approach to instrumentation, which provides opportunities for compile-time optimizations. We cannot compare directly to BGI because it targets the Windows kernel and no numbers were reported for the SFI microbenchmarks, but we would expect BGI to be faster than LXFI, because BGI's design carefully optimizes the runtime data structures to enable low-overhead checking.

Benchmark	Δ code size	Slowdown
`hotlist`	1.14×	0%
`lld`	1.12×	11%
`MD5`	1.15×	2%

Figure 11: Code size and slowdown of the SFI microbenchmarks.

Figure 11 summarizes the results from the measurements. We compare our result with the slowpath write-only overhead in XFI (Table 1 in [9]). For all benchmarks, the code size is 1.1x-1.2x larger with LXFI instrumentation, while with XFI the code size is 1.1x-3.9x larger. We believe that LXFI's instrumentation inserts less code

Test	Throughput		CPU %	
	Stock	**LXFI**	**Stock**	**LXFI**
TCP_STREAM TX	836 M bits/sec	828 M bits/sec	13%	48%
TCP_STREAM RX	770 M bits/sec	770 M bits/sec	29%	64%
UDP_STREAM TX	3.1 M/3.1 M pkt/sec	2.0 M/2.0 M pkt/sec	54%	100%
UDP_STREAM RX	2.3 M/2.3 M pkt/sec	2.3 M/2.3 M pkt/sec	46%	100%
TCP RR	9.4 K Tx/sec	9.4 K Tx/sec	18%	46%
UDP RR	10 K Tx/sec	8.6 K Tx/sec	18%	40%
TCP RR (1-switch latency)	16 K Tx/sec	9.8 K Tx/sec	24%	43%
UDP RR (1-switch latency)	20 K Tx/sec	10 K Tx/sec	23%	47%

Figure 12: Performance of `netperf` benchmark with stock and LXFI enabled `e1000` driver.

because LXFI does not employ fastpath checks (inlining memory-range tests for the module's data section to handle common cases [9]) as XFI does. Moreover, LXFI targets *x86_64*, which provides more registers, allowing the inserted instructions to be shorter.

Like XFI, LXFI adds almost no overhead for `hotlist`, because `hotlist` performs mostly read-only operations over a linked list, which LXFI does not instrument.

The performance of `lld` under LXFI (11% slowdown) is much better than for XFI (93% slowdown). This is because the code of `lld` contains a few trivial functions, and LXFI's compiler plugin effectively inlined them, greatly reducing the number of guards at function entries and exits. In contrast, XFI uses binary rewriting and therefore is unable to perform this optimization. Since BGI also uses a compiler plug-in, we would expect BGI to do as well or better than LXFI.

The slowdown of `MD5` is also negligible (2% compared with 27% for XFI). `oprofile` shows that most of the memory writes in `MD5` target a small buffer, residing in the module's stack frame. By applying optimizations such as inlining and loop unrolling, LXFI's compiler plugin detects that these writes are safe because they operate on constant offsets within the buffer's bound, and can avoid inserting checks. Similar optimizations are difficult to implement in XFI's binary rewriting design, but BGI again should be as fast or faster than LXFI.

8.4 Performance

To evaluate the overhead of LXFI on an isolated kernel module, we run `netperf` [14] to exercise the Linux `e1000` driver as a kernel module. We run LXFI on the same desktop described in §8.3. The other side of the network connection runs stock Linux 2.6.35 SMP on a desktop equipped with an Intel(R) Core(TM) i7-980X 3.33 GHz CPU, 24 GB memory, and a Realtek RTL8111/8168B PCIE Gigabit Ethernet card. The two machines are connected via a switched Gigabit network. In this section, "TX" means that the machine running LXFI sends packets, and "RX" means that the machine running LXFI receives packets from the network.

Figure 12 shows the performance of `netperf`. Each test runs for 10 seconds. The "CPU %" column reports the CPU utilization on the desktop running LXFI. The first test, TCP_STREAM, measures the TCP throughput of the `e1000` driver. The test uses a send buffer of 16,384 bytes, and a receive buffer of 87,370 bytes. The message size is 16,384 bytes. As shown in Figure 12, for both "TX" and "RX" workloads, LXFI achieves the same throughput as the stock `e1000` driver; the CPU utilization increases by 3.7× and 2.2× with LXFI, respectively, because of the added cost of capability operations.

UDP_STREAM measures UDP throughput. The UDP socket size is 126,976 bytes on the send side, and 118,784 bytes on the receive side. The test sends messages of 64 bytes. The two performance numbers report the number of packets that get sent and received. LXFI achieves 65% of the throughput of the stock version for TX, and achieves the same throughput for RX. The LXFI version cannot

achieve the same throughput for TX because the CPU utilization reaches 100%, so the system cannot generate more packets. We expect that using a faster CPU would improve the throughput for TX (although the CPU overhead would remain high).

We run TCP_RR and UDP_RR to measure the impact of LXFI on latency, using the same message size, send and receive buffer sizes as above. We conducted two tests, each with a different network configuration.

In the first configuration, the two machines are connected the same subnet, and there are a few switches between them (but no routers). As shown in the middle rows of Figure 12, with LXFI, the throughput of TCP_RR is almost the same as the stock version, and the CPU utilization increases by 2.6×. For UDP_RR, the throughput decreases by 14%, and the CPU utilization increases by 2.2×.

Part of the latency observed in the above test comes from the network switches connecting the two machines. To understand how LXFI performs in a configuration with lower network latency, we connect the two machines to a dedicated switch and run the test again. As Figure 12 shows, the CPU utilization and the throughput increase for both versions. The relative overhead of LXFI increases because the network latency is so low that the processing of the next incoming packets are delayed by capability actions, slowing down the rate of packets received per second. We expect that few real systems use a network with such low latencies, and LXFI provides good throughput when even a small amount of latency is available for overlap.

Guard type	Guards per pkt	Time per guard (ns)	Time per pkt (ns)
Annotation action	13.5	124	1,674
Function entry	7.1	16	114
Function exit	7.1	14	99
Mem-write check	28.8	51	1,469
Kernel ind-call all	9.2	64	589
Kernel ind-call e1000	3.1	86	267

Figure 13: Average number of guards executed by the LXFI runtime per packet, the average cost of each guard, and the total time spent in runtime guards per packet for UDP_STREAM TX benchmark.

To understand the sources of LXFI's overheads, we measure the average number of guards per packet that the LXFI runtime executes, and the average time for each guard. We report the numbers for the UDP_STREAM TX benchmark, because LXFI performs worst for this workload (not considering the 1-switch network configuration). Figure 13 shows the results. As expected, LXFI spends most of the time performing annotation actions (grant, revoke, and check), and checking permissions for memory writes. Both of them are the most frequent events in the system. "Kernel ind-call all" and "Kernel ind-call `e1000`" show that the core kernel performs 9.2 indirect function calls per packet, around 1/3 of which are calls to the `e1000` driver that involve transmitting packets. This suggests that our writer-set

126

tracking optimization is effective at eliminating 2/3 of checks for indirect function calls.

8.5 Discussion

The results suggests that LXFI works well for the modules that we annotated. The amount of work to annotate is modest, requiring 8–133 annotations per module, including annotations that are shared between multiple modules. Instrumenting a network driver with LXFI increases CPU usage by 2.2–3.7×, and achieves the same TCP throughput as an unmodified kernel. However, UDP throughput drops by 35%. It is likely that we can use design ideas for runtime data structures from BGI to reduce the overhead of checking. In terms of security, LXFI is less beneficial to modules that must perform privileged operations; an adversary who compromises such a module will be able to invoke the privileged operation that the modules is allowed to perform. It would be interesting to explore how to refactor such modules to separate privileges. Finally, some modules have complicated semantics and the LXFI annotation language is not rich enough; for example, file systems have setuid and file permission invariants that are difficult to capture with LXFI annotations. We would like to explore how to increase LXFI's applicability in future work.

9 RELATED WORK

LXFI is inspired by XFI [9] and BGI [4]. XFI, BGI, and LXFI use SFI [26] to isolate modules. XFI assumes that the interface between the module and the support interface is simple and static, and does not handle overly permissive support functions. BGI extends XFI to handle more complex interfaces by manually interposing on every possible interaction between the kernel and module, and uses access control lists to restrict the operations a module can perform. Manual interposition for BGI is feasible because the Windows Driver Model (WDM) only allows drivers to access kernel objects, or register callbacks, through well-defined APIs. In contrast, the Linux kernel exposes its internal data objects to module developers. For example, a buggy module may overwrite function pointers in the kernel object to trick the kernel into executing arbitrary code. To provide API integrity for these complex interfaces, LXFI provides a capability and annotation system that programmers can use to express the necessary contracts for API integrity. LXFI's capabilities are dual to BGI's access control lists. Another significant difference between LXFI and BGI is LXFI's support for principals to partition the privileges held by a shared module. Finally, LXFI shows that it can prevent real and synthesized attacks, whereas the focus of BGI is high-performance fault isolation.

Mondrix [27] shows how to implement fault isolation for several parts of the Linux kernel, including the memory allocator, several drivers, and the Unix domain socket module. Mondrix relies on specialized hardware not available in any processor today, whereas LXFI uses software-based techniques to run on commodity *x*86 processors. Mondrix also does not protect against malicious modules, which drives much of LXFI's design. For example, malicious kernel modules in Mondrix can invoke core kernel functions with incorrect arguments, or simply reload the page table register, to take over the entire kernel.

Loki [28] shows how to privilege-separate the HiStar kernel into mutually distrustful "library kernels". Loki's protection domains correspond to user or application protection domains (defined by HiStar labels), in contrast with LXFI's domains which are defined by kernel component boundaries. Loki relies on tagged memory, and also relies on HiStar's simple kernel design, which has no complex subsystems like network protocols or sound drivers in Linux that LXFI supports.

Full formal verification along the lines of seL4 [15] is not practical for Linux, both because of its complexity, and because of its ill-defined specification. It may be possible to use program analysis techniques to check some limited properties of LXFI itself, though, to ensure that an adversary cannot subvert LXFI.

Driver isolation techniques such as Sud [3], Termite [21], Dingo [20], and Microdrivers [10] isolate device drivers at user-level, as do microkernels [7, 11]. This requires significantly re-designing the kernel interface, or restricting user-mode drivers to well-defined interfaces that are amenable to expose through IPC. Many kernel subsystems, such as protocol modules like RDS, make heavy use of shared memory that would not work well over IPC. Although there has been a lot of interest in fault containment in the Linux kernel [16, 24], fault tolerance is a weaker property than stopping attackers.

A kernel runtime that provides type safety and capabilities by default, such as Singularity [13], can provide strong API contracts similar to LXFI. However, most legacy OSes including Linux cannot benefit from it since they are not written in a type-safe language like C#.

SecVisor [22] provides kernel code integrity, but does not guarantee data protection or API integrity. As a result, code integrity alone is not enough to prevent privilege escalation exploits. OSck [12] detects kernel rootkits by enforcing type safety and data integrity for operating system data at hypervisor level, but does not address API safety and capability issues among kernel subsystems.

Overshadow [6] and Proxos [25] provide security by interposing on kernel APIs from a hypervisor. The granularity at which these systems can isolate features is more coarse than with LXFI; for example, Overshadow can just interpose on the file system, but not on a single protocol module like RDS. Furthermore, techniques similar to LXFI would be helpful to prevent privilege escalation exploits in the hypervisor's kernel.

10 CONCLUSION

This paper presents an approach to help programmers capture and enforce *API integrity* of complex, irregular kernel interfaces like the ones found in Linux. LXFI introduces capabilities and annotations to allow programmers to specify these rules for any given interface, and uses *principals* to isolate privileges held by independent instances of the same module. Using software fault isolation techniques, LXFI enforces API integrity at runtime. Using a prototype of LXFI for Linux, we instrumented a number of kernel interfaces with complex contracts to run 10 different kernel modules with strong security guarantees. LXFI succeeds in preventing privilege escalation attacks through 5 known vulnerabilities, and imposes moderate overhead for a network-intensive benchmark.

ACKNOWLEDGMENTS

We thank the anonymous reviewers and our shepherd, Sam King, for their feedback. This research was partially supported by the DARPA Clean-slate design of Resilient, Adaptive, Secure Hosts (CRASH) program under contract #N66001-10-2-4089, by the DARPA UHPC program, and by NSF award CNS-1053143. Dong Zhou was supported by China 973 program 2007CB807901 and NSFC 61033001. The opinions in this paper do not necessarily represent DARPA or official US policy.

REFERENCES

[1] Common vulnerabilities and exposures. From http://cve.mitre.org/cgi-bin/cvekey.cgi?keyword=linux+kernel+2010.

[2] J. Arnold, T. Abbott, W. Daher, G. Price, N. Elhage, G. Thomas, and A. Kaseorg. Security impact ratings considered harmful. In *Proceedings of the 12th Workshop on Hot Topics in Operating Systems*, Monte Verita, Switzerland, May 2009.

[3] S. Boyd-Wickizer and N. Zeldovich. Tolerating malicious device drivers in Linux. In *Proceedings of the 2010 USENIX Annual Technical Conference*, pages 117–130, Boston, MA, June 2010.

[4] M. Castro, M. Costa, J. P. Martin, M. Peinado, P. Akritidis, A. Donnelly, P. Barham, and R. Black. Fast byte-granularity software fault isolation. In *Proceedings of the 22nd ACM Symposium on Operating Systems Principles*, Big Sky, MT, October 2009.

[5] H. Chen, Y. Mao, X. Wang, D. Zhou, N. Zeldovich, and M. F. Kaashoek. Linux kernel vulnerabilities: State-of-the-art defenses and open problems. In *Proceedings of the 2nd Asia-Pacific Workshop on Systems*, Shanghai, China, July 2011.

[6] X. Chen, T. Garfinkel, E. C. Lewis, P. Subrahmanyam, C. A. Waldspurger, D. Boneh, J. Dwoskin, and D. R. K. Ports. Overshadow: A virtualization-based approach to retrofitting protection in commodity operating systems. In *Proceedings of the 13th International Conference on Architectural Support for Programming Languages and Operating Systems*, Seattle, WA, March 2008.

[7] F. M. David, E. M. Chan, J. C. Carlyle, and R. H. Campbell. CuriOS: Improving reliability through operating system structure. In *Proceedings of the 8th Symposium on Operating Systems Design and Implementation*, San Diego, CA, December 2008.

[8] N. Elhage. CVE-2010-4258: Turning denial-of-service into privilege escalation. `http://blog.nelhage.com/2010/12/cve-2010-4258-from-dos-to-privesc/`, December 2010.

[9] U. Erlingsson, M. Abadi, M. Vrable, M. Budiu, and G. C. Necula. XFI: Software guards for system address spaces. In *Proceedings of the 7th Symposium on Operating Systems Design and Implementation*, Seattle, WA, November 2006.

[10] V. Ganapathy, M. Renzelmann, A. Balakrishnan, M. Swift, and S. Jha. The design and implementation of microdrivers. In *Proceedings of the 13th International Conference on Architectural Support for Programming Languages and Operating Systems*, Seattle, WA, March 2008.

[11] J. N. Herder, H. Bos, B. Gras, P. Homburg, and A. Tanenbaum. Fault isolation for device drivers. In *Proceedings of the 2009 IEEE Dependable Systems and Networks Conference*, Lisbon, Portugal, June–July 2009.

[12] O. Hofmann, A. Dunn, S. Kim, I. Roy, and E. Witchel. Ensuring operating system kernel integrity with OSck. In *Proceedings of the 16th International Conference on Architectural Support for Programming Languages and Operating Systems*, Newport Beach, CA, March 2011.

[13] G. C. Hunt, J. R. Larus, M. Abadi, M. Aiken, P. Barham, M. Fahndrich, C. Hawblitzel, O. Hodson, S. Levi, N. Murphy, B. Steensgaard, D. Tarditi, T. Wobber, and B. Zill. An overview of the Singularity project. Technical Report MSR-TR-2005-135, Microsoft, Redmond, WA, October 2005.

[14] R. Jones. Netperf: A network performance benchmark, version 2.45. `http://www.netperf.org`.

[15] G. Klein, K. Elphinstone, G. Heiser, J. Andronick, D. Cock, P. Derrin, D. Elkaduwe, K. Engelhardt, M. Norrish, R. Kolanski, T. Sewell, H. Tuch, and S. Winwood. seL4: Formal verification of an OS kernel. In *Proceedings of the 22nd ACM Symposium on Operating Systems Principles*, Big Sky, MT, October 2009.

[16] A. Lenharth, V. S. Adve, and S. T. King. Recovery domains: An organizing principle for recoverable operating systems. In *Proceedings of the 14th International Conference on Architectural Support for Programming Languages and Operating Systems*, pages 49–60, Washington, DC, March 2009.

[17] J. Oberheide. Linux kernel CAN SLUB overflow. `http://jon.oberheide.org/blog/2010/09/10/linux-kernel-can-slub-overflow/`, September 2010.

[18] D. Rosenberg. Econet privilege escalation exploit. `http://thread.gmane.org/gmane.comp.security.full-disclosure/76457`, December 2010.

[19] D. Rosenberg. RDS privilege escalation exploit. `http://www.vsecurity.com/download/tools/linux-rds-exploit.c`, October 2010.

[20] L. Ryzhyk, P. Chubb, I. Kuz, and G. Heiser. Dingo: Taming device drivers. In *Proceedings of the ACM EuroSys Conference*, Nuremberg, Germany, March 2009.

[21] L. Ryzhyk, P. Chubb, I. Kuz, E. L. Sueur, and G. Heiser. Automatic device driver synthesis with Termite. In *Proceedings of the 22nd ACM Symposium on Operating Systems Principles*, Big Sky, MT, October 2009.

[22] A. Seshadri, M. Luk, N. Qu, and A. Perrig. SecVisor: A tiny hypervisor to provide lifetime kernel code integrity for commodity OSes. In *Proceedings of the 21st ACM Symposium on Operating Systems Principles*, Stevenson, WA, October 2007.

[23] C. Small and M. I. Seltzer. Misfit: Constructing safe extensible systems. *IEEE Concurrency*, 6:34–41, 1998.

[24] M. M. Swift, B. N. Bershad, and H. M. Levy. Improving the reliability of commodity operating systems. *ACM Transactions on Computer Systems*, 22(4), November 2004.

[25] R. Ta-Min, L. Litty, and D. Lie. Splitting interfaces: Making trust between applications and operating systems configurable. In *Proceedings of the 7th Symposium on Operating Systems Design and Implementation*, pages 279–292, Seattle, WA, November 2006.

[26] R. Wahbe, S. Lucco, T. E. Anderson, and S. L. Graham. Efficient software-based fault isolation. In *Proceedings of the 14th ACM Symposium on Operating Systems Principles*, pages 203–216, Asheville, NC, December 1993.

[27] E. Witchel, J. Rhee, and K. Asanovic. Mondrix: Memory isolation for Linux using Mondriaan memory protection. In *Proceedings of the 20th ACM Symposium on Operating Systems Principles*, Brighton, UK, October 2005.

[28] N. Zeldovich, H. Kannan, M. Dalton, and C. Kozyrakis. Hardware enforcement of application security policies. In *Proceedings of the 8th Symposium on Operating Systems Design and Implementation*, pages 225–240, San Diego, CA, December 2008.

Thialfi: A Client Notification Service for Internet-Scale Applications

Atul Adya   Gregory Cooper   Daniel Myers   Michael Piatek

{adya, ghc, dsmyers, piatek}@google.com

Google, Inc.

ABSTRACT

Ensuring the freshness of client data is a fundamental problem for applications that rely on cloud infrastructure to store data and mediate sharing. Thialfi is a notification service developed at Google to simplify this task. Thialfi supports applications written in multiple programming languages and running on multiple platforms, e.g., browsers, phones, and desktops. Applications register their interest in a set of shared objects and receive notifications when those objects change. Thialfi servers run in multiple Google data centers for availability and replicate their state asynchronously. Thialfi's approach to recovery emphasizes simplicity: all server state is soft, and clients drive recovery and assist in replication. A principal goal of our design is to provide a straightforward API and good semantics despite a variety of failures, including server crashes, communication failures, storage unavailability, and data center failures.

Evaluation of live deployments confirms that Thialfi is scalable, efficient, and robust. In production use, Thialfi has scaled to millions of users and delivers notifications with an average delay of less than one second.

Categories and Subject Descriptors

C.2.4 [**Computer-Communications Networks**]: Distributed Systems; D.4.5 [**Operating Systems**]: Reliability

General Terms

Distributed Systems, Scalability, Reliability, Performance

1. INTRODUCTION

Many Internet-scale applications are structured around data shared between multiple users, their devices, and cloud infrastructure. Client applications maintain a local cache of their data that must be kept fresh. For example, if a user changes the time of a meeting on a calendar, that change should be quickly reflected on the devices of all attendees. Such scenarios arise frequently at Google. Although infrastructure services provide reliable storage, there is currently no general-purpose mechanism to notify clients that shared data has changed. In practice, many applications periodically poll to detect

changes, which results in lengthy delays or significant server load. Other applications develop custom notification systems, but these have proven difficult to generalize and cumbersome to maintain.

This paper presents Thialfi, a highly scalable notification system developed at Google for user-facing applications with hundreds of millions of users and billions of objects. Thialfi provides sub-second notification delivery in the common case and clear semantics despite failures, even of entire data centers. Thialfi supports applications written in a variety of languages (C++, Java, JavaScript) and running on a diverse set of platforms such as web browsers, mobile phones, and desktops. To achieve reliability, Thialfi relies on clients to drive recovery operations, avoiding the need for hard state at the server, and our API is structured so that error handling is incorporated into the normal operation of the application.

Thialfi models shared data as versioned objects, which are stored at a data center and cached at clients. Clients *register* with Thialfi to be notified when an object changes, and the application's servers notify Thialfi when updates occur. Thialfi propagates notifications to registered clients, which synchronize their data with application servers. Crucially, Thialfi delivers only the latest *version number* to clients, not application data, which simplifies our design and promotes scalability.

Thialfi's implementation consists of a library embedded in client applications and two types of servers that run in Google data centers. *Matchers* are partitioned by object and receive and forward notifications; *Registrars* are partitioned by client and manage client registration and presence state. The client library communicates with the servers over a variety of application-specific channels; Thialfi protocols provide end-to-end reliability despite channel losses or message reordering. Finally, a best-effort replication protocol runs between Thialfi data centers, and clients correct out-of-date servers during migration.

A principal feature of Thialfi's design is reliability in the presence of a wide variety of faults. The system ensures that clients eventually learn of the latest version of each registered object, even if the clients were unreachable at the time the update occurred. At large scale, ensuring even eventual delivery is challenging—Thialfi is designed to operate at the scale of hundreds of millions of clients, billions of objects, and hundreds of thousands of changes per second. Since applications are replicated across data centers for reliability, notifications may need to be routed over multiple unreliable communication channels to reach all clients. During propagation, a client may become unavailable or change its server affinity. Clients may be offline. Servers, storage systems, or even entire data centers may become temporarily unavailable. Thialfi handles these issues internally, freeing application developers from the need to cope with them as special cases. Indeed, Thialfi remains correct even when all server state is discarded. In our API, *all failures* manifest as signals that objects or registrations have become stale and should be refreshed, and this process reconstructs state at the server if necessary.

Like many infrastructure services, Thialfi is designed for operational simplicity: the same aspects of our design that provide reliability (e.g., tolerating data center failures) also make the system easier to run in production. Our techniques emphasize simplicity but do not provide perfect availability. While Thialfi remains correct, recovering from some failures results in partial unavailability, and we discuss these scenarios in our design.

Thialfi is a production service that is in active use by millions of people running a diverse set of Google's applications. We focus on two: Chrome and Contacts. These show the diversity of Thialfi usage, which includes desktop applications synchronizing data with the cloud (Chrome) as well as web/mobile applications sharing data between devices (Contacts). In both cases, Thialfi has simplified application design and improved efficiency substantially.

Further evaluation of Thialfi confirms its scalability, efficiency, and robustness. In production use, Thialfi has scaled to millions of users. Load testing shows that Thialfi's resource consumption scales directly with usage. Injecting failures shows that the cost of recovery is modest; despite the failure of an entire data center, Thialfi can rapidly migrate clients to remaining data centers with limited over-provisioning.

To summarize, we make the following contributions:

- We provide a system robust to the full and partial failures common to infrastructure services. Thialfi is one of the first systems to demonstrate robustness to the complete failure of a data center and to the partial unavailability of infrastructure storage.

- Our design provides reliability at Internet scale without hard server state. Thialfi ensures that clients eventually learn the latest versions of registered objects even if all server state is dropped.

- Thialfi's API unifies error recovery with ordinary operation. No separate error-handling code paths are required, greatly simplifying integration and reasoning about correctness.

- We integrate Thialfi with several Google applications and demonstrate the performance, scalability, and robustness of our design for millions of users and thousands of notifications per second.

2. MOTIVATION AND REQUIREMENTS

This section describes an abstraction for a notification service with requirements drawn from our experience at Google. Figure 1 shows the abstraction. Since Internet applications are separated into server and client components, the service includes both an infrastructure component and a client library. At the client, developers program against the library's API and make updates that modify shared data. At the server, applications publish notifications, which the service routes to appropriate clients. The remainder of this section describes how we arrived at this abstraction.

2.1 A Case for a Notification Service

Applications that share data among users and devices have a common need for notifications when data has changed. For example, the Google Contacts application allows users to create, edit, and

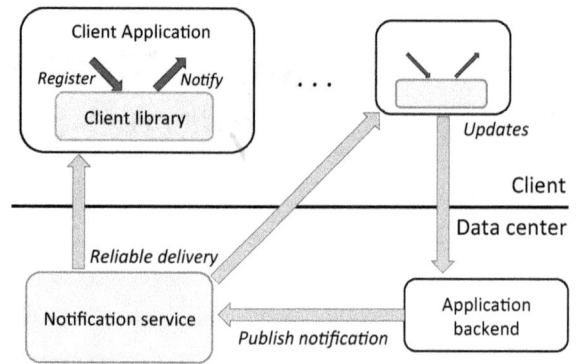

Figure 1: An abstraction for a client notification service.

share contact information through web, mobile, and desktop interfaces that communicate with servers running in Google's data centers. If a contact changes, other devices should learn of the change quickly. This is the essence of a notification service: informing interested parties of changes to data in a reliable and timely manner.

Throughout the paper, we refer to application data as *objects*: named, versioned entities for which users may receive notifications. For example, a contacts application might model each user's address book as an object identified by that user's email address, or the application may model each contact as a separate object. Contacts may be shared among users or a user's devices. When the contact list is changed, its version number increases, providing a simple mechanism to represent changes.

In the absence of a general service, applications have developed custom notification mechanisms. A widely used approach is for each client to periodically poll the server for changes. While conceptually simple and easy to implement, polling creates an unfortunate tension between timeliness and resource consumption. Frequent polling allows clients to learn of changes quickly but imposes significant load on the server. And, most requests simply indicate that no change has occurred.

An alternative is to push notifications to clients. However, ensuring reliability in a push system is difficult: a variety of storage, network, and server failures are common at Internet scale. Further, clients may be disconnected when updates occur and remain offline for days. Buffering messages indefinitely is infeasible. The server's storage requirements must be bounded, and clients should not be overwhelmed by a flood of messages upon wakeup.

As a result of these challenges, push systems at Google are generally best-effort; developers must detect and recover from errors. This is typically done via a low-frequency, backup polling mechanism, again resulting in occasional, lengthy delays that are difficult to distinguish from bugs.

2.2 Requirements

Summarizing our discussion above, a general notification service should satisfy at least four requirements.

- **Tracking.** The service should track which clients are interested in what data. Particularly for shared data, tracking a mapping between clients and objects is a common need.

- **Reliability.** Notifications should be reliable. To the extent pos-

Configuration	Choices
Channel	HTTP, XMPP, internal RPC (in DC)
Language	Java, C++, JavaScript
Platform	Web, mobile, native desktop apps
Storage	Storage with inter-DC sync or async replication

Table 1: Configurations supported by Thialfi.

sible, application developers should not be burdened with error detection and recovery mechanisms such as polling.

- **End-to-end.** Given an unreliable channel, the service must provide reliability in an end-to-end manner; i.e., it must include a client-side component.

- **Flexibility.** To be widely applicable, a notification service must impose few restrictions on developers. It should support web, desktop, and mobile applications written in a variety of languages for a variety of platforms. At the server, similar diversity in storage and communication dependencies precludes tight integration with a particular software stack. We show the variety of configurations that Thialfi supports in Table 1.

2.3 Design Alternatives

Before describing our system in detail, we first consider alternative designs for a notification service.

Integrating notifications with the storage layer: Thialfi treats each application's storage layer as opaque. Updates to shared objects must be explicitly published, and applications must explicitly register for notifications on shared objects. An alternative would be to track object sharing at the storage layer and automatically generate notifications when shared objects change. We avoid this for two reasons. The first is diversity: while many applications share a common need for notifications, applications use storage systems with diverse semantics, data models, and APIs customized to particular application requirements. We view the lack of a one-size-fits-all storage system as fundamental, leading us to design notifications as a separate component that is loosely coupled with the storage layer. The second reason is complexity. Even though automatically tracking object dependencies [22] may simplify the programming model when data dependencies are complex (e.g., constructing webpages on-the-fly with data joins), such application structures are difficult to scale and rare at Google. Requiring explicit object registrations and updates substantially simplifies our design, and our experience has been that reasoning about object registrations in our current applications is straightforward.

Reliable messaging from servers to clients: Reliable messaging is a familiar primitive for developers. We argue for a different abstraction: a reliable notification of the latest *version number* of an object. Why not reliable messaging? First, reliable messaging is inappropriate when clients are often unavailable. Lengthy queues accumulate while clients are offline, leading to a flood of messages upon wakeup, and server resources are wasted if offline clients never return. Second, message delivery is often application-specific. Delivering application data requires adhering to diverse security and privacy requirements, and different client devices require delivery in different formats (e.g., JSON for browsers, binary for phones). Instead of reliable messaging, Thialfi provides *reliable signaling*—the queue of notifications for each object is collapsed to a single message, and old clients may be safely garbage-collected without sacrificing reliability. Moreover, such an abstraction allows Thialfi to remain loosely coupled with applications.

3. OVERVIEW

This section gives an overview of the Thialfi architecture and its programming interface.

3.1 Model and Architecture

Thialfi models data in terms of object identifiers and their version numbers. Objects are stored in each application's backend servers, not by Thialfi. Each object is named using a variable length byte string of the application's choosing (typically less than 32 bytes), which resides in a private namespace for that application. Version numbers (currently 64-bit) are chosen by applications and included in the update published to Thialfi.

Application backends are required to ensure that version numbers are monotonically increasing to ensure reliable delivery; i.e., in order for Thialfi to reliably notify a client of an object's latest version, the latest version must be well-defined. Synchronous stores can achieve this by incrementing a version number after every update, for example. Asynchronous stores typically have some method of eventually reconciling updates and reaching a commit point; such stores can issue notifications to Thialfi afterwards. At Google, to avoid modifying existing asynchronous backend stores, some services simply inform Thialfi when updates reach one of the storage replicas, using the current time at that replica as the version number. Although such services run the risk of missing updates due to clock skew and conflicts, this is rare in practice. Clock skew in the data center is typically low, conflicts are infrequent for many applications, and replication delay is low (seconds).

As shown in Figure 1, Thialfi is comprised of a client library and server infrastructure. We describe these components in turn.

Client library: The client library provides applications with a programmatic interface for registering for shared objects and receiving notifications. The library speaks the Thialfi protocol and communicates with the Thialfi infrastructure service running in data centers. An application uses the Thialfi library to register for objects, and the library invokes callbacks to inform the application of registration changes and to deliver notifications. For each notification, Thialfi informs the application of the modified object's identifier and the latest version known. When the application receives a notification, it synchronizes object data by talking directly with its servers: Thialfi does not provide data synchronization.

Server infrastructure: In the data center, application servers apply updates and notify Thialfi when objects change. We provide a *Publisher* library that application backends can embed. The publisher library call:

Publish(objectId, version, source)

ensures that all Thialfi data centers are notified of the change. When present, the optional *source* parameter identifies the client that made the change. (This ID is provided by the application client at startup and is referred to as its *application* ID.) As an optimization, Thialfi omits delivery of the notification to this client, since the client already knows about the change.

Thialfi supports multiple communication channels to accommodate application diversity. For example, native applications may use XMPP [27], while web applications typically use persistent HTTP connections [17]. This support allows Thialfi to reuse an application's existing communication channel, an important capability given the high cost of maintaining a channel in certain con-

131

```
// Client actions
interface NotificationClient {
  Start(byte[] persistentState);
  Register(ObjectId objectId, long version);
  Unregister(ObjectId objectId);
}

// Client library callbacks
interface NotificationListener {
  Notify(ObjectId objectId, long version);

  NotifyUnknown(ObjectId objectId);

  RegistrationStatusChanged(ObjectId objectId,
      boolean isRegistered);

  RegistrationFailure(ObjectId objectId,
      boolean isTransient);

  ReissueRegistrations();

  WriteState(byte[] persistentState);
}
```

Figure 2: The Thialfi client API.

texts (e.g., mobile- or browser-based applications). Other than non-corruption, Thialfi imposes few requirements—messages may be dropped, reordered, or duplicated. Although rare, the channels most commonly used by applications exhibit all of these faults.

3.2 Security

Given the diversity of authorization and authentication techniques used by applications, Thialfi does not dictate a particular scheme for securing notifications. Instead, we provide hooks for applications to participate in securing their data at various points in the system. For example, Thialfi can make RPCs to application backends to authorize registrations. If required, Thialfi can also make authorization calls before sending notifications to clients.

Similarly, applications must provide a secure client-server channel if confidentiality is required. Thialfi does not mandate a channel security policy.

3.3 Client API and Usage

The Thialfi client library provides applications with the API shown in Figure 2, and we refer to these calls throughout our discussion.

The **NotificationClient** interface lists the actions available via the client library. The **Start**() method initializes the client, and the **Register**() and **Unregister**() calls can be used to register/unregister for object notifications. We point out that the client interface does not include support for generating notifications. **Publish**() calls must be made by the application backend.

The **NotificationListener** interface defines callbacks invoked by the client library to notify the user application of status changes. Application programmers using Thialfi's library implement these methods. When the library receives a notification from the server, it calls **Notify**() with that object's ID and new version number. In scenarios where Thialfi does not know the version number of the object (e.g., if Thialfi has never received any update for the object or has deleted the last known version value for it), the client library uses the **NotifyUnknown**() call to inform the application that it should refetch the object from the application store regardless of its cached version. Internally, such notifications are assigned a se-

quence number by the server so that they can be reliably delivered and acknowledged in the protocol.

The client library invokes **RegistrationStatusChanged**() to inform the application of any registration information that it receives from the server. It uses **RegistrationFailure**() to indicate a registration operation failure to the application. A boolean, **isTransient**, indicates whether the application should attempt to retry the operation. **ReissueRegistrations**() allows the client library to request all registrations from the application. This call can be used to ensure that Thialfi state matches the application's intent, e.g., after a loss of server state.

The **WriteState**() call is an optional method that provides Thialfi with persistent storage on the client, if available. Client data storage is application-specific; e.g., some applications have direct access to the filesystem while others are limited to a browser cookie. When a client receives its identifier from the server, the client library invokes **WriteState**() with an opaque byte string encoding the identifier, which is then stored by the application and provided to Thialfi during subsequent invocations of **Start**(). This allows clients to resume using existing registrations and notification state. Clients that do not support persistence are treated as new clients after each restart.

4. DESIGN AND IMPLEMENTATION

This section describes the design and implementation of Thialfi. We highlight several key techniques.

No hard server state: Thialfi operates on *registration state* (i.e., which clients care about which objects) and *notification state* (the latest known version of each object). The Thialfi client library is responsible for tracking the registration state and updating servers in the event of a discrepancy, so loss of server-side state does not jeopardize correctness. Moreover, while Thialfi makes a substantial effort to deliver "useful" notifications at specific version numbers, it is free to deliver spurious notifications, and notifications may be associated with an *unknown* version. This flexibility allows notification state to be discarded, provided the occurrence of the drop is noted.

Efficient I/O through multiple views of state: The registration and notification state in Thialfi consists of relations between clients and objects. There is no clear advantage to choosing either client ID or object ID as the primary key for this state: notifications update a single object and multiple clients, while registrations update a single client and multiple objects. To make processing of each operation type simple and efficient, we maintain two separate views of the state, one indexed by client ID and one by object ID, allowing each type of operation to be performed via a single write to one storage location in one view. The remaining view is brought up-to-date asynchronously.

Idempotent operations only: Thialfi is designed so that any server-side operation can be safely repeated. Every operation commits at the server after a single write to storage, allowing aggressive batching of writes. Any dependent changes are performed in the background, asynchronously. Avoiding overwrites fosters robustness; operations are simply retried until they succeed.

Buffering to cope with partial storage availability: While data corruption is uncommon, large-scale storage systems do not have perfect availability. Writes to some storage regions may fail tran-

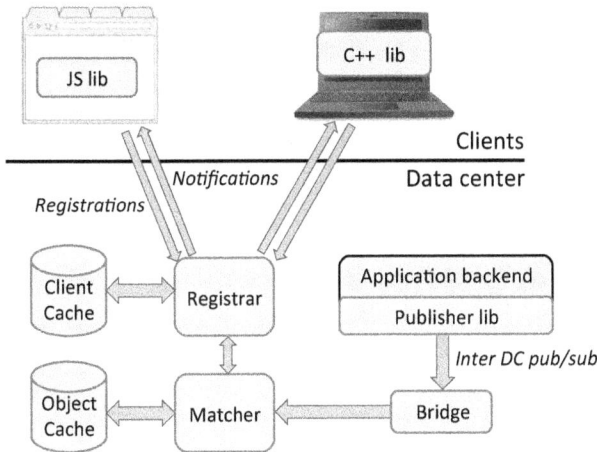

Figure 3: Overall architecture of Thialfi.

siently. To prevent this transient storage unavailability from cascading to application backends, Thialfi buffers failed notification writes at available storage locations, migrating buffered state to its appropriate location when possible.

Figure 3 shows the major components of Thialfi. **Bridge servers** are stateless, randomly load-balanced tasks that consume a feed of application-specific update messages from Google's infrastructure pub/sub service, translate them into a standard notification format, and assemble them into batches for delivery to Matcher tasks. **Matchers** consume notifications for objects, match them with the set of registered clients, and forward them to the Registrar for reliable delivery to clients. Matchers are partitioned over the set of objects and maintain a view of state indexed by object ID. **Registrars** track clients, process registrations, and reliably deliver notifications using a view of state indexed by client ID.

The remainder of this section describes our design in stages, starting with a simplified version of Thialfi that operates entirely in memory and in one data center only. We use this simplified design to explain the Thialfi protocol and to describe why discarding Thialfi's server state is safe. We then extend the in-memory design to use persistent storage, reducing the cost of recovering failed servers. Finally, we add replication in order to improve recovery from the failure of entire data centers.

4.1 In-memory Design

An in-memory version of Thialfi stores client and object state in the memory of the Registrar and Matcher servers. As mentioned above, clients are partitioned over Registrar servers, and objects are partitioned over Matcher servers. In order to ensure roughly uniform distribution of load, each client and object is assigned a *partitioning key*. This key is computed by prepending a hash of the client or object ID to the ID itself. We statically partition this keyspace into contiguous ranges; one range is assigned to each server. If a server crashes or reboots, its state is lost and must be reconstructed from scratch.

Aside from lack of persistence and support for multiple data centers, this design is identical to that deployed at Google. We next describe the specific state maintained.

4.1.1 In-memory State

Registrar: For each client, the Registrar servers maintain two sets: 1) *registrations* (objects of interest to the client) and 2) *pending notifications* (notifications not yet acknowledged by the client). They also maintain a monotonically-increasing *sequence number* for each client, used to pick an ordering for registration operations and to generate version numbers for unknown-version notifications.

Matcher: For each object, Matcher servers store the latest version number provided by the application backend. Matcher servers also maintain a copy of the registered clients for each object from the Registrar; this copy is updated asynchronously. We refer to the combined Matcher and Registrar state as the C/O-Cache (Client and Object cache).

Thialfi components that we call *Propagators* asynchronously propagate state between Matchers and Registrars. The *Registrar Propagator* copies client registrations to the Matcher, and the *Matcher Propagator* copies new notifications to the Registrar.

Both Matchers and Registrars maintain a set of pending operations to perform for objects and clients; i.e., propagation and delivery of (un)registrations and notifications. The state maintained by each server thus decomposes into two distinct parts: the C/O-Cache and a pending operation set.

4.1.2 Client Token Management

Thialfi identifies clients using *client tokens* issued by Registrars. Tokens are composed of two parts: *client identifiers* and *session identifiers*. Tokens are opaque to clients, which store them for inclusion in each subsequent message. A client identifier is unique and persists for the lifetime of the client's state. A session identifier binds a client to a particular Thialfi data center and contains the identity of the data center that issued the token.

A client acquires tokens via a handshake protocol, in which the Registrar creates an entry for the client's state. If the client later migrates to another data center, the Registrar detects that the token was issued elsewhere and informs the client to repeat the handshake protocol with the current data center. When possible, the new token reuses the existing client identifier. A client may thus acquire many session identifiers during its interactions with Thialfi, although it holds only one client token (and thus one session identifier) at any given time.

The Thialfi client library sends periodic heartbeat messages to the Registrar to indicate that it is online (a Registrar only sends notifications to online clients). In the current implementation, the heartbeat interval is 20 minutes, and the Registrar considers a client to be offline if it has not received any message from the client for 80 minutes. Certain channels inform Thialfi in a best-effort manner when a client disconnects, allowing the Registrar to mark the client offline more quickly. Superficially, these periodic heartbeats might resemble polling. However, they are designed to be extremely lightweight: the messages are small, and processing only requires a single in-memory operation in the common case when the client is already online. Thus, unlike application-level polling, they do not pose a significant scalability challenge.

4.1.3 Registration Operation

Once a client has completed the initial handshake, it is able to execute registrations. When an application calls **Register**(), the client

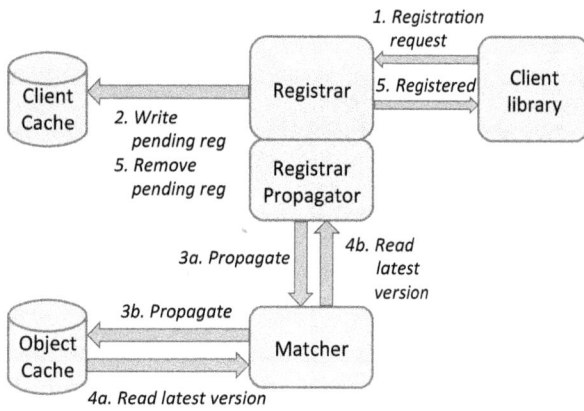

Figure 4: Object registration in Thialfi.

library queues a message to send to the Registrar. (As with all protocol messages, the application dispatches outgoing registrations asynchronously using its channel.) An overview of registration is shown in Figure 4.

1. The client library sends a registration message to the Registrar with the object identifier.
2. The Registrar picks an ordering for the registration by assigning it a sequence number, using the sequence number it maintains for the issuing client. The Registrar writes the registration to the client record and adds a new entry to the pending operation set.
3. Subsequently, the Registrar Propagator attempts to forward the registration and the application ID of the registering client to the Matcher responsible for the object via an RPC, and the Matcher updates the copy of the registration in its object cache. The Registrar Propagator repeats this until either propagation succeeds or its process crashes.
4. After propagation succeeds, the Registrar reads the latest version of the object from the Matcher (which reads the versions from its object cache) and writes a pending notification for it into the client cache (i.e., updates its copy of the latest version). We call this process *Registrar post-propagation*. If no version is known, the Registrar generates an unknown-version notification for the object with the version field set using the sequence number maintained for the client.
5. The Registrar sends a message to the client confirming the registration and removes the operation from the pending set.

Clients unregister using an analogous process. To keep the registrations at the client and the Registrar in sync, Thialfi uses a **Registration Sync Protocol**. Each message from the client contains a digest of the client's registered objects, and each message from the server contains the digest of the client's registrations known to the server (in our current implementation, we compute the digest using HMAC-SHA1 [10]). If the client or the server detects a discrepancy at any point, the client resends its registrations to the server. If the server detects the problem, it requests that the client resend them. To support efficient synchronization for large numbers of objects, we have implemented optional support for Merkle Trees [18], but no application currently using Thialfi has required this mechanism.

The client library keeps track of the application's intended registrations via registration/unregistration API calls. To preserve the registration state across application restarts, the library could write all registrations to the local disk using the **WriteState()** call (Section 3.3). To simplify persistence requirements, however, Thialfi relies on applications to restate intended registrations on restart.

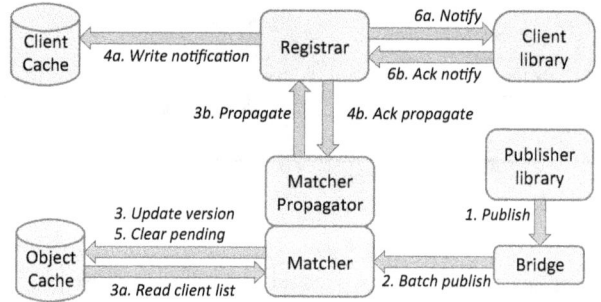

Figure 5: Notification delivery in Thialfi.

When a client restarts, the client library invokes **ReissueRegistrations()**. The library then recomputes the digest and sends it as part of the regular communication with the server (e.g., in heartbeats). Any discrepancy in the registrations is detected and resolved using the Registration Sync Protocol discussed above. In the normal case when digests match, no registrations are resent to the server.

4.1.4 Notification Operation

As users modify data, client applications send updates to application servers in the data center. Application servers apply the updates and publish notifications to be delivered by Thialfi. Figure 5 shows the sequence of operations by which Thialfi delivers notifications to registered clients.

1. The application server updates its authoritative copy of user data and notifies Thialfi of the new version number. Applications publish notifications using a library that ensures each published notification is received by all data centers running Thialfi. Currently, we use an internal Google infrastructure publish/subscribe service to disseminate messages to data centers. The pub/sub service acknowledges the Publisher library only after a reliable handoff, ensuring eventual delivery. (During periods of subscriber unavailability, the pub/sub service buffers notifications in a persistent log.)
2. Thialfi's Bridge component consumes the feed of published notifications in each data center and processes them in small batches. The Bridge delivers the update to the Matcher server responsible for the object.
3. The Matcher updates its record for the object with the new version number. Subsequently, using its copy of the registered client list, the Matcher propagator determines which Registrar servers have clients registered for the object. It sends RPCs to each Registrar server with (client, oid, version) tuples indicating which clients need to be notified. The client identifiers are used to index the Registrar's C/O-Cache efficiently.
4. Each Registrar receiving a message stores the pending notification for the appropriate clients and responds to the RPC.
5. When all Registrars have responded, the operation is removed from the Matcher pending operation set.
6. Periodically, the Registrars resend unacknowledged notifications for online clients. Currently, we use a 60-second retransmission interval.

4.1.5 Handling Server Failures

We now discuss how a server reconstructs its in-memory state after a restart (an independent infrastructure system at Google monitors and restarts services that have crashed or become unresponsive). For simplicity, consider a brute-force approach: if any server fails,

Registrar Table						
Row Key	Client State			Object State		Propagation State
	created	last-seqno	presence	reg-{oid}	log-{oid}	pending
hash(user):user:uuid	*appid@0*	*""@seqno*	*addr@seqno*	*""@seqno*	*""@version*	*""@seqno*

Matcher Table			
Row Key	Object State	Client State	Propagation State
	version	reg-{client-id}	pending
hash(object-id):object-id	*appid@version*	*appid@seqno*	*""@version*

Table 2: Bigtable layout for server-side state. *a@b* indicates a value *a* at timestamp *b*. *seqno* refers to the sequence number assigned by the Registrar for that particular client.

all servers restart, and the data center identifier is changed to a new value. Subsequent messages from clients with old tokens are detected by the Registrars, triggering a token update as described in §4.1.2. The Registration Sync Protocol then ensures that the clients reissue their registrations.

Client registration messages are sufficient to reconstruct the registration state at the Registrar. The latest-version data at the Matcher is not recovered (and pending notifications are lost) since there is no mechanism to fetch version information from the application backend. Nonetheless, correctness is not compromised. When processing client registrations, the Registrar will send unknown-version notifications for each registered object. This triggers client requests to the application backend to learn the latest version. Such an approach is conservative since the data may not have changed, but Thialfi cannot easily confirm this. After restart, Thialfi resumes normal processing of updates.

4.1.6 Handling Network Failures

There are three types of messages sent between the client and server: client token requests, registration changes, and notifications / acks. Any of these may be lost, reordered, or duplicated. Notifications are acknowledged and hence reliably delivered, and reordering and duplication are explicitly permitted by the semantics of Thialfi. All other messages are retried by the client as needed. Clients detect and ignore duplicate or reordered token grant messages from the Registrar using a nonce, and the Registration Sync Protocol ensures that client and server registration state eventually converge.

4.2 Persistent Storage

At the scale of millions of clients, recovering from failures by flushing and reconstructing state is impractical. *Some* retention of state is required to reduce work during recovery. In this section, we describe how Thialfi currently uses Bigtable [7] to address this issue. The main idea guiding our use of persistent storage is that updates to the C/O-Cache in the memory-only design translate directly into *blind writes* into a Bigtable; i.e., updating state without reading it. Because Bigtable is based on a log-structured storage system, writes are efficient and fast.

4.2.1 Bigtable Layout

Storage locations in a Bigtable (*Bigtable cells*) are named by {row key, column, version} tuples, and Bigtables may be sparse; i.e., there may be many cells with no value. We exploit this property in our storage layout to avoid overwrites. For example, in the Registrar table, for a particular client/object registration pair, we use a distinct row key (based on the client ID), column (based on the object ID), and version (based on the registration sequence number).

When querying the registration status for that client/object pair, we simply read the latest version.

Adapting our in-memory representation to Bigtable is straightforward. Registrar and Matcher state is stored in separate Bigtables. The partitioning keys used in the in-memory system become the row keys used in the Bigtables, distributing load uniformly. We continue to statically partition the keyspace over the Registrar and Matcher servers. Each server is thus assigned a contiguous range of Bigtable rows.

The Bigtable schema is summarized in Table 2. Each row of the Matcher table stores the latest known version for an object, the application ID of the client that created that version, and the set of clients registered for that object. Each Registrar row stores the client's application ID, the latest sequence number that was generated for the client by the Registrar, a channel-specific address if the client is online, the object IDs that the client is registered for, and the objects for which the client has an unacknowledged notification. Each table also contains a column for tracking which rows have pending information to propagate to the other table. Note that a cell is written in the last-seqno column whenever a sequence number is used for the client. This ensures that sequence numbers always increase.

4.2.2 In-memory State

In order to improve performance, we cache a small amount of state from Bigtable in Registrar and Matcher server memory. The Registrars cache the registration digest of each online client (but not the full set of registrations). The Matchers and Registrars also cache their pending operation sets. We rely on Bigtable's memory cache for fast reads of the registrations and pending notifications. Since our working set currently fits in Bigtable's memory cache, this has not created a performance problem. (We may revisit this decision if emerging workloads change our Bigtable memory cache profile.)

The outcome of these properties is that *the in-memory state of Thialfi servers corresponds to in-progress operations and limited data for online clients only*.

4.2.3 Pushing Notifications to Clients

As with the in-memory design, reliable notification delivery to clients is achieved by scanning for unacknowledged notifications. Instead of memory, the scan is over the Registrar Bigtable. For efficiency and performance, we also introduce a *fast path*: we unreliably send notifications to online clients during Matcher propagation. While channels are unreliable, message drops are rare, so this fast path typically succeeds. We confirm this in our evaluation (§6).

Realizing that a lengthy periodic scan adversely impacts the tail of the notification latency distribution, we are currently implementing a scheme that buffers undelivered notifications in Registrar memory to more quickly respond to failures.

4.2.4 Client Garbage Collection

If a client remains offline for an extended period (e.g., several days), Thialfi garbage-collects its Bigtable state. This involves deleting the client's row in the Registrar Bigtable and deleting any registration cells in the Matcher Bigtable. If the client later comes back online, our use of blind writes means that the client's row may be inadvertently recreated. Although rare, some mechanism is required to detect such an entry, remove it, and notify the client that it must restart with a fresh client ID.

In order to detect client resurrection after garbage collection, Thialfi maintains a *created* cell in the client's Registrar row (Table 2). The Registrar writes this cell when it assigns an ID for a client, and the garbage collector deletes it; no other operations modify this cell. If a garbage collected client comes back online as described above, its *created* cell will be absent from the recreated row. An asynchronous process periodically scans the Registrar Table for rows without created cells. When encountered, the 'zombie' client row is deleted. Also, if the client is online, it is informed that its ID is invalid. Upon receiving this message, the client discards its ID and reconnects as a new client. This message may be lost without compromising correctness; it will be resent by the asynchronous process if the client attempts further operations.

4.2.5 Recovery from Server Failures

We now describe how persistent storage reduces the burden of failure recovery. The server caches of Bigtable state and of pending operations are write-through caches, so they may be restored after a restart by simply scanning the Bigtable. Since each server is assigned a contiguous range, this scan is efficient. Additionally, scanning to recover pending operations yields a straightforward strategy for shedding load during periods of memory pressure: a server aborts in-progress propagations, evicts items from its pending operation set, and schedules a future scan to recover.

If required, all Bigtable state can be dropped, with recovery proceeding as in the in-memory design. In practice, this has simplified service administration significantly; e.g., when performing a Bigtable schema change, we simply drop all data, avoiding the complexity of migration.

4.2.6 Tolerating Storage Unavailability

A consequence of storing state in Bigtable is that Thialfi's overall availability is limited by that of Bigtable. While complete unavailability is extremely rare, a practical reality of large-scale storage is *partial unavailability*—the temporary failure of I/O operations for some rows, but not all. In our experience, minor Bigtable unavailability occurs several times per day. Our asynchronous approach to data propagation accommodates storage unavailability. I/O failures are skipped and retried, but do not prevent partial progress; e.g., clients corresponding to available regions will continue to receive notifications.

This covers the majority of Thialfi I/O with two exceptions: 1) the initial write when accepting a client operation, e.g., a registration, and 2) the write accepting a new version of an object at the Matcher. In the first case, the client simply retries the operation.

However, accepting new versions is more complex. One possibility is to have the Bridge delay the acknowledgment of a notification to the publish/subscribe service until the Matcher is able to perform the write. This approach quickly results in a backlog being generated for all notifications destined for the unavailable Matcher rows. Once a large backlog accumulates, the pub/sub service no longer delivers new messages, delaying notifications for *all* clients in the data center. Even in the absence of our particular pub/sub system, requiring application backends to buffer updates due to partial Thialfi storage unavailability would significantly increase their operational complexity.

Given the prevalence of such partial storage unavailability in practice, we have implemented a simple mechanism to prevent a backlog from being generated. To acknowledge a notification, the Bridge needs to record the latest version number *somewhere* in stable storage. It need not be written to the correct location immediately, so long as it is *eventually* propagated there. To provide robustness during these periods, we reissue failed writes to a distinct, scratch Bigtable. A scanner later retries the writes against the Matcher Bigtable. The Everest system [19] uses a similar technique to spread load; in Thialfi, such buffering serves to reduce cascading failures.

Specifically, for a given object, we deterministically compute a sequence of retry locations in a scratch Bigtable. These are generated by computing a salted hash over the object ID, using the retry count as the salt. This computation exploits Thialfi's relaxed semantics to reduce the amount of scratch storage required; successive version updates to the same object overwrite each other in the scratch table when the first scratch write succeeds. Storing failed updates in random locations—a simple alternative—would retain and propagate *all* updates instead of only the latest. While correct, this is inefficient, particularly for hot objects. Our scheme efficiently supports the common case: a series of Matcher writes fails, but the first attempt of each corresponding scratch write succeeds.

4.3 Supporting Multiple Data Centers

To meet availability requirements at Google, Thialfi must be replicated in multiple data centers. In this section, we describe the extensions required to support replication, completing the description of Thialfi's design. Our goal is to ensure that a site failure does not degrade reliability; i.e., notifications may be delayed, but not dropped. Clients migrate when a failure or load balancing event causes protocol messages to be routed from the Thialfi data center identified in the client's session token to a Thialfi instance in another data center.

We require that the application's channel provide client affinity; i.e., Thialfi messages from a given client should be routed to the same data center over short time scales (minutes). Over longer time scales, clients may migrate among data centers depending on application policies and service availability. Also, when a Thialfi data center fails, we require the application channel to re-route messages from clients to other data centers. These characteristics are typical for commonly used channels.

Even without replication of registration state, Thialfi can automatically migrate clients among data centers. When a client connects to a new data center, the Registrar instructs it to repeat the token-assignment handshake, by which it obtains a new token (§4.1.2). Since the new data center has no information about the client's registrations, the client and server registration digests will not match, triggering the Registration Sync Protocol. The client then reissues all of its registrations. While correct, this is expensive; a data center failure causes a flood of re-registrations. Thus, replication is designed as an optimization to decrease such migration load.

4.3.1 State Replication

Thialfi uses two forms of state replication: 1) reliable replication of notifications to all data centers and 2) best-effort replication of registration state. The pub/sub service acknowledges the Publisher library after a reliable handoff and ensures that each notification is reliably delivered to all Thialfi data centers; the Thialfi Matchers in each data center acknowledge the notification only after it has been written to stable storage.

When replicating registration state, we use a custom, asynchronous protocol that replicates only the state we must reconstruct during migration. Specifically, we replicate three Registrar operations between Thialfi data centers: 1) client ID assignment, 2) registrations, and 3) notification acknowledgements. Whenever a Registrar processes one of these operations, it sends best-effort RPC messages to the Registrars in other data centers. At each data center, *replication agents* in the Registrar consume these messages and replay the operations. (While we have implemented and evaluated this scheme, we have not yet deployed it in production.)

We initially attempted to avoid designing our own replication scheme. A previous design of Thialfi used a synchronous, globally consistent storage layer called Megastore [2]. Megastore provides transactional storage with consistency guarantees spanning data centers. Building on such a system is appealingly straightforward: simply commit a transaction that updates relevant rows in all data centers before acknowledging an operation. Unfortunately, microbenchmarks show that Megastore requires roughly 10 times more operations per write to its underlying Bigtables than a customized approach. For a write-intensive service like Thialfi, this overhead is prohibitive.

Although the Thialfi replication protocol is designed to make migration efficient, an outage still causes a spike in load. During a planned outage, we use an *anti-storm* technique to spread load. During a migration storm, Thialfi silently drops messages from a progressively-decreasing fraction of migrated clients at the surviving data centers, trading short-term unavailability for reduced load.

5. ACHIEVING RELIABLE DELIVERY

In this section, we describe Thialfi's notion of reliability and argue that our mechanisms provide it. We define reliable delivery as follows:

> **Reliable delivery property:** If a well-behaved client registers for an object X, Thialfi ensures that the client will always eventually learn of the latest version of X.

A well-behaved client is one that faithfully implements Thialfi's API and remains connected long enough to complete required operations, e.g., registration synchronization. In our discussion, we make further assumptions regarding integrity and liveness of dependent systems. First, we assume that despite transitory unavailability, Bigtable tablets will eventually be accessible and will not corrupt stored data. Second, we assume that the communication channel will not corrupt messages and will eventually deliver them given sufficient retransmissions.

As is typical for many distributed systems, Thialfi's reliability goal is *one-sided*. By this we mean that, while clients will learn the latest version of registered objects, notifications may be duplicated or reordered, and intermediate versions may be suppressed.

Thialfi achieves end-to-end reliability by ensuring that state changes in one component eventually propagate to all other relevant components of the system. We enumerate these components and their interactions below and discuss why state transfer between them eventually succeeds. We have not developed a formal model of Thialfi nor complete proofs of its safely or liveness; these are left as future work.

Registration state is determined by the client, from which it propagates to the Registrar and Matcher (subject to access control policies). The following mechanisms ensure the eventual synchronization of registration state across the three components:

- **Client ↔ Registrar:** Every message from the client includes a digest that summarizes all client registration state (§4.1.3). If the client-provided digest disagrees with the state at the Registrar, the synchronization protocol runs, after which client and server agree. Periodic heartbeat messages include the registration digest, ensuring that any disagreement will be detected.

- **Registrar → Matcher:** When the Registrar commits a registration state change to Bigtable, a pending work marker is also set atomically. This marker is cleared only after all dependent writes to the Matcher Bigtable have completed successfully. All writes are retried by the Registrar Propagator if any failure occurs. (Because all writes are idempotent, this repetition is safe.)

Notification state comes from the Publisher, which provides a reliable feed of object-version pairs via the pub/sub service. These flow reliably through the Bridge, Matcher, and Registrar to the client using the following mechanisms:

- **Bridge → Matcher:** Notifications are removed from the update feed by the Bridge only after they have been successfully written to either their appropriate location in the Matcher Bigtable or buffered in the Matcher scratch Bigtable. A periodic task in the Bridge reads the scratch table and resends the notifications to the Matcher, removing entries from the scratch table only after a successful Matcher write.

- **Matcher → Registrar:** When a notification is written to the Matcher Bigtable, a pending work marker is used to ensure eventual propagation. This mechanism is similar to that used for Registrar → Matcher propagation of registration state.

  Notification state also flows from the Matcher to the Registrar in response to registration state changes. After a client registers for an object, Registrar post-propagation will write a notification at the latest version into the client's Registrar row (§4.1.3). This ensures that the client learns of the latest version even if the notification originally arrived before the client's registration.

- **Registrar → Client:** The Registrar retains a notification for a client until either the client acknowledges it or a subsequent notification supersedes it. The Registrar periodically retransmits any outstanding notifications while the client is online, ensuring eventual delivery.

Taken together, local state propagation among components provides end-to-end reliability. Specifically:

- A client's registration eventually propagates to the Matcher, ensuring that the latest notification received for the registered object after the propagation will be sent to the client.
- Registrar post-propagation ensures that a client learns the version of the object known to Thialfi when its registration reached the Matcher. If no version was present at the Matcher, the client receives a notification at *unknown version*.

The preceding discussion refers to system operation within a single data center. In the case of multiple data centers, our Publisher Library considers notification publication complete only after the notification has been accepted by the Matcher or buffered in the persistent storage of Google's infrastructure publish/subscribe service in all data centers. Thus, each application's notifications are reliably replicated to all data centers. This is in contrast to Thialfi's registration state, which is replicated on a best-effort basis. However, so long as a client is not interacting with a given data center, there is no harm in the registration state being out-of-sync there. When the client migrates to a new data center, the Registration Sync Protocol (§4.1.3) ensures that the new Registrar obtains the client's current registration state. The propagation and post-propagation mechanisms described above also apply in the new data center, ensuring that the new Registrar will reliably inform the client of the latest version of each registered object. Taken together, these mechanisms provide reliable delivery when operating with multiple data centers.

6. EVALUATION

Thialfi is a production service that has been in active use at Google since the summer of 2010. We report performance from this deployment. Additionally, we evaluate Thialfi's scalability and fault tolerance for synthetic workloads at the scale of millions of users and thousands of updates per second. Specifically, we show:

- *Ease of adoption:* Applications can adopt Thialfi with minimal design and/or code changes. We describe a representative case study, the Chrome browser, for which a custom notification service was replaced with Thialfi. (§6.1)
- *Scalability:* In production use, Thialfi has scaled to millions of users. Load testing shows that resource consumption scales linearly with active users and notification rate while maintaining stable notification latencies. (§6.2)
- *Performance:* Measurements of our production deployment show that Thialfi delivers 88% of notifications in less than one second. (§6.3)
- *Fault-tolerance:* Thialfi is robust to the failure of an entire data center. In a synthetic fail-over experiment, we rapidly migrate over 100,000 clients successfully and quantify the over-provisioning required at remaining instances in order to absorb clients during fail-over. We also provide measurements of transient unavailability in production that demonstrate the practical necessity of coping with numerous short-term faults. (§6.4)

6.1 Chrome Sync Deployment

Chrome supports synchronizing client bookmarks, settings, extensions, and so on among all of a user's installations. Initially, this feature was implemented by piggy-backing on a previously-deployed chat service. Each online client registered its presence with the chat service and would broadcast a chat metadata message notifying online replicas that a change had committed to the back-end storage

infrastructure. Offline clients synchronized data on startup. While appealingly simple, this approach has three drawbacks:

- *Costly startup synchronization:* The combined load of synchronizing clients on startup is significant at large scale. Ideally, synchronization of offline clients would occur only after a change in application data, but no general-purpose signaling mechanism was available.
- *Unreliable chat delivery:* Although generally reliable, chat message delivery is best-effort. Even when a client is online, delivery is not guaranteed, and delivery failures may be silent. In some cases, this resulted in a delay in synchronization until the next browser restart.
- *Lack of fate-sharing between updates and notifications:* Since clients issue both updates and change notifications, the update may succeed while the notification fails, leading to stale replicas. Ensuring eventual broadcast of the notification with timeout and retry at the client is challenging; e.g., a user may simply quit the program before it completes.

While these issues might have been addressed with specific fixes, the complexity of maintaining a reliable push-based architecture is substantial. Instead, Chrome adopted a hybrid approach: best-effort push with periodic polling for reliability. Unfortunately, the back-end load arising from frequent polling was substantial. To control resource consumption, clients polled only once every few hours. This again gave rise to lengthy, puzzling delays for a small minority of users and increased complexity from maintaining separate code paths for polling and push updates.

These issues drove Chrome's adoption of Thialfi, which addresses the obstacles above. Thialfi clients are persistent; offline clients receive notifications on startup only if a registered object has changed or the client has been garbage collected. This eliminates the need for synchronization during every startup. Thialfi provides end-to-end reliability over the best-effort communication channel used by Chrome, thereby easing the porting process. Finally, Thialfi servers receive notifications directly from Chrome's storage service rather than from clients, ensuring that notification delivery is fate-shared with updates to persistent storage.

Migrating from custom notifications to Thialfi required modest code additions and replaced both the previous push and polling notification support. Chrome includes Thialfi's C++ client library, implements our API (Figure 2), and routes Thialfi notifications to appropriate Chrome components. In full, Chrome's Thialfi-specific code is 1,753 lines of commented C++ code (535 semicolons).

6.2 Scalability

We evaluate Thialfi's scalability in terms of resource consumption and performance. We show that resource consumption increases proportionally with increases in load. With respect to performance, we show that notification latencies are stable as load increases, provided sufficient resources. These measurements confirm our practical experience. To support increasing usage of Thialfi, we need only allocate an incremental amount of additional infrastructure resources. The two main contributors to Thialfi's load are 1) the number of active users and 2) the rate at which notifications are published. We consider each in turn, measuring synthetic workloads on shared Google clusters. While our experiments are not performance-isolated, the results presented are consistent over multiple trials.

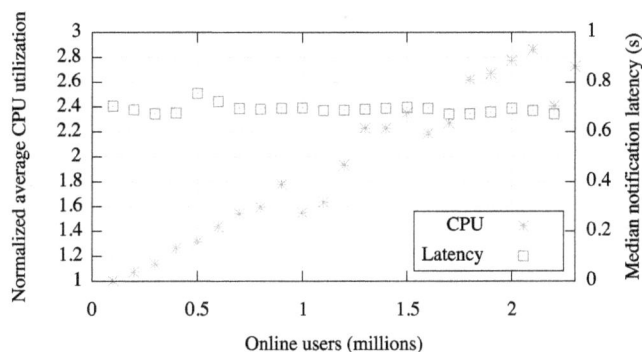

Figure 6: Resource consumption and notification latency as active users increase.

Increasing active users: Increasing the number of active users exercises registration, heartbeat processing, and client / session assignment. To measure this, we recorded the resource consumption of Thialfi in a single data center while adding 2.3 million synthetic users. Each user had one client (the number of clients per user does not impact performance in Thialfi). Clients arrived at a constant rate of 570 per second. Each registered for five distinct objects and issued a random notification every 8 minutes and a heartbeat message every 20 minutes. The version of each notification was set to the current time, allowing registered clients to measure the end-to-end latency upon receipt.

Figure 6 shows the results. As a proxy for overall resource consumption, we show the increasing CPU consumption as users arrive. Demand for other resources (network traffic, RPCs, memory) grows similarly. The CPU data is normalized by the amount required to support a baseline of 100,000 users. Overall, increasing active users 23-fold (from 100,000 to 2.3 million) requires ~3× the resources. Throughout this increase, median notification delays are stable, ranging between 0.6–0.7 seconds. (Because these synthetic clients are local to the data center, delays do not include wide-area messaging latency.)

Increasing notification rate: Increasing the notification rate stresses Matcher to Registrar propagation. In this case, we measure resource consumption while varying the notification rate for a fixed set of 1.4 million synthetic clients that have completed registrations and session assignment; all clients were online simultaneously for the duration of the experiment. As in the previous measurements, each client registered for five objects and each user had one client.

Figure 7 shows the results of scaling the notification rate. We report CPU consumption normalized by the amount required to support a baseline notification rate of 1,000 per second and increase the rate by 1,000 up to 13,000. As before, median notification delays remain stable with proportional resource consumption.

6.3 Performance

The previous measurements quantify median performance for synthetic workloads. We next examine the distribution of notification latencies observed in our production deployment. Each Thialfi component tracks internal propagation delays by appending a log of timestamps to each notification as it flows through the system.

Figure 8 shows a CDF of 2,514 notifications sampled over a 50-minute period from an active Thialfi cell. 88% of notifications are dispatched in less than one second. However, as is typical in asyn-

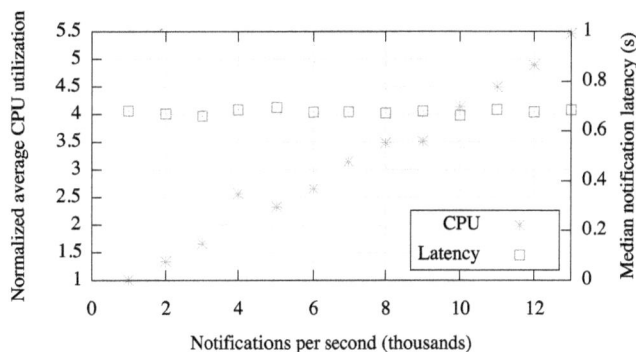

Figure 7: Resource consumption and notification latency as the notification rate increases.

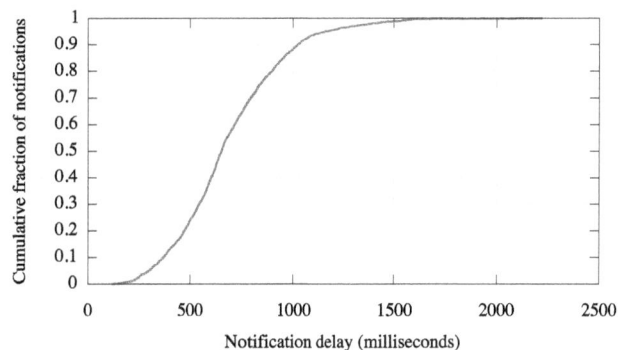

Figure 8: Cumulative distribution of notification latencies randomly sampled from our live deployment.

chronous distributed systems operating on shared infrastructure, a minority of messages may be delayed for much longer, exceeding two seconds in our measurements.

We point out that these delays do not include delivery and acknowledgements from clients themselves; we measure only the delay within Thialfi from the receipt of a notification to the first attempt to send it to an online client. End-to-end delays vary significantly due to the variable quality of channels and the lengthy delays incurred by offline clients. In practice, network propagation adds between 30–100 ms to overall notification latency.

In practice, the majority of Thialfi's delay is self-imposed. Our current implementation aggressively batches Bigtable operations and RPC dispatch to increase efficiency. This is illustrated in Figure 9, which shows the delay for each stage of notification delivery averaged over a 10-minute interval. This data is drawn from our production deployment. The Publisher library appends an initial timestamp when the notification is generated by the application, and its propagation delay to Thialfi's bridge is fundamental. Once received, the RPC sending a notification from the bridge to the Matcher is batched with a maximum delay of 500 ms. Matcher Bigtable writes are similarly batched. During propagation, the Matcher reads the active client list—this data is typically retrieved directly from Bigtable's in-memory cache. Finally, the propagation RPC to the Registrar has a batch delay of 200 ms.

The majority of our current applications use Thialfi as a replacement for lengthy polling, and the sub-second delays associated with batching are acceptable. But, as Figure 9 shows, we can further

139

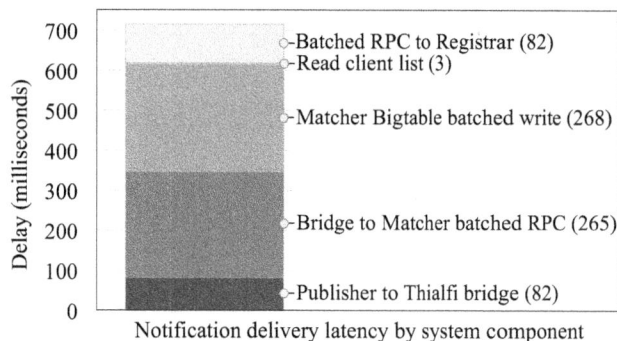

Figure 9: The average contribution to overall notification delay of each Thialfi system component.

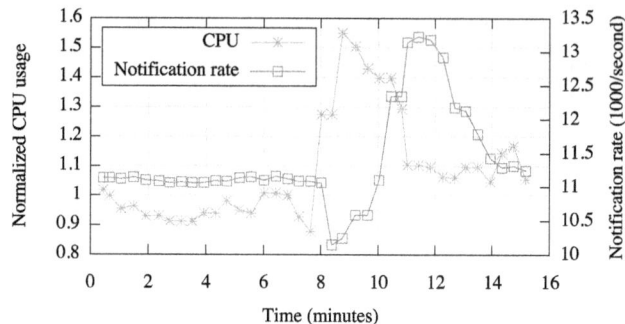

Figure 10: CPU usage and notification rate during the sudden failure of a Thialfi data center.

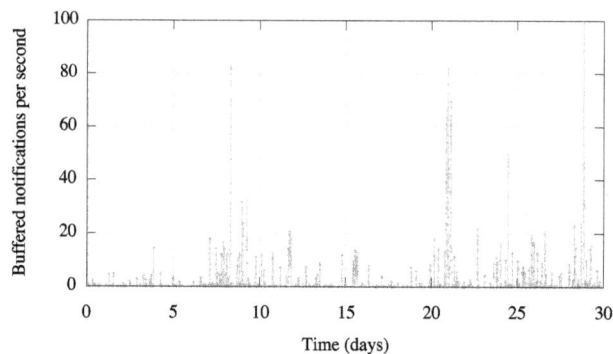

Figure 11: A month-long trace of notification buffering during Matcher unavailability or Matcher storage unavailability.

reduce Thialfi's delay by simply reducing the batching delay of relevant components. This increases resource demands but does not introduce any fundamental scalability bottlenecks.

6.4 Fault Tolerance

We evaluate fault tolerance in two ways. First, we examine failover of clients between data centers. This exercises our synchronization protocol and quantifies the over-provisioning required to cope with data center failure in practice. Second, we present a month-long trace of how often Thialfi buffers incoming notifications to cope with small periods of partial Matcher unavailability. This shows the practical necessity for our techniques.

Data center fail-over: The failure of a data center requires that clients be migrated to a new instance and their state synchronized with new servers. Migration can be expensive at the server; it requires reading the set of registered objects, computing the digest, sending pending notifications, and processing registration requests (if any). Applications with few updates and/or lengthy heartbeat intervals naturally spread migration load over a lengthy interval. Here, we consider a more challenging case: rapidly migrating tens of thousands of clients with very frequent heartbeats to ensure rapid fail-over.

We instantiated 380,000 clients spread uniformly across three distinct Thialfi data centers with a heartbeat interval of 30 seconds. Each client registered for five objects and generated random notifications yielding an incoming notification rate of roughly 11,000/sec across all clients. After allowing the system to stabilize, we halted the Thialfi instance of one data center while measuring the CPU consumption of the remaining two as well as the overall client notification rate. The failed data center was not restored for the duration of the experiment. Note that this experiment was performed using a prior version of the Registration Sync Protocol; rather than including the registration digest in each message, clients request the full registration list during migration. This modification has not significantly changed resource consumption in practice.

Figure 10 shows the results. We normalize CPU usage by the first observation taken in steady state. After several minutes, we fail one data center, which clients detect after three failed heartbeats. This is reflected by increased CPU consumption at the remaining instances and a sudden drop in notification receive rate corresponding to clients in the failed data center. As clients migrate, accumulated notifications are discharged as clients are brought up-to-date. Shortly after, the system stabilizes. To migrate 33% of clients over

several minutes, Thialfi requires over-provisioning by a factor of ~1.6.

Matcher unavailability: Thialfi's provisions for fault tolerance arise from practical experience. For example, our implementation buffers notifications to a temporary Bigtable to cope with transient unavailability (§4.2.6). This mechanism was added after our initial deployment in response to frequent manual intervention to respond to failures. Figure 11 shows a month-long trace of notification buffering, confirming the need for error handling in practice. After deploying this solution, the number of alerts that occurred due to a backlog disappeared completely. We point out that buffering occurs not only during storage unavailability but *any* unavailability of the Matcher, e.g., during software upgrades or restarts. Support for automatically buffering notifications without manual action during these periods has greatly simplified service administration.

7. RELATED WORK

The problem of scalable event notification has received significant attention in the distributed systems community, which we draw on in our design. Thialfi differs from existing work in two principal ways. The first is the constraints of our environment. Thialfi's design stems from the unique requirements of Internet applications, infrastructure services, and the failures they exhibit. The second difference is our goal. Our API and semantics provide developers with reliability that simplifies development, but Thialfi does not impose significant restrictions on an application's runtime environment or software stack.

Thialfi builds on existing infrastructure services widely used at Google. We use Bigtable [7] to store object and client data. The Chubby lock service [4] provides reliable, consistent naming and configuration of our server processes. While specific to Google, the functionality of these systems is being increasingly replicated by open source alternatives for which Thialfi's design could be adapted. For example, HBase [12] provides Bigtable-like structured storage atop the HDFS block store [13], and Zookeeper [15] provides a highly reliable group coordination service.

Thialfi's provisions for fault-tolerance draw on emerging practical experience with infrastructure services [3, 9, 11, 21]. Our experience with performance variability and communications failures is consistent with these observations. But, unlike many existing infrastructure services, Thialfi is explicitly designed to cope with the failure of entire data centers. Megastore [2] shares this goal, using synchronous replication with Paxos [16] to provide consistent structured data storage. While early designs of Thialfi were built atop Megastore to inherit its robustness to data center failure, we eventually adopted replication and fault-tolerance techniques specific to a notification service; these increase efficiency substantially.

Our goal of providing a scalable notification service is shared by a number of P2P notification and publish / subscribe systems, e.g., Bayeux [29], Scribe [23], and Siena [6]. These systems construct multicast trees on overlay routing substrates in order to efficiently disseminate messages. While Thialfi addresses a similar problem, differences between P2P and infrastructure environments necessitate radical differences in our design. For example, P2P message delivery requires direct browser-to-browser communication that is precluded by fundamental security policies [24]. Also, message delivery is best-effort, departing from our goal of maintaining reliable delivery of notifications. Significant additional work exists on publish / subscribe systems (e.g. [1, 20, 25, 26]), but these systems provide richer semantics and target lower scale.

For web applications, Thialfi addresses a longstanding limitation of HTTP—the need for polling to refresh data. Others have observed these problems; e.g., Cao and Liu [5] advocate the use of invalidations as an alternative to polling to maintain the freshness of web documents, but their proposed protocol extensions were not taken up. Yin et al. [28] study the efficiency of HTTP polling and propose an invalidation protocol that is conceptually similar to Thialfi, although it operates on a single HTTP server only. We reexamine these problems at much larger scale. Cowling et al. [8] mention the applicability of Census, a Byzantine-fault-tolerant group membership system, to the problem of large-scale cache invalidation, but they leave the design to future work.

More recently, practitioners have developed a number of techniques to work around the request / reply limitations of HTTP [17]. Many approaches rely on a common technique: each client maintains an in-flight request to the server, which replies to this outstanding request only when new data is available. More recently, web sockets [14] have been proposed as a standard enabling full-duplex HTTP messaging. Thialfi supports these channels transparently, separating the implementation details of achieving push messages from the semantics of the notification service.

8. LESSONS LEARNED

In the process of designing, implementing, and supporting Thialfi we learned several lessons about our design.

For many applications, the signal is enough. Our choice to provide applications with only a notification signal was contentious. In particular, developers have almost universally asked for richer features than Thialfi provides: e.g., support for data delivery, message ordering, and duplicate suppression. Absent these more compelling features, some developers are hesitant to adopt Thialfi. We have avoided these features, however, as they would significantly complicate both our implementation and API. Moreover, we have encountered few applications with a fundamental need for them. For example, applications that would prefer to receive data directly from Thialfi typically store the data in their servers and retrieve it after receiving a notification. While developers often express consternation over the additional latency induced by the retrieval, for many applications this does not adversely affect the user experience. In our view, reliable signaling strikes a balance between complexity and system utility.

Client library rather than client protocol. Perhaps more than any other component in the system, Thialfi's client library has undergone significant evolution since our initial design. Initially, we had no client library whatsoever, opting instead to expose our protocol directly. Engineers, however, strongly prefer to develop against native-language APIs. And, a high-level API has allowed us to evolve our client-server protocol without modifying application code.

Initially, the client library provided only a thin shim around RPCs, e.g., register, unregister, acknowledge. This API proved essentially unusable. While seemingly simple, this initial design exposed too many failure cases to application programmers, e.g., server crashes and data center migration. This experience lead us to our goal of unifying error handling with normal operations in Thialfi's API.

Complexity at the server, not the client. The presence of a client library creates a temptation to improve server scalability by offloading functionality. Our second client library took exactly this approach. For example, it detected data center switchover and drove the recovery protocol, substantially simplifying the server implementation. In many systems, this design would be preferable: server scalability is typically the bottleneck, and client resources are plentiful. But, a sophisticated client library is difficult to maintain. Thialfi's client library is implemented in multiple languages, and clients may not upgrade their software for years, if ever. In contrast, bug and performance fixes to data center code can be deployed in hours. Given these realities, we trade server resources for client simplicity in our current (third) client library.

Asynchronous events, not callbacks. Developers are accustomed to taking actions that produce results, and our initial client libraries tried to satisfy this expectation. For example, the register call took a registration callback for success or failure. Experience showed callbacks are not sufficient; e.g., a client may become spontaneously unregistered during migration. Given the need to respond to asynchronous events, callbacks are unnecessary and often misleading. Clients only need to know current state, not the sequence of operations leading to it.

Initial workloads have few objects per client. A key feature of Thialfi is its support for tens of thousands of objects per client. At present, however, no client application has more than tens of objects per client. We suspect this is because existing client applications were initially designed around polling solutions that work best with few objects per client. Emerging applications make use of fine-grained objects, and we anticipate workloads with high fanout and many objects per client.

9. SUMMARY

We have presented Thialfi, an infrastructure service that provides web, desktop, and mobile client applications with timely (sub-second) notifications of updates to shared state. To make Thialfi generally applicable, we provide a simple object model and client API that permit developers flexibility in communication, storage, and runtime environments. Internally, Thialfi uses a combination of server-side soft state, asynchronous replication, and client-driven recovery to tolerate a wide range of failures common to infrastructure services, including the failure of entire data centers. The Thialfi API is structured so that these failures are handled by the same application code paths used for normal operation. Thialfi is in production use by millions of people daily, and our measurements confirm its scalability, performance, and robustness.

Acknowledgements

We would like to thank the anonymous reviewers and our shepherd, Robert Morris, for their valuable feedback. We are also grateful to many colleagues at Google. John Pongsajapan and John Reumann offered valuable wisdom during design discussions, Shao Liu and Kyle Marvin worked on the implementation, and Fred Akalin and Rhett Robinson helped with application integration. Brian Bershad and Dan Grove have provided support and resources over the life of the project, and Steve Lacey provided encouragement and connections with application developers. Finally, we thank James Cowling, Xiaolan Zhang, and Elisavet Kozyri for helpful comments on the paper.

10. REFERENCES

[1] Y. Amir and J. Stanton. The Spread Wide Area Group Communication System. Technical Report CNDS 98-4, 1998.

[2] J. Baker, C. Bond, J. C. Corbett, J. Furman, A. Khorlin, J. Larson, J.-M. Léon, Y. Li, A. Lloyd, and V. Yushprak. Megastore: Providing scalable, highly available storage for interactive service. In *Proc. of CIDR*, 2011.

[3] T. Benson, A. Akella, and D. A. Maltz. Network traffic characteristics of data centers in the wild. In *Proc. of IMC*, 2010.

[4] M. Burrows. The Chubby lock service for loosely-coupled distributed systems. In *Proc. of OSDI*, 2006.

[5] P. Cao and C. Liu. Maintaining strong cache consistency in the world wide web. *IEEE Trans. Comput.*, 47:445–457, April 1998.

[6] A. Carzaniga, D. S. Rosenblum, and A. L. Wolf. Design and evaluation of a wide-area event notification service. *ACM Trans. Comput. Syst.*, 19:332–383, August 2001.

[7] F. Chang, J. Dean, S. Ghemawat, W. C. Hsieh, D. A. Wallach, M. Burrows, T. Chandra, A. Fikes, and R. E. Gruber. Bigtable: A distributed storage system for structured data. In *Proc. of OSDI*, 2006.

[8] J. Cowling, D. R. K. Ports, B. Liskov, R. A. Popa, and A. Gaikwad. Census: Location-aware membership management for large-scale distributed systems. In *Proc. of USENIX*, 2009.

[9] J. Dean. Designs, lessons and advice from building large distributed systems. In *LADIS Keynote*, 2009.

[10] D. E. Eastlake and P. E. Jones. US secure hash algorithm 1 (SHA1). Internet RFC 3174, 2001.

[11] D. Ford, F. Labelle, F. I. Popovici, M. Stokely, V.-A. Truong, L. Barroso, C. Grimes, and S. Quinlan. Availability in globally distributed storage systems. In *Proc. of OSDI*, 2010.

[12] HBase. http://hbase.apache.org/.

[13] Hadoop Distributed File System. http://hadoop.apache.org/hdfs/.

[14] I. Hickson. The WebSocket API. http://dev.w3.org/html5/websockets/.

[15] P. Hunt, M. Konar, F. P. Junqueira, and B. Reed. Zookeeper: Wait-free coordination for Internet-scale systems. In *Proc. of USENIX*, 2010.

[16] L. Lamport. The part-time parliament. *ACM Trans. Comput. Syst.*, 16:133–169, May 1998.

[17] P. McCarthy and D. Crane. *Comet and Reverse Ajax: The Next-Generation Ajax 2.0*. Apress, 2008.

[18] R. Merkle. *Secrecy, authentication and public key systems*. PhD thesis, Dept. of Electrical Engineering, Stanford University, 1979.

[19] D. Narayanan, A. Donnelly, E. Thereska, S. Elnikety, and A. Rowstron. Everest: Scaling down peak loads through i/o off-loading. In *Proc. of OSDI*, 2008.

[20] P. R. Pietzuch and J. Bacon. Hermes: A distributed event-based middleware architecture. In *Proc. ICDCS*, ICDCSW '02, pages 611–618, Washington, DC, USA, 2002. IEEE Computer Society.

[21] E. Pinheiro, W.-D. Weber, and L. A. Barroso. Failure trends in a large disk drive population. In *Proc. of FAST*, 2007.

[22] D. R. K. Ports, A. T. Clements, I. Zhang, S. Madden, and B. Liskov. Transactional consistency and automatic management in an application data cache. In *Proc. of OSDI*, 2010.

[23] A. I. T. Rowstron, A.-M. Kermarrec, M. Castro, and P. Druschel. SCRIBE: The design of a large-scale event notification infrastructure. In *Networked Group Communication*, pages 30–43, 2001.

[24] J. Ruderman. Same origin policy for JavaScript. https://developer.mozilla.org/En/Same_origin_policy_for_JavaScript.

[25] R. Strom, G. Banavar, T. Chandra, M. Kaplan, K. Miller, B. Mukherjee, D. Sturman, and M. Ward. Gryphon: An information flow based approach to message brokering. In *Proc. Intl. Symposium on Software Reliability Engineering*, 1998.

[26] R. van Renesse, K. P. Birman, and S. Maffeis. Horus: a flexible group communication system. *Commun. ACM*, 39:76–83, April 1996.

[27] Extensible Messaging and Presence Protocol. http://xmpp.org/xmpp-protocols.

[28] J. Yin, L. Alvisi, M. Dahlin, and A. Iyengar. Engineering server-driven consistency for large scale dynamic web services. In *Proc. of WWW*, 2001.

[29] S. Q. Zhuang, B. Y. Zhao, A. D. Joseph, R. H. Katz, and J. D. Kubiatowicz. Bayeux: An architecture for scalable and fault-tolerant wide-area data dissemination. In *Proc. of NOSSDAV*, 2001.

Windows Azure Storage: A Highly Available Cloud Storage Service with Strong Consistency

Brad Calder, Ju Wang, Aaron Ogus, Niranjan Nilakantan, Arild Skjolsvold, Sam McKelvie, Yikang Xu,
Shashwat Srivastav, Jiesheng Wu, Huseyin Simitci, Jaidev Haridas, Chakravarthy Uddaraju,
Hemal Khatri, Andrew Edwards, Vaman Bedekar, Shane Mainali, Rafay Abbasi, Arpit Agarwal,
Mian Fahim ul Haq, Muhammad Ikram ul Haq, Deepali Bhardwaj, Sowmya Dayanand,
Anitha Adusumilli, Marvin McNett, Sriram Sankaran, Kavitha Manivannan, Leonidas Rigas

Microsoft

Abstract

Windows Azure Storage (WAS) is a cloud storage system that provides customers the ability to store seemingly limitless amounts of data for any duration of time. WAS customers have access to their data from anywhere at any time and only pay for what they use and store. In WAS, data is stored durably using both local and geographic replication to facilitate disaster recovery. Currently, WAS storage comes in the form of Blobs (files), Tables (structured storage), and Queues (message delivery). In this paper, we describe the WAS architecture, global namespace, and data model, as well as its resource provisioning, load balancing, and replication systems.

Categories and Subject Descriptors

D.4.2 [**Operating Systems**]: Storage Management—*Secondary storage*; D.4.3 [**Operating Systems**]: File Systems Management—*Distributed file systems*; D.4.5 [**Operating Systems**]: Reliability—*Fault tolerance*; D.4.7 [**Operating Systems**]: Organization and Design—*Distributed systems*; D.4.8 [**Operating Systems**]: Performance—*Measurements*

General Terms

Algorithms, Design, Management, Measurement, Performance, Reliability.

Keywords

Cloud storage, distributed storage systems, Windows Azure.

1. Introduction

Windows Azure Storage (WAS) is a scalable cloud storage system that has been in production since November 2008. It is used inside Microsoft for applications such as social networking search, serving video, music and game content, managing medical records, and more. In addition, there are thousands of customers outside Microsoft using WAS, and anyone can sign up over the Internet to use the system.

WAS provides cloud storage in the form of Blobs (user files), Tables (structured storage), and Queues (message delivery). These three data abstractions provide the overall storage and

workflow for many applications. A common usage pattern we see is incoming and outgoing data being shipped via Blobs, Queues providing the overall workflow for processing the Blobs, and intermediate service state and final results being kept in Tables or Blobs.

An example of this pattern is an ingestion engine service built on Windows Azure to provide near real-time Facebook and Twitter search. This service is one part of a larger data processing pipeline that provides publically searchable content (via our search engine, Bing) within 15 seconds of a Facebook or Twitter user's posting or status update. Facebook and Twitter send the raw public content to WAS (e.g., user postings, user status updates, etc.) to be made publically searchable. This content is stored in WAS Blobs. The ingestion engine annotates this data with user auth, spam, and adult scores; content classification; and classification for language and named entities. In addition, the engine crawls and expands the links in the data. While processing, the ingestion engine accesses WAS Tables at high rates and stores the results back into Blobs. These Blobs are then folded into the Bing search engine to make the content publically searchable. The ingestion engine uses Queues to manage the flow of work, the indexing jobs, and the timing of folding the results into the search engine. As of this writing, the ingestion engine for Facebook and Twitter keeps around 350TB of data in WAS (before replication). In terms of transactions, the ingestion engine has a peak traffic load of around 40,000 transactions per second and does between two to three billion transactions per day (see Section 7 for discussion of additional workload profiles).

In the process of building WAS, feedback from potential internal and external customers drove many design decisions. Some key design features resulting from this feedback include:

Strong Consistency – Many customers want strong consistency: especially enterprise customers moving their line of business applications to the cloud. They also want the ability to perform conditional reads, writes, and deletes for optimistic concurrency control [12] on the strongly consistent data. For this, WAS provides three properties that the CAP theorem [2] claims are difficult to achieve at the same time: strong consistency, high availability, and partition tolerance (see Section 8).

Global and Scalable Namespace/Storage – For ease of use, WAS implements a global namespace that allows data to be stored and accessed in a consistent manner from any location in the world. Since a major goal of WAS is to enable storage of massive amounts of data, this global namespace must be able to address exabytes of data and beyond. We discuss our global namespace design in detail in Section 2.

Disaster Recovery – WAS stores customer data across multiple data centers hundreds of miles apart from each other. This redundancy provides essential data recovery protection against disasters such as earthquakes, wild fires, tornados, nuclear reactor meltdown, etc.

Multi-tenancy and Cost of Storage – To reduce storage cost, many customers are served from the same shared storage infrastructure. WAS combines the workloads of many different customers with varying resource needs together so that significantly less storage needs to be provisioned at any one point in time than if those services were run on their own dedicated hardware.

We describe these design features in more detail in the following sections. The remainder of this paper is organized as follows. Section 2 describes the global namespace used to access the WAS Blob, Table, and Queue data abstractions. Section 3 provides a high level overview of the WAS architecture and its three layers: Stream, Partition, and Front-End layers. Section 4 describes the stream layer, and Section 5 describes the partition layer. Section 6 shows the throughput experienced by Windows Azure applications accessing Blobs and Tables. Section 7 describes some internal Microsoft workloads using WAS. Section 8 discusses design choices and lessons learned. Section 9 presents related work, and Section 10 summarizes the paper.

2. Global Partitioned Namespace

A key goal of our storage system is to provide a single global namespace that allows clients to address all of their storage in the cloud and scale to arbitrary amounts of storage needed over time. To provide this capability we leverage DNS as part of the storage namespace and break the storage namespace into three parts: an account name, a partition name, and an object name. As a result, all data is accessible via a URI of the form:

http(s)://**AccountName**.<service>[1].core.windows.net/**PartitionName/ObjectName**

The **AccountName** is the customer selected account name for accessing storage and is part of the DNS host name. The AccountName DNS translation is used to locate the primary storage cluster and data center where the data is stored. This primary location is where all requests go to reach the data for that account. An application may use multiple AccountNames to store its data across different locations.

In conjunction with the AccountName, the **PartitionName** locates the data once a request reaches the storage cluster. The PartitionName is used to scale out access to the data across storage nodes based on traffic needs.

When a PartitionName holds many objects, the **ObjectName** identifies individual objects within that partition. The system supports atomic transactions across objects with the same PartitionName value. The ObjectName is optional since, for some types of data, the PartitionName uniquely identifies the object within the account.

This naming approach enables WAS to flexibly support its three data abstractions[2]. For Blobs, the full blob name is the PartitionName. For Tables, each entity (row) in the table has a

primary key that consists of two properties: the PartitionName and the ObjectName. This distinction allows applications using Tables to group rows into the same partition to perform atomic transactions across them. For Queues, the queue name is the PartitionName and each message has an ObjectName to uniquely identify it within the queue.

3. High Level Architecture

Here we present a high level discussion of the WAS architecture and how it fits into the Windows Azure Cloud Platform.

3.1 Windows Azure Cloud Platform

The Windows Azure Cloud platform runs many cloud services across different data centers and different geographic regions. The Windows Azure Fabric Controller is a resource provisioning and management layer that provides resource allocation, deployment/upgrade, and management for cloud services on the Windows Azure platform. WAS is one such service running on top of the Fabric Controller.

The Fabric Controller provides node management, network configuration, health monitoring, starting/stopping of service instances, and service deployment for the WAS system. In addition, WAS retrieves network topology information, physical layout of the clusters, and hardware configuration of the storage nodes from the Fabric Controller. WAS is responsible for managing the replication and data placement across the disks and load balancing the data and application traffic within the storage cluster.

3.2 WAS Architectural Components

An important feature of WAS is the ability to store and provide access to an immense amount of storage (exabytes and beyond). We currently have 70 petabytes of raw storage in production and are in the process of provisioning a few hundred more petabytes of raw storage based on customer demand for 2012.

The WAS production system consists of Storage Stamps and the Location Service (shown in Figure 1).

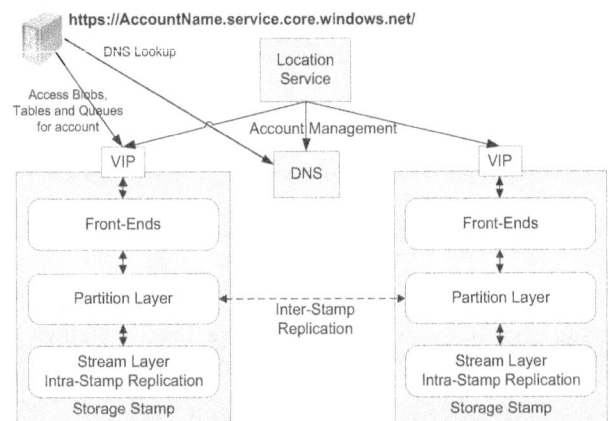

Figure 1: High-level architecture

Storage Stamps – A storage stamp is a cluster of N racks of storage nodes, where each rack is built out as a separate fault domain with redundant networking and power. Clusters typically range from 10 to 20 racks with 18 disk-heavy storage nodes per rack. Our first generation storage stamps hold approximately 2PB of raw storage each. Our next generation stamps hold up to 30PB of raw storage each.

---

[1] <service> specifies the service type, which can be **blob**, **table**, or **queue**.

[2] APIs for Windows Azure Blobs, Tables, and Queues can be found here: http://msdn.microsoft.com/en-us/library/dd179355.aspx

To provide low cost cloud storage, we need to keep the storage provisioned in production as highly utilized as possible. Our goal is to keep a storage stamp around 70% utilized in terms of capacity, transactions, and bandwidth. We try to avoid going above 80% because we want to keep 20% in reserve for (a) disk short stroking to gain better seek time and higher throughput by utilizing the outer tracks of the disks and (b) to continue providing storage capacity and availability in the presence of a rack failure within a stamp. When a storage stamp reaches 70% utilization, the location service migrates accounts to different stamps using inter-stamp replication (see Section 3.4).

Location Service (LS) – The location service manages all the storage stamps. It is also responsible for managing the account namespace across all stamps. The LS allocates accounts to storage stamps and manages them across the storage stamps for disaster recovery and load balancing. The location service itself is distributed across two geographic locations for its own disaster recovery.

WAS provides storage from multiple locations in each of the three geographic regions: North America, Europe, and Asia. Each location is a data center with one or more buildings in that location, and each location holds multiple storage stamps. To provision additional capacity, the LS has the ability to easily add new regions, new locations to a region, or new stamps to a location. Therefore, to increase the amount of storage, we deploy one or more storage stamps in the desired location's data center and add them to the LS. The LS can then allocate new storage accounts to those new stamps for customers as well as load balance (migrate) existing storage accounts from older stamps to the new stamps.

Figure 1 shows the location service with two storage stamps and the layers within the storage stamps. The LS tracks the resources used by each storage stamp in production across all locations. When an application requests a new account for storing data, it specifies the location affinity for the storage (e.g., US North). The LS then chooses a storage stamp within that location as the primary stamp for the account using heuristics based on the load information across all stamps (which considers the fullness of the stamps and other metrics such as network and transaction utilization). The LS then stores the account metadata information in the chosen storage stamp, which tells the stamp to start taking traffic for the assigned account. The LS then updates DNS to allow requests to now route from the name https://AccountName.service.core.windows.net/ to that storage stamp's virtual IP (VIP, an IP address the storage stamp exposes for external traffic).

3.3 Three Layers within a Storage Stamp

Also shown in Figure 1 are the three layers within a storage stamp. From bottom up these are:

Stream Layer – This layer stores the bits on disk and is in charge of distributing and replicating the data across many servers to keep data durable within a storage stamp. The stream layer can be thought of as a distributed file system layer within a stamp. It understands files, called "streams" (which are ordered lists of large storage chunks called "extents"), how to store them, how to replicate them, etc., but it does not understand higher level object constructs or their semantics. The data is stored in the stream layer, but it is accessible from the partition layer. In fact, partition servers (daemon processes in the partition layer) and stream servers are co-located on each storage node in a stamp.

Partition Layer – The partition layer is built for (a) managing and understanding higher level data abstractions (Blob, Table, Queue), (b) providing a scalable object namespace, (c) providing transaction ordering and strong consistency for objects, (d) storing object data on top of the stream layer, and (e) caching object data to reduce disk I/O.

Another responsibility of this layer is to achieve scalability by partitioning all of the data objects within a stamp. As described earlier, all objects have a PartitionName; they are broken down into disjoint ranges based on the PartitionName values and served by different partition servers. This layer manages which partition server is serving what PartitionName ranges for Blobs, Tables, and Queues. In addition, it provides automatic load balancing of PartitionNames across the partition servers to meet the traffic needs of the objects.

Front-End (FE) layer – The Front-End (FE) layer consists of a set of stateless servers that take incoming requests. Upon receiving a request, an FE looks up the AccountName, authenticates and authorizes the request, then routes the request to a partition server in the partition layer (based on the PartitionName). The system maintains a Partition Map that keeps track of the PartitionName ranges and which partition server is serving which PartitionNames. The FE servers cache the Partition Map and use it to determine which partition server to forward each request to. The FE servers also stream large objects directly from the stream layer and cache frequently accessed data for efficiency.

3.4 Two Replication Engines

Before describing the stream and partition layers in detail, we first give a brief overview of the two replication engines in our system and their separate responsibilities.

Intra-Stamp Replication (stream layer) – This system provides *synchronous replication* and is focused on making sure all the data written into a stamp is kept durable within that stamp. It keeps enough replicas of the data across different nodes in different fault domains to keep data durable within the stamp in the face of disk, node, and rack failures. Intra-stamp replication is done completely by the stream layer and is on the critical path of the customer's write requests. Once a transaction has been replicated successfully with intra-stamp replication, success can be returned back to the customer.

Inter-Stamp Replication (partition layer) – This system provides *asynchronous replication* and is focused on replicating data across stamps. Inter-stamp replication is done in the background and is off the critical path of the customer's request. This replication is at the object level, where either the whole object is replicated or recent delta changes are replicated for a given account. Inter-stamp replication is used for (a) keeping a copy of an account's data in two locations for disaster recovery and (b) migrating an account's data between stamps. Inter-stamp replication is configured for an account by the location service and performed by the partition layer.

Inter-stamp replication is focused on replicating objects and the transactions applied to those objects, whereas intra-stamp replication is focused on replicating blocks of disk storage that are used to make up the objects.

We separated replication into intra-stamp and inter-stamp at these two different layers for the following reasons. Intra-stamp replication provides durability against hardware failures, which occur frequently in large scale systems, whereas inter-stamp replication provides geo-redundancy against geo-disasters, which are rare. It is crucial to provide intra-stamp replication with low latency, since that is on the critical path of user requests; whereas the focus of inter-stamp replication is optimal use of network bandwidth between stamps while achieving an acceptable level of replication delay. They are different problems addressed by the two replication schemes.

Another reason for creating these two separate replication layers is the namespace each of these two layers has to maintain. Performing intra-stamp replication at the stream layer allows the amount of information that needs to be maintained to be scoped by the size of a single storage stamp. This focus allows all of the meta-state for intra-stamp replication to be cached in memory for performance (see Section 4), enabling WAS to provide fast replication with strong consistency by quickly committing transactions within a single stamp for customer requests. In contrast, the partition layer combined with the location service controls and understands the global object namespace across stamps, allowing it to efficiently replicate and maintain object state across data centers.

4. Stream Layer

The stream layer provides an internal interface used only by the partition layer. It provides a file system like namespace and API, except that all writes are append-only. It allows clients (the partition layer) to open, close, delete, rename, read, append to, and concatenate these large files, which are called streams. A stream is an ordered list of extent pointers, and an extent is a sequence of append blocks.

Figure 2 shows stream "//foo", which contains (pointers to) four extents (E1, E2, E3, and E4). Each extent contains a set of blocks that were appended to it. E1, E2 and E3 are sealed extents. It means that they can no longer be appended to; only the last extent in a stream (E4) can be appended to. If an application reads the data of the stream from beginning to end, it would get the block contents of the extents in the order of E1, E2, E3 and E4.

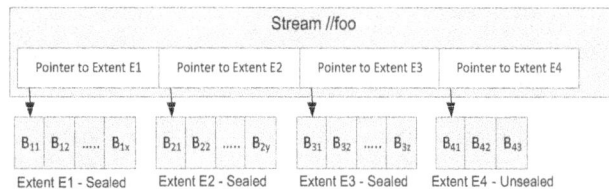

Figure 2: Example stream with four extents

In more detail these data concepts are:

Block – This is the minimum unit of data for writing and reading. A block can be up to N bytes (e.g. 4MB). Data is written (appended) as one or more concatenated blocks to an extent, where blocks do not have to be the same size. The client does an append in terms of blocks and controls the size of each block. A client read gives an offset to a stream or extent, and the stream layer reads as many blocks as needed at the offset to fulfill the length of the read. When performing a read, the entire contents of a block are read. This is because the stream layer stores its checksum validation at the block level, one checksum per block. The whole block is read to perform the checksum validation, and it is checked on every block read. In addition, all blocks in the system are validated against their checksums once every few days to check for data integrity issues.

Extent – Extents are the unit of replication in the stream layer, and the default replication policy is to keep three replicas within a storage stamp for an extent. Each extent is stored in an NTFS file

and consists of a sequence of blocks. The target extent size used by the partition layer is 1GB. To store small objects, the partition layer appends many of them to the same extent and even in the same block; to store large TB-sized objects (Blobs), the object is broken up over many extents by the partition layer. The partition layer keeps track of what streams, extents, and byte offsets in the extents in which objects are stored as part of its index.

Streams – Every stream has a name in the hierarchical namespace maintained at the stream layer, and a stream looks like a big file to the partition layer. Streams are appended to and can be randomly read from. A stream is an ordered list of **pointers to extents** which is maintained by the Stream Manager. When the extents are concatenated together they represent the full contiguous address space in which the stream can be read in the order they were added to the stream. A new stream can be constructed by concatenating extents from existing streams, which is a fast operation since it just updates a list of pointers. Only the last extent in the stream can be appended to. All of the prior extents in the stream are immutable.

4.1 Stream Manager and Extent Nodes

The two main architecture components of the stream layer are the Stream Manager (SM) and Extent Node (EN) (shown in Figure 3).

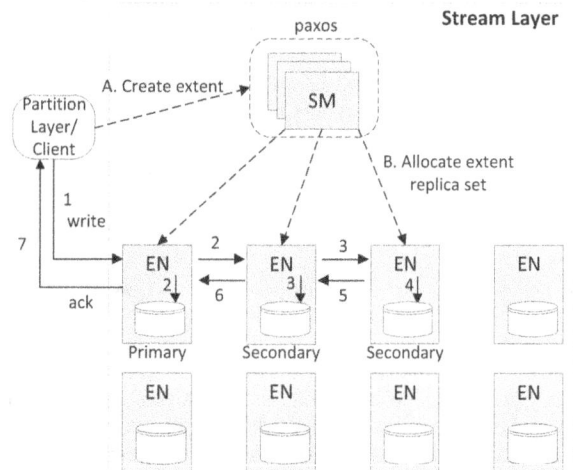

Figure 3: Stream Layer Architecture

Stream Manager (SM) – The SM keeps track of the stream namespace, what extents are in each stream, and the extent allocation across the Extent Nodes (EN). The SM is a standard Paxos cluster [13] as used in prior storage systems [3], and is off the critical path of client requests. The SM is responsible for (a) maintaining the stream namespace and state of all active streams and extents, (b) monitoring the health of the ENs, (c) creating and assigning extents to ENs, (d) performing the lazy re-replication of extent replicas that are lost due to hardware failures or unavailability, (e) garbage collecting extents that are no longer pointed to by any stream, and (f) scheduling the erasure coding of extent data according to stream policy (see Section 4.4).

The SM periodically polls (syncs) the state of the ENs and what extents they store. If the SM discovers that an extent is replicated on fewer than the expected number of ENs, a re-replication of the extent will lazily be created by the SM to regain the desired level of replication. For extent replica placement, the SM randomly chooses ENs across different fault domains, so that they are stored on nodes that will not have correlated failures due to power, network, or being on the same rack.

The SM does not know anything about blocks, just streams and extents. The SM is off the critical path of client requests and does not track each block append, since the total number of blocks can be huge and the SM cannot scale to track those. Since the stream and extent state is only tracked within a single stamp, the amount of state can be kept small enough to fit in the SM's memory. The only client of the stream layer is the partition layer, and the partition layer and stream layer are co-designed so that they will not use more than 50 million extents and no more than 100,000 streams for a single storage stamp given our current stamp sizes. This parameterization can comfortably fit into 32GB of memory for the SM.

Extent Nodes (EN) – Each extent node maintains the storage for a set of extent replicas assigned to it by the SM. An EN has N disks attached, which it completely controls for storing extent replicas and their blocks. An EN knows nothing about streams, and only deals with extents and blocks. Internally on an EN server, every extent on disk is a file, which holds data blocks and their checksums, and an index which maps extent offsets to blocks and their file location. Each extent node contains a view about the extents it owns and where the peer replicas are for a given extent. This view is a cache kept by the EN of the global state the SM keeps. ENs only talk to other ENs to replicate block writes (appends) sent by a client, or to create additional copies of an existing replica when told to by the SM. When an extent is no longer referenced by any stream, the SM garbage collects the extent and notifies the ENs to reclaim the space.

4.2 Append Operation and Sealed Extent

Streams can only be appended to; existing data cannot be modified. The append operations are atomic: either the entire data block is appended, or nothing is. Multiple blocks can be appended at once, as a single atomic "multi-block append" operation. The minimum read size from a stream is a single block. The "multi-block append" operation allows us to write a large amount of sequential data in a single append and to later perform small reads. The contract used between the client (partition layer) and the stream layer is that the multi-block append will occur atomically, and if the client never hears back for a request (due to failure) the client should retry the request (or seal the extent). This contract implies that the client needs to expect the same block to be appended more than once in face of timeouts and correctly deal with processing duplicate records. The partition layer deals with duplicate records in two ways (see Section 5 for details on the partition layer streams). For the metadata and commit log streams, all of the transactions written have a sequence number and duplicate records will have the same sequence number. For the row data and blob data streams, for duplicate writes, only the last write will be pointed to by the RangePartition data structures, so the prior duplicate writes will have no references and will be garbage collected later.

An extent has a target size, specified by the client (partition layer), and when it fills up to that size the extent is sealed at a block boundary, and then a new extent is added to the stream and appends continue into that new extent. Once an extent is **sealed** it can no longer be appended to. A sealed extent is immutable, and the stream layer performs certain optimizations on sealed extents like erasure coding cold extents. Extents in a stream do not have to be the same size, and they can be sealed anytime and can even grow arbitrarily large.

4.3 Stream Layer Intra-Stamp Replication

The stream layer and partition layer are co-designed to provide strong consistency at the object transaction level. The correctness of the partition layer providing strong consistency is built upon the following guarantees from the stream layer:

1. Once a record is appended and acknowledged back to the client, any later reads of that record from any replica will see the same data (the data is immutable).

2. Once an extent is sealed, any reads from any sealed replica will always see the same contents of the extent.

The data center, Fabric Controller, and WAS have security mechanisms in place to guard against malicious adversaries, so the stream replication does not deal with such threats. We consider faults ranging from disk and node errors to power failures, network issues, bit-flip and random hardware failures, as well as software bugs. These faults can cause data corruption; checksums are used to detect such corruption. The rest of the section discusses the intra-stamp replication scheme within this context.

4.3.1 Replication Flow

As shown in Figure 3, when a stream is first created (step A), the SM assigns three replicas for the first extent (one primary and two secondary) to three extent nodes (step B), which are chosen by the SM to randomly spread the replicas across different fault and upgrade domains while considering extent node usage (for load balancing). In addition, the SM decides which replica will be the primary for the extent. Writes to an extent are always performed from the client to the primary EN, and the primary EN is in charge of coordinating the write to two secondary ENs. The primary EN and the location of the three replicas never change for an extent while it is being appended to (while the extent is **unsealed**). Therefore, no leases are used to represent the primary EN for an extent, since the primary is always fixed while an extent is unsealed.

When the SM allocates the extent, the extent information is sent back to the client, which then knows which ENs hold the three replicas and which one is the primary. This state is now part of the stream's metadata information held in the SM and cached on the client. When the last extent in the stream that is being appended to becomes sealed, the same process repeats. The SM then allocates another extent, which now becomes the last extent in the stream, and all new appends now go to the new last extent for the stream.

For an extent, every append is replicated three times across the extent's replicas. A client sends all write requests to the primary EN, but it can read from any replica, even for unsealed extents. The append is sent to the primary EN for the extent by the client, and the primary is then in charge of (a) determining the offset of the append in the extent, (b) ordering (choosing the offset of) all of the appends if there are concurrent append requests to the same extent outstanding, (c) sending the append with its chosen offset to the two secondary extent nodes, and (d) only returning success for the append to the client after a successful append has occurred to disk for all three extent nodes. The sequence of steps during an append is shown in Figure 3 (labeled with numbers). Only when all of the writes have succeeded for all three replicas will the primary EN then respond to the client that the append was a success. If there are multiple outstanding appends to the same extent, the primary EN will respond success in the order of their offset (commit them in order) to the clients. As appends commit in order for a replica, the last append position is considered to be the current **commit length** of the replica. We ensure that the bits are the same between all replicas by the fact that the primary EN for an extent never changes, it always picks the offset for appends,

appends for an extent are committed in order, and how extents are sealed upon failures (discussed in Section 4.3.2).

When a stream is opened, the metadata for its extents is cached at the client, so the client can go directly to the ENs for reading and writing without talking to the SM until the next extent needs to be allocated for the stream. If during writing, one of the replica's ENs is not reachable or there is a disk failure for one of the replicas, a write failure is returned to the client. The client then contacts the SM, and the extent that was being appended to is sealed by the SM at its current commit length (see Section 4.3.2). At this point the sealed extent can no longer be appended to. The SM will then allocate a new extent with replicas on different (available) ENs, which makes it now the last extent of the stream. The information for this new extent is returned to the client. The client then continues appending to the stream with its new extent. This process of sealing by the SM and allocating the new extent is done on average within 20ms. A key point here is that the client can continue appending to a stream as soon as the new extent has been allocated, and it does not rely on a specific node to become available again.

For the newly sealed extent, the SM will create new replicas to bring it back to the expected level of redundancy in the background if needed.

4.3.2 Sealing

From a high level, the SM coordinates the sealing operation among the ENs; it determines the commit length of the extent used for sealing based on the commit length of the extent replicas. Once the sealing is done, the commit length will never change again.

To seal an extent, the SM asks all three ENs their current length. During sealing, either all replicas have the same length, which is the simple case, or a given replica is longer or shorter than another replica for the extent. This latter case can only occur during an append failure where some but not all of the ENs for the replica are available (i.e., some of the replicas get the append block, but not all of them). We guarantee that the SM will seal the extent even if the SM may not be able to reach all the ENs involved. When sealing the extent, the SM will choose the smallest commit length based on the available ENs it can talk to. This will not cause data loss since the primary EN will not return success unless all replicas have been written to disk for all three ENs. This means the smallest commit length is sure to contain all the writes that have been acknowledged to the client. In addition, it is also fine if the final length contains blocks that were never acknowledged back to the client, since the client (partition layer) correctly deals with these as described in Section 4.2. During the sealing, all of the extent replicas that were reachable by the SM are sealed to the commit length chosen by the SM.

Once the sealing is done, the commit length of the extent will never be changed. If an EN was not reachable by the SM during the sealing process but later becomes reachable, the SM will force the EN to synchronize the given extent to the chosen commit length. This ensures that once an extent is sealed, all its available replicas (the ones the SM can eventually reach) are bitwise identical.

4.3.3 Interaction with Partition Layer

An interesting case is when, due to network partitioning, a client (partition server) is still able to talk to an EN that the SM could not talk to during the sealing process. This section explains how the partition layer handles this case.

The partition layer has two different read patterns:

1. **Read records at known locations.** The partition layer uses two types of data streams (row and blob). For these streams, it always reads at specific locations (extent+offset, length). More importantly, the partition layer will only read these two streams using the location information returned from a previous successful append at the stream layer. That will only occur if the append was successfully committed to all three replicas. The replication scheme guarantees such reads always see the same data.

2. **Iterate all records sequentially in a stream on partition load.** Each partition has two additional streams (metadata and commit log). These are the only streams that the partition layer will read sequentially from a starting point to the very last record of a stream. This operation only occurs when the partition is loaded (explained in Section 5). The partition layer ensures that no useful appends from the partition layer will happen to these two streams during partition load. Then the partition and stream layer together ensure that the same sequence of records is returned on partition load.

At the start of a partition load, the partition server sends a "check for commit length" to the primary EN of the last extent of these two streams. This checks whether all the replicas are available and that they all have the same length. If not, the extent is sealed and reads are only performed, during partition load, against a replica sealed by the SM. This ensures that the partition load will see all of its data and the exact same view, even if we were to repeatedly load the same partition reading from different sealed replicas for the last extent of the stream.

4.4 Erasure Coding Sealed Extents

To reduce the cost of storage, WAS erasure codes sealed extents for Blob storage. WAS breaks an extent into N roughly equal sized fragments at block boundaries. Then, it adds M error correcting code fragments using Reed-Solomon for the erasure coding algorithm [19]. As long as it does not lose more than M fragments (across the data fragments + code fragments), WAS can recreate the full extent.

Erasure coding sealed extents is an important optimization, given the amount of data we are storing. It reduces the cost of storing data from three full replicas within a stamp, which is three times the original data, to only 1.3x – 1.5x the original data, depending on the number of fragments used. In addition, erasure coding actually increases the durability of the data when compared to keeping three replicas within a stamp.

4.5 Read Load-Balancing

When reads are issued for an extent that has three replicas, they are submitted with a "deadline" value which specifies that the read should not be attempted if it cannot be fulfilled within the deadline. If the EN determines the read cannot be fulfilled within the time constraint, it will immediately reply to the client that the deadline cannot be met. This mechanism allows the client to select a different EN to read that data from, likely allowing the read to complete faster.

This method is also used with erasure coded data. When reads cannot be serviced in a timely manner due to a heavily loaded spindle to the data fragment, the read may be serviced faster by doing a reconstruction rather than reading that data fragment. In this case, reads (for the range of the fragment needed to satisfy the client request) are issued to all fragments of an erasure coded extent, and the first N responses are used to reconstruct the desired fragment.

4.6 Spindle Anti-Starvation

Many hard disk drives are optimized to achieve the highest possible throughput, and sacrifice fairness to achieve that goal. They tend to prefer reads or writes that are sequential. Since our system contains many streams that can be very large, we observed in developing our service that some disks would lock into servicing large pipelined reads or writes while starving other operations. On some disks we observed this could lock out non-sequential IO for as long as 2300 milliseconds. To avoid this problem we avoid scheduling new IO to a spindle when there is over 100ms of expected pending IO already scheduled or when there is any pending IO request that has been scheduled but not serviced for over 200ms. Using our own custom IO scheduling allows us to achieve fairness across reads/writes at the cost of slightly increasing overall latency on some sequential requests.

4.7 Durability and Journaling

The durability contract for the stream layer is that when data is acknowledged as written by the stream layer, there must be at least three durable copies of the data stored in the system. This contract allows the system to maintain data durability even in the face of a cluster-wide power failure. We operate our storage system in such a way that all writes are made durable to power safe storage before they are acknowledged back to the client.

As part of maintaining the durability contract while still achieving good performance, an important optimization for the stream layer is that on each extent node we reserve a whole disk drive or SSD as a **journal drive** for all writes into the extent node. The journal drive [11] is dedicated solely for writing a single sequential journal of data, which allows us to reach the full write throughput potential of the device. When the partition layer does a stream append, the data is written by the primary EN while in parallel sent to the two secondaries to be written. When each EN performs its append, it (a) writes all of the data for the append to the journal drive and (b) queues up the append to go to the data disk where the extent file lives on that EN. Once either succeeds, success can be returned. If the journal succeeds first, the data is also buffered in memory while it goes to the data disk, and any reads for that data are served from memory until the data is on the data disk. From that point on, the data is served from the data disk. This also enables the combining of contiguous writes into larger writes to the data disk, and better scheduling of concurrent writes and reads to get the best throughput. It is a tradeoff for good latency at the cost of an extra write off the critical path.

Even though the stream layer is an append-only system, we found that adding a journal drive provided important benefits, since the appends do not have to contend with reads going to the data disk in order to commit the result back to the client. The journal allows the append times from the partition layer to have more consistent and lower latencies. Take for example the partition layer's commit log stream, where an append is only as fast as the slowest EN for the replicas being appended to. For small appends to the commit log stream without journaling we saw an average end-to-end stream append latency of 30ms. With journaling we see an average append latency of 6ms. In addition, the variance of latencies decreased significantly.

5. Partition Layer

The partition layer stores the different types of objects and understands what a transaction means for a given object type (Blob, Table, or Queue). The partition layer provides the (a) data model for the different types of objects stored, (b) logic and semantics to process the different types of objects, (c) massively scalable namespace for the objects, (d) load balancing to access objects across the available partition servers, and (e) transaction ordering and strong consistency for access to objects.

5.1 Partition Layer Data Model

The partition layer provides an important internal data structure called an Object Table (OT). An OT is a massive table which can grow to several petabytes. Object Tables are dynamically broken up into RangePartitions (based on traffic load to the table) and spread across Partition Servers (Section 5.2) in a stamp. A **RangePartition** is a contiguous range of rows in an OT from a given low-key to a high-key. All RangePartitions for a given OT are non-overlapping, and every row is represented in some RangePartition.

The following are the Object Tables used by the partition layer. The Account Table stores metadata and configuration for each storage account assigned to the stamp. The Blob Table stores all blob objects for all accounts in the stamp. The Entity Table stores all entity rows for all accounts in the stamp; it is used for the public Windows Azure Table data abstraction. The Message Table stores all messages for all accounts' queues in the stamp. The Schema Table keeps track of the schema for all OTs. The Partition Map Table keeps track of the current RangePartitions for all Object Tables and what partition server is serving each RangePartition. This table is used by the Front-End servers to route requests to the corresponding partition servers.

Each of the above OTs has a fixed schema stored in the Schema Table. The primary key for the Blob Table, Entity Table, and Message Table consists of three properties: AccountName, PartitionName, and ObjectName. These properties provide the indexing and sort order for those Object Tables.

5.1.1 Supported Data Types and Operations

The property types supported for an OT's schema are the standard simple types (bool, binary, string, DateTime, double, GUID, int32, int64). In addition, the system supports two special types – DictionaryType and BlobType. The DictionaryType allows for flexible properties (i.e., without a fixed schema) to be added to a row at any time. These flexible properties are stored inside of the dictionary type as (name, type, value) tuples. From a data access standpoint, these flexible properties behave like first-order properties of the row and are queryable just like any other property in the row. The BlobType is a special property used to store large amounts of data and is currently used only by the Blob Table. BlobType avoids storing the blob data bits with the row properties in the "row data stream". Instead, the blob data bits are stored in a separate "blob data stream" and a pointer to the blob's data bits (list of "extent + offset, length" pointers) is stored in the BlobType's property in the row. This keeps the large data bits separated from the OT's queryable row property values stored in the row data stream.

OTs support standard operations including insert, update, and delete operations on rows as well as query/get operations. In addition, OTs allows batch transactions across rows with the same PartitionName value. The operations in a single batch are committed as a single transaction. Finally, OTs provide snapshot isolation to allow read operations to happen concurrently with writes.

5.2 Partition Layer Architecture

The partition layer has three main architectural components as shown in Figure 4: a Partition Manager (PM), Partition Servers (PS), and a Lock Service.

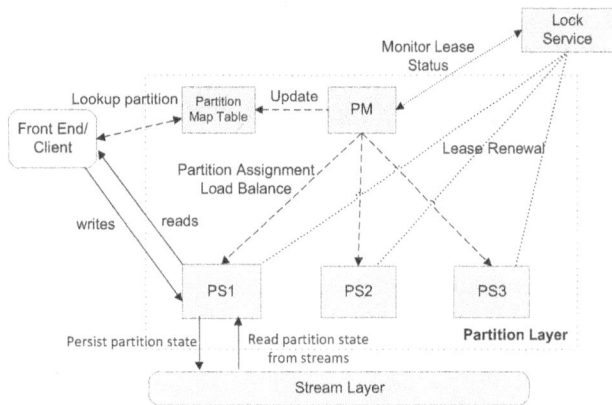

Figure 4: Partition Layer Architecture

Partition Manager (PM) – Responsible for keeping track of and splitting the massive Object Tables into RangePartitions and assigning each RangePartition to a Partition Server to serve access to the objects. The PM splits the Object Tables into N RangePartitions in each stamp, keeping track of the current RangePartition breakdown for each OT and to which partition servers they are assigned. The PM stores this assignment in the Partition Map Table. The PM ensures that each RangePartition is assigned to exactly one active partition server at any time, and that two RangePartitions do not overlap. It is also responsible for load balancing RangePartitions among partition servers. Each stamp has multiple instances of the PM running, and they all contend for a leader lock that is stored in the Lock Service (see below). The PM with the lease is the active PM controlling the partition layer.

Partition Server (PS) – A partition server is responsible for serving requests to a set of RangePartitions assigned to it by the PM. The PS stores all the persistent state of the partitions into streams and maintains a memory cache of the partition state for efficiency. The system guarantees that no two partition servers can serve the same RangePartition at the same time by using leases with the Lock Service. This allows the PS to provide strong consistency and ordering of concurrent transactions to objects for a RangePartition it is serving. A PS can concurrently serve multiple RangePartitions from different OTs. In our deployments, a PS serves on average ten RangePartitions at any time.

Lock Service – A Paxos Lock Service [3,13] is used for leader election for the PM. In addition, each PS also maintains a lease with the lock service in order to serve partitions. We do not go into the details of the PM leader election, or the PS lease management, since the concepts used are similar to those described in the Chubby Lock [3] paper.

On partition server failure, all N RangePartitions served by the failed PS are assigned to available PSs by the PM. The PM will choose N (or fewer) partition servers, based on the load on those servers. The PM will assign a RangePartition to a PS, and then update the Partition Map Table specifying what partition server is serving each RangePartition. This allows the Front-End layer to find the location of RangePartitions by looking in the Partition Map Table (see Figure 4). When the PS gets a new assignment it will start serving the new RangePartitions for as long as the PS holds its partition server lease.

5.3 RangePartition Data Structures

A PS serves a RangePartition by maintaining a set of in-memory data structures and a set of persistent data structures in streams.

5.3.1 Persistent Data Structure

A RangePartition uses a Log-Structured Merge-Tree [17,4] to maintain its persistent data. Each Object Table's RangePartition consists of its own set of streams in the stream layer, and the streams belong solely to a given RangePartition, though the underlying extents can be pointed to by multiple streams in different RangePartitions due to RangePartition splitting. The following are the set of streams that comprise each RangePartition (shown in Figure 5):

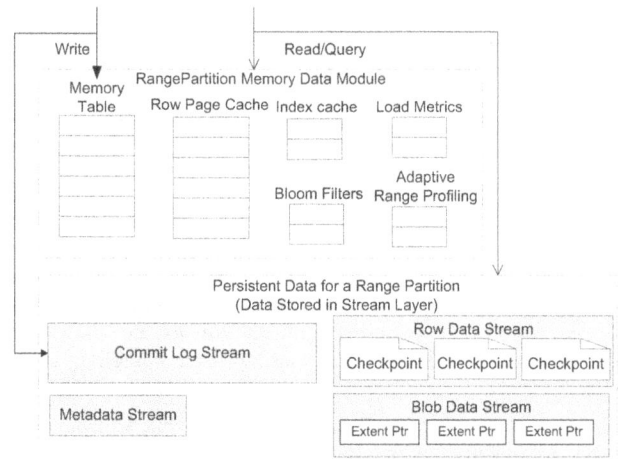

Figure 5: RangePartition Data Structures

Metadata Stream – The metadata stream is the root stream for a RangePartition. The PM assigns a partition to a PS by providing the name of the RangePartition's metadata stream. The metadata stream contains enough information for the PS to load a RangePartition, including the name of the commit log stream and data streams for that RangePartition, as well as pointers (extent+offset) into those streams for where to start operating in those streams (e.g., where to start processing in the commit log stream and the root of the index for the row data stream). The PS serving the RangePartition also writes in the metadata stream the status of outstanding split and merge operations that the RangePartition may be involved in.

Commit Log Stream – Is a commit log used to store the recent insert, update, and delete operations applied to the RangePartition since the last checkpoint was generated for the RangePartition.

Row Data Stream – Stores the checkpoint row data and index for the RangePartition.

Blob Data Stream – Is only used by the Blob Table to store the blob data bits.

Each of the above is a separate stream in the stream layer owned by an Object Table's RangePartition.

Each RangePartition in an Object Table has only one data stream, except the Blob Table. A RangePartition in the Blob Table has a "row data stream" for storing its row checkpoint data (the blob index), and a separate "blob data stream" for storing the blob data bits for the special BlobType described earlier.

5.3.2 In-Memory Data Structures

A partition server maintains the following in-memory components as shown in Figure 5:

Memory Table – This is the in-memory version of the commit log for a RangePartition, containing all of the recent updates that have not yet been checkpointed to the row data stream. When a lookup occurs the memory table is checked to find recent updates to the RangePartition.

Index Cache – This cache stores the checkpoint indexes of the row data stream. We separate this cache out from the row data cache to make sure we keep as much of the main index cached in memory as possible for a given RangePartition.

Row Data Cache – This is a memory cache of the checkpoint row data pages. The row data cache is read-only. When a lookup occurs, both the row data cache and the memory table are checked, giving preference to the memory table.

Bloom Filters – If the data is not found in the memory table or the row data cache, then the index/checkpoints in the data stream need to be searched. It can be expensive to blindly examine them all. Therefore a bloom filter is kept for each checkpoint, which indicates if the row being accessed *may* be in the checkpoint.

We do not go into further details about these components, since these are similar to those in [17,4].

5.4 Data Flow
When the PS receives a write request to the RangePartition (e.g., insert, update, delete), it appends the operation into the commit log, and then puts the newly changed row into the memory table. Therefore, all the modifications to the partition are recorded persistently in the commit log, and also reflected in the memory table. At this point success can be returned back to the client (the FE servers) for the transaction. When the size of the memory table reaches its threshold size or the size of the commit log stream reaches its threshold, the partition server will write the contents of the memory table into a checkpoint stored persistently in the row data stream for the RangePartition. The corresponding portion of the commit log can then be removed. To control the total number of checkpoints for a RangePartition, the partition server will periodically combine the checkpoints into larger checkpoints, and then remove the old checkpoints via garbage collection.

For the Blob Table's RangePartitions, we also store the Blob data bits directly into the commit log stream (to minimize the number of stream writes for Blob operations), but those data bits are not part of the row data so they are not put into the memory table. Instead, the BlobType property for the row tracks the location of the Blob data bits (extent+offset, length). During checkpoint, the extents that would be removed from the commit log are instead concatenated to the RangePartition's Blob data stream. Extent concatenation is a fast operation provided by the stream layer since it consists of just adding pointers to extents at the end of the Blob data stream without copying any data.

A PS can start serving a RangePartition by "loading" the partition. Loading a partition involves reading the metadata stream of the RangePartition to locate the active set of checkpoints and replaying the transactions in the commit log to rebuild the in-memory state. Once these are done, the PS has the up-to-date view of the RangePartition and can start serving requests.

5.5 RangePartition Load Balancing
A critical part of the partition layer is breaking these massive Object Tables into RangePartitions and automatically load balancing them across the partition servers to meet their varying traffic demands.

The PM performs three operations to spread load across partition servers and control the total number of partitions in a stamp:

Load Balance – This operation identifies when a given PS has too much traffic and reassigns one or more RangePartitions to less loaded partition servers.

Split – This operation identifies when a single RangePartition has too much load and splits the RangePartition into two or more smaller and disjoint RangePartitions, then load balances (reassigns) them across two or more partition servers.

Merge – This operation merges together cold or lightly loaded RangePartitions that together form a contiguous key range within their OT. Merge is used to keep the number of RangePartitions within a bound proportional to the number of partition servers in a stamp.

WAS keeps the total number of partitions between a low watermark and a high watermark (typically around ten times the partition server count within a stamp). At equilibrium, the partition count will stay around the low watermark. If there are unanticipated traffic bursts that concentrate on a single RangePartition, it will be split to spread the load. When the total RangePartition count is approaching the high watermark, the system will increase the merge rate to eventually bring the RangePartition count down towards the low watermark. Therefore, the number of RangePartitions for each OT changes dynamically based upon the load on the objects in those tables.

Having a high watermark of RangePartitions ten times the number of partition servers (a storage stamp has a few hundred partition servers) was chosen based on how big we can allow the stream and extent metadata to grow for the SM, and still completely fit the metadata in memory for the SM. Keeping many more RangePartitions than partition servers enables us to quickly distribute a failed PS or rack's load across many other PSs. A given partition server can end up serving a single extremely hot RangePartition, tens of lightly loaded RangePartitions, or a mixture in-between, depending upon the current load to the RangePartitions in the stamp. The number of RangePartitions for the Blob Table vs. Entity Table vs. Message Table depends upon the load on the objects in those tables and is continuously changing within a storage stamp based upon traffic.

For each stamp, we typically see 75 splits and merges and 200 RangePartition load balances per day.

5.5.1 Load Balance Operation Details
We track the load for each RangePartition as well as the overall load for each PS. For both of these we track (a) transactions/second, (b) average pending transaction count, (c) throttling rate, (d) CPU usage, (e) network usage, (f) request latency, and (g) data size of the RangePartition. The PM maintains heartbeats with each PS. This information is passed back to the PM in responses to the heartbeats. If the PM sees a RangePartition that has too much load based upon the metrics, then it will decide to split the partition and send a command to the PS to perform the split. If instead a PS has too much load, but no individual RangePartition seems to be too highly loaded, the PM will take one or more RangePartitions from the PS and reassign them to a more lightly loaded PS.

To load balance a RangePartition, the PM sends an offload command to the PS, which will have the RangePartition write a current checkpoint before offloading it. Once complete, the PS acks back to the PM that the offload is done. The PM then assigns the RangePartition to its new PS and updates the Partition Map Table to point to the new PS. The new PS loads and starts serving traffic for the RangePartition. The loading of the RangePartition on the new PS is very quick since the commit log is small due to the checkpoint prior to the offload.

5.5.2 Split Operation

WAS splits a RangePartition due to too much load as well as the size of its row or blob data streams. If the PM identifies either situation, it tells the PS serving the RangePartition to split based upon load or size. The PM makes the decision to split, but the PS chooses the key (AccountName, PartitionName) where the partition will be split. To split based upon size, the RangePartition maintains the total size of the objects in the partition and the split key values where the partition can be approximately halved in size, and the PS uses that to pick the key for where to split. If the split is based on load, the PS chooses the key based upon Adaptive Range Profiling [16]. The PS adaptively tracks which key ranges in a RangePartition have the most load and uses this to determine on what key to split the RangePartition.

To split a RangePartition (B) into two new RangePartitions (C,D), the following steps are taken.

1. The PM instructs the PS to split B into C and D.

2. The PS in charge of B checkpoints B, then stops serving traffic briefly during step 3 below.

3. The PS uses a special stream operation "MultiModify" to take each of B's streams (metadata, commit log and data) and creates new sets of streams for C and D respectively with the same extents in the same order as in B. This step is very fast, since a stream is just a list of pointers to extents. The PS then appends the new partition key ranges for C and D to their metadata streams.

4. The PS starts serving requests to the two new partitions C and D for their respective disjoint PartitionName ranges.

5. The PS notifies the PM of the split completion, and the PM updates the Partition Map Table and its metadata information accordingly. The PM then moves one of the split partitions to a different PS.

5.5.3 Merge Operation

To merge two RangePartitions, the PM will choose two RangePartitions C and D with adjacent PartitionName ranges that have low traffic. The following steps are taken to merge C and D into a new RangePartition E.

1. The PM moves C and D so that they are served by the same PS. The PM then tells the PS to merge (C,D) into E.

2. The PS performs a checkpoint for both C and D, and then briefly pauses traffic to C and D during step 3.

3. The PS uses the MultiModify stream command to create a new commit log and data streams for E. Each of these streams is the concatenation of all of the extents from their respective streams in C and D. This merge means that the extents in the new commit log stream for E will be all of C's extents in the order they were in C's commit log stream followed by all of D's extents in their original order. This layout is the same for the new row and Blob data stream(s) for E.

4. The PS constructs the metadata stream for E, which contains the names of the new commit log and data stream, the combined key range for E, and pointers (extent+offset) for the start and end of the commit log regions in E's commit log derived from C and D, as well as the root of the data index in E's data streams.

5. At this point, the new metadata stream for E can be correctly loaded, and the PS starts serving the newly merged RangePartition E.

6. The PM then updates the Partition Map Table and its metadata information to reflect the merge.

5.6 Partition Layer Inter-Stamp Replication

Thus far we have talked about an AccountName being associated (via DNS) to a single location and storage stamp, where all data access goes to that stamp. We call this the **primary stamp** for an account. An account actually has one or more **secondary stamps** assigned to it by the Location Service, and this primary/secondary stamp information tells WAS to perform inter-stamp replication for this account from the primary stamp to the secondary stamp(s).

One of the main scenarios for inter-stamp replication is to geo-replicate an account's data between two data centers for disaster recovery. In this scenario, a primary and secondary location is chosen for the account. Take, for example, an account, for which we want the primary stamp (P) to be located in US South and the secondary stamp (S) to be located in US North. When provisioning the account, the LS will choose a stamp in each location and register the AccountName with both stamps such that the US South stamp (P) takes live traffic and the US North stamp (S) will take only inter-stamp replication (also called geo-replication) traffic from stamp P for the account. The LS updates DNS to have hostname **AccountName**.service.core.windows.net point to the storage stamp P's VIP in US South. When a write comes into stamp P for the account, the change is fully replicated within that stamp using intra-stamp replication at the stream layer then success is returned to the client. After the update has been committed in stamp P, the partition layer in stamp P will asynchronously geo-replicate the change to the secondary stamp S using inter-stamp replication. When the change arrives at stamp S, the transaction is applied in the partition layer and this update fully replicates using intra-stamp replication within stamp S.

Since the inter-stamp replication is done asynchronously, recent updates that have not been inter-stamp replicated can be lost in the event of disaster. In production, changes are geo-replicated and committed on the secondary stamp within 30 seconds on average after the update was committed on the primary stamp.

Inter-stamp replication is used for both account geo-replication and migration across stamps. For disaster recovery, we may need to perform an abrupt failover where recent changes may be lost, but for migration we perform a clean failover so there is no data loss. In both failover scenarios, the Location Service makes an active secondary stamp for the account the new primary and switches DNS to point to the secondary stamp's VIP. Note that the URI used to access the object does not change after failover. This allows the existing URIs used to access Blobs, Tables and Queues to continue to work after failover.

6. Application Throughput

For our cloud offering, customers run their applications as a tenant (service) on VMs. For our platform, we separate computation and storage into their own stamps (clusters) within a data center since this separation allows each to scale independently and control their own load balancing. Here we examine the performance of a customer application running from their hosted service on VMs in the same data center as where their account data is stored. Each VM used is an extra-large VM with full control of the entire compute node and a 1Gbps NIC. The results were gathered on live shared production stamps with internal and external customers.

Figure 6 shows the WAS Table operation throughput in terms of the entities per second (y-axis) for 1-16 VMs (x-axis) performing random 1KB single entity get and put requests against a single 100GB Table. It also shows batch inserts of 100 entities at a time – a common way applications insert groups of entities into a WAS Table. Figure 7 shows the throughput in megabytes per second (y-axis) for randomly getting and putting 4MB blobs vs. the number of VMs used (x-axis). All of the results are for a single storage account.

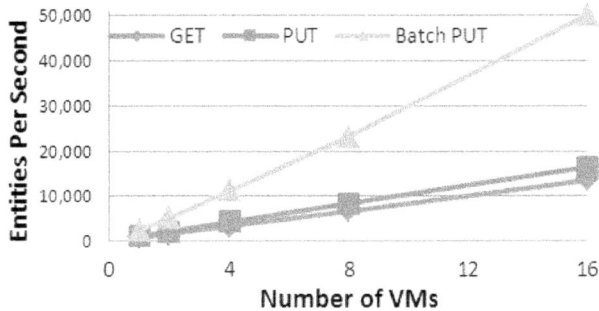

Figure 6 Table Entity Throughput for 1-16 VMs

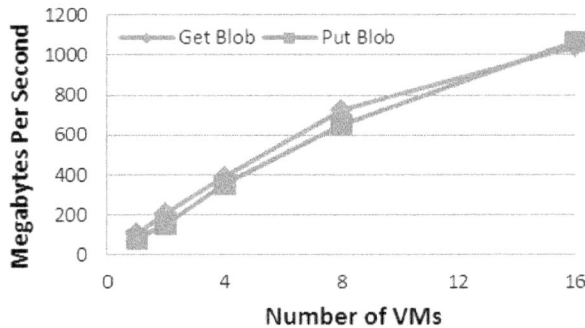

Figure 7: Blob Throughput for 1-16 VMs

These results show a linear increase in scale is achieved for entities/second as the application scales out the amount of computing resources it uses for accessing WAS Tables. For Blobs, the throughput scales linearly up to eight VMs, but tapers off as the aggregate throughput reaches the network capacity on the client side where the test traffic was generated. The results show that, for Table operations, batch puts offer about three times more throughput compared to single entity puts. That is because the batch operation significantly reduces the number of network roundtrips and requires fewer stream writes. In addition, the Table read operations have slightly lower throughput than write operations. This difference is due to the particular access pattern of our experiment, which randomly accesses a large key space on a large data set, minimizing the effect of caching. Writes on the other hand always result in sequential writes to the journal.

7. Workload Profiles

Usage patterns for cloud-based applications can vary significantly. Section 1 already described a near-real time ingestion engine to provide Facebook and Twitter search for Bing. In this section we describe a few additional internal services using WAS, and give some high-level metrics of their usage.

The XBox GameSaves service was announced at E3 this year and will provide a new feature in Fall 2011 for providing saved game data into the cloud for millions of XBox users. This feature will enable subscribed users to upload their game progress into the

WAS cloud storage service, which they can then access from any XBox console they sign into. The backing storage for this feature leverages Blob and Table storage.

The XBox Telemetry service stores console-generated diagnostics and telemetry information for later secure retrieval and offline processing. For example, various Kinect related features running on Xbox 360 generate detailed usage files which are uploaded to the cloud to analyze and improve the Kinect experience based on customer opt-in. The data is stored directly into Blobs, and Tables are used to maintain metadata information about the files. Queues are used to coordinate the processing and the cleaning up of the Blobs.

Microsoft's Zune backend uses Windows Azure for media file storage and delivery, where files are stored as Blobs.

Table 1 shows the relative breakdown among Blob, Table, and Queue usage across all (All) services (internal and external) using WAS as well as for the services described above. The table shows the breakdown of requests, capacity usage, and ingress and egress traffic for Blobs, Tables and Queues.

Notice that, the percentage of requests for all services shows that about 17.9% of all requests are Blob requests, 46.88% of the requests are Table operations and 35.22% are Queue requests for all services using WAS. But in terms of capacity, 70.31% of capacity is in Blobs, 29.68% of capacity is used by Tables, and 0.01% used by Queues. "%Ingress" is the percentage breakdown of incoming traffic (bytes) among Blob, Table, and Queue; "%Egress" is the same for outbound traffic (bytes). The results show that different customers have very different usage patterns. In term of capacity usage, some customers (e.g., Zune and Xbox GameSaves) have mostly unstructured data (such as media files) and put those into Blobs, whereas other customers like Bing and XBox Telemetry that have to index a lot of data have a significant amount of structured data in Tables. Queues use very little space compared to Blobs and Tables, since they are primarily used as a communication mechanism instead of storing data over a long period of time.

Table 1: Usage Comparison for (Blob/Table/Queue)

		%Requests	%Capacity	%Ingress	%Egress
All	Blob	17.9	70.31	48.28	66.17
	Table	46.88	29.68	49.61	33.07
	Queue	35.22	0.01	2.11	0.76
Bing	Blob	0.46	60.45	16.73	29.11
	Table	98.48	39.55	83.14	70.79
	Queue	1.06	0	0.13	0.1
XBox GameSaves	Blob	99.68	99.99	99.84	99.88
	Table	0.32	0.01	0.16	0.12
	Queue	0	0	0	0
XBox Telemetry	Blob	26.78	19.57	50.25	11.26
	Table	44.98	80.43	49.25	88.29
	Queue	28.24	0	0.5	0.45
Zune	Blob	94.64	99.9	98.22	96.21
	Table	5.36	0.1	1.78	3.79
	Queue	0	0	0	0

8. Design Choices and Lessons Learned

Here, we discuss a few of our WAS design choices and relate some of the lessons we have learned thus far.

Scaling Computation Separate from Storage – Early on we decided to separate customer VM-based computation from storage for Windows Azure. Therefore, nodes running a customer's service code are separate from nodes providing their storage. As a result, we can scale our supply of computation cores and storage independently to meet customer demand in a given data center. This separation also provides a layer of isolation between compute and storage given its multi-tenancy usage, and allows both of the systems to load balance independently.

Given this decision, our goal from the start has been to allow computation to efficiently access storage with high bandwidth without the data being on the same node or even in the same rack. To achieve this goal we are in the process of moving towards our next generation data center networking architecture [10], which flattens the data center networking topology and provides full bisection bandwidth between compute and storage.

Range Partitions vs. Hashing – We decided to use range-based partitioning/indexing instead of hash-based indexing (where the objects are assigned to a server based on the hash values of their keys) for the partition layer's Object Tables. One reason for this decision is that range-based partitioning makes performance isolation easier since a given account's objects are stored together within a set of RangePartitions (which also provides efficient object enumeration). Hash-based schemes have the simplicity of distributing the load across servers, but lose the locality of objects for isolation and efficient enumeration. The range partitioning allows WAS to keep a customer's objects together in their own set of partitions to throttle and isolate potentially abusive accounts.

For these reasons, we took the range-based approach and built an automatic load balancing system (Section 5.5) to spread the load dynamically according to user traffic by splitting and moving partitions among servers.

A downside of range partitioning is scaling out access to sequential access patterns. For example, if a customer is writing all of their data to the very end of a table's key range (e.g., insert key 2011-06-30:12:00:00, then key 2011-06-30:12:00:02, then key 2011-06-30:12:00:10), all of the writes go to the very last RangePartition in the customer's table. This pattern does not take advantage of the partitioning and load balancing our system provides. In contrast, if the customer distributes their writes across a large number of PartitionNames, the system can quickly split the table into multiple RangePartitions and spread them across different servers to allow performance to scale linearly with load (as shown in Figure 6). To address this sequential access pattern for RangePartitions, a customer can always use hashing or bucketing for the PartitionName, which avoids the above sequential access pattern issue.

Throttling/Isolation – At times, servers become overloaded by customer requests. A difficult problem was identifying which storage accounts should be throttled when this happens and making sure well-behaving accounts are not affected.

Each partition server keeps track of the request rate for AccountNames and PartitionNames. Because there are a large number of AccountNames and PartitionNames it may not be practical to keep track of them all. The system uses a Sample-Hold algorithm [7] to track the request rate history of the top N busiest AccountNames and PartitionNames. This information is used to determine whether an account is well-behaving or not (e.g., whether the traffic backs off when it is throttled). If a server is getting overloaded, it uses this information to selectively throttle the incoming traffic, targeting accounts that are causing the issue. For example, a PS computes a throttling probability of the incoming requests for each account based on the request rate history for the account (those with high request rates will have a larger probability being throttled, whereas accounts with little

traffic will not). In addition, based on the request history at the AccountName and PartitionName levels, the system determines whether the account has been well-behaving. Load balancing will try to keep the servers within an acceptable load, but when access patterns cannot be load balanced (e.g., high traffic to a single PartitionName, high sequential access traffic, repetitive sequential scanning, etc.), the system throttles requests of such traffic patterns when they are too high.

Automatic Load Balancing – We found it crucial to have efficient automatic load balancing of partitions that can quickly adapt to various traffic conditions. This enables WAS to maintain high availability in this multi-tenancy environment as well as deal with traffic spikes to a single user's storage account. Gathering the adaptive profile information, discovering what metrics are most useful under various traffic conditions, and tuning the algorithm to be smart enough to effectively deal with different traffic patterns we see in production were some of the areas we spent a lot of time working on before achieving a system that works well for our multi-tenancy environment.

We started with a system that used a single number to quantify "load" on each RangePartition and each server. We first tried the product of request latency and request rate to represent the load on a PS and each RangePartition. This product is easy to compute and reflects the load incurred by the requests on the server and partitions. This design worked well for the majority of the load balancing needs (moving partitions around), but it did not correctly capture high CPU utilization that can occur during scans or high network utilization. Therefore, we now take into consideration request, CPU, and network loads to guide load balancing. However, these metrics are not sufficient to correctly guide splitting decisions.

For splitting, we introduced separate mechanisms to trigger splits of partitions, where we collect hints to find out whether some partitions are reaching their capacity across several metrics. For example, we can trigger partition splits based on request throttling, request timeouts, the size of a partition, etc. Combining split triggers and the load balancing allows the system to quickly split and load balance hot partitions across different servers.

From a high level, the algorithm works as follows. Every N seconds (currently 15 seconds) the PM sorts all RangePartitions based on each of the split triggers. The PM then goes through each partition, looking at the detailed statistics to figure out if it needs to be split using the metrics described above (load, throttling, timeouts, CPU usage, size, etc.). During this process, the PM picks a small number to split for this quantum, and performs the split action on those.

After doing the split pass, the PM sorts all of the PSs based on each of the load balancing metrics - request load, CPU load and network load. It then uses this to identify which PSs are overloaded versus lightly loaded. The PM then chooses the PSs that are heavily loaded and, if there was a recent split from the prior split pass, the PM will offload one of those RangePartitions to a lightly loaded server. If there are still highly loaded PSs (without a recent split to offload), the PM offloads RangePartitions from them to the lightly loaded PSs.

The core load balancing algorithm can be dynamically "swapped out" via configuration updates. WAS includes scripting language support that enables customizing the load balancing logic, such as defining how a partition split can be triggered based on different system metrics. This support gives us flexibility to fine-tune the load balancing algorithm at runtime as well as try new algorithms according to various traffic patterns observed.

Separate Log Files per RangePartition – Performance isolation for storage accounts is critical in a multi-tenancy environment. This requirement is one of the reasons we used separate log streams for each RangePartition, whereas BigTable [4] uses a single log file across all partitions on the same server. Having separate log files enables us to isolate the load time of a RangePartition to just the recent object updates in that RangePartition.

Journaling – When we originally released WAS, it did not have journaling. As a result, we experienced many hiccups with read/writes contending with each other on the same drive, noticeably affecting performance. We did not want to write to two log files (six replicas) like BigTable [4] due to the increased network traffic. We also wanted a way to optimize small writes, especially since we wanted separate log files per RangePartition. These requirements led us to the journal approach with a single log file per RangePartition. We found this optimization quite effective in reducing the latency and providing consistent performance.

Append-only System – Having an append-only system and sealing an extent upon failure have greatly simplified the replication protocol and handling of failure scenarios. In this model, the data is never overwritten once committed to a replica, and, upon failures, the extent is immediately sealed. This model allows the consistency to be enforced across all the replicas via their commit lengths.

Furthermore, the append-only system has allowed us to keep snapshots of the previous states at virtually no extra cost, which has made it easy to provide snapshot/versioning features. It also has allowed us to efficiently provide optimizations like erasure coding. In addition, append-only has been a tremendous benefit for diagnosing issues as well as repairing/recovering the system in case something goes wrong. Since the history of changes is preserved, tools can easily be built to diagnose issues and to repair or recover the system from a corrupted state back to a prior known consistent state. When operating a system at this scale, we cannot emphasize enough the benefit we have seen from using an append-only system for diagnostics and recovery.

An append-based system comes with certain costs. An efficient and scalable garbage collection (GC) system is crucial to keep the space overhead low, and GC comes at a cost of extra I/O. In addition, the data layout on disk may not be the same as the virtual address space of the data abstraction stored, which led us to implement prefetching logic for streaming large data sets back to the client.

End-to-end Checksums – We found it crucial to keep checksums for user data end to end. For example, during a blob upload, once the Front-End server receives the user data, it immediately computes the checksum and sends it along with the data to the backend servers. Then at each layer, the partition server and the stream servers verify the checksum before continuing to process it. If a mismatch is detected, the request is failed. This prevents corrupted data from being committed into the system. We have seen cases where a few servers had hardware issues, and our end-to-end checksum caught such issues and helped maintain data integrity. Furthermore, this end-to-end checksum mechanism also helps identify servers that consistently have hardware issues so we can take them out of rotation and mark them for repair.

Upgrades – A rack in a storage stamp is a fault domain. A concept orthogonal to fault domain is what we call an upgrade domain (a set of servers briefly taken offline at the same time during a rolling upgrade). Servers for each of the three layers are spread evenly across different fault and upgrade domains for the storage service. This way, if a fault domain goes down, we lose at most 1/X of the servers for a given layer, where X is the number of fault domains. Similarly, during a service upgrade at most 1/Y of the servers for a given layer are upgraded at a given time, where Y is the number of upgrade domains. To achieve this, we use rolling upgrades, which enable us to maintain high availability when upgrading the storage service, and we upgrade a single upgrade domain at a time. For example, if we have ten upgrade domains, then upgrading a single domain would potentially upgrade ten percent of the servers from each layer at a time.

During a service upgrade, storage nodes may go offline for a few minutes before coming back online. We need to maintain availability and ensure that enough replicas are available at any point in time. Even though the system is built to tolerate isolated failures, these planned (massive) upgrade "failures" can be more efficiently dealt with instead of being treated as abrupt massive failures. The upgrade process is automated so that it is tractable to manage a large number of these large-scale deployments. The automated upgrade process goes through each upgrade domain one at a time for a given storage stamp. Before taking down an upgrade domain, the upgrade process notifies the PM to move the partitions out of that upgrade domain and notifies the SM to not allocate new extents in that upgrade domain. Furthermore, before taking down any servers, the upgrade process checks with the SM to ensure that there are sufficient extent replicas available for each extent outside the given upgrade domain. After upgrading a given domain, a set of validation tests are run to make sure the system is healthy before proceeding to the next upgrade domain. This validation is crucial for catching issues during the upgrade process and stopping it early should an error occur.

Multiple Data Abstractions from a Single Stack – Our system supports three different data abstraction from the same storage stack: Blobs, Tables and Queues. This design enables all data abstractions to use the same intra-stamp and inter-stamp replication, use the same load balancing system, and realize the benefits from improvements in the stream and partition layers. In addition, because the performance needs of Blobs, Tables, and Queues are different, our single stack approach enables us to reduce costs by running all services on the same set of hardware. Blobs use the massive disk capacity, Tables use the I/O spindles from the many disks on a node (but do not require as much capacity as Blobs), and Queues mainly run in memory. Therefore, we are not only blending different customer's workloads together on shared resources, we are also blending together Blob, Table, and Queue traffic across the same set of storage nodes.

Use of System-defined Object Tables – We chose to use a fixed number of system defined Object Tables to build Blob, Table, and Queue abstractions instead of exposing the raw Object Table semantics to end users. This decision reduces management by our system to only the small set of schemas of our internal, system defined Object Tables. It also provides for easy maintenance and upgrade of the internal data structures and isolates changes of these system defined tables from end user data abstractions.

Offering Storage in Buckets of 100TBs – We currently limit the amount of storage for an account to be no more than 100TB. This constraint allows all of the storage account data to fit within a given storage stamp, especially since our initial storage stamps held only two petabytes of raw data (the new ones hold 20-30PB). To obtain more storage capacity within a single data center, customers use more than one account within that location. This ended up being a reasonable tradeoff for many of our large customers (storing petabytes of data), since they are typically already using multiple accounts to partition their storage across different regions and locations (for local access to data for their customers). Therefore, partitioning their data across accounts within a given location to add more storage often fits into their existing partitioning design. Even so, it does require large services to have account level partitioning logic, which not all customers naturally have as part of their design. Therefore, we plan to increase the amount of storage that can be held within a given storage account in the future.

CAP Theorem – WAS provides high availability with strong consistency guarantees. This combination seems to violate the CAP theorem [2], which says a distributed system cannot have availability, consistency, and partition tolerance at the same time. However, our system, in practice, provides all three of these properties within a storage stamp. This situation is made possible through layering and designing our system around a specific fault model.

The stream layer has a simple append-only data model, which provides high availability in the face of network partitioning and other failures, whereas the partition layer, built upon the stream layer, provides strong consistency guarantees. This layering allows us to decouple the nodes responsible for providing strong consistency from the nodes storing the data with availability in the face of network partitioning. This decoupling and targeting a specific set of faults allows our system to provide high availability and strong consistency in face of various classes of failures we see in practice. For example, the type of network partitioning we have seen within a storage stamp are node failures and top-of-rack (TOR) switch failures. When a TOR switch fails, the given rack will stop being used for traffic — the stream layer will stop using that rack and start using extents on available racks to allow streams to continue writing. In addition, the partition layer will reassign its RangePartitions to partition servers on available racks to allow all of the data to continue to be served with high availability and strong consistency. Therefore, our system is designed to be able to provide strong consistency with high availability for the network partitioning issues that are likely to occur in our system (at the node level as well as TOR failures).

High-performance Debug Logging – We used an extensive debug logging infrastructure throughout the development of WAS. The system writes logs to the local disks of the storage nodes and provides a grep-like utility to do a distributed search across all storage node logs. We do not push these verbose logs off the storage nodes, given the volume of data being logged.

When bringing WAS to production, reducing logging for performance reasons was considered. The utility of verbose logging though made us wary of reducing the amount of logging in the system. Instead, the logging system was optimized to vastly increase its performance and reduce its disk space overhead by automatically tokenizing and compressing output, achieving a system that can log 100's of MB/s with little application performance impact per node. This feature allows retention of many days of verbose debug logs across a cluster. The high-performance logging system and associated log search tools are critical for investigating any problems in production in detail without the need to deploy special code or reproduce problems.

Pressure Point Testing – It is not practical to create tests for all combinations of all complex behaviors that can occur in a large scale distributed system. Therefore, we use what we call Pressure Points to aid in capturing these complex behaviors and

interactions. The system provides a programmable interface for all of the main operations in our system as well as the points in the system to create faults. Some examples of these pressure point commands are: checkpoint a RangePartition, combine a set of RangePartition checkpoints, garbage collect a RangePartition, split/merge/load balance RangePartitions, erasure code or un-erasure code an extent, crash each type of server in a stamp, inject network latencies, inject disk latencies, etc.

The pressure point system is used to trigger all of these interactions during a stress run in specific orders or randomly. This system has been instrumental in finding and reproducing issues from complex interactions that might have taken years to naturally occur on their own.

9. Related Work

Prior studies [9] revealed the challenges in achieving strong consistency and high availability in a poorly-connected network environment. Some systems address this by reducing consistency guarantees to achieve high availability [22,14,6]. But this shifts the burden to the applications to deal with conflicting views of data. For instance, Amazon's SimpleDB was originally introduced with an eventual consistency model and more recently added strongly consistent operations [23]. Van Renesse et. al. [20] has shown, via Chain Replication, the feasibility of building large-scale storage systems providing both strong consistency and high availability, which was later extended to allow reading from any replica [21]. Given our customer needs for strong consistency, we set out to provide a system that can provide strong consistency with high availability along with partition tolerance for our fault model.

As in many other highly-available distributed storage systems [6,14,1,5], WAS also provides geo-redundancy. Some of these systems put geo-replication on the critical path of the live application requests, whereas we made a design trade-off to take a classical asynchronous geo-replication approach [18] and leave it off the critical path. Performing the geo-replication completely asynchronously allows us to provide better write latency for applications, and allows more optimizations, such as batching and compaction for geo-replication, and efficient use of cross-data center bandwidth. The tradeoff is that if there is a disaster and an abrupt failover needs to occur, then there is unavailability during the failover and a potential loss of recent updates to a customer's account.

The closest system to ours is GFS [8,15] combined with BigTable [4]. A few differences from these prior publications are: (1) GFS allows relaxed consistency across replicas and does not guarantee that all replicas are bitwise the same, whereas WAS provides that guarantee, (2) BigTable combines multiple tablets into a single commit log and writes them to two GFS files in parallel to avoid GFS hiccups, whereas we found we could work around both of these by using journaling in our stream layer, and (3) we provide a scalable Blob storage system and batch Table transactions integrated into a BigTable-like framework. In addition, we describe how WAS automatically load balances, splits, and merges RangePartitions according to application traffic demands.

10. Conclusions

The Windows Azure Storage platform implements essential services for developers of cloud based solutions. The combination of strong consistency, global partitioned namespace, and disaster recovery has been important customer features in WAS's multi-tenancy environment. WAS runs a disparate set of workloads with various peak usage profiles from many customers on the same set of hardware. This significantly reduces storage cost since the amount of resources to be provisioned is significantly less than the sum of the peak resources required to run all of these workloads on dedicated hardware.

As our examples demonstrate, the three storage abstractions, Blobs, Tables, and Queues, provide mechanisms for storage and workflow control for a wide range of applications. Not mentioned, however, is the ease with which the WAS system can be utilized. For example, the initial version of the Facebook/Twitter search ingestion engine took one engineer only two months from the start of development to launching the service. This experience illustrates our service's ability to empower customers to easily develop and deploy their applications to the cloud.

Additional information on Windows Azure and Windows Azure Storage is available at http://www.microsoft.com/windowsazure/.

Acknowledgements

We would like to thank Geoff Voelker, Greg Ganger, and anonymous reviewers for providing valuable feedback on this paper.

We would like to acknowledge the creators of Cosmos (Bing's storage system): Darren Shakib, Andrew Kadatch, Sam McKelvie, Jim Walsh and Jonathan Forbes. We started Windows Azure 5 years ago with Cosmos as our intra-stamp replication system. The data abstractions and append-only extent-based replication system presented in Section 4 was created by them. We extended Cosmos to create our stream layer by adding mechanisms to allow us to provide strong consistency in coordination with the partition layer, stream operations to allow us to efficiently split/merge partitions, journaling, erasure coding, spindle anti-starvation, read load-balancing, and other improvements.

We would also like to thank additional contributors to Windows Azure Storage: Maneesh Sah, Matt Hendel, Kavitha Golconda, Jean Ghanem, Joe Giardino, Shuitao Fan, Justin Yu, Dinesh Haridas, Jay Sreedharan, Monilee Atkinson, Harshawardhan Gadgil, Phaneesh Kuppahalli, Nima Hakami, Maxim Mazeev, Andrei Marinescu, Garret Buban, Ioan Oltean, Ritesh Kumar, Richard Liu, Rohit Galwankar, Brihadeeshwar Venkataraman, Jayush Luniya, Serdar Ozler, Karl Hsueh, Ming Fan, David Goebel, Joy Ganguly, Ishai Ben Aroya, Chun Yuan, Philip Taron, Pradeep Gunda, Ryan Zhang, Shyam Antony, Qi Zhang, Madhav Pandya, Li Tan, Manish Chablani, Amar Gadkari, Haiyong Wang, Hakon Verespej, Ramesh Shankar, Surinder Singh, Ryan Wu, Amruta Machetti, Abhishek Singh Baghel, Vineet Sarda, Alex Nagy, Orit Mazor, and Kayla Bunch.

Finally we would like to thank Amitabh Srivastava, G.S. Rana, Bill Laing, Satya Nadella, Ray Ozzie, and the rest of the Windows Azure team for their support.

Reference

[1] J. Baker et al., "Megastore: Providing Scalable, Highly Available Storage for Interactive Services," in *Conf. on Innovative Data Systems Research*, 2011.

[2] Eric A. Brewer, "Towards Robust Distributed Systems. (Invited Talk)," in *Principles of Distributed Computing*, Portland, Oregon, 2000.

[3] M. Burrows, "The Chubby Lock Service for Loosely-Coupled Distributed Systems," in *OSDI*, 2006.

[4] F. Chang et al., "Bigtable: A Distributed Storage System for Structured Data," in *OSDI*, 2006.

[5] B. Cooper et al., "PNUTS: Yahoo!'s Hosted Data Serving Platform," *VLDB*, vol. 1, no. 2, 2008.

[6] G. DeCandia et al., "Dynamo: Amazon's Highly Available Key-value Store," in *SOSP*, 2007.

[7] Cristian Estan and George Varghese, "New Directions in Traffic Measurement and Accounting," in *SIGCOMM*, 2002.

[8] S. Ghemawat, H. Gobioff, and S.T. Leung, "The Google File System," in *SOSP*, 2003.

[9] J. Gray, P. Helland, P. O'Neil, and D. Shasha, "The Dangers of Replication and a Solution," in *SIGMOD*, 1996.

[10] Albert Greenberg et al., "VL2: A Scalable and Flexible Data Center Network," *Communications of the ACM*, vol. 54, no. 3, pp. 95-104, 2011.

[11] Y. Hu and Q. Yang, "DCD—Disk Caching Disk: A New Approach for Boosting I/O Performance," in *ISCA*, 1996.

[12] H.T. Kung and John T. Robinson, "On Optimistic Methods for Concurrency Control," *ACM Transactions on Database Systems*, vol. 6, no. 2, pp. 213-226, June 1981.

[13] Leslie Lamport, "The Part-Time Parliament," *ACM Transactions on Computer Systems*, vol. 16, no. 2, pp. 133-169, May 1998.

[14] A. Malik and P. Lakshman, "Cassandra: a decentralized structured storage system," *SIGOPS Operating System Review*, vol. 44, no. 2, 2010.

[15] M. McKusick and S. Quinlan, "GFS: Evolution on Fast-forward," *ACM File Systems*, vol. 7, no. 7, 2009.

[16] S. Mysore, B. Agrawal, T. Sherwood, N. Shrivastava, and S. Suri, "Profiling over Adaptive Ranges," in *Symposium on Code Generation and Optimization*, 2006.

[17] P. O'Neil, E. Cheng, D. Gawlick, and E. O'Neil, "The Log-Structured Merge-Tree (LSM-tree)," *Acta Informatica - ACTA*, vol. 33, no. 4, 1996.

[18] H. Patterson et al., "SnapMirror: File System Based Asynchronous Mirroring for Disaster Recovery," in *USENIX-FAST*, 2002.

[19] Irving S. Reed and Gustave Solomon, "Polynomial Codes over Certain Finite Fields," *Journal of the Society for Industrial and Applied Mathematics*, vol. 8, no. 2, pp. 300-304, 1960.

[20] R. Renesse and F. Schneider, "Chain Replication for Supporting High Throughput and Availability," in *USENIX-OSDI*, 2004.

[21] J. Terrace and M. Freedman, "Object Storage on CRAQ: High-throughput chain replication for read-mostly workloads," in *USENIX'09*, 2009.

[22] D. Terry, K. Petersen M. Theimer, A. Demers, M. Spreitzer, and C. Hauser, "Managing Update Conflicts in Bayou, A Weakly Connected Replicated Storage System," in *ACM SOSP*, 1995.

[23] W. Vogel, "All Things Distributed - Choosing Consistency," in *http://www.allthingsdistributed.com/2010/02/strong_consistency_simpledb.html*, 2010.

An Empirical Study on Configuration Errors in Commercial and Open Source Systems

Zuoning Yin*, Xiao Ma*, Jing Zheng†, Yuanyuan Zhou†, Lakshmi N. Bairavasundaram‡, and Shankar Pasupathy‡

*Univ. of Illinois at Urbana-Champaign, †Univ. of California, San Diego, ‡NetApp, Inc.

ABSTRACT

Configuration errors (i.e., misconfigurations) are among the dominant causes of system failures. Their importance has inspired many research efforts on detecting, diagnosing, and fixing misconfigurations; such research would benefit greatly from a real-world characteristic study on misconfigurations. Unfortunately, few such studies have been conducted in the past, primarily because historical misconfigurations usually have not been recorded rigorously in databases.

In this work, we undertake one of the first attempts to conduct a real-world misconfiguration characteristic study. We study a total of 546 real world misconfigurations, including 309 misconfigurations from a commercial storage system deployed at thousands of customers, and 237 from four widely used open source systems (CentOS, MySQL, Apache HTTP Server, and OpenLDAP). Some of our major findings include: (1) A majority of misconfigurations (70.0%~85.5%) are due to mistakes in setting configuration parameters; however, a significant number of misconfigurations are due to compatibility issues or component configurations (i.e., not parameter-related). (2) 38.1%~53.7% of parameter mistakes are caused by illegal parameters that clearly violate some format or rules, motivating the use of an automatic configuration checker to detect these misconfigurations. (3) A significant percentage (12.2%~29.7%) of parameter-based mistakes are due to inconsistencies between different parameter values. (4) 21.7%~57.3% of the misconfigurations involve configurations external to the examined system, some even on entirely different hosts. (5) A significant portion of misconfigurations can cause hard-to-diagnose failures, such as crashes, hangs, or severe performance degradation, indicating that systems should be better-equipped to handle misconfigurations.

Categories and Subject Descriptors: D.4.5 [Operating Systems]: Reliability

General Terms: Reliability, Management

Keywords: Misconfigurations, characteristic study

1. INTRODUCTION

1.1 Motivation

Configuration errors (i.e., misconfigurations) have a great impact on system availability. For example, a recent misconfiguration at Facebook prevented its 500 million users from accessing the website for several hours [15]. Last year, a misconfiguration brought down the entire ".se" domain for more than an hour [6], affecting almost 1 million hosts.

Not only do misconfigurations have high impact, they are also prevalent. Gray's pioneering paper on system faults [11] stated that administrator errors were responsible for 42% of system failures in high-end mainframes. Similarly, Patterson et al. [30] observed that more than 50% of failures were due to operator errors in telephone networks and Internet systems. Studies have also observed that a majority of operator errors (or administrator errors) are misconfigurations [23, 29]. Further, of the issues reported in COMP-A's[1] customer-support database (used in this study), around 27% are labeled as configuration-related (as shown later in Figure 1(a) in Section 3). This percentage is second only to hardware failures and is much bigger than that of software bugs.

Moreover, configuration errors are also expensive to troubleshoot. Kappor [16] found that 17% of the total cost of ownership of today's desktop computers goes toward technical support, and a large fraction of that is troubleshooting misconfigurations.

Given the data on the prevalence and impact of misconfigurations, several recent research efforts [3, 17, 18, 35, 38, 41] have proposed ideas to detect, diagnose, and automatically fix misconfigurations. For example, PeerPressure [38] uses statistics methods on a large set of configurations to identify single configuration parameter errors. Chronus [41] periodically checkpoints disk state and automatically searches for configuration changes that may have caused the misconfiguration. ConfAid [3] uses data flow analysis to trace the configuration error back to a particular configuration entry. AutoBash [35] leverages a speculative OS kernel to automatically try out fixes from a solution database in order to find a proper solution for a configuration problem. Further, ConfErr [17] provides a useful framework with which users can inject configuration errors of three types: typos, structural mistakes, and semantic mistakes. In addition to research efforts, various tools are available to aid users in managing

---

[1]We are required to keep the company anonymous.

Major Findings on Prevalence and Severity of Configuration Issues (Section 3)
Similar to results from previous studies [11, 29, 30], data from COMP-A shows that a significant portion (27%) of customer cases are related to configuration issues.
Configuration issues cause the largest percentage (31%) of high-severity support requests.

Major Findings on Misconfiguration Types (Section 4)
Configuration-parameter mistakes account for the majority (70.0%~85.5%) of the examined misconfigurations.
However, a significant portion (14.5%~30.0%) of the examined misconfigurations are caused by software compatibility issues and component configuration, which are not well addressed in literature.
38.1%~53.7% of parameter misconfigurations are caused by illegal parameters that violate formats or semantic rules defined by the system, and can be potentially detected by checkers that inspect against these rules.
A significant portion (12.2%~29.7%) of parameter mistakes are due to value-based inconsistency, calling for an inconsistency checker or a better configuration design that does not require users to worry about such error-prone consistency constraints.
Although most misconfigurations are located within each examined system, still a significant portion (21.7%~57.3%) involve configurations beyond the system itself or span over multiple hosts.

Major Findings on System Reactions to Misconfigurations (Section 5)
Only 7.2%~15.5% of the studied misconfiguration problems provide explicit messages that pinpoint the configuration error.
Some misconfigurations have caused the systems to crash, hang or have severe performance degradation, making failure diagnosis a challenging task.
Messages that pinpoint configuration errors can shorten the diagnosis time by 3 to 13 times as compared to the cases with ambiguous messages or by 1.2 to 14.5 times as compared to cases with no messages.

Major Findings on Causes of Misconfigurations (Section 6)
The majority of misconfigurations are related to first-time use of desired functionality. For more complex systems, a significant percentage (16.7%~32.4%) of misconfigurations were introduced into systems that used to work.
By looking into the 100 used-to-work cases (32.4% of the total) at COMP-A, 46% of them are attributed to configuration parameter changes due to routine maintenance, configuring for new functionality, system outages, etc, and can benefit from tracking configuration changes. The remainder are caused by non-parameter related issues such as hardware changes (18%), external environmental changes (8%), resource exhaustion (14%), and software upgrades(14%).

Major Findings on Impact of Misconfigurations (Section 7)
Although most studied misconfiguration cases only lead to partial unavailability of the system, 16.1%~47.3% of them make the systems to be fully unavailable or cause severe performance degradation.

Table 1: Major findings on misconfiguration characteristics. Please take our methodology into consideration when you interpret and draw any conclusions.

system configuration; for example, storage systems have provisioning tools [13, 14, 25, 26], misconfiguration-detection tools [24], and upgrade assistants that check for compatibility issues [24]. The above research directions and tools would benefit greatly from a characteristic study of real-world misconfigurations. Moreover, understanding the major types and root causes of misconfigurations may help guide developers to better design configuration logic and requirements, and testers to better verify user interfaces, thereby reducing the likelihood of configuration mistakes by users.

Unfortunately, in comparison to software bugs that have well-maintained bug databases and have benefited from many software bug characteristic studies [5, 19, 36, 37], a misconfiguration characteristic study is much harder, mainly because historical misconfigurations usually have not been recorded rigorously in databases. For example, developers record information about the context in the code for bugs, the causes of bugs, and how they were fixed; they also focus on eliminating or coalescing duplicate bug reports. On the other hand, the description of misconfigurations is user-driven, the fixes may be recorded simply as pointers to manuals and best-practice documents, and there is no duplicate elimination. As a result, analyzing and understanding misconfigurations is a much harder, and more importantly, manual task.

1.2 Our Contributions

In this paper, we perform one of the first characteristic studies of real-world misconfigurations in both commercial and open-source systems, using a total of 546 misconfiguration cases. The commercial system is a storage system from COMP-A deployed at thousands of customers. It has a well-maintained customer-issues database. The open-source systems include widely used system software: CentOS, MySQL, Apache, and OpenLDAP. The misconfiguration issues we examine are primarily user-reported. Therefore, our study is a manual analysis of user descriptions of misconfigurations, aided by discussions with developers, support engineers, and system architects of these systems to ensure correct understanding of these cases. Our study was approximately 21 person-months of effort, excluding the help from several COMP-A engineers and open-source developers.

We study the types, patterns, causes, system reactions, and impact of misconfigurations:

- We examine the prevalence and reported severity of configuration issues (includes, but not limited to misconfigurations) as compared to other support issues in COMP-A's customer-issues database.

- We develop a simple taxonomy of misconfiguration types: *parameter*, *compatibility*, and *component*, and identify the prevalence of each type. Given the prevalence of parameter-based misconfigurations, we further analyze its types and observable patterns.

- We identify how systems react to misconfigurations: whether error messages are provided, whether systems experience failures or severe performance issues, etc. Given that error messages are important for diagnosis and fixes, we also investigate the relationship between message clarity and diagnosis time.

- We study the frequency of different causes of misconfigurations such as first-time use, software upgrades, hardware changes, etc.

- Finally, we examine the impact of misconfigurations, including the impact on system availability and performance.

The major findings of the study are summarized in Table 1. While we believe that the misconfiguration cases we examined are fairly representative of misconfigurations in large system software, we do not intend to draw any general conclusions about all applications. In particular, we remind readers that all of the characteristics and findings in this study should be taken with the specific system types and our methodology in mind (discussed in Section 2).

We will release our open-source misconfiguration cases to share with the research community.

2. METHODOLOGY

This section describes our methodology for analyzing misconfigurations. There are unique challenges in obtaining and analyzing a large set of real-world misconfigurations. Historically, unlike bugs that usually have Bugzillas as repositories, misconfigurations are not recorded rigorously. Much of the information is in the form of unstructured textual descriptions and there is no systematic way to report misconfiguration cases. Therefore, in order to overcome these challenges, we manually analyzed reported misconfiguration cases by studying manuals, instructions, source code, and knowledge bases of each system. For some hard cases, we contacted the corresponding engineers through emails or phone calls to understand them thoroughly.

2.1 Data Sets

We examine misconfiguration data for one commercial system and four open-source systems. The commercial system is a storage system from COMP-A. The core software running in such system is proprietary to COMP-A. The four open-source systems include CentOS, MySQL, Apache HTTP server, and OpenLDAP. We select these software systems for two reasons: (1) they are mature and widely used, and (2) they have a large set of misconfiguration cases reported by users. While we cannot draw conclusions about any general system, our examined systems are representative of large, server-based systems. We focus only on software misconfigurations; we do not have sufficient data for hardware misconfigurations on systems running the open-source software.

COMP-A storage systems consist of multiple components including storage controllers, disk shelves, and interconnections between them (e.g., switches). These systems can be configured in a variety of ways for customers with different degrees of expertise. For instance, COMP-A offers tools that simplify system configuration. We cannot ascertain from the data whether users configured the systems directly or used tools for configuration.

The misconfiguration cases we study are from COMP-A's customer-issues database, which records problems reported

System	Total Cases	Sampled Cases	Used Cases
COMP-A	confidential	1000	309
CentOS	4338	521	60
MySQL	3340	720	55
Apache	8513	616	60
OpenLDAP	1447	472	62
Total	N/A	3329	546

Table 2: The systems we studied and the number of misconfiguration cases we identified for each of them.

by customers. For accuracy, we considered only closed cases, i.e. cases that COMP-A has provided a solution to the users. Also, to be as relevant as possible, we focused on only cases over the last two years. COMP-A's support process is rigorous, especially in comparison to open-source projects. For example, when a customer case is closed, the support engineer needs to record information about the root cause as well as resolution. Such information is very valuable for our study. There are many cases labeled as "Configuration-related" by support engineers and it is prohibitively difficult to study all of them. Therefore, we randomly sampled 1,000 cases labeled as related to configuration. Not all 1,000 cases are misconfigurations because more than half of them are simply customer questions related to how the system should be configured. Hence, we did not consider them as misconfigurations. We also pruned out a few cases for which we cannot determine whether a configuration error occurred. After careful manual examination, we identified 309 cases as misconfigurations, as shown in Table 2.

Besides COMP-A storage systems, we also study four open-source systems: CentOS, MySQL, Apache HTTP server, and OpenLDAP. All of them are mature software systems, well-maintained and widely used. CentOS is an enterprise-class Linux distribution, MySQL is a database server, Apache is a web server, and OpenLDAP is a directory server.

For open-source software, the misconfiguration cases come from three sources: official user-support forums, mailing lists, and ServerFault.com (a large question-answering website focusing on system administration). Whenever necessary, scripts were used to identify cases related to systems of interest, as well as to remove those that were not confirmed by users. We then randomly sampled from all the remaining candidate cases (the candidate set sizes and the sample set sizes are also shown in Table 2) and manually examined each case to check if it is a misconfiguration. Our manual examination yielded a total of 237 misconfiguration cases from these four open-source systems. The yield ratio (used cases/sampled cases) is low for these open-source projects because we observe a higher ratio of cases that are customer questions among the samples from open source projects as compared to the commercial data.

2.2 Threats to Validity and Limitations

Many characteristic studies suffer from limitations such as the systems or workloads not being representative of the entire population, the semantics of events such as failures differing across different systems, and so on. Given that misconfiguration cases have considerably less information than ideal to work with, and that we need to perform all of the analysis manually, our study has a few more limitations. We believe that these limitations do not invalidate our results; at the same time, we urge the reader to focus on

System	Parameter	Compatibility	Component	Total
COMP-A	246 (79.6±2.4%)	31 (10.0±1.8%)	32 (10.4±1.8%)	309
CentOS	42 (70.0±3.7%)	11 (18.3±3.1%)	7 (11.7±2.6%)	60
MySQL	47 (85.5±2.3%)	0	8 (14.5±2.3%)	55
Apache	50 (83.4±2.8%)	5 (8.3±2.1%)	5 (8.3±2.1%)	60
OpenLDAP	49 (79.0±3.0%)	7 (11.2±2.3%)	6 (9.7±2.2%)	62

Table 3: The numbers of misconfigurations of each type. Their percentages and the sampling errors are also shown.

overall trends and not on precise numbers. We expect that most systems and processes for configuration errors would have similar limitations to the ones we face. Therefore, we hope that the limitations of our methodology would inspire techniques and processes that can be used to record misconfigurations more rigorously and in a format amenable to automated analysis.

Sampling: To make the time and effort manageable, we sampled the data sets. As shown in Table 2, our sample rates are statistically significant and our collections are also large enough to be statistically meaningful [10]. In our result tables, we also show the confidence interval on ratios with a 95% confidence level based on our sampling rates.

Users: The sources from which we sample contain only user-reported cases. Users may choose not to report trivial misconfigurations. Also, it is more likely that novice users may report more misconfiguration problems. We do not have sufficient data to judge whether a user is a novice or an expert. But, with new systems or major revisions of an existing system deployed to the field, there will always be new users. Therefore, our findings are still valid.

User environment: Some misconfigurations may have been prevented, or detected and resolved automatically by the system or other tools. This scenario is particularly true for COMP-A systems. At the same time, some, but not all, COMP-A customers use the tools provided by COMP-A and we cannot distinguish the two in the data.

System versions: We do not differentiate between system versions. Given that software is constantly evolving, it is possible that some of the reported configuration issues may not apply to some versions, or have already been addressed in system development (e.g., automatically correcting configuration mistakes, providing better error messages, etc.).

Overall, our study is representative of user-reported misconfigurations that are more challenging, urgent, or important.

3. IMPORTANCE OF CONFIGURATION ISSUES

We first examine how prevalent configuration issues are in the field and how severely they impact users using data from the last two years from COMP-A's customer-issues database. There are five root causes classified by COMP-A engineers after resolving each customer-reported problem: *configuration* (configuration-related), *hardware failure*, *bug*, *customer environment* (cases caused by power supplies, cooling systems, or other environmental issues), and *user knowledge* (cases where customers request information about the system). Each case is also labeled with a severity level by customer-support engineers – from "1" to "4," based on how severe the problem is in the field; cases with severity level of

"1" or "2" are usually considered as high-severity cases that require prompt responses.

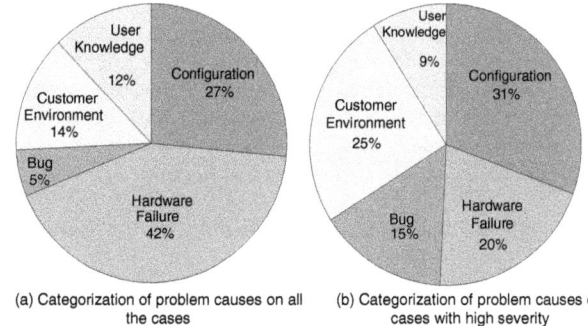

(a) Categorization of problem causes on all the cases
(b) Categorization of problem causes on cases with high severity

Figure 1: Root cause distribution among the customer problems reported to COMP-A

Figure 1(a) shows the distribution of customer cases based on different root causes. Figure 1(b) further shows the distribution of *high-severity* cases. We do not have the results for the open source systems due to unavailability of such labeled data (i.e., customer issues caused by hardware, software bugs, configurations, etc.).

Among all five categories, configuration-related issues contribute to 27% of the cases and are the second-most pervasive root cause of customer problems. While this number is potentially inflated by customer requests for information on configuration (as seen in our manual analysis), it shows that system configuration is nontrivial and of particular concern for customers. Furthermore, considering only high-severity cases, configuration-related issues become the most significant contributor to support cases; they contribute to 31% of high-severity cases. We expect that hardware issues are not as severe (smaller percentage of high-severity cases than of all cases) due to availability of redundancy and ease of fixes – the hardware can be replaced easily.

Finding 1.1: *Similar to the results from previous studies [11, 30, 29], data from COMP-A shows that a significant percentage (27%) of customer cases are related to configuration issues.*

Finding 1.2: *Configuration issues cause the largest percentage (31%) of high-severity support requests.*

4. MISCONFIGURATION TYPES
4.1 Distribution among Different Types

To examine misconfigurations in detail, we first look at the different types of misconfigurations that occur in the real world and their distributions. We classify the examined misconfiguration cases into three categories (as shown in Table 3). *Parameter* refers to configuration parameter mistakes; a parameter could be either an entry in a configuration file or a console command for configuring certain functionality. *Compatibility* refers to misconfigurations related to

| System | Legal | Illegal | | | | | |
| | | Format | | Value | | | |
		Lexical Mistakes	Syntax Mistakes	Typo	Value Inconsistent w/ Other Values	Value Inconsistent w/ Environment	Others
COMP-A	114(46.3±6.1%)	10(4.1±2.4%)	5(2.0±1.7%)	3(1.2±1.3%)	73 (29.7±5.6%)	32(13.0±4.1%)	9(3.7±2.3%)
CentOS	26 (61.9±13.8%)	1(2.4±4.4%)	0	2(4.8±6.0%)	6 (14.3±10.0%)	6(14.3±10.0%)	1(2.4±6.0%)
MySQL	24(51.1±12.7%)	1(2.1±3.6%)	0	0	7(14.9%±9.0%)	8(17.0%±9.5%)	7(14.9%±9.0%)
Apache	27(54.0±13.3%)	3(6.0±6.3%)	3(6.0±6.3%)	1(2.0±3.7%)	7(14.0±9.3%)	5(10.0±8.0%)	4(8.0±7.3%)
OpenLDAP	23(46.9±11.5%)	7(14.3±8.0%)	11(22.4±9.6%)	0	6(12.2±7.5%)	1(2.0±3.2%)	1(2.0±3.2%)

Table 4: The distribution of different types of parameter mistakes for each application.

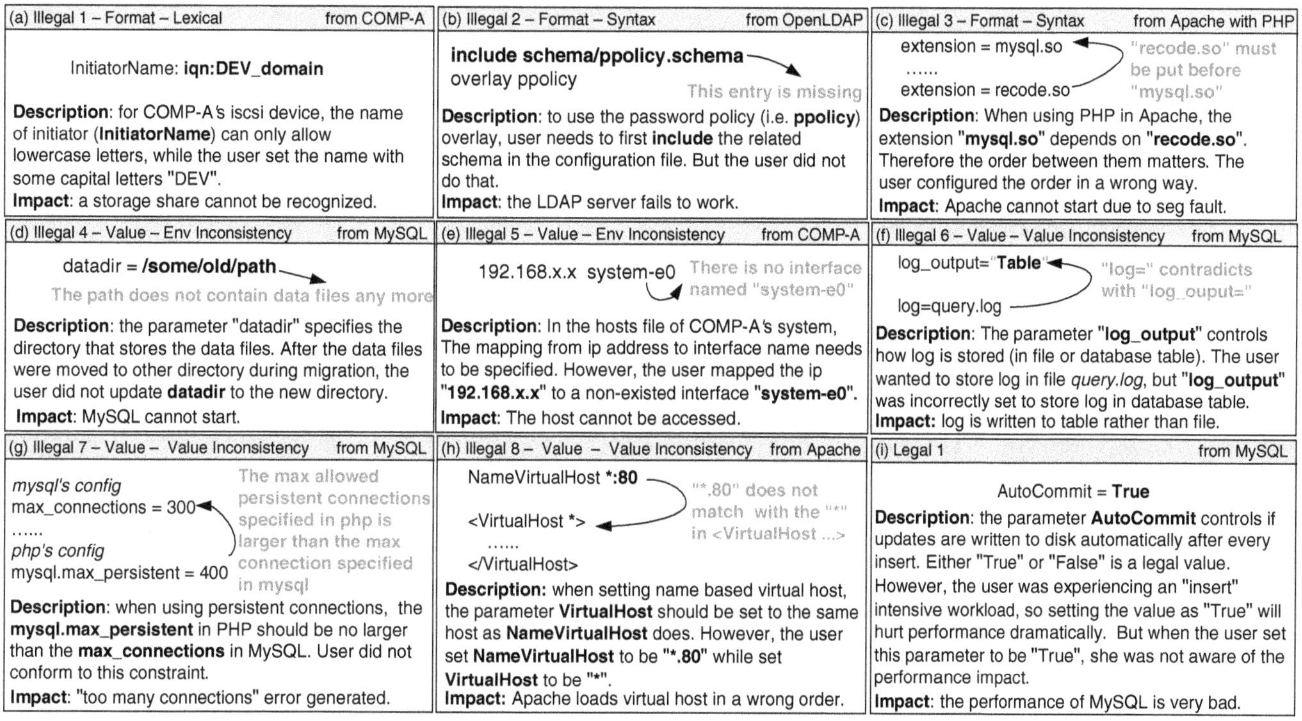

Figure 2: Examples of different types of configuration parameter related mistakes. (*legal* vs. *illegal*, *lexical error*, *syntax error* and *inconsistency error*)

software compatibility (i.e. whether different components or modules are compatible with each other). *Component* refers to other remaining software misconfigurations (e.g., a module is missing).

Finding 2.1: *Configuration parameter mistakes account for the majority (70.0%~85.5%) of the examined misconfigurations.*

Finding 2.2: *However, a significant portion (14.5%~30.0%) of the examined misconfigurations are caused by software compatibility and component configuration, which are not well addressed in literature.*

First, Finding 2.1 supports recent research efforts [3, 35, 38, 41] on detecting, diagnosing, or fixing parameter-based misconfigurations. Second, this finding perhaps indicates that system designers should have fewer "knobs" (i.e. parameters) for users to configure and tune. Whenever possible, auto-configuration [44] should be preferred because in many cases users may not be experienced enough to set the knobs appropriately.

While parameter-based misconfigurations are the most common, Finding 2.2 calls for attention to investigating solu-

tions dealing with non-parameter-based configurations such as software incompatibility, etc. For example, software may need to be shipped as a complete package, deployed as an appliance (either virtual or physical), or delivered as a service (SaaS) to reduce these incompatibilities and general configuration issues.

4.2 Parameter Misconfigurations

Given the prevalence of parameter-based mistakes, we study the different types of such mistakes (as shown in Table 4), the number of parameters needed for diagnosing or fixing a parameter misconfiguration, and the problem domain of these mistakes.

Types of mistakes in parameter configuration. First, we look at parameter mistakes that clearly violate some implicit or explicit configuration rules related to format, syntax, or semantics. We call them *illegal* misconfigurations because they are unacceptable to the examined system. Figures 2(a)~(h) show eight such examples. These types of misconfigurations may be detected automatically by checking against configuration rules.

In contrast, some other parameter mistakes are perfectly *legal*, but they are incorrect simply because they do not deliver the functionality or performance desired by users, like the example in Figure 2(i). These kinds of mistakes are difficult to detect unless users' expectation and intent can be specified separately and checked against configuration settings. More user training may reduce these kinds of mistakes, as can simplified system configuration logic, especially for things that can be auto-configured by the system.

Finding 3.1: *38.1%~53.7% of parameter misconfigurations are caused by illegal parameters that clearly violate some format or semantic rules defined by the system, and can be potentially detected by checkers that inspect against these rules.*

Finding 3.2: *However, a large portion (46.3% ~61.9%) of the parameter misconfigurations have perfectly legal parameters but do not deliver the functionality intended by users. These cases are more difficult to detect by automatic checkers and may require more user training or better configuration design.*

We subcategorize illegal parameter misconfigurations into *illegal format*, in which some parameters do not obey format rules such as lower case, field separators, etc.; and *illegal value*, in which the parameter format is correct but the value violates some constraints, e.g., the value of a parameter should be smaller than some threshold. We find that illegal-value misconfigurations are more common than illegal-format misconfigurations in most systems, perhaps because format is easier to test against and thereby avoid.

Illegal format misconfigurations include both *lexical* and *syntax* mistakes. Similar to lexical and syntax errors in program languages, a *lexical* mistake violates the grammar of a single parameter, like the example shown in Figure 2(a); a *syntax* mistake violates structural or order constraints of the format, like the example shown in Figure 2(b) and 2(c). As shown in Table 4, up to 14.3% of the parameter misconfigurations are lexical mistakes, and up to 22.4% are syntax mistakes.

Illegal value misconfigurations mainly consist of two type of mistakes, "*value inconsistency*" and "*environment inconsistency*". *Value inconsistency* means that some parameter settings violate some relationship constraints with some other parameters, while *environment inconsistency* means that some parameter's setting is inconsistent with the system environment (i.e., physical configuration). Figure 2(d) and 2(e) are two environment inconsistency examples. As shown in Table 4, value inconsistency accounts for 12.2%~29.7% of the parameter misconfigurations, while environment inconsistency contributes 2.0%~17.0%. Both can be detected by some well-designed checkers as long as the constraints are known and enforceable.

Figure 2(f), 2(g), and 2(h) present three value-inconsistency examples. In the first example, the name of the log file is specified while the log output is chosen to be database table. In the second example, two parameters from two *different* but related configuration files contradict each other. In the third example, two parameters, *NameVirtualHost* and *VirtualHost*, have unmatched values ("*.80" v.s. "*").

Finding 4: *A significant portion (12.2%~29.7%) of parameter mistakes are due to value-based inconsistency, calling for an inconsistency checker or a better configuration design that does not require users to worry about such error-prone consistency constraints.*

Number of erroneous parameters. As some previous work on detecting or diagnosing misconfiguration focuses on only *single* configuration parameter mistakes, we look into what percentages of parameter mistakes involve only a single parameter.

System	Number of Involved Parameters		
	One	Multiple	Unknown
COMP-A	117(47.6%±6.1%)	117(47.6%±6.1%)	12(4.8%±2.6%)
CentOS	30(71.4%±12.8%)	10(23.8%±12.1%)	2(4.8%±6.0%)
MySQL	35(74.5%±11.0%)	11(23.4%±10.7%)	1(2.1%±3.6%)
Apache	31(62.0%±13.0%)	16(32.0%±12.4%)	3(6.0%±6.3%)
OpenLDAP	18(36.7%±11.1%)	30(61.2%±11.2%)	1(2.0%±3.2%)

System	Number of Fixed Parameters		
	One	Multiple	Unknown
COMP-A	189(76.8%±5.1%)	44(17.9%±4.7%)	13(5.3%±2.7%)
CentOS	33(78.6%±11.7%)	7(16.7%±10.6%)	2(4.8%±6.1%)
MySQL	39(83.0%±9.5%)	7(14.9%±9.0%)	1(2.1%±3.6%)
Apache	33(66.0%±12.7%)	14(28.0%±12.0%)	3(6.0%±6.3%)
OpenLDAP	29(59.2%±11.3%)	17(34.7%±11.0%)	3(6.1%±5.5%)

Table 5: The number of parameters in the configuration parameter mistakes.

Table 5 shows the number of parameters involved in configuration as well as the number of parameters that were changed to fix the misconfiguration. These numbers may not be the same because a mistake may involve two parameters, but can be fixed by changing only one parameter. Our analysis indicates that about 23.4%~61.2% of the parameter mistakes involve multiple parameters. Examples of cases where multiple parameters are involved are cases with value inconsistencies (see above).

In comparison, about 14.9%~34.7% of the examined misconfigurations require fixing multiple parameters. For example, the performance of a system could be influenced by several parameters. To achieve the expected level of performance, all these parameters need to be considered and set correctly.

Finding 5.1: *The majority (36.7%~74.5%) of parameter mistakes can be diagnosed by considering only one parameter, and an even higher percentage(59.2%~83.0%) of them can be fixed by changing the value of only one parameter.*

Finding 5.2: *However, a significant portion (23.4%~61.2%) of parameter mistakes involve more than one parameter, and 14.9%~34.7% require fixing more than one parameter.*

Problem domains of parameter mistakes. We also study what problem domains each parameter mistake falls under. We decide the domain based on the functionality of the involved parameter. Four major problem domains – network, permission/privilege, performance, and devices – are observed. Overall, 18.3% of examined parameter mistakes relate to how the network is configured; 16.8% relate to permission/privilege; 7.1% relate to performance adjustment. For the COMP-A systems and CentOs (the OSes), 8.5%~26.2% of examined parameter mistakes are about device configurations.

4.3 Software Incompatibility

Besides parameter-related mistakes, software incompatibility is another major cause of misconfigurations (up to 18.3%, see Table 3). Software-incompatibility issues refer to improper combinations of components or their versions. They could be caused by incompatible libraries, applications, or even operating system kernels.

One may think that system upgrades are more likely to cause software-incompatibility issues, but we find that only 18.5% of the software-incompatibility issues are caused by upgrades. One possible reason is that both developers and users already put significant effort into the process of upgrades. For example, COMP-A provides a tool to help with upgrades that creates an easy-to-understand report of all known compatibility issues, and recommends ways to resolve them.

Some of the misconfiguration cases we analyze show that package-management systems (e.g., RPM [34] and Debian dpkg [8]) can help address many software-incompatibility issues. For example, in one of the studied cases, the user failed to install the *mod_proxy_html* module because the existing *libxml2* library was not compatible with this module.

Package-management systems may work well for systems with a standard set of packages. For systems that require multiple applications from different vendors to work together, it is more challenging. An alternative to package management systems is to use self-contained packaging, i.e. integrating dependent components into one installation package and minimizing the requirements on the target system. To further reduce dependencies, one could deliver a system as virtual machine images (e.g., Amazon Machine Image) or appliances (e.g., COMP-A's storage systems). The latter may even eliminate hardware-compatibility issues.

4.4 Component Misconfiguration

Subtype	Number of Cases
Missing component	15(25.9%)
Placement	13(22.4%)
File format	3(5.2%)
Insufficient resource	15(25.7%)
Stale data	3(5.2%)
Others	9(15.5%)

Table 6: Subtypes of component misconfigurations.

Component misconfigurations are configuration errors that are neither parameter mistakes nor compatibility problems. They are more related to how the system is organized and how resources are supplied. A sizable portion (8.3%~14.5%) of our examined misconfigurations are of this category. Here, we further classify them into the following five subtypes based on root causes: (1) *Missing component*: certain components (modules or libraries) are missing; (2) *Placement*: certain files or components are not in the place expected by the system; (3) *File format*: the format of a certain file is not acceptable to the system. For example, an Apache web server on a Linux host cannot load a configuration file because it is in the MS-DOS format with unrecognized new line characters. (4) *Insufficient resource*: the available resources are not enough to support the system functionality (e.g., not enough disk space); (5) *Stale data*: stale data in the system

prevents the new configuration. Table 6 shows the distribution of the subtypes of component misconfigurations. Missing components, placement issues, and insufficient resources are equally prominent.

4.5 Mistake Location

Table 7 shows the distribution of configuration error locations. Naturally, most misconfigurations are contained in the target application itself. However, many misconfigurations also span to places beyond the application. The administrators also need to consider other parts of the system, including file-system permissions/capacities, operating-system modules, other applications running in the system, network configuration, etc. So looking at only the application itself is not enough to diagnose and fix many configuration errors.

Finding 6: *Although most misconfigurations are located within each examined application, still a significant portion (21.7%~57.3%) of cases involve configurations beyond the application itself or span across multiple hosts.*

5. SYSTEM REACTION TO MISCONFIGURATIONS

In this section, we examine system reactions to misconfigurations, focusing on whether the system detects the misconfiguration and on the error messages issued by the system.

5.1 Do Systems Detect and Report Configuration Errors?

Proactive detection and informative reporting can help diagnose misconfigurations more easily. Therefore, we wish to understand whether systems detect and report configuration errors. We divide the examined cases into three categories based on how well the system handles configuration errors (Table 8). Cases where the systems and associated tools detect, report, recover from (or help the user correct) misconfigurations may not be reported by users. Therefore, the results in this section may be especially skewed by the available data. Nevertheless, there are interesting findings that arise from this analysis.

```
                                    from COMP-A
Symptom: the user cannot create new directories in
directory /vol/vol1/xxx/data
Root cause: the number of existing files in that
directory /vol/vol1/xxx/data/

Error message:
[COMP-A - dir.size.max:warning]:
Directory /vol/vol1/xxx/data/ reached
the maxdirsize limit. Reduce the number
of files or use the vol options command
to increase this limit
```

Figure 3: A misconfiguration case where the error message pinpoints the root cause and tells the user how to fix it.

We classify system reactions into *pinpoint reaction*, *indeterminate reaction*, and *quiet failure*.

A pinpoint reaction is one of the best system reactions to misconfigurations. The system not only detects a configuration error but also pinpoints the exact root cause in the error

System	Inside	FS	OS-Module	Network	Other App	Environment	Others
COMP-A	132(42.7±3.0%)	23(7.4±1.6%)	3(1.0±0.6%)	53(17.2±2.3%)	82(26.5±2.7%)	5(1.6±0.8%)	11(3.6±1.1%)
CentOS	26(43.3±4.0%)	2(3.3±1.4%)	12(20.0±3.2%)	4(6.7±2.0%)	11(18.3±3.1%)	2(3.3±1.4%)	3(5.0±1.8%)
MySQL	27(49.1±3.2%)	10(18.2±2.5%)	6(10.9±2.0%)	1(1.8±0.9%)	6(10.9±2.0%)	4(7.3±1.7%)	1(1.8±0.9%)
Apache	47(78.3±3.1%)	3(5.0±1.7%)	3(5.0±1.7%)	3(5.0±1.7%)	3(5.0±1.7%)	0	1(1.7±1.0%)
OpenLDAP	39(62.9±3.4%)	2(3.2±1.3%)	1(1.6±0.9%)	0	17(27.4±3.3%)	1(1.6±0.9%)	2(3.2±1.3%)

Table 7: The location of errors. "Inside": inside the target application. "FS": in file system. "OS-Module": in some OS modules like SELinux. "Network": in network settings. "Other App": in other applications. "Environment": other environment like DNS service.

System	Pinpoint Reaction	Indeterminate Reaction	Quiet Failure	Unknown
COMP-A	48(15.5±2.2%)	153(49.5±3.0%)	74(23.9±2.6%)	34(11.0±1.9%)
CentOS	7(11.7±2.4%)	33(55.0±3.7%)	16(26.7±3.3%)	4(6.7±1.9%)
MySQL	4(7.2±1.7%)	26(47.3±3.2%)	13(23.6±2.8%)	12(21.8±2.7%)
Apache	8(13.3±2.6%)	28(46.7±3.8%)	16(26.7±3.4%)	8(13.3±2.6%)
OpenLDAP	9(14.5±2.6%)	28(45.2±3.7%)	14(22.6±3.1%)	11(17.7±2.8%)

(a)

System	Mysterious Symptoms w/o Message
COMP-A	26(8.4±1.7%)
CentOS	4(6.7±1.9%)
MySQL	9(16.4±2.4%)
Apache	3(5.0±1.7%)
OpenLDAP	3(4.8±1.5%)

(b)

Table 8: How do systems react to misconfigurations? Table (a) presents the number of cases in each category of system reaction. Table (b) presents the number of cases that cause mysterious crashes, hangs, etc. but do not provide any messages.

message (see a COMP-A example in Figure 3). As shown in Table 8 (a), more than 85% of the cases do *not* belong to this category, indicating that systems may *not* react in a user-friendly way to misconfigurations. As previously discussed, the study includes only reported cases. Therefore, some misconfigurations with good error messages may have already been solved by users themselves and thus not reported. So in reality, the percentage of pinpoint reaction to misconfiguration may be higher. However, considering the total number of misconfigurations in the sources we selected is very large, there are still a significant number of misconfigurations for which the examined systems do not pinpoint the misconfigurations.

An indeterminate reaction is a reaction that a system does provide some information about the failure symptoms (i.e., manifestation of the misconfiguration), but does not pinpoint the root cause or guide the user on how to fix the problem. 45.2%~55.0% of our studied cases belong to this category.

A quiet failure refers to cases where the system does not function properly, and it further does not provide any information regarding the failure or the root cause. 22.6%~26.7% of the cases belong to this category. Diagnosing them is very difficult.

Finding 7: *Only 7.2%~15.5% of the studied misconfiguration problems provide explicit messages that pinpoint the configuration error.*

Quiet failures can be even worse when the misconfiguration causes the system to misbehave in a mysterious way (crash, hang, etc.) just like software bugs. We find that such behavior occurred in 5%~8% of the cases (Table 8 (b)).

Why would misconfigurations cause a system to crash or hang unexpectedly? The reason is intuitive: since configuration parameters can also be considered as a form of input, if a system does not perform validity checking and prepare for illegal configurations, it may lead to system misbehavior. We describe two such scenarios below.

Crash example: A web application used both *mod_python* and *mod_wsgi* modules in an Apache httpd server. These two modules used two different versions of Python, which caused segmentation fault errors when trying to access the web page.

Hang example: A server was configured to authenticate via LDAP with the *hard* bind policy, which made it keep connecting to the LDAP server until it succeeded. However, the LDAP server was not working, so the server hung when the user added new accounts.

Such misbehavior is very challenging to diagnose because users and support engineers may suspect these unexpected failures to have been caused by a bug in the system instead of a configuration issue (of course, one may argue that, in a way it can also be considered to be a bug). If the system is built to perform more thorough configuration validity-checking and avoid misconfiguration-caused misbehavior, both the cost of support and the diagnosis time can be reduced.

Finding 8: *Some misconfigurations have caused the systems to crash, hang, or have severe performance degradation, making failure diagnosis a challenging task.*

We further study if there is a correlation between the type of misconfiguration and the difficulty for systems to react. We find that it is more difficult to have an appropriate reaction for software-incompatibility issues. Only 9.3% of all the incompatibility issues have pinpoint reaction, while the same ratio for parameter mistakes and component misconfigurations is 14.3% and 15.5% respectively. This result is reasonable since global knowledge (e.g., the configuration of different applications) is often required to decide if there are incompatibility issues.

5.2 System Reaction to Illegal Parameters

Cases with illegal configuration parameters (defined in Section 4.2) are usually easier to be checked and pinpointed automatically. For example, Figure 4 is a patch from MySQL that prints a warning message when the user sets illegal (inconsistent) parameters.

166

System	Pinpoint Reaction	Indeterminate Reaction	Quiet Failure	Unknown
COMP-A	25(18.9%)	57(43.2%)	27(20.5%)	23(17.4%)
CentOS	4(25.0%)	7(43.8%)	5(31.3%)	0
MySQL	1(4.3%)	13(56.5%)	3(13.0%)	6(26.1%)
Apache	5(21.7%)	9(39.1%)	4(17.4%)	5(21.7%)
OpenLDAP	7(26.9%)	11(42.3%)	4(15.4%)	4(15.4%)

Table 9: How do systems react to illegal parameters? The reaction category is the same as in Table 8 (a).

```
From MySQL                              mysqld.cc
+if (opt_logname && !(log_output_options & LOG_FILE)
+   && !(log_output_options & LOG_NONE))
+   sql_print_warning("Although a path was specified
+   for the --log option, log tables are used. To enable
+   logging to files use the --log-output option.");
```

Figure 4: A patch from MySQL that adds an explicit warning message when an illegal configuration is detected. If parameter *log_output* (value stored in variable log_output_options) is set as neither "FILE" (i.e. output logs to files) nor "NONE" (i.e. not output logs) but parameter *log* (value stored in variable opt_logname) is specified with the name of a log file, a warning will be issued because these two parameters contradict each other.

Unfortunately, systems do not detect and pinpoint a majority of these configuration mistakes, as shown in Table 9.

Finding 9: *Among 220 cases with illegal parameters that could be easily detected and fixed, only 4.3%~26.9% of them provide explicit messages. Up to 31.3% of them do not provide any message at all, unnecessarily complicating the diagnosis process.*

5.3 Impact of Messages on Diagnosis Time

Do good error messages help engineers diagnose misconfiguration problems more efficiently? To answer this question, we calculate the diagnosis time, in hours, from the time when a misconfiguration problem was posted to the time when the correct answer was provided.

System	Explicit Message	Ambiguous Message	No Message
COMP-A	1x	13x	14.5x
CentOS	1x	3x	5.5x
MySQL	1x	3.4x	1.2x
Apache	1x	10x	3x
OpenLDAP	1x	5.3x	2.5x

Table 10: The *median* of diagnosis time for cases with and without messages (time is normalized for confidentiality reasons). *Explicit message* means that the error message directly pinpoints the location of the misconfiguration. The median diagnosis time of the cases with explicit messages is used as base. *Ambiguous message* means there are messages, but they do not directly identify the misconfiguration. *No message* is for cases where no messages are provided.

Table 10 shows that the misconfiguration cases with explicit messages are diagnosed much faster. Otherwise, engineers have to spend much more time on diagnosis, where the median of the diagnosis time is up to 14.5 times longer.

Finding 10: *Messages that pinpoint configuration errors can shorten the diagnosis time 3 to 13 times as compared to the cases with ambiguous messages or 1.2 to 14.5 times as compared to the cases with no messages.*

To improve error reporting, two types of approaches can be adopted. A white-box approach [43] uses program analysis to identify the state that should be captured at each logging statement in source code to minimize ambiguity in error messages. When source code is not available, a black-box approach, such as Clarify [12], can be taken instead. Clarify associates the program's runtime profile with ambiguous error report, which enables improved error reporting.

Interestingly, for some of the systems (Apache, MySQL, and OpenLDAP), engineers seem to spend more time (2~4 times longer) diagnosing cases with ambiguous messages than cases with no messages at all. There are several potential reasons. First, incorrect or irrelevant messages can sometimes mislead engineers, directing them down a wrong path. Figure 5 shows such an example. Based on the message provided by the client, both the support engineers and the customers thought the problem was on the client end, so they made several attempts to set certificates, but the root cause turned out to be a problem in the configuration on the server side. This indicates that the accuracy of messages is critical to the diagnosis process. Providing misleading messages may be worse than providing nothing at all.

```
                                    from COMP-A
Symptom: When the user tried to connect the admin
web site, the web browser (Firefox) threw a misleading
error message asking for new certificate.
Root cause: The "httpd.admin.ssl.enable" parameter
was set to be "on" in a COMP-A server.

Error message:
You have received an invalid certificate.
Please contact the administrator and get
a new certificate containing a unique
serial number.
(error code: sec_error_reused_issuer)
```

Figure 5: A misconfiguration case where the error message misled the customer and the support engineers.

Second, in some cases, symptoms and configuration-file content are already sufficient for support engineers or experts to resolve the problem. For these cases, whether there are error messages is less important. For example, many cases from MySQL related to performance degradation do not have error messages, but it was relatively easy for experts to solve those problems by looking only at the configuration file. However, even for these cases, if the system could give good-quality messages, users may be able to solve these problems themselves.

Finding 11: *Giving an irrelevant message may be worse than not giving message at all for diagnosing misconfiguration. Some irrelevant messages could mislead users to chase down the wrong path. In three of the five studied systems, statistical data shows that ambiguous messages may lead to longer diagnosis time compared to not having any message.*

We further performed a preliminary study on what kind of error messages are more useful in reducing diagnosis time. Specifically, we read through the misconfiguration cases that have explicit messages and are parameter mistakes (a total of 62 cases). Besides that all these cases pinpoint the root cause of the failure (which is our definition of *explicit*), 69.4% of them further mention the parameter name in the message; 6.5% of even further point out the parameter's location within the configuration file. However, we do not find strong correlation between the diagnosis time and this extra information (e.g., parameter name) in the explicit messages. A more comprehensive study on this topic is a good avenue for future work.

6. CAUSES OF MISCONFIGURATIONS

6.1 When Do Misconfigurations Happen?

There are many ways to look at the reasons that cause a misconfiguration. Here, we examine only a couple. First, when a misconfiguration happens, i.e. whether it happens at the user's first attempt to access certain functionality, or the system used to work but does not work any more due to various changes. Based on this, we categorize the misconfiguration cases into two categories (Table 11): (1) *Used-to-work* and (2) *First-time use*.

System	Used-to-Work	First-Time Use	Unknown
COMP-A	100(32.4±2.8%)	165(53.4±3.0%)	44(14.2±2.1%)
CentOS	10(16.7±3.0%)	40(66.6±3.8%)	10(16.7±3.0%)
MySQL	3(5.5±1.5%)	45(81.8±2.5%)	7(12.7±2.2%)
Apache	2(3.3±1.4%)	40(66.7±3.6%)	18(30.0±3.5%)
OpenLDAP	2(3.2±1.3%)	57(91.9±1.6%)	3(4.8±1.6%)

Table 11: The number of misconfigurations categorized by *used-to-work* and *first-time use*.

One may think that most misconfigurations happen when users configure a system for the first time. As our results show, it is indeed the case, especially for relatively simple systems (MySQL, Apache, and OpenLDAP). The causes for the misconfigurations during first-time use can be the inadequate knowledge of personnel, flawed design of the system, or even inconsistent user manuals [33].

However, for more complex systems, COMP-A and CentOS, a significant portion (16.7%~32.4%) of the misconfigurations happen in the middle of the system's lifetime. There could be two major reasons. First, these systems have more frequent changes (upgrades, reconfiguration, etc.) in their lifetime. Second, the configuration is more complicated, so it takes a long time for users to master.

Finding 12: *The majority of misconfigurations are related to first-time use of desired functionality. For more complex systems, a significant percentage (16.7%~32.4%) of misconfigurations were introduced into systems that used to work.*

6.2 Why Do Systems Stop Working?

To further examine the causes of used-to-work cases, we categorize the 100 cases of this category from COMP-A based on their root causes (Figure 6).

Collateral damage refers to cases when users made configuration changes for some new functionality but accidentally

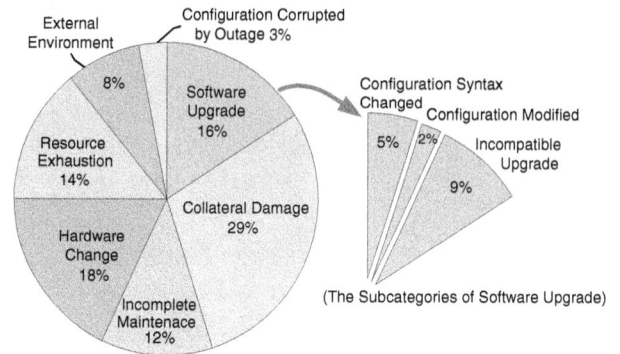

Figure 6: The cause distribution for the *used-to-work* misconfigurations at COMP-A (we also subcategorize the cases caused by *software upgrade*).

broke existing functionality. It accounts for 29.0% of the used-to-work cases from COMP-A. To avoid such collateral damages, it might be useful if users can be warned by the configuration management/change tool about the side-effects of their changes.

Incomplete maintenance refers to cases when some regular maintenance tasks introduced incomplete configuration changes. 12.0% of the used-to-work cases from COMP-A belong to this category. For example, when an administrator does a routine periodic password change to certain accounts but forgets to propagate it to all affected systems, some systems would not be able to authenticate these accounts.

In addition, configuration could also be *corrupted by outage* (3.0%) or be modified accidentally by some (2.0%) *software upgrades* (Figure 6). To sum up, 46% of the examined used-to-work misconfiguration cases from COMP-A are caused by configuration-parameter changes due to various reasons, including configuring other features, routine maintenance, system outages, or software upgrades. To diagnose and fix these cases, it is useful for systems to automatically keep track of configuration changes [24], and even better, help users to pinpoint which change is the culprit [41].

Another major cause is *hardware change* (18.0%). When customers upgrade, replace or reorganize hardware (e.g., moving a disk from one server to another), it can cause problems if they forget to change related configuration parameters accordingly.

Resource exhaustion (14.0%) can also affect a previously working system. For example, in one of the studied cases, a database system hung and did not work properly even after rebooting because the data disks became full.

Finally, *external environment* changes could also be harmful to previously working systems. They account for 8.0% of used-to-work cases from COMP-A. For example, in one of the studied cases, a system suffered from severe performance degradation because its primary DNS server went offline accidentally. Such changes are error prone and problematic, because different systems may be managed by different administrators who may not communicate with each other in a timely manner about their changes.

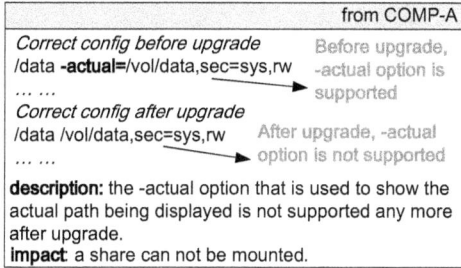

	from COMP-A
Correct config before upgrade /data **-actual**=/vol/data,sec=sys,rw	Before upgrade, -actual option is supported
Correct config after upgrade /data /vol/data,sec=sys,rw	After upgrade, -actual option is not supported

description: the -actual option that is used to show the actual path being displayed is not supported any more after upgrade.
impact: a share can not be mounted.

Figure 7: A misconfiguration example where the syntax of configuration files has changed after upgrade. A previously working NFS mounting configuration is no longer valid, because the option *actual* became deprecated after upgrade.

Software upgrades, as one may expect, is another major cause of misconfigurations that break a previously working system. It accounts for 16% of the "used-to-work" cases from COMP-A. We further subcategorize it into three types. First, a new software release may have changed the configuration file syntax or format requirements, making the old configuration file invalid. Figure 7 gives such an example. Second, some automatic upgrade processes may silently modify certain configuration parameters (e.g. set them to default values) without users' awareness. Third, software upgrades may cause incompatibilities among components.

In order to prevent misconfigurations caused by software upgrades, systems should provide automatic upgrade tools or at least detailed upgrade instructions [24, 7]. The upgrade process should also take users' existing configurations into consideration.

Finding 13: *By looking into the 100 used-to-work cases (32.4% of the total) at COMP-A, 46% of them are attributed to configuration parameter changes due to routine maintenance, configuring for new functionality, system outages, etc, and can benefit from tracking configuration changes. The remainder are caused by non-parameter related issues such as hardware changes (18%), external environmental changes (8%), resource exhaustion (14%), and software upgrades(14%).*

7. IMPACT OF MISCONFIGURATIONS

We analyzed the severity of customer-reported issues from COMP-A (Section 3) and found that a large percentage (31%) of high-impact issues were related to system configuration. In this section, we analyze the severity of the specific misconfiguration cases used in our study, particularly from the viewpoint of system availability and performance. We divide the misconfiguration cases into three categories, as shown in Table 12: (1) the system becomes *fully unavailable*; (2) the system becomes *partially unavailable*, i.e. it cannot deliver certain desired features; and (3) the system suffers from severe *performance degradation*. We do expect the results to be skewed towards the more severe, causing users to report them as issues more than simpler cases.

We find 9.7%~27.3% of the misconfigurations cause the system to become fully unavailable. This shows again that misconfigurations can be a severe threat to system availability.

System	Fully Unavailable	Partially Unavailable	Performance Degradation
COMP-A	41 (13.3±2.1%)	247 (79.9±2.4%)	21 (6.8±1.5%)
CentOS	12 (20.0±3.2%)	47 (78.3±3.3%)	1 (1.7±1.0%)
MySQL	15 (27.3±2.9%)	29 (52.7±3.2%)	11 (20.0±2.6%)
Apache	15 (25.0±3.3%)	44 (73.3±3.4%)	1 (1.7±1.0%)
OpenLDAP	6 (9.7±2.2%)	52 (83.9±2.7%)	4 (6.4±1.8%)

Table 12: The impact distribution of the misconfiguration cases from all the studied systems.

Moreover, up to 20.0% of the misconfigurations cause severe performance degradation, especially for systems such as database servers that are performance-sensitive and require some nontrivial tuning based on users' particular workloads, infrastructure, and data sizes. For example, the official performance tuning guides for MySQL and Oracle have more than 400 pages, and mention tens, even hundreds of configuration parameters that are related to performance. The percentage of misconfigurations causing performance issues here might be an underestimate of performance problems in the field, since some trivial performance issues introduced by misconfigurations may not be reported by the user.

Finding 14: *Although most studied misconfiguration cases only lead to partial unavailability of the system, 16.1%~47.3% of them make the systems fully unavailable or cause severe performance degradation.*

The next question is whether different types of misconfigurations have different impact characteristics. Therefore, we also examine the impact of each type of misconfiguration; the results are shown in Table 13.

Misconfig Type	Fully Unavailable	Partially Unavailable	Performance Degradation
Parameters	59 (**13.6%**)	342 (78.8%)	33 (7.6%)
Compatibility	14 (**25.9%**)	38 (70.4%)	2 (3.7%)
Component	16 (**27.6%**)	39 (67.2%)	3 (5.2%)

Table 13: The impact on different types of misconfiguration cases. The data is aggregated for all the examined systems. The percentage shows the ratio of a specific type of misconfiguration (e.g., parameter mistake) that leads to a specific impact level (e.g., full unavailability).

We find that, compared to configuration parameter mistakes, software compatibility and component configuration errors are more likely to cause full unavailability of the system. 25.9% of the software compatibility issues and 27.6% of the component configuration errors make systems fully unavailable, whereas this ratio is only 13.6% for parameter-related misconfigurations.

The above results are not surprising because what components are used and whether they are compatible can easily prevent systems from even being able to start. In contrast, configuration-parameter mistakes, especially if the parameter is only for certain functionality, tend to have a much more localized impact.

In addition to having a more severe impact, compatibility and component configuration mistakes can be more difficult to fix. They usually require greater expertise from users. For example, in one of the misconfiguration cases of CentOS, the user could not mount a newly created ReiserFS file system, because the kernel support for this ReiserFS file system was missing. The user needed to install a set of libraries and kernel modules and also modify configuration parameters in several places to get it to work.

8. RELATED WORK

Characteristic studies on operator errors: Several previous studies have examined the contribution of operation errors or administrator mistakes [11, 22, 23, 27, 29, 30]. For example, Jim Gray found that 42% of system failures are due to administration errors [11]. Patterson et al. [30] also observed a similar trend in telephone networks. Murphy et al. [22] found that the percentage of failures due to system management is increasing over time. Oppenheimer et al. [29] studied the failures of the Internet services and found that configuration errors are the largest category of operator errors. Nagaraja et al. [23] also had similar findings from a user study.

To the best of our knowledge, very few studies have analyzed misconfigurations in detail and examined the subtypes, root causes, impacts and system reactions to misconfigurations, especially in both *commercial* and open source systems with a large set of real-world misconfigurations.

Detection of misconfigurations: A series of efforts [9, 21, 24, 38, 40] in recent years have focused on detecting misconfigurations. The techniques used in PeerPressure [38] and its predecessor Strider [40] have been discussed in the Introduction. Microsoft Baseline Security Analyzer (MBSA) [21] detects common *security-related* misconfigurations by checking configuration files against predefined rules; security is one of the important impact categories we have not focused on in our study. NetApp's AutoSupport-based health management system [24] checks the validity of configurations against "golden templates", focusing on compatibility and component issues (which are likelier to cause full availability according to our study).

Diagnosis of misconfigurations: Besides detection, another series of research efforts [41, 35, 2, 3] focus on diagnosing problems after the errors happen. We have already discussed AutoBash [35], ConfAid [3], and Chronus [41] in the Introduction. The applicability of Chronus depends on how many misconfigurations belong to the "used-to-work" category; according to our study, it is a significant percentage for more complex systems. A follow-up work to AutoBash by Attariyan et al. [2] leverages system call information to track the causality relation, which overcomes the limitations of the Hamming distance comparison used in AutoBash to further enhance accuracy. Similar to [2], Yuan et al. [42] use machine learning techniques to correlate system call information to problem causes in order to diagnose configuration errors. Most of these works focused on parameter-related misconfigurations.

Tolerance of misconfigurations: Some research work [35, 4] can help fix or tolerate misconfigurations. In addition to AutoBash [35], Undo [4] uses checkpoints to allow administrators to have a chance to roll back if they made some misconfigurations. Obviously, it assumes that the system used to work fine, thus addressing a significant number of cases for more complex systems.

Avoidance of misconfigurations: One approach to avoid misconfiguration is to develop tools to configure the system automatically. SmartFrog [1] uses a declarative language to describe software components and configuration parameters, and how they should connect to each other. Configurations can then be automatically generated to greatly mitigate human errors. Similarly, Zheng et al. [44] leverage custom-specified templates to automatically generate the correct configuration for a system. Kardo [18] adopts machine learning techniques to automatically extract the solution operations out of the user's UI sequence and apply them automatically. The significant percentage of "illegal configuration parameters" provides some supporting evidence and also shows the benefits of the above approaches.

A more fundamental approach is to design better configuration logic/interface to avoid misconfigurations. Maxion et al. [20] discovered that many misconfigurations for NTFS permissions are due to the configuration interfaces not providing adequate information to users. Therefore, they proposed a new design of the interface with subgoal support that can effectively reduce the configuration errors on NTFS permissions by 94%.

Misconfiguration injection: As mentioned in the Introduction, a misconfiguration-injection framework like ConfErr [17] is very useful for evaluating techniques for detecting, diagnosing, and fixing misconfigurations. Our study can be beneficial for such framework to construct a more accurate misconfiguration model.

Online validation: Another avenue of work [7, 23, 27, 28] focus on validating the system for detecting operator mistakes. Nagaraja et al. [23] developed a validation framework which can detect operator mistakes before deployment by comparing against the comparator functions provided by users. A follow-up work by Oliveira et al. [27] validates database system administrations. Another follow-up work by Oliveira et al. [28] addresses the limitation of the previous validation system, which does not protect against human errors directly performed on the production system. Mirage [7] also has a subsystem for validating system upgrades.

Miscellaneous: Wang et al. [39] used reverse engineering to extract the security-related configuration parameters automatically. Users can leverage the approach to slice the configuration file and see if the security-related parameters are correct. Ramachandran et al. [32] extracted the correlations between parameters, which can be used to detect some of the inconsistent-parameter misconfigurations in our study. Rabkin et al. [31] found that the configuration space after canonicalization is not very big after having analyzed seven open source applications. Therefore a thorough test of different configuration parameters might be possible for certain applications if input is generated in a smart way.

As we discussed in the Introduction, our characteristic study of real-world misconfigurations would be useful in providing some guidelines to evaluate, improve, and extend some of the above work on detecting, diagnosing, fixing, and injecting misconfigurations.

9. CONCLUSIONS

System configuration lies in the gray zone between the developers of a system and its users. The responsibility for creating correct configurations lies with both parties; the developer should create intuitive configuration logic, build logic that detects errors, and convey configuration knowledge to users effectively; the user should imbibe the knowledge and manage cross-application or cross-vendor configurations. This shared responsibility is non-trivial to efficiently achieve. For example, there is no obviously "correct" way to build configuration logic; also, unlike fixing a bug once, every user of the system has to be educated on the right way to configure the system. Perhaps as a result, misconfigurations have been one of the dominant causes of system issues and is likely to continue so.

We have performed a comprehensive characteristic study on 546 randomly-sampled real-world misconfiguration cases from both a commercial system that is deployed to thousands of customers, and four widely used open-source systems, namely CentOS, MySQL, Apache, and OpenLDAP. Our study covers several dimensions of misconfigurations, including types, causes, impact, and system reactions. We hope that our study helps extend and improve tools that inject, detect, diagnose, or fix misconfigurations. Further, we hope that the study provides system architects, developers, and testers insights into configuration-logic design and testing, and also encourages support personnel to record field configuration problems more rigorously so that vendors can learn from historical mistakes.

10. ACKNOWLEDGMENTS

We would like to express our great appreciation to our shepherd, Emmett Witchel, who was very responsive and provided us with valuable suggestions to improve our work. We also thank the anonymous reviewers for their insightful comments and suggestions. Moreover, we thank Kiran Srinivasan, Puneet Anand, Scott Leaver, Karl Danz, and James Ayscue for their feedback and insights, and thank the support engineers and developers of COMP-A storage systems and the open-source systems used in the study for their help. Finally, we greatly appreciate Soyeon Park, Wei-wei Xiong, Jiaqi Zhang, Xiaoming Tang, Peng Huang, Yang Liu, Michael Lee, Ding Yuan, Zhuoer Wang, and Alexander Rasmussen for helping us proofread our work. This research is supported by NSF CNS-0720743 grant, NSF CCF-0325603 grant, NSF CNS-0615372 grant, NSF CNS- 0347854 (career award), NSF CSR Small 1017784 grant, and a NetApp Faculty Fellowship.

11. REFERENCES

[1] P. Anderson, P. Goldsack, and J. Paterson. SmartFrog meets LCFG Autonomous Reconfiguration with Central Policy Control. In *LISA*, August 2003.

[2] M. Attariyan and J. Flinn. Using causality to diagnose configuration bugs. In *USENIX*, June 2008.

[3] M. Attariyan and J. Flinn. Automating configuration troubleshooting with dynamic information flow analysis. In *OSDI*, October 2010.

[4] A. B. Brown and D. A. Patterson. Undo for Operators: Building an Undoable E-mail Store. In *USENIX*, June 2003.

[5] A. Chou, J. Yang, B. Chelf, S. Hallem, and D. Engler. An empirical study of operating systems errors. In *SOSP'01*.

[6] CircleID. Misconfiguration brings down entire .se domain in sweden. www.circleid.com/posts/misconfiguration_brings_down_entire_se_domain_in_sweden/.

[7] O. Crameri, N. Knezević, D. Kostić, R. Bianchini, and W. Zwaenepoel. Staged Deployment in Mirage, an Integrated Software Upgrade Testing and Distribution System. In *SOSP'07*, October 2007.

[8] Debian. The Debian GNU/Linux FAQ, Chapter 8: The Debian Package Management Tools. http://www.debian.org/doc/FAQ/ch-pkgtools.en.html.

[9] N. Feamster and H. Balakrishnan. Detecting BGP configuration faults with static analysis. In *NSDI*, May 2005.

[10] D. Freedman, R. Pisani, and R. Purves. *Statistics, 3rd Edition*. W. W. Norton & Company., 1997.

[11] J. Gray. Why do computers stop and what can be done about it? In *Symp. on Reliability in Distributed Software and Database Systems*, 1986.

[12] J. Ha, C. J. Rossbach, J. V. Davis, I. Roy, H. E. Ramadan, D. E. Porter, D. L. Chen, and E. Witchel. Improved Error Reporting for Software that Uses Black-Box Components. In *PLDI*, 2007.

[13] Hewlett-Packard. HP Storage Essentials SRM Software Suite. http://h18000.www1.hp.com/products/quickspecs/12191_na/12191_na.pdf.

[14] IBM Corp. IBM Tivoli Software. http://www-01.ibm.com/software/tivoli/.

[15] R. Johnson. More details on today's outage. http://www.facebook.com/notes/facebook-engineering/more-details-on-todays-outage/431441338919.

[16] A. Kappor. Web-to-host: Reducing total cost of ownership. In *Technical Report 200503, The Tolly Group*, May 2000.

[17] L. Keller, P. Upadhyaya, and G. Candea. ConfErr: A Tool for Assessing Resilience to Human Configuration Errors. In *DSN*, June 2008.

[18] N. Kushman and D. Katabi. Enabling Configuration-Independent Automation by Non-Expert Users. In *OSDI*, October 2010.

[19] S. Lu, S. Park, E. Seo, and Y. Zhou. Learning from mistakes – a comprehensive study on real world concurrency bug characteristics. In *ASPLOS*, March 2008.

[20] R. A. Maxion and R. W. Reeder. Improving user-interface dependability through mitigation of human error. *International Journal of Human-Computer Studies*, 63, July 2005.

[21] Microsoft Corp. Microsoft Baseline Security Analyzer. 2008. http://www.microsoft.com/technet/security/tools/MBSAHome.mspx.

[22] B. Murphy and T. Gent. Measuring system and software reliability using an automated data collection process. In *Quality and Reliability Engineering International, 11(5),*, 1995.

[23] K. Nagaraja, F. Oliveira, R. Bianchini, R. P. Martin, and T. D. Nguyen. Understanding and Dealing with Operator Mistakes in Internet Services. In *OSDI'04*,

October 2004.

[24] NetApp, Inc. Proactive Health Management with AutoSupport. http://media.netapp.com/documents/wp-7027.pdf.

[25] NetApp, Inc. Protection Manager. http://www.netapp.com/us/products/management-software/protection.html.

[26] NetApp, Inc. Provisioning Manager. http://www.netapp.com/us/products/management-software/provisioning.html.

[27] F. Oliveira, K. Nagaraja, R. Bachwani, R. Bianchini, R. P. Martin, and T. D. Nguyen. Understanding and Validating Database System Administration. In *USENIX'06*, 2006.

[28] F. Oliveira, A. Tjang, R. Bianchini, R. P. Martin, and T. D. Nguyen. Barricade: Defending Systems Against Operator Mistakes. In *EuroSys'10*, April 2010.

[29] D. Oppenheimer, A. Ganapathi, and D. A. Patterson. Why do Internet services fail, and what can be done about it? In *Proceedings of the 4th USENIX Symposium on Internet Technologies and Systems (USITS)*, March 2003.

[30] D. Patterson, A. Brown, P. Broadwell, G. Candea, M. Chen, J. Cutler, P. Enriquez, A. Fox, E. Kiciman, M. Merzbacher, D. Oppenheimer, N. Sastry, W. Tetzlaff, J. Traupman, and N. Treuhaft. Recovery Oriented Computing (ROC): Motivation, Definition, Techniques, and Case Studies. In *Technical Report UCB//CSD-02-1175, University of California, Berkeley*, March 2002.

[31] A. Rabkin and R. Katz. Static Extraction of Program Configuration Options. In *ICSE*, May 2011.

[32] V. Ramachandran, M. Gupta, M. Sethi, and S. R. Chowdhury. Determining Configuration Parameter Dependencies via Analysis of Configuration Data from Multi-tiered Enterprise Applications. In *ICAC*, June 2009.

[33] E. Reisner, C. Song, K.-K. Ma, J. S. Foster, and A. Porter. Using symbolic evaluation to understand behavior in configurable software systems. In *ICSE*, May 2010.

[34] RPM. Rpm package manager (rpm). http://rpm.org/.

[35] Y.-Y. Su, M. Attariyan, and J. Flinn. AutoBash: improving configuration management with operating system causality analysis. In *SOSP*, October 2007.

[36] M. Sullivan and R. Chillarege. Software defects and their impact on system availability: A study of field failures in operating systems. In *FTCS*, 1991.

[37] M. Sullivan and R. Chillarege. A comparison of software defects in database management systems and operating systems. In *International Symposium on Fault-Tolerant Computing*, 1992.

[38] H. J. Wang, J. C. Platt, Y. Chen, R. Zhang, and Y.-M. Wang. Automatic Misconfiguration Troubleshooting with PeerPressure. In *OSDI'04*, October 2004.

[39] R. Wang, X. Wang, K. Zhang, and Z. li. Towards Automatic Reverse Engineering of Software Security Configurations. In *CCS*, October 2008.

[40] Y.-M. Wang, C. Verbowski, J. Dunagan, Y. Chen, H. J. Wang, C. Yuan, and Z. Zhang. STRIDER: A Black-box, State-based Approach to Change and Configuration Management and Support. In *LISA'03*, October 2003.

[41] A. Whitaker, R. S. Cox, and S. D. Gribble. Configuration Debugging as Search: Finding the Needle in the Haystack. In *OSDI*, October 2004.

[42] C. Yuan, N. Lao, J.-R. Wen, J. Li, Z. Zhang, Y.-M. Wang, and W.-Y. Ma. Automated Known Problem Diagnosis with Event Traces. In *EuroSys*, April 2006.

[43] D. Yuan, J. Zheng, S. Park, Y. Zhou, and S. Savage. Improving Software Diagnosability via Log Enhancement. In *ASPLOS*, March 2011.

[44] W. Zheng, R. Bianchini, and T. D. Nguyen. Automatic Configuration of Internet Services. In *EuroSys*, March 2007.

Cells: A Virtual Mobile Smartphone Architecture

Jeremy Andrus, Christoffer Dall, Alexander Van't Hof, Oren Laadan, and Jason Nieh
{jeremya, cdall, alexvh, orenl, nieh}@cs.columbia.edu
Department of Computer Science
Columbia University

ABSTRACT

Smartphones are increasingly ubiquitous, and many users carry multiple phones to accommodate work, personal, and geographic mobility needs. We present *Cells*, a virtualization architecture for enabling multiple virtual smartphones to run simultaneously on the same physical cellphone in an isolated, secure manner. *Cells* introduces a usage model of having one foreground virtual phone and multiple background virtual phones. This model enables a new device namespace mechanism and novel device proxies that integrate with lightweight operating system virtualization to multiplex phone hardware across multiple virtual phones while providing native hardware device performance. *Cells* virtual phone features include fully accelerated 3D graphics, complete power management features, and full telephony functionality with separately assignable telephone numbers and caller ID support. We have implemented a prototype of *Cells* that supports multiple Android virtual phones on the same phone. Our performance results demonstrate that *Cells* imposes only modest runtime and memory overhead, works seamlessly across multiple hardware devices including Google Nexus 1 and Nexus S phones, and transparently runs Android applications at native speed without any modifications.

Categories and Subject Descriptors

C.0 [**Computer Systems Organization**]: General–System architectures; D.4.6 [**Operating Systems**]: Security and Protection; D.4.7 [**Operating Systems**]: Organization and Design; D.4.8 [**Operating Systems**]: Performance; H.5.2 [**Information Interfaces and Presentation**]: User Interfaces–User-centered design; I.3.4 [**Computer Graphics**]: Graphics Utilities–Virtual device interfaces

General Terms

Design, Experimentation, Measurement, Performance, Security

Keywords

Android, Smartphones, Virtualization

1. INTRODUCTION

The preferred platform for a user's everyday computing needs is shifting from traditional desktop and laptop computers toward mobile smartphone and tablet devices [4]. Smartphones are becoming an increasingly important work tool for professionals who rely on them for telephone, text messaging, email, Web browsing, contact and calendar management, news, and location-specific information. These same functions as well as the ability to play music, movies, and games also make smartphones a useful personal tool. In fact, hundreds of thousands of smartphone applications are available for users to download and try through various online application stores. The ease of downloading new software imposes a risk on users as malicious software can easily access sensitive data with the risk of corrupting it or even leaking it to third parties [35]. For this reason, smartphones given to employees for work use are often locked down resulting in many users having to carry separate work and personal phones. Application developers also carry additional phones for development to avoid having a misbehaving application prototype corrupt their primary phone. Parents sometimes wish they had additional phones when their children use the parent's smartphone for entertainment and end up with unexpected charges due to accidental phone calls or unintended in-app purchases.

Virtual machine (VM) mechanisms have been proposed that enable two separate and isolated instances of a smartphone software stack to run on the same ARM hardware [2,5,13, 22]. These approaches require substantial modifications to both user and kernel levels of the software stack. Paravirtualization is used in all cases since ARM is not virtualizable and proposed ARM virtualization extensions are not yet available in hardware. While VMs are useful for desktop and server computers, applying these hardware virtualization techniques to smartphones has two crucial drawbacks. First, smartphones are more resource constrained, and running an entire additional operating system (OS) and user space environment in a VM imposes high overhead and limits the number of instances that can run. Slow system responsiveness is less acceptable on a smartphone than on a desktop computer since smartphones are often used for just a few minutes or even seconds at a time. Second, smartphones incorporate a plethora of devices that applications expect to be able to use, such as GPS, cameras, and GPUs.

Existing approaches provide no effective mechanism to enable applications to directly leverage these hardware device features from within VMs, severely limiting the overall system performance and making existing approaches unusable on a smartphone.

We present *Cells*, a new, lightweight virtualization architecture for enabling multiple virtual phones (VPs) to run simultaneously on the same smartphone hardware with high performance. *Cells* does not require running multiple OS instances. It uses lightweight OS virtualization to provide virtual namespaces that can run multiple VPs on a single OS instance. *Cells* isolates VPs from one another, and ensures that buggy or malicious applications running in one VP cannot adversely impact other VPs. *Cells* provides a novel file system layout based on unioning to maximize sharing of common read-only code and data across VPs, minimizing memory consumption and enabling additional VPs to be instantiated without much overhead.

Cells takes advantage of the small display form factors of smartphones, which display only a single application at a time, and introduces a usage model having one foreground VP that is displayed and multiple background VPs that are not displayed at any given time. This simple yet powerful model enables *Cells* to provide novel kernel-level and user-level device namespace mechanisms to efficiently multiplex hardware devices across multiple VPs, including proprietary or opaque hardware such as the baseband processor, while maintaining native hardware performance. The foreground VP is always given direct access to hardware devices. Background VPs are given shared access to hardware devices when the foreground VP does not require exclusive access. Visible applications are always running in the foreground VP and those applications can take full advantage of any available hardware feature, such as hardware-accelerated graphics. Since foreground applications have direct access to hardware, they perform as fast as when they are running natively.

Cells uses a VoIP service to provide individual telephone numbers for each VP without the need for multiple SIM cards. Incoming and outgoing calls use the cellular network, not VoIP, and are routed through the VoIP service as needed to provide both incoming and outgoing caller ID functionality for each VP. *Cells* uses this combination of a VoIP server and the cellular network to allow users to make and receive calls using their standard cell phone service, while maintaining per-VP phone number and caller ID features.

We have implemented a *Cells* prototype that supports multiple virtual Android phones on the same mobile device. Each VP can be configured the same or completely different from other VPs. The prototype has been tested to work with multiple versions of Android, including the most recent open-source version, version 2.3.4. It works seamlessly across multiple hardware devices, including Google Nexus 1 and Nexus S phones. Our experimental results running real Android applications in up to five VPs on Nexus 1 and Nexus S phones demonstrate that *Cells* imposes almost no runtime overhead and only modest memory overhead. *Cells* scales to support far more phone instances on the same hardware than VM-based approaches. *Cells* is the first virtualization system that fully supports available hardware devices with native performance including GPUs, sensors, cameras, and touchscreens, and transparently runs all Android applications in VPs without any modifications.

We present the design and implementation of *Cells*. Section 2 describes the Cells usage model. Section 3 provides an overview of the system architecture. Sections 4 and 5 describe graphics and power management virtualization, respectively, using kernel device namespaces. Sections 6 and 7 describe telephony and wireless network virtualization, respectively, using user-level device namespaces. Section 8 presents experimental results. Section 9 discusses related work. Finally, we present some concluding remarks.

2. USAGE MODEL

Cells runs multiple VPs on a single hardware phone. Each VP runs a standard Android environment capable of making phone calls, running unmodified Android applications, using data connections, interacting through the touch screen, utilizing the accelerometer, and everything else that a user can normally do on the hardware. Each VP is completely isolated from other VPs and cannot inspect, tamper with, or otherwise access any other VP.

Given the limited size of smartphone screens and the ways in which smartphones are used, *Cells* only allows a single VP, the foreground VP, to be displayed at any time. We refer to all other VPs that are running but not displayed as, background VPs. Background VPs are still running on the system in the background and are capable of receiving system events and performing tasks, but do not render content on the screen. A user can easily switch among VPs by selecting one of the background VPs to become the foreground one. This can be done using a custom key-combination to cycle through the set of running VPs, or by swiping up and down on the home screen of a VP. Each VP also has an application that can be launched to see a list of available VPs, and to switch any of these to the foreground. The system can force a new VP to become the foreground VP as a result of an event, such as an incoming call or text message. For security and convenience reasons, a no-auto-switch can be set to prevent background VPs from being switched to the foreground without explicit user action, preventing background VPs from stealing input focus or device data. An auto-lock can be enabled forcing a user to unlock a VP using a passcode or gesture when it transitions from background to foreground. Section 3 discusses how the foreground-background usage model is fundamental to the *Cells* virtualization architecture.

VPs are created and configured on a PC and downloaded to a phone via USB. A VP can be deleted by the user, but its configuration is password protected and can only be changed from a PC given the appropriate credentials. For example, a user can create a VP and can decide to later change various options regarding how the VP is run and what devices it can access. On the other hand, IT administrators can also create VPs that users can download or remove from their phones, but cannot be reconfigured by users. This is useful for companies that may want to distribute locked down VPs.

Each VP can be configured to have different access rights for different devices. For each device, a VP can be configured to have no access, shared access, or exclusive access. Some settings may not be available on certain devices; shared access is, for example, not available for the framebuffer since only a single VP is displayed at any time. These per device access settings provide a highly flexible security model that can be used to accommodate a wide range of security policies.

No access means that applications running in the VP cannot access the given device at any time. For example, VPs with no access to the GPS sensor would never be able to track location despite any user acceptances of application requests to allow location tracking. Users often acquiesce to such privacy invasions because an application will not work without such consent even if the application has no need for such information. By using the no access option *Cells* enables IT administrators to create VPs that allow users to install and run such applications without compromising privacy.

Shared access means that when a given VP is running in the foreground, other background VPs can access the device at the same time. For example, a foreground VP with shared access to the audio device would allow a background VP with shared access to play music.

Exclusive access means that when a given VP is running in the foreground, other background VPs are not allowed to access the device. For example, a foreground VP with exclusive access to the microphone would not allow background VPs to access the microphone, preventing applications running in background VPs from eavesdropping on conversations or leaking information. This kind of functionality is essential for supporting secure VPs. Exclusive access may be used in conjunction with the no-auto-switch to ensure that events cannot cause a background VP to move to the foreground and gain access to devices as a means to circumvent the exclusive access rights of another VP.

In addition to device access rights, *Cells* leverages existing OS virtualization technology to prevent privilege escalation attacks in one VP from compromising the entire device. Both user credentials and process IDs are isolated between VPs; the root user in one VP has no relation to the root user in any other VP.

3. SYSTEM ARCHITECTURE

Figure 1 provides an overview of the *Cells* system architecture. We describe *Cells* using Android since our prototype is based on it. Each VP runs a stock Android user space environment. *Cells* leverages lightweight OS virtualization [3, 23] to isolate VPs from one another. *Cells* uses a single OS kernel across all VPs that virtualizes identifiers, kernel interfaces, and hardware resources such that several execution environments can exist side-by-side in virtual OS sandboxes. Each VP has its own private virtual namespace so that VPs can run concurrently and use the same OS resource names inside their respective namespaces, yet be isolated from and not conflict with each other. This is done by transparently remapping OS resource identifiers to virtual ones that are used by processes within each VP. File system paths, process identifiers (PIDs), IPC identifiers, network interface names, and user names (UIDs) must all be virtualized to prevent conflicts and ensure that processes running

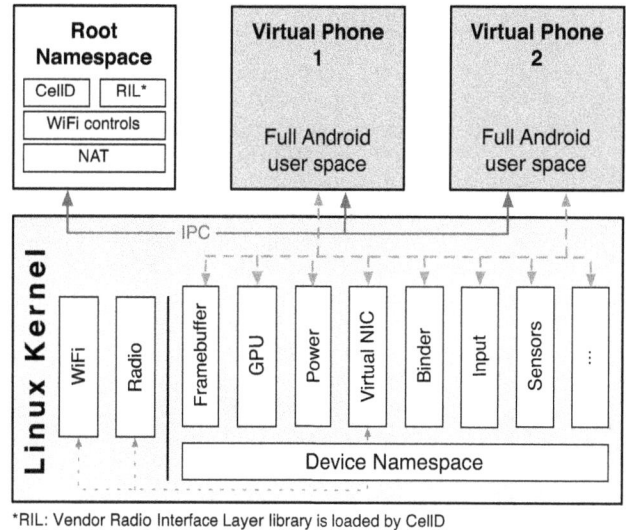

*RIL: Vendor Radio Interface Layer library is loaded by CellD

Figure 1: Overview of *Cells* architecture

in one VP cannot see processes in other VPs. The Linux kernel, including the version used by Android, provides virtualization for these identifiers through namespaces [3]. For example: the file system (FS) is virtualized using mount namespaces that allow different independent views of the FS and provide isolated private FS jails for VPs [16].

However, basic OS virtualization is insufficient to run a complete smartphone user space environment. Virtualization mechanisms have primarily been used in headless server environments with relatively few devices, such as networking and storage, which can already be virtualized in commodity OSes such as Linux. Smartphone applications, however, expect to be able to interact with a plethora of hardware devices, many of which are physically not designed to be multiplexed. OS device virtualization support is non-existent for these devices. For Android, at least the devices listed in Table 1 must be fully supported, which include both hardware devices and pseudo devices unique to the Android environment. Three requirements for supporting devices must be met: (1) support exclusive or shared access across VPs, (2) never leak sensitive information between VPs, and (3) prevent malicious applications in a VP from interfering with device usage by other VPs.

Cells meets all three requirements in the tightly integrated, and often proprietary, smartphone ecosystem. It does so by integrating novel kernel-level and user-level device virtualization methods to present a complete virtual smartphone OS environment. Kernel-level mechanisms provide transparency and performance. User-level mechanisms provide portability and transparency when the user space environment provides interfaces that can be leveraged for virtualization. For proprietary devices with completely closed software stacks, user-level virtualization is necessary.

3.1 Kernel-Level Device Virtualization

Cells introduces a new kernel-level mechanism, *device namespaces*, that provides isolation and efficient hardware resource multiplexing in a manner that is completely transparent to applications. Figure 1 shows how device names-

Device	Description
Alarm *	RTC-based alarms
Audio	Audio I/O (speakers, microphone)
Binder *	IPC framework
Bluetooth	Short range communication
Camera	Video and still-frame input
Framebuffer	Display output
GPU	Graphics processing unit
Input	Touchscreen and input buttons
LEDs	Backlight and indicator LEDs
Logger *	Lightweight RAM log driver
LMK *	Low memory killer
Network	Wi-Fi and Cellular data
Pmem *	Contiguous physical memory
Power *	Power management framework
Radio	Cellular phone (GSM, CDMA)
Sensors	Accelerometer, GPS

Table 1: Android devices
*custom Google drivers

paces are implemented within the overall *Cells* architecture. Unlike PID or UID namespaces in the Linux kernel, which virtualize process identifiers, a device namespace does not virtualize identifiers. It is designed to be used by individual device drivers or kernel subsystems to tag data structures and to register callback functions. Callback functions are called when a device namespace changes state. Each VP uses a unique device namespace for device interaction. *Cells* leverages its foreground-background VP usage model to register callback functions that are called when the VP changes between foreground and background state. This enables devices to be aware of the VP state and change how they respond to a VP depending on whether it is visible to the user and therefore the foreground VP, or not visible to the user and therefore one of potentially multiple background VPs. The usage model is crucial for enabling *Cells* to virtualize devices efficiently and cleanly.

Cells virtualizes existing kernel interfaces based on three methods of implementing device namespace functionality. The first method is to create a device driver wrapper using a new device driver for a virtual device. The wrapper device then multiplexes access and communicates on behalf of applications to the real device driver. The wrapper typically passes through all requests from the foreground VP, and updates device state and access to the device when a new VP becomes the foreground VP. For example, *Cells* use a device driver wrapper to virtualize the framebuffer as described in Section 4.1.

The second method is to modify a device subsystem to be aware of device namespaces. For example, the input device subsystem in Linux handles various devices such as the touchscreen, navigation wheel, compass, GPS, proximity sensor, light sensor, headset input controls, and input buttons. The input subsystem consists of the input core, device drivers, and event handlers, the latter being responsible for passing input events to user space. By default in Linux, input events are sent to any process that is listening for them, but this does not provide the isolation needed for supporting VPs. To enable the input subsystem to use device namespaces, *Cells* only has to modify the event handlers so that, for each process listening for input events, event handlers

first check if the corresponding device namespace is in the foreground. If it is not, the event is not raised to that specific process. The implementation is simple, and no changes are required to device drivers or the input core. As another example, virtualization of the power management subsystem is described in Section 5.

The third method is to modify a device driver to be aware of device namespaces. For example, Android includes a number of custom pseudo drivers which are not part of an existing kernel subsystem, such as the Binder IPC mechanism. To provide isolation among VPs, *Cells* needs to ensure that under no circumstances can a process in one VP gain access to Binder instances in another VP. This is done by modifying the Binder driver so that instead of allowing Binder data structures to reference a single global list of all processes, they reference device namespace isolated lists and only allow communication between processes associated with the same device namespace. A Binder device namespace context is only initialized when the Binder device file is first opened, resulting in almost no overhead for future accesses. While the device driver itself needs to be modified, pseudo device drivers are not hardware-specific and thus changes only need to be made once for all hardware platforms. In some cases, however, it may be necessary to modify a hardware-specific device driver to make it aware of device namespaces. For most devices, this is straightforward and involves duplicating necessary driver state upon device namespace creation and tagging the data describing that state with the device namespace. Even this can be avoided if the device driver provides some basic capabilities as described in Section 4.2, which discusses GPU virtualization.

3.2 User-Level Device Virtualization

In addition to kernel-level device namespace mechanisms, *Cells* introduces a user-level device namespace proxy mechanism that offers similar functionality for devices, such as the baseband processor, that are proprietary and entirely closed source. *Cells* also uses this mechanism to virtualize device configuration, such as Wi-Fi, which occurs in user space. Sections 6 and 7 describe how this user-level proxy approach is used to virtualize telephony and wireless network configuration.

Figure 1 shows the relationship between VPs, kernel-level device namespaces, and user-level device namespace proxies which are contained in a *root namespace*. *Cells* works by booting a minimal init environment in a root namespace which is not visible to any VP and is used to manage individual VPs. The root namespace is considered part of the trusted computing base and processes in the root namespace have full access to the entire file system. The init environment starts a custom process, CellD, which manages the starting and switching of VPs between operating in the background or foreground. Kernel device namespaces export an interface to the root namespace through the /proc filesystem that is used to switch the foreground VP and set access permissions for devices. CellD also coordinates user space virtualization mechanisms such as the configuration of telephony and wireless networking.

To start a new VP, CellD mounts the VP filesystem, clones itself into a new process with separate namespaces, and starts the VP's init process to boot up the user space environment. CellD also sets up the limited set of IPC sockets accessible to processes in the VP for communicating with the root namespace. These IPC sockets are the only ones that can be used for communicating with the root namespace; all other IPC sockets are internal to the respective VP. *Cells* also leverages existing Linux kernel frameworks for resource control to prevent resource starvation from a single VP [15].

3.3 Scalability and Security

Cells uses three scalability techniques to enable multiple VPs running the same Android environment to share code and reduce memory usage. First, the same base file system is shared read-only among VPs. To provide a read-write file system view for a VP, file system unioning [32] is used to join the read-only base file system with a writable file system layer by stacking the latter on top of the former. This creates a unioned view of the two: file system objects, namely files and directories, from the writable layer are always visible, while objects from the read-only layer are only visible if no corresponding object exists in the other layer. Second, when a new VP is started, *Cells* enables Linux Kernel Samepage Merging (KSM) for a short time to further reduce memory usage by finding anonymous memory pages used by the user space environment that have the same contents, then arranging for one copy to be shared among the various VPs [30]. Third, *Cells* leverages the Android low memory killer to increase the total number of VPs it is possible to run on a device without sacrificing functionality. The Android low memory killer kills background and inactive processes consuming large amounts of RAM. Android starts these processes purely as an optimization to reduce application startup-time, so these processes can be killed and restarted without any loss of functionality. Critical system processes are never chosen to be killed, and if the user requires the services of a background process which was killed, the process is simply restarted.

Cells uses four techniques to isolate all VPs from the root namespace and from one another, thereby securing both system and individual VP data from malicious reads or writes. First, user credentials, virtualized through UID namespaces, isolate the root user in one VP from the root user in the root namespace or any other VP. Second, kernel-level device namespaces isolate device access and associated data; no data or device state may be accessed outside a VP's device namespace. Third, mount namespaces provide a unique and separate FS view for each VP; no files belonging to one VP may be accessed by another VP. Fourth, CellD removes the capability to create device nodes inside a VP, preventing processes from gaining direct access to Linux devices or outside their environment, e.g., by re-mounting block devices. These isolation techniques secure *Cells* system data from each VP, and individual VP data from other VPs. For example, a privilege escalation or root attack compromising one VP has no access to the root namespace or any other VP, and cannot use device node creation or super-user access to read or write data in any other VP.

4. GRAPHICS

The display and its graphics hardware is one of the most important devices in smartphones. Applications expect to take full advantage of any hardware display acceleration or GPU available on the smartphone. Android relies on a standard Linux framebuffer (*FB*) which provides an abstraction to a physical display, including screen memory, memory dedicated to and controlled exclusively by the display device. For performance reasons, screen memory is mapped and written to directly both by processes and GPU hardware. The direct memory mapping and the performance requirements of the graphics subsystem present new challenges for virtualizing mobile devices.

4.1 Framebuffer

To virtualize *FB* access in multiple VPs, *Cells* leverages the kernel-level device namespace and its foreground-background usage model in a new multiplexing *FB* device driver, `mux_fb`. The `mux_fb` driver registers as a standard *FB* device and multiplexes access to a single physical device. The foreground VP is given exclusive access to the screen memory and display hardware while each background VP maintains virtual hardware state and renders any output to a virtual screen memory buffer in system RAM, referred to as the backing buffer. VP access to the `mux_fb` driver is isolated through its device namespace, such that a unique virtual device state and backing buffer is associated with each VP. `mux_fb` currently supports multiplexing a single physical frame buffer device, but more complicated multiplexing schemes involving multiple physical devices could be accomplished in a similar manner.

In Linux, the basic *FB* usage pattern involves three types of accesses: `mmaps`, standard control `ioctls`, and custom `ioctls`. When a process `mmaps` an open *FB* device file, the driver is expected to map its associated screen memory into the process' address space allowing the process to render directly on the display. A process controls and configures the *FB* hardware state through a set of standard control `ioctls` defined by the Linux framebuffer interface which can, for example, change the pixel format. Each *FB* device may also define custom `ioctls` which can be used to perform accelerated drawing or rendering operations.

Cells passes all accesses to the `mux_fb` device from the foreground VP directly to the hardware. This includes control `ioctls` as well as custom `ioctls`, allowing applications to take full advantage of any custom `ioctls` implemented by the physical device driver used, for example, to accelerate rendering. When an application running in the foreground VP `mmaps` an open `mux_fb` device, the `mux_fb` driver simply maps the physical screen memory provided by the hardware back end. This creates the same zero-overhead pass-through to the screen memory as on native systems.

Cells does not pass any accesses to the `mux_fb` driver from background VPs to the hardware back end, ensuring that the foreground VP has exclusive hardware access. Standard control `ioctls` are applied to virtual hardware state maintained in RAM. Custom `ioctls`, by definition, perform nonstandard functions such as graphics acceleration or memory allocation, and therefore accesses to these functions from background VPs must be at least partially handled by the same kernel driver which defined them. Instead of passing the `ioctl` to the hardware driver, *Cells* uses a new notification API that allows the original driver to appropriately virtualize the access. If the driver does not register for this new notification, *Cells* either returns an error code, or blocks the calling process when the custom `ioctl` is called from a background VP. Returning an error code was sufficient for both the Nexus 1 and Nexus S systems. When an application running in a background VP `mmaps` the framebuffer device, the `mux_fb` driver will map its backing buffer into the process' virtual address space.

Switching the display from a foreground VP to a background VP is accomplished in four steps, all of which must occur before any additional *FB* operations are performed: (1) screen memory remapping, (2) screen memory deep copy, (3) hardware state synchronization, and (4) GPU coordination. Screen memory remapping is done by altering the page table entries for each process which has mapped *FB* screen memory to redirect virtual addresses in each process to new physical locations. Processes running in the VP which is to be moved into the background have their virtual addresses remapped to backing memory in system RAM, and processes running in the VP which is to become the foreground have their virtual addresses remapped to physical screen memory. The screen memory deep copy is done by copying the contents of the screen memory into the previous foreground VP's backing buffer and copying the contents of the new foreground VP's backing buffer into screen memory. This copy is not strictly necessary if the new foreground VP completely redraws the screen. Hardware state synchronization is done by saving the current hardware state into the virtual state of the previous foreground VP and then setting the current hardware state to the new foreground VP's virtual hardware state. Because the display device only uses the current hardware state to output the screen memory, there is no need to correlate particular drawing updates with individual standard control `ioctls`; only the accumulated virtual hardware state is needed. GPU coordination, discussed in section 4.2, involves notifying the GPU of the memory address switch so that it can update any internal graphics memory mappings.

To better scale the *Cells FB* virtualization, the backing buffer in system RAM could be reduced to a single memory page which is mapped into the entire screen memory address region of background VPs. This optimization not only saves memory, but also eliminates the need for the screen memory deep copy. However, it does require the VP's user space environment to redraw the entire screen when it becomes the foreground VP. Redraw overhead is minimal, and Android conveniently provides this functionality through the `fbearlysuspend` driver discussed in Section 5.1.

4.2 GPU

Cells virtualizes the GPU by leveraging the GPU's independent graphics contexts together with the *FB* virtualization of screen memory described in Section 4.1. Each VP is given direct pass-through access to the GPU device. Because each process which uses the GPU executes graphics commands in its own context, processes are already isolated from each other and there is no need for further VP GPU isolation. The key challenge is that each VP requires *FB* screen memory on which to compose the final scene to be displayed, and in general the GPU driver can request and use this memory from within the OS kernel.

Cells solves this problem by leveraging its foreground-background usage model to provide a virtualization solution similar to *FB* screen memory remapping. The foreground VP will use the GPU to render directly into screen memory, but background VPs, which use the GPU, will render into their respective backing buffers. When the foreground VP changes, the GPU driver locates all GPU addresses which are mapped to the physical screen memory as well as the background VP's backing buffer in system RAM. It must then remap those GPU addresses to point to the new backing buffer and to the physical screen memory, respectively. To accomplish this remapping, *Cells* provides a callback interface from the `mux_fb` driver which provides source and destination physical addresses on each foreground VP switch.

While this technique necessitates a certain level of access to the GPU driver, it does not preclude the possibility of using a proprietary driver so long as it exposes three basic capabilities. First, it should provide the ability to remap GPU linear addresses to specified physical addresses as required by the virtualization mechanism. Second, it should provide the ability to safely reinitialize the GPU device or ignore re-initialization attempts as each VP running a stock user space configuration will attempt to initialize the GPU on startup. Third, it should provide the ability to ignore device power management and other non-graphics related hardware state updates, making it possible to ignore such events from a user space instance running in a background VP. Some of these capabilities were already available on the *Adreno* GPU driver, used in the Nexus 1, but not all. We added a small number of lines of code to the *Adreno* GPU driver and *PowerVR* GPU driver, used in the Nexus S, to implement these three capabilities.

While most modern GPUs include an MMU, there are some devices which require memory used by the GPU to be physically contiguous. For example, the *Adreno* GPU can selectively disable the use of the MMU. For *Cells* GPU virtualization to work under these conditions, the backing memory in system RAM must be physically contiguous. This can be done by allocating the backing memory either with `kmalloc`, or using an alternate physical memory allocator such as Google's `pmem` driver or Samsung's `s3c_mem` driver.

5. POWER MANAGEMENT

To provide *Cells* users the same power management experience as non-virtualized phones, we apply two simple virtualization principles: (1) background VPs should not be able to put the device into a low power mode, and (2) background VPs should not prevent the foreground VP from putting the device into a low power mode. We apply these principles to Android's custom power management, which is based on the premise that a mobile phone's preferred state should be suspended. Android introduces three interfaces which attempt to extend the battery life of mobile devices through extremely aggressive power management: *early suspend*, *fbearlysuspend*, and *wake locks*, also known as suspend blockers [33].

The *early suspend* subsystem is an ordered callback interface allowing drivers to receive notifications just before a device is suspended and after it resumes. *Cells* virtualizes this subsystem by disallowing background VPs from initiating suspend operations. The remaining two Android-specific power management interfaces present unique challenges and offer insights into aggressive power management virtualization.

5.1 Frame Buffer Early Suspend

The *fbearlysuspend* driver exports display device suspend and resume state into user space. This allows user space to block all processes using the display while the display is powered off, and redraw the screen after the display is powered on. Power is saved since the overall device workload is lower and devices such as the GPU may be powered down or made quiescent. Android implements this functionality with two `sysfs` files, `wait_for_fb_sleep` and `wait_for_-fb_wake`. When a user process opens and reads from one of these files, the read blocks until the framebuffer device is either asleep or awake, respectively.

Cells virtualizes fbearlysuspend by making it namespace aware, leveraging the kernel-level device namespace and foreground-background usage model. In the foreground VP, reads function exactly as a non-virtualized system. Reads from a background VP always report the device as sleeping. When the foreground VP switches, all processes in all VPs blocked on either of the two files are unblocked, and the return values from the read calls are based on the new state of the VP in which the process is running. Processes in the new foreground VP see the display as awake, processes in the formerly foreground VP see the display as asleep, and processes running in background VPs that remain in the background continue to see the display as asleep. This forces background VPs to pause drawing or rendering which reduces overall system load by reducing the number of processes using hardware drawing resources, and increases graphics throughput in the foreground VP by ensuring that its processes have exclusive access to the hardware.

5.2 Wake Locks

Wake locks are a special kind of OS kernel reference counter with two states: *active* and *inactive*. When a wake lock is "locked", its state is changed to active; when "unlocked," its state is changed to inactive. A wake lock can be locked multiple times, but only requires a single unlock to put it into the inactive state. The Android system will not enter suspend, or low power mode, until all wake locks are inactive. When all locks are inactive, a suspend timer is started. If it completes without an intervening lock then the device is powered down.

Wake locks in a background VP interfering with the foreground VP's ability to suspend the device coupled with their distributed use and initialization make wake locks a challenging virtualization problem. Wake locks can be created statically at compile time or dynamically by kernel drivers or user space. They can also be locked and unlocked from user context, kernel context (work queues), and interrupt context (IRQ handlers) independently, making determination of the VP to which a wake lock belongs a non-trivial task.

Cells leverages the kernel-level device namespace and foreground-background usage model to maintain both kernel and user space wake lock interfaces while adhering to the two virtualization principles specified above. The solution

is predicated on three assumptions. First, all lock and unlock coordination in the trusted root namespace was correct and appropriate before virtualization. Second, we trust the kernel and its drivers; when lock or unlock is called from interrupt context, we perform the operation unconditionally. Third, the foreground VP maintains full control of the hardware.

Under these assumptions, *Cells* virtualizes Android wake locks by allowing multiple device namespaces to independently lock and unlock the same wake lock. Power management operations are initiated based on the state of the set of locks associated with the foreground VP. The solution comprises the following set of rules:

1. When a wake lock is locked, a namespace "token" is associated with the lock indicating the context in which the lock was taken. A wake lock token may contain references to multiple namespaces if the lock was taken from those namespaces.
2. When a wake lock is unlocked from user context, remove the associated namespace token.
3. When a wake lock is unlocked from interrupt context or the root namespace, remove *all* lock tokens. This follows from the second assumption.
4. After a user context lock or unlock, adjust any suspend timeout value based only on locks acquired in the current device namespace.
5. After a root namespace lock or unlock, adjust the suspend timeout based on the foreground VP's device namespace.
6. When the foreground VP changes, reset the suspend timeout based on locks acquired in the newly active namespace. This requires per-namespace bookkeeping of suspend timeout values.

One additional mechanism was necessary to implement the *Cells* wake lock virtualization. The set of rules given above implicitly assumes that, aside from interrupt context, the lock and unlock functions are aware of the device namespace in which the operation is being performed. While this is true for operations started from user context, it is not the case for operations performed from kernel work queues. To address this issue, we introduced a mechanism which executes a kernel work queue in a specific device namespace.

6. TELEPHONY

Cells provides each VP with separate telephony functionality enabling per-VP call logs, and independent phone numbers. We first describe how *Cells* virtualizes the radio stack to provide telephony isolation among VPs, then we discuss how multiple phone numbers can be provided on a single physical phone using the standard carrier voice network and a single SIM.

6.1 RIL Proxy

The Android telephony subsystem is designed to be easily ported by phone vendors to different hardware devices. The Android phone application uses a set of Java libraries and services that handle the telephony state and settings such as displaying current radio strength in the status bar, and selection of different roaming options. The phone application, the libraries and the services all communicate via Binder

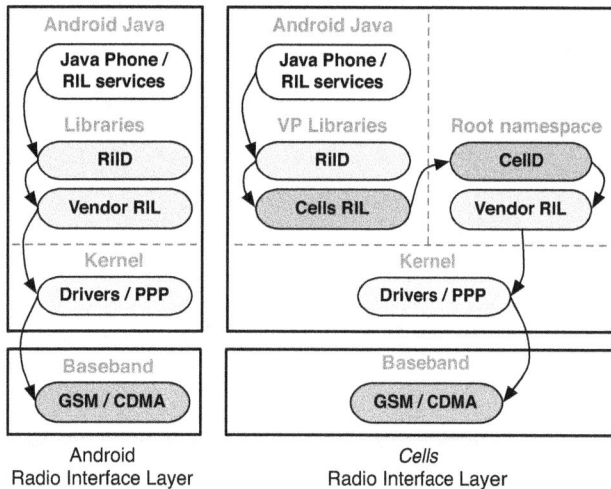

Figure 2: *Cells* Radio Interface Layer

Call	Class	Category
Dial Request	Solicited	
Set Screen State	Solicited	Foreground
Set Radio State	Solicited	
SIM I/O	Solicited	Initialization
Signal Strength	Unsolicited	Radio Info
Call State Changed	Unsolicited	
Call Ring	Unsolicited	Phone Calls
Get Current Calls	Solicited	

Table 2: Filtered RIL commands

IPC with the Radio Interface Layer (RIL) Daemon (RilD). RilD dynamically links with a library provided by the phone hardware vendor which in turn communicates with kernel drivers and the radio baseband system. The left side of Figure 2 shows the standard Android telephony system.

The entire radio baseband system is proprietary and closed source, starting from the user-level RIL vendor library down to the physically separate hardware baseband processor. Details of the vendor library implementation and its communication with the baseband are well-guarded secrets. Each hardware phone vendor provides its own proprietary radio stack. Since the stack is a complete black box, it would be difficult if not impossible to intercept, replicate, or virtualize any aspect of this system in the kernel without direct hardware vendor support. Furthermore, the vendor library is designed to be used by only a single RilD and the radio stack as a whole is not designed to be multiplexed.

As a result of these constraints, *Cells* virtualizes telephony using our user-level device namespace proxy in a solution designed to work transparently with the black box radio stack. Each VP has the standard Android telephony Java libraries and services and its own stock RilD, but rather than having RilD communicate directly with the hardware vendor provided RIL library, *Cells* provides its own proxy RIL library in each VP. The proxy RIL library is loaded by RilD in each VP and connects to CellD running in the root namespace. CellD then communicates with the hardware vendor library to use the proprietary radio stack. Since there can be only one radio stack, CellD loads the vendor RIL library on system startup and multiplexes access to it. We refer to the proxy RIL library together with CellD as the *RIL proxy*. The right side of Figure 2 shows the *Cells* Android telephony system, which has three key features. First, no hardware vendor support is required since it treats the radio stack as a black box. Second, it works with a stock Android environment since Android does not provide its own RIL library but instead relies on it being supplied by the system on which it will be used. Third, it operates at a well-defined interface, making it possible to understand exactly how communication is done between RilD and the RIL library it uses.

Cells leverages its foreground-background model to enable the necessary multiplexing of the radio stack. Since the user can only make calls from the foreground VP, because only its user interface is displayed, CellD allows only the foreground VP to make calls. All other forms of multiplexing are done in response to incoming requests from the radio stack through CellD. CellD uses the vendor RIL library in the same manner as Android's RilD, and can therefore provide all of the standard call multiplexing available in Android for handling incoming calls. For example, to place the current call in the foreground VP on hold while answering an incoming call to a background VP, CellD issues the same set of standard GSM commands RilD would have used.

The RIL proxy needs to support the two classes of function calls defined by the RIL, *solicited calls* which pass from RilD to the RIL library, and *unsolicited calls* which pass from the RIL library to RilD. The interface is relatively simple, as there are only four defined solicited function calls and two defined unsolicited function calls, though there are a number of possible arguments. Both the solicited requests and the responses carry structured data in their arguments. The structured data can contain pointers to nested data structures and arrays of pointers. The main complexity in implementing the RIL proxy is dealing with the implementation assumption in Android that the RIL vendor library is normally loaded in the RilD process so that pointers can be passed between the RIL library and RilD. In *Cells*, the RIL vendor library is loaded in the CellD process instead of the RilD process and the RIL proxy passes the arguments over a standard Unix Domain socket so all data must be thoroughly packed and unpacked on either side.

The basic functionality of the RIL proxy is to pass requests sent from within a VP unmodified to the vendor RIL library and to forward unsolicited calls from the vendor RIL library to RilD inside a VP. CellD filters requests as needed to disable telephony functionality for VPs that are configured not to have telephony access. However, even in the absence of such VP configurations, some solicited requests must be filtered from background VPs and some calls require special handling to properly support our foreground-background model and provide working isolated telephony. The commands that require filtering or special handling are shown in Table 2 and can be categorized as those involving the foreground VP, initialization, radio info, and phone calls.

Foreground commands are allowed only from the foreground VP. The *Dial Request* command represents outgoing calls, *Set Screen State* is used to suppress certain notifications like signal strength, and *Set Radio State* is used to turn the radio on or off. *Set Screen State* is filtered from background VPs by only changing a per-VP variable in CellD that suppresses notifications to the issuing background VP accordingly. *Dial Request* and *Set Radio State* are filtered from all background VPs by returning an error code to the calling background VP. This ensures that background VPs do not interfere with the foreground VP's exclusive ability to place calls.

Initialization commands are run once on behalf of the first foreground VP to call them. The *SIM I/O* command is used to communicate directly with the SIM card, and is called during radio initialization (when turning on the device or turning off airplane mode), and when querying SIM information such as the *IMSI*. The first time a VP performs a *SIM I/O* command, CellD records an ordered log of commands, associated data, and corresponding responses. This log is used to replay responses from the vendor RIL library when other VPs attempt *SIM I/O* commands. When the radio is turned off, the log is cleared, and the first foreground VP to turn on the radio will be allowed to do so, causing CellD to start recording a new log. CellD also records the radio state between each *SIM I/O* command to properly replay the state transitions.

Radio Info commands are innocuous and are broadcast to all VPs. *Signal Strength* is an unsolicited notification about the current signal strength generated by the vendor library. CellD re-broadcasts this information to all VPs with one exception. During initialization, a VP cannot be notified of the signal strength since that would indicate an already initialized radio and generate errors in the initializing VP.

The *Phone Call* commands, *Call State Changed*, *Call Ring*, and *Get Current Calls*, notify a VP of incoming calls and call state changes. When an incoming call occurs, a *Call State Changed* notification is sent, followed by a number of *Call Ring* notifications for as long as the call is pending. CellD inspects each notification and determines the VP to which it should forward the notification. However, this is somewhat complicated since neither notification is associated with a phone number. Therefore, CellD queues these notifications and issues a *Get Current Calls* command, mirroring the functionality of RilD, to receive a list of all incoming and active calls. Using tagging information encoded in the caller ID as discussed in Section 6.2, CellD determines the target VP and passes the queued notifications into the appropriate VP. When a VP issues a *Get Current Calls* request, CellD intercepts the data returned from the vendor library and only returns data from calls directed to, or initiated from the requesting VP.

CellD's architecture supports a highly configurable implementation, and there are many valid security configuration scenarios. For example, if the user switches the foreground VP during a call, CellD can either drop the call and switch to the new VP, keep the call alive and switch to a new VP (handling the active call in a background VP, or, deny switching to a new VP until the call is ended by the user. Under all configurations, *Cells* provides strict isolation between every VP by not allowing any information pertaining to a specific VP to be revealed to another VP including incoming and outgoing call information and the phone call voice data.

6.2 Multiple Phone Numbers

While some smartphones support multiple SIM cards, which makes supporting multiple phone numbers straightforward, most phones do not provide this feature. Since mobile network operators do not generally offer multiple phone numbers per SIM card or CDMA phone, we offer an alternative system to provide a distinct phone number for each VP on existing unmodified single SIM card phones, which dominate the market. Our approach is based on pairing *Cells* with a VoIP service that enables telephony with the standard cellular voice network and standard Android applications, but with separate phone numbers.

The *Cells* VoIP service consists of a VoIP server which registers a pool of subscriber numbers and pairs each of them with the carrier provided number associated with a user's SIM. The VoIP server receives incoming calls, forwards them to a user's actual phone number using the standard cellular voice network, and passes the incoming caller ID to the user's phone appending a digit denoting the VP to which the call should be delivered. When CellD receives the incoming call list, it checks the last digit of the caller ID and chooses a VP based on that digit. *Cells* allows users to configure which VP should handle which digit through the VoIP service interface. CellD strips the appended digit before forwarding call information to the receiving VP resulting in correctly displayed caller IDs within the VP. If the VP is not available, the VoIP service will direct the incoming call to a server-provided voice mail. We currently use a single digit scheme supporting a maximum of ten selectable VPs, which should be more than sufficient for any user. While it is certainly possible to spoof caller ID, in the worst case, this would simply appear to be a case of dialing the wrong phone number. Our VoIP service is currently implemented using an Asterisk [1] server as it provides unique functionality not available through other commercial voice services. For example, although Google Voice can forward multiple phone numbers to the same land line, it does not provide this capability for mobile phone numbers, and does not provide arbitrary control over outgoing caller ID [10].

The caller ID of outgoing calls should also be replaced with the phone number of the VP that actually makes the outgoing call instead of the mobile phone's actual mobile phone number. Unfortunately, the GSM standard does not have any facility to *change* the caller ID, only to either enable or disable showing the caller ID. Therefore, if the VP is configured to display outgoing caller IDs, *Cells* ensures that they are correctly sent by routing those calls through the VoIP server. CellD intercepts the *Dial Request*, dials the VoIP service subscriber number associated with the dialing VP, and passes the actual number to be dialed via DTMF tones. The VoIP server interprets the tones, dials the requested number, and connects the call.

7. NETWORKING

Mobile devices are most commonly equipped with an IEEE 802.11 wireless LAN (WLAN) adapter and cellular data connectivity through either a GSM or CDMA network. Each VP that has network access must be able to use either WLAN or cellular data depending on what is available to the user at any given location. At the same time, each VP must be completely isolated from other VPs. *Cells* integrates both kernel and user-level virtualization to provide necessary isolation and functionality, including core network resource virtualization and a unique wireless configuration management virtualization.

Cells leverages previous kernel-level work [27,28] that virtualizes core network resources such as IP addresses, network adapters, routing tables, and port numbers. This functionality has been largely built in to recent versions of the Linux kernel in the form of network namespaces [3]. Virtual identifiers are provided in VPs for all network resources, which are then translated into physical identifiers. Real network devices representing the WLAN or cellular data connection are not visible within a VP. Instead, a virtual Ethernet pair is setup from the root namespace where one end is present inside a VP and the other end is in the root namespace. The kernel is then configured to perform Network Address Translation (NAT) between the active public interface (either WLAN or cellular data) and the VP-end of an Ethernet pair. Each VP is then free to bind to any socket address and port without conflicting with other VPs. *Cells* uses NAT as opposed to bridged networking since bridging is not supported on cellular data connections and is also not guaranteed to work on WLAN connections. Note that since each VP has its own virtualized network resources, network security mechanisms are isolated among VPs. For example, VPN access to a corporate network from one VP cannot be used by another VP.

However, WLAN and cellular data connections use device-specific, user-level configuration which requires support outside the scope of existing core network virtualization. There exists little if any support for virtualizing WLAN or cellular data configuration. Current best practice is embodied in desktop virtualization products such as VMware Workstation [29] which create a virtual wired Ethernet adapter inside a virtual machine but leave the configuration on the host system. This model does not work on a mobile device where no such host system is available and a VP is the primary system used by the user. VPs rely heavily on network status notifications reflecting a network configuration that can frequently change, making it essential for wireless configuration and status notifications to be virtualized and made available to each VP. A user-level library called `wpa_supplicant` with support for a large number of devices is typically used to issue various `ioctls` and netlink socket options that are unique to each device. Unlike virtualizing core network resources which are general and well-defined, virtualizing wireless configuration in the kernel would involve emulating the device-specific understanding of configuration management which is error-prone, complicated, and difficult to maintain.

To address this problem, *Cells* leverages the user-level device namespace proxy and the foreground-background model to decouple wireless configuration from the actual network interfaces. A configuration proxy is introduced to replace the user-level WLAN configuration library and RIL libraries inside each VP. The proxy communicates with CellD running in the root namespace, which communicates with the user-level library for configuring WLAN or cellular data connections. In the default case where all VPs are allowed network access, CellD forwards all configuration requests from the foreground VP proxy to the user-level library, and ignores configuration requests from background VP proxies that would adversely affect the foreground VP's network access. This approach is minimally intrusive since user space phone environments, such as Android, are already designed to run on multiple hardware platforms and therefore cleanly interface with user space configuration libraries.

To virtualize Wi-Fi configuration management, *Cells* replaces `wpa_supplicant` inside each VP with a thin Wi-Fi proxy. The well-defined socket interface used by `wpa_supplicant` is simple to virtualize. The Wi-Fi proxy communicates with CellD running in the root namespace, which in turn starts and communicates with `wpa_supplicant` as needed on behalf of individual VPs. The protocol used by the Wi-Fi proxy and CellD is quite simple, as the standard interface to `wpa_supplicant` consists of only eight function calls each with text-based arguments. The protocol sends the function number, a length of the following message, and the message data itself. Replies are similar, but also contain an integer return value in addition to data. CellD ensures that background VPs cannot interfere with the operation of the foreground VP. For instance, if the foreground VP is connected to a Wi-Fi network and a background VP requests to disable the Wi-Fi access, the request is ignored. At the same time, inquiries sent from background VPs that do not change state or divulge sensitive information, such as requesting the current signal strength, are processed since applications such as email clients inside background VPs may use this information when checking for new email.

For virtualizing cellular data connection management, *Cells* replaces the RIL vendor library as described in Section 6, which is also responsible for establishing cellular data connections. As with Wi-Fi, CellD ensures that background VPs cannot interfere· with the operation of the foreground VP. For instance, a background VP cannot change the data roaming options causing the foreground VP to either lose data connectivity or inadvertently use the data connection. Cellular data is configured independently from the Wi-Fi connection and VPs can also be configured to completely disallow data connections. Innocuous inquiries from background VPs with network access, such as the status of the data connection (Edge, 3G, HSPDA, etc.) or signal strength, are processed and reported back to the VPs.

8. EXPERIMENTAL RESULTS

We have implemented a *Cells* prototype using Android and demonstrated its complete functionality across different Android devices, including the Google Nexus 1 [8] and Nexus S [9] phones. The prototype has been tested to work with multiple versions of Android, including the most recent open-source version, version 2.3.4. In UI testing while running multiple VPs on a phone, there is no user noticeable performance difference between running in a VP and running natively on the phone. For example, while running 4 VPs on Nexus 1 device, we simultaneously played the popular game *Angry Birds* [26] in one VP, raced around a dirt track in the *Reckless Racing* [24] game on a second VP, crunched some numbers in a spreadsheet using the *Office Suite Pro* [19] application in a third VP, and listened to some music using the Android music player in the fourth VP. Using *Cells* we were able to deliver native 3D acceleration to both game instances while seamlessly switching between and interacting with all four running VPs.

8.1 Methodology

We further quantitatively measured the performance of our unoptimized prototype running a wide range of applications in multiple VPs. Our measurements were obtained using a Nexus 1 (Qualcomm 1 GHz QSD8250, Adreno 200 GPU, 512 MB RAM) and Nexus S (Samsung Hummingbird 1 GHz Cortex A8, PowerVR GPU, 512 MB RAM) phones. The Nexus 1 uses an SD card for storage for some of the applications; we used a Patriot Memory class 10 16 GB SD card. Due to space constraints on the Nexus 1 flash device, all Android system files for all *Cells* configurations were stored on, and run from, the SD card.

The *Cells* implementation used for our measurements was based on the Android Open Source Project (AOSP) version 2.3.3, the most recent version available at the time our measurements were taken. Aufs version 2.1 was used for file system unioning [21]. A single read-only branch of a union file system was used as the /system and /data partitions of each VP. This saves megabytes of file system cache while maintaining isolation between VPs through separate writable branches. When one VP modified a file in the read-only branch, the modification is stored in its own private write branch of the file system. The implementation enables the Linux KSM driver for a period of time when a VP is booted. To maximize the benefit of KSM, CellD uses a custom system call which adds all memory pages from all processes to the set of pages KSM attempts to merge. While this potentially maximizes shared pages, the processing overhead required to hash and check all memory pages from all processes quickly outweighs the benefit. Therefore, CellD monitors the KSM statistics through the procfs interface and disables shared page merging after the merge rate drops below a pre-determined threshold.

We present measurements along three dimensions of performance: runtime overhead, power consumption, and memory usage. To measure runtime overhead, we compared the performance of various applications running with *Cells* versus running the applications on the latest manufacturer stock image available for the respective mobile devices (Android 2.3.3 build GRI40). We measured the performance of *Cells* when running 1 VP (1-VP), 2 VPs (2-VP), 3 VPs (3-VP), 4 VPs (4-VP), and 5 VPs (5-VP), each with a fully booted Android environment running all applications and system services available in such an environment. Since AOSP v2.3.3 was used as the system origin in our experiments, we also measured the performance of a baseline system (Baseline) created by compiling the AOSP v2.3.3 source and installing it unmodified.

We measured runtime overhead in two scenarios, one with a benchmark application designed to stress some aspect of the system, and the other with the same application running, but simultaneously with an additional background workload. The benchmark application was always run in the foreground VP and if a background workload was used, it was run in a single background VP when multiple VPs were used. For the benchmark application, we ran one of six Android applications designed to measure different aspects of

performance: CPU using Linpack for Android v1.1.7; file I/O using Quadrant Advanced Edition v1.1.1; 3D graphics using Neocore by Qualcomm; Web browsing using the popular SunSpider v0.9.1 JavaScript benchmark; and networking using the wget module in a cross-compiled version of BusyBox v1.8.1 to download a single 400 MB file from a dedicated Samsung nb30 laptop (1.66 GHz Intel Atom N450, Intel GMA 3150 GPU, 1 GB RAM). The laptop was running Windows 7, providing a WPA wireless access point via its Atheros AR9285 chipset and built-in Windows 7 SoftAP [18] functionality, and serving up the file through the HFS [11] file server v2.2f. To minimize network variability, a location with minimal external Wi-Fi network interference was chosen. Each experiment was performed from this same location with the phone connected to the same laptop access point. For the background workload, we played a music file from local storage in a loop using the standard Android music player. All results were normalized against the performance of the manufacturer's stock configuration without the background workload.

To measure power consumption, we compared the power consumption of the latest manufacturer stock image available for the respective mobile devices against that of Baseline and *Cells* in 1-VP, 2-VP, 3-VP, 4-VP, and 5-VP configurations. We measured two different power scenarios. In the first scenario, the device configuration under test was fully booted, all VPs started up and KSM had stopped merging pages, then the Android music player was started. In multiple VP configurations, the music player ran in the foreground VP, preventing the device from entering a low power state. The music player repeated the same song continuously for four hours. During this time we sampled the remaining battery capacity every 10 seconds. In the second power scenario, the device configuration under test was fully booted, and then the device was left idle for 12 hours. During the idle period, the device would normally enter a low power state, preventing intermediate measurements. However, occasionally the device would wake up to service timers and Android system alarms, and during this time we would take a measurement of the remaining battery capacity. At the end of 12 hours we took additional measurements of capacity. To measure power consumption due to *Cells* and avoid having those measurements completely eclipsed by Wi-Fi, cellular, and display power consumption, we disabled Wi-Fi and cellular communication, and turned off the display backlight for these experiments.

To measure memory usage, we recorded the amount of memory used for the Baseline and *Cells* in 1-VP, 2-VP, 3-VP, 4-VP, and 5-VP configurations. We measured two different memory scenarios. First, we ran a full Android environment without launching any additional applications other than those that are launched by default on system bootup (No Apps). Second, we ran the first scenario plus the Android Web browser, the Android email client, and the Android calendar application (Apps). In both scenarios, an instance of every application was running in all background VPs as well as the foreground VP.

8.2 Measurements

Figures 3a to 3f show measurement results. These are the first measurements we are aware of for running multiple An-

(a) Normalized Nexus 1 results

(b) Normalized Nexus S results

(c) Normalized Nexus 1 + music results

(d) Normalized Nexus S + music results

(e) Normalized battery capacity

(f) Memory usage in MB

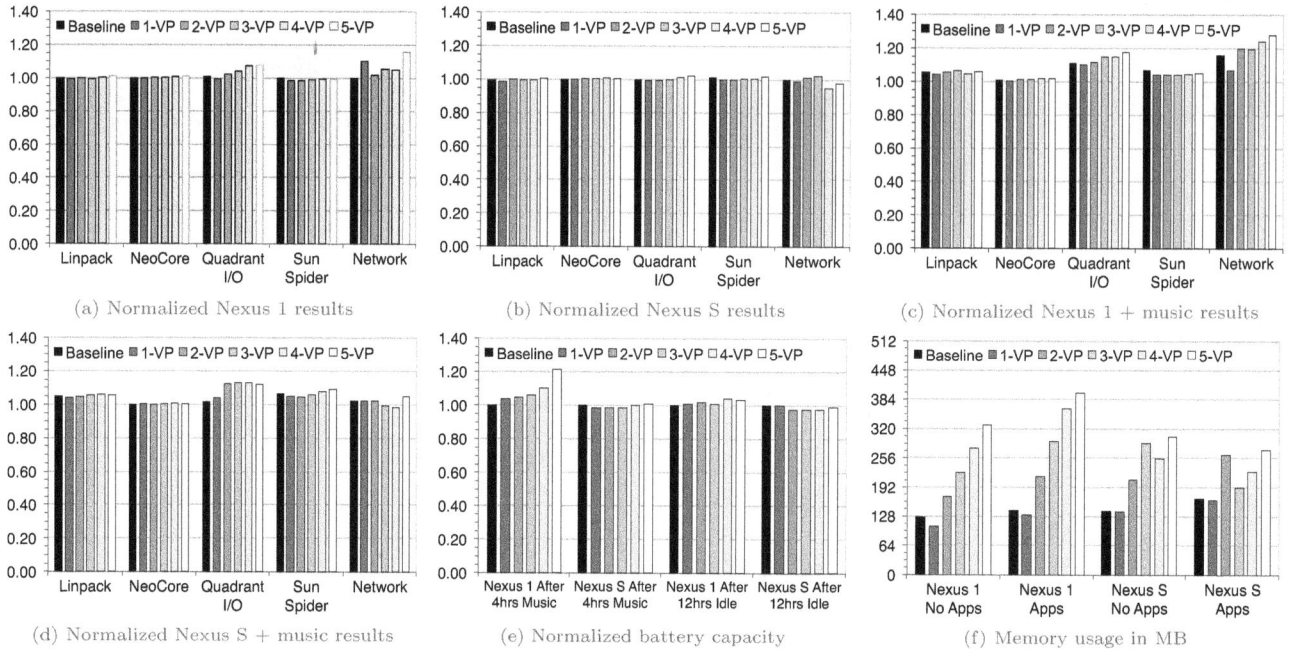

Figure 3: Experimental results

droid instances on a single phone. In all experiments, Baseline and stock measurements were within 1% of each other, so only Baseline results are shown.

Figures 3a and 3b show the runtime overhead on the Nexus 1 and Nexus S, respectively, for each of the benchmark applications with no additional background workload. *Cells* runtime overhead was small in all cases, even with up to 5 VPs running at the same time. *Cells* incurs less than than 1% overhead in all cases on the Nexus 1 except for Network and Quadrant I/O, and less than 4% overhead in all cases on the Nexus S. The Neocore measurements show that *Cells* is the first system that can deliver fully-accelerated graphics performance in virtual mobile devices. Quadrant I/O on the Nexus 1 has less than 7% overhead in all cases, though the 4-VP and 5-VP measurements have more overhead than the configurations with fewer VPs. This is likely due to the use of the slower SD card on the Nexus 1 for this benchmark instead of internal flash memory on the Nexus S coupled with the presence of I/O system background processes running in each VP.

The Network overhead measurements show the highest overhead on the Nexus 1 and the least overhead on the Nexus S. The measurements shown are averaged across ten experiments per configuration. The differences here are not reflective of any significant differences in performance as much as the fact that the results of this benchmark were highly variable; the variance in the results for any one configuration was much higher than any differences across configurations. While testing in a more tightly controlled environment would provide more stable numbers, any overhead introduced by *Cells* was consistently below Wi-Fi variability levels observed on the manufacturer's stock system and should not be noticeable by a user.

Figures 3c and 3d show the runtime overhead on the Nexus 1 and Nexus S, respectively, for each of the benchmark ap-

plications while running the additional background music player workload. All results are normalized to the performance of the stock system running the first scenario without a background workload to show the overhead introduced by the background workload. As expected, there is some additional overhead relative to a stock system not running a background workload, though the amount of overhead varies across applications. Relative to a stock system, Neocore has the least overhead, and has almost the same overhead as without the background workload because it primarily uses the GPU for 3D rendering which is not used by the music player. Linpack and SunSpider incur some additional overhead compared to running without the background workload, reflecting the additional CPU overhead of running the music player at the same time. Network runtime overhead while running an additional background workload showed the same level of variability in measurement results as the benchmarks run without a background workload. *Cells* network performance overhead is modest, as the variance in the results for any one configuration still exceeded the difference across configurations. Quadrant I/O overhead was the highest among the benchmark applications, reflecting the expected I/O contention between the I/O benchmark and the music player.

Comparing to the Baseline configuration with an additional background workload, *Cells* overhead remains small in all cases. It incurs less than 1% overhead in all cases on the Nexus 1 except for Network and Quadrant I/O, and less than 4% overhead in all cases on the Nexus S except for Quadrant I/O, although the majority of benchmark results on the Nexus S show nearly zero overhead. Quadrant I/O on the Nexus 1, while running an additional background workload, incurs a maximum overhead of 7% relative to Baseline performance. Quadrant I/O on the Nexus S has less than 2% overhead for the 1-VP configuration when compared to the Baseline configuration. However, configurations with more than 1 VP show an overhead of 10% relative to the Baseline due to higher I/O performance in the Nexus S baseline compared to the Nexus 1. The higher absolute performance of the Nexus S accentuates the virtualization overhead of running multiple VPs.

Figure 3e shows power consumption on the Nexus 1 and Nexus S, both while playing music with the standard Android music player for 4 hours continuously, and while letting the phone sit idle for 12 hours in a low power state. In both scenarios, the background VPs were the same as the foreground VP except that in the second scenario the music player was not running in the background VPs. Note that the graph presents normalized results, not absolute percentage difference in battery capacity usage, so lower numbers are better.

The power consumption attributable to *Cells* during the 4 hours of playing music on the Nexus 1 increased while running more VPs, which involved scheduling and running more processes and threads on the system and resulted in a higher power supply load variation. The nonlinearity in how this variation affects power consumption resulted in the 4-6% overhead in battery usage for 1-VP through 3-VP, and the 10-20% overhead for 4-VP and 5-VP. In contrast, the Nexus S showed no measurable increase in power consumption during the 4 hours of playing music, though the the noisy measurements had some slight variation. Because the Nexus S is a newer device, the better power management may be reflective of what could be expected when running *Cells* on newer hardware.

Nexus 1 power consumption after 12 hours of sitting idle was within 2% of Baseline. Similarly, Nexus S measurements showed no measurable increase in power consumption due to *Cells* after the 12 hour idle period. When the device sat idle, the Android wake lock system would aggressively put the device in a low power mode where the CPU was completely powered down. The idle power consumption results hold even when background VPs are running applications which would normally hold wake locks to prevent the device from sleeping such as a game like *Angry Birds* or the Android music player. This shows that the *Cells'* wake lock virtualization makes efficient use of battery resources.

Figure 3f shows memory usage on the Nexus 1 and Nexus S. These results show that by leveraging the KSM driver and file system unioning, *Cells* requires incrementally less memory to start each additional VP compared to running the first VP. Furthermore, the 1-VP configuration uses less memory than the Baseline configuration, also due to the use of the KSM driver. *Cells* device memory use increases linearly with the number of VPs running, but at a rate much less than the amount of memory required for the Baseline.

The Nexus 1 memory usage is reported for both memory scenarios, No Apps and Apps, across all six configurations. The No Apps measurements were taken after booting each VP and waiting until CellD disabled the KSM driver. The Apps measurements were taken after starting an instance of the Android Web browser, email client, and calendar program in each running VP. Leveraging the Linux KSM driver, *Cells* uses approximately 20% less memory for 1-VP than Baseline in the No Apps scenario. The No Apps measurements

show that the memory cost for *Cells* to start each additional VP is approximately 55 MB, which is roughly 40% of the memory used by the Baseline Android system and roughly 50% of the memory used to start the first VP. The reduced memory usage of additional VPs is due to *Cells'* use of file system unioning to share common code and data as well as KSM, providing improved scalability on memory-constrained phones.

As expected, the No Apps scenario uses less memory than the Apps scenario. Starting all three applications in the 1-VP Apps scenario consumes 24 MB. This memory scales linearly with the number of VPs because we disable the KSM driver before starting the applications. It may be possible to reduce the memory used when running the same application in all VPs by periodically enabling the KSM driver, however application heap usage would limit the benefit. For example, while *Cells* uses 20% less memory for 1-VP than Baseline in the No Apps scenario, this savings decreases in the Apps scenario because of application heap memory usage.

The Nexus S memory usage is reported under the same conditions described above for the Nexus 1. The memory cost of starting a VP on the Nexus S is roughly 70 MB. This is higher than the Nexus 1 due to increased heap usage by Android base applications and system support libraries. The memory cost of starting all three apps in the 1-VP Apps scenario is approximately the same as the Nexus 1, and also scales linearly with the number of running VPs.

However, the total memory usage for the Nexus S shown in Figure 3f does not continue to increase with the number of running VPs. This is due to the more limited available RAM on the Nexus S and the Android low memory killer. The Nexus S contains several hardware acceleration components which require dedicated regions of memory. These regions can be multiplexed across VPs, but reduce the total available system memory for general use by applications. As a result, although the Nexus 1 and Nexus S have the same amount of RAM, the RAM available for general use on the Nexus S is about 350 MB versus 400 MB for the Nexus 1. Thus, after starting the 4th VP in the No Apps scenario, and after starting the 3rd VP in the Apps scenario, the Android low memory killer begins to kill background processes to free system memory for new applications. While this allowed us to start and interact with 5 VPs on the Nexus S, it also slightly increased application startup time.

9. RELATED WORK

Virtualization on embedded and mobile devices is a relatively new area. Bare-metal hypervisors such as OKL4 Microvisor [22] and Red Bend's VLX [25] offer the potential benefit of a smaller trusted computing base, but the disadvantage of having to provide device support and emulation, an onerous requirement for smartphones which provide increasingly diverse hardware devices. For example, we are not aware of any OKL4 implementations that run Android on any phones other than the dated HTC G1. A hosted virtualization solution such as VMware MVP [2] can leverage Android device support to more easily run on recent hardware, but its trusted computing base is larger as it includes both the Android user space environment and host Linux OS. Xen for ARM [13] and KVM/ARM [5] are open-source virtualization solutions for ARM, but are both incomplete with respect to device support. All of these approaches require paravirtualization and require an entire OS instance in each VM adding to both memory and CPU overhead. This can significantly limit scalability and performance on resource constrained phones. For example, VMware MVP is targeted to run just one VM to encapsulate an Android virtual work phone on an Android host personal phone.

Cells' OS virtualization approach provides several advantages over existing hardware virtualization approaches on smartphones. First, it is more lightweight and introduces less overhead. Second, only a single OS instance is run to support multiple VPs as opposed to needing to run several OS instances on the same hardware, one per VM plus an additional host instance for hosted virtualization. Attempts have been made to run a heavily modified Android in a VM without the OS instance [12], but they lack support for most applications and are problematic to maintain. Third, OS virtualization is supported in existing commodity OSes such as Linux, enabling *Cells* to leverage existing investments in commodity software as opposed to building and maintaining a separate, complex hypervisor platform. Fourth, by running the same commodity OS already shipped with the hardware, we can leverage already available device support instead of needing to rewrite our own with a bare metal hypervisor.

Cells has two potential disadvantages versus hardware virtualization. First, the TCB necessary for ensuring security is potentially larger than a bare metal hypervisor, though no worse than hosted virtualization. We believe the benefits in ease of deployment from leveraging existing OS infrastructure are worth this tradeoff. Second, applications in VPs are expected to run on the same OS, for example VPs cannot run Apple iOS on an Android system. However, running a different OS using hardware virtualization would first need to overcome licensing restrictions and device compatibility issues that would prevent popular smartphone OSes such as iOS from being run on non-Apple hardware and hypervisors from being run on Apple hardware.

User-level approaches have also been proposed to support separate work and personal virtual phone environments on the same mobile hardware. This is done by providing either an Android work phone application [7] that also supports other custom work-related functions such as email, or a secure SDK on which applications can be developed [31]. While such solutions are easier to deploy, they suffer from the inability to run standard Android applications and a weaker security model.

Efficient device virtualization is a difficult problem on user-centric systems such as desktops and phones that must support a plethora of devices. Most approaches require emulation of hardware devices, imposing high overhead [34]. Dedicating a device to a VM can enable low overhead pass-through operation, but then does not allow the device to be used by other VMs [20]. Bypass mechanisms for network I/O have been proposed to reduce overhead [17], but require specialized hardware support used in high-speed network interfaces not present on most user-centric systems, including phones. GPU devices are perhaps the most diffi-

cult to virtualize. For example, VMware MVP simply cannot run graphics applications such as games within a VM with reasonable performance [VMware, personal communication]. There are two basic GPU virtualization techniques, API forwarding and back-end virtualization [6]. API forwarding adds substantial complexity and overhead to the TCB, and is problematic due to vendor-specific graphics extensions [14]. Back-end virtualization in a type-1 hypervisor offers the potential for transparency and speed, but unfortunately most graphics vendors keep details of their hardware trade-secret precluding any use of this virtualization method. In contrast, *Cells* leverages existing GPU graphics context isolation and takes advantage of the usage model of mobile devices to create a new device namespace abstraction that transparently virtualizes devices while maintaining native or near native device performance across a wide range of devices including GPU devices.

10. CONCLUSIONS

We have designed, implemented, and evaluated *Cells*, the first OS virtualization solution for mobile devices. Mobile devices have a different usage model than traditional computers. We use this observation to provide new device virtualization mechanisms, device namespaces and device namespace proxies, that leverage a foreground-background usage model to isolate and multiplex phone devices with near zero overhead. Device namespaces provide a kernel-level abstraction that is used to virtualize critical hardware devices such as the framebuffer and GPU while providing fully accelerated graphics. Device namespaces are also used to virtualize Android's complicated power management framework, resulting in almost no extra power consumption for *Cells* compared to stock Android. *Cells* proxy libraries provide a user-level mechanism to virtualize closed and proprietary device infrastructure, such as the telephony radio stack, with only minimal configuration changes to the Android user space environment. *Cells* further provides each virtual phone complete use of the standard cellular phone network with its own phone number and incoming and outgoing caller ID support through the use of a VoIP cloud service.

We have implemented a *Cells* prototype that runs the latest open-source version of Android on the most recent Google phone hardware, including both the Nexus 1 and Nexus S. The system can use virtual mobile devices to run standard unmodified Android applications downloadable from the Android market. Applications running inside VPs have full access to all hardware devices, providing the same user experience as applications running on a native phone. Performance results across a wide-range of applications running in up to 5 VPs on the same Nexus 1 and Nexus S hardware show that *Cells* incurs near zero performance overhead, and human UI testing reveals no visible performance degradation in any of the benchmark configurations.

11. ACKNOWLEDGMENTS

Qi Ding and Charles Hastings helped with running benchmarks to obtain many of the measurements in this paper. Kevin DeGraaf setup our Asterisk VoIP service. Philip Levis provided helpful comments on earlier drafts of this paper. This work was supported in part by NSF grants CNS-1018355, CNS-0914845, CNS-0905246, AFOSR MURI grant FA9550-07-1-0527, and a Google Research Award.

12. REFERENCES

[1] Asterisk. http://www.asterisk.org.

[2] K. Barr, P. Bungale, S. Deasy, V. Gyuris, P. Hung, C. Newell, H. Tuch, and B. Zoppis. The VMware Mobile Virtualization Platform: Is That a Hypervisor in Your Pocket? *ACM SIGOPS Operating Systems Review*, 44:124–135, Dec. 2010.

[3] S. Bhattiprolu, E. W. Biederman, S. Hallyn, and D. Lezcano. Virtual Servers and Checkpoint/Restart in Mainstream Linux. *ACM SIGOPS Operating Systems Review*, 42:104–113, July 2008.

[4] CNN. Industry First: Smartphones Pass PCs in Sales. http://tech.fortune.cnn.com/2011/02/07/idc-smartphone-shipment-numbers-passed-pc-in-q4-2010.

[5] C. Dall and J. Nieh. KVM for ARM. In *Proceedings of the Ottawa Linux Symposium*, Ottawa, Canada, June 2010.

[6] M. Dowty and J. Sugerman. GPU Virtualization on VMware's Hosted I/O Architecture. *ACM SIGOPS Operating Systems Review*, 43:73–82, July 2009.

[7] Enterproid, Inc. http://www.enterproid.com.

[8] Google. Nexus One - Google Phone Gallery, May 2011. http://www.google.com/phone/detail/nexus-one.

[9] Google. Nexus S - Google Phone Gallery, May 2011. http://www.google.com/phone/detail/nexus-s.

[10] Google Inc. Google Voice, Feb. 2011. http://www.google.com/googlevoice/about.html.

[11] HFS ~ HTTP File Server. http://www.rejetto.com/hfs/.

[12] M. Hills. Android on OKL4. http://www.ertos.nicta.com.au/software/androidokl4/.

[13] J. Hwang, S. Suh, S. Heo, C. Park, J. Ryu, S. Park, and C. Kim. Xen on ARM: System Virtualization using Xen Hypervisor for ARM-based Secure Mobile Phones. In *Proceedings of the 5th Consumer Communications and Newtork Conference*, Las Vegas, NV, Jan. 2008.

[14] Khronos Group. OpenGL Extensions – OpenGL.org. http://www.opengl.org/wiki/OpenGL_Extensions.

[15] K. Kolyshkin. Recent Advances in the Linux Kernel Resource Management. http://www.cse.wustl.edu/~lu/control-tutorials/im09/slides/virtualization.pdf.

[16] O. Laadan, R. Baratto, D. Phung, S. Potter, and J. Nieh. DejaView: A Personal Virtual Computer Recorder. In *Proceedings of the 21st Symposium on Operating Systems Principles*, Stevenson, WA, Oct. 2007.

[17] J. Liu, W. Huang, B. Abali, and D. K. Panda. High Performance VMM-bypass I/O in Virtual Machines. In *Proceedings of the 2006 USENIX Annual Technical Conference*, Boston, MA, June 2006.

[18] Microsoft. About the Wireless Hosted Network. http://msdn.microsoft.com/en-us/library/dd815243(v=vs.85).aspx.

[19] Mobile Systems. Office Suite Pro (Trial) – Android Market. https://market.android.com/details?id=com.mobisystems.editor.office_with_reg.

[20] NVIDIA Corporation. NVIDIA SLI MultiOS, Feb. 2011. http://www.nvidia.com/object/sli_multi_os.html.

[21] J. R. Okajima. AUFS. http://aufs.sourceforge.net/aufs2/man.html.

[22] Open Kernel Labs. OKL4 Microvisor, Mar. 2011. http://www.ok-labs.com/products/okl4-microvisor.

[23] S. Osman, D. Subhraveti, G. Su, and J. Nieh. The Design and Implementation of Zap: a System for Migrating Computing Environments. In *Proceedings of the 5th Symposium on Operating Systems Design and Implementation*, Boston, MA, Dec. 2002.

[24] polarbit. Reckless Racing – Android Market. https://market.android.com/details?id=com.polarbit.RecklessRacing.

[25] Red Bend Software. VLX Mobile Virtualization. http://www.redbend.com.

[26] Rovio Mobile Ltd. Angry Birds – Android Market. https://market.android.com/details?id=com.rovio.angrybirds.

[27] G. Su. *MOVE: Mobility with Persistent Network Connections*. PhD thesis, Columbia University, Oct. 2004.

[28] J. Sugerman, G. Venkitachalam, and B. Lim. Virtualizing I/O Devices on VMware Workstation's Hosted Virtual Machine Monitor. In *Proceedings of the 2001 USENIX Annual Technical Conference*, Boston, MA, June 2001.

[29] VMware, Inc. VMware Workstation. http://www.vmware.com/products/workstation/.

[30] C. A. Waldspurger. Memory Resource Management in VMware ESX Server. In *Proceedings of the 5th Symposium on Operating Systems Design and Implementation*, Boston, MA, Dec. 2002.

[31] WorkLight, Inc. WorkLight Mobile Platform. http://www.worklight.com.

[32] C. P. Wright, J. Dave, P. Gupta, H. Krishnan, D. P. Quigley, E. Zadok, and M. N. Zubair. Versatility and Unix Semantics in Namespace Unification. *ACM Transactions on Storage (TOS)*, 2:74–105, Feb. 2006.

[33] R. J. Wysocki. Technical Background of the Android Suspend Blockers Controversy. http://lwn.net/images/pdf/suspend_blockers.pdf.

[34] Xen Project. Architecture for Split Drivers Within Xen, 2011. http://wiki.xensource.com/xenwiki/XenSplitDrivers.

[35] ZDNet. Stolen Apps that Root Android, Steal Data and Open Backdoors Available for Download from Google Market. http://zd.net/gGUhOo.

Breaking Up is Hard to Do: Security and Functionality in a Commodity Hypervisor

Patrick Colp[†], Mihir Nanavati[†], Jun Zhu[‡], William Aiello[†],
George Coker[*], Tim Deegan[‡], Peter Loscocco[*], and Andrew Warfield[†]

[†]Department of Computer Science, University of British Columbia
[‡]Citrix Systems R&D, [*]National Security Agency

ABSTRACT

Cloud computing uses virtualization to lease small slices of large-scale datacenter facilities to individual paying customers. These *multi-tenant* environments, on which numerous large and popular web-based applications run today, are founded on the belief that the virtualization platform is sufficiently secure to prevent breaches of isolation between different users who are co-located on the same host. Hypervisors are believed to be trustworthy in this role because of their small size and narrow interfaces.

We observe that despite the modest footprint of the hypervisor itself, these platforms have a large aggregate trusted computing base (TCB) that includes a monolithic control VM with numerous interfaces exposed to VMs. We present *Xoar*, a modified version of Xen that retrofits the modularity and isolation principles used in microkernels onto a mature virtualization platform. Xoar breaks the control VM into single-purpose components called *service VMs*. We show that this componentized abstraction brings a number of benefits: sharing of service components by guests is configurable and auditable, making exposure to risk explicit, and access to the hypervisor is restricted to the least privilege required for each component. Microrebooting components at configurable frequencies reduces the temporal attack surface of individual components. Our approach incurs little performance overhead, and does not require functionality to be sacrificed or components to be rewritten from scratch.

1. INTRODUCTION

Datacenter computing has shifted the criteria for evaluating systems design from one that prioritizes peak capacity and offered load, to one that emphasizes the efficiency with which computing is delivered [2, 5, 47, 45]. This is particularly true for cloud hosting providers, who are motivated to reduce costs and therefore to multiplex and over-subscribe their resources as much as possible while still meeting customer service level objectives (SLOs).

While the efficiency of virtualization platforms remains a primary factor in their commercial success, their administrative features and benefits have been equally important. For example, hardware failures are a fact of life for large hosting environments; such envi-

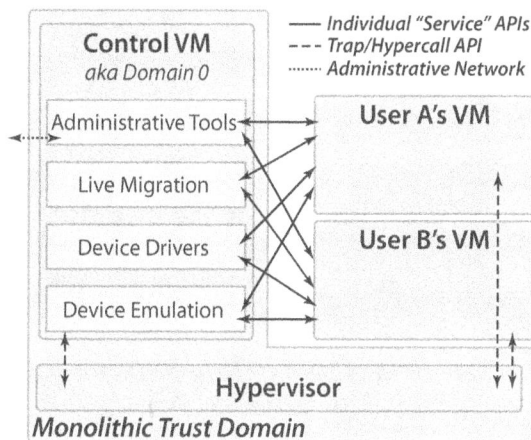

Figure 1: The control VM is often a full operating system install, has privilege similar to the hypervisor, and offers multiple services over numerous interfaces to guest VMs.

ronments rely on functionality such as live VM migration [13] for planned hardware replacements as well as unexpected failures [8, 15]. Hardware diversity is also inevitable in a large hosting facility; the use of hardware emulation and unified virtual devices means that a single VM image can be hosted on hardware throughout the facility without the need for device driver upgrades within customer VMs. Administrative benefits aside, the largest reason for the success of virtualization may be that it requires little or no change to existing applications. These three factors (resource utilization, administrative features, and the support of existing software) have allowed the emergence of large-scale hosting platforms, such as those offered by Amazon and Rackspace, that customers can trust to securely isolate their hosted virtual machines from those of other tenants despite physical co-location on the same physical hardware.

Are hypervisors worthy of this degree of trust? Proponents of virtualization claim that the small trusted computing base (TCB) and narrow interfaces afforded by a hypervisor provide strong isolation between the software components that share a host. In fact, the TCB of a mature virtualization platform is *larger* than that of a conventional server operating system. Even Type-1 hypervisors, such as Xen [4] and Hyper-V [22], rely on a privileged OS to provide additional shared services, such as drivers for physical devices, device emulation, and administrative tools. While the external interfaces to these services broaden the attack surface exposed to customer VMs, the internal interfaces *between* components within that OS are not as narrow or as carefully protected as those between components of the hypervisor itself. This large control VM is the "elephant in the room", often ignored in discussing the security of these systems.

While TCB size may not be a direct representation of risk, the shared control VM *is* a real liability for these systems. In Xen, for instance, this control VM houses a smorgasbord of functionality: device emulation and multiplexing, system boot, administrative toolstack, etc. Each of these services is presented to multiple customer VMs over different, service-specific interfaces (see Figure 1). As these services are all part of a single monolithic TCB, a compromise of any of them places the entire platform in danger.

The history of OS development shows us how to address the problem of a large TCB: break it into smaller pieces, isolate those pieces from each other, and reduce each one to the least privilege consistent with its task [43]. However, the history of OS deployment demonstrates that "secure by design" OSes often generate larger communities of readers than developers or users. In this vein, from-scratch hypervisors [38, 40, 42] have shown that particular security properties can be achieved by rearchitecting the platform, but they do not provide the rich set of features necessary for deployment in commercial hosting environments.

The work described in this paper avoids this compromise: we address the monolithic TCB presented by the control VM *without* reducing functionality. Instead, we hold the features of a mature, deployed hypervisor as a baseline and harden the underlying TCB. Our approach is to incorporate stronger isolation for the existing components in the TCB, increasing our ability to control and reason about exposure to risk. While full functionality is necessary, it is not sufficient for commercial deployment. Our approach adds only a small amount of performance overhead compared to our starting point full-featured virtualization platform.

1.1 Contributions

The primary contribution of this paper is to perform a component-based disaggregation of a mature, broadly deployed virtualization platform in a manner that is practical to incorporate and maintain. Our work takes advantage of a number of well-established mechanisms that have been used to build secure and reliable systems: the componentization of microkernels, freshening of component state using microreboots [10], and the use of recovery boxes [3] to allow a small set of explicitly designated state to survive reboots. The insight in this work is that these techniques can be applied to an existing system along the boundaries that already exist between processes and interfaces in the control VM.

We describe the challenges of decomposing Xen's control VM into a set of nine classes of *service VMs* while maintaining functional, performance, and administrative parity. The resulting system, which we have named *Xoar*, demonstrates a number of interesting new capabilities that are not possible without disaggregation:

- **Disposable Bootstrap.** Booting the physical computer involves a great deal of complex, privileged code. Xoar isolates this functionality in special purpose service VMs and destroys these VMs before the system begins to serve users. Other Xoar components are microrebooted to known-good snapshots, allowing developers to reason about a specific software state that is ready to handle a service request.

- **Auditable Configurations.** As the dependencies between customer VMs and service VMs are explicit, Xoar is able to record a secure audit log of all configurations that the system has been placed in as configuration changes are made. We

show that this log can be treated as a temporal database, enabling providers to issue forensic queries, such as asking for a list of VMs that depended on a known-vulnerable component.

- **Hardening of Critical Components.** While a core goal of our work has been to minimize the changes to source in order to make these techniques adoptable and maintainable, some critical components are worthy of additional attention. We identify *XenStore*, Xen's service for managing configuration state and inter-VM communication, as a sensitive and long-running component that is central to the security of the system. We show how isolation and microreboots allow Xen-Store to be rearchitected in a manner whereby an attacker must be capable of performing a stepping-stone attack across two isolated components in order to compromise the service.

We believe that Xoar represents a real improvement to the security of these important systems, in a manner that is practical to incorporate today. After briefly describing our architecture, we present a detailed design and implementation. We end by discussing the security of the system and evaluate the associated performance costs.

2. TCBS, TRUST, AND THREATS

This section describes the TCB of an enterprise virtualization platform and articulates our threat model. It concludes with a classification of relevant existing published vulnerabilities as an indication of threats that have been reported in these environments.

TCBs: Trust and Exposure. The TCB is classically defined as "the totality of protection mechanisms within a computer system — including hardware, firmware, and software — the combination of which is responsible for enforcing a security policy" [1]. In line with existing work on TCB reduction, we define the TCB of a subsystem S as "the set of components that S trusts not to violate the security of S" [21, 33].

Enterprise virtualization platforms, such as Xen, VMware ESX, and Hyper-V, are responsible for the isolation, scheduling, and memory management of guest VMs. Since the hypervisor runs at the highest privilege level, it forms, along with the hardware, part of the system's TCB.

Architecturally, these platforms rely on additional components. Device drivers and device emulation components manage and multiplex access to I/O hardware. Management toolstacks are required to actuate VMs running on the system. Further components provide virtual consoles, configuration state management, inter-VM communication, and so on. Commodity virtualization platforms, such as the ones mentioned above, provide all of these components in a monolithic domain of trust, either directly within the hypervisor or within a single privileged virtual machine running on it. Figure 1 illustrates an example of this organization as implemented in Xen.

A compromise of any component in the TCB affords the attacker two benefits. First, they gain the privileges of that component, such as access to arbitrary regions of memory or control of hardware. Second, they can access its interfaces to other elements of the TCB which allows them to attempt to inject malicious requests or responses over those interfaces.

Example Attack Vectors. We analyzed the CERT vulnerability database and VMware's list of security advisories, identifying a total of 44 reported vulnerabilities in Type-1 hypervisors.[1] Of the reported Xen vulnerabilities, 23 originated from within guest VMs,

---

[1]There were a very large number of reports relating to Type-2 hy-

11 of which were buffer overflows allowing arbitrary code execution with elevated privileges, while the other eight were denial-of-service attacks. Classifying by attack vector showed 14 vulnerabilities in the device emulation layer, with another two in the virtualized device layer. The remainder included five in management components and only two hypervisor exploits. 21 of the 23 attacks outlined above are against service components in the control VM.

Threat Model. We assume a well-managed and professionally administered virtualization platform that restricts access to both physical resources and privileged administrative interfaces. That is, we are not concerned with the violation of guest VM security by an administrator of the virtualization service. There are business imperatives that provide incentives for good behavior on the part of hosting administrators.

There is no alignment of incentives, however, for the guests of a hosting service to trust each other, and this forms the basis of our threat model. In a multi-tenancy environment, since guests may be less than well administered and exposed to the Internet, it is prudent to assume that they may be malicious. Thus, the attacker in our model is a guest VM aiming to violate the security of another guest with whom it is sharing the underlying platform. This includes violating the data integrity or confidentiality of the target guest or exploiting the code of the guest.

While we assume that the hypervisor of the virtualization platform is trusted, we also assume that the code instantiating the functionality of the control VM *will* contain bugs that are a potential source of compromise. Note that in the case of a privileged monolithic control VM, a successful attack on any one of its many interfaces can lead to innumerable exploits against guest VMs. Rather than exploring techniques that might allow for the construction of a bug-free platform, our more pragmatic goal is to provide an architecture that isolates functional components in space and time so that an exploit of one component is not sufficient to mount a successful attack against another guest or the underlying platform.

3. ARCHITECTURE OVERVIEW

Before explaining the design goals behind Xoar, it is worth providing a very high-level overview of the components, in order to help clarify the complexities of the control plane in a modern hypervisor and to establish some of the Xen-specific terminology that is used throughout the remainder of the paper. While our implementation is based on Xen, other commercial Type-1 hypervisors, such as those offered by VMware and Microsoft, have sufficiently similar structures that we believe the approach presented in this paper is applicable to them as well.

3.1 The Xen Platform

The Xen hypervisor relies on its control VM, Dom0, to provide a virtualized I/O path and host a system-wide registry and management toolstack.

Device Drivers. Xen delegates the control of PCI-based peripherals, such as network and disk controllers, to Dom0, which is responsible for exposing a set of abstract devices to guest VMs. These devices may either be virtualized, passed through, or emulated.

Virtualized devices are exposed to other VMs using a "split driver" model [17]. A backend driver, having direct control of the hardware,

exposes virtualized devices to frontend drivers in the guest VMs. Frontend and backend drivers communicate over a shared memory ring, with the backend multiplexing requests from several frontends onto the underlying hardware. Xen is only involved in enforcing access control for the shared memory and passing synchronization signals. ACLs are stored in the form of *grant tables*, with permissions set by the owner of the memory.

Alternatively, Xen uses direct device assignment to allow VMs other than Dom0 to directly interface with passed-through hardware devices. Dom0 provides a virtual PCI bus, using a split driver, to proxy PCI configuration and interrupt assignment requests from the guest VM to the PCI bus controller. Device-specific operations are handled directly by the guest. Direct assignment can be used to move physical device drivers out of Dom0, in particular for PCI hardware that supports hardware-based IO virtualization (SR-IOV) [28].

Unmodified commodity OSes, on the other hand, expect to run on a standard platform. This is provided by a device emulation layer, which, in Xen, is a per-guest Qemu [6] instance, running either as a Dom0 process or in its own VM [44]. It has privileges to map any page of the guest's memory in order to emulate DMA operations.

XenStore. XenStore is a hierarchical key-value store that acts as a system-wide registry and naming service. It also provides a "watch" mechanism which notifies registered listeners of any modifications to particular keys in the store. Device drivers and the toolstack make use of this for inter-VM synchronization and device setup.

XenStore runs as a Dom0 process and communicates with other VMs via shared memory rings. Since it is required in the creation and boot-up of a VM, it relies on Dom0 privileges to access shared memory directly, rather than using grant tables.

Despite the simplicity of its interface with VMs, the complex, shared nature of XenStore makes it vulnerable to DoS attacks if a VM monopolizes its resources [14]. Because it is the central repository for configuration state in the system and virtually all components in the system depend on it, it is a critical component from a security perspective. Exploiting XenStore allows an attacker to deny service to the system as a whole and to perform most administrative operations, including starting and stopping VMs, and possibly abusing interfaces to gain access to guest memory or other guest VMs.

Other systems (including previous versions of Xen) have used a completely message-oriented approach, either as a point-to-point implementation or as a message bus. Having implemented all of these at various points in the past (and some of them more than once), our experience is that they are largely isomorphic with regard to complexity and decomposability.

Toolstack. The toolstack provides administrative functions for the management of VMs. It is responsible for creating, destroying, and managing the associated resources and privileges of VMs. Creating a VM requires Dom0 privileges to map guest memory, in order to load a kernel or virtual BIOS and to set up initial communication channels with XenStore and the virtual console. In addition, the toolstack registers newly created guests with XenStore.

System Boot. In a traditional Xen system, the boot process is simple: the hypervisor creates Dom0 during boot-up, which proceeds to initialize hardware and bring up devices and their associated backend drivers. XenStore is started before any guest VM is created.

---

pervisors, most of which assume the attacker has access to the host OS and compromises known OS vulnerabilities — for instance, using Windows exploits to compromise VMware Workstation. These attacks are not representative of our threat model and are excluded.

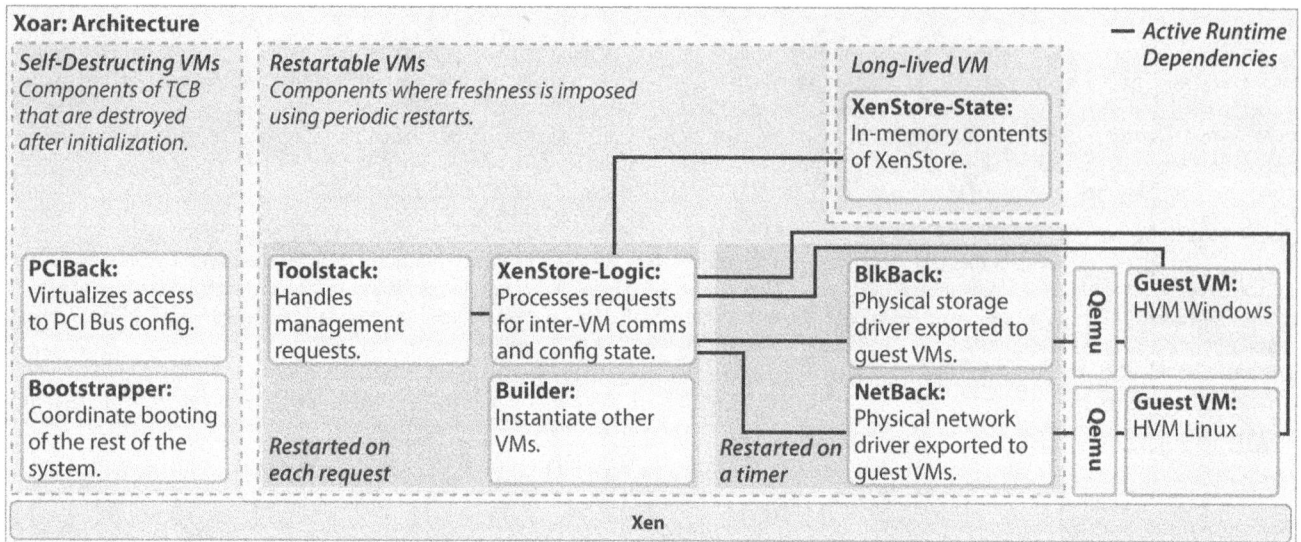

Figure 2: Architecture of Xoar. The figure above shows all the classes of service VMs along with the dependencies between them. For clarity, ephemeral dependencies (e.g., between the Builder and the VMs that it builds) are not shown. As suggested in the figure, a Qemu service VM is instantiated for the lifetime of each guest.

3.2 Xoar

Figure 2 shows the architecture of Xoar, and will be referred to throughout the remainder of this paper. In Xoar, the functionality of Xen's control VM has been disaggregated into nine classes of service VMs, each of which contains a single-purpose piece of control logic that has been removed from the original monolithic control VM. As is the case with the monolithic TCB, some components may have multiple instances, each serving different client VMs.

That these individual components may be instantiated more than once is important, as it allows them to be used as flexible building blocks in the deployment of a Xoar-based system. Figure 2 shows a single instance of each component other than the QemuVM. Later in the paper we will describe how multiple instances of these components, with differing resource and privilege assignments, can partition and otherwise harden the system as a whole.

From left to right, we begin with two start-of-day components that are closely tied to booting the hypervisor itself, *Bootstrapper* and *PCIBack*. These components bring up the physical platform and interrogate and configure hardware. In most cases this functionality is only required when booting the system and so these components are destroyed before any customer VMs are started. This is a useful property in that platform drivers and PCI discovery represent a large volume of complex code that can be removed prior to the system entering a state where it may be exposed to attacks.

While PCIBack is logically a start-of-day component, it is actually created after *XenStore* and *Builder*. XenStore is required to virtualize the PCI bus and the Builder is the only component capable of creating new VMs on the running system. PCIBack uses these components to create device driver VMs during PCI device enumeration by using `udev` [27] rules.

Three components are responsible for presenting platform hardware that is not directly virtualized by Xen. *BlkBack* and *NetBack* expose virtualized disk and network interfaces and control the specific PCI devices that have been assigned to them. For every guest VM running an unmodified OS, there is an associated *QemuVM* responsible for device emulation.

Once the platform is initialized, higher-level control facilities like the *Toolstacks* are created. The Toolstacks request the Builder to create guest VMs. As a control interface to the system, toolstacks are generally accessed over a private enterprise network, isolated from customer VM traffic.

As in Xen, a VM is described using a configuration file that is provided to the toolstack. This configuration provides runtime parameters such as memory and CPU allocations, and also device configurations to be provided to the VM. When a new VM is to be created, the toolstack parses this configuration file and writes the associated information into XenStore. Other components, such as driver VMs, have watches registered which are triggered by the build process, and configure connectivity between themselves and the new VM in response. While Xoar decomposes these components into isolated virtual machines, it leaves the interfaces between them unchanged; XenStore continues to be used to coordinate VM setup and tear down. The major difference is that privileges, both in terms of access to configuration state within XenStore and access to administrative operations in the hypervisor, are restricted to the specific service VMs that need them.

4. DESIGN

In developing Xoar, we set out to maintain functional parity with the original system and complete transparency with existing management and VM interfaces, including legacy support, without incurring noticeable overhead. This section discusses the approach that Xoar takes, and the properties that were considered in selecting the granularity and boundaries of isolation.

Our design is motivated by these three goals:

1. **Reduce privilege** Each component of the system should only have the privileges essential to its purpose; interfaces exposed by a component, both to dependent VMs and to the rest of the system, should be the minimal set necessary. This confines any successful attack to the limited capabilities and interfaces of the exploited component.

```
assign_pci_device (PCI_domain, bus, slot)
permit_hypercall (hypercall_id)
allow_delegation (guest_id)
```

Figure 3: Privilege Assignment API

2. **Reduce sharing** Sharing of components should be avoided wherever it is reasonable; whenever a component is shared between multiple dependent VMs, this sharing should be made explicit. This enables reasoning and policy enforcement regarding the exposure to risk introduced by depending on a shared component. It also allows administrators to securely log and audit system configurations and to understand exposure after a compromise has been detected.

3. **Reduce staleness** A component should only run for as long as it needs to perform its task; it should be restored to a known good state as frequently as practicable. This confines any successful attack to the limited execution time of the exploited component and reduces the execution state space that must be tested and evaluated for correctness.

To achieve these goals, we introduce an augmented version of the virtual machine abstraction: the *service VM*. Service VMs are the units of isolation which host the service components of the control VM. They differ from conventional virtual machines in that only service VMs can receive any extra privilege from the hypervisor or provide services to other VMs. They are also the only components which can be shared in the system, aside from the hypervisor itself.

Service VMs are entire virtual machines, capable of hosting full OSes and application stacks. Individual components of the control VM, which are generally either driver or application code, can be moved in their entirety out of the monolithic TCB and into a service VM. The hypervisor naturally assigns privilege at the granularity of the tasks these components perform. As such, there is little benefit, and considerable complexity, involved in finer-grained partitioning.

Components receiving heightened privilege and providing shared services are targets identified by the threat model discussed in Section 2. By explicitly binding their capabilities to a VM, Xoar is able to directly harden the riskiest portions of the system and provide service-specific enhancements for security. The remainder of this section discusses the design of Xoar with regard to each of these three goals.

4.1 Privilege: Fracture the Monolithic TCB

A service VM is designated as such using a `serviceVM` block in a VM config file. This block indicates that the VM should be treated as an isolated component and contains parameters that describe its capabilities. Figure 3 shows the API for the assignment of the three privilege-related properties that can be configured: direct hardware assignment, privileged hypercalls, and the ability to delegate privileges to other VMs on creation.

Direct hardware assignment is already supported by many x86 hypervisors, including Xen. Given a PCI domain, bus, and slot number, the hypervisor validates that the device is available to be assigned and is not already committed to another VM, then allows the VM to control the device directly.

Hypercall permissions allow a service VM access to some of the privileged functionality provided by the hypervisor. The explicit white-listing of hypercalls beyond the default set available to guest

```
resource =   [ provider, parameters,
              constraint_group=tag ]
```

Figure 4: Constraint Tagging API

```
SELECT e1, e2 FROM log e1, log e2 WHERE
  e1.name = e2.name AND
  e1.action = 'create' AND
  e2.action = 'destroy' AND
  e1.dependency = 'NameOfCompromisedNetBack' AND
  overlaps(period_intersect(e1.time, e2.time),
         compromise_period);


SELECT e1.name FROM log e1 WHERE
  e1.dependency = 'NetBack' AND
  e1.dependency_version = vulnerable_version;
```

Figure 5: Temporal queries which search for guest VMs that depended on a service VM that was compromised (top) or vulnerable (bottom).

VMs allows for least-privilege configuration of individual service VMs. These permissions are translated directly into a Flask [41] policy, which is installed into the hypervisor.

Access to resources is restricted by delegating service VMs to only those Toolstacks allowed to utilize those resources to support newly created VMs. Attempts to use undelegated service VMs are blocked by the hypervisor, enabling coarse-grained partitioning of resources. In the private cloud example presented at the end of this section, each user is assigned a private Toolstack, with delegated service VMs, and has exclusive access to the underlying hardware.

4.2 Sharing: Manage Exposure

Isolating the collection of shared services in service VMs confines and restricts attacks and allows an explicit description of the relationships between components in the system. This provides a clear statement of configuration constraints to avoid exposure to risk and enables mechanisms to reason about the severity and consequences of compromises after they occur.

Configuration Constraints. A guest can provide constraints on the service VMs that it is willing to use. At present, a single constraint is allowed, as shown in Figure 4. The `constraint_group` parameter provides an optional user-specified tag and may be appended to any line specifying a shared service in the VM's configuration. Xoar ensures that no two VMs specifying different constraint groups ever share the same service VM.

Effectively, this constraint is a user-specified coloring that prevents sharing. By specifying a tag on all of the devices of their hosted VMs, users can insist that they be placed in configurations where they only share service VMs with guest VMs that they control.

Secure Audit. Xoar borrows techniques from past forensics systems such as Taser [18]. The coarse-grained isolation and explicit dependencies provided by service VMs makes these auditing approaches easier to apply. Whenever the platform performs a guest-related configuration change (e.g., the creation, deletion, pausing, or unpausing of a VM), Xoar logs the resulting dependencies to an off-host, append-only database over a secure channel. Currently, we use the temporal extension for Postgres.

Two simple examples show the benefit of this approach. First, the

```
Calls from within the service VM:
vm_snapshot ()
recoverybox_balloc (size)

VM configuration for restart policy:
restart_policy ([(timer | event), parameters])
```

Figure 6: Microreboot API

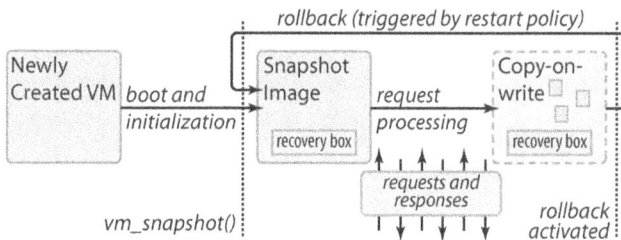

Figure 7: Rolling back to a known-good snapshot allows efficient microreboots of components.

top query in Figure 5 determines which customers could be affected by the compromise of a service VM by enumerating VMs that relied on that particular service VM at any point during the compromise. Second, providers frequently roll out new versions of OS kernels and in the event that a vulnerability is discovered in a specific release of a service VM after the fact, the audit log can be used to identify all guest VMs that were serviced by it.

4.3 Staleness: Protect VMs in Time

The final feature of service VMs is a facility to defend the *temporal* attack surface, preserving the freshness of execution state through the use of periodic restarts. This approach takes advantage of the observation from work on microreboots and "crash-only software" [10] that it is generally easier to reason about a program's correctness at the start of execution rather than over long periods of time.

Microreboots. Virtual machines naturally support a notion of rebooting that can be used to reset them to a known-good state. Further, many of the existing interfaces to control VM-based services already contain logic to reestablish connections, used when migrating a running VM from one physical host to another. There are two major challenges associated with microreboots. First, full system restarts are slow and significantly reduce performance, especially of components on a data path such as device drivers. Second, not all state associated with a service can be discarded since useful side-effects that have occurred during that execution will also be lost.

Snapshot and Rollback. Instead of fully restarting a component, it is snapshotted just after it has booted and been initialized, but before it has communicated with any other service or guest VM. The service VM is modified to explicitly snapshot itself at the time that it is ready to service requests (typically at the start of an event loop) using the API shown in Figure 6. Figure 7 illustrates the snapshot/rollback cycle. By snapshotting before any requests are served over offered interfaces, we ensure that the image is fresh. A complementary extension would be to measure and attest snapshot-based images, possibly even preparing them as part of a distribution and avoiding the boot process entirely.

We enable lightweight snapshots by using a hypervisor-based copy-on-write mechanism to trap and preserve any pages that are about to be modified. When rolling back, only these pages and the vir-

tual CPU state need be restored, resulting in very fast restart times — in our implementation, between 4 and 25 ms, depending on the workload.

Restart Policy. While it is obvious when to take the snapshot of a component, it is less clear when that component should be rolled back. Intuitively, it should be as frequently as possible. However, even though rollbacks are quick, the more frequently a component is restarted, the less time it has available to offer a useful service. Xoar specifies rollback policy in the service VM's configuration file and we currently offer two policies: notification-based and timer-based. Restart policy is associated with the VM when it is instantiated and is tracked and enforced by the hypervisor.

In our notification-based policy, the hypervisor interposes on message notifications *leaving* the service VM as an indication that a request transaction has completed, triggering a restart. For low-frequency, synchronous communication channels (e.g., those that access XenStore), this method isolates individual transactions and resets the service to a fresh state at the end of every processed request. In other words, every single request is processed by a fresh version of the service VM.[2]

The overhead of imposing a restart on every request would be too high for higher-throughput, concurrent channels, such as NetBack and BlkBack. For these service VMs, the hypervisor provides a periodic restart timer that triggers restarts at a configurable frequency.

Maintaining State. Frequent restarts suffer from the exact symptom that they seek to avoid: the establishment of long-lived state. In rolling back a service VM, any state that it introduces is lost. This makes it particularly hard to build services that depend on keeping in-memory state, such as configuration registries, and services that need to track open connections.

We address this issue by providing service VMs with the ability to allocate a "recovery box" [3]. Originally proposed as a technique for high availability, this is a block of memory that persists across restarts. Service VM code is modified to store any long-lived state in one of these allocations and to check and restore from it immediately after a snapshot call. Memory allocated using this technique is exempted from copy-on-write.

Maintaining state across restarts presents an obvious attack vector — a malicious user can attempt to corrupt the state that is reloaded after every rollback to repeatedly trigger the exploit and compromise the system. To address this, the service treats the recovery box as an untrusted input and audits its contents after the rollback. Xen also tracks the memory pages in the allocation and forcibly marks all virtual addresses associated with them as non-executable.

Driver VMs, like NetBack and BlkBack, automatically renegotiate both device state and frontend connections in cases of failures or restarts, allowing them to discard all state at every restart. In these performance-critical components, however, any downtime significantly affects the throughput of guests. This downtime can be reduced by caching a very small amount of device and frontend state in a recovery box. The desired balance between security and performance can be chosen, as discussed in Section 7.2.

Components like XenStore, on the other hand, maintain a large amount of long-lived state for other components in the system. In

---

[2]This mechanism leaves open the possibility that an exploited service VM might not send the event that triggers the rollback. To cover this attack vector, the hypervisor maintains a watchdog timer for each notification-based service VM. If a timer goes off, the VM is rolled back; if the restart is triggered normally, the timer is reset.

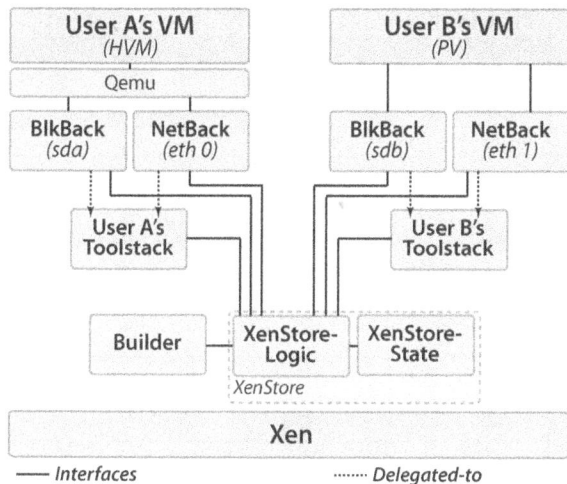

Figure 8: Partitioned configuration: In the configuration above, users A and B use isolated hardware and toolstacks and share interfaces only with XenStore and Xen itself.

such cases, this state can be removed from the service VM altogether and placed in a separate "state" VM that is accessible through a special-purpose interface. In Xoar, only XenStore, because of its central role in the correctness and security of the system, is refactored in this way (see Section 5.2). Only the processing and logic remain in the original service VM, making it amenable to rollbacks.

Per-request rollbacks force the attacker to inject exploit code into the state and have it triggered by another VM's interaction with XenStore. However, in the absence of further exploits, access control and guest ID authentication prevent the injection of such exploit code into sections of the state not owned by the attacking guest (see Section 5.2). Thus, an attack originating from a guest VM through XenStore requires an exploit of more than one service VM.

4.4 Deployment Scenarios

Public clouds, like Amazon Web Services, tightly pack many VMs on a single physical machine, controlled by a single toolstack. Partitioning the platform into service VMs, which can be judiciously restarted, limits the risks of sharing resources among potentially vulnerable and exposed VMs. Furthermore, dynamically restarting service VMs allows for in-place upgrades, reducing the window of exposure in the face of a newly discovered vulnerability. Finally, in the case of compromise, secure audit facilities allow administrators to reason, after the fact, about exposures that may have taken place.

Our design supports greater degrees of resource partitioning than this. Figure 8 shows a more conservative configuration, in which each user is assigned separate, dedicated hardware resources within the physical host and a personal collection of service VMs to manage them. Users manage their own service VMs and the device drivers using a private Toolstack with resource service VMs delegated solely to it.

5. IMPLEMENTATION

This section explains how the design described in Section 4 was implemented on the Xen platform. It begins with a brief discussion of how component boundaries were selected in fracturing the control VM and then describes implementation details and challenges faced during the development of Xoar.

5.1 Xoar Components

The division of service VMs in Xoar conforms to the design goals of Section 4; we reduce components into minimal, loosely coupled units of functionality, while obeying the principle of least privilege. As self-contained units, they have a low degree of sharing and inter-VM communication (IVC), and can be restarted independently. Existing software and interfaces are reused to aid development and ease future maintenance. Table 1 augments Figure 2 by describing the classes of service VMs in our decomposition of Dom0. While it is not the only possible decomposition, it satisfies our design goals without requiring an extensive re-engineering of Xen.

Virtualized devices mimic physical resources in an attempt to offer a familiar abstraction to guest VMs, making them ideal service VMs. Despite the lack of toolstack support, Xen has architectural support for driver VMs, reducing the development effort significantly. PCIBack virtualizes the physical PCI bus, while NetBack and BlkBack are driver VMs, exposing the required device backends for guest VMs. Further division, like separating device setup from the data path, yields no isolation benefits, since both components need to be shared simultaneously. This would also add a significant amount of IVC, conflicting with our design goals, and would require extensive modifications. Similarly, the serial controller is represented by a service VM that virtualizes the console for other VMs. Further details about virtualizing these hardware devices are discussed in Section 5.3 and Section 5.4.

Different aspects of the VM creation process require differing sets of privileges; placing them in the same service VM violates our goal of reducing privilege. These operations can largely be divided into two groups — those that need access to the guest's memory to set up the kernel, etc., and those that require access to XenStore to write entries necessary for the guest. Breaking this functionality apart along the lines of least privilege yields the Builder, a privileged service VM responsible for the hypervisor and guest memory operations, and the Toolstack, a service VM containing the management toolstack. While the Builder could be further divided into components for sub-operations, like loading the kernel image, setting up the page tables, etc., these would all need to run at the same privilege level and would incur high synchronization costs. The Builder responds to build requests issued by the Toolstack via XenStore. Once building is complete, the Toolstack communicates with XenStore to perform the rest of the configuration and setup process.

5.2 XenStore

Our refactoring of XenStore is the most significant implementation change that was applied to any of the existing components in Xen (and took the largest amount of effort). We began by breaking XenStore into two independent service VMs: XenStore-Logic, which contains the transactional logic and connection management code, and XenStore-State, which contains the actual contents of the store. This division allows restarts to be applied to request-handling code on a per-request basis, ensuring that exploits are constrained in duration to a single request. XenStore-State is a simple key-value store and is the only long-lived VM in Xoar.

Unfortunately, partitioning and per-request restarts are insufficient to ensure the security of XenStore. As XenStore-Logic is responsible for enforcing access control based on permissions in the store itself, a compromise of that VM may allow for arbitrary accesses to the contents of the store. We addressed this problem with two techniques. First, access control checks are moved into a small monitor module in XenStore-State; a compromise of XenStore-Logic is now limited to valid changes according to existing permissions in the

Component	P	Lifetime	OS	Parent	Depends On	Functionality
Bootstrapper	Y	Boot Up	nanOS	Xen	-	Instantiate boot service VMs
XenStore	N	Forever (R)	miniOS	Bootstrapper	-	System configuration registry
Console	N	Forever	Linux	Bootstrapper	XenStore	Expose physical console as virtual consoles to VMs
Builder	Y	Forever (R)	nanOS	Bootstrapper	XenStore	Instantiate non-boot VMs
PCIBack	Y	Boot Up	Linux	Bootstrapper	XenStore Builder Console	Initialize hardware and PCI bus, pass through PCI devices, and expose virtual PCI config space
NetBack	N	Forever (R)	Linux	PCIBack	XenStore Console	Expose physical network device as virtual devices to VMs
BlkBack	N	Forever (R)	Linux	PCIBack	XenStore Console	Expose physical block device as virtual devices to VMs
Toolstack	N	Forever (R)	Linux	Bootstrapper	XenStore Builder Console	Admin toolstack to manage VMs
QemuVM	N	Guest VM	miniOS	Toolstack	XenStore NetBack BlkBack	Device emulation for a single guest VM

Table 1: Components of Xoar. The "P" column indicates if the component is privileged. An "(R)" in the lifetime column indicates that the component can be restarted. Console is only mentioned for the sake of completeness. Since enterprise deployments typically disable console access, it is not part of the overall architecture.

store. Second, we establish the authenticity of accesses made by XenStore-Logic by having it declare the identity of the VM that it is about to service *before* reading the actual request. This approach effectively drops privilege to that of a single VM before exposing XenStore-Logic to any potentially malicious request, and makes the identity of the request made to XenStore-State unforgeable. The monitor refuses any request to change the current VM until the request has been completed, and an attempt to do so results in a restart of XenStore-Logic.

The monitor code could potentially be further disaggregated from XenStore-State and also restarted on a per-request basis. Our current implementation requires an attacker to compromise both XenStore-Logic and the monitor code in XenStore-State in succession, within the context of a single request, in order to make an unauthorized access to the store. Decoupling the monitor from XenStore-State would add limited extra benefit, for instance possibly easing static analysis of the two components, and still allow a successful attacker to make arbitrary changes in the event of the two successive compromises; therefore we have left the system is it stands.

5.3   PCI: A Shared Bus

PCIBack controls the PCI bus and manages interrupt routing for peripheral devices. Although driver VMs have direct access to the peripherals themselves, the shared nature of the PCI configuration space requires a single component to multiplex all accesses to it. This space is used during device initialization, after which there is no further communication with PCIBack. We remove PCIBack from the TCB entirely after boot by destroying it, reducing the number of shared components in the system.

Hardware virtualization techniques like SR-IOV [28] allow the creation of virtualized devices, where the multiplexing is performed in hardware, obviating the need for driver VMs. However, provisioning new virtual devices on the fly requires a persistent service VM to assign interrupts and multiplex accesses to the PCI configuration space. Ironically, although appearing to reduce the amount of sharing in the system, such techniques may increase the number of shared, trusted components.

5.4   Driver VMs: NetBack and BlkBack

Driver VMs, like NetBack and BlkBack, use direct device assignment to directly access PCI peripherals like NICs and disk controllers, and rely on existing driver support in Linux to interface with the hardware. Each NetBack or BlkBack virtualizes exactly one network or block controller, hosting the relevant device driver and virtualized backend driver. The Toolstack links a driver VM delegated to it to a guest VM by writing the appropriate frontend and backend XenStore entries during the creation of the guest, after which the guest and backend communicate directly using shared memory rings, without any further participation by XenStore.

Separating BlkBack from the Toolstack caused some problems as the existing management tools mount disk-based VM images as loopback devices with `blktap`, for use by the backend driver. After splitting BlkBack from the Toolstack, the disk images need to be created and mounted in BlkBack. Therefore, in Xoar, BlkBack runs a lightweight daemon that proxies requests from the Toolstack.

5.5   Efficient Microreboots

As described in Section 4.3, our snapshot mechanism copies memory pages which are dirtied as a service VM executes and restores the original contents of these pages during rollback, requiring a page allocation and deallocation and two copy operations for every dirtied page. Since many of the pages being modified are the same across several iterations, rather than deallocating the master copies of these pages after rollback, we retain them across runs, obviating the need for allocation, deallocation, and one copy operation when the same page is dirtied. However, this introduces a new problem: if a page is dirtied just once, its copy will reside in memory forever. This could result in memory being wasted storing copies of pages which are not actively required.

To address this concern, we introduced a "decay" value to the pages stored in the snapshot image. When a page is first dirtied after a rollback, its decay value is incremented by two, towards a maximum value. On rollback, each page's decay value is decremented. When this count reaches zero, the page is released.

5.6 Depriviledging Administrative Tools

XenStore and the Console require Dom0-like privileges to forcibly map shared memory, since they are required before the guest VM can set up its grant table mappings. To avoid this, Xoar's Builder creates grant table entries for this shared memory in each new VM, allowing these tools to use grant tables and function without any special privileges.

The Builder assigns VM management privileges to each Toolstack for the VMs that it requests to be built. A Toolstack can only manage these VMs, and an attempt to manage any others is blocked by the hypervisor. Similarly, it can only use service VMs that have been delegated to it. An attempt to use an undelegated service VM, for example a NetBack, for a new guest VM will fail. Restricting privileges this way allows for the creation of several Toolstack instances that run simultaneously. Different users, each with a private Toolstack, are able to partition their physical resources and manage their own VMs, while still guaranteeing strong isolation from VMs belonging to other users.

5.7 Developing with Minimal OSes

Bootstrapper and Builder are built on top of nanOS, a small, single-threaded, lightweight kernel explicitly designed to have the minimum functionality needed for VM creation. The small size and simplicity of these components leave them well within the realm of static analysis techniques, which could be used to verify their correctness. XenStore, on the other hand, demands more from its operating environment, and so is built on top of miniOS, a richer OS distributed with Xen.

Determining the correct size of OS to use is hard, with a fundamental tension between functionality and ease of use. Keeping nanOS so rigidly simple introduces a set of development challenges, especially in cases involving IVC. However, since these components have such high privilege, we felt that the improved security gained from reduced complexity is a worthwhile trade-off.

5.8 Implicit Assumptions about Dom0

The design of Xen does not mandate that all service components live in Dom0, however several components, including the hypervisor, implicitly hard-code the assumption that they do. A panoply of access control checks compare the values of domain IDs to the integer literal '0', the ID for Dom0. Many tools assume that they are running co-located with the driver backends and various paths in XenStore are hard-coded to be under Dom0's tree The toolstack expects to be able to manipulate the files that contain VM disk images, which is solved by proxying requests, as discussed in Section 5.4. The hypervisor assumes Dom0 has control of the hardware and configures signal delivery and MMIO and I/O-port privileges for access to the console and peripherals to Dom0. In Xoar, these need to be mapped to the correct VMs, with Console requiring the signals and I/O-port access for the console and PCIBack requiring the MMIO and remaining I/O-port privileges, along with access to the PCI bus.

6. SECURITY EVALUATION

Systems security is notoriously challenging to evaluate, and Xoar's proves no different. In an attempt to demonstrate the improvement to the state of security for commodity hypervisors, this section will consider a number of factors. First, we will evaluate the reduction in the size of the trusted computing base; this is an approach that we do not feel is particularly indicative of the security of a system, but has been used by a considerable amount of previous work and does provide some insight into the complexity of the system as a whole.

Permission	Bootstrapper	PCIBack	Builder	Toolstack	BlkBack	NetBack
Arbitrarily access memory	X		X			
Access and virtualize PCI devices		X				
Create VMs	X		X			
Manage VMs	X		X	X		
Manage assigned devices					X	X

Table 2: Functionality available to the service VMs in Xoar. Components with access to no privileged hypercalls are not shown. In Xen, Dom0 possesses all of these functionalities.

Component	Shared Interfaces
XenStore-Logic	XenStore-State, Console, Builder, PCIBack, NetBack, BlkBack, Guest
XenStore-State	XenStore-Logic
Console	XenStore-Logic
Builder	XenStore-Logic
PCIBack	XenStore-Logic, NetBack, BlkBack
NetBack	XenStore-Logic, PCIBack, Guest
BlkBack	XenStore-Logic, PCIBack, Guest
Toolstack	XenStore-Logic
Guest VM	XenStore-Logic, NetBack, BlkBack

Table 3: Interfaces shared between service VMs

Second, we consider how the attack surface presented by the control VM changes in terms of isolation, sharing, and per-component privilege in an effort to evaluate the exposure to risk in Xoar compared to other systems. Finally, we consider how well Xoar handles the existing published vulnerabilities first described in Section 2.

Much of this evaluation is necessarily qualitative: while we have taken efforts to evaluate against published vulnerabilities, virtualization on modern servers is still a sufficiently new technology with few disclosed vulnerabilities. Our sense is that these vulnerabilities may not be representative of the full range of potential attacks.

In evaluating Xoar's security, we attempt to characterize it from an attacker's perspective. One notable feature of Xoar is that in order for an adversary to violate our security claim, more than one service VM must have a vulnerability, and a successful exploit must be able to perform a stepping-stone attack. We will discuss why this is true, and characterize the nature of attacks that are still possible.

6.1 Reduced TCB

The Bootstrapper, PCIBack, and Builder service VMs are the most privileged components, with the ability to arbitrarily modify guest memory and control and assign the underlying hardware. These privileges necessarily make them part of the TCB, as a compromise of any one of these components would render the entire system vulnerable. Both Bootstrapper and PCIBack are destroyed after system initialization is complete, effectively leaving Builder as the only service VM in the TCB. As a result, the TCB is reduced from Linux's 7.6 million lines of code to Builder's 13,500 lines of code, both on top of the hypervisor's 280,000 lines of code.[3]

6.2 Attack Surface

Monolithic virtualization platforms like Xen execute service components in a single trust domain, with every component running at

---
[3]All lines of code were measured using David Wheeler's SLOC-Count from http://www.dwheeler.com/sloccount/

Component	Arbitrary Code Execution	DoS	File System Access
Hypervisor	0 / 1	0 / 1	0 / 0
Device Emulation	8 / 8	3 / 3	3 / 3
Virtualized Drivers	1 / 1	1 / 1	0 / 0
XenStore	0 / 0	1 / 1	0 / 0
Toolstack	1 / 1	2 / 2	1 / 1

Table 4: Vulnerabilities mitigated in Xoar. The numbers represent total mitigated over total identified.

Component	Memory	Component	Memory
XenStore-Logic	32 MB	XenStore-State	32 MB
Console	128 MB	PCIBack	256 MB
NetBack	128 MB	BlkBack	128 MB
Builder	64 MB	Toolstack	128 MB

Table 5: Memory requirements of individual components

the highest privilege level. As a result, the security of the entire system is defined by that of the weakest component, and a compromise of any component gives an attacker full control of the system.

Disaggregating service components into their own VMs not only provides strong isolation boundaries, it also allows privileges to be assigned on a per-component basis, reducing the effect a compromised service VM has on the entire system. Table 2 shows the privileges granted to each service VM, which corresponds to the amount of access that an attacker would have on successfully exploiting it.

Attacks originating from guest VMs can exploit vulnerabilities in the interfaces to NetBack, BlkBack, or XenStore (see Table 3). An attacker breaking into a driver VM gains access only to the degree that other VMs trust that device. Exploiting NetBack might allow for intercepting another VM's network traffic, but not access to arbitrary regions of its memory. On hosts with enough hardware, resources can be partitioned so that no two guests share a driver VM.

Where components reuse the same code, a single vulnerability could be sufficient to compromise them all. Service VMs like NetBack, BlkBack, Console, and Toolstack run the same core Linux kernel, with specific driver modules loaded only in the relevant component. As a result, vulnerabilities in the exposed interfaces are local to the associated service VM, but vulnerabilities in the underlying framework and libraries may be present in multiple components. For better code diversity, service VMs could use a combination of Linux, FreeBSD, OpenSolaris, and other suitable OSes.

Highly privileged components like the Builder have very narrow interfaces and cannot be compromised without exploiting vulnerabilities in multiple components, at least one of which is XenStore. Along with the central role it plays in state maintenance and synchronization, this access to Builder makes XenStore an attractive target. Compromising XenStore-Logic may allow an attacking guest to store exploit code in XenStore-State, which, when restoring state after a restart, re-compromises XenStore-Logic. The monitoring code described in Section 5.2, however, prevents this malicious state from being restored when serving requests from any other guest VM, ensuring that they interact with a clean copy of XenStore.

6.3 Vulnerability Mitigation

With a majority of the disclosed vulnerabilities against Xen involving privilege escalation against components in Dom0, Xoar proves to be successful in containing all but two of them. Table 4 taxonomizes the vulnerabilities discussed in Section 2 based on the vulnerable component and the type of vulnerability, along with the number that are successfully mitigated in Xoar.

The 14 device emulation attacks are completely mitigated, as the device emulation service VM has no rights over any VM except the one the attacker came from. The two attacks on the virtualized device layer and the three attacks against the toolstack would only affect those VMs that shared the same BlkBack, NetBack, and Toolstack components. The vulnerability present in XenStore did not exist in our custom version. Since Xoar does not modify the hyper-

visor, the two hypervisor vulnerabilities remain equally exploitable.

One of the vulnerabilities in the virtualized drivers is against the block device interface and causes an infinite loop which results in a denial of service. Periodically restarting BlkBack forces the attacker to continuously recompromise the system. Since requests from different guests are serviced on every restart, the device would continue functioning with low bandwidth, until a patch could be applied to prevent further compromises.

7. PERFORMANCE EVALUATION

The performance of Xoar is evaluated against a stock Xen Dom0 in terms of memory overhead, I/O throughput, and overall system performance. Each service VM in Xoar runs with a single virtual CPU; in stock Xen Dom0 runs with 2 virtual CPUs, the configuration used in the commercial XenServer [12] platform. All figures are the average of three runs, with 95% confidence intervals shown where appropriate.

Our test system was a Dell Precision T3500 server, with a quad-core 2.67 GHz Intel Xeon W3520 processor, 4 GB of RAM, a Tigon 3 Gigabit Ethernet card, and an Intel 82801JIR SATA controller with a Western Digital WD3200AAKS-75L9A0 320 GB 7200 RPM disk. VMX, EPT, and IOMMU virtualization are enabled. We use Xen 4.1.0 and Linux 2.6.31[4] pvops kernels for the tests. Identical guests running an Ubuntu 10.04 system, configured with two VCPUs, 1 GB of RAM and a 15 GB virtual disk are used on both systems. For network tests, the system is connected directly to another system with an Intel 82567LF-2 Gigabit network controller.

7.1 Memory Overhead

Table 5 shows the memory requirements of each of the components in Xoar. Systems with multiple network or disk controllers can have several instances of NetBack and BlkBack. Also, since users can select the service VMs to run, there is no single figure for total memory consumption. In commercial hosting solutions, console access is largely absent rendering the Console redundant. Similarly, PCIBack can be destroyed after boot. As a result, the memory requirements range from 512 MB to 896 MB, assuming a single network and block controller, representing a saving of 30% to an overhead of 20% on the default 750 MB Dom0 configuration used by XenServer. All performance tests compare a complete configuration of Xoar with a standard Dom0 Xen configuration.

7.2 I/O performance

Disk performance is tested using Postmark, with VMs' virtual disks backed by files on a local disk. Figure 9 shows the results of these tests with different configuration parameters.

Network performance is tested by fetching a 512 MB and a 2 GB file across a gigabit LAN using `wget`, and writing it either to disk, or to `/dev/null` (to eliminate performance artifacts due to disk performance). Figure 10 shows these results.

---

[4]Hardware issues forced us to use a 2.6.32 kernel for some of the components.

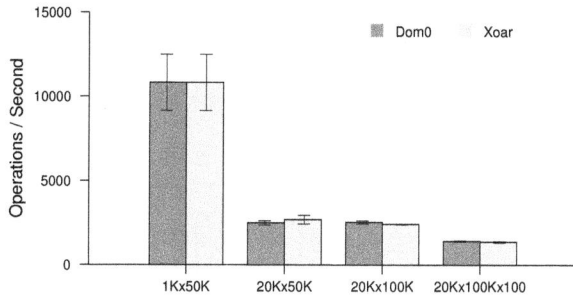

Figure 9: Disk performance using Postmark (higher is better). The x-axis denotes (files x transactions x subdirectories).

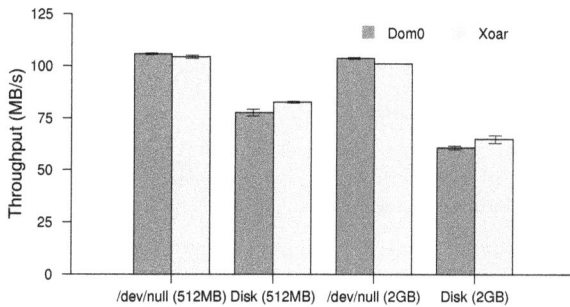

Figure 10: Network performance with `wget` **(higher is better)**

Overall, disk throughput is more or less unchanged, and network throughput is down by 1–2.5%. The combined throughput of data coming from the network onto the disk *increases* by 6.5%; we believe this is caused by the performance isolation of running the disk and network drivers in separate VMs.

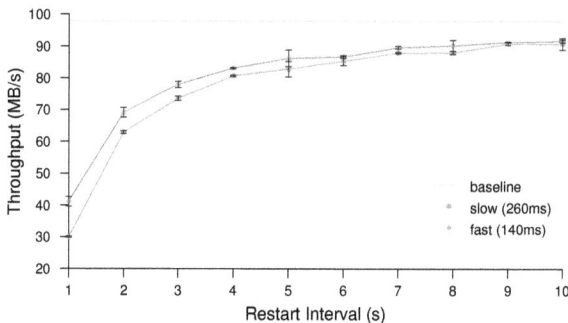

Figure 11: `wget` **throughput while restarting NetBack at different time intervals**

To measure the effect of microrebooting driver VMs, we ran the 2 GB `wget` to `/dev/null` while restarting NetBack at intervals between 1 and 10 seconds. Two different optimizations for fast microreboots are shown.

In the first (marked as "slow" in Figure 11), the device hardware state is left untouched during reboots; in the second ("fast"), some configuration data that would normally be renegotiated via Xen-

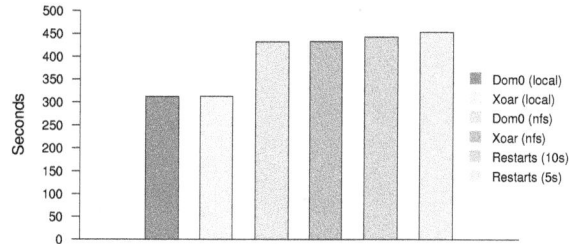

Figure 12: Linux kernel build run on Dom0 and Xoar, locally, over NFS and over NFS with NetBack restarts.

Store is persisted. In "slow" restarts the device downtime is around 260 ms, measuring from when the device is suspended to when it responds to network traffic again. The optimizations used in the "fast" restart reduce this downtime to around 140 ms.

Resetting every 10 seconds causes an 8% drop in throughput, as `wget`'s TCP connections respond to the breaks in connectivity. Reducing the interval to one second gives a 58% drop. Increasing it beyond 10 seconds makes very little difference to throughput. The faster recovery gives a noticeable benefit for very frequent reboots but is worth less than 1% for 10-second reboots.

7.3 Real-world Benchmarks

Figure 12 compares the time taken to build a Linux kernel, both in stock Xen and Xoar, off a local ext3 volume as well as an NFS mount. The overhead added by Xoar is much less than 1%.

The *Apache Benchmark* is used to gauge the performance of an Apache web server serving a 10 KB static webpage 100,000 times to five simultaneous clients. Figure 13 shows the results of this test against Dom0, Xoar, and Xoar with network driver restarts at 10, 5, and 1 second intervals. Performance decreases non-uniformly with the frequency of the restarts: an increase in restart interval from 5 to 10 seconds yields barely any performance improvements, while changing the interval from 5 seconds to 1 second introduces a significant performance loss.

Dropped packets and network timeouts cause a small number of requests to experience very long completion times — for example, for Dom0 and Xoar, the longest packet took only 8–9 ms, but with restarts, the values range from 3000 ms (at 5 and 10 seconds) to 7000 ms (at 1 second). As a result, the longest request interval is not shown in the figure.

Overall, the overhead of disaggregation is quite low. This is largely because driver VMs do not lengthen the data path between guests and the hardware: the guest VM communicates with NetBack or BlkBack, which drives the hardware. While the overhead of driver restarts is noticeable, as intermittent outages lead to TCP backoff, it can be tuned by the administrator to best match the desired combination of security and performance.

8. RELATED WORK

With the widespread use of VMs, the security of hypervisors has been studied extensively and several attempts have been made to address the problem of securing the TCB. This section looks at some of these techniques in the context of our functional requirements.

Build a Smaller Hypervisor. SecVisor [38] and BitVisor [40] are examples of tiny hypervisors, built with TCB size as a primary con-

Figure 13: Apache Benchmark run on Dom0, Xoar, and Xoar with network driver restarts at 10s, 5s, and 1s.

cern, that use the interposition capabilities of hypervisors to retrofit security features for commodity OSes. While significantly reducing the TCB of the system, they do not share the multi-tenancy goals of commodity hypervisors and are unsuitable for such environments.

Microkernel-based architectures like KeyKOS [20] and EROS [39], its x86-based successor, are motivated similarly to Xoar and allow mutually untrusting users to securely share a system. Our Builder closely resembles the *factory* in KeyKOS. While multiple, isolated, independently administered UNIX instances, rather like VMs, can be hosted on EROS, this requires modifications to the environment and arbitrary OSes cannot be hosted. More recently, NOVA [42] uses a similar architecture and explicitly partitions the TCB into several user-level processes within the hypervisor. Although capable of running multiple unmodified OSes concurrently, the removal of the control VM and requirement for NOVA-specific drivers sacrifice hardware support for TCB size. Also, it is far from complete: it cannot run Windows guests and has limited toolstack support.

NoHype [23] advocates removing the hypervisor altogether, using static partitioning of CPUs, memory, and peripherals among VMs. This would allow a host to be shared by multiple operating systems, but with none of the other benefits of virtualization. In particular, the virtualization layer could no longer be used for interposition, which is necessary for live migration [13], memory sharing and compression [19, 32], and security enhancements [11, 30, 46, 16].

Harden the Components of the TCB. The security of individual components of the TCB can be improved using a combination of improved code quality and access control checks to restrict the privileges of these components. Xen's XAPI toolstack is written in OCaml and benefits from the robustness that a statically typed, functional language provides [37]. Xen and Linux both have mechanisms to enforce fine-grained security policies [31, 36]. While useful, these techniques do not address the underlying concern about the size of the TCB.

Split Up the TCB, Reduce the Privilege of Each Part. Murray *et al.* [33] removed Dom0 userspace from the TCB by moving the VM builder into a separate privileged VM. While a step in the right direction, it does not provide functional parity with Xen or remove the Dom0 kernel from the TCB, leaving the system vulnerable to attacks on exposed interfaces, such as network drivers.

Driver domains [17] allow device drivers to be hosted in dedicated VMs rather than Dom0, resulting in better driver isolation. Qubes-OS [35] uses driver domains in a single-user environment, but does not otherwise break up Dom0. Stub domains [44] isolate the Qemu device model for improved performance and isolation. Xoar builds on these ideas and extends them to cover the entire control VM.

9. DISCUSSION AND FUTURE WORK

This idea of partitioning a TCB is hardly new, with software partitioning having been explored in a variety of contexts before. Microkernels remain largely in the domain of embedded devices with relatively small and focused development teams (e.g., [26]), and while attempts at application-level partitioning have demonstrated benefits in terms of securing sensitive data, they have also demonstrated challenges in implementation and concerns about maintenance [7, 9, 24, 34], primarily due to the mutability of application interfaces.

While fracturing the largely independent, shared services that run in the control VM above the hypervisor, we observe that these concerns do not apply to nearly the same degree; typically the components are drivers or application code exposing their dominant interfaces either to hardware or to dependent guests. Isolating such services into their own VMs was a surprisingly natural fit.

While it is tempting to attribute this to a general property of virtualization, we also think that it was particularly applicable to the architecture of Xen. Although implemented as a monolithic TCB, several of the components were designed to support further compartmentalization, with clear, narrow communication interfaces.

We believe the same is applicable to Hyper-V, which has a similar architecture to Xen. In contrast, KVM [25] converts the Linux kernel itself into a hypervisor, with the entire toolstack hosted in a Qemu process. Due to the tight coupling, we believe that disaggregating KVM this aggressively would be extremely hard, more akin to converting Linux into a microkernel.

9.1 Lessons

In the early design of the system our overall rule was to take a practical approach to hardening the hypervisor. As usual, with the hindsight of having built the system, some more specific guidelines are clear. We present them here as "lessons" and hope that they may be applied earlier in the design process of future systems.

Don't break functionality. From the outset, the work described in this paper has been intended to be applied upstream to the open source Xen project. We believe that for VM security improvements to be deployed broadly, they must not sacrifice the set of functionality that has made these systems successful, and would not expect a warm reception for our work from the maintainers of the system if we were to propose that facilities such as CPU overcommit simply didn't make sense in our design.

This constraint places enormous limitations on what we are able to do in terms of hardening the system, but it also reduces the major argument against accepting new security enhancements.

Don't break maintainability. Just as the users of a virtualization platform will balk if enhancing security costs functionality, developers will push back on approaches to hardening a system that require additional effort from them. For this reason, our approach to hardening the hypervisor has been largely a *structural* one: individual service VMs already existed as independent applications in the monolithic control VM and so the large, initial portion of our work was simply to break each of these applications out into its own virtual machine. Source changes in this effort largely improved the existing source's readability and maintainability by removing hard-coded values and otherwise generalizing interfaces.

By initially breaking the existing components of the control VM out into their own virtual machines, we also made it much easier for new, alternate versions of these components to be written and maintained as drop-in replacements: our current implementation uses largely unchanged source for most of the service VM code, but then chooses to completely reimplement XenStore. The original version of XenStore still works in Xoar, but the new one can be dropped in to strengthen a critical, trusted component of the system.

There isn't always a single best interface. The isolation of components into service VMs was achieved through multiple implementations: some service VMs use a complete Linux install, some a stripped-down "miniOS" UNIX-like environment, and some even smaller "nanOS", effectively a library for building small single-purpose VMs designed to be amenable to static analysis.

Preserving application state across microreboots has a similar diversity of implementation: driver VMs take advantage of a recovery-box-like API, while for the reimplementation of XenStore it became more sensible to split the component into two VMs, effectively building our own long-lived recovery box component.

Our experience in building the system is that while we might have built simpler and more elegant versions of each of the individual components, we probably couldn't have used fewer of them without making the system more difficult to maintain.

9.2 Future Work

The mechanism of rebooting components that automatically renegotiate existing connections allow many parts of the virtualization platform to be upgraded in place. An old component can be shut down gracefully, and a new, upgraded one brought up in its place with a minor modification of XenStore keys. Unfortunately, these are not applicable to long-lived components with state like XenStore and the hypervisor itself. XenStore could potentially be restarted by persisting its state to disk. Restarting Xen under executing VMs, however, is more challenging. We would like to explore techniques like those in ReHype [29], but using *controlled* reboots to safely replace Xen, allowing the complete virtualization platform to be upgraded and restarted without disturbing the hosted VMs.

Although the overall design allows for it, our current implementation does not include cross-host migration of VMs. We are in the process of implementing a new service VM that contains the live VM migration toolset to transmit VMs over the network. While this component is not currently complete, it has begun to demonstrate an additional benefit of disaggregation: the new implementation strikes a balance between the implementation of a feature that requires considerable privilege to map and monitor changes to a VM's memory in the control VM, and the proposal to completely internalize migration within the guest itself [13]. Xoar's live migration tool allows the guest to delegate access to map and monitor changes to its memory to a trusted VM, and allows that VM to run, much like the QemuVM, for as long as is necessary. We believe that this technique will further apply to other proposals for interposition-based services, such as memory sharing, compression, and virus scanning.

10. CONCLUSION

Advances in virtualization have spurred demand for highly-utilized, low-cost centralized hosting of systems in the cloud. The virtualization layer, while designed to be small and secure, has grown out of a need to support features desired by enterprises.

Xoar is an architectural change to the virtualization platform that looks at retrofitting microkernel-like isolation properties to the Xen hypervisor without sacrificing any existing functionality. It divides the control VM into a set of least-privilege service VMs, which not only makes any sharing dependencies between components explicit, but also allows microreboots to reduce the temporal attack surface of components in the system. We have achieved a significant reduction in the size of the TCB, and address a substantial percentage of the known classes of attacks against Xen, while maintaining feature parity and incurring very little performance overhead.

11. ACKNOWLEDGMENTS

We would like to thank our shepherd, Bryan Ford, the anonymous reviewers, Steve Hand, Derek Murray, Steve Gribble, Keir Fraser, David Lie, and the members of the systems research groups at the University of British Columbia and at the University of Cambridge for their suggestions and feedback. This work was partially supported through funding from the NSERC Internetworked Systems Security Network (ISSNet) and from the Communications Security Establishment Canada (CSEC).

12. REFERENCES

[1] *Department of Defense Trusted Computer System Evaluation Criteria*. DoD 5200.28-STD. U.S. Department of Defense, Dec. 1985.

[2] D. G. Andersen, J. Franklin, M. Kaminsky, A. Phanishayee, L. Tan, and V. Vasudevan. FAWN: A fast array of wimpy nodes. In *Proc. 22nd ACM SOSP*, pages 1–14, Oct. 2009.

[3] M. Baker and M. Sullivan. The recovery box: Using fast recovery to provide high availability in the UNIX environment. In *Proc. USENIX Summer Conference*, pages 31–43, June 1992.

[4] P. Barham, B. Dragovic, K. Fraser, S. Hand, T. Harris, A. Ho, R. Neugebauer, I. Pratt, and A. Warfield. Xen and the art of virtualization. In *Proc. 19th ACM SOSP*, pages 164–177, Oct. 2003.

[5] L. A. Barroso and U. Hölzle. The case for energy-proportional computing. *IEEE Computer*, 40:33–37, December 2007.

[6] F. Bellard. QEMU, a fast and portable dynamic translator. In *Proc. USENIX ATC*, pages 41–46, Apr. 2005.

[7] A. Bittau, P. Marchenko, M. Handley, and B. Karp. Wedge: splitting applications into reduced-privilege compartments. In *Proc. 5th USENIX NSDI*, pages 309–322, Apr. 2008.

[8] T. C. Bressoud and F. B. Schneider. Hypervisor-based fault tolerance. In *Proc. 15th ACM SOSP*, pages 1–11, Dec. 1995.

[9] D. Brumley and D. Song. Privtrans: automatically partitioning programs for privilege separation. In *Proc. 13th USENIX Security Symposium*, pages 57–72, Aug. 2004.

[10] G. Candea, S. Kawamoto, Y. Fujiki, G. Friedman, and A. Fox. Microreboot — a technique for cheap recovery. In *Proc. 6th USENIX OSDI*, pages 31–44, Dec. 2004.

[11] X. Chen, T. Garfinkel, E. C. Lewis, P. Subrahmanyam, C. A. Waldspurger, D. Boneh, J. Dwoskin, and D. R. Ports. Overshadow: a virtualization-based approach to retrofitting protection in commodity operating systems. In *Proc. 13th ASPLOS*, pages 2–13, Mar. 2008.

[12] Citrix Systems, Inc. *Citrix XenServer 5.6 Admininistrator's Guide*. June 2010.

[13] C. Clark, K. Fraser, S. Hand, J. G. Hansen, E. Jul, C. Limpach, I. Pratt, and A. Warfield. Live migration of virtual machines. In *Proc. 2nd USENIX NSDI*, pages 273–286, May 2005.

[14] P. Colp. [xen-devel] [announce] xen ocaml tools. http://lists.xensource.com/archives/html/xen-devel/2009-02/msg00229.html.

[15] B. Cully, G. Lefebvre, D. Meyer, M. Feeley, N. Hutchinson, and A. Warfield. Remus: high availability via asynchronous virtual machine replication. In *Proc. 5th USENIX NSDI*, pages 161–174, Apr. 2008.

[16] A. Dinaburg, P. Royal, M. Sharif, and W. Lee. Ether: malware analysis via hardware virtualization extensions. In *Proc. 15th ACM CCS*, pages 51–62, Oct. 2008.

[17] K. Fraser, S. Hand, R. Neugebauer, I. Pratt, A. Warfield, and M. Williamson. Safe hardware access with the Xen virtual machine monitor. In *Proc. 1st OASIS*, Oct. 2004.

[18] A. Goel, K. Po, K. Farhadi, Z. Li, and E. de Lara. The Taser intrusion recovery system. In *Proc. 20th ACM SOSP*, pages 163–176, Oct. 2005.

[19] D. Gupta, S. Lee, M. Vrable, S. Savage, A. C. Snoeren, G. Varghese, G. M. Voelker, and A. Vahdat. Difference engine: harnessing memory redundancy in virtual machines. In *Proc. 8th Usenix OSDI*, pages 85–93, Oct. 2008.

[20] N. Hardy. The KeyKOS architecture. *Operating Systems Review*, 19(4):8–25, October 1985.

[21] M. Hohmuth, M. Peter, H. Härtig, and J. S. Shapiro. Reducing TCB size by using untrusted components: small kernels versus virtual-machine monitors. In *Proc. 11th ACM SIGOPS EW*, Sept. 2004.

[22] K. Kappel, A. Velte, and T. Velte. *Microsoft Virtualization with Hyper-V*. McGraw-Hill, 1st edition, 2010.

[23] E. Keller, J. Szefer, J. Rexford, and R. B. Lee. NoHype: virtualized cloud infrastructure without the virtualization. In *Proc. 37th ACM ISCA*, pages 350–361, June 2010.

[24] D. Kilpatrick. Privman: A library for partitioning applications. In *Proc. USENIX ATC*, pages 273–284, June 2003.

[25] A. Kivity, Y. Kamay, D. Laor, U. Lublin, and A. Liguori. kvm: the Linux virtual machine monitor. In *Proc. Linux Symposium*, pages 225–230, July 2007.

[26] G. Klein, K. Elphinstone, G. Heiser, J. Andronick, D. Cock, P. Derrin, D. Elkaduwe, K. Engelhardt, R. Kolanski, M. Norrish, T. Sewell, H. Tuch, and S. Winwood. seL4: formal verification of an OS kernel. In *Proc. 22nd ACM SOSP*, pages 207–220, Oct. 2009.

[27] G. Kroah-Hartman. udev: A userspace implementation of devfs. In *Proc. Linux Symposium*, pages 263–271, July 2003.

[28] P. Kutch. PCI-SIG SR-IOV primer: An introduction to SR-IOV technology. Application note 321211-002, Intel Corporation, Jan. 2011.

[29] M. Le and Y. Tamir. ReHype: Enabling VM survival across hypervisor failures. In *Proc. 7th ACM VEE*, pages 63–74, Mar. 2011.

[30] L. Litty, H. A. Lagar-Cavilla, and D. Lie. Hypervisor support for identifying covertly executing binaries. In *Proc. 17th USENIX Security Symposium*, pages 243–258, July 2008.

[31] P. Loscocco and S. Smalley. Integrating flexible support for security policies into the Linux operating system. In *Proc. USENIX ATC*, pages 29–42, June 2001.

[32] G. Milos, D. G. Murray, S. Hand, and M. A. Fetterman. Satori: Enlightened page sharing. In *Proc. USENIX ATC*, pages 1–14, June 2009.

[33] D. G. Murray, G. Milos, and S. Hand. Improving Xen security through disaggregation. In *Proc. 4th ACM VEE*, pages 151–160, Mar. 2008.

[34] N. Provos, M. Friedl, and P. Honeyman. Preventing privilege escalation. In *Proc. 12th USENIX Security Symposium*, pages 231–242, Aug. 2003.

[35] J. Rutkowska and R. Wojtczuk. *Qubes OS Architecture*. Version 0.3. Jan. 2010. http://qubes-os.org/.

[36] R. Sailer, T. Jaeger, E. Valdez, R. Cáceres, R. Perez, S. Berger, J. L. Griffin, and L. van Doorn. Building a MAC-based security architecture for the Xen open-source hypervisor. In *Proc. 21st ACSAC*, pages 276–285, Dec. 2005.

[37] D. Scott, R. Sharp, T. Gazagnaire, and A. Madhavapeddy. Using functional frogramming within an industrial product group: perspectives and perceptions. In *Proc. 15th ICFP*, pages 87–92, Sept. 2010.

[38] A. Seshadri, M. Luk, N. Qu, and A. Perrig. SecVisor: a tiny hypervisor to provide lifetime kernel code integrity for commodity OSes. In *Proc. 21st ACM SOSP*, pages 335–350, Oct. 2007.

[39] J. S. Shapiro, J. M. Smith, and D. J. Farber. EROS: a fast capability system. In *Proc. 17th ACM SOSP*, pages 170–185, Dec. 1999.

[40] T. Shinagawa, H. Eiraku, K. Tanimoto, K. Omote, S. Hasegawa, T. Horie, M. Hirano, K. Kourai, Y. Oyama, E. Kawai, K. Kono, S. Chiba, Y. Shinjo, and K. Kato. BitVisor: a thin hypervisor for enforcing I/O device security. In *Proc. 5th ACM VEE*, pages 121–130, Mar. 2009.

[41] R. Spencer, S. Smalley, P. Loscocco, M. Hibler, D. Andersen, and J. Lepreau. The Flask security architecture: System support for diverse security policies. In *Proc. 8th USENIX Security Symposium*, pages 123–139, Aug. 1999.

[42] U. Steinberg and B. Kauer. NOVA: a microhypervisor-based secure virtualization architecture. In *Proc. 5th EuroSys*, pages 209–222, Apr. 2010.

[43] A. S. Tanenbaum, J. N. Herder, and H. Bos. Can we make operating systems reliable and secure? *IEEE Computer*, 39(5):44–51, May 2006.

[44] S. Thibault and T. Deegan. Improving performance by embedding HPC applications in lightweight Xen domains. In *Proc. 2nd HPCVIRT*, Mar. 2008.

[45] D. Tsirogiannis, S. Harizopoulos, and M. A. Shah. Analyzing the energy efficiency of a database server. In *Proc. ACM SIGMOD*, pages 231–242, June 2010.

[46] Z. Wang, X. Jiang, W. Cui, and P. Ning. Countering kernel rootkits with lightweight hook protection. In *Proc. 16th ACM CCS*, pages 545–554, Nov. 2009.

[47] J. Wilkes, J. Mogul, and J. Suermondt. Utilification. In *Proc. 11th ACM SIGOPS EW*, Sept. 2004.

CloudVisor: Retrofitting Protection of Virtual Machines in Multi-tenant Cloud with Nested Virtualization

Fengzhe Zhang, Jin Chen, Haibo Chen and Binyu Zang
Parallel Processing Institute
Fudan University
{fzzhang, chenjin, hbchen, byzang}@fudan.edu.cn

ABSTRACT

Multi-tenant cloud, which usually leases resources in the form of virtual machines, has been commercially available for years. Unfortunately, with the adoption of commodity virtualized infrastructures, software stacks in typical multi-tenant clouds are non-trivially large and complex, and thus are prone to compromise or abuse from adversaries including the cloud operators, which may lead to leakage of security-sensitive data.

In this paper, we propose a transparent, backward-compatible approach that protects the privacy and integrity of customers' virtual machines on commodity virtualized infrastructures, even facing a total compromise of the virtual machine monitor (VMM) and the management VM. The key of our approach is the separation of the resource management from security protection in the virtualization layer. A tiny security monitor is introduced underneath the commodity VMM using nested virtualization and provides protection to the hosted VMs. As a result, our approach allows virtualization software (e.g., VMM, management VM and tools) to handle complex tasks of managing leased VMs for the cloud, without breaking security of users' data inside the VMs.

We have implemented a prototype by leveraging commercially-available hardware support for virtualization. The prototype system, called CloudVisor, comprises only 5.5K LOCs and supports the Xen VMM with multiple Linux and Windows as the guest OSes. Performance evaluation shows that CloudVisor incurs moderate slow-down for I/O intensive applications and very small slowdown for other applications.

Categories and Subject Descriptors

D.4.6 [**Operating Systems**]: Security and Protection

General Terms

Design, Security, Performance

Keywords

Multi-tenant Cloud, Virtual Machine Security, Nested Virtualization

1. INTRODUCTION

Multi-tenant cloud has advantages of providing elastic and scalable computing resources and freeing users from the cumbersome tasks such as configuring, managing and maintaining IT resources. For example, Amazon's Elastic Compute Cloud (EC2) [6] platform provides flexible and resizable computing resources in the form of Xen-based VMs for a number of usage scenarios, including application hosting, content delivering, e-commerce and web hosting [6].

However, multi-tenant cloud also redefines the threat model of computing and raises new security challenges: the security of customers' sensitive data will be a key concern if being put into a third-party multi-tenant cloud. Unfortunately, current multi-tenant cloud platforms adopting commodity virtualization infrastructures usually provide limited assurance for the security of tenants' sensitive data. Many cloud providers only provide "security on your own" guarantee to users' content [8].

There are mainly two reasons for the poor security guarantee provided in current clouds. First, many cloud platforms usually adopt off-the-shelf virtualized infrastructures for the purpose of easing deployment and lowering costs. However, this also introduces the probability of security compromises of leased VMs from the virtualization stack. This is because, the trusted computing base (TCB) for commodity virtualized infrastructures, which includes *both the Virtual Machine Monitor (VMM) and the management VM*, is in the scale of several millions LOCs. Thus, the stack is prone to intrusions and "jail-breaks". For example, by December 2010, there have been 35 and 32 reported vulnerabilities from CVE [2] for VMware and Xen respectively.

Second, tenants from competitive companies or even the cloud operators themselves may be potential adversaries, which might stealthily make unauthorized access to unencrypted sensitive data. For example, a report assessing security risks of cloud computing from Gartner states that, one biggest challenge of cloud computing is "invisibly access unencrypted data in its facility" [26]. Google also recently fired two employees for breaching user privacy [63].

To ameliorate this problem, previous efforts have attempted to completely remove the virtualization layer [31], building a new micro-kernel like VMM [60], or protecting a VMM's control-flow integrity [68]. However, these approaches mostly only protect VMMs from attacks from a malicious guest VM, without consideration of preventing an operator with control of management tools and control VM from tampering with or stealing users' confidential data, especially external storage such as virtual disks. Further, they require changes to the core parts of a VMM [68] or even a complete reconstruction of VMMs [31, 60], thus may pose a notable barrier for adoption in commercially-successful virtualized cloud.

In this paper, we propose an alternative approach that protects leased virtual machines in a multi-tenant cloud. Our approach uses the concept of *nested virtualization* [23, 13] and introduces a tiny security monitor called CloudVisor underneath a mostly unmodified commodity VMM. Unlike previous approaches that incorporate nested virtualization functionality into a commodity VMM [13] for the purpose of multiple-level virtualization, Cloud-Visor decouples the functionality of nested virtualization from a commodity VMM and makes itself very lightweight in only supporting one VMM.

CloudVisor is responsible for protecting privacy and integrity of resources owned by VMs, while the VMM is still in charge of allocating and managing resources for VMs atop. Such a separation between security protection and resource management allows CloudVisor and the VMM to be independently designed, verified and evolved. As the essential protection logic for VM resources is quite fixed, CloudVisor can be small enough to verify its security properties (e.g., using formal verification methods [34]).

CloudVisor interposes interactions between a VMM and its guest VMs for privacy protection and integrity checking. To protect memory owned by a VM, CloudVisor tracks memory pages of a VM and encrypts page content upon unauthorized mappings from the VMM and other VMs. The privacy of Disk I/O data is protected using whole virtual disk encryption: disk I/O between VMM and guest VMs are intercepted and encrypted on disk write and decrypted on disk read. To defend against tampering with encrypted pages and persistent storage data, CloudVisor uses the MD5 hash algorithm and Merkle tree [42] to do integrity checking of disk data during decryption.

In the software stack, only CloudVisor is within the trusted computing base, while other software such as the VMM and the management VM are untrusted. The integrity of CloudVisor can be ensured using the authenticated boot provided by the trusted platform module (TPM) [66]. To simplify the development and deployment of CloudVisor, we leverage Intel Trusted eXecution Technology (TXT) [27], which allows launching and measuring the CloudVisor after the platform has been initialized. In this way, CloudVisor is freed from most hardware initialization work.

We have designed and implemented a prototype system, based on commercially-available hardware support for virtualization, including ISA virtualization (i.e., VT-x [45]), MMU virtualization (i.e., EPT), I/O virtualization (e.g., IOMMU [5], SR-IOV [18]) and dynamic platform measurement (e.g., Intel Trusted eXecution Technology [27]). CloudVisor comprises around 5.5K LOCs and supports running mostly unmodified[1] Xen VMM with multiple Linux and Windows as guest OSes. Our performance evaluation using a range of benchmarks shows that CloudVisor incurs moderate slowdown for I/O intensive applications (ranging from 4.5% to 54.5%) and very small slowdown for other applications (ranging from 0.1% to 16.8%) compared to vanilla Xen.

---

[1]An *optional* patch with about 100 LOCs to reduce unnecessary *VM exits*, similar to the optimization in Turtles [13].

In summary, this paper makes the following contributions:

- The case of using *nested virtualization* to separate security protection from resource management of virtualization, which is backward-compatible with commercial virtualization stack and significantly reduces the TCB size from millions lines of code to only several thousand lines of code.

- A set of protection techniques that provide whole VM protection against adversaries who are even with full control of a VMM and the management VM.

- A prototype implementation that leverages existing hardware support for virtualization, which is demonstrated with low performance overhead.

The rest of this paper is organized as follows. The next section identifies threats to virtualized multi-tenant cloud and describes the threat model under CloudVisor. Section 3 first discusses our design goals, and then describes our approaches as well as the overall architecture of CloudVisor. Section 4, 5 and 6 describe how CloudVisor secures CPU states, memory pages and disk storages accordingly. The implementation issues and status are discussed in section 7. We then present performance evaluation results in section 8, and discuss the current limitation and possible future work in section 9. Finally, section 10 relates CloudVisor with other literatures and section 11 concludes this paper.

2. MOTIVATION AND THREAT MODEL
This section first identifies the attack surface of a virtualized multi-tenant cloud and then discusses the threat model under CloudVisor.

2.1 Attack Surface of Virtualization Layer

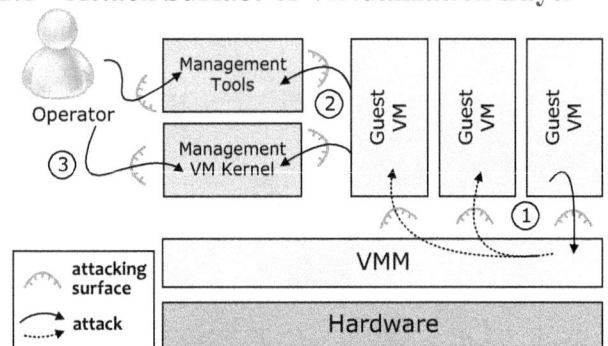

Figure 1: Typical virtualized architecture and attack surface in multiple tenant cloud.

Virtualization [24] has a good engagement with cloud computing due to its features in server consolidation, power saving and eased management. Many cloud providers have used virtualization in its cloud infrastructure and leasing resources to users in the form of virtual machine (a form of "Infrastructure as a Service" cloud), such as Amazon EC2 [6], Eucalyptus [46], FlexiScale [20] Nimbus [64] and RackSpace Cloud [62].

Virtualization might have both positive [16] and negative [22] impacts on the security and trustworthiness of the cloud. On the positive side, many "out-of-the-box" security techniques could now be implemented in the virtualization layers, making them more resilient to attacks to the VM [16]. On the negative side, commodity virtualization software stack is usually huge and most of them are within the trusted computing base.

Figure 1 depicts the typical (hostless) architecture of virtualization and the attack surface in a multi-tenant cloud. As tenant VMs are usually managed by the management tools via over-powerful privileged interfaces to the VMM, they could be arbitrarily inspected and tampered with by *not only the VMM but also the management tools in the management VM*. In principle, operators should be granted with only the least privilege and will not be able to tamper with tenant VMs. In practice, however, operators are usually granted with access rights more than they should have, as it is usually difficult to define the proper privilege precisely [35]. Consequently, improperly granting access rights to users' data could easily put users' data under threat (i.e., attack surface 3). For example, a cloud operator might leverage the internal maintenance interface to dump a VM's memory image for offline analysis, stealthily migrate/clone a VM to a shadow place for replaying, or even copy away all VM's virtual disks.

Worse even, as more and more functionalities being integrated into the virtualization layer such as live migration, security monitoring and snapshot, the TCB, which *includes VMM, management VM and management tools*, is exploding in both size and complexity. For example, the TCB size for Xen, including the VMM, management VM and tools has been steadily increasing across each major release, as shown in Table 1. An adversary could mount attacks to the virtualization layer by exploiting the inside security vulnerabilities (attack surface 1 and 2). Here, we deliberately separate internal (surface 3) and external attacks (surface 1 and 2) as in typical data-center there are usually physically separated network for internal operators and for external accesses. Usually, internal attacks are much more powerful and easy to mount if a cloud operator tends to be malicious.

However, most previous efforts only aim at protecting against attack surface 1 and 2 by securing [60, 68] or removing [31] the virtualization layer, without defending attackers leveraging attack surface 3. For example, they cannot defend against attacks leveraging legal maintenance operations such as dump/clone/migrate a VM or virtual disks. Further, they require a reconstruction of the cloud software stack. To this end, it is critical to provide multi-tenant cloud with an approach that defending against attackers penetrated through the three attack surfaces from tampering with tenant VMs, yet with a small trusted computing base, which motivates the design and implementation of CloudVisor.

	VMM	Dom0 Kernel	Tools	TCB
Xen 2.0	45K	4,136K	26K	4,207K
Xen 3.0	121K	4,807K	143K	5,071K
Xen 4.0	270K	7,560K	647K	8,477K

Table 1: TCB of Xen virtualization layer (by Lines of Code, counted by *sloccount*).

2.2 Assumptions and Threat Models

Adversaries: Given that there are multiple attack surfaces in a multi-tenant cloud, we consider both local adversaries and remote adversaries and assume that they have full control over the VM management stack including the commodity hypervisor, the management VM and tools. An adversary may leverage the powerful management interfaces to try to dump a tenant VM's memory, steal the VM's virtual disks, or even inject code to the VM.

Assumptions: We assume the *cloud provider* itself does not intend to be malicious or with the goal of tampering with or stealing its tenant's sensitive information. Instead, the threat may come from the intentional or unintentional mis-operations from its operators [26, 63]. Hence, we assume there will be no internal physical attacks such as placing probes into the buses and freezing all main memory and reading out the data. Actually, typical data-centers usually have strict control of physical accesses as well as surveillance cameras to monitor and log such accesses. However, as the disk storage might be easily accessible by operators through the VM management stack or even physical maintenance (such as disk replacements), we assume that the external disk storage is not trustworthy.

Security Guarantees: The goal of CloudVisor is to prevent the malicious VM management stack from inspecting or modifying a tenant's VM states, thus providing both *secrecy* and *integrity* to a VM's states, including CPU states, memory pages and disk I/O data. CloudVisor guarantees that all accesses not from a VM itself (e.g., the VMM, other VMs), such as DMA, memory dumping and I/O data, can only see the encrypted version of that VM's data. Upon illegal tampering with a VM's states, CloudVisor uses cryptographic approaches to verify the integrity, ordering and freshness of a VM's data and fail-stops a VM upon tampering.

A malicious VMM cannot issue arbitrary control transfers from the VMM to a tenant' VM. Instead, all control transfers between the VMM and a VM can only be done through a well-defined entry and exit points, which will be mediated by CloudVisor. The VMM cannot fake an execution context to let a VM run upon. Actually, a VM's execution context is securely saved and restored by CloudVisor during a control transfer.

With platform measurement techniques such as Intel Trusted eXecution Technology and TPM, CloudVisor allows cloud tenants to assure that their VMs are running "as is" on machines protected by CloudVisor. Hence, attackers cannot alter the booting environment or fool a tenant's VM to run in a wrong execution mode such as a para-virtualized mode and a different paging mode, which will be detected and refused by CloudVisor.

Non-Security Goals: As a tenant's VM still uses services provided by the VMM and its management VM and tools, CloudVisor cannot guarantee availability and execution correctness of a tenant's VM. However, we believe this is not an issue for multi-tenant cloud, as the primary goal of cloud providers is featuring utility-style computing resources to users with certain service-level agreement. Providing degraded or even wrong services will be easily discovered by customers and the misbehaving provider or operator will soon be dumped out of the market.

CloudVisor does not guard against side-channel attacks in the cloud [49], which may be hard to deploy and have very limited bandwidth to leak information. However, CloudVisor does leverage advanced hardware features like AES instructions in recent CPUs [4] to prevent leakage of crypto keys [56]. Further, many security-critical applications such as OpenSSL have builtin mechanism to defend against side-channel attacks.

CloudVisor also provides no protection to interactions of a VM with its outside environments. Hence, the security of a tenant's VM is ultimately limited by the VM itself. For example, an adversary may still be able to subvert a VM by exploiting security vulnerabilities inside the VM. This can be usually mitigated by leveraging the traditional security-enhancing mechanisms for applications and operating systems. CloudVisor does guarantee that, adversaries controlling a subverted VM or even having subverted the management software or the VMM, cannot further break the security protection by CloudVisor to other VMs in the same machine.

3. GOALS AND APPROACHES

This section first illustrates the design goals of CloudVisor, and then describes approaches to achieving the goals. Finally, we present the overall architecture of CloudVisor.

3.1 Design Consideration

The primary goal of CloudVisor is to provide transparent security protection to a whole VM under existing virtualized platforms, yet with minimal trusted computing base:

Whole-VM protection: We choose the protection granularity at the VM level for three considerations. First, many cloud platforms such as Amazon EC2 choose to provide tenants with resources in the form of VMs (i.e., Infrastructure as a Service). Second, the VM is with a simple and clean abstraction and the interactions between a VM and the VMM are well-defined, compared to those between a process and an operating system, which usually is with several hundreds to thousands of APIs with complex and subtle semantics (e.g., ioctl). Finally, protection at the VM level is transparent to guest OS above. By contrast, providing protection at the process level (e.g., CHAOS [15, 14], Overshadow [17] and SP^3 [71]) is usually closely coupled with a specific type of operating system and requires non-trivial efforts when being ported to other operating systems.

Non-intrusive with Commodity VMMs: It is important to design a security-enhancing approach to working non-intrusively with existing commercially-available virtualization stack. Hence, CloudVisor should require minimal changes to both the VMM and the management software. This could enable rapid integration and deployment of CloudVisor to existing cloud infrastructure. Further, CloudVisor can then be separately designed and verified, and be orthogonal to the evolvement of the VMM and management software.

Minimized TCB: Prior experiences show that a smaller code size usually indicates more trustworthy software [21, 58]. Hence, the TCB size for CloudVisor should be minimal so that CloudVisor could be verified for correctness. For example, recent formal verification effort [34] has shown its success in a general-purpose OS kernel with 8,700 LOCs.

3.2 Approach Overview

Unlike traditional virtualization systems, CloudVisor excludes a VMM and the management VM out of the TCB. Instead, CloudVisor executes in the most privileged mode of a machine and monitors the execution of and interactions between the VMM and the hosted VMs, both of which execute in less privileged modes. As the resources of a VM mainly comprise of CPU, memory and I/O devices, CloudVisor is designed to protect such resources accordingly (as shown in Table 2):

Transparent Interposition using Nested Virtualization: To make CloudVisor transparent with existing virtualization stack, we use nested virtualization [23, 13] to give the illusion that a VMM

Category	Protecting Approaches
CPU states	Interpose control transfers between VMM and VM Conceal CPU states from the VMM
Memory pages	Interpose address translation from guest physical address to host physical address
Persistent data	Transparent whole VM image encryption Decrypt/encrypt I/O data in CloudVisor
Bootstrap	Intel TXT to late launch CloudVisor Hash of CloudVisor is stored in TPM

Table 2: Methodologies to protect a tenant VM.

still controls all resources of VMs. To achieve this, CloudVisor interposes all control transfer events between the VMM and its VMs (section 4). Upon interposition, CloudVisor does necessary transformation and protection, and forwards the (virtualized) events to the VMM to handle. For example, upon an interrupt and depending on the context, CloudVisor will save general-purpose registers and only provide necessary ones to the VMM, to limit information being exposed to the VMM.

VM-based Memory Ownership Tracking: To protect a VM's memory from inspection by the VMM and the management VM, CloudVisor interposes address translation from guest physical address to host physical address. Specifically, CloudVisor tracks the ownership of each page and each page table maintained by the VMM (i.e., extended page table, EPT [2]) (section 5). CloudVisor disallows the VMM from directly overwriting the EPT. On intercepting updates to the VMM's page table, CloudVisor checks if the ownership of the page matches with that of the page table and encrypts the page content if there is a mismatch.

One alternative approach to protecting a guest VM's memory might be multi-shadowing [17], which provides both encrypted version (seen by the VMM) and plain version (seen by the guest VM) of a page. However, this would require two EPTs for each VM and two copies of some pages, which causes additional memory pressure. Further, the VMM sometimes needs to access some guest VMs' memory in plain form, which requires interposition and protection by CloudVisor (section 5.3). Simply providing encrypted versions of pages to the VMM would corrupt the whole system.

I/O Protection through Encryption: CloudVisor currently provides protection to virtual disks owned by a VM. For network devices, as typical security-sensitive applications have already used encrypted message channels such as SSL, CloudVisor does not provide cryptography protection to such devices. To protect virtual disks, CloudVisor transparently encrypts and decrypts data during each disk I/O access by a VM, including both port-based I/O and direct memory access (DMA) (detailed in section 6). The integrity of disk data is ensured using the MD5 hash algorithm and Merkle tree [42] to do integrity checking (section 6). To prevent a VM, the VMM or the management VM from issuing DMA attacks, CloudVisor maintains a per-VM I/O access permission table (i.e., by manipulating the IOMMU [3]) and only grants DMA accesses to their own memory regions.

Late Launch to Reduce CloudVisor Complexity: As CloudVi-

---

[2] Translates guest physical address to host physical address.
[3] IOMMU translates the guest physical I/O addresses to host physical addresses on an memory access issued by I/O devices.

sor runs underneath the VMM, CloudVisor has to implement many machine initialization procedures if it is booted before the VMM. This could increase the complexity and also the code base of CloudVisor. Hence, CloudVisor leverages existing hardware support for dynamic measurement [27, 9] and boots CloudVisor after the system has finished its booting process. Specifically, upon receiving requests of booting CloudVisor from the VMM, CloudVisor boots itself and the processor will issue a measurement on the integrity of CloudVisor, which prevents the VMM from booting a tampered version of CloudVisor. The measurement results will be used by cloud tenants as evidences in remote attestation.

3.3 The CloudVisor Architecture

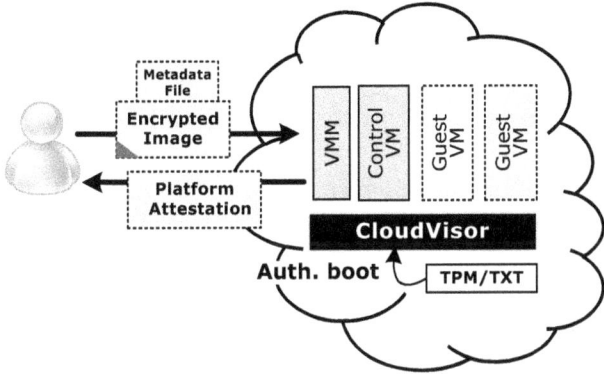

Figure 2: Overall architecture of CloudVisor.

Figure 2 shows the overall architecture of CloudVisor, which is a featherweight security monitor that runs at the most privileged level, while the commodity VMM is deprivileged into the less privileged mode together with the control VM and guest VMs. CloudVisor enforces the isolation and protection of resources used by each guest VM and ensures the isolation among the VMM and its guest VMs. Traditional virtualization functionalities, such as resource management, VM construction and destruction, scheduling, are still done by the VMM. CloudVisor transparently monitors how the VMM and the VMs use hardware resources to enforce the protection and isolation of resources used by each guest VM.

Figure 2 also depicts how cloud users could use CloudVisor to securely deploy their services. A cloud tenant may first authenticate the cloud platform by using TCG's attestation protocol with TPM to know if the platform is running a known version of CloudVisor. Then, the tenant may send VM images and the corresponding metadata file to run in the cloud. Similar to Amazon Machine Images [7], the image is encrypted using a random symmetric key. The public key will then be used to encrypt the symmetric key and the users will send both cipher-texts to CloudVisor. CloudVisor controls the private key of the platform and uses it to decrypt the images for booting. In the metadata file for the VM image, there is some information (such as hashes and initial vectors) guarding the integrity, ordering and freshness of the VM images. The metadata also contains information describing the execution modes (e.g., paging mode) of this VM. Upon launching of a VM, CloudVisor will use this information to ensure that the VM image is executed "as is".

4. SECURING CONTROL TRANSITION WITH NESTED VIRTUALIZATION

CloudVisor interposes control transitions between a VMM and its guest VMs. With hardware support for virtualization (i.e., VT-x [45] or SVM [9]), such control transitions are abstracted with *VM exit* (transitions from a VM to the VMM) and *VM entry* (transitions from the VMM back to a VM). CloudVisor transparently secures such transitions using nested virtualization [23, 13] by virtualizing such events and doing necessary security protection. This section first introduces the necessary background information with hardware-assisted (nested) virtualization using Intel's VT-x as an example, and then describes how CloudVisor leverages it to secure control transitions.

4.1 Hardware-assisted (Nested) Virtualization

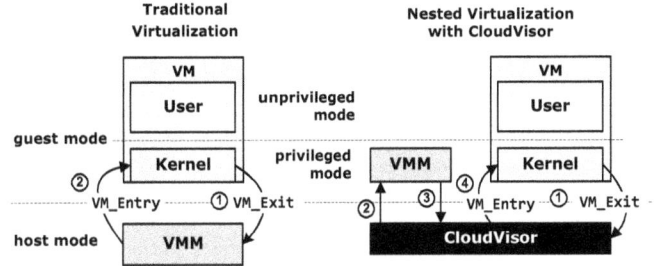

Figure 3: The general architecture of hardware-assisted virtualization (left) and how CloudVisor leverages it to secure control transfer using nested virtualization.

The left part of Figure 3 shows the general architecture of hardware-assisted virtualization, where the VMM runs in *host mode*, and the VMs run in *guest mode*. The former mode is used by the VMM and instructions are natively executed. The latter mode is used by guest VMs, where privileged instructions that access critical hardware resources (e.g., I/O resources) will cause a control transition from *guest mode* to *host mode* (a *VM exit*, step 1). The VMM will handle the event (e.g., by emulating the violating instruction) and then use *VM entry* to transfer the control back to *guest mode* (step 2), where the guest VM resumes its execution.

For each virtual CPU of a guest VM, an in-memory VM control structures (*VMCS* in Intel's terminology) is maintained by the VMM. The *VMCS* saves the states for the VMM and the guest VM, as well as controls which guest events should cause *VM exit*.

With nested virtualization, CloudVisor now runs in *host mode*, while both the VMM and the guest VMs are put in *guest mode*, as shown in the right part of Figure 3. To enforce isolation between a VMM and its guest VMs, the VMM runs in a separated context of *guest mode*. Note that, placing the VMM into a less privileged mode will not degrade the security of the VMM, as CloudVisor will ensure strict isolation among the VMM and its VMs.

4.2 Securing Control Transition with Nested Virtualization

Enabling Interposition: CloudVisor maintains a *VMCS* for the VMM to control the types of instructions or events that will cause *VM exit* when executing in the VMM's context. Currently, the VMM only gets trapped on three types of architectural events relating to resource isolation: 1) NPT/EPT faults, which are caused by faults on translation from guest physical address to host physical address; 2) Execution of instructions in the virtualization instruction set such as VMRead/VMWrite [4]; 3) IOMMU faults, which is caused by faults during the translation from device address to host physical address. Other architectural events like page faults and interrupts do not cause traps to CloudVisor and are directly delivered to the VMM.

The VMCS for each guest VM is still created and maintained by the VMM. When a VMCS is to be installed on the CPU, CloudVisor overwrites some critical control fields. For instance, the entry address of *VM exit* handler is specified in the *VMCS*. To interpose control transition, CloudVisor records the entry address and replaces it with the entry address of the handler in CloudVisor. As a result, all *VM exits* from a guest VM is first handled by CloudVisor and then propagated to the VMM.

Securing Control Transition: CloudVisor interposes between guest VMs and the VMM on *VM exit* for mainly three purposes: 1) protecting CPU register contexts when a VM is interrupted; 2) manipulating address translation to enforce memory isolation (detailed in section 5); 3) intercepting and parsing I/O instructions to determine the I/O buffer addresses in a VM (detailed in section 6).

As shown in the right part of Figure 3, CloudVisor interposes each *VM exit* event (step 1), protects CPU contexts and parses I/O instructions if necessary, and then forwards the *VM exit* event to the VMM (step 2). It then intercepts the *VM entry* request from the VMM (step 3), restores CPU contexts and resumes the execution of guest VM (step 4) accordingly.

Both external interrupts and certain instruction execution can cause *VM exits*. For external interrupts, the VMM does not need the general-purpose registers to handle the event. In that case, CloudVisor saves and clears the content of general-purpose registers before propagating the event to the VMM. On *VM entry*, CloudVisor restores the saved registers for the guest VM and resumes the VM.

For *VM exits* caused by synchronous instruction execution, CloudVisor only resets a part of the register contexts and keeps the states that are essential for the event handling. For instance, the program counter and some general-purpose registers in an I/O instruction should be exposed to the VMM.

CloudVisor ensures the CPU context on *VM entry* is exactly the same with the context on last *VM exit* for each virtual CPU. Hence, the VMM is unable to dump CPU register information by triggering arbitrary interrupts, redirect control to arbitrary code in the guest VM, or tamper with the CPU context of the guest VMs.

4.3 Dynamic Nested Virtualization

Though, CloudVisor runs underneath the VMM, CloudVisor does not contain machine bootstrap code for the sake of small TCB. Consequently, it is booted after the VMM and the management VM have been initialized. When CloudVisor boots, it runs in *host mode* and demotes the VMM to *guest mode*, thus effectively virtualizes the VMM on the fly. To ensure a tamper-proof dynamic nested virtualization, CloudVisor adopts dynamic root of trust (such as Intel TXT [27] and AMD SVM [9]) to ensure the processors are in a known clean state when they initialize CloudVisor. The SHA-1 hash of CloudVisor binary is calculated and stored in the TPM [66] for future remote attestation. This is done in the macro instruction

---

[4]VMRead and VMWrite instructions read/write VM control structures (*VMCS*)

such as SINIT (Intel TXT) and SKINIT (AMD SVM) that are hardwired in the processor. For multi-processor or multi-core platforms, all the processors are synchronized before launching CloudVisor to ensure the all the processors are nestedly virtualized simultaneously.

5. MEMORY ISOLATION

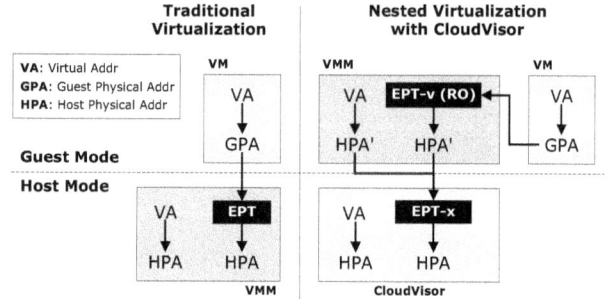

Figure 4: The general structure of extended paging (left) and how CloudVisor leverages it for memory isolation.

To provide efficient memory isolation among CloudVisor, the VMM and guest VMs, CloudVisor uses commercially-available extended paging or nested paging, which provides hardware support for MMU virtualization.

5.1 Isolation with Nested/Extended Paging

The left part of Figure 4 shows the intended usage of extended paging in virtualized systems: the VMM itself uses a translation table that directly converts virtual addresses (VA) to host physical addresses (HPA) and controls how VMs translate guest physical addresses (GPA) to HPA using an extended page table (EPT). The guest VM manages the address translation from VA to GPA with the conventional page table.

When CloudVisor is booted, the VMM is demoted to run in the *guest mode*. An extended page table (EPT) is created for the VMM and the address translation of the VMM is then configured to use a two-step address translation that uses page table (VA to GPA) and extended page table (EPT) (GPA to HPA). As shown in the right part of Figure 4, CloudVisor maintains an identity GPA-to-HPA mapping (i.e., HPA' equals to HPA) EPT for the VMM (called *EPT-x*). Thus, the VMM is unaware of the memory virtualization by CloudVisor. CloudVisor removes its own memory from EPT-x to isolate its memory space from the VMM. *EPT-x* is kept in the memory space of CloudVisor and is not accessible by the VMM. The VMM still maintains a GPA-to-HPA' mapping table (called *EPT-v*) for each VM, but is granted with only read permission.

In principle, a guest VM can be configured to use either software address translation such as shadow page table or hardware-assisted address translation. The support of software address translation should be technically doable in CloudVisor but might be more complex. For simplicity, CloudVisor currently only supports platforms with hardware-assisted address translation. If the VMM tricks a guest VM into using a software address translation mechanism, CloudVisor will refuse to attest for the VM.

5.2 Memory Ownership Tracking

To ensure memory isolation among the VMM and its guest VMs, CloudVisor maintains a table to track the ownership of each physical memory page. The value of the table is the owner ID of the page. Each VM is assigned with a unique ID when it is booted. The VMM's ID is fixed to zero. CloudVisor ensures that a physical memory page can only be assigned to be one owner at a time.

During system startup, all pages other than those in CloudVisor are owned by the VMM. When the EPT of a guest VM is loaded into the processor for the first time, CloudVisor walks through the whole EPT to find all the mapped pages. These pages are regarded as being assigned to the guest VM. CloudVisor changes the owner of these pages to the guest VM, and unmaps it from the EPT of the VMM so that the VMM cannot access the pages any more. When a page is unmapped from the EPT, the owner of the page is set to be the VMM and the page is mapped back in the EPT of the VMM.

Whenever the VMM updates the guest EPT, a page fault in the EPT (EPT violation in Intel's term) is raised. CloudVisor handles the fault by validating the page ownership. If a new mapping is to be established, CloudVisor ensures that the page to be mapped belongs to the VMM. CloudVisor unmaps it from the EPT of the VMM and changes the page owner to the guest VM. If an existing page is to be unmapped, CloudVisor encrypts the content of the page, maps it to the EPT of the VMM and changes the page owner to the VMM. CloudVisor does not allow a page to be mapped in the same EPT more than once. To remap a page, the VMM has to unmap it first, and then remap it to the new location.

DMA-capable devices can bypass memory access control enforced by MMU. To defend against malicious DMA requests, CloudVisor makes protected memory regions inaccessible from DMA devices using IOMMU by manipulating the translation from host physical address to device address. During system startup, CloudVisor unmaps its own memory in the IOMMU table to prevent DMA requests from accessing the memory. When a guest VM boots up, CloudVisor also unmaps the VM's memory in the IOMMU table used by DMA-capable devices. When the guest VM shuts down, the pages are returned to the VMM and CloudVisor remaps the pages in the IOMMU table. If a DMA request is setup to access memory pages in CloudVisor or guest VMs, an IOMMU fault is raised and handled by CloudVisor. Currently, CloudVisor simply denies the request.

5.3 Legal Memory Accesses

Memory isolation mechanism provided by CloudVisor ensures the entire memory space of a guest VM is inaccessible to the VMM and the management VM. However, there are several cases where the VMM and the management VM should be allowed to access some memory of guest VMs. In such cases, CloudVisor interposes and assists such accesses to ensure that only minimal insensitive information will be divulged.

Privileged instructions such as I/O instructions and accesses to control registers cause traps (i.e., *VM exits*) that are handled by the VMM. In some cases the VMM needs to get the instruction opcode in the guest VM memory to emulate it. During such traps, CloudVisor fetches the privileged opcode and feeds it to the VMM. As CloudVisor only allows fetching one opcode pointed by the program counter, the VMM is unable to trick CloudVisor into fetching arbitrary non-privileged opcode, nor can it arbitrarily trigger traps to access opcode.

On a trap, the program counter of the faulting instruction is a virtual address and the memory operands are also presented as virtual

addresses. The VMM needs to walk the page table in the guest VM to translate the virtual addresses to guest physical addresses, which are further translated to host physical addresses using the EPT. To handle this, CloudVisor temporarily allows the VMM to indirectly read the guest page table entries corresponding to the opcode and memory operands. Upon a trap caused by the execution of a privileged instruction, CloudVisor fetches the program counter of the instruction and parses the instruction to get the memory operand. CloudVisor walks the page table in the guest VM to get the page table entries required to translate the program counter and the memory operands. When the VMM accesses the page table, CloudVisor feeds it with the previously obtained page table entries. To reduce overhead associated with privileged instruction emulation, CloudVisor uses a buffer to cache the page table entries for privileged instructions for each VCPU.

The VMM also needs to get the contents of guest I/O buffers when emulating I/O accesses. When the VMM accesses I/O buffers, an EPT fault is raised and CloudVisor handles the fault by copying the data for the VMM. Specifically, when the VMM copies data to or from the guest VM, CloudVisor validates that the buffer address in the guest VM is a known I/O buffer and determines if the buffer is used for disk I/O (section 6.1).

6. DISK STORAGE PROTECTION

Virtual disks of a VM are also critical resources that demand both privacy and integrity protection. There are two alternative ways to protect a virtual disk. The first one is letting a cloud user use an encrypted file system that guard the disk I/O data at the file-system level, such as Bitlocker [1] and FileVault [3]. This requires no protection of disk I/O data by CloudVisor as the disk I/O only contains encrypted data and the file system itself will verify the integrity and freshness of disk data.

To provide transparent protection to tenant's VM, CloudVisor also provides full-disk encryption and hashing to protect disk data privacy and integrity. CloudVisor encrypts the data exchange between a VM and the VMM and verifies the integrity, freshness and ordering of disk I/O data.

6.1 Handling Data Exchange

Retrieving I/O configuration information: When a VM boots up, the guest VM usually probes its I/O configuration space (e.g., PCI) to identify I/O devices and their ports. The VMM usually virtualizes the I/O space and feeds the VM with information of the virtual devices. CloudVisor interposes the communication to gather the information of virtual devices plugged into the guest VM. In this way, CloudVisor knows the I/O ports used by the VM and their types. Among the I/O ports, CloudVisor treats disk I/O ports differently from others such as VGA, network and serial console. All data exchanged through disk I/O ports are encrypted and hashed before being copied to the VMM and decrypted before copying data to a guest VM. CloudVisor does not encrypt or decrypt data exchanges on other ports (such as NICs).

Interposing I/O requests: To determine if I/O data exchange between a guest VM and the VMM is legal, CloudVisor intercepts and parses I/O requests from the guest VM. CloudVisor does not emulate the I/O requests but only records the requests. By parsing I/O requests from the I/O instructions, CloudVisor retrieves the information of *I/O port*, *memory address* of the I/O buffer and the *buffer size* for further processing.

There are two alternative ways to process these I/O requests. The first one is to "trap and emulate" the requests. To ensure security, CloudVisor uses a *white-list* to record the I/O requests and then propagates them to the VMM, which will handle the requests by copying the data to/from buffers in the guest VM. The following data copying will trap (i.e., VM exit) to CloudVisor, which will use the *white-list* to validate the data copying. After the data exchange, the corresponding record will be removed from the list to prevent the VMM from revisiting the memory pages.

The second approach is using a *bounce buffer* in CloudVisor to assist the data exchange. When a guest VM tries to copy data to the VMM (i.e., an I/O write operation), CloudVisor intercepts the request, copies the data to the bounce buffer, and then provides the VMM with a modified I/O request to let the VMM read from the bounce buffer instead of the guest VM. Similarly, when a VMM tries to copy data to a guest VM, the data is first written to the bounce buffer and then read by the guest VM.

In principle, the first "trap and emulate" based approach can handle both port-based I/O and direct memory access (DMA). However, it will introduce a large amount of traps (i.e., VM exits) to CloudVisor if the data is copied in small chunks (e.g., 4 or 8 bytes). A DMA request that incurs multiple traps will cause non-trivial performance degradation for I/O intensive applications. Comparing to the first approach, the *bounce buffer* approach only incurs one additional data copy. Hence, CloudVisor uses the first approach for port-based I/O and the second approach for DMA.

6.2 Disk I/O Privacy and Integrity

CloudVisor uses the AES-CBC algorithm to encrypt and decrypt disk data in the granularity of disk sectors. A 128-bit AES key is generated by the user and passed to CloudVisor together with the encrypted VM image. The storage AES key is always maintained inside CloudVisor.

At VM bootup time, CloudVisor fetches all non-leaf nodes of hashes and IVs (Initial Vectors) in the Merkle hash tree and keeps them as in-memory cache. On disk reads, CloudVisor first hashes the data block to verify its integrity and then decrypts the disk sector using the AES storage key and the IV. On disk writes, an IV is generated for each disk sector if it has not been generated yet. The data block is hashed and then encrypted using the storage key and the IV.

As CloudVisor does not control the devices, it cannot read or write metadata on external storage space. One approach is let CloudVisor issue shadow DMA requests to the VMM. However, our experience shows that this sometimes could incur timeout for I/O requests in a guest VM. Instead, we provide a user-level agent in the management VM to assist metadata fetching, updating and caching. The agent is untrusted as it has the same privilege as other software in the management VM. If the agent refuses to function or functions incorrectly, CloudVisor can always detect the misbehavior by validating the metadata.

As shown in Figure 5, for each disk sector, a 128-bit MD5 hash and a 128-bit IV are stored in a file stored in the file system of the management VM. The hash is organized using a Merkle tree to guard the freshness and ordering of disk data. When launching a guest VM, the file is mapped into the memory of the agent. The agent fetches all the non-leaf hashes in the Merkle hash tree and sends them to CloudVisor. CloudVisor caches the hashes in memory to

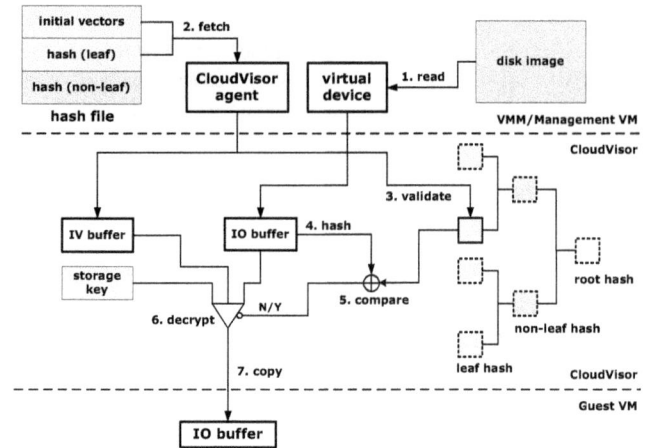

Figure 5: Data flow of disk I/O read.

eliminate further fetches.

On a disk I/O read, the virtual device driver first reads the requested disk block from the disk image of the VM (step 1). Then the agent fetches the hash and IV of the requested disk block and puts them in the hash and IV buffer provided by CloudVisor (step 2), and the integrity of the fetched hash is validated by CloudVisor (step 3). The MD5 hash of the cipher text is calculated (step 4) and compared with the fetched hash (step 5). If the computed hash matches with the store hash, CloudVisor decrypts the data using the fetched IV and the storage key (step 6). If the data is valid, CloudVisor copies it to the I/O buffer in the guest VM and removes the buffer address from the *white-list* if necessary (step 7). The disk I/O write operation is similar to read. The difference is that CloudVisor will generate the IVs and hashes and put it to metadata file.

The agent leverages the file cache of the operating system to buffer the most frequently used metadata. In the worst case, for a disk read, the agent needs two more disk access to fetch the corresponding hash and IV.

Sudden power loss may cause state inconsistency, as CloudVisor currently does not guarantee atomic updates of disk data, hashes and IVs. For simplicity, CloudVisor assumes the cloud servers are equipped with power supply backups and can shutdown the machine without data loss on power loss. Recent researchers [70] have also shown that providing atomicity and consistency in a secure file system is not very difficult. We plan to incorporate such support in future.

7. IMPLEMENTATION ISSUES AND STATUS

CloudVisor has been implemented based on commercially-available hardware support for virtualization, including VT-x [45], EPT [45], VT-d [5], and TXT [27]. To defend against cache-based side-channel attacks among VMs [56], CloudVisor uses the AES-NI instruction set in CPU [4] to do encryption. For simplicity, CloudVisor currently only supports hardware-assisted virtualization. CloudVisor supports Xen with both Linux and Windows as the guest operating systems and can run multiple uniprocessor and multiprocessor VMs.

7.1 Multiple VMs and Multicore Support

CloudVisor supports multiple VMs to run simultaneously atop a multiprocessor machine. To support multiprocessor, CloudVisor maintains one VMCS for each CPU core used by the VMM. All CPU cores shares one EPT for the VMM (i.e., EPT-x) and CloudVisor serializes accesses from multiple cores to EPT-x. During startup, SINIT/SKINIT uses IPIs (Inter-processor Interrupt) to broadcast to all CPU cores and launch CloudVisor on all the cores simultaneously.

7.2 VM Life-cycle Management

CloudVisor can transparently support VM construction and destruction, as well as VM save, restore and migration. The followings briefly describe the involved actions required by CloudVisor to provide protection to a VM on these operations:

VM construction and destruction: Even if the whole VM image is encrypted, VM construction can still be supported by CloudVisor in a transparent way. I/O data are transparently decrypted when it is copied to guest VM memory. On VM destruction, the access right of memory pages of the VM is restored to the VMM transparently.

VM snapshot, save, restore: In order to support VM snapshot, save and restore, guest VM memory integrity and privacy should be guaranteed when it is on storage space. CloudVisor uses per-page encryption and hashing to protect memory snapshot. Similar to the protection on the disk image, the memory contents are hashed at the granularity of page. The hashes are organized as a Merkle tree and stored together with an array of IVs.

When the management VM maps and copies the VM memory for saving, the operation is not initiated by I/O instructions of the VM itself. CloudVisor would not be able to find a corresponding entry in the *white-list*. In that case, CloudVisor would encrypt the requested page with the AES storage key and a newly generated IV. The VMM will get an encrypted memory image. When restoring the memory image, the VMM copies the encrypted memory image into guest memory space. CloudVisor finds the corresponding storage key of the VM, fetches the IVs and hashes of the memory image and decrypts the pages.

VM migration: VM migration procedure is similar to VM save and restore, but requires an additional key migration protocol. CloudVisor on the migration source and destination platform needs to verify each other before migrating the storage key and root hash. The verification procedure is similar to the remote attestation procedure between CloudVisor and the cloud user, which is a standard remote attestation protocol from TCG [52].

7.3 Performance Optimization

Boosting I/O with hardware support: CloudVisor currently supports virtualization-enabled devices such as SR-IOV NICs, direct assignment of devices to a VM and virtualizing traditional devices. For the first two cases, as most of operations are done in a VM itself without interventions from the VMM, CloudVisor mostly only needs to handle the initialization work and does very little work when the devices are functioning.

Reducing unnecessary VM exits: On Intel platform, we found that a large amount of *VM exit* events are due to *VM read* and *VM write* instructions. The VMM intensively uses these instructions to check and update the states of guest VMs. These instructions always cause *VM exits* if not being executed in *host mode*. The large amount of *VM exits* would bring notable performance overhead. To remedy this, CloudVisor provides an optional patch to Xen that replaces the *VM read* and *VM write* instructions with memory accesses to the *VMCS*, similar to the method used in [13]. Note that, adding an in-memory cache for VMCS will not introduce security vulnerabilities, as CloudVisor always validates the integrity of a *VMCS* when the VMCS is loaded into CPU.

7.4 Key Management

Currently, CloudVisor uses a simple key management scheme by using the cryptography key within VM images. The VM key is encrypted using the public key of a machine (e.g., storage root key) so that the VM images can only be decrypted and verified by a know version of CloudVisor verified using authenticated boot by the trusted platform module (TPM) [66] and Intel's TXT [27]. When a VM is being launched, the encrypted VM key will be loaded into CloudVisor's memory and decrypted using the public key of the platform (e.g., storage root key in TPM). The decrypted VM key will then be used to encrypt/decrypt the data exchange between the VMM and the guest VM. To ease users' deployment, we also provide a user-level tool to convert a normal VM image to the encrypted form and generate the metadata file. Note that the key management scheme is orthogonal to the protection means in CloudVisor and can be easily replaced with a more complex scheme.

7.5 Soft and Hard Reset

An attacker might issue a soft reset that does not reset memory and try to read the memory content owned by a leased VM. In such cases, the reset will send a corresponding *INIT* signal to the processor, which will cause a *VMX exit* to CloudVisor. CloudVisor will then scrub all memory owned by the leased VMs and self-destruct by scrubbing its own memory. Similarly, if the VMM or a VM crashes, CloudVisor will do the same scrubbing work upon intercepting the events. For a hard reset, as the memory will be lost due to power loss, CloudVisor simply post the hard rest signals to CPUs. In short, CloudVisor uses a fail-stop manner to defend against possible attacks during hard and soft reset as well as crashes.

7.6 Implementation Complexity

We have built a prototype of CloudVisor based on commercially-available hardware support for virtualization. Our prototype consists of a set of event handlers for privileged operations (e.g., *VM exit* and *EPT fault*), a tiny instruction interpreter, and an AES library for encryption. The code base is only around 5.5K lines of code (LOCs), which should be small and simple enough to verify. There is also an untrusted user-level CloudVisor agent in the QEMU module of Xen. The agent consists of around 200 LOCs and handles the management of hashes for pages and I/O data.

CloudVisor supports Xen with both Linux and Windows as the guest operating systems. CloudVisor is mostly transparent to Xen with an *optional* patch with about 100 LOCs to Xen for Intel platform. Multiple unmodified Linux and Windows VMs can run with uniprocessor or multiprocessor mode simultaneously atop CloudVisor. CloudVisor could also transparently support VMMs other than Xen, as it makes little assumption on the VMM, which will be our future work.

8. PERFORMANCE EVALUATION

We evaluated the performance overhead of CloudVisor by comparing it with vanilla Xen using a set of benchmarks. As we did not have a machine with all features required by the current implementation, we used two machines to demonstrate the functionalities of CloudVisor separately. The first machine is equipped with an Intel Core2 Quad processor. The chipset supports Intel TXT [27] and has a TPM chip installed, but without EPT support [45]. This machine is used to demonstrate how CloudVisor dynamically establishes a trusted execution environment after the boot of Xen. We use a Dell R510 server as the second machine, which is equipped with two SR-IOV NICs connected with one Gigabyte Ethernet. This machine has a 2.6 GHz 4-core/8-thread Intel processor with VT-x, EPT and AES-NI support and 8 GB physical memory. Although verified separately, the evaluation of functionality and performance should still be valid as TXT and TPM are only effective at booting time and VM launch time. CloudVisor has no interaction with TXT and TPM during normal execution time.

We compare the performance of Linux and Windows VMs runs upon CloudVisor, vanilla Xen-4.0.0. XenLinux-2.6.31.13 is used as Domain0 kernel. Each VM is configured with one or more virtual CPUs, 1 GB memory, a 4 GB virtual disk and a virtual NIC. The VMs run unmodified Debian-Linux with kernel version 2.6.31 and Windows XP with SP2, both are of x86-64 version.

The application benchmarks for Linux VMs include: 1) Kernel Build (*KBuild*) that builds a compact Linux kernel 2.6.31 to measure the slowdown for CPU-intensive workloads; 2) *Apache* benchmark (ab) on Apache web server 2.2.15 [10] for network I/O intensive workloads; 3) *memcached* 1.4.5 [19] for memory and network I/O intensive workloads; 4) *dbench* 3.0.4 [65] for the slowdown of disk I/O workloads. *SPECjbb* [59] is used to evaluate the server side performance of Java runtime environment in the Windows VM. To understand the overhead in encryption and hashing and the effect of the *VM read* and *VM write* optimization, we also present a detailed performance analysis using *KBuild* and *dbench*. We further evaluate the performance and scalability of CloudVisor by running *KBuild* in multicore and multi-VM configurations. Finally, we use *lmbench*-3.0 [41] to quantify the performance loss incurred in primitive operating system operations. Each test were ran five times and the average result using performance slowdown (calculated using (Time(new) - Time(old))/Time(old)) is reported. Throughout the evaluation, hardware cryptographic instructions (Intel AES-NI) are used to perform the AES encryption and decryption.

8.1 Performance of Uniprocessor VMs

We use two applications to quantify the performance slowdown of uniprocessor VMs underlying CloudVisor. For *KBuild*, we build a compact kernel by running "make allnoconfig" and record the time spent to complete the compilation. For *Apache*, we use Apache Benchmark (ab) to issue 10,000 requests with concurrency level 500 to request a 4 Kbyte file from a client machine, and collect its transfer rate. For *memcached*, we use a remote client to issue requests to a *memcached* server, which is listening to a UDP port. For *SPECjbb*, we use the standard testing script of *SPECjbb* to evaluate the average number of business operations for eight data warehouses on a Windows XP VM.

As shown in Figure 6, for *KBuild*, the performance slowdown is relatively high (6.0%), as there are some disk I/O requests associated when reading files from disks and writing files back. Disk I/O operations in CloudVisor requires interposition and cryptographic operations, which are the major source of slowdown. For *Apache*,

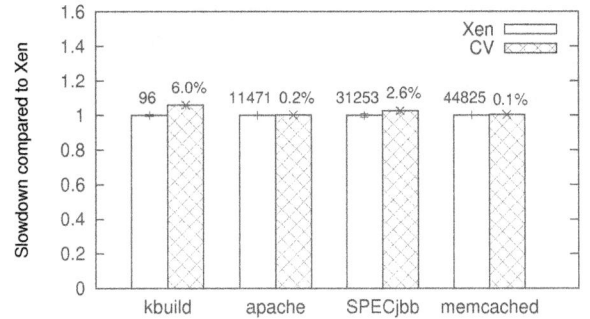

Figure 6: Slowdown for Kernel Build (*KBuild*), *Apache*, *SPECjbb* and *memcached*. The values shown in the bar indicate the execution time (s), transfer rate (KB/s), score and requests, accordingly.

as it mostly involves networked I/O which requires no intervention by CloudVisor, CloudVisor incurs only 0.2% slowdown. For *memcached*, the performance slowdown is also quite small (0.1%). This is because most of the operations are in memory and there are only a small amount of disk I/O requests. Hence, it rarely traps to CloudVisor. The performance overhead for *SPECjbb* is around 2.6% as it involes very few I/O operations. For all applications, most of the performance slowdown comes from the additional *VM exits* to CloudVisor and the emulation of some privileged instructions (such as disk I/O operations).

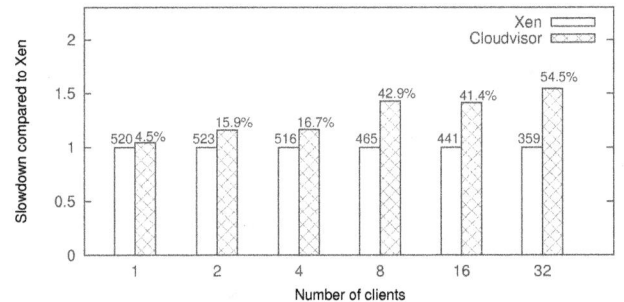

Figure 7: Performance slowdown of CloudVisor on *dbench* from 1 concurrent client to 32. The data on the left bar shows the raw throughput in MB/s.

I/O Performance: As disk I/O is likely a performance bottleneck in CloudVisor due to the cryptographic operations, we use *dbench* as a worst case benchmark to quantify the incurred slowdown. *dbench* mimics the I/O pattern of real applications that issues POSIX calls to the local filesystem, which taxes the I/O module in CloudVisor.

As shown in Figure 7, when the number of clients is small, *dbench* experiences relative small performance slowdown (4.5%, 15.9% and 16.7% for 1, 2 and 4 clients accordingly), due to the fact that the filesystem cache for IVs and hashes in the control VM has relatively better locality. However, when the number of clients is larger than four, the interference among clients causes worse locality for IVs and hashes, thus incurs large performance slowdown. This can either be fixed by increasing the filesystem cache in the control VM for a machine with abundant memory or integrating an intelligent cache in the untrusted user-level agent and CloudVisor.

Analyzing the Performance Slowdown: To understand the benefit of using the *VM exit* optimization, we profiled the execution of *KBuild*. We first collected the statistics of *VM exit* in CloudVisor and observed 4,717,658 *VM exits*, which accounted for around 3.31s out of 102s spent on *VM exit* handlers in CloudVisor. In contrast, before the *VM exit* optimization, we observed 9,049,852 *VM exits*. Hence, the optimization eliminated around 47.9% *VM exits*, which accounted for 2.11s in *VM exit* handlers.

As I/O intensive benchmarks stress the cryptographic module in CloudVisor, we used *dbench* running 32 concurrent clients to profile the slowdown caused by AES encryption/decryption and hashing. We replaced the AES cryptographic and/or hashing operations with NULL operations. Without encryption and hashing, the throughput of *dbench* is 270 MB/s. When only AES encryption for I/O data was turned on, the throughput is 255 MB/s, causing a relative slowdown of 5.9%. When both AES cryptographic and hashing were enabled, the throughput is 233 MB/s, causing a slowdown of around 9.4%. The evaluation showed that, with the new AES-NI instruction support, cryptographic operations incur only a small amount of slowdown, even when CloudVisor is highly stressed. Thus, the major overhead comes from the I/O interposition and metadata management, which are further worsened by poor locality due to interference among multiple clients.

8.2 Performance of Multiple VMs and Multi-core

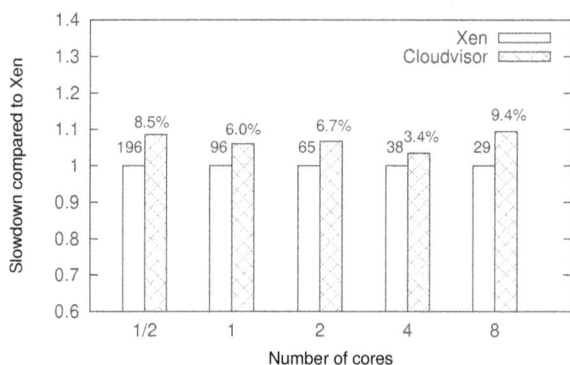

Figure 8: Slowdown of kernel build on a VM configured with 1/2, 1, 2, 4, 8 cores. When configured with 1/2 core, it means that there are two VMs runs on one core.

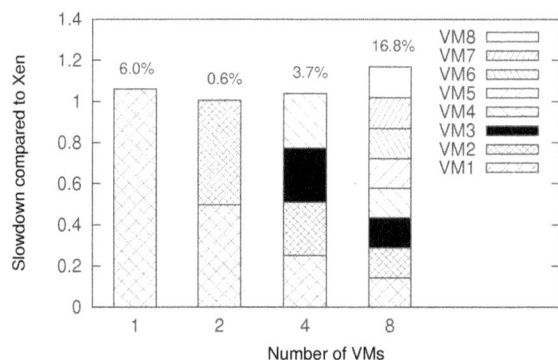

Figure 9: Slowdown of kernel build CloudVisor compared to Xen. The workload is concurrently run on multiple VMs.

To evaluate the performance of CloudVisor in multi-tenant cloud, we scaled up the system by increasing the number of cores managed by a VM or increasing the number of VMs. Figure 8 shows the scalability of a single VM running kbuild workloads on both Xen and CloudVisor. CloudVisor incurs at most 9.4% slowdown compared to Xen and the slowdown does not grow up much with the increase of processor cores. During the execution of a guest VM, *VM exits* are mainly caused by disk I/O requests.

The evaluation results of concurrent execution of *KBuild* on multiple VMs is shown in Figure 9. In the evaluation, each VM was configured with one core, 512 MB memory and one virtual disk. CloudVisor incurs at most 16.8% slowdown (8 VMs) compared to Xen. When the number of VMs is less than 8, the slowdown is moderate. In CloudVisor, disk I/O states of each guest VM are organized in the per-VM area that can be simultaneously accessed without lock protection. Multiple I/O requests can be handled by CloudVisor in parallel. However, with the increase of the number of VMs, the buffer cache used by the CloudVisor agent will be stressed. Although each guest VM has its own CloudVisor agent instance, the instances in the control VM share the file cache in the OS kernel.

8.3 OS Primitives:

app	Xen	CV	slowdown
ctx(16p/64k)	2.3	2.46	7.1%
stat	1.115	1.12	0.4%
mmap	2259	2287	1.2%
sh proc	1171	1437	22.7%
10k file(delete)	9.7	11.0	13.1%
Bcopy(hand)	3527	3443	2.4%
Bcopy(libc)	3565	3466	2.9%

Table 3: *The slowdown of OS primitives in CloudVisor (CV stands for CloudVisor).*

Lmbench is used to evaluate the slowdown of some primitive operating system operations. The results are shown in Table 3. CloudVisor does not cause much slowdown for primitives that do not trap to the VMM, like *stat*, *mmap* and *Bcopy*. *10k file delete* and *sh proc* incur relatively high slowdown. *10k file delete* tests the rate of file remove per second that involves inode updates in the filesystem. *sh proc* executes a binary that also involves expensive file operations.

8.4 Boot Time and Memory Overhead

As CloudVisor requires to do decryption and integrity checking when booting a guest VM, we also compared the time of completely booting a VM under CloudVisor and Xen. As expected, the VM booting time under CloudVisor suffered a 2.7X slowdown (33.3s vs. 9.1s) when booting up a VM with 1 GB memory. This is due to the frequent privilege instruction emulation, I/O interposition and cryptographic operations during system bootup. We believe that such overhead is worthwhile as CloudVisor ensures tamper-resistant bootstrap of a guest VM.

The major memory usage in CloudVisor is for the storage of non-leaf Merkle tree metadata for each guest VM and a bounce buffer. This counts up to 10 MB per VM. The memory consumption of the rest part of CloudVisor is less than 1 MB. Hence, for commodity server machines with abundant memory, the memory overhead of CloudVisor is negligible.

9. LIMITATION AND FUTURE WORK

CloudVisor is a first attempt to leverage the concept of nested virtualization [23, 13] for the case of TCB reduction and security protection of virtualized multi-tenant cloud. There are still ample improvement spaces over CloudVisor, which will be our further work:

Enhancing Protection: A common problem exists in CloudVisor and other similar systems when trying to protect from a hostile service provider [15, 17, 71, 40], as the service provider (e.g., OS or VMM) might mislead or even refuse to serve a client (e.g., an application or a VM). Specifically, a malicious VMM might try to mislead a VM by even discarding I/O requests from a VM. One possible mitigation technique is to let a VM or CloudVisor to proof-check services by the VMM.

We are also investigating the tradeoff in functionality division between hardware and software. As the functionality of CloudVisor is very simple and fixed, it might be feasible to implement Cloud-Visor in hardware or firmware (like Loki [72]).

Impact on VMM's Functionality: While CloudVisor is mostly compatible with existing operations in virtualization stack like save and restore, it does inhibit some VM introspection systems [30, 29] that require introspection of a VM's memory, as they can only see encrypted data. Further, CloudVisor follows a strict isolation policy among VMs, which may prevent some memory sharing systems [67, 25, 43] from working. This could be simply enabled by allowing some pages being shared read-only among VMs, and validating any changes to these pages in CloudVisor. Finally, Cloud-Visor currently uses a fail-stop approach against possible attacks or crashes. This can be replaced by a fail-safe approach to improving the reliability of VMs atop CloudVisor.

VMM Cooperation: Our currently system is designed to work with existing VMMs, to retain backward compatibility. As demonstrated by our optimization on *VM read* and *VM write*, slight changes to the Xen VMM to make it cooperative with CloudVisor may further improve the performance and reduce the complexity of CloudVisor.

Supporting Other VMMs: We currently only tested CloudVisor for the Xen VMM. A part of our further work includes the evaluation of CloudVisor on other VMMs (such as VMware, KVM and BitVisor [57]) and OSes (such as MAC OS and FreeBSD). Further, we will also investigate how the VMM could be adapted to support para-virtualization in CloudVisor.

Verification: CloudVisor is currently built with a very small code base, thus would be possible to formally verify its correctness and security properties [34] and verify its implementation with software model checking [28], which will be our further work.

10. RELATED WORK

Securing the Virtualization Layer: The increasing number of systems relying on trustworthiness of the virtualization layer makes the security of this layer more important than ever before. Hence, there are several efforts in improving or even reconstructing the virtualization layer to increase the security of the virtualization stack. For example, HyperSentry [11] and HyperSafe [68] both target at improving the security of the VMM by either measuring its integrity dynamically or enforcing control-flow integrity. NOVA [60] is micro-kernel based VMM that decouples the traditional monolithic VMM into a component-based system, and improves security

by introducing capability-based access control for different components in a VMM. The security of the management software in Xen [12] is also improved by moving the domain (i.e., VM) building utilities into a separate domain [44]. However, these systems aim at protecting the virtualization layer from external attacks to the VM stack, but without considering possible attacks that leverage legal maintenance operations from the cloud operators, which is a new requirement in multi-tenant cloud. Hence, such systems are orthogonal to CloudVisor and could reduce the possibility of compromises in the VMM.

NoHype [31] tries to address the trustworthiness of multi-tenant clouds by removing the virtualization layer during execution. However, removing the virtualization layer may also lose some useful features such as sharing resources across multiple VMs, which are key features of multi-tenant clouds. Further, NoHype still trusts the VM management software and requires changes to existing hardware and virtualization stack and there is no available implementation of such a system. By contrast, CloudVisor is backward-compatible with commercial virtualization software and is with a smaller trusted computing base.

Protecting Application Code: The threat model and goal of CloudVisor are similar to systems that provide protection of individual processes inside an untrustworthy operating system, such as CHAOS [15], Overshadow [17] and SP^3 [71]. Compared to systems providing protection at the process level, protection at the VM level is much simpler and results in a much smaller TCB. This is because the VM interface and abstraction is with less semantics and thus much simpler and cleaner than those at the process level. For example, there are more than 300 and 1000 system calls with rich semantics (e.g., *ioctl*) in Linux and Windows accordingly. Porting the protection mechanism from one OS to another is usually non-trivial. By contrast, the interface between the VM and VMM can mostly be expressed using the *VM exit* and *VM entry* primitives.

To ensure secure execution of specific code (e.g., SSL) in some applications, researchers proposed several systems to ensure code integrity and data secrecy of such code by leveraging trusted computing hardware [39, 38] and virtualization [40]. Compared to these systems that protect only a part of application software, CloudVisor provides protection at the whole VM level, which naturally fits with the context of multi-tenant cloud.

Virtualization-based Attacks and Defenses: On the positive side, virtualization provides a new playground for system security. Many prior literatures use special-purpose VMMs to improve security of operating systems [53, 69, 48], or extend existing VMMs with security-enhanced policies or mechanisms [30, 29] Compared to CloudVisor, these systems only protect a part of a program, while CloudVisor aims at protecting the entire virtual machine. The above systems could be incorporated with CloudVisor to prevent attacks from the network side, which may form a more secure cloud platform.

On the negative side, virtualization has also been used as a means to mount attack traditional operating systems and virtualization system [32, 50, 51]. When it is used to attack a VMM [51], the rootkit also needs to implement part of the nested virtualization to give the illusion that the VMM is running on bare metal.

Software and Hardware Support for Trusted Computing: Building more trustworthy software stack and platforms is always the concerns of researchers. The trusted computing groups have proposed the *Trusted Platform Module* [66] for the purpose of measuring a platform [52]. There is also several research on software-based remote attestation (e.g., Pioneer [54] and SWATT [55]). Such attestation techniques could be integrated into CloudVisor for remote attestation of code inside leased VMs to prevent from network-side attacks.

Machine partitioning using virtualization (e.g., Terra [21], NGSCB [47]) tries to satisfy the security requirements of diverse applications by providing different types of close-box and open-box VMs to applications. However, no defense against operators is provided in these systems.

There are also many architectural proposals that aim at providing security protection to applications. For examples, many architectural enhancements [36, 61] have been proposed to support trusted execution of an application within an untrusted operating system. System designers also leverage such support to build operating systems (e.g., XOMOS [37]).

Nested Virtualization: Researchers have investigated integrating nested virtualization into commodity VMMs, which forms an even larger TCB. For example, the recent Turtles project [13] investigates the design and implementation of nested virtualization to support multi-level virtualization in KVM [33]. In contrast, CloudVisor leverages nested virtualization to minimize TCB by separating the functionality for nested virtualization from the functionality for resource management, and further enhances the nested VMM with security protection of the hosted virtual machines.

11. CONCLUSION

Current multi-tenant cloud faces two major sources of threats: attacks to the virtualized infrastructure by exploiting possible security vulnerabilities in the relative large and complex virtualized software stack; and attacks originated from stealthy accesses to sensitive data from cloud operators. This paper presented a lightweight approach that introduces a tiny security monitor underneath the VMM to defend against these attacks. Our system, called CloudVisor, provides strong privacy and integrity guarantees even if the VMM and the management software are in control by adversaries. CloudVisor achieved this by exploiting commercially-available hardware support for virtualization and trusted computing. Performance evaluation showed that CloudVisor incurred moderate slowdown for I/O intensive applications and very small slowdown for other applications.

12. ACKNOWLEDGMENTS

We thank our shepherd Nickolai Zeldovich and the anonymous reviewers for their insightful comments. Cheng Tan, Yubin Xia and Rong Chen helped to prepare the final version of this paper. This work was funded by China National Natural Science Foundation under grant numbered 90818015 and 61003002, a grant from the Science and Technology Commission of Shanghai Municipality numbered 10511500100, Fundamental Research Funds for the Central Universities in China and Shanghai Leading Academic Discipline Project (Project Number: B114).

13. REFERENCES

[1] Bitlocker drive encryption technical overview. http://technet.microsoft.com/en-us/library/cc766200%28WS.10%29.aspx.

[2] Common vulnerabilities and exposures. http://cve.mitre.org/.

[3] Filevault in mac osx. http://www.apple.com/macosx/whats-new/features.html#filevault2.

[4] Intel advanced encryption standard instructions (aes-ni). http://software.intel.com/en-us/articles/intel-advanced-encryption-standard-instructions-aes-ni/, 2010.

[5] D. Abramson, J. Jackson, S. Muthrasanallur, G. Neiger, G. Regnier, R. Sankaran, I. Schoinas, R. Uhlig, B. Vembu, and J. Wiegert. Intel virtualization technology for directed I/O. *Intel technology journal*, 10(3):179–192, 2006.

[6] Amazon Inc. Amazon Elastic Compute Cloud (Amazon EC2). http://aws.amazon.com/ec2/, 2011.

[7] Amazon Inc. Amazon machine image. http://aws.amazon.com/amis, 2011.

[8] Amazon Inc. Amazon web service customer agreement. http://aws.amazon.com/agreement/, 2011.

[9] AMD Inc. Secure virtual machine architecture reference manual, 2005.

[10] Apache. ab - apache http server benchmarking tool. http://httpd.apache.org/docs/2.0/programs/ab.html, 2011.

[11] A. Azab, P. Ning, Z. Wang, X. Jiang, X. Zhang, and N. Skalsky. HyperSentry: enabling stealthy in-context measurement of hypervisor integrity. In *Proc. CCS*, pages 38–49, 2010.

[12] P. Barham, B. Dragovic, K. Fraser, S. Hand, T. Harris, A. Ho, R. Neugebauer, I. Pratt, and A. Warfield. Xen and the art of virtualization. In *Proc. SOSP*. ACM, 2003.

[13] M. Ben-Yehuda, M. D. Day, Z. Dubitzky, M. Factor, N. Har'El, A. Gordon, A. Liguori, O. Wasserman, and B.-A. Yassour. The turtles project: Design and implementation of nested virtualization. In *Proc. OSDI*, 2010.

[14] H. Chen, J. Chen, W. Mao, and F. Yan. Daonity-grid security from two levels of virtualization. *Information Security Technical Report*, 12(3):123–138, 2007.

[15] H. Chen, F. Zhang, C. Chen, Z. Yang, R. Chen, B. Zang, P. Yew, and W. Mao. Tamper-resistant execution in an untrusted operating system using a virtual machine monitor. *Parallel Processing Institute Technical Report, Number: FDUPPITR-2007-0801, Fudan University*, 2007.

[16] P. Chen and B. Noble. When virtual is better than real. In *Proc. HotOS*, 2001.

[17] X. Chen, T. Garfinkel, E. Lewis, P. Subrahmanyam, C. Waldspurger, D. Boneh, J. Dwoskin, and D. Ports. Overshadow: a virtualization-based approach to retrofitting protection in commodity operating systems. In *Proc. ASPLOS*, pages 2–13. ACM, 2008.

[18] Y. Dong, Z. Yu, and G. Rose. SR-IOV networking in Xen: Architecture, design and implementation. In *Proc. Workshop on I/O virtualization*. USENIX, 2008.

[19] B. Fitzpatrick. Distributed caching with memcached. *Linux journal*, 2004.

[20] Flexiant Inc. Flexiscale public cloud. http://www.flexiant.com/products/flexiscale/.

[21] T. Garfinkel, B. Pfaff, J. Chow, M. Rosenblum, and D. Boneh. Terra: A virtual machine-based platform for trusted computing. *ACM SIGOPS Operating Systems Review*, 37(5):206, 2003.

[22] T. Garfinkel and M. Rosenblum. When virtual is harder than real: Security challenges in virtual machine based computing environments. In *Proc. HotOS*, 2005.

[23] R. Goldberg. Architecture of virtual machines. In *Proceedings of the workshop on virtual computer systems*, pages 74–112, 1973.

[24] R. Goldberg. Survey of virtual machine research. *IEEE Computer*, 7(6):34–45, 1974.

[25] D. Gupta, S. Lee, M. Vrable, S. Savage, A. C. Snoeren, G. Varghese, G. M. Voelker, and A. Vahdat. Difference engine: harnessing memory redundancy in virtual machines. In *Proc. OSDI*, pages 309–322, 2008.

[26] J. Heiser and M. Nicolett. Assessing the security risks of cloud computing. http://www.gartner.com/DisplayDocument?id=685308, 2008.

[27] Intel Inc. Intel trusted execution technology. www.intel.com/technology/security/, 2010.

[28] R. Jhala and R. Majumdar. Software model checking. *ACM Computing Surveys (CSUR)*, 41(4):1–54, 2009.

[29] X. Jiang and X. Wang. Out-of-the-box monitoring of VM-based high-interaction honeypots. In *Proc. RAID*, pages 198–218, 2007.

[30] X. Jiang, X. Wang, and D. Xu. Stealthy malware detection through vmm-based out-of-the-box semantic view reconstruction. In *Proc. CCS*, pages 128–138. ACM, 2007.

[31] E. Keller, J. Szefer, J. Rexford, and R. Lee. NoHype: virtualized cloud infrastructure without the virtualization. In *Proc. ISCA*, pages 350–361, 2010.

[32] S. King, P. Chen, Y. Wang, C. Verbowski, H. Wang, and J. Lorch. SubVirt: Implementing malware with virtual machines. In *Proc. S&P (Oakland)*, 2006.

[33] A. Kivity, Y. Kamay, D. Laor, U. Lublin, and A. Liguori. kvm: the linux virtual machine monitor. In *Linux Symposium*, 2007.

[34] G. Klein, K. Elphinstone, G. Heiser, J. Andronick, D. Cock, P. Derrin, D. Elkaduwe, K. Engelhardt, R. Kolanski, M. Norrish, et al. seL4: Formal verification of an OS kernel. In *Proc. SOSP*, pages 207–220, 2009.

[35] M. Krohn, P. Efstathopoulos, C. Frey, F. Kaashoek, E. Kohler, D. Mazieres, R. Morris, M. Osborne, S. VanDeBogart, and D. Ziegler. Make least privilege a right (not a privilege). In *Proc. HotOS*, 2005.

[36] D. Lie, C. Thekkath, M. Mitchell, P. Lincoln, D. Boneh, J. Mitchell, and M. Horowitz. Architectural support for copy and tamper resistant software. In *Proc. ASPLOS*, pages 168–177, 2000.

[37] D. Lie, C. A. Thekkath, and M. Horowitz. Implementing an untrusted operating system on trusted hardware. In *Proc. SOSP*, pages 178–192, 2003.

[38] J. McCune, B. Parno, A. Perrig, M. Reiter, and H. Isozaki. Flicker: An execution infrastructure for TCB minimization. In *Proc. Eurosys*, pages 315–328, 2008.

[39] J. McCune, B. Parno, A. Perrig, M. Reiter, and A. Seshadri. Minimal TCB code execution. In *Proc. S&P (Oakland)*, pages 267–272, 2007.

[40] J. M. McCune, Y. Li, N. Qu, Z. Zhou, A. Datta, V. Gligor, and A. Perrig. TrustVisor: Efficient TCB Reduction and Attestation. In *Proc. S&P (Oakland)*, 2010.

[41] L. McVoy and C. Staelin. lmbench: Portable tools for performance analysis. In *Proc. Usenix ATC*, 1996.

[42] R. Merkle. Protocols for public key cryptosystems. In *Proc. S&P (Oakland)*, 1980.

[43] G. Miłós, D. G. Murray, S. Hand, and M. A. Fetterman. Satori: enlightened page sharing. In *Proc. Usenix ATC*, 2009.

[44] D. Murray, G. Milos, and S. Hand. Improving Xen security through disaggregation. In *Proc. VEE*, pages 151–160, 2008.

[45] G. Neiger, A. Santoni, F. Leung, D. Rodgers, and R. Uhlig. Intel virtualization technology: Hardware support for efficient processor virtualization. *Intel Technology Journal*, 10(3):167–177, 2006.

[46] D. Nurmi, R. Wolski, C. Grzegorczyk, G. Obertelli, S. Soman, L. Youseff, and D. Zagorodnov. The eucalyptus open-source cloud-computing system. In *Proc. CCGRID*, pages 124–131, 2009.

[47] M. Peinado, Y. Chen, P. England, and J. Manferdelli. NGSCB: A trusted open system. In *Information Security and Privacy*, pages 86–97, 2004.

[48] R. Riley, X. Jiang, and D. Xu. Guest-transparent prevention of kernel rootkits with vmm-based memory shadowing. In *Proc. RAID*, pages 1–20, 2008.

[49] T. Ristenpart, E. Tromer, H. Shacham, and S. Savage. Hey, you, get off of my cloud: exploring information leakage in third-party compute clouds. In *Proc. CCS*, pages 199–212. ACM, 2009.

[50] J. Rutkowska. Introducing Blue Pill. *The official blog of the invisiblethings. org. June*, 22, 2006.

[51] J. Rutkowska and A. Tereshkin. Bluepilling the Xen Hypervisor. *Black Hat USA*, 2008.

[52] R. Sailer, X. Zhang, T. Jaeger, and L. van Doorn. Design and implementation of a tcg-based integrity measurement architecture. In *Proc. USENIX Security*, 2004.

[53] A. Seshadri, M. Luk, N. Qu, and A. Perrig. SecVisor: A tiny hypervisor to provide lifetime kernel code integrity for commodity OSes. In *Proc. SOSP*, 2007.

[54] A. Seshadri, M. Luk, E. Shi, A. Perrig, L. Van Doorn, and P. Khosla. Pioneer: Verifying integrity and guaranteeing execution of code on legacy platforms. In *Proc. SOSP*, pages 1–16, 2005.

[55] A. Seshadri, A. Perrig, L. Van Doorn, and P. Khosla. SWATT: Software-based attestation for embedded devices. In *Proc. S&P (Oakland)*, pages 272–282, 2004.

[56] J. Shi, X. Song, H. Chen, and B. Zang. Limiting cache-based side-channel in multi-tenant cloud using dynamic page. In *Proc. HotDep*, 2011.

[57] T. Shinagawa, H. Eiraku, K. Tanimoto, K. Omote, S. Hasegawa, T. Horie, M. Hirano, K. Kourai, Y. Oyama, E. Kawai, et al. BitVisor: a thin hypervisor for enforcing i/o device security. In *Proc. VEE*, pages 121–130. ACM, 2009.

[58] L. Singaravelu, C. Pu, H. H "artig, and C. Helmuth. Reducing TCB complexity for security-sensitive applications: Three case studies. In *Proc. Eurosys*, 2006.

[59] SPEC. Specjbb 2005. http://www.spec.org/jbb2005/, 2005.

[60] U. Steinberg and B. Kauer. NOVA: A microhypervisor-based secure virtualization architecture. In *Proc. Eurosys*, pages 209–222. ACM, 2010.

[61] G. Suh, D. Clarke, B. Gassend, M. Van Dijk, and S. Devadas. AEGIS: architecture for tamper-evident and tamper-resistant processing. In *Proc. Supercomputing*, 2003.

[62] T. R. Team. Rackspace cloud. http://www.rackspacecloud.com/.

[63] TechSpot News. Google fired employees for breaching user privacy. http://www.techspot.com/news/40280-google-fired-employees-for-breaching-user-privacy.html, 2010.

[64] The Nimbus Team. Nimbus project. http://www.nimbusproject.org/.

[65] A. Tridgell. Dbench filesystem benchmark. http://samba.org/ftp/tridge/dbench/.

[66] Trusted Computing Group. Trusted platform module. http://www.trustedcomputinggroup.org/, 2010.

[67] C. A. Waldspurger. Memory resource management in vmware esx server. In *Proc. OSDI*, pages 181–194, 2002.

[68] Z. Wang and X. Jiang. HyperSafe: A lightweight approach to provide lifetime hypervisor control-flow integrity. In *Proc. S&P (Oakland)*, pages 380–395, 2010.

[69] Z. Wang, X. Jiang, W. Cui, and P. Ning. Countering kernel rootkits with lightweight hook protection. In *Proc. CCS*, pages 545–554. ACM, 2009.

[70] C. Weinhold and H. Härtig. jVPFS: Adding Robustness to a Secure Stacked File System with Untrusted Local Storage Components. In *Proc. Usenix ATC*, 2011.

[71] J. Yang and K. G. Shin. Using hypervisor to provide data secrecy for user applications on a per-page basis. In *Proc. VEE*, pages 71–80, 2008.

[72] N. Zeldovich, H. Kannan, M. Dalton, and C. Kozyrakis. Hardware enforcement of application security policies using tagged memory. In *Proc. OSDI*, pages 225–240, 2008.

Atlantis: Robust, Extensible Execution Environments for Web Applications

James Mickens
Microsoft Research
mickens@microsoft.com

Mohan Dhawan
Rutgers University
mdhawan@cs.rutgers.edu

ABSTRACT

Today's web applications run inside a complex browser environment that is buggy, ill-specified, and implemented in different ways by different browsers. Thus, web applications that desire robustness must use a variety of conditional code paths and ugly hacks to deal with the vagaries of their runtime. Our new exokernel browser, called Atlantis, solves this problem by providing pages with an extensible execution environment. Atlantis defines a narrow API for basic services like collecting user input, exchanging network data, and rendering images. By composing these primitives, web pages can define custom, high-level execution environments. Thus, an application which does not want a dependence on Atlantis' predefined web stack can selectively redefine components of that stack, or define markup formats and scripting languages that look nothing like the current browser runtime. Unlike prior microkernel browsers like OP, and unlike compile-to-JavaScript frameworks like GWT, Atlantis is the first browsing system to truly minimize a web page's dependence on black box browser code. This makes it much easier to develop robust, secure web applications.

Categories and Subject Descriptors

D.4.7 [**Operating Systems**]: Organization and Design; D.4.5 [**Operating Systems**]: Reliability; D.4.6 [**Operating Systems**]: Security and Protection

General Terms

Design, Reliability, Security

Keywords

Web browsers, microkernels, exokernels

1. INTRODUCTION

Modern web browsers have evolved into sophisticated computational platforms. Unfortunately, creating robust web applications is challenging due to well-known quirks and deficiencies in commodity browsers [41]. In theory, there are a

variety of standards that define the software stack for web applications [14, 19, 36, 52, 55]. In practice, the aggregate specification is so complex that it is difficult for any browser to implement it properly. To further complicate matters, browser vendors often add new features without consulting other vendors. Thus, each browser defines an idiosyncratic JavaScript interpreter, HTML parser, and layout engine.

These components are loosely compatible across different vendors, but fine-tuning an application for multiple browsers often means developing specialized application code intended for just one browser. For example:

- Writing a portable web-based GUI is challenging because different browsers handle mouse and keyboard events in different, buggy ways (§2.4.1).
- Web pages use CSS [52] to express complex visual styles. Some browsers do not support certain CSS elements, or do not implement them correctly (§2.4.3). When this happens, web developers must trick each browser into providing the proper layout by cobbling together CSS elements that the browser does understand.
- Browsers expose certain internal data structures as JavaScript objects that web pages can access. By introspecting these objects, pages can implement useful low-level services like logging/replay frameworks [31]. However, the reflection interface for internal browser objects is extremely brittle, making it challenging to implement low-level services in a reliable, portable fashion (§2.4.4).

All of these issues make it difficult for web developers to reason about the robustness and the security of their applications. JavaScript frameworks like jQuery [5] try to encapsulate browser incompatibilities, providing high-level services like GUI libraries atop an abstraction layer that hides conditional code paths. However, these frameworks cannot hide all browser bugs, or change the fundamental reality that some browsers support useful features that other browsers lack [27, 31]. Indeed, the abstraction libraries themselves may perform differently on different browsers due to unexpected incompatibilities [18, 28].

1.1 A Problem of Interface

These problems are problems of interface: web applications interact with the browser using a bloated, complex API that is hard to secure, difficult to implement correctly, and which often exposes important functionality in an obscure way, if at all. For example, a page's visual appearance depends on how the page's HTML and CSS are parsed, how the parsed output is translated into a DOM tree (§2.2), how the resulting DOM tree is geometrically laid out, and how the renderer draws that layout. A web page cannot directly interact with any step of this process. Instead, the page can only provide HTML and CSS to the browser and hope that the browser behaves in the intended fashion. Unfortunately, this is not guaranteed [15, 30, 39, 41]. Using an abstraction framework like jQuery does not eliminate the fundamentally black box nature of the browser's rendering engine.

Using Xax [13] or NaCl [56], developers can write native code web applications, regaining low-level control over the execution environment and unlocking the performance that results from running on the bare metal. However, most web developers who are proficient with JavaScript, HTML, and CSS do not want to learn a native code development environment. Instead, these developers want a more robust version of their current software stack, a stack which does have several advantages over native code, like ease of development and the ability to deploy to any device which runs a browser.

1.2 Our Solution: Atlantis

To address these issues, we have created a new microkernel web browser called Atlantis. Atlantis' design was guided by a fundamental insight: the modern web stack is too complicated to be implemented by any browser in a robust, secure way that satisfies all web pages. The Atlantis kernel only defines a narrow, low-level API that provides basic services like network I/O, screen rendering, and the execution of abstract syntax trees [1] that respect same-origin security policies. Each web page composes these basic services to define a richer high-level runtime that is completely controlled by that page.

The Atlantis kernel places few restrictions on such a runtime. We envision that in many cases, web pages will customize a third-party implementation of the current HTML/CSS stack that was written in pure JavaScript and compiled to Atlantis ASTs. However, a page is free to use a different combination of scripting and markup technologies. Atlantis is agnostic about the details of the application stack—Atlantis' main role is to enforce the same origin policy and provide fair allocation of low-level system resources. Thus, Atlantis provides web developers with an unprecedented ability to customize the runtime environment for their pages. For example:

- Writing robust GUIs is easy because the developer has access to low-level input events, and can completely define higher-level event semantics.
- Creating a specific visual layout is straightforward because the developer can define his own HTML and CSS parsers, and use Atlantis' bitmap rendering APIs to precisely control how content is displayed.
- Pages can now safely implement low-level services that introspect "internal" browser state. The introspection is robust because the internal browser state is completely managed by the page itself—the Atlantis kernel knows nothing about traditional browser data structures like the DOM tree.

Atlantis' extensibility and complete agnosticism about the application stack differentiates it from prior browsers like OP [25] and IBOS [46] that also use a small kernel. Those systems are tightly coupled to the current browser abstractions for the web stack. For example, OP pushes the JavaScript interpreter and the HTML renderer outside the kernel, isolating them in separate processes connected by a message passing interface. However, the DOM tree abstraction is still managed by native code that a web page cannot introspect or modify in a principled way. In Atlantis, applications do not have to take dependencies on such opaque code bases. Thus, in contrast to prior microkernel browsers, Atlantis is more accurately described as an exokernel browser [16] in which web pages supply their own "library OSes" that implement the bulk of the web stack.

1.3 Contributions

Atlantis' primary contribution is to show that exokernel principles can lead to a browser that is not just more *secure*, but that also provides a more *extensible* execution environment; in turn, this increased extensibility allows web pages to be more *robust*. We provide a demonstration web stack that is written in pure JavaScript and contains an HTML parser, a layout engine, a DOM tree, and so on. This stack takes advantage of our new scripting engine, called Syphon, which provides several language features that make it easier to create application-defined runtimes (§3.3). We show that our prototype Syphon engine is fast enough to execute application-defined layout engines and GUI event handlers. We also demonstrate how easy it is to extend our demonstration web stack. For example, we show that it is trivial to modify the DOM tree `innerHTML` feature so that a sanitizer [33] is automatically invoked on write accesses. This allows a page to prevent script injection attacks [38].

The rest of this paper is organized as follows. In Section 2, we describe modern browser architectures, explaining why current browsers, both monolithic and microkernel, impede application robustness by exposing brittle black box and grey box interfaces. This discussion motivates the exokernel design of Atlantis, which we describe in Section 3. After describing our prototype implementation (§4) and several practical deployment issues (§5), we evaluate our prototype in Section 6, demonstrating its extensibility and its performance on a variety of tasks. We then discuss related work in Section 7 before concluding.

2. BACKGROUND

The vast majority of lay people, and many computer scientists, are unaware of the indignities that web developers currently face as they try to create stable, portable web applications. In this section, we describe the architecture of a modern web browser, and explain why even new research browsers fail to address the fundamental deficiency of the web programming model, namely, that the aggregate "web API" is too complex for any browser to implement in a robust fashion.

2.1 Core Web Technologies

Modern web development uses four essential technologies: HTML, CSS, JavaScript, and plugins. HTML [55] is a declarative markup language that describes the basic content in a web page. HTML defines a variety of tags for including different kinds of data; for example, an `<img>` tag references an external image, and a `<b>` tag indicates a section of bold text. Tags nest using an acyclic parent-child structure. Thus, a page's tags form a tree which is rooted by a top-level `<html>` node.

Using tags like `<b>`, HTML supports rudimentary manipulation of a page's visual appearance. However, cascading style sheets (often abbreviated as CSS [52]) provide much richer control. Using CSS, a page can choose fonts and color schemes, and specify how tags should be visually positioned with respect to each other.

JavaScript [20] is the most popular language for client-side browser scripting. JavaScript allows web pages to dynamically modify their HTML structure and register handlers for GUI events. JavaScript also allows a page to asynchronously fetch new data from web servers.

JavaScript has traditionally lacked access to client-side hardware like web cameras and microphones. However, a variety of native code plugins like Flash and Silverlight provide access to such resources. These plugins run within the browser's address space and are often used to manipulate audio or video data. A web page instantiates a plugin using a special HTML tag like `<object>`.

2.2 Standard Browser Modules

Browsers implement the core web technologies using a standard set of software components. The idiosyncratic experience of "surfing the web" on a particular browser is largely governed by how the browser implements these standard modules.

- The *network stack* implements various transfer protocols like `http://`, `https://`, `file://`, and so on.
- The *HTML parser* validates a page's HTML. The *CSS parser* performs a similar role for CSS. Since malformed HTML and CSS are pervasive, parsers define rules for coercing ill-specified pages into a valid format.
- The browser internally represents the HTML tag tree using a data structure called the *DOM tree*. "DOM" is an abbreviation for the Document Object Model, a browser-neutral standard for describing HTML content [51]. The DOM tree contains a node for every HTML tag. Each node is adorned with the associated CSS data, as well as any application-defined event handlers for GUI activity.
- The *layout and rendering engine* traverses the DOM tree and determines the visual size and spatial positioning of each element. For complex web pages, the layout engine may require multiple passes over the DOM tree to calculate the associated layout.
- The *JavaScript interpreter* provides two services. First, it implements the core JavaScript runtime. The core runtime defines basic datatypes like strings, and provides simple library services like random number generation. Second, the interpreter reflects the DOM tree into the JavaScript namespace, defining JavaScript objects which are essentially proxies for internal browser objects. These internal objects are written in *native code* (typically C++). From the perspective of a web

application, the JavaScript wrappers for internal native objects should support the same programming semantics that are supported by application-defined objects. However, as we discuss later, browsers do not provide this equivalence in practice.

- The *storage layer* manages access to persistent data like cookies, cached web objects, and DOM storage [48], a new abstraction that provides each domain with several megabytes of key/value storage.

Even simple browser activities require a flurry of communication between the modules described above. For example, suppose that JavaScript code wants to dynamically add an image to a page. First, the JavaScript interpreter must send a fetch request to the network stack. Once the stack has fetched the image, it examines the response headers and caches the image if appropriate. The browser adds a new image node to the DOM tree, recalculates the layout, and renders the result. The updated DOM tree is then reflected into the JavaScript namespace, and the interpreter triggers any application-defined event handlers that are associated with the image load.

2.3 Isolating Browser Components

Figure 1(a) shows the architecture of a monolithic browser like Firefox or IE8. Monolithic browsers share two important characteristics. First, a browser "instance" consists of a process containing all of the components mentioned in Section 2.2. In some monolithic browsers, separate tabs receive separate processes; however, within a tab, browser components are not isolated.

The second characteristic of a monolithic browser is that, from the web page's perspective, all of the browser components are either black box or grey box. In particular, the HTML/CSS parser, layout engine, and renderer are all black boxes—the application has no way to monitor or directly influence the operation of these components. Instead, the application provides HTML and CSS as inputs, and receives a DOM tree and a screen repaint as outputs. The JavaScript runtime is grey box, since the JavaScript language provides powerful facilities for reflection and dynamic object modification. However, many important data structures are defined by native objects, and the JavaScript proxies for these objects are only partially compatible with JavaScript's ostensible object semantics. The reason is that these proxies are bound to hidden browser state that an application cannot directly observe. Thus, seemingly innocuous interactions with native code proxies may force internal browser structures into inconsistent states [31]. We provide examples of these problems in Section 2.4.

Figure 1(b) shows the architecture of the OP microkernel browser [25]. The core browser consists of a network stack, a storage system, and a user-interface system. Each component is isolated in a separate process, and they communicate with each other by exchanging messages through the kernel. A *web page instance* runs atop these core components. Each instance consists of an HTML parser/renderer, a JavaScript interpreter, an Xvnc [47] server, and zero or more plugins. All of these are isolated in separate processes and communicate via message passing. For example, the JavaScript interpreter sends messages to the HTML parser to

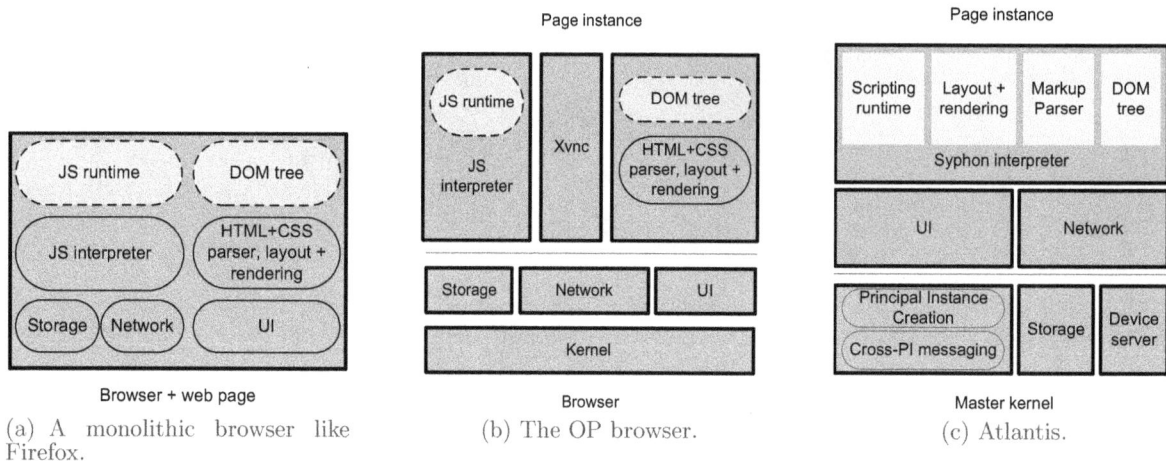

Figure 1: Browser architectures. Rectangles represent strong isolation containers (either processes or C#
AppDomains). Rounded rectangles represent modules within the same container. Solid borders indicate a lack
of extensibility. Dotted borders indicate partial extensibility, and no border indicates complete extensibility.

dynamically update a page's content; the parser sends screen
updates to the Xvnc server, which forwards them to the UI
component using the VNC protocol [47]. The kernel determines which plugins to load by inspecting the MIME types
of HTTP fetches (e.g., `application/x-shockwave-flash`).
The kernel loads each plugin in a separate process, and the
plugins use message passing to update the display or the
page's HTML content. IBOS [46] is another microkernel
browser that uses a philosophically similar isolation scheme.

OP and IBOS provide better security and fault isolation
than monolithic browsers. However, OP and IBOS still use
standard, off-the-shelf browser modules to provide the DOM
tree, the JavaScript runtime, and so on. Thus, these browsers still present web developers with the frustrations that we
describe next.

2.4   The Challenges of Web Development

Each browser provides its own implementation of the standard components. These implementation families are roughly
compatible with each other, but each one has numerous
quirks and bugs. Since a browser's components are weakly
introspectable at best, developers are forced to use conditional code paths and ad-hoc best practices to get sophisticated web applications running across different browsers. In
the remainder of this section, we provide concrete examples
of these development challenges.

2.4.1   Event Handling

To react to user inputs like mouse clicks, applications attach event handlers to DOM nodes. When the user generates an event, the browser creates a new JavaScript event
object and traces a path through the DOM tree, invoking
any event handlers along that path. The official DOM specification defines a three-phase propagation model. Let the
target node of the event be the DOM node whose GUI representation initiated the event; for example, the target for
a mouse click might be a `<button>` element. In the *capturing* phase, the browser delivers the event to nodes along the
path from the root `<html>` tag down to the `<button>` tag.

In the *target* phase, the `<button>`'s event handlers are invoked. In the *bubbling* phase, the event follows the reverse
path of the capturing phase, moving upwards towards the
DOM tree root. At any point, the event can be canceled by
an event handler. This stops the event from traversing the
rest of the propagation path.

IE9 supports the capturing phase, but IE8 does not—on IE8,
event propagation starts at the target. This makes some
web applications difficult to write on IE8 but easy to write
on IE9. For example, Mugshot [31] is a tool for logging and
replaying web applications. On browsers that support the
capturing phase, logging all GUI events is straightforward—
Mugshot simply installs capturing event handlers at the top
of the DOM tree. On IE8, Mugshot has to use an assort-
ment of hacks. Mugshot cannot just define top-level bubbling handlers, since these handlers would miss events that
were canceled earlier in the propagation process. Furthermore, whereas all events (are supposed to) have a capture
phase, the DOM specification states that some events do not
have a bubbling phase. IE8 adheres to this part of the specification, so bubbling-phase logging handlers would miss non-
bubbling events as well. To avoid these problems, Mugshot
uses DOM extensions [27]. Unfortunately, as we describe
later, DOM extensions are also problematic.

Another severe problem with event handling is that browsers
do not completely agree upon the set of events that should be
supported. Furthermore, even "cross-browser" events may
have different semantics on different browsers. For example:

- All popular browsers ostensibly support the `blur` event,
  which fires when the user shifts input focus away from
  a DOM node. Unfortunately, Chrome and Safari do
  not consistently fire the event for all types of DOM
  nodes. Opera sometimes generates multiple events for
  a single underlying blur [41].
- Browsers allow web pages to generate synthetic events.
  The browser is supposed to handle these fake events
  in the same way that it handles real ones. However,
  this does not happen in practice. For example, on

Firefox and IE, generating a fake `mouseup` event on a drop-down selection box will not cause an item to actually be selected. Similarly, generating synthetic keypress events on a text input will not actually cause the displayed text to change [31].

- IE fires an event when the user copies from or pastes to the clipboard. Other browsers do not support these events.

Abstraction libraries like jQuery [5] try to hide many of these differences, but some problems remain unfixable because they arise from browser functionality that is simply missing or fundamentally broken. Indeed, inconsistent cross-browser event policies can cause abstraction libraries themselves to behave differently on different browsers [28]. Furthermore, if a library's browser-sniffing algorithm has a bug, the library may execute the wrong conditional code paths for the actual browser being used [18].

2.4.2 Parsing bugs

Using the `document.write()` call, JavaScript code can insert new HTML tags into a document as that document is being parsed. This introduces race conditions into the parsing process, since the parser may or may not receive the new HTML tokens before it consumes the original token stream. Different browsers resolve this race in different ways [37].

Buggy parsers can also lead to security problems. Recent versions of Firefox, Chrome, Safari, and IE are vulnerable to a CSS parsing bug that allow an attacker to steal private data from authenticated web sessions [26]. Microsoft recently issued a patch for IE8 [32] which fixed a bug in the JSON [11] parser. In both of these cases, web developers who were aware of the security problems were reliant on browser vendors to implement fixes; the page developers themselves could not ship their pages with a patched execution environment.

2.4.3 Rendering bugs

All browsers have a variety of rendering quirks. For example, in Firefox 3.x and IE8 (but not prior versions of IE), negative values for the CSS `word-spacing` property are incorrectly coerced to zero, leading to problems with visual alignment [30]. Various hacks are needed to get IE to properly render semi-transparent elements [22]. Safari and Chrome can incorrectly calculate element dimensions that are specified as a percentage of the enclosing container's size [9]. Major browsers also define non-standard CSS attributes which are not universally implemented and whose use will cause web pages to render differently on different browsers [24].

2.4.4 JavaScript/DOM incompatibilities

JavaScript supports object inheritance using prototypes instead of classes [20]. A prototype object is an exemplar which defines properties for all objects using that prototype. Each object has exactly one prototype. Inheritance hierarchies are created by setting the prototype field for an object which itself is used as a prototype.

JavaScript is a dynamic language which permits runtime modification of prototype objects. In theory, this allows an application to arbitrarily extend the behavior of predefined objects. In practice, extending DOM objects is extremely brittle [27, 31] because the properties of DOM prototype objects are bound to opaque native code that is implemented in different ways on different browsers. Thus, wrapping old prototype properties, adding new ones, or deleting old ones may result in success on one browser but a runtime failure on another. Different browsers also define different prototype inheritance chains, meaning that modifying the same parent prototype on two browsers may lead to different property definitions for descendant prototypes. Although DOM extension is a powerful feature, it introduces so many corner cases that developers of the popular Prototype JavaScript framework [10] decided to abandon the technique for newer releases of the framework [27].

JavaScript allows applications to define getter and setter functions for object properties. These functions allow an application to intercept reads and writes to a property. Much like extending DOM prototypes, shimming the properties of native objects is difficult to do robustly, and it may disrupt the browser's event dispatch process [31]. Despite the danger of these techniques, they remain tantalizingly attractive because they allow a page to work around the deficiencies of a browser's DOM implementation.

In summary, it is easy to write a simple web page that looks the same in all browsers and has the same functionality in all browsers. Unfortunately, web pages of even moderate sophistication quickly encounter inconsistencies and bugs in browser runtimes. This observation motivates the Atlantis design, which we describe next.

3. ATLANTIS DESIGN

Figure 1(c) depicts Atlantis' architecture. At the bottom level is the switchboard process, the device server, and the storage manager; in aggregate, we refer to these components as the *master kernel*. The switchboard creates the isolation containers for web pages, and routes messages between these containers. The device server arbitrates access to non-essential peripheral devices like web cameras and microphones. The storage manager provides a key/value interface for persistent data.

The storage space is partitioned into a single public area and multiple, private, per-domain areas.[1] Any domain can read from or write to the public area, but the storage manager authenticates all requests for domain-private data. When the switchboard creates a new isolation container for domain X, it gives X an authentication token. It also sends a message to the storage manager that binds the token to X. Later, when X wishes to access private storage, it must include its authentication token in the request. In Section 3.2, we explain the usefulness of unauthenticated public storage.

In Atlantis, each instantiation of a web domain receives a separate isolation container. Following the terminology of Gazelle, we refer to these containers as principal instances. For example, if a user opens two separate tabs for the URL `http://a.com/foo.html`, Atlantis creates two separate principal instances. Each one contains a *per-instance Atlantis*

---

[1]A "domain" is synonymous with a `<protocol, host name, port>` origin as defined by the same-origin policy.

```
<environment>
  <compiler='http://a.com/compiler.syp'>
  <markupParser='http://b.com/parser.js'>
  <runtime='http://c.com/runtime.js'>
</environment>
```

Figure 2: To redefine its runtime, a web application puts an `<environment>` tag at the top of its markup.

kernel and a *script interpreter*. The instance kernel contains two modules. The network manager implements transfer protocols like `http://` and `file://`. The UI manager creates a new C# `Form` and registers handlers for low-level GUI events on that form. The UI manager forwards these events to the application-defined runtime, and updates the `Form`'s bitmap in response to messages from the page's layout engine.

The script interpreter executes abstract syntax trees which represent a new language called Syphon (§3.3). A web page installs a custom HTML/CSS parser, DOM tree, layout engine, and high-level script runtime by compiling the code to Syphon ASTs and submitting the ASTs for execution. The Syphon interpreter ensures that the code respects same-origin policies, but in all other regards, the interpreter is agnostic about what the code is doing. Thus, unlike in current browsers, the bulk of the web stack has no deep dependencies on internal browser state.

A principal instance's network stack, UI manager, and Syphon interpreter run in separate native threads. Thus, these components can run in parallel and take full advantage of multicore processors. Although these threads reside within a single process belonging to the principal instance, the threads are strongly isolated from each other using C# `AppDomains` [2]. `AppDomains` use the managed .NET runtime to enforce memory safety *within* a single process. Code inside an `AppDomain` cannot directly access memory outside its domain. However, domains can explicitly expose entry points that are accessible by other domains. The C# compiler translates these entry points into RPCs, serializing and deserializing data as necessary.

As shown in Figure 1(c), an application's runtime modules execute within the `AppDomain` of the interpreter. However, Syphon provides several language primitives which allow these modules to isolate themselves from each other. For example, an application can partition its Syphon code into privileged and unprivileged components, such that only privileged code can make kernel calls. We provide a detailed discussion of Syphon's protection features in Section 3.3. For now, we simply note that an application uses these isolation features to protect itself from itself—the Syphon interpreter is agnostic to the meaning of the protection domains that it enforces, and Atlantis' security guarantees do not depend on applications using Syphon-level protection mechanisms.

3.1 Initializing a New Principal Instance

When a new instance kernel starts, it receives a storage authentication token from the master kernel and then initializes its UI manager, network stack, and Syphon interpreter.

Once this is done, the instance kernel fetches the markup associated with its page's URL. Atlantis is agnostic about whether this markup is HTML or something else. However, pages that wish to redefine their runtime must include a special `<environment>` tag at the top of their markup. An example of this tag is shown in Figure 2. The tag contains at most three elements.

- The `<compiler>` element specifies the code that will translate a page's script source into Syphon ASTs. The compiler itself must already be compiled to Syphon. If no compiler is specified, Atlantis assumes that the page's runtime environment is directly expressed in Syphon.
- The `<markupParser>` element specifies the code that the page will use to analyze its post-`<environment>` tag markup.
- The `<runtime>` code provides the rest of the execution environment, e.g., the layout engine, the DOM tree, and the high-level scripting runtime.

The compiler code must define a standardized entry point called `compiler.compile(srcString)`. This method takes a string of application-specific script code as input, and outputs the equivalent Syphon code. The instance kernel invokes `compiler.compile()` to generate executable code for the markup parser and the runtime library. After installing this code, the kernel passes the application's markup to the standardized parser entry point `markup.parse(markupStr)`. At this point, Atlantis relinquishes control to the application. As the application parses its markup, it invokes the kernel to fetch additional objects, update the screen, and so on.

If the instance kernel does not find an `<environment>` prefix in the page's markup, it assumes that the page wishes to execute atop the traditional web stack. In this case, Atlantis loads its own implementation of the HTML/CSS/JavaScript environment. From the page's perspective, this stack behaves like the traditional stack, with the important exception that everything is written in pure JavaScript, with no dependencies on shadow browser state. This means that, for example, modifying DOM prototypes will work as expected (§2.4), and placing getters or setters on DOM objects will not break event propagation. Of course, Atlantis' default web stack might have bugs, *but the application can fix these bugs itself without fear of breaking the browser.*

3.2 The Kernel Interface

As the web application executes, it interacts with its instance kernel using the API in Figure 3. The API is largely self-explanatory, but we highlight a few of the subtler aspects in the text below.

To create a new frame or tab, the application invokes `createPI()`. If the new principal instance is a child frame, the instance kernel in the parent registers the parent-child relationship with the master kernel. Later, if the user moves or resizes the window containing the parent frame, the master kernel notifies the instance kernels in the descendant frames, allowing Atlantis to maintain the visual relationships between parents and children.

`createPI(url, width, height, topX,` `       topY, isFrame=false)`	Create a new principal instance. If `isFrame` is true, the new instance is the child of a parent frame. Otherwise, the new instance is placed in a new tab.
`registerGUICallback(dispatchFunc)`	Register an application-defined callback which the kernel will invoke when GUI events are generated.

`renderImage(pixelData, width, height,`
`       topX, topY, options)`
`renderText(textStr, width, height,`
`       topX, topY, options)`
`renderGUIwidget(widgetType, options)`
	The application's layout engine uses these calls to update the screen. Strictly speaking, `renderImage()` is sufficient to implement a GUI. However, web pages that want to mimic the native look-and-feel of desktop applications can use native fonts and GUI widgets using `renderText()` and `renderWidget()`.

`HTTPStream openConnection(url)`	Open an HTTP connection to the given domain. Returns an object supporting blocking writes and both blocking and non-blocking reads.
`sendToFrame(targetFrameUrl, msg)`	Send a message to another frame. Used to implement cross-frame communication like `postMessage()`.
`executeSyphonCode(ASTsourceCode)`	Tell the interpreter to execute the given AST.

`persistentStore(mimeType, key, value,`
`       isPublic, token)`
`string persistentFetch(mimeType, key,`
`       isPublic, token)`
	Access methods for persistent storage. The storage volume is partitioned into a single public area, and multiple, private, per-domain areas. The `token` argument is the authentication nonce created by the switchboard.

Figure 3: Primary Atlantis kernel calls.

Using the `sendToFrame()` kernel call, two frames can exchange messages. An application can implement JavaScript's `postMessage()` as a trivial wrapper around `sendToFrame()`. The application can also use `sendToFrame()` to support cross-frame namespace abstractions. For example, in the traditional web stack, if a child frame and a parent frame are in the same domain, they can reference each other's Java-Script state through objects like `window.parent` and `window.frames[childId]`. An Atlantis DOM implementation supports these abstractions by interposing on accesses to these objects and silently generating `postMessage()` RPCs which read or write remote variables. We describe how Syphon supports such interpositioning in Section 3.3.

The functions `persistentStore()` and `persistentFetch()` allow applications to implement abstractions like cookies and DOM storage [48], a new HTML5 facility which provides a public storage area and private, per-domain storage. Atlantis' persistent store exports a simple key/value interface, and like DOM storage, it is split into a single public space and multiple, private, per-domain areas. Accessing private areas requires an authentication token; accessing public areas does not. The standard browser cache is stored in the public area, with cached items keyed by their URL. However, only instance kernels can write to public storage using URL keys. This ensures that when the network stack is handling a fetch for an object, it can trust any cached data that it finds for that object.

The public storage area is useful for implementing asynchronous cross-domain message queues. In particular, public storage allows two domains to communicate without forcing them to use `postMessage()` (which only works when both domains have simultaneously active frames). Atlantis does not enforce mandatory access controls for the public storage volume, so domains that desire integrity and authenticity for public data must layer security protocols atop Atlantis' raw storage substrate.

3.3 Syphon: Atlantis ASTs

Applications pass abstract syntax trees to Atlantis for execution. However, we could have chosen for applications to pass low-level bytecodes ala applets. We eschewed this option for two reasons. First, it is easier to optimize ASTs than bytecodes, since bytecodes obscure semantic relationships that must be recreated before optimizations can take place [45]. Second, it is difficult to reconstruct source code from bytecode, whereas this is trivial for ASTs. This feature is useful when one is debugging an application consisting of multiple scripts from multiple authors.

Atlantis ASTs encode a new language that we call *Syphon*. The Syphon specification is essentially a superset of the recent ECMAScript JavaScript specification [14], albeit described with a generic tree syntax that is amenable to serving as a compilation target for higher-level languages that may or may not resemble JavaScript. In this section, we focus on the Syphon features that ease the construction of robust, application-defined runtimes.

Object shimming: JavaScript supports getter and setter functions which allow applications to interpose on reads and writes to object properties. Syphon supports these, but it also introduces *watcher functions* which can execute when any property on an object is accessed in any way, including attempted deletions.

Watchers are very powerful, and the default Atlantis web stack uses them extensively. As we describe in Section 6.2, watchers allow the web stack to place input sanitizers in the write path of sensitive runtime variables that deal with untrusted user inputs. As another example, consider cross-frame namespace accesses like `window.parent.objInParent`. To implement this operation, the web stack defines a watcher on the `window.parent` object and resolves property accesses by issuing `sendToFrame()` calls to a namespace server in the parent frame.

Method binding and privileged execution: The typical Atlantis application will consist of low-level code like the layout engine and the scripting runtime, and higher-level code which has no need to directly invoke the Atlantis kernel. Syphon provides several language features that allow applications to isolate the low-level code from the high-level code, effectively creating an application-level kernel. Like in JavaScript, a Syphon method can be assigned to an arbitrary object and invoked as a method of that object. However, Syphon supports the binding of a method to a specific object, thereby preventing the method from being invoked with an arbitrary `this` reference.

Syphon also supports the notion of *privileged execution*. Syphon code can only invoke kernel calls if the code belongs to a privileged method that has a privileged `this` reference. By default, Syphon creates all objects and functions as privileged. However, an application can call Syphon's `disableDefaultPriv()` function to turn off that behavior. Subsequently, only privileged execution contexts will be able to create new privileged objects.

Our demonstration web stack leverages privileged execution, method binding, and watchers to prevent higher-level application code from arbitrarily invoking the kernel or perturbing critical data structures in the DOM tree. However, the Atlantis kernel is agnostic as to whether the application takes advantage of features like privileged execution. These features have no impact on Atlantis' security guarantees—they merely help an application to protect itself from itself.

Strong typing: By default, Syphon variables are untyped, as in JavaScript. However, Syphon allows programs to bind variables to types, facilitating optimizations in which the script engine generates fast, type-specific code instead of slow, dynamic-dispatch code for handling generic objects.

Note that strong primitive types have straightforward semantics, but the meaning of a strong object type is unclear in a dynamic, prototype-based language in which object properties, including prototype references, may be fluid. To better support strong object types, Syphon supports ECMAScript v5 notions of *object freezing*. By default, objects are `Unfrozen`, meaning that their property list can change in arbitrary ways at runtime. An object which is `PropertyListFrozen` cannot have old properties deleted or new ones added. A `FullFreeze` object has a frozen property list, and all of its properties are read-only. An object's freeze status can change dynamically, but only in the stricter direction. By combining strong primitive typing with object freezing along a prototype chain, Syphon can simulate traditional classes in strongly typed languages.

Threading: Syphon supports a full threading model with locks and signaling. Syphon threads are more powerful than HTML5 web workers [50] for two reasons. First, web workers cannot access native objects like the DOM tree because this would interfere with the browser's internal locking strategies. In contrast, Syphon DOM trees reside in application-layer code; this means that, for example, an application can define a multi-threaded layout engine without fear of corrupting internal browser state.

The second disadvantage of web workers is that they are limited to communication via asynchronous message exchanges. To implement these exchanges, browsers must serialize and deserialize objects across threading containers and fire notification callbacks. Syphon threads avoid this overhead since they are just thin wrappers around native OS threads.

3.4 Hardware Access

JavaScript has traditionally lacked access to hardware devices like web cameras and microphones. Thus, web pages that wished to access such devices were forced to use native code plugins such as Flash and Silverlight. Like Gazelle and OP, Atlantis loads plugins in separate processes and restricts their behavior using same-origin checks. We refer the reader to other work for a more detailed discussion of plugin isolation [25, 49].

The HTML5 specification [55] exposes hardware to JavaScript programs through a combination of new HTML tags and new JavaScript objects. For example, the `<device>` tag [54] can introduce a web camera object into the JavaScript namespace; the JavaScript interpreter translates reads and writes of that object's properties into hardware commands on the underlying device. Similarly, the `navigator.geolocation` object exposes location data gathered from GPS, wireless signal triangulation, or IP address geolocation [53].

HTML5 has been welcomed by web developers because it finally gives JavaScript first-class access to hardware devices. However, HTML5 is problematic from the security perspective because it entrusts hardware security to the JavaScript interpreter of an unsandboxed browser. Interpreters are complex, buggy pieces of code. For example, there have been several attacks on the JavaScript garbage collectors in Firefox, Safari, and IE [12]. Once an HTML5 JavaScript interpreter is subverted, an attacker has full access to all of the user's hardware devices.

In contrast to HTML5, Atlantis sandboxes the Syphon interpreter, preventing it from directly accessing hardware. Instead, web pages use the Gibraltar AJAX protocol [3] to access hardware. The master kernel contains a *device server* running in an isolated process. The device server is a small program which directly manipulates hardware using native code, and exports a web server interface on the `localhost` address. Principal instances that wish to access hardware send standard AJAX requests to the device server. For example, a page that wants to access a web camera might send an AJAX request to `http://localhost/webCam`, specifying various device commands in the HTTP headers of the request. Users authorize individual web domains to access individual hardware devices, and the device server authenticates each hardware request by looking at its `referrer` HTTP header. This header identifies the URL (and thus the domain) that issued the AJAX request.

In Atlantis, each principal instance runs its own copy of the Syphon interpreter in a separate `AppDomain`. Thus, even if a malicious web page compromises its interpreter, it cannot learn which other domains have hardware access unless those domains willingly respond to `postMessage()` requests for that information. Even if domains collude in this fashion, the instance kernel implements the networking stack, so web pages cannot fake the referrer fields in their hardware requests unless they also subvert the instance kernel.

A variety of subtle authentication issues remain. There are also low-level engineering questions, such as how to facilitate device discovery, and how to create efficient device protocols atop HTTP. We defer a full discussion of these issues to other work [3].

4. PROTOTYPE IMPLEMENTATION

In this section, we briefly describe how we implemented our Atlantis prototype. We also describe some of the performance challenges that we faced. Many of these challenges will be obviated in the next version of Atlantis, which will use the advanced SPUR .NET environment [4]. Compared to the default .NET environment, SPUR has a faster core runtime and a more powerful JIT compiler.

The trusted computing base: The core Atlantis system contains 8634 lines of C# code. 4900 lines belong to the Syphon interpreter, 358 belong to the master kernel, and the remainder belong to the instance kernel and the messaging library shared by various components. We implemented the full kernel interface described in Section 3.2, but we have not yet ported any plugins to Atlantis.

The Syphon interpreter: The interpreter implements all of the language features mentioned in Section 3.3. The interpreter represents each type of Syphon object as a subclass of the SyphonObject C# class. SyphonObject implements the "object as dictionary" abstraction used by all non-primitive types; it also implements introspection interfaces like watcher shims.

Dynamic languages like Syphon allow applications to manipulate the namespace in rich ways at runtime. For example, programs can dynamically add and remove variables from a scope; programs can also create closures, which are functions that remember the values of nonlocal variables in the enclosing scope. Each scope in the scope chain is essentially a dynamically modifiable dictionary, so each namespace operation requires the modification of one or more hash tables.

These modifications can be expensive, so the Syphon interpreter performs several optimizations to minimize dictionary operations. For example, when a function references a variable for the first time, the interpreter searches the scope chain, retrieves the relevant object, and places it in a unified cache that holds variables from various levels in the scope hierarchy. This prevents the interpreter from having to scan a potentially deep scope chain for every variable access.

Each function call requires the interpreter to allocate and initialize a new scope dictionary, and each function return requires a dictionary to be torn down. To avoid these costs, the interpreter tries to inline functions, twizzling the names of their arguments and local variables, rewriting the function code to reference these twizzled variables, and embedding these variables directly in the name cache of the caller. The function call itself is implemented as a direct branch to the rewritten function code. When the inlined function returns, the interpreter must destroy the twizzled name cache entries,

but the overall cost of invoking an inlined function is still much smaller than the cost of invoking a non-inlined one. The interpreter will inline closures, but not functions that generate closures, since non-trivial bookkeeping is needed to properly bind closure variables.

The interpreter itself (and the enclosing browser) are written in C# and statically compiled to a CIL bytecode program. When the user invokes the browser, it is dynamically translated to x86 by the default .NET just-in-time compiler. In our current prototype, the Syphon interpreter compiles ASTs to high-level bytecodes, and then interprets those bytecodes directly. We did write another Syphon interpreter that directly compiled ASTs to CIL, but we encountered several challenges to making it fast. For example, to minimize the overhead of Syphon function calls, we wanted to implement them as direct branches to the starting CIL instructions of the relevant functions. Experiments showed that this kind of invocation was faster than placing the CIL for each Syphon function inside a C# function and then invoking that C# function using the standard CIL CallVirt instruction. Unfortunately, CIL does not support indirect branches. This made it tricky to implement function returns, since any given function can return to many different call sites. We had to implement function returns by storing call site program counters on a stack, and upon function return, using the topmost stack entry to index into a CIL switch where each case statement was a direct branch to a particular call site.

Unfortunately, this return technique does not work as described thus far. CIL is a stack-based bytecode, and the default .NET JIT compiler assumes that, for any instruction that is only the target of backward branches, the evaluation stack is empty immediately before that instruction executes [42]. This assumption was intended to simplify the JIT compiler, since it allows the compiler to determine the stack depth at any point in the program using a single pass through the CIL. Unfortunately, this assumption means that if a function return is a backwards branch to a call site, the CIL code after the call site must act as if the evaluation stack is initially empty; otherwise, the JIT compiler will declare the program invalid. If the evaluation stack is *not* empty before a function invocation (as is often the case), the application must manually save the stack entries to an application-defined data structure before branching to a function's first instruction.[2] Even with the overhead of manual stack management, branching function calls and returns were still faster than using the CallVirt instruction. However, this overhead did reduce the overall benefit of the technique, and the overhead would be avoidable with a JIT compiler that did not make the empty stack assumption.

We encountered several other challenges with the default JIT compiler. For example, we found that the JIT compiler was quick to translate the statically generated CIL for the Atlantis interpreter, but much slower to translate the dynamically generated CIL representing the Syphon application. For example, on several macrobenchmarks, we found that the CIL-emitting interpreter was spending twice as much time in JIT compilation as the high-level bytecode

---

[2]One could use forward branches to implement function returns, but then function *invocations* would have to use backwards branches, leading to a similar set of problems.

interpreter, even though the additional CIL to JIT (the CIL belonging to the Syphon program) was much smaller than the CIL for the interpreter itself.

Given these issues, our current prototype directly interprets the high-level bytecode. However, it is important to note that our challenges did not arise from an intrinsic deficiency in the .NET design, but from artifacts of the default .NET runtime, which is not optimized for our unusual demands. The SPUR project [4] has shown that significant performance gains can be realized by replacing the default .NET JIT engine with a custom one that can perform advanced optimizations like type speculation and trace-based JITing. We plan on using the SPUR framework in the next version of Atlantis.

The default web stack: If a web application does not provide its own high-level runtime, it will use Atlantis' default stack. This stack contains 5581 lines of JavaScript code which we compiled to Syphon ASTs using an ANTLR [40] tool chain. 65% of the code implements the standard DOM environment, providing a DOM tree, an event handling infrastructure, AJAX objects, and so on. The remainder of the code handles markup parsing, layout calculation, and rendering. Our DOM environment is quite mature, but our parsing and layout code is the target of active development; the latter set of modules are quite complex and require clever optimizations to run quickly.

5. EXOKERNEL BROWSERS: PRACTICAL ISSUES

Current web browsers must support an API that is hopelessly complex. This API is an uneasy conglomerate of disparate standards that define network protocols, markup formats, hardware interfaces, and more. Using exokernel principles [16], Atlantis allows each web page to ship with its own implementation of the web stack. Each page can tailor its execution environment to its specific needs; in doing so, the page liberates browser vendors from the futile task of creating a one-size-fits-all web stack.

Individual exokernel vendors might still produce buggy exokernel implementations. However, exokernel browsers are much simpler than their monolithic cousins; thus, their bugs should be smaller in number and easier to fix. Of course, an exokernel browser is only interesting when paired with a high-level runtime. In a certain sense, each high-level runtime represents yet another browser target with yet another set of quirks and incompatibilities that developers must account for. However, and importantly, *a page has complete control over its high-level runtime*. A page chooses which runtime it includes, and can modify that runtime as it sees fit. Thus, from the perspective of a web developer reasoning about portability challenges, the introduction of a new exokernel browser seems much less vexing than the introduction of a new monolithic browser.

Even if a single exokernel interface becomes the de facto browser design, there is always the danger that individual exokernel vendors will expand the narrow interface or introduce non-standard semantics for the sake of product differentiation. It seems impossible to prevent such feature creep by fiat. However, we believe that innovation at a low se-

mantic level happens more slowly than innovation at a high semantic level. For example, fundamentally new file system features are created much less frequently than new application types that happen to leverage the file system. Thus, we expect that cross-vendor exokernel incompatibilities will arise much less frequently than incompatibilities between different monolithic browsers.

Exokernel browsers allow individual web applications to define their own HTML parsers, DOM trees, and so on. Multiple implementations of each component will undoubtedly arise. By design or accident, these implementations may become incompatible with each other. Furthermore, certain classes of components may be rendered unnecessary for some web applications; for example, if an application decides to use SGML instead of HTML as its markup language, it has no need for an HTML parser. Incompatibilities above the exokernel layer are not problematic, and are encouraged by Atlantis in the sense that Atlantis enables web developers to customize their high-level runtimes as they see fit. In practice, most Atlantis developers will not create runtimes from scratch, in the same way that most web developers today do not create their own JavaScript GUI frameworks. Instead, most Atlantis applications will use stock runtimes that are written by companies or open-source efforts, and which are incorporated into applications with little or no modification. Only popular sites or those with uncommon needs will possess the desire and the technical skill needed to write a heavily customized runtime.

6. EVALUATION

In this section, we explore three issues. First, we discuss the security of the Atlantis browser with respect to various threats. Second, we demonstrate how easy it is to extend the demonstration Atlantis web stack. Finally, we examine the performance of Atlantis on several microbenchmarks and macrobenchmarks. We defer an evaluation of Atlantis' AJAX hardware protocol to other work [3].

6.1 Security

Prior work has investigated the security properties of microkernel browsers [25, 46, 49]. Here, we briefly summarize these properties in the context of Atlantis, and explain why Atlantis provides stronger security guarantees than prior microkernel browsers.

Trusted computing base: The core Atlantis runtime contains 8634 lines of trusted C# code. This code belongs to the Syphon interpreter, the instance kernel, the master kernel, and the IPC library. In turn, these modules depend on the .NET runtime which implements the garbage collector, the standard .NET data types, and so on. The .NET runtime is also included in Atlantis' trusted computing base. However, these libraries are type-safe and memory managed, in contrast to the millions of lines of non-type safe C++ code found in IE, Firefox, and other commodity browsers. Thus, we believe that Atlantis' threat surface is comparatively much smaller, particularly given its narrow microkernel interface.

Our Atlantis prototype also includes 5581 lines of JavaScript representing the demonstration web stack, and an ANTLR [40] tool chain which compiles JavaScript to Syphon ASTs. These components are not part of the trusted computing base, since Atlantis does not rely on information from the high-level web stack to guide security decisions.

Principal Isolation: Like other microkernel browsers, Atlantis strongly isolates principal instances from each other and the core browser components. This prevents a large class of attacks which exploit the fact that monolithic browsers place data from multiple domains in the same address space, and lack a centralized point of enforcement for same-origin checks [6]. By strongly isolating each plugin in a process and subjecting them to the same-origin checks experienced by other web content, Atlantis prevents the full browser compromise that results when a monolithic browser has a subverted plugin in its address space [25, 49].

Gazelle, OP, and IBOS use a single browser kernel which, although memory isolated, is shared by all principal instances. If this kernel is compromised, the entire browser is compromised. For example, a subverted Gazelle kernel can inspect all messages exchanged between principal instances, tamper with persistent data belonging to an arbitrary domain, and update the visual display belonging to an arbitrary domain. In contrast, Atlantis has a single master kernel and multiple, sandboxed per-instance kernels. A subverted instance kernel can draw to its own rendering area and create new rendering areas, but it cannot access or update the display of another instance. Similarly, a subverted instance kernel can only tamper with public persistent data (which is untrustworthy by definition) or private persistent data that belongs to the domain of the compromised principal instance. To tamper with resources belonging to arbitrary domains, the attacker must subvert the master kernel, which is strongly isolated from the instance kernels.

Enforcing the Same-origin Policy: Browsers define an object's origin as the server hostname, port, and protocol which are used to fetch the object. For example, a script named `https://x.com:8080/y.js` has a protocol of `https`, a port of 8080, and a hostname of `x.com`.

The same-origin policy constrains how documents and scripts from domain `X` can interact with documents and scripts from domain `Y`. For example, JavaScript in `X`'s pages cannot issue `XMLHttpRequests` for `Y`'s JavaScript files; this ostensibly prevents `X`'s pages from reading `Y`'s source code. `X` can execute (but not inspect) `Y`'s code by dynamically creating a `<script>` tag and setting its `src` attribute to an object in `Y`'s domain. This succeeds because HTML tags are exempt from same-origin checks.

Importantly, the same-origin policy does not prevent colluding domains from communicating. For example, if `X` and `Y` have frames within the same page, the frames cannot forcibly inspect each other's cookies, nor can they forcibly read or write each other's DOM tree or JavaScript state. However, colluding domains can exchange arbitrary data across frames using `postMessage()`. Domains can also leak data through `iframe` URLs. For example, `X` can dynamically create an `iframe` with a URL like `http://y.com?=PRIVATE_X_DATA`. Given all of this, the practical implication of the same-origin policy is that it prevents *non-colluding* domains from tampering with each other.

As a result of Atlantis' exokernel design, it can perform many, but not all, of the origin checks that current browsers perform. However, Atlantis provides the same *practical* level of domain isolation. Each principal instance resides in a separate process, so each frame belonging to each origin is separated by hardware-enforced memory protection. This prevents domains from directly manipulating each other's JavaScript state or window properties. The kernel also partitions persistent storage by domain, ensuring that pages cannot inspect the cookies, DOM storage, or other private data belonging to external domains.

In Atlantis, abstractions like HTML tags and `XMLHttpRequest` objects are implemented entirely outside the kernel. Thus, when the Atlantis kernel services an `openConnection()` request, it cannot determine whether the fetch was initiated by an HTML parser upon encountering a `<script>` tag, or by an `XMLHttpRequest` fetch. To ensure that `<script>` fetches work, Atlantis must also allow cross-domain `XMLHttpRequest` fetches of JavaScript. This violates a strict interpretation of the same-origin policy, but it does not change the practical security provided by Atlantis, since `X`'s pages can trivially learn `Y`'s JavaScript source by downloading the `.js` files through `X`'s web server. From the security perspective, it is not important to prevent the discovery of inherently public source code. Instead, it is important to protect the *user-specific client-side state* which is exposed through the browser runtime and persistent client-side storage. Atlantis protects these resources using strong memory isolation and partitioned local storage. This is the same security model provided by Gazelle [49], which assumes that principal instances will not issue cross-domain script fetches for the purposes of inspecting source code.

6.2 Extensibility
Atlantis' primary goal is to allow web pages to customize their runtime in a robust manner. To demonstrate Atlantis' extensibility, we produced two variants of the default Atlantis web stack.

Safe `innerHTML`: A DOM node's `innerHTML` property is a text string representing the contents of its associated HTML tag. Web pages like message boards often update themselves by taking user-submitted text and assigning it to an `innerHTML` property. Unfortunately, an attacker can use this vector to insert malicious scripts into the page [38]. To prevent this attack, we place a setter shim (§3.3) on `innerHTML` that invokes the Caja sanitizer library [33]. Caja strips dangerous markup from the text, and the setter assigns the safe markup to `innerHTML`.

Stopping drive-by downloads: Assigning a URL to a frame's `window.location` property makes the frame navigate to a new site. If a frame loads a malicious third party script, the script can manipulate `window.location` to trick users into downloading malware [8]. To prevent this, we place a setter on `window.location` that either prevents all assignments, or only allows assignments if the target URL is in a whitelist.

Implementing these extensions on Atlantis was trivial since the default DOM environment is written in pure JavaScript. Neither of these application-defined extensions are possible

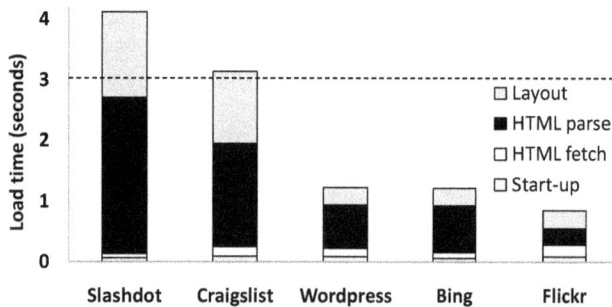

Figure 4: Atlantis page load times. The dotted line shows the three second window after which many users will become frustrated [21].

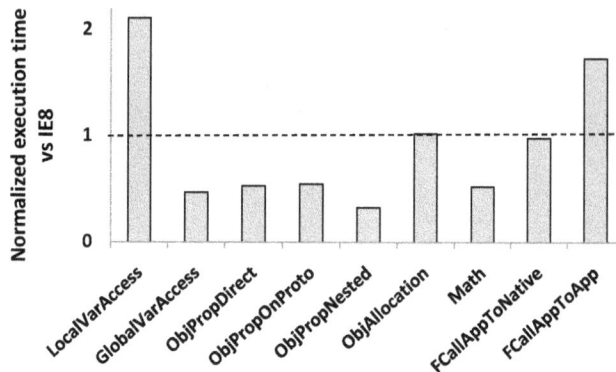

Figure 5: Execution speed versus IE8 (microbenchmarks).

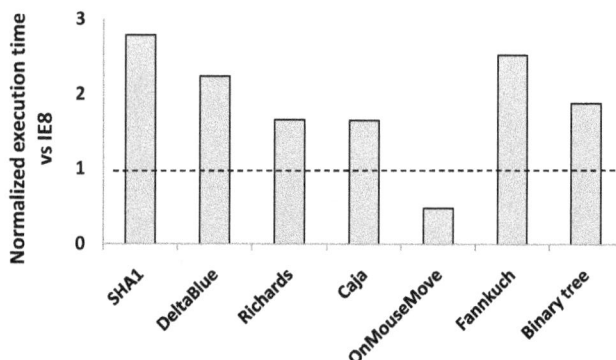

Figure 6: Execution speed versus IE8 (macrobenchmarks). All tests were CPU-bound except for On-MouseMove.

on a traditional browser. The design documents for popular browsers like IE and Firefox explicitly forbid applications from placing setters on `window` properties; placing setters on `innerHTML` is technically allowed, but actually doing so will break the browser's JavaScript engine [31].

6.3 Performance

To explore Atlantis' performance, we ran our prototype on a Lenovo Thinkpad laptop with 4 GB of RAM and a dual core 2.67 MHz processor. Our first experiment explored how quickly Atlantis could load several popular web pages. Figure 4 depicts the results. Each bar represents the average of five trials and contains four components: the start-up time between the user hitting "enter" on the address bar and the kernel issuing the fetch for the page's HTML; the time needed to fetch the HTML; the time needed to parse the HTML; and the time needed to calculate the layout and render the page. Note that layout time includes both pure computation time and the fetch delay for external content like images. To minimize the impact of network delays which Atlantis cannot control, Figure 4 depicts results for a warm browser cache. However, some objects were marked by their server as uncacheable and had to be refetched.

Given the unoptimized nature of our prototype scripting engine, we are encouraged by the results. In three of the five cases, Atlantis' load time is well below the three-second threshold at which users begin to get frustrated [21]. One page (Craiglist) is at the threshold, and another (Slashdot) is roughly a second over.

Figure 4 shows that Atlantis load times were often dominated by HTML parsing overhead. To better understand this phenomenon, we performed several microbenchmarks. The results are shown in Figure 5. Each bar represents Atlantis' relative execution speed with respect to IE8; standard deviations were less than 5% for each set of experiments. Figure 5 shows that in many cases, the Syphon interpreter is as fast or faster than IE's interpreter. In particular, Syphon is two to three times faster at accessing global variables, performing mathematical operations, and accessing object properties, whether they are defined directly on an object, on an object's prototype, or on a nested object four property accesses away.

The cost of application code invoking native functions like `String.indexOf()` is the same on both platforms. However, Atlantis is twice as slow to access local variables, and 1.7 times as slow to invoke application-defined functions from other application-defined functions. Given that Atlantis accesses global variables much faster than IE, its relative slowness in accessing local variables is surprising—both types of accesses should be assisted by Atlantis' name cache. We are currently investigating this issue further. Atlantis function invocation is slower because Atlantis performs several safety checks that IE does not perform. These checks help to implement the Syphon language features described in Section 3.3. For example, to support strongly typed variables, the Syphon interpreter has to compare the type metadata for function parameters with the type metadata for the arguments that the caller actually supplied. To enforce privilege constraints, the Syphon interpreter must also check whether the function to invoke and its "this" pointer are both privileged. These checks make HTML parsing slow on our current Atlantis prototype, since the parsing process requires the invocation of many different functions that process strings, create new DOM nodes, and so on.

Figure 6 shows Atlantis' performance on several macrobenchmarks from three popular benchmark suites (SunSpider, Dromaeo, and Google's V8). Figure 6 shows that in general, IE8 is 1.5–2.8 times faster than our Atlantis prototype. However, for the `OnMouseMove` program, which tracks the rate at which the browser can fire application event handlers when the user rapidly moves the cursor, Atlantis is actually about 50% faster. This is important, since recent empirical work has shown that most web pages consist of a large number of small callback functions that are frequently invoked [43]. Note that firing application-defined event handlers requires native code to invoke application-defined code. The `FCallAppToNative` experiment in Figure 5 measures the costs for application code to call native code.

In summary, our prototype Atlantis implementation is already fast enough to load many web pages and to dispatch events at a fast rate. As mentioned in Section 4, we expect Atlantis' performance to greatly improve when we transition the code base from the stock `.NET` runtime to the SPUR [4] runtime which is aggressively tuned for performance.

7. RELATED WORK

In Sections 1.2, 2.3, and 6.1, we provide a detailed discussion of OP [25] and IBOS [46], two prior microkernel browsers. Gazelle [49] is another microkernel browser; like Atlantis, Gazelle is agnostic about a web page's runtime environment. However, Atlantis differs from Gazelle in five important ways.

- First, Gazelle only isolates web domains from each other; in contrast, Atlantis also protects intra-domain components like HTML parsers and scripting engines from each other.
- Second, Gazelle only has a single kernel, and uses heavyweight processes to isolate this kernel from web page instances. In contrast, Atlantis uses lightweight C# `AppDomains` [2] to place a new kernel instance into each page's process. This maintains strong isolation between the kernel instance and the page while allowing Atlantis to sandbox individual kernel instances. Thus, unlike a Gazelle kernel subverted by domain X, a subverted Atlantis instance kernel can only tamper with data belonging to domain X.
- Third, Atlantis provides new, low-level runtime primitives (§3.3) which make it easier for web applications to define robust high-level runtimes.
- Fourth, Atlantis defines a bootstrapping process that allows a web page to automatically and dynamically load its own runtime environment. In contrast, Gazelle assumes that runtimes are manually installed using an out-of-band mechanism. Seamless dynamic loading is extremely important, since it allows page developers to change their runtime whenever they please without requiring action from the user.
- Finally, although the Gazelle kernel is agnostic to the web stack running above it, in practice, Gazelle uses an isolated version of Internet Explorer to provide that stack. In contrast, Atlantis provides a default web stack implemented in pure, extensible JavaScript. The stack includes a DOM tree, an HTML parser, a multi-pass layout algorithm, and a JavaScript runtime. This new stack provides web developers with unprecedented control over a runtime *implemented with their preferred software tools*: JavaScript and HTML.

The last point illuminates a primary contribution of this paper: whereas prior work leveraged microkernels solely to provide isolation, Atlantis leverages microkernels to also provide extensibility.

ServiceOS [34] is an extension of Gazelle that implements new policies for resource allocation. Architecturally, ServiceOS is very similar to Gazelle, so Atlantis has the same advantages over ServiceOS that it has over Gazelle.

JavaScript frameworks like jQuery [5] and Prototype [10] contain conditional code paths that try to hide browser incompatibilities. However, these libraries cannot hide all of these incompatibilities; furthermore, these libraries cannot make native code modules like layout engines amenable to introspection. Compile-to-JavaScript frameworks [7, 29] have similar limitations.

There are several JavaScript implementations of browser components like HTML parsers and JavaScript parsers [17, 23, 35, 44]. These libraries are typically used by a web page to analyze markup or script source before it is passed to the browser's actual parsing engine or JavaScript runtime. Using extensible web stacks, Atlantis lets pages extend and introspect the *real* application runtime. Atlantis' Syphon interpreter also provides new language primitives for making this introspection robust and efficient.

8. CONCLUSIONS

In this paper, we describe Atlantis, a new web browser which uses microkernels not just for security, but for extensibility as well. Whereas prior microkernel browsers reuse buggy, non-introspectable components from monolithic browsers, Atlantis allows each web page to define its own markup parser, layout engine, DOM tree, and scripting runtime. Atlantis gives pages the freedom to tailor their execution environments without fear of breaking fragile browser interfaces. Our evaluation demonstrates this extensibility, and shows that our Atlantis prototype is fast enough to render popular pages and rapidly dispatch event handlers. Atlantis also leverages multiple kernels to provide stronger security guarantees than previous microkernel browsers.

9. REFERENCES

[1] A. Aho, M. Lam, R. Sethi, and J. Ullman. *Compilers: Principles, Techniques, and Tools*. Addison-Wesley, 2nd edition, 2007.

[2] J. Albahari and B. Albahari. *C# 3.0 in a Nutshell*. O'Reilly Publishing, O'Reilly Media, Inc., 3rd edition, 2007.

[3] Anonymous. Paper title blinded. In submission.

[4] M. Bebenita, F. Brandner, M. Fahndrich, F. Logozzo, W. Schulte, N. Tillmann, and H. Venter. SPUR: A Trace-Based JIT Compiler for CIL. Microsoft Research Tech Report MSR-TR-2010-27, March 25, 2010.

[5] J. Chaffer and K. Swedberg. *jQuery 1.4 Reference Guide*. Packt Publishing, Birmingham, United Kingdom, 2010.

[6] S. Chen, D. Ross, and Y.-M. Wang. An Analysis of Browser Domain-Isolation Bugs and A Light-Weight Transparent Defense Mechanism. In *Proceedings of CCS*, Alexandria, VA, October 2007.

[7] R. Cooper and C. Collins. *GWT in Practice*. Manning Publications, Greenwich, CT, 2008.

[8] M. Cova, C. Kruegel, and G. Vigna. Detection and

Analysis of Drive-by-Download Attacks and Malicious JavaScript Code. In *Proceedings of WWW*, Raleigh, NC, April 2010.

[9] C. Coyier. Percentage Bugs in WebKit. *CSS-tricks Blog*. http://css-tricks.com/percentage-bugs-in-webkit/, August 30, 2010.

[10] D. Crane, B. Bibeault, and T. Locke. *Prototype and Scriptaculous in Action*. Manning Publications, Greenwich, CT, 2007.

[11] D. Crockford. The application/json Media Type for JavaScript Object Notation (JSON). RFC 4627, July 2006.

[12] M. Daniel, J. Honoroff, and C. Miller. Engineering Heap Overflow Exploits with JavaScript. In *Proceedings of USENIX Workshop on Offensive Technologies*, 2008.

[13] J. Douceur, J. Elson, J. Howell, and J. Lorch. Leveraging Legacy Code to Deploy Desktop Applications on the Web. In *Proceedings of OSDI*, San Diego, CA, December 2008.

[14] Ecma International. Ecmascript language specification, 5th edition, December 2009.

[15] H. Edskes. IE8 overflow and expanding box bugs. *Final Builds Blog*.http://www.edskes.net/ie/ie8overflowandexpandingboxbugs.htm, 2010.

[16] D. Engler, M. Kaashoek, and J. O. Jr. Exokernel: An Operating System Architecture for Application-Level Resource Management. In *Proceedings of SOSP*, Copper Mountain, CO, December 1995.

[17] Envjs Team. Envjs: Bringing the Browser. http://www.envjs.com/, 2010.

[18] eSpace Technologies. A tiny bug in Prototype JS leads to major incompatibility with Facebook JS client library. *eSpace.com blog*, April 23, 2008.

[19] Fielding, R., Gettys, J., Mogul, J.,Frystyk, H., Masinter, L., Leach, P., and Berners-Lee, T. Hypertext Transfer Protocol – HTTP/1.1. RFC 2616 (Draft Standard), June 1999.

[20] D. Flanagan. *JavaScript: The Definitive Guide*. O'Reilly Media, Inc., 5th edition, 2006.

[21] Forrester Consulting. *eCommerce Web Site Performance Today: An Updated Look At Consumer Reaction To A Poor Online Shopping Experience*. White paper, 2009.

[22] S. Galineau. The CSS Corner: Using Filters In IE8. *IBBlog*. http://blogs.msdn.com/b/ie/archive/2009/02/19/the-css-corner-using-filters-in-ie8.aspx, February 19, 2009.

[23] D. Glazman. JSCSSP: A CSS parser in JavaScript. http://www.glazman.org/JSCSSP/, 2010.

[24] Google. Fixing Google Chrome Compatibility bugs in WebSites. http://code.google.com/p/doctype/wiki/ArticleGoogleChromeCompatFAQ#Inline_elements_can%27t_enclose_block_elements, May 25, 2010.

[25] C. Grier, , S. Tang, and S. King. Secure Web Browsing with the OP Web Browser. In *Proceedings of IEEE Security*, Oakland, CA, May 2008.

[26] L.-S. Huang, Z. Weinberg, C. Evans, and C. Jackson. Protecting Browsers from Cross-Origin CSS Attacks. In *Proceedings of CCS*, Chicago, IL, October 2010.

[27] J. Zaytsev. What's wrong with extending the DOM. *Perfection Kills Website*. http://perfectionkills.com/whats-wrong-with-extending-the-dom, April 5, 2010.

[28] jQuery Message Forum. Focus() inside a blur() handler. https://forum.jquery.com/topic/focus-inside-a-blur-handler, January 2010.

[29] N. Kothari. Script#: Version 0.5.5.0.

[30] http://projects.nikhilk.net/ScriptSharp, 2009.

[30] L. Lazaris. CSS Bugs and Inconsistencies in Firefox 3.x. *Webdesigner Depot*. http://www.webdesignerdepot.com/2010/03/css-bugs-and-inconsistencies-in-firefox-3-x, March 15, 2010.

[31] J. Mickens, J. Howell, and J. Elson. Mugshot: Deterministic Capture and Replay for JavaScript Applications. In *Proceedings of NSDI*, San Jose, CA, April 2010.

[32] Microsoft. Update for Native JSON feature in IE8. http://support.microsoft.com/kb/976662, February 2010.

[33] M. Miller, M. Samuel, B. Laurie, I. Awad, and M. Stay. Caja: Safe active content in sanitized JavaScript. Draft specification, January 15, 2008.

[34] A. Moshchuk and H. J. Wang. Resource Management for Web Applications in ServiceOS. Microsoft Research Tech Report MSR-TR-2010-56, May 18, 2010.

[35] Mozilla Corporation. Narcissus javascript. http://mxr.mozilla.org/mozilla/source/js/narcissus/.

[36] Mozilla Developer Center. Gecko Plugin API Reference. https://developer.mozilla.org/en/Gecko_Plugin_API_Reference, 2010.

[37] Mozilla Developer Center. HTML5 Parser. https://developer.mozilla.org/en/HTML/HTML5/HTML5_Parser, July 29, 2010.

[38] National Vulnerability Database. CVE-2010-2301, 2010. Cross-site scripting vulnerability: innerHTML.

[39] T. Olsson. *The Ultimate CSS Reference*. Sitepoint, Collingwood, Victoria, Austraiia, 2008.

[40] T. Parr. *The Definitive ANTLR Reference*. Pragmatic Bookshelf, Raleigh, North Carolina, 2007.

[41] Peter-Paul Koch. QuirksMode–for all your browser quirks. http://www.quirksmode.org, 2011.

[42] J. Pobar, T. Neward, D. Stutz, and G. Shilling. Shared Source CLI 2.0 Internals. http://callvirt.net/blog/files/Shared%20Source%20CLI%202.0%20Internals.pdf, 2008.

[43] P. Ratanaworabhan, B. Livshits, and B. Zorn. JSMeter: Comparing the Behavior of JavaScript Benchmarks with RealWeb Applications. In *Proceedings of USENIX WebApps*, Boston, MA, June 2010.

[44] J. Resig. Pure JavaScript HTML Parser. http://ejohn.org/blog/pure-javascript-html-parser/, May 2008.

[45] C. Stork, P. Housel, V. Haldar, N. Dalton, and M. Franz. Towards language-agnostic mobile code. In *Proceedings of the Workshop on Multi-Language Infrastructure and Interoperability*, Firenze, Italy, 2001.

[46] S. Tang, H. Mai, and S. T. King. Trust and Protection in the Illinois Browser Operating System. In *Proceedings of OSDI*, 2010.

[47] C. Tyler. *X Power Tools*. O'Reilly Media, Inc., Cambridge, MA, 2007.

[48] W3C Web Apps Working Group. Web Storage: W3C Working Draft. http://www.w3.org/TR/2009/WD-webstorage-20091029, October 29, 2009.

[49] H. J. Wang, C. Grier, A. Moshchuk, S. T. King, P. Choudhury, and H. Venter. The Multi-principal OS Construction of the Gazelle Web Browser. In *Proceedings of USENIX Security*, 2009.

[50] Web Hypertext Application Technology Working Group (WHATWG). Web Workers (Draft Recommendation). http://www.whatwg.org/specs/web-workers/current-work/, September 10, 2010.

[51] World Wide Web Consortium. Document object model (DOM) level 2 core specification. W3C

Recommendation, November 13, 2000.

[52] World Wide Web Consortium. Cascading Style Sheets Level 2 Revision 1 (CSS 2.1) Specification. W3C Working Draft. `http://www.w3.org/TR/CSS2`, September 8, 2009.

[53] World Wide Web Consortium. Geolocation API Specification. `http://dev.w3.org/geo/api/spec-source.html`, February 10, 2010.

[54] World Wide Web Consortium. HTML Device: An addition to HTML. `http://dev.w3.org/html5/html-device/`, September 9, 2010.

[55] World Wide Web Consortium. HTML5: A vocabulary and associated APIs for HTML and XHTML. W3C Working Draft. `http://www.w3.org/TR/html5`, June 24, 2010.

[56] B. Yee, D. Sehr, G. Dardyk, J. B. Chen, R. Muth, T. Ormandy, S. Okasaka, N. Narula, and N. Fullagar. Native Client: A Sandbox for Portable, Untrusted x86 Native Code. In *Proceedings of IEEE Security*, Oakland, CA, May 2009.

PTask: Operating System Abstractions To Manage GPUs as Compute Devices

Christopher J. Rossbach
Microsoft Research
crossbac@microsoft.com

Jon Currey
Microsoft Research
jcurrey@microsoft.com

Mark Silberstein
Technion
marks@cs.technion.ac.il

Baishakhi Ray
University of Texas at Austin
bray@cs.utexas.edu

Emmett Witchel
University of Texas at Austin
witchel@cs.utexas.edu

ABSTRACT

We propose a new set of OS abstractions to support GPUs and other accelerator devices as first class computing resources. These new abstractions, collectively called the **PTask API**, support a dataflow programming model. Because a PTask graph consists of OS-managed objects, the kernel has sufficient visibility and control to provide system-wide guarantees like fairness and performance isolation, and can streamline data movement in ways that are impossible under current GPU programming models.

Our experience developing the PTask API, along with a gestural interface on Windows 7 and a FUSE-based encrypted file system on Linux show that the PTask API can provide important system-wide guarantees where there were previously none, and can enable significant performance improvements, for example gaining a 5× improvement in maximum throughput for the gestural interface.

Categories and Subject Descriptors

D.4.8 [**Operating systems**]: [Performance]; D.4.7 [**Operating systems**]: [Organization and Design]; I.3.1 [**Hardware Architecture**]: [Graphics processors]; D.1.3 [**Programming Techniques**]: [Concurrent Programming]

General Terms

OS Design, GPUs, Performance

Keywords

Dataflow, GPUs, operating systems, GPGPU, gestural interface, accelerators

1. INTRODUCTION

Three of the top five supercomputers on the TOP500 list for June 2011 (the most recent ranking) use graphics processing units (GPUs) [6]. GPUs have surpassed CPUs as a source of high-density computing resources. The proliferation of fast GPU hardware has been accompanied by the emergence of general purpose GPU (GPGPU)

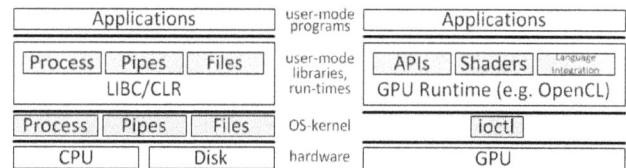

Figure 1: Technology stacks for CPU vs GPU programs. The 1-to-1 correspondence of OS-level and user-mode runtime abstractions for CPU programs is absent for GPU programs

frameworks such as DirectX, CUDA [59], and OpenCL [47], enabling talented programmers to write high-performance code for GPU hardware. However, despite the success of GPUs in supercomputing environments, GPU hardware and programming environments are not routinely integrated into many other types of systems because of programming difficulty, lack of modularity, and unpredictable performance artifacts.

Current software and system support for GPUs allows their computational power to be used for high-performance rendering or for a wide array of high-performance batch-oriented computations [26], but GPU use is limited to certain application domains. The GPGPU ecosystem lacks rich operating system (OS) abstractions that would enable new classes of compute-intensive interactive applications, such as gestural input, brain-computer interfaces, and interactive video recognition, or applications in which the OS uses the GPU for its own computation such as encrypted file systems. In contrast to interactive games, which use GPUs as rendering engines, these applications use GPUs as compute engines in contexts that require OS support. We believe these applications are not being built because of inadequate OS-level abstractions and interfaces. The time has come for OSes to stop managing graphics processing devices (GPUs) as I/O devices and start managing them as a computational devices, like CPUs.

Figure 1 compares OS-level support for traditional hardware to OS-level support for GPUs. In contrast to most common system resources such as CPUs and storage devices, kernel-level abstractions for GPUs are severely limited. While OSes provide a driver interface to GPUs, that interface locks away the full potential of the graphics hardware behind an awkward `ioctl`-oriented interface designed for reading and writing blocks of data to millisecond-latency disks and networks. Moreover, lack of a general kernel-facing interface severely limits what the OS can do to provide high-level abstractions for GPUs: in Windows, and other closed-source OSes, using the GPU from a kernel mode driver is not currently supported using any publicly documented APIs. Additionally, because the OS manages GPUs as peripherals rather than as shared compute resources, the OS leaves resource management for GPUs to vendor-supplied drivers and user-mode run-times. With no role in GPU resource-management, the OS cannot provide guarantees of fairness and performance isolation. For applications that rely on such guarantees, GPUs are consequently an impractical choice.

This paper proposes a set of kernel-level abstractions for managing interactive, high-compute devices. GPUs represent a new kind of peripheral device, whose computation and data bandwidth exceed that of the CPU. The kernel must expose enough hardware detail of these peripherals to allow programmers to take advantage of their enormous processing capabilities. But the kernel must hide programmer inconveniences like memory that is non-coherent between the CPU and GPU, and must do so in a way that preserves performance. GPUs must be promoted to first-class computing resources, with traditional OS guarantees such as fairness and isolation, and the OS must provide abstractions that allow programmers to write code that is both modular and performant.

Our new abstractions, collectively called the **PTask API**, provide a dataflow programming model in which the programmer writes code to manage a graph-structured computation. The vertices in the graph are called **ptasks** (short for **p**arallel **task**) which are units of work such as a shader program that runs on a GPU, or a code fragment that runs on the CPU or another accelerator device. PTask vertices in the graph have input and output **ports** exposing data sources and sinks in the code, and are connected by **channels**, which represent a data flow edge in the graph. The graph expresses both data movement and potential concurrency directly, which can greatly simplify programming. The programmer must express only *where* data must move, but not *how* or *when*, allowing the system to parallelize execution and optimize data movement without any additional code from the programmer. For example, two sibling ptasks in a graph can run concurrently in a system with multiple GPUs without additional GPU management code, and double buffering is eliminated when multiple ptasks that run on a single accelerator are dependent and sequentially ordered. Under current GPU programming models, such optimizations require direct programmer intervention, but with the PTask API, the same code adapts to run optimally on different hardware substrates.

A PTask graph consists of OS-managed objects, so the kernel has sufficient visibility and control to provide system-wide guarantees like fairness and performance isolation. The PTask runtime tracks GPU usage and provides a state machine for ptasks that allows the kernel to schedule them in a way similar to processes. Under current GPU frameworks, GPU scheduling is completely hidden from the kernel by vendor-provided driver code, and often implements simplistic policies such as round-robin. These simple policies can thwart kernel scheduling priorities, undermining fairness and inverting priorities, often in a dramatic way.

Kernel-level ptasks enable data movement optimizations that are impossible with current GPU programming frameworks. For example, consider an application that uses the GPU to accelerate real-time image processing for data coming from a peripheral like a camera. Current GPU frameworks induce excessive data copy by causing data to migrate back and forth across the user-kernel boundary, and by double-buffering in driver code. A PTask graph, conversely, provides the OS with precise information about data's origin(s) and destination(s). The OS uses this information to eliminate unnecessary data copies. In the case of real-time processing of image data from a camera, the PTask graph enables the elimination of two layers of buffering. Because data flows directly from the camera driver to the GPU driver, an intermediate buffer is unnecessary, and a copy to user space is obviated.

We have implemented the full PTask API for Windows 7 and PTask scheduling in Linux. Our experience using PTask to accelerate a gestural interface in Windows and a FUSE-based encrypted file system in Linux shows that kernel-level support for GPU abstractions provides system-wide guarantees, enables significant performance gains, and can make GPU acceleration practical in application domains where previously it was not.

This paper makes the following contributions.

- Provides quantitative evidence that modern OS abstractions are insufficient to support a class of "interactive" applications that use GPUs, showing that simple GPU programs can reduce the response times for a desktop that uses the GPU by nearly an order of magnitude.
- Provides a design for OS abstractions to support a wide range of GPU computations with traditional OS guarantees like fairness and isolation.
- Provides a prototype of the PTask API and a GPU-accelerated gestural interface, along with evidence that PTasks enable "interactive" applications that were previously impractical, while providing fairness and isolation guarantees that were previously absent from the GPGPU ecosystem. The data flow programming model supported by the PTask API delivers throughput improvements up to $4\times$ across a range of microbenchmarks and a $5\times$ improvement for our prototype gestural interface.
- Demonstrates a prototype of GPU-aware scheduling in the Linux kernel that forces GPU-using applications to respect kernel scheduling priorities.

2. MOTIVATION

This paper focuses on GPU support for interactive applications like gesture-based interfaces, neural interfaces (also called brain-computer interfaces or BCIs) [48], encrypting file systems and real-time audio/visual interfaces such as speech recognition. These tasks are computationally demanding, have real-time performance and latency constraints, and feature many data-independent phases of computation. GPUs are an ideal compute substrate for these tasks to achieve their latency deadlines, but lack of kernel support forces designers of these applications to make difficult and often untenable tradeoffs to use the GPU.

To motivate our new kernel abstractions we explore the problem of interactive gesture recognition as a case study. A gestural interface turns a user's hand motions into OS input events such as mouse movements or clicks [36]. Forcing the user to wear special gloves makes gesture recognition easier for the machine, but it is unnatural. The gestural interface we consider does not require the user to wear any special clothing. Such a system must be tolerant to visual noise on the hands, like poor lighting and rings, and must use cheap, commodity cameras to do the gesture sensing. A gestural interface workload is computationally demanding, has real-time latency constraints, and is rich with data-parallel algorithms, making it a natural fit for GPU-acceleration. Gesture recognition is similar to the computational task performed by Microsoft's Kinect, though that system has fewer cameras, lower data rates and grosser features. Kinect only runs a single application at a time (the current game), which can use all available GPU resources. An operating system must multiplex competing applications.

Figure 2 shows a basic decomposition of a gesture recognition system. The system consists of some number of cameras (in this example, photogrammetric sensors [28]), and software to analyze images captured from the cameras. Because such a system functions as a user input device, gesture events recognized by the system must be multiplexed across applications by the OS; to be us-

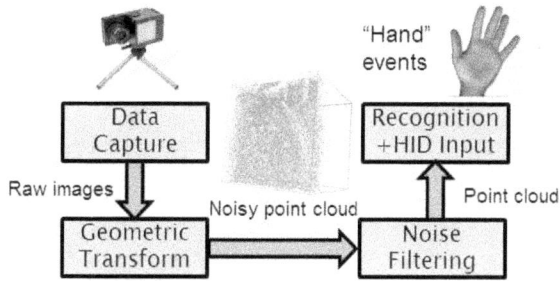

Figure 2: A gesture recognition system based on photogrammetric cameras

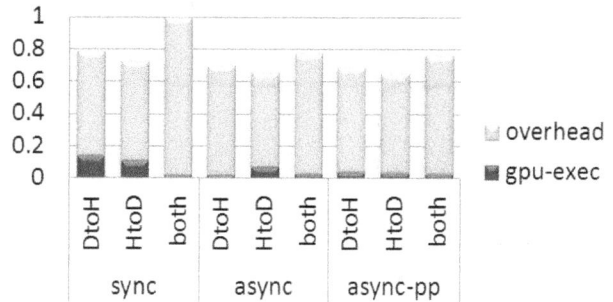

Figure 3: Relative GPU execution time and overhead (lower is better) for CUDA-based implementation of the xform program in our prototype system. sync uses synchronous communication of buffers between the CPU and GPU, async uses asynchronous communication, and async-pp uses both asynchrony and ping-pong buffers to further hide latency. Bars are divided into time spent executing on the GPU and system overhead. DtoH represents an implementation that communicates between the device and the host on every frame, HtoD the reverse, and both represent bi-directional communication for every frame. Reported execution time is relative to the synchronous, bi-directional case (sync-both).

able, the system must deliver those events with high frequency and low latency. The design decomposes the system into four components, implemented as separate programs:

- **catusb:** Captures image data from cameras connected on a USB bus. Short for "`cat /dev/usb`".
- **xform:** Perform geometric transformations to transform images from multiple camera perspectives to a single point cloud in the coordinate system of the screen or user. Inherently data-parallel.
- **filter:** Performs noise filtering on image data produced by the xform step. Inherently data-parallel.
- **hidinput:** Detects gestures in a point cloud and sends them to the OS as human interface device (HID) input. Not data parallel.

Given these four programs, a gestural interface system can be composed using POSIX pipes as follows:

```
catusb | xform | filter | hidinput &
```

This design is desirable because it is modular, (making its components easily reusable) and because it relies on familiar OS-level abstractions to communicate between components in the pipeline. Inherent data-parallelism in the **xform** and **filter** programs strongly argue for GPU acceleration. We have prototyped these computations and our measurements show they are not only a good fit for GPU-acceleration, they actually *require* it. If the system uses multiple cameras with high data rates and large image sizes, these algorithms can easily saturate a modern chip multi-processor (CMP). For example, our **filter** prototype relies on bilateral filtering [67]. A well-optimized implementation using fork/join parallelism is unable to maintain real-time frame rates on a 4-core CMP despite consuming nearly 100% of the available CPU. In contrast, a GPU-based implementation easily realizes frame rates above the real-time rate, and has minimal affect on CPU utilization because nearly all of the work is done on the GPU.

2.1 The problem of data movement

No direct OS support for GPU abstractions exists, so computing on a GPU for a gestural interface necessarily entails a user-level GPU programming framework and run-time such as DirectX, CUDA, or OpenCL. Implementing **xform** and **filter** in these frameworks yields dramatic speedups for the components operating in isolation, but the system composed with pipes suffers from excessive data movement across both the user-kernel boundary and through the hardware across the PCI express (PCIe) bus.

For example, reading data from a camera requires copying image buffers out of kernel space to user space. Writing to the pipe connecting **catusb** to **xform** causes the same buffer to be written back into kernel space. To run **xform** on the GPU, the system must read buffers out of kernel space into user space, where a user-mode runtime such as CUDA must subsequently write the buffer back into kernel space and transfer it to the GPU and back. This pattern repeats as data moves from the **xform** to the **filter** program and so on. This simple example incurs 12 user/kernel boundary crossings. Excessive data copying also occurs across hardware components. Image buffers must migrate back and forth between main memory and GPU memory repeatedly, increasing latency while wasting bandwidth and power.

Overheads introduced by run-time systems can severely limit the effectiveness of latency-hiding mechanisms. Figure 3 shows relative GPU execution time and system overhead per image frame for a CUDA-based implementation of the **xform** program in our prototype. The figure compares implementations that use synchronous and asynchronous communication as well as ping-pong buffers, another technique that overlaps communication with computation. The data illustrate that the system spends far more time marshaling data structures and migrating data than it does actually computing on the GPU. While techniques to hide the latency of communication improve performance, the improvements are modest at best.

User-level frameworks do provide mechanisms to minimize redundant hardware-level communication within a single process' address space. However, addressing such redundancy for cross-process or cross-device communication requires OS-level support and a programmer-visible interface. For example, USB data captured from cameras must be copied into system RAM before it can be copied to the GPU: with OS support, it could be copied directly into GPU memory.[1]

2.2 No easy fix for data movement

The problem of data migration between GPU and CPU memory spaces is well-recognized by the developers of GPGPU frameworks. CUDA, for example, supports mechanisms such as asyn-

---

[1]Indeed, NVIDIA GPU Direct [4] implements just such a feature, but requires specialized support in the driver of any I/O device involved.

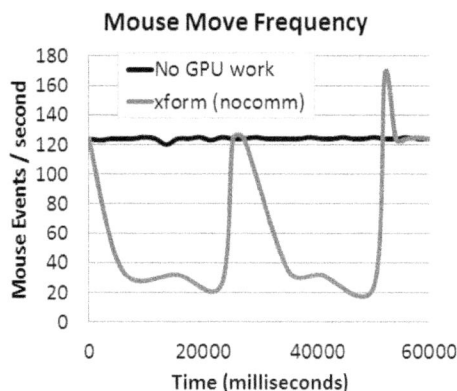

Figure 4: The effect of GPU-bound work on CPU-bound tasks The graph shows the frequency (in Hz) with which the OS is able to deliver mouse movement events over a period of 60 seconds during which a program makes heavy use of the GPU. Average CPU utilization over the period is under 25%.

chronous buffer copy, CUDA streams (a generalization of the latter), and pinning of memory buffers to tolerate data movement latency by overlapping computation and communication. However, to use such features, a programmer must understand OS-level issues like memory mapping. For example, CUDA provides APIs to pin allocated memory buffers, allowing the programmer to avoid a layer of buffering above DMA transfer. The programmer is cautioned to use this feature sparingly as it reduces the amount of memory available to the system for paging [59].

Using streams effectively requires a static knowledge of which transfers can be overlapped with which computations; such knowledge may not always be available statically. Moreover, streams can only be effective if there is available communication to perform that is independent of the current computation. For example, copying data for stream a_1 to or from the device for execution by kernel A can be overlapped with the execution of kernel B; attempts to overlap with execution of A will cause serialization. Consequently, modules that offload logically separate computation to the GPU must be aware of each other's computation and communication patterns to maximize the effectiveness of asynchrony.

New architectures may alter the relative difficulty of managing data across GPU and CPU memory domains, but software will retain an important role, and optimizing data movement will remain important for the foreseeable future. AMD's Fusion integrates the CPU and GPU onto a single die, and enables coherent yet slow access to the shared memory by both processors. However high performance is only achievable via non-coherent accesses or by using private GPU memory, leaving data placement decisions to software. Intel's Sandy Bridge, another CPU/GPU combination, is further indication that the coming years will see various forms of integrated CPU/GPU hardware coming to market. New hybrid systems, such as NVIDIA Optimus, have a power-efficient on-die GPU and a high-performance discrete GPU. Despite the presence of a combined CPU/GPU chip, such systems still require explicit data management. While there is evidence that GPUs with coherent access to shared memory may eventually become common, even a completely integrated virtual memory system requires system support for minimizing data copies.

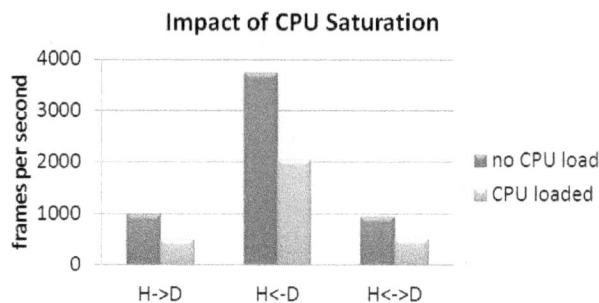

Figure 5: The effect of CPU-bound work on GPU-bound tasks. H→D is a CUDA workload that has communication from the host to the GPU device, while H←D has communication from the GPU to the host, and H↔D has bidirectional communication.

2.3 The scheduling problem

Modern OSes cannot currently guarantee fairness and performance for systems that use GPUs for computation. The OS does not treat GPUs as a shared computational resource, like a CPU, but rather as an I/O device. This design becomes a severe limitation when the OS needs to use the GPU for its own computation (e.g., as Windows 7 does with the Aero user interface). Under the current regime, watchdog timers ensure that screen refresh rates are maintained, but OS scheduling priorities are easily undermined by the GPU driver.

GPU work causes system pauses. Figure 4 shows the impact of GPU-bound work on the frequency with which the system can collect and deliver mouse movements. In our experiments, significant GPU-work at high frame rates causes Windows 7 to be unresponsive for seconds at a time. To measure this phenomenon, we instrument the OS to record the frequency of mouse events delivered through the HID class driver over a 60 second period. When no concurrent GPU work is executing, the system is able to deliver mouse events at a stable 120 Hz. However, when the GPU is heavily loaded, the mouse event rate plummets, often to below 20 Hz. The GPU-bound task is console-based (does not update the screen) and performs unrelated work in another process context. Moreover, CPU utilization is below 25%, showing that the OS has compute resources available to deliver events. A combination of factors are at work in this situation. GPUs are not preemptible, with the side-effect that in-progress I/O requests cannot be canceled once begun. Because Windows relies on cancelation to prioritize its own work, its priority mechanism fails. The problem is compounded because the developers of the GPU runtime use request batching to improve throughput for GPU programs. Ultimately, Windows is unable to interrupt a large number of GPU invocations submitted in batch, and the system appears unresponsive. The inability of the OS to manage the GPU as a first-class resource inhibits its ability to load balance the entire system effectively.

CPU work interferes with GPU throughput. Figure 5 shows the inability of Windows 7 to load balance a system that has concurrent, but fundamentally unrelated work on the GPU and CPUs. The data in the figure were collected on a machine with 64-bit Windows 7, Intel Core 2 Quad 2.66GHz, 8GB RAM, and an NVIDIA GeForce GT230 GPU. The figure shows the impact of a CPU-bound process (using all 4 cores to increment counter variables) on the frame rate of a shader program (the **xform** program from our prototype implementation). The frame rate of the GPU program drops by 2x, despite the near absence of CPU work in the program: **xform** uses the CPU only to trigger the next computation on the GPU device.

These results suggest that GPUs need to be treated as a first-class computing resource and managed by the OS scheduler like a normal CPU. Such abstractions will allow the OS to provide system-wide properties like fairness and performance isolation. User programs should interact with GPUs using abstractions similar to threads and processes. Current OSes provide no abstractions that fit this model. In the following sections, we propose abstractions to address precisely this problem.

3. DESIGN

We propose a set of new OS abstractions to support GPU programming called the PTask (**P**arallel **Task**) API. The PTask API consists of interfaces and runtime library support to simplify the offloading of compute-intensive tasks to accelerators such as GPUs. PTask supports a dataflow programming model in which individual tasks are assembled by the programmer into a directed acyclic graph: vertices, called **ptasks**, are executable code such as shader programs on the GPU, code fragments on other accelerators (e.g. a SmartNIC), or callbacks on the CPU. Edges in the graph represent data flow, connecting the inputs and outputs of each vertex. PTask is best suited for applications that have significant computational demands, feature both task- and data-level parallelism, and require both high throughput and low latency.

PTask was developed with three design goals. **(1)** Bring GPUs under the purview of a single (perhaps federated) resource manager, allowing that entity to provide meaningful guarantees for fairness and isolation. **(2)** Provide a programming model that simplifies the development of code for accelerators by abstracting away code that manages devices, performs I/O, and deals with disjoint memory spaces. In a typical DirectX or CUDA program, only a fraction of the code implements algorithms that run on the GPU, while the bulk of the code manages the hardware and orchestrates data movement between CPU and GPU memories. In contrast, PTask encapsulates device-specific code, freeing the programmer to focus on application-level concerns such as algorithms and data flow. **(3)** Provide a programming environment that allows code to be both modular and fast. Because current GPU programming environments promote a tight coupling between device-memory management code and GPU-kernel code, writing reusable code to leverage a GPU means writing both algorithm code to run on the GPU and code to run on the host that transfers the results of a GPU-kernel computation when they are needed. This approach often translates to sub-optimal data movement, higher latency, and undesirable performance artifacts.

3.1 Integrating PTask scheduling with the OS

The two chief benefits of coordinating OS scheduling with the GPU are efficiency and fairness (design goals (1) and (3)). By efficiency we mean both low latency between when a ptask is ready and when it is scheduled on the GPU, and scheduling enough work on the GPU to fully utilize it. By fairness we mean that the OS scheduler provides OS priority-weighted access to processes contending for the GPU, and balances GPU utilization with other system tasks like user interface responsiveness.

Separate processes can communicate through, or share a graph. For example, processes A and B may produce data that is input to the graph, and another process C can consume the results. The scheduler must balance thread-specific scheduling needs with PTask-specific scheduling needs. For example, gang scheduling the producer and consumer threads for a given PTask graph will maximize system throughput.

```
matrix gemm(A, B) {
  matrix res = new matrix();
  copyToDevice(A);
  copyToDevice(B);
  invokeGPU(gemm_kernel, A, B, res);
  copyFromDevice(res);
  return res;
}
matrix modularSlowAxBxC(A, B, C) {
  matrix AxB = gemm(A, B);
  matrix AxBxC = gemm(AxB, C);
  return AxBxC;
}
matrix nonmodularFastAxBxC(A, B, C) {
  matrix intermed = new matrix();
  matrix res = new matrix();
  copyToDevice(A);
  copyToDevice(B);
  copyToDevice(C);
  invokeGPU(gemm_kernel, A, B, intermed);
  invokeGPU(gemm_kernel, intermed, C, res);
  copyFromDevice(res);
  return res;
}
```

Figure 6: Pseudo-code to offload matrix computation $(A \times B) \times C$ to a GPU. This modular approach uses the `gemm` **subroutine to compute both** $A \times B$ **and** $(A \times B) \times C$**, forcing an unnecessary round-trip from GPU to main memory for the intermediate result.**

3.2 Efficiency vs. modularity

Consider the pseudo-code in Figure 6, which reuses a matrix multiplication subroutine called `gemm` to implement $((A \times B) \times C)$. GPUs typically have private memory spaces that are not coherent with main memory and not addressable by the CPU. To offload computation to the GPU, the `gemm` implementation must copy input matrices A and B to GPU memory. It then invokes a GPU-kernel called `gemm_kernel` to perform the multiplication, and copies the result back to main memory. If the programmer reuses the code for `gemm` to compose the product $((A \times B) \times C)$ as `gemm(gemm(A,B),C)` (`modularSlowAxBxC` in Figure 6), the intermediate result $(A \times B)$ is copied back from the GPU at the end of the first invocation of `gemm` only to be copied from main memory to GPU memory again for the second invocation. The performance costs for data movement are significant. The problem can be trivially solved by writing code specialized to the problem, such as the `nonmodularFastAxBxC` in the figure. However, the code is no longer as easily reused.

Within a single address space, such code modularity issues can often be addressed with a layer of indirection and encapsulation for GPU-side resources. However, the problem of optimizing data movement inevitably becomes an OS-level issue as other devices and resources interact with the GPU or GPUs. With OS-level support, computations that involves GPUs and OS-managed resources such as cameras, network cards, and file systems can avoid problems like double-buffering.

By decoupling data flow from algorithm, PTask eliminates difficult tradeoffs between modularity and performance (design goal (3)): the run-time automatically avoids unnecessary data movement (design goal (2)). With PTask, matrix multiplication is expressed as a graph with A and B as inputs to one `gemm` node; the output of that node becomes an input to another `gemm` node that also takes C as input. The programmer expresses only the structure of the computation and the system is responsible for materializing a consistent view of the data in a memory domain *only when it is ac-*

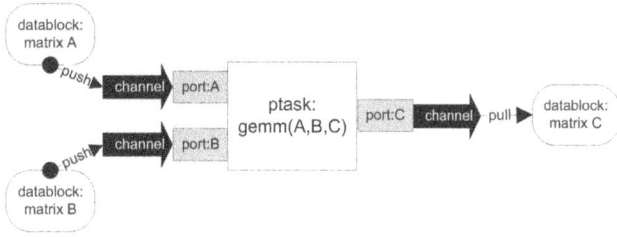

Figure 7: A dataflow graph for matrix multiplication.

tually needed. For example, the system knows that the intermediate result ($A \times B$) is both produced and consumed by the GPU, so it can avoid moving that intermediate result to and from CPU memory at run-time. The code for gemm remains modular, and there is no performance penalty for composition.

Dataflow is also an attractive programming model for GPUs and heterogeneous platforms because a DAG explicitly expresses concurrency without telling the system how to leverage that concurrency. On a machine with multiple GPUs, a PTask graph can take advantage of them with *no* modifications (see Section 6.4); current GPU frameworks require significant additional work from the programmer to use multiple GPUs.

3.3 Limitations

The PTask programming model is based on dataflow, and it allows only directed acyclic graphs, so some limitations are inherent. PTask does not support dynamic graphs, and consequently, problems that are not well-expressed as static graphs, such as those featuring recursion, are not easily expressed with PTask. Data-dependent loop iteration can be handled by unrolling loops into linear sections of the graph along with conditional execution of GPU code (i.e. if the graph represents an conservative unrolling of a loop, some vertices will not always execute). PTask does not fundamentally limit the programmer's ability to express algorithms that do not map easily to a data flow model, because the programmer can always work with PTask graphs containing only a single ptask. For example, an algorithm that requires data-dependent loop bounds can be expressed as a single-ptask graph, where iteration conditions are computed on the host, much as such programs are currently expressed.

4. PTASK API

The PTask API is built on the OS-level abstractions listed below. Supporting these new abstractions at the OS interface entails new system calls shown in Table 1. The additional system calls are analogous to the process API, inter-process communication API, and scheduler hint API in POSIX.

PTask. A ptask is analogous to the traditional OS process abstraction, but a ptask runs substantially on a GPU or other accelerator. A ptask requires some orchestration from the OS to coordinate its execution, but does not always require a user-mode host process. Each ptask has a list of input and output resources (analogous to the POSIX `stdin`, `stdout`, `stderr` file descriptors) that can be bound to ports.

Port. A port is an object in the kernel namespace that can be bound to ptask input and output resources. A port is a data source or sink for dynamically bound data and parameters in GPU code. Ports have sub-types **InputPort**, **OutputPort**, and **StickyPort**. The former two represent inputs and outputs respectively, while the latter represents an input which can retain its value across multiple invocations of a ptask.

PTask system call	Description
`sys_open_graph`	Create/open a graph
`sys_open_port`	Create/open a port
`sys_open_ptask`	Create/open a ptask
`sys_open_channel`	Create and bind a channel
`sys_open_template`	Create/open a template
`sys_push`	Write to a channel/port
`sys_pull`	Read from a channel/port
`sys_run_graph`	Run a graph
`sys_terminate_graph`	Terminate graph
`sys_set_ptask_prio`	Set ptask priority
`sys_set_geometry`	Set iteration space

Table 1: PTask API system calls.

Channel. A channel is analogous to a POSIX pipe: it connects a port to another port, or to other data sources and sinks in the system such as I/O buses, files, and so on. A channel can connect only a single source and destination port; InputPorts and StickyPorts can connect to only a single channel, while an OutputPort can connect to many channels.

Graphs. A graph is collection of ptasks whose ports are connected by channels. Multiple graphs may be created and executed independently, with the PTask runtime being responsible for scheduling them fairly.

Datablock and Template. A datablock represents a unit of data flow along an edge in a graph. A template provides meta-data describing datablocks, and helps map the raw data contained in datablocks to hardware threads on the GPU.

With the PTask API, ptasks encapsulate GPU code, and variables in GPU code are exposed with ports. The programmer composes computations by connecting ports to channels, indicating that data flowing through those channels should be bound dynamically to those variables. A ptask will execute when all its InputPorts have available data, and will produce data at its OutputPorts as a result. Figure 7 shows a PTask graph for the gemm multiplication computation discussed in Section 3.2. The variables for matrices A, B, and C in the gemm GPU code are exposed using ports:"port:A", "port:B", and "port:C". At run-time, datablocks containing input and output matrices are *pushed* by application code into input channels, causing the ptask to execute, and allowing a datablock containing the result matrix to be *pulled* from the output channel. A single template, which is not shown in the figure, provides meta-data describing the memory layout of matrices, allowing the runtime to orchestrate the computation.

4.1 Dataflow through the Graph

Data flows through a PTask graph as discrete datablocks, moving through channels, and arriving at ports which represent ptask inputs or outputs. When all a ptask's input ports have received data through a channel, the ptask can execute, producing output at its output ports.

Ports can be either "Occupied" or "Unoccupied", depending on whether the port holds a datablock or not. The three sub-types of Port behave differently. An InputPort reads datablocks from an associated up-stream channel. If Unoccupied, it will read the next datablock from the channel as soon as the channel is not empty. An OutputPort acts as a conduit: an Occupied port pushes its datablock to all its down-stream channels. Unlike the other port types, OutputPorts can be bound to multiple channels. The StickyPort type is a specialization of InputPort that retains its datablock and remains

238

in the Occupied state until a new datablock is written into its channel. The PTask run-time maintains a thread-pool from which it assigns threads to ptasks as necessary: port data movement (as well as GPU dispatch) is performed by threads from this pool. Ports have a *ptflags* member which indicates whether the port is bound to GPU-side resources or is consumed by the run-time. The *ptflags* also indicate whether datablocks flowing through that port are treated as in/out parameters by GPU code.

Channels have parameterizable (non-zero) *capacity*, which is the number of datablocks that the channel may queue between consuming them from its source and passing them to its destination in FIFO order. An application pushes data (using `sys_push`) into channels. If the channel is not ready (because it already has datablocks queued up to its capacity), the `sys_push` call blocks until the channel has available capacity. Likewise, a `sys_pull` call on a channel will block until a datablock arrives at that channel.

4.1.1 Datablocks and Templates

Data flows through a graph as discrete datablocks, even if the external input to and/or output from the graph is a continuous stream of data values. Datablocks refer to and are described by template objects (see below) which are meta-data describing the dimensions and layout of data in the block. The datablock abstraction provides a coherent view on data that may migrate between memory spaces. Datablocks encapsulate buffers in multiple memory spaces using a *buffer-map* property whose entries map memory spaces to device-specific buffer objects. The *buffer-map* tracks which buffer(s) represent the most up-to-date view(s) of the underlying data, enabling a datablock to materialize views in different memory spaces on demand. For example, a datablock may be created based on a buffer in CPU memory. When a ptask is about to execute using that datablock, the runtime will notice that no corresponding buffer exists in the GPU memory space where the ptask has been scheduled, and will create that view accordingly. The converse occurs for data written by the GPU—buffers in the CPU memory domain will be populated lazily based on the GPU version only when a request for that data occurs. Datablocks contain a *record-count* member, used to help manage downstream memory allocation for computations that work with record streams or variable-stride data (see below). Datablocks can be pushed concurrently into multiple channels, can be shared across processes, and are garbage-collected based on reference counts.

Iteration Space.

GPU hardware executes in a SIMT (**S**ingle **I**nstruction **M**ultiple **T**hread) fashion, allocating a hardware thread for each point in an iteration space.[2] Hence, the data items on which a particular GPU thread operates must be deduced in GPU code from a unique identifier assigned to each thread. For example, in vector addition, each hardware thread sums the elements at a single index; the iteration space is set of all vector indices, and each thread multiplies its identifier by the element stride to find the offset of the elements it will add. To execute code on the GPU, the PTask run-time must know the iteration space to correctly configure the number of GPU threads. For cases where the mapping between GPU threads and the iteration space is not straightforward (e.g. because threads compute on multiple points in the iteration space, or because input elements do not have fixed stride), the `sys_set_geometry` call allows the programmer to specify GPU thread parameters explic-

itly. In the common case, the run-time can infer the iteration space and GPU thread configuration from templates.

Templates.

Templates provide meta-data that describes the raw data in a datablock's buffers. A template contains a *dimensions* member (stride and three-dimensional array bounds), and a *dbtflags* member that indicates whether the data should be treated as an array of fixed-stride elements, a stream of variable-sized elements, or an opaque byte array. The *dbtflags* also indicate the type(s) of resource(s) the data will be bound to at execution time: examples include buffers in GPU global memory, buffers in GPU constant memory, or formal parameters. Templates serve several purposes. First, they allow the run-time to infer the iteration space when it is not specified by the programmer. In the common case, the iteration space is completely described by the product of the stride and array bounds, and the GPU should launch a hardware thread for every point in the iteration space. Second, templates bound to ports enable the run-time to allocate datablocks that will be consumed by internal and output channels in the graph. Finally, templates enable the run-time to give reasonable feedback to the programmer when API calls are mis-used. For example, constructing a channel requires a template; channel creation fails if either the source or destination port has a template that specifies an incompatible geometry. Similarly, attempts to push datablocks into channels also fail on any template mismatch.

4.1.2 Handling irregular data

Computations on data that lack a fixed stride require templates that describe a variable-geometry, meaning that data-layout is only available dynamically. In such cases, a template fundamentally can not carry sufficient information for the run-time to deduce the iteration space. Use of a variable-geometry channel requires an additional meta-data channel containing per-element geometry information. A meta-data channel carries, at some fixed stride, information that can be used by hardware threads as a map for data in the other channel. For example, if one input channel carries datablocks with records of variable length, its meta-data channel carries datablocks of integers indicating the offset and length of each record in datablocks received on the first channel.

PTask must use templates to allocate datablocks for downstream channels, because the programmer does not write code to allocate datablocks (except for those pushed into input channels), and because the runtime materializes device-side and host-side views of buffers on demand, typically after the datablock itself is allocated. For fixed-stride computations, allocating output datablocks is straightforward: the buffer size is the product of the stride and dimensions of the template. For computations that may produce a variable-length output (such as a select or join), the runtime needs additional information. To address this need, a template on an OutputPort with its variable-size record stream *ptflags* set contains a pointer to an InputPort which is designated to provide output size information. That InputPort's *ptflags* must indicate that it is bound to a run-time input, indicating it is used by the runtime and not by GPU-side code. The run-time generates an output size for each upstream invocation.

Computations with dynamically determined output sizes require this structure because memory allocated on the GPU must be allocated by a call from the host: dynamic memory allocation in GPU code is generally not possible.[3] Consequently, the canonical approach is to first run a computation on the GPU that determines

---

[2] The iteration space is the set of all possible assignments of control variables in a loop nest. Conceptually, GPUs execute subsets of an iteration space in parallel.

---

[3] Although some support for device-side memory allocation has

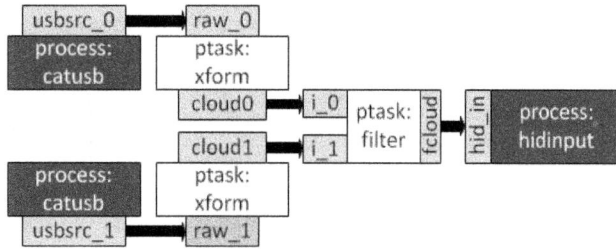

Figure 8: A dataflow graph for the gesture recognition system using the ptask, port, and channel abstractions.

output size and computes a map of offsets where each hardware thread writes its output. The map of offsets is used to allocate output buffers and is consumed as an additional input to the original computation [30, 34, 35]. In short, we argue that all variable-length GPU computations follow this type of structure, and while the pattern may be burdensome to the programmer, that burden is fundamental to GPU programming, and is not imposed by the PTask programming model. The PTask API enables any variable-geometry structures that are possible with other GPU programming frameworks.

4.2 PTask invocation

A ptask can be in one of four states: **Waiting** (for inputs), **Queued** (inputs available, waiting for a GPU), **Executing** (running on the GPU), or **Completed** (finished execution, waiting to have its outputs consumed). When all of a ptask's input ports are Occupied, the runtime puts the ptask on a run queue and transitions it from Waiting to Queued. A ptask is *invoked* when it is at the head of the run queue and a GPU is available that is capable[4] of running it: invocation is the transition from the Queued to Executing state. When a ptask is invoked, the runtime reads the Datablocks occupying that ptask's InputPorts. For any non-sticky InputPort, this will remove the datablock from the port and will cause the port to pull from its upstream channel; the port goes to the Unoccupied state if the upstream channel is empty. In contrast, a StickyPort remains in the Occupied state when the runtime reads its datablock. When the runtime identifies that it has compute resources available, it chooses a ptask in the Queued state. Scheduling algorithms are considered in more detail in Section 5.1. Upon completion of an invocation, the runtime sets a ptask's state to Completed, and moves its output datablocks to its OutputPorts, if and only if all the output ports are in the Unoccupied state. The ptask remains in the Completed state until all its output ports are occupied, after which it is returned to the Waiting state. The Completed state is necessary because channels have finite capacity. As a result it is possible for execution on the GPU to complete before a downstream channel drains.

4.3 Gestural Interface PTask Graph

The gestural interface system can be expressed as a PTask graph (see Figure 8), yielding multiple advantages. First, the graph eliminates unnecessary communication. A channel connects USB source ports (usbsrc_0, usbsrc_1) to image input ports (rawimg_0, rawimg_1). Data transfer across this channel eliminates double buffering by sharing a buffer between the USB device driver, PTask run-time, and GPU driver, or with hardware support, going directly

---

arrived with CUDA 4.0, GPUs and their programming frameworks in general do not support it.

[4]A system may have multiple GPUs with different features, and a ptask can only run on GPUs that supports all features it requires.

from the USB device to GPU memory, rather than taking an unnecessary detour through system memory. A channel connecting the output port of xform (cloud_*) to the inputs (i_*) port of the filter ptask can avoid data copying altogether by reusing the output of one ptask as the input of the next. Because the two **xform** ptasks and the **filter** ptasks run on the GPU, the system can detect that the source and destination memory domains are the same and elide any data movement as a result.

This PTask-based design also minimizes involvement of host-based user-mode applications to coordinate common GPU activities. For example, the arrival of data at the raw image input of the xform program can trigger the computation for the new frame using interrupt handlers in the OS, rather than waiting for a host-based program to be scheduled to start the GPU-based processing of the new frame. The only application-level code required to cause data to move through the system is the sys_pull call on the output channel of the **hidinput** process.

Under this design, the graph expresses concurrency that the runtime exploits without requiring the programmer to write code with explicit threads. Data captured from different camera perspectives can be processed in parallel. When multiple GPUs are present, or a single GPU with support for concurrent kernels [5], the two **xform** PTasks can execute concurrently. Regardless of what GPU-level support for concurrency is present in the system, the PTask design leverages the pipeline parallelism expressed in the graph, for example, by performing data movement along channels in parallel with ptask execution on both the host and the CPU. No code modifications are required by the programmer for the system to take advantage of any of these opportunities for concurrency.

5. IMPLEMENTATION

We have implemented the PTask design described in Section 3 on Windows 7, and integrated it both into a stand-alone user-mode library, and into the device driver for the photogrammetric cameras used in the gestural interface.

The stand-alone library allows us to evaluate the benefits of the model in isolation from the OS. The user-mode framework supports ptasks coded in HLSL (DirectX), CUDA, and OpenCL, implementing dataflow graph support on top of DirectX 11, the CUDA 4.0 driver-API, and the OpenCL implementation provided with NVIDIA's GPU Computing Toolkit 4.0.

The driver-integrated version emulates kernel-level support for ptasks. When ptasks run in the driver, we assign a range of ioctl codes in 1:1 correspondence with the system call interface shown in table 1, allowing applications other than the gestural interface to use the PTask API by opening a handle to the camera driver, and calling ioctl (DeviceIoControl in Windows). The driver-level implementation supports only ptasks coded in HLSL, and is built on top of DXGI, which is the system call interface Windows 7 provides to manage the graphics pipeline.

GPU drivers are vendor-specific and proprietary, so no kernel-facing interface exists to control GPUs. While this remains the case, kernel-level management of GPUs must involve some user-mode component. The Windows Driver Foundation [7] enables a layered design for drivers, allowing us to implement the camera driver as a combination kernel-mode (KMDF) and user-mode (UMDF) driver, where responsibilities of the composite driver are split between kernel- and user-mode components. The component that manages the cameras runs in kernel mode, while the component that implements PTask runs in user-mode. The two components avoid data copy across the user/kernel boundary by mapping the memory used to buffer raw data from the cameras into the address space of the user-mode driver. When the kernel-mode component has captured a new set of frames from a camera, it signals the user-mode component, which can begin working directly on the captured data without requiring buffer copy.

The PTask library comprises roughly 8000 lines of C and C++ code, and the camera driver is implemented in about 3000 lines of C. Code to assemble and manage the ptask graph for the gestural interface introduces approximately an additional 400 LOC.

5.1 PTask Scheduling

PTask scheduling faces several challenges. First, GPU hardware cannot currently be preempted or context-switched, ruling out traditional approaches to time-slicing hardware. Second, true integration with the process scheduler is not currently possible due to lack of an OS-facing interface to control the GPU in Windows. Third, when multiple GPUs are present in a system, data locality becomes the primary determinant of performance. Parallel execution on multiple GPUs may not always be profitable, because the increased latency due to data migration can be greater than the latency reduction gained through concurrency.

Our prototype implements four scheduling modes, **first-available**, **fifo**, **priority**, and **data-aware**. In **first-available** mode, every ptask is assigned a manager thread, and those threads compete for available accelerators. Ready ptasks are not queued in this mode, so when ready ptasks outnumber available accelerators, access is arbitrated by locks on the accelerator data structures. In the common case, with only a single accelerator, this approach is somewhat reasonable because dataflow signaling will wake up threads that need the lock anyway. The **fifo** policy enhances the **first-available** policy with queuing.

In **priority mode**, ptasks are enhanced with a static priority, and proxy priority. The proxy priority is the OS priority of the thread managing its invocation and data flows. Proxy priority allows the system to avoid *priority laundering*, where the priority of the requesting process is ineffective because requests run with the priority of threads in the PTask run-time rather than with the priority of the requester. Proxy priority avoids this by enabling a ptask's manager thread to assume the priority of a requesting process. A ptask's static and proxy priority can both be set with the `sys_set_ptask_prio` system call.

The scheduler manages a ready queue of ptasks, and a list of available accelerators. When any ptask transitions into Queued, Executing, or Completed state, a scheduler thread wakes up and computes an effective priority value for each ptask in the queue. The effective priority is the weighted sum of the ptask's static priority and boost values derived from its current wait time, its average wait time (computed with an exponential moving average), average run time, and its proxy priority. Weights are chosen such that, in general, a ptask's effective priority will increase if a) it has longer than average wait time, b) it has lower than average GPU run time, or c) its proxy priority is high. Boosting priority in response to long waits avoids starvation, boosting in response to short run times increases throughput by preferring low-latency PTasks, and boosting for high proxy priority helps the PTask scheduler respect the priority of the OS process scheduler. Pseudo-code for computing effective priority is shown in Figure 9. When the effective priority update is complete, the scheduler sorts the ready queue in descending order of effective priority.

To assign an accelerator to a ptask, the scheduler first considers the head of the queue, and chooses from the list of available accelerators based on *fitness* and *strength*. An accelerator's fitness is a function of whether the accelerator supports the execution environment and feature set required by the ptask: unfit accelerators are simply eliminated from the pool of candidates. The strength of the

```
void update_eff_prio(ptasks) {
  avg_gpu = avg_gpu_time(ptasks);
  avg_cwait = avg_current_wait(ptasks);
  avg_dwait = avg_decayed_wait(ptasks);
  avg_pprio = avg_proxy_prio(ptasks);
  foreach(p in ptasks) {
    boost = W_0*(p->last_cwait - avg_cwait);
    boost += W_1*(p->avg_wait - avg_dwait);
    boost += W_2*(p->avg_gpu - avg_gpu);
    boost += W_3*(p->proxy_prio - avg_pprio);
    p->eff_prio = p->prio + boost;
}}
gpu match_gpu(ptask) {
  gpu_list = available_gpus();
  remove_unfit(gpu_list, ptask);
  sort(gpu_list); // by descending strength
  return remove_head(gpu_list);
}
void schedule() {
  update_eff_prio(ptasks);
  sort(ptasks); // by descending eff prio
  while(gpus_available() && size(ptasks)>0) {
    foreach(p in ptasks) {
      best_gpu = match_gpu(p);
      if(best_gpu != null) {
        remove(ptasks, p);
        p->dispatch_gpu = best_gpu;
        signal_dispatch(p);
        return;
}}}}
```

Figure 9: Pseudo-code for algorithms used by PTask's priority scheduling algorithm.

accelerator is the product of the number of cores, the core clock speed, and the memory clock speed: in our experience, this is an imperfect but effective heuristic for ranking accelerators such that low-latency execution is preferred. The scheduler always chooses the strongest accelerator when a choice is available. If the scheduler is unable to assign an accelerator to the ptask at the head of the queue, it iterates over the rest of the queue until an assignment can be made. If no assignment can be made, the scheduler blocks. On a successful assignment, the scheduler removes the ptask from the queue, assigns the accelerator to it, moves the ptask to Executing state, and signals the ptask's manager thread that it can execute. The scheduler thread repeats this process until it runs out of available accelerators or ptasks on the run queue, and then blocks waiting for the next scheduler-relevant event. Pseudo-code for scheduling and matching accelerators to ptasks is shown in Figure 9 as the `schedule` and `match_gpu` functions respectively.

The **data-aware** mode uses the same effective priority system that the **priority** policy uses, but alters the accelerator selection algorithm to consider the memory spaces where a ptask's inputs are currently up-to-date. If a system supports multiple GPUs, the inputs required by a ptask may have been most recently written in the memory space of another GPU. The dataaware policy finds the accelerator where the majority of a ptask's inputs are up-to-date, designating it the ptask's preferred accelerator. If the preferred accelerator is available, the scheduler assigns it. Otherwise, the scheduler examines the ptask's effective priority to decide whether to schedule it on an accelerator that requires data migration. PTasks with high effective priority relative to a parameterizable threshold (empirically determined) will be assigned to the strongest fit available accelerator. If a ptask has low effective priority the scheduler will leave it on on the queue in hopes that its preferred accelerator will become available again soon. The policy is not work-conserving: it is possible that Queued ptasks do not execute even when accelerators are available. However, waiting for a preferred accelerator often incurs lower latency than migrating data between memory spaces. The system guarantees that a ptask will eventually execute, because long wait time will cause effective priority boosts that ultimately ensure it runs on its preferred accelerator or runs elsewhere.

5.2 Prototype limitations

It is the express vision of this work that all GPU computations use ptasks. This vision can only be enforced if all access to the GPU is mediated by a kernel-mode implementation of PTask. Because a substantial part of our prototype must run in user-mode, it remains possible for processes to access the GPU directly, potentially subverting the fairness and isolation mechanisms of our prototype. This limitation is a property of our prototype and is not fundamental to the proposed system.

The scheduling implementations in our prototype do not consider GPU memory demands that exceed the physical memory on GPUs. GPU drivers use swapping to virtualize GPU physical memory, but allow the programmer to create buffers in the GPU memory that cannot be swapped. Because our prototype mostly allocates unswappable resources, some additional memory management would be required to ensure that a PTask's inputs can always be materialized on the GPU under high memory load. Our prototype does not address this problem.

5.3 GPU scheduling on Linux

We do not port the PTask API to Linux, rather we exploit our control over the kernel and add GPU accounting state to Linux's `task_struct`, the data structure that holds information about a kernel thread. We add blocking system calls that inform the kernel about GPU activity. GPU kernel preemption is not supported by the hardware, which limits scheduling to non-preemptive policies enforced at GPU kernel boundaries. The GPU driver actually places computations on the GPU, but source code for commercial drivers for CUDA and OpenCL are not available, so we manually insert the Linux system calls into applications that use the GPU. By giving the kernel visibility into GPU use, it can enforce global properties, like fairness relative to scheduling priority.

The kernel uses a non-work-conserving scheduling algorithm similar to the token bucket algorithm. The choice of the algorithm is dictated by GPU execution being non-preemptive. Each process p using a GPU maintains its GPU budget B_p which reflects the current eligibility of a process to use the GPU. B_p is reduced by the execution time (t_p) used by p each time it executes on the GPU. B_p is incremented once per period T by quanta q to regain GPU access. If a process has a negative GPU budget, then the kernel will block any GPU invocation until the budget becomes positive. The actual GPU share of a process is governed by the maximum budget $Bmax_p$, which is set proportionally to the Linux priority n_p of the process p. The maximum budget $Bmax_p$ and the replenish period T are updated dynamically by the scheduler by taking into account dynamic GPU execution time and changes in the number of processes using a GPU. Namely, $Bmax_p = \frac{n_p}{\sum_{i \in P} n_i} \sum_{i \in P} t_i$ and $q = T = \alpha * \min_{i \in P} t_i$, where P denotes the set of kernel threads using a GPU and $\alpha \leq 1$ is a safety coefficient to avoid idling due to clock quantization. These values are updated upon every GPU completion, invocation or completion of a process using a GPU, and every 10 µsec, which is about an order of magnitude lower than the expected GPU kernel time.

The scheduler maintains the running average of the GPU usage time by each process. It assumes periodic GPU execution, which typically holds for GPU-bound workloads. TimeGraph [45] uses a similar scheduler but with statically assigned parameters.

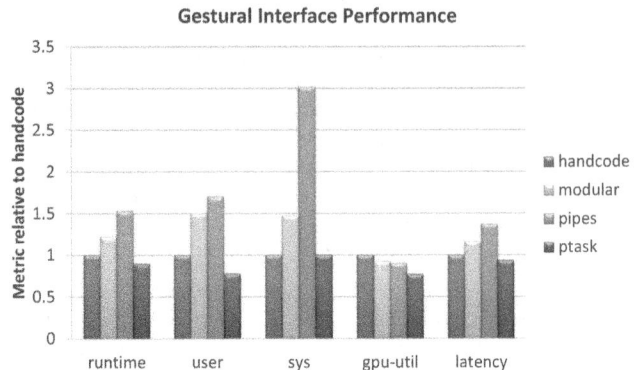

Gestural Interface Performance

Figure 10: Relative performance metrics for different gestural interface implementations. The runtime column shows the relative wall-clock time taken for each implementation to process 1000 frames. User, system, and gpu-util are the relative user time, system time, and gpu utilization. The latency column is the relative end-to-end latency for a single frame. In all columns, lower is better.

6. EVALUATION

In this section, we evaluate our PTask prototype using a gestural UI on Windows 7, an encrypted file system on Linux, and microbenchmarks. Our experience with the gestural interface shows that kernel-level management of objects in a PTask graph is necessary to provide optimal data movement in the general case. Our work with the encrypted file system in Linux shows that OS visibility into GPU usage is necessary for the OS to provide fairness and isolation.

6.1 Gestural interface

The primary benefits of leveraging a GPU for gestural interface come from offloading work to the GPU. In this section, we show that GPU-offload is required to make a gestural interface possible, and we quantify the costs incurred by the offload and supporting framework. To this end, we compare the performance of five gestural interface implementations: *host-based, handcode, pipes, modular*, and *ptask*.

The *host-based* implementation uses a Quad-Core CPU to perform all steps of the computation in the user-mode component of the camera driver. This implementation provides a performance baseline, and does not use the GPU. The *handcode* version is implemented in the user-mode component of the camera driver using DXGI system calls to offload work to the GPU. This version is hand-coded to avoid all needless data copy where subsequent GPU-kernels have a producer-consumer relationship. The *pipes* implementation uses four separate processes connected by pipes, as described in Section 2. To avoid double-buffering, raw camera data buffers used by the kernel-mode component of the camera driver are mapped into the address space of the `catusb` program, and the driver signals when new data is available. The `xform` and `filter` programs read data from pipes, invoke GPU-kernels and write results to pipes. We consider this implementation because it is modular and composable. The *modular* version is uses the same module design used to build the *pipes* version, but includes all components in a single process. This eliminates IPC overheads incurred by using pipes to communicate between modules, while still incurring overheads for migrating data to and from the GPU at module boundaries. The *PTask* implementation is described in detail in Section 5. It uses the PTask runtime in the camera driver, and

impl			fps	tput (MB/s)	lat (ms)	user	sys	gpu	gmem	thrds	ws-delta
Core2-Quad	host-based	real-time	20.2	35.8	36.6	78.1	3.9	–	–	1	–
GTX580	handcode	real-time	30	53.8	10.5	4.0	5.3	21.0	138	1	–
		unconstrained	138	248.2	–	2.4	6.4	41.8	138	1	–
	modular	real-time	30	53.8	12.2	6.0	8.1	19.4	72	1	0.8 (1%)
		unconstrained	113	202.3	–	5.7	8.6	55.7	72	1	0.9 (1%)
	pipes	real-time	30	53.8	14.4	6.8	16.6	18.9	72	3	45.3 (58%)
		unconstrained	90	161.9	–	12.4	24.6	55.4	76	3	46.3 (59%)
	ptask	real-time	30	53.8	9.8	3.1	5.5	16.1	71	7	0.7 (1%)
		unconstrained	154	275.3	–	4.9	8.8	65.7	79	7	1.4 (2%)

Table 2: Gestural interface performance on a Core-2 Quad, and an NVIDIA GTX 580 GPU. PTasks achieve higher maximum throughput than a hand-coded implementation and can support real-time data rates with low CPU utilization. The fps column is camera frames-per-second, tput is throughput in MB/s, lat is end-to-end latency (time from capture to delivered user-input). CPU utilization is broken down into user and kernel (sys) percentages. The gpu and gmem columns are GPU utilization and GPU memory usage. The thrds column is number of threads, and ws-delta is the increase (in MB) of the main memory footprint over the handcode version. The host-based implementation cannot deliver real-time frame rates, so the real-time and unconstrained implementations have identical performance.

uses ptasks to perform the **xform** and **filter** steps of on the GPU. The **hidinput** step is performed on the CPU in the camera driver.

We compare these four implementations in a "real-time" mode and an "unconstrained" mode. The former is the deployment target: the two cameras in the system drive all data flow. In "unconstrained", the system is driven by in-memory recordings of 1,000 frames of raw camera data, allowing us to measure maximum throughput for implementations that would otherwise be I/O bound. In "real-time" mode we are primarily concerned with utilization and end-to-end latency, while for "unconstrained", throughput is the primary metric.

The PTask infrastructure incurs overheads: additional memory to represent the graph (ports, channels, ptasks, the scheduler), and additional threads to drive the system. We measure the total number of threads used by the system as well as the change in memory footprint over the simplest hand-coded implementation. Table 2 and Figure 10 characterize the performance of the gestural interface system running on the Core2-Quad, and on an NVIDIA GTX580 GPU. The data include frames-per-second, throughput, end-to-end latency, CPU utilization (broken down into user/kernel), gpu utilization, the number of threads, and memory footprint delta.

The PTask implementation outperforms all others. The CPU-based implementation achieves a frame rate of only 20 frames per second, a mere 67% of the real-time frame rate of the cameras, using 82% of the CPU to do so. The bilateral filtering in the **filter** step is the primary bottleneck. The *pipes* version achieves real-time frame rates, using more than 23% of the CPU to do it, consuming about 45% more memory than the hand-coded and *ptask*. Both the *handcode* and *ptask* implementations deliver very low CPU utilization at real-time frame rates (9.3% and 8.6% respectively) but *ptask* achieves the highest throughput, outstripping *handcode* by 11.6%. Outperforming *handcode* is significant because the *handcode* system enjoys all the data movement optimizations that the *ptask* version enjoys: *ptask* has higher throughput because it overlaps communication and computation in ways the *handcode* system does not. The PTask implementation is not only significantly lower in code complexity, but retains a level of modularity that the handcode version sacrifices.

6.2 GPU sharing on Linux

We ran EncFS [29], a FUSE-based encrypted file system for Linux, modified to use a GPU for AES encryption and decryption. We used an NVIDIA GTX470 GPU and Intel Core i5 3.20GHz CPU, on a machine with 12GB of RAM and two SATA SSD 80GB drives connected in striped RAID configuration using the standard Linux software raid driver (md). We implemented AES with the XTS chaining mode, which is suitable for parallel hardware without compromising the cipher strength, and is now the standard mode used for encryption of storage devices [3]. We configured FUSE to pass data blocks of up to 1MB from the kernel, and we modified EncFS to pass the entire buffer to the GPU for encryption or decryption. The larger block size amortizes the cost of moving the data to and from the GPU and enables higher degree of parallelism.

A sequential read and write of a 200MB file are 17% and 28% faster for the version of EncFS that uses the GPU than the version that uses the SSL software library implementation (Table 3), with results averaged over five executions.

On Linux, using the GPU can completely defeat the kernel's scheduling priority. With several processes periodically contending for the GPU, the one invoking longer GPU kernels will effectively monopolize the GPU regardless of its OS priority. Our GPU scheduling mechanism in the kernel (§5.3), here called PTSched, eliminates this problem.

Table 3 shows the results of running EncFS concurrently with one or two competing background GPU-bound tasks (a loop of 19ms CUDA program invocations). To evaluate the Linux scheduler in the most favorable light, the GPU-bound tasks are set to the minimum scheduling priority (nice +19) while the EncFS process and its clients have the highest priority (-20). The tasks invoke GPU kernels in a tight loop, which challenges the scheduler. The results show that if Linux is not informed about GPU use, then GPU use can invert scheduling priority, leading to a drastic degradation of file system performance (e.g., a 30× slowdown). Once the kernel is informed of GPU use (the PTSched column), a relatively simple scheduling algorithm restores consistent, system-wide kernel scheduling priority.

Another experiment shows the effort needed to maintain global scheduling priorities (Table 4). We modified EncFS to propagate the client's OS scheduling priority to the EncFS worker thread that services that client's request. Each experiment has two EncFS

	CPU	1 GPU task Linux	1 GPU task PTSched	2 GPU tasks Linux	2 GPU tasks PTSched
read	247 MB/s	$-10.0\times$	$1.16\times$	$-30.9\times$	$1.16\times$
write	82 MB/s	$-8.2\times$	$1.21\times$	$-10.0\times$	$1.20\times$

Table 3: Bandwidth measurements for sequential read or write of a 200MB file on an encrypted file system, relative to the CPU performing encryption (CPU column). Negative numbers indicate reduced bandwidth. There are one or two concurrently executing background GPU-heavy tasks, running with the default Linux scheduler (Linux) or our scheduler (PTSched).

r/w (nice)	MB/s Linux	MB/s PTSched
read (0)	170	132
read (-20)	171	224
write (0)	58	51
write (-20)	58	75

Table 4: Bandwidth measurements for sequential read or write of a 200MB file on an encrypted file system by two EncFS clients that have different nice values (0 or -20).

threads of different nice values doing a read or write concurrently on two CPUs, but contending for the GPU. Without our GPU OS scheduling (Linux), the client throughput is not affected by the client's nice level. With PTSched, the client with higher priority (nice -20) achieves higher throughput at the expense of reduced throughput for the lower priority client. Note the aggregate throughput of this experiment is about 25% higher than the above experiment (e.g., 356 MB/s read bandwidth vs. 286 MB/s) because it uses two CPUs and EncFS has significant CPU work.

6.3 Microbenchmarks: benefits of dataflow

To demonstrate that PTask can improve performance and eliminate unnecessary data migration, we show that composition of basic GPU-accelerated programs into a dataflow graph can outperform not only designs that rely on IPC mechanisms such as pipes, but can also outperform programs that are hand-coded to minimize data movement.

The micro-benchmarks we measure are shown in Table 5. The benchmarks include bitonic `sort`, matrix multiplication (`gemm`), matrix additions (`madd`), and matrix copy (`mcopy`) kernels. To explore the impact on performance of different graph shapes, and relative costs of data copy and GPU-execution latency, we consider a range of data sizes (matrices ranging from 64×64 through 1024×1024), and graphs structured both as binary trees (for example, $((A \times B) \times (C \times D))$) and graphs structured as "rectangles", where each column is an independent computation (for example, $((A \times B) \times C)$ running concurrently with with $((D \times E) \times F)$ is a rectangular graph 2 columns wide and 2 rows deep). This allows us to explore a range of graph sizes and shapes for `gemm`, `madd`, and `mcopy`.

To illustrate the generality of PTask, we also consider four higher-level benchmarks including bitonic `sort`, `fdtd`, `pca`, and `grpby`. Bitonic sort is an example of a workload where the shape and size of the graph is fundamentally tied to the input dimensions. Bitonic sort is performed on a GPU as a series of pair-wise sort steps, alternated with transposition steps that effectively change the stride of the pairwise comparisons in the subsequent sort step. We express this as a linear graph connected by channels of 41 ptasks that implement either the sort or the transposition. The `pca` workload

bnc	description	P_{min}	P_{max}	C_{min}	C_{max}
gemm	matrix multiply	4	60	14	190
sort	bitonic sort	13	41	29	84
madd	matrix addition	4	60	14	190
mcopy	matrix copy	2	30	7	95
fdtd	3d stencil	30	60	85	170
pca	principal components	229	1197	796	4140
grpby	group by	7	7	13	13

Table 5: Micro-benchmarks evaluated across a range of PTask graph sizes and shapes. P_{min} and P_{max} are the number of ptasks, while C_{min} and C_{max} are the number of channels in the smallest and largest graphs.

implements the iterative principal components analysis described by Andrecut [9]. We compute the first three components for each matrix with 10 and 54 iterations per component, which exceeds 95% and 99% convergence respectively for all cases. The graph for 10 iterations uses 229 ptasks and 796 channels, while the 54 iteration graph uses 1197 ptasks and 4140 channels. The `grpby` workload uses a graph of 7 ptasks and 9 channels to implement a "group by" operation over a range of integers (0.5, 1, and 2 million) and a known number of unique keys (128, 256, and 512). The `fdtd` workload is an electromagnetic analysis tool implementing a Finite Difference Time Domain model of a hexahedral cavity with conducting walls [44], running 10 iterations over a stream of inputs of lengths 5 and 10.

For each benchmark, we compare the performance of four different implementations: single-threaded modular, modular, hand-coded, and PTask. The *single-threaded modular* implementation performs the equivalent computation as a sequence of calls to a subroutine that encapsulates the calling of the underlying operation on the GPU. For example, for matrix addition, a single-thread makes a sequence of calls to a subroutine called `matrix_add`, which copies two matrices to the GPU, performs the addition, and copies the result back to host memory. The configuration is called modular because the subroutine can be freely composed, but as we saw in Figure 6, this modularity comes at the cost of unnecessary data copies to and from the GPU. The *modular* implementation performs the equivalent computation using the same strategy for encapsulating operations on the GPU that is used in the *single-threaded modular* implementation, but makes liberal use of multi-threading to attempt to hide the latency of data movement, overlapping data copy to and from the GPU with execution on the GPU. This approach entails a significant level of code complexity for thread management and producer/consumer synchronization, but it does give us a lower bound on the performance of a composed, IPC based implementation (for example `matrix_add A B | matrix_add C`). The *handcode* implementation represents a single-threaded implementation handcoded to minimize data copy, at the expense of sacrificing composability. We consider this case to represent the most likely solution an expert CUDA programmer would choose. The *PTask* implementation executes the workload as a data flow graph as described above. In the case of `pca`, our *handcode* implementation is based on the CUBLAS [58] implementation described in [8].

Performance measurements were taken on a Windows 7 x64 desktop machine with a 4-core Intel Xeon running at 2.67 GHz, 6GB of RAM, and an NVIDIA GeForce GTX 580 GPU which features 512 processing cores and 1.5GB of memory. Data are averaged over

PTask micro-benchmark performance

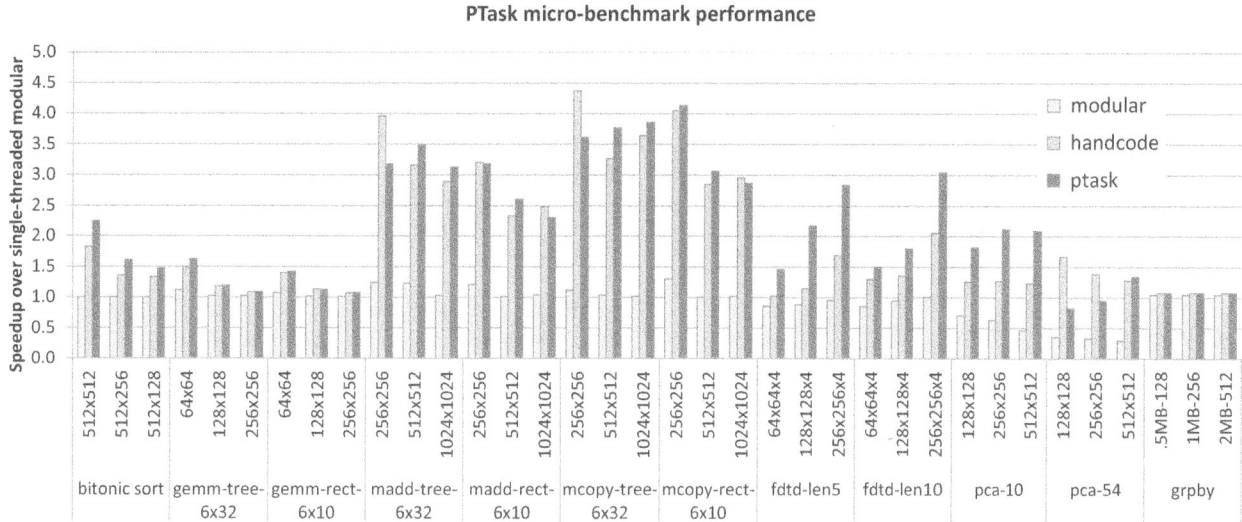

Figure 11: Speedup of various GPU-accelerated implementations of our benchmarks over single-thread, modular GPU-based implementations, for input matrix and image sizes ranging from 64x64 through 1024x1024. The PTask implementation has geometric mean speedup of 10% over handcoded, and $1.93\times$ over modular implementation.

three runs. Figure 11 shows speedup over the single-threaded modular implementation for our modular, handcode, and PTask implementations. The single-threaded modular implementation induces considerable unnecessary data copy, and cannot hide transfer latency, so it is always the slowest. In general, the PTask implementations out-perform the handcode versions because a PTask graph can take advantage of inherent pipeline parallelism to lower end-to-end latency. In some instances the handcode version outperforms PTask (e.g. tree, matrix addition for 6x32 sized graphs). In these cases, PTask overheads such as additional threading, GPU scheduling, and synchronization outstrip performance gains from overlapping GPU-execution and data transfer. The modular implementation is strictly less performant than PTask and handcode, due to unnecessary data migration. The `grpby` workload relies on device-side memory allocation that has to be cleaned up between GPU invocations. Consequently, communication and invocation are synchronous both for PTask and handcode, and PTask's additional overheads make it slightly slower.

Overall, *PTask* has geometric mean speedup of 10% over handcode, and $1.93\times$ over modular implementation, showing that performing these computations in a dataflow manner is worthwhile both in terms of performance and in terms of preserving modularity.

6.4 PTask Scheduling

To evaluate the efficacy of PTask scheduling policies, we add a second GTX 580 to the system described in Section 6.3. Figure 12 shows speedup on 2 GPUs over execution on a single GPU, for three of the scheduling policies defined in Section 5.1: **first-available**, **priority**, and **data-aware** (**fifo** is omitted because it is similar to **first-available**). The data shown represent rectangular graphs of matrix multiplication and addition kernels. All graphs have a breadth of 8, and depth from 1 to 6. Producer-consumer relationships exist only along the vertical axis. The data show that data-aware scheduling is effective at providing scalability. As the PTask graph gets deeper, priority scheduling alone actually hurts performance due to data-oblivious ptask assignment. Migrating a datablock across GPUs must be done through main memory, incur-

Multi-GPU scheduling

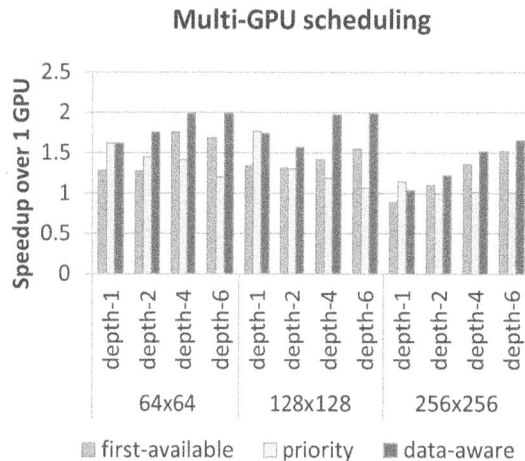

Figure 12: Speedup of PTask using 2 GTX580 GPUs over PTask using 1 GTX580 GPU, for a range of graph sizes using matrix multiplication ptasks. Data for the fifo scheduling policy is omitted because it is similar to that for first-available.

ring high latency. Because the priority algorithm does not consider locality, it induces frequent data-block transfers, making the system slower than the single GPU case for deep graphs. The rate of GPU-GPU migration goes from from an average over all workloads of 3.71% for **first-available** to 14.6% for **priority**. By contrast, the data-aware policy avoids needless data movement, bringing the average over all workloads down to 0.6%. Consequently, scalability generally improves as graph depth improves, because the scheduler can almost always make an assignment that preserves locality.

Figure 13 compares the throughput of our scheduling policies for 4 concurrently running PTask graphs (each of 36 ptasks) on a single GPU. Data for the data-aware policy are omitted because the data-aware and priority policies are identical with just one GPU. The first-available and fifo policies ignore priority completely, but

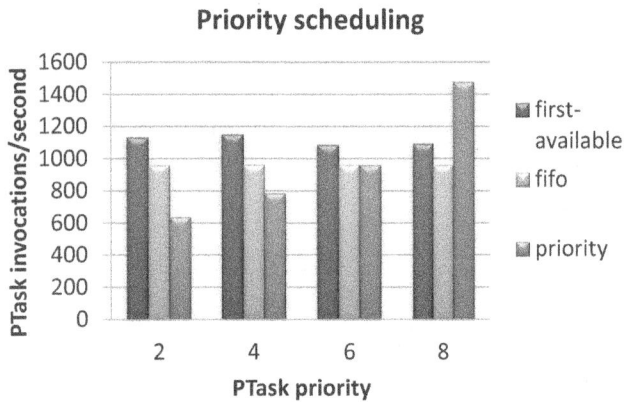

Figure 13: Number of ptask invocations per second on 1 GTX580 GPU for four competing PTask graphs with different ptask priorities (2,4,6,8) using 6x6 rectangular graphs of matrix multiplication ptasks. The trends are the same independent of graph size, shape, or ptask composition. Data for the data-aware policy is not shown because the the priority and data-aware policies are identical when only 1 GPU is present.

the priority policy is able to deliver throughput that increases near-linearly with the priority of the graph.

7. RELATED WORK

General-purpose GPU computing. The research community has focused considerable effort on the problem of providing a general-purpose programming interface to the specialized hardware supported by GPUs (GPGPU). GPGPU computing frameworks such as CUDA [59], OpenCL [47], and others [16,20,33,54,68] provide an expressive platform, but are implemented using heavy-weight user-mode libraries and run-times combined with proprietary GPU device drivers. These systems integrate poorly with the operating system. The programming interfaces provided by these frameworks can be implemented on top of the PTask API.

Offloading. A large body of research has been dedicated to offloading techniques such as channel processors [1], smart disks [22, 46,63], and TCP offload [24]. PTasks make it easier to create applications that offload work to a programmable device by exposing kernel abstractions. The Hydra framework [69] also provides a graph-based dataflow programming model for offloading tasks to peripheral devices. Unlike our work, the Hydra model requires components to communicate using RPC through a common run-time and an API that cannot be supported by current GPU hardware. Hydra cannot provide the fairness and isolation guarantees of PTasks.

OS support and architectural support. The Synthesis kernel [53] orchestrates threads of execution to form a dataflow graph, using *switches* and *pumps* to connect producers and consumers, and allowing interrupts to start threads at nodes in the graph. Synthesis uses dynamic construction of code to orchestrate data movement; in contrast, our abstractions are implemented on top of events, deferred procedure calls, and work queues. PTasks are exposed through the system call interface. The Helios [57] OS supports *satellite kernels*, which communicate via RPC. The Barrelfish OS [15] treats the hardware as a network of independent, heterogeneous cores communicating using RPC. Unlike our model, both Helios and Barrelfish propose abstractions that cannot be supported by current GPUs, which lack the architectural features to run OS code or communicate via RPC.

The Scout operating system [55] supports the construction of optimized code paths, with the goals of enabling modularity while eliminating wasted data copy and improving scheduling by providing the scheduler with richer information about interdependences between modules along a path. PTask's ptasks and ports share some similar to Scout's routers and services respectively. Scout's paths are different from PTask's graphs in that a path is a single path of data through a series of modules, while a graph represents potentially many paths contributing to a single computation. Unlike Scout, PTask graphs can handle fan-out.

The SPIN operating system [19] allows applications to change the OS interface and specialize OS behavior to improve performance. With similar motivation to PTask's channel specialization, SPIN enables data movement optimizations such as direct data streaming between disk and network to eliminate redundant buffering (such as `sendfile`). In SPIN, applications must implement these specializations explicitly, while a major goal of PTask is letting the system take advantage of optimization opportunities where they arise, without programmer intervention.

Gelado et al. propose ADSM [27]—an asymmetric distributed shared memory abstraction, in which in-memory data structures required by GPUs are automatically identified and marshalled to the GPU local memory and back, eliminating unnecessary data transfers. Unlike PTask, ADSM addresses only the data management issues without dealing with GPU scheduling.

Scheduling for heterogeneous processors. The TimeGraph [45] GPU scheduler provides isolation and prioritization capabilities for GPU resource management, targeting real-time environments. Time-Graph does not propose OS abstractions to manage GPUs: priorities are set statically in a file in `/etc/`, making TimeGraph unable to integrate with process priority. The design space of scheduling algorithms and policies for heterogeneous systems [13, 14, 17, 43] has received considerable research attention, along with approaches to dynamic selection between CPU and GPU execution [11, 12, 23, 64]. In contrast, ptasks are bound to either a class of accelerators or a CPU, and can not re-target dynamically.

Dataflow and streaming. Hardware systems such as Intel IXP [40] Imagine [2], and SCORE [21] enable programmers or compilers to express parallel computation as a graph of routines whose edges represent data movement. The classic data flow abstractions proposed for Monsoon and Id [61] target environments in which dataflow execution is supported directly by the processor hardware. A Stream-It [66] application is a graph of nodes which send and receive items to each other over channels. DirectShow [51] supports graph-based parallelism through "filter graphs" in which filters are connected to each other with input and output pins. StreamIt and DirectShow are programming models with dedicated compiler and user-mode runtime support. PTask is a streaming programming model that focuses on integration with OS abstractions.

Dryad [41] is a graph-based fault-tolerant programming model for distributed parallel execution in data center. PTask targets an entirely different execution environment. The Click modular router [49] provides a graph-based programming model. Click is always single-threaded, while PTask makes extensive use of threading to manage execution on and communication with the GPU. CODE2 [56], and P-RIO [52] use similar techniques to PTask to express computation as a graph with the goal of explicitly separating communication from computation at the programmer interface: neither system addresses problems of heterogeneity or OS support.

Sponge [38] is a compilation framework for GPUs using synchronous dataflow (SDF) streaming languages, addressing problems of portability for GPU-side code across different generations of GPUs and CPUs, as well abstracting hardware details such as memory hierarchy and threading models. Like other SDF languages [50] such as LUSTRE [31] and ESTEREL [18], Sponge provides a static schedule, while PTask does not. More importantly, Sponge is primarily concerned with optimizing compiler-generated GPU-side code, while PTask addresses systems-level issues. A PTask-based system could benefit from Sponge support, and vice-versa.

Liquid Metal [39] and Lime [10] provide programming environments for heterogeneous targets such as systems comprising CPUs and FGPAs. Lime's filters, and I/O containers allow a computation to be expressed (by the compiler, in intermediate form) as a pipeline, while PTask's graph-structured computation is expressed explicitly by the programmer. Lime's buffer objects provide a similar encapsulation of data movement across memory domains to that provided by PTask's channels and datablocks. Flextream [37] is compilation framework for the SDF model that dynamically adapts applications to target architectures in the face of changing availability of FPGA, GPU, or CPU resources. Like PTask, Flextream applications are represented as a graph. As language-level tools, Liquid Metal, Lime and Flextream provide no OS-level support and therefore cannot address isolation/fairness guarantees, and cannot address data sharing across processes or in contexts where accelerators do not have the required language-level support. PTask is not coupled with a particular language or user-mode runtime.

I/O and data movement. PacketShader [32] is a software router that accelerates packet processing on GPUs and SSLShader [42] accelerates a secure sockets layer server by offloading AES and RSA computations to GPUs. Both SSLShader and PacketShader rely heavily on batching (along with overlap of computation/communication with the GPU) to address the overheads of I/O to the GPU and concomitant kernel/user switches. The PTask system could help by reducing kernel/user switches and eliminating double buffering between the GPU and NIC. IO-Lite [60] supports unified buffering and caching to minimize data movement. Unlike IO-Lite's *buffer aggregate* abstraction, PTask's datablocks are mutable, but PTask's channel implementations share IO-Lite's technique of eliminating double-buffering with memory-mapping (also similar to *fbufs* [25], Container Shipping [62], and zero-copy mechanisms proposed by Thadani et. al [65]). While IO-Lite addresses data-movement across protection domains, it does not address the problem of data movement across disjoint/incoherent memory spaces, such as those private to a GPU or other accelerator.

8. CONCLUSION

This paper proposes a new set of OS abstractions for accelerators such as GPUs called the PTask API. PTasks expose only enough hardware detail as is required to enable programmers to achieve good performance and low latency, while providing abstractions that preserve modularity and composability. The PTask API promotes GPUs to a general-purpose, shared compute resource, managed by the OS, which can provide fairness and isolation.

9. ACKNOWLEDGEMENTS

We thank Ashwin Prasad for implementation of the **fdtd** and **grpby** microbenchmarks. This research is supported by NSF Career award CNS-0644205, NSF award CNS-1017785, and a 2010 NVIDIA research grant. We thank our shepherd, Steve Hand for his valuable and detailed feedback.

10. REFERENCES

[1] *IBM 709 electronic data-processing system: advance description.* I.B.M., White Plains, NY, 1957.

[2] *The Imagine Stream Processor*, 2002.

[3] Recommendation for block cipher modesl of operation: the xts-aes mode for confidentiality on block-oriented storage devices. *National Institute of Standards and Technology, Special Publication 800-e8E*, 2009.

[4] NVIDIA GPUDirect. 2011.

[5] NVIDIA's Next Generation CUDATM Compute Architecture: Fermi. 2011.

[6] Top 500 supercomputer sites. 2011.

[7] Windows Driver Foundation (WDF). 2011.

[8] M. Andrecut. Parallel GPU Implementation of Iterative PCA Algorithms. *ArXiv e-prints*, Nov. 2008.

[9] M. Andrecut. Parallel GPU Implementation of Iterative PCA Algorithms. *Journal of Computational Biology*, 16(11), Nov. 2009.

[10] J. S. Auerbach, D. F. Bacon, P. Cheng, and R. M. Rabbah. Lime: a java-compatible and synthesizable language for heterogeneous architectures. In *OOPSLA*. ACM, 2010.

[11] C. Augonnet and R. Namyst. StarPU: A Unified Runtime System for Heterogeneous Multi-core Architectures.

[12] C. Augonnet, S. Thibault, R. Namyst, and M. Nijhuis. Exploiting the Cell/BE Architecture with the StarPU Unified Runtime System. In *SAMOS '09*, pages 329–339, 2009.

[13] R. M. Badia, J. Labarta, R. Sirvent, J. M. Pérez, J. M. Cela, and R. Grima. Programming Grid Applications with GRID Superscalar. *Journal of Grid Computing*, 1:2003, 2003.

[14] C. Banino, O. Beaumont, L. Carter, J. Ferrante, A. Legrand, and Y. Robert. Scheduling strategies for master-slave tasking on heterogeneous processor platforms. 2004.

[15] A. Baumann, P. Barham, P.-E. Dagand, T. Harris, R. Isaacs, S. Peter, T. Roscoe, A. Schüpbach, and A. Singhania. The multikernel: a new OS architecture for scalable multicore systems. In *SOSP*, 2009.

[16] A. Bayoumi, M. Chu, Y. Hanafy, P. Harrell, and G. Refai-Ahmed. Scientific and Engineering Computing Using ATI Stream Technology. *Computing in Science and Engineering*, 11(6):92–97, 2009.

[17] P. Bellens, J. M. Perez, R. M. Badia, and J. Labarta. CellSs: a programming model for the cell BE architecture. In *SC 2006*.

[18] G. Berry and G. Gonthier. The esterel synchronous programming language: design, semantics, implementation. *Sci. Comput. Program.*, 19:87–152, November 1992.

[19] B. N. Bershad, S. Savage, P. Pardyak, E. G. Sirer, M. E. Fiuczynski, D. Becker, C. Chambers, and S. Eggers. Extensibility safety and performance in the spin operating system. *SIGOPS Oper. Syst. Rev.*, 29:267–283, December 1995.

[20] I. Buck, T. Foley, D. Horn, J. Sugerman, K. Fatahalian, M. Houston, and P. Hanrahan. Brook for GPUs: Stream Computing on Graphics Hardware. *ACM TRANSACTIONS ON GRAPHICS*, 2004.

[21] E. Caspi, M. Chu, R. Huang, J. Yeh, J. Wawrzynek, and A. DeHon. Stream computations organized for reconfigurable execution (score). FPL '00, 2000.

[22] S. C. Chiu, W.-k. Liao, A. N. Choudhary, and M. T. Kandemir. Processor-embedded distributed smart disks for I/O-intensive workloads: architectures, performance models and evaluation. *J. Parallel Distrib. Comput.*, 65(4):532–551, 2005.

[23] C. H. Crawford, P. Henning, M. Kistler, and C. Wright. Accelerating computing with the cell broadband engine processor. In *CF 2008*, 2008.

[24] A. Currid. TCP offload to the rescue. *Queue*, 2(3):58–65, 2004.

[25] P. Druschel and L. L. Peterson. Fbufs: a high-bandwidth cross-domain transfer facility. *SIGOPS Oper. Syst. Rev.*, 27:189–202, December 1993.

[26] M. Garland, S. Le Grand, J. Nickolls, J. Anderson, J. Hardwick, S. Morton, E. Phillips, Y. Zhang, and V. Volkov. Parallel Computing Experiences with CUDA. *Micro, IEEE*, 28(4):13–27, 2008.

[27] I. Gelado, J. E. Stone, J. Cabezas, S. Patel, N. Navarro, and W.-m. W. Hwu. An asymmetric distributed shared memory model for heterogeneous parallel systems. ASPLOS '10, 2010.

[28] S. B. Gokturk, H. Yalcin, and C. Bamji. A time-of-flight depth sensor - system description, issues and solutions. In CVPRW, 2004.

[29] V. Gough. EncFs. http://www.arg0.net/encfs.

[30] N. K. Govindaraju, B. Lloyd, W. Wang, M. Lin, and D. Manocha. Fast computation of database operations using graphics processors. In ACM SIGGRAPH 2005 Courses, SIGGRAPH '05, New York, NY, USA, 2005. ACM.

[31] N. Halbwachs, P. Caspi, P. Raymond, and D. Pilaud. The synchronous dataflow programming language lustre. In Proceedings of the IEEE, pages 1305–1320, 1991.

[32] S. Han, K. Jang, K. Park, and S. Moon. Packetshader: a GPU-accelerated software router. SIGCOMM Comput. Commun. Rev., 40:195–206, August 2010.

[33] T. D. Han and T. S. Abdelrahman. hiCUDA: a high-level directive-based language for GPU programming. In GPGPU 2009.

[34] B. He, W. Fang, Q. Luo, N. K. Govindaraju, and T. Wang. Mars: a mapreduce framework on graphics processors. In Proceedings of the 17th international conference on Parallel architectures and compilation techniques, PACT '08, pages 260–269, New York, NY, USA, 2008. ACM.

[35] B. He, K. Yang, R. Fang, M. Lu, N. Govindaraju, Q. Luo, and P. Sander. Relational joins on graphics processors. SIGMOD '08, 2008.

[36] M. Hirsch, D. Lanman, H. Holtzman, and R. Raskar. BiDi screen: a thin, depth-sensing LCD for 3D interaction using light fields. ACM Trans. Graph., 28(5):1–9, 2009.

[37] A. Hormati, Y. Choi, M. Kudlur, R. M. Rabbah, T. Mudge, and S. A. Mahlke. Flextream: Adaptive compilation of streaming applications for heterogeneous architectures. In PACT, pages 214–223. IEEE Computer Society, 2009.

[38] A. H. Hormati, M. Samadi, M. Woh, T. Mudge, and S. Mahlke. Sponge: portable stream programming on graphics engines. In Proceedings of the sixteenth international conference on Architectural support for programming languages and operating systems (ASPLOS), 2011.

[39] S. S. Huang, A. Hormati, D. F. Bacon, and R. M. Rabbah. Liquid metal: Object-oriented programming across the hardware/software boundary. In ECOOP, pages 76–103, 2008.

[40] Intel Corporation. Intel IXP 2855 Network Processor.

[41] M. Isard, M. Budiu, Y. Yu, A. Birrell, and D. Fetterly. Dryad: distributed data-parallel programs from sequential building blocks. In EuroSys 2007.

[42] K. Jang, S. Han, S. Han, S. Moon, and K. Park. Sslshader: cheap ssl acceleration with commodity processors. In Proceedings of the 8th USENIX conference on Networked systems design and implementation, NSDI'11, pages 1–1, Berkeley, CA, USA, 2011. USENIX Association.

[43] V. J. Jiménez, L. Vilanova, I. Gelado, M. Gil, G. Fursin, and N. Navarro. Predictive runtime code scheduling for heterogeneous architectures. In HiPEAC 2009.

[44] P. G. Joisha and P. Banerjee. Static array storage optimization in matlab. In In ACM SIGPLAN Conference on Programming Language Design and Implementation, pages 258–268, 2003.

[45] S. Kato, K. Lakshmanan, R. Rajkumar, and Y. Ishikawa. Timegraph: GPU scheduling for real-time multi-tasking environments. In Proceedings of the 2011 USENIX conference on USENIX annual technical conference, Berkeley, CA, USA, 2011. USENIX Association.

[46] K. Keeton, D. A. Patterson, and J. M. Hellerstein. A case for

[47] Khronos Group. The OpenCL Specification, Version 1.0, 2009.

[48] S.-P. P. Kim, J. D. Simeral, L. R. Hochberg, J. P. Donoghue, and M. J. Black. Neural control of computer cursor velocity by decoding motor cortical spiking activity in humans with tetraplegia. Journal of neural engineering, 5(4):455–476, December 2008.

[49] E. Kohler, R. Morris, B. Chen, J. Jannotti, and M. F. Kaashoek. The click modular router. ACM Trans. Comput. Syst., 18, August 2000.

[50] E. A. Lee and D. G. Messerschmitt. Static scheduling of synchronous data flow programs for digital signal processing. IEEE Trans. Comput., 36:24–35, January 1987.

[51] M. Linetsky. Programming Microsoft Directshow. Wordware Publishing Inc., Plano, TX, USA, 2001.

[52] O. Loques, J. Leite, and E. V. Carrera E. P-rio: A modular parallel-programming environment. IEEE Concurrency, 6:47–57, January 1998.

[53] H. Massalin and C. Pu. Threads and input/output in the synthesis kernal. In SOSP '89: Proceedings of the twelfth ACM symposium on Operating systems principles, pages 191–201, New York, NY, USA, 1989. ACM.

[54] M. D. McCool and B. D'Amora. Programming using RapidMind on the Cell BE. In SC '06: Proceedings of the 2006 ACM/IEEE conference on Supercomputing, page 222, New York, NY, USA, 2006. ACM.

[55] D. Mosberger and L. L. Peterson. Making paths explicit in the scout operating system. pages 153–167, 1996.

[56] P. Newton and J. C. Browne. The code 2.0 graphical parallel programming language. In Proceedings of the 6th international conference on Supercomputing, ICS '92, pages 167–177, New York, NY, USA, 1992. ACM.

[57] E. B. Nightingale, O. Hodson, R. McIlroy, C. Hawblitzel, and G. Hunt. Helios: heterogeneous multiprocessing with satellite kernels. In SOSP 2009.

[58] NVIDIA. CUDA Toolkit 4.0 CUBLAS Library, 2011.

[59] NVIDIA. NVIDIA CUDA Programming Guide, 2011.

[60] V. S. Pai, P. Druschel, and W. Zwaenepoel. Io-lite: A unified i/o buffering and caching system. 1997.

[61] G. M. Papadopoulos and D. E. Culler. Monsoon: an explicit token-store architecture. In Proceedings of the 17th annual international symposium on Computer Architecture (ISCA), 1990.

[62] J. Pasquale, E. Anderson, S. Diego, I. K. Muller, T. Global, and I. Solutions. Container shipping: Operating system support for i/o-intensive applications. IEEE Computer, 27:84–93, 1994.

[63] E. Riedel, C. Faloutsos, G. A. Gibson, and D. Nagle. Active disks for large-scale data processing. Computer, 34(6):68–74, 2001.

[64] S. Ryoo, C. I. Rodrigues, S. S. Baghsorkhi, S. S. Stone, D. B. Kirk, and W.-m. Hwu. Optimization principles and application performance evaluation of a multithreaded GPU using CUDA. In PPoPP 2008.

[65] M. N. Thadani and Y. A. Khalidi. An efficient zero-copy i/o framework for unix. Technical report, 1995.

[66] W. Thies, M. Karczmarek, and S. P. Amarasinghe. StreamIt: A Language for Streaming Applications. In CC 2002.

[67] C. Tomasi and R. Manduchi. Bilateral filtering for gray and color images. In ICCV 1998.

[68] S.-Z. Ueng, M. Lathara, S. S. Baghsorkhi, and W.-M. W. Hwu. CUDA-Lite: Reducing GPU Programming Complexity. In LCPC 2008.

[69] Y. Weinsberg, D. Dolev, T. Anker, M. Ben-Yehuda, and P. Wyckoff. Tapping into the fountain of CPUs: on operating system support for programmable devices. In ASPLOS 2008.

intelligent disks (IDISKs). SIGMOD Rec., 27(3):42–52, 1998.

Logical Attestation: An Authorization Architecture for Trustworthy Computing

Emin Gün Sirer   Willem de Bruijn†   Patrick Reynolds‡
Alan Shieh   Kevin Walsh   Dan Williams   Fred B. Schneider
Computer Science Department, Cornell University   †Google, Inc   ‡BlueStripe Software
{egs,wdb,reynolds,ashieh,kwalsh,djwill,fbs}@cs.cornell.edu

ABSTRACT

This paper describes the design and implementation of a new operating system authorization architecture to support trustworthy computing. Called *logical attestation*, this architecture provides a sound framework for reasoning about run time behavior of applications. Logical attestation is based on attributable, unforgeable statements about program properties, expressed in a logic. These statements are suitable for mechanical processing, proof construction, and verification; they can serve as credentials, support authorization based on expressive authorization policies, and enable remote principals to trust software components without restricting the local user's choice of binary implementations.

We have implemented logical attestation in a new operating system called the Nexus. The Nexus executes natively on x86 platforms equipped with secure coprocessors. It supports both native Linux applications and uses logical attestation to support new trustworthy-computing applications. When deployed on a trustworthy cloud-computing stack, logical attestation is efficient, achieves high-performance, and can run applications that provide qualitative guarantees not possible with existing modes of attestation.

Categories and Subject Descriptors

D.4 [**Operating Systems**]: Security and Protection

General Terms

Trusted Platform Module, Logic, Credentials-Based Authorization

1. Introduction

Secure coprocessors, such as industry standard Trusted Platform Modules (TPMs), are becoming ubiquitous. This hardware can provide a foundation for software systems that offer strong guarantees about run time behavior. Yet, there is a big semantic gap between the primitives provided by TPMs and what assurance secure applications actually require. The key primitive provided by secure coprocessors is *hash-based attestation*, whereby the platform generates a certificate that captures the binary launch-time hash of all components comprising the software stack. To identify trustworthy software configurations through their hashes necessitates software whitelisting, and that can restrict users to a limited set of applications due to platform lock-down [52]. Further, software certificates that divulge hashes compromise privacy [40]. Finally, launch-time program hashes do not adequately characterize programs whose behavior depends on inputs or external data. Much of the public backlash against trusted computing can, in fact, be traced to limitations of hash-based attestation.

Hash-based attestation forces all trust decisions to be *axiomatic*, because principals are trusted by fiat. Access control lists that enumerate principals by name, digital signatures to certify that a particular piece of code was vetted by a particular vendor, and authorization based on program hashes are all instances of the axiomatic basis for trust.

An alternative method of establishing trust is to employ an *analysis* that predicts whether certain behaviors by a program are possible. Proof carrying code [35], in which a program is accompanied by a proof that its execution satisfies certain properties, instantiates this analytical basis for trust. Similarly, systems that employ typecheckers and domain-specific languages, in which code snippets are loaded and executed only if the code is deemed safe, are employing analysis for establishing trust.

Finally, a *synthetic* basis for trust is involved when a program is transformed prior to execution and the transformation produces an artifact that can be trusted in ways that the original could not. Sandboxing [16], SFI [54], inlined reference monitors [11, 50], and other program rewriting techniques employ a synthetic basis for trust.

Today's operating systems provide disparate, ad hoc mechanisms to implement these three bases of trust. A unifying authorization architecture that can support all under the same rubric has not been undertaken. Moreover, establishing trust in practical settings often relies on a combination of these bases. For instance, a JVM enforces type correctness through both a static typechecker (an analytic basis) and code generation that adds run-time checks (a synthetic basis). The challenge, then, is to build an *authorization infrastructure*, by which we mean a system for generating, managing, and checking the credentials of principals in a computer system, that incorporates all three bases for trust. Our experience in designing such a unifying authorization architecture, implementing it in an operating system, and building system services to enable its use is the subject of this paper.

We propose a new authorization architecture, called *logical attestation*, that supports all three bases for trust. In logical attestation, a *labeling function* is used to generate an attributed statement called a *label* and expressed in a constructive logic of beliefs. Labels are unforgeable, machine-parseable statements of the form "*LF* says *S*" that capture information relevant to trust decisions. A bitstring that encodes a label is known as a *credential*. Since labeling functions can be provided by third parties and labels are logical statements, a rich set of properties can be available for logical attestation. These properties can incorporate references to dynamic system state, including the current time, current resource availability, and even history. Labels used in proofs demonstrate, through logical inference, reasons why a principal should be trusted; they are consumed by *guards* that verify proofs to make authorization decisions.

We have implemented a new operating system, called Nexus, designed around logical attestation. Nexus executes on x86 platforms equipped with a TPM, supports much of the Posix API, and natively executes many Linux applications. To our knowledge, Nexus is the first operating system to implement logic-based authorization with dynamic system state, the first to implement operating system capabilities [7] based on statements issued by a TPM, and first to support all three bases for trust in a single unified framework. Logical attestation enables novel authorization functionality, as we illustrate, and provides strong and useful guarantees today's systems cannot provide.

We illustrate the power of our new authorization architecture by implementing a cloud computing application, called Fauxbook, that implements guarantees about safety, confidentiality, and resource control. Fauxbook provides a familiar social networking experience, where users publicly post and exchange status messages. Even Fauxbook developers are blocked, by our authorization architecture, from examining or data-mining the information Fauxbook handles. Moreover, logical attestation enables the cloud-infrastructure operator to guarantees certain forms of resource availability to Fauxbook developers. Experiments show that the cost of authentication with logical attestation in Fauxbook is on the order of 1ms, and it can be reduced to 20 cycles with proof caching, an optimization we describe later.

The rest of this paper is structured as follows. The next section describes the elements of logical attestation. Section 3 discusses operating system services required to support expressive, flexible logical attestation. Section 4 describes Fauxbook. Section 5 evaluates Nexus in terms of authorization efficiency, Section 6 reviews related work, and Section 7 summarizes and concludes.

2. Logical Attestation

Logical attestation is based on the generation, communication and use of attributable property descriptions represented as logical formulas. It builds on much past work that uses logical inference for authorization, known as credentials-based authorization (CBA) [57, 2, 26, 1].

The key idea in credentials-based authorization is that each request is accompanied by credentials, which are statements that can be attributed to principals. Accesses to resources are protected by a guard, a reference monitor that enforces a resource-specific authorization policy. The guard allows a request to proceed if credentials are available that imply a *goal statement* embodying the requisite authorization policy.

Credentials-based authorization provides for better expressiveness than traditional access control mechanisms. For instance, whereas Unix file systems perform access control based only on owner/group/other permissions, a CBA system might enable a file containing an expense report to be restricted to, say, "*users who have successfully completed accounting training*," where a user can acquire such a credential by successfully completing an online course. Users of such a system need not contact an administrator in order to be placed in a special user-group. So, CBA enables decision-making authority to be removed from the guard (which now consists solely

of a general-purpose proof-checker), and relocated to (potentially remote) unprivileged credential-granting entities, better suited for the task. CBA's flexibility provides clients with the ability to select a convenient way of discharging an access control policy. For instance, a CBA policy that limits access to "*a user whose identity is vetted by any two of: a stored password service, a retinal scan service, and an identity certificate stored on a USB dongle*" provides the client with the freedom to pick the most convenient method for gaining access [23]. Note that CBA credentials are self-documenting—they include all of the evidence used to reach a conclusion, a feature well-suited for logging and auditing.

Yet implementing credentials-based authorization in a real system poses significant challenges. First, there is the semantic gap between credentials and the actual state an operating system embodies. For instance, the seemingly innocuous credential "*Filesystem says User A is consuming less than 80% of her quota*" illustrates two fundamental problems: (1) the statement may become invalid even as the credential continues to be used in authorization decisions, and (2) a badly-implemented filesystem could issue credentials attesting to conflicting statements (e.g., in the case of statements issued before and after the the user exceeds 80% of her quota) that together imply false. Past work in CBA has tried to bridge this semantic gap between logic and OS state, either by limiting credentials to conveying irrevocable truths, or by replicating real world facts in logic variables (which creates inconsistencies stemming from the duplication of state).

The second set of challenges relates to the generation, manipulation, and management of credentials. To reap the benefits of CBA, an operating system must provide mechanisms for capturing relevant credentials. Specifically, the OS must support general-purpose mechanisms for performing analysis as well as synthesis. It must enable an application that possesses a particular property to acquire relevant credentials that can be forwarded and trusted by remote parties.

The final set of challenges relate to performance. The performance overhead of the mechanisms required for checking credentials and validating proofs of goals from credentials must not be prohibitive. And the performance impact of supporting the analysis and synthesis mechanisms must be small.

The rest of this section describes the mechanisms and abstractions supported by the Nexus operating system to address these challenges.

2.1 Logic Labels and NAL

Logical attestation bases all authorization decisions on *labels*. A label is a logical formula P says S that attributes some statement S to a principal P. Labels are expressed in Nexus Authorization Logic (NAL). The design of the logic is discussed in detail elsewhere [45]; here, we summarize why NAL is suitable for use in an OS setting.

First, to preserve justification in all authorization decisions, NAL is a constructive logic—a logic that restricts deduction to formulas that are derived solely from facts observed by a witness. In such a logic, tautologies such as double negation elimination ($\neg\neg p \Rightarrow p$) are not axioms. Where classical logics preserve only the truth of statements, proofs in constructive logics leave an audit trail for their inferences, making them well suited to reasoning about authorization.

Second, NAL is a logic of belief. Its formulas attribute facts and deductions to individual principals. Each NAL principal has a *worldview*, a set of formulas that principal believes to hold. The NAL formula P says S is interpreted to mean: S is in the worldview of P. All deduction in NAL is local. So we can derive from A says *false* the statement A says G for any G, but A says *false* cannot be used to derive B says G in NAL if B and A are unrelated principals. This local inference property limits the damage an untrustworthy principal can cause. It also enables each Nexus application independently to specify which entities it trusts; the system does not require a superuser, a shared set of privileged principals, or an absolute universal frame of reference.

Finally, NAL supports group principals and subprincipals, as well as a `speaksfor` operator for characterizing delegation between principals. If A `speaksfor` B holds and A `says` S, then B `says` S for all statements S. Semantically, if A `speaksfor` B holds, then the worldview of A is a subset of the worldview of B. A subprincipal $A.\tau$ of A, by definition, satisfies A `speaksfor` $A.\tau$. This allows NAL to characterize dependencies between OS abstractions. For example, processes implemented by a kernel are all subprincipals of the kernel, which itself is a subprincipal of the hardware platform it executes on. So, strictly speaking, we should be writing *HW.kernel.process23* as the principal to which a statement by *process 23* would be attributed. For clarity, we elide the the prefix of dependencies in a principal's name whenever that prefix would be clear from the context. The NAL `speaksfor` operator optionally supports an "on" modifier that can restrict the scope of the delegation. For example, *Server* `says` *NTP* `speaksfor` *Server* on *TimeNow* delegates to *NTP* authority on statements for *Server* involving the time, but does not attribute to *Server* any other utterances by *NTP*.

The rest of this section traces label creation and usage for a time-sensitive content scenario. Here, a file on local disk is assumed to contain sensitive information that should be accessed before a fixed date. The contents of this file must not be overtly leaked over channels to the disk or network.

2.2 Label Creation

Labels are created in Nexus by invoking the **say** system call. This system call takes a string argument that encodes a NAL statement. Nexus imposes no semantic restrictions on the terms and predicates appearing in a statement. For instance, in the label *TypeChecker* `says` *isTypeSafe(PGM)*, *isTypeSafe* is a predicate introduced by the *TypeChecker*, whose meaning is presumed to be understood by a principal that imports this statement into its worldview. This flexibility enables third parties to define types of credentials that may not have been envisioned by the OS designers. Moreover, because all reasoning is local to a principal, separate applications need not subscribe to a common nomenclature or semantics for labels; for instance, the predicate *isTypeSafe* might be used by both a JVM and CLR, but denote different properties.

In our time-sensitive file example, the process that wants to read the file must acquire some credential certifying that its execution will not leak the sensitive information to the disk or network. One potential approach may use labels like:

Company `says` *isTrustworthy*(**Client**)
$\wedge$ *Nexus* `says` */proc/ipd/12* `speaksfor` **Client**

Here, **Client** is the well-known SHA1 hash of a program that some third party *Company* has certified to exhibit the properties sought. The second label, provided by the Nexus, indicates that the named process `speaksfor` its launch-time hash.

An alternative set of labels to accomplish the same task but without the disadvantages of axiomatic trust is:

Nexus `says` */proc/ipd/30* `speaksfor` **IPCAnalyzer**
$\wedge$ */proc/ipd/30* `says` ¬*hasPath*(*/proc/ipd/12,* **Filesystem***)*
$\wedge$ */proc/ipd/30* `says` ¬*hasPath*(*/proc/ipd/12,* **Nameserver***)*

Here, a separate program IPCAnalyzer, running as process 30, used an analytic basis to enumerate the transitive IPC connection graph using the Nexus introspection interface (for simplicity, we have replaced process identifiers with the strings **Filesystem** and **Nameserver**—hashes, signatures, or other labels may be used to relate these process identifiers to known principals). Since the disk and network drivers in Nexus operate in user space and rely on IPC for communication, a transitive IPC connection graph that has no links to these drivers demonstrates that there is no existing channel to the disk or network.

2.3 Labelstores

A simple way to implement labels is to use digital signatures. A process that controls a key stored in the TPM can direct the TPM to create such a signed credential. Alternatively, a process that stores a key in its address space can digitally sign statements; this is sensible only when the key resides in an address space (called an *isolated protection domain* (IPD) in Nexus terminology) that is not shared. Such credentials are sometimes used in Nexus, but because cryptographic operations are expensive, whether performed by TPM hardware or in software, the kernel provides a new abstraction that helps eliminate their overhead.

The *labelstore* is implemented by the Nexus for storing labels generated by user programs. A user process can issue labels by invoking the **say** system call, passing in a NAL statement S, and naming the labelstore into which the statement should be placed. The returned *handle* can be used to request manipulation of the label. The speaker P associated with the label is, by default, the name of the process that invoked the **say** system call. Once in a labelstore, labels can be transferred between labelstores, externalized into a standard cryptographically-signed certificate format (X.509), imported from that format into a labelstore, and deleted.

Since labels are generated directly by invoking the **say** system call, there exists a secure channel from the user program to the operating system during label creation. The presence of this channel obviates the need for cryptographic operations. In our time-sensitive file example, the labels mentioned above are emitted directly into the labelstore and stored as strings, without any costly cryptographic signatures.

2.4 Label Communication

A label *P says S* that is cryptographically signed is not vulnerable to misattribution and misquotation, but is computationally expensive to generate and verify. So the Nexus allows principals to exchange labels efficiently over secure system channels. Specifically, the kernel exposes IPC channels, and it authoritatively binds IPC ports to owning processes by producing a label *Nexus* `says` *IPC.x* `speaksfor` */proc/ipd/process.y*.

Externalized labels must convey context about principals named in labels. All Nexus principals are subprincipals of the TPM's secret key EK, associated permanently with that TPM at the time of manufacture. On first boot, the Nexus kernel uses the TPM to generate a Nexus key NK that is bound to the current contents of the TPM's platform configuration registers (PCRs) at boot time. NK serves as a principal associated with that version of the Nexus. And an attacker that boots a modified version of the kernel in order to access this NK will be unable to gain access to the private key due to the PCR mismatch. The kernel also generates a Nexus boot key (NBK) that identifies the unique boot instantiation of that Nexus installation. All processes are sub-principals of NK concatenated with the hash of the public component of the NBK, are named in full in X.509, signed with the NK, and are accompanied by another X.509 certificate attesting to NK using the TPM. So, when a label is externalized into X.509 format, the exported statements are, informally, of the form *"TPM says kernel says labelstore says processid says S."* In cases where TPMs are accompanied by certificates from the TPM manufacturer attesting to the chip and the PC hardware manufacturer attesting to the chip's integration on the motherboard, Nexus can furnish these to establish trust in the complete hardware platform; support for such certificates is currently vendor-dependent.

2.5 Goal Formulas

Nexus enables a *goal formula* to be associated with any operation on any system resource. The goal formula specifies what must be discharged for a client to be authorized to perform the given operation. A **setgoal** system call specifies the resource (e.g. process, thread, memory map, page, IPC port, files and directories), the operation on that resource, a goal formula and, optionally, the IPC channel to a designated guard. Following a successful **setgoal** call, all subsequent operations on that resource are vectored to the designated guard, which checks client-supplied labels against the specified goal formula.

Goal formulas, like labels, are expressed in NAL. A goal formula documents its trust assumptions by specifying speaksfor relationships in a preamble. For instance, a goal formula of the form "*Owner* says *TimeNow < Mar19*" requires the client to obtain a credential from a time server trusted by the file owner that attests that the deadline has not yet passed.[1] Specifically, this goal formula can be discharged by acquiring credentials:

Filesystem says *NTP* speaksfor *Filesystem* on *TimeNow*
∧ *NTP* says *TimeNow < Mar19*

Setting a goal formula is itself an operation that must be authorized. A goal formula that is separate (and often, distinct) from the one used for object access is involved. Typically, a goal formula for a shared object (e.g. a nameserver or a mail spool directory) will permit a wide range of principals to perform regular operations on the object, while restricting the **setgoal** call to an entity privileged enough to own or maintain that resource.[2]

For our time-sensitive file example, a suitable goal formula that embodies the desired policy is:

Owner says *TimeNow < Mar19*
∧ $\mathcal{X}$ says *openFile(filename)*
∧ *SafetyCertifier* says *safe($\mathcal{X}$)*

Here, calligraphic font is used for a class of identifiers that are instantiated for guard evaluation.

Typically, Nexus goal formulas involve the owner of a resource explicitly permitting an operation. Labels issued to the entity seeking access are used in conjunction with auxiliary labels issued by the resource owner to demonstrate that the conditions for access are satisfied. For instance, the *SafetyCertifier* above might examine the labelstore and issue additional labels of the form:

SafetyCertifier says *safe($\mathcal{X}$)*

for each IPD $\mathcal{X}$ when the following labels are also found in the labelstore:

Nexus says $\mathcal{Z}$ speaksfor **IPCAnalyzer**
∧ $\mathcal{Z}$ says *¬hasPath($\mathcal{X}$, **Filesystem**)*
∧ $\mathcal{Z}$ says *¬hasPath($\mathcal{X}$, **Nameserver**)*

---

[1] We discuss the details of handling credentials that refer to mutable state in Section 2.7.

[2] It is technically possible, in our current implementation, for a bad applicaton to set goal formulas on a resource that prohibit every entity, including itself, from ever interacting with that resource. This feature is the inevitable consequence of the lack of a superuser. If desired, one can modify the kernel to always permit operations by a designated superuser process or one of its delegates.

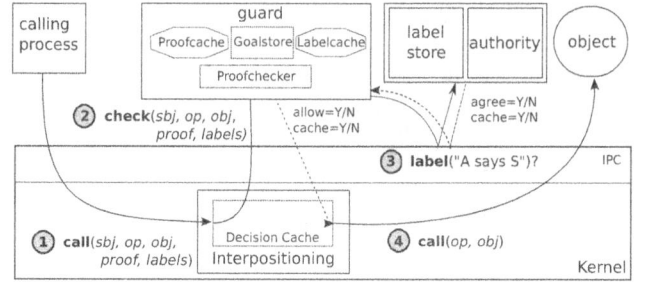

Figure 1: Logical Attestation in Nexus: To perform an operation on an object, an access control subject (1) passes a proof and set of labels that satisfy the associated goal formula. The kernel calls a guard process (2), that evaluates the proof and verifies authenticity of labels, referring (3) to external label-stores and authorities for unknown labels. The call is permitted to proceed (4) if the proof discharges the goal.

This is equivalent to the definition:

$$safe(\mathcal{X}) \triangleq \neg hasPath(\mathcal{X}, \textbf{Filesystem}) \wedge$$
$$\neg hasPath(\mathcal{X}, \textbf{Nameserver})$$

and an alternative would have been simply to include this definition in the guard.

2.6 Guards

Authorization decisions are determined by performing a logical inference that derives a goal formula from a set of credentials.

Since proof derivation in logics like NAL is undecidable, the Nexus places the onus on the client to construct a proof and present it when invoking an operation on an object. The guard need only check the proof and authenticity of credentials, both of which are tractable problems and, as we will demonstrate later, cheap. Figure 1 depicts all of the steps in the authorization process.

Kernel resources implemented by the Nexus, including threads, IPDs, IPC channels, network sockets, files and directories, are managed by a kernel-designated guard. The choice of default policy for such resources is tricky, since one has to ensure that a nascent object for which a goal policy has not yet been established is protected from access by unauthorized parties. The kernel-designated guard implements a simple default policy to solve this bootstrapping problem: it interprets the absence of a goal formula as the policy *resource-manager.object* says *operation*, which is only satisfiable by the object or its superprincipal, the resource manager that created the object. To pass object ownership to a third party, the resource manager issues a label *resource-manager* says *third-party* speaksfor *object*. For instance, when */proc/ipd/6* creates a file called */dir/file*, the fileserver *FS* creates the file on behalf of */proc/ipd/6* and deposits the label *FS* says */proc/ipd/6* speaksfor *FS./dir/file* in the labelstore for that process.

2.7 State and Authorities

A trustworthy principal should refrain from producing statements in transferable form if these statements might subsequently become invalid. For instance, a statement by *NTP* that assures the bearer of the current time would quickly expire, causing others to conclude that *NTP* is an untrustworthy principal. Nevertheless, realistic authorization policies often refer to non-monotonic dynamic state, such as user input and resource utilization. Therefore, logical attestation supports an *authority* abstraction for querying dynamic state without incurring the problems of invalidated credentials.

Nexus authorities attest to the veracity of a label only when asked, and they never issue credentials that are both transferable and can become invalidated. Specifically, an authority is implemented by a process listening on an attested IPC port i. That process authoritatively answers whether it currently believes statement *IPC.i* `says` S holds; its answer can only be observed by the principal posing the query. The default labels Nexus provides for IPC channels thus enable such a statement to be attributed to the authority process. So, over an attested IPC channel, the Nexus implements the following protocol: a guard that wants to validate a label sends the label to the port. The process listening on the port returns a binary answer that is authoritative (by virtue of the IPC channel), thus conveying the validity but not in a way that can be stored or further communicated. For example, in our time-sensitive file application, a trustworthy system clock service would refuse to sign labels, but would subscribe to a small set of arithmetic statements related to time, such as *NTP* `says` *TimeNow* $\leq$ *March 19*. The guard process can establish the veracity of such a claim by querying the system clock service on each time-dependent check.

By partitioning trusted statements into indefinitely cacheable labels and untransferable yes/no responses from authorities, we obviate the need in Nexus for an additional, system-provided revocation infrastructure. For instance, a software developer A wishing to implement her own revocation check for a statement S can, instead of issuing the label A `says` S, issue A `says` *Valid(S)* $\Rightarrow$ S. This design enables third-parties to implement the revocation service as an authority to the statement A `says` *Valid(S)*.

2.8 The Decision Cache

Since guard invocations are expensive, the overhead entailed by credential checks needs to be reduced whenever possible. To this end, the Nexus implements a cache in the kernel that stores previously observed guard decisions, called the *decision cache*.

The goal of the decision cache is to avoid expensive proof checking and validation operations when they are unnecessary. To support the decision cache, the guard-kernel interface is amended with a bit to signify whether a validation is cacheable. NAL's structure makes it easy to mechanically and conservatively determine those proofs that do not have references to dynamic system state and, thus, are safe to cache.

The decision cache is implemented as a hashtable indexed by the access control tuple of subject, operation, and object. Because the cache is a performance optimization, its contents can be marked invalid and the cache can be resized at runtime.

Authorization decisions are invalidated as a system executes. When a process updates a goal or proof, the kernel must invalidate corresponding entries in its decision cache. The kernel therefore interposes on the guard control IPC to monitor updates. On a proof update, the kernel clears a single entry in the decision cache. A **setgoal** operation, on the other hand, might affect many entries that, due to hashing, may spread across the memory implementing the decision cache. To avoid clearing the whole decision cache on each such update, the hash function we use was designed to hash all entries with the same operation and object into the same subregion. Subregion size is a configurable parameter that trades-off invalidation cost to collision rate. Only when the kernel has no cached decision, does it consult an IPC port lookup table and make an upcall to a guard process.

The decision cache has a significant impact on performance. As we discuss later, the decision cache can reduce proof checking latency on a minimal system call from 2100% of unguarded invocation latency down to 3%.

2.9 Guard Cache

To amortize proof-checking cost across principals and invocations, guards internally cache as much proof-checking as possible.

Caching valid credentials cannot cause a vulnerability, because labels are valid indefinitely. Even when proofs depend partially on dynamic state, they often have pieces that can be replaced by lemmas whose outcome may be cached safely. So, a cache in the guard can enable some parts of a proof to be checked quickly, reducing authorization to a few checks and subsequent consultation with designated authorities.

Since all information in the guard cache constitutes soft state and can be re-checked when needed, evictions from the guard cache cannot impact the correctness of access control decisions. To provide some measure of performance isolation between principals, the default Nexus guard, in response to a new request from a given principal, preferentially evicts cache entries from that same principal. To limit exhaustion attacks due to incessant spawning of new processes and thus principals, quotas are attached to the principal that is the root of an entire process tree.

3. Operating System Services

To effectively build secure applications using logical attestation, additional OS mechanisms are necessary.

3.1 Introspection

For supporting an analytic basis for trust, Nexus implements an extensible namespace through which principals can query the state of the kernel. Similar to Plan 9's /proc filesystem [38], this greybox information service allows components to publish application-defined *key=value* bindings. Logically, each node in the introspection service is the same as a label *process.i* `says` *key = value*. These key-value pairs indicate kernel state information. Each process and the kernel are linked against an in-memory fileserver. The fileserver has default mechanisms for rendering data contained in hashtables, queues, and other kernel datastructures. Using these tools, the Nexus kernel exposes a live view of its mutable state, including lookup tables for processes, IPC ports, and guard ports. Applications, such as the Python interpreter, similarly publish their state information, such as the list of currently loaded modules and executing files.

Introspection of metadata offers a portable alternative to property attestation by unique hash. For instance, a labeling function can verify, by analyzing information exported through introspection, that a language runtime is not executing unsafe code, that a device driver has its I/O mediated by a reference monitor, or that a keyboard driver detected physical keypresses. All of these, in fact, are used by the example applications in Section 4.

Two properties of NAL's term language are essential to meaningful label generation. First, the uniform naming scheme provided by the introspection service enables labeling functions to identify entities in the system in a portable manner. Second, the filesystem interface presents standard, well known, mechanisms for term access control and change notification. Associating goal formulas to information exported through the /proc filesystem enables the kernel to impose access control on sensitive kernel data.

3.2 Interpositioning

Not all properties are fully analyzable prior to execution. But even if it might be a priori undecidable to determine whether an application will open a particular file or execute a particular code path, it could still be trivial to monitor and detect such behavior dynamically. In this case, a synthetic basis for trust is achieved by actively interposing on all I/O of an untrusted process and transforming that I/O into safe actions, in effect rendering the untrusted process trustworthy.

Nexus provides an interpositioning service by which a reference monitor can be configured to intercept IPC operations originated by a particular process. Specifically, the **interpose** system call provides a way for a particular process to bind itself to a given IPC channel. As with every Nexus system call, an **interpose** call only succeeds if the reference monitor can satisfy some goal formula, typically by presenting a credential obtained from the process to be monitored. Thus, interposition is subject to consent, but a reference monitor, once installed, has access to each monitored IPC call. The reference monitor can inspect and modify IPC arguments and results, and at its discretion, block the IPC. Since all system calls in Nexus go through the IPC interface, a reference monitor can inspect, modify and block *all* interaction of a process with its surrounding environment, to the extent it is permitted to do so.

Interposition is implemented by using an redirector table in the kernel. Upon an IPC invocation, the kernel consults the redirector and reroutes the call to the interceptor, passing the subject, operation, and object. The interceptor can access the arguments passed to the intercepted call by issuing further system calls, and it may also modify them if it has credentials to do so. On completion, the monitor notifies the kernel about whether the call should be permitted to continue. If the call does continue as normal, then the kernel will later make an upcall when the return for that IPC occurs, so that the interceptor can modify response parameters.

Interpositioning is a composable operation. Multiple processes can be interpositioned on a given IPC channel, and the interposition system call itself can be monitored by an interposition agent.

3.3 Attested Storage

Data confidentiality and integrity can be important in many high-integrity applications. Password authenticators, capability managers, and file systems often need to retain confidential data in a manner that prohibits unauthorized access, avoids replay attacks, and detects tampering. Although hardware attacks against the TPM is beyond the capabilities of most attackers, attacking the storage system while a given machine is powered down can be as trivial as duplicating and replaying a disk image. Yet it is infeasible to store all sensitive information on a TPM, because the TPM provides only a small amount of secure on-chip storage. To guard against attacks on the storage system, a trustworthy operating system needs to offer integrity and confidentiality protection, even across reboots. Nexus does this by providing an abstraction called *Secure Storage Regions* (SSRs) that enable the limited TPM storage resources to be multiplexed in a way that provides integrity- and confidentiality-protected, replay-proof, persistent storage.

SSRs create the illusion of an unlimited amount of secure storage that is backed by the TPM. This can be achieved with TPM v1.1, which provides only two 20-byte registers (called Data Integrity Registers, or DIRs) for storage, or with TPM v1.2, which provides only a finite amount of secure NVRAM. Each SSR is an integrity-protected and optionally encrypted data store on a secondary storage device. Applications can **create**, **read**, **write** and **destroy** their SSRs. SSRs can be used by applications to store arbitrary data that demands integrity, and optionally, confidentiality guarantees, such as authentication tokens, keys, cookies, and other persistent and sensitive information. And guards can use SSRs to store the state of security automata [44], which may include counters, expiration dates, and summary of past behaviors.

The integrity of an SSR is protected by a hash. When the number of SSRs is small relative to the amount of storage on the TPM, their hashes can be stored by the TPM. Thereafter, attempts to replay old values of SSRs, for instance, by re-imaging a disk, would fail, because the hash of the (replayed) SSR would not match the (modified, current) hash stored in the TPM.

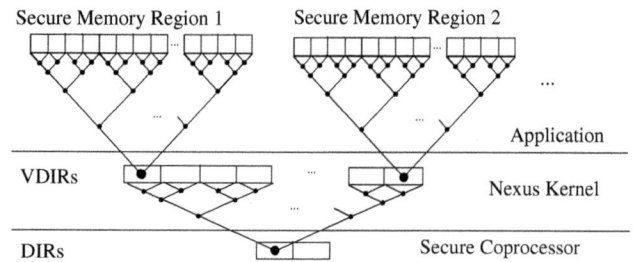

Figure 2: The SSR interface enables applications to provide integrity- and confidentiality-protection for data at rest.

In order to provide these same guarantees for an arbitrary number of SSRs, the Nexus utilizes a kernel-managed Merkle hash tree [33, 34] to store hashes of all SSRs. A Merkle hash tree divides a file into small blocks whose hashes form the leaves of a binary tree and, thus, somewhat decouples the hashing cost from the size of the file. Inner nodes in the tree store hashes computed by concatenating and hashing the values of their child nodes, resulting in a single root hash that protects the entire file. SSRs are implemented at user-level; they use a Nexus kernel abstraction, called Virtual Data Integrity Registers (VDIRs), to hold hashes. The Nexus kernel stores VDIR contents in a hash tree kept in memory and stored on secondary storage (between boots), with the root hash of the hash tree stored in the TPM. Any attempt to change or replay the contents of this tree by modifying the contents while it is dormant on a secondary storage device will be caught during boot through a mismatch of the root hash. Similarly, replay or modification attacks to an application's SSRs produces a mismatch against the hashes stored in the kernel-managed Merkle hash tree.

Writes to the storage system and to the TPM are not atomic, and a power failure may interrupt the system between or during these operations, so care must be taken when updating the kernel-managed Merkle hash tree. The Nexus uses an update protocol that can withstand asynchronous system shutdown and that requires no more than the two 160-bit hardware registers as provided by the TPM v1.1 standard. These TPM data integrity registers (DIRs), which we will call DIR_{cur} and DIR_{new} for clarity, are set up such that they cannot be accessed unless the state of certain platform configuration registers (PCRs) match a sequence that corresponds to the Nexus. The protocol additionally employs two state files /proc/state/current and /proc/state/new on disk to store the contents of the kernel hash tree.

When an application performs a write to a VDIR, the Nexus effectively creates an in-memory copy of the kernel hash tree and updates it to reflect the modification to that VDIR. It then follows a four step process to flush the contents to disk; namely: (1) write the new kernel hash tree to disk under /proc/state/new, (2) write the new root hash into DIR_{new}, (3) write the new root hash into DIR_{cur}, (4) write the kernel hash tree to /proc/state/current. A success indication is returned to the user application only after all four steps complete without failure.

On boot, the Nexus reads both state files, computes their hashes, and checks them against the contents of the two DIR registers. If only one of the DIR entries matches the corresponding file contents, the contents of the corresponding file are read and used to initialize all VDIRs; if both match, then /proc/state/new contains the latest state; and if neither matches, indicating that the on-disk storage was modified while the kernel was dormant, the Nexus boot is aborted. This sequence ensures that the current copy of the VDIR contents always resides on disk and can be located even in the presence of machine failures that may leave the files or the DIR registers in an undefined state. If it is desirable to protect against failures of the secondary storage device that may affect the files at rest, then more copies could be made at steps (2) and (3).

Nexus provides confidentiality guarantees for SSRs using kernel abstractions called Virtual Keys (VKEYs). Whereas VDIRs provide a mechanism to virtualize the limited data integrity storage on the TPM, VKEYs virtualize the limited encryption key storage. The VKEY interface provides methods for creating, destroying, externalizing, and internalizing key material, in addition to standard cryptographic operations suited for the type of key. VKEYs are stored in protected memory in the kernel. During externalization, a VKEY can optionally be encrypted with another VKEY to which a program has access; the Nexus uses the TPM to generate a default Nexus key, and sets it up to be accessible only to a kernel whose platform configuration registers (PCRs) match those for the Nexus. Specifically, SSRs use a symmetric counter-mode AES block cipher on the data blocks that comprise an SSR. Counter-mode encryption allows regions of files to be encrypted independently, decoupling operation time from the size of the file. Unlike most block-chaining modes, a counter-mode ciphertext block does not depend on its predecessor, obviating the need to recalculate all successor ciphertexts after an update to some plaintext block. This mechanism allows Nexus to retrieve and verify only the relevant blocks from the filesystem, and it enables demand paging for reading data blocks in an SSR.

Since all operations on VKEYs and VDIRs can be protected using logical attestation, complex policies about the uses of cryptographic keys and stored data are easy to express. Group signatures, for instance, can be implemented by creating a VKEY and setting an appropriate goal formula on the **sign** operation that can be discharged by members of the group. Further, by associating a different goal formula with the **externalize** operation, an application can separate the group of programs that can sign for the group from those that perform key management and transfer keys for the group. Similarly, goal formulas can be used to limit access to VDIRs and the corresponding SSRs. For instance, an SSR that holds sensitive data subject to policy controls such as Sorbanes-Oxley, HIPAA, and the like, can be restricted for access solely to those applications that have been certified, analyzed, or synthesized by appropriate authorities to uphold that policy.

3.4 Nexus Boot

Integrating the additional kernel abstractions and mechanisms described above with the TPM requires only modest modifications to the boot sequence. On power-up, the TPM initializes its platform configuration registers (PCR) to known values, and the system BIOS extends PCRs with a firmware hash and the firmware extends PCRs with the boot loader hash. A trusted boot loader extends PCRs with a hash over the Nexus kernel image. This provides a measurement over the entire kernel image; it forms a static root of trust for the Nexus kernel. We adopted this simple approach for establishing the root of trust because it makes minimal assumptions about the processor hardware; recent hardware extensions to support a dynamic root of trust, which can reduce TCB size even further by dynamically providing a safe execution environment for snippets of code, could also have been employed.

After the kernel is loaded, the Nexus boot sequence attempts to initialize the TPM to a known good state and to recover the kernel's internal state. If this is the first Nexus boot, then the Nexus forces the TPM to generate a new Storage Root Key (SRK) associated with the current PCR state by taking ownership of the coprocessor. If this is not the first boot, then it uses the protocol described in the preceding section to decrypt the VDIR and VKEY contents.

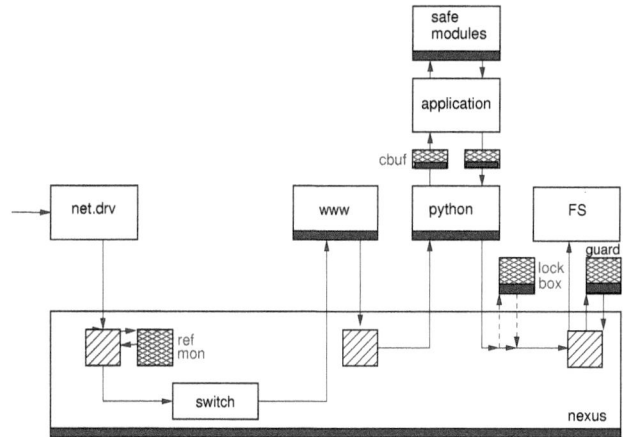

Figure 3: The Fauxbook multi-tier webserver. Cross-hatched boxes denote enforcement mechanisms, shaded boxes identify decision caches and thick borders indicate hash attestation.

This is performed through a TPM unseal operation that depends on the SRK and the PCR values. Consequently, the Nexus state can only be restored by the kernel that initially took ownership; attempts to boot a modified kernel to acquire access to the SRK and, consequently, decrypt the VDIR and VKEY contents, are prevents because a modified kernel that permits such unsafe operations will lead to different PCR values.

An early version of the Nexus kernel investigated mechanisms for acquiring a privacy-preserving kernel key from a Nexus Privacy Authority that can be used in lieu of TPM-based keys, and therefore mask the precise identity of the TPM. Techniques for implementing such privacy authorities (also known as trust brokers) are well-established and could be employed in settings where the identity of the TPM cannot be revealed.

4. Applications

The combination of operating system level interpositioning, introspection, and logical attestation enables the Nexus to support applications that enforce guarantees about state and history, and prove these guarantees to third parties.

4.1 Fauxbook

To illustrate these capabilities, we implemented a privacy-preserving social network application called Fauxbook. Unlike many, Fauxbook enforces user-defined policies on data dissemination. Fauxbook is a three-tier web service built from a standard Lighttpd webserver, Python application server with SQLite, and Posix filesystem. Figure 3 depicts how a web request flows through the system.

Logical attestation enables Fauxbook to provide novel guarantees. There are three kinds of entities in cloud computing environments, each demanding different guarantees: cloud providers who operate the cloud infrastructure and house tenants; developers who deploy applications on the cloud infrastructure and act as tenants to cloud providers; and users of the deployed applications. To the cloud provider, it guarantees that developers remain confined to a sandbox, obviating the need to use virtual machines or other mechanisms for isolation. To developers, Fauxbook guarantees that the underlying cloud provider actually provides levels of resources contracted. And to ordinary users, Fauxbook ensures that data shared with friends in the Fauxbook social network is protected from inspection, datamining, and display to unauthorized third-parties, including to Fauxbook developers themselves. Fauxbook implements these guarantees by combining axiomatic, analytical, and synthetic bases for trust.

Resource Attestation. Fauxbook employs logical attestation on kernel resources in order to guarantee that cloud providers deliver agreed-upon levels of service to the Fauxbook application. Oversubscription is a long-standing problem in shared environments, like the cloud. Clients might contract for some desired level of service from the underlying platform, but conventional systems provide few mechanisms for enforcing such service-level agreements (SLAs). Where SLAs involve externally-observable performance metrics, such as latency or throughput, enforcement typically requires continuous end-to-end measurement. And there is a class of SLAs, pertaining to the availability of reserved resources, such as backup links in the network, that are difficult or impossible to measure from an application's vantage point; such service must be evaluated using exogenous, ad hoc mechanisms, such as reputation and feedback measures on web forums. All of these approaches are costly, difficult, and incomplete.

If the cloud provider executes the cloud platform on top of the Nexus, a labeling function can examine the internal state of resource allocators in the kernel. Labels can then vouch for reservations of service. For instance, we implemented a proportional-share CPU scheduler that maintains a list of all active clients, which it exports through the introspection interface. A file in each tenant's directory stores the weight assigned to that tenant, while goal statements ensure that file is not readable by other tenants. Therefore, a labeling function that measures the resource reservations from each of the hosts on which the tenant code is deployed ensures that the tenant receives an agreed-upon fraction of the CPU.

Safety Guarantees. Fauxbook uses logical attestation to guarantee that tenant code will remain confined to a sandbox, thus obviating the need for other, potentially expensive, isolation mechanisms. A labeling function uses analysis and synthesis to ensure that mutually distrusting tenant applications can be executed safely within the same address space. Specifically, the labeling function performs static analysis to ensure that tenant applications are legal Python and that tenants import only a limited set of Python libraries. This restriction, by itself, is not sufficient to achieve the desired level of isolation, because Python provides rich reflection mechanisms that could be used to access the import function provided by the language. That import function could in turn allow a rogue application to invoke arbitrary (and potentially unsafe) code. To defend against this attack, a second labeling function rewrites every reflection-related call such that it will not invoke the import function. The two labeling functions in combination ensure that the resulting tenant application can only invoke a constrained set of legal Python instructions and libraries.

Confidentiality Guarantees. Fauxbook employs logical attestation to guarantee users that their data is shared only with people they have authorized through the social networking service. Even Fauxbook developers are blocked from accessing users' shared content; developers are not able to examine, data-mine, or misappropriate user data, even though, as developers, they are intimately involved in manipulating and servicing such data. These guarantees were motivated by well-publicized incidents where developers of social networking systems abused their power [12].

The observation we leverage to protect users from developers is that, in this particular application, actions are, in a sense, data independent. Collecting personal information comprising status updates, photos and videos from users, storing this information for later use, and collating it for display to other users, does not require the ability to examine that data—it just requires copying and displaying it. Thus, Fauxbook treats user information as indistinguishable from opaque blobs, and the Fauxbook code is restricted to store, manipulate, and merge such blobs without seeing their content.

The central data structure in any social networking application is a social network graph. Nodes represent users, and edges correspond to friend relationships. Fauxbook guarantees that this graph (1) only contains edges explicitly authorized by the user, and (2) data flows from one node to another only if there is an edge between the two nodes. More complex authorization policies, perhaps involving friends-of-friends or various subsets of nodes belonging to different circles of friends, are also possible, but they do not raise substantially new security or implementation issues, so we concentrate on this simpler authorization policy for clarity.

Fauxbook attests to these two guarantees about the social network graph by presenting to its users a set of labels concerning properties of the software components that comprise the application. These properties are gleaned through analysis based on introspection and through synthesis based on interpositioning. Coupled with axiomatic trust in the Nexus kernel, the labels together demonstrate to Fauxbook users that their data will be handled in a way that achieves the properties discussed above.

Credentials conveying externalized forms of these labels currently reside at a public url in X.509 form (e.g. similar to where the privacy policy for a web application would be located) and can be queried by a user prior to signing-up with Fauxbook. An alternative implementation would involve transferring these certificates to the client during SSL connection setup; in addition to the traditional SSL certificate which binds a name to an IP address, these certificates would provide the groundwork for the client to be convinced that the software connected to the socket has certain properties that together uphold the desired privacy policy. In both cases, the guarantees about the behavior of tenant applications stem from trust in the infrastructure operated by the cloud provider, which in turn proscribes the behavior of the applications deployed in the cloud.

The operation of Fauxbook depends on several software components. A user-level device driver manages a network interface card. A `lighttpd` web server receives HTTP requests from users and dispatches them to URL handlers supported by a web framework, in addition to extracting the HTTP stream into TCP/IP packets (since networking is done in user level in the Nexus). The web framework provides the execution environment for web applications deployed in the cloud by developers. It provides libraries for user management and authenticating sessions, as well as the dispatch loop for generic applications. Finally, the Fauxbook application provides the logic required to implement a simple social network.

The cloud environment precludes certain simplifying assumptions. First, we cannot assume that application code is monolithic, public, or unchanging. If it were, then certifying its behavior would be a simple task of certifying its binary hash and making its code public. We instead expect that applications deployed in the cloud cannot have their source code made public and will change too frequently for their behavior to be manually certified. Second, we cannot assume a web framework having functionality that is specific to Fauxbook or any other particular application. A web framework typically is operated by the cloud provider and designed to support any generic application. Therefore, it cannot be tightly coupled with application code provided by third-party developers. Finally, we cannot assume that users possess unique cryptographic keys, because they don't.

The privacy guarantees of Fauxbook derive from the properties of each of the components involved in managing user data. Below, we describe each of these components and how they guarantee these properties.

The network device driver needs to ensure that user data is delivered solely to its intended recipient. A driver that copies information from packets could potentially also exfiltrate authentication information, such as submitted passwords and returned authenticating cookies, to third parties who then could impersonate the user, as well as directly copying personal information from the user for use by others. Our device driver can demonstrate that it is unable to perform these actions. Like most user-level drivers, the Nexus NIC device drivers operate by allocating memory pages, granting these to the NIC, setting up DMA registers to point to these pages, and handling device interrupts. Unlike other device drivers, Nexus device drivers operate under control of a device driver reference monitor (DDRM) [56] that can constrain access to the device and to memory. So the driver provides the aforementioned assurance by demonstrating that it is operating in a DDRM with no read or write privileges for any of the pages the driver manages. In fact, the driver can perform the DMA setup and other device functionality without access to page contents, so it does not actually need that access. In addition, it operates under a second reference monitor that blocks all but a small set of systems calls governing I/O ports, memory, and IPC. In particular, the reference monitor only allows sending and receiving packets to and from a particular IPC channel connected to the web server process. In sum, the network driver provides labels, based on synthesis and provided by the reference monitor, certifying that the reference monitor only forwards unmodified data between network device and the web server, and that it cannot modify message contents, either by copying between sessions or by forcing transmission to untrustworthy hosts.

The trustworthiness of the web server rests on both axiomatic and synthetic bases for trust. The web server forwards packets from the device driver to the web framework, and vice versa. Unlike the device driver, the web server requires read/write access to data, because it must translate IP packets into HTTP requests and, subsequently, into FastCGI messages. This task requires only IPC-related system calls in addition to polling, synchronization, and memory allocation. To prove that it will not leak information to other entities, the web server relinquishes the right to execute all other system calls after initialization. And it provides labels that demonstrate that it lacks the ability to communicate with other processes besides the device driver and the web framework, and that it is bound by hash to a well known binary version of analyzable open source software.

The web framework provides guarantees (1) that it will provide libraries for creating, deleting, and authenticating users, (2) that user authentication information is stored in a file to which the web framework has exclusive access, (3) that it will dispatch the correct handler for each web application, and, most importantly, (4) it will constrain each such application to not leak user information except as authorized by the users. Since the web framework code is relatively static, the first three guarantees can be obtained through hash-based attestation. The fourth guarantee forms the critical link to the overall security properties of Fauxbook, since it means that, even though the application code is provided by Fauxbook developers and is tasked with storing and assembling the web pages a user sees when visiting the Fauxbook social networking site, the very same code is unable to parse and examine the contents of the data, such as status updates and images, submitted by users.

The web framework enforces guarantees by constraining Fauxbook application code to access user data through a restricted interface called *cobuf*, for *constrained buffers*. Cobufs enable untrusted applications to manipulate user-supplied data without allowing that data to be examined. A cobuf comprises a byte array that stores data and an identifier that identifies the principal owning that information; the result is an attributed buffer that may be used only for content-oblivious string manipulations. Applications running on the web framework can store, retrieve, concatenate, and slice cobufs but lack the ability to act on cobuf contents. Akin in functionality to homomorphic encryption, cobufs permit operations on data without revealing that data, but the functionality is achieved using low-overhead language-based access control techniques rather than by expensive crytography.

By design, cobufs are useful only for data-independent applications, yet much of the functionality of a social networking application is data-independent. Because the cobuf interface does not support data dependent branches, it is not Turing-complete—certain functionality, such as vote tallying, which is inherently dependent on the data values submitted by clients cannot be implemented using cobufs. But, in some cases, it may be possible to create new cobuf-like objects that perform the requisite computation while bounding the amount of information that may leak in the worst case. The design of such extensions to the cobuf interface is beyond the scope of this paper.

A modification of the Python loader analyzes code during loading and ensures that Fauxbook code cannot use Python reflection mechanisms for peeking at object fields. Every cobuf is tagged with an owner identifier that is assigned on a session basis following a successful user authentication, and cobuf contents may only be collated if the recipient cobuf's owner speaks for the owner of the cobuf from which the data is copied.

Cobufs are used to protect the integrity of the underlying social network graph. Because the owner identifier is attached in the web server layer, Fauxbook application code cannot forge cobufs on behalf of a user. This prohibits the application from adding impostors that leak sensitive data. A legitimate, user-initiated friend addition into the Fauxbook social network invokes a method in the user authentication library that generates the requisite link in the social graph corresponding to that `speaksfor` relationship.

Fauxbook stores user data in the Nexus filesystem. Goal formulas associated with each file constrain user access in accordance with the social graph. Moreover, Fauxbook files reside in a directory that can be accessed only by a process with the expected web framework process and Python code hashes. Additionally, each operation on each file in this directory has a policy: private, public, or friends. Private data of user a Alice is only accessible if an authority embedded in the web server attests to label *name.webserver* `says` *user=alice*. Alice can only read the files of her friend Bob if an embedded authority attests to the label *name.python* `says` *alice in bob.friends*. To verify whether this holds, the authority introspects on the contents of a publically readable friend file. This operation is trustworthy, because only the web framework can update the value of the current user and only the web framework acting on behalf of Bob can modify his friend file.

Taken together, the statements embedded in the labels described above attest to an environment in which the Fauxbook code cannot directly inspect personal information provided by its users. And even though the Nexus has no built-in notion of social networks or web users, the flexibility of the logical attestation framework was able to provide such privacy guarantees, demonstrating the generality and power of the logical attestation framework.

4.2 Other Applications

We have built other applications based on logical attestation. We outline their operation to provide a broader view on how labels can be used to prove desired characteristics to remote parties.

Movie Player. Platform lock-down is a long-standing and widely reviled problem with binary hash-based attestation. Yet, without any form of attestation, content owners are justifiably wary of distributing high-value digital content, such as movies, that can easily be copied and redistributed widely. With conventional approaches to attestation, a content owner wanting to ensure that her movies are not illegally copied would create a whitelist of known-to-be-trustworthy media players, demand a binary hash attestation, and stream content only if the player is on a list of trusted players. As a result, the user either needs to use a precertified player and operating system or forgo watching the movie.

Logical attestation makes it possible to offer much greater choice to users yet still satisfy the content owner's needs. Specifically, the user, instead of furnishing a binary attestation certificate, exports a label that says an IPC channel-connectivity analyzer has determined that user's program (whose hash need not be divulged in the certificate or elsewhere) lacks the ability to write to the disk or the network. We have built and implemented such a general-purpose IPC connectivity analyzer, though one could also imagine the content owner furnishing that labeling function to the user. In either case, the label provides a basis for a content provider to decide whether the user can be trusted with the data, but the user now has the flexibility to pick any player that can be analyzed and shown to satisfy the desired security policy.

Java Object Store. Unlike filesystem access control lists, logical attestation makes it possible to restrict access to a class of programs that possess an intrinsically-described capability. This can have far-reaching impact, including for performance optimization. For instance, Java virtual machines have long suffered object deserialization overhead. Because the Java runtime is typesafe and because data coming from the external world cannot be trusted, a number of type invariants needs to be checked dynamically during deserialization.

Logical attestation can be used to obviate such checking in cases where the object to be deserialized was generated by another typesafe Java virtual machine. Take, for instance, a Java object store, where the objects are stored on disk and later downloaded onto a separate computer. If the downloader can be assured that the entity producing that database was another Java virtual machine satisfying the same typesafety invariants, then the slow parts of sanity checking every byte of data can be skipped when reinstating an object. This is an instance of a class of applications based on transitive integrity verification [49].

Not-A-Bot. A recent proposal aims to combat email spam with certificates attached to each message that indicate whether that message originated from a human or from an automated script [17]. Using logical attestation, we have prototyped this approach. An email program was modified to obtain a certificate from the keyboard driver, where that certificate attests to the number of keypresses it received. Such a TPM-backed certificate then serves as an input to a SPAM classification algorithm.

TruDocs and CertiPics. Recent public scandals, such as those involving published pictures that were altered in significant ways and intelligence reports quoted in a manner that distorted their meaning, demonstrate the need to ensure important data is handled in accordance with appropriate guidelines. And there are many settings where such guidelines not only exist but, also, have been specified in a manner amenable to mechanistic enforcement [45]. To demonstrate that the logical attestation machinery is sufficient to implement such applications, we built TruDocs and CertiPics, two document handling systems that ensure that modifications comply with desired policies. There are many different ways in which the

different bases for trust can be used to implement these applications. We describe some implementation choices, which cover the spectrum.

CertiPics is an image editing suite whose goal is to ensure that images to be used in publications conform to standards. CertiPics consists of a user interface that executes without privilege and a set of image processing elements, such as crop, color transform, resize, clone, and other manipulations supported by the portable bitmap suite of tools, that execute on the Nexus. In addition to generating a desired image from a given source, CertiPics concurrently generates a certified, unforgeable log of the transformations performed. This log, coupled with the source and final images, make it possible for analyzers to determine if a disallowed modification, such as cloning, was applied to the image.

TruDocs is a document display system whose goal is to ensure that a given excerpt conveys the beliefs intended in the original document. Implemented as a set of extensions to the OpenOffice suite, this application issues a certificate attesting that an excerpt speaks for the original document if the excerpt satisfies a given *use policy*. Supported use policies can admit changing typecase, replacing certain text fragments with ellipses, and inserting editorial comments in square brackets, while limiting the length and total number of excerpts.

Protocol Verifiers. The BGP protocol is widely deployed, critical to Internet routing, and suffers from vulnerability to misbehaving participants. A naive approach to ensuring that a given BGP speaker is trustworthy would involve equipping all BGP speakers with TPMs and attesting to their launch-time hashes; an instance of axiomatic trust. Such an effort would not only incur tremendous hardware costs to replace legacy hardware but would also entail a tremendous software certification effort to determine which, if any, of the many different versions of BGP software is correct.

Applying the logical attestation approach to this problem, using synthetic trust, yields a far simpler approach. We have designed a BGP protocol verifier by coupling a BGP parser with a set of minimal BGP safety rules that identify route fabrication and false origination attacks [39]. The verifier straddles a legacy BGP speaker whose inputs and outputs it monitors by acting as a proxy between the legacy speaker and other speakers. It ensures that every outgoing BGP advertisement or withdrawal conforms to the BGP safety rules; for instance, by ensuring that a host cannot advertise an n hop route to a destination for which the shortest advertisement that it itself received is m, for $n < m$. While the details of this application, such as how such verifiers can be connected into an overlay, how they react to non-conforming BGP messages, and how they admit local policy preferences, is beyond the scope of this paper, this application is an exemplar for the use of synthetic trust in a network setting.

5. Evaluation

This section reports measurements of costs for logical attestation. We first quantify costs imposed by the base Nexus microkernel, by logical attestation operations, and by system services. Next, we measure the cumulative cost this architecture imposes on our Fauxbook application.

Benchmarks presented in this section represent the median of at least 100 measurements when we observed a maximal deviation of upper and lower quartiles below 2.5% each, unless otherwise stated. Application benchmarks have the same bound, showing the median of at least 10 runs, each of at least 1000 requests. All performance data was obtained on a Dell Optiplex 745 containing a 2.13 GHz Intel E6400 CPU with 2MB of L2 cache and 2 GB of

	Nexus Bare	Nexus	Linux
null	352	808	*n/a*
null (block)	*n/a*	624	*n/a*
getppid	360	824	688
gettimeofday	640	1112	978
yield	736	1128	1328
open		8752	3240
close		4672	1816
read		3600	1808
write		11792	3900

Table 1: **System call overhead, in cycles, comparing Nexus with Linux. System calls are cheaper in Nexus when interpositioning is disabled; when enabled, low-level operations have comparable performance, while high-level filesystem operations have higher overheads because their implementation employs multiple user-level servers.**

component	lines	component	lines
kernel core	9904	headers	5020
IPC	1217	label mgmt	621
interpositioning	67	introspection	981
VDIR/VKEY	1165	networking	1357
generic guard†	4157	malloc	158 / 3322
filesystem†	1810	debug†	356
Xen†	9678	kernel drivers†	27238
posix library†	3953	user drivers†	24830
TCB	20490		

Table 2: **Lines of Code. Items marked † are optional. Nexus has a small TCB, enabled by factoring device drivers out of the kernel.**

main memory running in 32bit uniprocessor mode. This system has an Intel 82540EM network adapter and Atmel v1.2 compatible TPM. Linux results were obtained with a Ubuntu 10.10 installation with the default 2.6.35-23 kernel.

5.1 Microbenchmarks

The Nexus system architecture implements services in user-space whenever possible, in order to reduce the size of the trusted computing base (TCB). Such a microkernel design inevitably adds overhead due to longer communication paths. System call interpositioning imposes further overhead for parameter marshaling at every kernel-mode switch.

To establish the cost of these design decisions, we compare invocation cost of common operations both with and without interpositioning directly to Linux. To establish size of the TCB, we calculate the number of lines of code contributing to each essential Nexus component.

Kernel Operations. Table 1 shows system call costs for a modified Nexus without interpositioning, standard Nexus, and Linux. Invocation of an empty `null` call gives an upper bound of interpositioning overhead, at $808 - 352 = 456$ extra cycles. An interposed call that is blocked returns earlier than a completed call, after only 624 cycles in total. Nexus executes the Posix calls `getppid`, `gettimeofday` and `yield` faster than Linux (1.5-2x) when interpositioning is disabled. When enabled, performance is comparable (0.8-1.2x). We conclude that parameter marshaling required for interpositioning does not significantly impact basic call overhead. File operations are between 2 and 3x more expensive, on the other hand, at least in part due to the communication imposed by the client-server microkernel architecture.

TCB Size. Table 2 reports the size of the TCB, using David Wheeler's `sloc` counter.

At less than 25 thousand lines, the kernel is larger than some microkernels but smaller than many device drivers. Device driver reference monitors (DDRMs) [56] enable the Nexus device drivers, comprising keyboard, mouse, pci, network (e1000, pcnet32, and tg3), sound (i810 and es1370), storage (ide) and tpm (atmel 1.1, nsc 1.1, and emulator 1.2) drivers, to execute in user space. Shown in the table as `user drivers`, they operate without privilege and are constrained throughout execution by a device driver safety policy designed to protect the isolation guarantees provided by Nexus IPDs, even in the presence of misbehaving and malicious drivers. We maintain implementations of a VESA video driver, a TG3 net-

work driver, and a PCI driver in the kernel (`kernel drivers`) for debugging and for performance comparison purposes.

The filesystem functionality in Nexus is spread over three components. Basic namespace services are provided by the kernel core, while a RAM-based store (`filesystem`) provides transient data storage. In addition, the networking module provides TFTP and NFS-based file and directory access. Even though these networking protocols do not provide security guarantees and the data resides on physically remote disks, the SSR implementation ensures that application data as well as the Nexus kernel's private VDIRs and VKEYs contents are tamper- and replay-proof.

The generic guard used by default for kernel resources is less than 5000 lines of code. For comparison, the Broadcom network driver alone measures 16920 lines (version tg3-3.110g). Note that the generic guard implementation is optional; applications can use alternative guards for their resources.

We have biult a few additional components to support legacy applications. A Posix library provides a familiar API for Nexus applications operating directly on the Nexus. Similar to past work on VM-based secure systems [9, 14], Xen support enables the Nexus to execute monolithic legacy systems in isolated virtual machines. A compact malloc library provides in-kernel memory management. Auxiliary libraries that are used by Nexus applications but are not specific to the Nexus kernel, such as μClibc and OpenSSL, are not shown.

5.2 Logical Attestation

Logical attestation can be prohibitively expensive without caching and system-backed credentials. We quantify the run-time cost of guard invocation and the effects of caching, measure scalability with proof complexity, and compare control operations overhead of system-backed and cryptographically implemented labels.

Invocation. Authorization cost depends on how many checks have to be performed. Figure 4 compares these costs for a bare system call invocation. To establish a baseline, we give the cost of evaluating a trivial proof consisting of a single assumption. From left to right, the figure presents runtime for the case where (a) authorization is disabled (`system call`), (b) a default ALLOW goal is set (`no goal`), (c) a real goal is set, but no proof was supplied by the subject (`no proof`), (d) the supplied proof is not sound (`not sound`), (e) the proof is sound and all premises are supported (`pass`), (f) the proof lacks a credential (`no cred`), (g) the proof depends on an embedded authority (`embed auth`), and (h) the proof depends on an external authority (`auth`). Solid bars depict execution time with the kernel decision cache enabled; dashed bars with it disabled. The upcall into the guard increases cost of authorizing

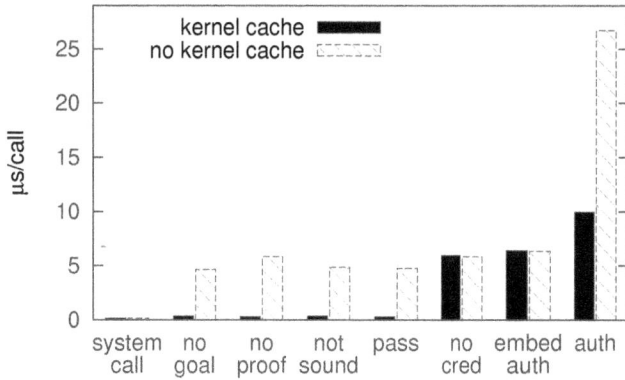

Figure 4: Authorization Cost. Cached decisions add around 456 cycles, keeping total runtime well below one μsecond. Upcalls into the guard are 16-20x as expensive.

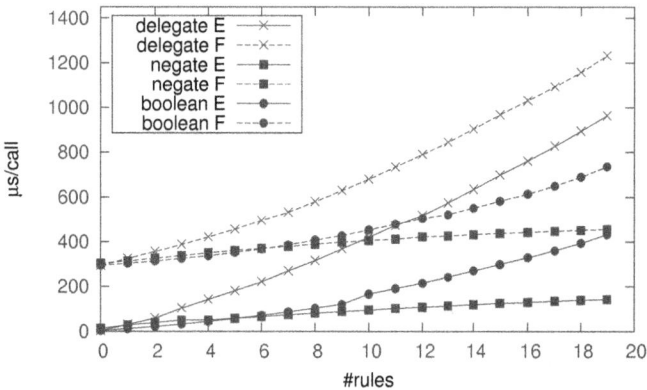

Figure 5: Proof Evaluation Cost. With caching, access control cost is reduced to tens of cycles.

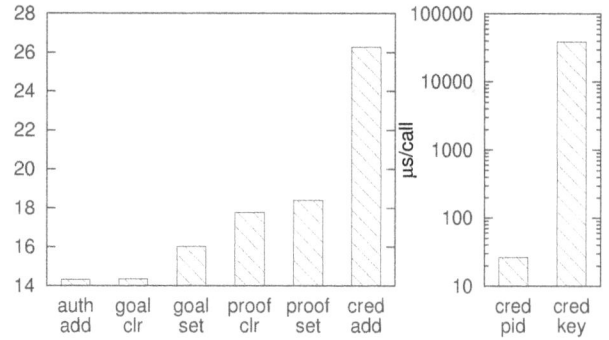

Figure 6: Authorization Control Overhead. Avoidance of cryptography reduces cost by 3 orders of magnitude.

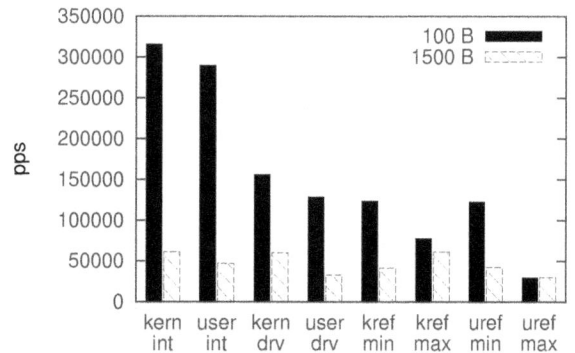

Figure 7: Overhead of interpositioning. Caching decisions decrease packet processing rate by less than 6%.

an operation from 624 to 12424 cycles. In general, guard operations are between 16 and 20x as expensive as kernel decisions. Cases (a)–(e) indicate the effectiveness of decision caching. The jump between (e) and (f) clearly delineates the set of cacheable proofs. Operations that cannot be cached are credential matching (20% overhead over `pass`) and invocation of an embedded (31%) or external authority (106%). The last case is exceptionally expensive with caching disabled, due to the cumulative effect of interposing on all system calls made by the authority process.

Proof Evaluation. When decisions cannot be cached, time spent in proof evaluation depends on proof size. Figure 5 shows proof checking time for proofs of increasing length, measured as the number of inference rules applied. It presents execution time for application of the simplest NAL rule, double negation introduction, together with two common NAL deduction rules: `speaksfor` delegation and disjunction elimination. The solid lines show the isolated cost of proof checking, while the dashed lines show total execution time, which also incorporates the time to check labels and look up authorities. Both curves show the same trend, with a different constant cost that reflects the overhead of IPCs and scheduling the processes that implement the label store and authority. Overall, the proof checker executes all proofs shorter than 15 steps in less than 1ms. All practical proofs that we have written in our applications involve less than 15 steps.

Control Operations. Logical attestation requires management of goals, proofs, and labels. Nexus is optimized for efficient invocation, even if it meant increased cost for these less-frequently executed operations. Figure 6 summarizes control-operation execution times. System-backed and cryptographic operations are displayed at difference scales, because of the huge gap in execution times. The left-hand figure shows cost of operations without cryptography at linear scale: authority registration (`auth add`), goal deletion and insertion (`goal clr/set`), proof deletion and insertion (`proof clr/set`), and credential insertion (`cred add`). The credential insertion operation is twice as expensive as the next slowest, because each label has to be parsed to verify that the caller is allowed to make the statement. The right-hand figure compares this same system-backed credential insertion call (`cred pid`) to insertion of a cryptographically signed label, using a logarithmic scale. Verification of the signed label is three orders of magnitude more expensive than the same operation for its system-backed equivalent, substantiating our view that cryptographic operations should be avoided if possible.

5.3 Operating System Services

Introspection and interpositioning are essential to using our logical attestation framework. Since introspection, whose performance is comparable to the file I/O numbers shown in Table 1, typically does not lie on the critical path, its performance overhead is unlikely to affect benchmarks. Interpositioning, on the other hand, introduces dynamic checks that could prove prohibitive, especially

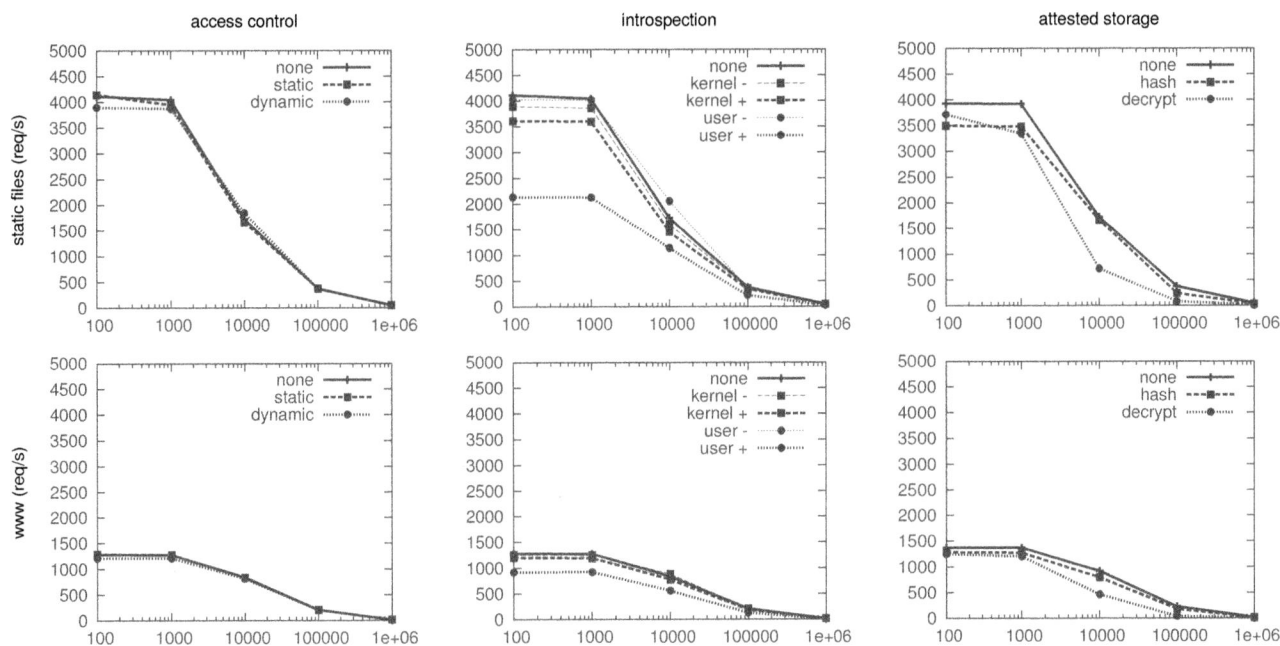

Figure 8: Application evaluation: impact of access control (col. 1), reference monitors (col. 2) and attested storage (col. 3) on a webserver serving static files (row 1) and dynamic Python content (row 2). Filesize varies from 100B to 1MB, the x-axis is plotted in logarithmic scale.

on highly active communication paths.

Interpositioning. To calculate an upper bound on overhead from dynamic checks, we install progressively more demanding reference monitors and measure maximally obtained throughput for a trivial application: a UDP echo server written in 27 lines of C. Figure 7 plots throughput in packets per second for increasing levels of protection, for both small and large size packets. For this test, quartiles lie within 5% of the median, except for the first measurement, which lies within 18%.

Figure 7 illustrates the causes of interpositioning overhead by progressively enabling more of the interpositioning machinery. The first two cases (`kern-int` and `user-int`) show throughput when the driver directly responds to requests from within the interrupt handler, bypassing all interpositioning. While a kernel driver achieves 17% higher rate than its user-level equivalent, executing untrusted application code within the device driver interrupt handler is not practical without substantial additional measures. Cases `kern-drv` and `user-drv` show the more realistic scenario of an independent server application that communicates with the driver through kernel IPC. The 2x drop in throughput is due to IPC, scheduling, routing, and the user-level TCP/IP stack. In cases `kref` and `uref`, reference monitors, located in the kernel and at user-level, respectively, are installed on the userspace driver to ensure compliance with a device driver safety policy. The measurements for `min` and `max` show the throughput with and without caching, respectively. While cache misses during reference monitoring can reduce throughput by 50%, caching can reduce monitoring overhead to as little as 4% for small packets. When user-space reference monitors are employed, the impact on throughput is as high as 77%, but the decision cache can reduce the overhead to less than 5%.

5.4 Application

In the worst case, overhead of logical attestation can be three orders of magnitude over functional cost if credentials are imple-

mented by using cryptographic labels. The Nexus architecture is based on the assumption that caching can reduce such overhead to negligible levels. To test this hypothesis, we measure the effects of the Nexus mechanisms on a demanding workload: throughput of the Fauxbook web application. We measure the impact of access control, interpositioning, and attested storage on throughput—both in the case of static file serving and dynamic Python execution. Figure 8 shows these three sources of cost, from left to right. Each figure plots HTTP requests per second versus filesize at logarithmic scale. The top row of graphs presents throughput for a static fileserver, the bottom row displays the same numbers for a dynamic server running Python.

The curves in graphs compare throughput under three types of access control: `none` performs no authorization checks, `static` evaluates a cacheable proof, and `dynamic` invokes an external authority. Figure 4 showed considerable cost at the micro level. At the application level, worst-case overhead is 6% for a minimal page with guard invocation. Comparing the two rows shows that overhead is consistently less pronounced for the multi-tier server with Python than for the simpler fileserver. Interpositioning cost, displayed in the middle column, significantly decreases throughput without caching. Worst case throughput is roughly 50% with the user-space reference monitor. With caching, this overhead is only 6%.

Hashing and encryption are expensive. Encryption decreases throughput by up to 85%; hashing up to 38%. Small file hashing suffers from a large 1 kB blocksize, requiring padding for the smallest files. Eventually, efficiency consistently decreases with larger file sizes as the per byte cost of hashing increases, while per request costs stay constant: the worst case occurs at the largest size. When files are accessed through Python, the overheads remain similar, with a worst case of 85% at the largest filesize.

6. Related Work

Hash-based attestation was initially proposed in security architectures for secure bootstrapping [15, 22, 3]. Logical attestation differs from this work in that credentials can capture properties that are not derived from the launch-time hash of a program. Like logical attestation, semantic remote attestation [18] and property-based attestation [40] suggest encoding meaningful application-level properties. Unlike logical attestation, their protocol formats are application-specific or unspecified, and they do not provide a corresponding implementation in an operating system. Nexus is the first OS to offer semantically rich attestation as a system service and demonstrate an efficient implementation.

TCGLinux [42] proposes to add attestation capabilities to a conventional Linux system. This approach is problematic due to Linux's large TCB and lack of strong isolation. Software-based attestation [47, 46] derives its correctness from assumptions about execution time, requiring intricate knowledge of target hardware. Hardware-based approaches do not have this constraint. BIND [49] offers fine-grained attestation on an untrusted OS through monitoring and sandboxing by a trusted software module. Flicker [32] extends the approach to legacy systems. Logical attestation is not inconsistent with such isolation, independent of the OS. The system-level implementation in Nexus avoids costly repeated state serialization, however, rendering per-call interpositioning feasible and offering assurance to all system objects.

To secure legacy systems, trusted hardware has been combined with virtualization, in the form of trusted hypervisors [41, 14], mediated TPM access [10], and full TPM virtualization [4]. Multiplexing the TPM hardware interface in software does not solve the problems stemming from limitations of the binary hash-based attestation interface provided by the hardware. Some approaches refine or replace the hardware interface: property-based virtualization [40] supports variations on the TPM Quote function, Not-a-Bot [17] presents human presence attestations, and TrustVisor exposes the isolated process interface of Flicker [31]. Even higher-level VMMs protection is inherently limited by the system interface, whereas operating system protection extends to all primitives, including files and users.

Microkernels offer another path to TCB minimization. seL4 demonstrated formal verification of correctness of microkernels [24]. L4 [21] has been proposed as a a small TCB [37, 20, 19]. Nizza [20] extends it with trusted wrappers, similar to how TrustVisor adapts VMMs. Nexus is a similarly small OS, but Nexus integrates a comprehensive authorization architecture. EROS [48] is another capability-based microkernel OS for mutually distrusting users. Like Nexus, it caches state in the kernel. EROS uses kernel-protected numerical capabilities that are not suitable for remote attestation and policies are not as flexible as arbitrary proofs. Flask [51] introduced an authorization architecture that supports these features and caches security decisions in the kernel. In this model, Nexus implements and evaluates a complete, expressive, policy mechanism.

The NGSCB [9] splits the system software into a large untrusted and smaller trusted compartment. XOMOS [29] treats the OS as an untrusted compartment from which trusted processes are shielded using hypothesized CPU extensions. Logical attestation replaces this duality with a delegated trust model that extends to multiparty environments. Wedge [5] splits applications into least-privilege compartments to isolate internal secrets, similar to the authenticated interpreter in the Nexus cloud stack, though this does not extend to multiple processes and system objects, such as files. HiStar [58] assures systemwide data confidentiality and integrity by enforcing information flow constraints on Asbestos [8] labels.

TPMs also support implementation of trustworthy abstractions that are independent of the operating system. Monotonic counters [43, 27] and append-only logs [6] are examples of trustworthy computing abstractions rooted in specialized hardware. Storage services on untrusted servers use TPMs [28, 55], possibly through virtual counters [53] and other cryptographic operations [30, 13]. An operating system such as the Nexus can offer the collective primitives and assurances in a single system, but requires more pervasive software changes than any individual system.

A recent survey reviews the state of the art in trusted computing in more depth than we can here [36]. Proof based authorization is not limited to trusted computing. Lampson argued for combining logics, reference monitors, and chains of trust to construct secure systems [25]. NAL borrows ideas and notation from Taos [57] and CDD [1] (among others [45]). Proof carrying authorization [2] introduces distributed decision based on logic proof evaluation. Alpaca [26] generalizes the approach to include common credential formats and cryptographic primitives.

For any credential issued by an operating system to be trustworthy, the system implementation must be free of bugs. The construction of a verifiable OS kernel is an area of active research [24], while efforts to reduce the kernel footprint [56] are synergistic.

7. Conclusions

Logical attestation offers strong operating system authorization by deriving trustworthiness from unforgeable system properties. It incorporates software analysis and containment as sources for trust decisions and captures the results in what we call labels: meaningful, unforgeable, and attributable statements written in a high-level logic. Labels serve as facts in proof-based authorization to offer rational decision making and incontestable audit trails. A comprehensive operating system architecture combines efficient and secure means for label generation, communication, and consumption with system services for introspection, interpositioning, and secure persistent storage.

We have implemented logical attestation in Nexus, a trustworthy operating system that combines a small TCB with a strong root of trust in the form of a TPM secure coprocessor. Evaluation shows that strong isolation and trust are compatible with high performance: multilevel caching amortizes authorization cost to offer system operations on level footing with Linux; cryptography avoidance reduces distributed decision making cost by three orders of magnitude. Even with full isolation, Nexus mechanisms impose modest overhead on policy-rich cloud computing applications.

Acknowledgments

The authors would like to thank the anonymous reviewers and our shepherd, Adrian Perrig, for their insightful feedback. This work was supported in part by ONR grant N00014-09-1-0652, AFOSR grant F9550-06-0019, NSF grants 0430161, 0964409, CNS-1111698 and CCF-0424422 (TRUST), and a gift from Microsoft Corporation.

8. References

[1] Martín Abadi. Variations in Access Control Logic. In *Proc. of the Conference on Deontic Logic in Computer Science*, Luxembourg, July 2008.

[2] Andrew W. Appel and Edward W. Felten. Proof-carrying authentication. In *Proc. of the Conference on Computer and Communications Security*, Singapore, November 1999.

[3] William A. Arbaugh, David J. Farber, and Jonathan M. Smith. A Secure and Reliable Bootstrap Architecture. In

Proc. of the IEEE Symposium on Security and Privacy, Oakland, CA, May 1997.

[4] Stefan Berger, Ramón Cáceres, Kenneth A. Goldman, Ronald Perez, Reiner Sailer, and Leendert van Doorn. vTPM: Virtualizing the Trusted Platform Module. In *Proc. of the USENIX Security Symposium*, Vancouver, Canada, August 2006.

[5] Andrea Bittau, Petr Marchenko, Mark Handley, and Brad Karp. Wedge: Splitting Applications into Reduced-privilege Compartments. In *Proc. of the Symposium on Networked System Design and Implementation*, San Francisco, CA, April 2008.

[6] Byung-Gon Chun, Petros Maniatis, Scott Shenker, and John Kubiatowicz. Attested append-only memory: Making adversaries stick to their word. In *Proc. of the Symposium on Operating System Principles*, Stevenson, WA, October 2007.

[7] Jack B. Dennis and Earl C. Van Horn. Programming semantics for multiprogrammed computations. *Comm. of the ACM*, 9:143–155, March 1966.

[8] Petros Efstathopoulos, Maxwell Krohn, Steve VanDeBogart, Cliff Frey, David Ziegler, Eddie Kohler, David Mazières, M. Frans Kaashoek, and Robert T. Morris. Labels and Event Processes in the Asbestos Operating System. In *Proc. of the Symposium on Operating Systems Principles*, Brighton, UK, October 2005.

[9] Paul England, Butler Lampson, John Manferdelli, Marcus Peinado, and Bryan Willman. A Trusted Open Platform. *Computer*, 36(7):55–62, July 2003.

[10] Paul England and Jork Loeser. Para-Virtualized TPM Sharing. In *Proc. of the International Conference on Trusted Computing and Trust in Information Technologies*, Villach, Austria, 2008.

[11] Ùlfar Erlingsson and Fred B. Schneider. IRM Enforcement of Java Stack Inspection. In *Proc. of the IEEE Symposium on Security and Privacy*, Oakland, CA, May 2000.

[12] Electronic Frontier Foundation. Facebook's New Privacy Changes: The Good, The Bad, and The Ugly. http://www.eff.org/deeplinks/2009/12/facebooks-new-privacy-changes-good-bad-and-ugly.

[13] Kevin Fu, M. Frans Kaashoek, and David Mazières. Fast and Secure Distributed Read-Only File System. In *Proc. of the Symposium on Operating Systems Design and Implementation*, San Diego, CA, October 2000.

[14] Tal Garfinkel, Ben Pfaff, Jim Chow, Mendel Rosenblum, and Dan Boneh. Terra: A Virtual Machine-Based Platform for Trusted Computing. In *Proc. of the Symposium on Operating Systems Principles*, Bolton Landing, NY, October 2003.

[15] Morrie Gasser, Andy Goldstein, Charlie Kaufman, and Butler Lampson. The Digital Distributed System Security Architecture. In *Proc. of the National Computer Security Conference*, Baltimore, MD, October 1989.

[16] Li Gong. Java Security: Present and Near Future. *IEEE Micro*, 17(3):14–19, May/June 1997.

[17] Ramakrishna Gummadi, Hari Balakrishnan, Petros Maniatis, and Sylvia Ratnasamy. Not-a-Bot: Improving Service Availability in the Face of Botnet Attacks. In *Proc. of the Symposium on Networked System Design and Implementation*, Boston, MA, April 2009.

[18] Vivek Haldar, Deepak Chandra, and Michael Franz. Semantic Remote attestation: A Virtual Machine Directed Approach to Trusted Computing. In *Proc. of the USENIX Virtual Machine Research and Technology Symposium*, San

Jose, CA, May 2004.

[19] Hermann Härtig. Security Architectures Revisited. In *Proc. of the SIGOPS European Workshop*, Saint-Emilion, France, September 2002.

[20] Hermann Härtig, Michael Hohmuth, Norman Feske, Christian Helmuth, Adam Lackorzynski, Frank Mehnert, and Michael Peter. The Nizza Secure-System Architecture. In *Proc. of the International Conference on Collaborative Computing*, San Jose, CA, December 2005.

[21] Hermann Härtig, Michael Hohmuth, Jochen Liedtke, and Sebastian Schönberg. The Performance of μ-Kernel-Based Systems. In *Proc. of the Symposium on Operating Systems Principles*, Saint Malo, France, October 1997.

[22] Hermann Härtig and Oliver Kowalski and Winfried Kühnhauser. The BirliX Security Architecture. *Journal of Computer Security*, 2(1):5–21, 1993.

[23] William K. Josephson, Emin Gün Sirer, and Fred B. Schneider. Peer-to-Peer Authentication With a Distributed Single Sign-On Service. In *Proc. of the Workshop on Peer-to-Peer Systems*, San Diego, CA, February 2004.

[24] Gerwin Klein, Kevin Elphinstone, Gernot Heiser, June Andronick, David Cock, Philip Derrin, Dhammika Elkaduwe, Kai Engelhardt, Michael Norrish, Rafal Kolanski, Thomas Sewell, Harvey Tuch, and Simon Winwood. seL4: Formal Verification of an OS Kernel. In *Proc. of the Symposium on Operating Systems Principles*, Big Sky, MT, October 2009.

[25] Butler Lampson. Computer Security in the Real World. *IEEE Computer*, 37(6), 2004.

[26] Chris Lesniewski-Laas, Bryan Ford, Jacob Strauss, Robert Morris, and Frans M. Kaashoek. Alpaca: Extensible Authorization for Distributed Services. In *Proc. of the Conference on Computer and Communications Security*, Alexandria, VA, October 2007.

[27] Dave Levin, John R. Douceur, Jacob R. Lorch, and Thomas Moscibroda. TrInc: Small Trusted Hardware for Large Distributed Systems. In *Proc. of the Symposium on Networked System Design and Implementation*, Boston, MA, April 2009.

[28] Jinyuan Li, Maxwell Krohn, David Mazières, and Dennis Shasha. Secure Untrusted Data Repository. In *Proc. of the Symposium on Operating Systems Design and Implementation*, San Francisco, CA, December 2004.

[29] David Lie, Chandramohan A. Thekkath, and Mark Horowitz. Implementing an Untrusted Operating System on Trusted Hardware. In *Proc. of the Symposium on Operating Systems Principles*, Bolton Landing, NY, October 2003.

[30] Umesh Maheshwari, Radek Vingralek, and William Shapiro. How to Build a Trusted Database System on Untrusted Storage. In *Proc. of the Symposium on Operating Systems Design and Implementation*, San Diego, CA, October 2000.

[31] Jonathan M. McCune, Yanlin Li, Ning Qu, Zongwei Zhou, Anupam Datta, Virgil Gligor, and Adrian Perrig. TrustVisor: Efficient TCB Reduction and Attestation. In *Proc. of the IEEE Symposium on Security and Privacy*, Oakland, CA, May 2010.

[32] Jonathan M. McCune, Bryan J. Parno, Adrian Perrig, Michael K. Reiter, and Hiroshi Isozaki. Flicker: An Execution Infrastructure for TCB Minimization. In *Proc. of the European Conference on Computer Systems*, Glasgow, Scotland, April 2008.

[33] Ralph C. Merkle. Protocols for Public Key Cryptosystems.

In *Proc. of the IEEE Symposium on Security and Privacy*, Oakland, CA, May 1980.

[34] Ralph C. Merkle. A Certified Digital Signature. In *Proc. of the International Cryptology Conference*, Santa Barbara, CA, August 1989.

[35] George C. Necula. Proof-Carrying Code. In *Proc. of the Symposium on Principles of Programming Languages*, pages 106–119, Paris, France, 1997.

[36] Bryan Parno, Jonathan M. McCune, and Adrian Perrig. Bootstrapping Trust in Commodity Computers. In *Proc. of the IEEE Symposium on Security and Privacy*, Oakland, CA, May 2010.

[37] Birgit Pfitzmann, James Riordan, Christian Stüble, Michael Waidner, and Arnd Weber. The PERSEUS System Architecture. Technical Report RZ3335 (93381), IBM Research Division, Zurich, April 2001.

[38] Rob Pike, Dave Presotto, Sean Dorward, Bob Flandrena, Ken Thompson, Howard Trickey, and Phil Winterbottom. Plan 9 from Bell Labs. *Computing Systems*, 8(3):221–254, Summer 1995.

[39] Patrick Reynolds, Oliver Kennedy, Emin Gün Sirer, and Fred B. Schneider. Securing Bgp Using External Security Monitors. Technical Report TR2006-2065, Cornell University, Computing and Information Science, Ithaca, New York, December 2006.

[40] Ahmad-Reza Sadeghi, Christian Stüble, and Marcel Winandy. Property-Based TPM Virtualization. In *Proc. of the International Conference on Information Security*, Hyderabad, India, December 2008.

[41] Reiner Sailer, Enriquillo Valdez, Trent Jaeger, Ronald Perez, Leendert van Doorn, John Linwood Griffin, and Stefan Berger. sHype: Secure Hypervisor Approach to Trusted Virtualized Systems. Technical Report RC23511 (W0502-006), IBM Research Division, Thomas J. Watson Research Center, Yorktown Heights, NY, February 2005.

[42] Reiner Sailer, Xiaolan Zhang, Trent Jaeger, and Leendert van Doorn. Design and Implementation of a TCG-based Integrity Measurement Architecture. In *Proc. of the USENIX Security Symposium*, San Diego, CA, August 2004.

[43] Luis F. G. Sarmenta, Marten van Dijk, Charles W. O'Donnell, Jonathan Rhodes, and Srinivas Devadas. Virtual Monotonic Counters and Count-limited Objects Using a TPM without a Trusted OS. In *Proc. of the Workshop on Scalable Trusted Computing*, Fairfax, VA, November 2006.

[44] Fred B. Schneider, Kevin Walsh, and Emin Gün Sirer. Enforceable Security Policies. *ACM Transactions on Information and System Security*, 1(3), February 2000.

[45] Fred B. Schneider, Kevin Walsh, and Emin Gün Sirer. Nexus Authorization Logic: Design Rationale and Applications. *ACM Transactions on Information and System Security*, 14(1), May 2011.

[46] Arvind Seshadri, Mark Luk, Elaine Shi, Adrian Perrig, Leendert van Doorn, and Pradeep Khosla. Pioneer: Verifying Integrity and Guaranteeing Execution of Code on Legacy Platforms. In *Proc. of the Symposium on Operating Systems Principles*, Brighton, UK, October 2005.

[47] Arvind Seshadri, Adrian Perrig, Leendert van Doorn, and Pradeep Khosla. SWATT: Software-based Attestation for Embedded Devices. In *Proc. of the IEEE Symposium on Security and Privacy*, Oakland, CA, May 2004.

[48] Jonathan S. Shapiro, Jonathan M. Smith, and David J. Farber. EROS: A Fast Capability System. In *Proc. of the Symposium on Operating Systems Principles*, Kiawah Island, SC, December 1999.

[49] Elaine Shi, Adrian Perrig, and Leendert van Doorn. BIND: A Fine-Grained Attestation Service for Secure Distributed Systems. In *Proc. of the Symposium on Security and Privacy*, 2005.

[50] Emin Gün Sirer, Robert Grimm, Arthur J. Gregory, and Brian N. Bershad. Design and Implementation of a Distributed Virtual Machine for Networked Computers. In *Proc. of the Symposium on Operating Systems Principles*, Kiawah Island, SC, December 1999.

[51] Ray Spencer, Stephen Smalley, Peter Loscocco, Mike Hibler, David Andersen, and Jay Lepreau. The Flask Security Architecture: System Support for Diverse Security Policies. In *Proc. of the USENIX Security Symposium*, Washington, DC, August 1999.

[52] Richard Stallman. Can You Trust Your Computer? Available at http://www.gnu.org/philosophy/can-you-trust.html.

[53] Marten van Dijk, Jonathan Rhodes, Luis F. G. Sarmenta, and Srinivas Devadas. Offline Untrusted Storage with Immediate Detection of Forking and Replay Attacks. In *Proc. of the Workshop on Scalable Trusted Computing*, Alexandria, VA, November 2007.

[54] Robert Wahbe, Steven Lucco, Thomas E. Anderson, and Susan L. Graham. Efficient Software-Based Fault Isolation. *ACM SIGOPS Operating Systems Review*, 27(5):203–216, December 1993.

[55] Carsten Weinhold and Hermann Härtig. VPFS: Building a Virtual Private File System with a Small Trusted Computing Base. In *Proc. of the European Conference on Computer Systems*, Glasgow, Scotland, April 2008.

[56] Dan Williams, Patrick Reynolds, Kevin Walsh, Emin Gün Sirer, and Fred B. Schneider. Device driver safety through a reference validation mechanism. In *Proc. of the Symposium on Operating System Design and Implementation*, San Diego, CA, December 2008.

[57] Edward Wobber, Martín Abadi, Michael Burrows, and Butler Lampson. Authentication in the Taos operating system. *Transactions on Computer Systems*, 12(1), 1994.

[58] Nickolai Zeldovich, Silas Boyd-Wickizer, Eddie Kohler, and David Mazières. Making Information Flow Explicit in HiStar. In *Proc. of the Symposium on Operating Systems Design and Implementation*, Seattle, WA, November 2006.

Practical Software Model Checking via Dynamic Interface Reduction

Huayang Guo*†   Ming Wu†   Lidong Zhou†   Gang Hu*†   Junfeng Yang°   Lintao Zhang†

* Tsinghua University   † Microsoft Research Asia   ° Columbia University

{huayang.guo,henry.hu.sh}@gmail.com   {miw,lidongz,lintaoz}@microsoft.com

junfeng@cs.columbia.edu

ABSTRACT

Implementation-level software model checking explores the state space of a system implementation directly to find potential software defects without requiring any specification or modeling. Despite early successes, the effectiveness of this approach remains severely constrained due to poor scalability caused by state-space explosion. DEMETER makes software model checking more practical with the following contributions: (i) proposing *dynamic interface reduction*, a new state-space reduction technique, (ii) introducing a framework that enables dynamic interface reduction in an existing model checker with a reasonable amount of effort, and (iii) providing the framework with a distributed runtime engine that supports parallel distributed model checking.

We have integrated DEMETER into two existing model checkers, MACEMC and MODIST, each involving changes of around 1,000 lines of code. Compared to the original MACEMC and MODIST model checkers, our experiments have shown state-space reduction from a factor of five to up to five orders of magnitude in representative distributed applications such as PAXOS, Berkeley DB, CHORD, and PASTRY. As a result, when applied to a deployed PAXOS implementation, which has been running in production data centers for years to manage tens of thousands of machines, DEMETER manages to explore *completely* a logically meaningful state space that covers both phases of the PAXOS protocol, offering higher assurance of software reliability that was not possible before.

Categories and Subject Descriptors

D.2.4 [**Software Engineering**]: Software/Program Verification— *Model checking, Reliability*; D.2.5 [**Software Engineering**]: Testing and Debugging—*Testing tools*

General Terms

Algorithms, Reliability

Keywords

Software model checking, state space reduction, dynamic interface reduction

SOSP '11, October 23-26, 2011, Cascais, Portugal.
Copyright © 2011 ACM 978-1-4503-0977-6/11/10 ... $10.00.

1. INTRODUCTION

Reliability has become an increasingly important attribute for computer systems, as we are witnessing growing dependencies on computer systems that run continuously on commodity hardware despite adversity in the environment. Complete verification of system implementations has been a daunting job, if not infeasible for complex real-world systems. Implementation-level software model checking [18, 36, 32, 41, 40, 33, 29, 38, 39] proves to be a viable approach for improving reliability. It has advanced to a stage where it can be applied directly to a system implementation and can find rare program bugs by exploring a system's state space systematically to detect system misbehavior such as crashes, exceptions, and assertion failures. Despite this success, these model checkers are often unable to explore *completely* any non-trivial logically bounded state space (e.g., a normal single execution of consensus), making it hard to provide any degree of assurance for reliability. State-space explosion is a major obstacle to their effectiveness.

In this paper, we introduce *dynamic interface reduction* (DIR), a new state-space reduction technique for software model checking. DIR is based on two principles.

First, *check components separately*. A common practice to manage software complexity is to encapsulate the complexity using well-defined interfaces. Leveraging this common practice, a model checker considers a target software system as consisting of a set of *components*, each with a well-defined *interface* to the rest of the system. For example, a typical distributed system is comprised of a set of processes interacting with each other through message exchanges. The set of message-exchange sequences, or *message traces*, between a component and the rest of the system defines the *interface behavior* for that component. In general, all behavior such as shared memory, failure correlations, or other implicit channels that cause one component to affect another is captured by interface behavior. Any behavior other than interface behavior is locally contained. Given the interface behavior of each component, DIR can check its local state-space separately, avoiding unnecessary (and expensive) exploration of the global state-space when possible.

Second, *discover interface behavior dynamically*. Model checking each component separately requires knowing the interface behavior of the component. DIR discovers this behavior dynamically during its state-space exploration, by running the target components for real and combining their discovered interface behavior. This process is often efficient because it ignores intra-component complexity that does not propagate through interfaces. Moreover, this process is completely automated, so that developers do not have to specify interface behavior manually [22, 31], which may be tedious, error-prone, and inaccurate. A last benefit is that this process discovers only the true interface behavior that may actually occur in practice, not made-up ones [23], thus avoiding difficult-to-diagnose false positives.

We incorporate the DIR technique into DEMETER, a model checking framework that includes an algorithm that progressively explores the local state-space of each component, while discovering interface behavior between components. DEMETER adopts a modular design as a framework to enable DIR in existing model checkers with a reasonably small amount of engineering effort. Its design can reuse the key modules for modeling a system and for state-space exploration in an existing model checker; DEMETER further defines a set of common data structures and APIs to encapsulate the implementation details of an existing model checker. The key DIR algorithm can then be implemented independently of any specific model checker and is accordingly reusable.

DEMETER implements a distributed runtime for DIR-enabled model checking that leverages the inherent parallelism of DIR, as local explorations for components with respect to given interface behavior are largely independent. As a result, DEMETER scales nicely when running on more machines, and is capable of tapping into any distributed system or cloud infrastructure that is becoming prevalent today to push model checking capabilities further.

To demonstrate the practicality of DEMETER, we have incorporated DIR into MACEMC and MODIST, two independently developed model checkers. Despite their fundamental differences in implementing model checking, each requires changes of only around 1,000 lines of code, thanks to the framework provided by DEMETER. The resulting model checkers take advantage of not only the new reduction technique, but also of the distributed runtime to run model checking in parallel on a cluster of machines.

The resulting checkers have been used to check representative applications, ranging from PASTRY and CHORD, two classic peer-to-peer protocols, to Berkeley DB (BDB), a widely used open source database, and to MPS, a deployed PAXOS implementation that has been running in production data centers for years to manage tens of thousands of machines. Our experiments show up to a 10^5 speedup in estimated state-space exploration, thanks to the effectiveness of interfaces in hiding local non-determinism related to thread interleaving and coordination. Furthermore, DEMETER's runtime shows nearly perfect scalability as we increase worker machines from 4 to 32. This significantly improved model-checking capability from both state-space reduction and parallelism translates directly to increased confidence in the reliability of systems that survive extensive checking: in our experiment with MPS, DEMETER was able to explore a complete sub-space, where three servers execute both phases in the PAXOS protocol. DEMETER was also able to explore a complete sub-space for CHORD on MACE with three servers until all have joined. To the best of our knowledge, neither would be possible for any published implementation-level model checker without DIR.

The rest of the paper is organized as follows. Section 2 presents an overview with an example system we use throughout the paper. Section 3 presents an overview of DIR and the algorithm. Section 4 outlines DEMETER's system architecture and how MACEMC and MODIST are integrated with DEMETER. Evaluations of and experiences with DEMETER are the subject of Section 5, followed by discussions in Section 6. We survey related work in Section 7 and conclude in Section 8.

```
Client                  Primary/Secondary
                        //Main thread      //Checkpoint thread
if (Choose(2)==0){      while (n=Recv()) {  Lock();
    Send(P,1);              Lock();         Log(sum);  ⎫ Ckpt
    Send(P,2);              sum+=n;  ⎫ Sum  Unlock();  ⎭
} else {                    Unlock(); ⎭
    Send(P,1);          if (isPrimary)
    Send(P,3);              Send(S,n);
}                       }
```

Figure 1: Code example for a contrived distributed accumulator composed of a client C, a primary server P, and a secondary server S.

2. OVERVIEW AND AN EXAMPLE

Dynamic interface reduction in DEMETER considers a system consisting of a set of components, each with a well-defined interface to interact with the rest of the system. For example, a distributed system can have processes running on each machine as a component, with a sequence of message exchanges between components forming a *message trace* as interface behavior. (We assume no interactions occur via any means other than messages.) State-space exploration is then divided into a set of local explorations, one for each component, and a global exploration that explores the interactions between components; e.g., in the form of message traces. During the exploration, DEMETER tracks and builds up the interface behavior (e.g., message traces) between each component and the rest of the system. By dynamically discovering interface behavior, DEMETER removes the need for users to model interactions beforehand through manual or static-analysis methods, and follows closely the philosophy of implementation-level software model checking with no specification or modeling.

Before presenting the details of the system model, the DIR algorithm, the architecture, and the implementation of DEMETER, in this section, we use a simple code example to describe at a high level the work flow of DEMETER with DIR and what kind of reduction it can achieve. For simplicity, we focus on distributed systems where an execution *trace* captures the non-deterministic events such as thread interleaving, message send, and message receive operations in an execution, while a *message trace*, which includes only the message send and receive operations in an execution, captures the interface behavior across components.

2.1 An Example

Figure 1 shows the pseudo code of a contrived distributed accumulator composed of three components: a client, a primary server, and a secondary server. The client (left of Figure 1) calls function Choose(2) [18, 39, 40, 29], which non-deterministically returns 0 or 1. In practice, this can be used to imitate the effect of timeout, failure, or a random function. Depending on the returned value of the Choose function, the client code sends two different sequences of numbers to the primary, which then sums them up and forwards them to the secondary. A checkpoint thread writes the sum to disk. We label the critical sections in these two threads as Sum and Ckpt, respectively. Both the primary and the secondary run the same code (right of Figure 1), except that the secondary has isPrimary set to false. As a result, the secondary receives the numbers from the primary, but does not forward the numbers further.

Our example does only simple summation for clarity. However,

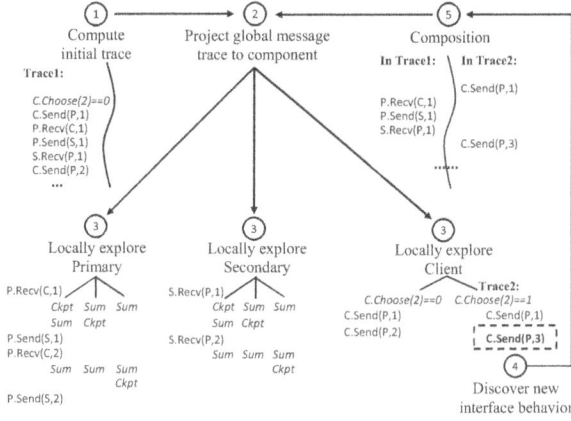

Figure 2: Work flow of DeMeter with DIR on the example in Figure 1. The work flow has five key steps, as explained in §2.2.

it still mimics real distributed systems in many aspects. For instance, it is built on top of common techniques that real distributed systems use, such as replication, message passing, multi-threading, and checkpointing. Moreover, it has a well-defined component interface that hides the implementation details (e.g., when the checkpoint thread of the server interleaves with the main thread) within a component. Because these local choices do not propagate outside of component interfaces, we can check them locally without resorting to expensive global exploration of all components.

2.2 DIR Work Flow

At a high level, the work flow of DeMeter with DIR alternates between a *global explorer* enumerating the global message traces across components and a set of *local explorers*, one per component, enumerating the local execution traces within each component. Figure 2 illustrates this work flow using the example in Figure 1. The DIR work flow has five key steps:

1. To bootstrap the checking process, the global explorer first performs a global execution including all components to discover an initial global execution trace, and the corresponding global message trace that keeps only the message send and receive operations. As shown in the figure, the global explorer first explores the choice of Choose(2) returning 0 in the client. The client then sends the sequence 1 and 2 to the primary, which forwards it to the secondary, resulting in the global trace Trace1. A corresponding global message trace can be obtained by removing all intra-component events from Trace1. The goal of the global explorer is to discover all global message traces.

2. The global explorer *projects* a newly discovered global message trace down to each component's local message trace by keeping only the message exchanges that are either sent or received by that component. It then sends to each component the corresponding projected message trace. Step 3 in Figure 2 shows the results of this projection for each component. As the global explorer discovers more and more global message traces, it keeps generating such projections, increasingly capturing the interface behavior of each component.

3. Checking now shifts to local explorers. A local explorer enumerates non-deterministic choices within the corresponding component. Because the local explorer does not control the execution of other components, whenever the component attempts to interact with other components, the local explorer will match

any outgoing messages with those in the local message trace and replay any incoming messages according to the local message trace. As shown in step 3 of Figure 2, the local explorer for the primary (similarly for the secondary) explores the different interleavings of the Sum and Ckpt operations while matching the Send operations and replaying the Recv.

4. If a local explorer causes the component to send a new message that deviates from the local message trace, it can no longer follow the message traces it already knows, and has to report this deviation to the global explorer. For instance, as shown in Figure 2, when the local explorer of the client explores the choice of Choose(2) returning 1, it encounters a new interface operation Send(P,3) (boxed) deviating from the known message traces of the client. We label the new trace Trace2.

5. The global explorer then composes the new message trace with existing global message traces to construct new global message traces. For instance, in Figure 2, the global explorer locates the deviating points in the global message trace derived from Trace1 and stitches the unchanged portion together with Trace2 to form a new global message trace. (For details of this composition process, see Section 3.3.) Then, the global explorer goes back to step 2 and repeats until no new message trace is discovered and all the local explorations against the known message traces have finished.

2.3 Reduction Analysis

For the example in Figure 1, each component has two different message traces (one for each value returned by Choose(2) at the client). The client has one local execution trace per message trace. The primary and the secondary each have three different local traces per message trace, because Sum and Ckpt can interleave differently and lead to different local states (see Figure 2), but the changed local state does not propagate across the component interfaces. Thus, DeMeter with DIR explores $2 * (1 + 3 + 3) = 14$ different executions.

In contrast, a model checker without DIR has to re-explore the entire system whenever the local state of a component changes. The reason is that, without dividing a whole system into components and monitoring the interface behavior, a model checker has to assume that a local change may affect the rest of the system. Thus, it must re-explore all non-deterministic choices in the rest of the system under this local change. For instance, when the primary's main thread interleaves differently with its checkpoint thread and results in a different local state, a model checker without DIR would have to re-explore unnecessarily the choices in both the client and the secondary. As a result, it would explore a total of $2 * 3 * 3 = 18$ executions.

Analytically, DIR achieves exponential state-space reduction. To illustrate, consider a modified example where the client sends one sequence of n numbers and the primary forwards the numbers to $(m - 1)$ replicas. Each server (primary or replica) has exactly one message trace (since the client sends only one sequence of numbers). Under this message trace, each server has $(n + 1)$ different thread interleavings. Therefore, DeMeter would explore $1 + m * (n + 1)$ executions, whereas a model checker without DIR would explore $(n + 1)^m$ executions.

From a system perspective, the reduction of DIR can be intuitively viewed as a result of caching. Consider a system where a component has many local non-deterministic choices but always sends the same message to the other components. When exploring this com-

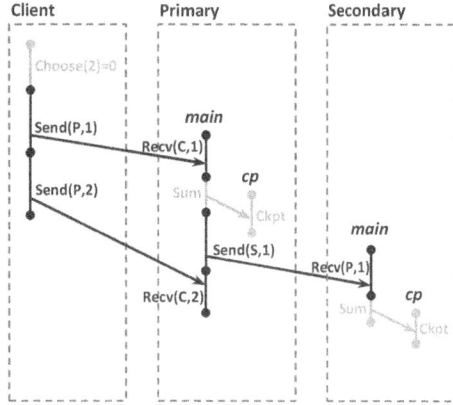

Figure 3: A trace τ of the example code in Figure 1. *main* and *cp* **refer to the main and the checkpoint threads, respectively.**

ponent, the first time we discover an outgoing message, we have to explore the effects of this message on the other components, which can be expensive. However, as we keep exploring this component, we discover that it sends the same message again in a different execution, and we can thus safely skip the expensive exploration of the other components under this same message. In other words, we effectively get a "cache hit." Following this intuition, we expect DIR to work well for any system where there are well-defined interfaces to hide implementation details. This is common for practically all real systems, especially loosely coupled distributed systems that are designed to reduce the amount of inter-process communication for performance reasons.

3. DYNAMIC INTERFACE REDUCTION

In this section, we present the system model we assume for DIR and the detailed algorithm.

3.1 System Model

DEMETER checks standard concurrent/distributed systems as defined previously in software model checking [16, 18]. Abstractly, a system starts from an initial state and at each step performs a *transition* into the next state. A transition is *enabled* if it is not blocked and can be scheduled to execute on the current state. The *environment* is used to model the *non-determinism* as different choices of enabled transitions at a state. Such non-determinism includes thread/process scheduling, message ordering, timers, failures, and other randomness in the system.

Implementation-level software model checkers work directly on actual implementations of target systems. They typically consist of two major pieces. The first is a *system wrapper* that exposes an underlying system and enables the control of non-determinism in the environment. The second is an *exploration mechanism* that builds on top of the system wrapper to explore the system state space by capturing and controlling non-determinism in order to find software defects such as unintended exceptions and crashes, assertion failures, and other safety violations.

In DEMETER, a system is divided into a static set $\mathscr{C}$ of components. Components interact with each other through *interface objects*, such as communication channels or shared objects. We classify transitions as *internal* transitions if they do not read or write interface objects, or *interface* transitions if they access and/or update interface objects. An interface transition is further an *output*

transition if it updates an interface object (e.g., sending a message or updating a shared object); or an *input* transition if it reads an interface object (e.g., receiving a message or reading a shared object).

Two transitions are *dependent* if their executions interfere with each other: one could enable/disable the other, or executing them in a different order could change the final outcome. Examples are two lock operations on the same lock, a write operation and read/write operations on the same shared variable, and a message send operation and the corresponding receive are dependent. Starting from an initial state, a system execution is modeled as a *trace* that captures all transitions taken by the system and the partial order ($\preceq$) between those transitions based on transition dependencies. Partial-order equivalent traces are considered the same. Given a trace τ and an enabled transition t at the state after executing τ, we can extend τ to a new trace $\tau \circ t$ by carrying out transition t. We can further define a *prefix* relation between traces as follows. A trace τ_p is a prefix of τ if and only if any transition in τ_p is in τ and, for any transition t in τ_p and any $t_p \preceq t$ in τ, t_p must be in τ_p and $t_p \preceq t$ in τ_p holds.

Each transition belongs to a particular component. A global trace τ can be *projected* onto a component C to obtain a *local trace* by preserving only transitions that belong to component C (including output transitions from C to other components) and output transitions from other components to C, along with their partial order. The result is referred to as $proj_c(\tau)$. To capture interface behavior in a trace, we construct a *global skeleton* from a global trace τ by keeping only interface transitions and their partial order in the trace. We refer to the resulting skeleton as $skel(\tau)$. Similarly, a *local skeleton* $skel(proj_c(\tau))$ can be defined on local trace $proj_c(\tau)$ for component c. A local skeleton captures the interface behavior between c and the rest of the system. Two global traces τ and τ' are *interface-equivalent* with respect to component c if and only if their local skeletons on c are the same; that is, $skel(proj_c(\tau)) = skel(proj_c(\tau'))$ holds.

Figure 3 shows an example trace τ of the example code in Figure 1. Each segment corresponds to a transition, while arrows represent inter-thread/process communications, which also imply the happen-before relation between transitions. A partial order ($\preceq$) is defined between transitions in the same thread, between a send transition and its corresponding receive transition across threads and processes, and is transitive. Examples include P.Recv(C,1) $\preceq$ P.Sum, P.Sum $\preceq$ P.Ckpt, P.Send(S,1) $\preceq$ S.Recv(P,1). All Send and Recv transitions (marked in bold) are interface transitions, while Choose, Sum, and Ckpt are internal transitions corresponding to local non-deterministic choices. The corresponding global skeleton of τ in Figure 3 contains the 6 interface transitions and their partial order as in the original trace. The local trace with a projection to the client contains Choose(2)=0, C.Send(P,1), and C.Send(P,2). The corresponding local skeleton contains only transitions C.Send(P,1) and C.Send(P,2).

3.2 Partial-Replay Local System

The first core idea of DIR is to check each component separately. Checking a component c is possible with a local skeleton that specifies all the interface behavior between c and the rest of the system. This is done through a *partial-replay local system*. In theory, it is possible to replay just the interface transitions on a local skeleton (e.g., by supplying received messages recorded in the local skeleton). In reality, replaying only the interface transitions is difficult. For example, in order to replay message-exchange transitions, the underlying network channels (sockets) must be set up correctly.

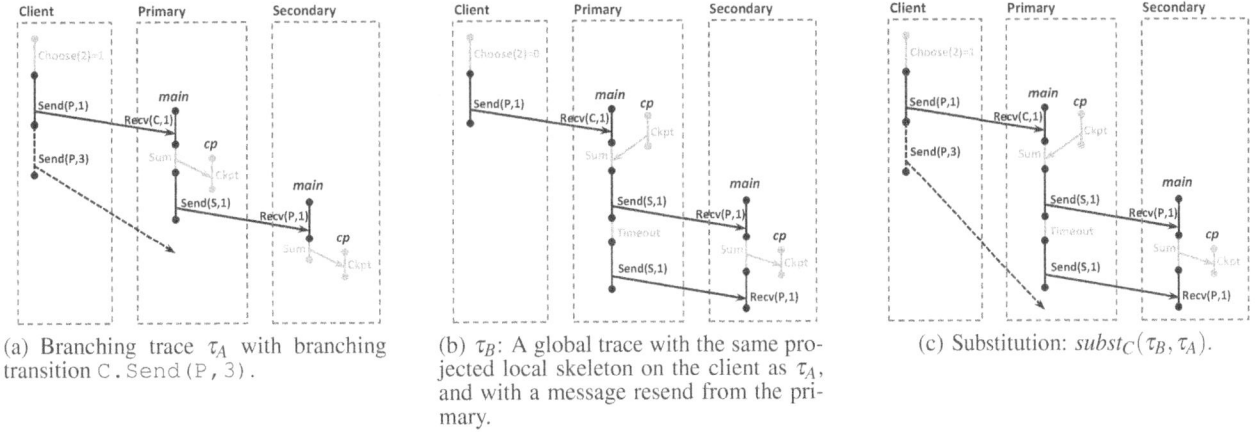

(a) Branching trace τ_A with branching transition C.Send(P,3).

(b) τ_B: A global trace with the same projected local skeleton on the client as τ_A, and with a message resend from the primary.

(c) Substitution: $subst_C(\tau_B, \tau_A)$.

Figure 4: Composition by Substitution: an Example.

This could involve earlier operations such as *bind*. Such internal dependencies might be hard to identify thoroughly; the process is often error-prone. Simulating network behavior for replaying is also a significant undertaking, as done in model checkers such as MODIST. Therefore, a partial-replay local system replays not only interface transitions, but also any other transitions in the rest of the system. This choice leads to a simple and modular design, albeit at the cost of running transitions in other components.

More precisely, given a local skeleton κ_c and a representative trace τ satisfying $proj_c(skel(\tau)) = \kappa_c$, a partial-replay local system tries to enumerate transitions in c, while *replaying* the behavior of the rest of the system (denoted as R) according to τ. Starting from the initial state, in each step the partial-replay local system either picks an enabled transition from component c or replays τ's transitions in R. A transition t made by R in $proj_R(\tau)$ can be replayed if and only if any transition in $proj_R(\tau)$ that t depends on has already been replayed.

A partial-replay local system could make an output transition in c that deviates from κ_c. Such a deviating output transition is called a *branching transition*. When a branching transition t_b is encountered, let τ_b be the trace explored right before taking the branching transition, the partial-replay local system reports $\langle t_b, \tau_b \rangle$ in order for DEMETER to discover new global and local skeletons through composition by substitution, which we describe next.

3.3 Composition by Substitution

The second core idea of DIR is to discover interface behavior dynamically. This is the responsibility of the *global explorer* through composition by substitution. The global explorer maintains the set G containing the pair $\langle \kappa, \tau \rangle$ for each discovered global skeleton κ and a corresponding global trace τ, where $\kappa = skel(\tau)$. The global explorer further maintains a set B of all discovered branching transition/trace pairs ($\langle t_b, \tau_b \rangle$) reported by partial-replay local systems.

Intuitively, the global explorer's process of discovering interface behavior can be thought of as a state-space exploration of a new transition system with only the interface transitions of the original system. The global explorer essentially builds up the transition system with the global skeletons captured in G, where the branching transitions captured in B are the transitions in that system. For a branching transition from component c, the local skeleton $\kappa_c = proj_c(skel(\tau_b))$ defines when that branching transition is

enabled: for any global skeleton κ, the branching transition is enabled if and only if $proj_c(\kappa) = \kappa_c$ holds, in which case we can carry out that branching transition to extend κ to a new global skeleton.

This process is described more precisely through the following composition by substitution on traces, which uses the *subst* operation defined as follows. If two traces τ and τ' are interface-equivalent with respect to component c, $\tau_s = subst_c(\tau, \tau')$ defines a new trace by replacing all c's transitions in τ with c's transitions in τ' while preserving the partial order in the original traces; that is, for any transitions t and t' in τ_n, if t and t' are both in τ or both in τ' with $t \preceq t'$, then $t \preceq t'$ holds in τ_s. Such a substitution is possible because τ and τ' are interface-equivalent with respect to c: c's transitions in τ and τ' are indistinguishable to the rest of the system because they present the same interface behavior (i.e., local skeleton).

Given $\langle t_b, \tau_b \rangle \in B$ and $\langle \kappa_g, \tau_g \rangle \in G$, where τ_b and τ_g are interface-equivalent with respect to component c, we compose a new global trace $\tau_s = subst_c(\tau_g, \tau_b)$ through substitution, construct $\tau_n = \tau_s \circ t_b$ by taking the branching transition t_b, and add $\langle skel(\tau_n), \tau_n \rangle$ into G.

Figure 4 illustrates the process of composition by substitution. We enrich the example in Figure 1 slightly by enabling the primary to resend its message if a local timeout for that message is triggered. The secondary ignores the resent message if it has already received the previous one. The extension creates more variations in global skeletons and helps illustrate how composition by substitution creates new global skeletons. Figure 4(a) shows a global trace τ_A (containing all transitions in solid lines) with a branching transition $t_b = $ C.Send(P, 3) (in dotted lines), when the client has Choose(2) set to 1, rather than 0. Figure 4(b) shows another global trace τ_B that has the same local skeleton for the client as τ_A. It is a prefix of a complete trace when the client has Choose(2) set to 0. The local traces of τ_A and τ_B for the primary are different in the order between Sum and Ckpt. The global skeletons of the two are also different: in τ_B, the primary resends the message with value 1. The differences in τ_A and τ_B are however invisible to the client. Further assume that τ_B and its global skeleton have already been discovered in G. When the branching transition in Figure 4(a) is reported, a composition is performed to yield a new trace $subst_C(\tau_B, \tau_A)$, where the branching transition is also enabled, as shown in Figure 4(c). $subst_C(\tau_B, \tau_A) \circ t_b$ is then a new global trace.

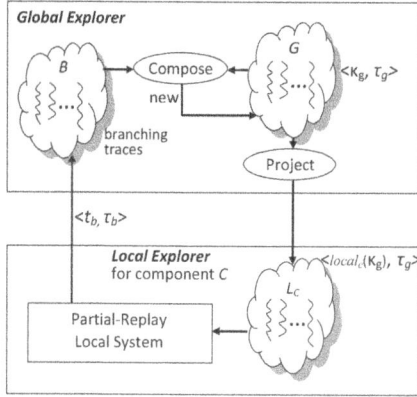

Figure 5: Interactions between global and local explorers.

3.4 Global and Local Explorers

The DIR algorithm consists of two types of cooperative progressive tasks that are running concurrently. Whereas the *global explorer* maintains a set G to track global skeletons and a set B to track branching transitions, a *local explorer* for component c maintains $L_c = \{\langle proj_c(\kappa), \tau \rangle \mid \langle \kappa, \tau \rangle \in G\}$ to track local skeletons for component c. Figure 5 illustrates the interactions between the global explorer and the local explorers. Local explorers use partial-replay local systems to explore each component separately and reports branching to the global explorer, while the global explorer uses composition by substitution to discover new global skeletons.

Local Explorer

1. Local explorer c initiates a partial-replay local system with respect to each $\langle \kappa_c, \tau \rangle \in L_c$.
2. When a partial-replay local system detects a branching transition t_b at trace τ_b, the local explorer backtracks and reports $\langle t_b, \tau_b \rangle$ to the global explorer to be added into B.

Global Explorer

1. Perform composition by substitution whenever B or G is updated until reaching a fixed point. For any $\langle \kappa_g, \tau_g \rangle \in G$, and $\langle t_b, \tau_b \rangle \in B$ satisfying $skel(proj_c(\tau_b)) = proj_c(\kappa_g)$, where t_b is a transition from component c, let $\tau_n = subst_c(\tau_g, \tau_b) \circ t_b$, add $\langle skel(\tau_n), \tau_n \rangle$ into G.
2. For each component c, update $L_c = \{\langle proj_c(\kappa), \tau \rangle \mid \langle \kappa, \tau \rangle \in G\}$ whenever G is updated.

Optimizations. It is worth noting that our presentation of the algorithm ignores certain obvious optimizations for simplicity and clarity. For example, any prefix of a global skeleton/trace can be subsumed because any prefix of a valid global skeleton/trace is a valid global skeleton/trace. We just need to record the longest ones. Also, to avoid an excessive number of branching transitions, when a new global skeleton is constructed, the global explorer will attempt to continue running the corresponding global trace to completion, including all system components. Similarly, the algorithm starts by having the global explorer perform a global execution including all system components to discover initial global traces, in order to initialize G with some global skeletons and associated global traces.

Correctness. A state-space reduction technique must be both sound and complete. In the context of DIR, soundness requires that every

local trace explored by the algorithm is a projection of a valid global trace, while completeness states that, for any valid global trace τ, our algorithm discovers $skel(\tau)$ in the global explorer (G) and finds $proj_c(\tau)$ in the local explorer for every component c.

Intuitively, the soundness hinges on the following fundamental *substitution rule*: if two valid traces τ and τ' are interface-equivalent with respect to component c, $subst_c(\tau, \tau')$ is also a valid trace. The substitution rule derives directly from the notion of interface equivalence and reflects the following observation. A component's interface behavior, captured by its local skeletons, isolates a component from the rest of the system. For an execution of a single component, changes in the rest of the system are irrelevant as long as the behavior at the interface (as captured in local skeletons) remains the same. Conversely, if two executions of a component conform to the same local skeleton, they are indistinguishable from the rest of the system.

DIR upholds soundness because, during both the partial-replay local exploration and the composition in global exploration, each discovered local or global skeleton complies with a valid global trace due to the substitution rule. The completeness is guaranteed through the cooperation of local and global explorers, as the local exploration can find all the local states and discover all the possible branching transitions with respect to given local skeletons, while the global explorer can construct all new global skeletons through composition for given sets of global skeletons and branching transitions. A proof sketch for the soundness and completeness is described in Appendix A.

4. ARCHITECTURE AND IMPLEMENTATION

In this section, we present the layered architecture of DEMETER that is specifically designed to facilitate incorporation of DIR into an existing model checker, followed by notes on some implementation details and on how we retrofit MACEMC and MODIST to integrate DEMETER.

4.1 A Model Checking Framework

We design DEMETER as a model-checking framework, which can embed an existing software model-checker in order to enable DIR for it. We refer to the model checker embedded in DEMETER as *eMC*. This design significantly reduces the amount of work to build model checkers with DEMETER and avoids having DIR trapped in a particular model checking implementation.

Turning DEMETER into a model-checking framework requires a careful modular design. Figure 6 shows the layered architecture

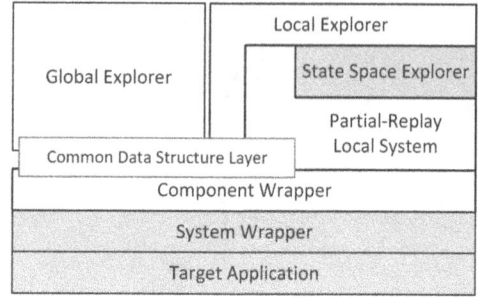

Figure 6: DEMETER Layering Architecture.

of DeMeter, where the shaded rectangles correspond to the layering in *eMC*. These modules (system wrapper and state-space explorer) are unmodified when plugged into DeMeter. In particular, DeMeter is able to leverage *eMC*'s state-space explorer because it adds a partial-replay local system layer that gives the state-space explorer an illusion of a stand-alone complete system, similar to the original application. The partial-replay local system layer further uses a *component wrapper*, which defines component boundaries and interface transitions. To isolate the specific implementation details of *eMC*, DeMeter defines a common set of *eMC*-neutral data structures/API and implements a *Common Data Structure Layer* that converts between these common data structures and those used in a particular *eMC*. Consequently, the global explorer and the part of the local explorer built on top of the Common Data Structure Layer are reusable across different *eMC*s.

Partial-Replay Local System. As shown in Figure 6, DeMeter builds a partial-replay local system by reusing *eMC*'s state-space explorer and system wrapper. The partial-replay local system takes a component c, a local skeleton, and a corresponding global trace τ, and runs the entire system on the original system wrapper except that it checks whether a transition is local to c or not (provided by the component wrapper) and replays any transitions in the rest of the system R following τ. The replay of R's transitions in τ is done by instructing *eMC*'s state-space explorer to take the designated transitions, but all the choices within component c are left to *eMC*'s state-space explorer.

Common data structures and APIs. Conceptually, the global explorer can be regarded as performing model checking of components with only interface transitions. However, reusing either *eMC*'s system wrapper or state-space explorer is difficult partly because this higher-level system must be constructed with transitions not known beforehand.

We opt for simplicity and build the global explorer on a small set of common data structures and APIs. In particular, we model the basic concurrency unit of a system as a thread. A transition is represented by a simple data structure with the following core fields: (i) its thread identifier, (ii) its unique identifier, (iii) its vector clock, (iv) interface transition flag, and (v) additional information about the transition. The additional information is mainly for converting this data structure to any original trace representation in *eMC*. A trace is defined as a set of transitions organized by their partial order (according to vector clocks). A skeleton is defined as a kind of trace that contains only interface transitions. Common operations can be defined on those data structures, such as projection from global trace to local trace, extraction of interface skeleton from a trace, and composition of a branching trace and a global trace. All of these operations are independent from *eMC*.

We have further implemented the following core functions on top of *eMC*'s system wrapper for global explorer: (i) reset system to the initial state, (ii) execute a particular transition at the current trace prefix, and (iii) run a trace prefix to completion (after the prefix, any completion of a global trace is sufficient). For local explorer, the partial-replay local system also provides a simple API to set up and run a partial replay. Implementing the global explorer and part of the local explorer on this set of common data structures and APIs makes its core logic reusable as it is made independent from *eMC*. The common data structure layer in Figure 6 is responsible for providing the data-structures and the APIs.

4.2 Interface Equivalence and Vector Clock

Interface equivalence defined on the equality of two skeletons is a key concept in DeMeter and is widely used in the implementation of DIR. For example, the local explorer needs to check equality between branching traces and local skeletons so that it can decide whether an encountered branching trace or local skeleton is new or not; when performing composition, the global explorer also needs to check whether two traces are interface-equivalent.

Interface equivalence can be judged by comparing interface transitions in skeletons. An interface transition in a skeleton is identified through the following four properties: (i) the component it belongs to, (ii) the communication object it accesses, (iii) its operation and arguments (e.g., a *send* operation with its message content), and (iv) partial order information which can be expressed in vector clocks that capture the happen-before relation between transitions.

Special care must be taken when vector clocks are used for interface-equivalence checking. Using vector clocks on traces directly might be problematic because the vector clocks also take into account internal transitions that are not included in skeletons. DeMeter therefore recomputes a skeleton vector clock for each trace. It first extracts the interface transitions and their dependencies from the original trace to build a dependency graph of the interface transitions. Based on the dependency graph, DeMeter re-computes the vector clock for the skeleton.

To expedite frequently-used interface-equivalence checking, DeMeter first imposes the same canonical representation on partial-order equivalent skeletons and computes a *signature* for a skeleton by applying a hash on that canonical representation. The equality of two skeletons is then the same as the equality of their signatures.

4.3 Distributed Runtime

The architecture of DeMeter enables a fair degree of parallelism. Model checking in DeMeter involves a global explorer and a set of local explorers, one for each component. Each local explorer is responsible for one component of the model-checked system and has no direct interactions with others. For each local skeleton of the component, the local explorer starts an *MC Worker* that executes the partial-replay local system for that component with respect to that local skeleton.

In our current implementation, the global explorer is the only major centralized task in the whole execution flow of DeMeter. Its core task, composition by substitution, is independent for each matching pair from G and B and can be executed separately, with its complexity linear to the length of the input traces. The complexity of finding matching pairs in G and B is in the worst case quadratic to the number of elements in the sets, although better data structures can be used to speed up the process of finding matching pairs. The size of G could grow exponentially with the number of components. In our experiments, we have not observed the global explorer becoming a bottleneck for the scalability of the entire exploration of DeMeter (see Section 5.2), largely because there are only a small number of components. We do not focus on cases where there are a large number of components because, as will be discussed in Section 6.1, it is possible to keep the number of components (at each level) small by organizing a system into a hierarchy of components.

All state changes on the global explorer are logged and persisted so that it can be re-started after failures. No replication is enabled, although doing so is straightforward. Because the global explorer always checks whether a reported branching trace is new, having duplicate branching traces sent to the global explorer is acceptable. As a result, any MC Worker can be re-started without causing any correctness problem. In the worst case, an MC Worker can be re-started (possibly on a different machine) and the previously explored local state space would be re-explored. Because it uses an existing model checker for local exploration, its ability to re-start from failure is determined by that underlying model checker. Ideally, each MC Worker leverages a checkpoint/recovery mechanism in the underlying model checker to avoid redundant exploration due to failures.

4.4 Integration with Existing Model Checkers

CompWrap DEMETER is designed to integrate with existing model checkers, and we have enabled DIR for MACEMC and MODIST using DEMETER. Table 1 shows line-number counts for the common parts of DEMETER, as well as those specifically for MACEMC and MODIST. The common DEMETER modules include the following: the global explorer, part of the local explorer that is responsible for coordinating with partial-replay local systems and with the global explorer, the common data structure and API, and other utilities, such as the network library, cross-OS utilities, and message-digest modules. For MACEMC and MODIST individually, we need to implement a partial-replay local system (PRLocal), a component wrapper (CompWrap), and a converter for the Common Data Structure Layer. The converters are simple in both: they take less than 100 lines of code and are integrated with other pieces.

	MACEMC	MODIST
PRLocal	1,006	574
CompWrap	108	183
Total	1,114	757
DEMETER Common	7,279	

Table 1: Development cost as lines of code for DEMETER, DEMETER-MACEMC, and DEMETER-MODIST.

MACEMC Integration. MACEMC is a software model checker for systems implemented using the MACE compiler and C++ language extensions. MACE models each node as a state machine with atomic event handlers for events such as message reception and timeouts. MACEMC treats a target application as a single program that composes every node with a simulated network environment for distributed applications. With such a system wrapper, at any time, MACEMC selects a node and one of its pending events to call the corresponding event handler to transition the system to the next state. This is considered one transition; each pending event therefore corresponds to an enabled transition. Control returns to MACEMC when a transition completes, while a transition could introduce new events to the system. MACEMC repeats this process as long as there are pending events.

For state-space exploration, MACEMC must control all sources of non-determinism, such as the scheduling of pending events, the use of a special Toss command in event handlers, or the use of time-outs in event handlers. In the implementation of MACEMC, the *RandomUtil* module in MACE controls such non-determinism in the system. Nodes in MACE interact with each other via TCP/UDP services. Each transition could trigger send operations that will enable corresponding receive events on receiving nodes. Transitions containing send or receive operations are candidates for interface transitions.

MACEMC's *system wrapper* therefore exposes and controls *RandomUtil*, as well as send and receive operations. Because the information associated with send and receive operations is insufficient (e.g., for identifying the destination of a send operation), a *component wrapper* has to trace it down in MACE to fill the needed information for interface transitions. In some cases, depending on how a component is defined, a send or receive operation might not be an interface transition. This happens when the receiving node is in the same component as the sender.

Data-structure conversion between MACEMC and DEMETER is relatively simple. Nodes in MACE are units of execution and we use node id as the thread identifier. Events in MACE have information about corresponding transitions. DEMETER does require recording any non-deterministic choices within an event handler. In fact, DEMETER enumerates all such choices to find out the set of possible transitions because different non-deterministic choices correspond to different transitions for the processing of an event. Each transition in MACE may contain multiple network operations that DEMETER must store to define interface transitions appropriately. MACEMC does not track partial-order dependencies. Without making any internal changes within MACEMC, DEMETER tracks dependencies for interface transitions conservatively where any two transitions from the same node are assumed to be dependent. As shown in Section 5, this conservative way of defining partial order has significant implications on the effectiveness of DIR.

MACEMC implements two search algorithms. The first is a depth-first search (DFS) that enumerates all possible execution paths with an execution depth bound and is used to verify safety properties in a limited state space. The other one is a random walk algorithm that is used to detect potential liveness bugs. We apply DEMETER only to improve the DFS part of MACEMC since its random exploration does not check whether a randomly executed transition introduces a redundant trace, and hence it gives up any hope of reducing redundancies or achieving any notion of completeness.

MODIST Integration. MODIST is a software model checker that detects bugs due to non-determinism in distributed applications. In MODIST, any concurrent program behavior can be modeled as different invocation orders of Win32 APIs, such as *EnterCriticalSection* and *WaitForSingleObject*. MODIST provides a module called *dist_sys* that maintains the application state and captures most Win32 API invocations of a target application, including synchronization, network, and file-system operations. This module constitutes the system wrapper for MODIST.

In MODIST, a transition is defined as an execution between two consecutive invocations of system APIs. There is a straightforward mapping between MODIST's data structures and DEMETER's. Process Id and thread Id are combined to identify a thread, while the operation of each transition can be identified by the MODIST id of the corresponding Win32 API. MODIST itself maintains traces as a partial order and its vector clock can be used directly in DEMETER's common data structure.

MODIST's state-space exploration uses DFS with dynamic partial-order reduction. This algorithm is designed for a general transition system and requires a partial-order dependency relation between transitions. Local explorers in DEMETER directly use this state-space exploration algorithm in their partial-replay local system.

5. EXPERIMENTS AND EVALUATIONS

In this section, we describe our experiments on DEMETER and report findings of our evaluation results on DEMETER-MACEMC and DEMETER-MODIST, two real model checkers that we have built in DEMETER by incorporating MACEMC and MODIST. We conduct all of our experiments on a cluster of machines (Intel Xeon x5550 2.67GHz CPU, 12GB main memory) on a 1Gb Ethernet.

Our experiments use representative applications for DEMETER-MACEMC and DEMETER-MODIST. For DEMETER-MACEMC, we check PASTRY and CHORD, two well-known peer-to-peer distributed hash-table implementations on MACE, as well as PAM, an unoptimized PAXOS implementation on MACE for a single consensus decision. PAM was independently developed by a student. For DEMETER-MODIST, we choose MPS, a production PAXOS implementation that has been running in Microsoft data centers for years and contains about 53K lines of code. We also check Berkeley DB (BDB), a widely used open-source transactional storage engine that supports replication for applications requiring high availability. We check its release version 4.7.25.NC as done with the original MODIST [39]. We use an example application `ex_rep_mgr` that comes with BDB as the test driver. This application manages its data using the replication manager of BDB. During the test, the multiple replicas first run an election. Once completed, the elected primary creates worker threads to modify the replicated database simultaneously. We have also implemented the standard *Dining Philosophers Problem* (DPhi) mostly for validation/debugging because we know the expected results in this case.

Our experiments are designed to evaluate the following three key aspects: (i) on effectiveness, how effective is DIR for reducing state spaces, and what factors could affect its effectiveness? (ii) on performance, cost, and parallelism, how much overhead does the extra complexity of DEMETER incur in model checking and how does the capability of state-space exploration increase with the use of more machines? (iii) on experience with verification and bug finding using DEMETER, does the state-space reduction translate into improved ability to cover a meaningful logical state space completely, and does it help find bugs more effectively?

5.1 Effectiveness

To estimate the effectiveness of DIR, we run DEMETER on target applications and record the number of local traces that have been explored by the local explorers. We then compute the number of global traces that are covered by those local traces. The computation is performed as follows: for each global skeleton κ, let n_c be the number of local traces in component c that are interface-equivalent with κ on c's interface. These local traces can compose across components to create global traces, whose number is then $\Pi_{c \in \mathscr{C}}(n_c)$. Let n_g be the sum on the number of global traces over all global skeletons. We then compute the *reduction ratio* as n_g divided by the number of explored local traces on all the local explorers.

Table 2 reports the reduction ratio (*Red-Ratio*), the actual number of global skeletons discovered, and the number of local traces explored. We run target applications in different settings in terms of the number of nodes (components) and perform each model checking for hours. App-n refers to the application running with n nodes (components), except that DPhi-n has n components with each containing 8 philosophers. Overall, we are seeing significant state-space reduction with the reduction ratio ranging from 5 to over 500,000. We see a significant increase when moving from a 2-node

to a 3-node system due to the multiplicative factor. Notice that all the applications in Table 2 except MPS, BDB, and CHORD-3 can also be fully checked by the original model checker. For those applications, we have validated the calculated value of n_g used for reduction ratio with the number of traces explored by the original model checker. This confirms that DEMETER with DIR upholds completeness and provides the justification to use calculated n_g for reduction ratio when the state space is too large to be fully explored by the original model checker.

Appli-cation	Red-Ratio	Global Skel	Local Trace	RT-Ratio	Speed-up
DPhi-2	41.7	6	1,510	2.0	20.9
DPhi-3	7,098.0	25	2.236	1.2	5,915.0
MPS-2	487.9	5	5,599	3.2	152.5
MPS-3	542,944.0	457	377,965	2.5	217,177.6
BDB-2	277.2	527	25,113	5.6	49.5
BDB-3	278,481.2	664	50,592	6.3	44,203.4
Pam-2	5.4	39	856	2.3	2.3
Pam-3	97.8	65	6,081	5.2	18.9
Pastry-2	4.9	48	713	1.5	3.3
Pastry-3	132.4	2,220	7,360	9.7	13.6
Chord-2	19.0	48	3,282	2.7	7.0
Chord-3	1,587.0	1,326	17,384	2.9	547.2

Table 2: State-space reduction and cost reduction of DEME-TER. The applications in top-half of the table are checked by DEMETER-MODIST, while the ones in bottom-half are checked by DEMETER-MACEMC.

The reduction ratios for MPS and BDB are particularly impressive. For MPS, each node is implemented with multiple threads that have to synchronize with others using *EnterCriticalSection*, e.g., to access a shared message queue. A significant portion of such different interleaving does not lead to changes in the interface, thereby resulting in state-space reduction. Most of such interleaving is in the underlying common network library, which is fairly complicated as it supports various forms of networking (e.g., AsyncIO with completion port). Similarly, BDB employs multiple threads to handle the delivered messages and update shared database or replication-related data structures. It also uses *WSAEventSelect* to process asynchronous network events. Again, most of the complex internal non-determinisms do not propagate across interfaces.

Although respectable, the reduction ratios for applications in MACE are relatively low. Our investigation shows that numbers of local traces for each global skeleton are relatively small in part because of our conservative partial-order tracking for DEMETER-MACEMC: two send transitions from the same node are always considered to have dependencies. Different orders of two inherently concurrent sends (on two separate threads, for example) would lead to different global skeletons. If their dependencies were accurately modeled, as MODIST does, they would be considered independent and their relative order due to intra-node non-determinism would not matter to other nodes, which would lead to a smaller number of global skeletons and better reduction.

5.2 Performance, Cost, and Parallelism

The reduction ratio tells only part of the story. The cost of exploring a trace in DEMETER can be noticeably higher due to the extra complexity related to DIR, which includes the extra cost in the partial-replay local system of the local explorer (e.g., computing the signature of the local skeleton for each local trace to check whether it is a branching trace), as well as the cost of composition and projection in the global explorer. In our experiment, we compute *RT-Ratio* as the relative cost of exploring a local trace in DEMETER

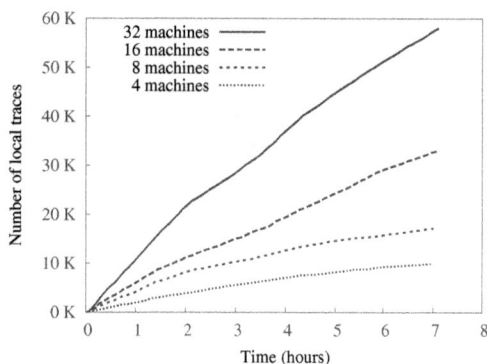

Figure 7: Numbers of explored local traces over time for MPS-3, with different numbers of worker machines.

with respect to the cost of exploring a global trace in the original model checker. The cost of exploring a local trace in DEMETER is the total amount of time spent on all the local explorers and the global explorer, amortized over the total number of explored local traces. As shown in Table 2, the *RT-Ratios* are significantly less than the *Red-Ratios*, which means that, although for the execution of a given trace, DEMETER is slower than original model checkers, it wins by exploring far fewer executions. We measure the effective speedup, without considering any potential parallelism in DEME-TER, as *Red-Ratio* divided by *RT-Ratio*. These results are shown as *Speedup* in Table 2. For MPS-3, we are seeing an effective speedup of over 10^5, while for PAM-2 the speedup is only about 2.

While having a small number of nodes is sufficient to discover many protocol-level issues, in order to understand how the reduction effectiveness and the composition cost scale with the number of components, we did also run MPS with 5 nodes for 1.5 hours (without completely searching local state spaces for each global skeleton): the reduction ratio and speedup already reached 10^9, confirming the trend of increased effectiveness with increased number of components. We also noticed a significant increase in the cost of composition: an order of magnitude increase from MPS-3. We are likely to run into scalability issues at some point with the global explorer. Section 6.1 discusses how we might address those issues.

Scalability. *RT-Ratio* and *Red-Ratio* do not take into account the effect of distributed and parallel execution. We further evaluated the inherent parallelism in DEMETER by deploying it on a cluster of machines. The goal of the experiment is to understand the increased effectiveness in state-space exploration as it uses more machines. We use DEMETER-MODIST on MPS as the showcase and vary the number of machines running MC Workers. Separately, we have one machine running the global explorer and three more as the local explorers, one for each component, coordinating MC Workers.

We run each experiment for about 7 hours. Figure 7 shows the numbers of discovered local traces over time with different numbers of worker machines. In each case, DEMETER is able to explore new local traces linearly over time and we also see near-perfect scalability as the number of machines goes up. This demonstrates (i) partial-replay local systems are embarrassingly parallel and (ii) composition by the global explorer does not become a bottleneck and can always dispatch enough local skeletons to make each worker machine busy when the local workers can discover and report enough new branching traces for composition in a short period of initial time.

5.3 Experiences

It is natural to ask whether or not the observed significant state-space reduction translates into any tangible benefits for improving system reliability. In particular, we look at two aspects: (i) DEME-TER's ability to explore completely a meaningful logically bounded state space of a system implementation for a higher degree of reliability assurance and (ii) how DEMETER improves our ability to find bugs.

Our experiment shows that DEMETER is capable of *completely* exploring a logically meaningful state space of a 3-node CHORD and MPS without any artificial bound on exploration depths. We do have to make the system finite: for CHORD, the system ends as soon as all three nodes join successfully with timeout fired at most once at each node. For MPS, we bound ballot numbers (to 2) and decree numbers (to 1). Such logical bounds still allow for a vast number of scenarios covering both phases of the PAXOS protocol. To see why previous model checkers do not come close to finishing the exploration, our CHORD exploration took 3 hours, exploring 17,384 local traces that correspond to 27,588,408 global traces, which would take more than 2 months for MACEMC to explore. Similarly, the exploration of DEMETER on MPS took 18 hours, exploring 182,689 local traces that correspond to 7,743,820,726 global traces, which would take about 34 years for MODIST to explore, even with its already significant partial-order methods for state-space reduction.

We believe the ability to explore thoroughly a meaningful logical state-space of a real implementation is significant. It offers a higher degree of assurance for system reliability as basic implementation-level protocol behaviors have now been "verified". Such kind of *coverage* statement for implementation was not possible before with the existing implementation-level model checkers and with the existing state-space exploration and reduction strategies on any non-trivial real production system.

Bug Finding. DEMETER naturally looks for safety bugs through state-space exploration. Finding liveness bugs often require a special set of strategies, as was done with MACEMC [29]. Those strategies are often incompatible with DIR, although they might still benefit from DIR. Our investigation focuses on safety bugs, while leaving liveness bugs to future work.

Our experiences with DEMETER on finding safety bugs are mixed, as significant state-space reduction does *not* translate automatically to proportional increases in bug-finding effectiveness. On the positive side, we have found two serious bugs in PAM: the depths at which those bugs were found are beyond the capability of the DFS search in MACEMC. The first bug arises due to loss of protocol state during replica recovery. In a 3-node replica system with nodes a, b, and c, replica a initially becomes a leader and passes a decree by getting the supporting vote from b only. Then b restarts from a failure and incorrectly votes with c to pass a different decree, because b has lost its state (related to a's earlier actions) during failure/recovery. DEMETER found this bug in a trace with a total depth of 27. The second bug is due to an incorrect vote message. When a leader receives accepted values in phase 1, it must vote in phase 2 the accepted value with the highest ballot number. The initial implementation incorrectly chose the first received value instead. This bug appears only when two different values were accepted on two different nodes and in our experiment involves a trace with a total depth of 43.

On the negative side, we did not find any new bugs when running DEMETER on MPS, BDB, PASTRY, and CHORD through a simple brute-force search. We found only the first bug in PAM. Bug finding turns out to be significantly different from covering a state space. When a state space is large, it is more effective to cover as many interesting scenarios as possible. Bug finding is therefore best guided with application-specific knowledge and DEMETER offers a more powerful tool for this guided process. For example, rather than focusing on the initial phase and running a system for a long time, we periodically stop the system to get a checkpoint and start a new exploration from that checkpoint if we think that checkpoint state is "interesting" (e.g., having replicas with inconsistent states). We essentially do *vertical decomposition* of system execution and prune out "uninteresting" branches. This allows DEMETER to explore longer traces more effectively. The second PAM bug was found this way through 3 "inconsistent" checkpoints as stepping stones. The final buggy path is the result of concatenation of these sub-paths.

6. DISCUSSIONS
This section discusses three subtle issues that affect the effectiveness of DIR: how to define components, how to check global properties, and how to avoid branching redundancies.

6.1 Defining Components
The effectiveness of DIR depends on how a target system is partitioned into components. One natural way is to make each process a component. In our experience, this simple approach is effective because processes in a distributed system tend to communicate with each other through message passing, where the design tends to minimize communication between them for performance reasons. Application logic within a process is often implemented with multiple threads and asynchronous I/O for high performance, which introduces substantial sources of non-determinism in it. Therefore, interactions between processes can be significantly simpler than nondeterminism within each process, leading to significant state-space reduction when explored with DIR.

It is also possible to group multiple processes together to form a component. Even with processes running the same code, different groupings often have different effects, due to different roles the processes play in an application. For example, in dining philosophers, it makes sense to group consecutive philosophers together because doing so will lead to an interface with only two forks no matter how many philosophers are included in that component. In the worst case, if philosophers are divided into two components in alternation, all forks will become interface objects. Even for the 3-node cases of PASTRY and CHORD, nodes 1 and 2 have more interactions between them. Our experiments show better reduction ratios when grouping those two into a group, compared to grouping nodes 2 and 3 in a component, although having three components yields the best reduction ratios.

The decision of whether certain processes should be grouped together as one component depends on a number of factors. Tightly coupled processes should ideally be grouped together, although this will increase the complexity of partial-replay local systems. When the number of components is high, the number of global skeletons goes up exponentially, which increases the overhead on the global explorer. We have developed an algorithm called *hierarchical dynamic interface reduction* to address this issue further. It reduces the overhead on the global explorer by recursively dividing a system into a small number of components at each level. We have shown the effectiveness of this method on dining philosophers,

which leads to exponential state-space reduction in theory. We have yet to show that the added complexity brings significant practical benefits on real applications. Peer-to-peer protocols such as PASTRY and CHORD are ideal targets.

6.2 Global Property Checking
Not only can DEMETER discover local assertion failures and misbehavior during state-space exploration, but can also be used to check global safety properties. The ideal place to perform global property checking is at the global explorer as it has a global view on a system via global skeletons and global traces. To facilitate global property checking, each component has to expose not only interface transitions but also any local states that are referenced by the specified global property. Updates to local variables referenced will have to be reported. Those states are taken into account when assessing whether an execution creates a branching trace, although local skeletons for the local explorers do not have to contain such states because they are not used in partial-replay local systems. All such information is incorporated into global skeletons during the composition process. The global explorer can then enumerate all the consistent snapshots of those state variables on all the global skeletons to check global properties. From our experience, adding global property checking into DEMETER-MODIST is natural as MODIST has the mechanism to expose states. Adding the same functionality to DEMETER-MACEMC is harder because the state variables are not easily exposed in MACEMC.

6.3 Branching Redundancy
DEMETER builds a partial-replay local system for each local skeleton. A branching trace is not part of a local state space, but should be counted as overhead for local exploration. We have observed that some trace prefixes are explored in multiple partial-replay local systems for different skeletons, once as part of local traces in one, and again as part of branching traces in another. This leads to redundant state-space exploration by partial-replay local systems for different local skeletons. DEMETER could explore a branching trace multiple times since it does not know whether that branching trace is already explored in other partial-replay systems. One solution to this problem is to have DEMETER explore all partial-replay systems of a component on a single worker to avoid such redundancies as the redundancies are among MC Workers for the same component. As a result, DEMETER's parallel granularity is now limited to the number of components. However, we can accelerate the exploration by parallelizing the exploring algorithm itself. For example, it is possible to have a different worker exploring a sub-tree space of a particular local-state partial-replay system. One caveat is the potential interactions with the state-space exploration strategy in an *eMC*: for example, MODIST uses dynamic partial order reduction, where the exploration of a sub-tree space might need to add new transitions to the execution points above that subtree.

7. RELATED WORK
Model Checking. Model checkers have previously been used to find bugs in both the design and implementation of software. Traditional model checkers require that users transform a target system into an abstract model beforehand [11, 34, 2, 14, 26, 27]. This process is often expensive and error-prone, thereby limiting the use of these tools for large-scale software systems. Implementation-level software model checkers [18, 36, 32, 41, 40, 39, 33, 29, 38] can instead work directly on implementations of software systems by systematically controlling executions and exploring non-determinisms in a system implementation.

Both traditional model checkers and software model checkers have to face the problem of state-space explosion. Based on the observation that complex large-scale systems normally consist of loosely-coupled components, compositional reasoning techniques [6, 35, 12, 4, 22, 31] have been proposed and applied for effective state-space reduction. Such methods check each component of a system in isolation and infer global system properties appropriately. However, all of the previous proposals target only traditional model checkers. Some of them need substantial human effort [22, 31], and hence are not scalable. Others [6, 35, 12], although automatic, require eagerly constructing an abstract component acting as the environment of a component being checked, making it impractical for complex large-scale systems. In contrast, DEMETER applies DIR to software model checkers by lazily and dynamically discovering all interface interactions among components, thereby significantly reducing the amount of human effort and removing any need for static program analysis to transform a system implementation or its environment into an abstract model.

Alur and Yannakakis [1] applied model checking on hierarchical state machines where the state nodes of a state machine can be ordinary states or state machines themselves. Their method leverages this hierarchical structure of the state machines to avoid exploring the same sub-state-machine multiple times. Their method applies to formal sequential hierarchical state-machine specifications only, whereas DIR targets implementation-level model checking of concurrent and distributed systems without formal specifications.

The most related method was proposed recently by Guerraoui and Yabandeh [23] to separate the exploration of system states (i.e., the combination of node-local states) and network states. The proposed method takes an optimistic approach and does not model dependencies between network transitions. This imprecision leads to loss of soundness, which has to be addressed using a compensatory validity check. In contrast, our approach tracks dependencies explicitly and ensures soundness during exploration.

State-Space Reduction. Other state-space reduction techniques, such as partial order reduction [17, 16], symmetry reduction [28], and abstraction [25, 10, 3, 13, 21], have been proposed and investigated. Those techniques are orthogonal to DIR and can often be applied together. For example, the analysis presented in Section 2.3 on the example in Figure 1 helps to show why DIR is orthogonal to partial order reduction (POR). POR states that it is sufficient to explore only one permutation order of a set of independent operations. For instance, only one order of the Sum in the primary and the Ckpt in the secondary need be explored because they are independent. Fundamentally, POR still views a system as a whole. Thus, when the Sum and Ckpt operations within one server interleave differently, POR has to re-explore the entire system. Nonetheless, combining the two reduction techniques is easy as both the global explorer and the local explorers in DIR can use POR to reduce the number of executions they explore. In fact, when integrating with MODIST, we have effectively enabled both POR and DIR. It is an interesting future direction to see whether other state-space reduction techniques are compatible with the architecture of DEMETER.

Error-Detection Techniques. Recently, symbolic execution [8, 7, 20, 9] has been used to detect errors in real systems. This technique takes program inputs as symbolic values and explores all possible execution paths by solving the corresponding path conditions. Similar to model checking, symbolic execution also confronts the problem of state-space explosion. SMART [19] applied *composi-tion* in symbolic execution at function granularity. It checks functions in isolation, encoding the results as function summaries expressed using input preconditions and output postconditions, and then re-using those summaries when checking higher-level functions. However, their idea cannot be applied in checking concurrent/distributed systems. Zamfir and Candea [42] further enhanced symbolic execution to support concurrent systems by making thread-scheduling decisions symbolic. It is again an interesting future research direction to understand whether an idea similar to DIR would help in this scenario.

Software Verification. Many attempts have been made to verify software implementations [30, 37, 5, 24, 3, 15]. BLAST [24] and SLAM [3] combine predicate abstraction and model checking techniques to analyze and verify specific safety properties of device drivers. Model checking is complementary in that it can be used to check a bounded small state space thoroughly and to provide some assurance by attempting to find defects when complete verification is infeasible.

8. CONCLUSIONS

DEMETER provides early validation on dynamic interface reduction and closes the gap between a theoretically interesting algorithm and a practical model checking framework that demonstrates its effectiveness on representative distributed systems with real model checkers. Experiences with DEMETER further shed lights on several interesting future directions. First, removing any scalability hurdle to applying DEMETER to a large number of components could further unleash the power of this reduction. Second, further pushing the boundary of state spaces that can be completely explored could make model checking a useful tool for software reliability assurance. Third, finding bugs effectively with DEMETER requires a different thinking from covering a state sub-space completely and might need guidance with domain knowledge.

9. ACKNOWLEDGEMENTS

We thank Tisheng Chen and Yi Yang for their help at the early stage of this project, and our colleagues at System Research Group in Microsoft Research Asia for their comments and support. Sean McDirmid helped greatly in improving the writing of this paper. Charles E. Killian, Jr. provided valuable information on MACEMC. We would also thank Lorenzo Alvisi, Robbert van Renesse, and Geoffrey M. Voelker for their comments on the paper. We are grateful to the anonymous reviewers for their valuable feedback. We are particularly in debt to our shepherd Petros Maniatis for his detailed guidance and constructive suggestions. Junfeng was supported in part by NSF grants CNS-1117805, CNS-1054906 (CAREER), CNS-1012633, and CNS-0905246; and AFRL FA8650-10-C-7024 and FA8750-10-2-0253.

10. REFERENCES

[1] R. Alur and M. Yannakakis. Model checking of hierarchical state machines. *ACM Transactions on Programming Languages and Systems (TOPLAS)*, 23(3):273–303, 2001.

[2] T. Ball and S. K. Rajamani. Automatically validating temporal safety properties of interfaces. In *Proceedings of the Eighth International SPIN Workshop on Model Checking of Software (SPIN '01)*, pages 103–122, May 2001.

[3] T. Ball and S. K. Rajamani. The SLAM project: debugging system software via static analysis. In *POPL '02: Proceedings of the 29th ACM SIGPLAN-SIGACT symposium on Principles of programming languages*, pages 1–3, New York, NY, USA, 2002. ACM.

[4] S. Berezin, S. V. A. Campos, and E. M. Clarke. Compositional reasoning in model checking. In *COMPOS'97: Revised Lectures from*

the *International Symposium on Compositionality: The Significant Difference*, pages 81–102, London, UK, 1998. Springer-Verlag.

[5] W. Bevier. Kit: A study in operating system verification. *IEEE Transactions on Software Engineering*, pages 1382–1396, 1989.

[6] J. Burch, E. M. Clarke, and D. Long. Symbolic model checking with partitioned transition relations. In *VLSI*, pages 49–58. North-Holland, 1991.

[7] C. Cadar, D. Dunbar, and D. Engler. KLEE: Unassisted and automatic generation of high-coverage tests for complex systems programs. In *Proceedings of the Eighth Symposium on Operating Systems Design and Implementation (OSDI '08)*, pages 209–224, Dec. 2008.

[8] C. Cadar, V. Ganesh, P. M. Pawlowski, D. L. Dill, and D. R. Engler. EXE: automatically generating inputs of death. In *Proceedings of the 13th ACM conference on Computer and communications security (CCS '06)*, pages 322–335, Oct.–Nov. 2006.

[9] V. Chipounov, V. Georgescu, C. Zamfir, and G. Candea. Selective symbolic execution. In *Workshop on Hot Topics in Dependable Systems*, 2009.

[10] E. Clarke, D. Kroening, and F. Lerda. A tool for checking ANSI-C programs. In K. Jensen and A. Podelski, editors, *Tools and Algorithms for the Construction and Analysis of Systems (TACAS 2004)*, volume 2988 of *Lecture Notes in Computer Science*, pages 168–176. Springer, 2004.

[11] E. M. Clarke and E. A. Emerson. Design and synthesis of synchronization skeletons using branching-time temporal logic. In *Logic of Programs, Workshop*, pages 52–71, London, UK, 1982. Springer-Verlag.

[12] E. M. Clarke, D. Long, and K. L. McMillan. Compositional model checking. In *Proceedings of the Fourth Annual Symposium on Logic in computer science*, pages 353–362, Piscataway, NJ, USA, 1989. IEEE Press.

[13] B. Cook, A. Podelski, and A. Rybalchenko. Termination proofs for systems code. In *PLDI '06: Proceedings of the 2006 ACM SIGPLAN conference on Programming language design and implementation*, pages 415–426, New York, NY, USA, 2006. ACM.

[14] J. C. Corbett, M. B. Dwyer, J. Hatcliff, S. Laubach, C. S. Păsăreanu, Robby, and H. Zheng. Bandera: Extracting finite-state models from Java source code. In *Proceedings of the 22nd International Conference on Software Engineering (ICSE '00)*, pages 439–448, June 2000.

[15] M. Emmi, R. Jhala, E. Kohler, and R. Majumdar. Verifying reference counting implementations. *Tools and Algorithms for the Construction and Analysis of Systems*, pages 352–367, 2009.

[16] C. Flanagan and P. Godefroid. Dynamic partial-order reduction for model checking software. In *Proceedings of the 32nd Annual Symposium on Principles of Programming Languages (POPL '05)*, pages 110–121, Jan. 2005.

[17] P. Godefroid. *Partial-Order Methods for the Verification of Concurrent Systems: An Approach to the State-Explosion Problem*, volume 1032 of LNCS. 1996.

[18] P. Godefroid. Model checking for programming languages using verisoft. In *POPL '97: Proceedings of the 24th ACM SIGPLAN-SIGACT symposium on Principles of programming languages*, pages 174–186, New York, NY, USA, 1997. ACM.

[19] P. Godefroid. Compositional dynamic test generation. In *POPL '07: Proceedings of the 34th annual ACM SIGPLAN-SIGACT symposium on Principles of programming languages*, pages 47–54, New York, NY, USA, 2007. ACM.

[20] P. Godefroid, N. Klarlund, and K. Sen. DART: directed automated random testing. In *PLDI '05: Proceedings of the 2005 ACM SIGPLAN conference on Programming language design and implementation*, pages 213–223, New York, NY, USA, 2005. ACM.

[21] S. Graf and H. Saïdi. Construction of abstract state graphs with pvs. In *CAV '97: Proceedings of the 9th International Conference on Computer Aided Verification*, pages 72–83, London, UK, 1997. Springer-Verlag.

[22] O. Grumberg and D. Long. Model checking and modular verification, May 1994.

[23] R. Guerraoui and M. Yabandeh. Model checking a networked system without the network. In *Proceedings of the 8th USENIX conference on Networked Systems Design and Implementation*, NSDI'11, Berkeley, CA, USA, 2011. USENIX Association.

[24] T. Henzinger, R. Jhala, R. Majumdar, and G. Sutre. Software verification with BLAST. In *Proceedings of the 10th international conference on Model checking software*, pages 235–239. Springer-Verlag, 2003.

[25] T. A. Henzinger, R. Jhala, R. Majumdar, and G. Sutre. Lazy abstraction. In *Proceedings of the 29th Annual Symposium on Principles of Programming Languages*, pages pp. 58–70. ACM Press, 2002.

[26] G. J. Holzmann. The model checker SPIN. *Software Engineering*, 23(5):279–295, 1997.

[27] G. J. Holzmann. From code to models. In *Proceedings of the Second International Conference on Applications of Concurrency to System Design (ACSD '01)*, June 2001.

[28] C. N. Ip and D. L. Dill. Better verification through symmetry. *Form. Methods Syst. Des.*, 9(1-2):41–75, 1996.

[29] C. Killian, J. W. Anderson, R. Jhala, and A. Vahdat. Life, death, and the critical transition: Finding liveness bugs in systems code. In *Proceedings of the Fourth Symposium on Networked Systems Design and Implementation (NSDI '07)*, pages 243–256, April 2007.

[30] G. Klein, K. Elphinstone, G. Heiser, J. Andronick, D. Cock, P. Derrin, D. Elkaduwe, K. Engelhardt, R. Kolanski, M. Norrish, T. Sewell, H. Tuch, and S. Winwood. seL4: Formal verification of an OS kernel. In *Proceedings of the ACM SIGOPS 22nd Symposium on Operating Systems Principles*, pages 207–220. ACM, 2009.

[31] K. Laster and O. Grumberg. Modular model checking of software. In *TACAS '98: Proceedings of the 4th International Conference on Tools and Algorithms for Construction and Analysis of Systems*, pages 20–35, 1998.

[32] M. Musuvathi, D. Y. Park, A. Chou, D. R. Engler, and D. L. Dill. CMC: A pragmatic approach to model checking real code. In *Proceedings of the Fifth Symposium on Operating Systems Design and Implementation (OSDI '02)*, pages 75–88, Dec. 2002.

[33] M. Musuvathi and S. Qadeer. Iterative context bounding for systematic testing of multithreaded programs. In *Proceedings of the ACM SIGPLAN 2007 Conference on Programming Language Design and Implementation (PLDI '07)*, June 2007.

[34] J.-P. Queille and J. Sifakis. Specification and verification of concurrent systems in cesar. In *Proceedings of the 5th Colloquium on International Symposium on Programming*, pages 337–351, London, UK, 1982.

[35] H. J. Touati, H. Savoj, B. Lin, R. K. Brayton, and A. Sangiovanni-Vincentelli. Implicit state enumeration of finite state machines using BDD's. In *IEEE Int. Conf. Computer-Aided Design*, pages 130–133, 1990.

[36] W. Visser, K. Havelund, G. Brat, S. Park, and F. Lerda. Model checking programs. *Automated Software Engineering*, 10(2):203–232, 2003.

[37] B. Walker, R. Kemmerer, and G. Popek. Specification and verification of the UCLA Unix security kernel. *Communications of the ACM*, 23(2):131, 1980.

[38] M. Yabandeh, N. Knezevic, D. Kostic, and V. Kuncak. CrystalBall: Predicting and preventing inconsistencies in deployed distributed systems. In *Proceedings of the Sixth Symposium on Networked Systems Design and Implementation (NSDI '09)*, Apr. 2009.

[39] J. Yang, T. Chen, M. Wu, Z. Xu, X. Liu, H. Lin, M. Yang, F. Long, L. Zhang, and L. Zhou. Modist: Transparent model checking of unmodified distributed systems. In *Proceedings of the Sixth Symposium on Networked Systems Design and Implementation (NSDI '09)*, Apr. 2009.

[40] J. Yang, C. Sar, and D. Engler. Explode: A lightweight, general system for finding serious storage system errors. In *Proceedings of the Seventh Symposium on Operating Systems Design and Implementation (OSDI '06)*, pages 131–146, Nov. 2006.

[41] J. Yang, P. Twohey, D. Engler, and M. Musuvathi. Using model checking to find serious file system errors. In *Proceedings of the Sixth Symposium on Operating Systems Design and Implementation (OSDI '04)*, pages 273–288, Dec. 2004.

[42] C. Zamfir and G. Candea. Execution synthesis: A technique for automated software debugging. In *Proceedings of the 5th European conference on Computer systems*, pages 321–334. ACM, 2010.

APPENDIX
A. PROOF SKETCH

In this section, we prove that the algorithms for the global explorer and the local explorer in Section 3.4 preserve both soundness and completeness. The proofs use the substitution rule introduced in Section 3.4 as an "axiom" that follows directly from the definitions of components, interfaces, and interface equivalence.

A.1 Soundness

Lemma A.1. *With respect to $\langle \kappa_c, \tau \rangle \in L_c$, where τ is a valid global trace, the partial-replay local system produces a valid global trace in every exploration step. A global trace is valid if its execution can occur in a real run of the checked system.*

Proof. Consider a system consisting of component c and the rest of the system R. A partial-replay local system for component c with respect to $\langle \kappa_c, \tau \rangle \in L_c$ starts from the initial state and in each step either picks an enabled transition from component c or replays τ's transitions in R. To enable replaying, the partial-replay local system tracks which of τ's transitions in R can be replayed: a transition t in τ can be replayed if and only if t is a transition from R and any transition $t' \neq t$ in $proj_R(\tau)$ satisfying $t' \preceq t$ has been replayed in previous steps. The transitions replayed in R and the interface transitions from component c always form a prefix of $proj_R(\tau)$. Therefore, at any step, there exists a prefix τ_p of τ such that $proj_R(\tau_p)$ captures all replayed transitions projected to R (including both R's internal transitions and interface transitions) and their partial order.

The partial-replay local system preserves the partial order between transitions in $proj_c$ as in the original system and between transitions in $proj_R(\tau)$ as in τ. By definition, the transitions taken in c and the interface transitions related to c form a projection of some valid trace τ_1 (i.e., $proj_c(\tau_1)$ captures all transitions in c and all the interface transitions for c). The trace that the partial-replay local system produces is therefore $subst_c(\tau_p, \tau_1)$. Due to the substitution rule, it is a valid trace.

$\square$

Lemma A.2. *(i) For each $\langle \kappa, \tau \rangle \in G$, τ is a valid global trace, (ii) for each $\langle t_b, \tau_b \rangle \in B$, τ_b is a valid global trace, and (iii) for each $\langle \kappa_c, \tau \rangle \in L_c$ for any component c, τ is a valid global trace.*

Proof. Prove by induction on the order of the entries added into sets G, B, and L_c's.

Initially, the algorithm uses a real global execution to find a global trace to add to G. That global trace is valid by construction. For the induction step, assume that all entries in G, B, and L_c satisfy the conditions. We consider the following cases:

Case 1: A new entry $\langle \kappa_c, \tau \rangle$ is added into L_c. There must exist some $\langle \kappa, \tau \rangle \in G$ satisfying $proj_c(\kappa) = \kappa_c$. By the induction hypothesis, τ is a valid global trace.

Case 2: A new entry $\langle t_b, \tau_b \rangle$ is added to B. This is because t_b is a branching transition at trace τ_b when executing a partial-replay local system for c with respect to some $\langle \kappa_c, \tau \rangle \in L_c$ for some component c. By the induction hypothesis, τ is a valid trace. τ_b is a valid trace by the construction of the partial-replay local system due to Lemma A.1.

Case 3: A new entry $\langle \kappa_n, \tau_n \rangle$ is added into G. This is because there exists $\langle t_b, \tau_b \rangle \in B$ and $\langle \kappa_g, \tau_g \rangle \in G$ satisfying $proj_c(\kappa_g) = skel(proj_c(\tau_b))$, $\tau_n = subst_c(\tau_g, \tau_b) \circ t_b$, and $\kappa_n = skel(\tau_n)$. By the induction hypothesis, τ_b is a valid global trace and τ_g is a valid global trace. Following the substitution rule, $subst_c(\tau_g, \tau_b)$ is a valid trace. By the construction of $\langle t_b, \tau_b \rangle$, t_b is a valid transition in $subst_c(\tau_g, \tau_b)$ because it is an enabled transition from c in τ_b. Therefore, $\tau_n = subst_c(\tau_g, \tau_b) \circ t_b$ is a valid trace. $\square$

Theorem A.3. *For any local trace τ_c that the local explorer for component c discovers, there exists a valid global trace τ, such that $\tau_c = proj_c(\tau)$.*

Proof. Follows directly from Lemma A.1 and Lemma A.2. $\square$

A.2 Completeness

Theorem A.4. *Assume a local explorer with the eMC and the partial-replay local system explores completely the enabled transitions in a component, for any valid global trace τ_g, the global explorer eventually adds $\langle skel(\tau_g), \tau \rangle$ into G for some global trace τ. For every component c, the local explorer discovers $proj_c(\tau_g)$.*

Proof. Assume there exists a valid global trace τ_g that invalidates the theorem, i.e., either some of its projected local traces for components cannot be explored by the local explorers, or its corresponding global skeleton cannot be discovered by the global explorer. There must be a longest prefix τ_p of this global trace τ_g that satisfies the following properties: (i) the local trace $\tau_x = proj_x(\tau_p)$ for any component x has been explored by the local explorer of x and (ii) there exists a global trace τ_p^g, such that $\langle skel(\tau_p), \tau_p^g \rangle$ has been discovered by the global explorer and is therefore in G.

Let t be the subsequent transition of τ_p in τ_g: by definition of τ_p and τ_g, such a transition must exist. Without loss of generality, let t be a transition belonging to a component c. Transition t will be enabled during the local exploration of c against $\tau_c = proj_c(\tau_p)$ according to the substitution rule. We consider two cases.

Case 1: t is an internal transition. We show that $\tau_p \circ t$ satisfies (i) and (ii) as τ_p does. Because t is enabled at τ_c, the local explorer for c will take this transition, reaching the projection of $\tau_p \circ t$ to c. For any other component, the projection of $\tau_p \circ t$ is the same as that of τ_p. Because t is an internal transition, $skel(\tau_p \circ t)$ is also the same as $skel(\tau_p)$. Because $\tau_p \circ t$ is a prefix of τ_g longer than τ_p, we have a contradiction with the definition of τ_p.

Case 2: t is an interface transition. Because t is enabled at τ_c, the local explorer will take this transition. Again, we show that $\tau_p \circ t$ satisfies (i) and (ii) as τ_p does. The part of the proof about (i) is the same as in Case 1. For (ii), we need to show that the global explorer discovers $skel(\tau_p \circ t)$ through composition by substitution. Let τ_b be the global trace that the partial-replay local system constructs when reaching τ_c. We have $\tau_c = proj_c(\tau_b)$. Pair $\langle t, \tau_b \rangle$ will be reported to the global explorer. Because $\langle skel(\tau_p), \tau_p^g \rangle \in G$ and $proj_c(skel(\tau_p)) = skel(proj_c(\tau_b))$ hold, the global explorer will construct a new global trace $\tau_n = subst_c(\tau_p^g, \tau_b) \circ t$ and discovers $skel(\tau_n)$. By construction, we have $skel(subst_c(\tau_p^g, \tau_b)) = skel(\tau_p)$. Therefore, we have $skel(\tau_n) = skel(\tau_p \circ t)$, which means that (ii) holds for $\tau_p \circ t$. Again, because $\tau_p \circ t$ is a prefix of τ_g longer than τ_p, we have a contradiction with the definition of τ_p.

$\square$

Detecting failures in distributed systems
with the FALCON spy network

Joshua B. Leners*   Hao Wu*   Wei-Lun Hung*   Marcos K. Aguilera†   Michael Walfish*

*The University of Texas at Austin   †Microsoft Research Silicon Valley

ABSTRACT

A common way for a distributed system to tolerate crashes is to explicitly detect them and then recover from them. Interestingly, detection can take much longer than recovery, as a result of many advances in recovery techniques, making failure detection the dominant factor in these systems' unavailability when a crash occurs.

This paper presents the design, implementation, and evaluation of Falcon, a failure detector with several features. First, Falcon's common-case detection time is sub-second, which keeps unavailability low. Second, Falcon is reliable: it never reports a process as down when it is actually up. Third, Falcon sometimes kills to achieve reliable detection but aims to kill the smallest needed component. Falcon achieves these features by coordinating a network of *spies*, each monitoring a layer of the system. Falcon's main cost is a small amount of platform-specific logic. Falcon is thus the first failure detector that is fast, reliable, and viable. As such, it could change the way that a class of distributed systems is built.

Categories and Subject Descriptors: C.2.4 [Computer-Communication Networks]: Distributed Systems—Client/Server; Distributed applications; D.4.5 [Operating Systems]: Reliability—fault-tolerance

General Terms: Algorithms, Design, Experimentation, Performance, Reliability

Keywords: Failure detectors, high availability, reliable detection, layer-specific monitors, layer-specific probes, STONITH

1 INTRODUCTION

Many distributed systems must handle crash failures, such as application crashes, operating system crashes, device driver crashes, application deadlocks, application livelocks, and hardware failures. A common way to handle crashes involves two steps: (1) Detect the failure; and (2) Recover, by restarting or failing over the crashed component. Failure recovery has received much attention. For instance, using periodic checkpoints, an entire VM can be failed over in one second [22]; finer-grained components such as processes or threads can be restarted even faster [15, 16]. Interestingly, failure detection has received less attention, perhaps because it is a hard problem. The fundamental difficulty is that uncertain communication delay and execution time make it hard to distinguish a crashed process from one that is merely slow.

Given this difficulty, current approaches to failure detection use a blunt instrument: an end-to-end timeout set to tens of seconds. As a result, after a crash, a system can be unavailable for a long time,

waiting for the timer to fire. Indeed, we (and everyone else) are personally familiar with the hiccups that occur when a distributed system freezes until a timeout expires. More technically, examples of timeouts in real systems include 60 seconds for GFS [29], at least 12 seconds for Chubby [14], 30 seconds for Dryad [32], and 60 seconds for NFS. Of course, one could set a shorter timeout—and thereby increase the risk of falsely declaring a working node as down. We discuss end-to-end timeouts further in Section 2.2 and for now just assert that there are no good end-to-end timeout values.

This paper introduces Falcon (Fast And Lethal Component Observation Network), a failure detector that leverages internal knowledge from various system layers to achieve a new combination in failure detection: sub-second crash detection time, reliability, and little disruption. With these features, Falcon can (1) improve applications' availability and (2) reduce their complexity. The target applications are those in data centers and enterprise networks.

A failure detector is a service that reports the status of a remote process as UP or DOWN. A failure detector should ideally have three properties. First, it should be a *reliable failure detector (RFD)*: when a process is up, it is reported as UP, and when it crashes, it is reported as DOWN after a while. Second, the failure detector should be *fast*: the time taken to report DOWN, known as the *detection time*, should be short (less than a second), so as not to delay recovery. Third, the failure detector should cause *little disruption*.

The above properties are in tension with each other and with other desired properties. For instance, a short detection time based on timeouts would compromise reliability, since the detector would report as DOWN a process that is up. As an alternative, a detector could ensure reliability and a short detection time by killing processes [6, 27] at the slightest provocation, but that would be disruptive. Also, short detection times often require probing the target incessantly, which is costly. Another challenge is comprehensiveness: how can the detector maximize its coverage of failures?

The starting point in the design of Falcon is the observation that many crash failures can be observed readily—by looking at the right layer of the system. As examples, a process that core dumps will disappear from the process table; after an operating system panics, it stops scheduling processes; and if a machine loses power, it stops communicating with its attached network switch. In fact, if the failure detector infiltrates various layers in the system, it can provide reliable failure detection using local instead of end-to-end timeouts and sometimes without using any timeouts.

To infiltrate the system, Falcon relies on a network of *spy modules* or *spies*. At the cost of a small amount of platform-specific logic, spies use inside information to learn whether layers are alive. If a layer seems crashed, the spies kill it so that Falcon can report DOWN with confidence. However, killing is a last resort and is *surgical*: Falcon aims to kill the smallest possible layer.

A challenge that we address in Falcon is to provide a careful, thorough, and general design for the collection of spies, to maximize detection coverage and to avoid disruption. Spies are arranged in a chained network, where the spy in one layer monitors the spy at the next layer up (e.g., the OS spy monitors the application spy). Thus, in the common case, if any layer in the system crashes, some spy will observe it. There are, however, two limiting cases in Falcon. First, Falcon cannot assume that spies will detect every failure. Thus, Falcon includes a backstop: a large end-to-end timeout to cover (the ideally rare) cases that the spies missed. Second, to report DOWN reliably, Falcon must be able to communicate with the remote system. Thus, if a network partition happens, Falcon pauses until the network heals, which we think is acceptable since a partition likely disrupts most services anyway.

We have implemented and evaluated Falcon. In its current implementation, Falcon deploys spies on four layers: application, OS, virtual machine monitor (VMM),[1] and network switch. We find that for a range of failures, Falcon has sub-second detection time, which is one or two orders of magnitude faster than baseline approaches. This yields higher availability: adding Falcon to ZooKeeper [31] (which provides configuration management, naming, and group membership) and to a replication library [44] reduces unavailability after some crashes by roughly 6×. Falcon's CPU overhead and per-platform requirements are small, and it can be integrated into an application with tens of lines of code. Finally, Falcon can simplify applications that use a failure detector: with RFDs, such applications can shed complex logic that handles failure detector errors (e.g., a replicated state machine can be implemented with primary-backup [9] instead of Paxos [35], thereby using 21% less code, in our rough estimate).

The contributions of this work are as follows:

- *The first viable and fast RFD.* Previous RFDs (§2.2, §7) have drawbacks that make them impractical: large timeouts (to avoid killing aggressively) or disruption from small timeouts. Perhaps for this reason, the conventional wisdom is that a viable RFD cannot be built (§6.1), and indeed, most current failure detectors are unreliable (i.e., not RFDs). Yet, a viable RFD could change the way that we build a class of distributed systems (§6.5).
- *Spies, a spy network, and their composition with existing techniques (§2.3).* Many of Falcon's elements are not new; for instance, killing to achieve reliability has been proposed before and so, for that matter, have end-to-end timeouts, which Falcon uses as a backstop. The new aspects of Falcon are (a) layer-specific monitors (spies); (b) a network of chained spies, where a spy monitors the spy in the next higher layer; and (c) composing these two with existing techniques. We note that the purpose of (a) and (b) is not just fast failure detection; they also reduce false suspicion and kill surgically.
- *The design of Falcon (§3).* We provide a concrete, complete, and sound design for Falcon, based on the key high-level ideas above.
- *The implementation and evaluation of Falcon (§4, §5).*

2 PROBLEM, PERILS, AND PRINCIPLES

2.1 Problem statement and setting

A reliable failure detector (RFD) is a service that, upon being queried about the operational status of a (possibly remote) process p, reports p as UP or DOWN, such that [19]:

- if the RFD reports p as DOWN, then p has crashed;
- if p crashes, then the RFD eventually reports p as DOWN (and does so ever after).

If p crashes, the second property above allows the RFD to report p as UP for some time—called the *detection time*—before it reports DOWN. A *fast* RFD is one with short detection time. We wish to build a fast RFD that is *viable*, meaning that it uses few resources, and that *minimizes disruption*, meaning that it kills only if necessary and, when it does so, kills only the smallest needed component.

Our target setting is a data center or enterprise system. The target applications range from small-scale Web applications that use primary-backup replication [9]; to large-scale storage systems like GFS [29] and Dynamo [25]; to distributed systems that perform batch computations (e.g., MapReduce [24], Dryad [32], and Hadoop [1]); to services, such as Chubby [14] and ZooKeeper [31], that provide common distributed systems functions (group membership, leases, locks, etc.) to other applications.

We assume that (limited) modifications to the software stack are permissible; this assumption holds in our target setting, in which there is a single administrative domain, and may hold in other controlled settings as well. Likewise, we assume that users are trustworthy; access control is orthogonal and could be added to our design. Our approach handles crash failures of any kind; handling Byzantine failures is future work. Also, we design for monitoring within a single data center (though our solution could be used across data centers, with some drawbacks, as discussed in Section 6.4).

2.2 Why is failure detection vexing?

The fundamental difficulty in failure detection is that it is hard to make judgments that are both quick and accurate—a problem that exists in many intelligence contexts. This difficulty leads to a choose-two-of-three situation, in which it is hard to achieve all three of the goals of fast detection, reliability, and little disruption but straightforward to achieve any two of them.

For instance, a failure detector (FD) can achieve accuracy and little disruption by dithering in its reply until there is no question of failure. Alternatively, an FD can achieve a fast detection time if it is willing to jump to conclusions, sometimes producing inaccurate suspicions of failure, at which point there are two ways to handle the inaccuracy. First, the FD can back up its misjudgments by killing the target; however, in converting bad calls into needless kills, this approach sacrifices the goal of little disruption. Second, the FD can give wrong answers, sacrificing reliability; such FDs are *unreliable failure detectors* (UFDs) and force applications—if they are to be responsible—to deal with added complexity, as we elaborate below.

We now highlight the above trade-offs in the context of existing approaches to failure detection; Section 2.3 describes the high-level ideas that we use to break the impasse. The prevalent approach to failure detection uses end-to-end timeouts. The problem is: how does one choose the timeout value? Small values lead to premature timeouts, while large timeouts lead to large detection times. In fact, there may not *be* a perfect timeout value: the difference in latency between normal and delayed requests in data center applications can be several orders of magnitude (e.g., [24]). And while adaptive timeouts (e.g., [11, 21, 30]) might seem promising, adaptation requires time; thus, if system responsiveness changes rapidly (e.g., from bursty load), one does not obtain an RFD.

To get an RFD, the failure detector can kill the process's machine (or virtual machine [5]) before reporting the process as DOWN (e.g., [6, 27]); this killing-based discipline is known as STONITH (for Shoot The Other Node In The Head).[2] Unfortunately, this approach causes disruption: what used to be too-short timeouts convert to

---

[1] Our current implementation is geared to a system with virtualization, but Falcon can be applied to a system with no virtual machines (§6.3).

[2] STONITH is folklore knowledge that appears to have been around since the 1970s but not in published form.

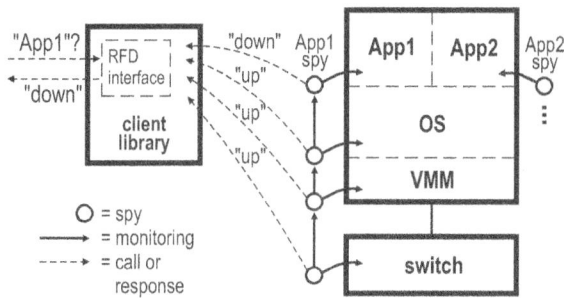

Figure 1—Architecture of Falcon. The application spy provides accurate information about whether the application is up; this spy is the only one that can observe that the application is working. The next spy down provides accurate information not only about its layer but also about whether the application spy is up; more generally, lower-level spies monitor higher-level ones.

needless killing. Other RFD approaches include special hardware (e.g., [52, 53]) or real-time synchronous systems built to bound delays in every case. Such systems are expensive and inappropriate for large data centers, where cost is a key consideration.

Why not give up on RFDs and instead implement an unreliable failure detector (UFD), which is explicitly allowed to make mistakes? UFDs require applications to implement distributed algorithms that handle the case that the UFD reports DOWN when a process is up (and just slow). Unfortunately, such algorithms carry added complexity. An example is Paxos-based consensus [35], used in various systems [13, 14, 18, 31, 33, 39, 43, 49]. Under Paxos, replicas never diverge, even if the system incorrectly detects a crash of the current leader and thereby obtains multiple leaders. Yet Paxos's complexity is well known, as evidenced by the many published papers that try to explain it [18, 34, 36, 37, 40, 45].

Developers have embraced UFDs because of the conventional wisdom that it is impossible to implement a fast RFD that is viable (§6.1). In this paper, we demonstrate that this wisdom is misleading, at least in the context of data centers.

2.3 Design principles

The design principles underlying Falcon are as follows.

Make it reliable. With a *reliable* failure detector, other layers need not handle failure detector mistakes and the resulting complexity.

Avoid end-to-end timeouts as the primary detection mechanism. End-to-end timeouts can serve as a catch-all to detect unforeseen failures, but they take too long to detect common failures.

Peek inside the layers. Layer-specific knowledge can indicate crashes accurately and quickly. For example, if a process disappears from the OS's process table, it is dead, or if a key thread exits, the process is as good as dead. Extracting this information requires a module, which we call a *spy*, at each layer. A spy may use timeouts on internal events (e.g., the main loop has not executed in 1 second), but those timeouts are better informed and shorter than end-to-end timeouts, as they reflect local, more predictable behavior.

Kill surgically, if needed. A spy may not always observe failures correctly, but it must be reliable. Thus, it may kill when it suspects a crash (e.g., the layer is acting erratically or a local timeout has fired). Killing is expensive, so the RFD should kill the smallest necessary component, rather than the entire machine, as in [27, 51, 53]. Such surgical killing conserves resources (e.g., a process is killed while others in the same machine are not) and improves recovery

function	description
init(target)	register with spies
uninit()	deregister with spies
query()	query the operational status
set_callback(callback)	install callback function
clear_callback()	cancel callback function
start_timeout(timeout)	start end-to-end timeout timer
stop_timeout()	stop end-to-end timeout timer

Figure 2—Falcon RFD interface to clients.

time (e.g., only the process must be restarted, not the machine). A similar argument was made by [15, 16] in the context of reboot.

Monitor the monitors. Spies are embedded in layers and can crash with them, so spies too should be monitored. This calls for a *spy network*, in which lower-level spies monitor higher-level ones.

3 DESIGN OF FALCON

Figure 1 depicts Falcon's architecture. Falcon consists of a *client library* as well as several *spy modules* (or *spies*) deployed at various layers of the system. The client library provides the RFD interface to the client, and it coordinates the spies. Roughly speaking, the client library takes as input the identifier of a *target*, which specifies a process whose operational status the client would like to know, and returns UP or DOWN. A spy is a layer-specific monitor. A spy is named by the layer monitored (e.g., the OS spy monitors the OS) but may have parts running at several layers. The layers monitored by our current implementation are application, OS, virtual machine monitor (VMM), and network. Falcon assumes that lower layers enclose higher ones, meaning that if a lower layer crashes, the layers above it also crash or stop responding. This assumption holds by design. As an example, if the VMM crashes, then both the OS and application crash; as another example, if the network crashes, then the higher layers become unresponsive.

The high-level difficulty in realizing Falcon out of spies is how it should interact with them and use their knowledge to meet the desired properties. Our experience is that ad-hoc approaches lead to erroneous designs or ones that do not simultaneously achieve reliability, fast detection, and minimal disruption (§6.2). Achieving these properties together requires carefully addressing the following questions: what interfaces are exposed by the RFD and the spies, what spies do and how, how to orchestrate spies, and how to handle various corner cases. The next sections address these questions in turn, focusing on aspects common to all spies. Section 4 describes the details of the spies in our implementation.

3.1 RFD interface

The RFD interface that Falcon presents to clients is shown in Figure 2. Function *init* indicates the target to be monitored, which identifies each layer (process name, VM id, VMM IP address, switch IP address). Function *query* returns UP or DOWN for the target. However, a client may wish to monitor the target continuously while waiting for a response or another event. Thus, rather than invoking *query* repeatedly, it may be more efficient for the client to use a callback interface. To that end, function *set_callback* installs a callback function to be called when a spy reports LAYER_DOWN or the application spy reports LAYER_UP. Function *clear_callback* uninstalls the callback function. To support end-to-end timeouts, Falcon needs to know when to start and stop the timeout timer, which the client indicates by calling functions *start_timeout* and *stop_timeout*.

281

3.2 Objective and operation of spies

A given layer is supposed to perform some activity, and if the layer is performing it, then the layer is alive by definition. In a Web server, for example, activity may mean receiving HTTP requests or an indication that there are no requests; for a map-reduce task, activity may mean reading and processing from the disk; for a numerical application, activity may mean finishing a small stage of the computation; for a generic server, it may mean placing requests on an internal work queue and waiting for a response; for the OS, it may mean scheduling a ready-to-run process; and for a VMM, it may mean scheduling virtual machines and executing internal functions.

The purpose of a spy is to sense the presence or absence of such activity using specialized knowledge—which we sometimes call "inside information". A spy exposes three remote procedures:

- *register*() to register a remote callback (which is distinct from the callback to the client in §3.1: the one here goes from a spy to the client library);
- *cancel*() to cancel it; and
- *kill*() to kill the monitored layer.

If the layer that the spy is monitoring crashes, the spy immediately calls back the client library, reporting LAYER_DOWN; if the layer is operational, the spy calls back the client library periodically, reporting LAYER_UP.

A spy is designed to recognize the common case when the monitored layer is clearly crashed or healthy. What if the spy is uncertain? To support reliable failure detection, a report of LAYER_DOWN must be correct, always. (No exceptions!) Thus, if the spy is inclined to report LAYER_DOWN but is not sure, the spy resorts to killing: it terminates the layer that it is monitoring and *then* reports LAYER_DOWN. (Section 4 explains how spies at each layer kill reliably; the basic idea is to use a component below the layer to be killed.) Of course, spies should be designed to avoid killing.

Figure 3 gives the pseudocode for our spies. UP-INTERVAL is the minimum duration to wait before a spy indicates that the layer is up, to prevent the spy from wasting resources with too frequent LAYER_UP reports; a reasonable value for UP-INTERVAL is 30 seconds. The value of UP-INTERVAL does not affect detection time: a spy reports that the layer is down as soon as it knows.

Below, in Section 3.3, we describe how the client library coordinates the spies, assuming that (1) spies are ideal and (2) network partitions do not happen. Sections 3.4 and 3.5 back off of these two assumptions in turn.

3.3 Orchestration: spies spying on spies

To report the operational status of the target, the client library uses the following algorithm. On initialization, it registers callbacks at each spy at the target and sets a local status variable to UP. If the client library receives a LAYER_DOWN callback from any of the spies, it sets the status variable to DOWN. When the client library receives a query from the application, it returns the value of the status variable.

To see why this algorithm works, first note that if the target application is responsive then none of the spies returns LAYER_DOWN—because we are assuming ideal spies—and therefore the client library reports the status of the target correctly. If the target application crashes but the application spy remains alive, then the application spy returns LAYER_DOWN and subsequently the client library reports the status of the target correctly. However, the application spy may never return, because it might have crashed. In that case, we rely on the spy at the next level—the OS spy—to sense this problem: in fact, the role of the layer-*L* spy can be seen as monitor-

```
remote-procedure register()
    add caller to Clients
    return ACK

remote-procedure cancel()
    remove caller from Clients
    return ACK

remote-procedure kill()
    kill layer we are spying on and wait to confirm kill
    return ACK

background-task monitor()
    while true
        sense layer and set rc accordingly
        if rc = CERTAINLY_DOWN then
            callback(LAYER_DOWN)
        if rc = CERTAINLY_UP then
            if have not called callback within UP-INTERVAL then
                callback(LAYER_UP)
        if rc = SUSPECT_CRASH then
            kill()
            callback(LAYER_DOWN)

function callback(status)
    for each client ∈ Clients do
        send status to client
```

Figure 3—Pseudocode for spies.

ing the layer-(*L*+1) spy, as shown in Figure 1. So here, the OS spy is monitoring the application spy, and if the application spy is crashed, the OS spy will eventually return LAYER_DOWN—provided the OS spy itself is alive. If the OS spy is not alive, this procedure continues at the spy at the next level, and so on. The ultimate result is that if a spy never responds, a lower-level spy will sense the unresponsive spy and will report LAYER_DOWN, causing the client library to report DOWN to the client.

We have not yet said how the spy on layer *L* + 1 is monitored by the spy on layer *L*. The spy on layer *L* + 1 has a component at layer *L*, for killing and for responding to queries. Given this component, the spy on layer *L* can monitor the spy on layer *L* + 1 by *monitoring layer L itself*. This avoids the complexity of a signaling protocol among spies. It works because, assuming ideal spies, the spy on layer *L* + 1 is down (permanently unresponsive) if and only if layer *L* is down.

3.4 Coping with imperfect spies

The last section assumed ideal spies. In this section, we identify the types of mistakes that a spy can make, and we explain how Falcon deals with these mistakes. While Falcon may take drastic actions (killing or waiting for a long time), we expect them to be rare.

There are four types of spy errors that we consider, as shown in Figure 4. Error A happens when a spy does not recognize a rare failure condition and thus wrongly thinks that a layer is up; for instance, an OS spy thinks that the OS is up because it shows some signs of life, yet the OS has stopped scheduling requests. Error B happens when there is a violation in the assumption from Section 3.3 that a layer *L* is up if and only if the spy on layer *L* + 1 is responsive. Error C is a spy's reporting LAYER_DOWN when either the monitored layer is up or any spy above the monitored layer is up. Error D occurs when none of the spies responds, because of a network problem such as a partition.

Errors A and B cause the *query* function to always return UP despite the application's being down. To address this problem, Falcon has a backstop: an end-to-end timeout started by the client. If this end-to-end timeout expires, Falcon kills the highest layer that it can and subsequently reports the target as DOWN.

Error C is not handled by Falcon and in fact Falcon is expressly designed *not* to have this error: when a spy reports LAYER_DOWN, it must absolutely ensure that the layer is down, which means disconnected from the outside world. Error D is addressed in Section 3.5.

Figure 5 describes the client library's pseudocode. There are several points to note here. First, end-to-end timeouts are used to indicate a failure only in the unlikely case that none of the spies can determine that a layer is up or down. Second, each spy's *kill* procedure is invoked by the client library when the end-to-end timeout expires. This procedure attempts to kill the highest layer and, if not successful after SPY-RETRY-INTERVAL, targets each lower layer successively. In this manner, killing is surgical. A reasonable value for SPY-RETRY-INTERVAL is 3 seconds; this parameter affects detection time (by imposing a floor) but only when a large end-to-end timeout expires, an event that we expect to be rare.

3.5 Network partition

We said above that lower-level spies monitor higher-level ones, but no spy monitors the lowest level spy. Is that a problem? No, because that spy inspects the network switch attached to the target, so it is conceptually a spy on the target's network connectivity. Thus, if the client library does not hear from that spy, then the network is slow or partitioned. (Our current implementation assumes that a machine is attached to one switch; we briefly discuss the case of multiple switches in Section 6.4.)

There are three ways to handle network partition. First, the client library can block until it hears from the switch; this is what our implementation does. This is reasonable because during a network partition, other vital services (DNS, file servers, etc) are likely blocked as well, making the system unusable. Second, the client library can, after the client-supplied timeout expires, call back with "I don't know"; this is an implementation convenience that is conceptually identical to blocking. Third, the client library can report DOWN *after* it is sure that a watchdog timer on the switch has disconnected the target; meanwhile, in ordinary operation, the watchdog is serviced by heartbeats from the client library to the switch.

3.6 Application restart

If the application crashes or exits, and restarts, the client library should not report the application as UP because clients typically want to know about the restart (e.g., the application may have lost part of its state in a crash). Therefore, when the application restarts, Falcon treats it as a different instance to be monitored, and the original crashed instance is reported DOWN.

To implement the above, the spy on a layer labels the layer with a generation number, and the spy includes this number in messages to the client library. Upon initialization, the client library records each layer's generation number. If it receives a mismatched generation number from a spy, then the associated layer has restarted and

```
function init(target)
    for L ← 1 to N do
        invoke register() at spy in target[L]
    Target ← target
    Status ← UP
    Callback ← dummy_function

function uninit()
    for L ← 1 to N do
        invoke cancel() at spy in Target[L]

function query()
    return Status

function set_callback(callback)
    Callback ← callback

function clear_callback()
    Callback ← dummy_function

function start_timeout(timeout)
    start countdown timer with value timeout

function stop_timeout()
    stop countdown timer

upon receiving callback (status) from spy in Target[L] do
    if status = LAYER_DOWN then
        Status ← DOWN
        Callback(DOWN)
    if status = LAYER_UP and L = N then Callback(UP)

upon expiration of countdown timer do
    for L ← N downto 1 do
        invoke kill() at spy in Target[L]
        if L ≠ 1 then wait for reply for SPY_RETRY_INTERVAL
        else wait for reply        // blocks on network partition; see §3.5
        if got reply then
            Status ← DOWN
            Callback(DOWN)
            return
```

Figure 5—Pseudocode for the client library. N is the number of monitored layers and the layer number of the application.

the client library considers the monitored instance as down. (Generation numbers are omitted from the pseudocode for brevity.)

Implementing generation numbers carries a subtlety: the generation number of a layer needs to increase if any layer below it restarts. Thus, a spy at layer L constructs its generation number as follows. It takes the entire generation number of layer $L - 1$, left shifts it 32 bits, and sets the low-order 32 bits to a counter that it increments on every restart. (The base case is the generation number of the lowest layer, which is just a counter.) At the application level, therefore, the generation number is a concatenation of 32-bit counters, one for each layer. 32 bits are sufficient because a problem occurs only if (a) the counter wraps around very quickly as crashes occur rapidly, and then (b) the counter suddenly stops exactly where it was the last time that the client library checked.

tag	error / limiting case	cause	effect
A	layer L is down, layer $L - 1$ is up, but spy on layer L reports LAYER_UP	bug in layer-L spy	triggers end-to-end timeout and kills
B	layer L is down, layer $L - 1$ is up, but spy on layer L is unresponsive	bug in layer-L spy	triggers end-to-end timeout and kills
C	layer L is up, but spy on layer L or below reports LAYER_DOWN	should not happen	would compromise RFD properties
D	none of the spies responds	network partition	RFD blocks or watchdog timer fires

Figure 4—Errors and limiting cases in Falcon, and their effects.

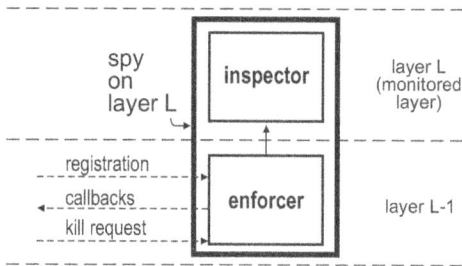

Figure 6—Architecture of spies. A spy has two components: an *inspector* that gathers inside information and an *enforcer* that ensures the reliability of LAYER_DOWN reports (and may also use inside information). The client library communicates with the enforcer.

4 DETAILS OF SPIES

The previous section described Falcon's high-level design. This section gives details of four classes of spies that we have built: application spies, an OS spy, a virtual machine monitor (VMM) spy, and a network connectivity spy. We emphasize that these spies are illustrative reference designs, not the final word; one can extend spies based on design-time application knowledge or on failures observed in a given system. Nevertheless, the spies that we present should serve as an existence proof that it is possible to react to a large class of failures.

As shown in Figure 6, a spy has two components:

1. *Inspector*: This component is embedded in the monitored layer and gathers detailed inside information to infer the operational status, for example by inspecting the appropriate data structures.

2. *Enforcer*: This component communicates with the client library and is responsible for killing the monitored layer; for these reasons, it resides one layer below the monitored layer. This component may also use inside information.

A spy has only two technical requirements (§3.2): it must eventually detect crashes of the layer that it is monitoring (and even then, Falcon handles the case that the spy fails in this charge, per §3.4), and it must be reliable, meaning that its LAYER_DOWN answers are accurate. However, in practice, a spy should be more ambitious; it should provide guarantees that are broader than the letter of its contract implies. To explain these guarantees and how they are achieved, we answer the questions below for each spy in our implementation, which is depicted in Figure 7.

- *What are the spy's components, and how do they communicate?* There is a lot of latitude here, but we discuss in Section 6.3 the possibility of a uniform intra-spy interface.
- *How does the spy detect crashes with sub-second detection time?* Although a spy is required to detect crashes of the monitored layer only eventually, it is most useful if it does so quickly.
- *How does the spy avoid false suspicions of crashes and the resulting needless kills?* Avoiding false suspicion is not an explicit requirement of a spy, but it is far better if the resulting needless kills are kept to a minimum, to meet our goal of little disruption.
- *How does the spy give a reliable answer?* We break this question into two: How does the spy know for sure when its layer is down? If the spy is unsure, how does it kill the layer to become sure?
- *What are the implementation details of the spy?* Spies are unavoidably platform-specific, and we try to give a flavor of that specificity as we describe the implementation details. Section 6.3 discusses how Falcon might work with a different set of layers (e.g., with a JVM and nested VMs, or without VMs) and different instances of each layer (e.g., Windows instead of Linux).

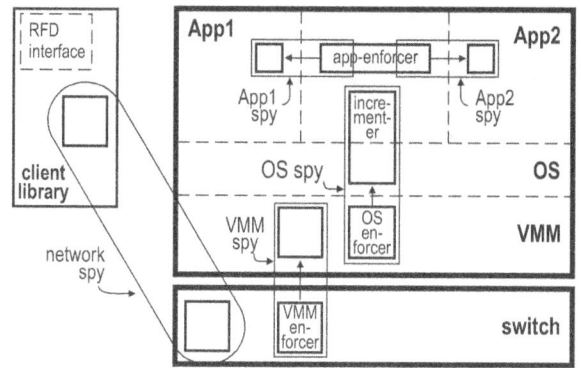

Figure 7—Our implementation of Falcon.

Application spies. All of our application spies have a common organization and approach.

Components. The inspector is a dedicated thread inside the application; it calls a function $f()$, whose implementation depends on the application. For example, in our primary-backup application spy, $f()$ checks whether the main event loop is processing events; in our ZooKeeper [31] spy, $f()$ tests whether a client request has been recently processed, while a separate component submits no-op client requests at a low rate.

The enforcer is a distinguished high-priority process, the *app-enforcer*, which serves as the enforcer for all monitored applications on the same OS. An assumption is that if the OS is up, then so is the app-enforcer; this is an instance of the assumption, from Section 3.3, that "if layer-L is up, then so is the spy on layer-$(L+1)$". As discussed in Section 3.4, if the assumption is violated (which is unlikely), then Falcon relies on an end-to-end timeout. The enforcer communicates with each inspector over a connected inter-process communication (IPC) channel.

Sub-second detection time. If the inspector locally detects a problem, it closes its handle to the connected IPC channel, causing the enforcer to suspect a crash immediately (which it then handles per *Reliability*, below). Similarly, if the application process exits or crashes, then it brings the inspector down with it, again causing an immediate notification along IPC.

In addition, every $T_{app\text{-}check}$ time units, the enforcer queries the inspector thread, which invokes $f()$. The enforcer infers a crash if $f()$ returns "down", if the IPC handle returns an error, or if the inspector thread does not respond within an application specific $T_{app\text{-}resp}$ time; the enforcer again handles these cases per *Reliability*, below. We note that $f()$ can use timing considerations apart from $T_{app\text{-}resp}$ and $T_{app\text{-}check}$ to return "down" (e.g., the inspector might know that if a given request is not removed from an internal queue within 10 ms, then the application is effectively down).

The periodic queries from enforcer to inspector achieve subsecond detection time in the usual cases because our implementation sets $T_{app\text{-}check}$ to 100 ms. While the precise choice is arbitrary, the order of magnitude (tens or hundreds of milliseconds) is not. Checking does not involve the network, and it is inexpensive—less than 0.02% CPU overhead per check in our experiments (see Figure 14, Section 5.4 and divide by 10 to scale per check). That is, we accept a minimal processing cost to get rapid detection time in the usual cases. The remaining case is covered by $T_{app\text{-}resp}$, which our implementation sets to 100 ms of CPU time, yielding sub-second detection time under light to medium load.

Avoiding false suspicions. The application spy avoids false suspicion in two ways. First, as mentioned above, the enforcer measures $T_{app\text{-}resp}$ by the CPU time consumed by the monitored application, not real time; this is an example of inside information and avoids the case that the enforcer declares an unresponsive application down when in fact the application is temporarily slow because of load. We note that this approach does not undermine any higher-level (human or application) deadlines since those are expressed and enforced by Falcon's end-to-end timeout (§3.4).

A second use of inside information is that $T_{app\text{-}resp}$ is set by the application itself. (Indeed, as mentioned in Section 2.3, timeouts are ideally local and application-specific.) One choice is $T_{app\text{-}resp} = \infty$; in that case, if the app inspector is unresponsive, then Falcon relies on the end-to-end timeout. Or, an application might expect to be able to reply quickly, given CPU cycles, in which case it can set a smaller value of $T_{app\text{-}resp}$ for faster detection when the application process is unexpectedly stuck.

Reliability. If the enforcer suspects a crash, it inspects the process table. If the application process is not there, the enforcer no longer has doubt and reports LAYER_DOWN to the client library. On the other hand, if the process is in the process table, then the enforcer kills it (by asking the OS to do so) and waits for confirmation (by polling the process table every 5 ms) before reporting LAYER_DOWN. If the process does not leave the process table, then Falcon relies on the end-to-end timeout.

Implementation details. The inspector and app-enforcer run on Linux, and we assign app-enforcer the maximum real-time priority. We also mlock it (to prevent swap out). The inspector is implemented in a library; using the library requires only supplying f() and a value of $T_{app\text{-}resp}$. The IPC channel between inspector and app-enforcer is a Unix domain socket. The enforcer kills by sending a SIGKILL. We are assuming that process ids are not recycled during the (short) process table polling interval; if a pid *is* recycled, the end-to-end timeout applies.

OS spy. Our OS spy currently assumes virtualization; Section 6.3 discusses how Falcon could handle alternate layerings.

Components. The inspector consists of (a) a kernel module that, when invoked, increments a counter in the OS's address space and (b) a high-priority process, the *incrementer*, that invokes this kernel module every $T_{OS\text{-}inc}$ time units, set to 1 ms in our implementation. The enforcer is a module inside the VMM. The communication between the enforcer and the inspector is implicit: the enforcer infers that there was a crash if the counter is not incremented. Before detailing this process, we briefly consider an alternate OS spy: the enforcer could inspect a kernel counter like jiffies, instead of a process-incremented counter. We rejected this approach because an observation of increasing jiffies does not imply a functional OS. With our approach, in contrast, if the counter is increasing, then the enforcer knows that at least the high priority incrementer process is being scheduled. The cost of this higher-level assurance is an extra point of failure: if the incrementer crashes (which is unlikely), then Falcon treats it as an OS crash. Specifically, the OS enforcer would detect the lack of increments, kill, and report LAYER_DOWN.

Sub-second detection time. Every $T_{OS\text{-}check}$ time units, the enforcer checks the OS. To do so, it first checks whether the VM of the OS is running. If not, the enforcer reports LAYER_DOWN to the client library. Otherwise, it checks whether the counter has incremented at least once over an interval of $T_{OS\text{-}resp}$ time units. If not, the enforcer suspects that the OS (or virtual machine) has crashed, which it handles per *Reliability* below. This approach achieves sub-second detection time by choosing $T_{OS\text{-}check}$ and $T_{OS\text{-}resp}$ to be tens or hundreds of milliseconds; our implementation sets them to 100 ms.

Avoiding false suspicions. Given the detection mechanism above, a false suspicion happens when the counter is not incremented, yet the VM is up. This case is most likely caused by temporary slowness of the VM, which in turn results from load on the whole machine. To ensure that the OS spy does not wrongly declare failure in such situations, we carefully choose $T_{OS\text{-}inc}$, $T_{OS\text{-}check}$, and $T_{OS\text{-}resp}$ to avoid premature local timeouts most of the time, even in extreme cases. This approach is inexact, as the VM could in theory slow down arbitrarily—say, due to a flood of hardware interrupts—triggering a premature local timeout. However, we do not expect this case to happen frequently; if it happens, the enforcer will kill the OS, but the spy will not return incorrect information.

We validate our choice of parameters by running a fork+exec bomb inside a guest OS, observing that in a 30 minute period (18,000 checks) the enforcer sees, per check, a mean of 97.8 increments, with a standard deviation of 3.9, and a minimum of 34 (where one increment would have sufficed to satisfy the enforcer). Of course, the operators of a production deployment would have to validate the parameters more extensively, using an actual peak workload. We note that these kinds of local timing parameters have to be validated only once and are likely to be accurate; this is an example of inside information (§2.3) and does not have the disadvantages of end-to-end timeouts (§2.2).

Reliability. If the VM is no longer being scheduled, the enforcer can verify that case, using its access to the VMM. If the enforcer suspects a crash, it asks the VMM to stop scheduling the VM and waits for confirmation.

Implementation details. Like the app-enforcer, the incrementer is a Linux process to which we assign the maximum real-time priority and which we mlock. Our VMM is standard Linux; the VMs are QEMU/KVM [46] instances. The enforcer runs alongside these instances and communicates with them through the libvirtd daemon, which exposes the libvirt API, an interface to common virtualization functions [41]. We extend this API with a call to check the incrementer's activity. Since all calls into libvirtd are blocking, we split the OS enforcer into two types of processes. A singleton main process communicates with the client library and forks a worker process, one per VM, sharing a pipe with the worker process. The workers use the libvirt API to examine the guests' virtual memory, kill guest VMs, and confirm kills.

VMM spy. Our implementation assumes the ability to deploy new functionality on the switch. We believe this assumption to be reasonable in our target environment of data centers and enterprise networks (§2.1), particularly given the trend toward programmable switches. We also assume that the target is connected to the network through a single interface; Section 6.4 discusses how this assumption could be relaxed.

Components. The inspector is a module in the VMM, while the enforcer is a software module that runs on the switch to which the VMM host is attached. The enforcer infers that the VMM is crashed if, after a period of time in which the switch has not received network packets through the port to which the VMM is connected, the enforcer cannot reach the inspector (this detection method saves network bandwidth, versus more active pinging). The two communicate by RPC over UDP.

Sub-second detection time. Every $T_{VMM\text{-}check}$ time units, the enforcer performs an aliveness check. This check takes one of two forms. Usually, the enforcer checks whether the switch has received network packets from the VMM over the prior interval. If this check fails, or if an interval of $T_{VMM\text{-}check\text{-}2}$ time units (set to 5 seconds in our implementation) has passed since the last probe, the enforcer probes the inspector with an RPC. If it does not get a response

Falcon goal	larger benefit	evaluation result	section
fast detection	availability	• Even simple spies are powerful enough to detect a range of common failures.	§5.1
		• For these failure modes, Falcon's 99th percentile detection time is several hundred ms; existing failure detectors take one or two orders of magnitude longer.	§5.1
		• Augmenting ZooKeeper [31] and a replication library (PMP) [44] with Falcon (minus killing) reduces unavailability by roughly 6× (or more, for PMP) for crashes below application level.	§5.2
little disruption	availability	• For a range of failures, Falcon kills the smallest problematic component that it can.	§5.3
		• Falcon avoids false suspicions (and kills) even when the target is unresponsive end-to-end.	§5.3
reliability	simplicity	• As an RFD, Falcon enables primary-backup replication [9], which has 50% less replica overhead than Paxos [35], and which requires less complexity (21% less code in our comparison).	§5.5
inexpensive	viability	• Falcon's CPU costs at each layer are single digits (or less) of percentage overhead.	§5.4
		• Falcon requires per-platform code: ≈2300 lines in our implementation. However, the added code is likely simpler than the application logic that can be removed by using an RFD.	§5.5
		• Falcon can be introduced into an application with tens or hundreds of lines of code.	§5.2, §5.5

Figure 8—Summary of main evaluation results.

within $T_{VMM\text{-}resp}$ time units (set to 20 ms in our implementation), it does $N_{VMM\text{-}retry}$ more tries (set to 5 in our implementation), for a total waiting period of $T_{VMM\text{-}resp} \cdot (N_{VMM\text{-}retry} + 1)$ time units (120 ms in our implementation). After this period, the enforcer suspects a crash and handles that case per *Reliability*, below. Similar to the other spies, this one achieves sub-second detection time by choice of $T_{VMM\text{-}check}$: 100 ms in our implementation.

Avoiding false suspicions. First, our enforcer test is conservative: most of the time, any traffic from the VMM host placates the enforcer. Second, we validate our choice of parameters by running an experiment where 2000 processes on the VMM contend for CPU. We set the enforcer to query the inspector 100,000 times, observing a mean response time of 397 μs, with standard deviation of 80 μs, and a maximum of 12.6 ms, which suffices to satisfy the enforcer. As with the OS spy, the operators would need to do more extensive parameter validation for production. Finally, although $N_{VMM\text{-}retry}$ is a constant in our implementation, a better implementation would set $N_{VMM\text{-}retry}$ proportionately to the traffic into the VMM. Then the test would permit more retransmissions under higher load, accommodating a message's lower likelihood of getting through.

Reliability. If it suspects a crash, the enforcer "kills" the VMM, by shutting down the network port to which the VMM is connected. The enforcer has no doubt once it has shut down the port, at which point it reports LAYER_DOWN to the client library.

Implementation details. The VMM inspector runs as a process on the VMM (which is standard Linux, as described above). The VMM enforcer is a daemon process that we run on the DD-WRT open router platform [23], which we modified to map connected hosts to physical ports and to run our software.

Network spy. The inspector is a software module that runs on the network switch connected to the target, and the enforcer is a module in the client library. However, under our current configuration and implementation of Falcon, the network spy does not check for failures and does not affect Falcon's end-to-end behavior or our experimental results. The reason is as follows. Falcon's knowledge of the network is limited to the switch attached to the target, so Falcon has no way to (a) know whether the switch is crashed or just slow, and (b) kill the switch if it is in doubt. The consequence is that Falcon blocks when the switch is unresponsive.

Localizing network failures via modules in multiple switches is future work (§6.4). For now, we leave the network spy in our design as a placeholder for this extension.

5 EVALUATION OF FALCON

To evaluate our Falcon implementation, we ask to what degree it satisfies our desired features for a failure detector (FD)—short detection time, reliability, little disruption—and at what cost. We also translate those features into higher-level benefits for the applications that are clients of Falcon. To do so, we experiment with Falcon, with other failure detectors [11, 21, 30] as a baseline, with ZooKeeper, with ZooKeeper modified to use Falcon, with a minimal Paxos-based replication library [44], with that library modified to use Falcon, and with a primary-backup-based replication library that uses Falcon. Figure 8 summarizes our evaluation results.

Most of our experiments involve two panels. The first is a *failure panel* with 12 kinds of model failures that we inject to evaluate Falcon's ability to detect them (the kernel failures are from [42]). The second is a *transient condition panel* with seven kinds of imposed load conditions, which are *not* failures, to evaluate Falcon's ability to avoid false suspicions. The failure panel is listed in Figure 9, and the transient condition panel is detailed in Section 5.3. Since the panels are synthetic, our evaluation should be viewed as an initial validation of Falcon, one within the means of academic research. An extended validation requires deploying Falcon in production environments and exposing it to failures in-the-wild.

Our testbed is three hosts connected to a switch. The switch is an ASUS RT-N16. The software on the switch is the DD-WRT v24-sp [23] platform (essentially Linux), extended with our VMM enforcer (§4). Our hosts are Dell PowerEdge T310, each with a quad-core Intel Xeon 2.4 GHz processor, 4 GB of RAM, and two Gigabit Ethernet ports. Each host runs an OS natively that serves as a VMM. The native (host) OS is 64-bit Linux (2.6.36-gentoo-r5), compiled with the kvm module [46], running QEMU (v0.13.0) and a modified libvirt [41] (v0.8.6). The virtual machines (guests) run 32-bit Linux (2.6.34-gentoo-r6), extended with a kernel module and accompanying kernel patch (for the OS inspector).

5.1 How fast is Falcon?

Method. We compare Falcon to a set of *baseline* failure detectors (FDs), focusing on detection times under the failure panel.

Figure 10 describes the baselines. These FDs are used in production or deployed systems (the ϕ-accrual FD is used by the Cassandra key-value store [17], static timers are used in many systems, etc.); we borrow the code to implement them from [55]. All of these FDs work as follows: the client pings the target according to a fixed

where injected?	what is the failure?	what does the failure model?
application	forced crash	app. memory error, assert failure, or condition that causes exit
application	app inspector reports LAYER_DOWN	inside information that indicates an application crash
application/ Falcon itself	non-responsive app inspector	since the app inspector is a thread inside the application, this models a buggy application (or app inspector) that cannot run but has not exited
kernel	infinite loop	kernel hang or liveness problem
kernel	stack overflow	runaway kernel code
kernel	kernel panic	unexpected condition that causes assert failure in kernel
VMM/host	VMM error; causes guest termination	VMM memory error, assert failure, or condition that causes guest exit
VMM/host	`ifdown eth0` on host	hardware crash (machine is separated from network)
Falcon itself	crash of app enforcer	bug in Falcon app spy
Falcon itself	crash of incrementer	bug in Falcon OS spy
Falcon itself	crash of OS enforcer	bug in Falcon OS spy
Falcon itself	crash of VMM inspector	bug in Falcon VMM spy

Figure 9—Panel of synthetic failures in our evaluation. The failures are at multiple layers of the stack and model various error conditions.

baseline FD	T: timeout (ms)	error	parameters
Static Timer	10,000	0.0	timer $= 10,000$
Chen [21]	5,001	0.0	$\alpha = 1$ ms
Bertier [11]	5,020	0.0	$\beta = 1, \phi = 4, \gamma = 0.1$, mod_step $= 0$
ϕ-accrual [30]	4,946	0.01	$\phi = 0.4297$
ϕ-accrual [30]	4,995	0.001	$\phi = 0.4339$

Figure 10—Baseline failure detectors that we compare to Falcon. The implementations are from [55]. We set their ping intervals as $p = 5$ seconds, which is aggressive and favors the baseline FDs. For all but Static Timer, the timeout value T is a function of network characteristics and various parameters, which we set to make the error, e, small (e is the fraction of ping intervals for which the FD declares a premature timeout). We set ϕ-accrual for different e; in our experiments with no network delay, Chen and Bertier have no observable error.

ping interval parameter p, and if the client has not heard a response by a *deadline*, the client declares a failure. We define the *timeout* T to be the duration from when the last ping was received until the deadline for the following ping. The difference in these FDs is in the algorithm that adjusts the timeout or deadline (based on empirical round-trip delay and/or on configured error tolerance).

We configure the baselines with $p = 5$ seconds, which is pessimistic for Falcon, as this setting allows the baselines to detect failures more quickly than they would in data center applications, where ping intervals are tens of seconds [14, 29, 32], as noted in the introduction. Likewise, we configure the ϕ-accrual failure detector to allow many more premature timeouts (one out of every 100 and 1000 ping intervals) than would be standard in a real deployment, which also decreases its timeout and hence its detection time.

We configure Falcon with an end-to-end timeout of 5 minutes; Falcon can afford this large backstop because it detects common failures much faster. For a like-to-like comparison between the baselines (which are UFDs) and Falcon (which is an RFD), we also experiment with a UFD version of Falcon called *Falcon-NoKill*, which is identical to Falcon except that it does not kill.

Each experiment holds constant the FD and the failure from the panel, and has 200 iterations. In each iteration, we choose the failure time uniformly at random inside an FD's periodic monitoring interval of duration p (for the baselines, p is the ping interval and for Falcon it is 100 ms, per §4). To produce a failure, a failure generator running at the FD client sends an RPC to one of the *failure servers* that we deploy at different layers on the target.

For convenience, our experiments measure detection time at the

FD client, as the elapsed time from when the client sends the RPC to the failure server to when the FD declares the failure. This approach adds one-way network delay to the measurement. However, we verified through separate experiments with synchronized clocks that the added delay is 2–3 orders of magnitude smaller than the detection times.

Experiments and results. We measure the detection times of the baseline FDs and of Falcon-NoKill, for a range of failures. Under constant network delay, we expect the baseline FDs' detection times to be uniformly distributed over $[T - p + d, T + d]$;[3] here, T and p are the timeout and ping interval, as defined above and quantified in Figure 10, and d is the one-way network delay. We hypothesize that Falcon's detection times will be on the order of 100 ms, given spies' periodic checks (§4).

Figure 11 depicts the 1st, 50th, and 99th percentile detection times, under no network delay ($d = 0$). The baselines behave as expected. For application crashes, Falcon's median detection time is larger than we had expected: 369 ms. The cause is the time taken by the Java Virtual Machine (JVM) to shut down, which we verified to be several hundred milliseconds on average. For the failure in which the app inspector reports LAYER_DOWN, Falcon's median detection time is 75.5 ms. This is in line with expectations: the app-enforcer polls the app inspector every $T_{app\text{-}check} = 100$ ms, so we expect an average detection time of 50 ms plus processing delays.

For the kernel hang, kernel overflow, and kernel panic failures, Falcon's median detection times are 204 ms, 197 ms, and 207 ms, respectively. The expected value here is 150 ms plus processing delays: every $T_{OS\text{-}check} = 100$ ms, the OS enforcer checks whether the prior interval saw OS activity (§4), so the OS enforcer in expectation has to wait at least 50 ms (the duration from the failure until the end of the prior interval) plus 100 ms (the time until the OS enforcer sees no activity). The processing delays in our unoptimized implementation are higher than we would like: 15 ms per check, for a total of 30 ms per failure, plus tens of milliseconds from supporting libraries and the client. Nevertheless, these delays, plus the expected value of 150 ms, explain the observations.

---

[3]The largest detection time occurs when the target fails just after replying to a ping; the client receives the ping reply after d time and declares the failure at the next deadline after T time, for a detection time of $T + d$. The smallest detection time occurs when the target fails just before replying to a ping; after d time (when the ping reply would have arrived), the client waits for $T - p$ time longer, then declares the failure, for a detection time of $T - p + d$.

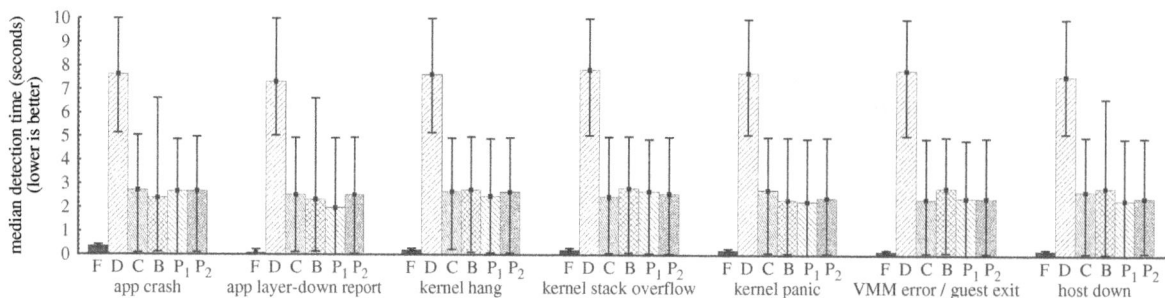

Figure 11—Detection time of Falcon (F) and baseline failure detectors under various failures. The baselines are Static Timer (D), Chen (C), Bertier (B), ϕ-accrual with 0.01 error (P_1), and ϕ-accrual with 0.001 error (P_2); see Figure 10 for details. Rectangle heights depict medians, and the bars depict 1st and 99th percentiles. The baseline FDs wait for multiple-second timers to fire. In contrast, Falcon has sub-second detection time, owing to inside information and callbacks. Moreover, the comparison is pessimistic for Falcon: with ping intervals that would mirror a real deployment, the baselines' bars would be higher while Falcon's would not change.

For the guest exit and host crash failures, Falcon's median detection times are 160 ms and 197 ms, respectively. For the guest exit, the observed detection time matches an expected 50 ms (since $T_{OS\text{-}check} = 100$ ms) plus cleanup by the VMM of 90 ms plus processing delays of tens of milliseconds. Likewise, for the host crash, the observed detection time matches an expected 50 ms (since $T_{VMM\text{-}check} = 100$ ms) plus the 120 ms of waiting (see §4), plus processing delays.

Falcon's detection time is an order of magnitude faster than that of the baseline FDs, for two reasons. First, inside information reveals the crash soon after it happens; second, the spies call back the client library when they detect a crash. With larger ping intervals p (which would be more realistic), the baselines' detection times would be even worse.

Our depicted measurements, here and ahead, are under no network delay (roughly modeling an uncongested network in a data center). However, we ran some of our experiments under injected delays ($d > 0$) and found, as expected, that Falcon's detection time increased by d. We did not experiment with the baselines under network delay; our prediction of their detection times (distributed over $[T - p + d, T + d]$) is stated above. We did not experiment under non-constant delay; based on their algorithms, we predict that the baselines, except for Static Timer, would react to network variation by increasing their timeout T. Falcon, meanwhile, would continue to detect crashes quickly, improving its relative performance.

5.2 What is Falcon's effect on availability?

We now consider the effect of improved detection time on system availability. We incorporate Falcon into two Paxos-based [35] applications that use failure detectors based on static timers: ZooKeeper [31] (ZK) and a replication library [44] (PMP). The modifications are straightforward: roughly 150 lines of Java and 100 lines of C, respectively. We compare unavailability of these systems and their unmodified versions, in the case of a leader crash.

To apply Falcon, we use the spy for ZooKeeper, as described in Section 4, and a PMP spy that checks whether the main event loop is running; in both cases, we use Falcon-NoKill, as both systems' unmodified failure detectors are unreliable. The unmodified ZK detects a crashed leader either via a ten-second timeout or if the leader's host closes the transport session with the followers. The unmodified PMP runs with its default of a ten-second timeout.

We configure ZK to use 4 nodes: 3 servers and 1 client (our testbed has 3 hosts, so the client and a server run on the same VMM). ZK partitions the servers into 1 leader and 2 followers. The ZK client sends requests to one of the followers (alternating

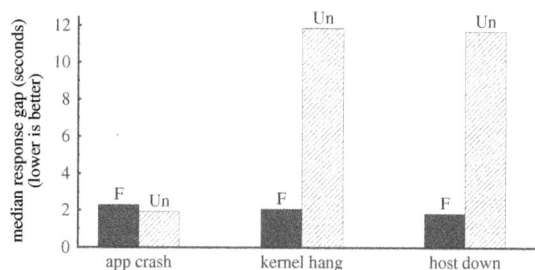

Figure 12—Median response gap (unavailability) of ZooKeeper [31] with Falcon-NoKill (F) and unmodified (Un) under injected failures at the leader. In unmodified ZooKeeper, followers quickly detect application crashes but not kernel- or host/VMM-level crashes. Under the latter types, Falcon reduces median ZooKeeper unavailability by roughly a factor of 6. In all cases, unavailability is several seconds on top of detection time because of ZooKeeper's recovery time.

`create()`s and `delete()`s) when it gets a response to its last one, recording the time of every response. For each of three failure types and the two ZKs, we perform 10 runs. In each run, we inject a failure into the leader at a time selected uniformly at random between 3 and 4 seconds after the run begins. The result is a gap in the response times. Example runs look like this:

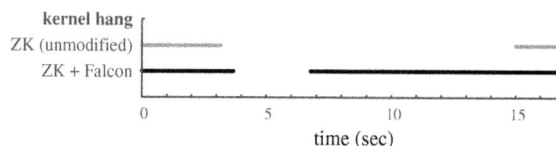

Figure 12 depicts the durations of those response gaps. Under application failures, ZK reacts relatively quickly because the follower explicitly loses its transport session with the leader. Though the median of ZK+Falcon is 350 ms slower than with unmodified ZK, this difference appears due to experimental variation (ZK+Falcon also experiences transport session loss, and the standard deviations are 566 ms for ZK+Falcon and 762 ms for unmodified ZK). Under kernel and VMM/host failures, the ZK follower receives no word that the system is leaderless, so it infers failure—and initiates leader election—only after not having heard from the leader for 10 seconds. Under all failures, Falcon's detection time is sub-second. However, unavailability is detection time plus recovery time, and in all of the depicted cases, recovery takes roughly 2 seconds: the ZK follower, in connecting to the new leader, usually requires two attempts separated by one second, and the client also has a retry discipline that imposes delays of one second or more.

failure	action taken by Falcon
app crash	app enforcer detects failure
app layer-down report	app enforcer kills application
app inspector hangs	app enforcer kills application
kernel hang	OS enforcer kills guest OS
kernel stack overflow	OS enforcer kills guest OS
kernel panic	OS enforcer kills guest OS
VMM error / guest exit	OS enforcer detects failure
host down	VMM enforcer kills VMM/host
crashed app enforcer + app crash	E2E timeout kills guest OS
crashed incrementer	OS enforcer kills guest OS
crashed OS enforcer + OS crash	E2E timeout kills VMM/host
crashed VMM inspector	VMM enforcer kills VMM/host

transient condition	action taken by Falcon
hung system call	none
CPU contention within guest	none
CPU contention across guests	none
memory contention within guest	none
memory contention across guests	OS enforcer kills guest OS
packet flood between guests	none
packet flood between VMMs	VMM enforcer kills VMM/host

Figure 13—Falcon's actions under the failure panel and transient condition panel. (Falcon-specific failures are augmented with target failures because otherwise the Falcon failure has no effect.) Under the failures, Falcon kills surgically while STONITH, for example, would kill more coarsely. Under the transient conditions, Falcon correctly holds its fire in most cases but sometimes suspects falsely and thus kills.

We run analogous experiments for PMP, and the results are similar: tens of seconds of unavailability without Falcon and less than one second with Falcon.

5.3 How disruptive is Falcon?

We now ask whether Falcon achieves its goal of little disruption, which has two aspects: (1) If Falcon must kill, it should kill the smallest possible component, and (2) Falcon should not kill if not required (e.g., if the target is momentarily slow); that is, Falcon should avoid false suspicions. To evaluate these aspects, we run Falcon against our two panels, failures and transient conditions, reporting the component killed, if any. Figure 13 tabulates the results.

For aspect (1), Falcon's reactions to the injected failures match our expectations. If the failure is in the target, Falcon detects it and, if needed, kills the smallest component of the target. If, however, the failure is in Falcon itself (the last four injected failures), then there are two cases. Either Falcon falls back on the end-to-end timeout, killing the layer at which the spy failure occurred, or else Falcon interprets the spy's failure as a layer failure and kills the layer quickly (e.g., as mentioned in Section 4, Falcon treats an incrementer crash as an OS crash). Falcon's surgical approach to reliability should be contrasted with STONITH, which kills the entire machine (though some implementations can target the virtual machine [5]).

For aspect (2), we apply the panel of transient conditions, listed in the bottom part of Figure 13. We expected Falcon to hold its fire in all of these cases, but there are two for which it does not. First, when guests contend for memory, the VMM (Linux) swaps QEMU processes that contain guests, to the point where there are intervals of duration $T_{OS\text{-}check}$ when some guests—and their embedded incrementers—do not run, causing the OS enforcer to kill. An improved OS enforcer would incorporate further inside information, not penalizing a guest in cases when the guest is ready to run but starved for cycles. Second, when the network is heavily loaded,

component (§4)	CPU overhead (percent of a core's cycles)	
	app uses no CPU	app uses 90% CPU
app inspector	0.06	0.04
app enforcer	0.11	0.07
incrementer	0.58	0.31
VM total	**0.75%**	**0.42%**
OS enforcer (main)	0.01	0.01
OS enforcer (worker)	0.04	0.03
libvirtd	0.91	0.95
QEMU	6.92	1.79
VMM inspector	0.39	0.27
VMM total	**8.27%**	**3.07%**
VMM enforcer	0.00	0.00
switch total	**0.00%**	**0.00%**

Figure 14—Background CPU overhead of our Falcon implementation, under an idle dummy application and under one that consumes 90% of its CPU. Each enforcer performs a local check 10 times per second. The switch's CPU overhead is less than one part in 10,000 so displays as 0. QEMU's contribution to the overhead is explained in the text.

the communication channel between VMM enforcer and VMM inspector degrades, causing the VMM enforcer sometimes (in 4 out of 15 of our runs) to infer death and kill. As mentioned in Section 4, a better design would set $N_{VMM\text{-}retry}$ adaptively. In the other cases, Falcon's inside information prevents it from killing. For example, the app-enforcer measures $T_{app\text{-}resp}$ based on CPU time (§4), so a long block (e.g., the "hung system call" row) does not cause a kill.

5.4 What are Falcon's computational costs?

Falcon's benefits derive from infiltrating the layers of a system. Such platform-specific logic incurs computational costs and programmer effort. We address the former in this section and the latter in the next one.

Falcon's main computational cost is CPU time to execute periodic local checks (described in Section 4). To assess this overhead we run a Falcon-enabled target with an idle dummy application for 15 minutes, inducing no failures. We then run the same target and application but with the Falcon components disabled (and with QEMU and libvirtd enabled). In both cases, we measure the accumulated CPU time over the run, reporting the CPU overhead of Falcon as the difference between the accumulated CPU times divided by the run length.

Figure 14 tabulates the results. For the most part, Falcon's CPU overhead is small (less than 1% per component). The exception is the QEMU process in the VMM layer. Two factors contribute to this overhead. First, the Falcon-enabled virtual machine is scheduled more frequently than the Falcon-disabled virtual machine (because of Falcon's multiple checks per second in the former case versus an idle application in the latter case). To control for this effect, we perform the same experiment above, except that we run another application, alongside the dummy, that uses 90% of the CPU. Under these conditions, as depicted in Figure 14, QEMU contributes only 1.8% overhead in the Falcon-enabled case. Second, the remaining overhead is from QEMU's reading guest virtual memory inefficiently (when requested by the OS enforcer; see §4). We verified this by separately running the experiment above (Falcon enabled, 90% CPU usage by the dummy application) except that memory reads by the OS enforcer were disabled. The difference in QEMU's CPU usage was 1.4%, explaining nearly all of the CPU usage difference between the Falcon-enabled and Falcon-disabled cases.

To mitigate the overhead of QEMU's guest memory reads, we

module (§4)	spy component (§4)	lines of code
platform-independent modules		
thread in app; glue (C++)	app inspector	101
thread in app; glue (Java)	app inspector	241
shared enforcer code	all enforcers	465
client library	client library	1287
client library glue (Java)	client library	310
platform-independent total		**2404**
platform-specfic modules		
app-enforcer process	app enforcer	403
incrementer	OS inspector	43
kernel module	OS inspector	39
libvirt extensions	OS enforcer	606
OS enforcer (main)	OS enforcer	509
OS enforcer (worker)	OS enforcer	83
libvirtd extensions	OS enforcer	53
RPC module	VMM inspector	103
DD-WRT extension	VMM enforcer	450
platform-specific total		**2289**
application-specific modules		
f() for Paxos (from [44])	app inspector	17
f() for primary-backup	app inspector	42
f() for ZooKeeper [31]	app inspector	159

Figure 15—The modules in our Falcon implementation and their lines of code. The platform-independent modules assume a POSIX system.

could increase $T_{OS\text{-}check}$ (which would reduce the number of checks but increase detection time) or improve the currently unoptimized implementation of guest memory reads.

5.5 What is the code and complexity trade-off?

Although we can use Falcon in legacy software (as in §5.2, where the gain was availability), Falcon provides an additional benefit to the applications that use it: shedding complexity. However, this is not "moving code around": the platform-specific logic required by Falcon has a simple function (detect a crashed layer and kill it if necessary) while the logic shed in applications is complex (tolerate mistakes in an unreliable failure detector).

Figure 15 tabulates the lines of code in our implementation, according to [54]. (We do not count external libraries in our implementation: sfslite for RPC functions, yajl for JSON functions, and libbridge for functions on the switch.) The platform-specific total is fewer than 2300 lines. The application-specific code is much smaller, for our sample implementations of f() (though a production application might wish to embed more intelligence in its f()).

Next, we assess the gain to applications that use failure detectors (FDs). Examples of such applications are ZooKeeper, Chubby, state machine replication libraries, and systems that use end-to-end timeouts based on pings of remote hosts.[4] As noted in Section 2.2, if the FD is a UFD, then the application needs complex algorithms that can handle FD mistakes; for example, it might use Paxos [35] for replication. However, if the application has access to an RFD (as provided by Falcon), then it can use simpler approaches; for example it can use primary-backup [9] for replication. Measuring simplicity is difficult, but we compare the lines of code in (1) PMP, which uses a static timer as an FD and Paxos for replication (see §5.2), and (2) a replication library that we implemented, which uses Falcon as an FD and primary-backup for replication. To make

replication approach	lines of code	# replicas/witnesses
Paxos (from [44])	1759	3
Primary-backup	1388	2

Figure 16—Comparison of two different approaches to replicating state machines: Paxos [35], as implemented in [44], and primary-backup [9], as implemented by us. The Paxos row excludes FD code and generated RPCs. The primary-backup approach is fewer lines of code because it is simpler: it does not tolerate unreliable failure detection. Primary-backup also has 50% lower replication overhead in the usual case.

the comparison like-to-like, we exclude PMP's FD code from the count.

Figure 16 lists the numbers, again according to [54]. The difference is only 371 lines, but this is 21% of the original code base. And the percentage may be deceptively low: using Paxos in a real system can require intricate engineering [18] whereas primary-backup deployments are not known to suffer similarly. Moreover, primary-backup has lower replication overhead than Paxos: to tolerate a crash, Paxos requires three replicas (or two replicas and a witness), while primary-backup requires just two replicas.

Assessing Falcon's reliability. The simplification results only if Falcon is truly reliable, meaning that it reports DOWN only if the target is down. Falcon's spies are carefully designed and implemented *not* to violate this property, and in our experience, Falcon has never reported an up target as DOWN. However, we cannot fully guarantee reliability without formally verifying our implementation.

6 DISCUSSION, EXTENSIONS, AND OUTLOOK

This section discusses how Falcon relates to the conventional wisdom that RFDs cannot be built (§6.1), why we favored Falcon over alternatives (§6.2), how one might apply Falcon to other systems (§6.3), what we see as future work (§6.4), and how Falcon might affect distributed systems more broadly (§6.5).

6.1 Is the conventional wisdom wrong?

The conventional wisdom holds that a viable fast RFD cannot be built, except with specialized hardware. So how did we build Falcon? We explain the arguments for this wisdom by both practitioners and theoreticians, and how Falcon overcomes them.

Practitioners argue that there is an inherent trade-off between detection time and either accuracy or little disruption (§2.2). This trade-off also applies to Falcon: for instance, by reducing the local timeouts of spies, we can get even faster detection and more frequent killing. However, by using inside information, Falcon shifts the trade-off curve to a point where it becomes almost insignificant: even when Falcon is configured to be relatively unaggressive, it often has very fast detection time (§5.1).

Theoreticians argue that RFDs cannot be implemented in asynchronous systems subject to failures because RFDs can be used to solve consensus, and consensus is impossible in such systems [28].[5] Falcon does not contradict this: the theoretical result holds in a model in which processes cannot infer crashes, and part of our point is that processes *can* infer crashes, using inside information. Furthermore, real systems are not asynchronous—a point that we and others have made before [8]. Of course, a system can sometimes experience large delays, thereby behaving like an asynchronous system; this causes Falcon to block temporarily, but that may be tolerable (§3.5).

---

[4]A non-example is an application that uses ZooKeeper, Chubby, or another higher-level service that itself incorporates FDs. In these cases, the simplicity benefit of Falcon accrues to the higher-level service, not its user. We discuss ZooKeeper and Chubby further in Section 7.

[5]Even in partially synchronous systems [26], where consensus can be solved, one can prove that RFDs cannot be implemented [38].

6.2 Alternatives to Falcon

Falcon has two backstops: an end-to-end timeout, to catch unexpected conditions, and a chained spy structure, where the spy on a layer monitors the spy on the next layer, to catch the death of spies themselves. An alternate design would be to eliminate the chained structure by not insisting that spies be monitored: there would be a set of ad-hoc spies, each tuned to a particular vulnerability. We did not pursue this design because a problem that both crashed a spy and triggered the vulnerability monitored by the spy would not be detected until the end-to-end timeout expired. Falcon, in contrast, can often detect this case quickly.

Falcon uses local timeouts within each layer. One might wonder if the local timeouts could be replaced with an end-to-end timeout that is the minimum or the sum of the local timeouts. The answer is no: with the minimum, there would be more frequent killing, and with the sum, the detection time would be much larger. In fact, even with the sum, there would be more frequent killing relative to Falcon: spies can avoid killing based on internal signs of life that are not visible end-to-end. One might wonder how this observation relates to the end-to-end argument [47]. The end-to-end argument states that functionality should be implemented at the end hosts (the highest layers), when it is possible to do so completely and correctly. In our context, however, the desired functionality—detecting failures quickly and reliably—can be provided only by infiltrating the layers.

Another design alternative concerns the handling of *intermittent failures*, such as temporary slowness of the target. We designed Falcon to avoid reporting an intermittent failure as a crash whenever possible, but an alternative is to conflate both problems. We eschewed that design for three reasons. First, clients may want to distinguish a crash from an intermittent failure, because the former requires recovery with non-zero cost, while the latter is self-healing. Second, to report an intermittent failure as a crash, an RFD must kill, causing possibly unnecessary disruption. Third, by using Falcon and a timer, a client can infer an intermittent failure, by observing that the target is unresponsive while Falcon deems it operational. However, a service that reports *where* the intermittent failure is, without calling it a crash, might be useful and would be an instance of an FD with richer failure indication (§6.4).

6.3 Applying Falcon to different platforms

Although Falcon's implementation targets a particular platform, we think that its overall design is general. With a different platform, Falcon needs to be tailored for two reasons. (1) The layers may be different: the platform may or may not have VMs, nested VMs [10], Java Virtual Machines (JVMs), etc. (2) A layer may have a different instantiation: the OS layer could be Windows instead of Linux, the VMM could be VMware instead of Linux with QEMU/KVM, etc.

We believe that we can keep small the tailoring from (1). The key is to standardize the communication between enforcer and inspectors, which would let us build different spy networks with minimal changes to the spies. With standardization, we could handle the case of no VMM by moving the OS enforcer to the network driver and leaving the OS inspector unchanged. Or we could insert into the JVM layer a JVM inspector and an enforcer for Java applications and leave unchanged the current app enforcer and app inspectors.

Reason (2), in contrast, requires reimplementing spies. However, because there are few OSs and VMMs, a small number of OS and VMM spies could cover most platforms. And while the application and network spy need to be implemented for each target, this cost is modest (see Section 5.5 for counts of lines of code).

Falcon is only as good as its spies, so how can a developer design useful new spies? Here are three guidelines. First and foremost, do not kill aggressively. Even if the spy monitors few conditions, if it does not kill aggressively, Falcon will fare better than an FD based on end-to-end timeouts alone because Falcon detects the failures monitored by the spy quickly and other failures as fast as the end-to-end timeout. Second, optimize for monitoring the common failures because therein lies the most benefit. Third, design the spy as an iterative process, as the common failures may be unknown at first. That is, the designer should first develop and deploy a simple spy based on some rough knowledge of failures; then observe that the spy fails to detect some common problem quickly (in which case the end-to-end timeout fires); then enhance the spy, redeploy it, and iterate until it catches all common problems. We used this process to design some of the spies in Section 4.

6.4 Future work

Richer failure indication. When a crash occurs, Falcon outputs a simple failure indication, but its spy network has much more information: which layer failed and what problem was observed in that layer. It would be useful to extend the FD interface to expose this data to help applications recover.

Monitoring across data centers. We have been assuming that the client library and the target are in the same physical data center. If they are in separate data centers but in the same administrative domain, our implementation still works, with the proviso that Falcon would block more often, since blocking happens if the client library cannot communicate with the target's switch (§3.5,§4). If they are in different administrative domains, Falcon would need to incorporate access control and permissions.

Scalable monitoring. Our focus has been one process monitoring another, but Falcon also works if $n > 1$ processes monitor each other. However, there will be $O(n^2)$ monitoring pairs, which should give us pause. Nevertheless, the actual resources consumed can be made efficient. When a layer fails, the detecting spy sends only $O(n)$ LAYER_DOWN reports. To avoid $O(n^2)$ messages during healthy times, one option is to eliminate LAYER_UP reports; another is to extend Falcon with techniques such as gossiping [50].

Targets with multiple network interfaces. Falcon currently assumes that the target's host is connected to a single switch, so that the VMM enforcer can kill the VMM by disabling the port of the target's host on the switch. If the target's host is connected to multiple switches, we need to deploy a VMM enforcer at each switch to disconnect all the ports of the target's host.

Network failure localization. Ultimately, we would like to extend Falcon's spy network downward, into the network, to enable failure localization. While one can imagine deploying spies on switches en route from client library to target, this approach raises complex questions related to the algorithms for detection, the approach to remediation (killing will not be viable in many scenarios), and the model for access control and administration.

6.5 Outlook

We finish by considering Falcon's potential effect on distributed systems, based on our expectations, postulations, and speculations.

The key features of Falcon are faster detection and reliability. With faster detection, Falcon may change distributed systems in four ways. First, it can improve availability by removing the periods when the system freezes for several seconds waiting for an end-to-end timeout to expire. Second, because detection is faster, the system has extra time to recover, so it can try multiple recovery strategies. For example, there may be enough time to restart and retry the failed component before taking the more drastic failover action. Third, with extra time to recover, the system could spend fewer resources during normal operation. For example, there may be no need to keep a warm backup or to checkpoint the state as often. Fourth, the system can afford more frequent failures while maintaining the same availability, which allows for cheaper components and less redundancy.

Besides fast detection, Falcon provides reliable detection, which could simplify the design of some distributed systems and algorithms—a point discussed in Sections 2.2 and 5.5 and which we now briefly elaborate. There are many abstractions to help build distributed systems including atomic registers, atomic broadcast, leader election, group membership, view synchrony, and transactions. However, these abstractions bring difficulty: materializing them has required much thought and work in both theory and practice. The difficulty arises because distributed systems have many sources of uncertainty: failures, slow messages and processes, concurrency, etc. Falcon does not remove all sources of uncertainty, but in its target domain—crash failures in data centers and enterprise networks—it eliminates a vexing one: the ambiguity between slowness and failures.

7 RELATED WORK

Before describing other approaches to failure detection, we give context. A formal theory of failure detectors, including definitions for several classes of FDs (reliable, different kinds of unreliable, etc.), was given by Chandra and Toueg [19]. That work established that, with RFDs (as opposed to UFDs), simpler solutions for consensus and atomic (totally-ordered) broadcast were possible. Subsequently, the theoretical advantages of *fast* RFDs were established [7]. Despite this body of theory, it was not known how to build an inexpensive failure detector that is reliable, fast, and minimally disruptive, so we organize related work in terms of the trade-offs among these characteristics.

We begin with unreliable FDs. Chen et al. [21] propose a failure detector based on freshness points and end-to-end timeouts, where the value is chosen adaptively based on delay and loss measurements. Such end-to-end timeouts could be set using other techniques too [11]. These approaches provide a binary indication of failure. Accrual failure detectors [30], in contrast, output a numerical value such that, roughly, the higher the value, the higher the chance that the process has crashed. In practice, applications consider the output to be an indication of failure if it is above a certain threshold. There has also been a strand of work on scaling the failure detector to a large number of processes, with gossiping [50]. This approach also uses end-to-end timeouts, again resulting in a UFD. Each of the above UFDs must trade detection time and accuracy, and none yields an RFD: end-to-end timeouts can be premature, and the guarantees of accrual FDs are probabilistic.

To realize an affordable RFD, one could augment any of the unreliable FDs above by backing up suspicion of failure with killing. In that case, the tradeoff becomes fast detection versus disruption, as what used to be false FD suspicions become needless kills. Such reliable failure detectors can be implemented using watchdogs [27], where the watchdog resets the machine based on an end-to-end timeout. Likewise, the Linux-HA project [6] provides a service called Heartbeat, which provides a failure detection service based on end-to-end timeouts and can be configured to use a hardware watchdog, or STONITH of real or virtual machines. Similarly, with

virtual synchrony [12] there is a notion of a process group (which corresponds to the set of operational processes), and if a process becomes very slow, it is excluded from the group via an end-to-end timeout, which is akin to killing. In contrast to all of these approaches, Falcon provides surgical killing and uses fine-grained inside information to detect failures faster than an end-to-end timeout would allow.

Surgical killing and fine-grained monitoring have appeared before but in different contexts. Candea et al. [16] articulated the benefits of surgical killing (faster recovery time, less disruption), and we concur. However, that work focuses on the application layer only, and it solves an orthogonal problem to detection, namely recovery. Fine-grained information is used in cluster monitoring, which collects information about the current condition of hosts in a cluster (e.g., [2–4]), possibly using application-specific data (load, queue lengths, etc.). In contrast to Falcon, these services peek inside only one layer (the application), monitor machines using an end-to-end timeout, and do not have a license to kill (which is needed to get an RFD). Fine-grained information is also used in the leader election service of [48], which enhances a timeout-based failure detector by suspecting a target if its pipe to a local module is broken. Here too, the fine-grained information is limited to one layer, and the failure detector does not kill.

A technique that does involve killing, which is used to increase the availability of Web servers and other services, is to deploy a local script that periodically checks if the application process is running. If not, or if the process has erratic behavior (such as very high CPU usage), the script restarts the application, killing it first if necessary. This technique is limited to one layer (nothing monitors the script) and does not report the failure status to a remote process.

A system that can provide information about failures is ZooKeeper [31], a service for configuration management, naming, and group membership. Its *ephemeral objects*—objects that disappear when the creator is deemed to have crashed—allow other clients to detect the creator's failure status. However, to implement these objects, ZooKeeper internally needs a bona fide failure detector. It uses a UFD (§2.2) for this purpose, so its ephemeral objects provide unreliable detection. However, we replaced its UFD here with Falcon, and though we did not experiment much in this configuration, the change makes ephemeral objects reliable and fast.

Another distributed systems building block is Chubby [14], a lock service with named objects, sessions, and other features. Chubby can address some of the problems that Falcon does. For example, Chubby can avoid two active primaries in some applications. This is done with locks: the primary owns a lock and has a session with Chubby. If the primary fails, Chubby releases the lock only after the primary has lost its session. For this purpose, Chubby uses large end-to-end timeouts and complex session management logic; if incorporated into Chubby, Falcon could replace the former and simplify the latter.

Other production services could also replace their failure detectors, which are based on end-to-end timeouts, with Falcon. For example, GFS [29] uses a timeout of 60 seconds for the primary of a chunk. BigTable [20] uses end-to-end timeouts for sessions with Chubby; it also uses timeouts to expire tablet servers. Dynamo [25] uses end-to-end timeouts in its gossip protocol and between communicating nodes.

8 SUMMARY AND CONCLUSION

We began by observing that tolerating crashes requires not only recovering from them—a problem that has been extensively studied—but also detecting them in the first place, a problem that has received comparatively less attention. This problem brings challenges, whose ultimate cause is the difficulty of quickly and accurately classifying what is truly happening at a remote target. To lift the fog of war, Falcon infiltrates the layers of a remote system with spies, chains spies into a spy network, and combines these with existing techniques (reliability by killing, end-to-end timeouts as a backstop, etc.). To us, the most interesting aspect of Falcon is not any of its individual techniques but rather that it composes them into a system that achieves—as an ad-hoc design would not, judging by our own discarded designs and revised reasoning—sub-second detection, reliability, little disruption, and tolerable expense. This combination is the key contribution of Falcon, and having made it, Falcon now has the chance, we hope, to yield broader benefits: distributed systems that for the user are more responsive and for the designer are more tractable.

Our implementation and experimental configurations are available at: http://www.cs.utexas.edu/falcon

Acknowledgments

An early prototype by James Kneeland inspired some of our implementation choices. This paper was improved by careful, detailed comments by Hari Balakrishnan, Allen Clement, Russ Cox, Trinabh Gupta, Carmel Levy, J.-P. Martin, Venugopalan Ramasubramanian, Chao Ruan, Srinath Setty, Sam Toueg, Edmund Wong, Emmett Witchel, the anonymous reviewers, and our shepherd, Marvin Theimer. The research was supported in part by AFOSR grant FA9550-10-1-0073 and NSF grants 1055057 and 1040083.

REFERENCES

[1] http://hadoop.apache.org.

[2] http://www.managementsoftware.hp.com.

[3] http://www.bmc.com/products/brand/patrol.html.

[4] http://www.ibm.com/software/tivoli.

[5] DomUClusters – Linux-HA. linux-ha.org/wiki/DomUClusters.

[6] Linux-HA, High-Availability software for Linux. http://www.linux-ha.org.

[7] M. K. Aguilera, G. L. Lann, and S. Toueg. On the impact of fast failure detectors on real-time fault-tolerant systems. In *International Conference on Distributed Computing (DISC)*, pages 354–370, Oct. 2002.

[8] M. K. Aguilera and M. Walfish. No time for asynchrony. In *Workshop on Hot Topics in Operating Systems (HotOS)*, May 2009.

[9] P. A. Alsberg and J. D. Day. A principle for resilient sharing of distributed resources. In *International Conference on Software Engineering (ICSE)*, pages 562–570, 1976.

[10] M. Ben-Yehuda, M. D. Day, Z. Dubitzky, M. Factor, N. Har'El, A. Gordon, A. Liguori, O. Wasserman, and B.-A. Yassour. The Turtles project: Design and implementation of nested virtualization. In *Symposium on Operating Systems Design and Implementation (OSDI)*, pages 423–436, Oct. 2010.

[11] M. Bertier, O. Marin, and P. Sens. Implementation and performance evaluation of an adaptable failure detector. In *International Conference on Dependable Systems and Networks (DSN)*, pages 354–363, June 2002.

[12] K. P. Birman and T. A. Joseph. Exploiting virtual synchrony in distributed systems. In *ACM Symposium on Operating Systems Principles (SOSP)*, pages 123–138, Nov. 1987.

[13] W. J. Bolosky, D. Bradshaw, R. B. Haagens, N. P. Kusters, and P. Li. Paxos replicated state machines as the basis of a high-performance data store. In *Symposium on Networked Systems Design and Implementation (NSDI)*, pages 141–154, Apr. 2011.

[14] M. Burrows. The Chubby lock service for loosely-coupled distributed systems. In *Symposium on Operating Systems Design and Implementation (OSDI)*, pages 335–350, Dec. 2006.

[15] G. Candea, J. Cutler, and A. Fox. Improving availability with recursive microreboots: A soft-state system case study. *Performance Evaluation Journal*, 56(1–4):213–248, Mar. 2004.

[16] G. Candea, S. Kawamoto, Y. Fujiki, G. Friedman, and A. Fox. Microreboot—a technique for cheap recovery. In *Symposium on Operating Systems Design and Implementation (OSDI)*, pages 31–44, Dec. 2004.

[17] The Apache Cassandra project. http://wiki.apache.org/cassandra/ArchitectureInternals#Failure_detection.

[18] T. Chandra, R. Griesemer, and J. Redstone. Paxos made live: An engineering perspective. In *ACM Symposium on Principles of Distributed Computing (PODC)*, pages 398–407, Aug. 2007.

[19] T. D. Chandra and S. Toueg. Unreliable failure detectors for reliable distributed systems. *Journal of the ACM*, 43(2):225–267, Mar. 1996.

[20] F. Chang, J. Dean, S. Ghemawat, W. C. Hsieh, D. A. Wallach, M. Burrows, T. Chandra, A. Fikes, and R. E. Gruber. Bigtable: A distributed storage system for structured data. In *Symposium on Operating Systems Design and Implementation (OSDI)*, pages 205–218, Nov. 2006.

[21] W. Chen, S. Toueg, and M. K. Aguilera. On the quality of service of failure detectors. *IEEE Transactions on Computers*, 51(5):561–580, May 2002.

[22] B. Cully, G. Lefebvre, D. Meyer, M. Feeley, N. Hutchinson, and A. Warfield. Remus: High availability via asynchronous virtual machine replication. In *Symposium on Networked Systems Design and Implementation (NSDI)*, pages 161–174, Apr. 2008.

[23] DD-WRT firmware. http://www.dd-wrt.com.

[24] J. Dean and S. Ghemawat. MapReduce: Simplified data processing on large clusters. In *Symposium on Operating Systems Design and Implementation (OSDI)*, pages 137–150, Dec. 2004.

[25] G. DeCandia, D. Hastorun, M. Jampani, G. Kakulapati, A. Lakshman, A. Pilchin, S. Sivasubramanian, P. Vosshall, and W. Vogels. Dynamo: Amazon's highly available key-value store. In *ACM Symposium on Operating Systems Principles (SOSP)*, pages 205–220, Oct. 2007.

[26] C. Dwork, N. A. Lynch, and L. Stockmeyer. Consensus in the presence of partial synchrony. *Journal of the ACM*, 35(2):288–323, Apr. 1988.

[27] C. Fetzer. Perfect failure detection in timed asynchronous systems. *IEEE Transactions on Computers*, 52(2):99–112, Feb. 2003.

[28] M. J. Fischer, N. A. Lynch, and M. S. Paterson. Impossibility of distributed consensus with one faulty process. *Journal of the ACM*, 32(2):374–382, Apr. 1985.

[29] S. Ghemawat, H. Gobioff, and S.-T. Leung. The Google file system. In *ACM Symposium on Operating Systems Principles (SOSP)*, pages 29–43, Oct. 2003.

[30] N. Hayashibara, X. Défago, R. Yared, and T. Katayama. The ϕ accrual failure detector. In *IEEE Symposium on Reliable Distributed Systems (SRDS)*, pages 66–78, Oct. 2004.

[31] P. Hunt, M. Konar, F. P. Junqueira, and B. Reed. ZooKeeper: Wait-free coordination for Internet-scale systems. In *USENIX Annual Technical Conference*, pages 145–158, June 2010.

[32] M. Isard, M. Budiu, Y. Yu, A. Birrell, and D. Fetterly. Dryad: Distributed data-parallel programs from sequential building blocks. In *European Conference on Computer Systems (EuroSys)*, pages 59–72, Mar. 2007.

[33] J. P. John, E. Katz-Bassett, A. Krishnamurthy, T. Anderson, and A. Venkataramani. Consensus routing: The Internet as a distributed system. In *Symposium on Networked Systems Design and Implementation (NSDI)*, pages 351–364, Apr. 2008.

[34] J. Kirsch and Y. Amir. Paxos for system builders: an overview. In *International Workshop on Large Scale Distributed Systems and Middleware (LADIS)*, Sept. 2008.

[35] L. Lamport. The part-time parliament. *ACM Transactions on Computer Systems (TOCS)*, 16(2):133–169, May 1998.

[36] L. Lamport. Paxos made simple. *Distributed Computing Column of ACM SIGACT News*, 32(4):51–58, Dec. 2001.

[37] B. Lampson. The ABCD's of Paxos. In *ACM Symposium on Principles of Distributed Computing (PODC)*, page 13, Aug. 2001.

[38] M. Larrea, A. Fernández, and S. Arévalo. On the impossibility of implementing perpetual failure detectors in partially synchronous systems. In *Euromicro Workshop on Parallel, Distributed and Network-based Processing*, pages 99–105, Jan. 2002.

[39] E. K. Lee and C. Thekkath. Petal: Distributed virtual disks. In *International Conference on Architectural Support for Programming Languages and Operating Systems (ASPLOS)*, pages 84–92, Dec. 1996.

[40] H. C. Li, A. Clement, A. S. Aiyer, and L. Alvisi. The Paxos register. In *IEEE Symposium on Reliable Distributed Systems (SRDS)*, pages 114–126, Oct. 2007.

[41] libvirt: The virtualization API. `http://libvirt.org/`.

[42] Linux kernel dump test module. `http://kernel.org/doc/Documentation/fault-injection/provoke-crashes.txt`.

[43] J. MacCormick, N. Murphy, M. Najork, C. A. Thekkath, and L. Zhou. Boxwood: Abstractions as the foundation for storage infrastructure. In *Symposium on Operating Systems Design and Implementation (OSDI)*, pages 105–120, Dec. 2004.

[44] D. Mazières. Paxos made practical. `http://www.scs.stanford.edu/~dm/home/papers/paxos.pdf`, as of Sept. 2011.

[45] R. D. Prisco, B. Lampson, and N. Lynch. Revisiting the Paxos algorithm. *Theoretical Computer Science*, 243(1–2):35–91, July 2000.

[46] Kernel based virtual machine. `http://www.linux-kvm.org/`.

[47] J. H. Saltzer, D. P. Reed, and D. D. Clark. End-to-end arguments in system design. *ACM Transactions on Computer Systems (TOCS)*, 2(4):277–288, Nov. 1984.

[48] N. Schiper, S. Toueg, and D. Ivan. Leader elector source code. `http://www.inf.usi.ch/phd/schiper/LeaderElection`.

[49] J. Stribling, Y. Sovran, I. Zhang, X. Pretzer, J. Li, M. F. Kaashoek, and R. Morris. Flexible, wide-area storage for distributed systems with WheelFS. In *Symposium on Networked Systems Design and Implementation (NSDI)*, pages 43–58, Apr. 2009.

[50] R. van Renesse, Y. Minsky, and M. Hayden. A gossip-style failure detection service. In *International Middleware Conference (Middleware)*, pages 55–70, Sept. 1998.

[51] P. Veríssimo. Uncertainty and predictability: Can they be reconciled? In *Future Directions in Distributed Computing (FuDiCo)*, pages 108–113. Springer-Verlag LNCS 2584, May 2003.

[52] P. Veríssimo and A. Casimiro. The Timely Computing Base model and architecture. *IEEE Transactions on Computers*, 51(8):916–930, Aug. 2002.

[53] P. Veríssimo, A. Casimiro, and C. Fetzer. The Timely Computing Base: Timely actions in the presence of uncertain timeliness. In *International Conference on Dependable Systems and Networks (DSN)*, pages 533–542, June 2000.

[54] D. A. Wheeler. SLOCCount. `http://www.dwheeler.com/sloccount/`.

[55] GSoC 2010: ZooKeeper Failure Detector model. `http://wiki.apache.org/hadoop/ZooKeeper/GSoCFailureDetector`.

Secure Network Provenance

Wenchao Zhou
University of Pennsylvania

Qiong Fei
University of Pennsylvania

Arjun Narayan
University of Pennsylvania

Andreas Haeberlen
University of Pennsylvania

Boon Thau Loo
University of Pennsylvania

Micah Sherr
Georgetown University

ABSTRACT

This paper introduces *secure network provenance (SNP)*, a novel technique that enables networked systems to explain to their operators *why* they are in a certain state – e.g., why a suspicious routing table entry is present on a certain router, or where a given cache entry originated. SNP provides network forensics capabilities by permitting operators to track down faulty or misbehaving nodes, and to assess the damage such nodes may have caused to the rest of the system. SNP is designed for adversarial settings and is robust to manipulation; its tamper-evident properties ensure that operators can detect when compromised nodes lie or falsely implicate correct nodes.

We also present the design of SNOOPY, a general-purpose SNP system. To demonstrate that SNOOPY is practical, we apply it to three example applications: the Quagga BGP daemon, a declarative implementation of Chord, and Hadoop MapReduce. Our results indicate that SNOOPY can efficiently explain state in an adversarial setting, that it can be applied with minimal effort, and that its costs are low enough to be practical.

Categories and Subject Descriptors

C.2.4 [**Computer Systems Organization**]: Computer-Communication Networks—*Distributed Systems*; D.4.5 [**Software**]: Operating Systems—*Reliability*

General Terms

Algorithms, Design, Reliability, Security

Keywords

Accountability, Byzantine faults, Distributed systems, Evidence, Provenance, Security

1. INTRODUCTION

Operators of distributed systems often find themselves needing to answer a diagnostic or forensic question. Some part of the system is found to be in an unexpected state – for example, a suspicious routing table entry is discovered, or a

proxy cache is found to contain an unusually large number of advertisements. The operators must determine the *causes* of this state before they can decide on an appropriate response. On the one hand, there may be an innocent explanation: the routing table entry could be the result of a misconfiguration, and the cache entries could have appeared due to a workload change. On the other hand, the unexpected state may be the symptom of an ongoing attack: the routing table entry could be the result of route hijacking, and the cache entries could be a side-effect of a malware infection. If an attack or misconfiguration is discovered, the operators must determine its *effects*, such as corrupted state or configuration changes on other nodes, so that these nodes can be repaired and the system brought back to a correct state.

In this paper, we consider forensics in an *adversarial* setting, that is, we assume that a faulty node does not necessarily crash but can also change its behavior and continue operating. To be conservative, we assume that faults can be Byzantine [24], i.e., a faulty node can behave arbitrarily. This covers a wide range of faults and misbehavior, e.g., cases where a malicious adversary has compromised some of the nodes, but also more benign faults, such as hardware failures or misconfigurations. Getting correct answers to forensic queries in an adversarial setting is difficult because the misbehaving nodes can lie to the querier. For example, the adversary can attempt to conceal his actions by causing his nodes to fabricate plausible (but incorrect) responses to forensic queries, or he can attempt to frame correct nodes by returning responses that blame his own misbehavior on them. Thus, the adversary can gain valuable time by misdirecting the operators and/or causing them to suspect a problem with the forensic system itself.

Existing forensic systems are either designed for non-adversarial settings [43, 51] or require some trusted components, e.g., a trusted virtual-machine monitor [3, 21], a trusted host-level monitor [27], a trusted OS [29], or trusted hardware [7]. However, most components that are available today are not fully trustworthy; OSes and virtual machine monitors have bugs, which a powerful adversary could exploit, and even trusted hardware is sometimes compromised [20]. We argue that it is useful to have alternative techniques available that do not require this type of trust.

We introduce *secure network provenance (SNP)*, a technique for building forensic systems that can operate in a *completely untrusted* environment. We assume that the adversary may have compromised an arbitrary subset of the nodes, and that he may have complete control over these nodes. On the one hand, this very conservative threat model requires some compromises: an SNP system can only answer queries about observable network state—i.e., state that has directly or indirectly affected at least one correct node—and its responses can be incomplete, although the missing parts are always clearly identified. On the other hand, an SNP system provides strong, provable guarantees: it ensures that an observable symptom of a fault or an attack can always be traced to a specific event—passive evasion or active misbehavior—on at least one faulty node, even when an adversary attempts to prevent this.

Two existing concepts, data provenance and tamper-evident logging, can provide a starting point for building SNP systems. Data provenance [4, 51] tracks and records data dependencies as data flows through the system. In the context of distributed systems, network provenance [51] is captured as a global dependency graph, where vertices are data items that represent state at a particular node, and edges represent local processing or message transmissions across nodes. This graph can then be used to answer forensic queries. Tamper-evident logging [17] can record data in such a way that forgeries, omissions, and other forms of tampering can be detected and proven to a third party.

However, as is often the case in computer security, a simple layering of these two concepts fails to achieve the desired goal. If an existing network provenance system, say ExSPAN [51], were combined with a system like PeerReview [17] that supports tamper-evident logging, an adversary could potentially subvert the resulting system by attacking it twice. The first attack would corrupt the system's internal data structures; this would require a protocol violation that PeerReview could detect, but not diagnose or repair. With the data structures suitably damaged, the adversary could then carry out the second attack without further protocol violations, and without leaving visible traces in the provenance system. Thus, the second attack would be invisible.

We have designed SNOOPY, a system that provides secure network provenance by combining evidence-based distributed query processing with a novel provenance model that is specially designed with fault detection in mind. We have formalized SNP's security properties, and we have proven that SNOOPY satisfies them. To demonstrate SNOOPY's practicality and generality, we have implemented a prototype, and we have applied it to three example applications: the Quagga BGP daemon [35], a declarative implementation of Chord [26], and Hadoop MapReduce [12]. Our evaluation demonstrates SNOOPY's ability to solve real-world forensic problems, such as finding the causes and effects of BGP misconfigurations, DHT routing attacks, and corrupt Hadoop mappers; our results also show that SNOOPY's costs (additional bandwidth, storage, and computation) vary with the application but are low enough to be practical. In summary, we make the following contributions:

- A provenance graph for causal, dynamic, and historical provenance queries that is suitable for SNP (Section 3);
- SNP, a method to securely construct network provenance graphs in untrusted environments (Section 4);
- The design of SNOOPY, a system that implements SNP for the provenance graph presented earlier (Section 5);
- A proof of correctness for SNOOPY (sketched here, and included in the extended version of this paper [50]);
- An application of SNOOPY to Quagga, Chord, and Hadoop MapReduce (Section 6); and
- A quantitative evaluation (Section 7).

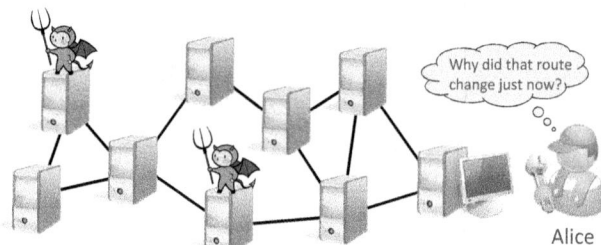

Figure 1: Motivating scenario. Alice is running a distributed system and observes some unexpected behavior that may indicate a fault or an attack.

2. OVERVIEW

Figure 1 illustrates the scenario that we are addressing in this paper. An administrator, here called Alice, is operating a distributed system – perhaps a cluster, a corporate network, or a content distribution system. At some point, Alice observes some unexpected behavior in the system and decides to investigate whether the behavior is legitimate or perhaps a symptom of a fault or an attack. Our goal is to enable Alice to query the system about the causes and effects of the unexpected behavior, and to obtain reliable results.

To achieve this goal, we extend each node in the system with a monitoring component that maintains some forensic information. We refer to the system that is being monitored as the *primary system* and to our additional components as the *provenance system*. To be useful to Alice, the provenance system should have the following two high-level properties:

- When the queried behavior is legitimate, the system should return a complete and correct explanation.

- When the queried behavior is a symptom of a fault or misbehavior, the explanation should tie it to a specific event on a faulty or misbehaving node.

By behavior, we mean a state change or a message transmission on any node. We assume that Alice knows what behavior is legitimate, e.g., because she knows which software the system was expected to run.

2.1 Threat model

Since we would like to enable Alice to investigate a wide range of problems, ranging from simple misconfigurations to hardware faults and even clandestine attacks, we conservatively assume Byzantine faults [24], i.e., that an adversary may have compromised an unknown subset of the nodes, and that he has complete control over them. Thus, the non-malicious problems are covered as a special case. We assume that the adversary can change both the primary system and the provenance system on these nodes, and he can read, forge, tamper with, or destroy any information they are holding. We also assume that no nodes or components of the system are inherently safe, i.e., Alice does not a priori trust any node other than her own local machine.

Handling such a broad range of faults is challenging because Alice cannot be sure that any data she is receiving is actually correct. When she queries a compromised node, the adversary can cause that node to lie or equivocate. In particular, he can try to forge a plausible explanation for the symptoms Alice has observed, or he can try to make it appear as if the symptoms were caused by a different node. If this is not prevented, Alice could overlook the attack entirely or waste time trying to repair the wrong nodes.

2.2 Approach

Our approach to this challenge is to construct a distributed data structure called the *provenance graph* which, at a high level, tracks how data flows through the system. Data provenance itself is not a new concept—it has been explored by the database and the system community [4, 10, 19, 29, 47, 51]—but most existing provenance systems are designed for non-adversarial settings and lack features that are necessary for forensics. For example, existing systems focus on explaining state that exists at query time ("Why does τ exist?"), which would allow an adversary to thwart Alice's investigation simply by deleting data that implicates him. To support forensics, we additionally provide *historical queries* ("Why did τ exist at time t?") and *dynamic queries* ("Why did τ (dis)appear?'); to assist with recovery, we also provide *causal queries* ("What state on other nodes was derived from τ?"), which can be used to determine which parts of the system have been affected and require repair.

Our key contribution, however, is to *secure* the provenance graph. Ideally, we would like to correctly answer Alice's queries even when the system is under attack. However, given our conservative threat model, this is not always possible. Hence, we make the following two compromises: first, we only demand that the system answer provenance queries about behavior that is *observable by at least one correct node* [15]; in other words, if some of the adversary's actions never affect the state of any correct node, the system is allowed to omit them. Second, we accept that the system may sometimes return an answer that is incorrect or incomplete, as long as Alice can a) tell which parts of the answer are affected, and she can b) learn the identity of at least one faulty node. In a forensic setting, this seems like a useful compromise: any unexpected behavior that can be noticed by Alice is observable by definition, and even a partial answer can help Alice to determine whether a fault or misbehavior has occurred, and which parts of the system have been affected.

2.3 Provenance and confidentiality

If Alice can query any datum on any node, she can potentially learn the full state of the entire system. Throughout this paper, we will assume that Alice is authorized to have this information. In centrally managed systems, there are typically at least some individuals (e.g., the system administrators) who have that authority. Examples of such systems include academic or corporate networks as well as infrastructure services—such as Akamai's CDN—that are physically distributed but controlled by a single entity.

In systems without central management, it is sometimes possible to partition the state among different managers. For example, in Amazon's Elastic MapReduce service, the owner of a given MapReduce job could be authorized to issue queries about that specific job while being prevented from querying jobs that belong to other customers. In other cases, abstractions can be used to hide confidential details from unauthorized queriers. SNP includes extensions to the provenance graph that can selectively conceal how certain parts of a node's state were derived. As discussed in Section 3.4, the resulting graph can be queried without disclosing the node's actual computation.

2.4 Strawman solutions

It is natural to ask whether our goals could be achieved by using some combination of an existing fault detection system, such as PeerReview [17], and/or an existing network provenance system, such as ExSPAN [51]. However, a simple combination of these two systems is insufficient for the following reasons.

Individually. In isolation, neither of the two systems can achieve our goals. PeerReview can detect when nodes deviate from the algorithm they are expected to run, but it provides no mechanisms for detecting or diagnosing problems that result from interactions between multiple nodes (such as an instance of BadGadget [11] in interdomain routing), or problems that are related to nodes lying about their local inputs or deliberately slowing down their execution. ExSPAN captures the interactions among nodes via provenance, but cannot detect when compromised nodes lie about provenance.

Layering. A natural approach to addressing ExSPAN's security vulnerabilities is simply to layer ExSPAN over PeerReview. However, this approach also fails to achieve the desired security guarantees. First, PeerReview reports faults with a certain delay; thus, a compromised node has a window of opportunity in which it can corrupt the provenance graph. Even if detection is nearly instantaneous, simply identifying the faulty node is not sufficient: since the graph is itself distributed, effects of the corruption can manifest in parts of the provenance graph that are stored on other nodes, and there is no way for the layered approach to detect this easily. This means that once a fault is detected by PeerReview, the results of further provenance queries (e.g., to find other compromised nodes, or to locate corrupted state) can no longer be trusted, and the entire provenance system is rendered unusable.

Our integrated solution. Achieving hard guarantees for secure provenance requires rethinking both ExSPAN and PeerReview. Instead of layering one system over the other, we tightly integrate the process of provenance generation and querying with the underlying fault detection system. Providing secure network provenance involves a fundamental redesign of ExSPAN's query and provenance model to enable tamper-evident query processing and the generation of evidence against faulty nodes, which can be used for further investigations.

In the following sections, we not only demonstrate that our integrated approach achieves the desired high-level properties introduced earlier at a cost that is low enough to be practical, we also experimentally validate its usefulness by performing forensic analysis on several existing applications. An additional benefit of this tight integration and our richer provenance model is that we can naturally support richer forensic queries, such as historical, dynamic, and causal provenance queries.

3. PROVENANCE GRAPH

In this section, we introduce our system model, and we define an 'ideal' provenance graph G, based on the true actions of each node. Of course, if faulty nodes can lie about their actions or suppress information, a correct node that is processing a provenance query may not be able to reconstruct G entirely. However, as we will show in the following sections, SNP can reconstruct a close approximation G_ν of G.

3.1 System model

For ease of exposition, we adopt a system model that is commonly used in database systems to reason about data provenance. In this model, the state of the primary system is represented as *tuples*, and its algorithm is represented as *derivation rules* [51], which describe how tuples are derived from the system's inputs. Few practical systems are explicitly built in terms of tuples and derivation rules, but this is not required to apply SNP: in Section 5.3, we describe three general techniques for extracting tuples and derivations from existing systems, and in Section 6 we report how we applied these techniques to Quagga, Chord, and Hadoop MapReduce.

Each node in a distributed system has its own set of tuples, and derivation rules can span multiple nodes. For example, the state of a router r might consist of tuples such as `link(@r,a)` to show that r has a link to a, or `route(@r,b,c)` to show that r knows a route to b on which the next hop is c. Here, `link` and `route` are the names of specific relations, and `@r` indicates that the tuple is maintained on r. The lower-case letters are constants; we later use upper-case letters for variables. Where the specific relation does not matter, we simply write $\tau @ n$ to denote a tuple τ on a node n.

Tuples can either be *base tuples* or *derived tuples*. Base tuples correspond to local inputs that are assumed to be true without derivations, e.g., a list of physical links that is input to a routing protocol. Derived tuples are obtained from other tuples through a derivation rule of the form $\tau @ n \leftarrow \tau_1 @ n_1 \wedge \tau_2 @ n_2 \wedge \cdots \wedge \tau_k @ n_k$. This is interpreted as a conjunction: tuple τ should be derived on n whenever all τ_i exist on their respective nodes n_i, and τ should then continue to exist until at least one of the τ_i disappears. (If a tuple has more than one derivation, we can distinguish between them using a logical reference counter.) When a derivation rule spans multiple nodes, the nodes must notify each other of relevant tuple changes: if a node i has a rule that depends on a tuple $\tau @ j$, j must send a message $+\tau$ to i whenever τ is derived or inserted as a base tuple, and j must send $-\tau$ to i whenever τ is underived or removed. We require that all derivations are finite and have no cyclic dependencies. This can be achieved by carefully writing the derivation rules, and it holds for our three example applications.

We assume that each node applies its rules deterministically. Thus, we can model the expected behavior of a node i as a state machine A_i, whose inputs are incoming messages and changes to base tuples, and whose outputs are messages that need to be sent to other nodes. An *execution* of the system can then be represented as a sequence of message transmissions, message arrivals, base tuple insertions, and base tuple deletions. We say that a node i is *correct* in an execution e if i's outputs in e are legal, given A_i and i's inputs in e. Otherwise we say that i is *faulty* in e.

Routing example. The derivation rule `route(@R,C,B)` ← `link(@R,B)` ∧ `route(@B,C,D)` expresses network reachability in a router: a router R has route to C via B (`route(@R,C,B)`) whenever it has a link to another router B (`link(@R,B)`) that already has a route to C via some third router D (`route(@B,C,D)`). Here, R, B, C, and D are variables that can refer to any router. If we declare the `link` tuples to be base tuples and add another rule to say that each router has a route to its immediate neighbors, the resulting system implements a simplified form of path-vector routing [26].

3.2 Vertices and edges

Having explicit derivation rules makes it very easy to see the provenance of a tuple: if a tuple τ was derived from other tuples $\tau_1, \ldots, \tau_k$, then τ's immediate provenance simply consists of all the τ_i taken together. To capture transitive provenance, we can define, for any execution e, a *provenance graph* $G(e) = (V(e), E(e))$, in which each vertex $v \in V(e)$ represents a state or state change, and each edge (v_1, v_2) indicates that v_1 is part of the provenance of v_2. The complete explanation for the existence of a tuple τ in e would then be a subtree that is embedded in $G(e)$ and rooted at the vertex that corresponds to τ. The leaves of this subtree consist of base tuple insertions or deletions, which require no further explanation.

$V(e)$ consists of twelve vertex types. The following seven types are used to represent local states and state changes:

- INSERT(n, τ, t) and DELETE(n, τ, t): Base tuple τ was inserted/deleted on node n at time t;
- APPEAR(n, τ, t) and DISAPPEAR(n, τ, t): Tuple τ appeared/disappeared on node n at time t;
- EXIST$(n, \tau, [t_1, t_2])$: Tuple τ existed on node n during interval $[t_1, t_2]$; and
- DERIVE(n, τ, R, t) and UNDERIVE(n, τ, R, t): Tuple τ was derived/underived on n via rule R at time t.

In contrast to other provenance graphs, such as the one in [51], the graph G we present here has an explicit representation for state changes, which is useful to support dynamic queries. G also retains information about tuples that no longer exist, which is necessary for historic queries; note particularly that vertices such as DELETE, UNDERIVE, and DISAPPEAR would not be necessary in a provenance graph that contains only extant tuples. The timestamps t should be interpreted relative to node n.

The remaining five vertex types are used to represent interactions between nodes. For the purposes of SNP, it is important that each vertex v has a specific node that is 'responsible' for it. (We will refer to this node as HOST(v).) To achieve this property, derivations and underivations from remote tuples must be broken up into a sequence of smaller steps that can each be attributed to a specific node. For example, when a rule $\tau_1 @ i \leftarrow \tau_2 @ j$ is triggered, we do not simply connect τ_1's DERIVE vertex to τ_2's APPEAR vertex; rather, we say that the provenance of τ_1's derivation was i's *belief* that τ_2 had appeared on j, which was caused by the arrival of $+\tau_2$ on i, the transmission of $+\tau_2$ by j, and finally the appearance of τ_2 on j. Thus, if j's message is later found to be erroneous, i's belief—and thus its derivation—is still legitimate, and the error can be attributed to j. The specific vertex types are the following:

- SEND$(n, n', \pm\tau, t)$: At time t, node n sent a notification to node n' that tuple τ has appeared/disappeared; and
- RECEIVE$(n, n', \pm\tau, t)$: At time t, node n received a message from node n' that tuple τ has appeared/disappeared.
- BELIEVE-APPEAR(n, n', τ, t) and BELIEVE-DISAPPEAR (n, n', τ, t): At time t, node n learned of the (dis)appearance of tuple τ on node n';
- BELIEVE$(n, n', \tau, [t_1, t_2])$: During $[t_1, t_2]$, node n believed that tuple τ existed on node n';

Finally, we introduce a *color* for each vertex $v \in V(e)$. Colors are used to indicate whether a vertex is legitimate: correct vertices are black, and faulty vertices are red. For example, if a faulty node i has no tuple τ but nevertheless sends a message $+\tau$ to another node, $\tau@i$ has no legitimate provenance, so we use a red SEND vertex to represent the transmission of $+\tau$. In Section 4.2, we will introduce a third color, yellow, for vertices whose true color is not yet known.

3.3 Example: Minimum cost routing

As a simple example, consider the network depicted on the right, which consists of five routers that are connected by links of different costs. Each router attempts to find the lowest-cost path to router d using a MinCost protocol. There are three types of tuples: link(@X,Y,K) indicates that router X has a direct link to router Y with cost K; cost(@X,Y,Z,K) indicates that X knows a path to Y via Z with total cost K; and bestCost(@X,Y,K) indicates that the cheapest path known by X to Y has cost K. The link tuples are base tuples because they are part of the static configuration of the routers (we assume that routers have *a priori* knowledge of their local link costs, and that links are symmetric), whereas cost and bestCost tuples are derived from other tuples according to one of three derivation rules: each router knows the cost of its direct links (R1); it can learn the cost of an advertised route from one of its neighbors (R2); and it chooses its own bestCost tuple according to the lowest-cost path it currently knows (R3).

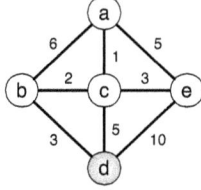

Figure 2 shows an example of a provenance tree for the tuple bestCost(@c,d,5). This tuple can be derived in two different ways. Router c knows its direct link to d via link(@c,d,5), which trivially produces cost(@c,d,d,5). Similarly, router b derives cost(@b,d,d,3) via its direct link with d, and since no other path from b to d offers a lower cost, b produces the tuple bestCost(@b,d,3). b then combines the knowledge along with link(@b,c,2) to derive cost(@c,d,b,5) and communicates it to c.

3.4 Constraints and 'maybe' rules

We now introduce two extensions to the provenance graph. The first extension is a second type of rule, called a *'maybe' rule* and written $\tau@n \xleftarrow{maybe} \tau_1@n_1 \land \ldots \land \tau_k@n_k$, which stipulates that the tuple τ on node n *may* be derived from tuples $\tau_1@n_1, \ldots, \tau_k@n_k$, but that the derivation is optional. In other words, as long as all of the underlying tuples are present, node n is free to decide whether or not to derive τ, and it is free to change its decision while the underlying tuples still exist. The rule merely describes τ's provenance if and when it exists.

There are at least two situations in which 'maybe' rules are useful. The first involves a node on which some rules or tuples are confidential. In this case, the node can be assigned *two* sets of rules: one full set for the actual computation (without 'maybe' rules) and another to define provenance, in which the confidential computation is replaced by 'maybe' rules. The second set can then be safely revealed to queriers. Another situation involves a node with a black-box computation, for which only the general dependencies are known. For example, a node n might choose a tuple τ from a set of other tuples, but the details of the decision process might

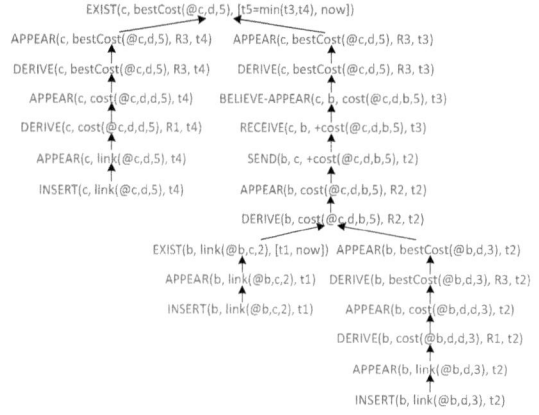

Figure 2: **Provenance of** bestCost(@c,d,5) **at** c

not be known (e.g., because it is performed by a third-party binary). In this case, 'maybe' rules can be used to infer provenance by observing the set of tuples: if all the τ_i exist, we cannot predict whether τ will appear, but if τ *does* appear, it must have been derived from the τ_i.

The second extension is intended for applications where the presence of *constraints* prevents us from modeling the state as completely independent tuples. For example, given tuples α and β, an application might derive *either* a tuple γ or a tuple δ, but not both. Modeling this with disjunctive rules would lose important information: if tuple δ replaces tuple γ, the appearance of δ and the disappearance of γ are not merely independent events, they are causally related. Thus, the explanation of δ's appearance should include the disappearance of γ. In G, we represent this by a direct edge between the corresponding APPEAR and DISAPPEAR vertices.

3.5 Graph construction

Conceptually, we can think of the provenance graph $G(e)$ as being constructed incrementally as the execution e unfolds – each new derivation, tuple insertion or deletion, or message transmission/arrival causes some new vertices to be added and/or existing BELIEVE and EXIST vertices to be updated. In practice, our implementation does not store the vertices and edges themselves; rather, it records only enough information to securely construct the subgraphs of $G(e)$ that are relevant to a given query.

The extended version of this paper [50] specifies an algorithm that computes $G(e)$ for any execution e. We do not present this algorithm here due to lack of space, but we briefly state three of its key properties. The first property says that the graph can be constructed incrementally:

Theorem 1 *If an execution e_1 is a prefix of an execution e_2, then $G(e_1)$ is a subgraph of $G(e_2)$.*

This holds because, at least conceptually, $G(e)$ contains vertices and edges for all tuples that have ever existed; vertices can be added but not removed. (Of course, our practical implementation has only limited storage and must eventually 'forget' about old vertices and edges.) Theorem 1 makes it possible to answer queries while the system is still running, without risking an inaccurate result. Graph construction is also compositional:

Theorem 2 *To construct the vertices $v \in V(e)$ with HOST$(v) = i$, it is sufficient to run the algorithm on the events that have occurred on i.*

Briefly, this holds because G has been carefully designed to be partitionable by nodes, and because derivations from remote tuples (which span multiple nodes) have been split into several steps that can each be attributed to a specific node. Compositionality is crucial for a scalable implementation because it implies that each node's subgraph of G can be reconstructed independently. Thus, we need only reconstruct those subgraphs that are relevant for a given query.

Finally, the graph construction algorithm uses the colors appropriately:

Theorem 3 *All the vertices v in $G(e)$ with* HOST$(v) = i$ *are black if, and only if, i is correct in e.*

Thus, if we encounter a red vertex in the provenance graph, we know that the corresponding node is faulty or has misbehaved. The proofs for these theorems are included in [50].

4. SECURE NETWORK PROVENANCE

The definition of the provenance graph G in the previous section assumes that, at least conceptually, the entire execution e of the primary system is known. However, in a distributed system without trusted components, no single node can have this information, especially when nodes are faulty and can tell lies. In this section, we define SNP, which constructs an approximation G_ν of the 'true' provenance graph G that is based on information available to correct nodes.

4.1 Using evidence to approximate G

Although each node can observe only its own local events, nodes can use messages from other nodes as *evidence* to reason about events on these nodes. Since we have assumed that messages can be authenticated, each received message m is evidence of its own transmission. In addition, we can demand that nodes attach some additional information $\varphi(m)$, such as an explanation for the transmission of m. Thus, when a provenance query is issued on a correct node, that node can collect some evidence ϵ, such as messages it has locally received, and/or messages collected from other nodes. It can then use this evidence to construct an approximation $G_\nu(\epsilon)$ of $G(e)$, from which the query can be answered. For the purposes of this section, we will assume that $\varphi(m)$ describes the sender's entire execution prefix, i.e., all of its local events up to and including the transmission of m. Of course, this would be completely impractical; our implementation in Section 5 achieves a similar effect in a more efficient way.

4.2 Limitations

When faulty nodes are present, we cannot always guarantee that $G_\nu(\epsilon) = G(e)$. There are four fundamental reasons for this. First, $\varphi(m)$ can be incorrect; for example, a faulty node can tell lies about its local inputs. As a human investigator, Alice may be able to recognize such lies (so there is still value in displaying all the available information), but it is not possible to detect them automatically, since nodes cannot observe each other's inputs. Thus, the corresponding vertices do not appear red in G_ν. Note, however, that a faulty node cannot lie arbitrarily; for example, it cannot forge messages from other nodes.

Second, $\varphi(m)$ can be incomplete. For example, if two faulty nodes secretly exchange messages but otherwise act normally, we cannot guarantee that these messages will appear in G_ν because the correct nodes cannot necessarily obtain any evidence about them. We *can*, however, be sure that

detectable faults [16] are represented in the graph. Briefly, a detectable fault is one that directly or indirectly affects a correct node through a message, or a chain of messages. Recall that, in our motivating scenario, we have assumed that Alice has observed some symptom of the fault; any fault of this type is detectable by definition.

Third, faulty nodes can equivocate, i.e., there can be two messages m_1 and m_2 such that $\varphi(m_1)$ is inconsistent with $\varphi(m_2)$. If a correct node encounters both m_1 and m_2, it can detect the inconsistency, but it is not clear which of them (if any) is correct and should appear in G_ν. One approach is to liberally use the color red for each vertex that is involved in an inconsistency. However, this can lead to an excessive amount of red coloring on equivocating nodes, which limits the usefulness of G_ν. Another approach, which we adopt here, is to arbitrarily accept one of the explanations as true, e.g., the one that appears first in ϵ, and to allow black for the corresponding vertices. Alice can influence this choice by reordering the messages in ϵ.

Finally, if φ is evaluated on demand, $\varphi(m)$ can be unavailable. For example, a correct node that is trying to evaluate a provenance query on ϵ might ask the sender of some $m \in \epsilon$ for $\varphi(m)$ but might not receive a response. This situation is ambiguous and does not necessarily indicate a fault – for example, the queried node could be slow, or the response could be delayed in the network – so it is not a good basis on which to color a vertex red. However, the only way to avoid it reliably would be to proactively attach $\varphi(m)$ to every message, which would be prohibitively expensive. Instead, SNP uses a third color (yellow) for vertices whose color is not yet known. Yellow vertices turn black or red when the response arrives. If a vertex v remains yellow, this is a sign that HOST(v) is refusing to respond and is therefore faulty.

4.3 Definition: SNP

We say that an approximation G_ν of G is *monotonic* if $G_\nu(\epsilon)$ is a subgraph of $G_\nu(\epsilon + \epsilon')$ for additional evidence ϵ'. This is an important property because it prevents G_ν from changing fundamentally once additional evidence becomes available, which could invalidate responses to earlier queries.

We define *secure network provenance (SNP)* to be a monotonic approximation G_ν of a provenance graph G that has the following two properties in an untrusted setting. G_ν is *accurate* if it faithfully reproduces all the vertices on correct nodes; in other words, if a vertex v on a correct node appears in $G_\nu(\epsilon)$ then v must also exist in G, be colored black, and have the same predecessors and successors. G_ν is *complete* if, given sufficient evidence ϵ from the correct nodes, a) each vertex in G on a correct node also appears in $G_\nu(\epsilon)$, and b) for each detectably faulty node, $G_\nu(\epsilon)$ contains at least one red or yellow vertex.

We also define a primitive called MICROQUERY that can be used to navigate a SNP graph.[1] MICROQUERY has two arguments: a vertex v, and evidence ϵ such that $v \in G_\nu(\epsilon)$. MICROQUERY returns one or two *color notifications* of the form BLACK(v), YELLOW(v), or RED(v). If two notifications are returned, the first one must be YELLOW(v). MICROQUERY can also return two sets P_v and S_v that contain the predecessors and successors of v in $G_\nu(\epsilon)$, respectively. Each set consists of elements (v_i, ϵ_i), where ϵ_i is additional evidence such that v_i and the edge between v_i and v appear

---

[1] MICROQUERY returns a single vertex; provenance queries must invoke it repeatedly to explore G_ν. Hence the name.

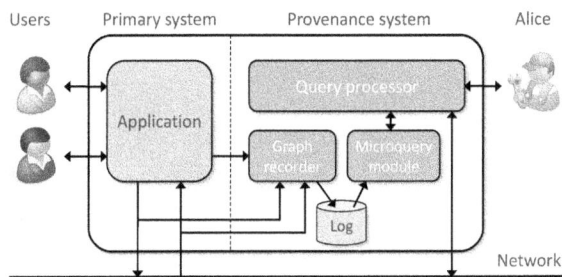

Figure 3: Architecture of a single SNOOPY node

in $G_\nu(\epsilon + \epsilon_i)$; this makes it possible to explore all of G_ν by invoking MICROQUERY recursively. We also require that MICROQUERY preserve accuracy, that is, if HOST(v) is correct, it must return BLACK(v), as well as P_v and S_v.

4.4 Discussion

MICROQUERY is sufficient to achieve the goals we stated in Section 2. Any system behavior that Alice can observe (such as derivations, messages, or extant tuples) corresponds to some vertex v in the provenance graph. Alice can then recursively invoke MICROQUERY to learn the causes or effects of v. To learn the causes of v, Alice can start at v and navigate the graph backwards until she arrives at the legitimate root causes (i.e., base tuples) or at some vertex that is colored red. To learn the effects of v, Alice can navigate the graph in the forward direction. The completeness of SNP ensures that, when a detectable fault has occurred, even an adversary cannot prevent Alice from discovering it. The accuracy of SNP ensures that the adversary cannot cause Alice to believe that a correct node is faulty.

Note that, if v is a vertex on a faulty node, it is possible that MICROQUERY returns only YELLOW(v), and nothing else. This is a consequence of the final limitation from Section 4.2, and it can prevent Alice from identifying *all* faulty nodes, since she may not be able to navigate 'past' a yellow vertex. However, Alice can still discover that a fault exists, and she can identify at least one faulty or misbehaving node. At worst, this provides a starting point for a more detailed investigation by supplying evidence against the faulty node. If the faulty node is able to be repaired and its prior observable actions can be verified to conform to its expected behavior, then the node can be recolored black, and subsequent MICROQUERYs will identify whether faults exist(ed) on other nodes.

5. THE SNOOPY SYSTEM

We next present the design of SNOOPY, a system that implements secure network provenance for the provenance graph G that was defined earlier in Section 3.

5.1 Architecture

SNOOPY consists of three major building blocks: a *graph recorder*, a *microquery module*, and a *query processor* (Figure 3). The graph recorder extracts provenance information from the actions of the primary system (Section 5.3) and stores it in a tamper-evident log (Section 5.4). The microquery module (Section 5.5) uses the information in this log to implement MICROQUERY; it uses authenticators as a specific form of evidence.

The query processor accepts higher-level (macro) queries, such as simple provenance queries, but also causal, historical, or dynamic queries, and answers them by repeatedly invoking MICROQUERY to retrieve the relevant part of the provenance graph. In some primary systems, this graph can be very large; therefore, queries can be parametrized with a *scope k*, which causes the query processor to return only vertices that are within distance k of the queried vertex. For a discussion of scope in an actual usage scenario, see Section 7.3.

5.2 Assumptions and requirements

SNOOPY makes the following assumptions:

1. A message sent from one correct node to another is eventually received, if retransmitted sufficiently often;

2. Each node i has a certificate that securely binds a key-pair to the node's identity;

3. Nodes have access to a cryptographic hash function, and the signature of a correct node cannot be forged;

4. In the absence of an attack, messages are typically received within at most time T_{prop};

5. Each node has a local clock, and clocks are synchronized to within Δ_{clock};

6. Apart from the 'maybe' rules, the computation on each node is deterministic; and

7. Queriers are allowed to see any vertex and any edge in the provenance graph.

The first three assumptions are needed for the tamper-evident log. Assumption 2 prevents faulty nodes from changing their identity and from creating fictitious nodes; it could be satisfied by installing each node with a certificate that is signed by an offline CA. Assumption 3 is commonly assumed to hold for algorithms like RSA and SHA-1. The next two assumptions are for simplicity; there are ways to build tamper-evident logs without them [17]. Both T_{prop} and Δ_{clock} can be large, e.g., on the order of seconds. The sixth assumption is needed to efficiently store and verify the provenance graph; it is also required for certain BFT systems [6], and it can be enforced for different types of applications [17], including legacy binaries [13]. The final assumption was already discussed in Section 2.3.

5.3 Extracting provenance

To generate the provenance graph, SNOOPY must extract information about events from the application to which it is applied. Provenance extraction (or the more general problem of correlating changes to network state based on incoming/outgoing messages) is an ongoing area of active research [29, 30] that is largely orthogonal to the main focus of this paper. In SNOOPY, we have found the following three techniques useful for extracting provenance for the target applications that we have examined:

Method #1: Inferred provenance. SNOOPY can infer provenance by transparently tracking data dependencies as inputs flow through the system. Inferred provenance can be applied when the dependencies are already explicitly captured in the programming language. We have applied this method to a version of the Chord DHT written in a declarative language (Section 6.1).

Method #2: Reported provenance. Following the approach from [29], applications can explicitly call methods in

301

SNooPy to report data dependencies. This requires modifications to the source code; also, key parts of the application must be deterministic to enable the querier to verify that provenance was reported correctly. We have applied this method to the Hadoop MapReduce system (Section 6.2).

Method #3: External specification. When black-box applications cannot use either of the previous two approaches, SNooPy can rely on an external specification of how the application's outputs are derived from its inputs. SNooPy can then generate the provenance graph by observing the inputs and outputs. We have applied this method to the Quagga BGP daemon (Section 6.3).

5.4 Graph recorder

The graph recorder stores the extracted provenance information securely at runtime, so that it can later be used by the microquery module when a query is issued.

Recall from Section 3 that our provenance graph $G = (V, E)$ is designed so that each vertex $v \in V$ can be attributed to a specific node $\text{HOST}(v)$. Thus, we can partition the graph so that each $v \in V$ is stored on $\text{HOST}(v)$. To ensure accuracy, we must additionally keep evidence for each cross-node edge, i.e., $(v_1, v_2) \in E$ with $\text{HOST}(v_1) \neq \text{HOST}(v_2)$. Specifically, $\text{HOST}(v_1)$ must be able to prove that $\text{HOST}(v_2)$ has committed to v_2, and vice versa, so that each node can prove that its own vertex is legitimate, even if the other node is compromised. Finally, according to assumption 6, each node's subgraph of G is completely determined by its inputs, its outputs, and the behavior of its 'maybe' rules; hence, it is sufficient to store messages, changes to base tuples, and any (un)derivations that directly involve a 'maybe' rule. When necessary, the microquery module can reconstruct the node's subgraph of G from this information.

In the following, we will write $\sigma_i(x)$ to indicate a signature on x with i's private key, and $\pi_i(x, y)$ to indicate a check whether x is a valid signature on y with i's private key. $H(\cdot)$ stands for the hash function, and $||$ for concatenation.

Logs and authenticator sets: SNooPy's log is a simplified version of the log from PeerReview [17]. The log λ_i of a node i consists of entries of the form $e_k := (t_k, y_k, c_k)$, where t_k is a timestamp, y_k is an entry type, and c_k is some type-specific content. There are five types of entries: SND and RCV record messages, ACK records acknowledgments, and INS and DEL record insertions and deletions of base tuples and, where applicable, tuples derived from 'maybe' rules. Note that log entries are different from vertex types. Each entry is associated with a hash value $h_k = H(h_{k-1} || t_k || y_k || c_k)$ with $h_0 := 0$. Together, the h_k form a hash chain. A node i can issue an *authenticator* $a_k := (t_k, h_k, \sigma_i(t_k || h_k))$, which is a signed commitment that e_k (and, through the hash chain, $e_1, \ldots, e_{k-1}$) must exist in λ_i. Each node i stores the authenticators it receives from another node j in its *authenticator set* $U_{i,j}$.

Commitment: When a node i needs to send a message m (+τ or -τ) to another node j, it first appends a new entry $e_x := (t_x, \text{SND}, (m, j))$ to its local log. Then it sends $(m, h_{x-1}, t_x, \sigma_i(t_x || h_x))$ to j. When a node j receives a message (m, a, b, c), j calculates $h'_x := H(a || b || \text{SND} || (m, j))$ and then checks whether the authenticator is properly signed, i.e., $\pi_i(c, (b || h'_x))$, and whether t_x is within $\Delta_{\text{clock}} + \text{T}_{\text{prop}}$ of its local time. If not, j discards the message. Otherwise, j adds (t_x, h'_x, c) to its authentica-

tor set $U_{j,i}$, appends an entry $e_y := (k, \text{RCV}, (m, i, a, b, c))$ to λ_j, and sends $(\text{ACK}, t_x, h_{y-1}, t_y, \sigma_j(t_y || h_y))$ back to i.

Once i receives (ACK, a, b, c, d) from j, it first checks its log to see whether there is an entry $e_x = (a, \text{SND}, (m, j))$ in its log that has not been acknowledged yet. If not, it discards the message. i then calculates $h'_y := H(b || c || \text{RCV} || (m, i, h_{x-1}, t_x, \sigma_i(t_x || h_x)))$, and checks $\pi_j(d, (c || h'_y))$ and t_y is within $\Delta_{\text{clock}} + \text{T}_{\text{prop}}$ of its local time. If not, i discards the message. Otherwise, i adds (c, h'_y, d) to its authenticator set $U_{i,j}$ and appends an entry $e_z := (t, \text{ACK}, a, b, c, d)$ to its log.

If i does not receive a valid acknowledgment within $2 \cdot \text{T}_{\text{prop}}$, it immediately notifies the maintainer of the distributed system. Any such notification is a clear indication of a fault: at least one of i, j, or the connection between them must be faulty. Once the maintainer acknowledges the notification, the problem is known and can be ignored for the purposes of forensics. However, if the maintainer has *not* received a notification and a query later uncovers a SND without a matching ACK, SNooPy can color the corresponding SEND vertex red because the sender is clearly faulty. Without the notification mechanism, this situation would be ambiguous and could not be reliably attributed to i or j.

Retrieval: The graph recorder implements a primitive $\text{RETRIEVE}(v, a_k^i)$ which, when invoked on $i := \text{HOST}(v)$ with a vertex v and an authenticator a_k^i of i, returns the prefix[2] of the log in which v was generated. In essence, RETRIEVE implements the function φ from Section 4 but evaluates it on demand. Typically, the prefix RETRIEVE returns is the prefix authenticated by a_k^i, but if v is an EXIST or BELIEVE vertex that exists at e_k, the prefix is extended to either a) the point where v ceases to exist, or b) the current time. (The special case is necessary because an existing or believed tuple can be involved in further derivations between e_k and the time it disappears, so its vertex may acquire additional outbound edges.) If the prefix extends beyond e_k, i must also return a new authenticator that covers the entire prefix. A correct node can always comply with such a request.

5.5 Microquery module

The microquery module implements $\text{MICROQUERY}(v, \epsilon)$. At a high level, this works by 1) using ϵ to retrieve a log prefix from $\text{HOST}(v)$, 2) replaying the log to regenerate $\text{HOST}(v)$'s partition of the provenance graph G, and 3) checking whether v exists in it. If v exists and was derived correctly, its predecessors and successors are returned, and v is colored black; otherwise v is colored red.

More formally, the evidence for a vertex v is an authenticator from $\text{HOST}(v)$ that covers a log prefix in which v existed. When $\text{MICROQUERY}(v, \epsilon)$ is invoked on a node i, i first outputs $\text{YELLOW}(v)$ to indicate that v's real color is not yet known, and then invokes $\text{RETRIEVE}(v, \epsilon)$ on $j := \text{HOST}(v)$. If j returns a log prefix that matches ϵ, i replays the prefix to regenerate j's partial provenance subgraph $G_\nu(\epsilon) | j$. This is possible because we have assumed that the computation is deterministic. If $G_\nu(\epsilon) | j$ does not contain v or replay fails (i.e., the sent messages do not match the SEND entries in the log, a SEND does not have a matching ACK, or the authenticators in the RECV and ACK entries do not satisfy the conditions from Section 5.4), i outputs $\text{RED}(v)$; otherwise it outputs $\text{BLACK}(v)$ and returns the predecessors

---

[2] In practice, SNooPy usually does not return an entire prefix; see Section 5.6 for a list of optimizations.

and successors of v in $G_\nu(\epsilon)$. The additional evidence that is returned for a SEND predecessor and a RECEIVE successor consists of the authenticator from the RCV and ACK entries, respectively; the additional evidence for all other vertices is the authenticator returned by RETRIEVE, if any.

Consistency check: As described so far, the algorithm colors a vertex v red when HOST(v) does not have a correct 'explanation' (in the form of a log prefix), and it colors v yellow if HOST(v) does not return any explanation at all. The only remaining case is the one in which v's explanation is inconsistent with the explanation for one of its other vertices. To detect this, i performs the following check: it determines the interval I during which v existed during replay, and asks all nodes with which j could have communicated during I (or simply all other nodes) to return any authenticators that were a) signed by j, and b) have timestamps in I. If such authenticators are returned, i checks whether they are consistent with the log prefix it has retrieved earlier; if not, i outputs RED(v).

5.6 Optimizations

As described so far, each SNOOPY node cryptographically signs every single message and keeps its entire log forever, and each microquery retrieves and replays an entire log prefix. Most of the corresponding overhead can be avoided with a few simple optimizations. First, nodes can periodically record a checkpoint of their state in the log, which must include a) all currently extant or believed tuples and b) for each tuple, the time when it appeared. Thus, it is sufficient for MICROQUERY(v, ϵ) to retrieve the log segment that starts at the last checkpoint before v appeared, and start replay from there. Note that this does not affect correctness because, if a faulty node adds a nonexistent tuple τ to its checkpoint, this will be discovered when the corresponding EXIST or BELIEVE vertex is queried, since replay will then begin before the checkpoint and end after it. If the node omits an extant or believed tuple that affects a queried tuple, this will cause replay to fail.

Second, nodes can be required to keep only the log segment that covers the most recent T_{hist} hours in order to decrease storage costs. To speed up queries, the querier can cache previously retrieved log segments, authenticators, and even previously regenerated provenance graphs. As we show in Section 7, this reduces the overhead to a practical level.

Third, the overhead of the commitment protocol can be reduced by sending messages in batches. This can be done using a variant of Nagle's algorithm that was previously used in NetReview [14]: each outgoing message is delayed by a short time T_{batch}, and then processed together with any other messages that may have been sent to the same destination within this time window. Thus, the rate of signature generations/verifications is limited to $1/T_{batch}$ per destination, regardless of the number of messages. The cost is an increase in message latency by up to T_{batch}.

5.7 Correctness

Next, we argue that, given our assumptions from Section 5.2, SNOOPY provides secure network provenance as defined in Section 4.3—that is, monotonicity, accuracy, and completeness. For lack of space, we present only informal theorems and proof sketches here; the formal theorems and the proofs can be found in the extended version of this paper [50].

Theorem 4 SNOOPY *is monotonic: if ϵ is a set of valid authenticators and a_k^i a valid authenticator, $G_\nu(\epsilon)$ is a subgraph of $G_\nu(\epsilon + a_k^i)$.*

Proof sketch: There are four cases we must consider. First, the new authenticator a_k^i can be the first authenticator from node i that the querying node has seen. In this case, the querying node will RETRIEVE the corresponding log segment, replay it, and add the resulting vertices to G_ν. Since the graph construction is compositional, this can only add to the graph, and the claim holds. Second, a can belong to a log segment SNOOPY has previously retrieved; in this case, G_ν already contains the corresponding vertices and remains unchanged. Third, a can correspond to an extension of an existing log segment. In this case, the additional events are replayed and the corresponding vertices added, and the claim follows because the graph construction is compositional and incremental. Finally, a's log segment can be inconsistent with an existing segment; in this case, the consistency check will add a red SEND vertex to G_ν. □

Theorem 5 SNOOPY *is accurate: any vertex v on a correct node that appears in $G_\nu(\epsilon)$ must a) also appear in G, with the same predecessors and successors, and b) be colored black.*

Proof sketch: Claim a) follows fairly directly from the fact that $i :=$ HOST(v) is correct and will cooperate with the querier. In particular, i will return the relevant segment of its log, and since the graph construction is deterministic, the querier's replay of this log will faithfully reproduce a subgraph of G that contains v. Any predecessors or successors v' of v with HOST(v') $= i$ can be taken from this subgraph. This leaves the case where HOST(v') $\neq v$. If v' is a predecessor, then it must be a SEND vertex, and its existence can be proven with the authenticator from the corresponding SND entry in λ. Similarly, if v' is a successor, then it must be a RECV vertex, and the evidence is the authenticator in the corresponding ACK entry in λ.

Now consider claim b). Like all vertices, v is initially yellow, but it must turn red or black as soon as $i :=$ HOST(v) responds to the querier's invocation of RETRIEVE, which will happen eventually because i is correct. However, v can only turn red for a limited number of reasons—e.g., because replay fails, or because i is found to have tampered with its log—but each of these is related to some form of misbehavior and cannot have occurred because i is correct. Thus, since v cannot turn red and cannot remain yellow, it must eventually turn (and remain) black. □

Theorem 6 SNOOPY *is complete: given sufficient evidence ϵ from the correct nodes, a) each vertex in G on a correct node also appears in $G_\nu(\epsilon)$, and b) when some node is detectably faulty, recursive invocations of MICROQUERY will eventually yield a red or yellow vertex on a faulty node.*

Proof sketch: Claim a) follows if we simply choose ϵ to include the most recent authenticator from each correct node, which the querying node can easily obtain. Regarding claim b), the definition of a detectable fault implies the existence of a chain of causally related messages such that the fault is apparent from the first message and the last message m is received by a correct node j. We can choose v' to be the RECV vertex that represents m's arrival. Since causal relationships correspond to edges in G, G_ν must contain a path $v' \rightarrow^* v$. By recursively invoking MICROQUERY on v' and its predecessors, we retrieve a subgraph of G_ν that contains this path, so the vertices on the path are queried in turn. Now consider some vertex v'' along the path. When v'' is queried, we either obtain the next vertex on the path, along with valid evidence, or v'' must turn red or yellow. Thus, either this color appears before we reach v, or we eventually obtain evidence of v. □

5.8 Limitations

By design, SNooPy is a forensic system; it cannot actively detect faults, but rather relies on a human operator to spot the initial symptom of an attack, which can then be investigated using SNooPy. Investigations are limited to the part of the system that is being monitored by SNooPy. We do not currently have a solution for partial deployments, although it may be possible to use the approach adopted by NetReview [14] at the expense of slightly weaker guarantees. SNooPy also does not have any built-in redundancy; if the adversary sacrifices one of his nodes and destroys all the provenance state on it, some parts of the provenance graph may no longer be reachable via queries (though any disconnection points will be marked yellow in the responses). This could be mitigated by replicating each log on some other nodes, although, under our threat model, the problem cannot be avoided entirely because we have assumed that any set of nodes—and thus any replica set we may choose—could be compromised by the adversary. Finally, SNooPy does not provide negative provenance, i.e., it can only explain the existence of a tuple (or its appearance or disappearance), but not its absence. Negative provenance is known to be a very difficult problem that is actively being researched in the database community [28]. We expect that SNooPy can be enhanced to support negative provenance by incorporating recent results from this community.

5.9 Prototype implementation

We have built a SNooPy prototype based on components from ExSPAN [51] and PeerReview [17], with several modifications. We completely redesigned ExSPAN's provenance graph according to Section 3, added support for constraints and 'maybe' rules, and implemented the graph recorder and the microquery module. Unlike ExSPAN, the provenance graph is not maintained at runtime; rather, the prototype records just enough information to reconstruct relevant parts of the graph on demand when a query is issued. This is done using deterministic replay, but with additional instrumentation to capture provenance. Since auditing in SNooPy is driven by the forensic investigator, PeerReview's witnesses are not required, so we disabled this feature. It would not be difficult to connect the prototype to a visualizer for provenance graphs, e.g., VisTrails [45].

Macroqueries are currently expressed in *Distributed Datalog* (*DDlog*), a distributed query language for maintaining and querying network provenance graphs. All three methods from Section 5.3 for extracting provenance are supported: since the prototype is internally based on *DDlog*, it can directly infer provenance from any *DDlog* program, but it also contains hooks for reporting provenance, as well as an API for application-specific proxies.

6. APPLICATIONS

To demonstrate that SNooPy is practical, we have applied our prototype implementation to three existing applications, using a different provenance extraction method each time.

6.1 Application #1: Chord

To test SNooPy's support for native *DDlog* programs, we applied it to a declarative implementation [26] of the Chord distributed hash table that uses RapidNet [37]. There are several known attacks against DHTs, so this seems like an attractive test case for a forensic system. Since ExSPAN can automatically transform any *DDlog* program into an equivalent one that automatically reports provenance, and since RapidNet is already deterministic, no modifications were required to the Chord source code.

6.2 Application #2: Hadoop MapReduce

To test SNooPy's support for reported provenance, we applied it to Hadoop MapReduce [12]. We manually instrumented Hadoop to report provenance to SNooPy at the level of individual key-value pairs.

Our prototype considers input files to be base tuples. The provenance of an intermediate key-value pair consists of the arguments of the corresponding `map` invocation, and the provenance of an output consists of the arguments of the corresponding `reduce` invocation. The set of intermediate key-value pairs sent from a map task to a reduce task constitutes a message that must be logged; thus, if there are m map tasks and r reduce tasks, our prototype sends up to $2mr$ messages (a request and a response for each pair). To avoid duplication of the large data files, we apply a trivial optimization: rather than copying the files in their entirety into the log, we log their hash values, which is sufficient to authenticate them later during replay. Since we are mainly interested in tracking the provenance of key-value pairs, we treat inputs from the JobTracker as base tuples. It would not be difficult to extend our prototype to the JobTracker as well.

Individual `map` and `reduce` tasks are already deterministic in Hadoop, so replay required no special modifications. We did, however, add code to replay `map` and `reduce` tasks separately, as well as a switch for enabling provenance reporting (recall that this is only needed during replay). More specifically, we assign a unique identifier (UID) [19] to each of the input, output and intermediate tuples, based on its content and execution context (which indicates, for example, a tuple τ is an input of `map` task m). The Hadoop implementation is instrumented to automatically track *cross-stage* causalities. This is achieved by adding edges between corresponding vertices when tuples are communicated across stages (e.g. from a `map` output file to a reducer). For the causalities *within* a stage, users need to *report* them using a provided API, which takes as arguments the UID of the output tuple, the UIDs of the input tuples that contribute to the output, and the execution context. The reported provenance information is then passed to and maintained in the graph recorder.

Altogether, we added or modified less than 100 lines of Java code in Hadoop itself, and we added another 550 lines for the interface to SNooPy.

6.3 Application #3: Quagga

To test SNooPy's support for application-specific proxies, we applied it to the Quagga BGP daemon. BGP interdomain routing is plagued by a variety of attacks and malfunctions [32], so a secure provenance system seems useful for diagnostics and forensics. SNooPy could complement secure routing protocols such as S-BGP [40]: it cannot actively prevent routing problems from manifesting themselves, but it can investigate a wider range of problems, including route equivocation (i.e., sending conflicting route announcements to different neighbors), replaying of stale routes, and failure to withdraw a route, which are not addressed by S-BGP.

Rather than instrumenting Quagga for provenance and deterministic replay, we treated it as a 'black box' and implemented a small proxy that a) transparently intercepts Quagga's BGP messages and converts them into SNOOPY tuples, and b) converts incoming tuples back to BGP messages. The proxy uses a small *DDlog* specification of only four rules. The first rule specifies how announcements propagate between networks, and the next two express the constraint that a network can export at most one route to each prefix at any given time, as required by BGP. The fourth rule is a 'maybe' rule (Section 3.4); it stipulates that each route must either be originated by the network itself, or extend the path of a route that was previously advertised to it. Due to the 'maybe' rule, we did not need to model the details of Quagga's routing policy (which may be confidential); rather, the proxy can infer the essential dependencies between routes from the incoming and outgoing BGP messages it observes.

In addition to the four rules, we wrote 626 lines of code for the proxy. Much of this code is generic and could be reused for other black-box applications. We did not modify any code in Quagga.

6.4 Summary

Our three application prototypes demonstrate that SNOOPY can be applied to different types of applications with relatively little effort. Our prototypes cover all three provenance extraction methods described in Section 5.3. Moreover, the three applications generate different amounts of communication, process different amounts of data, have different scalability requirements, etc., so they enable us to evaluate SNOOPY across a range of scenarios.

7. EVALUATION

In this section, we evaluate SNOOPY using our three applications in five different scenarios. Since we have already proven that SNOOPY correctly provides secure network provenance, we focus mostly on overheads and performance. Specifically, our goal is to answer the following high-level questions: a) can SNOOPY answer useful forensic queries? b) how much overhead does SNOOPY incur at runtime? and c) how expensive is it to ask a query?

7.1 Experimental setup

We examine SNOOPY's performance across five application configurations: a Quagga routing daemon (version 0.99.16) deployment, two Chord installations (derived from Rapid-Net [37] v0.3), and two Hadoop clusters (version 0.20.2).

Our **Quagga** experiment is modeled after the setup used for NetReview [14]. We instantiated 35 unmodified Quagga daemons, each with the SNOOPY proxy from Section 6.3, on an Intel machine running Linux 2.6. The daemons formed a topology of 10 ASes with a mix of tier-1 and small stub ASes, and both customer/provider and peering relationships. The internal topology was a full iBGP mesh. To ensure that both the BGP traffic and the routing table sizes were realistic, we injected approximately 15,000 updates from a RouteViews [39] trace. The length of the trace, and thus

the duration of the experiment, was 15 minutes. In all experiments, each node was configured with a 1,024-bit RSA key.

We evaluated the Chord prototype (Section 6.1) in two different configurations: **Chord-Small** contains 50 nodes and **Chord-Large** contains 250 nodes. The experiments were performed in simulation, with stabilization occurring every 50 seconds, optimized finger fixing every 50 seconds, and keep-alive messages every 10 seconds. Each simulation ran for 15 minutes of simulated time.

In the **Hadoop-Small** experiment, we ran the prototype described in Section 6.2 on 20 c1.medium instances on Amazon EC2 (in the us-east-1c region). The program we used (WordCount) counts the number of occurrences of each word in a 1.2 GB Wikipedia subgraph from WebBase [46]. We used 20 mappers and 10 reducers; the total runtime was about 79 seconds. Our final experiment, **Hadoop-Large**, used 20 c1.medium instances with 165 mappers, 10 reducers, and a 10.3 GB data set that consisted of the same Wikipedia data plus the 12/2010 Newspapers crawl from WebBase [46]; the runtime for this was about 255 seconds.

Quagga, Chord, and Hadoop have different characteristics that enable us to study SNOOPY under varying conditions. For instance, Quagga and Chord have small messages compared to Hadoop, while Quagga has a large number of messages. In terms of rate of system change, Quagga has the highest, with approximately 1,350 route updates per minute. In all experiments, the actual replay during query evaluation was carried out on an Intel 2.66GHz machine running Linux with 8GB of memory.

7.2 Example queries

To evaluate SNOOPY's ability to perform a variety of forensic tasks as well as to measure its query performance, we tested SNOOPY using the following provenance queries, each of which is motivated by a problem or an attack that has been previously reported in the literature:

Quagga-Disappear is a dynamic query that asks why an entry from a routing table has disappeared. In our scenario, the cause is the appearance of an alternative route in another AS j, which replaces the original route in j but, unlike the original route, is filtered out by j's export policy. This is modeled after a query motivated in Teixeira *et al.* [44]; note that, unlike Omni, SNOOPY works even when nodes are compromised. **Quagga-BadGadget** query asks for the provenance of a 'fluttering' route; the cause is an instance of BadGadget [11], a type of BGP configuration problem.

Chord-Lookup is a historical query that asks which nodes and finger entries were involved in a given DHT lookup, and **Chord-Finger** returns the provenance of a given finger table entry. Together, these two queries can detect an Eclipse attack [42], in which the attacker gains control over a large fraction of the neighbors of a correct node, and is then able to drop or reroute messages to this node and prevent correct overlay operation.

Hadoop-Squirrel asks for the provenance of a given key-value pair in the output; for example, if WordCount produces the (unlikely) output (`squirrel,10000`) to indicate that the word 'squirrel' appeared 10,000 times in the input, this could be due to a faulty or compromised mapper. Such queries are useful to investigate computation results on outsourced Cloud databases [34].

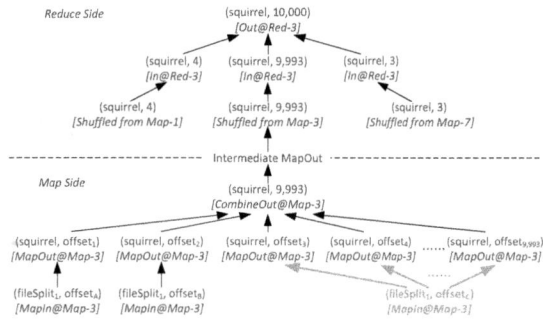

Figure 4: Example result of the Hadoop-Squirrel macroquery (in a simplified notation).

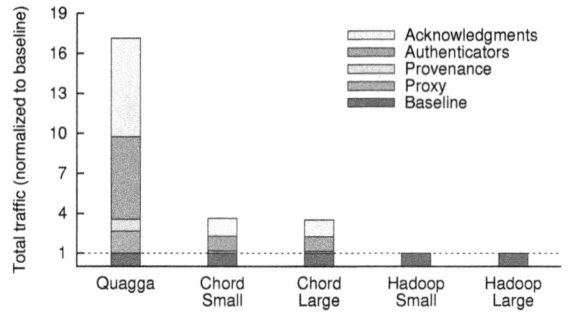

Figure 5: Network traffic with SNooPy, normalized to a baseline system without provenance.

7.3 Usability

In addition to the formal guarantees in Section 4, we also need to demonstrate that SNooPy is a useful forensic tool *in practice*. For this purpose, we executed each of the above queries twice – once on a correct system and once on a system into which we had injected a corresponding fault. Specifically, we created an instance of BadGadget in our Quagga setup, we modified a Chord node to mount an Eclipse attack by always returning its own ID in response to lookups, and we tampered with a Hadoop map worker to make it return inaccurate results. For all queries, SNooPy clearly identified the source of the fault.

To illustrate this, we examine one specific example in more detail. Figure 4 shows the output of the Hadoop-Squirrel macroquery in which one of the mappers (Map-3) was configured to misbehave: in addition to emitting (`word`, `offset`) tuples for each word in the text, it injected 9,991 additional (`squirrel`, `offset`) tuples (shown in red). A forensic analyst who is suspicious of the enormous prevalence of squirrels in this dataset can use SNooPy to query the provenance of the (`squirrel`, `10000`) output tuple. To answer this query, SNooPy selectively reconstructs the provenance subgraph of the corresponding reduce task by issuing a series of microqueries, one for each immediate predecessor of the (`squirrel`, `10000`) tuple, and then assembles the results into a response to the analyst's macroquery. Seeing that one mapper output 9,993 squirrels while the others only reported 3 or 4, she can 'zoom in' further by requesting the provenance of the (`squirrel`, `9993`) tuple, at which point SNooPy reconstructs the provenance subgraph of the corresponding map task. This reveals two legitimate occurrences and lots of additional bogus tuples, which are colored red.

Once the faulty tuples are identified, SNooPy can be used to determine their effects on the rest of the system, e.g., to identify other outputs that may have been affected by key-value pairs from the corrupted `map` worker.

In this example, the analyst repeatedly issues queries with a small scope and inspects the results before deciding which query to issue next. This matches the usage pattern of provenance visualization tools, such as VisTrails [5], which allow the analyst to navigate the provenance graph by expanding and collapsing vertices. The analyst could also use a larger scope directly, but this would cause more subgraphs to be reconstructed, and most of the corresponding work would be wasted because the analyst subsequently decides to investigate a different subtree.

7.4 Network traffic at runtime

SNooPy increases the network traffic of the primary system because messages must contain an authenticator and be acknowledged by the recipient. To quantify this overhead, we ran all five experiments in two configurations. In the *baseline* configuration, we ran the original Hadoop, Quagga, or declarative Chord in RapidNet with no support for provenance. In the SNooPy-enabled prototype, we measured the additional communication overhead that SNooPy adds to the baseline, broken down by cause, i.e., authenticators, acknowledgments, provenance, and proxy.

Figure 5 shows the SNooPy results, normalized to the baseline results. The overhead ranges between a factor of 16.1 for Quagga and 0.2% for Hadoop. The differences are large because SNooPy adds a fixed number of bytes for each message – 22 bytes for a timestamp and a reference count, 156 bytes for an authenticator, and 187 bytes for an acknowledgment. Since the average message size is small for Quagga (68 bytes) and very large for Hadoop (1.08 MB), the relative overhead for Quagga is higher, although in absolute terms, the Quagga traffic is still low (78.2 Kbps with SNooPy). Chord messages are 145 bytes on average, and hence its overhead factor is in between Quagga and Hadoop.

The relative overhead of the Quagga proxy is high in part because, unlike the original BGP implementation in Quagga, the proxy does not combine BGP announcements and (potentially multiple) withdrawals into a single message. However, the overhead can be reduced by enabling the message batching optimization from Section 5.6. With a window size of $T_{batch} = 100$ ms, the number of messages decreases by more than 80%, and the normalized overhead drops from 16.1 to 4.8, at the expense of delaying messages by up to T_{batch}.

In summary, SNooPy adds a constant number of bytes to each message. Thus, the absolute overhead depends on how many messages the primary system sends. The relative increase in network traffic depends on the primary system's average message size.

7.5 Storage

Each SNooPy node requires some local storage for the graph recorder's log. Since the microquery module uses deterministic replay to partially reconstruct the provenance graph on demand, we should generally expect the log to be at least as large as a replay log, although SNooPy can sometimes save space by referencing data that is already kept for other

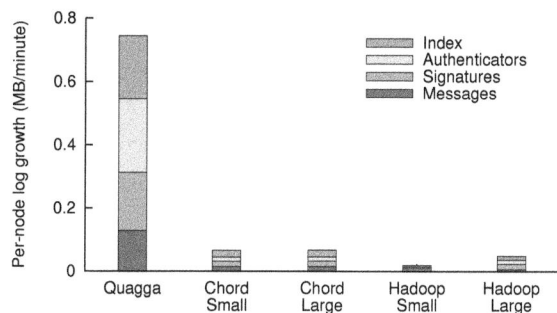

Figure 6: Per-node log growth in SNOOPY, excluding checkpoints.

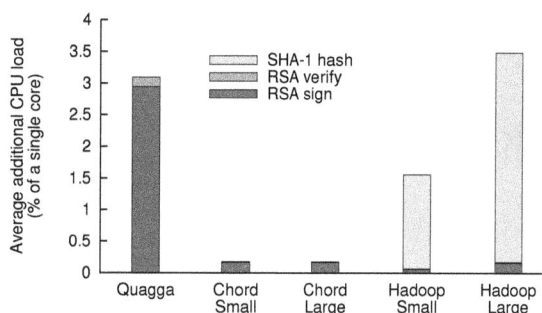

Figure 7: Additional CPU load for generating and verifying signatures, and for hashing.

reasons. To quantify the incremental storage cost, we ran our five experiments in the SNOOPY configuration, and we measured the size of the resulting logs.

Figure 6 shows the average amount of log data that each node produced per minute, excluding checkpoints. In absolute terms, the numbers are relatively low; they range from 0.066 MB/min (Chord-Small) to 0.74 MB/min (Quagga). We expect that most forensic queries will be about fairly recent events, e.g., within one week. To store one week's worth of data, each node would need between 7.3 GB (Quagga) and 665 MB (Chord-Small). Note that, in contrast to proactive detection systems like PeerReview [17], this data is merely archived locally at each node and is only sent over the network when a query is issued. Also, it should be possible to combine SNOOPY with state-of-the-art replay techniques such as ODR [1], which produce very small logs.

The log contains copies of all received messages (for Hadoop, references to files), authenticators for each sent and received message, and acknowledgments. Thus, log growth depends both on the number of messages and their size distribution. As a result, Figure 6 shows that log growth was fastest for Quagga, given that its baseline system generates the largest number of messages. In the case of Hadoop, our proxy benefits from the fact that Hadoop already retains copies of the input files unless the user explicitly deletes them. Thus, the proxy can save space by merely referencing these files from the log, and the *incremental* storage cost is extremely low (less than 0.1 MB/minute). The size of the input files was 1.2 GB for Small and 10.3 GB for Large. If these files were not retained by Hadoop, they would have to be copied to the log.

As described in Section 5.6, SNOOPY can additionally keep checkpoints of the system state. The size of a typical checkpoint is 25 kB for Chord and 64 MB for Quagga. Since replay starts at checkpoint, more checkpoints result in faster queries but consume more space. For Hadoop, the equivalent of a checkpoint is to keep the intermediate files that are produced by the Map tasks, which requires 207 MB for Small and 682 MB for Large.

7.6 Computation

We next measured the computation cost imposed by SNOOPY. We expect the cost to be dominated by signature generation and verification and, in the case of Hadoop, hashing the input and output files (see Section 6.2). To verify this, we used `dstat` to measure the overall CPU utilization of a Quagga node with and without the SNOOPY proxy; the

log and the checkpoints were written to a RAM disk to isolate computation from I/O overhead. Our results show an average utilization of 5.4% of one core with SNOOPY, and 0.9% without. As expected, more than 70% of the overhead can be explained by the cost of signature generation and verification alone (in our setup, 1.3 ms and 66 μs per 1,024-bit signature); the rest is due to the proxy logic.

To get a more detailed breakdown of the crypto overhead in our three applications, we counted the number of crypto operations in each configuration, and we multiplied the counts with the measured cost per operation to estimate the average additional CPU load they cause. As our results in Figure 7 show, the average additional CPU load is below 4% for all three applications. For Quagga and Chord, the increase is dominated by the signatures, of which two are required for each message – one for the authenticator and the other for the acknowledgment. Hadoop sends very few messages (one from each mapper to each reducer) but handles large amounts of data, which for SNOOPY must be hashed for commitment. Note that we do not include I/O cost for the hashed data because the data would have been written by the unmodified Hadoop as well; SNOOPY merely adds a SHA-1 hash operation, which can be performed on-the-fly as the data is written.

The message batching optimization from Section 5.6 can be used to reduce the CPU load. To evaluate this, we performed an additional experiment with Quagga, and we found that a window size of $T_{batch} = 100$ ms reduced the total number of signatures by a factor of six. Message batching also prevents the CPU load from spiking during message bursts, since it limits the rate at which signatures are generated to at most $1/T_{batch}$ per destination.

7.7 Query performance

Next, we evaluate how quickly SNOOPY can answer queries, and how much data needs to be downloaded. Since the answer depends on the query, we performed several different queries in different systems. For each query, we measured a) how much data (log segments, authenticators, and checkpoints) was downloaded, b) how long it took to verify the log against the authenticators, and c) how much time was needed to replay the log and to extract the relevant provenance subgraph. Figure 8 shows our results. Note that the query turnaround time includes an estimated download time, based on an assumed download speed of 10 Mbps.

The results show that both the query turnaround times and the amount of data downloaded can vary consider-

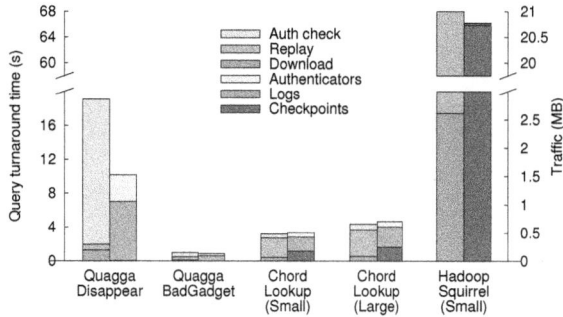

Figure 8: Query turnaround time (left bar) and data downloaded to answer the query (right bar).

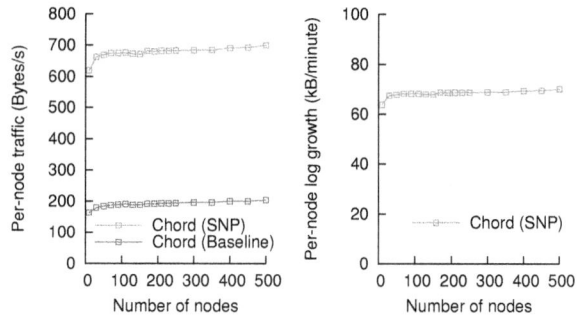

Figure 9: Scalability for Chord: Total traffic (left) and log size (right)

ably with the query. The Chord and Quagga-BadGadget queries were completed in less than five seconds; the Quagga-Disappear query took 19 seconds, of which 14 were spent verifying partial checkpoints using a Merkle Hash Tree; and the Hadoop-Squirrel query required 68 seconds, including 51 for replay. The download varied between 133 kB for Quagga-BadGadget and 20.8 MB for Hadoop-Squirrel. The numbers for Hadoop are larger because our prototype does not create checkpoints *within* map or reduce tasks, and so must replay a node's entire task to reconstruct a vertex on that node. Fine-grained checkpoints could be added but would require more changes to Hadoop. Generally, there is a tradeoff between storage and query performance: finer-grained checkpoints require more storage but reduce the size of the log segments that need to be downloaded and replayed.

In summary, the downloads and query turnaround times vary between queries but generally seem low enough to be practical for interactive forensics.

7.8 Scalability

In our final experiment, we examine how SNOOPY's overhead scales with the number of nodes N. We ran our Chord experiment with a range of different system sizes between $N = 10$ and $N = 500$ nodes, and we measured two of the main overheads, traffic and log size, for each N. Figure 9 shows our results, plus the baseline traffic for comparison.

The results show that both overheads increase only slowly with the system size. This is expected because, as discussed in Sections 7.4 and 7.5, the overhead is a function of the number and size of the messages sent. If the per-node traffic of the application did not depend on N, the runtime overhead would not depend on N either; however, recall that Chord's traffic increases with $O(\log N)$, as illustrated here by the baseline traffic results, so the SNOOPY overheads in this experiment similarly grow with $O(\log N)$.

Note the contrast to accountability systems like PeerReview [17] where the overhead itself grows with the system size. This is because PeerReview uses witnesses to ensure that each pair of authenticators from a given node is seen by at least one correct node. SNOOPY relies on the querier's node for this property (see Section 5.5) and, as a forensic system, it does not audit proactively.

In summary, SNOOPY does not reduce the scalability of the primary system; its per-node overheads mainly depend upon the number of messages sent.

7.9 Summary

SNOOPY's runtime costs include a fixed-size authenticator and acknowledgment for each message, processing power to generate and verify the corresponding signatures, and storage space for a per-node log with enough information to reconstruct that node's recent execution. Some part of the log needs to be downloaded and replayed when a query is issued. In the three different applications we evaluated, these costs are low enough to be practical. We have also described several example queries that can be used to investigate attacks previously reported in the literature, and we have demonstrated that SNOOPY can answer them within a few seconds.

8. RELATED WORK

Debugging and forensics: The main difference between SNP and existing forensic systems is that SNP does not require trust in any components on the compromised nodes. For example, Backtracker [21, 22] and PASS [29] require a trusted kernel, cooperative ReVirt [3] a trusted VMM, and A2M [7] trusted hardware. ForNet [41] and NFA [48] assume a trusted infrastructure and collaboration across domains. Other systems, such as the P2 debugger [43], ExSPAN [51], Magpie [2], D3S [25], QI [33], Friday [9], and Pip [38] are designed to diagnose non-malicious faults, such as bugs or race conditions. When nodes have been compromised by an adversary, these systems can return incorrect results.

Accountability: Systems like PeerReview [17] and NetReview [14] can automatically detect when a node deviates from the algorithm it is expected to run. Unlike SNP, these systems cannot detect problems that arise from interactions between multiple nodes, such as BadGadget [11] in interdomain routing, or problems that are related to inputs or unspecified aspects of the algorithm. Also, accountability systems merely report that a node is faulty, whereas SNP also offers support for diagnosing faults and for assessing their effects on other nodes.

Fault tolerance: An alternative approach to the problem of Byzantine faults is to mask their effects, e.g., using techniques like PBFT [6]. Unlike SNP, these techniques require a high degree of redundancy and a hard bound on the number of faulty nodes, typically one third of the total. The two approaches are largely complementary and could be combined.

Proofs of misbehavior: Many systems that are designed to handle non-crash faults internally use proofs of misbehavior, such as the signed confessions in Ngan *et al.* [31], a set of conflicting tickets in SHARP [8], or the POM message in Zyzzyva [23]. In SNP, any evidence that creates a red vertex in G_ν essentially constitutes a proof of misbehavior, but SNP's evidence is more general because it proves misbehavior with respect to the (arbitrary) primary system, rather than with respect to SNP or its implementation, e.g., SNOOPY. Systems like PeerReview [17] can generate protocol-independent evidence as well, but, unlike SNP's evidence, PeerReview's evidence is not diagnostic: it only shows that a node is faulty, but not what went wrong.

Network provenance: Systems like ExSPAN [51] describe the history and derivations of network state that results from the execution of a distributed protocol. SNP extends network provenance to adversarial environments, and enhances the traditional notion of network provenance by adding support for dynamic provenance and historical queries. The support for historical queries includes some features from an earlier workshop paper [49].

Secure provenance: McDaniel *et al.* [27] outlines requirements for secure network provenance, emphasizing the need for provenance to be tamper-proof and non-repudiable. Sprov [18] implements secure chain-structured provenance for individual documents; however, it lacks essential features that are required in a distributed system, e.g., a consistency check to ensure that nodes are processing messages in a way that is consistent with their current state. Pedigree [36] captures provenance at the network layer in the form of per-packet *tags* that store a history of all nodes and processes that manipulated the packet. It assumes a trusted environment, and its set-based provenance is less expressive compared to SNP's graph-based dependency structure.

9. CONCLUSION

This paper introduces secure network provenance (SNP), a technique for securely constructing network provenance graphs in untrusted environments with Byzantine faults. SNP systems can help forensic analysts by answering questions about the causes and effects of specific system states. Since faulty nodes can tell lies or suppress information, SNP systems cannot always determine the exact provenance of a given system state, but they can approximate it and give strong, provable guarantees on the quality of the approximation.

SNOOPY, our implementation of a SNP system, can query not only the provenance of an extant state, but also the provenance of a past state or a state change, which should be useful in a forensic setting. For this, it relies on a novel, SNP-enabled provenance graph that has been augmented with additional vertex types to capture the necessary information. To demonstrate that SNP and SNOOPY are general, we have evaluated a SNOOPY prototype with three different example applications: the Quagga BGP daemon, a declarative implementation of Chord, and Hadoop MapReduce. Our results show that the costs vary with the application but are low enough to be practical.

Acknowledgments

We thank our shepherd, Petros Maniatis, and the anonymous reviewers for their comments and suggestions. We also thank Joe Hellerstein, Bill Marczak, Clay Shields, and Atul Singh for helpful comments on earlier drafts of this paper. This work was supported by NSF grants IIS-0812270, CNS-0845552, CNS-1040672, CNS-1054229, CNS-1064986, CNS-1065130, AFOSR MURI grant FA9550-08-1-0352, and DARPA SAFER award N66001-11-C-4020. Any opinions, findings, and conclusions or recommendations expressed herein are those of the authors and do not necessarily reflect the views of the funding agencies.

10. REFERENCES

[1] G. Altekar and I. Stoica. ODR: Output-deterministic replay for multicore debugging. In *Proc. ACM Symposium on Operating Systems Principles (SOSP)*, Oct. 2009.

[2] P. Barham, A. Donnelly, R. Isaacs, and R. Mortier. Using Magpie for request extraction and workload modelling. In *Proc. USENIX Symposium on Operating System Design and Implementation (OSDI)*, Dec. 2004.

[3] M. Basrai and P. M. Chen. Cooperative ReVirt: adapting message logging for intrusion analysis. Technical Report University of Michigan CSE-TR-504-04, Nov 2004.

[4] P. Buneman, S. Khanna, and W.-C. Tan. Why and where: A characterization of data provenance. In *Proc. International Conference on Database Theory (ICDT)*, Jan. 2001.

[5] S. Callahan, J. Freire, E. Santos, C. Scheidegger, C. Silva, and H. Vo. VisTrails: Visualization meets data management. In *Proc. ACM SIGMOD Conference*, June 2006.

[6] M. Castro and B. Liskov. Practical Byzantine fault tolerance and proactive recovery. *ACM Transactions on Computer Systems (TOCS)*, 20(4):398–461, 2002.

[7] B.-G. Chun, P. Maniatis, S. Shenker, and J. Kubiatowicz. Attested append-only memory: Making adversaries stick to their word. In *Proc. ACM Symposium on Operating Systems Principles (SOSP)*, Oct. 2007.

[8] Y. Fu, J. Chase, B. Chun, S. Schwab, and A. Vahdat. SHARP: An architecture for secure resource peering. In *Proc. ACM Symposium on Operating Systems Principles (SOSP)*, Oct. 2003.

[9] D. Geels, G. Altekar, P. Maniatis, T. Roscoe, and I. Stoica. Friday: Global comprehension for distributed replay. In *Proc. USENIX Symp. on Networked Systems Design and Implementation (NSDI)*, Apr. 2007.

[10] T. J. Green, G. Karvounarakis, Z. G. Ives, and V. Tannen. Update exchange with mappings and provenance. In *Proc. International Conference on Very Large Data Bases (VLDB)*, Sept. 2007.

[11] T. G. Griffin, F. B. Shepherd, and G. Wilfong. The stable paths problem and interdomain routing. *IEEE/ACM Transactions on Networking (ToN)*, 10(2):232–243, Apr. 2002.

[12] Hadoop. http://hadoop.apache.org/.

[13] A. Haeberlen, P. Aditya, R. Rodrigues, and P. Druschel. Accountable virtual machines. In *Proc. USENIX Symposium on Operating System Design and Implementation (OSDI)*, Oct. 2010.

[14] A. Haeberlen, I. Avramopoulos, J. Rexford, and P. Druschel. NetReview: Detecting when interdomain routing goes wrong. In *Proc. USENIX Symposium on Networked Systems Design and Implementation (NSDI)*, Apr. 2009.

[15] A. Haeberlen and P. Kuznetsov. The Fault Detection Problem. In *Proc. Intl. Conference on Principles of Distributed Systems (OPODIS)*, Dec. 2009.

[16] A. Haeberlen, P. Kuznetsov, and P. Druschel. The case for Byzantine fault detection. In *Proc. Workshop on Hot Topics in System Dependability (HotDep)*, Nov. 2006.

[17] A. Haeberlen, P. Kuznetsov, and P. Druschel. PeerReview: Practical accountability for distributed systems. In *Proc. ACM Symposium on Operating Systems Principles (SOSP)*, Oct. 2007.

[18] R. Hasan, R. Sion, and M. Winslett. Preventing history forgery with secure provenance. *ACM Transactions on Storage (TOS)*, 5(4):1–43, 2009.

[19] R. Ikeda, H. Park, and J. Widom. Provenance for generalized map and reduce workflows. In *Proc. Conference on Innovative Data Systems Research (CIDR)*, Jan. 2011.

[20] B. Kauer. OSLO: Improving the security of Trusted Computing. In *Proc. 16th USENIX Security Symposium*, Aug 2007.

[21] S. T. King and P. M. Chen. Backtracking intrusions. *ACM Transactions on Computer Systems (TOCS)*, 23(1):51–76, 2005.

[22] S. T. King, Z. M. Mao, D. Lucchetti, and P. Chen. Enriching intrusion alerts through multi-host causality. In *Proc. Annual Network and Distributed Systems Security Symposium (NDSS)*, Feb. 2005.

[23] R. Kotla, L. A. M. Dahlin, A. Clement, and E. Wong. Zyzzyva: Speculative Byzantine fault tolerance. *ACM Trans. on Comp. Syst. (TOCS)*, 27(4), Dec. 2009.

[24] L. Lamport, R. Shostak, and M. Pease. The Byzantine generals problem. *ACM Trans. on Prog. Lang. and Systems (TOPLAS)*, 4(3):382–401, 1982.

[25] X. Liu, Z. Guo, X. Wang, F. Chen, X. Lian, J. Tang, M. Wu, M. F. Kaashoek, and Z. Zhang. D3S: debugging deployed distributed systems. In *Proc. USENIX Symposium on Networked Systems Design and Implementation (NSDI)*, Apr. 2008.

[26] B. T. Loo, T. Condie, M. Garofalakis, D. E. Gay, J. M. Hellerstein, P. Maniatis, R. Ramakrishnan, T. Roscoe, and I. Stoica. Declarative Networking. *CACM*, 2009.

[27] P. McDaniel, K. Butler, S. McLaughlin, R. Sion, E. Zadok, and M. Winslett. Towards a Secure and Efficient System for End-to-End Provenance. In *Proc. USENIX Workshop on the Theory and Practice of Provenance (TaPP)*, Feb. 2010.

[28] A. Meliou, W. Gatterbauer, K. M. Moore, and D. Suciu. The complexity of causality and responsibility for query answers and non-answers. In *Proc. International Conference on Very Large Data Bases (VLDB)*, Aug. 2011.

[29] K.-K. Muniswamy-Reddy, D. A. Holland, U. Braun, and M. Seltzer. Provenance-aware storage systems. In *Proc. USENIX Annual Technical Conference*, 2006.

[30] J. Newsome and D. Song. Dynamic taint analysis for automatic detection, analysis, and signature generation of exploits on commodity software. In *Proc. Annual Network and Distributed Systems Security Symposium (NDSS)*, Feb. 2005.

[31] T.-W. Ngan, D. Wallach, and P. Druschel. Enforcing fair sharing of peer-to-peer resources. In *Proc.*

International Workshop on Peer-to-Peer Systems (IPTPS), Feb. 2003.

[32] O. Nordstroem and C. Dovrolis. Beware of BGP attacks. *ACM Comp. Comm. Rev. (CCR)*, Apr 2004.

[33] A. J. Oliner and A. Aiken. A query language for understanding component interactions in production systems. In *Proc. International Conference on Supercomputing (ICS)*, June 2010.

[34] H. Pang and K.-L. Tan. Verifying Completeness of Relational Query Answers from Online Servers. *ACM Transactions on Information and System Security (TISSEC)*, 11:5:1–5:50, May 2008.

[35] Quagga Routing Suite. http://www.quagga.net/.

[36] A. Ramachandran, K. Bhandankar, M. Bin Tariq, and N. Feamster. Packets with provenance. Technical Report GT-CS-08-02, Georgia Tech, 2008.

[37] RapidNet. http://netdb.cis.upenn.edu/rapidnet/.

[38] P. Reynolds, C. Killian, J. L. Wiener, J. C. Mogul, M. A. Shah, and A. Vahdat. Pip: Detecting the unexpected in distributed systems. In *Proc. USENIX Symposium on Networked Systems Design and Implementation (NSDI)*, May 2006.

[39] RouteViews project. http://www.routeviews.org/.

[40] Secure BGP. http://www.ir.bbn.com/sbgp/.

[41] K. Shanmugasundaram, N. Memon, A. Savant, and H. Bronnimann. ForNet: A distributed forensics network. In *Proc. Intl. Workshop on Mathematical Methods, Models and Architectures for Computer Networks Security (MMM-ACNS)*, Sept. 2003.

[42] A. Singh, M. Castro, P. Druschel, and A. Rowstron. Defending against the Eclipse attack in overlay networks. In *Proc. ACM SIGOPS European Workshop*, Sept. 2004.

[43] A. Singh, P. Maniatis, T. Roscoe, and P. Druschel. Using queries for distributed monitoring and forensics. In *Proc. EuroSys Conference*, Apr. 2006.

[44] R. Teixeira and J. Rexford. A measurement framework for pin-pointing routing changes. In *Proc. SIGCOMM Network Troubleshooting Workshop*, Sep 2004.

[45] Vistrails. http://www.vistrails.org/.

[46] The Stanford WebBase Project. http://diglib.stanford.edu/~testbed/doc2/WebBase/.

[47] J. Widom. Trio: A system for integrated management of data, accuracy, and lineage. In *Proc. Conference on Innovative Data Systems Research (CIDR)*, Jan. 2005.

[48] Y. Xie, V. Sekar, M. Reiter, and H. Zhang. Forensic analysis for epidemic attacks in federated networks. In *Proc. IEEE International Conference on Network Protocols (ICNP)*, Nov. 2006.

[49] W. Zhou, L. Ding, A. Haeberlen, Z. Ives, and B. T. Loo. TAP: Time-aware provenance for distributed systems. In *Proc. USENIX Workshop on the Theory and Practice of Provenance (TaPP)*, June 2011.

[50] W. Zhou, Q. Fei, A. Narayan, A. Haeberlen, B. T. Loo, and M. Sherr. Secure network provenance. Technical Report MS-CIS-11-14, University of Pennsylvania, 2011. Available at http://snp.cis.upenn.edu/.

[51] W. Zhou, M. Sherr, T. Tao, X. Li, B. T. Loo, and Y. Mao. Efficient querying and maintenance of network provenance at Internet-scale. In *Proc. ACM SIGMOD Conference*, June 2010.

Fay: Extensible Distributed Tracing from Kernels to Clusters

Úlfar Erlingsson
Google Inc.*

Marcus Peinado
Microsoft Research
Extreme Computing Group

Simon Peter
ETH Zurich*
Systems Group

Mihai Budiu
Microsoft Research
Silicon Valley

ABSTRACT

Fay is a flexible platform for the efficient collection, processing, and analysis of software execution traces. Fay provides dynamic tracing through use of runtime instrumentation and distributed aggregation within machines and across clusters. At the lowest level, Fay can be safely extended with new tracing primitives, including even untrusted, fully-optimized machine code, and Fay can be applied to running user-mode or kernel-mode software without compromising system stability. At the highest level, Fay provides a unified, declarative means of specifying what events to trace, as well as the aggregation, processing, and analysis of those events.

We have implemented the Fay tracing platform for Windows and integrated it with two powerful, expressive systems for distributed programming. Our implementation is easy to use, can be applied to unmodified production systems, and provides primitives that allow the overhead of tracing to be greatly reduced, compared to previous dynamic tracing platforms. To show the generality of Fay tracing, we reimplement, in experiments, a range of tracing strategies and several custom mechanisms from existing tracing frameworks.

Fay shows that modern techniques for high-level querying and data-parallel processing of disaggregated data streams are well suited to comprehensive monitoring of software execution in distributed systems. Revisiting a lesson from the late 1960's [15], Fay also demonstrates the efficiency and extensibility benefits of using safe, statically-verified machine code as the basis for low-level execution tracing. Finally, Fay establishes that, by automatically deriving optimized query plans and code for safe extensions, the expressiveness and performance of high-level tracing queries can equal or even surpass that of specialized monitoring tools.

Categories and Subject Descriptors

D.4.8 [**Performance**]: Monitors; D.2.5 [**Software Engineering**]: Testing and Debugging—*Tracing*

General Terms

Design, Languages, Measurement, Experimentation, Performance

---

*Work done while at Microsoft Research Silicon Valley.

1. INTRODUCTION

Fay takes a new approach to the collection, processing, and analysis of software execution traces within a machine or across a cluster. The dictionary definition of Fay is "a fairy," as a noun, or "to join tightly or closely," as a verb. In our work, Fay is a comprehensive tracing platform that provides both expressive means for querying software behavior and also the mechanisms for the efficient execution of those queries. Our Fay platform implementation shows the appeal of the approach and can be applied to live, unmodified production systems running current x86-64 versions of Windows.

At its foundation, Fay provides highly-flexible, efficient mechanisms for the inline generation and general processing of trace events, via dynamic instrumentation and safe machine-code execution. These mechanisms allow pervasive, high-frequency tracing of functions in both kernel and user-mode address spaces to be applied dynamically, to executing binaries, without interruption in service. At the point of each trace event generation, Fay safely allows custom processing of event data and computation of arbitrary summaries of system state. Through safe execution of native machine code and through inline code invocation (not using hardware traps), Fay provides primitives with an order-of-magnitude less overhead than those of DTrace or SystemTap [11, 45].

At its topmost level, Fay provides a high-level interface to systems tracing where runtime behavior of software is modeled as a distributed, dynamically-generated dataset, and trace collection and analysis is modeled as a data-parallel computation on that dataset. This query interface provides a flexible, unified means for specifying large-scale tracing of distributed systems. High-level queries also allow the Fay platform to automatically optimize trace event collection and analysis in ways that often greatly reduce overhead.

Below is an example of a complete high-level Fay query that specifies both what to trace and also how to process and combine trace events from different CPUs, threads, and machines:

```
from io in cluster.Function("iolib!Read")
  where io.time < Now.AddMinutes(5)
  let size = io.Arg(2)    // request size in bytes
  group io by size/1024 into g
  select new { sizeInKilobytes = g.Key,
               countOfReadIOs = g.Count() };
```

This query will return, for an entire cluster of machines, an aggregate view over 5 minutes of the read sizes seen in a module `iolib`, for all uses of that module in user-mode or in the kernel. In our Fay implementation, such declarative queries are written in a form of LINQ [29]. From these queries, Fay automatically derives efficient code for distributed query execution, optimizing for factors such as early trace data aggregation and reduced network communication.

Fay can also be accessed through other, more traditional means. In particular, in our implementation, Fay can be used through scripts in the PowerShell system administration scripting language [55], as well as directly through standard command-line tools. However it is used, Fay retains the best features of prior tracing systems, such as efficient trace event collection, low overhead—proportional to tracing activity, and zero by default—and stateful *probes* that can process event data directly at a tracepoint. Fay also provides strong safety guarantees that allow probes to be extended in novel ways with new, high-performance primitives.

1.1 Implementation and Experience

For now, Fay has been implemented only for the current x86-64 variants of Windows. However, the Fay approach is generally applicable, and could be used for distributed software execution tracing on most operating systems platforms. In particular, a Fay implementation for Linux should be achievable by modifying existing mechanisms such as Ftrace [48], Native Client [64], and the FlumeJava or Hadoop data-parallel execution frameworks [2, 13].

Although the specifics will vary, any Fay implementation will have to overcome most of the same challenges that we have addressed in our implementation for Windows. First, Fay must preserve all the relevant software invariants—such as timing constraints, reentrancy and thread safety, locking disciplines, custom calling conventions, paging and memory access controls, and the execution states of threads, processes, and the kernel—and these are often hard-to-enumerate, implicit properties of systems platforms.

Specifically, Fay must correctly manage tracepoints and probes and reliably modify machine code to invoke probes inline at tracepoints—which is made especially challenging by preemptive thread scheduling and hardware concurrency [1]. As described in Section 3, Fay meets these challenges with generally-applicable techniques that include machine-wide code-modification barriers, non-reentrant dispatching, lock-free or thread-local state, and the use of time-limited, safe machine code to prevent side effects. In particular, Fay offers the lesson that reliable machine-code modification is a good basis for implementing platform mechanisms, as well as to install tracepoints.

Second, Fay must provide mechanisms for safe machine-code extensibility, in a manner that balances tradeoffs between simplicity, performance, high assurance, applicability to legacy code, compatibility with low-level runtime environments, debuggability, ease-of-use, etc. As described in Section 3.3, the safety of our Fay extensions is based on XFI mechanisms, which are uniquely well suited to low-level, kernel-mode machine code [18]. We have developed several variants of XFI, over a number of years, and applied them to different purposes. Our experience is that specializing mechanisms like XFI to the target application domain, and its constraints, results in the best tradeoffs. Thus, Fay's XFI variant is relatively simple, and is tuned for thread-local, run-to-completion execution of newly-written, freshly ported, or synthesized Fay extensions, either in user-mode processes or the kernel.

Third, as the last major hurdle, to efficiently support high-level queries, a Fay tracing platform must correctly integrate with new or existing query languages and data-parallel execution frameworks. In particular, Fay query-plan generation, optimizations, and task scheduling must correctly consider the difference between persistent, redundantly-stored trace event data and tracepoint-generated data—which is available only at an online, ephemeral source, since

a tracepoint's thread, process, or machine may halt at any time. Section 4.2 describes how our Fay implementation meets this challenge, by using a simple, fixed policy for scheduling the processing of ephemeral trace events, by using explicitly-flushed, constant-size (associative) arrays as the single abstraction for their data, and by applying incremental-view-update techniques from databases to query planning and optimization.

We have applied Fay tracing to a variety of execution monitoring tasks and our experience suggests that Fay improves upon the expressiveness and efficiency of previous dynamic tracing platforms, as well as of some custom tracing mechanisms. In particular, we have found no obstacles to using data-parallel processing of high-level queries for distributed systems monitoring. Although Fay query processing is disaggregated—collecting and partially analyzing trace events separately on different CPU cores, user-mode processes, threads, and machines—in practice, Fay can combine collected trace events into a sufficiently global view of software behavior to achieve the intended monitoring goals. We have found no counterexamples, ill-suited to Fay tracing, in our review of the execution tracing literature, in our searches of the public forums and repositories of popular tracing platforms, or in our experiments using Fay tracing to reimplement a wide range of tracing strategies, described in Section 5. Thus, while data-parallel processing is not a natural fit for all computations, it seems well-suited to the mechanisms, strategies, and queries of distributed systems tracing.

Our experiences also confirm the benefits of extensibility through safe, statically-verified machine code—benefits first identified four decades ago in the Informer profiler [15]. Safe extensions are key to the flexibility of Fay tracing, since they allow any untrusted user to utilize new, native-code tracing primitives without increased risk to system integrity or reliability. As described in Section 4.2, they also enable practical use of high-level, declarative Fay tracing queries, by allowing Fay to synthesize code for efficient, query-specific extensions that it can use for early aggregation and processing in optimized Fay query plans.

In the rest of this paper we outline the motivation, design, and high-level interfaces of Fay tracing and describe the details of its mechanisms. We report on benchmarks, measurements, and use cases in order to establish the scalability, efficiency, and flexibility of Fay tracing and to show its benefits to investigations of software behavior. In particular, we show that Fay tracing can replicate and extend a variety of powerful, custom strategies used on existing distributed software monitoring platforms.

2. GOALS AND LANGUAGE INTERFACES

Fay is motivated by an idealized model of software execution tracing for distributed systems, outlined in Figure 1. The goals can be summarized as follows: The tracing platform should allow arbitrary high-level, side-effect-free *queries* about any aspect of system behavior. At each *tracepoint*—i.e., when the traced behavior occurs at runtime—the platform should allow arbitrary processing across all current system state. Such general processing *probes* should be allowed to maintain state, and used to perform early data reduction (such as filtering or aggregation) before emitting *trace events*.

Ideally, tracing should incur low overhead when active and should have zero overhead when turned off. The total overhead should be proportional to the frequency of tracepoints and to the complexity of probe processing. Tracing should be optimized for efficiency, in particular by favoring early data reduction and aggregation; this

FayLINQ tracing a single machine:

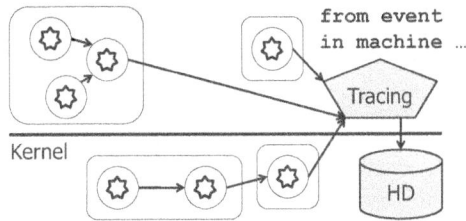

FayLINQ tracing a cluster:

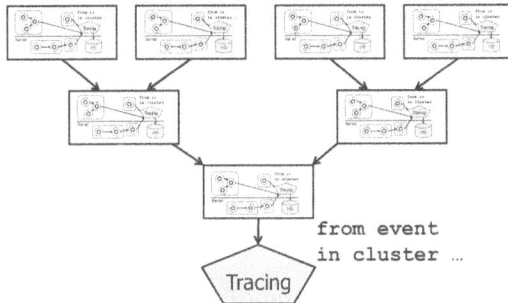

Figure 1: Tracing of an operating system and a machine cluster, as implemented in FayLINQ. Stars represent tracepoints, circles are probes, rounded rectangles are address spaces or modules, rectangles are machines, and pentagons denote final aggregation and processing. Arrows show data flow, optimized for early data reduction within each module, process, or machine; redundant copying for fault tolerance is not indicated.

optimization should apply to all communication, including that between probes, between traced modules, and between machines in the system. Finally, trace events may be ephemeral, since software or hardware may fail at any time; however, once a trace event has been captured, further trace processing should be lossless, and fault-tolerant.

To achieve these goals for Fay tracing, our implementation integrates with two high-level-language platforms: PowerShell scripting [55] and the DryadLINQ system for distributed computing [66]. Figure 2 and Figure 3 show examples of how Fay tracing can be specified on these platforms.

FayLINQ is a high-level interface to Fay tracing that allows analysis of strongly-typed sequences of distributed trace events. FayLINQ is implemented by extending DryadLINQ and derives its expressive programming model from Language INtegrated Queries, or LINQ [29]. FayLINQ's programming model allows a flexible combination of object-oriented, imperative code and high-level declarative data processing [65, 66]. A FayLINQ query can simultaneously express trace collection, trace event analysis, and even the persisting of trace event logs.

FayLINQ queries operate on the entire dataset of all possible tracepoints, and their associated system state, but hide the distributed nature of this dataset by executing as if it had been collected to a central location. In practice, queries are synthesized into data-parallel computations that enable tracing only at relevant tracepoints, and perform early data selection, filtering, and aggregation of trace events. FayLINQ makes use of modified mechanisms from DryadLINQ—described in Section 4.2—to handle query optimiza-

```
$probe = {
  process {
    switch( $([Fay]::Tracepoint()) ) {
      $([Fay]::Kernel("ExAllocate*"))
        { $count = $count + 1; }
    }
  }
  end { Write-FayOutput $count; }
}
Get-FayTrace $probe -StopAfterMinutes 5 `
  | select count `
  | measure -Sum
```

Figure 2: A Fay PowerShell script that counts the invocation of certain memory-allocation functions in a 5-minute interval, on all CPUs of a Windows kernel. Here, $probe uses a switch to match tracepoints to awk-like processing (counting) and specifies the output of aggregated data (the count). A separately-specified pipeline combines the outputs (into a final sum).

```
cluster.Function(kernel, "ExAllocate*")
.Count(event => (event.time < Now.AddMinutes(5)));
```

Figure 3: An example FayLINQ query to perform the same count as in Figure 2 across an entire cluster. From this, Fay can generate optimized query plans and efficient code for local processing (counting) and hierarchical aggregation (summing).

tion, data distribution, and fault-tolerance [65, 66]. In particular, analysis and rewriting of the query plan allows FayLINQ to automatically derive optimized code that runs within the finite space and time constraints of simple probe processing, and can be used even in the operating system kernel.

There is little room for optimization in script-based tracing systems such as Fay PowerShell, or the popular DTrace and SystemTap platforms [11, 45]. These scripting interfaces share inefficiencies that can also be seen in Figure 2. Trace events are generated by executing imperative probes that are specified separately, in isolation from later processing, and this barrier between event generation and analysis prevents most automatic optimizations. Furthermore, by default, for final analysis, trace events must be collected in a fan-in fashion onto a single machine.

In comparison, FayLINQ is able to give the illusion of tracing a single system, through a unified, coherent interface, even when multiple computers, kernels, or user-level processes are involved. Only a few limitations remain, such as that tracing may slightly perturb timing, and that probes can access only state in the address space they are tracing.

Fay tracing may sometimes be best done directly on the command line, or through a PowerShell script, despite the limited opportunity for optimization, In particular, PowerShell is part of the standard Windows monitoring toolset, and is well suited to processing and analysis of object sequences such as trace events [55]. Furthermore, PowerShell exposes Windows secure remote access features that allow Fay scripts to be executed even across machines in heterogeneous administrative domains.

Even so, the benefits of FayLINQ over PowerShell are made clear by the example query of Figure 3. This query shows how simple and intuitive tracing a cluster of machines can be with FayLINQ—

313

especially when compared against the more traditional script in Figure 2, which applies to one machine only. Using FayLINQ, this query will also be executed in an efficient, optimized fashion. In particular, counts will be aggregated, per CPU, in each of the operating system kernels of the cluster; per-machine counts will then be aggregated locally, persisted to disk—redundantly, to multiple machines for fault-tolerance—and finally aggregated in a tree-like fashion for a final query result.

3. FUNDAMENTAL MECHANISMS

At the core of Fay tracing are safe, efficient, and easily extensible mechanisms for tracing kernel and user-mode software behavior within a single machine.

3.1 Tracing and Probing

The basis of the Fay platform is dynamic instrumentation that adds function tracing to user-level processes or the operating system kernel. Fay instrumentation is minimally intrusive: only the first machine-code instruction of a function is changed, temporarily, while that function is being traced.

Notably, Fay instrumentation uses inline invocations that avoid the overhead of hardware trap instructions. However, such inline invocations, and their resulting state updates, are necessarily confined to a single process, or to the kernel, forcing each address space to be traced separately. Therefore, Fay treats even a single machine as a distributed system composed of many isolated parts.

3.1.1 Tracepoints

Fay provides *tracepoints* at the entry, normal return, and exceptional exit of the traced functions in a target address space. All Fay trace events are the result of such function boundary tracing. Fay can also support asynchronous or time-based tracepoints, as long as they eventually result in a call to an instrumentable function.

When a tracepoint is triggered at runtime, execution is transferred inline to the Fay *dispatcher*. The dispatcher, in turn, invokes one or more probe functions, or *probes*, that have been associated with the tracepoint. A probe may be associated with one or more tracepoints, and any number of probe functions may be associated with each tracepoint. Further details of the Fay dispatcher are described in Section 3.2 and illustrated in Figure 5.

To enable tracing of an address space, the base Fay platform module must be loaded into the address space to be traced. This platform module then installs probes by loading *probe modules* into the target address space.

3.1.2 Probe Modules

Fay probe modules are kernel drivers or user-mode libraries (DLLs). For both FayLINQ and PowerShell, source-to-source translation is used to automatically generate compiled probe modules. (Our implementation uses the freely available, state-of-the-art optimizing C/C++ compiler in the Windows Driver Kit [36].)

Figure 4 outlines how Fay probe modules are used for tracing in the kernel address space. A high-level query is evaluated and compiled into a safe probe module; then, that driver binary is installed into the kernel. At a kernel function tracepoint, Fay instrumentation ensures that control is transferred to the Fay dispatcher, which invokes one or more probes at runtime. Finally the probe outputs (partially) processed trace events for further aggregation and analysis.

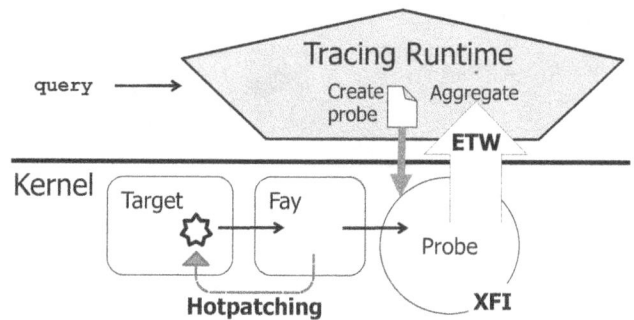

Figure 4: Overview of how Fay makes use of probes when tracing the kernel address space. Visual representations are as in Figure 1—e.g., the star is a tracepoint. Kernel arrows show probe module installation (going down), dynamic instrumentation (going left), the dispatch of a tracepoint to a probe function (going right), as well as the flow of trace event data (going up).

Probe modules are subject to the standard Windows access control checks. In particular, only system administrators can trace the kernel or other system address spaces, and kernel probe modules must be cryptographically signed for the x86-64 platform. However, this is not enough: bad compiler setup, malicious input data, or other factors might easily lead to the creation of a flawed probe that would impair system security and reliability. Therefore, subsequent to their generation, probe module binaries are rewritten and processed to establish that they can be safely loaded and used within the traced address space. This processing is based on a variant of XFI: a Software-based Fault Isolation (SFI) technique that is uniquely applicable to both kernel-mode and user-mode code [61, 64, 18]. Section 3.3 gives the details of the simplified XFI mechanisms used in our Fay platform.

Fay probe modules can be written from scratch, in C or C++, ported from legacy code, or even hand-crafted in assembly code. Fay can also be extended with new computations or data structures, similarly specified as low-level or native code. Such Fay probe *extensions* might, for example, include hash functions for summarizing state, or code for maintaining representative samples of data. Extensions allow enhancing Fay with new primitives without any changes to the platform—and can be used even from FayLINQ or other high-level queries. Extensions are compiled with probes, and are subject to the same safety checks; therefore, they raise no additional reliability or security concerns.

Fay resolves symbolic target-module references by making use of debug information emitted at compile time for executable binaries. (Much the same is done in other tracing systems [11, 45].) On the Windows platform, such "PDB files" are available, and easily accessible through a public network service, for all components and versions of Windows.

3.1.3 Probe Processing

When triggered at a tracepoint, a probe will typically perform selection, filtering, and aggregation of trace data. For instance, a probe may count how often a function returns with an error code, or collect a histogram of its argument values. However, probes are not limited to this; instead, they may perform arbitrary processing.

In particular, probes might summarize a large, dynamic data structure in the traced address space using expensive pointer chasing—

but do so only when certain, exceptional conditions hold true. Fay probe *extensions* for such data traversal may even be compiled from the same code as is used in the target system. Thus, Fay tracing can make it practical to perform valuable, deep tracing of software corner cases, and to gather all their relevant system state and execution context when they occur.

Fay probes can invoke an *accessor* support routine to examine the state of the system. Multiple accessors are available in a runtime library and can be used to obtain function arguments and return values, the current CPU, process, and thread identity, CPU cycle counts, etc. A `TryRead` accessor allows attempted reading from any memory address, and thereby arbitrary inspection of the address space. All accessors are simple, and self-contained, in order to prevent probe activity from perturbing the traced system.

3.1.4 Probe State

For maintaining summaries of system behavior, Fay provides each probe module with its own local and global memories. This mutable state is respectively private to each thread (or CPU, in the kernel), or global to each probe module. These two types of state allow efficient, lock-free, thread-local data maintenance, as well as communication between probe functions in the same address space—globally across the CPUs and threads of the target system.

Both types of mutable probe state are of constant, fixed size, set at the start of tracing. However, probes may at any time send a *trace event* with their collected data, and flush mutable state for reuse, which alleviates the limitations of constant-size state. To reduce the frequency of such trace event generation, probes can make use of space-efficient data structures (e.g., our Fay implementation makes use of cuckoo hashtables [19]).

To initialize global and local state, probe modules can define special *begin* and *end* probe functions, invoked at the start and end of tracing. These "begin" and "end" probe functions are also invoked at thread creation and termination, e.g., to allow thread-local state to be captured into a trace event for higher-level analysis.

In combination, the above mechanisms allow Fay probes to efficiently implement—from first principles—tracing features such as predicated tracing, distributed aggregation, and speculative tracing [11]. In addition, they make it easy to extend Fay tracing with new primitives, such as sketches [7]. These features are exposed through the high-level Fay language interfaces, and can be considered during both the optimization of Fay tracing queries and during their execution. Section 5 describes some of our experiences implementing such extended Fay tracing features.

3.1.5 Limitations of Fay Tracepoints and Probes

Compared to popular, mature tracing platforms, our Fay implementation has some limitations that stem from its early stage of development. For example, while Fay tracing can be used for live, online execution monitoring (e.g., as in Figure 7), the batch-driven nature of the Dryad runtime prevents streaming of FayLINQ query results. Also, currently, users of Fay tracing must manually choose between `call` and `jmp` dispatchers, and whether trace events are logged to disk, first, or whether per-machine analysis happens in a real-time, machine-local Fay aggregation process.

On the other hand, the Fay primitives in our implementation are fundamentally limited to function-boundary tracing of specially-compiled binary modules, for which debug information is available. Other tracing platforms also rely on debug information to offer full functionality, and are applied mostly to properly-compiled or system binaries. Less common is Fay's lack of support for tracing arbitrary instructions. However, although supported by both DTrace and SystemTap, per-instruction tracing can affect system stability and is also fragile when instructions or line numbers change, or are elided, as is common in optimized production code. Thus, this feature is not often used, and its omission should not greatly affect the utility of Fay tracing.

To confirm that per-instruction tracing is rarely-used, we performed an extensive review of the public discussion forums and available collections of tracing scripts and libraries for both DTrace and SystemTap. Typical of the per-instruction tracing we could find are examples such as counting the instructions executed by a process or a function [17], or the triggering of a tracing probe upon a change to a certain variable [57]. This type of tracing is not likely to be common, since it requires extensive instrumentation and incurs correspondingly high overhead, and since its goals are more easily achieved using hardware performance counters or memory tracepoints. Programmer addition of new debugging messages to already-compiled code is the one example we could find where per-instruction tracing seemed practical [56]; however, the same can also be achieved by running under a debugger or, if recompilation is an option, by the addition of calls to empty functions, which Fay could then trace. Therefore, we have no current plans to extend Fay beyond function-boundary tracing.

Fay supports only disaggregated tracing, even within a single machine: Fay probes have only a disjoint view of the activity in different address spaces, i.e., the kernel or each user-mode process, which is then combined by higher-level Fay trace-event processing. Existing tracing platforms such as DTrace [11] support imperative operations on per-machine shared state, and use hardware-trap-based instrumentation to access this shared state from both the kernel and any user-mode address space. We have considered, but decided against, adding Fay support for machine-global probe state, accessible across all address spaces, implemented via memory mapping or a software device driver. So far, the distributed nature of Fay tracing has made it sufficiently convenient to get visibility into user-mode activity by combining trace events from user and kernel address spaces.

3.2 Dispatching Tracepoints to Probes

Fay tracing uses inline invocations to a Fay probe dispatcher, through a call or jump instruction inserted directly into the target machine code. Some other platforms dynamically insert a kernel transition, or faulting instruction, to perform tracing [11, 45]. Compared to this alternative, Fay inline tracing offers greater efficiency, by avoiding hardware traps; similarly, the Ftrace facility recently added to Linux also uses inline tracing for kernel functions [48].

Fay repurposes Windows *hotpatching* in a novel manner to modify the machine code at a function entry point, so that control is transferred to the Fay probe dispatcher. Windows function hotpatching is an existing operating systems facility, designed to allow incorrect or insecure functions to be replaced on a running system, without a reboot or process shutdown [34]. Hotpatching performs reliable, atomic code modification with all CPUs in a well-defined state (e.g., not executing the code being hotpatched). Previously, hotpatching has been rarely used: since its introduction in 2003, we are not aware of a generally-available software update from Microsoft that makes use of hotpatching.

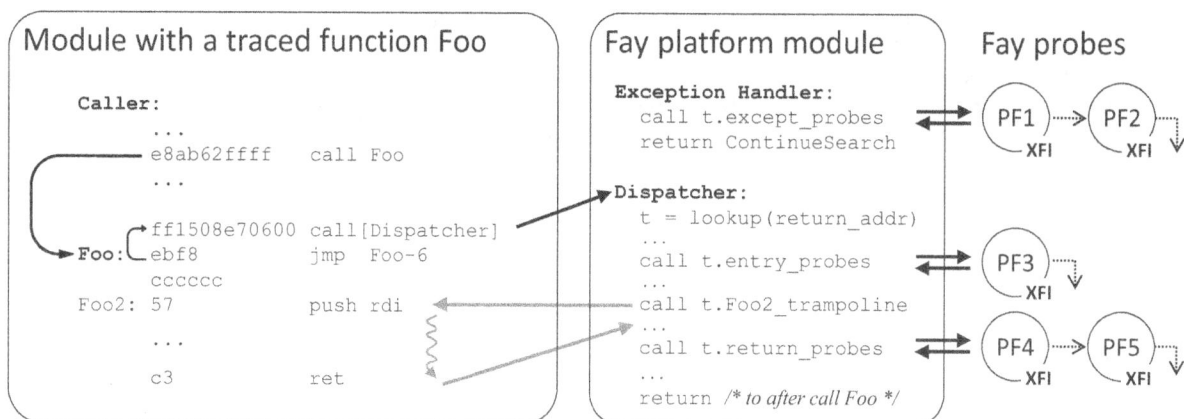

Figure 5: Fay dynamic instrumentation of a function Foo, with five separate, safe probe functions invoked at its entry, return, and exception tracepoints. Rounded rectangles show the relevant binary modules in the traced address space (the kernel, or a user-mode process). Arrows indicate control flow, starting at the original call to Foo (no arrow is shown for the return to that original call site). The lighter arrows, colored blue, show the nested call to Foo from the Fay dispatcher—via a trampoline that executes Foo's original first instruction and then jumps to its second instruction.

Fay uses the hotpatching mechanism to insert, at the start of functions, inline invocations to the Fay probe dispatcher. This permitted, but unintended use of hotpatching allows Fay to be used for the pervasive tracing of existing, unmodified production systems.

All currently supported Windows binaries are hotpatch enabled. Hotpatching constrains machine-code at function entry: six unused bytes must be present before the function, and its first instruction must be at least two bytes long, and be drawn from a small set of opcodes. Each binary must also contain a number of *hotpatch data slots* for pointers to new function versions; a normal binary module has only 31 such slots, while the kernel has 127. In Fay, these constraints on hotpatch data slots do not limit the number of tracepoints: Fay tracing is scalable to an arbitrary number of functions.

Figure 5 shows the machine code of a function Foo after Fay has used hotpatching to modify Foo to enable its entry, return, and exceptional exit tracepoints. The first instruction of Foo has been replaced with a two-byte instruction that jumps backwards by six bytes. At the six-bytes-earlier address, a new instruction has been written that calls the Fay dispatcher. The call is indirect, through one of the hotpatch data slots of the target module being traced (this indirection allows loading the Fay platform module anywhere in the 64-bit address space).

As Figure 5 indicates, upon entry the Fay dispatcher looks up a descriptor for the current tracepoint (shown as t in the figure). Tracepoint descriptors control what probes are triggered and provide the crucial first instruction that allows the dispatcher to call the traced function. Fay looks up these descriptors in a space-efficient hashtable [19], and the use of a simpler hashtable, with significantly more memory, could reduce the cost of this lookup. For threads not being traced, the lookup and use of descriptors might even be eliminated by using a Fay dispatcher with multiple entry points—one for each possible first instruction—since different preamble code at each distinct entry point could instruct the Fay dispatcher how to emulate the effects of a traced function's first instruction before passing control to the rest of the function. Fay does not yet implement such elaborations, since we have found the current lookup efficient enough (about 40 cycles in our measurements).

A Fay tracepoint descriptor contains lists of probe functions to be invoked, as well as other relevant information—such as the global and local state to be used for each probe. Dispatching is lock free, but runs with (most) interrupts disabled; descriptor updates are atomically applied at an all-CPU synchronization barrier.

If the current thread is to be traced, the Fay dispatcher will invoke probe functions both before and after the traced function as indicated in the tracepoint descriptor lists—subjecting the execution of each probe to the necessary safety and reliability constraints.

The Fay dispatcher also invokes the traced function itself. For this, the dispatcher creates a new stack frame with copies of the function's arguments. Then, the dispatcher uses a pointer from the tracepoint descriptor to transfer control to a function-specific, executable trampoline that contains a copy of the traced function's first instruction, followed by a direct jump to its second instruction.

The Fay dispatcher also registers an exception handler routine, for capturing any exceptional exit of the function being traced. Fay invokes exceptional exit probes when an exception is unwound past this handler; once the probes have executed, Fay forwards the exception on to higher stack frames.

Actually, Fay provides multiple dispatcher implementations whose performance and scalability differs. In particular, depending on the traced function, Fay can save different sets of registers: functions synthesized through whole-program optimizations require preserving all registers, while stable, externally-accessible functions require saving only a small, non-volatile set of registers.

Figure 5 shows the slowest and most scalable version of the Fay dispatcher. This version hotpatches a call instruction before the traced function. That call pushes Foo's address on the stack for descriptor lookup. This dispatcher is scalable since it requires only one hotpatch data slot (out of the very limited number of slots). However, the call places a superfluous return address on the stack, which the dispatcher must eliminate before returning (at the /**/ comment). Unfortunately, on modern CPU architectures, such stack manipulations can have an adverse performance impact

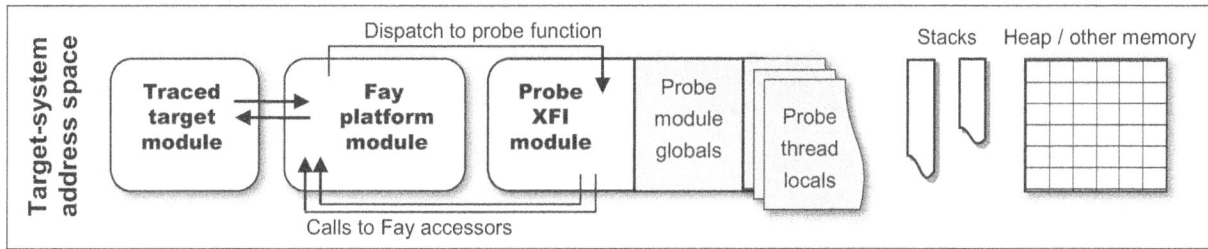

Figure 6: The layout of a traced address space, with a Fay probe XFI module. Probe functions may invoke only a restricted set of Fay accessor support routines. Probe functions may write only to the shaded memory areas—and only to the thread-local memory of the current thread. A probe may attempt to read any memory address via a Fay accessor that prevents faults due to invalid addresses. XFI safeguards the integrity of the execution stacks, privileged hardware registers, and other critical host-address-space state.

by disrupting dynamic branch prediction [51]. Therefore, when only a limited number of functions are traced, Fay will use a faster dispatcher, where hotpatching places a `jmp` instruction to a dispatch trampoline. Both dispatchers have low overheads; Section 5 compares their performance.

3.3 Reliability and Safety

Reliability is the paramount goal of the Fay dispatcher and other Fay mechanisms; these must be correct, and are designed and implemented defensively, with the goal of allowing target systems to always make progress, and fail gracefully, in the worst case. However, Fay relies crucially on the safety of probe processing: to the rest of the system, probes must always appear as (almost) side-effect-free, pure functions—whether written by hand, compiled in an uncertain environment, or even when crafted by a malicious attacker. To ensure probe safety, previous tracing systems have used safe interpreters or trusted compilers [11, 45].

Fundamentally, Fay ensures probe safety through use of XFI: one of the recently-developed, low-overhead SFI mechanisms that are suitable to x86-64 CPUs [18, 61, 64]. XFI is the only SFI mechanism to be applicable even to machine code that runs as part of privileged, low-level systems software. Thus, Fay can rely on XFI to provide comprehensive constraints on machine code probes, including flexible access controls and strong integrity guarantees, and yet allow probes to be utilized in any address space, including the kernel. As in all SFI systems, safety is enforced through a combination of inline software guards and static verification of machine code. Below, we outline the characteristics of the Fay variant of XFI; more details about its underlying policies and mechanisms can be found in the original XFI paper [18].

Like previous variants, Fay XFI is implemented using Vulcan [54]. However, Fay XFI aims for simplicity, and avoids complexities—such as "fastpath guards" [18]—as long as doing so retains acceptable performance. Instead of being fully inlined, Fay XFI guards reside in separate functions, but are invoked inline with arguments pushed on the stack. While slightly less efficient, this style leads to minimal code perturbation, which both simplifies XFI rewriting and also facilities debugging and understanding of probe machine code.

Fay XFI is also customized to its task of enforcing safety properties for Fay probes. Figure 6 shows a Fay XFI probe module in a target address space (cf. Figure 1 in [18]). Fay probes should be side-effect-free, and execute only for short periods—to completion, without interruption, serially on each (hardware) thread—using only the fixed-size memory regions of their local and global state,

and making external invocations only to Fay accessor routines. Thus, upon a memory access, Fay XFI memory-range guards can compare against only one thread-local and one static region, and need not consult slowpath permission tables—and, similar, fixed tables can be consulted upon use of a software call gate.

Fay probes are not unmodified legacy code—they are either newly written, newly ported, or automatically generated. Therefore, Fay XFI does not allow arbitrary C, C++, or assembly code, but imposes some restrictions on how probes are written. Fay probes may not use recursive code, dynamically allocate memory on the stack frame, or make use of function pointers or virtual methods; these restrictions make XFI enforcement of control-flow integrity trivial, and also reduce the number of stack-overflow guards necessary, by allowing worst-case stack usage to be computed statically. Also, Fay probes may not use code that generates or handles exceptions, or use other stack context saving functionality; such probe code would be very difficult to support at low levels of the kernel and we have removed the associated XFI host-system support. Finally, Fay probes may not access stack memory through pointers, so probe code must be converted to use thread-local probe state instead of stack-resident variables; this simplifies XFI rewriting and verification, and eliminates the need for XFI allocation stacks. These restrictions do not prevent any functionality, and although they may result in greater porting efforts for some Fay probe extensions, this is not onerous, since Fay probes necessarily execute relatively small amounts of code and this code is often automatically generated.

Despite the above simplifications, Fay XFI still enforces all the safety properties of XFI [18]—for instance, constraining machine-code control flow, preventing use of dangerous instructions, restricting memory access, and thwarting violations of stack integrity.

3.3.1 Thread-local Tracking for Reliability

To ensure reliability, the interactions between Fay and the software it is tracing must always be benign. Thus, the operation of the Fay dispatcher, probes, and accessors must be self-contained, since Fay's invocation of an external subsystem might adversely affect the integrity of that subsystem, or result in deadlock. For example, while Fay accessor routines may read system state, they must never invoke system functions with negative side effects.

A thread that is performing Fay dispatching must be treated differently by both the Fay platform and the system itself. In particular, Fay tracing must not be applied recursively, such as might happen if Fay were used to trace system functions that are themselves used by code in a Fay accessor routine. This scenario might happen, e.g., if Fay tracing was applied to mechanisms for trace event transport.

To prevent recursive tracing, Fay maintains a thread-local flag that is set only while a probe is executing, and that is checked during dispatching. (In the kernel, a small amount of thread-local storage is available in the CPU control block; in user mode, arbitrary thread-local storage is available.) A similar flag allows Fay to efficiently support thread-specific tracing: the common scenario where some threads are traced, but not others. Depending on the state of these flags for the current thread, the Fay dispatcher may skip all probes and invoke only the traced function. Fay keeps a count of lost tracing opportunities due to the Fay dispatcher being invoked recursively on a flagged thread.

Fay does not enforce any confidentiality policy: no secrets can be held from kernel probes. Even so, Fay kernel probes are subject to an unusual form of memory access control. A probe may write only to its global or local state, and may only read those regions when dereferencing a memory address. In addition, probes may use a special `TryRead` accessor to try to read a value from any (potentially invalid) memory address; this functionality can be used by probes that perform pointer chasing, for example. The `TryRead` accessor sets a thread-local flag that changes pagefault behavior on invalid memory accesses and prevents the kernel from halting (Section 3.5 gives further details on its implementation). However, Fay will prevent even `TryRead` from accessing the memory of hardware control registers, since such accesses could cause side effects.

Finally, probes must be prevented from executing too long. In the kernel, a special tracing probe is added by Fay to one of the Windows kernel functions that handles timer interrupts, to detect runaway probes. This special probe maintains state that allows it to detect if a hardware thread is still running the same probe as at the previous timer interrupt—and will trigger an exception if a Fay probe runs for too many timer interrupts in a row.

3.4 Transporting Trace Events

Fay uses Event Tracing for Windows, (*ETW*) [41] to collect and persist trace events in a standard log format. ETW is a high-functionality Windows system mechanism that provides general-purpose, structured definitions for trace events, efficient buffering of trace events, support for real-time trace consumers as well as efficient persistent logging and access to tracelog files, support for dynamic addition and removal of producers, consumers, and trace sessions, as well as the automatic provisioning of timestamps and other metadata.

ETW tracing is lock free and writes trace events to CPU-local buffers. Also, ETW is lossless, in that the number of outstanding buffers is dynamically adjusted to the rate of event generation—and in the unlikely case that no buffer space is available, an accurate count of dropped events is still provided. Finally, the standard, manifest-based ETW tracelog formats allows Fay trace events to be consumed and processed by a wide range of utilities on the Windows platform.

3.5 Practical Deployment Issues

Our Fay implementation has been crafted to ensure that it can be installed even on production systems, without a reboot. In particular, we have carefully (and painfully) avoided dependencies on system internals, and on features that vary across Windows versions. For this, our Fay implementation sometimes makes use of side-effect-free tracing of system functions such as in our support for asynchronous tracepoints. In one case we had to change the behavior of Windows: Fay hotpatches the kernel page fault handler with a

new variant that throws an exception (instead of halting execution) when invalid kernel-mode addresses are accessed during execution of the `TryRead` accessor.

The use of Fay tracing is subject to some limitations. In particular, Fay requires that target binary modules have been compiled with hotpatching support; while this holds true for binaries in Windows and Microsoft server products, it is not the case for all software. Also, kernel tracing with the more scalable Fay probe dispatcher will require rebooting with kernel debugging automatically enabled; otherwise, PatchGuard [35] will bugcheck Windows after detecting an unexpected `call` instruction, which it disallows in machine-code hotpatches.

Finally, even for Windows system binaries, Fay is currently not able to trace variable-argument functions—since the Fay dispatcher would then have to create a stack frame of unbounded size for its invocation of the traced function.

4. LANGUAGES FOR FAY TRACING

We have integrated Fay with PowerShell to provide a traditional scripting interface to tracing, and also created FayLINQ to provide a LINQ query interface and a declarative, data-parallel approach to distributed tracing. Both these popular high-level language platforms provide flexible, efficient means of specifying tracing, in a manner that feels natural—thereby removing the need to introduce a domain-specific language, as done in other dynamic tracing platforms [11, 45].

We have implemented several Fay support mechanisms that can be utilized both in PowerShell and FayLINQ, since both are managed code platforms. In particular, these provide for optimized compilation of probe modules, their installation into the kernel, or injection into a user-mode process. These mechanisms also give access to debug information (from PDBs) for currently executing software—e.g., to allow symbolic identification of tracepoints in a target binary module, as well as the global variables, types, enums, etc., of that module. Finally, these mechanisms allow real-time consumption of ETW trace events, and the custom, type-driven unmarshalling of their contents.

4.1 Fay PowerShell Scripting

Here we give a brief outline of Fay PowerShell scripting. PowerShell is structured around *cmdlets*, which are similar to awk scripts operating on streams of objects, and augmented with administration and monitoring features. In PowerShell, Fay probes are just regular cmdlets, with a few natural changes in semantics: `begin{}` blocks execute at the start of tracing, `process{}` executes at each tracepoint, variables such as `$global:var` live in global state, whereas regular variables are thread local, etc.

When used with Fay support cmdlets, such as `Get-FayTrace`, tracing scripts are converted to C code, using source-to-source translation, and compiled and processed into binary XFI probe modules. Fay makes use of partial evaluation to resolve symbolic reference in PowerShell scripts, as well as to identify tracepoints and define a specialized probe function for each tracepoint. We have used PowerShell mostly as a convenient means for ad hoc Fay tracing, like that in Figure 7.

4.2 FayLINQ Queries

FayLINQ integrates the fundamental Fay mechanisms with the LINQ language, as well as the optimizations and large-scale data

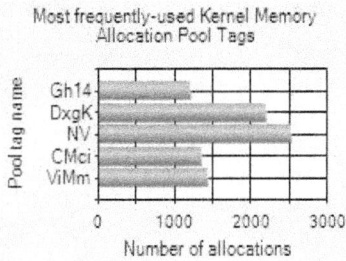

Figure 7: Output of a 20-line Fay PowerShell script that every second updates a visual histogram of the five most common types (or "tags") of memory allocations from non-paged kernel memory. The greatest number of memory allocations are of type 'NV', indicating they are due to the NVidia display driver.

processing capabilities of DryadLINQ [66]. This combination allows high-level queries about distributed systems behavior to be applied to—and executed on—the same cluster of computers.

On both a single machine, and on a cluster, FayLINQ input is naturally modeled as operations on a concatenated set of trace event streams. Fundamentally, Fay tracing generates multiple, disjoint streams of ordered trace events, with a separate trace event stream output by each thread in each address space. Therefore, FayLINQ tracing consists of the execution of LINQ queries on an unordered, merged collection of these ordered streams.

Concretely, the FayLINQ implementation proceeds from a single, high-level query to generate an efficient set of tracepoints, and code for Fay probes that perform extraction, processing, and early aggregation of trace event data. FayLINQ also produces optimized DryadLINQ query plans and processing code for both machine-local and cluster-level aggregation and analysis.

The example in Figure 8 helps explain how FayLINQ operates, and give an overview of query execution. In the query, `kernelAllocations` constrains the set of tracepoints to those at the entry of the primary kernel memory allocation function—with the `Function` extension method operating like a `Where` clause. Then, from each tracepoint, the query retrieves the time property and the size of the allocation, which is the second argument of `ExAllocatePool` (unfortunately, PDB files do not contain symbolic argument names). Then, `allocIntervalSizePairs` is used to collect, for each tracepoint, which `period`-length interval it fell into, and integer $\log_2$ of its allocation size. These events are then grouped together into `results`, and a separate count is made of each group where both the time and $\log_2$ allocation sizes are equal, with these triples output as strings. Importantly, this final grouping applies to events from all machines, and is implemented in two phases: first on each machine, and then across all cluster machines.

Distributed tracing can be straightforwardly implemented by emitting trace events for each tracepoint invocation and collecting and processing those events centrally. One approach would be to use a flat, wide schema (the union of all possible output fields) to allow the same trace events to be output at any probe and at any tracepoint. Probes may be very simple, and need only fill out fields in the schema. Unfortunately, this is not a very viable strategy: flattened schemas lead to large trace events, and the output of trace events at

```
// Get the disaggregated set of kernel allocation trace events.
var kernelAllocations =
    PartitionedTable<FayTracepoint>
    .Get("fay://clustername")
    .Function(kernel, "ExAllocatePool");

// For the next 10 minutes, map each allocation to a coarser period-based
// timeline of intervals and to log2 of the requested allocation size.
var allocIntervalSizePairs =
    from event in kernelAllocations
    where event.time < Now.AddMinutes(10)
    let allocSize = event.Arg(2)  // NumberOfBytes
    select new { interval = event.time/period,
                 size = log2(allocSize)) };

// Group allocations by interval and log2 of the size and count each group.
var results =
    from pair in allocIntervalSizePairs
    group pair by pair into reduction
    select new { interval = reduction.Key.interval,
                 logsize = reduction.Key.size,
                 count = reduction.Count() };

// Map each interval/log2size/count triple to a string for output.
var output =
    results.Select( r => r.ToString() );
```

Figure 8: A FayLINQ query that summarizes the rate of different-sized kernel memory allocation requests over 10 minutes. The output indicates, for each `period`-length interval, how often allocation sizes of different magnitude were seen.

high-frequency tracepoints will incur significant load, which may easily skew measurements or even swamp the system.

Instead of the above, naive implementation approach, FayLINQ performs a number of steps to optimize the execution of queries like that in Figure 8. At a coarse granularity, these steps are:

Generic Optimizations. First, FayLINQ performs basic DryadLINQ query optimizations, like dead code removal—notably moving filtering and selection to the leaves of the query plan—i.e., towards the source of trace event data, the tracepoints.

Second, since a `fay://` data source is used, FayLINQ creates an optimized query plan, which collects trace events from Fay probes. Like with PowerShell, the query is analyzed (using a form of partial evaluation) to discover what machines, address spaces, processes, and threads, and what functions should be traced by Fay.

Greedy Optimizations. Third, the query plan optimizer greedily tries to move operations into Fay probe functions—as many as possible. For the query in Figure 8, nearly all work can be pushed into Fay probes at the query plan leaves, since the `GroupBy` operator can be decomposed into a local and a global aggregation [65].

Fourth, by default, the plan is modified to materialize Fay probe output, to make trace events persistent and fault tolerant. Fifth, a DryadLINQ plan is built for all remaining query parts. For Figure 8, this is the final, global aggregation and the computation of the `output` strings. Sixth, the code for the Fay probes, and their installation and use, is emitted as a synthetic Dryad input vertex [26].

Query Execution. Figure 9 shows how FayLINQ will efficiently execute the example in Figure 8. Figure 10 shows the term-rewriting rules used to generate this optimized query plan.

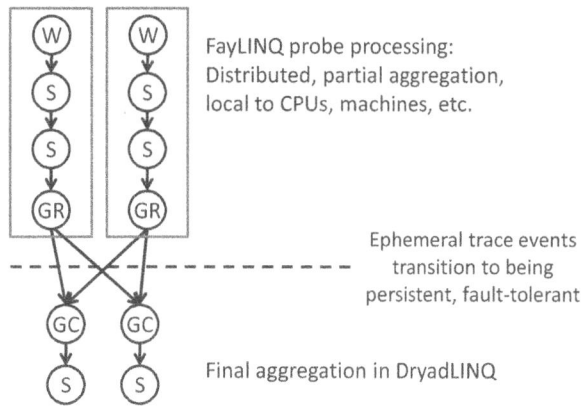

Figure 9: Optimized plan for the query in Figure 8. Symbols are as in Figure 10 and its legend (e.g., arrows show data flow).

The dotted line in Figure 9 marks the separation between Fay and DryadLINQ. At runtime, Dryad input vertices execute, start Fay tracing, and then enter a loop processing the trace events output by Fay probes. The Fay probes will usually perform some aggregation. The results of the aggregation are periodically encapsulated in ETW events and flushed to the cluster-level aggregation pipeline. Normally the aggregation results are flushed when the internal fixed-size hashtables are filled. However, the user can control the message frequency by specifying that aggregated event statistics should be flushed at least every k probe invocations. The payload of the ETW events is unmarshalled and decoded into .NET objects, which are further transported using the standard DryadLINQ transport mechanisms using reliable Dryad channels. The DryadLINQ part of the query runs on the cluster, taking full advantage of the fault-tolerance, scheduling and optimizations of the Dryad runtime, which is proven to scale to large clusters.

4.2.1 Probe Code Generation

The FayLINQ implementation optimizes the query plan to move data filtering, transformation, and aggregation (including GroupBy-Aggregate) from the LINQ query into Fay probes. Currently, the following LINQ statements can be executed by Fay probes: `Where`, `Select`, `Aggregate`, and `GroupBy`—as well as the many special cases of these operators, such as `Sum`, `Count`, `Average`, `Distinct`, `Take`, etc. Query parts that cannot be executed by probes are executed by DryadLINQ, on the cluster. This includes the aggregates of data from multiple machines—which, DryadLINQ will automatically perform in a tree-like fashion, when that improves performance [65].

In our current implementation, not all uses of the above LINQ operators can be transformed to execute in Fay probes. The operators must use only values (basic types and structures) and must only call static methods for which a Fay accessor or extension is available. However, Fay probes can invoke any lambda expression that uses only these basic primitives. For example, sketch-based tracing (similar to that in Chopstix [7]) can be expressed simply as

```
clusterTraceEvents
  .Where(event => HCA(event.time/period, event))
```

where HCA is a function in an optimized, native-code Fay extension that sketches all events in each distinct time period, by updating mutable probe state. Section 5.2.3. describes further how Fay extensions can implement tracing primitives such as sketching.

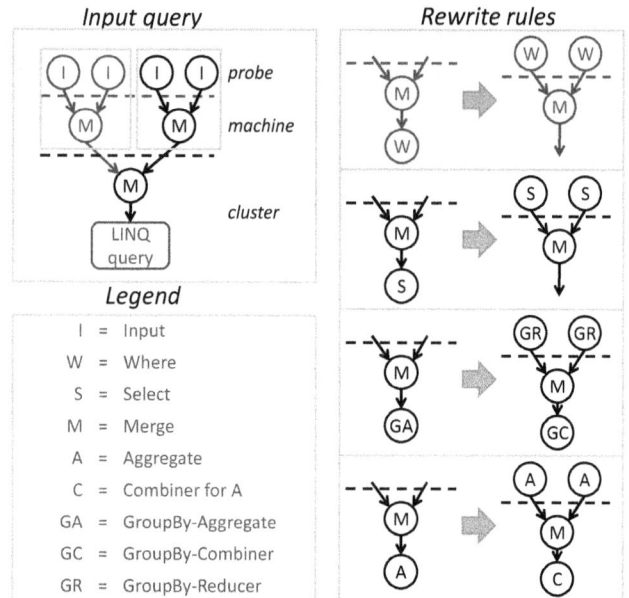

Figure 10: Term-rewriting from LINQ to Fay probes, with circles and arrows representing operators and data flow. The input operation merges the trace events from tracepoints and performs user-specified computations on that merged stream. Term-rewriting optimizations push operations closer to data sources. The first and second rewrite rules push filtering and selection ahead of merging. The last rewrite rule transforms counting into a sum of partial counts; the third rule generalizes this last one and rewrites aggregations on partial groups.

FayLINQ generates C code using syntax-directed translation from the optimized LINQ query plan. The translation proceeds naturally—e.g., `Where` translates to `if` statements, etc. More interestingly, at each tracepoint invocations, the C code may modify probe state to perform incremental updates. Since LINQ queries are essentially database views, this implementation of FayLINQ query evaluation is much like an optimized incremental view update, and makes use of database-like mechanisms [24, 65]. For example, in the query of Figure 8, at each probe invocation, the time interval and log(allocation size) are computed immediately and used to update counts in a hashtable.

Notably, `GroupBy`, when followed by aggregation, can often be translated using Fay hashtable updates. As mentioned above, this pattern—often known as map-reduce [14]—can often be decomposed into a local and global `GroupBy` operations [65]. The local reduction may then be Fay hashtable updates, while the global reduction remains in DryadLINQ. Importantly, fixed-size hashtables may be used for local aggregation, since the global aggregation can "fix" incomplete aggregations. When the hashtables are full, and insertion fails, Fay probes can output a trace event containing the hashtable data and clear it out for reuse.

5. EXPERIMENTS AND EVALUATION

We have used Fay to diagnose system behavior on both single machines and on medium-size clusters. For example, as we started using Fay we immediately noticed a performance issue where the built-in Windows command shell was CPU-bound doing continuous system calls for no good reason. Below, we retell our diagnosis of this issue as a detailed, anecdotal case study of using Fay tracing.

Windows System Call	Count	Callers
NtRequestWaitReplyPort	1,515,342	cmd.exe conhost
NtAlpcSendWaitReceivePort	764,503	CSRSS
NtQueryInformationProcess	758,933	CSRSS
NtReplyWaitReceivePort	757,934	conhost

Table 1: The processes in the command shell case study, and a count of how often they made the relevant system calls. The two calling `NtRequestWaitReplyPort` did so about equally often.

The utility of tracing and monitoring platforms has long since been established through both published results as well as through previous anecdotal case studies. In many cases, such as in the DTrace study in Section 9 of [10], an issue is first raised by some external monitoring tool that can be applied continuously to live production systems (such as an offline log analysis tool or a low-overhead, statistical profiler [9]). After such initial identification by other means, dynamic tracing may be used for detailed, manual or semi-automatic behavior analysis. Even then, tracing overheads may be too high for production systems, which often forces the issue to be reproduced on non-critical systems before it can be analyzed.

Fay tracing can be efficient enough to overturn the above paradigm and allow continuous dynamic tracing of live production systems, both before and during the analysis of any detected issues. With this in mind, the Fay primitives have been used to extend the existing tracing mechanisms in one of Microsoft's mature, scalable enterprise transaction platforms. This platform performs transactions on separate threads and, during normal operation, Fay tracing allows the properties of a random sample of transactions to be closely monitored with very low overhead. Fay tracing has little global performance impact (e.g., it does not force kernel traps), and threads that are not being traced spend few extra CPU cycles at each tracepoint, thanks to thread-specific Fay dispatching. If an issue arises, and needs to be analyzed, Fay tracing can be dynamically directed to detailed behavior analysis, and more functions and threads, usually at only a modest, acceptable increase in overhead.

The rest of this section starts off with a Fay case study, presented in the informal, anecdotal style of studies in the literature [10]. Instead of enumerating further tracing applications, we subsequently examine the flexibility of Fay tracing through the implementation of a variety of different distributed software monitoring strategies. Finally, we present experimental measurements that establish the efficiency of the Fay tracing primitives, the scalability of the Fay platform to fully-loaded clusters, and the benefits of FayLINQ query optimizations.

5.1 A Fay Performance-diagnosis Case Study

In some of our earliest Fay tracing experiments, we interactively used the Windows command shell (cmd.exe) while observing a live, real-time chart of machine-wide system-call frequencies much like that in Figure 7. Surprisingly, we observed very high frequencies for some tasks where we expected to see few system calls, such as `copy * NUL`, or `type large.txt` in a minimized window, or `dir /S >NUL`. We used Fay to investigate, as described below, and to ensure reproducibility we used only public information available outside Microsoft, such as public symbol files.

Outputting a 16 MB file of ASCII text in a minimized console window, using `type`, produced around 3.75 million system calls, and

was CPU bound for a significant amount of time. We used a Fay query to aggregate by calling process, with Table 1 showing the dominant four system calls. To see how these three processes interacted, we combined their system calls and arguments into a single view, using a Fay query for a temporal join (see Section 5.2.4 and [5]). The query showed a repeated pattern: cmd.exe blocks on a port request to conhost; then, conhost blocks on a port request to the CSRSS service, which queries for process information; then, CSRSS blocks on a port send to conhost, which unblocks it; finally, conhost makes a request back to cmd.exe, unblocking it. These were clearly Windows Local Procedure Calls (LPC) spanning the three processes [49].

Fay tracing showed some LPC rounds to be a result of the well-documented `WriteConsole` function outputting a line (of 80 characters or less) to the console, However, we saw an even greater number of LPC rounds caused by a function `FileIsConsole`. By Fay tracing of arguments, we could establish that, for every single line of output, the command shell would check twice whether `stdout` was directed to the console window, or not, at the cost of two LPC rounds and many context switches and system calls. Even more surprisingly, we saw those checks and LPC rounds continue to occur when output was directed to a file—causing nearly a million system calls when we used `type` to output our 16 MB text file to the special file `NUL`, for example.

We also used Fay tracing to investigate other frequent system calls, by collecting and counting their distinct arguments, return values, and user-mode stack traces. This data indicated that the calls to `NtQueryInformationProcess` in Table 1 were due to an internal CSRSS function, `IsConhost`, inspecting an undocumented property (number 49) of the cmd.exe process. The arguments and return values strongly indicated that CSRSS was retrieving this property, on every LPC round, to verify that an intermediary conhost was still hosting the console for an originating cmd.exe.

The above behavior also occurs for commands run in shell scripts, which often redirect large amounts of output to files or to `NUL`. The most frequent system calls simply retrieve information from the kernel, and user-mode processes can typically cache such data or read it via a "shared user data page" (like the one exposed by the Windows kernel) that gives a read-only, up-to-date view of data maintained elsewhere [49]. Thus, concretely, our Fay case study identified potential reductions in the LPC rounds and context switches required for each line of command shell output, which could eliminate most of the system calls in Table 1. However, command shell output is usually not a critical performance issue, and its implementation in Windows appears tuned for reliability and simplicity; thus, while insightful, our observations are not sufficient to justify immediate changes to user-mode or kernel-mode code.

5.2 Reimplementing Tracing Strategies

To stress the generality of Fay tracing, we reimplemented several existing, custom tracing strategies on top of the Fay tracing platform. This reimplementation was done with minimal effort, by leveraging Fay extensions and the high-level queries of FayLINQ. We used two DryadLINQ clusters: one with 12 machines with dual 2GHz AMD Opteron 246 processors and 8GB of memory, and another with 128 machines with two 2.1GHz quad-core AMD Opteron 2373EE processors and 16GB of memory, both running Windows Server 2008 R2 Enterprise. Below we describe our implementations and (in some cases) the results of applying these monitoring strategies to our clusters.

5.2.1 Distributed Performance Counters

A common strategy for distributed monitoring is to count the events generated across all machines of a cluster. Fay tracing can trivially implement this strategy by applying the appropriate aggregation operations to any metrics on the trace events available to probes on a single machine. Unlike traditional performance counters, Fay tracing allows both user-controllable and efficient aggregation. For instance, with small changes, the query shown on page 1 can provide per-process, per-thread, and per-module statistics on all cluster activity in both user-mode and the kernel. Such monitoring of memory allocation cannot be achieved with traditional Windows performance counters, even on a single machine.

5.2.2 Automatic Analysis of Cluster Behavior

Several recent systems have applied automatic machine-learning techniques to extract useful information from activity signatures collected across a cluster [30, 63]. We used FayLINQ to perform an analysis similar to that of Fmeter [30] on our cluster, while it executed an unrelated map-reduce workload (N-gram generation).

A single FayLINQ query sufficed to express the entire trace collection, the k-means clustering of the collected traces, and the analysis of the traced workload using those machine-learning results. This query collects periodic system-call-frequency histograms for the 402 system calls in the Windows kernel, at a granularity of around 1 second. Collecting this information does not measurably affect CPU utilization or machine performance, since FayLINQ synthesizes efficient, stateful kernel probes that maintain counts per system call. The data-analysis part of the FayLINQ query reduced the dataset dimensionality by applying k-means clustering (with k set to 5) on the histograms, using published distributed machine-learning techniques for DryadLINQ [33]. Then, the FayLINQ query associated the workload activity in each period with the closest of the five centroids resulting from the k-means clustering. Finally, the FayLINQ query output results into a visualization tool to produce the chart in Figure 11.

Figure 11 shows activity on all machines, during execution of the map-reduce workload. All activity periods are associated with their most similar k-means centroid, each of which has a unique color and a (manually-added) label: io, idle, memory, cpu, or outlier. By comparing against the map-reduce job plan, it can be seen that Figure 11 precisely captures the workload's different processing stages, as annotated at the bottom of the figure—including the use of five machines in the first stage, and ten machines for the second, and the final stages of io-intensive data reduction. Here, we compared against ground truth from a known map-reduce job plan. However, in most cases, no such explicit plan exists, and similar FayLINQ analysis could clarify the processing phases of even complex, opaque distributed services.

5.2.3 Predicated and Windowed Trace Processing

Some systems implement stateful or non-deterministic tracing primitives that are not so easily expressed as pure, functional LINQ queries. Nonetheless, FayLINQ can utilize Fay's extensibility to provide such primitives and incorporate their results into tracing queries. Concretely, users of FayLINQ can implement any probe extension by providing an arbitrary C function, or make use of our library of such extensions.

Fay extensions can use optimized machine code to evaluate the state of a traced system in any manner, whether complex or stateful. Thus, Fay can offer a efficient, general form of predication and

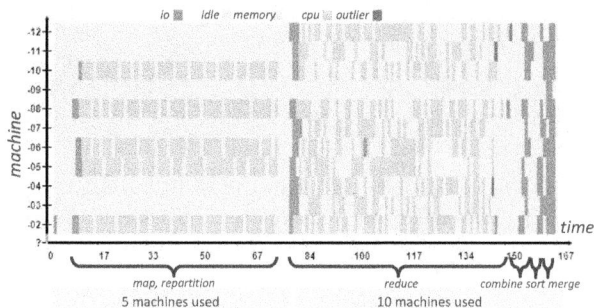

Figure 11: The result of FayLINQ analysis of cluster behavior while executing a map-reduce job. This 2D plot shows the results of automatic k-means clustering of system-call histograms collected periodically across all machines. The X axis shows time, machines are on the Y axis, and each period is colored according to its representative k-means centroid.

speculation, and support tracing that cannot even be expressed in language-restricted platforms like DTrace [11]. To achieve similar functionality, other tracing platforms require the evaluation code to be fully trusted—thereby leaving the traced system fully exposed to any reliability and security issues in that code.

In particular, we have implemented Fay probe extension functions for Chopstix sketches [7], to provide statistical, non-uniform sampling of low- and high-frequency events with low overhead. FayLINQ sketching uses a hashtable of counters to ensure that trace events are output in logarithmic proportion to the total number of occurrences. While our sketching library implementation hides some complexity, FayLINQ users need only invoke a simple HCA function to use the library, much as in the code on page 10.

We have also implemented probe extensions for temporal processing on trace event streams, such as windowed (sliding or staggered) computations. For example, our simple MovingAverage extension for computing moving averages is used in the below query, which emits all kernel memory allocations that are 10 times larger than the current local moving average:

```
cluster.Function("ExAllocatePoolWithTag")
.Select(event => GetArg(2)) // allocation size
.Select(sizeArg => new {
                average = MovingAverage(sizeArg),
                size = sizeArg })
.Where(alloc => alloc.size > 10*alloc.average);
```

5.2.4 Tracking Work Across Distributed Systems

Several distributed monitoring platforms track all the activity performed for work items, as those items are processed by different parts of the system [5, 50]. Often, such tracking is done via passive, distributed monitoring, combined with "temporal joins" to infer dynamic dependencies and flow of work items. Fay tracing can easily support such monitoring, by encoding temporal joins as recursive queries that transitively propagate information, and by iterating to convergence. We have used FayLINQ to track work in a distributed system by monitoring and correlating sent and received network packets, to analyze the traffic matrix of DryadLINQ workloads.

5.2.5 Tracing Across Software Abstractions

We used Fay to redo a study of the Windows timer interfaces and mechanisms; the original study [43] was done by modifying Win-

Experiment	Fay	Solaris DTrace	OS X DTrace	Fedora STap
km	220	1717	1805	1129
um `call`	197	1557	2565	9009
um `jmp`	155			
um `call` **deep**	431	1683	2813	9384
um `jmp` **deep**	268			

Table 2: Overhead in CPU cycles per call to a traced function. Here, km is kernel mode, um is user mode, and deep builds a 20-deep stack before each call. Fay dispatches using inline `call` or `jmp` instructions; other platforms trap to the kernel.

dows source code. Starting with the low-level, kernel timer interfaces `KeSetTimer`, `KeSetTimerEx`, and `KeCancelTimer`, we used FayLINQ to trace timer usage. For each use, we grouped by return addresses on the call stack and sorted to identify common callers, thereby identifying the small number of modules and functions that are the primary users of `KeSetTimer`, etc. We then iterated, by creating a larger, recursive FayLINQ query, predicated to generate trace events only in certain contexts, and discovered 13 sets of timer interfaces in Windows, such as `ZwUserSetTimer`. Close, manual inspection revealed that those interfaces were based on five separate timer wheel implementations [59].

5.3 Performance Evaluation

To assess the efficiency and scalability of our Fay implementation, we measured the performance of Fay tracing and its mechanisms for instrumentation, inline dispatching, and safe probe execution. The experiments ran on an iMac with a 3.06GHz Intel E7600 CPU and 8GB of RAM. We configured this machine to run 64-bit versions of Windows 7 Enterprise, Mac OS X v10.6, Fedora 15 Linux (kernel version 2.6.40-4.fc15), and Oracle Solaris 11 Express, in order to directly compare Fay tracing against DTrace, on two platforms, and against SystemTap (version 1.5/0.152) on Linux.

5.3.1 Microbenchmarks

To measure the cost of dispatching and executing an empty probe, we created a user-mode microbenchmark that contains an empty function `foo`, which it calls in a tight loop. We measured its running time both with, and without, Fay tracing of `foo` using an empty probe. We also created a microbenchmark that invokes a trivial system call in a tight loop, and where we traced the kernel-mode system call handler. (We used the `getpid` system call, except on Windows where we used `NtQuerySystemInformation` with an invalid parameter to minimize the work it performed.)

We also wanted to measure the effects of branch-misprediction caused by the stack manipulation of the Fay `call` dispatcher (see Section 3.2). Therefore, we created variants of the microbenchmarks that call `foo` via a sequence of 20 nested functions—forcing 20 extra stack frames to be unwound at each `foo` tracepoint.

Table 2 shows the results of our microbenchmarks, with time measurements converted to CPU cycle counts. Fay takes around 200 cycles per call and, as expected, dispatching using `jmp` is noticeably faster than Fay `call` dispatcher. If a thread is not being traced, this work can be cut in half, and the Fay `call` dispatcher adds only about 107 cycles per call. In both of these cases, the hashtable lookup of tracepoint descriptors accounts for roughly 40 cycles. The experiments for DTrace and SystemTap were run using

	MD5	lld	hotlist
Measured Fay XFI slowdown	184%	552%	1387%
XFI slowdown from [18]	101%	346%	798%

Table 3: Slowdown due to XFI for three benchmarks. The Fay XFI variant is much simpler, but has nearly twice the overhead.

	Fay	Solaris DTrace	OS X DTrace
Traced functions	8001	31998	9341
Function calls (millions)	60	253	306
Running time w/tracing	28.0	103.2	149.6
Slowdown	2.8x	17.2x	26.7x

Table 4: Instrumenting all kernel functions to test scalability.

function boundary tracing and per-CPU collection and aggregation. Compared to Fay, the other tracing platforms generally required a bit less than an order-of-magnitude more cycles.

Next, we compare the execution time of three benchmark probes with and without XFI rewriting, summarizing the results in Table 3. This experiment replicates parts of Table 1 in [18] (slowpath with read and write protection). Our overhead is larger than that in [18], which is not surprising, since we targeted simplicity in our implementation. However, Fay XFI performance still compares favorably to that of safe interpreters like those used in DTrace [47].

5.3.2 Scalability and Impact of Optimizations

We have used Fay to trace all the 8,001 hotpatchable functions in the Windows kernel and increment a per-CPU counter at each tracepoint, to count the total kernel function invocations. Such tracing does not occur often, but can be useful. An example application, that has seen practical use in other tracing platforms, is the tracing of all kernel activity due to a specific kernel module, such as a network driver, or a specific interrupt handler [17], and the generation of function call graphs for later visualization [16].

Table 4 displays the results of tracing a workload that copied all the RFC text files between ramdisk directories, deleted the new copies, and repeated this a fixed number of times. Fay scales very well, and using it to trace the vast majority of Windows kernel functions leaves the machine perfectly responsive and about 2.8 times slower on a benchmark that spends 75% of its time executing kernel code. Notably, the scale of this experiment creates a worst-case scenario for Fay performance: the Fay `call` dispatcher adds an extra stack frame on every kernel function invocation, and suffers a branch-prediction miss on every function return.

The slowdown factors for DTrace are significantly higher, on both Solaris and Mac OS X. However, slowdown factors are not directly comparable, since Fay and DTrace are instrumenting different operating systems. Trying to repeat the experiment with SystemTap resulted in a hung Linux kernel, apparently due to a long-standing, well-known SystemTap bug [58].

We tested the scalability, robustness, and optimizations of Fay tracing by utilizing our 128-machine, 1024-core cluster for a benchmark that makes 50 million memory allocations per machine. In the benchmark, each thread allocates and clears 10 heap-memory regions, of a random size between 1 byte and 16 kilobytes, yields with a `Sleep(0)`, clears and frees the 10 regions, and then loops.

We measured all configurations of partitioning per-machine work over 1, 2, 5, or 10 processes and 1, 5, 10, 50, 100, 500, or 1000 concurrent threads in each process. These configurations ran on the entire, dedicated cluster, spreading 6.4 billion allocations between 128 to 1,280,000 threads, each at 100% CPU utilization when running. The benchmark took between 30 seconds and 4 minutes to run, depending on the configuration—not counting unpredictable delays and high variance caused by the cluster's job scheduler.

Using a FayLINQ query to measure total allocated memory added an overhead of 1% to 11% (mean 7.8%, std.dev. 3.8%) to the benchmark running time. The numbers matched our expectation: per allocation, the benchmark spent approximately a couple of thousand cycles, to which Fay tracing added a couple of hundred cycles, as per Figure 2—but, as the number of processes and threads grew, increased context switches and other costs started masking some of Fay's overhead. The time to initialize tracing, and install Fay probes, grew as processes increased from 1 to 10, going from 1.5 to 7 seconds. Whether or not Fay tracing was enabled, the benchmark had similar variance in CPU time (mean std.dev. 2%, max std.dev. 6%) and wall-clock time (mean std.dev. 10%, max std.dev. 33%), both per-process and per-thread.

We exercised the fault-tolerance of Fay tracing by randomly killing threads, processes, or machines running the benchmark. When a thread dies, all its thread-local Fay probe state is lost, if it has not already been sent as a trace event. Machine-local Fay aggregation continued unimpeded by failure of benchmark threads or processes. Even upon the failure of machines, the Dryad fault-tolerance mechanisms would ensure that cluster-level aggregation continued. Thus, the results of our FayLINQ query were perturbed in proportion to our violence. In addition, the data lost for any thread could be bounded by having Fay probes periodically send off their data as ETW trace events. For our benchmark FayLINQ query, probe state was sent as trace events every 100 memory allocations, at the cost of 1% extra Fay tracing overhead.

In the limit, a trace event might need to be sent at every tracepoint invocation, if the work of a tracing query was completely unsuited to Fay probe processing. To assess the benefits of early aggregation and FayLINQ optimizations, we modified our benchmark to measure such high-frequency trace events. With nearly half-a-million Fay trace events a second, and no probe processing, the benchmark's tracing overhead increased to between 5% and 163% (average 67%, std.dev. 45%). However, most of those trace events were lost, and not accounted for in the result of our FayLINQ query.

These lost trace events were surprising, since our Fay implementation minimizes the risk of data loss, both by dynamically tuning ETW buffer size, and also by running time-critical Fay activity like trace-event processing on Windows threads with high enough priority. Upon inspection, we discovered that the real-time, machine-local FayLINQ aggregation process that converts ETW trace events to .NET objects—rather slowly, on a single thread—was completely unable to handle the high event rate. FayLINQ can be manually directed to stream trace events directly to disk, into ETW log files, processed by later, batch-processing parts of the query plan. We attempted this next, but failed again: each ETW log file record is about 100 bytes, which at 50 million events, in less than four minutes, exceeded our disk bandwidth. Even though consuming data at high rates is intrinsically difficult, these results clearly indicated that FayLINQ was lacking in its support for high-event-rate tracing. So, we enhanced Fay with a custom, real-time

ETW consumer thread that efficiently streams just the Fay payload of ETW events (4 bytes in our benchmark) directly to disk. After this, FayLINQ could return correct query results, by generating a plan that processes the disk files subsequent to the benchmark run.

To further evaluate the benefits of FayLINQ query-plan optimizations, we reran the experiment from Section 5.2.2 with the term-rewriting in Figure 10 turned off. While Fay tracing previously had no measurable performance effects, unoptimized tracing significantly increased the workload completion time, e.g., due to the addition of (a near-constant) 10% of CPU time being spent on kernel-mode trace event processing. Also, the lack of early-aggregation optimizations lead to a high event rate (more than 100,000 events/second, for some phases of the workload). Thus, we again had to direct FayLINQ to create query plans that stored trace events first on disk, and finished processing later. Even then, several times more data was received and processed at the higher-levels of the FayLINQ aggregation pipeline.

6. RELATED WORK

Fay is motivated by the many attractive benefits of the DTrace platform [11], while Fay's fundamental primitives are more like those of SystemTap [45] and Ftrace [48].

Fay makes use of, and integrates with a number of technologies from Microsoft Windows [49], including Event Tracing for Windows [41], PowerShell [55], Vulcan [54], Hotpatching [34], Structured Exception Handling [44], and the Driver Model [40].

Dynamic Instrumentation Systems Fay is related to several systems that perform dynamic instrumentation: KLogger [20], PinOS [8], Valgrind [39], scalable tracing on K42 [62], Ftrace and SystemTap on Linux [45, 48], Solaris DTrace [11], the NTrace prototype [42], and Detours for the Win32 interface [25].

The Fay probe dispatcher is related to new tracing tools that make use of inline mechanisms, not traps. On Linux, Ftrace [48] provides tracing based on fast, inline hooks placed by compiling the kernel with special flags. On Windows, the NTrace research project leverages hotpatching [42], but does so via a custom, modified kernel. Compared to Fay, the Ftrace and NTrace mechanisms offer more limited functionality, are likely to be less efficient, and provide neither safe extensibility nor a high-level query interface.

Safe Operating Systems Extensions Fay is an example of a system that implements safe operating systems extensions using software-based techniques [6]. This is not a new idea. Indeed, Fay has striking similarities to the SDS-940 Informer profiler developed at the end of the 1960's [15]. Other systems and techniques for providing safe system extensibility include Typed Assembly Language [37], Proof-Carrying Code [38], as well as Software-based Fault Isolation (SFI) [61], and its implementations in MiSFIT [52], Native Client [64], and similar systems [18].

Declarative Tracing and Debugging The Fay integration with DryadLINQ is related to several prior efforts to support declarative or relational queries of software execution traces. In particular, Fay is related to declarative tracepoints [12], PQL [31], and PTQL [23], and also to work in aspect-oriented programming [3].

In the trade-off between creating a domain-specific language and using a generic language, such as LINQ, we have opted towards the latter. Embedded knowledge about the semantics of traces (e.g., time, procedure nesting, etc.) can make the evaluation of some queries more efficient. Probes should be able to aggregate and reduce data as much as possible, while relegating expensive computations to external systems. Here, we believe that FayLINQ strikes a good balance.

Large-scale, Distributed Tracing Large-scale, distributed tracing, data collection and debugging [28, 53] is a highly active area, with several existing, attractive systems, and one deployed across a billion machines [22]. Of particular relevance are recent systems, like Chopstix [7], and Flight data recorder [60], as well as their predecessor DCPI [9] and its recent distributed analogue GWP [46]. Similarly, earlier work such as Magpie [5] on tracing requests across activities has recently been extended to the datacenter [50]. Finally, also highly relevant is work from the high-performance community for tracing in parallel systems [27, 32], and the techniques of stream-processing platforms [4]. Flume [21] is a log collection system that allows the transformation and filtering of log data, similar in some aspects to simple FayLINQ queries.

7. CONCLUSIONS

Fay is a flexible platform for the dynamic tracing of distributed systems. Fay is applicable to both user- and kernel-mode activity; our Fay implementation for x86-64 Windows can be applied even to live, unmodified production systems. Users can utilize Fay tracing through several means, which include traditional scripting. Fay users can also safely extend Fay with new, efficient tracing primitives, without affecting the reliability of traced systems.

Distinguishing Fay from previous tracing platforms is its disaggregated execution, even within a single machine, as well as its safe, efficient extensibility, and its deep integration with a high-level language and distributed runtime in FayLINQ—all of which facilitate large-scale execution trace collection and analysis.

Building on the above, FayLINQ provides a unified, declarative means of specifying what events to trace, as well as the aggregation, processing, and analysis of those events. As such, FayLINQ holds the potential to greatly simplify the investigation of performance, functionality, or reliability issues in distributed systems. Through benchmarks and experiments, we have demonstrated the efficiency and flexibility of Fay distributed tracing, and also shown how a few simple FayLINQ queries can offer the same functionality as that provided by custom mechanisms in other tracing platforms.

Acknowledgments

We thank the SOSP PC for their useful comments and our shepherd, Greg Ganger, for his gracious help. Fay's hotpatch-based instrumentation was designed and implemented in collaboration with the Microsoft Windows Fundamentals group: Anshul Dhir, Haifeng He, Bradford Neuman, and Dragoş Sâmbotin contributed directly to the implementation, starting from a prototype by Neeraj Singh. Gloria Mainar-Ruiz helped with the Fay XFI implementation and experiments. Jacob Gorm Hansen and Jorrit Herder worked on previous XFI variants and applications in Windows, respectively, for KMDF device drivers and for safe kernel-mode interrupt handlers for UMDF device drivers. The DryadLINQ integration benefited from work by Pradeep Kumar Gunda. Jon Currey helped with cluster-experiment infrastructure. Michael Vrable provided camera-ready support. The up-to-date version of SystemTap that we measured was provided by William Cohen, of Red Hat, Inc.

8. REFERENCES

[1] J. Ansel, P. Marchenko, Ú. Erlingsson, E. Taylor, B. Chen, D. L. Schuff, D. Sehr, C. L. Biffle, and B. Yee. Language-independent sandboxing of just-in-time compilation and self-modifying code. In *PLDI*, 2011.

[2] Apache. Hadoop project. http://hadoop.apache.org/.

[3] P. Avgustinov, J. Tibble, E. Bodden, L. Hendren, O. Lhotak, O. de Moor, N. Ongkingco, and G. Sittampalam. Efficient trace monitoring. In *OOPSLA*, 2006.

[4] M. Balazinska, H. Balakrishnan, S. Madden, and M. Stonebraker. Fault-tolerance in the Borealis distributed stream processing system. In *SIGMOD*, 2005.

[5] P. Barham, A. Donnelly, R. Isaacs, and R. Mortier. Using Magpie for request extraction and workload modelling. In *OSDI*, 2004.

[6] B. N. Bershad, S. Savage, P. Pardyak, D. Becker, M. Fiuczynski, and E. G. Sirer. Protection is a software issue. In *HotOS*, 1995.

[7] S. Bhatia, A. Kumar, M. E. Fiuczynski, and L. Peterson. Lightweight, high-resolution monitoring for troubleshooting production systems. In *OSDI*, 2008.

[8] P. P. Bungale and C.-K. Luk. PinOS: A programmable framework for whole-system dynamic instrumentation. In *VEE*, 2007.

[9] M. Burrows, Ú. Erlingsson, S.-T. A. Leung, M. T. Vandevoorde, C. A. Waldspurger, K. Walker, and W. E. Weihl. Efficient and flexible value sampling. In *ASPLOS*, 2000.

[10] B. Cantrill. Hidden in plain sight. *ACM Queue*, 4, 2006.

[11] B. M. Cantrill, M. W. Shapiro, and A. H. Leventhal. Dynamic instrumentation of production systems. In *USENIX Annual Technical Conf.*, 2004.

[12] Q. Cao, T. Abdelzaher, J. Stankovic, K. Whitehouse, and L. Luo. Declarative tracepoints: A programmable and application independent debugging system for wireless sensor networks. In *SenSys*, 2008.

[13] C. Chambers, A. Raniwala, F. Perry, S. Adams, R. R. Henry, R. Bradshaw, and N. Weizenbaum. FlumeJava: Easy, efficient data-parallel pipelines. In *PLDI*, 2010.

[14] J. Dean and S. Ghemawat. MapReduce: A flexible data processing tool. *Comm. ACM*, 53(1), 2010.

[15] P. Deutsch and C. A. Grant. A flexible measurement tool for software systems. In *IFIP*, 1971.

[16] Eclipse. Callgraph plug-in. http://wiki.eclipse.org/Linux_Tools_Project/Callgraph/User_Guide.

[17] F. C. Eigler. Systemtap tutorial, Dec. 2010. http://sourceware.org/systemtap/tutorial/.

[18] Ú. Erlingsson, M. Abadi, M. Vrable, M. Budiu, and G. C. Necula. XFI: Software guards for system address spaces. In *OSDI*, 2006.

[19] Ú. Erlingsson, M. Manasse, and F. McSherry. A cool and practical alternative to traditional hash tables. In *Workshop on Distributed Data and Structures*, 2006.

[20] Y. Etsion, D. Tsafrir, S. Kirkpatrick, and D. G. Feitelson. Fine grained kernel logging with KLogger: Experience and insights. In *EuroSys*, 2007.

[21] Flume: Open source log collection system. http://github.com/cloudera/flume.

[22] K. Glerum, K. Kinshumann, S. Greenberg, G. Aul, V. Orgovan, G. Nichols, D. Grant, G. Loihle, and G. Hunt.

Debugging in the (very) large: Ten years of implementation and experience. In *SOSP*, 2009.

[23] S. F. Goldsmith, R. O'Callahan, and A. Aiken. Relational queries over program traces. In *OOPSLA*, 2005.

[24] A. Gupta, I. S. Mumick, and V. S. Subrahmanian. Maintaining views incrementally. In *ACM Intl. Conf. on Management of Data*, 1993.

[25] G. Hunt and D. Brubacher. Detours: Binary interception of Win32 functions. In *USENIX Windows NT Symposium*, 1998.

[26] M. Isard, M. Budiu, Y. Yu, A. Birrell, and D. Fetterly. Dryad: Distributed data-parallel programs from sequential building blocks. In *EuroSys*, 2007.

[27] G. L. Lee, M. Schulz, D. H. Ahn, A. Bernat, B. R. de Supinskil, S. Y. Ko, and B. Rountree. Dynamic binary instrumentation and data aggregation on large scale systems. *Intl. Journal on Parallel Programming*, 35(3), 2007.

[28] B. Liblit, A. Aiken, A. X. Zheng, and M. I. Jordan. Bug isolation via remote program sampling. *PLDI*, 38(5), 2003.

[29] F. Marguerie, S. Eichert, and J. Wooley. *LINQ in action*. Manning Publications Co., 2008.

[30] T. Marian, A. Sagar, T. Chen, and H. Weatherspoon. Fmeter: Extracting Indexable Low-level System Signatures by Counting Kernel Function Calls. Technical Report http://hdl.handle.net/1813/23568, Cornell University, Computing and Information Science, 2011.

[31] M. Martin, B. Livshits, and M. S. Lam. Finding application errors and security flaws using PQL: A program query language. In *OOPSLA*, 2005.

[32] M. L. Massie, B. N. Chun, and D. E. Culler. The Ganglia distributed monitoring system: Design, implementation and experience. *Intl. Journal on Parallel Computing*, 30, 2003.

[33] F. McSherry, Y. Yu, M. Budiu, M. Isard, and D. Fetterly. *Scaling Up Machine Learning*. Cambridge U. Press, 2011.

[34] Microsoft Corp. Introduction to hotpatching. *Microsoft TechNet*, 2003.

[35] Microsoft Corp. Kernel patch protection: Frequently asked questions. *Windows Hardware Developer Central*, 2006. http://www.microsoft.com/whdc/driver/kernel/64bitpatch_FAQ.mspx.

[36] Microsoft Corp. WDK and developer tools. *Windows Hardware Developer Central*, 2010. http://www.microsoft.com/whdc/DevTools/default.mspx.

[37] G. Morrisett, D. Walker, K. Crary, and N. Glew. From System F to typed assembly language. In *POPL*, 1998.

[38] G. C. Necula. Proof-carrying code. In *POPL*, 1997.

[39] N. Nethercote and J. Seward. Valgrind: A framework for heavyweight dynamic binary instrumentation. In *PLDI*, 2007.

[40] W. Oney. *Programming the Microsoft Windows Driver Model*. Microsoft Press, 2002.

[41] I. Park and R. Buch. Improve debugging and performance tuning with ETW. *MSDN Magazine*, April 2007.

[42] J. Passing, A. Schmidt, M. von Lowis, and A. Polze. NTrace: Function boundary tracing for Windows on IA-32. In *Working Conference on Reverse Engineering*, 2009.

[43] S. Peter, A. Baumann, T. Roscoe, P. Barham, and R. Isaacs. 30 seconds is not enough!: A study of operating system timer usage. In *EuroSys*, 2008.

[44] M. Pietrek. A crash course on the depths of Win32 structured exception handling. *Microsoft Systems Journal*, 1997.

[45] V. Prasad, W. Cohen, F. C. Eigler, M. Hunt, J. Keniston, and

B. Chen. Locating system problems using dynamic instrumentation. In *Ottawa Linux Symposium*, 2005.

[46] G. Ren, E. Tune, T. Moseley, Y. Shi, S. Rus, and R. Hundt. Google-wide profiling: A continuous profiling infrastructure for data centers. *IEEE Micro*, 30(4), 2010.

[47] T. H. Romer, D. Lee, G. M. Voelker, A. Wolman, W. A. Wong, J.-L. Baer, B. N. Bershad, and H. M. Levy. The structure and performance of interpreters. In *ASPLOS*, 1996.

[48] S. Rostedt. Debugging the kernel using Ftrace. *lwn.net*, 2009.

[49] M. E. Russinovich, D. A. Solomon, and A. Ionescu. *Microsoft Windows Internals*. Microsoft Press, 2009.

[50] B. H. Sigelman, L. A. Barroso, M. Burrows, P. Stephenson, M. Plakal, D. Beaver, S. Jaspan, and C. Shanbhag. Dapper, a large-scale distributed systems tracing infrastructure. Technical Report 2010-1, Google Inc., 2010.

[51] K. Skadron, P. S. Ahuja, M. Martonosi, and D. W. Clark. Improving prediction for procedure returns with return-address-stack repair mechanisms. In *MICRO*, 1998.

[52] C. Small and M. I. Seltzer. MiSFIT: Constructing safe extensible systems. *IEEE Concurrency: Parallel, Distributed and Mobile Computing*, 6(3), 1998.

[53] T. Sookoor, T. Hnat, P. Hooimeijer, W. Weimer, and K. Whitehouse. Macrodebugging: Global views of distributed program execution. In *SenSys*, 2009.

[54] A. Srivastava, A. Edwards, and H. Vo. Vulcan: Binary transformation in a distributed environment. Technical Report MSR-TR-2001-50, Microsoft Research, 2001.

[55] W. Stanek. *Windows PowerShell(TM) 2.0 Administrator's Pocket Consultant*. Microsoft Press, 2009.

[56] M. Strosaker. Sample real-world use of SystemTap. http://zombieprocess.wordpress.com/2008/01/03/sample-real-world-use-of-systemtap/.

[57] SystemTap. Examples. http://sourceware.org/systemtap/examples/.

[58] SystemTap. Bug 2725: function("*") probes sometimes crash & burn, June 2006. http://sources.redhat.com/bugzilla/show_bug.cgi?id=2725.

[59] G. Varghese and A. Lauck. Hashed and hierarchical timing wheels. *IEEE/ACM Transactions on Networking*, 5(6), 1997.

[60] C. Verbowski, E. Kiciman, A. Kumar, B. Daniels, S. Lu, J. Lee, Y.-M. Wang, and R. Roussev. Flight data recorder: Monitoring persistent-state interactions to improve systems management. In *OSDI*, 2006.

[61] R. Wahbe, S. Lucco, T. E. Anderson, and S. L. Graham. Efficient software-based fault isolation. In *SOSP*, 1993.

[62] R. W. Wisniewski and B. Rosenburg. Efficient, unified, and scalable performance monitoring for multiprocessor operating systems. In *Supercomputing*, 2003.

[63] D. B. Woodard and M. Goldszmidt. Model-based clustering for online crisis identification in distributed computing. Technical Report TR-2009-131, MSR, 2009.

[64] B. Yee, D. Sehr, G. Dardyk, J. B. Chen, R. Muth, T. Ormandy, S. Okasaka, N. Narula, and N. Fullagar. Native client: A sandbox for portable, untrusted x86 native code. *Comm. ACM*, 53(1):91–99, 2010.

[65] Y. Yu, P. K. Gunda, and M. Isard. Distributed aggregation for data-parallel computing: Interfaces and implementations. In *SOSP*, 2009.

[66] Y. Yu, M. Isard, D. Fetterly, M. Budiu, Ú. Erlingsson, P. G. Kumar, and J. Currey. DryadLINQ: A system for general-purpose distributed data-parallel computing using a high-level language. In *OSDI*, 2008.

DTHREADS: Efficient Deterministic Multithreading

Tongping Liu   Charlie Curtsinger   Emery D. Berger

Dept. of Computer Science
University of Massachusetts, Amherst
Amherst, MA 01003

Abstract

Multithreaded programming is notoriously difficult to get right. A key problem is non-determinism, which complicates debugging, testing, and reproducing errors. One way to simplify multithreaded programming is to enforce deterministic execution, but current deterministic systems for C/C++ are incomplete or impractical. These systems require program modification, do not ensure determinism in the presence of data races, do not work with general-purpose multithreaded programs, or run up to 8.4× slower than `pthreads`.

This paper presents DTHREADS, an efficient deterministic multithreading system for unmodified C/C++ applications that replaces the `pthreads` library. DTHREADS enforces determinism in the face of data races and deadlocks. DTHREADS works by exploding multithreaded applications into multiple processes, with private, copy-on-write mappings to shared memory. It uses standard virtual memory protection to track writes, and deterministically orders updates by each thread. By separating updates from different threads, DTHREADS has the additional benefit of eliminating false sharing. Experimental results show that DTHREADS substantially outperforms a state-of-the-art deterministic runtime system, and for a majority of the benchmarks evaluated here, matches and occasionally exceeds the performance of `pthreads`.

1. Introduction

The advent of multicore architectures has increased the demand for multithreaded programs, but writing them remains painful. It is notoriously far more challenging to write concurrent programs than sequential ones because of the wide range of concurrency errors, including deadlocks and race conditions [16, 20, 21]. Because thread interleavings are non-deterministic, different runs of the same multithreaded program can unexpectedly produce different results. These "Heisenbugs" greatly complicate debugging, and eliminating them requires extensive testing to account for possible thread interleavings [2, 11].

Instead of testing, one promising alternative approach is to attack the problem of concurrency bugs by eliminating its source: non-determinism. A fully *deterministic multithreaded system* would prevent Heisenbugs by ensuring that executions of the same program with the same inputs always yield the same results, even in the face of race conditions in the code. Such a system would not only dramatically simplify debugging of concurrent programs [13] and reduce testing overhead, but would also enable a number of other applications. For example, a deterministic multithreaded system would greatly simplify record and replay for multithreaded programs by eliminating the need to track memory operations [14, 19], and it would enable the execution of multiple replicas of multithreaded applications for fault tolerance [4, 7, 10, 23].

Several recent software-only proposals aim at providing deterministic multithreading for C/C++ programs, but these suffer from a variety of disadvantages. Kendo ensures determinism of synchronization operations with low overhead, but does not guarantee determinism in the presence of data races [22]. Grace prevents all concurrency errors but is limited to fork-join programs. Although it can be efficient, it often requires code modifications to avoid large runtime overheads [6]. CoreDet, a compiler and runtime system, enforces deterministic execution for arbitrary multithreaded C/C++ programs [3]. However, it exhibits prohibitively high overhead, running up to 8.4× slower than `pthreads` (see Section 6) and generates thread interleavings at arbitrary points in the code, complicating program debugging and testing.

Contributions

This paper presents **DTHREADS**, a deterministic multithreading (DMT) runtime system with the following features:

- DTHREADS guarantees deterministic execution of multithreaded programs even in the presence of data races. Given the same sequence of inputs or OS events, a program using DTHREADS always produces the same output.

- DTHREADS is straightforward to deploy: it replaces the `pthreads` library, requiring no recompilation or code changes.

- DTHREADS is *robust* to changes in inputs, architectures, and code, enabling `printf` debugging of concurrent programs.

- DTHREADS eliminates cache-line *false sharing*, a notorious performance problem for multithreaded applications.

- DTHREADS is efficient. It nearly matches or even exceed the performance of `pthreads` for the majority of the benchmarks examined here.

DTHREADS works by exploding multithreaded applications into multiple processes, with private, copy-on-write mappings to shared memory. It uses standard virtual memory protection to track writes, and deterministically orders updates by each thread. By separating updates from different threads, DTHREADS has the additional benefit of eliminating false sharing.

Our key insight is counterintuitive: the runtime costs and benefits of DTHREADS' mechanisms (processes, protection faults, copying and diffing, and false sharing elimination) balance out, for the majority of applications we evaluate here, the costs and benefits of `pthreads` (threads, no protection faults, and false sharing).

By committing changes only when needed, DTHREADS amortizes most of its costs. For example, because it only uses virtual memory protection to track the first write to a page, DTHREADS amortizes the cost of a fault over the length of a transaction.

DTHREADS provides deterministic execution while performing as well as or even better than `pthreads` for the majority of applications examined here, including much of the PARSEC benchmark suite (designed to be representative of next-generation shared-memory programs for chip-multiprocessors). DTHREADS isn't suitable for all applications: DTHREADS intercepts communication using the `pthreads` API, so programs using ad-hoc synchronization will not work with DTHREADS. Other application characteristics make it impossible for DTHREADS to amortize the costs of isolation and synchronization, resulting in poor performance. Despite these and other limitations, which we discuss in-depth in Section 7.2, DTHREADS still outperforms the previous state-of-the-art deterministic system by between 14% and 11.2× when evaluated using 14 parallel benchmarks.

DTHREADS marks a significant advance over the state of the art in deployability and performance, and provides promising evidence that fully deterministic multithreaded programming may be practical.

2. Related Work

The area of deterministic multithreading has seen considerable recent activity. Due to space limitations, we focus here on software-only, non language-based approaches.

Grace prevents a wide range of concurrency errors, including deadlocks, race conditions, ordering and atomicity violations by imposing sequential semantics on threads with speculative execution [6]. DTHREADS borrows Grace's threads-as-processes paradigm to provide memory isolation, but differs from Grace in terms of semantics, generality, and performance.

Because it provides the effect of a serial execution of all threads, one by one, Grace rules out all interthread communication, including updates to shared memory, condition variables, and barriers. Grace supports only a restricted class of multithreaded programs: fork-join programs (limited to thread create and join). Unlike Grace, DTHREADS can run most general-purpose multithreaded programs while guaranteeing deterministic execution.

DTHREADS enables far higher performance than Grace for several reasons: It deterministically resolves conflicts, while Grace must rollback and re-execute threads that update any shared pages (requiring code modifications to avoid serialization); DTHREADS prevents false sharing while Grace exacerbates it; and DTHREADS imposes no overhead on reads.

CoreDet is a compiler and runtime system that represents the current state-of-the-art in deterministic, general-purpose software multithreading [3]. It uses alternating parallel and serial phases, and a token-based global ordering that we adapt for DTHREADS. Like DTHREADS, CoreDet guarantees deterministic execution in the presence of races, but with different mechanisms that impose a far higher cost: on average 3.5× slower and as much as 11.2× slower than DTHREADS (see Section 6). The CoreDet compiler instruments all reads and writes to memory that it cannot prove by static analysis to be thread-local. CoreDet also serializes *all* external library calls, except for specific variants provided by the CoreDet runtime.

CoreDet and DTHREADS also differ semantically. DTHREADS only allows interleavings at synchronization points, but CoreDet relies on the count of instructions retired to form quanta. This approach makes it impossible to understand a program's behavior by examining the source code—the only way to know what a program does in CoreDet (or dOS and Kendo, which rely on the same mechanism) is to execute it on the target machine. This instruction-based commit schedule is also brittle: even small changes to the input or program can cause a program to behave differently, effectively ruling out `printf` debugging. DTHREADS uses synchronization operations as boundaries for transactions, so changing the code or input does not affect the schedule as long as the sequence of synchronization operations remains unchanged. We call this more stable form of determinism *robust determinism*.

dOS [4] is an extension to CoreDet that uses the same deterministic scheduling framework. dOS provides deterministic process groups (DPGs), which eliminate all internal non-determinism and control external non-determinism by recording and replaying interactions across DPG boundaries. dOS is orthogonal and complementary to DTHREADS, and in principle, the two could be combined.

Determinator is a microkernel-based operating system that enforces system-wide determinism [1]. Processes on Determinator run in isolation, and are able to communicate only at explicit synchronization points. For programs that use condition variables, Determinator emulates a legacy thread API with quantum-based determinism similar to CoreDet. This legacy support suffers from the same performance and robustness problems as CoreDet.

Like Determinator, DTHREADS isolates threads by running them in separate processes, but natively supports all `pthreads` communication primitives. DTHREADS is a drop-in replacement for `pthreads` that needs no special operating system support.

Finally, some recent proposals provide limited determinism. Kendo guarantees a deterministic order of lock acquisitions on commodity hardware ("weak determinism"); Kendo only enforces full ("strong") determinism for race-free programs [22]. TERN [15] uses code instrumentation to memoize safe thread schedules for applications, and uses these memoized schedules for future runs on the same input. Unlike these systems, DTHREADS guarantees full determinism even in the presence of races.

3. DTHREADS Overview

We begin our discussion of how DTHREADS works with an example execution of a simple, racy multithreaded program, and explain at a high level how DTHREADS enforces deterministic execution.

Figure 1 shows a simple multithreaded program that, because of data races, non-deterministically produces the outputs "1,0," "0,1" and "1,1." With `pthreads`, the order in which these modifications occur can change from run to run, resulting in non-deterministic output.

With DTHREADS, however, this program *always* produces the same output, ("1,1"), which corresponds to exactly one possible thread interleaving. DTHREADS ensures determinism using the following key approaches, illustrated in Figure 2:

Isolated memory access: In DTHREADS, threads are implemented using separate processes with private and shared views of memory, an idea introduced by Grace [6]. Because processes have separate address spaces, they are a convenient mechanism to isolate memory accesses between threads. DTHREADS uses this isolation to control the visibility of updates to shared memory, so each "thread" operates independently until it reaches a synchronization point (see below). Section 4.1 discusses the implementation of this mechanism in depth.

Deterministic memory commit: Multithreaded programs often use shared memory for communication, so DTHREADS must propagate one thread's writes to all other threads. To ensure deterministic execution, these updates must be applied at deterministic times, and in a deterministic order.

DTHREADS updates shared state in sequence at synchronization points. These points include thread creation and exit; mutex lock and unlock; condition variable wait and signal; posix sigwait and signal; and barrier waits. Between synchronization points, all

```
int a = b = 0;                          void * t1 (void *) {        void * t2 (void *) {
main() {                                  if (b == 0) {               if (a == 0) {
  pthread_create(&p1, NULL, t1, NULL);      a = 1;                      b = 1;
  pthread_create(&p2, NULL, t2, NULL);    }                           }
  pthread_join(&p1, NULL);                return NULL;                return NULL;
  pthread_join(&p2, NULL);              }                           }
  printf ("%d,%d\n", a, b);
}
```

Figure 1. A simple multithreaded program with data races on a and b. With `pthreads`, the output is non-deterministic, but DTHREADS guarantees the same output on every execution.

code effectively executes within an atomic *transaction*. This combination of memory isolation between synchronization points with a deterministic commit protocol guarantees deterministic execution even in the presence of data races.

Deterministic synchronization: DTHREADS supports the full array of `pthreads` synchronization primitives. Because current operating systems make no guarantees about the order in which threads will acquire locks, wake from condition variables, or pass through barriers, DTHREADS re-implements these primitives to guarantee a deterministic ordering. Details on the DTHREADS implementations of these primitives are given in Section 4.3.

Twinning and diffing: Before committing updates, DTHREADS first compares each modified page to a "twin" (copy) of the original shared page, and then writes only the modified bytes (diffs) into shared state (see Section 5 for optimizations that avoid copying and diffing). This algorithm is adapted from the distributed shared memory systems TreadMarks and Munin [12, 17]. The order in which threads write their updates to shared state is enforced by a single global token passed from thread to thread; see Section 4.2 for full details.

Fixing the data race example

Returning to the example program in Figure 1, we can now see how DTHREADS' memory isolation and a deterministic commit order ensure deterministic output. DTHREADS effectively isolates each thread from each other until it completes, and then orders updates by thread creation time using a deterministic last-writer-wins protocol.

At the start of execution, thread 1 and thread 2 have the same view of shared state, with $a = 0$ and $b = 0$. Because changes by one thread to the value of a or b will not be made visible to the other until thread exit, both threads' checks on line 2 will be true. Thread 1 sets the value of a to 1, and thread 2 sets the value of b to 1. These threads then commit their updates to shared state and exit, with thread 1 always committing before thread 2. The main thread then has an updated view of shared memory, and prints "1, 1" on every execution.

This determinism not only enables record-and-replay and replicated execution, but also effectively converts Heisenbugs into "Bohr" bugs, making them reproducible. In addition, DTHREADS optionally reports any conflicting updates due to racy writes, further simplifying debugging.

4. DTHREADS Architecture

This section describes DTHREADS' key algorithms—memory isolation, deterministic (diff-based) memory commit, deterministic synchronization, and deterministic memory allocation—as well as other implementation details.

4.1 Isolated Memory Access

To achieve deterministic memory access, DTHREADS isolates memory accesses among different threads between commit points, and commits the updates of each thread deterministically.

DTHREADS achieves cross-thread memory isolation by replacing threads with processes. In a multithreaded program running with `pthreads`, threads share all memory except for the stack. Changes to memory immediately become visible to all other threads. Threads share the same file descriptors, sockets, device handles, and windows. By contrast, because DTHREADS runs threads in separate processes, it must manage these shared resources explicitly.

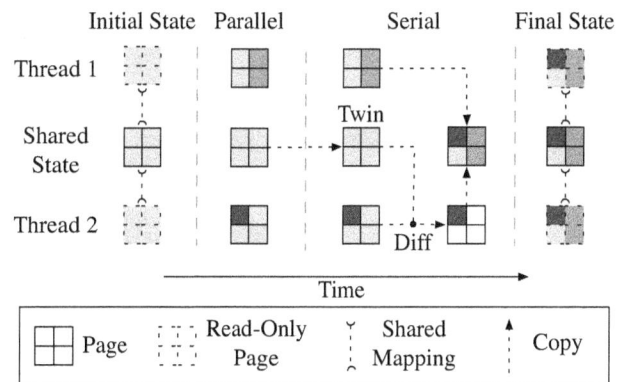

Figure 2. An overview of DTHREADS execution.

4.1.1 Thread Creation

DTHREADS replaces the `pthread_create()` function with the `clone` system call provided by Linux. To create processes that have disjoint address spaces but share the same file descriptor table, DTHREADS uses the `CLONE_FILES` flag. DTHREADS shims the `getpid()` function to return a single, globally-shared identifier.

4.1.2 Deterministic Thread Index

POSIX does not guarantee deterministic process or thread identifiers; that is, the value of a process id or thread id is not deterministic. To avoid exposing this non-determinism to threads running as processes, DTHREADS shims `pthread_self()` to return an internal thread index. The internal thread index is managed using a single global variable that is incremented on thread creation. This unique thread index is also used to manage per-thread heaps and as an offset into an array of thread entries.

4.1.3 Shared Memory

To create the illusion of different threads sharing the same address space, DTHREADS uses memory mapped files to share memory across processes (globals and the heap, but not the stack; see Section 7).

DTHREADS creates two different mappings for both the heap and the globals. One is a *shared* mapping, which is used to hold shared state. The other is a *private*, copy-on-write (COW) per-process mapping that each process works on directly. Private mappings are linked to the shared mapping through a single fixed-size memory-mapped file. Reads initially go directly to the shared mapping, but after the first write operation, both reads and writes are entirely private.

Memory allocations from the shared heap use a scalable per-thread heap organization loosely based on Hoard [5] and built using HeapLayers [8]. DTHREADS divides the heap into a fixed number of sub-heaps (currently 16). Each thread uses a hash of its deterministic thread index to find the appropriate sub-heap.

4.2 Deterministic Memory Commit

Figure 3 illustrates the progression of parallel and serial phases. To guarantee determinism, DTHREADS isolates memory accesses in the parallel phase. These accesses work on private copies of memory; that is, updates are not shared between threads during the parallel phase. When a synchronization point is reached, updates are applied (and made visible) in a deterministic order. This section describes the mechanism used to alternate between parallel and serial execution phases and guarantee deterministic commit order, and the details of commits to shared memory.

4.2.1 Fence and Token

The boundary between the parallel and serial phases is the internal fence. We implement this fence with a custom barrier, because the standard `pthreads` barrier does not support a dynamic thread count (see Section 4.3).

Threads wait at the internal fence until all threads from the previous fence have departed. Waiting threads must block until the departure phase. If the thread is the last to enter the fence, it initiates the departure phase and wakes all waiting threads. As threads leave the fence, they decrement the waiting thread count. The last thread to leave sets the fence to the arrival phase and wakes any waiting threads.

To reduce overhead, whenever the number of running threads is less than or equal to the number of cores, waiting threads block by spinning rather than by invoking relatively expensive cross-process `pthreads` mutexes. When the number of threads exceeds the number of cores, DTHREADS falls back to using `pthreads` mutexes.

A key mechanism used by DTHREADS is its global token. To guarantee determinism, each thread must wait for the token before it can communicate with other threads. The token is a shared pointer that points to the next runnable thread entry. Since the token is unique in the entire system, waiting for the token guarantees a global order for all operations in the serial phase.

DTHREADS uses two internal subroutines to manage tokens. The `waitToken` function first waits at the internal fence and then waits to acquire the global token before entering serial mode. The `putToken` function passes the token to the next waiting thread.

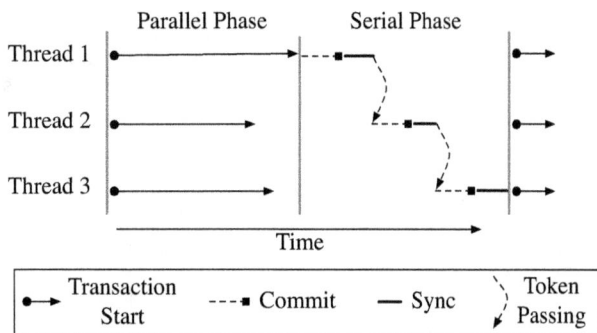

Figure 3. An overview of DTHREADS phases. Program execution with DTHREADS alternates between parallel and serial phases.

To guarantee determinism (see Figure 3), threads leaving the parallel phase must wait at the internal fence before they can enter into the serial phase (by calling `waitToken`). Note that it is crucial that threads wait at the fence even for a thread which is guaranteed to obtain the token next, since one thread's commits can affect another threads' behavior if there is no fence.

4.2.2 Commit Protocol

Figure 2 shows the steps taken by DTHREADS to capture modifications to shared state and expose them in a deterministic order. At the beginning of the parallel phase, threads have a read-only mapping for all shared pages. If a thread writes to a shared page during the parallel phase, this write is trapped and re-issued on a private copy of the shared page. Reads go directly to shared memory and are not trapped. In the serial phase, threads commit their updates one at a time. The first thread to commit to a page can directly copy its private copy to the shared state, but subsequent commits must copy only the modified bytes. DTHREADS computes diffs from a twin page, an unmodified copy of the shared page created at the beginning of the serial phase. At the end of the serial phase, private copies are released and these addresses are restored to read-only mappings of the shared memory.

At the start of every transaction (that is, right after a synchronization point), DTHREADS starts by write-protecting all previously-written pages. The old working copies of these pages are then discarded, and mappings are then updated to reference the shared state.

Just before every synchronization point, DTHREADS first waits for the global token (see below), and then commits all changes from the current transaction to the shared pages in order. DTHREADS maintains one "twin" page (a snapshot of the original) for every modified page with more than one writer. If the version number of the private copy matches the shared page, then the current thread must be the first thread to commit. In this case, the working copy can be copied directly to the shared state. If the version numbers do not match, then another thread has already committed changes to the page and a diff-based commit must be used.

Once changes have been committed, the number of writers to the page is decremented and the shared page's version number is incremented. If there are no writers left to commit, the twin page is freed.

4.3 Deterministic Synchronization

DTHREADS enforces determinism for the full range of synchronization operations in the `pthreads` API, including locks, condition variables, barriers and various flavors of thread exit.

4.3.1 Locks

DTHREADS uses a single global token to guarantee ordering and atomicity during the serial phase. When acquiring a lock, threads must first wait for the global token. Once a thread has the token it can attempt to acquire the lock. If the lock is currently held, the thread must pass the token and wait until the next serial phase to acquire the lock. It is possible for a program run with DTHREADS to deadlock, but only for programs that can also deadlock with `pthreads`.

Lock acquisition proceeds as follows. First, DTHREADS checks to see if the current thread is already holding any locks. If not, the thread first waits for the token, commits changes to shared state by calling `atomicEnd`, and begins a new atomic section. Finally, the thread increments the number of locks it is currently holding. The lock count ensures that a thread does not pass the token on until it has released all of the locks it acquired in the serial phase.

`pthread_mutex_unlock`'s implementation is similar. First, the thread decrements its lock count. If no more locks are held, any local modifications are committed to shared state, the token

330

is passed, and a new atomic section is started. Finally, the thread waits on the internal fence until the start of the next round's parallel phase. If other locks are still held, the lock count is just decreased and the running thread continues execution with the global token.

4.3.2 Condition Variables

Guaranteeing determinism for condition variables is more complex than for mutexes because the operating system does not guarantee that processes will wake up in the order they waited for a condition variable.

When a thread calls `pthread_cond_wait`, it first acquires the token and commits local modifications. It then removes itself from the token queue, because threads waiting on a condition variable do not participate in the serial phase until they are awakened. The thread decrements the live thread count (used for the fence between parallel and serial phases), adds itself to the condition variable's queue, and passes the token. While threads are waiting on DTHREADS condition variables, they are suspended on a `pthreads` condition variable. When a thread is awakened (signalled), it busy-waits on the token before beginning the next transaction. Threads must acquire the token before proceeding because the condition variable wait function must be called within a mutex's critical section.

In the DTHREADS implementation of `pthread_cond_signal`, the calling thread first waits for the token, and then commits any local modifications. If no threads are waiting on the condition variable, this function returns immediately. Otherwise, the first thread in the condition variable queue is moved to the head of the token queue and the live thread count is incremented. This thread is then marked as ready and woken up from the real condition variable, and the calling thread begins another transaction.

To impose an order on signal wakeup, DTHREADS signals actually call `pthread_cond_broadcast` to wake all waiting threads, but then marks only the logically next one as ready. The threads not marked as ready will wait on the condition variable again.

4.3.3 Barriers

As with condition variables, DTHREADS must ensure that threads waiting on a barrier do not disrupt token passing among running threads. DTHREADS removes threads entering into the barrier from the token queue and places them on the corresponding barrier queue.

In `pthread_barrier_wait`, the calling thread first waits for the token to commit any local modifications. If the current thread is the last to enter the barrier, then DTHREADS moves the entire list of threads on the barrier queue to the token queue, increases the live thread count, and passes the token to the first thread in the barrier queue. Otherwise, DTHREADS removes the current thread from the token queue, places it on the barrier queue, and releases token. Finally, the thread waits on the actual `pthreads` barrier.

4.3.4 Thread Creation and Exit

To guarantee determinism, thread creation and exit are performed in the serial phase. Newly-created threads are added to the token queue immediately after the parent thread. Creating a thread does not release the token; this approach allows a single thread to quickly create multiple child threads without having to wait for a new serial phase for each child thread.

When creating a thread, the parent first waits for the token. It then creates a new process with shared file descriptors but a distinct address space using the `clone` system call. The newly created child obtains the global thread index, places itself in the token queue, and notifies the parent that the child has registered itself in the active list. The child thread then waits for the next parallel phase before proceeding.

Similarly, DTHREADS' `pthread_exit` first waits for the token and then commits any local modifications to memory. It then removes itself from the token queue and decreases the number of threads required to proceed to the next phase. Finally, the thread passes its token to the next thread in the token queue and exits.

4.3.5 Thread Cancellation

DTHREADS implements thread cancellation in the serial phase. A thread can only invoke `pthread_cancel` while holding the token. If the thread being cancelled is waiting on a condition variable or barrier, it is removed from the queue. Finally, to cancel the corresponding thread, DTHREADS kills the target process with a call to `kill(tid, SIGKILL)`.

4.4 Deterministic Memory Allocation

Programs sometimes rely on the addresses of objects returned by the memory allocator intentionally (for example, by hashing objects based on their addresses), or accidentally. A program with a memory error like a buffer overflow will yield different results for different memory layouts.

This reliance on memory addresses can undermine other efforts to provide determinism. For example, CoreDet is unable to fully enforce determinism because it relies on the Hoard scalable memory allocator [5]. Hoard was not designed to provide determinism and several of its mechanisms, thread id based hashing and non-deterministic assignment of memory to threads, lead to non-deterministic execution in CoreDet for the `canneal` benchmark.

To preserve determinism in the face of intentional or inadvertent reliance on memory addresses, we designed the DTHREADS memory allocator to be fully deterministic. DTHREADS assigns subheaps to each thread based on its thread index (deterministically assigned; see Section 4.1.2). In addition to guaranteeing the same mapping of threads to subheaps on repeated executions, DTHREADS allocates superblocks (large chunks of memory) deterministically by acquiring a lock (and the global token) on each superblock allocation. Thus, threads always use the same subheaps, and these subheaps always contain the same superblocks on each execution. The remainder of the memory allocator is entirely deterministic. The superblocks themselves are allocated via `mmap`: while DTHREADS could use a fixed address mapping for the heap, we currently simply disable ASLR to provide deterministic `mmap` calls. If a program does not use the absolute address of any heap object, DTHREADS can guarantee determinism even with ASLR enabled. Hash functions and lock-free algorithms frequently use absolute addresses, and any deterministic multithreading system must disable ASLR to provide deterministic results for these cases.

4.5 OS Support

DTHREADS provides shims for a number of system calls both for correctness and determinism (although it does not enforce deterministic arrival of I/O events; see Section 7).

System calls that write to or read from buffers on the heap (such as `read` and `write`) will fail if the buffers contain protected pages. DTHREADS intercepts these calls and touches each page passed in as an argument to trigger the copy-on-write operation before issuing the real system call. DTHREADS conservatively marks all of these pages as modified so that any updates made by the system will be committed properly.

DTHREADS also intercepts other system calls that affect program execution. For example, when a thread calls `sigwait`, DTHREADS behaves much like it does for condition variables. It removes the calling thread from the token queue before issuing the system call, and after being awakened the thread must re-insert itself into the token queue and wait for the token before proceeding.

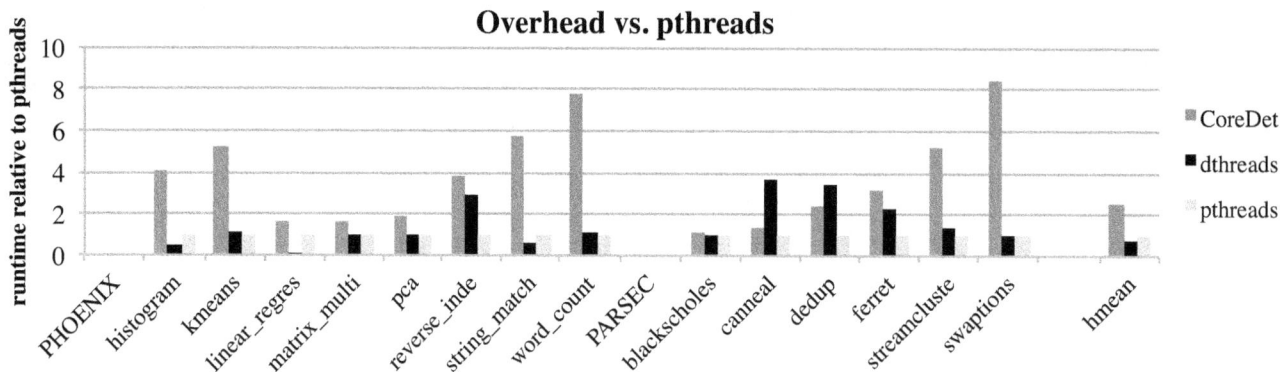

Figure 4. Normalized execution time with respect to `pthreads` (lower is better). For 9 of the 14 benchmarks, DTHREADS runs nearly as fast or faster than `pthreads`, while providing deterministic behavior.

5. Optimizations

DTHREADS employs a number of optimizations that improve its performance.

Lazy commit: DTHREADS reduces copying overhead and the time spent in the serial phase by *lazily* committing pages. When only one thread has ever modified a page, DTHREADS considers that thread to be the page's owner. An owned page is committed to shared state only when another thread attempts to read or write this page, or when the owning thread attempts to modify it in a later phase. DTHREADS tracks reads with page protection and signals the owning thread to commit pages on demand. To reduce the number of read faults, pages holding global variables (which we expect to be shared) and any pages in the heap that have ever had multiple writers are all considered unowned and are not read-protected.

Lazy twin creation and diff elimination: To further reduce copying and memory overhead, a twin page is only created when a page has multiple writers during the same transaction. In the commit phase, a single writer can directly copy its working copy to shared state without performing a diff. DTHREADS does this by comparing the local version number to the global page version number for each dirtied page. At commit time, DTHREADS directly copies its working copy for each page whenever its local version number equals its global version number. This optimization saves the cost of a twin page allocation, a page copy, and a diff in the common case where just one thread is the sole writer of a page.

Single-threaded execution: Whenever only one thread is running, DTHREADS stops using memory protection and treats certain synchronization operations (locks and barriers) as no-ops. In addition, when all other threads are waiting on condition variables, DTHREADS does not commit local changes to the shared mapping or discard private dirty pages. Updates are only committed when the thread issues a signal or broadcast call, which wakes up at least one thread and thus requires that all updates be committed.

Lock ownership: DTHREADS uses lock ownership to avoid unnecessary waiting when threads are using distinct locks. Initially, all locks are unowned. Any thread that attempts to acquire a lock that it does not own must wait until the serial phase to do so. If multiple threads attempt to acquire the same lock, this lock is marked as shared. If only one thread attempts to acquire the lock, this thread takes ownership of the lock and can acquire and release it during the parallel phase.

Lock ownership can result in starvation if one thread continues to re-acquire an owned lock without entering the serial phase. To avoid this, each lock has a maximum number of times it can be acquired during a parallel phase before a serial phase is required.

Parallelization: DTHREADS attempts to expose as much parallelism as possible in the runtime system itself. One optimization takes place at the start of trasactions, where DTHREADS performs a variety of cleanup tasks. These include releasing private page frames, and resetting pages to read-only mode by calling the `madvise` and `mprotect` system calls. If all this cleanup work is done simultaneously for all threads in the beginning of parallel phase (Figure 3), this can hurt performance for some benchmarks.

Since these operations do not affect other the behavior of other threads, most of this work can be parallelized with other threads' commit operations without holding the global token. With this optimization, the token is passed to the next thread as soon as possible, saving time in the serial phase. Before passing the token, any local copies of pages that have been modified by other threads must be discarded, and the shared read-only mapping is restored. This ensures all threads have a complete image of this page which later transactions may refer to. In the actual implementation, this cleanup occurs at the end of each transaction.

6. Evaluation

We perform our evaluation on an Intel Core 2 dual-processor CPU system equipped with 16GB of RAM. Each processor is a 4-core 64-bit Xeon running at 2.33GHZ with a 4MB L2 cache. The operating system is CentOS 5.5 (unmodified), running with Linux kernel version 2.6.18-194.17.1.el5. The glibc version is 2.5. Benchmarks were built as 32-bit executables with version 2.6 of the LLVM compiler.

6.1 Methodology

We evaluate the performance and scalability of DTHREADS versus CoreDet and `pthreads` across the PARSEC [9] and Phoenix [24] benchmark suites. We do not include results for `bodytrack`, `fluidanimate`, `x.264`, `facesim`, `vips`, and `raytrace` benchmarks from PARSEC, since they do not currently work with DTHREADS (note that many of these also do not work for CoreDet).

In order to compare performance directly against CoreDet, which relies on the LLVM infrastructure [18], all benchmarks are compiled with the LLVM compiler at the "-O3" optimization level [18]. Each benchmark is executed ten times on a quiescent machine. To reduce the effect of outliers, the lowest and highest execution times for each benchmark are discarded, so each result is the average of the remaining eight runs.

Tuning CoreDet: The performance of CoreDet [3] is extremely sensitive to three parameters: the granularity for the ownership table (in bytes), the quantum size (in number of instructions retired), and the choice between full and reduced serial mode. We performed an extensive search of the parameter space to find the one that

Scalability

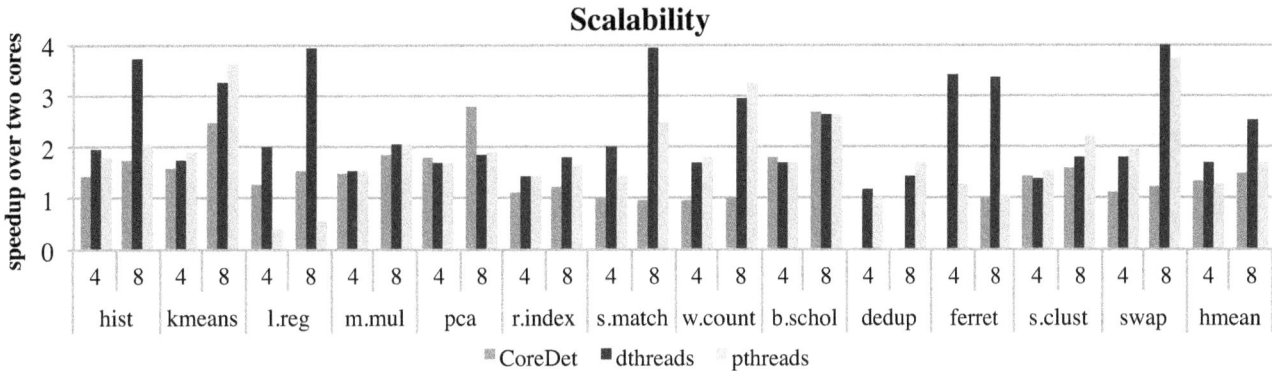

Figure 5. Speedup with four and eight cores relative to two cores (higher is better). DTHREADS generally scales nearly as well or better than `pthreads` and almost always as well or better than CoreDet. CoreDet was unable to run `dedup` with two cores and `ferret` with four cores, so some scalability numbers are missing.

yielded the lowest average normalized runtimes (using six possible granularities and eight possible quanta for each benchmark), and found that the best settings on our system were 64-byte granularity and a quantum size of 100,000 instructions, in full serial mode.

Unsupported Benchmarks: We were unable to evaluate DTHREADS on seven of the PARSEC benchmarks: `vips` and `raytrace` would not build as 32-bit executables; `bodytrack`, `facesim`, and `x264` depend on sharing of stack variables; `fluidanimate` uses ad-hoc synchronization, so it will not run without modifications; and `freqmine` does not use `pthreads`.

For all scalability experiments, we logically disable CPUs using Linux's CPU hotplug mechanism, which allows us to disable or enable individual CPUs by writing "0" (or "1") to a special pseudo-file (`/sys/devices/system/cpu/cpuN/online`).

6.2 Determinism

We first experimentally verify DTHREADS' ability to ensure determinism by executing the *racey* determinism tester [22]. This stress test is extremely sensitive to memory-level non-determinism. DTHREADS reports the same results for 2,000 runs. We also compared the schedules and outputs of all benchmarks used to ensure that every execution is identical.

6.3 Performance

We next compare the performance of DTHREADS to CoreDet and `pthreads`. Figure 4 presents these results graphically (normalized to `pthreads`).

DTHREADS outperforms CoreDet on 12 out of 14 benchmarks (between 14% and 11.2× faster); for 8 benchmarks, DTHREADS matches or outperforms `pthreads`. DTHREADS results in good performance for several reasons:

- Process invocation is only slightly more expensive than thread creation. This is because both rely on the `clone` system call. Copy-on-write semantics allow process creation without expensive copying.

- Context switches between processes are more expensive than for threads because of the required TLB shootdown. The number of context switches was minimized by running on a quiescent system with the number of threads matched to the number of cores whenever possible.

- DTHREADS incurs no read overhead and very low write overhead (one page fault per written page), but commits are expensive. Most of our benchmarks (and many real applications) result in small, infrequent commits.

- DTHREADS isolates updates in separate processes, which can improve performance by eliminating false sharing. Because threads actually execute in different address spaces, there is no coherence traffic between synchronization points.

By eliminating catastrophic false sharing, DTHREADS dramatically improves the performance of the `linear_regression` benchmark, running 7× faster than `pthreads` and 11.2× faster than CoreDet. The `string_match` benchmark exhibits a similar, if less dramatic, false sharing problem: with DTHREADS, it runs almost 40% faster than `pthreads` and 9.2× faster than CoreDet. Two benchmarks also run faster with DTHREADS than with `pthreads` (`histogram`, 2× and `swaptions`, 5%; respectively 8.5× and 8.9× faster than with CoreDet). We believe but have not yet verified that the reason is false sharing.

For some benchmarks, DTHREADS incurs modest overhead. For example, unlike most benchmarks examined here, which create long-lived threads, the `kmeans` benchmark creates and destroys over 1,000 threads over the course of one run. While Linux processes are relatively lightweight, creating and tearing down a process is still more expensive than the same operation for threads, accounting for a 5% performance degradation of DTHREADS over `pthreads` (though it runs 4.9× faster than CoreDet).

DTHREADS runs substantially slower than `pthreads` for 4 of the 14 benchmarks examined here. The `ferret` benchmark relies on an external library to analyze image files during the first stage in its pipelined execution model; this library makes intensive (and in the case of DTHREADS, unnecessary) use of locks. Lock acquisition and release in DTHREADS imposes higher overhead than ordinary `pthreads` mutex operations. More importantly in this case, the intensive use of locks in one stage forces DTHREADS to effectively serialize the other stages in the pipeline, which must repeatedly wait on these locks to enforce a deterministic lock acquisition order. The other three benchmarks (`canneal`, `dedup`, and `reverse_index`) modify a large number of pages. With DTHREADS, each page modification triggers a segmentation violation, a system call to change memory protection, the creation of a private copy of the page, and a subsequent copy into the shared space on commit. We note that CoreDet also substantially degrades performance for these benchmarks, so much of this slowdown may be inherent to any deterministic runtime system.

6.4 Scalability

To measure the scalability cost of running DTHREADS, we ran our benchmark suite (excluding `canneal`) on the same machine with eight cores, four corse, and just two cores enabled. Whenever possible without source code modifications, the number of threads was matched to the number of CPUs enabled. We have found that DTHREADS scales at least as well as pthreads for 9 of 13 benchmarks, and scales as well or better than CoreDet for all but one benchmark where DTHREADS outperforms CoreDet by 3.5×. Detailed results of this experiment are presented in Figure 5 and discussed below.

The canneal benchmark was excluded from the scalability experiment because it matches the workload to the number of threads, making the comparison between different numbers of threads invalid. DTHREADS hurts scalability relative to pthreads for the kmeans, word_count, dedup, and streamcluster benchmarks, although only marginally in most cases. In all of these cases, DTHREADS scales better than CoreDet.

DTHREADS is able to match the scalability of pthreads for three benchmarks: matrix_multiply, pca, and blackscholes. With DTHREADS, scalability actually *improves* over pthreads for 6 out of 13 benchmarks. This is because DTHREADS prevents false sharing, avoiding unnecessary cache invalidations that normally hurt scalability.

6.5 Performance Analysis

6.5.1 Benchmark Characteristics

The data presented in Table 1 are obtained from the executions running on all 8 cores. Column 2 shows the percentage of time spent in the serial phase. In DTHREADS, all memory commits and actual synchronization operations are performed in the serial phase. The percentage of time spent in the serial phase thus can affect performance and scalability. Applications with higher overhead in DTHREADS often spend a higher percentage of time in the serial phase, primarily because they modify a large number of pages that are committed during that phase.

Column 3 shows the number of transactions in each application and Column 4 provides the average length of each transaction (ms). Every synchronization operation, including locks, condition variables, barriers, and thread exits demarcate transaction boundaries in DTHREADS. For example, reverse_index, dedup, ferret and streamcluster perform numerous transactions whose execution time is less than 1ms, imposing a performance penalty for these applications. Benchmarks with longer (or fewer) transactions run almost the same speed as or faster than pthreads, including histogram or pca. In DTHREADS, longer transactions amortize the overhead of memory protection and copying.

Column 5 provides more detail on the costs associated with memory updates (the number and total volume of dirtied pages). From the table, it becomes clear why canneal (the most notable outlier) runs much slower with DTHREADS than with pthreads. This benchmark updates over 3 million pages, leading to the creation of private copies, protection faults, and commits to the shared memory space. Copying alone is quite expensive: we found that copying one gigabyte of memory takes approximately 0.8 seconds when using memcpy, so for canneal, copying overhead alone accounts for at least 20 seconds of time spent in DTHREADS (out of a total execution time of 39 seconds).

Conclusion: For the few benchmarks that perform large numbers of short-lived transactions, modify a large number of pages per-transaction, or both, DTHREADS can result in substantial overhead. Most benchmarks examined here run fewer, longer-running transactions with a modest number of modified pages. For these applications, overhead is amortized. With the side-effect of eliminating false sharing, DTHREADS can sometimes even outperform pthreads.

6.5.2 Performance Impact Analysis

To understand the performance impact of DTHREADS, we re-ran the benchmark suite on two individual components of DTHREADS: deterministic synchronization and memory protection.

Benchmark	Serial (% time)	Transactions Count	Time (ms)	Dirtied Pages
histogram	0	23	15.47	29
kmeans	0	3929	3.82	9466
linear_reg.	0	24	23.92	17
matrix_mult.	0	24	841.2	3945
pca	0	48	443	11471
reverseindex	17%	61009	1.04	451876
string_match	0	24	82	41
word_count	1%	90	26.5	5261
blackscholes	0	24	386.9	991
canneal	26.4%	1062	43	3606413
dedup	31%	45689	0.1	356589
ferret	12.3%	11282	1.49	147027
streamcluster	18.4%	130001	0.04	131992
swaptions	0	24	163	867

Table 1. Benchmark characteristics.

Sync-only: This configuration enforces only a deterministic synchronization order. Threads have direct access to shared memory with no isolation. Overhead from this component is largely due to load imbalance from the deterministic scheduler.

Prot-only: This configuration runs threads in isolation, with commits at synchronization points. The synchronization and commit order is not controlled by DTHREADS. This configuration eliminates false sharing, but also introduces isolation and commit overhead. The lazy twin creation and single-threaded execution optimizations are disabled here because they are unsafe without deterministic synchronization.

The results of this experiment are presented in Figure 6 and discussed below.

- The reverse_index, dedup, and ferret benchmarks show significant load imbalance with the *sync-only* configuration. Additionally, these benchmarks have high overhead from the *prot-only* configuration because of a large number of transactions.

- Both string_match and histogram run faster with the *sync-only* configuration. The reason for this is not obvious, but may be due to the per-thread allocator.

- Memory isolation in the *prot-only* configuration eliminates false sharing, which resulted in speedups for histogram, linear_regression, and swaptions.

- Normally, the performance of DTHREADS is not better than the *prot-only* configuration. However, both ferret and canneal run faster with deterministic synchronization enabled. Both benchmarks benefit from optimizations described in Section 5 that are only safe with deterministic synchronization enabled. ferret benefits from the single threaded execution optimization, and canneal sees performance gains due to the shared twin page optimization.

7. Discussion

All DMT systems must impose an order on updates to shared memory and synchronization operations. The mechanism used to isolate updates affects the limitations and performance of the system. DTHREADS represents a new point in the design space for DMT systems with some inherent advantages and limitations which we discuss below.

7.1 Design Tradeoffs

CoreDet and DTHREADS both use a combination of parallel and serial phases to execute programs deterministically. These two sys-

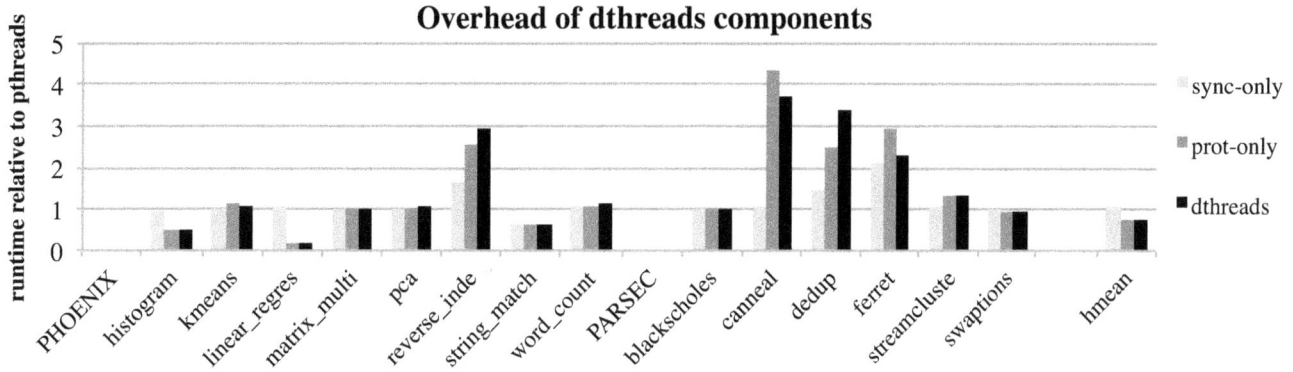

Figure 6. Normalized execution time with respect to `pthreads` (lower is better) for three configurations. The *sync-only* and *prot-only* configurations are described in Section 6.5.2.

tems take different approaches to isolation during parallel execution, as well as the transitions between phases:

Memory isolation: CoreDet orders updates to shared memory by instrumenting all memory accesses that could reference shared data. Synchronization operations and updates to shared memory must be performed in a serial phase. This approach results in high instrumentation overhead during parallel execution, but incurs no additional overhead when exposing updates to shared state.

DTHREADS takes an alternate approach: updates to shared state proceed at full speed, but are isolated using hardware-supported virtual memory. When a serial phase is reached, these updates must be exposed in a deterministic order with the twinning and diffing method described in Section 4.2.2.

A pleasant side-effect of this approach is the elimination of false sharing. Because threads work in separate address spaces, there is no need to keep caches coherent between threads during the parallel phase. For some programs this results in a performance improvement as large as 7× when compared to `pthreads`.

Phases: CoreDet uses a quantum-based scheduler to execute the serial phase. After the specified number of instructions is executed, the scheduler transitions to the serial phase. This approach bounds the waiting time for any threads that are blocked until a serial phase. One drawback of this approach is that transitions to the serial phase do not correspond to static program points. Any code changes (and most inputs) will result in a new, previously-untested schedule.

Transitions between phases are static in DTHREADS. Any synchronization operation will result in a transition to a serial phase, and parallel execution will resume once all threads have executed their critical sections. This makes DTHREADS susceptible to delays due to load imbalance between threads but results in more robust determinism. With DTHREADS, only the order of synchronization operations affects the schedule. For most programs this means that different inputs, and even many code changes, will not change the schedule produced by DTHREADS.

7.2 Limitations

External non-determinism: DTHREADS provides only internal determinism. It does not guarantee determinism when a program's behavior depends on external events, such as system time or the arrival order of network packets. The dOS framework is a proposed OS mechanism that provides system-level determinism [4]. dOS provides Deterministic Process Groups and a deterministic replay shim for external events, but uses CoreDet to make each individual process deterministic. DTHREADS could be used instead CoreDet within the dOS system, which would add support for controlling external non-determinism.

Unsupported programs: DTHREADS supports programs that use the `pthreads` library, but does not support programs that bypass it by rolling their own *ad hoc* synchronization operations. While *ad hoc* synchronization is common, it is also a notorious source of bugs; Xiong et al. show that 22–67% of the uses of *ad hoc* synchronization lead to bugs or severe performance issues [25].

DTHREADS does not write-share the stack across threads, so any updates to stack variables are only locally visible. While sharing of stack variables is supported by `pthreads`, this practice is error-prone and relatively uncommon. Support for shared stack variables could be added to DTHREADS by handling stack memory like the heap and globals, but this would require additional optimizations to avoid poor performance in the common case where stack memory is unshared.

Memory consumption: DTHREADS creates private, per-process copies of modified pages between commits. Because of this, it can increase a program's memory footprint by the number of modified pages between synchronization operations. This increased footprint does not pose a problem in practice, both because the number of modified pages is generally far smaller than the number of pages read, and because it is transitory: all private pages are relinquished to the operating system (via `madvise`) at the end of every commit.

Memory consistency: DTHREADS provides a form of release consistency for parallel programs, where updates are exposed at static program points. CoreDet's DMP-B mode also uses release consistency, but the update points depend on when the quantum counter reaches zero. To the best of our knowledge, DTHREADS cannot produce an output that is not possible with `pthreads`, although for some cases it will result in unexpected output. When run with DTHREADS, the example in Figure 1 will always produce the output "1,1." This ouptut is also possible with `pthreads`, but is much less likely (occurring in just 0.01% of one million runs) than "1,0" (99.43%) or "0,1" (0.56%). Of course, the same unexpected output will be produced on every run with DTHREADS, making it easier for developers to track down the source of the problem than with `pthreads`.

8. Conclusion

DTHREADS is a deterministic replacement for the `pthreads` library that supports general-purpose multithreaded applications. It is straightforward to deploy: DTHREADS resuires no source code, and operates on commodity hardware. By converting threads into processes, DTHREADS leverages process isolation and virtual memory protection to track and isolate concurrent memory updates with low overhead. Changes are committed deterministically at natural synchronization points in the code, rather than at boundaries based on hardware performance counters. DTHREADS not only ensures full internal determinism—eliminating data races as well as deadlocks—but does so in a way that is portable and easy to understand. Its software architecture prevents false sharing, a notorious performance problem for multithreaded applications running on multiple, cache-coherent processors. The combination of these approaches enables DTHREADS to match or even exceed the performance of `pthreads` for the majority of the benchmarks examined here, making DTHREADS a safe and efficient alternative to `pthreads` for many applications.

9. Acknowledgements

The authors thank Robert Grimm, Sam Guyer, Shan Lu, Tom Bergan, Daan Leijen, Dan Grossman, Yannis Smaragdakis, the anonymous reviewers, and our shepherd Steven Hand for their invaluable feedback and suggestions which helped improve this paper. We acknowledge the support of the Gigascale Systems Research Center, one of six research centers funded under the Focus Center Research Program (FCRP), a Semiconductor Research Corporation entity. This material is based upon work supported by Intel, Microsoft Research, and the National Science Foundation under CCF-1012195 and CCF-0910883. Any opinions, findings, and conclusions or recommendations expressed in this material are those of the author(s) and do not necessarily reflect the views of the National Science Foundation.

References

[1] A. Aviram, S.-C. Weng, S. Hu, and B. Ford. Efficient system-enforced deterministic parallelism. In *OSDI'10: Proceedings of the 9th Conference on Symposium on Opearting Systems Design & Implementation*, pages 193–206, Berkeley, CA, USA, 2010. USENIX Association.

[2] T. Ball, S. Burckhardt, J. de Halleux, M. Musuvathi, and S. Qadeer. Deconstructing concurrency heisenbugs. In *ICSE Companion*, pages 403–404. IEEE, 2009.

[3] T. Bergan, O. Anderson, J. Devietti, L. Ceze, and D. Grossman. CoreDet: a compiler and runtime system for deterministic multithreaded execution. In *Proceedings of the fifteenth edition of ASPLOS on Architectural support for programming languages and operating systems*, ASPLOS '10, pages 53–64, New York, NY, USA, 2010. ACM.

[4] T. Bergan, N. Hunt, L. Ceze, and S. D. Gribble. Deterministic process groups in dOS. In *OSDI'10: Proceedings of the 9th Conference on Symposium on Opearting Systems Design & Implementation*, pages 177–192, Berkeley, CA, USA, 2010. USENIX Association.

[5] E. D. Berger, K. S. McKinley, R. D. Blumofe, and P. R. Wilson. Hoard: A scalable memory allocator for multithreaded applications. In *Proceedings of the International Conference on Architectural Support for Programming Languages and Operating Systems (ASPLOS-IX)*, pages 117–128, Cambridge, MA, Nov. 2000.

[6] E. D. Berger, T. Yang, T. Liu, and G. Novark. Grace: safe multithreaded programming for C/C++. In *OOPSLA '09: Proceeding of the 24th ACM SIGPLAN conference on Object oriented programming systems languages and applications*, pages 81–96, New York, NY, USA, 2009. ACM.

[7] E. D. Berger and B. G. Zorn. DieHard: Probabilistic memory safety for unsafe languages. In *Proceedings of the 2006 ACM SIGPLAN Conference on Programming Language Design and Implementation (PLDI)*, pages 158–168, New York, NY, USA, 2006. ACM Press.

[8] E. D. Berger, B. G. Zorn, and K. S. McKinley. Composing high-performance memory allocators. In *Proceedings of the 2001 ACM SIGPLAN Conference on Programming Language Design and Implementation (PLDI)*, Snowbird, Utah, June 2001.

[9] C. Bienia and K. Li. Parsec 2.0: A new benchmark suite for chip-multiprocessors. In *Proceedings of the 5th Annual Workshop on Modeling, Benchmarking and Simulation*, June 2009.

[10] T. C. Bressoud and F. B. Schneider. Hypervisor-based fault tolerance. In *SOSP '95: Proceedings of the fifteenth ACM symposium on Operating systems principles*, pages 1–11, New York, NY, USA, 1995. ACM Press.

[11] S. Burckhardt, P. Kothari, M. Musuvathi, and S. Nagarakatte. A randomized scheduler with probabilistic guarantees of finding bugs. In J. C. Hoe and V. S. Adve, editors, *ASPLOS*, ASPLOS '10, pages 167–178, New York, NY, USA, 2010. ACM.

[12] J. B. Carter, J. K. Bennett, and W. Zwaenepoel. Implementation and performance of Munin. In *SOSP '91: Proceedings of the thirteenth ACM symposium on Operating systems principles*, pages 152–164, New York, NY, USA, 1991. ACM.

[13] R. H. Carver and K.-C. Tai. Replay and testing for concurrent programs. *IEEE Softw.*, 8:66–74, March 1991.

[14] J.-D. Choi and H. Srinivasan. Deterministic replay of Java multithreaded applications. In *Proceedings of the SIGMETRICS symposium on Parallel and distributed tools*, SPDT '98, pages 48–59, New York, NY, USA, 1998. ACM.

[15] H. Cui, J. Wu, C. Tsa, and J. Yang. Stable deterministic multithreaded through schedule memoization. In *OSDI'10: Proceedings of the 9th Conference on Symposium on Opearting Systems Design & Implementation*, pages 207–222, Berkeley, CA, USA, 2010. USENIX Association.

[16] J. W. Havender. Avoiding deadlock in multitasking systems. *IBM Systems Journal*, 7(2):74–84, 1968.

[17] P. Keleher, A. L. Cox, S. Dwarkadas, and W. Zwaenepoel. Treadmarks: distributed shared memory on standard workstations and operating systems. In *Proceedings of the USENIX Winter 1994 Technical Conference on USENIX Winter 1994 Technical Conference*, pages 10–10, Berkeley, CA, USA, 1994. USENIX Association.

[18] C. Lattner and V. Adve. LLVM: A Compilation Framework for Lifelong Program Analysis & Transformation. In *Proceedings of the 2004 International Symposium on Code Generation and Optimization (CGO'04)*, Palo Alto, California, Mar 2004.

[19] T. J. LeBlanc and J. M. Mellor-Crummey. Debugging parallel programs with instant replay. *IEEE Trans. Comput.*, 36:471–482, April 1987.

[20] C. E. McDowell and D. P. Helmbold. Debugging concurrent programs. *ACM Comput. Surv.*, 21(4):593–622, 1989.

[21] R. H. B. Netzer and B. P. Miller. What are race conditions?: Some issues and formalizations. *ACM Lett. Program. Lang. Syst.*, 1(1):74–88, 1992.

[22] M. Olszewski, J. Ansel, and S. Amarasinghe. Kendo: efficient deterministic multithreading in software. In *ASPLOS '09: Proceedings of the 14th International Conference on Architectural Support for Programming Languages and Operating Systems*, pages 97–108, New York, NY, USA, 2009. ACM.

[23] J. Pool, I. Sin, and D. Lie. Relaxed determinism: Making redundant execution on multiprocessors practical. In *Proceedings of the 11th Workshop on Hot Topics in Operating Systems (HotOS 2007)*, May 2007.

[24] C. Ranger, R. Raghuraman, A. Penmetsa, G. Bradski, and C. Kozyrakis. Evaluating MapReduce for multi-core and multiprocessor systems. In *HPCA '07: Proceedings of the 2007 IEEE 13th International Symposium on High Performance Computer Architecture*, pages 13–24, Washington, DC, USA, 2007. IEEE Computer Society.

[25] W. Xiong, S. Park, J. Zhang, Y. Zhou, and Z. Ma. Ad hoc synchronization considered harmful. In *OSDI'10: Proceedings of the 9th Conference on Symposium on Opearting Systems Design & Implementation*, pages 163–176, Berkeley, CA, USA, 2010. USENIX Association.

Efficient Deterministic Multithreading through Schedule Relaxation

Heming Cui, Jingyue Wu, John Gallagher, Huayang Guo, Junfeng Yang
{heming, jingyue, jmg, huayang, junfeng}@cs.columbia.edu
Department of Computer Science
Columbia University

ABSTRACT

Deterministic multithreading (DMT) eliminates many pernicious software problems caused by nondeterminism. It works by constraining a program to repeat the same thread interleavings, or *schedules*, when given same input. Despite much recent research, it remains an open challenge to build *both deterministic and efficient* DMT systems for general programs on commodity hardware. To deterministically resolve a data race, a DMT system must enforce a deterministic schedule of shared memory accesses, or *mem-schedule*, which can incur prohibitive overhead. By using schedules consisting only of synchronization operations, or *sync-schedule*, this overhead can be avoided. However, a sync-schedule is deterministic only for race-free programs, but most programs have races.

Our key insight is that races tend to occur only within minor portions of an execution, and a dominant majority of the execution is still race-free. Thus, we can resort to a mem-schedule only for the "racy" portions and enforce a sync-schedule otherwise, combining the efficiency of sync-schedules and the determinism of mem-schedules. We call these combined schedules *hybrid schedules*.

Based on this insight, we have built PEREGRINE, an efficient deterministic multithreading system. When a program first runs on an input, PEREGRINE records an execution trace. It then *relaxes* this trace into a hybrid schedule and reuses the schedule on future compatible inputs efficiently and deterministically. PEREGRINE further improves efficiency with two new techniques: *determinism-preserving slicing* to generalize a schedule to more inputs while preserving determinism, and *schedule-guided simplification* to precisely analyze a program according to a specific schedule. Our evaluation on a diverse set of programs shows that PEREGRINE is deterministic and efficient, and can frequently reuse schedules for half of the evaluated programs.

Categories and Subject Descriptors:

D.4.5 [**Operating Systems**]: Threads, Reliability D.2.4 [**Software Engineering**]: Software/Program Verification;

General Terms:

Algorithms, Design, Reliability, Performance

Keywords:

Deterministic Multithreading, Program Slicing, Program Simplification, Symbolic Execution

1 Introduction

Different runs of a multithreaded program may show different behaviors, depending on how the threads interleave. This *nondeterminism* makes it difficult to write, test, and debug multithreaded programs. For instance, testing becomes less assuring because the schedules tested may not be the ones run in the field. Similarly, debugging can be a nightmare because developers may have to reproduce the exact buggy schedules. These difficulties have resulted in many "heisenbugs" in widespread multithreaded programs [39].

Recently, researchers have pioneered a technique called *deterministic multithreading (DMT)* [9, 10, 12, 19, 20, 42]. DMT systems ensure that the same input is always processed with the same deterministic schedule, thus eliminating heisenbugs and problems due to nondeterminism. Unfortunately, despite these efforts, an open challenge [11] well recognized by the DMT community remains: how to build *both deterministic and efficient* DMT systems for general multithreaded programs on commodity multiprocessors. Existing DMT systems either incur prohibitive overhead, or are not fully deterministic if there are data races.

Specifically, existing DMT systems enforce two forms of schedules: (1) a *mem-schedule* is a deterministic schedule of shared memory accesses [9, 10, 20], such as `load/store` instructions, and (2) a *sync-schedule* is a deterministic order of synchronization operations [19, 42], such as `lock()/unlock()`. Enforcing a mem-schedule is truly deterministic even for programs with data races, but may incur prohibitive overhead (*e.g.*, roughly 1.2X-6X [9]). Enforcing a sync-schedule is efficient (*e.g.*, average 16% slowdown [42]) because most code does not control synchronization and can still run in parallel, but a sync-schedule is only deterministic for race-free programs, when, in fact, most real programs have races, harmful or benign [39, 54]. The dilemma is, then, to pick either determinism or efficiency but not both.

Our key insight is that although most programs have races, these races tend to occur only within minor portions of an execution, and the majority of the execution is still race-free. Thus, we can resort to a mem-schedule only for the "racy" portions of an execution and enforce a sync-schedule otherwise, combining both the efficiency of sync-schedules and the determinism of mem-schedules. We call these combined schedules *hybrid schedules*.

Based on this insight, we have built PEREGRINE, an efficient deterministic multithreading system to address the aforementioned open challenge. When a program first runs on an input, PEREGRINE records a detailed execution trace including memory accesses in case the execution runs into races. PEREGRINE then *relaxes* this detailed trace into a hybrid schedule, including (1) a total order of synchronization operations and (2) a set of execution order constraints to deterministically resolve each occurred race. When the same input is provided again, PEREGRINE can reuse this schedule deterministically and efficiently.

Reusing a schedule only when the program input matches exactly is too limiting. Fortunately, the schedules PEREGRINE computes are often "coarse-grained" and reusable on a broad range of inputs. Indeed, our previous work has shown that a small number of sync-schedules can often cover over 90% of the workloads for real programs such as Apache [19]. The higher the reuse rates, the more efficient PEREGRINE is. Moreover, by reusing schedules, PEREGRINE makes program behaviors more *stable* across different inputs, so that slight input changes do not lead to vastly different schedules [19] and thus "*input-heisenbugs*" where slight input changes cause concurrency bugs to appear or disappear.

Before reusing a schedule on an input, PEREGRINE must check that the input satisfies the *preconditions* of the schedule, so that (1) the schedule is feasible, *i.e.*, the execution on the input will reach all events in the same deterministic order as in the schedule and (2) the execution will not introduce new races. (New races may occur if they are *input-dependent*; see §4.1.) A naïve approach is to collect preconditions from all input-dependent branches in an execution trace. For instance, if a branch instruction inspects input variable X and goes down the true branch, we collect a precondition that X must be nonzero. Preconditions collected via this approach ensures that an execution on an input satisfying the preconditions will always follow the path of the recorded execution in all threads. However, many of these branches concern thread-local computations and do not affect the program's ability to follow the schedule. Including them in the preconditions thus unnecessarily decreases schedule-reuse rates.

How can PEREGRINE compute sufficient preconditions to avoid new races and ensure that a schedule is feasible? How can PEREGRINE filter out unnecessary branches to increase schedule-reuse rates? Our previous work [19] requires developers to grovel through the code and mark the input affecting schedules; even so, it does not guarantee full determinism if there are data races.

PEREGRINE addresses these challenges with two new program analysis techniques. First, given an execution trace and a hybrid schedule, it computes sufficient preconditions using *determinism-preserving slicing*, a new precondition slicing [18] technique designed for multithreaded programs. Precondition slicing takes an execution trace and a *target* instruction in the trace, and computes a *trace slice* that captures the instructions required for the execution to reach the target with equivalent operand values. Intuitively, these instructions include "branches whose outcome matters" to reach the target and "mutations that affect the outcome of those branches" [18]. This trace slice typically has much fewer branches than the original execution trace, so that we can compute more relaxed preconditions. However, previous work [18] does not compute correct trace slices for multithreaded programs or handle multiple targets; our slicing technique correctly handles both cases.

Our slicing technique often needs to determine whether two pointer variables may point to the same object. *Alias analysis* is the standard static technique to answer these queries. Unfortunately, one of the best alias analyses [52] yields overly imprecise results for 30% of the evaluated programs, forcing PEREGRINE to reuse schedules only when the input matches almost exactly. The reason is that standard alias analysis has to be conservative and assume all possible executions, yet PEREGRINE cares about alias results according only to the executions that reuse a specific schedule. To improve precision, PEREGRINE uses *schedule-guided simplification* to first simplify a program according to a schedule, then runs standard alias analysis on the simplified program to get more precise results. For instance, if the schedule dictates eight threads, PEREGRINE can clone the corresponding thread function eight times, so that alias analysis can separate the results for each thread, instead of imprecisely merging results for all threads.

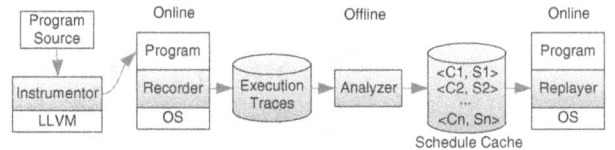

Figure 1: PEREGRINE *Architecture: components and data structures are shaded (and in green).*

We have built a prototype of PEREGRINE that runs in user-space. It automatically tracks main() arguments, data read from files and sockets, and values returned by random()-variants as input. It handles long-running servers by splitting their executions into *windows* and reusing schedules across windows [19]. The hybrid schedules it computes are fully deterministic for programs that (1) have no nondeterminism sources beyond thread scheduling, data races, and inputs tracked by PEREGRINE and (2) adhere to the assumptions of the tools PEREGRINE uses.

We evaluated PEREGRINE on a diverse set of 18 programs, including the Apache web server [6]; three desktop programs, such as PBZip2 [3], a parallel compression utility; implementations of 12 computation-intensive algorithms in the popular SPLASH2 and PARSEC benchmark suites; and racey [29], a benchmark with numerous intentional races for evaluating deterministic execution and replay systems. Our results show that PEREGRINE is both deterministic and efficient (executions reusing schedules range from 68.7% faster to 46.6% slower than nondeterministic executions); it can frequently reuse schedules for half of the programs (*e.g.*, two schedules cover all possible inputs to PBZip2 compression as long as the number of threads is the same); both its slicing and simplification techniques are crucial for increasing schedule-reuse rates, and have reasonable overhead when run offline; its recording overhead is relatively high, but can be reduced using existing techniques [13]; and it requires no manual efforts except a few annotations for handling server programs and for improving precision.

Our main contributions are the schedule-relaxation approach and PEREGRINE, an efficient DMT system. Additional contributions include the ideas of hybrid schedules, determinism-preserving slicing, and schedule-guided simplification. To our knowledge, our slicing technique is the first to compute correct (non-trivial) preconditions for multithreaded programs. We believe these ideas apply beyond PEREGRINE (§2.2).

The remainder of this paper is organized as follows. We first present a detailed overview of PEREGRINE (§2). We then describe its core ideas: hybrid schedules (§3), determinism-preserving slicing (§4), and schedule-guided simplification (§5). We then present implementation issues (§6) and evaluation (§7). We finally discuss related work (§8) and conclude (§9).

2 PEREGRINE Overview

Figure 1 shows the architecture of PEREGRINE. It has four main components: the instrumentor, recorder, analyzer, and replayer. The *instrumentor* is an LLVM [2] compiler plugin that prepares a program for use with PEREGRINE. It instruments synchronization operations such as pthread_mutex_lock(), which the recorder and replayer control at runtime. It marks the main() arguments, data read from read(), fscanf(), and recv(), and values returned by random()-variants as inputs. We chose LLVM [2] as our instrumentation framework for its compatibility with GCC and easy-to-analyze intermediate representation (IR). However, our approach is general and should apply beyond LLVM. For clarity, we will present our examples and algorithms at the source level, instead of the LLVM IR level.

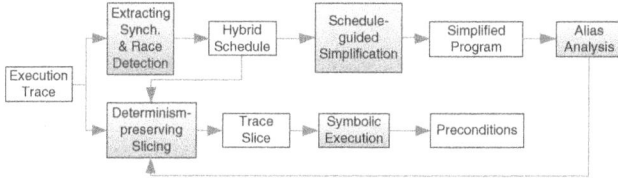

Figure 2: *Analyses performed by the analyzer.*

The *recorder* is similar to existing systems that deterministically record executions [13, 22, 33]. Our current recorder is implemented as an LLVM interpreter. When a program runs, the recorder saves the LLVM instructions interpreted for each thread into a central log file. The recorder does not record external input data, such as data read from a file, because our analysis does not need this information. To schedule synchronization operations issued by different threads, the recorder can use a variety of DMT algorithms [19].

The *analyzer* is a stand-alone program that computes (1) a hybrid schedule S and (2) the preconditions C required for reusing the schedule on future inputs. It does so using a series of analyses, shown in Figure 2. To compute a hybrid schedule, the analyzer first extracts a total order of synchronization operations from the execution trace. It then detects data races according to this synchronization order, and computes additional *execution order* constraints to deterministically resolve the detected races. To compute the preconditions of a schedule, the analyzer first *simplifies* the program according to the schedule, so that alias analysis can compute more precise results. It then slices the execution trace into a trace slice with instructions required to avoid new races and reach all events in the schedule. It then uses *symbolic execution* [31] to collect preconditions from the input-dependent branches in the slice. The trace slice is typically much smaller than the execution trace, so that the analyzer can compute relaxed preconditions, allowing frequent reuses of the schedule. The analyzer finally stores $\langle C, S \rangle$ into the schedule cache, which conceptually holds a set of such tuples. (The actual representation is tree-based for fast lookup [19].)

The *replayer* is a lightweight user-space scheduler for reusing schedules. When an input arrives, it searches the schedule cache for a $\langle C, S \rangle$ tuple such that the input satisfies the preconditions C. If it finds such a tuple, it simply runs the program enforcing schedule S efficiently and deterministically. Otherwise, it forwards the input to the recorder.

In the remainder of this section, we first use an example to illustrate how PEREGRINE works, highlighting the operation of the analyzer (§2.1). We then describe PEREGRINE's deployment and usage scenarios (§2.2) and assumptions (§2.3).

2.1 An Example

Figure 3 shows our running example, a simple multithreaded program based on the real ones used in our evaluation. It first parses the command line arguments into `nthread` (line L1) and `size` (L2), then spawns `nthread` threads including the main thread (L4–L5) and processes `size/nthread` bytes of data in each thread. The thread function `worker()` allocates a local buffer (L10), reads data from a file (L11), processes the data (L12–L13), and sums the results into the shared variable `result` (L14–L16). The `main()` function may further update `result` depending on `argv[3]` (L7–L8), and finally prints out `result` (L9). This example has read-write and write-write races on `result` due to missing `pthread_join()`. This error pattern matches some of the real errors in the evaluated programs such as PBZip2.

Instrumentor. To run this program with PEREGRINE, we first compile it into LLVM IR and instrument it with the instrumentor.

```
int size; // total size of data
int nthread; // total number of threads
unsigned long result = 0;

      int main(int argc, char *argv[]) {
L1:       nthread = atoi(argv[1]);
L2:       size = atoi(argv[2]);
L3:       assert(nthread>0 && size>=nthread);
L4:       for(int i=1; i<nthread; ++i)
L5:           pthread_create(..., worker, NULL);
L6:       worker(NULL);
          // NOTE: missing pthread_join()
L7:       if(atoi(argv[3]) == 1)
L8:           result += ...; // race with line L15
L9:       printf("result = %lu\n", result); // race with line L15
          ...
      }

      void *worker(void *arg) {
L10:      char *data = malloc(size/nthread);
L11:      read(..., data, size/nthread);
L12:      for(int i=0; i<size/nthread; ++i)
L13:          data[i] = ...; // compute using data
L14:      pthread_mutex_lock(&mutex);
L15:      result += ...; // race with lines L8 and L9
L16:      pthread_mutex_unlock(&mutex);
          ...
      }
```

Figure 3: *Running example.* It uses the common divide-and-conquer idiom to split work among multiple threads. It contains write-write (lines L8 and L15) and read-write (lines L9 and L15) races on `result` because of missing `pthread_join()`.

The instrumentor replaces the synchronization operations (lines L5, L14, and L16) with PEREGRINE-provided wrappers controlled by the recorder and replayer at runtime. It also inserts code to mark the contents of `argv[i]` and the data from `read()` (line L11) as input.

Recorder: execution trace. When we run the instrumented program with arguments "2 2 0" to spawn two threads and process two bytes of data, suppose that the recorder records the execution trace in Figure 4. (This figure also shows the hybrid schedule and preconditions PEREGRINE computes, explained later in this subsection.) This trace is just one possible trace depending on the scheduling algorithm the recorder uses.

Analyzer: hybrid schedule. Given the execution trace, the analyzer starts by computing a hybrid schedule. It first extracts a sync-schedule consisting of the operations tagged with (1), (2), ..., (8) in Figure 4. It then detects races in the trace according to this sync-schedule, and finds the race on `result` between L15 of thread t_1 and L9 of t_0. It then computes an execution order constraint to deterministically resolve this race, shown as the dotted arrow in Figure 4. The sync-schedule and execution order constraint together form the hybrid schedule. Although this hybrid schedule constrains the order of synchronization and the last two accesses to `result`, it can still be efficiently reused because the core computation done by `worker` can still run in parallel.

Analyzer: simplified program. To improve analysis precision, the analyzer simplifies the program according to the hybrid schedule. For instance, based on the number of `pthread_create()` operations in the schedule, the analyzer clones function `worker()` to give each thread a copy, so that the alias analysis separates different threads and determines that the two instances of L13 in t_0 and t_1 access different `malloc`'ed locations and never race.

Analyzer: trace slice. The analyzer uses determinism-preserving slicing to reduce the execution trace into a trace slice, so that it can compute relaxed preconditions. The final trace slice consists of the instructions not crossed out in Figure 4. The ana-

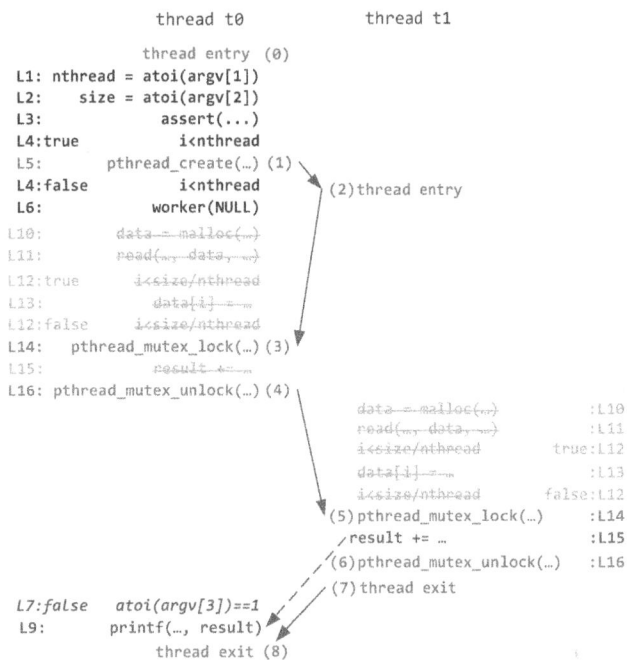

```
           thread t0          thread t1
                 thread entry (0)
L1: nthread = atoi(argv[1])
L2:    size = atoi(argv[2])
L3:            assert(...)
L4:true          i<nthread
L5:          pthread_create(…) (1)
L4:false         i<nthread         (2)thread entry
L6:            worker(NULL)
L10:          data = malloc(…)
L11:          read(…, data, …)
L12:true         i<size/nthread
L13:             data[i] = …
L12:false        i<size/nthread
L14:    pthread_mutex_lock(…) (3)
L15:             result +=…
L16: pthread_mutex_unlock(…) (4)

                      data = malloc(…)          :L10
                      read(…, data, …)          :L11
                      i<size/nthread        true:L12
                      data[i] = …               :L13
                      i<size/nthread       false:L12
                  (5)pthread_mutex_lock(…)       :L14
                     result += …                :L15
                  (6)pthread_mutex_unlock(…)     :L16
                  (7)thread exit

L7:false    atoi(argv[3])==1
L9:         printf(…, result)
                 thread exit (8)
```

Figure 4: *Execution trace, hybrid schedule, and trace slice.* An execution trace of the program in Figure 3 on arguments "2 2 0" is shown. Each executed instruction is tagged with its static line number Li. Branch instructions are also tagged with their outcome (true or false). Synchronization operations (green), including thread entry and exit, are tagged with their relative positions in the synchronization order. They form a sync-schedule whose order constraints are shown with solid arrows. L15 of thread t_1 and L9 of thread t_0 race on result, and this race is deterministically resolved by enforcing an execution order constraint shown by the dotted arrow. Together, these order constraints form a hybrid schedule. Instruction L7 of t_0 (italic and blue) is included in the trace slice to avoid new races, while L6, L4:false, L4:true, L3, L2, and L1 of t_0 are included due to intra-thread dependencies. Crossed-out (gray) instructions are elided from the slice.

lyzer computes this trace slice using inter-thread and intra-thread steps. In the inter-thread step, it adds instructions required to avoid new races into the slice. Specifically, for t_0 it adds the false branch of L7, or L7:false, because if the true branch is taken, a new race between L8 of t_0 and L15 of t_1 occurs. It ignores branches of line L12 because alias analysis already determines that L13 of t_0 and L13 of t_1 never race.

In the intra-thread step, the analyzer adds instructions required to reach all instructions identified in the inter-thread step (L7:false of t_0 in this example) and all events in the hybrid schedule. It does so by traversing the execution trace backwards and tracking control- and data-dependencies. In this example, it removes L15, L13, L12, L11, and L10 because no instructions currently in the trace slice depend on them. It adds L6 because without this call, the execution will not reach instructions L14 and L16 of thread t_0. It adds L4:false because if the true branch is taken, the execution of t_0 will reach one more pthread_create(), instead of L14, pthread_mutex_lock(), of t_0. It adds L4:true because this branch is required to reach L5, the pthread_create() call. It similarly adds L3, L2, and L1 because later instructions in the trace slice depend on them.

Analyzer: preconditions. After slicing, all branches from L12 are gone. The analyzer joins the remaining branches together as the preconditions, using a version of KLEE [15] augmented with thread support [19]. Specifically, the analyzer marks input data as *symbolic*, and then uses KLEE to track how this symbolic data is

$$(atoi\_argv_1 = 2) \wedge (atoi\_argv_2 \geq atoi\_argv_1) \wedge (atoi\_argv_3 \neq 1)$$

Figure 5: *Preconditions computed from the trace slice in Figure 4.* Variable $atoi\_argv_i$ represents the return of atoi(arg[i]).

propagated and observed by the instructions in the trace slice. (Our PEREGRINE prototype runs symbolic execution within the recorder for simplicity; see §6.1.) If a branch instruction inspects symbolic data and proceeds down the true branch, the analyzer adds the precondition that the symbolic data makes the branch condition true. The analyzer uses symbolic summaries [18] to succinctly generalize common library functions. For instance, it considers the return of atoi(arg) symbolic if arg is symbolic.

Figure 5 shows the preconditions the analyzer computes from the trace slice in Figure 4. These preconditions illustrate two key benefits of PEREGRINE. First, they are sufficient to ensure deterministic reuses of the schedule. Second, they only loosely constrain the data size ($atoi\_argv_2$) and do not constrain the data contents (from read()), allowing frequent schedule-reuses. The reason is that L10–L13 are all sliced out. One way to leverage this benefit is to populate a schedule cache with small workloads to reduce analysis time, and then reuse the schedules on large workloads.

Replayer. Suppose we run this program again on different arguments "2 1000 8." The replayer checks the new arguments against the preconditions in Figure 5 using KLEE's constraint checker, and finds that these arguments satisfy the preconditions, despite the much larger data size. It can therefore reuse the hybrid schedule in Figure 4 on this new input by enforcing the same order of synchronization operations and accesses to result.

2.2 Deployment and Usage Scenarios

PEREGRINE runs in user-space and requires no special hardware, presenting few challenges for deployment. To populate a schedule cache, a user can record execution traces from real workloads; or a developer can run (small) representative workloads to pre-compute schedules before deployment. PEREGRINE efficiently makes the behaviors of multithreaded programs more repeatable, even across a range of inputs. We envision that users can use this repeatability in at least four ways.

Concurrency error avoidance. PEREGRINE can reuse well-tested schedules collected from the testing lab or the field, reducing the risk of running into untested, buggy schedules. Currently PEREGRINE detects and avoids only data races. However, combined with the right error detectors, PEREGRINE can be easily extended to detect and avoid other types of concurrency errors.

Record and replay. Existing deterministic record-replay systems tend to incur high CPU and storage overhead (*e.g.*, 15X slowdown [13] and 11.7 GB/day storage [22]). A record-replay system on top of PEREGRINE may drastically reduce this overhead: for inputs that hit the schedule cache, we do not have to log any schedule.

Replication. To keep replicas of a multithreaded program consistent, a replication tool often records the thread schedules at one replica and replays them at others. This technique is essentially *online* replay [35]. It may thus incur high CPU, storage, and bandwidth overhead. With PEREGRINE, replicas can maintain a consistent schedule cache. If an input hits the schedule cache, all replicas will automatically select the same deterministic schedule, incurring zero bandwidth overhead.

Schedule-diversification. Replication can tolerate hardware or network failures, but the replicas may still run into the same concurrency error because they all use the same schedules. Fortunately, many programs are already "mostly-deterministic" as they either compute the same correct result or encounter heisenbugs. We can thus run PEREGRINE to deterministically diversify the schedules at different replicas (*e.g.*, using different scheduling algorithms or schedule caches) to tolerate *unknown* concurrency errors,

Applications of individual techniques. The individual ideas in PEREGRINE can also benefit other research efforts. For instance, hybrid schedules can make the sync-schedule approach deterministic without recording executions, by coupling it with a sound static race detector. Determinism-preserving slicing can (1) compute input filters to block bad inputs [18] causing concurrency errors and (2) randomize an input causing a concurrency error for use with anonymous bug reporting [16]. Schedule-guided simplification can transparently improve the precision of many existing static analyses: simply run them on the simplified programs. This improved precision may be leveraged to accurately detect errors or even verify the correctness of a program according to a set of schedules. Indeed, from a verification perspective, our simplification technique helps *verify* that executions reusing schedules have *no* new races.

2.3 Assumptions

At a design level, we anticipate the schedule-relaxation approach to work well for many programs/workloads as long as (1) they can benefit from repeatability, (2) their schedules can be frequently reused, (3) their races are rare, and (4) their nondeterminism comes from the sources tracked by PEREGRINE. This approach is certainly not designed for every multithreaded program. For instance, like other DMT systems, PEREGRINE should not be used for parallel simulators that desire nondeterminism for statistical confidence. For programs/workloads that rarely reuse schedules, PEREGRINE may be unable to amortize the cost of recording and analyzing execution traces. For programs full of races, enforcing hybrid schedules may be as slow as mem-schedules. PEREGRINE addresses nondeterminism due to thread scheduling and data races. It mitigates input nondeterminism by reusing schedules on different inputs. It currently considers command line arguments, data read from a file or a socket, and the values returned by `random()`-variants as inputs. PEREGRINE ensures that schedule-reuses are fully deterministic if a program contains only these nondeterminism sources, an assumption met by typical programs. If a program is nondeterministic due to other sources, such as functions that query physical time (*e.g.*, `gettimeofday()`), pointer addresses returned by `malloc()`, and nondeterminism in the kernel or external libraries, PEREGRINE relies on developers to annotate these sources.

The underlying techniques that PEREGRINE leverages make assumptions as well. PEREGRINE computes preconditions from a trace slice using the symbolic execution engine KLEE, which does not handle floating point operations; though recent work [17] has made advances in symbolic execution of floating point programs. (Note that floating point operations not in trace slices are not an issue.) We explicitly designed PEREGRINE's slicing technique to compute sufficient preconditions, but these preconditions may still include unnecessary ones, because computing the *weakest* (most relaxed) preconditions in general is undecidable [4]. The alias analysis PEREGRINE uses makes a few assumptions about the analyzed programs [8]; a "sounder" alias analysis [28] would remove these assumptions. These analyses may all get expensive for large programs. For server programs, PEREGRINE borrows the windowing idea from our previous work [19]; it is thus similarly limited (§6.3).

At an implementation level, PEREGRINE uses the LLVM framework, thus requiring that a program is in either source (so we can compile using LLVM) or LLVM IR format. PEREGRINE ignores inline x86 assembly or calls to external functions it does not know. For soundness, developers have to lift x86 assembly to LLVM IR and provide summaries for external functions. (The external function problem is alleviated because KLEE comes with a Libc imple-

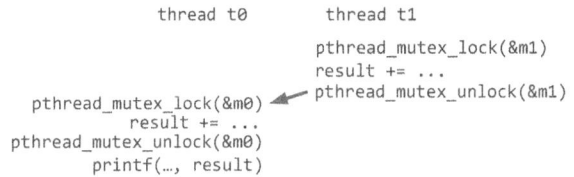

```
      thread t0          thread t1
                         pthread_mutex_lock(&m1)
                         result += ...
pthread_mutex_lock(&m0)◄─ pthread_mutex_unlock(&m1)
        result += ...
pthread_mutex_unlock(&m0)
      printf(…, result)
```

Figure 6: *No* PEREGRINE *race with respect to this schedule.*

mentation.) Currently PEREGRINE works only with a single process, but previous work [10] has demonstrated how DMT systems can be extended to multiple processes.

3 Hybrid Schedules

This section describes how PEREGRINE computes (§3.1) and enforces (§3.2) hybrid schedules.

3.1 Computing Hybrid Schedules

To compute a hybrid schedule, PEREGRINE first extracts a total order of synchronization operations from an execution trace. Currently, it considers 28 `pthread` operations, such as `pthread_mutex_lock()` and `pthread_cond_wait()`. It also considers the entry and exit of a thread as synchronization operations so that it can order these events together with other synchronization operations. These operations are sufficient to run the programs evaluated, and more can be easily added. PEREGRINE uses a total, instead of a partial, order because previous work has shown that a total order is already efficient [19, 42].

For determinism, PEREGRINE must detect races that occurred during the recorded execution and compute execution order constraints to deterministically resolve the races. An off-the-shelf race detector would flag too many races because it considers the original synchronization constraints of the program, whereas PEREGRINE wants to detect races according to a sync-schedule [44, 45]. To illustrate, consider Figure 6, a modified sync-schedule based on the one in Figure 4. Suppose the two threads acquire different mutex variables, and thread t_1 acquires and releases its mutex before t_0. Typical lockset-based [47] or happens-before-based [34] race detectors would flag a race on `result`, but our race detector does not: the sync-schedule in the figure deterministically resolves the order of accesses to `result`. Sync-schedules anecdotally reduced the number of possible races greatly, in one extreme case, from more than a million to four [44].

Mechanically, PEREGRINE detects occurred races using a happens-before-based algorithm. It flags two memory accesses as a race iff (1) they access the same memory location and at least one is a `store` and (2) they are *concurrent*. To determine whether two accesses are concurrent, typical happens-before-based detectors use vector clocks [40] to track logically when the accesses occur. Since PEREGRINE already enforces a total synchronization order, it uses a simpler and more memory-efficient logical clock representation.

Specifically, given two adjacent synchronization operations within one thread with relative positions m and n in the sync-schedule, PEREGRINE uses $[m, n]$ as the logical clock of all instructions executed by the thread between the two synchronization operations. For instance, in Figure 4, all instructions run by thread t_0 between the `pthread_mutex_unlock()` operation and the thread exit have clock $[4, 8]$. PEREGRINE considers two accesses with clocks $[m_0, n_0]$ and $[m_1, n_1]$ concurrent if the two clock ranges overlap, *i.e.*, $m_0 < n_1 \wedge m_1 < n_0$. For instance, $[4, 8]$ and $[5, 6]$ are concurrent.

To deterministically resolve a race, PEREGRINE enforces an execution order constraint $inst_1 \rightarrow inst_2$ where $inst_1$ and $inst_2$ are

thread t0   thread t1

inst1
inst2 ──────► inst3   - - - - -► Subsumed
              inst4

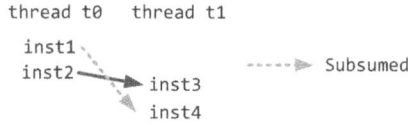

Figure 7: *Example subsumed execution order constraint.*

the two dynamic instruction instances involved in the race. PERE-GRINE identifies a dynamic instruction instance by $\langle sid, tid, nbr \rangle$ where sid refers to the unique ID of a static instruction in the executable file; tid refers to the internal thread ID maintained by PEREGRINE, which always starts from zero and increments deterministically upon each `pthread_create()`; and nbr refers to the number of control-transfer instructions (branch, call, and return) locally executed within the thread from the last synchronization to instruction $inst_i$. For instance, PEREGRINE represents the execution order constraint in Figure 4 as $\langle L15, t_1, 0 \rangle \rightarrow \langle L9, t_0, 2 \rangle$, where the branch count 2 includes the return from `worker` and the branch L7 of thread t_0. We must distinguish different dynamic instances of a static instruction because some of these dynamic instances may be involved in races while others are not. We do so by counting branches because if an instruction is executed twice, there must be a control-transfer between the two instances [22]. We count branches starting from the last synchronization operation because the partial schedule preceding this operation is already made deterministic.

If one execution order constraint subsumes another, PEREGRINE does not add the subsumed one to the schedule. Figure 7 shows a subsumed constraint example. Algorithmically, PEREGRINE considers an execution order constraint $inst_1 \rightarrow inst_4$ subsumed by $inst_2 \rightarrow inst_3$ if (1) $inst_1$ and $inst_2$ have the same logical clock (so they must be executed by the same thread) and $inst_2$ occurs no earlier than $inst_1$ in the recorded execution trace; (2) $inst_3$ and $inst_4$ have the same logical clock and $inst_3$ occurs no later than $inst_4$ in the trace. This algorithm ignores transitive order constraints, so it may miss some subsumed constraints. For instance, it does not consider $inst_1 \rightarrow inst_4$ subsumed if we replace constraint $inst_2 \rightarrow inst_3$ with $inst_2 \rightarrow inst_{other}$ and $inst_{other} \rightarrow inst_3$ where $inst_{other}$ is executed by a third thread.

3.2   Enforcing Hybrid Schedules

To enforce a synchronization order, PEREGRINE uses a technique called *semaphore relay* [19] that orders synchronization operations with per-thread semaphores. At runtime, a synchronization wrapper (recall that PEREGRINE instruments synchronization operations for runtime control) waits on the semaphore of the current thread. Once it is woken up, it proceeds with the actual synchronization operation, then wakes up the next thread according to the synchronization order. For programs that frequently do synchronization operations, the overhead of semaphore may be large because it may cause a thread to block. Thus, PEREGRINE also provides a spin-wait version of semaphore relay called *flag relay*. This technique turns out to be very fast for many programs evaluated (§7.2).

To enforce an execution order constraint, PEREGRINE uses program instrumentation, avoiding the need for special hardware, such as the often imprecise hardware branch counters [22]. Specifically, given a dynamic instruction instance $\langle sid, tid, nbr \rangle$, PEREGRINE instruments the static instruction sid with a semaphore `up()` or `down()` operation. It also instruments the branch instructions counted in nbr so that when each of these branch instructions runs, a per-thread branch counter is incremented. PEREGRINE activates the inserted semaphore operation for thread tid only when the thread's branch counter matches nbr. To avoid interference and unnecessary contention when there are multiple order constraints,

```
void slot(int sid) { // sid is static instruction id
    if(instruction sid is branch)
        nbr[self()] ++; // increment per-thread branch counter
    // get semaphore operations for current thread at instruction sid
    my_actions = actions[sid][self()];
    for action in my_actions
        if nbr[self()] == action.nbr // check branch counter
            actions.do(); // perform up() or down()
}
```

Figure 8: *Instrumentation to enforce execution order constraints.*

PEREGRINE assigns a unique semaphore to each constraint.

PEREGRINE instruments a program by leveraging a fast instrumentation framework we previously built [53]. It keeps two versions of each basic block: a normally compiled, fast version, and a slow backup padded with calls to a `slot()` function before each instruction. As shown in Figure 8, the `slot()` function interprets the actions (semaphore `up`/`down`) to be taken at each instruction. To instrument an instruction, PEREGRINE simply updates the actions for that instruction. This instrumentation may be expensive, but fortunately, PEREGRINE leaves it off most of the time and turns it on only at the last synchronization operation before an inserted semaphore operation.

PEREGRINE turns on/off this instrumentation by switching a per-thread flag. Upon each function entry, PEREGRINE inserts code to check this flag and determine whether to run the normal or slow version of the basic blocks. PEREGRINE also inserts this check after each function returns in case the callee has switched the per-thread flag. The overhead of these checks tend to be small because the flags are rarely switched and hardware branch predication works well in this case [53].

One potential issue with branch-counting is that PEREGRINE has to "fix" the partial path from the last synchronization to the dynamic instruction instance involved in a race so that the branch-counts match between the recorded execution and all executions reusing the extracted hybrid schedule, potentially reducing schedule-reuse rates. Fortunately, races are rare, so this issue has not reduced PEREGRINE's schedule-reuse rates based on our evaluation.

4   Determinism-Preserving Slicing

PEREGRINE uses determinism-preserving slicing to (1) compute sufficient preconditions to avoid new races and ensure that a schedule is feasible, and (2) filter many unnecessary preconditions to increase schedule-reuse rates. It does so using inter- and intra-thread steps. In the inter-thread step (§4.1), it detects and avoids *input-dependent* races that do not occur in the execution trace, but may occur if we reuse the schedule on a different input. In the intra-thread step (§4.1), the analyzer computes a *path slice* per thread by including instructions that may affect the events in the schedule or the instructions identified in the inter-thread step.

4.1   Inter-thread Step

In the inter-thread step, PEREGRINE detects and avoids input-dependent races with respect to a hybrid schedule. An example input-dependent race is the one between lines L8 and L15 in Figure 3, which occurs when `atoi(argv[3])` returns 1 causing the true branch of L7 to be taken. Figure 9 shows two more types of input-dependent races.

```
// thread t1        // thread t2          // thread t1      // thread t2
                                          if(input1==0)     if(input2==0)
a[input1]++;        a[input2] = 0;            a++;              a = 0;
           (a)                                         (b)
```

Figure 9: *Input-dependent races.* Race (a) occurs when `input1` and `input2` are the same; Race (b) occurs when both true branches are taken.

```
// detect input-dependent races, and add involved dynamic instruction
// instances to slicing_targets used by the inter-thread step. r1 and
// r2 are two concurrent regions
void detect_input_dependent_races(r1, r2) {
    // iterate through all instruction pairs in r1, r2
    for (i1, i2) in (r1, r2) {
        if (neither i1 nor i2 is a branch instruction) {
            if(mayrace(i1, i2)) {
                slicing_targets.add(i1); // add i1 to slicing targets
                slicing_targets.add(i2); // add i2 to slicing targets
            }
        } else if (exactly one of i1, i2 is a branch instruction) {
            br = branch instruction in i1, i2;
            inst = the other instruction in i1, i2;
            nottaken = the not taken branch of br in the execution trace;
            if(mayrace_br(br, nottaken, inst)) {
                // add the taken branch of br to slicing targets
                taken = the taken branch of br in trace;
                slicing_targets.add_br(br, taken);
            }
        } else { // both i1, i2 are branches
            nottaken1 = the not taken branch of i1 in trace;
            nottaken2 = the not taken branch of i2 in trace;
            if(mayrace_br_br(i1, nottaken1, i2, nottaken2) {
                taken1 = the taken branch of i1 in trace;
                slicing_targets.add_br(i1, taken1);
            }
        }
    }
}
// return true if instructions i1 and i2 may race
bool mayrace(i1, i2) {
    // query alias analysis
    return mayalias(i1, i2) && ((i1 is a store) || (i2 is a store));
}
// return true if the not-taken branch of br may race with inst
bool mayrace_br(br, nottaken, inst) {
    for i in (instructions in the nottaken branch of br) {
        if(mayrace(i, inst))
            return true;
    }
    return false;
}
// return true if the not-taken branch of br1 may race with the
// not-taken branch of br2
bool mayrace_br_br(br1, nottaken1, br2, nottaken2) {
    for inst in (instructions in the nottaken2 branch of br2) {
        if(mayrace_br(br1, nottaken1, inst))
            return true;
    }
    return false;
}
```

Figure 10: *Input-dependent race detection algorithm.*

To detect such races, PEREGRINE starts by refining the logical clocks computed based on the sync-schedule (§3.1) with execution order constraints because it will also enforce these constraints. PEREGRINE then iterates through all pairs of concurrent *regions*, where a region is a set of instructions with an identical logical clock. For each pair, it detects input-dependent races, and adds the racy instructions to a list of *slicing targets* used by the intra-thread step.

Figure 10 shows the algorithm to detect input-dependent races for two concurrent regions. The algorithm iterates through each pair of instructions respectively from the two regions, and handles three types of input-dependent races. First, if neither instruction is a branch instruction, it queries alias analysis to determine whether the instructions *may* race. If so, it adds both instructions to slicing_targets and adds additional preconditions to ensure that the pointers dereferenced are different, so that reusing the schedule on a different input does not cause the may-race to become a real race. Figure 9(a) shows a race of this type.

Second, if exactly one of the instructions is a branch instruction, the algorithm checks whether the instructions contained in the not-taken branch[1] of this instruction may race with the other instruction. It must check the not-taken branch because a new execution may well take the not-taken branch and cause a race. To avoid such a race, PEREGRINE adds the taken branch into the trace slice so that executions reusing the schedule always go down the taken branch. For instance, to avoid the input-dependent race between lines L8 and L15 in Figure 3, PEREGRINE includes the false branch of L7 in the trace slice.

Third, if both instructions are branch instructions, the algorithm checks whether the not-taken branches of the instructions may race, and if so, it adds either taken branch to slicing_targets. For instance, to avoid the race in Figure 9(b), PEREGRINE includes one of the false branches in the trace slice.

For efficiency, PEREGRINE avoids iterating through all pairs of instructions from two concurrent regions because instructions in one region often repeatedly access the same memory locations. Thus, PEREGRINE computes memory locations read or written by all instructions in one region, then checks whether instructions in the other region also read or write these memory locations. These locations are static operands, not dynamic addresses [14], so that PEREGRINE can aggressively cache them per static function or branch. The complexity of our algorithm thus drops from $O(MN)$ to $O(M+N)$ where M and N are the numbers of memory instructions in the two regions respectively.

4.2 Intra-thread Step

In the intra-thread step, PEREGRINE leverages a previous algorithm [18] to compute a per-thread path slice, by including instructions required for the thread to reach the slicing_targets identified in the inter-thread step and the events in the hybrid schedule. To do so, PEREGRINE first prepares a per-thread ordered target list by splitting slicing_targets and events in the hybrid schedule and sorting them based on their order in the execution trace.

PEREGRINE then traverses the execution trace backwards to compute path slices. When it sees a target, it adds the target to the path slice of the corresponding thread, and starts to track the control- and data-dependencies of this target.[2] PEREGRINE adds a branch instruction to the path slice if taking the opposite branch may cause the thread not to reach any instruction in the current (partial) path slice; L3 in Figure 4 is added for this reason. It adds a non-branch instruction to the path slice if the result of this instruction may be used by instructions in the current path slice; L1 in Figure 4 is added for this reason.

A "load p" instruction may depend on an earlier "store q" if p and q may alias even though p and q may not be the same in the execution trace, because an execution on a different input may cause p and q to be the same. Thus, PEREGRINE queries alias analysis to compute such *may*-dependencies and include the depended-upon instructions in the trace slice.

Our main modification to [18] is to slice toward multiple ordered targets. To illustrate this need, consider branch L4:false of t_0 in Figure 4. PEREGRINE must add this branch to thread t_0's slice, because otherwise, the thread would reach another

---

[1]PEREGRINE computes instructions contained in a not-taken branch using an interprocedural *post-dominator analysis* [4].
[2]For readers familiar with precondition slicing, PEREGRINE does not always track data-dependencies for the operands of a target. For instance, consider instruction L9 of thread t_0 in Figure 4. PEREGRINE's goal is to deterministically resolve the race involving L9 of t_0, but it allows the value of result to be different. Thus, PEREGRINE does not track dependencies for the value of result; L15 of t_0 is elided from the slice for this reason.

`pthread_create()`, a different synchronization operation than the `pthread_mutex_lock()` operation in the schedule.

The choice of LLVM IR has considerably simplified our slicing implementation. First, LLVM IR limits memory access to only two instructions, `load` and `store`, so that our algorithms need consider only these instructions. Second, LLVM IR uses an unlimited number of virtual registers, so that our analysis does not get poisoned by stack spilling instructions. Third, each virtual register is defined exactly once, and multiple definitions to a variable are merged using a special instruction. This representation (*static single assignment*) simplifies control- and data-dependency tracking. Lastly, the type information LLVM IR preserves helps improving the precision of the alias analysis.

5 Schedule-Guided Simplification

In both the inter- and intra-thread steps of determinism-preserving slicing, PEREGRINE frequently queries alias analysis. The inter-thread step needs alias information to determine whether two instructions may race (`mayalias()` in Figure 10). The intra-thread step needs alias information to track potential dependencies.

We thus integrated `bddbddb` [51, 52], one of the best alias analyses, into PEREGRINE by creating an LLVM frontend to collect program facts into the format `bddbddb` expects. However, our initial evaluation showed that `bddbddb` sometimes yielded overly imprecise results, causing PEREGRINE to prune few branches, reducing schedule-reuse rates (§7.3). The cause of the imprecision is that standard alias analysis is purely static, and has to be conservative and assume all possible executions. However, PEREGRINE requires alias results only for the executions that may reuse a schedule, thus suffering from unnecessary imprecision of standard alias analysis.

To illustrate, consider the example in Figure 3. Since the number of threads is determined at runtime, static analysis has to abstract this unknown number of dynamic thread instances, often coalescing results for multiple threads into one. When PEREGRINE slices the trace in Figure 4, `bddbddb` reports that the accesses to `data` (L13 instances) in different threads may alias. PEREGRINE thus has to add them to the trace slice to avoid new races (§4.1). Since L13 depends on L12, L11, and L10, PEREGRINE has to add them to the trace slice, too. Eventually, an imprecise alias result snowballs into a slice as large as the trace itself. The preconditions from this slice constrains the data size to be exactly 2, so PEREGRINE cannot reuse the hybrid schedule in Figure 4 on other data sizes.

To improve precision, PEREGRINE uses schedule-guided simplification to simplify a program according to a schedule, so that alias analysis is less likely to get confused. Specifically, PEREGRINE performs three main simplifications:

1. It clones the functions as needed. For instance, it gives each thread in a schedule a copy of the thread function.
2. It unrolls a loop when it can determine the loop bound based on a schedule. For instance, from the number of the `pthread_create()` operations in a schedule, it can determine how many times the loop at lines L4–L5 in Figure 3 executes.
3. It removes branches that contradict the schedule. Loop unrolling can be viewed as a special case of this simplification.

PEREGRINE does all three simplifications using one algorithm. From a high level, this algorithm iterates through the events in a schedule. For each pair of adjacent events, it checks whether they are "at the same level," *i.e.*, within the same function and loop iteration. If so, PEREGRINE does not clone anything; otherwise, PEREGRINE clones the mismatched portion of instructions between the events. (To find these instructions, PEREGRINE uses an interprocedural reachability analysis by traversing the control flow graph of the program.) Once these simplifications are applied, PERE-

GRINE can further simplify the program by running stock LLVM transformations such as constant folding. It then feeds the simplified program to `bddbddb`, which can now distinguish different thread instances (*thread-sensitivity* in programing language terms) and precisely reports that L13 of t_0 and L13 of t_1 are not aliases, enabling PEREGRINE to compute the small trace slice in Figure 4.

By simplifying a program, PEREGRINE can automatically improve the precision of not only alias analysis, but also other analyses. We have implemented *range analysis* [46] to improve the precision of alias analysis on programs that divide a global array into disjoint partitions, then process each partition within a thread. The accesses to these disjoint partitions from different threads do not alias, but `bddbddb` often collapses the elements of an array into one or two abstract locations, and reports the accesses as aliases. Range analysis can solve this problem by tracking the lower and upper bounds of the integers and pointers. With range analysis, PEREGRINE answers alias queries as follows. Given two pointers (`p+i`) and (`q+i`), it first queries `bddbddb` whether `p` and `q` may alias. If so, it queries the more expensive range analysis whether `p+i` and `q+j` may be equal. It considers the pointers as aliases only when both queries are true. Note that our simplification technique is again key to precision because standard range analysis would merge ranges of different threads into one.

While schedule-guided simplification improves precision, PEREGRINE has to run alias analysis for each schedule, instead of once for the program. This analysis time is reasonable as PEREGRINE's analyzer runs offline. Nonetheless, the simplified programs PEREGRINE computes for different schedules are largely the same, so a potential optimization is to *incrementally* analyze a program, which we leave for future work.

6 Implementation Issues

6.1 Recording an Execution

To record an execution trace, PEREGRINE can use one of the existing deterministic record-replay systems [13, 22, 33] provided that PEREGRINE can extract an instruction trace. For simplicity, we have built a crude recorder on top of the LLVM interpreter in KLEE. When an program calls the PEREGRINE-provided wrapper to `pthread_create(..., func, args)`, the recorder spawns a thread to run `func(args)` within an interpreter instance. These interpreter instances log each instruction interpreted into a central file. For simplicity, PEREGRINE does symbolic execution during recording because it already runs KLEE when recording an execution and pays the high overhead of interpretation. A faster recorder would enable PEREGRINE to symbolically execute only the trace slices instead of the typically larger execution traces. Since deterministic record-replay is a well studied topic, we have not focused our efforts on optimizing the recorder.

6.2 Handling Blocking System Calls

Blocking system calls are natural scheduling points, so PEREGRINE includes them in the schedules [19]. It currently considers eight blocking system calls, such as `sleep()`, `accept()`, and `read()`. For each blocking system call, the recorder logs when the call is issued and when the call is returned. When PEREGRINE computes a schedule, it includes these blocking system call and return operations. When reusing a schedule, PEREGRINE attempts to enforce the same call and return order. This method works well for blocking system calls that access local state, such as `sleep()` or `read()` on local file descriptors. However, other blocking system calls receive input from the external world, which may or may not arrive each time a schedule is reused. Fortunately, programs that use these operations tend to be server programs, and PEREGRINE handles this class of programs differently.

6.3 Handling Server Programs

Server programs present two challenges for PEREGRINE. First, they are more prone to timing nondeterminism than batch programs because their inputs (client requests) arrive nondeterministically. Second, they often run continuously, making their schedules too specific to reuse.

PEREGRINE addresses these challenges with the *windowing* idea from our previous work [19]. The insight is that server programs tend to return to the same quiescent states. Thus, instead of processing requests as they arrive, PEREGRINE breaks a continuous request stream down into windows of requests. Within each window, it admits requests only at fixed points in the current schedule. If no requests arrive at an admission point for a predefined timeout, PEREGRINE simply proceeds with the partial window. While a window is running, PEREGRINE buffers newly arrived requests so that they do not interfere with the running window. With windowing, PEREGRINE can record and reuse schedules across windows.

PEREGRINE requires developers to annotate points at which request processing begins and ends. It also assumes that after a server processes all current requests, it returns to the same quiescent state. That is, the input from the requests does not propagate further after the requests are processed. The same assumption applies to the data read from local files. For server programs not meeting this assumption, developers can manually annotate the functions that observe the changed server state, so that PEREGRINE can consider the return values of these functions as input. For instance, since Apache caches client requests, we made it work with PEREGRINE by annotating the return of `cache_find()` as input.

One limitation of applying our PEREGRINE prototype to server programs is that our current implementation of schedule-guided simplification does not work well with thread pooling. To give each thread a copy of the corresponding thread function, PEREGRINE identifies `pthread_create(...,func,...)` operations in a program and clones function `func`. Server programs that use thread pooling tend to create worker threads to run generic thread functions during program initialization, then repeatedly use the threads to process client requests. Cloning these generic thread functions thus helps little with precision. One method to solve this problem is to clone the relevant functions for processing client requests. We have not implemented this method because the programs we evaluated include only one server program, Apache, on which slicing already performs reasonably well without simplification (§7.3).

6.4 Skipping Wait Operations

When reusing a schedule, PEREGRINE enforces a total order of synchronization operations, which subsumes the execution order enforced by the original synchronization operations. Thus, for speed, PEREGRINE can actually skip the original synchronization operations as in [19]. PEREGRINE currently skips sleep-related operations such as `sleep()` and wait-related operations such as `pthread_barrier_wait()`. These operations often unconditionally block the calling thread, incurring context switch overhead, yet this blocking is unnecessary as PEREGRINE already enforces a correct execution order. Our evaluation shows that skipping blocking operations significantly speeds up executions.

6.5 Manual Annotations

PEREGRINE works automatically for most of the programs we evaluated. However, as discussed in §6.3, it requires manual annotations for server programs. In addition, if a program has nondeterminism sources beyond what PEREGRINE automatically tracks, developers should annotate these sources with `input(void* addr, size_t nbyte)` to mark `nbyte` of data starting from `addr` as input, so that PEREGRINE can track this data.

Developers can also supply optional annotations to improve PEREGRINE's precision in four ways. First, for better alias results, developers can add custom memory allocators and `memcpy`-like functions to a configuration file of PEREGRINE. Second, they can help PEREGRINE better track ranges by adding `assert()` statements. For instance, a function in the FFT implementation we evaluated uses bit-flip operations to transform an array index into another, yet both indexes have the same range. The range analysis we implemented cannot precisely track these bit-flip operations, so it assumes the resultant index is unbounded. Developers can fix this problem by annotating the range of the index with an assertion "`assert(index<bound)`." Third, they can provide *symbolic summaries* to help PEREGRINE compute more relaxed constraints. For instance, consider Figure 5 and a typical implementation of `atoi()` that iterates through all characters in the input string and checks whether each character is a digit. Without a summary of `atoi()`, PEREGRINE would symbolically execute the body of `atoi()`. The preconditions it computes for `argv[3]` would be $(argv_{3,0} \neq 49) \wedge (argv_{3,1} < 48 \vee argv_{3,1} > 57)$, where $argv_{3,i}$ is the ith byte of `argv[3]` and 48, 49, and 57 are ASCII codes of '0', '1', and '9'. These preconditions thus unnecessarily constrain `argv[3]` to have a valid length of one. Another example is string search. When a program calls `strstr()`, it often concerns whether there exists a match, not specifically where the match occurs. Without a symbolic summary of `strstr()`, the preconditions from `strstr()` would constrain the exact location where the match occurs. Similarly, if a trace slice contains complex code such as a decryption function, users can provide a summary of this function to mark the decrypted data as symbolic when the argument is symbolic. Note that complex code not included in trace slices, such as the `read()` in Figure 3, is not an issue.

7 Evaluation

Our PEREGRINE implementation consists of 29,582 lines of C++ code, including 1,338 lines for the recorder; 2,277 lines for the replayer; and 25,967 lines for the analyzer. The analyzer further splits into 7,845 lines for determinism-preserving slicing, 12,332 lines for schedule-guided simplification, and 5,790 lines for our LLVM frontend to bddbddb.

We evaluated our PEREGRINE implementation on a diverse set of 18 programs, including Apache, a popular web server; PBZip2, a parallel compression utility; aget, a parallel wget-like utility; pfscan, a parallel grep-like utility; parallel implementations of 13 computation-intensive algorithms, 10 in SPLASH2 and 3 in PARSEC; and racey, a benchmark specifically designed to exercise deterministic execution and replay systems [29]. All SPLASH2 benchmarks were included except one that we cannot compile, one that our current prototype cannot handle due to an implementation bug, and one that does not run correctly in 64-bit environment. The chosen PARSEC benchmarks (blackscholes, swaptions and streamcluster) include the ones that (1) we can compile, (2) use threads, and (3) use no x86 inline assemblies. These programs were widely used in previous studies (*e.g.*, [12, 39, 54]).

Our evaluation machine was a 2.67 GHz dual-socket quad-core Intel Xeon machine with 24 GB memory running Linux 2.6.35. When evaluating PEREGRINE on Apache and aget, we ran the evaluated program on this machine and the corresponding client or server on another to avoid contention between the programs. These machines were connected via 1Gbps LAN. We compiled all programs to machine code using `llvm-gcc -O2` and the LLVM com-

Program	Race Description
Apache	Reference count decrement and check against 0 are not atomic, resulting in a program crash.
PBZip2	Variable `fifo` is used by one thread after being freed by another thread, resulting in a program crash.
barnes	Variable `tracktime` is read by one thread before assigned the correct value by another thread.
fft	`initdonetime` and `finishtime` are read by one thread before assigned the correct values by another thread.
lu-non-contig	Variable `rf` is read by one thread before assigned the correct value by another thread.
streamcluster	PARSEC has a custom barrier implementation that synchronizes using a shared integer flag `is_arrival_phase`.
racey	Numerous intentional races caused by multiple threads reading and writing global arrays `sig` and `m` without synchronization.

Table 1: *Programs used for evaluating* PEREGRINE's *determinism.*

Program	Races	Order Constraints
Apache	0	0
PBZip2	4	3
barnes	5	1
fft	10	4
lu-non-contig	10	7
streamcluster	0	0
racey	167974	9963

Table 2: *Hybrid schedule statistics.* Column **Races** shows the number of races detected according the corresponding sync-schedule, and Column **Order Constraints** shows the number of execution order constraints PEREGRINE adds to the final hybrid schedule. The latter can be smaller than the former because PEREGRINE prunes subsumed execution order constraints (§3). PEREGRINE detected no races for Apache and streamcluster because the corresponding sync-schedules are sufficient to resolve the races deterministically; it thus adds no order constraints for these programs.

Program	Deterministic?	
	sync-schedule	hybrid schedule
Apache	✔	✔
PBZip2	✘	✔
barnes	✘	✔
fft	✘	✔
lu-non-contig	✘	✔
streamcluster	✔	✔
racey	✘	✔

Table 3: *Determinism of sync-schedules v.s. hybrid schedules.*

piler `llc`. We used eight worker threads for all experiments.

Unless otherwise specified, we used the following workloads in our experiments. For Apache, we used `ApacheBench` [1] to repeatedly download a 100 KB webpage. For PBZip2, we compressed a 10 MB randomly generated text file. For `aget`, we downloaded a 77 MB file (`Linux-3.0.1.tar.bz2`). For `pfscan`, we scanned the keyword `return` from 100 randomly chosen files in GCC. For SPLASH2 and PARSEC programs, we ran workloads which typically completed in 1-100 ms.

In the remainder of this section, we focus on four questions:

§7.1: Is PEREGRINE deterministic if there are data races? Determinism is one of the strengths of PEREGRINE over the sync-schedule approach.

§7.2: Is PEREGRINE fast? For typical multithreaded programs that have rare data races, PEREGRINE should be roughly as fast as the sync-schedule approach. Efficiency is one of the strengths of PEREGRINE over the mem-schedule approach.

§7.3: Is PEREGRINE stable? That is, can it frequently reuse schedules? The higher the reuse rate, the more repeatable program behaviors become and the more PEREGRINE can amortize the cost of computing hybrid schedules.

§7.4: Can PEREGRINE significantly reduce manual annotation overhead? Recall that our previous work [19] required developers to manually annotate the input affecting schedules.

7.1 Determinism

We evaluated PEREGRINE's determinism by checking whether PEREGRINE could deterministically resolve races. Table 1 lists the seven racy programs used in this experiment. We selected the first five because they were frequently used in previous studies [37, 39, 43, 44] and we could reproduce their races on our evaluation machine. We selected the integer flag race in PARSEC to test whether PEREGRINE can handle ad hoc synchronization [54]. We selected racey to stress test PEREGRINE: each run of racey may have thousands of races, and if any of these races is resolved differently, racey's final output changes with high probability [29].

For each program with races, we recorded an execution trace and computed a hybrid schedule from the trace. Table 2 shows for each

program (1) the number of dynamic races detected according to the sync-schedule and (2) the number of execution order constraints in the hybrid schedule. The reduction from the former to the latter shows how effectively PEREGRINE can prune redundant order constraints (§3). In particular, PEREGRINE prunes 94% of the constraints for racey. For Apache and streamcluster, their races are already resolved deterministically by their sync-schedules, so PEREGRINE adds no execution order constraints.

To verify that the hybrid schedules PEREGRINE computed are deterministic, we first manually inspected the order constraints PEREGRINE added for each program except racey (because it has too many races for manual verification). Our inspection results show that these constraints are sufficient to resolve the corresponding races. We then re-ran each program including racey 1000 times while enforcing the hybrid schedule and injecting delays; and verified that each run reused the schedule and computed equivalent results. (We determined result equivalence by checking either the output or whether the program crashed.)

We also compared the determinism of PEREGRINE to our previous work [19] which only enforces sync-schedules. Specifically, we reran the seven programs with races 50 times enforcing only the sync-schedules and injecting delays, and checked whether the reuse runs computed equivalent results as the recorded run. As shown in Table 3, sync-schedules are unsurprisingly deterministic for Apache and streamcluster, because no races are detected according to the corresponding sync-schedules. However, they are not deterministic for the other five programs, illustrating one advantage of PEREGRINE over the sync-schedule approach.

7.2 Efficiency

Replayer overhead. The most performance-critical component is the replayer because it operates within a deployed program. Figure 11 shows the execution times when reusing hybrid schedules; these times are normalized to the nondeterministic execution time. (The next paragraph compares these times to those of sync-schedules.) For Apache, we show the throughput (TPUT) and response time (RESP). All numbers reported were averaged over 500 runs. PEREGRINE has relatively high overhead on `water-nsquared` (22.6%) and `cholesky` (46.6%) because these programs do a large number of mutex operations within tight loops. Still, this overhead is lower than the reported 1.2X-6X overhead of a mem-schedule DMT system [9]. Moreover, PEREGRINE speeds up `barnes`, `lu-non-contig`, `radix`, `water-spatial`, and `ocean` (by up to 68.7%) because it safely skips synchronization and sleep

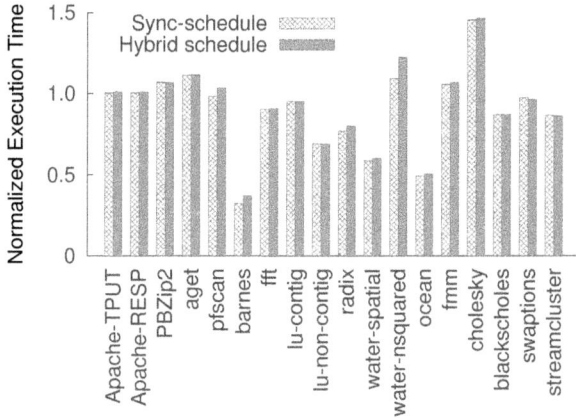

Figure 11: *Normalized execution time when reusing sync-schedules v.s. hybrid schedules.* A time value greater than 1 indicates a slowdown compared to a nondeterministic execution without PEREGRINE. We did not include `racey` because it was not designed for performance benchmarking.

operations (§6.4). For the other programs, PEREGRINE's overhead or speedup is within 15%. (Note that increasing the page or file sizes of the workload tends to reduce PEREGRINE's relative overhead because the network and disk latencies dwarf PEREGRINE's.)

For comparison, Figure 11 shows the normalized execution time when enforcing just the sync-schedules. This overhead is comparable to our previous work [19]. For all programs except `water-nsquared`, the overhead of enforcing hybrid schedules is only slightly larger (at most 5.4%) than that of enforcing sync-schedules. This slight increase comes from two sources: (1) PEREGRINE has to enforce execution order constraints to resolve races deterministically for `PBZip2`, `barnes`, `fft`, and `lu-non-contig`; and (2) the instrumentation framework PEREGRINE uses also incurs overhead (§3.2). The overhead for `water-nsquared` increases by 13.4% because it calls functions more frequently than the other benchmarks, and our instrumentation framework inserts code at each function entry and return (§3.2).

Figure 12 shows the speedup of flag relay (§3.2) and skipping blocking operations (§6.4). Besides `water-nsquared` and `cholesky`, a second group of programs, including `barnes`, `lu-non-contig`, `radix`, `water-spatial`, and `ocean`, also perform many synchronization operations, so flag relay speeds up both groups of programs significantly. Moreover, among the synchronization operations done by the second group of programs, many

Program	Trace	Det	Sli	Sim	Sym
Apache	449	0.4	885.32	n/a	5.8
PBZip2	2,227	0.1	587.9	317.8	19.7
aget	233	0.4	78.8	60.1	13.2
pfscan	46,602	1.1	1,601.4	2,047.9	1,136.6
barnes	324	0.2	300.5	481.5	56.9
fft	39	0.0	2.1	3,661.7	0.4
lu-contig	44,799	19.9	1,271.5	124.9	1,126.7
lu-non-contig	41,302	21.2	1,999.8	14,243.8	1,201.0
radix	3,110	1.5	46.2	96.4	182.9
water-spatial	7,508	1.0	1,407.0	9,628.1	120.6
water-nsquared	12,381	1.7	962.3	1,841.4	215.7
ocean	55,247	26.4	2,259.3	5,902.8	2,062.1
fmm	13,772	8.3	260.5	1,107.5	151.3
cholesky	47,200	28.8	3,102.9	6,350.1	685.5
blackscholes	62,024	16.5	539.9	542.9	3,284.8
swaptions	1,366	0.0	23.2	87.3	1.2
streamcluster	259	0.1	1.4	1.9	4.9

Table 4: *Analysis time.* **Trace** shows the number of thousand LLVM instructions in the execution trace of the evaluated programs, the main factor affecting the execution time of PEREGRINE's various analysis techniques, including race detection (**Det**), slicing (**Sli**), simplification and alias analysis (**Sim**), and symbolic execution (**Sym**). The execution time is measured in seconds. The `Apache` trace is collected from one window of eight requests. `Apache` uses thread pooling which our simplification technique currently does not handle well (§6.3); nonetheless, slicing without simplification works reasonably well for `Apache` already (§7.3).

are `pthread_barrier_wait()` operations, so PEREGRINE further speeds up these programs by skipping these wait operations.

Analyzer and recorder overhead. Table 4 shows the execution time of PEREGRINE's various program analyses. The execution time largely depends on the size of the execution trace. All analyses typically finish within a few hours. For `PBZip2` and `fft`, we used small workloads (compressing 1 KB file and transforming a 256X256 matrix) to reduce analysis time and to illustrate that the schedules learned from small workloads can be efficiently reused on large workloads. The simplification and alias analysis time of `fft` is large compared to its slicing time because it performs many multiplications on array indexes, slowing down our range analysis. Although `lu-non-contig` and `lu-contig` implement the same scientific algorithm, their data access patterns are very different (§7.3), causing PEREGRINE to spend more time analyzing `lu-non-contig` than `lu-contig`.

As discussed in §6.1, PEREGRINE currently runs KLEE to record executions. Column Sym is also the overhead of PEREGRINE's recorder. This crude, unoptimized recorder can incur large slowdown compared to the normal execution of a program. However, this slowdown can be reduced to around 10X using existing record-replay techniques [13, 33]. Indeed, we have experimented with a preliminary version of a new recorder that records an execution by instrumenting `load` and `store` instructions and saving them into per-thread logs [13]. Figure 13 shows that this new recorder incurs roughly 2-35X slowdown on eight programs, comparable to existing record-replay systems. Due to time constraints, we have not

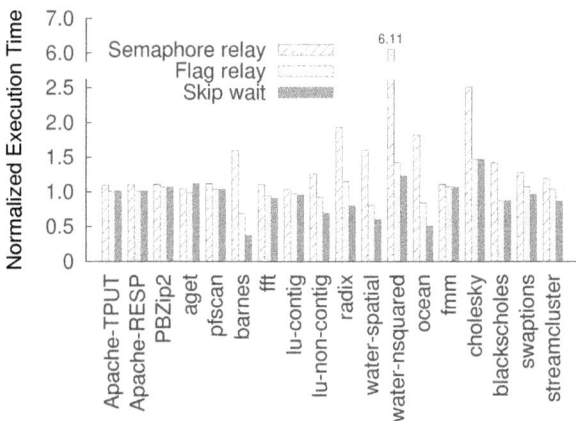

Figure 12: *Speedup of optimization techniques.* Note that Y axis is broken.

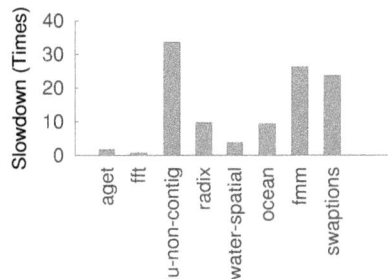

Figure 13: *Overhead of recording* `load` *and* `store` *instructions.*

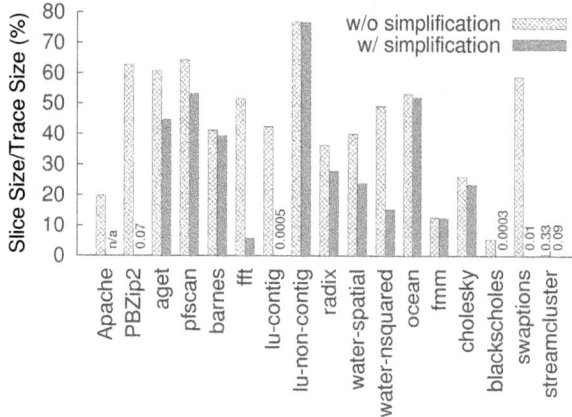

Figure 14: *Slicing ratio after applying determinism-preserving slicing alone (§4) and after further applying schedule-guided simplification (§5).*

integrated this new recorder with PEREGRINE.

7.3 Stability

Stability measures how frequently PEREGRINE can reuse schedules. The more frequently PEREGRINE reuses schedules, the more efficient it is, and the more repeatable a program running on top of PEREGRINE becomes. While PEREGRINE achieves determinism and efficiency through hybrid schedules, it may have to pay the cost of slightly reduced reuse rates compared to a manual approach [19].

A key factor determining PEREGRINE's schedule-reuse rates is how effectively it can slice out irrelevant instructions from the execution traces. Figure 14 shows the ratio of the slice size over the trace size for PEREGRINE's determinism-preserving slicing technique, with and without schedule-guided simplification. The slicing technique alone reduces the trace size by over 50% for all programs except PBZip2, aget, pfscan, fft, lu-non-contig, ocean, and swaptions. The slicing technique combined with scheduled-guide simplification vastly reduces the trace size for PBZip2, aget, fft, lu-contig, and swaptions.

Recall that PEREGRINE computes the preconditions of a schedule from the input-dependent branches in a trace slice. The fewer branches included in the slice, the more general the preconditions PEREGRINE computes tend to be. We further measured the number of such branches in the trace slices. Table 5 shows the results, together with a upper bound determined by the total number of input-dependent branches in the execution trace, and a lower bound determined by only including branches required to reach the recorded synchronization operations. This lower bound may not be tight as we ignored data dependency. For barnes, fft, blackscholes, swaptions, and streamcluster, slicing with simplification (Column "Slicing+Sim") achieves the best possible reduction. For PBZip2, aget, pfscan, and lu-contig, the number of input-dependent branches in the trace slice is close to the lower bound. In the remaining programs, Apache, fmm, and cholesky also enjoy large reduction, while the other five programs do not. This table also shows that schedule-guided simplification is key to reduce the number of input-dependent branches for PBZip2, fft, lu-contig, blackscholes, and swaptions, and to reach the lower bound for blackscholes, swaptions, and streamcluster.

We manually examined the preconditions PEREGRINE computed from the input-dependent branches for these programs. We category these programs below.

Best case: PBZip2, fft, lu-contig, blackscholes, swaptions, and streamcluster. PEREGRINE computes the weakest (*i.e.*, most relaxed) preconditions for these programs. The

Program	UB	PEREGRINE		LB
		Slicing	Slicing+Sim	
Apache	4,522	624	n/a	56
PBZip2	913	865	101	94
aget	20,826	18,859	9,514	9,491
pfscan	1,062,047	992,524	992,520	992,501
barnes	92	52	52	52
fft	2,266	1,568	17	17
lu-contig	2,823,379	2,337,431	131	128
lu-non-contig	2,962,621	2,877,877	2,876,364	128
radix	175,679	98,750	89,732	75
water-spatial	98,054	77,567	76,763	233
water-nsquared	89,348	76,786	76,242	1,843
ocean	2,605,185	2,364,538	2,361,256	400
fmm	299,816	57,670	56,532	1,642
cholesky	7,459	1,627	1,627	1,233
blackscholes	421,909	409,618	10	10
swaptions	35,584	35,005	21	21
streamcluster	20,851	75	42	42

Table 5: *Effectiveness of program analysis techniques.* **UB** shows the total number of input-dependent branches in the corresponding execution trace, an upper bound on the number included in the trace slice. **Slicing** and **Slicing+Sim** show the number of input-dependent branches in the slice after applying determinism-preserving slicing alone (§4) and after further applying schedule-guided simplification (§5). **LB** shows a lower bound on the number of input-dependent branches, determined by only including branches required to reach the recorded synchronization operations. This lower bound may not be tight as we ignored data dependency when computing it.

preconditions often allow PEREGRINE to reuse one or two schedules for each number of threads, putting no or few constraints on the data processed. Schedule-guided simplification is crucial for these programs; without simplification, the preconditions would fix the data size and contents.

Slicing limitation: Apache and aget. The preconditions PEREGRINE computes for Apache fix the URL length; they also constrain the page size to be within an 8 KB-aligned range if the page is not cached. The preconditions PEREGRINE computes for aget fix the positions of "/" in the URL and narrow down the file size to be within an 8 KB-aligned range. These preconditions thus unnecessarily reduce the schedule-reuse rates. Nonetheless, they can still match many different inputs, because they do not constrain the page or file contents.

Symbolic execution limitation: barnes. barnes reads in two floating point numbers from a file, and their values affect schedules. Since PEREGRINE cannot symbolically execute floating point instructions, it currently does not collect preconditions from them.

Alias limitation: lu-non-contig, radix, water-spatial, water-nsquared, ocean, and cholesky. Even with simplification, PEREGRINE's alias analysis sometimes reports may-alias for pointers accessed in different threads, causing PEREGRINE to include more instructions than necessary in the slices and compute preconditions that fix the input data. For instance, each thread in lu-non-contig accesses disjoint regions in a global array, but the accesses from one thread are *not* continuous, confusing PEREGRINE's alias analysis. (In contrast, each thread in lu-contig accesses a contiguous array partition.)

Programs that rarely reuse schedules: pfscan and fmm. For instance, pfscan searches a keyword in a set of files using multiple threads, and for each match, it grabs a lock to increment a counter. A schedule computed on one set of files is unlikely to suit another.

7.4 Ease of Use

Table 6 shows the annotations (§6.5) we added to make the evaluated programs work with PEREGRINE. For most programs, PEREGRINE works out of the box. Apache uses its own library functions for common tasks such as memory allocation, so we annotated 21

Program	LOC	PEREGRINE	TERN
Apache	464 K	24	6
PBZip2	7,371	1	3
aget	834	0	n/a
pfscan	776	0	n/a
barnes	1,954	0	9
fft	1,403	1	4
lu-contig	991	0	n/a
lu-non-contig	1,265	0	3
radix	661	0	4
water-spatial	1,573	0	9
water-nsquared	1,188	0	10
ocean	6,494	0	5
fmm	3,208	0	9
cholesky	3,683	0	4
blackscholes	1,275	0	n/a
swaptions	1,110	0	n/a
streamcluster	1,963	0	n/a
racey	124	0	n/a

Table 6: *Source annotation requirements of* PEREGRINE *v.s.* TERN. **PERE-GRINE** represents the number of annotations added for PEREGRINE, and **TERN** counts annotations added for TERN. Programs not included in the TERN evaluation are labeled n/a. LOC of PBZip2 also includes the lines of code of the compression library libbz2.

such functions. We added two annotations to mark the boundaries of client request processing and one to expose the hidden state in Apache (§6.3). PBZip2 decompression uses a custom search function (memstr) to scan through the input file for block boundaries. We added one annotation for this function to relax the preconditions PEREGRINE computes. (PEREGRINE works automatically with PBZip2 compression.) We added one assertion to annotate the range of a variable in fft (§6.5).

For comparison, Table 6 also shows the annotation overhead of our previous DMT system TERN [19]. For all programs except Apache, PEREGRINE has fewer number of annotations than TERN. Although the number of annotations that TERN has is also small, adding these annotations may require developers to manually reconstruct the control- and data-dependencies between instructions.

In order to make the evaluated programs work with PEREGRINE, we had to fix several bugs in them. For aget, we fixed an off-by-one write in revstr() which prevented us from tracking constraints for the problematic write, and a missing check on the return value of pwrite() which prevented us from computing precise ranges. We fixed similar missing checks in swaptions, streamcluster, and radix. We did not count these modifications in Table 6 because they are real bug fixes. (This interesting side-effect illustrates the potential of PEREGRINE as an error detection tool: the precision gained from simplification enables PEREGRINE to detect real races in well-studied programs.)

8   Related Work

Deterministic execution. By reusing schedules, PEREGRINE mitigates input nondeterminism and makes program behaviors repeatable across inputs. This method is based on the *schedule-memoization* idea in our previous work TERN [19], but PEREGRINE largely eliminates manual annotations, and provides stronger determinism guarantees than TERN. To our knowledge, no other DMT systems mitigate input nondeterminism; some actually aggravate it, potentially creating "input-heisenbugs."

PEREGRINE and other DMT systems can be complementary: PEREGRINE can use an existing DMT algorithm when it runs a program on a new input so that it may compute the same schedules at different sites; existing DMT systems can speed up their pathological cases using the schedule-relaxation idea.

Determinator [7] advocates a new, radical programming model

that converts all races, including races on memory and other shared resources, into exceptions, to achieve pervasive determinism. This programming model is not designed to be backward-compatible. dOS [10] provides similar pervasive determinism with backward compatibility, using a DMT algorithm first proposed in [20] to enforce mem-schedules. While PEREGRINE currently focuses on multithreaded programs, the ideas in PEREGRINE can be applied to other shared resources to provide pervasive determinism. PEREGRINE's hybrid schedule idea may help reduce dOS's overhead. Grace [12] makes multithreaded programs with fork-join parallelism behave like sequential programs. It detects memory access conflicts efficiently using hardware page protection. Unlike Grace, PEREGRINE aims to make general multithreaded programs, not just fork-join programs, repeatable.

Concurrent to our work, DTHREADS [36] is another efficient DMT system. It tracks memory modifications using hardware page protection and provides a protocol to deterministically commit these modifications. In contrast to DTHREADS, PEREGRINE is software-only and does not rely on page protection hardware which may be expensive and suffer from false sharing; PEREGRINE records and reuses schedules, thus it can handle programs with ad hoc synchronizations [54] and make program behaviors stable.

Program analysis. Program slicing [49] is a general technique to prune irrelevant statements from a program or trace. Recently, systems researchers have leveraged or invented slicing techniques to block malicious input [18], synthesize executions for better error diagnosis [57], infer source code paths from log messages for post-mortem analysis [56], and identify critical inter-thread reads that may lead to concurrency errors [59]. Our determinism-preserving slicing technique produces a correct trace slice for multithreaded programs and supports multiple ordered targets. It thus has the potential to benefit existing systems that use slicing.

Our schedule-guided simplification technique shares similarity with SherLog [56] such as the removal of branches contradicting a schedule. However, SherLog starts from log messages and tries to compute an execution trace, whereas PEREGRINE starts with a schedule and an execution trace and computes a simplified yet runnable program. PEREGRINE can thus transparently improve the precision of many existing analyses: simply run them on the simplified program.

Replay and re-execution. Deterministic replay [5, 21, 22, 26, 27, 32, 33, 41, 44, 48, 50] aims to replay the exact recorded executions, whereas PEREGRINE "replays" schedules on different inputs. Some recent deterministic replay systems include Scribe, which tracks page ownership to enforce deterministic memory access [33]; Capo, which defines a novel software-hardware interface and a set of abstractions for efficient replay [41]; PRES and ODR, which systematically search for a complete execution based on a partial one [5, 44]; SMP-ReVirt, which uses page protection for recording the order of conflicting memory accesses [22]; and Respec [35], which uses online replay to keep multiple replicas of a multithreaded program in sync. Several systems [35, 44] share the same insight as PEREGRINE: although many programs have races, these races tend to occur infrequently.

PEREGRINE can help these systems reduce CPU, disk, or network bandwidth overhead, because for inputs that hit PEREGRINE's schedule cache, these systems do not have to record a schedule.

Retro [30] shares some similarity with PEREGRINE because it also supports "mutated" replay. When repairing a compromised system, Retro can replay legal actions while removing malicious ones using a novel dependency graph and *predicates* to detect when changes to an object need not be propagated further. PEREGRINE's determinism-preserving slicing algorithm may be used to automatically compute these predicates, so that Retro does not have to rely on programmer annotations.

Concurrency errors. The complexity in developing multi-threaded programs has led to many concurrency errors [39]. Much work exists on concurrency error detection, diagnosis, and correction (*e.g.*, [23–25, 38, 43, 55, 58, 59]). PEREGRINE aims to make the executions of multithreaded programs repeatable, and is complementary to existing work on concurrency errors. PEREGRINE may use existing work to detect and fix the errors in the schedules it computes. Even for programs free of concurrency errors, PEREGRINE still provides value by making their behaviors repeatable.

9 Conclusion and Future Work

PEREGRINE is one of the first efficient and fully deterministic multithreading systems. Leveraging the insight that races are rare, PEREGRINE combines sync-schedules and mem-schedules into hybrid schedules, getting the benefits of both. PEREGRINE reuses schedules across different inputs, amortizing the cost of computing hybrid schedules and making program behaviors repeatable across inputs. It further improves efficiency using two new techniques: determinism-preserving slicing to generalize a schedule to more inputs while preserving determinism, and schedule-guided simplification to precisely analyze a program according to a dynamic schedule. Our evaluation on a diverse set of programs shows that PEREGRINE is both deterministic and efficient, and can frequently reuse schedules for half of the evaluated programs.

PEREGRINE's system and ideas have broad applications. Our immediate future work is to build applications on top of PEREGRINE, such as fast deterministic replay, replication, and diversification systems. We will also extend our approach to system-wide deterministic execution by computing inter-process communication schedules and preconditions. PEREGRINE enables precise program analysis according to a set of inputs and dynamic schedules. We will leverage this capability to accurately detect concurrency errors and verify concurrency-error-freedom for real programs.

Acknowledgement

We thank Cristian Cadar, Bryan Ford (our shepherd), Ying Xu, and the anonymous reviewers for their many helpful comments, which have substantially improved the content and presentation of this paper. We thank Dawson Engler, Yang Tang, and Gang Hu for proofreading. This work was supported in part by AFRL FA8650-10-C-7024 and FA8750-10-2-0253, and NSF grants CNS-1117805, CNS-1054906 (CAREER), CNS-1012633, and CNS-0905246.

References

[1] ab - Apache HTTP server benchmarking tool. http://httpd.apache.org/docs/2.2/programs/ab.html.

[2] The LLVM Compiler Framework. http://llvm.org.

[3] Parallel BZIP2 (PBZIP2). http://compression.ca/pbzip2/.

[4] A. V. Aho, M. S. Lam, R. Sethi, and J. D. Ullman. *Compilers: Principles, Techniques, and Tools (2nd Edition)*. Addison-Wesley, 2006.

[5] G. Altekar and I. Stoica. ODR: output-deterministic replay for multicore debugging. In *Proceedings of the 22nd ACM Symposium on Operating Systems Principles (SOSP '09)*, pages 193–206, Oct. 2009.

[6] Apache Web Server. http://www.apache.org.

[7] A. Aviram, S.-C. Weng, S. Hu, and B. Ford. Efficient system-enforced deterministic parallelism. In *Proceedings of the Ninth Symposium on Operating Systems Design and Implementation (OSDI '10)*, Oct. 2010.

[8] D. Avots, M. Dalton, V. B. Livshits, and M. S. Lam. Improving software security with a C pointer analysis. In *Proceedings of the 27th International Conference on Software Engineering (ICSE '05)*, pages 332–341, May 2005.

[9] T. Bergan, O. Anderson, J. Devietti, L. Ceze, and D. Grossman. CoreDet: a compiler and runtime system for deterministic multithreaded execution. In *Fifteenth International Conference on Architecture Support for Programming Languages and Operating Systems (ASPLOS '10)*, pages 53–64, Mar. 2010.

[10] T. Bergan, N. Hunt, L. Ceze, and S. D. Gribble. Deterministic process groups in dOS. In *Proceedings of the Ninth Symposium on Operating Systems Design and Implementation (OSDI '10)*, pages 1–16, Oct. 2010.

[11] T. Bergan, J. Devietti, N. Hunt, and L. Ceze. The deterministic execution hammer: how well does it actually pound nails? In *The 2nd Workshop on Determinism and Correctness in Parallel Programming (WODET '11)*, Mar. 2011.

[12] E. Berger, T. Yang, T. Liu, D. Krishnan, and A. Novark. Grace: safe and efficient concurrent programming. In *Conference on Object-Oriented Programming Systems, Languages, and Applications (OOPSLA '09)*, pages 81–96, Oct. 2009.

[13] S. Bhansali, W.-K. Chen, S. de Jong, A. Edwards, R. Murray, M. Drinić, D. Mihocka, and J. Chau. Framework for instruction-level tracing and analysis of program executions. In *Proceedings of the 2nd International Conference on Virtual Execution Environments (VEE '06)*, pages 154–163, June 2006.

[14] P. Boonstoppel, C. Cadar, and D. Engler. RWset: attacking path explosion in constraint-based test generation. In *Proceedings of the Theory and practice of software, 14th international conference on Tools and algorithms for the construction and analysis of systems*, pages 351–366, Mar. 2008.

[15] C. Cadar, D. Dunbar, and D. Engler. KLEE: unassisted and automatic generation of high-coverage tests for complex systems programs. In *Proceedings of the Eighth Symposium on Operating Systems Design and Implementation (OSDI '08)*, pages 209–224, Dec. 2008.

[16] M. Castro, M. Costa, and J.-P. Martin. Better bug reporting with better privacy. In *Thirteenth International Conference on Architecture Support for Programming Languages and Operating Systems (ASPLOS '08)*, pages 319–328, Mar. 2008.

[17] P. Collingbourne, C. Cadar, and P. H. Kelly. Symbolic crosschecking of floating-point and SIMD code. In *Proceedings of the 6th ACM European Conference on Computer Systems (EUROSYS '11)*, pages 315–328, Apr. 2011.

[18] M. Costa, M. Castro, L. Zhou, L. Zhang, and M. Peinado. Bouncer: securing software by blocking bad input. In *Proceedings of the 21st ACM Symposium on Operating Systems Principles (SOSP '07)*, pages 117–130, Oct. 2007.

[19] H. Cui, J. Wu, C.-C. Tsai, and J. Yang. Stable deterministic multithreading through schedule memoization. In *Proceedings of the Ninth Symposium on Operating Systems Design and Implementation (OSDI '10)*, Oct. 2010.

[20] J. Devietti, B. Lucia, L. Ceze, and M. Oskin. DMP: deterministic shared memory multiprocessing. In *Fourteenth International Conference on Architecture Support for Programming Languages and Operating Systems (ASPLOS '09)*, pages 85–96, Mar. 2009.

[21] G. Dunlap, S. T. King, S. Cinar, M. Basrat, and P. Chen. ReVirt: enabling intrusion analysis through virtual-machine logging and replay. In *Proceedings of the Fifth Symposium on Operating Systems Design and Implementation (OSDI '02)*, pages 211–224, Dec. 2002.

[22] G. W. Dunlap, D. G. Lucchetti, M. A. Fetterman, and P. M. Chen. Execution replay of multiprocessor virtual machines. In *Proceedings of the 4th International Conference on Virtual Execution Environments (VEE '08)*, pages 121–130, Mar. 2008.

[23] D. Engler and K. Ashcraft. RacerX: effective, static detection of race conditions and deadlocks. In *Proceedings of the 19th ACM Symposium on Operating Systems Principles (SOSP '03)*, pages 237–252, Oct. 2003.

[24] P. Fonseca, C. Li, and R. Rodrigues. Finding complex concurrency bugs in large multi-threaded applications. In *Proceedings of the 6th ACM European Conference on Computer Systems (EUROSYS '11)*, pages 215–228, Apr. 2011.

[25] Q. Gao, W. Zhang, Z. Chen, M. Zheng, and F. Qin. 2ndStrike: towards manifesting hidden concurrency typestate bugs. In *Sixteenth International Conference on Architecture Support for Programming Languages and Operating Systems (ASPLOS '11)*, pages 239–250, Mar. 2011.

[26] D. Geels, G. Altekar, P. Maniatis, T. Roscoe, and I. Stoica. Friday: global comprehension for distributed replay. In *Proceedings of the Fourth Symposium on Networked Systems Design and Implementation (NSDI '07)*, Apr. 2007.

[27] Z. Guo, X. Wang, J. Tang, X. Liu, Z. Xu, M. Wu, M. F. Kaashoek, and Z. Zhang. R2: An application-level kernel for record and replay. In *Proceedings of the Eighth Symposium on Operating Systems Design and Implementation (OSDI '08)*, pages 193–208, Dec. 2008.

[28] B. Hackett and A. Aiken. How is aliasing used in systems software? In *Proceedings of the 14th ACM SIGSOFT International Symposium on Foundations of Software Engineering (SIGSOFT '06/FSE-14)*, pages 69–80, Nov. 2006.

[29] M. D. Hill and M. Xu. Racey: A stress test for deterministic execution. http://www.cs.wisc.edu/~markhill/racey.html.

[30] T. Kim, X. Wang, N. Zeldovich, and M. F. Kaashoek. Intrusion recovery using selective re-execution. In *Proceedings of the Ninth Symposium on Operating Systems Design and Implementation (OSDI '10)*, pages 1–9, Oct. 2010.

[31] J. C. King. A new approach to program testing. In *Proceedings of the international conference on Reliable software*, pages 228–233, 1975.

[32] R. Konuru, H. Srinivasan, and J.-D. Choi. Deterministic replay of distributed Java applications. In *Proceedings of the 14th International Symposium on Parallel and Distributed Processing (IPDPS '00)*, pages 219–228, May 2000.

[33] O. Laadan, N. Viennot, and J. Nieh. Transparent, lightweight application execution replay on commodity multiprocessor operating systems. In *Proceedings of the ACM SIGMETRICS Conference on Measurement and Modeling of Computer Systems (SIGMETRICS '10)*, pages 155–166, June 2010.

[34] L. Lamport. Time, clocks, and the ordering of events in a distributed system. *Comm. ACM*, 21(7):558–565, 1978.

[35] D. Lee, B. Wester, K. Veeraraghavan, S. Narayanasamy, P. M. Chen, and J. Flinn. Respec: efficient online multiprocessor replayvia speculation and external determinism. In *Fifteenth International Conference on Architecture Support for Programming Languages and Operating Systems (ASPLOS '10)*, pages 77–90, Mar. 2010.

[36] T. Liu, C. Curtsinger, and E. D. Berger. DTHREADS: efficient deterministic multithreading. In *Proceedings of the 23rd ACM Symposium on Operating Systems Principles (SOSP '11)*, Oct. 2011.

[37] S. Lu, J. Tucek, F. Qin, and Y. Zhou. AVIO: detecting atomicity violations via access interleaving invariants. In *Twelfth International Conference on Architecture Support for Programming Languages and Operating Systems (ASPLOS '06)*, pages 37–48, Oct. 2006.

[38] S. Lu, S. Park, C. Hu, X. Ma, W. Jiang, Z. Li, R. A. Popa, and Y. Zhou. Muvi: automatically inferring multi-variable access correlations and detecting related semantic and concurrency bugs. *SIGOPS Oper. Syst. Rev.*, 41(6):103–116, 2007.

[39] S. Lu, S. Park, E. Seo, and Y. Zhou. Learning from mistakes: a comprehensive study on real world concurrency bug characteristics. In *Thirteenth International Conference on Architecture Support for Programming Languages and Operating Systems (ASPLOS '08)*, pages 329–339, Mar. 2008.

[40] F. Mattern. Virtual time and global states of distributed systems. In *Proceedings of the International Workshop on Parallel and Distributed Algorithms*, pages 215–226. 1988.

[41] P. Montesinos, M. Hicks, S. T. King, and J. Torrellas. Capo: a software-hardware interface for practical deterministic multiprocessor replay. In *Fourteenth International Conference on Architecture Support for Programming Languages and Operating Systems (ASPLOS '09)*, pages 73–84, Mar. 2009.

[42] M. Olszewski, J. Ansel, and S. Amarasinghe. Kendo: efficient deterministic multithreading in software. In *Fourteenth International Conference on Architecture Support for Programming Languages and Operating Systems (ASPLOS '09)*, pages 97–108, Mar. 2009.

[43] S. Park, S. Lu, and Y. Zhou. CTrigger: exposing atomicity violation bugs from their hiding places. In *Fourteenth International Conference on Architecture Support for Programming Languages and Operating Systems (ASPLOS '09)*, pages 25–36, Mar. 2009.

[44] S. Park, Y. Zhou, W. Xiong, Z. Yin, R. Kaushik, K. H. Lee, and S. Lu. PRES: probabilistic replay with execution sketching on multiprocessors. In *Proceedings of the 22nd ACM Symposium on Operating Systems Principles (SOSP '09)*, pages 177–192, Oct. 2009.

[45] M. Ronsse and K. De Bosschere. Recplay: a fully integrated practical record/replay system. *ACM Trans. Comput. Syst.*, 17(2):133–152, 1999.

[46] R. Rugina and M. Rinard. Symbolic bounds analysis of pointers, array indices, and accessed memory regions. In *Proceedings of the ACM SIGPLAN 2000 Conference on Programming Language Design and Implementation (PLDI '00)*, pages 182–195, June 2000.

[47] S. Savage, M. Burrows, G. Nelson, P. Sobalvarro, and T. E. Anderson. Eraser: A dynamic data race detector for multithreaded programming. *ACM Trans. Comput. Syst.*, pages 391–411, Nov. 1997.

[48] S. M. Srinivasan, S. Kandula, C. R. Andrews, and Y. Zhou. Flashback: A lightweight extension for rollback and deterministic replay for software debugging. In *Proceedings of the USENIX Annual Technical Conference (USENIX '04)*, pages 29–44, June 2004.

[49] F. Tip. A survey of program slicing techniques. *Journal of Programming Languages 3(3)*, pages 121–189, 1995.

[50] VMWare Virtual Lab Automation. http://www.vmware.com/solutions/vla/.

[51] J. Whaley. bddbddb Project. http://bddbddb.sourceforge.net. URL http://bddbddb.sourceforge.net.

[52] J. Whaley and M. S. Lam. Cloning-based context-sensitive pointer alias analysis using binary decision diagrams. In *Proceedings of the ACM SIGPLAN 2004 Conference on Programming Language Design and Implementation (PLDI '04)*, pages 131–144, June 2004.

[53] J. Wu, H. Cui, and J. Yang. Bypassing races in live applications with execution filters. In *Proceedings of the Ninth Symposium on Operating Systems Design and Implementation (OSDI '10)*, Oct. 2010.

[54] W. Xiong, S. Park, J. Zhang, Y. Zhou, and Z. Ma. Ad hoc synchronization considered harmful. In *Proceedings of the Ninth Symposium on Operating Systems Design and Implementation (OSDI '10)*, Oct. 2010.

[55] Y. Yu, T. Rodeheffer, and W. Chen. RaceTrack: efficient detection of data race conditions via adaptive tracking. In *Proceedings of the 20th ACM Symposium on Operating Systems Principles (SOSP '05)*, pages 221–234, Oct. 2005.

[56] D. Yuan, H. Mai, W. Xiong, L. Tan, Y. Zhou, and S. Pasupathy. SherLog: error diagnosis by connecting clues from run-time logs. In *Fifteenth International Conference on Architecture Support for Programming Languages and Operating Systems (ASPLOS '10)*, pages 143–154, Mar. 2010.

[57] C. Zamfir and G. Candea. Execution synthesis: a technique for automated software debugging. In *Proceedings of the 5th ACM European Conference on Computer Systems (EUROSYS '10)*, pages 321–334, Apr. 2010.

[58] W. Zhang, C. Sun, and S. Lu. ConMem: detecting severe concurrency bugs through an effect-oriented approach. In *Fifteenth International Conference on Architecture Support for Programming Languages and Operating Systems (ASPLOS '10)*, pages 179–192, Mar. 2010.

[59] W. Zhang, J. Lim, R. Olichandran, J. Scherpelz, G. Jin, S. Lu, and T. Reps. ConSeq: detecting concurrency bugs through sequential errors. In *Sixteenth International Conference on Architecture Support for Programming Languages and Operating Systems (ASPLOS '11)*, pages 251–264, Mar. 2011.

Pervasive Detection of Process Races in Deployed Systems

Oren Laadan, Nicolas Viennot, Chia-Che Tsai,
Chris Blinn, Junfeng Yang, and Jason Nieh
orenl@cs.columbia.edu, nviennot@cs.columbia.edu, chiache.tsai@gmail.com,
cpb2114@columbia.edu, junfeng@cs.columbia.edu, nieh@cs.columbia.edu
Department of Computer Science
Columbia University

ABSTRACT

Process races occur when multiple processes access shared operating system resources, such as files, without proper synchronization. We present the first study of real process races and the first system designed to detect them. Our study of hundreds of applications shows that process races are numerous, difficult to debug, and a real threat to reliability. To address this problem, we created RACEPRO, a system for automatically detecting these races. RACEPRO checks deployed systems *in-vivo* by recording live executions then deterministically replaying and checking them later. This approach increases checking coverage beyond the configurations or executions covered by software vendors or beta testing sites. RACEPRO records multiple processes, detects races in the recording among system calls that may concurrently access shared kernel objects, then tries different execution orderings of such system calls to determine which races are harmful and result in failures. To simplify race detection, RACEPRO models under-specified system calls based on load and store micro-operations. To reduce false positives and negatives, RACEPRO uses a *replay and go-live* mechanism to distill harmful races from benign ones. We have implemented RACEPRO in Linux, shown that it imposes only modest recording overhead, and used it to detect a number of previously unknown bugs in real applications caused by process races.

Categories and Subject Descriptors:

D.2.4 [**Software Engineering**]: Software/Program Verification;
D.4.5 [**Operating Systems**]: Reliability

General Terms:

Design, Reliability, Verification

Keywords:

Record-replay, Debugging, Race Detection, Model Checking

1 Introduction

While thread races have drawn much attention from the research community [9, 11, 30, 36, 38], little has been done for *process races*, where multiple processes access an operating system (OS) resource such as a file or device without proper synchronization. Process races are much broader than time-of-check-to-time-of-use (TOCTOU) races or signal races [39]. A typical TOCTOU race is an atomicity violation where the permission check and the use of a resource are not atomic, so that a malicious process may slip in. A signal race is often triggered when an attacker delivers two signals consecutively to a process to interrupt and reenter a non-reentrant signal handler. In contrast, a process race may be any form of race. Some real examples include a shutdown script that unmounts a file system before another process writes its data, `ps | grep X` shows N or $N + 1$ lines depending on the timing of the two commands, and `make -j` failures.

To better understand process races, we present the first study of real process races. We study hundreds of real applications across six Linux distributions and show that process races are numerous and a real threat to reliability and security. For example, a simple search on Ubuntu's software management site [2] returns hundreds of process races. Compared to thread races that typically corrupt volatile application memory, process races are arguably more dangerous because they often corrupt persistent and system resources. Our study also reveals that some of their characteristics hint towards potential detection methods.

We then present RACEPRO, the first system for automatically detecting process races beyond TOCTOU and signal races. RACEPRO faces three key challenges. The first is scope: process races are extremely heterogeneous. They may involve many different programs. These programs may be written in different programming languages, run within different processes or threads, and access diverse resources. Existing detectors for thread or TOCTOU races are unlikely to work well with this heterogeneity.

The second challenge is coverage: although process races are numerous, each particular process race tends to be highly elusive. They are timing-dependent, and tend to surface only in rare executions. Arguably worse than thread races, they may occur only under specific software, hardware, and user configurations at specific sites. It is hopeless to rely on a few software vendors and beta testing sites to create all possible configurations and executions for checking.

The third challenge is algorithmic: what race detection algorithm can be used for detecting process races? Existing algorithms assume well-defined load and store instructions and thread synchronization primitives. However, the effects of system calls are often under-specified and process synchronization primitives are very different from those used in shared memory. For instance, what shared objects does `execve` access? In addition to reading the inode of the executed binary, an obvious yet incomplete answer, `execve` also conceptually writes to `/proc`, which is the root cause of the `ps | grep X` race (§5). Similarly, a thread-join returns only when the thread being waited for exits, but `wait` may return when any child process exits or any signal arrives. Besides fork-wait, processes can also synchronize using pipes, signals, `ptrace`, etc. Missing the (nuanced) semantics of these system calls can lead to false positives where races that do not exist are mistakenly identified and, even worse, false negatives where harmful races are not detected.

RACEPRO addresses these challenges with four ideas. First, it checks deployed systems *in-vivo*. While a deployed system is running, RACEPRO records the execution without doing any checking. RACEPRO then systematically checks this recorded execution for races *offline*, when the deployed system is idle or by replicating the execution to a dedicated checking machine. By checking deployed systems, RACEPRO mitigates the coverage challenge because all user machines together can create a much larger and more diverse set of configurations and executions for checking. Alternatively, if a configuration or execution never occurs, it is probably not worth checking. By decoupling recording and checking [7], RACEPRO reduces its performance overhead on the deployed systems.

Second, RACEPRO records a deployed system as a system-wide, deterministic execution of multiple processes and threads. RACE-PRO uses lightweight OS mechanisms developed in our previous work [17] to transparently and efficiently record nondeterministic interactions such as related system calls, signals, and shared memory accesses. No source code or modifications of the checked applications are required, mitigating the scope challenge. Moreover, since processes access shared OS resources through system calls, this information is recorded at the OS level so that RACEPRO can use it to detect races regardless of higher level program semantics.

Third, to detect process races in a recorded execution, RACE-PRO models each system call by what we call *load and store micro-operations* to shared kernel objects. Because these two operations are well-understood by existing race detection algorithms, RACE-PRO can leverage these algorithms, mitigating the algorithmic challenge. To reduce manual annotation overhead, RACEPRO automatically infers the micro-operations a system call does by tracking how it accesses shared kernel objects, such as inodes. Given these micro-operations, RACEPRO detects *load-store races* when two concurrent system calls access a common kernel object and at least one system call stores to the object. In addition, it detects *wait-wakeup races* such as when two child processes terminate simultaneously so that either may wake up a waiting parent. To our knowledge, no previous algorithm directly handles wait-wakeup races.

Fourth, to reduce false positives and negatives, RACEPRO uses *replay and go-live* to validate detected races. A race detected based on the micro-operations may be either *benign* or *harmful*, depending on whether it leads to a *failure*, such as a segmentation fault or a program abort. RACEPRO considers a change in the order of the system calls involved in a race to be an *execution branch*. To check whether this branch leads to a failure, RACEPRO replays the recorded execution until the *reordered* system calls then resumes live execution. It then runs a set of built-in or user-provided checkers on the live execution to detect failures, and emits a bug report only when a real failure is detected. By checking many execution branches, RACEPRO reduces false negatives. By reporting only harmful races, it reduces false positives.

We have implemented RACEPRO in Linux as a set of kernel components for record, replay, and go-live, and a user-space explo-ration engine for systematically checking execution branches. Our experimental results show that RACEPRO can be used in production environments with only modest recording overhead, less than 2.5% for server and 15% for desktop applications. Furthermore, we show that RACEPRO can detect 10 real bugs due to process races in widespread Linux distributions.

This paper is organized as follows. §2 presents a study of process races and several process race examples. §3 presents an overview of the RACEPRO architecture. §4 describes the execution recording mechanism. §5 describes the system call modeling using micro-operations and the race detection algorithm. §6 describes how replay and go-live are used to determine harmful races. §7 presents experimental results. §8 discusses related work. Finally, §9 presents some concluding remarks and directions for future work.

2 Process Race Study

We conducted a study of real process races with two key questions in mind. First, are process races a real problem? Second, what are their characteristics that may hint towards how to detect them? We collected bugs from six widespread Linux distributions, namely Ubuntu, RedHat, Fedora, Gentoo, Debian, and CentOS. For each distribution, we launched a search query of "race" on the distribution's software management website. We manually examined a random sample of the returned pages, identified all unique bugs in the sampled pages, and classified these bugs based on whether they resulted in process or thread races. Raw data of the studied bugs is available [1]. §2.1 presents our findings. §2.2 describes four process race examples from the most serious to the least.

2.1 Findings

Table 1 summarizes the collected pages and bugs; Fedora and Red-hat results are combined as they share the same management website. For each distribution, we show the number of pages returned for our query (Returned), the number of pages sampled and manually examined (Sampled), the number of process races (Process) and the subset of which were TOCTOU races, the number of thread races (Thread), and the total number of bugs in the sampled pages (Total).

Process races are numerous. Of the 150 sampled bugs, 109 resulted in process races, a dominating majority; the other 41 bugs resulted in thread races. However, thread races are likely under-represented because the websites we searched are heavily used by Linux distribution maintainers, not developers of individual applications. Of the 109 process races, 84 are not TOCTOU races and therefore cannot be detected by existing TOCTOU detectors. Based on this sample, the 7,498 pages that our simple search returned may extrapolate to over 1,500 process races. Note that our counting is very conservative: the sampled pages contain an additional 58 likely process races, but the pages did not contain enough information for us to understand the cause, so we did not include them in Table 1.

Distribution	Pages		Bugs		
	Returned	Sampled	Total	Process	Thread
Ubuntu	3330	300	45	42 (1)	3
Fedora/RedHat	1070	100	52	30 (10)	22
Gentoo	2360	60	31	23 (10)	8
Debian	768	40	17	12 (4)	5
CentOS	1500	40	5	2 (0)	3
Total	9028	540	150	109 (25)	41

Table 1: *Summary of collected pages and bugs.*

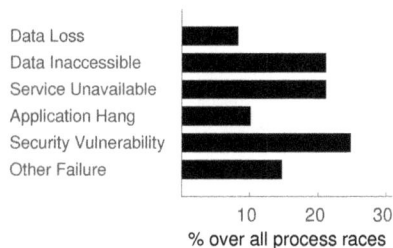

Figure 1: *Process races breakdown by effects.*

Process races are dangerous. Compared to thread races that typically corrupt volatile application memory, process races are arguably more dangerous because they often corrupt persistent and system resources. Indeed, the sampled process races caused security breaches, files and databases to become corrupted, programs to read garbage, and processes to get stuck in infinite loops. Figure 1 summarizes the effects of all process races from Table 1.

Process races are heterogeneous. The sampled process races spread across over 200 programs, ranging from server applications such as MySQL, to desktop applications such as OpenOffice, to shell scripts in Upstart [4], an event-driven replacement of System V init scripts. Figure 2 breaks down the process races by packages, processes, and programming languages involved. Over half of the 109 process races, including all examples described in §2.2, require interactions of at least two programs. These programs are written in different programming languages such as C, Java, PHP, and shell scripts, run in multiple processes, synchronize via `fork` and `wait`, pipes, sockets, and signals, and access resources such as files, devices, process status, and mount points.

This heterogeneity makes it difficult to apply existing detection methods for thread races or TOCTOU races to process races. For instance, static thread race detectors [11] work only with one program written in one language, and dynamic thread race detectors [38] work only with one process. To handle this heterogeneity, RACE-PRO's race detection should be system-wide.

Process races are highly elusive. Many of the process races, including Bug 1 and 3 described in §2.2, occur only due to site-specific software, hardware, and user configurations. Moreover, many of the sampled process races, including all of those described in §2.2, occur only due to rare runtime factors. For example, Bug 1 only occurs when a database shutdown takes longer than usual, and Bug 2 only occurs when a signal is delivered right after a child process exited. These bugs illustrate the advantage of checking deployed systems, so that we can rely on real users to create the diverse configurations and executions to check.

Process race patterns. Classified by the causes, the 109 process races fall into two categories. Over two thirds (79) are execution order violations [20], such as Bug 1, 3, and 4 in §2.2, where a set of events are supposed to occur in a fixed order, but no synchronization operations enforce the order. Less than one third (30) are atomicity violations, including all TOCTOU bugs; most of them are the simplest load-store races, such as Bug 2 in §2.2. Few programs we studied use standard locks (*e.g.*, `flock`) to synchronize file system accesses among processes. These patterns suggest that a lockset-based race detection algorithm is unlikely to work well for detecting process races. Moreover, it is crucial to use an algorithm that can detect order violations.

2.2 Process Race Examples

Bug 1: Upstart-MySQL. `mysqld` does not cleanly terminate during system shutdown, and the file system becomes corrupted. This failure is due to an execution order violation where `S20sendsigs`, the shutdown script that terminates processes, does not wait long enough for MySQL to cleanly shutdown. The script then fails to unmount the file system which is still in use, so it proceeds to reboot the system without cleanly unmounting the file system. Its occurrence requires a combination of many factors, including the mixed use of Systems V initialization scripts and Upstart, a misconfiguration so that `S20sendsigs` does not wait for daemons started by Upstart, insufficient dependencies specified in MySQL's Upstart configuration file, and a large MySQL database that takes a long time to shut down.

Bug 2: dash-MySQL. The shell wrapper `mysql_safe` of the MySQL server daemon `mysqld` goes into an infinite loop with 100% CPU usage after a MySQL update. This failure is due to an atomicity violation in `dash`, a small shell Debian uses to run daemons [3]. It occurs when `dash` is interrupted by a signal unexpectedly. Figure 3 shows the event sequence causing this race. To run a new background job, `dash` forks a child process and adds it to the job list of `dash`. It then calls `setjmp` to save an execution context and waits for the child to exit. After the child exits, `wait` returns, and `dash` is supposed to remove the child from the job list. However, if a signal is delivered at this time, `dash`'s signal handler will call `longjmp` to go back to the saved context, and the subsequent `wait` call will fail because the child's exit status has been collected by the previous `wait` call. The job list is still not empty, so `dash` gets stuck waiting for the nonexistent child to exit. Although this bug is in `dash`, it is triggered in practice by a combination of `dash`, the `mysql_safe` wrapper, and `mysqld`.

Bug 3: Mutt-OpenOffice. OpenOffice displays garbage when a user tries to open a Microsoft (MS) Word attachment in the Mutt mail client. This failure is due to an execution order violation when `mutt` prematurely overwrites the contents of a file before OpenOffice uses this file. It involves a combination of Mutt, OpenOffice, a user configuration entry in Mutt, and the `openoffice` shell script wrapper. The user first configures Mutt to use the `openoffice`

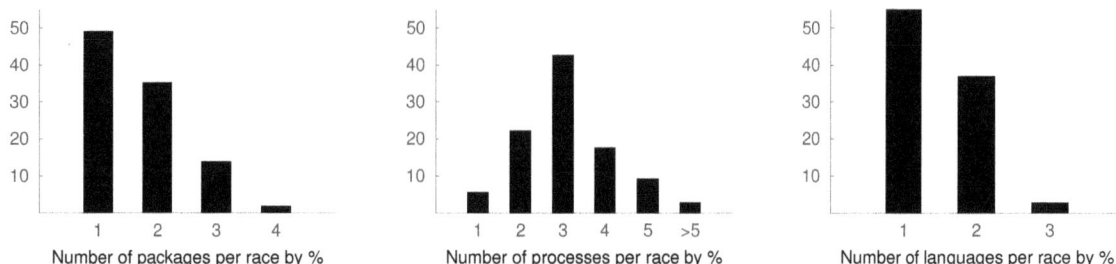

Figure 2: *Process races breakdown.* X axis shows the number of software packages, processes, or programming languages involved. Y axis shows the percentage of process races that involve the specific number of packages, processes, or languages. To avoid inflating the number of processes, we count a run of a shell script as one process. (Each external command in a script causes a `fork`.)

```
child = fork()
setjmp(loc)
p = wait(...) [blocks...]
...              // ← child exits
p = wait(...) [...returns]
...              // ← signaled
longjmp(loc)
p = wait(...) // error (no child)
```

Figure 3: *dash-MySQL race.*

```
fd = open(H,RDONLY);
read(fd, buf, ...);
close(fd);
... // update buf
... // do work
fd = open(H,WRONLY|TRUNC);
write(fd, buf, ...);
close(fd);
```

Figure 4: *bash race.*

wrapper to open MS Word attachments. To show an attachment, `mutt` saves the attachment to a temporary file, spawns the configured viewer in a new process, and waits for the viewer process to exit. The `openoffice` wrapper spawns the actual OpenOffice binary and exits at once. `mutt` mistakes this exit as the termination of the actual viewer, and overwrites the temporary file holding the attachment with all zeros, presumably for privacy reasons.

Bug 4: bash. The `bash` shell history is corrupted. This failure is due to an atomicity violation when multiple `bash` shells write concurrently to `.bash_history` without synchronization. When `bash` appends to the history file, it correctly uses `O_APPEND`. However, it also occasionally reads back the history file and overwrites it, presumably to keep the history file under a user-specified size. Figure 4 shows this problematic sequence of system calls. `bash` also runs this sequence when it exits. When multiple `bash` processes exit at the same time, the history file may be corrupted.

3 Architecture Overview

RACEPRO is designed to automatically detect process races using the workflow shown in Figure 5. It consists of three steps, the first of which runs on the deployed system, while the latter two can run elsewhere on a separate replay system to avoid any performance impact on the deployed system. First, a *recorder* records the execution of a deployed system while the system is running and stores the recording in a log file. Second, an *explorer* reads the log and detects load-store and wait-wakeup races in the recorded execution. Third, each race is validated to determine if it is harmful. An execution branch of the recorded execution corresponding to each race is computed by systematically changing the order of system calls involved in the race. For each execution branch, a modified log is constructed that is used to replay execution with the changed order of system calls. A *replayer* replays the respective modified log up to the occurrence of the race, then causes it to resume live execution from that point onward. A set of built-in and user-provided *checkers* then check whether the execution results in misbehavior or a failure such as a segmentation fault. By examining the effects of a live execution, we distinguish harmful races from false or be-

nign ones, thus reducing false positives [25, 30]. The live part of the re-execution is also recorded, so that users can deterministically replay detected bugs for debugging.

Figure 6 shows the RACEPRO architecture used to support its workflow. Of the four main architectural components, the recorder and the replayer run in kernel-space, and the explorer and checkers run in user-space. We will describe how RACEPRO records executions (§4) and detects (§5) and validates (§6) races using these components.

4 Recording Executions

RACEPRO's record-replay functionality builds on our previous work on lightweight OS-level deterministic replay on multiprocessors [17]. This approach provides four key benefits for detecting process races. First, RACEPRO's recorder can record the execution of multiple processes and threads with low overhead on a deployed system so that the replayer can later deterministically replay that execution. This makes RACEPRO's *in-vivo* checking approach possible by minimizing the performance impact of recording deployed systems. Second, RACEPRO's record-replay is application-transparent; it does not require changing, relinking, or recompiling applications or libraries. This enables RACEPRO to detect process races that are extremely heterogeneous involving many different programs written in different program languages. Third, RACEPRO's recorder operates at the OS level to log sufficiently fine-grained accesses to shared kernel objects so that RACEPRO's explorer can detect races regardless of high-level program semantics (§5). Finally, RACEPRO's record-replay records executions such that it can later transition from controlled replay of the recording to live execution at any point. This enables RACEPRO to distinguish harmful races from benign ones by allowing checkers to monitor an application for failures (§6.2).

To record the execution of multiprocess and multithreaded applications, RACEPRO records all nondeterministic interactions between applications and the OS and saves the recording as a log file. We highlight how key interactions involving system calls, signals, and shared memory are handled.

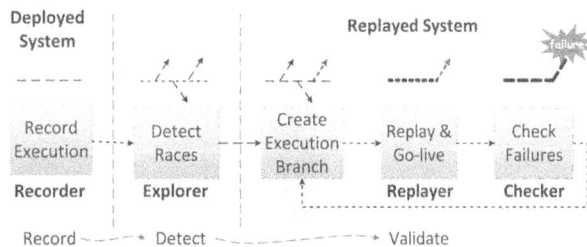

Figure 5: RACEPRO *Workflow.* Thin solid lines represent recorded executions; thick solid lines represent replayed executions. Dashed arrows represent potentially buggy execution branches. The dotted thick arrow represents the branch RACEPRO selects to explore.

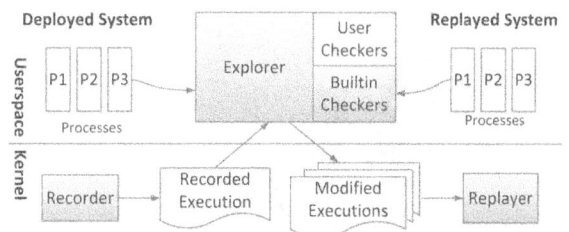

Figure 6: RACEPRO *Architecture.* Components are shaded. The recorder and the replayer run in kernel-space, and the explorer and the checkers run in user-space. Recorded executions and modified executions are stored in files.

Object	Description
inode	file, directory, socket, pipe, tty, pty, device
file	file handle of an open file
file-table	process file table
mmap	process memory map
cred	process credentials and capabilities, *e.g.*, user ID
global	system-wide properties (*e.g.*, hostname, mounts)
pid	process ID (access to process and /proc)
ppid	parent process ID (synchronize exit/getppid)

Table 2: *Shared kernel objects tracked.*

System calls. Unlike previous work [15, 31] that records and replays a total order of system calls, RACEPRO records and replays a partial order of system calls for speed. RACEPRO enforces no ordering constraints among system calls during record-replay unless they access the same kernel object and at least one of them modifies it, such as a write and a read on the same file. In that case, RACEPRO records the order in the kernel in which the object is accessed by the system calls and later replays the exact same order of accesses. This is done by piggybacking on the synchronization code that the kernel already has for serializing accesses to shared objects. These tracked accesses also help detect process races in a recorded execution (§5).

Table 2 lists the kernel objects tracked by RACEPRO. Most of the entries correspond one-to-one to specific low-level kernel resources, including inodes, files, file-tables, memory maps, and process credentials. The global entry corresponds to system-wide kernel objects, such as the hostname, file system mounts, system time, and network interfaces. For each such system-wide resource there is a unique global kernel object used to track accesses to that resource. The last two entries in the table, pid and ppid, provide a synchronization point to track dependencies on process states. For example, the pid entry of a process is used to track instances where the process is referenced by another process, *e.g.*, through a system call that references the process ID or through the /proc file system. The ppid entry is used to track when an orphan process is re-parented, which is visible through the getppid system call. Both pid and ppid correspond to identifiers that are visible to processes but cannot be modified explicitly by processes.

The recorder only tracks kernel objects whose state is visible to user-space processes, either directly or indirectly. For example, inode state is accessible via the system call lstat, and file-table state is visible through resolving of file descriptor in many system calls. RACEPRO does not track accesses to kernel objects which are entirely invisible to user-space. This avoids tracking superfluous accesses that may pollute the race detection results with unnecessary dependencies. For example, both the fork and exit system calls access the kernel process table, but the order is unimportant to user-space. It only matters that the lifespan of processes is observed correctly, which is already tracked and enforced via the pid resource. If RACEPRO tracked accesses to the kernel process table, it would mistakenly conclude that every two fork system calls are "racy" because they all modify a common resource (§5). One complication with this approach is that if the kernel object in question controls assignment of identifiers (*e.g.*, process ID in the fork example), it may assign different identifiers during replay because the original order of accesses is not enforced. To address this problem, RACEPRO virtualizes identifiers such as process IDs to ensure the same values are allocated during replay as in the recording.

Signals. Deterministically replaying signals is hard since they must be delivered at the exact same instruction in the target execution flow as during recording. To address this problem, RACE-

PRO uses *sync points* that correspond to synchronous kernel entries such as system calls. Sending a signal to a target process may occur at any time during the target process's execution. However, RACE-PRO defers signal delivery until sync points occur to make their timing deterministic so they are easier to record and replay efficiently. Unlike previous approaches, sync points do not require hardware counters or application modifications, and do not adversely impact application performance because they occur frequently enough in real server and desktop applications due to OS activities.

Shared memory. RACEPRO combines page ownership with sync points to deterministically record and replay the order of shared memory accesses among processes and threads. Each shared memory page is assigned an owner process or thread for some time interval. The owner can exclusively modify that page during the interval and treat it like private memory, avoiding the need to track all memory accesses during such ownership periods. Transitioning page ownership from one process or thread to another is done using a concurrent read, exclusive write (CREW) protocol [10, 19]. To ensure that ownership transitions occur at precisely the same location in the execution during both record and replay, RACEPRO defers such transitions until the owner reaches a sync point. When a process tries to access an owned page, it triggers a page fault, notifies the owner, and blocks until access is granted. Conversely, each owner checks for pending requests at every sync point and, if necessary, gives up ownership. Page faults due to the memory interleaving under the CREW protocol are synchronous kernel entries that deterministically occur on replay and hence are also used as sync points.

5 Detecting Process Races

RACEPRO flags a set of system calls as a race if (1) they are *concurrent* and therefore could have executed in a different order than the order recorded, (2) they access a common resource such that reordering the accesses may change the outcome of the execution. To determine whether a set of system calls are concurrent, RACEPRO constructs a happens-before [18] graph for the recorded execution (§5.1). To determine whether a set of system calls access common resources, RACEPRO obtains the shared kernel resources accessed by system calls from the log file and models the system calls as *load* and *store* micro-operations (§5.2) on those resources. RACEPRO then runs a set of happens-before based race detection algorithms to detect load-store and wait-wakeup races (§5.3).

5.1 The Happens-Before Graph

We define a partial ordering on the execution of system calls called *inherent* happens-before relations. We say that system call S_1 *inherently* happens-before system call S_2 if (1) S_1 accesses some resource before S_2 accesses that resource, (2) there is a dependency such that S_2 would not occur or complete unless S_1 completes, and (3) the dependency must be inferable from the system call semantics. For example, a fork that creates a child process inherently happens-before any system call in the child process, and a write to a pipe inherently happens-before a blocking read from the pipe. On the other hand, there is no inherent happens-before relation between a read and subsequent write to the same file.

RACEPRO constructs the happens-before graph using only inherent happens-before relations, as they represent the basic constraints on the ordering of system calls. Given a recorded execution, RACE-PRO constructs a happens-before graph for all recorded system call events by considering pairs of such events. If two events S_1 and S_2 occur in the same process and S_2 is the next system call event that occurs after S_1, RACEPRO adds a directed edge $S_1 \rightarrow S_2$ in the happens-before graph. If two events S_1 and S_2 occur in two

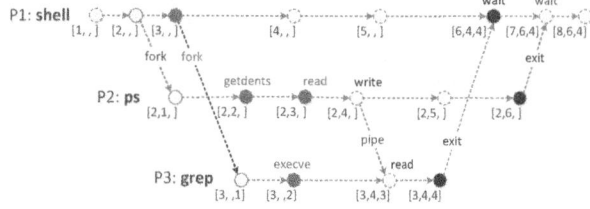

Figure 7: *The Happens-before graph and respective vector-clocks (in brackets) for ps | grep X. $P_{i=1,2,3}$ represent the processes involved. The* read *of process P_2 and the* execve *of P_3 form a load-store race (§5.3.1), and so do the second* fork *of P_1 and the* getdents *(read directory entries) of P_2. The first* wait *of P_1 and the* exits *of P_2 and P_3 form a wait-wakeups race (§5.3.2). For clarity, not all system calls are shown.*

different processes, RACEPRO adds a directed edge $S_1 \rightarrow S_2$ in four cases:

1. S_1 is a fork call, and S_2 is the corresponding fork return in the child process;
2. S_1 is the exit of a child process, and S_2 is the corresponding wait in the parent;
3. S_1 is a kill call, and S_2 is the corresponding signal delivery in the target process; or
4. S_1 is a stream (*e.g.*, pipe or socket) write, and S_2 is a read from the same stream and the data written and the data read overlap.

We say that event S_1 *happens-before* S_2 with respect to a happens-before graph iff there is a directed path from S_1 to S_2 in the happens-before graph. Two events are *concurrent* with respect to a happens-before graph iff neither happens before the other.

RACEPRO also computes the vector-clocks [22] for all the system calls in the happens-before graph. By definition, the vector-clock of S_1 is earlier than the vector-clock of S_2 iff S_1 *happens-before* S_2 with respect to the graph, so comparing the vector-clocks of system calls is a fast and efficient way to test whether they are concurrent.

Our definition of inherent happens-before does not capture all dependencies that may constrain execution ordering. It may be missing happens-before edges that depend on the behavior of the application but cannot be directly inferred from the semantics of the system calls involved. For example, the graph does not capture dependencies between processes via shared memory. It also does not capture dependencies caused by contents written to and read from files. For example, one can implement a fork-join primitive using read and write operations on a file. In some cases, such inaccuracies may make RACEPRO more conservative in flagging racy system calls and thereby identify impossible races. However, such cases will be filtered later by RACEPRO's validation step (§6) and will not be reported.

Figure 7 shows the happens-before graph for the example command ps | grep X. This command creates two child processes that access grep's entry in the /proc directory: the process that runs grep modifies its command-line data when executed, and the process that runs ps reads that data. A race exists because both processes access the common resource in an arbitrary order, and the end result can be either N or $N + 1$ lines depending on that order.

Consider the execve system call in process P_3 and the read system call in process P_2. These two system calls are concurrent because there is no directed path between them in the graph. They both access a shared resource, namely, the inode of the file cmd_line in the directory corresponding to P_3 in /proc. Therefore, these system calls are racy: depending on the precise execu-

tion order, read may or may not observe the new command line with the string "X". Similarly, the second fork in process P_1 and the getdents in process P_3 are also racy: getdents may or may not observe the newly created entry for process P_3 in the /proc directory.

In contrast, consider the pipe between P_2 and P_3. This pipe is a shared resource accessed by their write and read system calls, respectively. However, these two system calls are not racy because they are not concurrent. There exists a happens-before edge in the graph because a read from the pipe will block until data is available after a write to it.

5.2 Modeling Effects of System Calls

Existing algorithms for detecting memory races among threads rely on identifying concurrent load and store instructions to shared memory. To leverage such race detection algorithms, RACEPRO models the effects of a system call on the kernel objects that it may access using two micro-operations: *load* and *store*. These micro-operations are analogous to the traditional load and store instructions that are well-understood by the existing algorithms, except our micro-operations refer to shared kernel objects, such as inodes and memory maps, instead of an application's real shared memory.

More formally, we associate an abstract memory range with each kernel object. The effect of a system call on a kernel object depends on its semantics. If the system call only observes the object's state, we use a *load(obj,range)* operation. If it may also modify the object's state, we use a *store(obj,range)* operation. The argument *obj* indicates the affected kernel object, and the argument *range* indicates the ranges being accessed within that object's abstract memory. A single system call may access multiple kernel objects or even the same kernel object multiple times within the course of its execution.

We use a memory range for a shared kernel object instead of a single memory location because system calls often access different properties of an object or ranges of the object data. For instance, lstat reads the meta-data of files, while write writes the contents of files. They access a common object, but because they access distinct properties of that object, we do not consider them to race. Likewise, read and write system calls to non-overlapping regions in the same file do not race.

Memory ranges are particularly useful to model pathnames. Pathname creation and deletion change the parent directory structure and may race with reading its contents, but pathname creation, deletion, and lookup may only race with each other if given the same pathname. For example, both creat(/tmp/a) and unlink(/tmp/b) may race with a getdents on /tmp, but are unrelated to each other or to an lstat(/tmp/c). Modeling all pathname accesses using a single location on the parent directory's inode is too restrictive. Instead, we assign a unique memory location in the parent directory's inode for each possible pathname. We then model pathname creation and deletion system calls as stores to the designated location, pathname lookup system calls as loads from that location, and read directory system calls as loads from the entire pathname space under that directory.

Memory ranges are also useful to model *wait system calls* which may block on events and *wakeup system calls* which may trigger events. Example wait and wakeup system calls include wait and exit, respectively, and a blocking read from a pipe and a write to the pipe, respectively. To model the effect of wait and wakeup system calls, we use a special location in the abstract memory of the resource involved. Wait system calls are modeled as *loads* from that location, and wakeup system calls are modeled as *stores* to that location. For instance, the exit system call does a *store* to

Syscall	Micro-Op	Kernel Object
open	*store*	file-table
	load	inodes of path components
	store	inode of directory, if O_CREAT
	load	inode of file, if no O_CREAT
	store	data of file (range), if O_TRUNC
write	*load*	process file-table
	store	file handle of file
	store	inode of file
	store	data of file (range)
read	*load*	process file-table
	store	file handle of file
	load	inode of file, if regular file
	store	inode of file, if a stream
	load	data of file (range)
getdents	*load*	process file-table
	store	file handle of directory
	load	inode of directory
	load	data of directory (range)
execve	*load*	inodes of path components
	store	data of `/proc/self/status`
	store	data of `/proc/self/cmdline`
clone	*load*	process memory map
	store	data of `/proc` directory
exit	*store*	'pid' of self
	store	'ppid' of re-parented children
wait	*store*	data of /proc directory
	load	'pid' of reaped child
getppid	*load*	'ppid' of self

Table 3: *Micro-operations of common system calls.*

the special location associated with the parent process ID, and the getppid system call does a *load* from the same location.

Table 3 shows the template of micro-operations that RACEPRO uses to model nine common system calls: open, write, read, getdents, execve, clone (fork a process), exit, wait, and getppid. The open system call accesses several resources. It stores to the process file-table to allocate a new file descriptor, loads from the inodes of the directories corresponding to the path components, stores to the inode of the parent directory if the file is being created or loads from the file's inode otherwise, and stores to the entire data range of the inode if the file is being truncated.

The write, read, and getdents system calls access three resources: process file-table, file handle, and inode. write loads from the process file-table to locate the file handle, stores to the file handle to update the file position, stores to the meta-data of the file's inode in the file system, and stores to the affected data range of the file's inode. The last two micro-operations both affect the file's inode, but at different offsets. read from a regular file and getdents are similar to write, except that they load from the respective file's or directory's inode. read from a stream, such as a socket or a pipe, is also similar, except that it consumes data and thus modifies the inode's state, so it is modeled as a store to the corresponding inode.

The execve system call accesses several resources. It loads from the inodes of the directories corresponding to the path components. It also stores to the inodes of the status and cmdline files in the /proc directory entry of the process, to reflect the newly executed program name and command line.

The clone, exit, and wait system calls access two resources. clone loads from the process's memory map to create a copy for the newborn child, and stores to the /proc directory inode to reflect

the existence of a new entry in it. exit stores to the pid resource of the current process to set the zombie state, and stores to the ppid resource of its children to reparent them to init. wait stores to the reaped child's pid resource to change its state from zombie to dead, and stores to the /proc directory inode to remove the reaped child's entry. RACEPRO detects races between exit and wait based on accesses to the exiting child's pid resource. Similarly, getppid loads from the current process's ppid resource, and RACEPRO detects races between exit and getppid based on accesses to the ppid resource.

To account for system calls that operate on streams of data, such as reads and writes on pipes and sockets, we maintain a virtual write-offset and read-offset for such resources. These offsets are advanced in response to write and read operations, respectively. Consider a stream object with write-offset L_W and read-offset L_R. A write(fd,buf,n) is modeled as a *store* to the memory range $[L_W..L_W + n]$ of the object, and also advances L_W by n. A read(fd,buf,n) is modeled as a *load* from the memory range $[L_R..L_R + \tilde{n}]$, where $\tilde{n} = min(L_W - L_R, n)$, and also advances L_R by $\tilde{n}$.

To account for the effects of signal delivery and handling, we model signals in a way that reflects the possibility of a signal to affect any system call, not just the one system call that was actually affected in the recording. We associate a unique abstract memory location with each signal. A kill system call that sends a signal is modeled as a *store* to this location. Each system call in the target process is considered to access that location, and therefore modeled as a *load* from all the signals. This method ensures that any system call that may be affected by a signal would access the shared object that represents that signal.

5.3 Race Detection Algorithms

Building on the happens-before graph and the modeling of system calls as micro-operations, RACEPRO detects three types of process races: load-store races (§5.3.1), wait-wakeups races (§5.3.2), and wakeup-waits races (§5.3.3). RACEPRO may also be extended to detect other types of races (§5.3.4).

5.3.1 Load-Store Races

A load-store race occurs when two system calls concurrently access the same shared object and at least one is a *store* operation. In this case, the two system calls could have executed in the reverse order. RACEPRO flags two system calls as a load-store race if (1) they are concurrent; (2) they access the same shared kernel object, and (3) at least one access is a *store*. In the ps | grep X example shown in Figure 7, the system calls read and execve are flagged as a race because they are concurrent, they access the same resource, and at least one, execve, does a *store*. In contrast, the system call exit of P_3 also stores to the same resource, but is not flagged as a race because it is not concurrent with any of them as read happens-before exit and execve happens-before exit.

RACEPRO detects load-store races using a straightforward happens-before-based race detection algorithm. We chose a happens-before over lockset because processes rarely use standard locks (§2). RACEPRO iterates through all the shared kernel objects in the recording. For each shared object, it considers the set of all accesses to that object by all system calls, and divides this set into per-process lists, such that the list L_i of process P_i contains all the accesses performed by that process. RACEPRO now looks at all pairs of processes, P_i, P_j, $i \neq j$, and considers their accesses to the object. For each access $S_n \in L_i$, it scans through the accesses $S_m \in L_j$. If the vector-clocks of S_n and S_m are concurrent, the pair of system calls is marked as a race. If $S_n \to S_m$, then $S_n \to S_{m+k}$, so the scan is aborted and the next access $S_{n+1} \in L_i$

is considered. If $S_m \rightarrow S_n$, then $S_m \rightarrow S_{n+k}$, so $S_{m+1} \in L_j$ is saved so that the next scan of accesses from L_j will start from S_{m+1}, since we know that earlier events happened-before all remaining accesses in L_i.

Because system calls may access more than one shared object during their execution, it is possible that the same pair of system calls will be marked more than once. For example, two `write` system calls from different processes to the same location in the same file will be marked twice, once when the meta-data of the inode is considered, and once when the data of the file is considered. Because RACEPRO detects and later validates (§6) races at the granularity of system calls, it only reports the respective pair of system calls once.

RACEPRO may produce a myriad of races, which can take a long time to produce and later validate. To address this concern, RACEPRO prioritizes which races to examine in two ways. First, RACEPRO may defer or entirely skip races that are less likely to prove harmful, depending on the system calls and resource involved. For example, when analyzing the execution of a parallel compilation, resources related to visual output may be skipped: although many processes may be writing to the standard output, races, if they exist, are likely to be benign. Second, RACEPRO ranks pairs of system calls according to their distance from each other in the happens-before graph, and examines nearer system calls first.

5.3.2 Wait-Wakeups Races

A wait-wakeups race occurs when a wait system call may be woken up by more than a single matching wakeup system call. If the wakeup system calls executed in a different order, the wait system call could have picked a different wakeup than in the original execution. Wait-wakeups races involve at least three system calls. For instance, a `wait` system call which does not indicate a specific process identifier to wait for will complete if any of its children terminate. Likewise, a blocking `read` from a stream will complete after any `write` to the stream.

In these cases, the wait system call essentially uses a *wildcard* argument for the wakeup condition so that there can be multiple system calls that match the wakeup condition depending on their order of execution. The wait-wakeups race requires a wildcard, otherwise there is only a single matching system call, and thus a single execution order. For instance, a `wait` system call that requests a specific process identifier must be matched by the exit of that process. In this case, the wait-wakeup relationship implies an inherent happens-before edge in the happens-before graph, since the two system calls must always occur in that order.

RACEPRO flags three system calls as a wait-wakeups race if (1) one is a wait system call, (2) the other two are wakeup system calls that match the wait condition, and (3) the wait system call did not happen-before any of the wakeup system calls. In the `ps | grep X` example shown in Figure 7, the two `exit` system calls of P_2 and P_3 and the first `wait` system call of P_1 are flagged as a wait-wakeups race since both `exit` calls are concurrent and can match the `wait`. In contrast, the `write` and `read` system calls to and from the pipe are not flagged as a race, because there does not exist a second wakeup system call that matches the `read`.

RACEPRO detects wait-wakeups races using an algorithm that builds on the load-store race detection algorithm, with three main differences. First, the algorithm considers only those accesses that correspond to wait and wakeup system calls by looking only at locations in the abstract memory reserved for wait and wakeup actions. Second, it considers only pairs of accesses where one is a *load* and the other is a *store*, corresponding to one wait and one wakeup system calls. The wait system call must not happen-before the wakeup

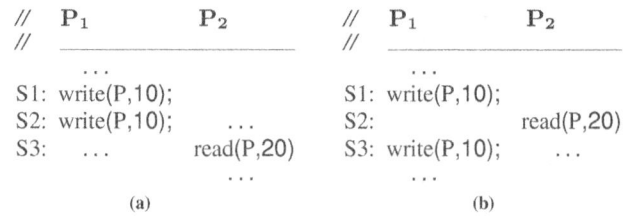

```
//  P₁              P₂          //  P₁              P₂
// ──────────────────────      // ──────────────────────
      . . .                           . . .
S1: write(P,10);                S1: write(P,10);
S2: write(P,10);    . . .       S2:              read(P,20)
S3:    . . .     read(P,20)      S3: write(P,10);    . . .
      . . .                           . . .
         (a)                             (b)
```

Figure 8: *Wait-wakeups races in streams.*

system call. Third, for each candidate pair of wait and wakeup system calls S_1 and S_2, RACEPRO narrows its search to the remaining wakeup system calls that match the wait system call by looking for system calls that store to the same abstract memory location. For each matching wakeup system call S_3, RACEPRO checks whether it would form a wait-wakeups race together with S_1 and S_2.

The relative order of the wakeup system calls may matter if their effect on the resource is cumulative. For instance, Figure 8 depicts a cumulative wait-wakeups scenario in which the order of two `write` system calls to the same stream determines what a matching `read` would observe. A `read` from a stream may return less data than requested if the data in the buffer is insufficient. In Figure 8a, a blocking `read` occurs after two `writes` and consumes their cumulative data. However, in Figure 8b, the `read` occurs before the second `write` and returns the data only from the first `write`. Note that S_2 and S_3 in Figure 8a do not form a load-store race as S_2 inherently happens-before S_3. Thus, RACEPRO flags either case as a wait-wakeups race. The relative order of the wakeup system calls does not matter if their effect on the resource is not cumulative, such as with `wait` and `exit` system calls.

5.3.3 Wakeup-Waits Races

A wakeup-waits race occurs when a wakeup system call may wake up more than a single matching wait system call. Like wait-wakeups races, wakeup-waits races involve at least three system calls. For example, a `connect` system call to a listening socket will wake up any processes which may have a pending `accept` on that socket; the popular Apache Web server uses this method to balance incoming requests. As another example, a signal sent to a process may interrupt the process during a system call. Depending on the exact timing of events, the signal may be delivered at different times and interrupt different system calls.

Some wakeup system calls only affect the first matching wait system call that gets executed; that system call "consumes" the wakeup and the remaining wait system calls must wait for a subsequent wakeup. Examples include `connect` and `accept` system calls, and `read` and `write` system calls on streams. In contrast, when two processes monitor the same file using the `select` system call, a file state change will notify both processes equally. Even in this case, a race exists as the behavior depends on which wait system calls executes first.

RACEPRO flags three system calls as a wakeup-waits race if (1) one is a wakeup system call, (2) the other two are wait system calls that match the wakeup, (3) the wait system calls did not happen-before the wakeup system call. To detect wakeup-waits races, RACEPRO builds on the wait-wakeups race detection algorithm with one difference. For each candidate pair of wait and wakeup system calls S_1 and S_2, RACEPRO narrows its search to the remaining wait system calls that match the wakeup system call by looking for system calls that load from the same abstract memory location. For each matching wait system call S_3, RACEPRO checks whether it would form a wakeup-waits race together with S_1 and S_2.

5.3.4 Many-System-Calls Races

RACEPRO's algorithms handle races that involve two system calls for load-store races, and three system calls for both wait-wakeups and wakeup-waits races. However, it is also possible that a race involves more system calls. For example, consider a load-store race that comprises a sequence of four system calls that only if executed in the reverse order, from last to first, will produce a bug. RACEPRO's algorithm will not detect this load-store race since it only considers one pair of system calls at a time. To detect such races, the algorithms can be extended to consider more system calls at a time and more complex patterns of races. An alternative approach is to apply RACEPRO's analysis recursively on modified executions (§6.2).

6 Validating Races

A detected process race may be either benign or harmful, depending on whether it leads to a failure. For instance, consider the `ps | grep X` example again which may output either N or $N + 1$ lines. When run from the command line, this race is usually benign since most users will automatically recognize and ignore the difference. However, for applications that rely on one specific output, this race can be harmful and lead to a failure (§7).

To avoid false positives, RACEPRO validates whether detected races are harmful and reports only harmful races as bugs. For each race, it creates an execution branch in which the racy system calls, which we refer to as *anchor* system calls, would occur in a different order from the original recorded execution (§6.1). It replays the modified execution until the race occurs, then makes the execution go-live (§6.2). It checks the live execution for failures (§6.3), and, if found, reports the race as a bug.

6.1 Creating Execution Branches

RACEPRO does not replay the original recorded execution, but instead replays an execution branch built from the original execution in a controlled way. The execution branch is a truncated and modified version of the original log file. Given a detected race which, based on its type, involves two or three anchor system calls, RACE-PRO creates an execution branch in two steps. First, it copies the sequence of log events from the original execution recording *up to* the anchor system calls. Then, it adds the anchor system calls with suitable ordering constraints so that they will be replayed in an order that makes the race resolve differently than in the original recorded execution. The rest of the log events from the original execution are not included in the modified version.

A key requirement in the first step above is that the definition of *up to* must form a *consistent cut* [22] across all the processes to avoid deadlocks in replay. A consistent cut is a set of system calls, one from each process, that includes the anchor system calls, such that all system calls and other log events that occurred before this set are on one side of the cut. For instance, if S_1 in process P_1 happens-before S_2 in process P_2 and we include S_2 in the consistent cut, then we must also include S_1 in the cut.

To compute a consistent cut for a set of anchor system calls, RACEPRO simply merges the vector-clocks of the anchor system calls into a unified vector-clock by taking the latest clock value for each process. In the resulting vector-clock, the clock value for each process indicates the last observed happens-before path from that process to any of the anchor system calls. By definition, the source of this happens-before edge is also the last system call of that process that must be included in the cut. For instance, the unified vector-clock for the `read` and `execve` race in Figure 7 is $[3, 3, 2]$, and the consistent cut includes the second `fork` of P_1, `read` of P_2, and `execve` of P_3.

Given a consistent cut, RACEPRO copies the log events of each process, except the anchor system calls, until the clock value for that process is reached. It then adds the anchors in a particular order. For load-store races, there are two anchor system calls. To generate the execution branch, RACEPRO simply flips the order of the anchors compared to the original execution; it first adds the system call that occurred *second* in the original execution, followed by the one that occurred *first*. It also adds an ordering constraint to ensure that they will be replayed in that order.

For wait-wakeups races, there are three anchor system calls: two wakeup system calls and a wait system call. To generate the execution branch, RACEPRO first adds both wakeup system calls, then adds a modified version of the wait system call in which its wildcard argument is replaced with a specific argument that will match the wakeup system call that was *not* picked in the original execution. For example, consider a race with two child processes in `exit`, either of which may wake up a parent process in `wait`. RACEPRO first adds both `exit` system calls, then the `wait` system call modified such that its wildcard argument is replaced by a specific argument that will cause this `wait` to pick the `exit` of the child that was not picked in the original execution. It also adds a constraint to ensure that the parent will execute after that child's `exit`. The other child is not constrained.

For wakeup-waits races, there are also three anchor system calls: one wakeup system call and two wait system calls. To generate the execution branch, RACEPRO simply flips the order of the two wait system calls compared to the original execution. Races that involve signals, which may be delivered earlier or later than in the original execution, are handled differently. To generate an execution branch for a signal to be delivered earlier, RACEPRO simply inserts the signal delivery event at an earlier location which is thereby considered one of the anchors of the consistent cut. In contrast, delivering a signal arbitrarily later is likely to cause replay divergence (§6.2). Instead, RACEPRO only considers delivering a signal later if it interrupted a system call in the recorded execution, in which case the signal is instead delivered promptly after the corresponding system call completes when replayed.

Reordering of the anchor system calls may also imply reordering of additional system calls that also access the same resources. Consider the execution scenario depicted in Figure 9, which involves three processes and five system calls that access the same resource. The system calls S_1 and S_5 form a load-store race. To generate the modified execution for this race, RACEPRO will make the following changes: (1) it will include S_1 but not S_2, because system calls following the anchors remain outside the cut and are truncated; (2) it will reorder S_5, and therefore S_4 too, with respect to S_1; and (3) depending on the consistent cut, it will either exclude S_3 or reorder S_3 with respect to S_1. RACEPRO adjusts the modified recording so that it will enforce the new partial order of system calls instead of the partial order of system calls in the original execution.

6.2 Replaying Execution Branches and Going Live

RACEPRO's replayer provides deterministic replay of the originally recorded execution and also ensures that successful replay of a modified execution is also deterministic. Given a modified execution, RACEPRO replays each recorded event while preserving the partial order indicated by the recording. The last events replayed are the anchor system calls. To force races to resolve as desired, RACE-PRO replays the anchor system calls serially, one by one, while holding the remaining processes inactive. From that point onward, it allows the processes to go live to resume normal execution.

Go Live. The ability to go live by resuming live execution from a replay is fundamental for allowing RACEPRO to validate whether

```
//   P1          P2          P3
//   ─────────────────────────────
       ...
S1:  syscall(R);
S2:  syscall(R);
S3:     ...        ...     syscall(R);
S4:             syscall(R)    ...
S5:             syscall(R)
                   ...
```

Figure 9: *Replay divergence due to reordering.*

```
//   P1          P2            //   P1          P2
//   ──────────────────       //   ──────────────────
       ...                            ...
S1:  creat(F);   ...          S1:  write(F,x);   ...
S2:     ...    r=unlink(F);   S2:     ...      read(F,b);
               if (r==0)                       if (b=='x')
S3:            creat(F);      S3:              write(F,y);
                   ...                             ...
          (a)                           (b)
```

Figure 10: *Replay divergence examples.*

races manifest into real bugs or not, and thereby avoid reporting false-positives. To go live, RACEPRO faces two challenges. First, RACEPRO must ensure that replayed processes perceive the underlying system to be the same as at the time of recording. For example, system identifiers such as process IDs must remain the same for processes to run correctly after they transition to live execution. RACEPRO leverages OS virtualization to encapsulate processes in a virtual execution environment that provides the same private, virtualized view of the system when the session is replayed or goes live as when it was recorded [17]. Processes only see virtual identifiers that always stay the same so that the session can go live at any time. Second, RACEPRO needs to not only replay the application state in user-space, but also the corresponding state that is internally maintained by the operating system for the processes. For example, actions such as creating a pipe and writing to it must be done as is so that the pipe exists and has suitable state should the process transition to live execution.

RACEPRO works best when a go-live execution requests no inputs from users or external processes; such executions include parallel make, parallel boot, and executions of non-interactive programs. If a go-live execution requests external inputs, RACEPRO tries to replay the inputs recorded from the original execution. Currently RACEPRO replays standard inputs from users and pipe or socket data received from external processes. It does not replay data read from the file system. Instead, it checkpoints the file system before recording an execution and restores to this checkpoint before each replay, using unionfs [29], which has low overhead. Replaying inputs may not always work because the go-live execution differs from the original execution, but we have not found it a problem in our evaluation because tightly coupled processes should be recorded together anyway.

RACEPRO can be applied recursively to detect races involving more system calls (§5.3.4). Since it already records the go-live portion of modified executions, doing so is as easy as running the same detection logic on these new recordings. This essentially turns RACEPRO into a model checker [12]. However, we leave this mode off by default because exhaustive model checking is quite expensive and it is probably more desirable to spend limited checking resources on real executions over the fake checking-generated executions.

Replay Divergence. RACEPRO's replayer may not be able to replay some execution branches due to *replay divergence*. This can result from trying to replay a modified recording instead of the original recording. Replay divergence occurs when there is a mismatch between the actual actions of a replayed process and what is scripted in the execution recording. The mismatch could be between the actual system call and the expected system call or, even if the system calls match, between the resources actually accessed by the system call and the resources expected to be accessed. When a divergence failure occurs for some execution branch, RACEPRO does not flag the corresponding race as a bug because it lacks evidence to that end.

Divergence is commonly caused when the reordering of the anchor system calls implies reordering of additional system calls that also access the same resources. Consider again the execution scenario depicted in Figure 9 in which the system calls S_1 and S_5 form a load-store race and the modified execution branch reorders the systems calls as S_3, S_4, S_5, and S_1 while dropping S_2 as being outside the cut. A replay divergence may occur if the execution of S_5 depended on S_2 which was dropped out, or if the execution of S_4 depends on S_1 which was reordered with respect to S_4. Figure 10a illustrates the former scenario. Reordering the two creat system calls would cause P_2 to call unlink before P_1's creat. The call will fail and P_2 will not call creat and thus diverge from the recorded execution.

Divergence can also be caused when processes rely on a specific execution ordering of system calls in a way that is not tracked by RACEPRO. Figure 10b illustrates one such scenario where process P_1 executes system call S_1 to write data to a file, and process P_2's execution depends on data read from file by S_2. If P_2 depends on the specific data written by S_1, then reordering S_1 and S_2 will almost certainly cause a divergence. Were the dependency on the file's content considered an inherent happens-before $S_1 \rightarrow S_2$, RACEPRO's explorer would not have flagged the race in the first place. However, it is prohibitively expensive, and in some cases impossible, to track generic semantics of applications.

Another cause for divergence is use of shared memory. Recall that shared memory accesses are tracked by the recorder and enforced by the replayer. However, reordering of system calls may lead to reordering of shared memory accesses as well, which will certainly lead to replay divergence. RACEPRO mitigates this effect by permitting *relaxed* execution from where the reordering takes place. In this mode the replayer does not enforce memory access ordering, but continues to enforce other ordering constraints such as partial ordering of system calls. This improves the chances that the replayed execution reach the point of go-live. However, accesses to shared memory may now resolve arbitrarily and still cause divergence. For this reason RACEPRO is likely to be less effective in finding races on OS resources between threads of the same process. We believe that such races are relatively unlikely to occur.

Replay divergence is reportedly a serious problem for a previous race classifier [25], where it can occur for two reasons: the race being validated does occur and causes the execution to run code or access data not recorded originally, or the race being validated cannot occur and is a false positive. In contrast, replay divergence actually *helps* RACEPRO to distinguish root-cause races from other races. By relying on a replay followed by transition to live execution, RACEPRO is no longer concerned with the first scenario. If replay diverges, RACEPRO can tell that the race is a false positive and discard it.

Moreover, if the divergence is not due to untracked interactions or shared memory discussed above (or file locking, also untracked by RACEPRO), then there must exist another race that is "tighter" than the one being validated. The other race may involve the same

Bug ID	Description
debian-294579	concurrent `adduser` processes read and write `/etc/passwd` without synchronization, corrupting this file
debian-438076	`mv` unlinks the target file before calling atomic `rename`, violating the atomicity requirement on `mv`
debian-399930	`logrotate` creates a new file then sets it writable, but deamons may observe it without write permissions
redhat-54127	`ps	grep` race causes a wrong version of `licq 7.3` to be started
launchpad-596064	`upstart` does not wait until `smbd` creates a directory before spawning `nmbd`, which requires that directory
launchpad-10809	`bash` updates the history file without synchronization, corrupting this file
new-1	`tcsh 6.17` updates the history file without synchronization, even when "savehist merge" is set
new-2	`updatedb` removes old database before renaming the new one, so `locate` finds nothing (`findutils 4.4.2`)
new-3	concurrent `updatedb` processes may cause the database to be empty
new-4	incorrect dependencies in Makefile of `abr2gbr 1.0.3` may causes compilation failure

Table 4: *Bugs found by* RACEPRO. Bugs are identified by "distribution - bug ID". New bugs are identified as "new - bug number"

resource or a different one. For example, in Figure 10b the race between S_1 and S_3 causes divergence because of another race between S_1 and S_2. The latter race is "tighter" in the sense that S_2 is closer to S_1 because $S_2 \rightarrow S_3$; the race between S_1 and S_2 subsumes the race between S_1 and S_3. In other words, discarding races that cause replay divergence helps RACEPRO to find root-cause races. We believe the go-live mechanism can benefit existing replay-based thread-race classifiers.

6.3 Checking Execution Branches

When the replay of an execution branch switches to live execution, RACEPRO no longer controls the execution. Rather, it records the execution from that point on, and activates a checker to monitor the execution for failures or incorrect behavior. If the checker detects a failure that did not occur during recording, it reports a bug and saves the combined execution recording, consisting of the original recording followed by the new recording, so that users can deterministically replay it for debugging.

RACEPRO provides a set of built-in checkers to detect bad application behavior. The built-in checker can detect erroneous behavior such as segmentation faults, infinite loops (via timeouts), error messages in system logs, and failed commands with non-zero exit status. In addition, RACEPRO can also run system-provided checker programs such as `fsck`.

Moreover, RACEPRO allows users to plug in domain-specific checkers. To do so, a user need only provide a program or even a shell script that will run concurrently along the live execution. For instance, such scripts could compare the output produced by a modified execution to that of the original execution, and flag significant differences as errors. It is also possible to use existing test-suites already provided with many application packages. These test-suites are particularly handy if the target application is a server. For instance, both the Apache web server and the MySQL database server are shipped with basic though useful test suites, which could be executed against a modified server. Finally it may also compare the output of the go-live execution with a linearized run [13].

By running checkers on live executions, RACEPRO guarantees that observed failures always correspond to real executions, thus eliminating false positives if the checkers are accurate. Moreover, the process races RACEPRO detects are often the root cause of the failures, aiding developers in diagnosis. In rare cases, after a modified execution goes live, it may encounter an unrelated bug. RACEPRO still provides an execution recording useful for debugging, but without pointing out the root-cause.

As in many other checking frameworks, RACEPRO can detect only what is checked. Although its built-in checkers can detect many errors (§7.1), it may miss domain-specific "silent" corruptions. Fortunately, recent work has developed techniques to check advanced properties such as conflict serializability or linearizability [13], which RACEPRO can leverage.

RACEPRO may have false negatives. A main source is that RACEPRO is a dynamic tool, thus it may miss bugs in the executions that do not occur. Fortunately, by checking deployed systems, RACEPRO increases its checking coverage. A second source is checker inaccuracy. If a checker is too permissive or no checker is provided to check for certain failures, RACEPRO would miss bugs.

7 Experimental Results

We have implemented a RACEPRO prototype in Linux. The prototype consists of Linux kernel components for record, replay, and go-live, and a Python user-space exploration engine for detecting and validating races. The current prototype has several limitations. For replaying executions and isolating the side effects of replay, RACEPRO must checkpoint system states. It currently checkpoints only file system states, though switching to better checkpoint mechanism [27] is straightforward. RACEPRO detects idle state simply by reading `/proc/loadavg`, and can benefit from a more sophisticated idle detection algorithm [34].

Using the RACEPRO prototype, we demonstrated its functionality in finding known and unknown bugs, and measured its performance overhead. For our experiments, the software used for RACEPRO was Linux kernel 2.6.35, Python 2.6.6, Cython 0.14, Networkx 1.1-2, and UnionFs-Fuse 0.23.

7.1 Bugs Found

We evaluated RACEPRO's effectiveness by testing to see if it could find both known and unknown bugs. To find known bugs, we used RACEPRO on 6 bugs from our study. Bugs were selected based on whether we could find and compile the right version of the software and run it with RACEPRO. Some of the bugs in §2 are in programs that we cannot compile, so we excluded them from the experiments. For each known bug, we wrote a shell script to perform the operations described in the bug report, without applying any stress to make the bug easily occur. We ran this shell script without RACEPRO 50 times, and observed that the bug never occurred. We then ran RACEPRO with the script to detect the bug.

To find unknown bugs, we used four commonly used applications. We applied RACEPRO to the `locate` utility and `updatedb`, a utility to create a database for `locate`. These two utilities are commonly used and well tested, and they touch a shared database of file names, thus they are likely to race with each other. Inspired by the history file race in `bash`, we applied RACEPRO to `tcsh`. `tcsh` has a "savehist merge" option, which should supposedly merge history files from different windows and sessions. Because compilation of software packages often involves multiple concurrent and interdependent processes, we also applied RACEPRO to the `make -j` command.

Table 4 shows all the bugs RACEPRO found. RACEPRO found a total of 10 bugs, including all of the known bugs selected and 4 previously unknown bugs. We highlight a few interesting bugs. Of the

Name	Statistics			Number of Races				Execution Times [seconds/race]			
	Processes	Syscalls	Resources	Detected	Diverged	Benign	Harmful	Record	Replay	Generate	Validate
debian-294579	19	5275	658	4232	3019	1171	42	2.47	2.43	3.42	2.92
debian-438076	21	1688	213	50	0	46	4	3.76	0.75	0.84	2.87
debian-399930	10	1536	279	17	0	13	4	0.59	0.57	0.75	0.84
redhat-54127	14	1298	229	35	15	16	4	0.27	0.25	0.66	0.41
launchpad-596064	34	5564	722	272	267	3	2	21.45	3.11	2.49	1.70
launchpad-10809	13	1890	205	143	117	16	10	0.27	0.25	0.81	0.44
new-1	12	2569	201	137	90	33	14	0.56	0.54	1.52	0.76
new-2	47	2621	467	82	13	27	42	0.89	0.88	1.44	1.16
new-3	30	4361	2981	17	0	13	4	2.63	2.61	2.34	2.98
new-4	19	4672	716	8	0	7	1	1.01	0.98	4.81	1.35

Table 5: *Bug detection statistics.* **Processes** is the number of processes, **Syscalls** the number of system calls occured, and **Resources** the number of distinct shared resources tracked in the recorded executions. For races, **Detected** is the number of races detected by RACEPRO, **Diverged** the races for which the replay diverged (*i.e.*, false positive), **Benign** the benign races, and **Harmful** harmful races that led to failures. **Record** and **Replay** are the times to record and replay the executions, respectively. **Generate** is the average time to generate an execution branch and **Validate** the average time to validate a race.

known bugs, the debian-294579 bug is the most serious: it leads to corruption of /etc/passwd since adduser does not synchronize concurrent reads and writes of /etc/passwd. This bug was triggered when an administrator tried to import users from OpenLDAP to a local machine.

The redhat-54127 bug is due to the ps | grep X race. Instant messenger program licq uses ps | grep to detect whether KDE or Gnome is running. Due to the race in ps | grep, licq sometimes believes a windows manager is running when it in fact is not, thus loading the wrong version of licq.

The 4 previously unknown bugs were named new-1, new-2, new-3, and new-4. In the new-1 bug, RACEPRO found that tcsh writes to its history file without proper synchronization, even when "savehist merge" is set. This option is supposed to merge history across windows and sessions, but unfortunately, it is not implemented correctly.

In the new-2 bug, RACEPRO found that when locate and updatedb run concurrently, locate may observe an empty database and return zero results. The reason is that updatedb unlinks the old database, before calling rename to replace it with the new database. This unlink is unnecessary as rename guarantees atomic replacement of the destination link.

In the new-3 bug, RACEPRO found that when multiple instances of updatedb run concurrently, the resultant database may be corrupted. Multiple updatedb processes may exist, for example, when users manually run one instance while cron is running another. While updatedb carefully validates the size of the new database before using it to replace the old one, the validation and replacement are not atomic, and the database may still be corrupted.

In the new-4 bug, RACEPRO found that in the compilation of abr2gbr, a package to convert between image formats, the build process may fail when using make -j for parallel compilation. The reason is that the dependencies defined in the Makefile are incomplete, which produces a race condition between the creation of an $OBJDIR directory and the use of that directory to store object files from the compilation.

7.2 Bug Statistics

Table 5 shows various statistics for each detected bug, including the number of processes involved (Processes), the number of system calls recorded (Syscalls), the number of unique shared resources tracked (Resources), the total number of races detected (Races), the number of races in which the replay diverged (Diverged), the number of benign races (Benign), and the number of harmful races

(Harmful). The number of processes tends to be large because when running a shell script, the shell forks a new process for each external command. The number of system calls in the recorded executions ranges from 1,298 to 5,564. The number of distinct shared resources accessed by these system calls ranges from 201 to 2,981.

The number of races that RACEPRO detects varies across different bugs. For instance, RACEPRO detected only 17 races for debian-399930, but it detected over 4,000 races for debian-294579. Typically only a small number of races are harmful, while the majority are benign, as shown by the Benign column. In addition, RACEPRO effectively pruned many false positives as shown by the Diverged column. These two columns together illustrate the benefit of the replay and go-live approach.

The mapping between harmful races and bugs is generally many-to-one. There are multiple distinct races that produce the same or similar failures due to a common logical bug. There are two main reasons why a single programming error may result in multiple races. First, a bug may occur in a section of the code that is executed multiple times, for instance in a loop, or in a function called from multiple sites. Thus, there can be multiple races involving distinct instances of the same resource type; RACEPRO will detect and validate each independently. Second, a bug such as missing locks around critical sections may incorrectly allow reordering of more than two system calls, and each pair of reordered system calls could produce a distinct race.

In most cases, we relied on built-in checkers in RACEPRO to detect the failures. For instance, RACEPRO caught bug launchpad-596064 by using grep to find error messages in standard daemon logs, and it caught bugs debian-438076, debian-399930, new-2, new-3, and new-4 by checking for the exit status of programs. Writing checkers to detect other cases was also easy, and required just one line in all cases. For example, for debian-294579, launchpad-10809, and new-1, we detected the failures simply using a diff of the old and new versions of the affected file.

7.3 Performance Overhead

Low recording overhead is crucial because RACEPRO runs with deployed systems. Low replay overhead is desirable because RACEPRO can check more execution branches within the same amount of time. To evaluate RACEPRO's record and replay overhead, we applied it to a wide range of real applications on an IBM HS20 eServer BladeCenter, each blade with dual 3.06 GHz Intel Xeon CPUs with hyperthreading, 2.5 GB RAM, a 40 GB local disk, interconnected with a Gigabit Ethernet switch. These applications include

(1) server applications such as Apache in multi-process and multi-threaded configurations, MySQL, an OpenSSH server, (2) utility programs such as SSH clients, make, untar, compression programs such as gzip and lzma, and a vi editor, and (3) graphical desktop applications such as Firefox, Acrobat Reader, MPlayer, and OpenOffice. To run the graphical applications on the blade which lacks a monitor, we used VNC to provide a virtual desktop. For application workloads that required clients and a server, we ran the clients on one blade and the server on another. Our results show that RACE-PRO's recording overhead was under 2.5% for server and under 15% for desktop applications. Replay speed was in all cases at least as fast as native execution and in some cases up to two orders of magnitude faster. This speedup is particularly useful for enabling rapid race validation. Replay speedup stems from omitted in-kernel work due to system calls partially or entirely skipped, and waiting time skipped at replay. Applications that do neither operations perform the same work whether recording or replaying, and sustain speedups close to 1.

We also measured various overhead statistics involved in finding the bugs listed in Table 5. These measurements were done on an HP DL360 G3 server with dual 3.06 GHz Intel Xeon CPUs, 4 GB RAM, and dual 18 GB local disks. For each bug, Table 5 shows the time to record the execution (Record) and to replay it (Replay), the average time to generate an execution branch for a race from a recorded execution (Generate), and the average time to validate an execution branch for a race (Validate).

In all cases, recording execution times were within 3% of the original execution times without recording, and replaying the execution took less time than the original recorded execution. Replay time for each recording ranged from 250 ms to 1.8 s, providing an upper limit on the time to replay execution branches. Replaying execution branches is generally faster because those branches are truncated versions of the original execution. Replay speedup was near 1 in most cases, but was as high as 7 times for launchpad-596064 due to very long idle times as part of starting up the workload. These results are in line with our other record-replay results for desktop and server applications. In particular, the results demonstrate that RACEPRO recording overhead is low enough to enable its use on deployed systems.

The time for our unoptimized prototype to detect all races was under 350 ms for most bugs, but in some cases as much as 3.8 s. This time correlates roughly with the number of unique shared kernel objects tracked and the number of processes involved. For example, detecting all races for launchpad-596064 took 2.5 s, or less than 0.5 ms per race. The average time to generate an execution branch for a race ranged from 0.66 s to 4.81 s. This time correlates roughly with the number of system calls. The average time to validate a race ranged from 0.44 s to 2.98 s. This time correlates roughly with the replay time.

In most cases, the average time to validate a race was somewhat larger than the time to replay the original execution by 0.3 s to 2 s. The time to validate a race is longer because, in addition to the time to replay the execution branch, it also includes the time to run the go-live execution, run the checker, and perform setup and cleanup work between races. Replaying an execution branch which ends at the anchor system calls is faster than replaying the whole original execution. However, during validation, the remainder of the recorded execution now runs live, which is usually slower than replayed execution. In one case, launchpad-596064, validation was faster then original execution replay because nearly all of the execution branches resulted in replay divergence relatively early, eliminating the additional time it would take to replay the entire execution branches and have them go live.

The Generate and Validate times are averaged per race, so the total time to generate execution branches and validate races will grow with the number of races. However, races are independent of one another, so these operations can be easily done in parallel on multiple machines to speed them up significantly. Overall, the results show that RACEPRO can detect harmful process races not only automatically without human intervention, but efficiently.

8 Related Work

We previously presented in a workshop paper [16] a preliminary design of RACEPRO, without the full design, implementation, and evaluation described in this paper. In the remainder of this section, we discuss closely related work to RACEPRO.

Thread races. Enormous work has been devoted to detecting, diagnosing, avoiding, and repairing thread races (e.g., [11, 24, 25, 30, 36, 38]). However, as discussed in §1, existing systems for detecting thread races do not directly address the challenges of detecting process races. For instance, existing static race detectors work with programs written in only one language [11, 24]; the dynamic ones detect races within only one process and often incur high overhead (e.g., [23]). In addition, no previous detection algorithms as we know of explicitly detect wait-wakeup races, a common type of process races.

Nonetheless, many ideas in these systems apply to process races once RACEPRO models system call effects as *load* and *store* micro-operations. For instance, we may leverage the algorithm in AVIO [21] to detect atomicity violations involving multiple processes; the consequence-oriented method in ConSeq [40] to guide the detection of process races; and serializability or linearizability checking [13].

A recent system, 2ndStrike [14], detects races that violate complex access order constraints by tracking the *typestate* of each shared object. For instance, after a thread calls `close(fd)`, 2ndStrike transits the file descriptor to a "closed" state; when another thread calls `read(fd)`, 2ndStrike flags an error because reads are allowed only on "open" file descriptors. RACEPRO may borrow this idea to model system calls with richer effects, but we have not found the need to do so for the bugs RACEPRO caught.

RACEPRO leverages the replay-classification idea [25] to distill harmful races from false or benign ones. The go-live mechanism in RACEPRO improves on existing work by turning a replayed execution into a real one, thus avoiding replay divergence when a race does occur and changes the execution to run code not recorded.

We anticipate that ideas in RACEPRO can help thread race detection, too. For instance, thread wait and wakeup operations may also pair up in different ways, such as a `sem_post` waking up multiple `sem_down` calls. Similarly, the go-live mechanism can enable other race classifiers to find "root races" instead of derived ones.

TOCTOU races. TOCTOU race detection [32, 33, 35] has been a hot topic in the security community. Similar to RACEPRO, these systems often perform OS-level detection because file accesses are sanitized by the kernel. However, TOCTOU races often refer to specific types of races that allow an attacker to access unauthorized files bypassing permission checks. In contrast, RACEPRO focuses on general process races and resources not only files. Nonetheless, RACEPRO can be used to detect TOCTOU races *in-vivo*, which we leave for future work.

Checking deployed systems. Several tools can also check deployed systems. CrystalBall [37] detects and avoids errors in a deployed distributed system using an efficient global state collection and exploration technique. Porting CrystalBall to detect process races is difficult because it works only with programs written in a special language, and it does checking while the deployed system is running, relying on network delay to hide the checking overhead. In-vivo testing [8] uses live program states, but it focuses on unit testing and lacks concurrency support.

To reduce the overhead on a deployed system, several systems decouple execution recording from dynamic analysis [7, 26]. RACEPRO leverages this approach to check process races. One difference is that RACEPRO uses OS-level record and replay, which has lower overhead than [7] and, unlike Speck [26], RACEPRO works with both multiprocess and multithreaded applications. In addition, a key mechanism required for validating races is that RACEPRO can faithfully replay an execution and make it go-live at any point, which neither previous system can do.

OS support for determinism and transaction. Our idea to pervasively detect process races is inspired by operating system transactions in TxOS [28] and pervasive determinism in Determinator [5] and dOS [6]. TxOS provides transaction support for heterogeneous OS resources, efficiently and consistently solving many concurrency problems at the OS level. For instance, it can prevent file system TOCTOU attacks. However, as pointed out in [20], even with transaction support, execution order violations may still occur. Determinator advocates a new, radical programming model that converts all races, including thread and process races, into exceptions. A program conforming to this model runs deterministically in Determinator. dOS makes legacy multithreaded programs deterministic even in the presence of races on memory and other shared resources. None of these systems aim to detect process races.

9   Conclusion and Future Work

We have presented the first study of real process races, and the first system, RACEPRO, for effectively detecting process races beyond TOCTOU and signal races. Our study has shown that process races are numerous, elusive, and a real threat. To address this problem, RACEPRO automatically detects process races, checking deployed systems *in-vivo* by recording live executions and then checking them later. It thus increases checking coverage beyond the configurations or executions covered by software vendors or beta testing sites. First, RACEPRO records executions of multiple processes while tracking accesses to shared kernel resources via system calls. Second, it detects process races by modeling recorded system calls as load and store micro-operations to shared resources and leveraging existing memory race detection algorithms. Third, for each detected race, it modifies the original recorded execution to reproduce the race by changing the order of system calls involved in the races. It replays the modified recording up to the race, allows it to resume live execution, and checks for failures to determine if the race is harmful. We have implemented RACEPRO, shown that it has low recording overhead so that it can be used with minimal impact on deployed systems, and used it with real applications to effectively detect 10 process races, including several previously unknown bugs in shells, databases, and makefiles.

Detection of process races is only the first step. Given an execution where a process race surfaces, developers still have to figure out the cause of the race. Fixing process races take time, and before developers produce a fix, systems remain vulnerable. Exploring the possibility of automatically fixing process races and providing better operating system primitives to eliminate process races are important areas of future work.

Acknowledgements

Our shepherd Tim Harris and the anonymous reviewers provided many helpful comments, which have substantially improved the content and presentation of this paper. Peter Du helped with the process race study. Dawson Engler provided early feedback on the ideas of this paper. This work was supported in part by AFRL FA8650-10-C-7024 and FA8750-10-2-0253, AFOSR MURI FA9550-07-1-0527, and NSF grants CNS-1117805, CNS-1054906 (CAREER), CNS-1012633, CNS-0914845, and CNS-0905246.

10   References

[1] All resource races studied. http://rcs.cs.columbia.edu/projects/racepro/.

[2] Launchpad Software Collaboration Platform. https://launchpad.net/.

[3] The Debian Almquist Shell. http://gondor.apana.org.au/~herbert/dash/.

[4] Upstart: an Event-Based Replacement for System V Init Scripts. http://upstart.ubuntu.com/.

[5] A. Aviram, S.-C. Weng, S. Hu, and B. Ford. Efficient System-Enforced Deterministic Parallelism. In *Proceedings of the 9th Symposium on Operating Systems Design and Implementation (OSDI '10)*, Oct. 2010.

[6] T. Bergan, N. Hunt, L. Ceze, and S. D. Gribble. Deterministic Process Groups in dOS. In *Proceedings of the 9th Symposium on Operating Systems Design and Implementation (OSDI '10)*, Oct. 2010.

[7] J. Chow, T. Garfinkel, and P. M. Chen. Decoupling Dynamic Program Analysis from Execution in Virtual Environments. In *Proceedings of the USENIX Annual Technical Conference (USENIX '08)*, June 2008.

[8] M. Chu, C. Murphy, and G. Kaiser. Distributed In Vivo Testing of Software Applications. In *Proceedings of the First IEEE International Conference on Software Testing, Verification, and Validation (ICST '08)*, Apr. 2008.

[9] H. Cui, J. Wu, C.-C. Tsai, and J. Yang. Stable Deterministic Multithreading through Schedule Memoization. In *Proceedings of the 9th Symposium on Operating Systems Design and Implementation (OSDI '10)*, Oct. 2010.

[10] G. W. Dunlap, D. G. Lucchetti, M. A. Fetterman, and P. M. Chen. Execution Replay of Multiprocessor Virtual Machines. In *Proceedings of the 4th International Conference on Virtual Execution Environments (VEE '08)*, Mar. 2008.

[11] D. Engler and K. Ashcraft. RacerX: Effective, Static Detection of Race Conditions and Deadlocks. In *Proceedings of the 19th ACM Symposium on Operating Systems Principles (SOSP '03)*, Oct. 2003.

[12] C. Flanagan and P. Godefroid. Dynamic Partial-Order Reduction for Model Checking Software. In *Proceedings of the 32nd Annual Symposium on Principles of Programming Languages (POPL '05)*, Jan. 2005.

[13] P. Fonseca, C. Li, and R. Rodrigues. Finding Complex Concurrency Bugs in Large Multi-Threaded Applications. In *Proceedings of the 6th ACM European Conference on Computer Systems (EUROSYS '11)*, Apr. 2011.

[14] Q. Gao, W. Zhang, Z. Chen, M. Zheng, and F. Qin. 2ndStrike: Towards Manifesting Hidden Concurrency Typestate Bugs. In *Proceedings of the 16th International Conference on Architecture Support for Programming Languages and Operating Systems (ASPLOS '11)*, Mar. 2011.

[15] Z. Guo, X. Wang, J. Tang, X. Liu, Z. Xu, M. Wu, M. F. Kaashoek, and Z. Zhang. R2: An Application-Level Kernel for Record and Replay. In *Proceedings of the 8th Symposium on Operating Systems Design and Implementation (OSDI '08)*, Dec. 2008.

[16] O. Laadan, C.-C. Tsai, N. Viennot, C. Blinn, P. S. Du,

J. Yang, and J. Nieh. Finding Concurrency Errors in Sequential Code—OS-level, In-vivo Model Checking of Process Races. In *Proceedings of the 13th USENIX Workshop on Hot Topics in Operating Systems (HOTOS '11)*, May 2011.

[17] O. Laadan, N. Viennot, and J. Nieh. Transparent, Lightweight Application Execution Replay on Commodity Multiprocessor Operating Systems. In *Proceedings of the ACM SIGMETRICS Conference on Measurement and Modeling of Computer Systems (SIGMETRICS '10)*, June 2010.

[18] L. Lamport. Time, Clocks, and the Ordering of Events in a Distributed System. *Comm. ACM*, 21(7):558–565, 1978.

[19] T. J. LeBlanc and J. M. Mellor-Crummey. Debugging Parallel Programs with Instant Replay. *IEEE Trans. Comput.*, 36(4):471–482, 1987.

[20] S. Lu, S. Park, E. Seo, and Y. Zhou. Learning from Mistakes: a Comprehensive Study on Real World Concurrency Bug Characteristics. In *Proceedings of the 13th International Conference on Architecture Support for Programming Languages and Operating Systems (ASPLOS '08)*, Mar. 2008.

[21] S. Lu, J. Tucek, F. Qin, and Y. Zhou. AVIO: Detecting Atomicity Violations via Access Interleaving Invariants. In *Proceedings of the 12th International Conference on Architecture Support for Programming Languages and Operating Systems (ASPLOS '06)*, Oct. 2006.

[22] F. Mattern. Dynamic Partial-Order Reduction for Model Checking Software. In *Proceedings of the 32nd Annual Symposium on Principles of Programming Languages (POPL '05)*. Oct. 1988.

[23] M. Musuvathi, S. Qadeer, T. Ball, G. Basler, P. A. Nainar, and I. Neamtiu. Finding and Reproducing Heisenbugs in Concurrent Programs. In *Proceedings of the 8th Symposium on Operating Systems Design and Implementation (OSDI '08)*, Dec. 2008.

[24] M. Naik, A. Aiken, and J. Whaley. Effective Static Race Detection For Java. In *Proceedings of the ACM SIGPLAN 2006 Conference on Programming Language Design and Implementation (PLDI '06)*, 2006.

[25] S. Narayanasamy, Z. Wang, J. Tigani, A. Edwards, and B. Calder. Automatically Classifying Benign and Harmful Data Racesallusing Replay Analysis. In *Proceedings of the ACM SIGPLAN 2007 Conference on Programming Language Design and Implementation (PLDI '07)*, June 2007.

[26] E. B. Nightingale, D. Peek, P. M. Chen, and J. Flinn. Parallelizing Security Checks on Commodity Hardware. In *Proceedings of the 13th International Conference on Architecture Support for Programming Languages and Operating Systems (ASPLOS '08)*, Mar. 2008.

[27] S. Osman, D. Subhraveti, G. Su, and J. Nieh. The Design and Implementation of Zap: A System for Migrating Computing Environments. In *Proceedings of the 5th Symposium on Operating Systems Design and Implementation (OSDI '02)*, Dec. 2002.

[28] D. E. Porter, O. S. Hofmann, C. J. Rossbach, A. Benn, and E. Witchel. Operating System Transactions. In *Proceedings of the 22nd ACM Symposium on Operating Systems Principles (SOSP '09)*, Oct. 2009.

[29] D. P. Quigley, J. Sipek, C. P. Wright, and E. Zadok. UnionFS: User- and Community-oriented Development of a Unification Filesystem. In *Proceedings of the 2006 Linux Symposium*, July 2006.

[30] K. Sen. Race Directed Random Testing of Concurrent Programs. In *Proceedings of the ACM SIGPLAN 2008 Conference on Programming Language Design and Implementation (PLDI '08)*, June 2008.

[31] S. M. Srinivasan, S. Kandula, C. R. Andrews, and Y. Zhou. Flashback: A Lightweight Extension for Rollback and Deterministic Replay for Software Debugging. In *Proceedings of the USENIX Annual Technical Conference (USENIX '04)*, June 2004.

[32] D. Tsafrir, T. Hertz, D. Wagner, and D. Da Silva. Portably Solving File TOCTTOU Races with Hardness Amplification. In *Proceedings of the 6th USENIX Conference on File and Storage Technologies (FAST '08)*, Feb. 2008.

[33] E. Tsyrklevich and B. Yee. Dynamic Detection and Prevention of Race Conditions in File Accesses. In *Proceedings of the 12th Conference on USENIX Security Symposium*, Aug. 2003.

[34] University of California at Berkeley. Open-Source Software for Volunteer Computing and Grid Computing. http://boinc.berkeley.edu/.

[35] J. Wei and C. Pu. TOCTTOU Vulnerabilities in UNIX-Style File Systems: an Anatomical Study. In *Proceedings of the 4th USENIX Conference on File and Storage Technologies (FAST '05)*, Dec. 2005.

[36] J. Wu, H. Cui, and J. Yang. Bypassing Races in Live Applications with Execution Filters. In *Proceedings of the 9th Symposium on Operating Systems Design and Implementation (OSDI '10)*, Oct. 2010.

[37] M. Yabandeh, N. Knezevic, D. Kostic, and V. Kuncak. CrystalBall: Predicting and Preventing Inconsistencies in Deployed Distributed Systems. In *Proceedings of the 6th Symposium on Networked Systems Design and Implementation (NSDI '09)*, Apr. 2009.

[38] Y. Yu, T. Rodeheffer, and W. Chen. RaceTrack: Efficient Detection of Data Race Conditions via Adaptive Tracking. In *Proceedings of the 20th ACM Symposium on Operating Systems Principles (SOSP '05)*, Oct. 2005.

[39] M. Zalewski. Delivering Signals for Fun and Profit. Bindview Corporation, 2001.

[40] W. Zhang, J. Lim, R. Olichandran, J. Scherpelz, G. Jin, S. Lu, and T. Reps. ConSeq: Detecting Concurrency Bugs through Sequential Errors. In *Proceedings of the 16th International Conference on Architecture Support for Programming Languages and Operating Systems (ASPLOS '11)*, Mar. 2011.

Detecting and Surviving Data Races using Complementary Schedules

Kaushik Veeraraghavan, Peter M. Chen, Jason Flinn, and Satish Narayanasamy
University of Michigan
{kaushikv,pmchen,jflinn,nsatish}@umich.edu

ABSTRACT

Data races are a common source of errors in multithreaded programs. In this paper, we show how to protect a program from data race errors at runtime by executing multiple replicas of the program with complementary thread schedules. Complementary schedules are a set of replica thread schedules crafted to ensure that replicas diverge only if a data race occurs and to make it very likely that harmful data races cause divergences. Our system, called Frost[1], uses complementary schedules to cause at least one replica to avoid the order of racing instructions that leads to incorrect program execution for most harmful data races. Frost introduces outcome-based race detection, which detects data races by comparing the state of replicas executing complementary schedules. We show that this method is substantially faster than existing dynamic race detectors for unmanaged code. To help programs survive bugs in production, Frost also diagnoses the data race bug and selects an appropriate recovery strategy, such as choosing a replica that is likely to be correct or executing more replicas to gather additional information.

Frost controls the thread schedules of replicas by running all threads of a replica non-preemptively on a single core. To scale the program to multiple cores, Frost runs a third replica in parallel to generate checkpoints of the program's likely future states — these checkpoints let Frost divide program execution into multiple epochs, which it then runs in parallel.

We evaluate Frost using 11 real data race bugs in desktop and server applications. Frost both detects and survives all of these data races. Since Frost runs three replicas, its utilization cost is 3x. However, if there are spare cores to absorb this increased utilization, Frost adds only 3–12% overhead to application runtime.

[1] Our system is named after the author of the poem "The Road Not Taken". Like the character in the poem, our second replica deliberately chooses the schedule not taken by the first replica.

Categories and Subject Descriptors

D.4.5 [**Operating Systems**]: Reliability; D.4.8 [**Operating Systems**]: Performance

General Terms

Design, Performance, Reliability

Keywords

Data race detection, Data race survival, Uniparallelism

1. INTRODUCTION

The prevalence of multicore processors has encouraged the use of multithreaded software in a wide range of domains, including scientific computing, network servers, desktop applications, and mobile devices. Unfortunately, multithreaded software is vulnerable to bugs due to data races, in which two instructions in different threads (at least one of which is a write) access the same memory location without being ordered by synchronization operations. Many concurrency bugs are due to data races. These bugs are difficult to find in development and can cause crashes or other program errors at runtime. Failures due to races can be catastrophic, as shown by the 2003 Northeastern United States power blackout [33] and radiation overdoses from the Therac-25 [25].

Researchers have proposed various solutions that attempt to eliminate or identify data races in the development process, including disciplined languages [5, 7], static race analysis [13], and dynamic race analysis [15, 40, 42]. Despite these attempts, data races continue to plague production code and are a major source of crashes, incorrect execution, and computer intrusions.

To help address the problem of data race bugs, we propose running multiple replicas of a program and forcing two of these replicas to follow *complementary schedules*. Our goal in using complementary schedules is to force replicas to diverge if and only if there is a potentially harmful data race. We do this by exploiting a sweet spot in the space of possible thread schedules. First, we ensure that all replicas see identical inputs and use thread schedules that obey the same program ordering constraints imposed by synchronization events and system calls. This guarantees that replicas that do not execute a pair of racing instructions will not diverge [37]. Second, while obeying the previous constraint, we attempt to make the thread schedules executed by the two replicas as dissimilar as possible. Specifically, we try to maximize the probability that any two instructions executed by different threads and not ordered by a synchronization operation or system call are executed in opposite orders by the replicas. For all harmful data races we have studied in actual applications, this strategy causes replica divergence.

Our system, called Frost, uses complementary schedules to achieve two goals: detecting data races at low overhead and increasing availability by masking the effects of harmful data races at runtime. Frost introduces a new method to detect races: *outcome-based data-race detection*. While traditional methods detect races by analyzing the events executed by a program, outcome-based race detection detects the *effects* of a data race by comparing the states of different replicas executed with complementary schedules. Outcome-based race detection achieves lower overhead than traditional dynamic data race detectors, but it can fail to detect some races, e.g., data races that require a preemption to cause a failure and that generate identical correct outcomes using multiple non-preemptive schedules (See Section 3.4 for a full discussion). However, in our evaluation of real programs, Frost detects all potentially harmful data races detected by a traditional data race detector. While prior work [31] compared the outcomes of multiple orderings of instructions for *known* data races in order to classify those races as either benign or potentially malign, Frost is the first system to construct multiple schedules to detect and survive *unknown* data races. Frost thus faces the additional challenge of constructing useful schedules without first knowing which instructions race. A benefit that Frost inherits from the prior classification work is that it automatically filters out most benign races that are reported by a traditional dynamic race detector.

For production systems, Frost moves beyond detection to also diagnose and survive harmful data races. Since a concurrency bug due to a data race manifests only under a specific order of racing memory accesses, executing complementary schedules makes it extremely likely that one of the replicas survives the ill effects of a data race. Thus, once Frost detects a data race, it analyzes the outcomes of the various replicas and chooses a strategy that is likely to mask the failure, such as identifying and resuming execution from the correct replica or creating additional replicas to help identify a correct replica.

To generate complementary thread schedules, Frost must control tightly the execution of each replica. To do this, Frost timeslices the threads of a replica onto a single processor and switches between threads only at synchronization points (i.e., it uses non-preemptive scheduling). Running threads on a single processor without preemptions has another benefit: it prevents bugs that require preemptions (e.g., atomicity violations) from manifesting, thereby increasing availability. Because running all threads on a single processor prevents a replica from scaling to take advantage of multiple cores, Frost uses *uniparallelism* [44] to parallelize a uniprocessor execution by running multiple *epochs* (time intervals) of that execution on separate cores simultaneously.

Frost helps address the problem of data races in several scenarios. During testing, it can serve as a fast dynamic data race detector that also classifies races as benign or potentially harmful in the observed execution. For a beta or production system with active users, both detection and availability are important goals. Frost masks many data race failures while providing developers with reports of data races that could lead to potential failures.

This paper makes the following contributions. First, it proposes the idea of complementary schedules, which guar-antees that replicas do not diverge in the absence of data races and makes it very likely that replicas do diverge in the presence of harmful data races. Second, it shows a practical and low-latency way to run two replicas with complementary thread schedules by using a third replica to accelerate the execution of the two complementary replicas. Third, it shows how to analyze the outcomes of the three replicas to craft a strategy for surviving data races. Fourth, it introduces a new way to detect data races that has lower overhead than traditional dynamic data race detectors.

We evaluate the effectiveness of complementary thread schedules on 11 real data race bugs in desktop and server applications. Frost detects and survives all these bugs in every trial. Frost's overhead is at worst 3x utilization to run three replicas, but it has only 3–12% overhead if there are sufficient cores or idle CPU cycles to run all replicas.

2. COMPLEMENTARY SCHEDULES

The key idea in Frost is to execute two replicas with complementary schedules in order to detect and survive data race bugs. A data race is comprised of two instructions (at least one of which is a write) that access the same data, such that the application's synchronization constraints allow the instructions to execute in either order. For harmful data races, one of those orders leads to a program error (if both orders lead to an error, then the root cause of the error is not the lack of synchronization). We say that the order of two instructions that leads to an error is a *failure requirement*. A data race bug may involve multiple failure requirements, all of which must be met for the program to fail.

As an example, consider the simple bug in Figure 1(a). If thread 1 sets fifo to NULL before thread 2 dereferences the pointer, the program fails. If thread 2 accesses the pointer first, the program executes correctly. The arrow in the figure shows the failure requirement. Figure 1(b) shows a slightly more complex atomicity violation. This bug has two failure requirements; i.e., both data races must execute in a certain order for the failure to occur.

To explain the principles underlying the idea of complementary schedules, we first consider an interval of execution in which at most one data race bug occurs and which contains no synchronization operations that induce an ordering constraint on the instructions (we call such an interval *synchronization-free*). For such regions, complementary schedules provide hard guarantees for data race detection and survival. We discuss these guarantees in this section. However, real programs do not consist solely of such regions, so in Section 3.4 we discuss how generalizing the range of scenarios affects Frost's guarantees.

The goal of executing two replicas with complementary schedules is to ensure that one replica avoids the data race bug. We say that two replicas have perfectly complementary schedules if and only if, for every pair of instructions a and b executed by different threads that are not ordered by application synchronization, one replica executes a before b, and the other executes b before a.

Since a failure requirement orders two such instructions, use of perfectly complementary schedules guarantees that for any failure requirement, one replica will execute a schedule that fulfills the requirement and one will execute a schedule that does not. This guarantees that one of the two replicas does not experience the failure.

Eliminating preemptions is essential to achieving perfectly

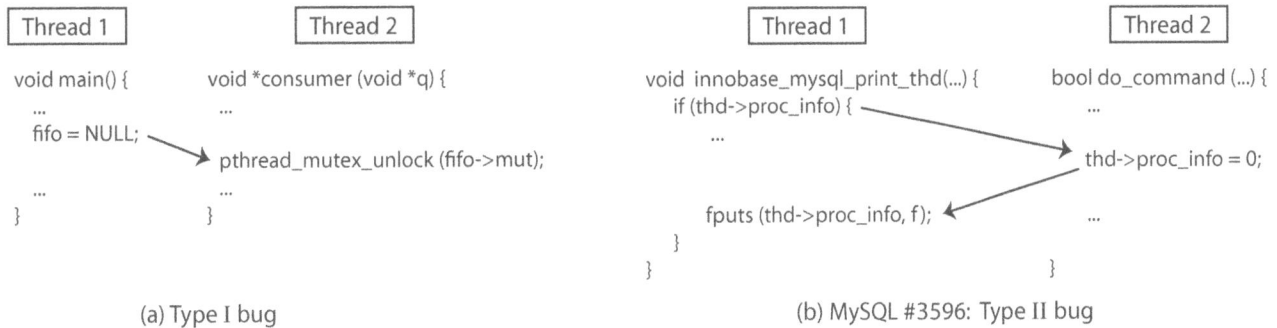

Thread 1	Thread 2
void main() {	void *consumer (void *q) {
...	...
fifo = NULL;	pthread_mutex_unlock (fifo->mut);
...	...
}	}

(a) Type I bug

Thread 1	Thread 2
void innobase_mysql_print_thd(...) {	bool do_command (...) {
if (thd->proc_info) {	...
...	thd->proc_info = 0;
fputs (thd->proc_info, f);	...
}	}
}	

(b) MySQL #3596: Type II bug

Figure 1: Data race examples

complementary schedules. To understand why this is so, consider a canonical schedule with a preemption: thread A executes an instruction a_0, then thread B preempts thread A and executes an instruction b_0, then thread A resumes and executes a_1. It is impossible to generate a perfectly complementary schedule for this schedule. In such a schedule, a_1 would precede b_0, and b_0 would precede a_0. However, this would require a_1 to precede a_0, which would violate the sequential order of executing instructions within a thread.

In contrast, without preemptions, constructing a perfectly complementary schedule for two threads in a synchronization-free interval is trivial—one schedule simply executes all of thread A's instructions before thread B's instructions; the other schedule executes all of thread B's instructions before thread A's instructions. For more than two threads, one schedule executes the threads in some order, and the other executes the threads in the reverse order.

Thus, to guarantee that at least one replica avoids a particular data race bug in a synchronization-free interval, we execute two replicas, use non-preemptive scheduling for these replicas, and reverse the scheduling order of thread execution between the two replicas.

The above algorithm provides even stronger properties for some common classes of data race bugs. For instance, consider the atomicity violation in Figure 1(b). Because the failure requirements point in opposite directions, each of the two replica schedules will fulfill one constraint but not the other. Since failure requires that both requirements be fulfilled, the proposed algorithm guarantees that *both* replicas avoid this failure.

In general, given n threads, we must choose an arbitrary order of those threads for one schedule and reverse that order in the complementary schedule. Visualizing the threads arrayed according to the order chosen, if all failure requirements point in the same direction, then the proposed algorithm guarantees that one replica avoids the failure. In the rest of the paper, we will refer to bugs in this category as *Type I*. If any two failure requirements point in the opposite direction, the proposed algorithm provides the stronger guarantee that both replicas avoid the failure. We will refer to bugs in this category as *Type II*.

3. DESIGN AND IMPLEMENTATION

Frost uses complementary schedules to detect and survive data races. This section describes several challenges, including approximating the ideal behavior for intervals of execution with synchronization operations and multiple bugs, scaling performance via multicore execution, and implementing heuristics for identifying correct and faulty replicas. It concludes with a discussion of specific scenarios in which Frost can fail to detect or survive races and the steps Frost takes to minimize the effect of those scenarios.

3.1 Constructing complementary schedules

Frost divides program execution into time-slices called *epochs*. For each epoch, it runs multiple replicas and controls the thread schedule of each to achieve certain properties.

The first property that Frost enforces is that each replica follows the same partial order of system calls and synchronization operations. In other words, certain pairs of events such as lock and unlock on a mutex lock, signal and wait on a condition variable, or read and write on a pipe represent a happens-before order of events in the two threads; e.g., events following the lock in one thread cannot occur until after the other thread calls unlock. By ensuring that all threads have the same happens-before order of such events, Frost guarantees that two replicas can diverge in output or final memory and register state only if a data race occurs within the epoch [37]. Further, all replicas will encounter the same pair of racing instructions.

The second property that Frost tries to achieve is that two replicas have thread schedules that are as complementary as possible, given that the first property has to be upheld. As discussed in Section 2, this property is intended to ensure that at least one of the two replicas with complementary thread schedules does not fail due to a particular data race.

Frost must execute a replica to observe the happens-before order of synchronization operations and system calls before it can enforce an identical order over the same operations in other replicas. Frost observes this order by using a modified glibc and Linux kernel that maintain a vector clock for each thread and for synchronization entities such as locks and condition variables. Each value in the vector represents a thread's virtual time. Synchronization events and system calls increment the calling thread's value in its local vector clock. Operations such as unlock set the vector clock of the lock to the maximum of its previous value and the vector clock of the unlocking thread. Operations such as lock set the vector clock of the locking thread to the maximum of its previous value and the vector clock of the lock. Similarly, we modified kernel entities to contain vector clocks and propagate this information on relevant system calls. For instance, since system calls such as map and munmap do not commute,

Frost associates a vector clock with the address space of the process to enforce a total order over address-space-modifying system calls such as `mmap`.

When the first replica executes, Frost logs the vector clocks of all system calls and synchronizations in a log. Other replicas read the logged values and use them to follow the same happens-before order. Each replica maintains a *replay vector clock* that is updated when a thread performs a synchronization operation or system call. A thread may not proceed with its next operation until the replay vector clock equals or exceeds the value logged for the operation by the first replica. This ensures, for example, that one thread does not return from `lock` until after another thread calls `unlock` if there was a happens-before order between the two operations in the original replica. More than one replica can execute an epoch concurrently; however, all other replicas typically are slightly behind the first replica since they cannot execute a synchronization operation or system call until the same operation is completed by the first replica.

Given a happens-before order, Frost uses the following algorithm to construct schedules for two replicas that complement each other as much as possible without modifying the application. Frost chooses an order over all threads within a replica and assigns the reverse order to those threads in a second replica. For example, if three threads are ordered [A, B, C] in one replica, they are ordered [C, B, A] in the other. Frost executes all threads within each replica on a single core so that two threads do not run simultaneously. A thread is eligible to run as long as it is not waiting to satisfy a happens-before constraint and it has not yet completed the current epoch. The Frost kernel always runs the eligible thread that occurs first in its replica's scheduling order. A thread runs until it reaches the end of the epoch, it blocks to enforce a happens-before constraint, or a thread earlier in the replica's scheduling order becomes eligible to run.

3.2 Scaling via uniparallelism

As described so far, the use of complementary schedules does not allow a program to scale to use multiple cores because all threads of a replica must run sequentially on a single core. If multiple threads from a replica were to concurrently execute two instructions on different cores, those two instructions cannot be ordered by a happens-before constraint and are thus potentially racing. In this case, the two replicas should execute these instructions in different orders. However, determining the order of these instructions and enforcing the opposite order on the other replica implies that the instructions execute sequentially, not concurrently.

Frost uses uniparallelism [44] to achieve scalability. Uniparallelism is based on the observation that there exists at least two methods to scale a multithreaded program to run on multiple cores. The first method, termed *thread parallelism*, runs multiple threads on different cores — this is the traditional method for exploiting parallelism. The second method, termed *epoch parallelism*, runs multiple time-slices of the application concurrently.

Uniparallel execution runs a thread-parallel and one or more epoch-parallel executions of a program concurrently. It further constrains each epoch-parallel execution so that all its threads execute on a single core. This strategy allows the epoch-parallel execution to take advantage of the properties that come with running on a uniprocessor. Our original use

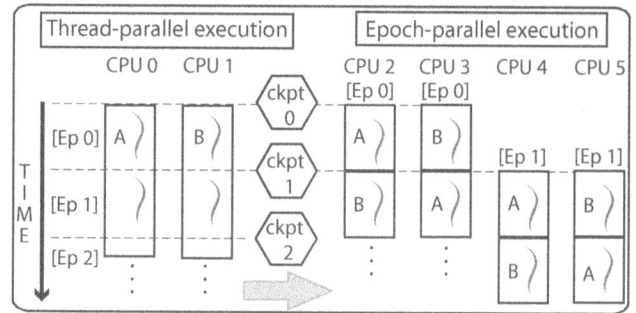

Figure 2: Frost: Overview

of uniparallelism in a system called DoublePlay provided efficient software-only deterministic replay [44]. Frost is built on a modified version of the DoublePlay infrastructure, but it uses uniparallelism for a different purpose, namely the execution of replicas with complementary schedules and identical happens-before constraints.

As shown in Figure 2, to run epochs in parallel, a uniparallel execution generates checkpoints from which to start each epoch. It must generate these checkpoints early enough to start future epochs before prior ones finish. Thus, the thread-parallel execution runs ahead of the epoch-parallel execution and generates checkpoints from which to start future epochs. Multiple epochs execute in parallel, in a manner similar to a processor pipeline — this allows an epoch-parallel execution to scale with the number of available cores.

In summary, Frost executes three replicas for each epoch: a thread-parallel replica that is used to record the happens-before constraints for the epoch and generate checkpoints to speculatively parallelize the other two replicas, and two epoch-parallel replicas with complementary schedules. Replicas use copy-on-write sharing to reduce overall memory usage. Frost uses online deterministic replay [24] to ensure that all replicas receive the same non-deterministic input and to enforce the same happens-before constraints in all replicas. It logs the result of all system calls and synchronization operations as the thread-parallel replica executes. When the epoch-parallel replicas later execute the same operations, Frost's modified kernel and glibc library do not re-execute the operations but rather return the logged values. Signals are also logged during the thread-parallel execution and delivered at the same point in the epoch-parallel executions. Because Frost logs and replays all forms of non-determinism except data races, only data races can cause replicas to diverge. Online replay has an additional performance benefit — the epoch-parallel executions do not block on I/O since the results have already been obtained by the thread-parallel execution.

When replicas diverge during an epoch, Frost chooses one of several actions. First, it may decide to accept the results of one of the replica executions, which we refer to as *committing* that replica. If it chooses to commit the thread-parallel replica, it simply discards the checkpoint taken at the beginning of the epoch. If it chooses to commit an epoch-parallel replica, and the memory and register state of that replica is different from that of the thread-parallel replica, then subsequent epochs in the pipeline are invalid. Effectively, the checkpoint from which the execution of the next epoch began was an incorrect hint about the future state of the application. Frost first discards the checkpoint taken at the beginning of the committed epoch. Then, it quashes all epochs subsequent to the one just committed and begins anew with fresh thread-parallel and epoch-parallel replicas using the state of the committed replica.

Frost may also choose to execute additional replicas to learn more about the epoch that led to the divergence. It starts additional thread-parallel and/or epoch-parallel executions from the checkpoint taken at the beginning of the epoch that led to the divergence — we refer to this process as *rolling back* the epoch. Frost could later decide to commit one of the original replicas or one of the new ones, though currently only new replicas are ever committed.

Since replicas may produce different output, Frost does not externalize any output until it decides which replica to commit. It uses speculative execution (implemented via Speculator [32]) to defer the output. This leads to a trade-off among correctness, overhead, and output latency when choosing how long an epoch should last. Longer epochs offer better correctness properties, as discussed in Section 3.4.3, and also lower overhead. Shorter epochs yield lower latency for output. Frost balances these constraints by using an adaptive epoch length. For CPU-bound applications that issue no external output, epoch length grows up to one second. However, when the application executes a system call that produces external output, Frost immediately starts to create a new epoch. Thus, server applications we have evaluated often see the creation of hundreds of epochs per second. Additionally, as will be discussed in Section 3.3.1, the epoch length is varied depending on the number of data races observed during execution — epochs without a data race gradually increase the epoch length (by 50 ms at a time), while epochs with a data race decrease the epoch length (by up to a factor of 20). After Frost decides to start an epoch, it waits for all threads to reach a system call or synchronization operation. It then checkpoints the process and allows threads to proceed.

3.3 Analyzing epoch outcomes

After all three replicas finish executing an epoch, the Frost kernel compares their executions to detect and survive data races. Since the Frost control code and data are in the kernel, the following logic cannot be corrupted by application-level bugs.

First, Frost determines if a replica has crashed or entered an infinite loop. We call this a *self-evident* failure because Frost can declare such a replica to have failed without considering the results of other replicas. Frost detects if a replica crashes or aborts by interposing on kernel signal-handling routines. It detects if a replica has entered an infinite loop via a timeout-based heuristic (we have not yet had the need to implement more sophisticated detection).

Other classes of failures are not self-evident; e.g., a replica may produce incorrect output or internal state. One way to detect this type of failure is to require a detailed specification of the correct output. Yet, for complex programs such as databases and Web servers, composing such a specification is quite daunting. Addressing this challenge in practice requires a method of detecting incorrect output that does not rely on program semantics or hand-crafted specifications.

Frost infers the potential presence of failures that are not

self-evident by comparing the output and program state of the three replicas. During execution, Frost compares the sequence and arguments of the system calls produced by each replica. Frost also compares the memory and register state of all replicas at the end of epoch execution. To reduce the performance impact of comparing memory state, Frost only compares pages dirtied or newly allocated during the epoch. Frost declares two replicas to have different outcomes if either their output during the epoch or their final states at the end of the epoch differ.

To detect and survive data races, Frost must infer whether a data race has occurred and which replica(s) failed. Frost first considers whether each replica has experienced a self-evident failure. If the replica has not experienced a self-evident failure, Frost considers the memory and register state of the replica at the end of an epoch, and the output produced by the replica during that epoch.

There are 11 combinations of results among the three replicas, which are shown in the left column of Table 1. The result of each replica is denoted by a letter: F means the replica experienced a self-evident failure; A-C refer to a particular value for the final state and output produced by the replica for the epoch. We use the same letter, A, B, or C, for replicas that produced the same state and output. To simplify the explanation, we do not distinguish between different types of failures in this exposition. The first letter shows the result of the thread-parallel execution; the next two letters show the outcomes of the epoch-parallel executions. For example, the combination F-AA indicates that the thread-parallel execution experienced a self-evident failure, but the two epoch-parallel executions did not experience a self-evident failure and produced the same state and output.

As an aside, two replicas may produce the same output and reach the same final state, yet take different execution paths during the epoch due to a data race. Due to Frost's complementary scheduling algorithm, it is highly likely that the data race was benign, meaning that both replicas are correct. Allowing minor divergences during an epoch is thus a useful optimization for filtering out benign races. Frost lets an epoch-parallel replica execute a different system call (if the call does not have side effects) or a different synchronization operation when it can supply a reasonable result for the operation. For instance, it allows an epoch-parallel replica to perform a nanosleep or a getpid system call not performed by the thread-parallel replica. It also allows self-canceling pairs of operations such as a lock followed by an unlock. While further optimizations are possible, the total number of benign races currently filtered through such optimizations is relatively small. Thus, adding more optimizations may not be worth the implementation effort. Consequently, when a divergence cannot be handled through any of the above optimizations, Frost declares the two replicas to have different output.

3.3.1 Using the epoch outcome for survival

Frost diagnoses results by applying Occam's razor: it chooses the simplest explanation that could produce the observed results. Specifically, Frost chooses the explanation that requires the fewest data race bugs in an epoch. Among explanations with the same number of bugs, Frost chooses the explanation with the fewest failure requirements. The middle column in Table 1 shows the explanation that Frost associates with each combination of results, and the right

Epoch Results	Likely Bug	Survival Strategy
A-AA	None	Commit A
F-FF	Non-Race Bug	Rollback
A-AB/A-BA	Type I	Rollback
A-AF/A-FA	Type I	Commit A
F-FA/F-AF	Type I	Commit A
A-BB	Type II	Commit B
A-BC	Type II	Commit B or C
F-AA	Type II	Commit A
F-AB	Type II	Commit A or B
A-BF/A-FB	Multiple	Rollback
A-FF	Multiple	Rollback

The left column shows the possible combinations of results for three replicas; the first letter denotes the result of the thread-parallel run, and the other two letters denote the results of the epoch-parallel replicas. F denotes a self-evident failure; A, B, or C denote the result of a replica with no self-evident failure. We use the same letter when replicas produce identical output and state.

Table 1: A taxonomy of epoch outcomes

column shows the action that Frost takes based on that explanation.

The simplest possible explanation is that the epoch was free of data race bugs. Because all replicas obey the same happens-before constraints, an epoch that is free of data races must produce the same results in all replicas, so this explanation can apply only to the combinations A-AA and F-FF. For A-AA epochs, Frost concludes that the epoch executed correctly on all replicas and commits it. For F-FF epochs, Frost concludes that the epoch failed on all replicas due to a non-race bug. In this case, Frost rolls back and retries execution from the beginning of the epoch in the hope that the failure is non-deterministic and might be avoided in a different execution, e.g., due to different happens-before constraints.

The next simplest explanation is that the epoch experienced a single Type I data race bug. A single Type I bug can produce at most two different outcomes (one for each order of the racing instructions) and the outcome of the two epoch-parallel executions should differ because they execute the racing instructions in different order. For a Type I bug, one of these orders will not meet the failure requirement and will thereby work correctly. The other order will meet the failure requirement and may lead to a self-evident failure, incorrect state, or incorrect output. The following combinations have two different outcomes among the two epoch-parallel replicas (one of which is correct) and at most two outcomes among all three replicas: A-AB (and the isomorphic A-BA), A-AF (and the isomorphic A-FA), and F-AF (and the isomorphic F-FA).

For epochs that result in A-AF and F-AF, a replica that does not experience the self-evident failure is likely correct, so Frost commits that replica. For epochs that produce A-AB, it is unclear which replica is correct (or if both are correct due to a benign race), so Frost gathers additional information by executing an additional set of three replicas starting from the checkpoint at the beginning of the epoch. In this manner, Frost first tries to find a execution in which a happens-before constraint prevents the race from occurring;

our hypothesis is that for a reasonably well-tested program, such an execution is likely to be correct. For the data races we have tested so far, Frost typically encounters such a constraint after one or two rollbacks. This results in a different combination of results (e.g., A-AA, in which case Frost can commit the epoch and proceed). If Frost encounters the same data race on every execution, we plan to use the heuristic that most natural executions are likely to be correct and have Frost choose the thread-parallel execution that occurs most often in such executions. Note that because epoch-parallel executions use artificially-perturbed schedules, they should not be given much weight; for this reason, we would not consider an A-BA to be two votes for A and one vote for B, but rather would consider it to be a single vote for A.

If a combination of results cannot be explained by a single Type I bug, the next simplest explanation is a single Type II bug. A Type II bug can produce the following combination of results: A-BB, A-BC, F-AA, and F-AB. None of these should be produced by a single Type I bug because the epoch-parallel replicas generate the same answer (A-BB or F-AA) or because there are three outcomes (A-BC or F-AB). In the latter case, it is impossible for the outcome to have been produced by a single Type I bug, whereas in the first case, the outcome is merely unlikely. Any epoch-parallel execution should avoid a Type II bug because its non-preemptive execution invalidates one of the bug's failure requirements. For instance, atomicity violation bugs are Type II bugs that are triggered when one thread interposes between two events in another thread. Because threads are not preempted in the epoch-parallel replicas, both replicas avoid such bugs.

We have found that it is common for a single type II bug to result in three different outcomes (e.g., A-BC or F-AB). For example, consider two threads both logging outputs in an unsynchronized manner. The thread-parallel replica incorrectly garbles the outputs by mixing them together (outcome A), one epoch-parallel replica correctly outputs the first value in its entirety before the second (outcome B), and the remaining epoch-parallel replica outputs the second value in its entirety before the first (outcome C), which is also correct. Similar situations arise when inserting or removing elements from an unsynchronized shared data structure. Thus, when Frost sees an A-BC outcome, it commits one of the epoch-parallel replicas.

The remaining combinations (A-BF, the isomorphic A-FB, and A-FF) cannot be explained by a single data race bug. A-BF has more than two outcomes, which rules out a single Type I bug. A-BF also includes a failing epoch-parallel run, which rules out a single Type II bug. Both epoch-parallel replicas fail in A-FF, and this is also not possible from a single Type I or Type II bug. We conclude that these combinations are caused by multiple data race bugs in a single epoch. Frost rolls back to the checkpoint at the beginning of the epoch and executes with a shorter epoch length (trying to encounter only one bug at a time during re-execution).

3.3.2 Using the epoch outcome for race detection

Using epoch outcomes for data race detection is more straightforward than using those outcomes to survive races. Any outcome that shows a divergence in system calls executed (which includes all external output), synchronization operations executed, or final state at the end of the epoch indicates that a data race occurred during the epoch. Because all three replicas obey the same happens-before order, a data race is the only cause of replica divergence. Further, that data race must have occurred during the epoch being checked because all replicas start from the same initial memory and register state.

Because Frost's data race detection is outcome-based, not all data races that occur during the epoch will be reported. This is a useful way to filter out benign races, which are sometimes intentionally inserted by programmers to improve performance. In particular, an ad-hoc synchronization may never cause a memory or output divergence, or a race may lead to a temporary divergence, such as in values in the stack that are soon overwritten. If Frost explores both orders for a pair of racing instructions and does not report a race, then the race is almost certainly benign, at least in this execution of the program. The only exception, discussed in Section 3.4.4, occurs when multiple bugs produce identical-but-incorrect program state or output.

Since Frost allows replicas to diverge slightly during an epoch, it sometimes observes a difference between replicas in system calls or synchronization operations executed, but it does not observe a difference in output or final replica state. Such races are also benign. Frost reports the presence of such races but adds an annotation that the race had no observable effect on program behavior. A developer can choose whether or not to deal with such races.

Because Frost is implemented on top of the DoublePlay framework for deterministic record and replay, it inherits DoublePlay's ability to reproduce any execution of an epoch-parallel replica [44]. Thus, in addition to reporting the existence of each race, Frost also can reproduce on demand an entire execution of the program that leads to each reported race, allowing a developer to employ his or her favorite debugging tools. For instance, we have implemented a traditional dynamic data race detector based on the design of DJIT+ [34] that replays a divergent epoch to precisely identify the set of racing instructions.

3.3.3 Sampling

Some recent race detection tools use sampling to reduce overhead at the cost of missing some data races [6, 14, 29]. We added a similar option to Frost. When the user specifies a target sampling rate, Frost creates epoch-parallel replicas for only some epochs; we call these the *sampled epochs*. Frost does not execute epoch-parallel replicas for other epochs, meaning that it neither detects nor survives races during those epochs. Frost dynamically chooses which epochs are sampled such that the ratio of the execution time of the sampled epochs to the overall execution time of the program is equal to the sampling rate. While it is possible to use more sophisticated heuristics to choose which epochs to sample, this strategy has the property that the relative decrease in Frost's ability to survive and detect dynamic data races will be roughly proportional to the sampling rate.

3.4 Limitations

Section 2 discussed the guarantees that complementary scheduling provides for data race survival and detection in synchronization-free code regions that contain no more than one data race. We now describe the limitations on these guarantees for epochs that do not conform to those properties. We also describe the steps that Frost takes to mitigate these limitations. As the results in Section 4.1.2 show, these limitations did not compromise Frost's survival or detection properties in practice when we evaluated Frost with real application bugs.

3.4.1 Multiple bugs in an epoch

Although we posit that data race bugs are rare, an epoch could contain more than one bug. If multiple bugs occur in one epoch, Frost's diagnosis might explain the epoch outcome but be incorrect for that execution. This would affect both survival and detection guarantees.

Survival requires that at least one replica execute correctly. Adding any number of Type II bugs to an epoch does not affect survival since neither epoch-parallel replica will fail due to such bugs. Thus, one replica will be correct for a synchronization-free region that contains zero or one Type I bugs and any number of Type II bugs. However, the presence of multiple Type I bugs can cause both replicas to fail. Typically, different bugs will cause the program to fail in different ways. The symptom of failure (e.g., crash or abort) might be different, or the memory and register state may be different at the time of failure. Thus, Frost can still take corrective action such as rolling back and executing additional replicas, especially if such failures are self-evident. When Frost rolls back, it substantially reduces the epoch length to separate out different bugs during re-execution. This is a form of search.

It is conceivable, though unlikely, that two different Type I bugs have the same effect on program state, in which case the replicas with complementary schedules could reach the same final state. If the failure is not self-evident, Frost will mis-classify the epoch and commit faulty state.

For the purpose of data race detection, multiple data races are only a problem if all races have an identical effect on program state. Otherwise, replicas will diverge and Frost will report a race for the epoch. The presence of multiple data races will subsequently be discovered by the developer when replaying the epoch in question.

3.4.2 Priority inversion

The presence of happens-before constraints within an epoch may cause Frost to fail to survive or detect a data race within that epoch. For epochs in which only pairs of threads interact with one another, Frost's algorithm for complementary schedule generation will construct schedules in which the order of all potentially racing instructions differ. Non-racing instructions may execute in the same order, but, by definition, this does not affect any guarantees about data races.

When more than two threads interact in an epoch, a situation similar to priority inversion may arise and prevent Frost from constructing schedules that change the order of all non-racing instructions. For instance, consider Figure 3. The epoch contains three threads, a happens-before constraint due to application synchronization, and a failure requirement caused by two racing instructions. If Frost's assigns the order ABC to threads in one replica, the serial order of execution in the two schedules is $\{ a_0, b, c_0, a_1, c_1 \}$ in one replica and $\{ c_0, c_1, b, a_0, a_1 \}$ in the other. All pairs of code segments that occur in different threads execute in a different order in the two schedules, with two exceptions. c_0 executes before a_1 in both schedules. However, this order is required by application synchronization, and that synchronization prevents these instructions from racing. Additionally, b executes before a_1 in both schedules. If the Type I bug shown in the figure occurs, then both replicas will fail.

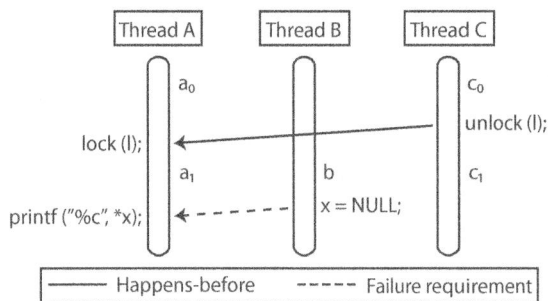

Figure 3: Priority inversion scenario

This may prevent Frost from surviving or detecting the race if the failure does not occur in the thread-parallel execution and is not self-evident.

Note that Frost could have guaranteed both survival and detection by choosing another set of priorities for the three threads, such as BAC. Based on this observation, we have implemented a heuristic that helps choose thread priorities that avoid priority inversion. As a program executes, Frost counts the number of happens-before constraints between each pair of threads. It uses a greedy algorithm to place the two threads with the most frequent constraints in adjacent slots in the priority order, then place the thread with the most frequent constraints with one of those two threads adjacent to the thread with which it shares the most constraints, and so on. Since priority inversion can happen only when a constraint occurs between two non-adjacent threads in the priority order, this heuristic reduces the possibility of priority inversion happening as long as the constraints seen earlier in a program are a good predictor of future constraints.

In some cases, the thread-parallel execution of an epoch may complete before the epoch-parallel executions begin. In such cases, Frost can observe the exact set of happens-before constraints during that epoch and choose thread priorities accordingly. We have not yet implemented this further optimization.

3.4.3 Epoch boundaries

Frost separates execution into epochs to achieve scalability via multicore execution. Each epoch represents an ordering constraint (a barrier) that was not present in the original program. If a failure requirement crosses an epoch barrier (i.e., one of the instructions occurs in a prior epoch and one occurs in a subsequent epoch), the order of these two instructions is fixed in all replicas. For a Type I bug, all replicas will fail together or all will avoid failure.

Frost takes two steps to mitigate this limitation. First, it creates epochs infrequently. Second, it creates an epoch such that all threads are executing a system call at the point the epoch is created. For a data race such as the atomicity violation in Figure 1(b), this guarantees that no replica will fail unless the program issues a system call in the region that must be atomic.

All systems (including Frost) that are used to survive harmful races must commit state before externalizing output, and externalizing output is often required for forward progress. To avoid a bug due to a harmful race, such systems must also roll back to some committed state that pre-

cedes the race. This committed state may artificially order instructions before and after the commit point, and this ordering constraint may force the program to experience a harmful ordering of racing instructions [26].

When Frost is used only to detect races and not to survive them (e.g., during testing), there may be no need to keep the external output consistent after a data race occurs. Thus, we have implemented an optimization when Frost is used for data race detection in which external output does not cause the creation of a new epoch. This optimization is used only in Section 4.2 and not elsewhere in the evaluation.

3.4.4 Detection of Type II bugs

Frost's outcome-based race detection may not detect certain Type II bugs. Detection requires that any two replicas differ in system calls or synchronization operations executed, or that two replicas have a different memory or register state at the end of the epoch. As previously mentioned, certain benign races may have this property — filtering out such races is an advantage of outcome-based race detection. In addition, a code region may exhibit this property if the effects of two or more sets of racing instructions are identical. This is most likely to happen for a Type II bug in which both epoch-parallel replicas are correct and finish the epoch in identical states. However, in our experience so far with actual programs, Type II bugs have always led to some difference in program state or output.

4. EVALUATION

Our evaluation answers the following questions:

- How effectively does Frost survive data race bugs?
- How effectively does Frost detect such bugs?
- What is Frost's overhead?

4.1 Detecting and surviving races

4.1.1 Methodology

We evaluated Frost's ability to survive and detect data races using a 8-core server with two 2.66 GHz quad-core Xeon processors and 4 GB of DRAM. The server ran CentOS Linux 5.3, with a Linux 2.6.26 kernel and GNU library version 2.5.1, both modified to support Frost.

We used 11 actual concurrency bugs in our evaluation. We started by reproducing all data race bugs from an online collection of concurrency bugs [50] in Apache, MySQL, and pbzip2 compiled form several academic sources [27, 49, 51] and BugZilla databases. Out of the 12 concurrency bugs in the collection, we reproduced all 9 data race bugs. In addition, we reproduced a data race bug in the application pfscan that has been previously used in academic literature [51]. Finally, during our tests, Frost detected a previously unknown, potentially malign data race in glibc, which we added to our test suite. Table 2 lists the bugs and describes their effects.

For each bug, we ran 5 trials in which the bug manifests while the application executes under Frost's shepherding. The fourth column in Table 2 shows the replica outcomes for the epoch containing the bug. The fifth column shows the percentage of trials in which Frost survives the bug by producing output equivalent to a failure-free execution. The next column shows the percentage of trials in which Frost detects the bug via divergence in replica output or state. The

Application	Bug number	Bug manifestation	Outcome	% survived	% detected	Recovery time (sec)
pbzip2	N/A	crash	F-AA	100%	100%	0.01 (0.00)
apache	21287	double free	A-BB or A-AB	100%	100%	0.00 (0.00)
apache	25520	corrupted output	A-BC	100%	100%	0.00 (0.00)
apache	45605	assertion	A-AB	100%	100%	0.00 (0.00)
MySQL	644	crash	A-BC	100%	100%	0.02 (0.01)
MySQL	791	missing output	A-BC	100%	100%	0.00 (0.00)
MySQL	2011	corrupted output	A-BC	100%	100%	0.22 (0.09)
MySQL	3596	crash	F-BC	100%	100%	0.00 (0.00)
MySQL	12848	crash	F-FA	100%	100%	0.29 (0.13)
pfscan	N/A	infinite loop	F-FA	100%	100%	0.00 (0.00)
glibc	12486	assertion	F-AA	100%	100%	0.01 (0.00)

Results are the mean of five trials. Values in parentheses show standard deviations.

Table 2: Data race detection and survival

final column shows how long Frost takes to recover from the bug — this includes the cost of rolling back and executing new replicas.

4.1.2 Results

The main result of these experiments is that Frost both survives and detects all 11 bugs in all 5 trials for each bug. For these applications, surviving a bug adds little overhead to application execution time, mostly because epochs are short for server applications such as MySQL and Apache, and the bugs in other applications occurred close to the end of execution, so little work was lost due to quashing future epochs. We next provide more detail about each bug.

The pbzip2 data race can trigger a `SIGSEGV` when a worker thread dereferences a pointer that the main thread has freed. This is a Type II bug because the dereference must occur after the deallocation but before the main thread exits. This failure is self-evident, leading to the `F-AA` epoch outcome.

Apache bug #21287 is caused by lack of atomicity in updating and checking the reference count on cache objects, typically leading to a double free. This is a latent bug: the data race leads to an incorrect value for the reference count, which typically manifests later as an application fault. Frost detects this bug via a memory divergence at the end of the epoch in which the data race occurs, which is typically much earlier than when the fault is exhibited. Early detection allows Frost to avoid externalizing any output corrupted by the data race. The bug may manifest as either a Type I or Type II bug, depending on the order of cache operations.

Apache bug #25520 is a Type II atomicity violation in which two threads concurrently modify a shared variable in an unsafe manner. This leads to garbled output in Apache's access log. Frost detects a memory divergence since the log data is buffered before it is written to the log. The epoch classification is `A-BC` because the failure is not self-evident and the two epoch-parallel executions produce a different order of log messages (both orders are correct since the logged operations execute concurrently).

Apache bug #45605 is an atomicity violation that occurs when the dispatcher thread fails to recheck a condition after waiting on a condition variable. For this bug to manifest, the dispatcher thread must spin multiple times through a loop and accept multiple connections. Frost prevents this bug from manifesting in any replica because of its requirement

that output not be released prior to the end of an epoch. Since `accept` is a synchronous network operation, two `accepts` cannot occur in the same epoch. Thus, Frost converts the bug to a benign data race, which it detects. Even when the requirement for multiple `accepts` is removed, Frost detects the bug as a Type II race and survives it.

MySQL bug #644 is a Type II atomicity violation that leads to an incorrect loop termination condition. This causes memory corruption that eventually may cause MySQL to crash. Frost detects this bug as a memory divergence at the end of the buggy epoch. Thus, it recovers before memory corruption causes incorrect output.

MySQL bug #791 is a Type II atomicity violation that causes MySQL to fail to log operations. In a manner similar to Apache bug #25520, Frost sees an `A-BC` outcome for the buggy epoch, although the difference occurs in external output rather than memory state. As with the Apache bug, the outputs in the two epoch-parallel replicas are different, but both are correct.

MySQL bug #2011 is a Type II multi-variable atomicity violation that occurs when MySQL rotates its relay logs. This leads MySQL to fail an error check, leading to incorrect behavior. Frost detects the bug as an `A-BC` outcome.

MySQL bug #3596 is the Type II bug shown in Figure 1(b). The NULL pointer dereference generates a self-evident failure. The two epoch-parallel replicas avoid the race and take correct-but-divergent paths depending on how the condition is evaluated. Frost therefore sees the epoch outcome as `F-BC`.

MySQL bug #12848 exposes an incorrect intermediate cache size value during a cache resizing operation, leading MySQL to crash. Although this variable is protected by a lock for most accesses, one lock acquisition is missing, leading to an incorrect order of operations that results in a Type I bug. Since the crash occurs immediately, the failure is self-evident.

A Type I bug in pfscan causes the main thread to enter a spin-loop as it waits for worker threads to exit. Frost detects the spin-loop as a self-evident failure and classifies the epoch as `F-FA`. The third replica avoids the spin-loop by choosing an order of racing instructions that violates the bug's failure requirement.

While reproducing the prior bugs, Frost detected an additional, unreported data race bug in glibc. Multiple threads

App	Bug Number	Harmful Race Detected?		Benign Races	
		Traditional	Frost	Traditional	Frost
pbzip2	N/A	5	5	3	1
apache	21287	0	0	55	2
apache	25520	3	3	61	2
apache	45605	3	3	65	2
MySQL	644	4	4	2899	2
MySQL	791	3	3	808	1
MySQL	2011	0	0	1414	1
MySQL	3596	0	0	658	2
MySQL	12848	0	0	1449	2
pfscan	N/A	5	5	0	0
glibc	12486	6	6	9	3

The third column shows the number of runs in which a full-coverage, traditional dynamic race detector identifies the harmful race and the fourth column shows the number of runs in which Frost identifies the harmful race. The last two columns report the number of benign races detected for that benchmark in our runs.

Table 3: Comparison of data race detection coverage

concurrently update `malloc` statistics counters without synchronization, leading to possibly incorrect values. When debugging is enabled, additional checks on these variables trigger assertions. If a data race causes invalid statistics, the assertion can trigger incorrectly. We wrote a test program that triggers this bug reliably. Since the assertion happens in the same epoch as the data race, the failure is self-evident. We have reported this data race to the glibc developer's mailing list and are awaiting confirmation.

In summary, for a diverse set of application bugs, Frost both detects and survives all bugs in all trials with minimal time needed for recovery. For latent bugs that corrupt application state, Frost detects the failure in the epoch that contains the data race bug rather than when the program exhibits a self-evident symptom of failure and thereby avoids externalizing buggy output.

4.2 Stand-alone race detection

We next compare the coverage of Frost's data race detector to that of a traditional happens-before dynamic data race detector. Section 4.1.2 showed that Frost detects (and survives) all harmful data races in our benchmarks. However, in those experiments, we considered only scenarios in which the race manifests in a harmful manner. This may have made it easier for Frost to detect these races by making it more likely for replicas to diverge.

In this section, we repeat the experiments of Section 4.1.2, but we make no special effort to have the bug manifest. That is, we simply execute a sequence of actions that could *potentially* lead to a buggy interleaving of racing instructions. For comparison, we built a data race detector based on the design of DJIT+ [34]. Although it is slow, this data race detector provides full coverage; in other words, it detects all data races that occur during program execution. Since modern data race detectors often compromise coverage for speed (e.g., by sampling), a full-coverage data race detector such as the one we used provides the strongest competition.

Comparing the coverage of race detection tools is challenging since there is ordinarily no guarantee that each tool will observe the same sequence of instructions and synchronization operations during different executions of the program.

Fortunately, because Frost is built using the DoublePlay infrastructure, we can use DoublePlay to record the execution of the application and deterministically replay the same execution later. When we execute a dynamic race detector on the replayed execution, it is guaranteed to see the same happens-before order of synchronization operations as observed by both the thread-parallel and epoch-parallel executions. Further, the sequence of instructions executed by each thread is guaranteed to be the same up to the first data race. This ensures an apples-to-apples comparison.

Table 3 compares the coverage of Frost to that of the traditional dynamic race detector. We evaluated each benchmark for the same amount of testing time; the table shows cumulative results for all runs.

For each run for which the traditional data race detector identified a harmful race, Frost also identified the same race. The third column in Table 3 lists the number of runs for which the traditional data race detector identified the harmful race. The fourth column shows the number of runs for which Frost identified the same race. For some harmful races, neither Frost nor the traditional data race detector detect the race during our preset testing duration; this is expected since dynamic data race detectors must see instructions execute without synchronization to report a race.

We also evaluated the benefit of the ordering heuristic described in Section 3.4.2. When we executed Frost with the heuristic disabled, it detected all harmful races detected in Table 3 except for the harmful race in pbzip2. We verified that Frost does not report this race without the heuristic due to a priority inversion.

The last two columns in Table 3 list the number of benign races identified by the traditional data race detector and Frost for each benchmark. We manually classified 79 benign races reported by the traditional race detector in the pbzip2, Apache, pfscan and glibc benchmarks, according to a previously-proposed taxonomy [31], with the following results: (a) user-constructed synchronization (42 races): for example, Apache uses custom synchronization that the traditional race detector is unaware of without annotation and so the traditional race detector incorrectly identifies correctly synchronized accesses as racing, (b) redundant writes (8 races): two threads write identical values to the same location, (c) double checks (11 races): a variable is intentionally checked without acquiring a lock and re-checked if a test fails, and (d) approximate computation (18 races): for example, glibc's malloc routines maintain statistics and some threads concurrently log the order in which they service requests without synchronization. We also classified MySQL #644 and found that user-constructed synchronization accounted for 2619 benign data races, redundant writes for 71, double checks for 153 and approximate computation for 156. Due to the effort required, we have not classified the other MySQL benchmarks.

In contrast, Frost reports many fewer benign races. For example, if a race leads to transient divergence (e.g., an idempotent write-write race), Frost does not flag the race if the replica states converge before the end of the epoch. Frost also need not be aware of custom synchronization if that synchronization ensures that synchronized instructions have identical effects on all replicas. In our benchmarks, Frost identified only 8 benign races (2 double checks and 6 approximate computations). Thus, almost half of the races identified by Frost were harmful, while less than 0.25% of the

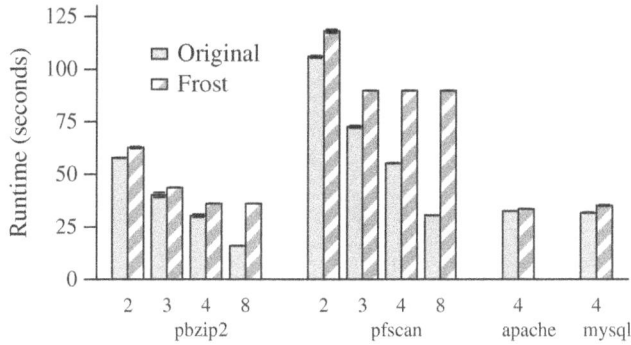

This figure shows how Frost affects execution time for four benchmarks on an 8-core machine. We show results for 2, 3, 4 and 8 threads for pbzip2 and pfscan. Apache and MySQL are I/O bound, so results are the same between 2 and 8 threads; we show the 4 thread results as a representative sample. Results are the mean of five trials; error bars are 90% confidence intervals. Frost adds a small amount of overhead (3-12%) when there are sufficient cores to run the extra replicas. When the number of worker threads exceeds 3 (pfscan) or 4 (pbzip2), Frost cannot hide the cost of running additional replicas.

Figure 4: Execution time overhead

races identified by the traditional race detector were harmful (with most benign races due to custom synchronization in MySQL).

4.3 Performance

4.3.1 Methodology

Our previous experiment demonstrated Frost's ability to survive and detect data races in pbzip2, pfscan, Apache and MySQL. We next measured the throughput overhead introduced by Frost for these 4 applications by comparing the execution time with Frost on the same 8-core server running our modified Linux kernel and glibc to the execution time running without Frost (i.e., running the same kernel and glibc versions without the Frost modifications).

We evaluate pbzip2 compressing a 498 MB log file in parallel. We use pfscan to search for a string in a directory with 935 MB of log files. We extended the benchmark to perform 150 iterations of the search so that we could measure the overhead of Frost over a longer run while ensuring that data is in the file cache (otherwise, our benchmark would be disk-bound). We tested Apache using ab (Apache Bench) to simultaneously send 5000 requests for a 70 KB file from multiple clients on the same local network. We evaluate MySQL using sysbench version 0.4.12. This benchmark uses multiple client threads to generate 2600 total database queries on a 9.8 GB myISAM database; 2000 queries are read-only and 600 update the database.

For these applications, the number of worker threads controls the maximum number of cores that they can use effectively. For each benchmark, we varied the number of worker threads from two to eight. Some benchmarks have additional control threads which do little work during the execution; we do not count these in the number of threads. Pbzip2 uses two additional threads: one to read file data and one to write the output; these threads are also not counted in the number of threads shown. All results are the mean of five trials.

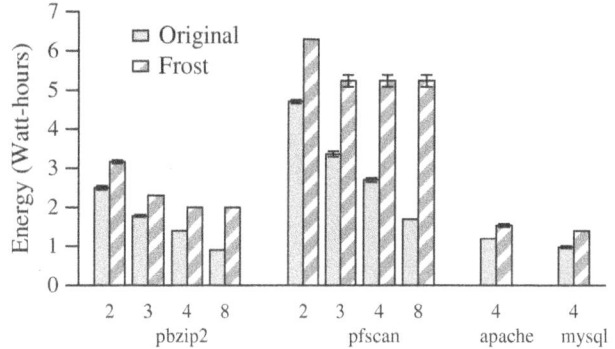

This figure shows Frost's energy overhead. We show results for 2, 3, 4 and 8 threads for pbzip2 and pfscan, and 4 threads for Apache and MySQL. Results are the mean of five trials; error bars are 90% confidence intervals.

Figure 5: Energy overhead

4.3.2 Throughput

The primary factor affecting Frost's performance for CPU-bound applications is the availability of unused cores. As Figure 4 shows, Frost adds a reasonable 8% overhead for pbzip2 and a 12% overhead for pfscan when these applications use only 2 cores. The reason that Frost's execution time overhead is low is that the server has spare resources to run its additional replicas.

To measure how Frost's overhead varies with the amount of spare cores, we gradually increased the number of threads used by the application up to the full capacity of the 8-core machine. Frost performance for pfscan stops improving at 3 worker threads, which is expected since running 3 replicas with 3 worker threads each requires 9 cores (1 more than available on this computer). Frost performance continues to scale up to 4 worker threads for pbzip2 due to application-specific behavior. A data race in pbzip2 sometimes leads to a spin-loop containing a call to `nanosleep`. One replica does not consume CPU time when this happens. As expected, if these two CPU-bound applications use all 8 cores, Frost adds slightly less than a 200% overhead. As with all systems that use active replication, Frost cannot hide the cost of running additional replicas when there are no spare resources available for their execution.

In contrast, we found the server applications Apache and MySQL do not scale with additional cores and are hence less affected by Frost's increased utilization. Specifically, we find that Apache is bottlenecked on network I/O and MySQL is bottlenecked on disk I/O. Since Apache and MySQL are not CPU-bound, neither the original nor Frost's execution time is affected as we vary the number of threads from 2 to 8. For this reason, we simply show the results for 4 threads. As shown in Figure 4, Frost only adds 3% overhead for Apache and 11% overhead for MySQL.

4.3.3 Energy use

Even when spare resources can hide the performance impact of executing multiple replicas, the additional execution has an energy cost. On perfectly energy-proportional hardware, the energy overhead would be approximately 200%. We were interested to know the energy cost on current hardware, which is not particularly energy-proportional.

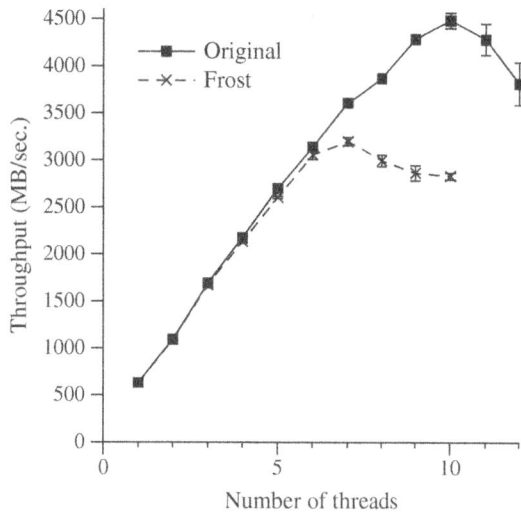

This figure shows pfscan throughput (MB of data scanned per second) with and without Frost. We vary the number of pfscan worker threads. Results are the mean of five trials; error bars are 90% confidence intervals.

Figure 6: Scalability on a 32-core server

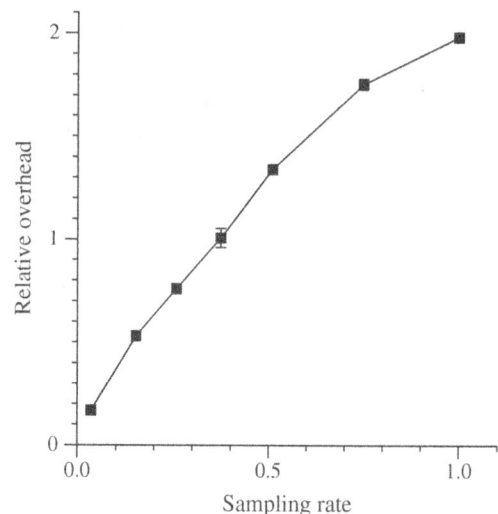

This figure shows Frost's relative overhead running pfscan at various sampling rates. A sampling rate of 0.25 means that Frost detects and survives races in 1 out of 4 epochs. Results are the mean of five trials; error bars are 90% confidence intervals.

Figure 7: Effect of sampling on relative overhead

We used a Watts Up? .Net power meter to measure the energy consumed by the 8-core machine when running the throughput benchmarks with and without Frost. As Figure 5 shows, Frost adds 26% energy overhead for pbzip2 and 34% overhead for pfscan when run with 2 threads. The energy cost increases to 122% and 208% respectively when the applications use 8 worker threads. Frost adds 28% energy overhead for Apache and 43% overhead for MySQL, independent of the number of worker threads.

4.3.4   Scalability

As the 8-core machine runs out of CPU resources with only 2-3 worker threads, we next evaluate how Frost scales on a 32-core server with four 2.27 GHz 8-core Xeon X7560 processors and 1.8 GB of RAM. This server ran the same software as in the previous experiments. We look at pfscan in these experiments as it showed the highest 8-core overhead. We scaled up the benchmark by increasing the number of data scans by a factor of 100. We report the throughput, measured by the amount of data scanned by pfscan per second.

As Figure 6 shows, pfscan scales well without Frost until it reaches 10 cores. At this point, we conjecture that it is using all the available memory bandwidth for the 32-core computer. Frost scales well up to 6 cores on this computer, with overhead less than 4%. Frost's execution of pfscan achieves maximum throughput at 7 cores. We conjecture that it hits the memory wall sooner due to executing multiple replicas. Because replicas execute the same workload, cache effects presumably mitigate the fact that the combined replicas access 3 times as much data as the original execution.

4.3.5   Sampling

As described in Section 3.3.3, Frost can be configured to sample only a portion of a program's execution. Sampling reduces overhead, but Frost will only detect and/or survive data races in the sampled intervals for which it executes epoch-parallel replicas. Thus, Frost will experience a de-

crease in its survival and detection rates for dynamic data races that is proportional to the sampling rate.

We re-ran the CPU-bound pfscan benchmark with 8 worker threads on the 8-core computer used in our previous experiments. We varied the percentage of epochs sampled and measured the relative overhead that Frost adds to application execution time. Figure 7 shows that with a sampling rate of 3.5%, Frost adds only 17% relative overhead to the benchmark. As the sampling rate increases, Frost's relative overhead scales roughly linearly up to approximately 200% when no sampling is employed.

4.4   Discussion

In summary, Frost detects all harmful races detected by a full-coverage dynamic race detector and survives those races in our experiments. While these results are quite positive, we believe there are a small set of scenarios that Frost will fail to handle correctly, as described in Section 3.4. Frost's overhead ranges from 3–12% for the applications we measured when spare resources are available to execute additional replicas. When spare resources are not available, the cost of executing additional replicas cannot be masked. Frost scales well with the number of cores, though it may experience limitations in other resources such as memory bandwidth if that resource is the bottleneck for the application being executed.

Frost's measured overhead is slightly less than that reported for the DoublePlay system on which it is built [44] due to code optimizations added after the reporting of the DoublePlay results. Uniparallel execution, as used by both Frost and DoublePlay, can have substantially higher overheads for benchmarks that dirty memory pages very rapidly. For example, by far the worst case overhead we measured for DoublePlay was the `ocean` benchmark in the SPLASH-2 suite (121% with spare cores); we expect Frost would have similar overhead with spare cores and 3x that overhead without spare cores.

These measured overheads are substantially less than those reported for dynamic data race detectors that handle non-managed code. As with other systems that use multiple replicas, Frost offers a tradeoff between reliability and utilization. During the software life cycle, one may choose to employ Frost at different times as priorities change; e.g., one can use Frost when software is newly released or updated to survive and detect data race bugs, then disable Frost or sample a subset of epochs to reduce overhead when software is believed to be race-free. Additionally, since it is inherently difficult to scale many workloads (e.g., those that are I/O bound), spare cores may often be available in production, in which case Frost can mask its extra utilization. One could, for instance, use a variation of sampling that only runs extra replicas when spare cores are available.

5. RELATED WORK

As Frost can serve as a tool for either surviving or detecting data races, we discuss related work in both areas.

5.1 Data race survival

The idea of using replication to survive errors dates back to the early days of computing [45, 28]. In active (state-machine) replication, replicas run in parallel and can be used to detect errors and vote on which result is correct [41]. In passive (primary-backup) replication, a single replica is used until an error is detected, then another replica is started from a checkpoint of a known-good state [8]. Passive replication incurs lower run-time overhead than active replication but cannot detect errors by comparing replicas. Frost uses active replication to detect and survive programming bugs.

In 1985, Jim Gray observed that just as transient hardware errors could be handled by retrying the operation (a type of passive replication), some software errors (dubbed Heisenbugs) could be handled in the same manner. Researchers have extended this idea in many ways, such as retrying from successively older states [47], proactively restarting to eliminate latent errors [20], shrinking the part of the system that needs to be restarted [9], and reducing the cost of running multiple replicas [19].

A general technique to increase the chance of survival in replication-based systems is to use *diverse* replicas to reduce the probability of all replicas failing at the same time. Many types of diversity can be added, including changing the layout of memory [4, 17, 36], changing the instruction set [2, 22], or even running multiple independently-written versions of the program [1]. Our focus on ensuring at least one correct replica is similar to work in security that creates replicas with disjoint exploitation sets [11, 39].

The replication-based systems most closely related to Frost are those that add diversity by changing the scheduling of various events, such as changing the order in which messages or signals are delivered [36, 47] or changing the priority order of processes [36]. Frost contributes to the domain of replica diversity by introducing the idea of complementary schedules, describing how complementary schedules enable data race detection, and showing how to produce complementary schedules efficiently via non-preemptive scheduling and uniparallelism.

The idea of controlling thread schedules has also been used to explore the space of possible thread interleavings in model checking and program testing [18, 30]. The goal of such prior work is to explore the space of the possible behaviors to find bugs. In contrast, the primary goal of Frost is to ensure that at least one of the thread schedules executes racy accesses in the correct order. This difference changes the algorithm used to create schedules and leads to the design choice in Frost to use two complementary schedules instead of many schedules. Like Frost, CHESS [30] uses non-preemptive scheduling to tightly control the thread schedule. However, because CHESS is used only for testing, it has no need to parallelize the execution of non-preemptive runs as Frost does.

Past research has examined several approaches that do not require active replication for surviving concurrency bugs that cause deadlocks [21, 46]. Frost is complementary to these techniques as it targets a different class of concurrency bugs due to data races. Instead of detecting concurrency bugs and then recovering from them, recent research proposes to actively avoid untested thread interleavings and thereby reduce the chance of triggering concurrency bugs. This approach, however, incurs high overhead [12] or requires processor support [51]. Other researchers have observed that some concurrency bugs can be eliminated by minimizing preemptions and providing sequential semantics [3]. Other systems [48] avoid known bugs by avoiding thread schedules that lead to the buggy behavior; unlike Frost, these systems do not survive the first occurrence of unknown bugs.

5.2 Data race detection

In addition to its survival functionality, Frost can also be used as a dynamic race detection tool, targeted either at production or test environments. Data race detectors can be compared along many dimensions, including overhead, coverage (how many data races are detected), accuracy (how many false positives are reported), and fidelity (how much data about each race is provided).

Static race detectors (e.g., [13]) try to prove that a program is free of data races; they incur no runtime overhead but report many false positives (lowering accuracy) due to the limits of static analysis, especially for less-structured languages such as C. On the other hand, dynamic race detectors seek only to detect when a specific run experiences a data race; they must observe potentially racing instructions execute in order to report a race. Prior dynamic data race detectors are mostly based on two basic techniques: happens-before analysis [23, 42] and lockset analysis [40]. Both techniques analyze the synchronization and memory operations issued by a program to determine whether a data race may have occurred. Because memory operations occur frequently, dynamic race detectors have historically slowed programs by an order of magnitude. In a recent study, Flanagan and Freund [15] compared several state-of-the-art dynamic data race detectors and showed that their best Java implementation is about 8.5x slower than native execution. Implementations that check for data races in less-structured, optimized code running outside of a virtual machine (such as C and C++ programs) may have even higher overhead, as exemplified by recently-released industrial strength race detectors from Intel [38] and Google [43], which incur more than 30x performance overhead.

Dynamic race detectors can use language-specific or runtime-specific features to reduce overhead. RaceTrack [52] runs CPU-intensive benchmark in Microsoft's CLR 2.6-3.2x slower, but limits coverage by not checking for races involving native code, which represents a non-negligible number of methods. RaceTrack also leverages the object-oriented nature of the checked code to employ a clever refinement strategy in which it first checks for races at object granularity, then subsequently checks accesses to the object for races at field granularity. Object-granularity checks may have substantial false positives, so are reported at lower priority. However, unless a particular pair of instructions races twice for the same object, RaceTrack cannot report the race with high confidence. Overhead can also be reduced by eliminating checks that are shown to be unnecessary via a separate static analysis phase [10]. However, these optimizations are difficult to implement precisely for unsafe languages.

Frost executes applications 3–12% slower if spare cores are available to parallelize replica execution, and approximately 3x slower if spare cores are not available. This compares very favorably with all prior dynamic race detection tools for general code running outside of a virtual machine, and also with most tools for managed code. While Frost may miss races that are detected by the higher-overhead happens-before race detectors, in practice Frost has detected all harmful races that would be reported by such detectors.

Several recent race detectors use sampling to trade coverage for reduced overhead by monitoring only a portion of a program's execution. PACER [6] uses random sampling, so has coverage approximately equal to the sampling rate used. At a 3% sampling rate, PACER runs CPU-intensive applications 1.6-2.1x slower. However, PACER reports only 2–20% of all dynamic races at that sampling rate. LiteRace [29] uses a heuristic (adaptive bursty thread-local sampling that biases execution toward cold code) to increase the expected number of races found, but the same heuristic may systematically bias against finding certain races (such as those executed along infrequent code paths in frequently-executed functions). LiteRace runs CPU-intensive applications 2.4x slower to find 70% of all races and 50% of rare races.

Sampling is orthogonal to most data race detection techniques. Frost implements sampling by checking only a portion of epochs. At a slightly greater than 3% sampling rate, Frost's overhead is only 17% for a CPU-bound benchmark. It would also be possible to use heuristics similar to those used by LiteRace, but the application is complicated by the granularity of Frost's epochs. Whereas LiteRace toggles instrumentation at function granularity, Frost can only toggle instrumentation at epoch granularity. However, Frost could benefit from its thread-parallel execution, for example by measuring the percentage of cold code executed before deciding which epochs to check via epoch-parallel execution.

It is possible to reduce dynamic data race detection overhead further through the use of custom hardware [35]. Data Collider [14] repurposes existing hardware (watchpoints) to implement a novel dynamic race detection technique. Data Collider samples memory accesses by pausing the accessing thread and using watchpoints to identify unsynchronized accesses to the memory location made by other threads. The paucity of hardware watchpoints on existing processors (4 in their experiments) limits the number of memory locations that can be sampled simultaneously. Data Collider can thus achieve very low overhead (often less than 10%) but may not have suitable coverage to detect rare races since the sampling rate (only 4 memory locations at a time) is very low. It is also not clear how Data Collider will scale as the number of cores increases because the number of watchpoints per core

does not increase and sampling an address requires an IPI to all cores to set a watchpoint.

Most data races are not bugs. Prior work has shown that comparing execution outcomes for schedules with different orderings of conflicting memory accesses can be used to classify data races as benign or potentially harmful [31]. This can be viewed as a method of improving accuracy. Frost's design applies this filtering technique. In contrast to the prior work that assumed that the data race was known in order to generate thread schedules, Frost uses complementary schedules to detect races that are *unknown* at the time that the schedules are generated.

Frost has extremely high fidelity because it can deterministically replay the execution of a program up to the first data race in an epoch (and often beyond that). This allows Frost to re-generate any diagnostic information, such as stack traces, required by a developer. We use this capability, for example, in Section 4.2 to implement a complete dynamic race detector. Other tools such as Intel's Thread-Checker [38] provide stack traces for both threads participating in a data race, and some tools, such as RaceTrack [52] can guarantee a stack trace for only one thread.

Pike [16] also uses multiple replicas to test for concurrency bugs by comparing executions with interleaved requests with executions with serialized requests (which are assumed to be correct). Pike requires that the application provide a cononicalized representation of its state that is independent of thread interleavings, which could be time-consuming to develop. Pike has high overhead (requiring a month to test one application) but can find more types of concurrency bugs than just data race bugs. TightLip [53] compares the output of a replica with access to sensitive data with that of a replica without such access to detect information leaks.

6. CONCLUSION

Frost introduces two main ideas to mitigate the problem of data races: complementary schedules and outcome-based race detection. Running multiple replicas with complementary schedules ensures that, for most types of data race bugs, at least one replica avoids the order of racing instructions that leads to incorrect program execution. This property enables a new, faster dynamic data race detector, which detects races by comparing outcomes of different replicas rather than analyzing the events executed. After Frost detects a data race, it analyzes the combination of results and selects the strategy that is most likely to survive the bug.

Acknowledgments

We thank the anonymous reviewers and our shepherd, Tim Harris, for comments that improved this paper. Jie Hou and Jessica Ouyang helped gather data used in the paper. The work is supported by the National Science Foundation under awards CNS-0905149 and CCF-0916770. The views and conclusions contained in this document are those of the authors and should not be interpreted as representing the official policies, either expressed or implied, of NSF, the University of Michigan, the U.S. government, or industrial sponsors.

7. REFERENCES

[1] A. Avizienis. The N-version approach to fault-tolerant software. *IEEE Transactions on Software Engineering*, SE-11(12):1491–1501, December 1985.

[2] E. Barrantes, D. Ackley, S. Forrest, T. Palmer, D. Stefanovic, and D. Zovi. Randomized instruction set emulation to disrupt binary code injection attacks. In *Proceedings of the 10th ACM Conference on Computer and Communications Security (CCS)*, Washington, DC, October 2003.

[3] E. D. Berger, T. Yang, T. Liu, and G. Novark. Grace: Safe multithreaded programming for C/C++. In *Proceedings of the International Conference on Object Oriented Programming Systems, Languages, and Applications*, pages 81–96, Orlando, FL, October 2009.

[4] E. D. Berger and B. G. Zorn. DieHard: Probabilistic memory safety for unsafe languages. In *Proceedings of the ACM SIGPLAN 2006 Conference on Programming Language Design and Implementation*, Ottawa, Canada, June 2006.

[5] R. L. Bocchino, Jr., V. S. Adve, D. Dig, S. V. Adve, S. Heumann, R. Komuravelli, J. Overbey, P. Simmons, H. Sung, and M. Vakilian. A type and effect system for deterministic parallel Java. In *Proceedings of the International Conference on Object Oriented Programming Systems, Languages, and Applications*, pages 97–116, Orlando, FL, October 2009.

[6] M. D. Bond, K. E. Coons, and K. S. McKinley. PACER: Proportional detection of data races. In *Proceedings of the ACM SIGPLAN 2010 Conference on Programming Language Design and Implementation*, Toronto, Canada, June 2010.

[7] C. Boyapati, R. Lee, and M. Rinard. Ownership types for safe programming: preventing data races and deadlocks. In *Proceedings of the 17th Annual ACM Conference on Object Oriented Programming Systems, Languages, and Applications*, pages 211–230, Seattle, WA, November 2002.

[8] N. Budhiraja, K. Marzullo, F. B. Schneider, and S. Toueg. *The primary-backup approach*. Addison-Wesley, 1993. in Distributed Systems, edited by Sape Mullender.

[9] G. Candea, S. Kawamoto, Y. Fujiki, G. Friedman, and A. Fox. Microreboot – A technique for cheap recovery. In *Proceedings of the 6th Symposium on Operating Systems Design and Implementation*, pages 31–44, San Francisco, CA, December 2004.

[10] J.-D. Choi, K. Lee, A. Loginov, R. O'Callahan, V. Sarkar, and M. Sridharan. Efficient and precise datarace detection for multithreaded object-oriented programs. In *Proceedings of the ACM SIGPLAN 2002 Conference on Programming Language Design and Implementation*, Berlin, Germany, June 2002.

[11] B. Cox, D. Evans, A. Filipi, J. Rowanhill, W. Hu, J. Davidson, J. Knight, A. Nguyen-Tuong, and J. Hiser. N-variant systems: A secretless framework for security through diversity. In *USENIX Security*, August 2006.

[12] H. Cui, J. Wu, C.-C. Tsai, and J. Yang. Stable deterministic multithreading through schedule memoization. In *Proceedings of the 9th Symposium on Operating Systems Design and Implementation*, Vancouver, BC, October 2010.

[13] D. Engler and K. Ashcraft. RacerX: Efficient static detection of race conditions and deadlocks. In *Proceedings of the 19th ACM Symposium on Operating Systems Principles*, pages 237–252, Bolton Landing, NY, 2003.

[14] J. Erickson, M. Musuvathi, S. Burckhardt, and K. Olynyk. Effective data-race detection for the kernel. In *Proceedings of the 9th Symposium on Operating Systems Design and Implementation*, Vancouver, BC, October 2010.

[15] C. Flanagan and S. Freund. FastTrack: Efficient and precise dynamic race detection. In *Proceedings of the ACM SIGPLAN 2009 Conference on Programming Language Design and Implementation*, pages 121–133, Dublin, Ireland, June 2009.

[16] P. Fonseca, C. Li, and R. Rodrigues. Finding complex concurrency bugs in large multi-threaded applications. In *Proceedings of the European Conference on Computer Systems*, Salzburg, Austria, April 2011.

[17] S. Forrest, A. Somayaji, and D. Ackley. Building diverse computer systems. In *Proceedings of the 6th Workshop on Hot Topics in Operating Systems*, pages 67–72, Cape Cod, MA, May 1997.

[18] P. Godefroid. Model checking for programming languages using VeriSoft. In *Proceedings of the 24th ACM SIGPLAN-SIGACT Symposium on Principles of Programming Languages*, pages 174–186, Paris, France, January 1997.

[19] R. Huang, D. Y. Den, and G. E. Suh. Orthrus: Efficient software integrity protection on multi-cores. In *Proceedings of the 15th International Conference on Architectural Support for Programming Languages and Operating Systems*, pages 371–383, Pittsburgh, PA, March 2010.

[20] Y. Huang, C. Kintala, N. Kolettis, and N. D. Fulton. Software rejuvenation: Analysis, module and applications. In *Proceedings of the 25th International Symposium of Fault-Tolerant Computing*, pages 381–390, Pasadena, CA, June 1995.

[21] H. Jula, D. Tralamazza, C. Zamfir, and G. Candea. Deadlock immunity: Enabling systems to defend against deadlocks. In *Proceedings of the 8th Symposium on Operating Systems Design and Implementation*, pages 294–308, San Diego, CA, December 2008.

[22] G. S. Kc, A. D. Keromytis, and V. Prevelakis. Countering code-injection attacks with instruction-set randomization. In *Proceedings of the 10th ACM Conference on Computer and Communications Security (CCS)*, Washington, DC, October 2003.

[23] L. Lamport. Time, clocks, and the ordering of events in a distributed system. *Communications of the ACM*, 21(7):558–565, 1978.

[24] D. Lee, B. Wester, K. Veeraraghavan, P. M. Chen, J. Flinn, and S. Narayanasamy. Respec: Efficient online multiprocessor replay via speculation and external determinism. In *Proceedings of the 15th International Conference on Architectural Support for Programming Languages and Operating Systems*, pages 77–89, Pittsburgh, PA, March 2010.

[25] N. G. Leveson and C. S. Turner. Investigation of the Therac-25 accidents. *IEEE Computer*, 26(7):18–41, 1993.

[26] D. E. Lowell, S. Chandra, and P. M. Chen. Exploring failure transparency and the limits of generic recovery. In *Proceedings of the 4th Symposium on Operating Systems Design and Implementation*, San Diego, CA, October 2000.

[27] S. Lu, S. Park, E. Seo, and Y. Zhou. Learning from mistakes — a comprehensive study on real world concurrency bug characteristics. In *Proceedings of the 13th International Conference on Architectural Support for Programming Languages and Operating Systems*, pages 329–339, 2008.

[28] R. E. Lyons and W. Vanderkulk. The use of triple-modular redundancy to improve computer reliability. *IBM Journal of Research and Development*, 6(2):200–209, 1962.

[29] D. Marino, M. Musuvathi, and S. Narayanasamy. LiteRace: efficient sampling for lightweight data-race detection. In *Proceedings of the ACM SIGPLAN 2009 Conference on Programming Language Design and Implementation*, Dublin, Ireland, June 2009.

[30] M. Musuvathi, S. Qadeer, T. Ball, G. Basler, P. A. Nainar, and I. Neamtiu. Finding and reproducing Heisenbugs in concurrent programs. In *Proceedings of the 8th Symposium on Operating Systems Design and Implementation*, pages 267–280, San Diego, CA, December 2008.

[31] S. Narayanasamy, Z. Wang, J. Tigani, A. Edwards, and B. Calder. Automatically classifying benign and harmful data races using replay analysis. In *Proceedings of the ACM SIGPLAN 2007 Conference on Programming Language Design and Implementation*, San Diego, CA, June 2007.

[32] E. B. Nightingale, P. M. Chen, and J. Flinn. Speculative execution in a distributed file system. In *Proceedings of the*

20th ACM Symposium on Operating Systems Principles, pages 191–205, Brighton, United Kingdom, October 2005.

[33] K. Poulsen. Software bug contributed to blackout. *SecurityFocus*, 2004.

[34] E. Pozniansky and A. Schuster. Efficient on-the-fly data race detection in multithreaded C++ programs. In *Proceedings of the 9th ACM SIGPLAN Symposium on Principles and Practice of Parallel Programming*, pages 179–190, San Diego, CA, June 2003.

[35] M. Prvulovic and J. Torrellas. ReEnact: using thread-level speculation mechanisms to debug data races in multithreaded codes. In *Proceedings of the 30th Annual International Symposium on Computer architecture*, pages 110–121, San Diego, California, 2003.

[36] F. Qin, J. Tucek, J. Sundaresan, and Y. Zhou. Rx: Treating bugs as allergies—a safe method to survive software failures. In *ACM Symposium on Operating Systems Principles*, pages 235–248, Brighton, United Kingdom, October 2005.

[37] M. Ronsse and K. De Bosschere. RecPlay: A fully integrated practical record/replay system. *ACM Transactions on Computer Systems*, 17(2):133–152, May 1999.

[38] P. Sack, B. E. Bliss, Z. Ma, P. Petersen, and J. Torrellas. Accurate and efficient filtering for the Intel thread checker race detector. In *Proceedings of the 1st Workshop on Architectural and System Support for Improving Software Dependability*, pages 34–41, San Jose, CA, October 2002.

[39] B. Salamat, T. Jackson, A. Gal, and M. Franz. Orchestra: Intrusion detection using parallel execution and monitoring of program variants in user-space. In *Proceedings of the European Conference on Computer Systems*, April 2009.

[40] S. Savage, M. Burrows, G. Nelson, P. Sobalvarro, and T. Anderson. Eraser: A dynamic data race detector for multithreaded programs. *ACM Transactions on Computer Systems*, 15(4):391–411, November 1997.

[41] F. B. Schneider. Implementing fault-tolerant services using the state machine approach: a tutorial. *ACM Computing Surveys*, 22(4):299–319, December 1990.

[42] E. Schonberg. On-the-fly detection of access anomalies. In *Proceedings of the ACM SIGPLAN 1989 Conference on Programming Language Design and Implementation*, Portland, OR, June 1989.

[43] K. Serebryany and T. Iskhodzhanov. ThreadSanitizer: Data race detection in practice. In *Proceedings of the Workshop on Binary Instrumentation and Applications*, December 2009.

[44] K. Veeraraghavan, D. Lee, B. Wester, J. Ouyang, P. M. Chen, J. Flinn, and S. Narayanasamy. DoublePlay: Parallelizing sequential logging and replay. In *Proceedings of the 16th International Conference on Architectural Support for Programming Languages and Operating Systems*, Long Beach, CA, March 2011.

[45] J. von Neumann. Probabilistic logics and the synthesis of reliable organisms from unreliable components. *Automata Studies*, pages 43–98, 1956.

[46] Y. Wang, T. Kelly, M. Kudlur, S. Lafortune, and S. Mahlke. Gadara: Dynamic deadlock avoidance for multithreaded programs. In *Proceedings of the 8th Symposium on Operating Systems Design and Implementation*, pages 281–294, San Diego, CA, December 2008.

[47] Y.-M. Wang, Y. Huang, and W. K. Fuchs. Progressive retry for software error recovery in distributed systems. In *Proceedings of the 23rd Annual International Symposium on Fault-Tolerant Computing*, Toulouse, France, June 1993.

[48] J. We, H. Cui, and J. Yang. Bypassing races in live applications with execution filters. In *Proceedings of the 9th Symposium on Operating Systems Design and Implementation*, Vancouver, BC, October 2010.

[49] M. Xu, R. Bodik, and M. D. Hill. A serializability violation detector for shared-memory server programs. In *Proceedings of the ACM SIGPLAN 2005 Conference on Programming Language Design and Implementation*, Chicago, IL, June 2005.

[50] J. Yu. Collection of concurrency bugs. http://www.eecs.umich.edu/ jieyu/bugs.html.

[51] J. Yu and S. Narayanasamy. A case for an interleaving constrained shared-memory multi-processor. In *Proceedings of the 36th Annual International Symposium on Computer Architecture*, pages 325–336, June 2009.

[52] Y. Yu, T. Rodeheffer, and W. Chen. RaceTrack: Efficient detection of data race conditions via adaptive tracking. In *Proceedings of the 20th ACM Symposium on Operating Systems Principles*, pages 221–234, Brighton, United Kingdom, October 2005.

[53] A. R. Yumerefendi, B. Mickle, and L. P. Cox. TightLip: Keeping applications from spilling the beans. In *Proceedings of the 4th Symposium on Networked Systems Design and Implementation*, pages 159–172, Cambridge, MA, April 2007.

Transactional storage for geo-replicated systems

Yair Sovran*   Russell Power*   Marcos K. Aguilera†   Jinyang Li*
*New York University   †Microsoft Research Silicon Valley

ABSTRACT

We describe the design and implementation of Walter, a key-value store that supports transactions and replicates data across distant sites. A key feature behind Walter is a new property called *Parallel Snapshot Isolation* (PSI). PSI allows Walter to replicate data asynchronously, while providing strong guarantees within each site. PSI precludes write-write conflicts, so that developers need not worry about conflict-resolution logic. To prevent write-write conflicts and implement PSI, Walter uses two new and simple techniques: preferred sites and counting sets. We use Walter to build a social networking application and port a Twitter-like application.

Categories and Subject Descriptors: C.2.4 [Computer-Communication Networks]: Distributed Systems—client/server; distributed applications; distributed databases; D.4.5 [Operating Systems]: Reliability—fault-tolerance; H.3.4 [Information Storage and Retrieval]: Systems and Software—distributed systems

General Terms: Algorithms, Design, Experimentation, Performance, Reliability

Keywords: Transactions, asynchronous replication, geo-distributed systems, distributed storage, key-value store, parallel snapshot isolation

1. INTRODUCTION

Popular web applications such as Facebook and Twitter are increasingly deployed over many data centers or *sites* around the world, to provide better geographic locality, availability, and disaster tolerance. These applications require a storage system that is *geo-replicated*—that is, replicated across many sites—to keep user data, such as status updates, photos, and messages in a social networking application. An attractive storage choice for this setting is a key-value store [16], which provides good performance and reliability at low cost.

We describe Walter, a geo-replicated key-value store that supports *transactions*. Existing geo-distributed key-value stores provide no transactions or only restricted transactions (see Section 9). Without transactions, an application must carefully coordinate access to data to avoid race conditions, partial writes, overwrites, and other hard problems that cause erratic behavior. Developers must address these same problems for many applications. With transactions, developers are relieved from concerns of atomicity, consistency, isolation, durability, and coordination. For example, in a social networking application, one may want to remove user A from B's friends list and vice versa. Without transactions, developers must write code carefully to prevent one removal from happening without the other. With transactions, developers simply bundle

those updates in a transaction.

Transactions in Walter ensure a new isolation property called *Parallel Snapshot Isolation* (PSI), which provides a balance between consistency and latency [22, 54], as appropriate for web applications. In such applications, a user might log into the site closest to her, where she accesses application servers, ad servers, authentication servers, etc. These hosts should observe a consistent storage state. For example, in a social network, a user expects to see her own posts immediately and in order. For that reason, the storage system should provide a strong level of consistency among hosts in her site. Across sites, weaker consistency is *acceptable*, because users can tolerate a small delay for their actions to be seen by other users. A weaker consistency is also *desirable*, so that transactions can be replicated across sites asynchronously (lazy replication).

Eventual consistency [44, 47] is often the property provided by asynchronous replication. When different sites update the same data concurrently, there is a conflict that must be resolved by application logic. This logic can be complex, and we want to avoid forcing it upon developers.

With PSI, hosts within a site observe transactions according to a consistent snapshot and a common ordering of transactions. Across sites, PSI enforces only causal ordering, not a global ordering of transactions, allowing the system to replicate transactions asynchronously across sites. With causal ordering, if Alice posts a message that is seen by Bob, and Bob posts a response, no user can see Bob's response without also seeing Alice's original post. Besides providing causal ordering, PSI precludes write-write conflicts (two transactions concurrently writing to the same object) so that developers need not write conflict resolution logic.

To prevent write-write conflicts and implement PSI, Walter relies on two techniques: *preferred sites* and *counting sets*. In web applications, writes to an object are often made by the user who owns the object, at the site where this user logs into. Therefore, we assign each object to a *preferred site*, where objects can be written more efficiently. For example, the preferred site for the wall posts of a user is the site closest to the user. Preferred sites are less restrictive than primary sites, as we discuss in Section 2.

Preferred sites may not always suffice. For example, a friends list can be updated by users in many sites. The second technique in Walter to avoid conflicts is to use a new simple data type called a *counting set* (cset), inspired by commutative data types [29]. A cset is like a set, except that each element has an integer count. Unlike sets, csets operations are commutative, and so they never conflict [25]. Therefore, transactions with csets can commit without having to check for conflicts across sites. When developing applications for Walter, we used csets extensively to store friend lists, message walls, photo albums, and message timelines. We found that csets were versatile and easy to use.

Walter uses multi-version concurrency control within each site, and it can quickly commit transactions that write objects at their preferred sites or that use csets. For other transactions, Walter resorts to two-phase commit to check for conflicts. We found that the latter type of transaction can be avoided in the applications we built.

Using Walter as the storage system, we build WaltSocial, a Facebook-like social networking application, and we port a third-party Twitter-clone called ReTwis [2]. We find that the transactions provided by Walter are effective and efficient. Experiments on four geographic locations on Amazon EC2 show that transactions have low latency and high throughput. For example, the operation to post a message on a wall in WaltSocial has a throughput of 16500 ops/s and the 99.9-percentile latency is less than 50 ms.

In summary, our contributions are the following:

- We define Parallel Snapshot Isolation, an isolation property well-suited for geo-replicated web applications. PSI provides a strong guarantee within a site; across sites, PSI provides causal ordering and precludes write-write conflicts.
- We describe the design and implementation of Walter, a geo-replicated transactional key-value store that provides PSI. Walter can avoid common write-write conflicts without cross-site communication using two simple techniques: preferred sites and csets.
- We give distributed protocols to execute and commit transactions in Walter.
- We use Walter to build two applications and demonstrate the usefulness of its transactional guarantees. Our experience indicates that Walter transactions simplify application development and provide good performance.

2. OVERVIEW

Setting. A geo-replicated storage system replicates objects across multiple sites. The system is managed by a single administrative entity. Machines can fail by crashing; addressing Byzantine failures is future work. Network partitions between sites are rare: sites are connected by highly-available links (e.g., private leased lines or MPLS VPNs) and there are redundant links to ensure connectivity during planned periods of link maintenance (e.g., using a ring topology across sites). We wish to provide a useful back-end storage system for web applications, such as social networks, web email, social games, and online stores. The storage system should provide reliability, a simple interface and semantics, and low latency.

Why transactions? We illustrate the benefit of transactions in a social networking application, where users post photos and status updates, befriend other users, and write on friends' walls. Each site has one or more application servers that access shared user data. When Alice adds a new photo album, the application creates an object for the new album, posts a news update on Alice's wall, and updates her album set. With transactions, the application groups these writes into an atomic unit so that failures do not leave behind partial writes (atomicity) and concurrent access by other servers are not intermingled (isolation). Without transactions, the application risks exposing undesirable inconsistent state to end users. For example, Bob may see the wall post that Alice has a new album but not find the album. Developers can sometimes alleviate these inconsistencies manually, by finding and ensuring proper ordering of writes. For example, the application can create the new album and wait for it to be replicated before posting on the wall. Then, concurrent access by Bob is not a problem, but a failure may leave behind an orphan album not linked to any user. The developer can deal with this problem by logging and replaying actions—which amounts to implementing rudimentary transactions—or garbage collecting dangling structures. This non-transactional approach places significant burden on developers.

We are not the first to point out the benefits of transactions to data center applications. Sinfonia uses transactions for infrastructure services [3, 4], while Percolator [38] uses them for search indexing. Both systems target applications on a single site, whereas we target geo-replicated applications that span many sites.

One way to provide transactions in a geo-replicated setting is to partition the data across several databases, where each database has its primary at a different site. The databases are replicated asynchronously across all sites, but each site is the primary for only one of the partitions. Unfortunately, with this solution, transactions cannot span multiple partitions, limiting their utility to applications.

Key features. Walter provides a unique combination of features to support geo-replicated web applications:

- *Asynchronous replication across sites.* Transactions are replicated lazily in the background, to reduce latency.
- *Efficient update-anywhere for certain objects.* Counting sets can be updated efficiently anywhere, while other objects can be updated efficiently at their preferred site.
- *Freedom from conflict-resolution logic,* which is complex and burdensome to developers.
- *Strong isolation within each site.* This is provided by the PSI property, which we cover below.

Existing systems do not provide some of the above features. For instance, eventually consistent systems such as [44, 47] require conflict-resolution logic; primary-copy database systems do not support any form of update-anywhere. We discuss related work in more detail in Section 9.

Overview of PSI. Snapshot isolation [8] is a popular isolation condition provided by commercial database systems such as Oracle and SQLServer. Snapshot isolation ensures that (a) transactions read from a snapshot that reflects a single commit ordering of transactions, and (b) if two concurrent transactions have a write-write conflict, one must be aborted. By imposing a single commit ordering, snapshot isolation forces implementations to coordinate transactions on commit, even when there are no conflicts (Section 3.1).

Parallel snapshot isolation extends snapshot isolation by allowing different sites to have different commit orderings. For example, suppose site A executes transactions T_1, T_2 and site B executes transactions T_3, T_4. PSI allows site A to first incorporate just T_1, T_2 and later T_3, T_4, while site B first incorporates T_3, T_4 and later T_1, T_2. This flexibility is needed for asynchronous replication: site A (or site B) can commit transactions T_1, T_2 (or T_3, T_4) without coordinating with the other site and later propagate the updates.

Although PSI allows different commit orderings at different sites, it still preserves the property of snapshot isolation that committed transactions have no write-write conflicts, thereby avoiding the need for conflict resolution. Furthermore, PSI preserves causal ordering: if a transaction T_2 reads from T_1 then T_1 is ordered before T_2 at every site. We give a precise specification of PSI in Section 3.

We believe PSI provides strong guarantees that are well-suited for web applications. Intuitively, PSI provides snapshot isolation for all transactions executed within a single site. PSI's relaxation over snapshot isolation is acceptable for web applications where each user communicates with one site at a time and there is no need for a global ordering of all actions across all users. In a social networking application, Alice in site A may post a message at the same time as Bob in site B. Under PSI, Alice may see her message first before seeing Bob's message, and Bob sees the opposite ordering, which is reasonable since Alice and Bob post concurrently. As another example, in an auction application, PSI allows bids on different objects to be committed in different orders at different sites. (In contrast, snapshot isolation requires the same ordering at all sites.)

Such relaxation is acceptable since the auction application requires bid ordering on each object separately, not across all objects.

Avoiding conflicts efficiently. To avoid write-write conflicts across sites, and implement PSI, Walter uses two techniques.

- *Preferred sites.* Each object is assigned a *preferred site*, which is the site where writes to the object can be committed without checking other sites for write conflicts. Walter executes and commits a transaction quickly if all the objects that it modifies have a preferred site where the transaction executes. Objects can be updated at any site, not just the preferred site. In contrast, some database systems have the notion of a *primary site*, which is the only site that can update the data. This notion is more limiting than the notion of a preferred site. For instance, suppose objects O_1 and O_2 are both replicated at sites 1 and 2, but the primary of O_1 is site 1 while the primary of O_2 is site 2. A transaction executing on site 1 can *read* both objects (since they are both replicated at site 1), but because the primary of O_2 is not site 1, the transaction can *write* only O_1—which is limiting to applications. In practice, this limitation is even more severe because database systems assign primary sites at the granularity of the whole database, and therefore non-primary sites are entirely read-only.

- *Conflict-free counting set objects.* Sometimes an object is modified frequently from many sites and hence does not have a natural choice for a preferred site. We address this problem with counting set (cset) objects. Transactions in Walter support not just read and write operations, but also operations on csets. Csets have the desirable property that transactions concurrently accessing the cset object never generate write-write conflicts. A cset is similar to a multiset in that it keeps a count for each element. But, unlike a multiset, the count could be negative [25]. A cset supports an operation $add(x)$ to add element x, which increments the counter of x in the cset; and an operation $rem(x)$ to remove x, which decrements the counter of x. Because increment and decrement commute, *add* and *rem* also commute, and so operations never conflict.

  For example, a group of concurrent cset operations can be ordered as $add(x)$, $add(y)$, $rem(x)$ at one site, and ordered as $rem(x)$, $add(x)$, $add(y)$ at another site. Both reach the final state containing just y with count 1. Note that removing element x from an empty cset results in -1 copies of element x, which is an *anti-element*: later addition of x to the cset results in the empty cset.

3. PARALLEL SNAPSHOT ISOLATION

In this section, we precisely specify PSI—the guarantee provided by Walter—and we discuss its properties and implications. We start by reviewing snapshot isolation and explaining the framework that we use to specify properties (Section 3.1). Then, we give the exact specification of PSI and discuss its properties (Section 3.2). We next explain how to extend PSI to include set operations (Section 3.3). We then explain how developers can use PSI (Section 3.4) and csets (Section 3.5) to build their applications.

3.1 Snapshot isolation

We specify snapshot isolation by giving an abstract specification code that an implementation must emulate. The specification code is centralized to make it as simple as possible, whereas an implementation can be distributed, complex, and more efficient. An implementation code satisfies the specification code if both codes produce the same output given the same input (e.g., [32]). The input

```
operation startTx(x)
    x.startTs ← new monotonic timestamp
    return OK

operation write(x, oid, data)
    append ⟨oid, DATA(data)⟩ to x.updates
    return OK

operation read(x, oid)
    return state of oid from x.updates and Log up to timestamp x.startTs

operation commitTx(x)
    x.commitTs ← new monotonic timestamp
    x.status ← chooseOutcome(x)
    if x.status = COMMITTED
    then append x.updates to Log with timestamp x.commitTs
    return x.status
```

Figure 1: Specification of snapshot isolation.

```
function chooseOutcome(x)
    if some write-conflicting transaction has committed after x started
    then return ABORTED
    else if some write-conflicting transaction has aborted after x started
        or is currently executing
    then return (either ABORTED or COMMITTED)    // non-deterministic choice
    else return COMMITTED
```

Figure 2: Transaction outcome in snapshot isolation.

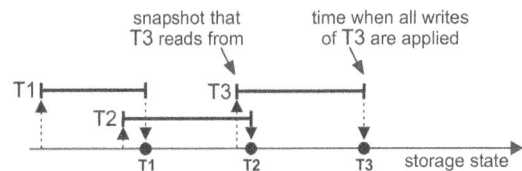

Figure 3: Depiction of snapshot isolation. The writes of T_1 are seen by T_3 but not T_2 as T_2 reads from a snapshot prior to T_1's commit.

is given by calls to operations to start a transaction, read or write data, commit a transaction, etc. The output is the return value of these operations. Many clients may call the operations of the specification concurrently, resulting possibly in many outstanding calls; however, the body of each operation is executed one at a time, using a single thread.

The specification is given in Figures 1 and 2 and depicted in Figure 3. It is assumed that clients start a transaction x with x initially $\bot$, then perform a sequence of reads and/or writes, and then try to commit the transaction. The behavior is unspecified if any client fails to follow this discipline, say by writing to a transaction that was never started. To start transaction x, the code obtains a new monotonically increasing timestamp, called the *start timestamp* of x. The timestamp is stored as an attribute of x; in the code, x is passed by reference. To write an object in transaction x, the code stores the object id and data in a temporary update buffer. To read an object, the code uses the update buffer—to check for any updates to the object written by the transaction itself—as well as a snapshot of the state when the transaction began. To determine the snapshot, the code maintains a *Log* variable with a sequence of object ids, data, and timestamps for the writes of previously-committed transactions. Only committed transactions are in the log, not outstanding ones. A read of an object reflects the updates in *Log* up to the transaction's start timestamp. To commit transaction x, the code obtains a new monotonically increasing timestamp, called the *commit timestamp* of x. It then determines the outcome of a transaction according to the function in Figure 2. This function indicates the cases when the outcome is abort, commit, or either one chosen nonde-terministically.[1] The code considers what happens after x started: if some write-conflicting transaction committed then the outcome is abort, where a *write-conflicting transaction* is one that writes an object that x also writes. Otherwise if some write-conflicting trans-action has aborted or is currently executing—meaning it has started but its outcome has not been chosen—then the outcome is either abort or commit, chosen nondeterministically. Otherwise, the out-come is commit. If the outcome is commit, the writes of x are appended to *Log* with x's commit timestamp.

Note that the specification keeps internal variables—such as the log, timestamps, and other attributes of a transaction—but an im-plementation need not have these variables. It needs to emulate only the return values of each operation.

The above specification of snapshot isolation implies that any implementation must satisfy two key properties [51, Page 362]:

SI PROPERTY 1. *(Snapshot Read) All operations read the most recent committed version as of the time when the transaction began.*

SI PROPERTY 2. *(No Write-Write Conflicts) The write sets of each pair of committed concurrent transactions must be disjoint.*

Here, we say that two committed transactions are *concurrent* if one of them has a commit timestamp between the start and commit timestamp of the other.

Snapshot isolation is inadequate for a system replicated at many sites, due to two issues. First, to define snapshots, snapshot iso-lation imposes a total ordering of the commit time of all transac-tions, even those that do not conflict[2]. Establishing such an ordering when transactions execute at different sites is inefficient. Second, the writes of a committed transaction must be immediately visible to later transactions. Therefore a transaction can commit only after its writes have been propagated to all remote replicas, thereby pre-cluding asynchronous propagation of its updates.[3] We define PSI to address these problems.

3.2 Specification of PSI

We define PSI as a relaxation of snapshot isolation so that trans-actions can propagate asynchronously and be ordered differently across sites. Note that the PSI specification does not refer to pre-ferred sites, since they are relevant only to the implementation of PSI. The specification code is given in Figures 4 and 5 and de-picted in Figure 6. As before, the specification is abstract and centralized—there is a single thread that executes the code with-out interleaving—but we expect that implementations will be dis-tributed. Each transaction x has a site attribute denoted $site(x)$. There is a log per site, kept in a vector *Log* indexed by sites. A transaction has one commit timestamp per site. A transaction first commits locally, by writing its updates to the log at its site; sub-sequently, the transaction propagates to and commits at the remote sites. This propagation is performed by the **upon** statement which, at some non-deterministic time, picks a committed transaction x and a site s to which x has not been propagated yet, and then writes the updates of x to the log at s. (For the moment, we ignore the second line of the upon statement in the code.) As Figure 5 shows,

---

[1]Nondeterminism in specifications allows implementations to have either behavior.

[2]For example, suppose $A=B=0$ initially and transaction T_1 writes $A \leftarrow 1$, transac-tion T_2 writes $B \leftarrow 1$, and both commit concurrently. Then T_1 and T_2 do not conflict and can be ordered arbitrarily, so either $(A=1, B=0)$ or $(A=0, B=1)$ are valid snapshots for transactions to read. However, it is illegal for both snapshots to occur, because snapshot isolation either orders T_1 before T_2 or vice versa.

[3]A variant called weak snapshot isolation [15] allows a transaction to remain invisible to others even after it commits, but that does not address the first issue above.

```
operation startTx(x)
   x.startTs ← new monotonic timestamp
   return OK

operation write(x, oid, data)
   append ⟨oid, DATA(data)⟩ to x.updates
   return OK

operation read(x, oid)
   return state of oid from x.updates and Log[site(x)] up to timestamp x.startTs

operation commitTx(x)
   x.commitTs[site(x)] ← new monotonic timestamp
   x.status ← chooseOutcome(x)
   if x.outcome = COMMITTED
      append x.updates to Log[site(x)] with timestamp x.commitTs[site(x)]
   return x.status

upon [∃x, s: x.status = COMMITTED and x.commitTs[s] = ⊥ and
        ∀y such that y.commitTs[site(x)] < x.startTs : y.commitTs[s] ≠ ⊥]
   x.commitTs[s] ← new monotonic timestamp
   append x.updates to Log[s] with timestamp x.commitTs[s]
```

Figure 4: Specification of PSI.

```
function chooseOutcome(x)
   if some write-conflicting transaction has committed at site(x) after x started
      or is currently propagating to site(x)   // text has definition of "propagating"
   then return ABORTED
   else if some write-conflicting transaction has aborted after x started
           or is currently executing
   then return (either ABORTED or COMMITTED)
   else return COMMITTED
```

Figure 5: Transaction outcome in PSI.

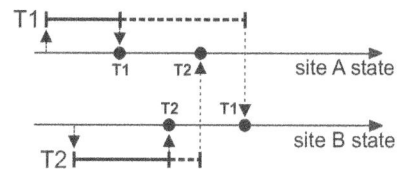

Figure 6: PSI allows a transaction to have different commit times at different sites. At site A, committed transactions are ordered as T1, T2. Site B orders them differently as T2, T1.

a transaction is aborted if there is some write-conflicting transac-tion that has committed at $site(x)$ after x started or that is currently *propagating* to $site(x)$; a transaction y is propagating to a site s if its status is committed but it has not yet committed at site s—that is, $y.status$=COMMITTED and $y.commitTs[s]$=⊥. Otherwise, if there is some concurrent write-conflicting transaction that has not committed, the outcome can be abort or commit. Otherwise, the outcome is commit. The outcome of a transaction is decided only once: if it commits at its site, the transaction is not aborted at the other sites. In Section 5.7, we discuss what to do when a site fails.

The above specification contains code that may be expensive to implement directly, such as monotonic timestamps and checks for write conflicts of transactions in different sites. We later give a distributed implementation that can avoid these inefficiencies.

From the specification, it can be seen that PSI replaces property 1 of snapshot isolation with the following:

PSI PROPERTY 1. *(Site Snapshot Read) All operations read the most recent committed version at the transaction's site as of the time when the transaction began.*

Intuitively, a transaction reads from a snapshot established at its site. In addition, PSI essentially preserves property 2 of snapshot

```
operation setAdd(x, setid, id)
    append ⟨setid, ADD(id)⟩ to x.updates
    return OK

operation setDel(x, setid, id)
    append ⟨setid, DEL(id)⟩ to x.updates
    return OK

operation setRead(x, setid)
    return state of setid from x.updates and Log[site(x)] up to timestamp x.startTs
```

Figure 7: Set operations in PSI specification.

isolation. To state the exact property, we say two transactions T_1 and T_2 are *concurrent at site s* if one of them has a commit timestamp at s between the start and commit timestamp of the other at s. We say the transactions are *somewhere-concurrent* if they are concurrent at $site(T_1)$ or at $site(T_2)$.

PSI PROPERTY 2. *(No Write-Write Conflicts) The write sets of each pair of committed somewhere-concurrent transactions must be disjoint.*

This property prevents the lost update anomaly (Section 3.4). The specification of PSI also ensures causal ordering:

PSI PROPERTY 3. *(Commit Causality Across Sites) If a transaction T_1 commits at a site A before a transaction T_2 starts at site A, then T_1 cannot commit after T_2 at any site.*

This property is ensured by the second line of the **upon** statement in Figure 4: x can propagate to a site s only if all transactions that committed at x's site before x started have already propagated to s. The property prevents a transaction x from committing before y at a remote site when x has observed the updates of y. The property also implies that write-conflicting transactions are committed in the same order at all sites, to prevent the state at different sites from diverging permanently.

3.3 PSI with cset objects

In the specification of PSI in Section 3.2, transactions operate on objects via read and write operations, but it is possible to extend the specification to support objects with other operations. We give the extension for cset objects, but this extension should apply to any object with commutative operations. To add an element to a cset, the code appends an entry ⟨setid, ADD, id⟩ to the transaction's update buffer (x.updates) and, on commit, appends this entry to the log. Similarly, to remove an element from a cset, the code appends entry ⟨setid, DEL, id⟩. To read a cset, the code computes the state of the cset: for each element, it sums the number of ADD minus the number of DEL in the log and the update buffer, thus obtaining a count for each element. Only elements with a non-zero count are returned by the read operation. Because the operations to add and remove elements in a cset commute, these operations do not cause a write conflict. Note that a cset object does not support a write operation since it does not commute with ADD. Figure 7 shows the code of the specification.

A cset may have many elements, and reading the entire cset could return large amounts of data. It is easy to extend the specification with an operation *setReadId* to return the count of a chosen element on a cset, by simply computing the state of the cset (using the log) to extract the count of that element.

3.4 Using PSI

One way to understand an isolation property is to understand what type of anomalous behavior it allows, so that developers know

Anomaly	Serializability	Snapshot Isolation	PSI	Eventual Consistency
Dirty read	No	No	No	Yes
Non-repeatable read	No	No	No	Yes
Lost update	No	No	No	Yes
Short fork	No	Yes	Yes	Yes
Long fork	No	No	Yes	Yes
Conflicting fork	No	No	No	Yes

Dirty read. A transaction reads the update made by another transaction that has not yet committed; the other transaction may later abort or rewrite the object, making the data read by the first transaction invalid. *Example.* Initially $A=0$. T_1 writes $A\leftarrow1$ and $A\leftarrow2$ and commits; concurrently, T_2 reads $A=1$.
Non-repeatable read. A transaction reads the same object twice—once before and once after another transaction commits an update to it—obtaining different results. *Example.* Initially $A=0$. T_1 writes $A\leftarrow1$ and commits; concurrently T_2 reads $A=0$ and then reads $A=1$.
Lost update. Transactions make concurrent updates to some common object, causing one transaction to lose its updates. *Example.* Initially $A=0$. T_1 reads $A=0$, writes $A\leftarrow1$, and commits. Concurrently, T_2 reads $A=0$, writes $A\leftarrow2$, and commits.
Short fork. Transactions make concurrent disjoint updates causing the state to fork. After committing, the state is merged back. *Example.* Initially $A=B=0$. T_1 reads $A=B=0$, writes $A\leftarrow1$, and commits. Concurrently, T_2 reads $A=B=0$, writes $B\leftarrow1$, and commits. Subsequently, T_3 reads $A=B=1$.

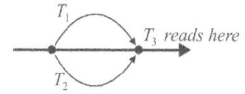

Long fork. Transactions make concurrent disjoint updates causing the state to fork. After they commit, the state may remain forked but it is later merged back. *Example.* Initially $A=B=0$. T_1 reads $A=B=0$, writes $A\leftarrow1$, and commits; then T_2 reads $A=1$, $B=0$. T_3 and T_4 execute concurrently with T_1 and T_2, as follows. T_3 reads $A=B=0$, writes $B\leftarrow1$, and commits; then T_4 reads $A=0$, $B=1$. Finally, after $T_1, \ldots, T_4$ finish, T_5 reads $A=B=1$.

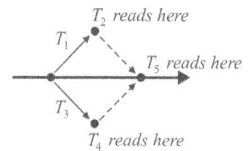

Conflicting fork. Transactions make concurrent conflicting updates causing the state to fork in a way that requires application-specific or ad-hoc rules to merge back. *Example.* Initially $A=0$. T_1 writes $A\leftarrow1$ and commits. Concurrently, T_2 writes $A\leftarrow2$ and commits. Some external logic determines that the value of A should be 3, and subsequently T_3 reads $A=3$.

Figure 8: Anomalies allowed by each isolation property.

what to expect. In this section, we consider PSI from that standpoint, and we compare it against snapshot isolation and serializability. It is well-known that the weaker a property is, the more anomalous behaviors it has, but at the same time, the more efficiently it can be implemented. The anomalies allowed by PSI can be seen as the price to pay for allowing asynchronous replication.

Figure 8 shows various anomalies and whether each isolation property has those anomalies. Eventual consistency is very weak and allows all anomalies. The first three anomalies are well-known (e.g., [24]). Snapshot isolation and PSI prevent dirty and non-repeatable reads, because a transaction reads from a snapshot, and they prevent lost updates because there are no write-write conflicts. Snapshot isolation allows the state to fork, because two or more transactions may read from the same snapshot and make concurrent updates to different objects. We call this a *short fork*, also known as *write skew*, because the state merges after transactions commit. With PSI, the state may remain forked after transactions commit (when they execute in different sites), but the state is later merged when the transactions propagate across sites. Due to its longer duration, we call this a *long fork*. A *conflicting fork* occurs when the states diverges due to conflicting updates, which is not allowed by PSI.

Long forks are acceptable in web applications when users in a site do not expect their updates to be instantly visible across all sites. If the user wants to know that her updates are visible everywhere, she can wait for her transaction to commit at all sites. In some cases, the fork may be noticeable to users: say, Alice posts a message on her social network wall saying that she is the first to flag a new promotion; she then confirms her statement by reading her friend's walls and seeing nothing there. With a long fork, Bob could be simultaneously doing the same thing from a different site, so that both Alice and Bob believe they posted their message first. One way to avoid possible confusion among users is for the application to show an "in-flight" mark on a freshly posted message; this mark is removed only when the message has been committed at all sites. Then, when Alice sees the mark, she can understand that her in-flight message may not yet be visible to all her friends.

Having discussed the anomalies of PSI, we now discuss ways that an application can use and benefit from PSI.

Multi-object atomic updates. With PSI, updates of a transaction occur together, so an application can use a transaction to modify many objects without exposing partial updates on each object.

Snapshots. With PSI, a transaction reads from a fixed consistent snapshot, so an application can use a transaction to ensure that it is reading consistent versions of different objects.

Read-modify-write operations. Because PSI disallows write-write conflicts, a transaction can implement any atomic read-modify-write operation, which reads an object and writes a new value based on the value read. Such operations include atomic increment and decrement of counters, atomic appends, and atomic edits.

Conditional writes. A particularly useful type of read-modify-write operation is a conditional write, which writes an object only if its content or version matches a value provided by the application. With PSI, this is performed by reading the object, evaluating the condition and, if it is satisfied, writing the object. This scheme can be extended to check and write many objects at once.

3.5 Using cset operations

A cset is a mapping from ids to counts, possibly negative. The mapping indicates how many times the element with a given id appears in the cset. There are two ways to use csets. First, when the count is useful to the application, a cset can be used as is. For example, a cset can keep the number of items in a shopping cart or inventory, the number of accesses to a data item, or the number of references to an object.

The second way to use a cset is as a conventional set, by hiding the counts from the user. For example, a cset can keep a list of friends, messages, active users, or photo albums. In these cases, the count has no meaning to the user. The application should be designed to keep the counts of elements at zero or one: the application should not add an element to a cset when the element is already present, or remove an element from a cset when the element is not there. In some cases, however, concurrent updates may cause the count to raise above one or drop below zero. For example, a user may add the same friend to her friends list, and do so concurrently at two different sites: the application sees a count of zero in both sites, and so it adds the friend once at each site. This situation is rare, because there must be updates to the *same* element in the *same* cset, and those updates must be concurrent, but it may happen. This

is addressed by treating a count of one or more as present in the set, and count of zero or less as absent from the set. For example, when showing the list to the user, friends with negative counts are excluded. When the user adds a friend, if the count is negative, the application adds the friend enough times for the count to be one. When removing a friend, the application removes her enough times for the count to be zero. This is done by the application, transparently to the user.

4. SERVICE

This section describes how clients view and use Walter. Each site contains a Walter server and one or more application clients. Walter stores key-value object pairs grouped in containers (Section 4.1), where each container is replicated across multiple sites. The Walter client interface is exposed as a user-level library with functions to start transactions, read and write data, and commit transactions (Section 4.2). Walter provides fault tolerance by replicating data across sites (Section 4.3), and it allows users to trade-off durability for availability (Section 4.4).

4.1 Objects and containers

Walter stores objects, where an object has a key and a value. There are two types of objects: regular and cset. In a regular object, the value is an uninterpreted byte sequence, while in cset object, the value is a cset.

Each object is stored in a *container*, a logical organization unit that groups objects with some common purpose. For example, in a Web application, each user could have a container that holds all of her objects. To reduce space overhead, all objects in a container have the same preferred site, and Walter stores this information only once, as an attribute of the container. Administrators choose the preferred site to be the site most likely to modify the objects. For example, each user may have a designated site where she logs into the system (if she tries to log into a different site, she is redirected), and this would be the preferred site of her objects.

Object ids consist of a container id and a local id. The container id indicates to which container the object belongs, and the local id differentiates objects within a container. Since the container id is part of the object id, the container of an object cannot be changed.

4.2 Interface

Walter provides a client library for starting a transaction, manipulating objects, and committing a transaction, with the PSI semantics and operations explained in Sections 3.2 and 3.3. For regular objects, the available operations are read and write; for cset objects, the available operations are read, add element, and delete element.

Walter replicates transactions asynchronously, and the interface allows a client to receive a callback when (a) the transaction is disaster-safe durable (Section 4.4), and (b) the transaction is globally visible, meaning it has been committed at all sites.

4.3 Replication

Walter provides both durability and availability by replicating data within a single site and across multiple sites. Replication is transparent to clients: all the replicas of an object have the same object id, and the system accesses the replica closest to the client. An object need not be replicated at all sites and clients can read objects even if they are not replicated at the local site, in which case Walter fetches the data from a remote site.[4] A transaction commits

---

[4]In the PSI specification, data is replicated at every site, but an implementation need not do that, as long as it behaves identically in terms of responses to operations.

at every site, even where it is not replicated, following the semantics of PSI in Section 3.2: once a transaction is committed at a site, reads from that site see the effects of the transaction. Administrators choose how many replicas and where they are. These settings are stored as attributes of a container, so all objects of a container are replicated similarly.

4.4 Durability and availability

Walter provides two levels of durability:

(Normal Durability) When a transaction commits at its site, writes have been logged to a replicated cluster storage system [21, 28, 40, 48], so writes are not lost due to power failures. Data may be lost if an entire data center is wiped out by a disaster.

(Disaster-safe Durability) A transaction is considered *disaster-safe durable* if its writes have been logged at $f+1$ sites, where parameter f determines the desired fault tolerance level: up to f sites may fail without causing data loss. The default value of f is 1.

If an entire site s fails temporarily or is unreachable due to cross-site network issues, it may have transactions that were locally committed but not yet propagated to other sites. In that case, the application has two choices:

(Conservative) Wait for the site s to come back online, so that it can propagate the missing transactions. But then clients cannot write to objects whose preferred site is s until s comes back online—a loss of availability for some writes.

(Aggressive) Sacrifice the durability of a few committed transactions at site s for better availability, by replacing site s and abandoning its non-propagated transactions. Technically, this choice violates PSI, but one could extend the PSI definition to allow for lost committed transactions when a site fails or disconnects. Applications can wait for important transactions to be marked disaster-safe durable before confirming them to users.

Availability within a site comes from the availability of the cluster storage system: if the Walter server at a site fails, the system starts a new server, which can access the same cluster storage system. Availability under network partitions or disasters comes from cross-site replication. If a site fails, an application can warn users before they are redirected to another site, because users may see a different system state at the new site due to the semantics of PSI. In practice, the state at different sites diverges by only a few seconds.

5. DESIGN AND ALGORITHMS

This section describes Walter's design, emphasizing the protocols for executing and committing transactions. We first give an overview of the basic architecture (Section 5.1) and object versioning (Section 5.2). We then explain how to execute transactions (Section 5.3) and how to commit certain common transactions quickly (Section 5.4). Next, we explain how to commit other transactions (Section 5.5) and how transactions are replicated asynchronously (Section 5.6). Lastly, we consider failure recovery (Section 5.7) and scalability (Section 5.8).

5.1 Basic architecture

There are multiple sites numbered $1, 2, \ldots$ Each site contains a local Walter server and a set of clients. A client communicates with the server via remote procedure calls implemented by the API library. The server executes the actual operations to start and commit transactions, and to access objects.

Walter employs a separate *configuration service* to keep track of the currently active sites, and the preferred site and replica set

At *Server$_i$*: // i denotes the site number
CurrSeqNo$_i$: integer with last assigned local sequence number
CommittedVTS$_i$: vector indicating for each site how many transactions of that site have been committed at site i
History$_i$[oid]: a sequence of updates of the form $\langle data, version \rangle$ to *oid*, where *version* $= \langle j{:}n \rangle$ for some j, n
GotVTS$_i$: vector indicating for each site how many transactions of that site have been received by site i

Figure 9: Variables at server on each site.

for each object container. The configuration service tolerates failures by running as a Paxos-based state machine replicated across multiple sites. A Walter server confirms its role in the system by obtaining a lease from the configuration service, similar to what is done in [12, 46]. The lease assigns a set of containers to a preferred site, and it is held by the Walter server at that site. A Walter server caches the mapping from a container to its replica sites to avoid contacting the configuration service at each access. Incorrect cache entries do not affect correctness because a server rejects requests for which it does not hold the corresponding preferred site lease.

5.2 Versions and vector timestamps

The PSI specification is centralized and uses a monotonic timestamp when a transaction starts and commits. But monotonic timestamps are expensive to produce across multiple sites. Thus, to implement PSI, Walter replaces them with version numbers and vector timestamps. A version number (or simply *version*) is a pair $\langle site, seqno \rangle$ assigned to a transaction when it commits; it has the site where the transaction executed, and a sequence number local to that site. The sequence number orders all transactions within a site. A vector timestamp represents a snapshot; it contains a sequence number for each site, indicating how many transactions of that site are reflected in the snapshot. A transaction is assigned a vector timestamp *startVTS* when it starts. For example, if *startVTS* $= \langle 2, 4, 5 \rangle$ then the transaction reads from the snapshot containing 2 transactions from site 1, 4 from site 2, and 5 from site 3.

Given a version $v = \langle site, seqno \rangle$ and a vector timestamp *startVTS*, we say that v is *visible* to *startVTS* if $seqno \leq startVTS[site]$. Intuitively, the snapshot of *startVTS* has enough transactions from *site* to incorporate version v.

Figure 9 shows the variables at the server at site i. Variable *CurrSeqNo$_i$* has the last sequence number assigned by the server, and *CommittedVTS$_i$[j]* has the sequence number of the last transaction from each site j that was committed at site i. We discuss *History$_i$* and *GotVTS$_i$* in Sections 5.3 and 5.6.

5.3 Executing transactions

To execute transactions, the server at each site i maintains a history denoted *History$_i$[oid]* with a sequence of writes/updates for each object *oid*, where each update is tagged with the version of the responsible transaction. This history variable is similar to variable *Log* in the PSI specification, except that it keeps a list per object, and it has versions not timestamps. When a transaction x starts, Walter obtains a new start vector timestamp *startVTS* containing the sequence number of the latest transactions from each site that were committed at the local site. To write an object, add to a cset, or remove from a cset, Walter stores this update in a temporary buffer *x.updates*. To read an object, Walter retrieves its state from the snapshot determined by *startVTS* and any updates in *x.updates*. Specifically, for a regular object, Walter returns the last update in *x.updates* or, if none, the last update in the history visible to *startVTS*. For a cset object, Walter computes its state by

```
At Server_i:                                    // i denotes the site number
operation startTx(x)
    x.tid ← unique transaction id
    x.startVTS ← CommittedVTS_i
    return OK

operation write(x, oid, data): add ⟨oid, DATA(data)⟩ to x.updates; return OK
operation setAdd(x, setid, id): add ⟨setid, ADD(id)⟩ to x.updates; return OK
operation setDel(x, setid, id): add ⟨setid, DEL(id)⟩ to x.updates; return OK

operation read(x, oid)
    if oid is locally replicated
    then return state of oid reflecting x.updates and
        all versions in History_i[oid] visible to x.startVTS
    else return state of oid reflecting x.updates,
        the versions in History_site(oid)[oid] visible to x.startVTS, and
        the versions in History_i[oid] visible to x.startVTS

operation setRead(x, setid): same as read(x, oid)
```

Figure 10: Executing transactions.

```
At Server_i:                                    // i denotes the site number
function unmodified(oid, VTS): true if oid unmodified since VTS
function update(updates, version)
    for each ⟨oid, X⟩ ∈ updates do add ⟨X, version⟩ to History_i[oid]

operation commitTx(x)
    x.writeset ← { oid : ⟨oid, DATA(*)⟩ ∈ x.updates }       // * is a wildcard
    if ∀oid ∈ x.writeset : site(oid) = i then return fastCommit(x)
    else return slowCommit(x)

function fastCommit(x)
  | if ∀oid ∈ x.writeset : unmodified(oid, startVTS) and oid not locked then
  |     x.seqno ← ++CurrSeqNo_i           // vertical bar indicates atomic region
  |     update(x.updates, ⟨i, x.seqno⟩)
  |     wait until CommittedVTS_i[i] = x.seqno−1
  |     CommittedVTS_i[i] ← x.seqno
  |     x.outcome ← COMMITTED
  |     fork propagate(x)
    else x.outcome ← ABORTED
    return x.outcome
```

Figure 11: Fast commit.

applying the updates in the history visible to *startVTS* and the updates in $x.updates$.

The above explanation assumes an object is replicated locally. If not, its local history $History_i[oid]$ will not have all of the object's updates (but it may have some recent updates). Therefore, to read such an object, Walter retrieves the data from the object's preferred site and merges it with any updates in the local history and in $x.updates$. To write, Walter buffers the write in $x.updates$ and, upon commit, stores the update in the local history while it is being replicated to other sites; after that, the local history can be garbage collected. Figure 10 shows the detailed pseudocode executed by a server. Recall that clients invoke the operations at the local server using a remote procedure call (not shown). The code is multi-threaded and we assume that each line is executed atomically.

5.4 Fast commit

For transactions whose write-set has only objects with a local preferred site, Walter uses a fast commit protocol. The write-set of a transaction consists of all oids to which the transaction writes; it excludes updates to set objects. To fast commit a transaction x, Walter first determines if x can really commit. This involves two checks for conflicts. The first check is whether all objects in the write-set are unmodified since the transaction started. To perform this check, Walter uses the start vector timestamp: specifically, we say that an object oid is *unmodified since $x.startVTS$* if all versions of oid in the

```
At Server_i:                                    // i denotes the site number
function slowCommit(x)
    // run 2pc among preferred sites of updated objects
    sites ← {site(oid) : oid ∈ x.writeset}
    pfor each s ∈ sites do                      // pfor is a parallel for
        vote[s] ← remote call prepare(x.tid,
            {oid ∈ x.writeset : site(oid) = s}, x.startVTS)
    if ∀s ∈ sites : vote[s] = YES then
  |     x.seqno ← ++CurrSeqNo_i           // vertical bar indicates atomic region
  |     update(x.updates, ⟨i, x.seqno⟩)
  |     wait until CommittedVTS_i[i] = x.seqno − 1
  |     CommittedVTS_i[i] ← x.seqno
  |     release locks (at this server) with owner x.tid
  |     x.outcome ← COMMITTED
  |     fork propagate(x)
    else
        pfor each s ∈ sites such that vote[s] = YES do remote call abort(x.tid)
        x.outcome ← ABORTED
    return x.outcome

function prepare(tid, localWriteset, startVTS)
  | if ∀oid ∈ localWriteset : oid not locked and unmodified(oid, startVTS) then
  |     for each oid ∈ localWriteset do lock oid with owner tid
  |     return YES
    else return NO

function abort(tid)
    release locks (at this server) with owner tid
```

Figure 12: Slow commit.

history of the local site are visible to $x.startVTS$. The second check is whether all objects in the write-set of x are unlocked; intuitively, a locked object is one being committed by the slow commit protocol (Section 5.5). If either check fails, then x is aborted. Otherwise, Walter proceeds to commit x, as follows. It assigns a new local sequence number to x, and then applies x's updates to the histories of the modified objects. Walter then waits until the local transaction with preceding sequence number has been committed. This typically happens quickly, since sequence numbers are assigned in commit order. Finally, transaction x is marked as committed and Walter propagates x to remote sites asynchronously as described in Section 5.6. Figure 11 shows the detailed pseudocode. The notation $site(oid)$ denotes the preferred site of oid. As before, we assume that each line is executed atomically. A vertical bar indicates a block of code with multiple lines that is executed atomically.

5.5 Slow commit

Transactions that write a regular object whose preferred site is not local must be committed using the slow commit protocol, which employs a type of two-phase commit among the preferred sites of the written objects (not across all replicas of the objects). The purpose of two-phase commit is to avoid conflicts with instances of fast commit and other instances of slow commit. To commit a transaction x, the server at the site of the transaction acts as the coordinator in the two-phase protocol. In the first phase, the coordinator asks the (servers at the) preferred sites of each written object to vote based on whether those objects are unmodified and unlocked. If an object is modified at the preferred site, then an instance of fast commit conflicts with x; if the object is locked at the preferred site, then another instance of slow commit conflicts with x. If either case occurs, the site votes "no", otherwise the site locks the objects and votes "yes". If any vote is "no", the coordinator tells the sites to release the previously acquired locks. Otherwise, the coordinator proceeds to commit x as in the fast commit protocol: it assigns a sequence number to x, applies x's updates to the object histories, marks x as committed, and propagates x asynchronously. When x

```
At Server_i:                                    // i denotes the site number
function propagate(x)
  send ⟨PROPAGATE, x⟩ to all servers
  wait until ∀oid∈x.writeset: received ⟨PROPAGATE-ACK, x.tid⟩
       from f+1 sites replicating oid including site(oid)
  mark x as disaster-safe durable
  send ⟨DS-DURABLE, x⟩ to all servers
  wait until received ⟨VISIBLE, x.tid⟩ from all sites
  mark x as globally visible

when received ⟨PROPAGATE, x⟩ from Server_j and
     GotVTS_i ≥ x.startVTS and GotVTS_i[j] = x.seqno−1 do
  if i ≠ j then update(items in x.updates replicated in this site, ⟨j : x.seqno⟩)
  // when i = j, update has been applied already when transaction committed
  GotVTS_i[j] = x.seqno
  send ⟨PROPAGATE-ACK, x.tid⟩ to Server_j

when received ⟨DS-DURABLE, x⟩ and ⟨PROPAGATE, x⟩ from Server_j and
     CommittedVTS_i ≥ x.startVTS and CommittedVTS_i[j] = x.seqno−1 do
  CommittedVTS_i[j] ← x.seqno
  release all locks with owner x.tid
  send ⟨VISIBLE, x.tid⟩ to Server_j
```

Figure 13: Transaction replication.

commits, a site releases the acquired locks when x is propagated to it. Figure 12 shows the detailed pseudocode.

5.6 Asynchronous propagation

After a transaction commits, it is propagated asynchronously to other sites. The propagation protocol is simple: the site of a transaction x first copies the objects modified by x to the sites where they are replicated. The site then waits until *sufficiently many sites* indicate that they received (a) transaction x, (b) all transactions that causally precede x according to $x.startVTS$, and (c) all transactions of x's site with a smaller sequence number. "Sufficiently many sites" means at least $f+1$ sites replicating each object including the object's preferred site, where f is the disaster-safe tolerance parameter (Section 4.4). At this point, x is marked as disaster-safe durable and all sites are notified. Transaction x commits at a remote site j when (a) site j learns that x is disaster-safe durable, (b) all transactions that causally precede x are committed at site j, and (c) all transactions of x's site with a smaller sequence number are committed at site j. When x has committed at all sites, it is marked as globally visible. The pseudocode is shown in Figure 13. Vector $GotVTS_i$ keeps track of how many transactions site i has received from each other site. Note that when a site i receives a remote transaction and updates the history of its objects, the transaction is not yet committed at i: it commits only when $CommittedVTS_i[j]$ is incremented. The code omits simple but important optimizations: when server i propagates transaction x to a remote server, it should not send all the updates of x, just those updates replicated at the remote server. Similarly, when it sends a DS-DURABLE message, a server need not include the updates of x again.

5.7 Handling failures

Recovering from client or server failure. If a client crashes, its outstanding transactions are aborted and any state kept for those transactions at the server is garbage collected. Each server at a site stores its transaction log in a replicated cluster storage system. When a Walter server fails, the replacement server resumes propagation for those committed transactions that have not yet been fully propagated.

Handling a site failure. An entire site s may fail due to a disaster or a power outage. Such failure is problematic because there may be committed transactions at s that were not yet replicated at other sites. As explained in Section 4.4, Walter offers two site recovery options: conservative and aggressive. Recall that the conservative option is to wait for s to come back online, while the aggressive option is to remove s and reassign the preferred site of its containers to another site. To remove a failed site, Walter uses the configuration service (Section 5.1). Each configuration indicates what sites are active. Before switching to a new configuration that excludes site s, the configuration service must find out the transactions committed by s that will survive across the configuration change. Transaction x of site s survives if x and all transactions that causally precede x and all transactions of s with a smaller sequence number have been copied to a site in the new configuration. The configuration service queries the sites in the new configuration to discover what transactions survive. Then, it asks each site to discard the replicated data of non-surviving transactions and, in the background, it completes the propagation of surviving transactions that are not yet fully replicated. Finally, the configuration service reassigns the preferred site of containers of s to another site, by having another site take over the appropriate leases. While reconfiguration is in progress, sites that are still active continue to commit transactions, except transactions that write to objects whose preferred site was s, which are postponed until those objects get a new preferred site.

Re-integrating a previously failed site. When a previously removed site s recovers, it must be re-integrated into the system. The configuration service starts a new reconfiguration that includes s. To switch to the new configuration, s must first synchronize with its replacement site s' to integrate modifications committed by s'. Once synchronization is finished, s takes over the lease for being the preferred site for the relevant containers, and the new configuration takes effect.

5.8 Scalability

Walter relies on a single server per site to execute and commit transactions, which can become a scalability bottleneck. A simple way to scale the system is to divide a data center into several "local sites", each with its own server, and then partition the objects across the local sites in the data center. This is possible because Walter supports partial replication *and* allows transactions to operate on an object not replicated at the site—in which case, the transaction accesses the object at another site within the same data center. We should note that PSI allows sites to diverge; to avoid exposing this divergence to users, applications can be designed so that a user always log into the same local site in the data center. Another approach to scalability, which we do not explore in this paper, is to employ several servers per site and replace the fast commit protocol of Section 5.4 with distributed commit.

6. IMPLEMENTATION

The Walter implementation has a client-side library and a server, written in C++, with a total of 30K lines of code. There is also a PHP interface for web development with 600 lines of code. The implementation differs from the design as follows. First, each Walter server uses direct-attached storage devices, instead of a cluster storage system. Second, we have not implemented the scheme to reintegrate a failed site (Section 5.7): currently, the administrator must invoke a script manually to do that. Third, the client interface, shown in Figure 14, differs cosmetically from the specification in Section 3.2, due to the specifics of C++ and PHP. In C++, there is a Transaction class and operations are methods of this class. Functions read, setRead, and setReadId return the data via a parameter (the C++ return value is a success indication). setRead provides an

Method	Description
void start()	start transaction
int commit()	try to commit
int abort()	abort
int read(Oid o, char **buf)	read object
int write(Oid o, char *buf, int len)	write object
Oid newid(ContainerId cid, OType otype)	get new oid
int setAdd(Oid cset, Id id)	add *id* to *cset*
int setDel(Oid cset, Id id)	delete *id* from *cset*
int setRead(Oid cset, IdSetIterator **iter)	read *cset*
int setReadId(Oid cset, Id id, int *answer)	read *id* in *cset*

```
C++ Example:
  Tx x;
  x.start();
  len = x.read(o1, &buf);
  err = x.write(o2, buf, len);
  ...
  res = x.commit();

PHP Example:
  $x = waStartTx();
  $buf = waRead($x, $o1);
  $err = waWrite($x, $o2, $buf);
  ...
  $res = waCommit($x);
```

Figure 14: Basic C++ API for Walter and C++ and PHP examples.

iterator for the ids in a cset. setReadId indicates the count of an identifier in a cset. commit can optionally inform the client via supplied callbacks—not shown—when the transaction is disaster-safe durable and globally visible (i.e., committed at all sites). There is a function newid to return a fresh oid, explained below.

There are no specialized functions to create or destroy objects. Conceptually, all objects always exist and are initialized to *nil*, without any space allocated to them. If a client reads a never-written object, it obtains *nil*. Function *newid* returns a unique oid of a never-written object of a chosen type (regular or cset) in a chosen container. Destroying a regular object corresponds to writing *nil* to it, while destroying a cset object corresponds to updating its elements so that they have zero count. There are some additional functions (not shown), including (a) management functions for initialization, shutdown, creating containers, and destroying containers; and (b) functions that combine multiple operations in a single RPC to the server, to gain performance; these include functions for reading or writing many objects, and for reading all objects whose ids are in a cset. The functions to create and destroy containers run outside a transaction; we expect them to be used relatively rarely. Identifiers for containers and objects are currently restricted to a fixed length, but it would be easy to make them variable-length.

The server stores object histories in a persistent log and maintains an in-memory cache of recently-used objects. The persistent log is periodically garbage collected to remove old entries. The entries in the in-memory cache are evicted on an LRU basis. Since it is expensive to reconstruct csets from the log, the eviction policy prefers to evict regular objects rather than csets. There is an in-memory index that keeps, for each object, a list of updates to the object, ordered from most to least recent, where each update includes a pointer to the data in the persistent log and a flag of whether the data is in the cache. To speed up system startup and recovery, Walter periodically checkpoints the index to persistent storage; the checkpoint also describes transactions that are being replicated. Checkpointing is done in the background, so it does not block transaction processing. When the server starts, it reconstructs the index from the checkpointed state and the data in the log after the checkpoint.

To improve disk efficiency, Walter employs group commit to flush many commit records to disk at the same time. To reduce the number of threads, the implementation makes extensive use of asynchronous calls and callbacks when it invokes blocking and slow operations. To enhance network efficiency, Walter propagates transactions in periodic batches, where each batch remotely copies all transactions that committed since the last batch.

```
Tx x;
x.start();
x.read(oidA, &profileA);
x.read(oidB, &profileB);
(* continues in next column *)

x.setAdd(profileA.friendlist, oidB);
x.setAdd(profileB.friendlist, oidA);
success = x.commit();
```

Figure 15: Transaction for *befriend* operation in WaltSocial.

The protocol for slow commit may starve because of repeated conflicting instances of fast commit. A simple solution to this problem is to mark objects that caused the abort of slow commit and briefly delay access to them in subsequent fast commits: this delay would allow the next attempt of slow commit to succeed. We have not implemented this mechanism since none of our applications use slow commit.

7. APPLICATIONS

Using Walter, we built a social networking web site (WaltSocial) and ported a third-party Twitter-like application called *ReTwis* [2]. Our experience suggests that it is easy to develop applications using Walter and run them across multiple data centers.

WaltSocial. WaltSocial is a complete implementation of a simple social networking service, supporting the common operations found in a system such as Facebook. These include *befriend, status-update, post-message, read-info* as well as others. In WaltSocial, each user has a profile object for storing personal information (e.g., name, email, hobbies) and several cset objects: a *friend-list* has oids of the profile objects of friends, a *message-list* has oids of received messages, an *event-list* has oids of events in the user's activity history, and an *album-list* has oids of photo albums, where each photo album is itself a cset with the oids of photo objects.

WaltSocial uses transactions to access objects and maintain data integrity. For example, when users A and B *befriend* each other, a transaction adds A's profile oid to B's friend-list and vice versa (Figure 15). To *post-message* from A to B, a transaction writes an object *m* with the message contents and adds its oid to B's message-list and to A's event-list.

Each user has a container that stores her objects. The container is replicated at all sites to optimize for reads. The system directs a user to log into the preferred site of her container. User actions are confirmed when transactions commit locally.

ReTwis. ReTwis is a Twitter-clone written in PHP using the Redis key-value store [1]. Apart from simple get/put operations, this application makes extensive use of Redis's native support for certain atomic operations, such as adding to or removing from a list, and adding or subtracting from an integer. In Redis, cross-site replication is based on a master-slave scheme. For our port of ReTwis, we replace Redis with Walter, so that ReTwis can update data on multiple sites. We use Walter transactions and csets to provide the equivalent atomic integer and list operation in Redis.

For each user, ReTwis has a timeline that tracks messages posted by the users that the user is following. In the original implementation, a user's timeline is stored in a Redis list. When a user posts a message, ReTwis performs an atomic increment on a sequence number to generate a postID, stores the message under the postID, and appends the postID to each of her followers' timelines. When a user checks postings, ReTwis displays the 10 most recent messages from her timeline. To port ReTwis to use Walter, we make several changes: we use a cset object to represent each user's timeline so that different sites can add posts to a user's timeline without conflicts. To post a message, we use a transaction that writes a message under a unique postID, and adds the postID to the timeline of every follower of the user.

We found the process of porting ReTwis to Walter to be quite simple and straightforward: a good programmer without previous Walter experience wrote the port in less than a day. Transactions allow the data structure manipulations built into Redis to be implemented by the application, while providing competitive performance (Section 8.7).

8. EVALUATION

We evaluate the performance of Walter and its applications (Walt-Social, ReTwis) using Amazon's EC2. The highlights of our results are the following:

- Transactions that modify objects at their preferred sites commit quickly, with a 99.9-percentile latency of 27ms on EC2. Committed transactions are asynchronously replicated to remote sites within twice the network round-trip latency.
- Transactions that modify csets outside of their preferred sites also commit quickly without cross-site coordination. Walt-Social uses csets extensively and processes user requests with a 99.9-percentile latency under 50ms.
- The overhead for supporting transactions in Walter is reasonable. ReTwis running on Walter has a throughput 25% smaller than running on Redis in a single site, but Walter allows ReTwis to scale to multiple sites.

8.1 Experimental setup

Unless stated otherwise, experiments run on Amazon's EC2 cloud platform. We use machines in four EC2 sites: Virginia (VA), California (CA), Ireland (IE), and Singapore (SG), with the following average round-trip latencies within and across sites (in ms):

	VA	CA	IE	SG
VA	0.5	82	87	261
CA		0.3	153	190
IE			0.5	277
SG				0.3

Within a site, the bandwidth between two hosts is over 600 Mbps; across sites, we found a bandwidth limit of 22 Mbps.

We use extra-large EC2 virtual machine instances, with 7 GB of RAM and 8 virtual cores, each equivalent to a 2.5 GHz Intel Xeon processor. Walter uses write-ahead logging, where commit logs are flushed to disk at commit time. Since one cannot disable write-caching at the disk on EC2, where indicated we run experiments on a private cluster outside of EC2, with machines with two quad core Intel Xeon E5520 2.27 GHz processors and 8 GB of RAM.

Each EC2 site has a Walter server, and we run experiments with different numbers of sites and replication levels, as shown below:

Experiment name	Sites	Replication level
1-site	VA	none
2-sites	VA, CA	2
3-sites	VA, CA, IE	3
4-sites	VA, CA, IE, SG	4

Our microbenchmark workload (Sections 8.2–8.5) consists of transactions that read or write a few randomly chosen 100-byte objects. (Changing the object size from 100 bytes to 1 KB yields similar results.) We choose to evaluate small transactions because our applications, WaltSocial and ReTwis, only access a few small objects in each transaction. We consider a transaction to be disaster-safe durable when it is committed at all sites in the experiment.

8.2 Base performance

We first evaluate the base performance of Walter, and compare it against Berkeley DB 11gR2 (BDB), a commercial open-source developer database library. The goal is to understand if Walter provides a usable base performance.

Benchmark setup. We configure BDB to use B-trees with default pagesize and snapshot isolation; parameters are chosen for the best performance. We configure BDB to have two replicas with asynchronous replication. Since BDB allows updates at only one replica (the primary), we set up the Walter experiment to also update at one site. To achieve good throughput in BDB, we must use many threads at the primary to achieve high concurrency. However, with many threads, EC2 machines perform noticeably worse than private machines. Therefore, we run the primary BDB replica in our private cluster (with write-caching at the disk enabled), and the other replica at the CA site of EC2. We do the same for Walter. Clients and the server run on separate hosts. For BDB, we use an RPC server to receive and execute client requests.

The workload consists of either read or write transactions each accessing one 100-byte object. We populate BDB and Walter with 50,000 keys, which fits in the 1 GB cache of both systems. Walter includes an optimization to reduce the number of RPCs, where the start and commit of each transaction are piggybacked onto the first and last access, respectively. Thus, transactions with one access require just one RPC in Walter and in BDB.

Results. Figure 16 shows that throughput of read and write transactions of Walter is comparable to that of BDB. Read throughput is CPU-bound and mainly limited by the performance of our RPC library in both systems. Walter's read throughput is slightly lower because it does more work than BDB by acquiring a local lock and assigning a start timestamp vector when a transaction starts. The commit and replication latency of BDB and Walter are also similar and not shown here (see Section 8.3 for Walter's latency).

8.3 Fast commit on regular objects

This microbenchmark evaluates the performance of transactions on regular objects, using fast commit.

Benchmark setup. The experiments involve one to four sites. Objects are replicated at all sites, and their preferred sites are assigned evenly across sites. At each site, we run multiple clients on different hosts to issue transactions as fast as possible to its local Walter server. There are several workloads: *read-only*, *write-only*, and *mixed*. Read-only or write-only transactions access one or five 100-byte objects. The mixed workload consists of 90% read-only transactions and 10% write-only transactions.

Result: throughput. Figure 17 shows Walter's aggregate throughput across sites as the number of sites varies. Read throughput is bounded by the RPC performance and scales linearly with the number of sites, reaching 157 Ktps (thousands of transactions per second) with 4 sites. Write throughput is lower than read throughput due to lock contention within a Walter server. Specifically, when a transaction commits, a thread needs to acquire a highly contended lock to check for transaction conflicts. Moreover, write throughput does not scale as well as read throughput as the number of

Name	Read Tx throughput	Write Tx throughput
Walter	72 Ktps	33.5 Ktps
Berkeley DB	80 Ktps	32 Ktps

Figure 16: Base read and write transaction throughput.

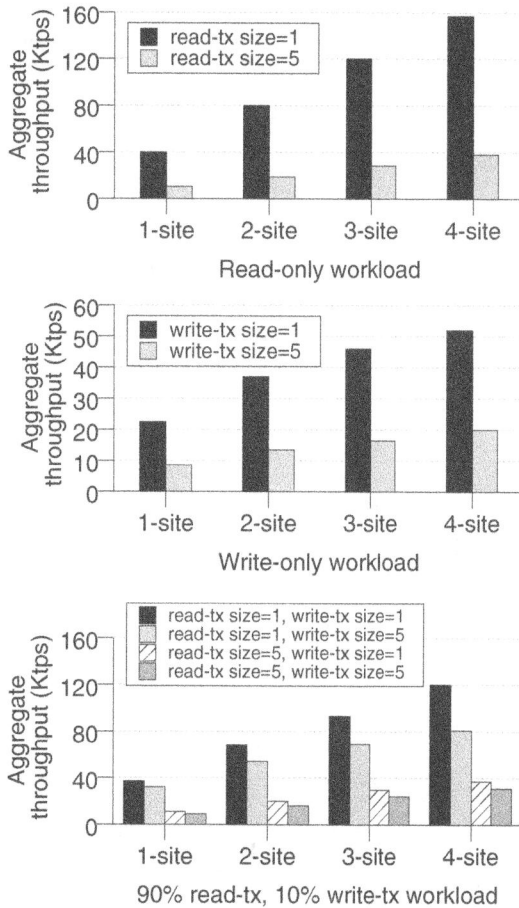

Figure 17: Aggregate transaction throughput on EC2.

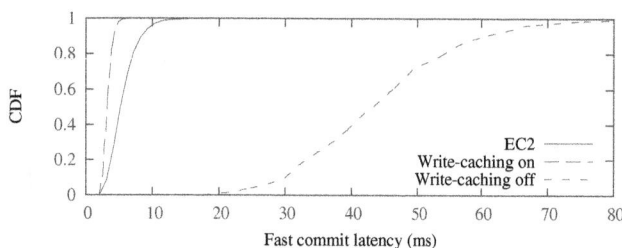

Figure 18: Fast commit latency on EC2 and our private cluster.

sites increases. This is because data is replicated at all sites, so the amount of work per write transaction grows with the number of sites. Yet, the cost of replication is lower than that of committing because replication is done in batches. Thus, the write throughput still grows with the number of sites, but not linearly. Note that the read and write throughput for transactions of size 1 in Figure 17 is only 50–60% of that in Figure 16 as a result of running this experiment on EC2 instead of the private cluster. In the mixed workload, performance is mostly determined by how many operations a transaction issues on average. For example, when there are 90% read-only transactions each reading one object and 10% write-only transactions each writing 5 objects, a transaction issues on average only 1.4 requests to the server. As a result, a relatively high aggregate throughput of 80 Ktps is reached across 4 sites.

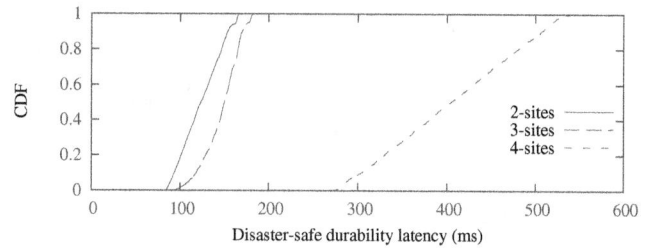

Figure 19: Replication latency for disaster-safe durability.

Result: latency. We measure the fast commit latency for write-only transactions accessing 5 objects. We record the time elapsed between issuing a commit and having the server acknowledge the commit completion. Figure 18 shows the latency distribution measured on EC2, and in our private cluster with and without write caching at the disk. The measurements were taken for a moderate workload in which clients issued enough requests to achieve 70% of maximal throughput. The points at the lower-end of the distributions in Figure 18 show latencies that we observe in a lightly loaded system.

Because there is no cross-site coordination, fast commit is quick: On EC2 the 99-percentile latency is 20 ms and the 99.9-percentile is 27 ms. Since the network latency within a site is low at 0.5 ms, the commit latency is dominated by the effects of queuing inside the Walter server and of flushing the commit log to disk when committing transactions at a high throughput. Figure 18 also shows the effect of disabling write-caching at the disk, measured on our private cluster. Even in that case, the 99.9-percentile latency of a fast commit is under 90 ms.

The latency for a committed transaction to become disaster-safe durable is dominated by the network latency across sites. As shown in Figure 19, the latency is distributed approximately uniformly between $[RTT_{max}, 2 * RTT_{max}]$ where RTT_{max} is the maximum round-trip latency between VA and the other three sites. This is because Walter propagates transactions in batches to maximize throughput, so a transaction must wait for the previous batch to finish.

The latency for a committed transaction to become globally visible is an additional RTT_{max} after it has become disaster-safe durable (not shown).

8.4 Fast commit on cset objects

We now evaluate transactions that modify csets.

Benchmark setup. We run the 4-site experiment in which each transaction modifies two 100-byte objects at the preferred site and adds an id to a cset with a remote preferred site.

Results. The latency distribution curve for committing transactions (not shown) is similar to the curve corresponding to EC2 in Figure 18. This is because transactions modifying csets commit via the same fast commit protocol as transactions modifying regular objects at their preferred site. Across 4 sites, the aggregate throughput is 26 Ktps, which is lower than the single-write transaction throughput of 52 Ktps shown in Figure 17. This is because the cset transactions issue 4 RPCs (instead of 1 RPC for the transactions in Figure 17), to write two objects, modify a cset, and commit.

8.5 Slow commit

We now evaluate the slow commit protocol for transactions modifying objects with different preferred sites. Unlike fast commit, slow commit requires cross-site coordination.

Benchmark setup. We run the 4-site experiments and have clients

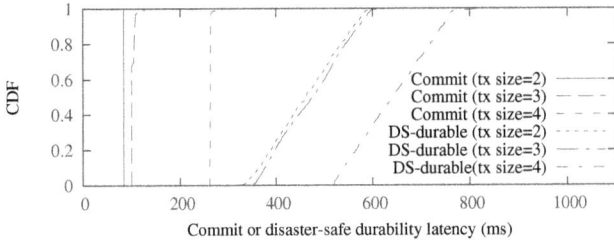

Figure 20: Latency of slow commit and replication.

Operation	# objs+csets read	# objs written	# of csets written	Throughput (1000 ops/s)
read-info	3	0	0	40
befriend	2	0	2	20
status-update	1	2	2	18
post-message	2	2	2	16.5
mix1	2.9	0.5	0.3	34
mix2	2.8	0.7	0.5	32

Figure 21: Transaction size and throughput for Waltsocial operations.

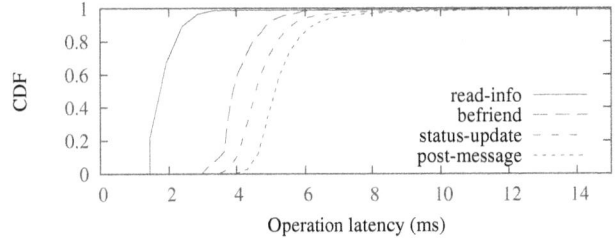

Figure 22: Latency of WaltSocial operations.

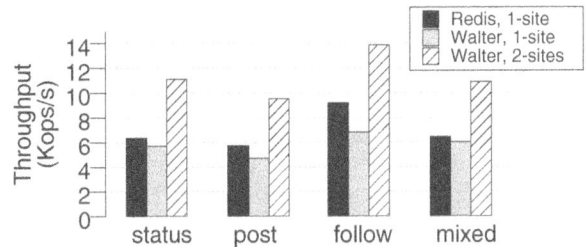

Figure 23: Throughput of ReTwis using Redis and Walter.

issue write-only transactions at the VA site. We vary the size of a transaction from 2 to 4 objects. Each object written has a different preferred site: the first, second, third, and fourth object's preferred sites are VA, CA, IE, and SG respectively.

Results. Figure 20 shows the commit latency (left-most three lines) and the latency for achieving disaster-safe durability (right-most three lines). The commit latency is determined by the round-trip time between VA and the farthest preferred site of objects in the writeset. This is because slow commit runs a two-phase protocol among the preferred sites of the objects in the writeset. For example, for transactions of size 3, the commit latency is 87 ms, which is the round-trip time from VA to IE. The latency for disaster-safe durability is the commit latency plus the replication latency. The replication latency is the same as for fast commit: it is uniformly distributed between $[RTT_{max}, 2 * RTT_{max}]$, where RTT_{max} is the round-trip time between VA and SG.

To optimize performance, applications should minimize the use of slow commits. Both WaltSocial and ReTwis avoid slow commits by using csets.

8.6 WaltSocial performance

Transactions make it easy to develop WaltSocial. Our experiments also show that WaltSocial achieves good performance.

Workload setup. The WaltSocial experiments involve 4 sites in EC2. We populate Walter with $400,000$ users, each with 10 status updates and 10 wall postings from other users. We run many application clients at each site, where each client issues WaltSocial operations. An operation corresponds to a user action, and it is implemented by executing and committing a transaction that reads and/or writes several data objects (Section 7). We measure the latency and aggregate throughput for each operation. We also evaluate two mixed workloads: mix1 consists of 90% *read-info* operations and 10% update operations including *status-update*, *post-message* and *befriend*; mix2 contains 80% *read-info* operations and 20% update operations.

Operation throughput. Figure 21 shows the throughput in thousands operations per second (Kops/s) for each WaltSocial operation and for the mixed workloads. The *read-info* operation issues read-only transactions; it has the highest aggregate throughput at 40 Kops/s. The other operations issue transactions that update objects; their throughput varies from 16.5 Kops/s to 20 Kops/s, depending on the number of objects read and written in the transactions. The mixed workloads are dominated by *read-info* operations, hence their throughput values are closer to that of *read-info*. The achieved throughput is likely sufficient for small or medium social networks. To handle larger deployments, one might deploy several sites per data center to scale the system (Section 5.8) .

Operation latency. Figure 22 shows the latency of WaltSocial operations when the system has a moderate load. Operations finish

quickly because the underlying transactions involve no cross-site communication: transactions always read a local replica for any object and transactions that update data use cset objects. The 99.9-percentile latency of all operations in Figure 22 is below 50 ms. As each WaltSocial operation issues read/write requests to Walter in series, the latency is affected by the number of objects accessed by different WaltSocial operations. The *read-info* operation involves fewest objects and hence is faster than other operations.

8.7 ReTwis performance

We compare the performance of ReTwis using Walter and Redis as the storage system, to assess the cost of Walter.

Workload setup. The Walter experiments involve one or two sites. Redis does not allow updates from multiple sites, so the Redis experiments involve one site. Since Redis is a semi-persistent key-value store optimized for in-memory operations, we configure both Walter and Redis to commit writes to memory. We run multiple front-end web servers (Apache 2.2.14 with PHP 5.3.2) and client emulators at each site. We emulate $500,000$ users who issue requests to post a message (*post*), follow another user (*follow*), or read postings in their own timeline (*status*). The mixed workload consists of 85% *status*, 7.5% *post* and 7.5% *follow* operations.

Throughput comparison. Figure 23 shows the aggregate throughput (Kops/s) for different workloads when running ReTwis with Walter and Redis. As can be seen, with one site, ReTwis with Walter has similar performance as ReTwis with Redis: the slowdown is no more than 25%. For example, the throughput of the *post* operation for Walter (1 site) is 4713 ops/s, compared to 5740 ops/s for

Redis. But ReTwis with Walter can use multiple sites to scale the throughput. For example, the throughput of *post* using ReTwis with Walter on two sites is 9527 ops/s—twice the throughput of one site.

9. RELATED WORK

Transactions in data centers. Early transactional storage for data centers include Bigtable [12], Sinfonia [4], Percolator [38], and distributed B-trees [3]. Unlike Walter, these systems were designed for a single data center only.

Storage systems that span many data centers often do not provide transactions (e.g., Dynamo [16]), or support only restricted transactional semantics. For example, PNUTS [14] supports only one-record transactions. COPS [31] provides only read-only transactions. Megastore [7] partitions data and provides the ACID properties within a partition but, unlike Walter, it fails to provide full transactional semantics for reads across partitions.

Transactions in disconnected or wide-area systems. Perdis [19] is an object store with a check-out/check-in model for wide-area operations: it creates a local copy of remote data (check-out) and later reconciles local changes (check-in), relying on manual repair when necessary. For systems with mobile nodes, tentative update transactions [23] can commit at a disconnected node. Tentative commits may be aborted later due to conflicts when the hosts re-connect to servers, which requires reconciliation by an external user. In contrast to the above systems, Walter does not require burdensome operations for manual repair or reconciliation. Mariposa [45] is a wide-area system whose main focus is on incentivizing a site to run third-party *read-only queries*.

Database replication. There is much work on database replication, both commercially and academically. Commercial database systems support master-slave replication across sites: one site is the primary, the others are mirrors that are often read-only and updated asynchronously. When asynchronous mirrors are writable, applications must provide logic to resolve conflicts. On the academic side, the database replication literature is extensive; here we summarize relevant recent work. Replication schemes are classified on two axes [23]: (1) who initiates updates (primary-copy vs update-anywhere), and (2) when updates propagate (eager vs lazy). With *primary-copy*, objects have a master host and only the master initiates updates; with *update-anywhere*, any host may initiate updates. With *eager replication*, updates propagate to the replicas before commit; with *lazy replication*, replicas receive updates asynchronously after commit. All four combinations of these two dimensions are possible. Eager replication is implemented using distributed two-phase commit [9]. Later work considers primary-copy lazy replication and provides serializability by restricting the placement of each object's primary [13], or controlling when secondary nodes are updated [10, 36]. Update-anywhere lazy replication is problematic because conflicting transactions can commit concurrently at different replicas. Thus, recent work considers hybrids between eager and lazy replication: updates propagate after commit (lazy), but replicas also coordinate during transaction execution or commit to deal with conflicts (eager). This coordination may involve a global graph to control conflicts [6, 11], or atomic broadcast to order transactions [27, 37]. Later work considers snapshot isolation as a more efficient alternative to serializability [15, 17, 18, 30, 39, 52]. Walter differs from the above works because they ensure a stronger isolation property—serializability or snapshot isolation—which inherently requires coordination across sites

to commit, whereas Walter commits common transactions without such coordination.

Federated transaction management considers techniques to execute transactions that span multiple database systems [41]. This work differs from Walter because it does not consider issues involving multiple sites and its main concern is to minimize changes to database systems, rather than avoiding coordination across sites.

Relaxed consistency. Some systems provide weaker consistency, where concurrent updates cause diverging versions that must be reconciled later by application-specific mechanisms [16, 34, 47]. *Eventual consistency* permits replicas to diverge but, if updates stop, replicas eventually converge again. Weak consistency may be tolerable [49], but it can lead to complex application logic. Inconsistency can also be quantified and bounded [5, 26, 54], to improve the user experience. Fork consistency [33] allows the observed operation history to fork and not converge again; it is intended for honest clients to detect the misbehavior of malicious servers rather than to provide efficient replication across sites.

Commutative data types. Prior work has shown how to exploit the semantics of data types to improve concurrency. In [50], abstract data types (such as sets, FIFO queues, and a bank account) are characterized using a table of commutativity relations where two operations conflict when they do not commute. In [20, 42], a lock compatibility table is used to serialize access to abstract data types, such as directory, set or FIFO queue, by exploiting the commutativity of their operations. Because these works aim to achieve serializability, not all operations on a set object are conflict-free (e.g., testing the membership of element a conflicts with the insertion of a in the set). As a result, operating on sets require coordination to check for potential conflicts. In contrast, since we aim to achieve the weaker PSI property, operations on Walter's cset objects are always free of conflicts, allowing each data center to read and modify these csets without any remote coordination.

Letia et al. [29] have proposed the use of commutative replicated data types to avoid concurrency control and conflict resolution in replicated systems. Their work has inspired our use of csets. Subsequent recent work [43] provides a theoretical treatment for such data types and others—which are together called conflict-free replicated data types or CRDTs—proposing sufficient conditions for replica convergence under a newly-defined strong eventual consistency model. While that work concerns replication of single operations/objects at a time, not transactions, one could imagine using general CRDTs with PSI and our protocols to replicate transactions efficiently. U-sets [43, 53] are a type of set in which commutativity is achieved by preventing a removed element from being added again. In contrast, csets achieve commutativity by augmenting elements with counts. Csets are similar to Z-relations [25], which are mappings from tuples to integers, used to allow for decidability of equivalence of queries in the context of query optimization.

Escrow transactions [35] update numeric data, such as account balances, by holding some amount in escrow to allow concurrent commutative updates. By exploiting commutativity, such transactions resemble transactions with csets, but they differ in two ways. First, escrow transactions operate on numeric data. Second, escrow transactions must coordinate among themselves to check the amounts in escrow, which does not serve our goal of avoiding coordination across distant sites.

10. CONCLUSION

Walter is a transactional geo-replicated key-value store with properties that make it appealing as the storage system for web applications. A key feature behind Walter is Parallel Snapshot Isolation (PSI), a precisely-stated isolation property that permits asynchronous replication across sites without the need for conflict resolution. Walter relies on techniques to avoid conflicts across sites, thereby allowing transactions to commit locally in a site. PSI thus permits an efficient implementation, while also providing strong guarantees to applications. We have demonstrated the usefulness of Walter by building a Facebook-like social networking application and porting a third-party Twitter clone. Both applications were simple to implement and achieved reasonable performance.

Acknowledgements

We are grateful to many people who helped us improve this work. Our shepherd Robbert van Renesse and the anonymous reviewers provided much useful feedback throughout the paper. Margo Seltzer made many suggestions on how to tune the performance of Berkeley DB. Frank Dabek, Wilson Hsieh, Frans Kaashoek, Christopher Mitchell, Rama Ramasubramanian, Mehul Shah, Chandramohan Thekkath, Michael Walfish, and Lidong Zhou provided several comments that helped us improve the presentation. This work was partially supported by NSF Award CNS-0720644.

References

[1] Redis: an open-source advanced key-value store. http://redis.io.

[2] A Twitter clone for the Redis key-value database. http://retwis.antirez.com.

[3] M. K. Aguilera, W. Golab, and M. A. Shah. A practical scalable distributed B-tree. In *International Conference on Very Large Data Bases*, pages 598–609, Aug. 2008.

[4] M. K. Aguilera, A. Merchant, M. Shah, A. Veitch, and C. Karamanolis. Sinfonia: A new paradigm for building scalable distributed systems. *ACM Transactions on Computer Systems*, 27(3):5:1–5:48, Nov. 2009.

[5] R. Alonso, D. Barbará, and H. Garcia-Molina. Data caching issues in an information retrieval system. *ACM Transactions on Database Systems*, 15(3):359–384, Sept. 1990.

[6] T. Anderson, Y. Breitbart, H. F. Korth, and A. Wool. Replication, consistency, and practicality: are these mutually exclusive? In *International Conference on Management of Data*, pages 484–495, June 1998.

[7] J. Baker et al. Megastore: Providing scalable, highly available storage for interactive services. In *5th Conference on Innovative Data Systems Research*, pages 223–234, Jan. 2011.

[8] H. Berenson et al. A critique of ANSI SQL isolation levels. In *International Conference on Management of Data*, pages 1–10, May 1995.

[9] P. A. Bernstein, V. Hadzilacos, and N. Goodman. *Concurrency Control and Recovery in Database Systems*. Addison-Wesley, 1987.

[10] Y. Breitbart et al. Update propagation protocols for replicated databases. In *International Conference on Management of Data*, pages 97–108, June 1999.

[11] Y. Breitbart and H. F. Korth. Replication and consistency in a distributed environment. *Journal of Computer and System Sciences*, 59(1):29–69, Aug. 1999.

[12] F. Chang et al. Bigtable: A distributed storage system for structured data. In *Symposium on Operating Systems Design and Implementation*, pages 205–218, Nov. 2006.

[13] P. Chundi, D. J. Rosenkrantz, and S. S. Ravi. Deferred updates and data placement in distributed databases. In *International Conference on Data Engineering*, pages 469–476, Feb. 1996.

[14] B. F. Cooper et al. PNUTS: Yahoo!'s hosted data serving platform. In *International Conference on Very Large Data Bases*, pages 1277–1288, Aug. 2008.

[15] K. Daudjee and K. Salem. Lazy database replication with snapshot isolation. In *International Conference on Very Large Data Bases*, pages 715–726, Sept. 2006.

[16] G. DeCandia et al. Dynamo: Amazon's highly available key-value store. In *ACM Symposium on Operating Systems Principles*, pages 205–220, Oct. 2007.

[17] S. Elnikety, S. Dropsho, and F. Pedone. Tashkent: Uniting durability with transaction ordering for high-performance scalable database replication. In *European Conference on Computer Systems*, pages 117–130, Apr. 2006.

[18] S. Elnikety, S. Dropsho, and W. Zwaenepoel. Tashkent+: Memory-aware load balancing and update filtering in replicated databases. In *European Conference on Computer Systems*, pages 399–412, Mar. 2007.

[19] P. Ferreira et al. Perdis: design, implementation, and use of a persistent distributed store. In *Recent Advances in Distributed Systems*, volume 1752 of *LNCS*, chapter 18. Springer-Verlag, Feb. 2000.

[20] H. Garcia-Molina. Using semantic knowledge for transaction processing in a distributed database. *ACM Transactions on Database Systems*, 8(2):186–213, June 1983.

[21] S. Ghemawat, H. Gobioff, and S.-T. Leung. The Google file system. In *ACM Symposium on Operating Systems Principles*, pages 29–43, Oct. 2003.

[22] S. Gilbert and N. Lynch. Brewer's conjecture and the feasibility of consistent, available, partition tolerant web services. *ACM SIGACT News*, 33(2):51–59, June 2002.

[23] J. Gray, P. Helland, P. O'Neil, and D. Shasha. The dangers of replication and a solution. In *International Conference on Management of Data*, pages 173–182, June 1996.

[24] J. Gray and A. Reuter. *Transaction processing: concepts and techniques*. Morgan Kaufmann Publishers, 1993.

[25] T. J. Green, Z. G. Ives, and V. Tannen. Reconcilable differences. In *International Conference on Digital Telecommunications*, pages 212–224, Mar. 2009.

[26] H. Guo et al. Relaxed currency and consistency: How to say "good enough" in SQL. In *International Conference on Management of Data*, pages 815–826, June 2004.

[27] B. Kemme and G. Alonso. A new approach to developing and implementing eager database replication protocols. *ACM Transactions on Database Systems*, 25(3):333–379, Sept. 2000.

[28] E. K. Lee and C. A. Thekkath. Petal: Distributed virtual disks. In *International Conference on Architectural Support for Programming Languages and Operating Systems*, pages 84–92, Oct. 1996.

[29] M. Letia, N. Preguiça, and M. Shapiro. Consistency without concurrency control in large, dynamic systems. In *International Workshop on Large Scale Distributed Systems and Middleware*, Oct. 2009.

[30] Y. Lin, B. Kemme, M. P. no Martínez, and R. Jiménez-Peris. Middleware based data replication providing snapshot isolation. In *International Conference on Management of Data*, pages 419–430, June 2005.

[31] W. Lloyd, M. Freedman, M. Kaminsky, and D. Andersen. Don't settle for eventual: Stronger consistency for wide-area

storage with cops. In *ACM Symposium on Operating Systems Principles*, Oct. 2011.

[32] N. A. Lynch. *Distributed Algorithms*. Morgan Kaufmann Publishers, 1996.

[33] D. Mazières and D. Shasha. Building secure file systems out of byzantine storage. In *ACM Symposium on Principles of Distributed Computing*, pages 108–117, July 2002.

[34] L. B. Mummert, M. R. Eblig, and M. Satyanarayanan. Exploiting weak connectivity for mobile file access. In *ACM Symposium on Operating Systems Principles*, pages 143–155, Dec. 1995.

[35] P. E. O'Neil. The escrow transactional method. *ACM Transactions on Database Systems*, 11(4):405–430, Dec. 1986.

[36] E. Pacitti, P. Minet, and E. Simon. Fast algorithms for maintaining replica consistency in lazy master replicated databases. In *International Conference on Very Large Data Bases*, pages 126–137, Sept. 1999.

[37] M. Patino-Martinez, R. Jiménez-Peris, B. Kemme, and G. Alonso. MIDDLE-R: Consistent database replication at the middleware level. *ACM Transactions on Computer Systems*, 23(4):375–423, Nov. 2005.

[38] D. Peng and F. Dabek. Large-scale incremental processing using distributed transactions and notifications. In *Symposium on Operating Systems Design and Implementation*, pages 251–264, Oct. 2010.

[39] C. Plattner and G. Alonso. Ganymed: Scalable replication for transactional web applications. In *International Middleware Conference*, pages 155–174, Oct. 2004.

[40] Y. Saito et al. FAB: building distributed enterprise disk arrays from commodity components. In *International Conference on Architectural Support for Programming Languages and Operating Systems*, pages 48–58, Oct. 2004.

[41] R. Schenkel et al. Federated transaction management with snapshot isolation. In *Workshop on Foundations of Models and Languages for Data and Objects, Transactions and Database Dynamics*, pages 1–25, Sept. 1999.

[42] P. Schwarz and A. Spector. Synchronizing shared abstract types. *ACM Transactions on Computer Systems*, 2(3):223–250, Aug. 1984.

[43] M. Shapiro, N. Preguiça, C. Baquero, and M. Zawirski. Conflict-free replicated data types. In *International Symposium on Stabilization, Safety, and Security of Distributed Systems*, Oct. 2011.

[44] A. Singh, P. Fonseca, P. Kuznetsov, R. Rodrigues, and P. Maniatis. Zeno: Eventually consistent byzantine fault tolerance. In *Symposium on Networked Systems Design and Implementation*, pages 169–184, Apr. 2009.

[45] M. Stonebraker et al. Mariposa: a wide-area distributed database system. In *International Conference on Very Large Data Bases*, pages 48–63, Jan. 1996.

[46] J. Stribling, Y. Sovran, I. Zhang, X. Pretzer, J. Li, F. Kaashoek, and R. Morris. Simplifying wide-area application development with WheelFS. In *Symposium on Networked Systems Design and Implementation*, pages 43–58, Apr. 2009.

[47] D. B. Terry et al. Managing update conflicts in Bayou, a weakly connected replicated storage system. In *ACM Symposium on Operating Systems Principles*, pages 172–183, Dec. 1995.

[48] C. A. Thekkath, T. Mann, and E. K. Lee. Frangipani: A scalable distributed file system. In *ACM Symposium on Operating Systems Principles*, pages 224–237, Oct. 1997.

[49] W. Vogels. Data access patterns in the amazon.com technology platform. In *International Conference on Very Large Data Bases*, page 1, Sept. 2007.

[50] W. Weihl. Commutativity-based concurrency control for abstract data types. *IEEE Transactions on Computers*, 37(12):1488–1505, Dec. 1988.

[51] G. Weikum and G. Vossen. *Transactional Information Systems: Theory, Algorithms, and the Practice of Concurrency Control and Recovery*. Morgan Kaufmann, 2009.

[52] S. Wu and B. Kemme. Postgres-R(SI): Combining replica control with concurrency control based on snapshot isolation. In *International Conference on Data Engineering*, pages 422–433, Apr. 2005.

[53] G. T. J. Wuu and A. J. Bernstein. Efficient solutions to the replicated log and dictionart problems. In *ACM Symposium on Principles of Distributed Computing*, pages 233–242, Aug. 1984.

[54] H. Yu and A. Vahdat. Design and evaluation of a conit-based continuous consistency model for replicated services. *ACM Transactions on Computer Systems*, 20(3):239–282, Aug. 2002.

Don't Settle for Eventual:
Scalable Causal Consistency for Wide-Area Storage with COPS

Wyatt Lloyd*, Michael J. Freedman*, Michael Kaminsky†, and David G. Andersen‡

*Princeton University, †Intel Labs, ‡Carnegie Mellon University

ABSTRACT

Geo-replicated, distributed data stores that support complex online applications, such as social networks, must provide an "always-on" experience where operations always complete with low latency. Today's systems often sacrifice strong consistency to achieve these goals, exposing inconsistencies to their clients and necessitating complex application logic. In this paper, we identify and define a consistency model—causal consistency with convergent conflict handling, or *causal+*—that is the strongest achieved under these constraints.

We present the design and implementation of COPS, a key-value store that delivers this consistency model across the wide-area. A key contribution of COPS is its scalability, which can enforce causal dependencies between keys stored across an entire cluster, rather than a single server like previous systems. The central approach in COPS is tracking and explicitly checking whether causal dependencies between keys are satisfied in the local cluster before exposing writes. Further, in COPS-GT, we introduce get transactions in order to obtain a consistent view of multiple keys without locking or blocking. Our evaluation shows that COPS completes operations in less than a millisecond, provides throughput similar to previous systems when using one server per cluster, and scales well as we increase the number of servers in each cluster. It also shows that COPS-GT provides similar latency, throughput, and scaling to COPS for common workloads.

Categories and Subject Descriptors

C.2.4 [**Computer Systems Organization**]: Distributed Systems

General Terms

Design, Experimentation, Performance

Keywords

Key-value storage, causal+ consistency, scalable wide-area replication, ALPS systems, read transactions

SOSP '11, October 23-26, 2011, Cascais, Portugal.
Copyright © 2011 ACM 978-1-4503-0977-6/11/10 ... $10.00.

1. INTRODUCTION

Distributed data stores are a fundamental building block of modern Internet services. Ideally, these data stores would be strongly consistent, always available for reads and writes, and able to continue operating during network partitions. The CAP Theorem, unfortunately, proves it impossible to create a system that achieves all three [13, 23]. Instead, modern web services have chosen overwhelmingly to embrace availability and partition tolerance at the cost of strong consistency [16, 20, 30]. This is perhaps not surprising, given that this choice also enables these systems to provide low latency for client operations and high scalability. Further, many of the earlier high-scale Internet services, typically focusing on web search, saw little reason for stronger consistency, although this position is changing with the rise of interactive services such as social networking applications [46]. We refer to systems with these four properties—**A**vailability, low **L**atency, **P**artition-tolerance, and high **S**calability—as ALPS systems.

Given that ALPS systems must sacrifice strong consistency (i.e., linearizability), we seek the strongest consistency model that is achievable under these constraints. Stronger consistency is desirable because it makes systems easier for a programmer to reason about. In this paper, we consider *causal consistency with convergent conflict handling*, which we refer to as *causal+ consistency*. Many previous systems believed to implement the weaker causal consistency [10, 41] actually implement the more useful causal+ consistency, though none do so in a scalable manner.

The causal component of causal+ consistency ensures that the data store respects the causal dependencies between operations [31]. Consider a scenario where a user uploads a picture to a web site, the picture is saved, and then a reference to it is added to that user's album. The reference "depends on" the picture being saved. Under causal+ consistency, these dependencies are always satisfied. Programmers never have to deal with the situation where they can get the reference to the picture but not the picture itself, unlike in systems with weaker guarantees, such as eventual consistency.

The convergent conflict handling component of causal+ consistency ensures that replicas never permanently diverge and that conflicting updates to the same key are dealt with identically at all sites. When combined with causal consistency, this property ensures that clients see only progressively newer versions of keys. In comparison, eventually consistent systems may expose versions out of order. By combining causal consistency and convergent conflict handling, causal+ consistency ensures clients see a causally-correct, conflict-free, and always-progressing data store.

Our COPS system (Clusters of Order-Preserving Servers) provides causal+ consistency and is designed to support complex online applications that are hosted from a small number of large-scale datacenters, each of which is composed of front-end servers (clients of

COPS) and back-end key-value data stores. COPS executes all put and get operations in the local datacenter in a linearizable fashion, and it then replicates data across datacenters in a causal+ consistent order in the background.

We detail two versions of our COPS system. The regular version, COPS, provides scalable causal+ consistency between individual items in the data store, even if their causal dependencies are spread across many different machines in the local datacenter. These consistency properties come at low cost: The performance and overhead of COPS is similar to prior systems, such as those based on log exchange [10, 41], even while providing much greater scalability.

We also detail an extended version of the system, COPS-GT, which also provides *get transactions* that give clients a consistent view of multiple keys. Get transactions are needed to obtain a consistent view of multiple keys, even in a fully-linearizable system. Our get transactions require no locks, are non-blocking, and take at most two parallel rounds of intra-datacenter requests. To the best of our knowledge, COPS-GT is the first ALPS system to achieve non-blocking scalable get transactions. These transactions do come at some cost: compared to the regular version of COPS, COPS-GT is less efficient for certain workloads (e.g., write-heavy) and is less robust to long network partitions and datacenter failures.

The scalability requirements for ALPS systems creates the largest distinction between COPS and prior causal+ consistent systems. Previous systems required that all data fit on a single machine [2, 12, 41] or that all data that potentially could be accessed together fit on a single machine [10]. In comparison, data stored in COPS can be spread across an arbitrary-sized datacenter, and dependencies (or get transactions) can stretch across many servers in the datacenter. To the best of our knowledge, COPS is the first scalable system to implement causal+ (and thus causal) consistency.

The contributions in this paper include:

- We explicitly identify four important properties of distributed data stores and use them to define ALPS systems.
- We name and formally define causal+ consistency.
- We present the design and implementation of COPS, a *scalable* system that efficiently realizes the causal+ consistency model.
- We present a non-blocking, lock-free get transaction algorithm in COPS-GT that provides clients with a consistent view of multiple keys in at most two rounds of local operations.
- We show through evaluation that COPS has low latency, high throughput, and scales well for all tested workloads; and that COPS-GT has similar properties for common workloads.

2. ALPS SYSTEMS AND TRADE-OFFS

We are interested in infrastructure that can support many of today's largest Internet services. In contrast with classical distributed storage systems that focused on local-area operation in the small, these services are typically characterized by wide-area deployments across a few to tens of datacenters, as illustrated in Figure 1. Each datacenter includes a set of application-level clients, as well as a back-end data store to which these clients read and write. For many applications—and the setting considered in the paper—data written in one datacenter is replicated to others.

Often, these clients are actually webservers that run code on behalf of remote browsers. Although this paper considers consistency from the perspective of the application client (i.e., the webserver), if the browser accesses a service through a single datacenter, as we expect, it will enjoy similar consistency guarantees.

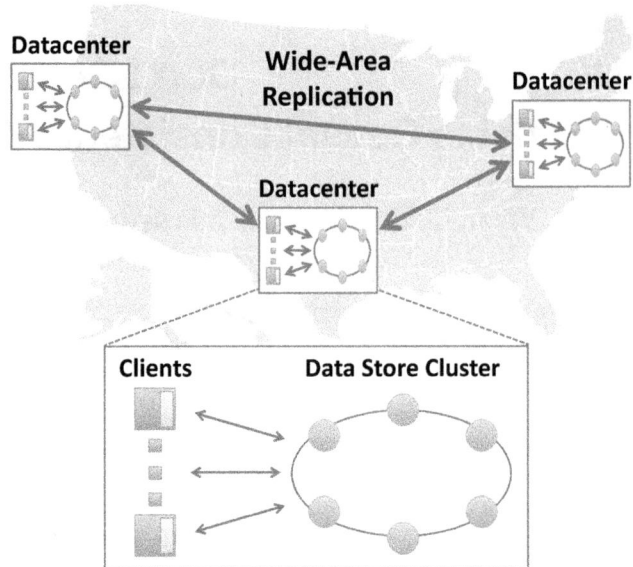

Figure 1: The general architecture of modern web services. Multiple geographically distributed datacenters each have application clients that read and write state from a data store that is distributed across all of the datacenters.

Such a distributed storage system has multiple, sometimes competing, goals: *availability*, *low latency*, and *partition tolerance* to provide an "always on" user experience [16]; *scalability* to adapt to increasing load and storage demands; and a sufficiently strong *consistency* model to simplify programming and provide users with the system behavior that they expect. In slightly more depth, the desirable properties include:

1. Availability. All operations issued to the data store complete successfully. No operation can block indefinitely or return an error signifying that data is unavailable.

2. Low Latency. Client operations complete "quickly." Commercial service-level objectives suggest average performance of a few milliseconds and worse-case performance (i.e., 99.9th percentile) of 10s or 100s of milliseconds [16].

3. Partition Tolerance. The data store continues to operate under network partitions, e.g., one separating datacenters in Asia from the United States.

4. High Scalability. The data store scales out linearly. Adding N resources to the system increases aggregate throughput and storage capacity by $O(N)$.

5. Stronger Consistency. An ideal data store would provide *linearizability*—sometimes informally called *strong consistency*—which dictates that operations appear to take effect across the entire system at a single instance in time between the invocation and completion of the operation [26]. In a data store that provides linearizability, as soon as a client completes a write operation to an object in one datacenter, read operations to the same object in all other datacenters will reflect its newly written state. Linearizability simplifies programming—the distributed system provides a single, consistent image—and users experience the storage behavior they expect. Weaker, eventual consistency models, common in many large distributed systems, are less intuitive: Not only might subsequent reads not reflect the latest value, reads across multiple objects might reflect an incoherent mix of old and new values.

The CAP Theorem proves that a shared-data system that has availability and partition tolerance cannot achieve linearizability [13,

Client 1   put(x,1) ⟶ put(y,2) ⟶ put(x,3)
                                    ↓
Client 2   get(y)=2 ⟶ put(x,4)
                                        ↓
Client 3   get(x)=4 ⟶ put(z,5)

Time   --->

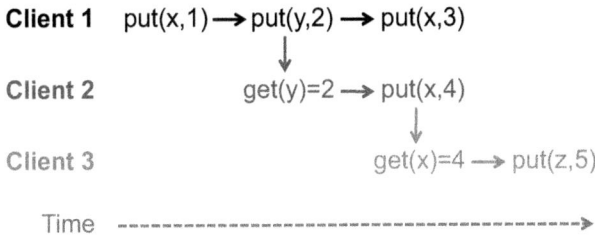

Figure 2: Graph showing the causal relationship between operations at a replica. An edge from a to b indicates that $a \rightsquigarrow b$, or b depends on a.

23]. Low latency—defined as latency less than the maximum wide-area delay between replicas—has also been proven incompatible with linearizability [34] and sequential consistency [8]. To balance between the requirements of ALPS systems and programmability we define an intermediate consistency model in the next section.

3. CAUSAL+ CONSISTENCY

To define *causal consistency with convergent conflict handling* (causal+ consistency), we first describe the abstract model over which it operates. We restrict our consideration to a key-value data store, with two basic operations: put(key,val) and get(key)=val. These are equivalent to write and read operations in a shared-memory system. Values are stored and retrieved from logical *replicas*, each of which hosts the entire key space. In our COPS system, a single *logical* replica corresponds to an entire local cluster of nodes.

An important concept in our model is the notion of *potential causality* [2, 31] between operations. Three rules define potential causality, denoted $\rightsquigarrow$:

1. **Execution Thread.** If a and b are two operations in a *single thread of execution*, then $a \rightsquigarrow b$ if operation a happens before operation b.
2. **Gets From.** If a is a put operation and b is a get operation that returns the value written by a, then $a \rightsquigarrow b$.
3. **Transitivity.** For operations a, b, and c, if $a \rightsquigarrow b$ and $b \rightsquigarrow c$, then $a \rightsquigarrow c$.

These rules establish potential causality between operations within the same execution thread and between operations whose execution threads interacted through the data store. Our model, like many, does not allow threads to communicate directly, requiring instead that all communication occur through the data store.

The example execution in Figure 2 demonstrates all three rules. The *execution thread* rule gives get(y)=2 $\rightsquigarrow$ put(x,4); the *gets from* rule gives put(y,2) $\rightsquigarrow$ get(y)=2; and the *transitivity* rule gives put(y,2) $\rightsquigarrow$ put(x,4). Even though some operations follow put(x,3) in real time, no other operations depend on it, as none read the value it wrote nor follow it in the same thread of execution.

3.1 Definition

We define causal+ consistency as a combination of two properties: causal consistency and convergent conflict handling. We present intuitive definitions here and the formal definitions in Appendix A.

Causal consistency requires that values returned from get operations at a replica are consistent with the order defined by $\rightsquigarrow$ (causality) [2]. In other words, it must appear the operation that writes a value occurs after all operations that causally precede it.

For example, in Figure 2, it must appear put(y,2) happened before put(x,4), which in turn happened before put(z,5). If client 2 saw get(x)=4 and then get(x)=1, causal consistency would be violated.

Causal consistency does not order concurrent operations. If $a \not\rightsquigarrow b$ and $b \not\rightsquigarrow a$, then a and b are concurrent. Normally, this allows increased efficiency in an implementation: Two unrelated put operations can be replicated in any order, avoiding the need for a serialization point between them. If, however, a and b are both puts to the same key, then they are in *conflict*.

Conflicts are undesirable for two reasons. First, because they are unordered by causal consistency, conflicts allow replicas to diverge forever [2]. For instance, if a is put(x,1) and b is put(x,2), then causal consistency allows one replica to forever return 1 for x and another replica to forever return 2 for x. Second, conflicts may represent an exceptional condition that requires special handling. For example, in a shopping cart application, if two people logged in to the same account concurrently add items to their cart, the desired result is to end up with both items in the cart.

Convergent conflict handling requires that all conflicting puts be handled in the same manner at all replicas, using a handler function h. This handler function h must be associative and commutative, so that replicas can handle conflicting writes in the order they receive them and that the results of these handlings will converge (e.g., one replica's $h(a, h(b, c))$ and another's $h(c, h(b, a))$ agree).

One common way to handle conflicting writes in a convergent fashion is the last-writer-wins rule (also called Thomas's write rule [50]), which declares one of the conflicting writes as having occurred later and has it overwrite the "earlier" write. Another common way to handle conflicting writes is to mark them as conflicting and require their resolution by some other means, e.g., through direct user intervention as in Coda [28], or through a programmed procedure as in Bayou [41] and Dynamo [16].

All potential forms of convergent conflict handling avoid the first issue—conflicting updates may continually diverge—by ensuring that replicas reach the same result after exchanging operations. On the other hand, the second issue with conflicts—applications may want special handling of conflicts—is only avoided by the use of more explicit *conflict resolution* procedures. These explicit procedures provide greater flexibility for applications, but require additional programmer complexity and/or performance overhead. Although COPS can be configured to detect conflicting updates explicitly and apply some application-defined resolution, the default version of COPS uses the last-writer-wins rule.

3.2 Causal+ vs. Other Consistency Models

The distributed systems literature defines several popular consistency models. In decreasing strength, they include: linearizability (or strong consistency) [26], which maintains a global, real-time ordering; sequential consistency [32], which ensures at least a global ordering; causal consistency [2], which ensures partial orderings between dependent operations; FIFO (PRAM) consistency [34], which only preserves the partial ordering of an execution thread, not between threads; per-key sequential consistency [15], which ensures that, for each individual key, all operations have a global order; and eventual consistency, a "catch-all" term used today suggesting eventual convergence to some type of agreement.

The causal+ consistency we introduce falls between sequential and causal consistency, as shown in Figure 3. It is weaker than sequential consistency, but sequential consistency is provably not achievable in an ALPS system. It is stronger than causal consistency

Figure 3: A spectrum of consistency models, with stronger models on the left. Bolded models are provably incompatible with ALPS systems.

and per-key sequential consistency, however, and it *is* achievable for ALPS systems. Mahajan et al. [35] have concurrently defined a similar strengthening of causal consistency; see Section 7 for details.

To illustrate the utility of the causal+ model, consider two examples. First, let Alice try to share a photo with Bob. Alice uploads the photo and then adds the photo to her album. Bob then checks Alice's album expecting to see her photo. Under causal and thus causal+ consistency, if the album has a reference to the photo, then Bob must be able to view the photo. Under per-key sequential and eventual consistency, it is possible for the album to have a reference to a photo that has not been written yet.

Second, consider an example where Carol and Dan both update the starting time for an event. The time was originally set for 9pm, Carol changed it to 8pm, and Dan concurrently changed it to 10pm. Regular causal consistency would allow two different replicas to forever return different times, even after receiving both put operations. Causal+ consistency requires that replicas handle this conflict in a convergent manner. If a last-writer-wins policy is used, then either Dan's 10pm or Carol's 8pm would win. If a more explicit conflict resolution policy is used, the key could be marked as in conflict and future gets on it could return both 8pm and 10pm with instructions to resolve the conflict.

If the data store was sequentially consistent or linearizable, it would still be possible for there to be two simultaneous updates to a key. In these stronger models, however, it is possible to implement mutual exclusion algorithms—such as the one suggested by Lamport in the original sequential consistency paper [32]—that can be used to avoid creating a conflict altogether.

3.3 Causal+ in COPS

We use two abstractions in the COPS system, *versions* and *dependencies*, to help us reason about causal+ consistency. We refer to the different values a key has as the *versions* of a key, which we denote key$_{version}$. In COPS, versions are assigned in a manner that ensures that if $x_i \rightsquigarrow y_j$ then $i < j$. Once a replica in COPS returns version i of a key, x_i, causal+ consistency ensures it will then only return that version or a causally later version (note that the handling of a conflict is causally later than the conflicting puts it resolves).[1] Thus, each replica in COPS always returns non-decreasing versions of a key. We refer to this as causal+ consistency's *progressing property*.

Causal consistency dictates that all operations that causally precede a given operations must appear to take effect before it. In other words, if $x_i \rightsquigarrow y_j$, then x_i must be written before y_j. We call these preceding values *dependencies*. More formally, we say y_j **depends on** x_i if and only if $\text{put}(x_i) \rightsquigarrow \text{put}(y_j)$. These dependencies are in essence the reverse of the causal ordering of writes. COPS provides causal+ consistency during replication by writing a version only after writing all of its dependencies.

---

[1]To see this, consider by contradiction the following scenario: assume a replica first returns x_i and then x_k, where $i \neq k$ and $x_i \not\rightsquigarrow x_k$. Causal consistency ensures that if x_k is returned after x_i, then $x_k \not\rightsquigarrow x_i$, and so x_i and x_k conflict. But, if x_i and x_k conflict, then convergent conflict handling ensures that as soon as both are present at a replica, their handling $h(x_i,x_k)$, which is causally after both, will be returned instead of either x_i or x_k, which contradicts our assumption.

3.4 Scalable Causality

To our knowledge, this paper is the first to name and formally define causal+ consistency. Interestingly, several previous systems [10, 41] believed to achieve causal consistency in fact achieved the stronger guarantees of causal+ consistency.

These systems were not designed to and do not provide *scalable* causal (or causal+) consistency, however, as they all use a form of log serialization and exchange. All operations at a logical replica are written to a single log in serialized order, commonly marked with a version vector [40]. Different replicas then exchange these logs, using version vectors to establish potential causality and detect concurrency between operations at different replicas.

Log-exchange-based serialization inhibits replica scalability, as it relies on a single serialization point in each replica to establish ordering. Thus, either causal dependencies between keys are limited to the set of keys that can be stored on one node [10, 15, 30, 41], or a single node (or replicated state machine) must provide a commit ordering and log for all operations across a cluster.

As we show below, COPS achieves scalability by taking a different approach. Nodes in each datacenter are responsible for different partitions of the keyspace, but the system can track and enforce dependencies between keys stored on different nodes. COPS explicitly encodes dependencies in metadata associated with each key's version. When keys are replicated remotely, the receiving datacenter performs dependency checks before committing the incoming version.

4. SYSTEM DESIGN OF COPS

COPS is a distributed storage system that realizes causal+ consistency and possesses the desired ALPS properties. There are two distinct versions of the system. The first, which we refer to simply as COPS, provides a data store that is causal+ consistent. The second, called COPS-GT, provides a superset of this functionality by also introducing support for *get transactions*. With get transactions, clients request a set of keys and the data store replies with a consistent snapshot of corresponding values. Because of the additional metadata needed to enforce the consistency properties of get transactions, a given deployment must run exclusively as COPS or COPS-GT.

4.1 Overview of COPS

COPS is a key-value storage system designed to run across a small number of datacenters, as illustrated in Figure 4. Each datacenter has a local COPS *cluster* with a complete replica of the stored data.[2] A *client* of COPS is an application that uses the COPS *client library* to call directly into the COPS key-value store. Clients communicate only with their local COPS cluster running in the same datacenter.

Each local COPS cluster is set up as a linearizable (strongly consistent) key-value store [5, 48]. Linearizable systems can be implemented scalably by partitioning the keyspace into N linearizable partitions (each of which can reside on a single node or a single chain of nodes) and having clients access each partition independently. The composability of linearizability [26] ensures that the resulting system as a whole remains linearizable. Linearizability is acceptable locally because we expect very low latency and no

---

[2]The assumption of full replication simplifies our presentation, though one could imagine clusters that replicate only part of the total data store and sacrifice low latency for the rest (according to configuration rules).

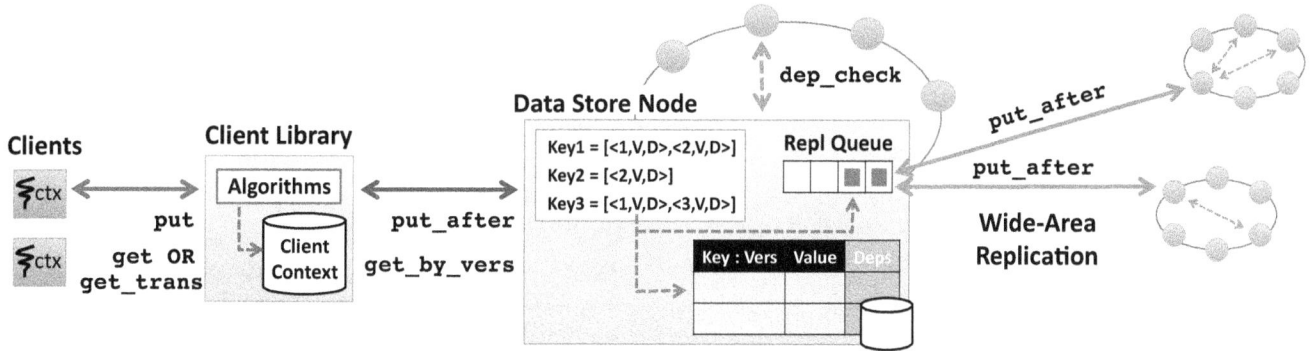

Figure 4: The COPS architecture. A client library exposes a put/get interface to its clients and ensures operations are properly labeled with causal dependencies. A key-value store replicates data between clusters, ensures writes are committed in their local cluster only after their dependencies have been satisfied, and in COPS-GT, stores multiple versions of each key along with dependency metadata.

partitions within a cluster—especially with the trend towards redundant paths in modern datacenter networks [3, 24]—unlike in the wide-area. On the other hand, replication *between* COPS clusters happens asynchronously to ensure low latency for client operations and availability in the face of external partitions.

System Components. COPS is composed of two main software components:

- *Key-value store.* The basic building block in COPS is a standard key-value store that provides linearizable operations on keys. COPS extends the standard key-value store in two ways, and COPS-GT adds a third extension.

  1. Each key-value pair has associated metadata. In COPS, this metadata is a version number. In COPS-GT, it is both a version number and a list of dependencies (other keys and their respective versions).

  2. The key-value store exports three additional operations as part of its key-value interface: get_by_version, put_after, and dep_check, each described below. These operations enable the COPS client library and an asynchronous replication process that supports causal+ consistency and get transactions.

  3. For COPS-GT, the system keeps around old versions of key-value pairs, not just the most recent put, to ensure that it can provide get transactions. Maintaining old versions is discussed further in Section 4.3.

- *Client library.* The client library exports two main operations to applications: reads via get (in COPS) or get_trans (in COPS-GT), and writes via put.[3] The client library also maintains state about a client's current dependencies through a *context* parameter in the client library API.

Goals. The COPS design strives to provide causal+ consistency with resource and performance overhead similar to existing eventually consistent systems. COPS and COPS-GT must therefore:

- *Minimize overhead of consistency-preserving replication.* COPS must ensure that values are replicated between clusters in a causal+ consistent manner. A naive implementation, however, would require checks on all of a value's dependencies. We present a mechanism that requires only a small number of such checks by leveraging the graph structure inherent to causal dependencies.

---
[3]This paper uses different fixed-width fonts for client-facing API calls (e.g., get) and data store API calls (e.g., get_by_version).

- *(COPS-GT) Minimize space requirements.* COPS-GT stores (potentially) multiple versions of each key, along with their associated dependency metadata. COPS-GT uses aggressive garbage collection to prune old state (see Section 5.1).

- *(COPS-GT) Ensure fast get_trans operations.* The get transactions in COPS-GT ensure that the set of returned values are causal+ consistent (all dependencies are satisfied). A naive algorithm could block and/or take an unbounded number of get rounds to complete. Both situations are incompatible with the availability and low latency goals of ALPS systems; we present an algorithm for get_trans that completes in at most two rounds of local get_by_version operations.

4.2 The COPS Key-Value Store

Unlike traditional ⟨*key, val*⟩–tuple stores, COPS must track the versions of written values, as well as their dependencies in the case of COPS-GT. In COPS, the system stores the most recent version number and value for each key. In COPS-GT, the system maps each key to a list of version entries, each consisting of ⟨*version, value, deps*⟩. The *deps* field is a list of the version's zero or more dependencies; each dependency is a ⟨*key, version*⟩ pair.

Each COPS cluster maintains its own copy of the key-value store. For scalability, our implementation partitions the keyspace across a cluster's nodes using consistent hashing [27], through other techniques (e.g., directory-based approaches [6, 21]) are also possible. For fault tolerance, each key is replicated across a small number of nodes using chain replication [5, 48, 51]. Gets and puts are linearizable across the nodes in the cluster. Operations return to the client library as soon as they execute in the *local* cluster; operations between clusters occur asynchronously.

Every key stored in COPS has one *primary* node in each cluster. We term the set of primary nodes for a key across all clusters as the *equivalent nodes* for that key. In practice, COPS's consistent hashing assigns each node responsibility for a few different key ranges. Key ranges may have different sizes and node mappings in different datacenters, but the total number of equivalent nodes with which a given node needs to communicate is proportional to the number of datacenters (i.e., communication is *not* all-to-all between nodes in different datacenters).

After a write completes locally, the primary node places it in a replication queue, from which it is sent asynchronously to remote equivalent nodes. Those nodes, in turn, wait until the value's dependencies are satisfied in their local cluster before locally committing

```
# Alice's Photo Upload
ctx_id = createContext()    // Alice logs in
put(Photo, "Portuguese Coast", ctx_id)
put(Album, "add &Photo", ctx_id)
deleteContext(ctx_id)       // Alice logs out

# Bob's Photo View
ctx_id = createContext()    // Bob logs in
"&Photo" ← get(Album, ctx_id)
"Portuguese Coast" ← get(Photo, ctx_id)
deleteContext(ctx_id)       // Bob logs out
```

Figure 5: Snippets of pseudocode using the COPS programmer interface for the photo upload scenario from Section 3.2. When using COPS-GT, each get would instead be a get_trans on a single key.

the value. This dependency checking mechanism ensures writes happen in a causally consistent order and reads never block.

4.3 Client Library and Interface

The COPS client library provides a simple and intuitive programming interface. Figure 5 illustrates the use of this interface for the photo upload scenario. The client API consists of four operations:

1. $ctx\_id \leftarrow$ createContext()
2. bool $\leftarrow$ deleteContext(ctx_id)
3. bool $\leftarrow$ put (key, $value$, ctx_id)
4. $value \leftarrow$ get (key, ctx_id) [In COPS]

or

4. $\langle values \rangle \leftarrow$ get_trans ($\langle keys \rangle$, ctx_id) [In COPS-GT]

The client API differs from a traditional key-value interface in two ways. First, COPS-GT provides get_trans, which returns a consistent view of multiple key-value pairs in a single call. Second, all functions take a context argument, which the library uses internally to track causal dependencies across each client's operations [49]. The context defines the causal+ "thread of execution." A single process may contain many separate threads of execution (e.g., a web server concurrently serving 1000s of independent connections). By separating different threads of execution, COPS avoids false dependencies that would result from intermixing them.

We next describe the state kept by the client library in COPS-GT to enforce consistency in get transactions. We then show how COPS can store significantly less dependency state.

COPS-GT Client Library. The client library in COPS-GT stores the client's context in a table of $\langle key, version, deps \rangle$ entries. Clients reference their context using a *context ID* (ctx_id) in the API.[4] When a client gets a key from the data store, the library adds this key and its causal dependencies to the context. When a client puts a value, the library sets the put's dependencies to the most recent version of each key in the current context. A successful put into the data store returns the version number v assigned to the written value. The client library then adds this new entry, $\langle key, v, D \rangle$, to the context.

The context therefore includes all values previously read or written in the client's session, as well as all of those dependencies' dependencies, as illustrated in Figure 6. This raises two concerns about the potential size of this causality graph: (i) state requirements for storing these dependencies, both in the client library and in the

---
[4]Maintaining state in the library and passing in an ID was a design choice; one could also encode the entire context table as an opaque blob and pass it between client and library so that the library is stateless.

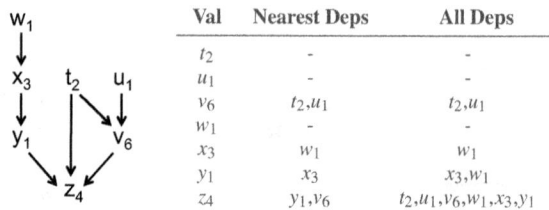

Val	Nearest Deps	All Deps
t_2	-	-
u_1	-	-
v_6	t_2, u_1	t_2, u_1
w_1	-	-
x_3	w_1	w_1
y_1	x_3	x_3, w_1
z_4	y_1, v_6	$t_2, u_1, v_6, w_1, x_3, y_1$

Figure 6: A sample graph of causal dependencies for a client context. Arrows indicate causal relationships (e.g., x_3 depends on w_1). The table lists all dependencies for each value and the "nearest" dependencies used to minimize dependency checks.

data store, and (ii) the number of potential checks that must occur when replicating writes between clusters, in order to ensure causal consistency. To mitigate the client and data-store state required to track dependencies, COPS-GT provides garbage collection, described in Section 5.1, that removes dependencies once they are committed to all COPS replicas.

To reduce the number of dependency checks during replication, the client library identifies several potential optimizations for servers to use. Consider the graph in Figure 6. y_1 depends on x_3 and, by transitivity, on w_1. If the storage node committing y_1 determines that x_3 has been committed, then it can infer that w_1 has also been committed, and thus, need not check for it explicitly. Similarly, while z_4 depends directly on t_2 and v_6, the committing node needs only check v_6, because v_6 itself depends on t_2.

We term dependencies that *must* be checked the *nearest* dependencies, listed in the table in Figure 6.[5] To enable servers to use these optimizations, the client library first computes the nearest dependencies within the write's dependency list and marks them accordingly when issuing the write.

The nearest dependencies are sufficient for the key-value store to provide causal+ consistency; the full dependency list is only needed to provide get_trans operations in COPS-GT.

COPS Client Library. The client library in COPS requires significantly less state and complexity because it only needs to learn the nearest, rather than all, dependencies. Accordingly, it does not store or even retrieve the dependencies of any value it gets: The retrieved value is nearer than any of its dependencies, rendering them unnecessary.

Thus, the COPS client library stores only $\langle key, version \rangle$ entries. For a get operation, the retrieved $\langle key, version \rangle$ is added to the context. For a put operation, the library uses the current context as the nearest dependencies, clears the context, and then repopulates it with only this put. This put depends on all previous key-version pairs and thus is nearer than them.

4.4 Writing Values in COPS and COPS-GT

Building on our description of the client library and key-value store, we now walk through the steps involved in writing a value to COPS. All writes in COPS first go to the client's local cluster and then propagate asynchronously to remote clusters. The key-value store exports a single API call to provide both operations:

$\langle bool, vers \rangle \leftarrow$ put_after (key, val, $[deps]$, $nearest$, $vers=\emptyset$)

---
[5]In graph-theoretic terms, the nearest dependencies of a value are those in the causality graph with a *longest* path to the value of length one.

Writes to the local cluster. When a client calls put (*key*,*val*,*ctx_id*), the library computes the complete set of dependencies *deps*, and identifies some of those dependency tuples as the value's *nearest* ones. The library then calls put_after without the *version* argument (i.e., it sets *version*=0). In COPS-GT, the library includes *deps* in the put_after call because dependencies must be stored with the value; in COPS, the library only needs to include *nearest* and does not include *deps*.[6] The key's primary storage node in the local cluster assigns the key a version number and returns it to the client library. We restrict each client to a single outstanding put; this is necessary because later puts must know the version numbers of earlier puts so they may depend on them.

The put_after operation ensures that *val* is committed to each cluster only *after* all of the entries in its dependency list have been written. In the client's local cluster, this property holds automatically, as the local store provides linearizability. (If *y* depends on *x*, then put(*x*) must have been committed before put(*y*) was issued.) This is not true in remote clusters, however, which we discuss below.

The primary storage node uses a Lamport timestamp [31] to assign a unique version number to each update. The node sets the version number's high-order bits to its Lamport clock and the low-order bits to its unique node identifier. Lamport timestamps allow COPS to derive a single global order over all writes for each key. This order implicitly implements the last-writer-wins convergent conflict handling policy. COPS is also capable of explicitly detecting and resolving conflicts, which we discuss in Section 5.3. Note that because Lamport timestamps provide a partial ordering of all distributed events in a way that respects potential causality, this global ordering is compatible with COPS's causal consistency.

Write replication between clusters. After a write commits locally, the primary storage node asynchronously replicates that write to its equivalent nodes in different clusters using a stream of put_after operations; here, however, the primary node includes the key's version number in the put_after call. As with local put_after calls, the *deps* argument is included in COPS-GT, and not included in COPS. This approach scales well and avoids the need for a single serialization point, but requires the remote nodes receiving updates to commit an update only after its dependencies have been committed to the same cluster.

To ensure this property, a node that receives a put_after request from another cluster must determine if the value's *nearest* dependencies have already been satisfied locally. It does so by issuing a check to the local nodes responsible for the those dependencies:

bool ← dep_check (*key*, *version*)

When a node receives a dep_check, it examines its local state to determine if the dependency value has already been written. If so, it immediately responds to the operation. If not, it blocks until the needed version has been written.

If all dep_check operations on the nearest dependencies succeed, the node handling the put_after request commits the written value, making it available to other reads and writes in its local cluster. (If any dep_check operation times out the node handling the put_after reissues it, potentially to a new node if a failure occurred.) The way that *nearest* dependencies are computed ensures that *all* dependencies have been satisfied before the value is committed, which in turn ensures causal consistency.

---

[6]We use bracket notation ([]) to indicate an argument is optional; the optional arguments are used in COPS-GT, but not in COPS.

4.5 Reading Values in COPS

Like writes, reads are satisfied in the local cluster. Clients call the get library function with the appropriate context; the library in turn issues a read to the node responsible for the key in the local cluster:

⟨*value*, *version*, *deps*⟩ ← get_by_version (*key*, *version*=LATEST)

This read can request either the latest version of the key or a specific older one. Requesting the latest version is equivalent to a regular single-key get; requesting a specific version is necessary to enable get transactions. Accordingly, get_by_version operations in COPS always request the latest version. Upon receiving a response, the client library adds the ⟨*key*,*version*[,*deps*]⟩ tuple to the client context, and returns *value* to the calling code. The *deps* are stored only in COPS-GT, not in COPS.

4.6 Get Transactions in COPS-GT

The COPS-GT client library provides a get_trans interface because reading a set of dependent keys using a single-key get interface cannot ensure causal+ consistency, even though the data store itself is causal+ consistent. We demonstrate this problem by extending the photo album example to include access control, whereby Alice first changes her album ACL to "friends only", and then writes a new description of her travels and adds more photos to the album.

A natural (but incorrect!) implementation of code to read Alice's album might (1) fetch the ACL, (2) check permissions, and (3) fetch the album description and photos. This approach contains a straightforward "time-to-check-to-time-to-use" race condition: when Eve accesses the album, her get(ACL) might return the old ACL, which permitted anyone (including Eve) to read it, but her get(album contents) might return the "friends only" version.

One straw-man solution is to require that clients issue single-key get operations in the reverse order of their causal dependencies: The above problem would not have occurred if the client executed get(album) before get(ACL). This solution, however, is *also* incorrect. Imagine that after updating her album, Alice decided that some photographs were too personal, so she (3) deleted those photos and rewrote the description, and then (4) marked the ACL open again. This straw-man has a different time-of-check-to-time-of-use error, where get(album) retrieves the private album, and the subsequent get(ACL) retrieves the "public" ACL. In short, there is no correct canonical ordering of the ACL and the album entries.

Instead, a better programming interface would allow the client to obtain a causal+ consistent view of multiple keys. The standard way to achieve such a guarantee is to read and write all related keys in a transaction; this, however, requires a single serialization point for all grouped keys, which COPS avoids for greater scalability and simplicity. Instead, COPS allows keys to be written independently (with explicit dependencies in metadata), and provides a get_trans operation for retrieving a consistent view of multiple keys.

Get transactions. To retrieve multiple values in a causal+ consistent manner, a client calls get_trans with the desired set of keys, e.g., get_trans(⟨ACL, album⟩). Depending on when and where it was issued, this get transaction can return different combinations of ACL and album, but never ⟨ACL$_{public}$, Album$_{personal}$⟩.

The COPS client library implements the get transactions algorithm in two rounds, shown in Figure 7. In the first round, the library issues *n* concurrent get_by_version operations to the local cluster, one for each key the client listed in get_trans. Because

```
# @param  keys     list of keys
# @param  ctx_id   context id
# @return values   list of values

function get_trans(keys, ctx_id):
  # Get keys in parallel (first round)
  for k in keys
    results[k] = get_by_version(k, LATEST)

  # Calculate causally correct versions (ccv)
  for k in keys
    ccv[k] = max(ccv[k], results[k].vers)
    for dep in results[k].deps
      if dep.key in keys
        ccv[dep.key] = max(ccv[dep.key], dep.vers)

  # Get needed ccvs in parallel (second round)
  for k in keys
    if ccv[k] > results[k].vers
      results[k] = get_by_version(k, ccv[k])

  # Update the metadata stored in the context
  update_context(results, ctx_id)

  # Return only the values to the client
  return extract_values(results)
```

Figure 7: Pseudocode for the get_trans algorithm.

COPS-GT commits writes locally, the local data store guarantees that each of these explicitly listed keys' dependencies are already satisfied—that is, they have been written locally and reads on them will immediately return. These explicitly listed, independently retrieved values, however, may not be consistent with one another, as shown above. Each get_by_version operation returns a ⟨*value*, *version*, *deps*⟩ tuple, where *deps* is a list of keys and versions. The client library then examines every dependency entry ⟨*key*, *version*⟩. The causal dependencies for that result are satisfied if either the client did not request the dependent key, or if it did, the version it retrieved was ≥ the version in the dependency list.

For all keys that are not satisfied, the library issues a second round of concurrent get_by_version operations. The version requested will be the newest version seen in any dependency list from the first round. These versions satisfy all causal dependencies from the first round because they are ≥ the needed versions. In addition, because dependencies are transitive and these second-round versions are all depended on by versions retrieved in the first round, they do not introduce any new dependencies that need to be satisfied. This algorithm allows get_trans to return a consistent view of the data store as of the time of the latest timestamp retrieved in first round.

The second round happens only when the client must read newer versions than those retrieved in the first round. This case occurs only if keys involved in the get transaction are updated during the first round. Thus, we expect the second round to be rare. In our example, if Eve issues a get_trans concurrent with Alice's writes, the algorithms first round of gets might retrieve the public ACL and the private album. The private album, however, depends on the "friends only" ACL, so the second round would fetch this newer version of the ACL, allowing get_trans to return a causal+ consistent set of values to the client.

The causal+ consistency of the data store provides two important properties for the get transaction algorithm's second round. First, the get_by_version requests will succeed immediately, as the requested version must already exist in the local cluster. Second, the new get_by_version requests will not introduce any new dependencies, as those dependencies were already known in the first

round due to transitivity. This second property demonstrates why the get transaction algorithm specifies an explicit version in its second round, rather than just getting the latest: Otherwise, in the face of concurrent writes, a newer version could introduce still newer dependencies, which could continue indefinitely.

5. GARBAGE, FAULTS, AND CONFLICTS

This section describes three important aspects of COPS and COPS-GT: their garbage collection subsystems, which reduce the amount of extra state in the system; their fault tolerant design for client, node, and datacenter failures; and their conflict detection mechanisms.

5.1 Garbage Collection Subsystem

COPS and COPS-GT clients store metadata; COPS-GT servers additionally keeps multiple versions of keys and dependencies. Without intervention, the space footprint of the system would grow without bound as keys are updated and inserted. The COPS garbage collection subsystem deletes unneeded state, keeping the total system size in check. Section 6 evaluates the overhead of maintaining and transmitting this additional metadata.

Version Garbage Collection. (COPS-GT only)
What is stored: COPS-GT stores multiple versions of each key to answer get_by_version requests from clients.
Why it can be cleaned: The get_trans algorithm limits the number of versions needed to complete a get transaction. The algorithm's second round issues get_by_version requests only for versions later than those returned in the first round. To enable prompt garbage collection, COPS-GT limits the total running time of get_trans through a configurable parameter, *trans_time* (set to 5 seconds in our implementation). (If the timeout fires, the client library will restart the get_trans call and satisfy the transaction with newer versions of the keys; we expect this to happen only if multiple nodes in a cluster crash.)
When it can be cleaned: After a new version of a key is written, COPS-GT only needs to keep the old version around for *trans_time* plus a small delta for clock skew. After this time, no get_by_version call will subsequently request the old version, and the garbage collector can remove it.
Space Overhead: The space overhead is bounded by the number of old versions that can be created within the *trans_time*. This number is determined by the maximum write throughput that the node can sustain. Our implementation sustains 105MB/s of write traffic per node, requiring (potentially) a non-prohibitive extra 525MB of buffer space to hold old versions. This overhead is per-machine and does not grow with the cluster size or the number of datacenters.

Dependency Garbage Collection. (COPS-GT only)
What is stored: Dependencies are stored to allow get transactions to obtain a consistent view of the data store.
Why it can be cleaned: COPS-GT can garbage collect these dependencies once the versions associated with old dependencies are no longer needed for correctness in get transaction operations.

To illustrate when get transaction operations no longer need dependencies, consider value z_2 that depends on x_2 and y_2. A get transaction of x, y, and z requires that if z_2 is returned, then $x_{\geq 2}$ and $y_{\geq 2}$ must be returned as well. Causal consistency ensures that x_2 and y_2 are written before z_2 is written. Causal+ consistency's progressing property ensures that once x_2 and y_2 are written, then either they or some later version will always be returned by a get operation. Thus, once z_2 has been written in all datacenters and the *trans_time* has passed, any get transaction returning z_2 will return $x_{\geq 2}$ and $y_{\geq 2}$, and thus z_2's dependencies can be garbage collected.

When it can be cleaned: After *trans_time* seconds after a value has been committed in *all* datacenters, COPS-GT can clean a value's dependencies. (Recall that committed enforces that its dependencies have been satisfied.) Both COPS and COPS-GT can further set the value's *never-depend* flag, discussed below. To clean dependencies each remote datacenter notifies the originating datacenter when the write has committed and the timeout period has elapsed. Once all datacenters confirm, the originating datacenter cleans its own dependencies and informs the others to do likewise. To minimize bandwidth devoted to cleaning dependencies, a replica only notifies the originating datacenter if this version of a key is the newest after *trans_time* seconds; if it is not, there is no need to collect the dependencies because the entire version will be collected.[7]

Space Overhead: Under normal operation, dependencies are garbage collected after *trans_time* plus a round-trip time. Dependencies are only collected on the most recent version of the key; older versions of keys are already garbage collected as described above.

During a partition, dependencies on the most recent versions of keys cannot be collected. This is a limitation of COPS-GT, although we expect long partitions to be rare. To illustrate why this concession is necessary for get transaction correctness, consider value b_2 that depends on value a_2: if b_2's dependence on a_2 is prematurely collected, some later value c_2 that causally depends on b_2—and thus on a_2—could be written without the explicit dependence on a_2. Then, if a_2, b_2, and c_2 are all replicated to a datacenter in short order, the first round of a get transaction could obtain a_1, an earlier version of a, with c_2, and then return these two values to the client, precisely because it did not know c_2 depends on the newer a_2.

Client Metadata Garbage Collection. (COPS + COPS-GT)

What is Stored: The COPS client library tracks all operations during a client session (single thread of execution) using the *ctx_id* passed with all operation. In contrast to the dependency information discussed above which resides in the key-value store itself, the dependencies discussed here are part of the client metadata and are store in the client library. In both systems, each get since the last put adds another nearest dependency. Additionally in COPS-GT, all new values and their dependencies returned in get_trans operations and all put operations add normal dependencies. If a client session lasts for a long time, the number of dependencies attached to updates will grow large, increasing the size of the dependency metadata that COPS needs to store.

Why it can be cleaned: As with the dependency tracking above, clients need to track dependencies only until they are guaranteed to be satisfied everywhere.

When it can be cleaned: COPS reduces the size of this client state (the context) in two ways. First, as noted above, once a put_after commits successfully to all datacenters, COPS flags that key version as *never-depend*, in order to indicate that clients need not express a dependence upon it. get_by_version results include this flag, and the client library will immediately remove a *never-depend* item from the list of dependencies in the client context. Furthermore, this process is transitive: Anything that a *never-depend* key depended on must have been flagged *never-depend*, so it too can be garbage collected from the context.

Second, the COPS storage nodes remove unnecessary dependencies from put_after operations. When a node receives a put_after, it checks each item in the dependency list and removes items with version numbers older than a *global checkpoint time*. This checkpoint time is the newest Lamport timestamp that is satisfied at *all* nodes across the entire system. The COPS key-value store returns this checkpoint time to the client library (e.g., in response to a put_after), allowing the library to clean these dependencies from the context.[8]

To compute the global checkpoint time, each storage node first determines the oldest Lamport timestamp of any *pending* put_after in the key range for which it is primary. (In other words, it determines the timestamp of its oldest key that is not guaranteed to be satisfied at all replicas.) It then contacts its equivalent nodes in other datacenters (those nodes that handle the same key range). The nodes pair-wise exchange their minimum Lamport times, remembering the oldest observed Lamport clock of any of the replicas. At the conclusion of this step, all datacenters have the same information: each node knows the globally oldest Lamport timestamp in its key range. The nodes within a datacenter then gossip around the per-range minimums to find the minimum Lamport timestamp observed by any one of them. This periodic procedure is done 10 times a second in our implementation and has no noticeable impact on performance.

5.2 Fault Tolerance

COPS is resilient to client, node, and datacenter failures. For the following discussion, we assume that failures are fail-stop: components halt in response to a failure instead of operating incorrectly or maliciously, and failures are detectable.

Client Failures. COPS's key-value interface means that each client request (through the library) is handled independently and atomically by the data store. From the storage system's perspective, if a client fails, it simply stops issuing new requests; no recovery is necessary. From a client's perspective, COPS's dependency tracking makes it easier to handle failures of other clients, by ensuring properties such as referential integrity. Consider the photo and album example: If a client fails after writing the photo, but before writing a reference to the photo, the data store will still be in a consistent state. There will never be an instance of the reference to the photo without the photo itself already being written.

Key-Value Node Failures. COPS can use any underlying fault-tolerant linearizable key-value store. We built our system on top of independent clusters of FAWN-KV [5] nodes, which use chain replication [51] *within* a cluster to mask node failures. Accordingly, we describe how COPS can use chain replication to provide tolerance to node failures.

Similar to the design of FAWN-KV, each data item is stored in a chain of R consecutive nodes along the consistent hashing ring. put_after operations are sent to the head of the appropriate chain, propagate along the chain, and then commit at the tail, which then acknowledges the operation. get_by_version operations are sent to the tail, which responds directly.

Server-issued operations are slightly more involved because they are issued from and processed by different chains of nodes. The tail in the local cluster replicates put_after operations to the head in each remote datacenter. The remote heads then send dep_check operations, which are essentially read operations, to the appropriate

---

[7]We are currently investigating if collecting dependencies in this manner provides a significant enough benefit over collecting them after the global checkpoint time (discussed below) to justify its messaging cost.

[8]Because of outstanding reads, clients and servers must also wait *trans_time* seconds before they can use a new global checkpoint time.

tails in their local cluster. Once these return (if the operation does not return, a timeout will fire and the `dep_check` will be reissued), the remote head propagates the value down the (remote) chain to the remote tail, which commits the value and acknowledges the operation back to the originating datacenter.

Dependency garbage collection follows a similar pattern of interlocking chains, though we omit details for brevity. Version garbage collection is done locally on each node and can operate as in the single node case. Calculation of the global checkpoint time, for client metadata garbage collection, operates normally with each tail updating its corresponding key range minimums.

Datacenter Failures. The partition-tolerant design of COPS also provides resiliency to entire datacenter failures (or partitions). In the face of such failures, COPS continues to operate as normal, with a few key differences.

First, any `put_after` operations that originated in the failed datacenter, but which were not yet copied out, will be lost. This is an inevitable cost of allowing low-latency local writes that return faster than the propagation delay between datacenters. If the datacenter is only partitioned and has not failed, no writes will be lost. Instead, they will only be delayed until the partition heals.[9]

Second, the storage required for replication queues in the active datacenters will grow. They will be unable to send `put_after` operations to the failed datacenter, and thus COPS will be unable to garbage collect those dependencies. The system administrator has two options: allow the queues to grow if the partition is likely to heal soon, or reconfigure COPS to no longer use the failed datacenter.

Third, in COPS-GT, dependency garbage collection cannot continue in the face of a datacenter failure, until either the partition is healed or the system is reconfigured to exclude the failed datacenter.

5.3 Conflict Detection

Conflicts occur when there are two "simultaneous" (i.e., not in the same context/thread of execution) writes to a given key. The default COPS system avoids conflict detection using a last-writer-wins strategy. The "last" write is determined by comparing version numbers, and allows us to avoid conflict detection for increased simplicity and efficiency. We believe this behavior is useful for many applications. There are other applications, however, that become simpler to reason about and program with a more explicit conflict-detection scheme. For these applications, COPS can be configured to detect conflicting operations and then invoke some application-specific convergent conflict handler.

COPS with conflict detection, which we refer to as COPS-CD, adds three new components to the system. First, all put operations carry with them *previous version* metadata, which indicates the most recent previous version of the key that was visible at the local cluster at the time of the write (this previous version may be null). Second, all put operations now have an implicit dependency on that previous version, which ensures that a new version will only be written after its previous version. This implicit dependency entails an additional `dep_check` operation, though this has low overhead and always executes on the local machine. Third, COPS-CD has an application-specified convergent conflict handler that is invoked when a conflict is detected.

System	Causal+	Scalable	Get Trans
LOG	Yes	No	No
COPS	Yes	Yes	No
COPS-GT	Yes	Yes	Yes

Table 1: Summary of three systems under comparison.

COPS-CD follows a simple procedure to determine if a put operation *new* to a key (with previous version *prev*) is in conflict with the key's current visible version *curr*:

$$prev \neq curr \text{ if and only if } new \text{ and } curr \text{ conflict.}$$

We omit a full proof, but present the intuition here. In the forward direction, we know that *prev* must be written before *new*, $prev \neq curr$, and that for *curr* to be visible instead of *prev*, we must have $curr > prev$ by the progressing property of causal+. But because *prev* is the most recent causally previous version of *new*, we can conclude $curr \not\leadsto new$. Further, because *curr* was written before *new*, it cannot be causally after it, so $new \not\leadsto curr$ and thus they conflict. In the reverse direction, if *new* and *curr* conflict, then $curr \not\leadsto new$. By definition, $prev \leadsto new$, and thus $curr \neq prev$.

6. EVALUATION

This section presents an evaluation of COPS and COPS-GT using microbenchmarks that establish baseline system latency and throughput, a sensitivity analysis that explores the impact of different parameters that characterize a dynamic workload, and larger end-to-end experiments that show scalable causal+ consistency.

6.1 Implementation and Experimental Setup

COPS is approximately 13,000 lines of C++ code. It is built on top of FAWN-KV [5, 18] (~8500 LOC), which provides linearizable key-value storage within a local cluster. COPS uses Apache Thrift [7] for communication between all system components and Google's Snappy [45] for compressing dependency lists. Our current prototype implements all features described in the paper, excluding chain replication for local fault tolerance[10] and conflict detection.

We compare three systems: LOG, COPS, and COPS-GT. LOG uses the COPS code-base but excludes all dependency tracking, making it simulate previous work that uses log exchange to establish causal consistency (e.g., Bayou [41] and PRACTI [10]). Table 1 summarizes these three systems.

Each experiment is run on one cluster from the VICCI testbed [52]. The cluster's 70 servers give users an isolated Linux VServer. Each server has 2x6 core Intel Xeon X5650 CPUs, 48GB RAM, 3x1TB Hard Drives, and 2x1GigE network ports.

For each experiment, we partition the cluster into multiple logical "datacenters" as necessary. We retain full bandwidth between the nodes in different datacenters to reflect the high-bandwidth backbone that often exists between them. All reads and writes in FAWN-KV go to disk, but most operations in our experiments hit the kernel buffer cache.

The results presented are from 60-second trials. Data from the first and last 15s of each trial were elided to avoid experimental artifacts, as well as to allow garbage collection and replication mechanisms to ramp up. We run each trial 15 times and report the median; the minimum and maximum results are almost always within 6% of

---

[9]It remains an interesting aspect of future work to support flexibility in the number of datacenters required for committing within the causal+ model.

[10]Chain replication was not fully functional in the version of FAWN-KV on which our implementation is built.

System	Operation	Latency (ms)			Throughput (Kops/s)
		50%	99%	99.9%	
Thrift	ping	0.26	3.62	12.25	60
COPS	get_by_version	0.37	3.08	11.29	52
COPS-GT	get_by_version	0.38	3.14	9.52	52
COPS	put_after (1)	0.57	6.91	11.37	30
COPS-GT	put_after (1)	0.91	5.37	7.37	24
COPS-GT	put_after (130)	1.03	7.45	11.54	20

Table 2: Latency (in ms) and throughput (in Kops/s) of various operations for 1B objects in saturated systems. put_after(x) includes metadata for x dependencies.

the median, and we attribute the few trials with larger throughput differences to the shared nature of the VICCI platform.

6.2 Microbenchmarks

We first evaluate the performance characteristics for COPS and COPS-GT in a simple setting: two datacenters, one server per datacenter, and one colocated client machine. The client sends put and get requests to its local server, attempting to saturate the system. The requests are spread over 2^{18} keys and have 1B values—we use 1B values for consistency with later experiments, where small values are the worst case for COPS (see Figure 11(c)). Table 2 shows the median, 99%, and 99.9% latencies and throughput.

The design decision in COPS to handle client operations locally yields low latency for all operations. The latencies for get_by_version operations in COPS and COPS-GT are similar to an end-to-end RPC ping using Thrift. The latencies for put_after operations are slightly higher because they are more computationally expensive; they need to update metadata and write values. Nevertheless, the median latency for put_after operations, even those with up to 130 dependencies, is around 1 ms.

System throughput follows a similar pattern. get_by_version operations achieve high throughput, similar to that of Thrift ping operations (52 vs. 60 Kops/s). A COPS server can process put_after operations at 30 Kops/s (such operations are more computationally expensive than gets), while COPS-GT achieves 20% lower throughput when put_after operations have 1 dependency (due to the cost of garbage collecting old versions). As the number of dependencies in COP-GT put_after operations increases, throughput drops slightly due to the greater size of metadata in each operation (each dependency is ~12B).

6.3 Dynamic Workloads

We model a dynamic workload with interacting clients accessing the COPS system as follows. We set up two datacenters of S servers each and colocate S client machines in one of the two datacenters. The clients access storage servers in the local datacenter, which replicates put_after operations to the remote datacenter. We report the *sustainable* throughput in our experiments, which is the maximum throughput that both datacenters can handle. In most cases, COPS becomes CPU-bound at the local datacenter, and that COPS-GT becomes CPU-bound at the remote one.

To better stress the system and more accurately depict real operation, each client machine emulates multiple logical COPS clients. Each time a client performs an operation, it randomly executes a put or get operation, according to a specified put:get ratio. All operations in a given experiment use fixed-size values.

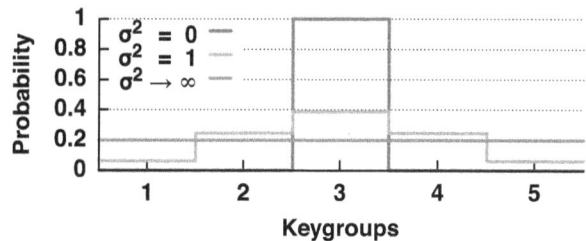

Figure 8: In our experiments, clients choose keys to access by first selecting a keygroup according to some normal distribution, then randomly selecting a key within that group according to a uniform distribution. Figure shows such a stepped normal distribution for differing variances for client #3 (of 5).

The key for each operation is selected to control the amount of dependence between operations (i.e., from fully isolated to fully intermixed). Specifically, given N clients, the full keyspace consists of N keygroups, $R_1 \ldots R_N$, one per client. Each keygroup contains K keys, which are randomly distributed (i.e., they do not all reside on the same server). When clients issue operations, they select keys as follows. First, they pick a keygroup by sampling from a normal distribution defined over the N keygroups, where each keygroup has width 1. Then, they select a key within that keygroup uniformly at random. The result is a distribution over keys with equal likelihood for keys within the same keygroup, and possibly varying likelihood across groups.

Figure 8 illustrates an example, showing the keygroup distribution for client #3 (of 5 total) for variances of 0, 1, and the limit approaching ∞. When the variance is 0, a client will restrict its accesses to its "own" keygroup and never interact with other clients. In contrast, when the variance $\rightarrow \infty$, client accesses are distributed uniformly at random over all keys, leading to maximal inter-dependencies between put_after operations.

The parameters of the dynamic workload experiments are the following, unless otherwise specified:

Parameter	Default	Parameter	Default
datacenters	2	put:get ratio	1:1 or 1:4
servers / datacenter	4	variance	1
clients / server	1024	value size	1B
keys / keygroup	512		

As the state space of all possible combinations of these variables is large, the following experiments explore parameters individually.

Clients Per Server. We first characterize the system throughput as a function of increasing delay between client operations (for two different put:get ratios).[11] Figure 9(a) shows that when the inter-operation delay is low, COPS significantly outperforms COPS-GT. Conversely, when the inter-operation delay approaches several hundred milliseconds, the maximum throughputs of COPS and COPS-GT converge. Figure 9(b) helps explain this behavior: As the inter-operation delay increases, the number of dependencies per operation *decreases* because of the ongoing garbage collection.

---

[11]For these experiments, we do not directly control the inter-operation delay. Rather, we increase the number of logical clients running on each of the client machines from 1 to 2^{18}; given a fixed-size thread pool for clients in our test framework, each logical client gets scheduled more infrequently. As each client makes one request before yielding, this leads to higher average inter-op delay (calculated simply as $\frac{throughput}{\# \text{ of clients}}$). Our default setting of 1024 clients/server yields an average inter-op delay of 29 ms for COPS-GT with a 1:0 put:get ratio, 11ms for COPS with 1:0, 11ms for COPS-GT with 1:4, and 8ms for COPS with 1:4.

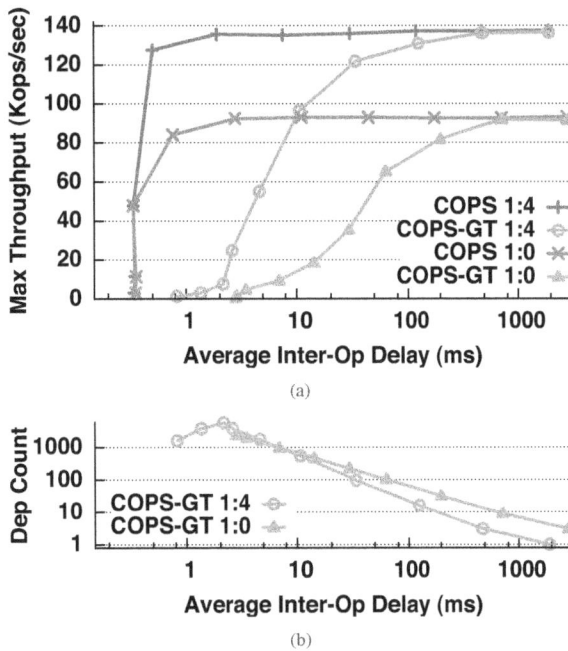

Figure 9: Maximum throughput and the resulting average dependency size of COPS and COPS-GT for a given inter-put delay between consecutive operations by the same logical client. The legend gives the put:get ratio (i.e., 1:0 or 1:4).

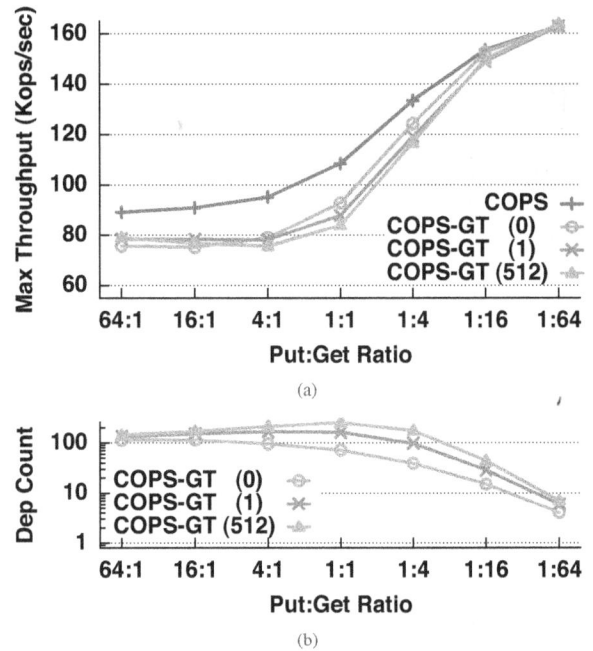

Figure 10: Maximum throughput and the resulting average dependency size of COPS and COPS-GT for a given put:get ratio. The legend gives the variance (i.e., 0, 1, or 512).

To understand this relationship, consider the following example. If the global-checkpoint-time is 6 seconds behind the current time and a logical client is performing 100 puts/sec (in an all-put workload), each put will have $100 \cdot 6 = 600$ dependencies. Figure 9(b) illustrates this relationship. While COPS will store only the single nearest dependency (not shown), COPS-GT must track all dependencies that have not been garbage collected. These additional dependencies explain the performance of COPS-GT: When the inter-put time is small, there are a large number of dependencies that need to be propagated with each value, and thus each operation is more expensive.

The global-checkpoint-time typically lags ~6 seconds behind the current time because it includes both the *trans_time* delay (per Section 5.1) and the time needed to gossip checkpoints around their local datacenter (nodes gossip once every 100ms). Recall that an agreed-upon *trans_time* delay is needed to ensure that currently executing get_trans operations can complete, while storage nodes use gossiping to determine the oldest uncommitted operation (and thus the latest timestamp for which dependencies can be garbage collected). Notably, round-trip-time latency *between* datacenters is only a small component of the lag, and thus performance is not significantly affected by RTT (e.g., a 70ms wide-area RTT is about 1% of a 6s lag for the global-checkpoint-time).

Put:Get Ratio. We next evaluate system performance under varying put:get ratios and key-access distributions. Figure 10(a) shows the throughput of COPS and COPS-GT for put:get ratios from 64:1 to 1:64 and three different distribution variances. We observe that throughput increases for read-heavier workloads (put:get ratios < 1), and that COPS-GT becomes competitive with COPS for read-mostly workloads. While the performance of COPS is identical under different variances, the throughput of COPS-GT *is* affected by variance. We explain both behaviors by characterizing the relationship be-

tween put:get ratio and the number of dependencies (Figure 10(b)); fewer dependencies translates to less metadata that needs to be propagated and thus higher throughput.

When different clients access the same keys (variance > 0), we observe two distinct phases in Figure 10(b). First, as the put:get ratio decreases from 64:1 to 1:1, the number of dependencies *increases*. This increase occurs because each get operation increases the likelihood a client will inherit new dependencies by getting a value that has been recently put by another client. For instance, if client₁ puts a value v_1 with dependencies d and client₂ reads that value, then client₂'s future put will have dependencies on both v_1 and d. Second, as the put:get ratio then decreases from 1:1 to 1:64, the number of dependencies *decreases* for two reasons: (i) each client is executing fewer put operations and thus each value depends on fewer values previously written by this client; and (ii) because there are fewer put operations, more of the keys have a value that is older than the global-checkpoint-time, and thus getting them introduces no additional dependencies.

When clients access independent keys (variance = 0), the number of dependencies is strictly decreasing with the put:get ratio. This result is expected because each client accesses only values in its own keygroup that it previously wrote and already has a dependency on. Thus, no get causes a client to inherit new dependencies.

The average dependency count for COPS (not shown) is always low, from 1 to 4 dependencies, because COPS needs to track only the nearest (instead of all) dependencies.

Keys Per Keygroup. Figure 11(a) shows the effect of keygroup size on the throughput of COPS and COPS-GT. Recall that clients distribute their requests uniformly over keys in their selected keygroup. The behavior of COPS-GT is nuanced; we explain its varying throughput by considering the likelihood that a get operation will inherit new dependencies, which in turn reduces throughput. With the default variance of 1 and a low number of keys/keygroup, most

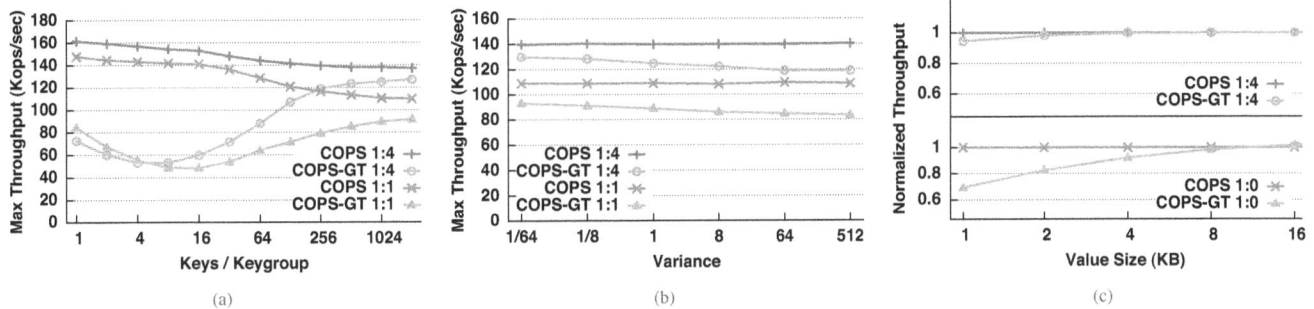

Figure 11: Maximum system throughput (using put:get ratios of 1:4, 1:1, or 1:0) for varied keys/keygroup, variances, and value sizes.

clients access only a small number of keys. Once a value is retrieved and its dependencies inherited, subsequent gets on that same value do not cause a client to inherit any new dependencies. As the number of keys/keygroup begins to increase, however, clients are less likely to get the same value repeatedly, and they begin inheriting additional dependencies. As this number continues to rise, however, garbage collection can begin to have an effect: Fewer gets retrieve a value that was recently written by another client (e.g., after the global checkpoint time), and thus fewer gets return new dependencies. The bowed shape of COPS-GT's performance is likely due to these two contrasting effects.

Variance. Figure 11(b) examines the effect of variance on system performance. As noted earlier, the throughput of COPS is unaffected by different variances: Get operations in COPS never inherit extra dependencies, as the returned value is always "nearer," by definition. COPS-GT has an increased chance of inheriting dependencies as variance increases, however, which results in decreased throughput.

Value Size. Finally, Figure 11(c) shows the effect of value size on system performance. In this experiment, we normalize the systems' maximum throughput against that of COPS (the COPS line at exactly 1.0 is shown only for comparison). As the size of values increases, the relative throughput of COPS-GT approaches that of COPS.

We attribute this to two reasons. First, the relative cost of processing dependencies (which are of fixed size) decreases compared to that of processing the actual values. Second, as processing time per operation increases, the inter-operation delay correspondingly increases, which in turn leads to fewer dependencies.

6.4 Scalability

To evaluate the scalability of COPS and COPS-GT, we compare them to LOG. LOG mimics systems based on log serialization and exchange, which can only provide causal+ consistency with single node replicas. Our implementation of LOG uses the COPS code, but excludes dependency tracking.

Figure 12 shows the throughput of COPS and COPS-GT (running on 1, 2, 4, 8, or 16 servers/datacenter) normalized against LOG (running on 1 server/datacenter). Unless specified otherwise, all experiments use the default settings given in Section 6.3, including a put:get ratio of 1:1. In all experiments, COPS running on a single server/datacenter achieves performance almost identical to LOG. (After all, compared to LOG, COPS needs to track only a small number of dependencies, typically ≤ 4, and any dep_check operations in the remote datacenter can be executed as local function calls.) More importantly, we see that COPS and COPS-GT scale well in all scenarios: as we double the number of servers per datacenter, throughput almost doubles.

In the experiment with all default settings, COPS and COPS-GT scale well relative to themselves, although COPS-GT's throughput is only about two-thirds that of COPS. These results demonstrate that the default parameters were chosen to provide a non-ideal workload for the system. However, under a number of different conditions—and, indeed, a workload more common to Internet services—the performance of COPS and COPS-GT is almost identical.

As one example, the relative throughput of COPS-GT is close to that of COPS when the inter-operation delay is high (achieved by hosting 32K clients per server, as opposed to the default 1024 clients; see Footnote 11). Similarly, a more read-heavy workload (put:get ratio of 1:16 vs. 1:1), a smaller variance in clients' access distributions (1/128 vs. 1), or larger-sized values (16KB vs. 1B)—controlling for all other parameters—all have the similar effect: the throughput of COPS-GT becomes comparable to that of COPS.

Finally, for the "expected workload" experiment, we set the parameters closer to what we might encounter in an Internet service such as social networking. Compared to the default, this workload has a higher inter-operation delay (32K clients/server), larger values (1KB), and a read-heavy distribution (1:16 ratio). Under these settings, the throughput of COPS and COPS-GT are very comparable, and both scale well with the number of servers.

7. RELATED WORK

We divide related work into four categories: ALPS systems, causally consistent systems, linearizable systems, and transactional systems.

ALPS Systems. The increasingly crowded category of ALPS systems includes eventually consistent key-value stores such as Amazon's Dynamo [16], LinkedIn's Project Voldemort [43], and the popular memcached [19]. Facebook's Cassandra [30] can be configured to use eventual consistency to achieve ALPS properties, or can sacrifice ALPS properties to provide linearizability. A key influence for our work was Yahoo!'s PNUTS [15], which provides per-key sequential consistency (although they name this per-record timeline consistency). PNUTS does not provide any consistency between keys, however; achieving such consistency introduces the scalability challenges that COPS addresses.

Causally Consistent Systems. Many previous system designers have recognized the utility of causal consistency. Bayou [41] provides a SQL-like interface to single-machine replicas that achieves causal+ consistency. Bayou handles all reads and writes locally; it does not address the scalability goals we consider.

TACT [53] is a causal+ consistent system that uses order and numeric bounding to limit the divergence of replicas in the system. The ISIS [12] system exploits the concept of virtual synchrony [11] to provide applications with a causal broadcast primitive (CBcast).

Normalized Throughput

Legend: LOG, COPS, COPS-GT

Y-axis values: 16, 8, 4, 2, 1, 0.5

Categories:
- All Defaults
- High Inter-Op Delay
- 1:16 Put:Get
- 1/128 Variance
- 16KB Values
- Expected Workload

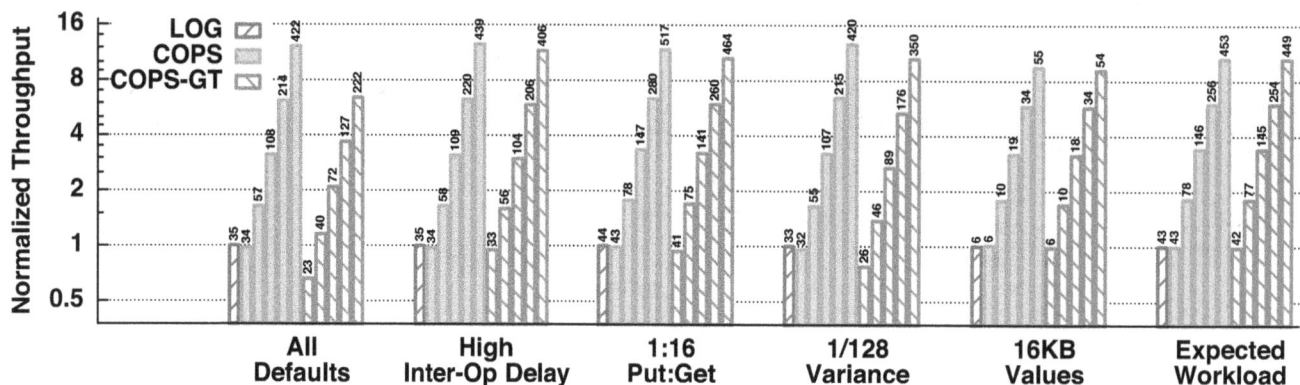

Figure 12: Throughput for LOG with 1 server/datacenter, and COPS and COPS-GT with 1, 2, 4, 8, and 16 servers/datacenter, for a variety of scenarios. Throughput is normalized against LOG for each scenario; raw throughput (in Kops/s) is given above each bar.

CBcast could be used in a straightforward manner to provide a causally consistent key-value store. Replicas that share information via causal memory [2] can also provide a causally consistent ALP key-value store. These systems, however, all require single-machine replicas and thus do not provide scalability.

PRACTI [10] is a causal+ consistent ALP system that supports partial replication, which allows a replica to store only a subset of keys and thus provides some scalability. However, each replica—and thus the set of keys over which causal+ consistency is provided—is still limited to what a single machine can handle.

Lazy replication [29] is closest to COPS's approach. Lazy replication explicitly marks updates with their causal dependencies and waits for those dependencies to be satisfied before applying them at a replica. These dependencies are maintained and attached to updates via a front-end that is an analog to our client library. The design of lazy replication, however, assumes that replicas are limited to a single machine: Each replica requires a single point that can (i) create a sequential log of all replica operations, (ii) gossip that log to other replicas, (iii) merge the log of its operations with those of other replicas, and finally (iv) apply these operations in causal order.

Finally, in concurrent theoretical work, Mahajan et al. [35] define real-time causal (RTC) consistency and prove that it is the strongest achievable in an always-available system. RTC is stronger than causal+ because it enforces a real-time requirement: if causally-concurrent writes do not overlap in real-time, the earlier write may not be ordered after the later write. This real-time requirement helps capture potential causality that is hidden from the system (e.g., out-of-band messaging [14]). In contrast, causal+ does not have a real-time requirement, which allows for more efficient implementations. Notably, COPS's efficient last-writer-wins rule results in a causal+ but not RTC consistent system, while a "return-them-all" conflict handler would provide both properties.

Linearizable Systems. Linearizability can be provided using a single commit point (as in primary-copy systems [4, 39], which may *eagerly* replicate data through two-phase commit protocols [44]) or using distributed agreement (e.g., Paxos [33]). Rather than replicate content everywhere, quorum systems ensure that read and write sets overlap for linearizability [22, 25].

As noted earlier, CAP states that linearizable systems cannot have latency lower than their round-trip inter-datacenter latency; only recently have they been used for wide-area operation, and only when the low latency of ALPS can be sacrificed [9]. CRAQ [48] can complete reads in the local-area when there is little write contention, but otherwise requires wide-area operations to ensure linearizability.

Transactions. Unlike most filesystems or key-value stores, the database community has long considered consistency across multiple keys through the use of read *and* write transactions. In many commercial database systems, a single master executes transactions across keys, then *lazily* sends its transaction log to other replicas, potentially over the wide-area. Typically, these asynchronous replicas are read-only, unlike COPS's write-anywhere replicas. Today's large-scale databases typically partition (or shard) data over multiple DB instances [17, 38, 42], much like in consistent hashing. Transactions are applied only within a single partition, whereas COPS can establish causal dependencies across nodes/partitions.

Several database systems support transactions across partitions and/or datacenters (both of which have been viewed in the database literature as independent *sites*). For example, the R* database [37] uses a tree of processes and two-phase locking for multi-site transactions. This two-phase locking, however, prevents the system from guaranteeing availability, low latency, or partition tolerance. Sinfonia [1] provides "mini" transactions to distributed shared memory via a lightweight two-phase commit protocol, but only considers operations within a single datacenter. Finally, Walter [47], a recent key-value store for the wide-area, provides transactional consistency across keys (including for writes, unlike COPS), and includes optimizations that allow transactions to execute within a single site, under certain scenarios. But while COPS focuses on availability and low-latency, Walter stresses transactional guarantees: ensuring causal relationships between keys can require a two-phase commit across the wide-area. Furthermore, in COPS, scalable datacenters are a first-order design goal, while Walter's sites currently consist of single machines (as a single serialization point for transactions).

8. CONCLUSION

Today's high-scale, wide-area systems provide "always on," low-latency operations for clients, at the cost of weak consistency guarantees and complex application logic. This paper presents COPS, a scalable distributed storage system that provides causal+ consistency without sacrificing ALPS properties. COPS achieves causal+ consistency by tracking and explicitly checking that causal dependencies are satisfied before exposing writes in each cluster. COPS-GT builds upon COPS by introducing get transactions that enable clients to obtain a consistent view of multiple keys; COPS-GT incorporates optimizations to curtail state, minimize multi-round protocols, and reduce replication overhead. Our evaluation demonstrates that COPS and COPS-GT provide low latency, high throughput, and scalability.

Acknowledgments. We owe a particular debt both to the SOSP program committee and to our shepherd, Mike Dahlin, for their extensive comments and Mike's thoughtful interaction that substantially improved both the presentation of and, indeed, our own view of, this work. Jeff Terrace, Erik Nordström, and David Shue provided useful comments on this work; Vijay Vasudevan offered helpful assistance with FAWN-KV; and Sapan Bhatia and Andy Bavier helped us run experiments on the VICCI testbed. This work was supported by NSF funding (CAREER CSR-0953197 and CCF-0964474), VICCI (NSF Award MRI-1040123), a gift from Google, and the Intel Science and Technology Center for Cloud Computing.

REFERENCES

[1] M. K. Aguilera, A. Merchant, M. Shah, A. Veitch, and C. Karamanolis. Sinfonia: A new paradigm for building scalable distributed systems. *ACM TOCS*, 27(3), 2009.

[2] M. Ahamad, G. Neiger, P. Kohli, J. Burns, and P. Hutto. Causal memory: Definitions, implementation, and programming. *Distributed Computing*, 9(1), 1995.

[3] M. Al-Fares, A. Loukissas, and A. Vahdat. A scalable, commodity data center network architecture. In *SIGCOMM*, Aug. 2008.

[4] P. Alsberg and J. Day. A principle for resilient sharing of distributed resources. In *Conf. Software Engineering*, Oct. 1976.

[5] D. G. Andersen, J. Franklin, M. Kaminsky, A. Phanishayee, L. Tan, and V. Vasudevan. FAWN: A fast array of wimpy nodes. In *SOSP*, Oct. 2009.

[6] T. E. Anderson, M. D. Dahlin, J. M. Neefe, D. A. Patterson, D. S. Roselli, and R. Y. Wang. Serverless network file systems. *ACM TOCS*, 14(1), 1996.

[7] Apache Thrift. http://thrift.apache.org/, 2011.

[8] H. Attiya and J. L. Welch. Sequential consistency versus linearizability. *ACM TOCS*, 12(2), 1994.

[9] J. Baker, C. Bond, J. C. Corbett, J. Furman, A. Khorlin, J. Larson, J.-M. Leon, Y. Li, A. Lloyd, and V. Yushprakh. Megastore: Providing scalable, highly available storage for interactive services. In *CIDR*, Jan. 2011.

[10] N. Belaramani, M. Dahlin, L. Gao, A. Nayate, A. Venkataramani, P. Yalagandula, and J. Zheng. PRACTI replication. In *NSDI*, May 2006.

[11] K. P. Birman and T. Joseph. Exploiting virtual synchrony in distributed systems. In *SOSP*, Nov. 1987.

[12] K. P. Birman and R. V. Renesse. *Reliable Distributed Computing with the ISIS Toolkit*. IEEE Comp. Soc. Press, 1994.

[13] E. Brewer. Towards robust distributed systems. PODC Keynote, July 2000.

[14] D. R. Cheriton and D. Skeen. Understanding the limitations of causally and totally ordered communication. In *SOSP*, Dec. 1993.

[15] B. F. Cooper, R. Ramakrishnan, U. Srivastava, A. Silberstein, P. Bohannon, H.-A. Jacobsen, N. Puz, D. Weaver, and R. Yerneni. PNUTS: Yahoo!'s hosted data serving platform. In *VLDB*, Aug. 2008.

[16] G. DeCandia, D. Hastorun, M. Jampani, G. Kakulapati, A. Lakshman, A. Pilchin, S. Sivasubramanian, P. Vosshall, and W. Vogels. Dynamo: Amazon's highly available key-value store. In *SOSP*, Oct. 2007.

[17] D. DeWitt, S. Ghandeharizadeh, D. Schneider, A. Bricker, H.-I. Hsiao, and R. Rasmussen. The gamma database machine project. *Knowledge and Data Engineering*, 2(1), 1990.

[18] FAWN-KV. https://github.com/vrv/FAWN-KV, 2011.

[19] B. Fitzpatrick. Memcached: a distributed memory object caching system. http://memcached.org/, 2011.

[20] A. Fox, S. D. Gribble, Y. Chawathe, E. A. Brewer, and P. Gauthier. Cluster-based scalable network services. In *SOSP*, Oct. 1997.

[21] S. Ghemawat, H. Gobioff, and S.-T. Leung. The Google file system. In *SOSP*, Oct. 2003.

[22] D. K. Gifford. Weighted voting for replicated data. In *SOSP*, Dec. 1979.

[23] S. Gilbert and N. Lynch. Brewer's conjecture and the feasibility of consistent, available, partition-tolerant web services. *ACM SIGACT News*, 33(2), 2002.

[24] A. Greenberg, J. R. Hamilton, N. Jain, S. Kandula, C. Kim, P. Lahiri, D. A. Maltz, P. Patel, and S. Sengupta. VL2: A scalable and flexible data center network. In *SIGCOMM*, Aug. 2009.

[25] M. Herlihy. A quorum-consensus replication method for abstract data types. *ACM TOCS*, 4(1), Feb. 1986.

[26] M. P. Herlihy and J. M. Wing. Linearizability: A correctness condition for concurrent objects. *ACM TOPLAS*, 12(3), 1990.

[27] D. Karger, E. Lehman, F. Leighton, M. Levine, D. Lewin, and R. Panigrahy. Consistent hashing and random trees: Distributed caching protocols for relieving hot spots on the World Wide Web. In *STOC*, May 1997.

[28] J. Kistler and M. Satyanarayanan. Disconnected operation in the Coda file system. *ACM TOCS*, 10(3), Feb. 1992.

[29] R. Ladin, B. Liskov, L. Shrira, and S. Ghemawat. Providing high availability using lazy replication. *ACM TOCS*, 10(4), 1992.

[30] A. Lakshman and P. Malik. Cassandra – a decentralized structured storage system. In *LADIS*, Oct. 2009.

[31] L. Lamport. Time, clocks, and the ordering of events in a distributed system. *Comm. ACM*, 21(7), 1978.

[32] L. Lamport. How to make a multiprocessor computer that correctly executes multiprocess programs. *IEEE Trans. Computer*, 28(9), 1979.

[33] L. Lamport. The part-time parliament. *ACM TOCS*, 16(2), 1998.

[34] R. J. Lipton and J. S. Sandberg. PRAM: A scalable shared memory. Technical Report TR-180-88, Princeton Univ., Dept. Comp. Sci., 1988.

[35] P. Mahajan, L. Alvisi, and M. Dahlin. Consistency, availability, and convergence. Technical Report TR-11-22, Univ. Texas at Austin, Dept. Comp. Sci., 2011.

[36] J. Misra. Axioms for memory access in asynchronous hardware systems. *ACM TOPLAS*, 8(1), Jan. 1986.

[37] C. Mohan, B. Lindsay, and R. Obermarck. Transaction management in the R* distributed database management system. *ACM Trans. Database Sys.*, 11(4), 1986.

[38] MySQL. http://www.mysql.com/, 2011.

[39] B. M. Oki and B. H. Liskov. Viewstamped replication: A general primary copy. In *PODC*, Aug. 1988.

[40] D. S. Parker, G. J. Popek, G. Rudisin, A. Stoughton, B. J. Walker, E. Walton, J. M. Chow, D. Edwards, S. Kiser, and C. Kline. Detection of mutual inconsistency in distributed systems. *IEEE Trans. Software Eng.*, 9(3), 1983.

[41] K. Petersen, M. Spreitzer, D. Terry, M. Theimer, and A. Demers. Flexible update propagation for weakly consistent replication. In *SOSP*, Oct. 1997.

[42] PostgresSQL. http://www.postgresql.org/, 2011.

[43] Project Voldemort. http://project-voldemort.com/, 2011.

[44] D. Skeen. A formal model of crash recovery in a distributed system. *IEEE Trans. Software Engineering*, 9(3), May 1983.

[45] Snappy. http://code.google.com/p/snappy/, 2011.

[46] J. Sobel. Scaling out. Engineering at Facebook blog, Aug. 20 2008.

[47] Y. Sovran, R. Power, M. K. Aguilera, and J. Li. Transactional storage for geo-replicated systems. In *SOSP*, Oct. 2011.

[48] J. Terrace and M. J. Freedman. Object storage on CRAQ: High-throughput chain replication for read-mostly workloads. In *USENIX ATC*, June 2009.

[49] D. B. Terry, A. J. Demers, K. Petersen, M. Spreitzer, M. Theimer, and B. W. Welch. Session guarantees for weakly consistent replicated data. In *Conf. Parallel Distributed Info. Sys.*, Sept. 1994.

[50] R. H. Thomas. A majority consensus approach to concurrency control for multiple copy databases. *ACM Trans. Database Sys.*, 4(2), 1979.

[51] R. van Renesse and F. B. Schneider. Chain replication for supporting high throughput and availability. In *OSDI*, Dec. 2004.

[52] VICCI. http://vicci.org/, 2011.

[53] H. Yu and A. Vahdat. Design and evaluation of a continuous consistency model for replicated services. In *OSDI*, Oct. 2000.

A. FORMAL DEFINITION OF CAUSAL+

We first present causal consistency with convergent conflict handling (causal+ consistency) for a system with only get and put operations (reads and writes), and we then introduce get transactions. We use a model closely derived from Ahamad et al. [2], which in turn was derived from those used by Herlihy and Wing [26] and Misra [36].

Original Model of Causal Consistency [2] with terminology modified to match this paper's definitions:

A system is a finite set of threads of execution, also called threads, that interact via a key-value store that consists of a finite set of keys. Let $T = \{t_1, t_2, \ldots, t_n\}$ be the set of threads. The local history L_i of a thread i is a sequence of get and put operations. If operation σ_1 precedes σ_2 in L_i, we write $\sigma_1 \xrightarrow{i} \sigma_2$. A history $H = \langle L_1, L_2, \ldots, L_n \rangle$ is the collection of local histories for all threads of execution. A serialization S of H is a linear sequence of all operations in H in which each get on a key returns its most recent preceding put (or $\perp$ if there does not exist any preceding put). The serialization S respects an order $\rightarrow$ if, for any operation σ_1 and σ_2 in S, $\sigma_1 \rightarrow \sigma_2$ implies σ_1 precedes σ_2 in S.

The *puts-into* order associates a put operation, put(k,v), with each get operation, get(k)=v. Because there may be multiple puts of a value to a key, there may be more than one puts-into order.[12] A puts-into order $\mapsto$ on H is any relation with the following properties:

- If $\sigma_1 \mapsto \sigma_2$, then there is a key k and value v such that operation $\sigma_1 := \text{put}(k,v)$ and $\sigma_2 := \text{get}(k)=v$.
- For any operation σ_2, there exists at most one σ_1 for which $\sigma_1 \mapsto \sigma_2$.
- If $\sigma_2 := \text{get}(k)=v$ for some k,v and there exists no σ_1 such that $\sigma_1 \mapsto \sigma_2$, then v = $\perp$. That is, a get with no preceding put must retrieve the initial value.

Two operations, σ_1 and σ_2, are related by a causal order $\leadsto$ if and only if one of the following holds:

- $\sigma_1 \xrightarrow{i} \sigma_2$ for some t_i (σ_1 precedes σ_2 in L_i);
- $\sigma_1 \mapsto \sigma_2$ (σ_2 gets the value put by σ_1); or
- There is some other operation σ' such that $\sigma_1 \leadsto \sigma' \leadsto \sigma_2$.

Incorporating Convergent Conflict Handling. Two operations on the same key, $\sigma_1 := \text{put}(k,v_1)$ and $\sigma_2 := \text{put}(k,v_2)$, are in *conflict* if they are not related by causality: $\sigma_1 \not\leadsto \sigma_2$ and $\sigma_2 \not\leadsto \sigma_1$.

A *convergent conflict handling function* is an associative, commutative function that operates on a set of conflicting operations on a key to eventually produce one (possibly new) final value for that key. The function must produce the same final value independent of the order in which it observes the conflicting updates. In this way, once every replica has observed the conflicting updates for a key, they will all independently agree on the same final value.

We model convergent conflict handling as a set of *handler* threads that are distinct from normal client threads. The handlers operate on a pair of conflicting values (v_1, v_2) to produce a new value *newval* = $h(v_1, v_2)$. By commutativity, $h(v_1, v_2) = h(v_2, v_1)$. To produce the new value, the handler thread had to read both v_1 and v_2 before putting the new value, and so *newval* is causally ordered after both original values: $v_1 \leadsto newval$ and $v_2 \leadsto newval$.

With more than two conflicting updates, there will be multiple invocations of handler threads. For three values, there are several possible orders for resolving the conflicting updates in pairs:

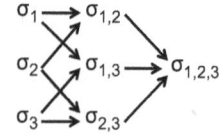

The commutativity and associativity of the handler function ensures that regardless of the order, the final output will be identical. Further, it will be causally ordered after all of the original conflicting writes, as well as any intermediate values generated by the application of the handler function. If the handler observes multiple pairs of conflicting updates that produce the same output value (e.g., the final output in the figure above), it must output only one value, not multiple instances of the same value.

To prevent a client from seeing and having to reason about multiple, conflicting values, we restrict the put set for each **client** thread to be conflict free, denoted p_{cf_i}. A put set is *conflict free* if $\forall \sigma_j, \sigma_k \in p_{cf_i}$, σ_j and σ_k are not in conflict; that is, either they are puts to different keys or causally-related puts to the same key. For example, in the three conflicting put example, p_{cf_i} might include σ_1, $\sigma_{1,2}$, and $\sigma_{1,2,3}$, but not σ_2, σ_3, $\sigma_{1,3}$, or $\sigma_{2,3}$. The conflict-free property applies to client threads and not handler threads purposefully. Handler threads must be able to get values from conflicting puts so they may reason about and resolve them; client threads should not see conflicts so they do not have to reason about them.

Adding handler threads models the new functionality that convergent conflict handling provides. Restricting the put set strengthens consistency from causal to causal+. There are causal executions that are not causal+: for example, if σ_1 and σ_2 conflict, a client may get the value put by σ_1 and then the value put by σ_2 in a causal, but not causal+, system. On the other hand, there are no causal+ executions that are not causal, because causal+ only introduces an additional restriction (a smaller put set) to causal consistency.

If H is a history and t_i is a thread, let $A_{i+p_{cf_i}}^H$ comprise all operations in the local history of t_i, and a conflict-free set of puts in H, p_{cf_i}. A history H is *causally consistent with convergent conflict handling* (causal+) if it has a causal order $\leadsto$, such that

Causal+: For each *client* thread of execution t_i, there is a serialization S_i of $A_{i+p_{cf_i}}^H$ that respects $\leadsto$.

A data store is *causal+ consistent* if it admits only causal+ histories.

Introducing Get Transactions. To add get transactions to the model, we redefine the puts-into order so that it associates N put operations, put(k,v), with each get transaction of N values, get_trans($[k_1, \ldots, k_N]$)=$[v_1, \ldots, v_N]$. Now, a puts-into order $\mapsto$ on H is any relation with the following properties:

- If $\sigma_1 \mapsto \sigma_2$, then there is a k and v such that $\sigma_1 := \text{put}(k,v)$ and $\sigma_2 := \text{get\_trans}([\ldots,k,\ldots])=[\ldots,v,\ldots]$. That is, for each component of a get transaction, there exists a preceding put.
- For each component of a get transaction σ_2, there exists at most one σ_1 for which $\sigma_1 \mapsto \sigma_2$.
- If $\sigma_2 := \text{get\_trans}([\ldots,k,\ldots])=[\ldots,v,\ldots]$ for some k,v and there exists no σ_1 such that $\sigma_1 \mapsto \sigma_2$, then v=$\perp$. That is, a get with no preceding put must retrieve the initial value.

---

[12] The COPS system uniquely identifies values with version numbers so there is only one puts-into order, but this is not necessarily true for causal+ consistency in general.